WEBSTER'S
Dictionary
&
Thesaurus

**The Rotary Club of
Columbia Patuxent**

The Four-Way Test
of the things we think, say or do:

1. Is it the TRUTH?
2. Is it FAIR to all concerned?
3. Will it build GOOD WILL and
   BETTER FRIENDSHIPS?
4. Will it be BENEFICIAL to all
   concerned?

www.columbiarotary.com

WEBSTER'S
Dictionary
&
Thesaurus

Created in Cooperation with the Editors of
MERRIAM-WEBSTER

property
of
Connie
Bell

FEDERAL
STREET
PRESS

A Division of Merriam-Webster, Incorporated
Springfield, Massachusetts

This 2016 edition published by
Federal Street Press
A Division of Merriam-Webster, Incorporated
P.O. Box 281
Springfield, MA 01102

ISBN 13   978-1-59695-085-6

Printed in Canada

1st Printing   Webcom, Toronto, ON   8/2016

Dictionary

Preface

This new dictionary contains more than 19,000 words that represent the very core of the language. It is intended to serve as a quick reference for spelling, hyphenation, and meaning of the words in everyday use. Conciseness of presentation necessarily requires special treatment of entries, and this book has a number of special features all its own.

Entry words appear in **boldface type** with raised periods to indicate where they can be hyphenated at the end of a line in writing. Words that begin an entry paragraph are **main entry words** and are followed by definitions or cross-references to related entries.

> **aard·vark** . . . **:** ant-eating African mammal
> **abroad** . . . **1:** over a wide area **2 :** outside one's country
> **ate** *past of* EAT

Variant spellings of bold words are shown following a comma.

> **blond, blonde** . . . **1 :** fair in complexion

Labels indicating a word's grammatical function in the sentence **(part of speech)** are shown as abbreviations in italics after the bold word.

> **cam·era** *n* **:** box with a lens for taking pictures . . .
> **cam·ou·flage** *vb* **:** hide by disguising . . .
> **can·did** *adj* **1 :** frank **2 :** not posed . . .
> **— can·did·ly** *adv* . . .

Within an entry paragraph, derived words with the same spelling but a different part of speech are represented by a **swung dash** and are provided with their own definitions.

> **di·rect** *vb* **1 :** address **2 :** cause to move or to follow a certain course . . .
> **~** *adj* **1 :** leading to or coming from a point without deviation or interruption . .

Derived words are run on undefined at the end of the entry when their meanings are self-evident from the definitions preceding. This treatment allows for the saving of space to permit many more words to be entered and at the same time shows word relationships.

> **ex·haust** *vb* **1 :** draw out or develop completely **2 :** use up . . .
> **~** *n* **:** waste steam or gas from an engine . . . **— ex·haus·tion** *n*
> **— ex·haus·tive** *adj*

Main entries with the same spelling but not derived from one another are entered separately, marked with a superscript numeral.

> **¹file** *n* **:** tool for smoothing or sharpening . . .
> **²file** *vb* **1 :** arrange in order **2 :** enter or record officially . . .
> **³file** *n* **:** row of persons or things one behind the other

Plurals of nouns, principal parts of verbs, and comparative and superlative forms of adjectives (and adverbs) are know as **inflected forms.** Those formed by the regular addition of a suffix (such as *-s, -ed, -ing, -er, -est*) are well-known regular formations and are not shown in this dictionary. Inflections formed by an internal change in the spelling of the word (or no change) are shown inside parentheses. For nouns, the forms shown will be plurals (*pl*); for verbs, the forms shown will be past tense (*past*) and past participle (*past part*). The past and past participle are separated by a semicolon. If variant spellings are shown for any inflected form, that spelling is set off by a slash (*/*).

> **grow** *vb* **grew; grown 1 :** come into existence and develop to maturity
> **knife** *n* **knives :** sharp blade with a handle . . .
> **¹lie** *vb* **lay; lain 1 :** be in, rest in, or assume a horizontal position . . .
> **moose** *n* **moose :** large heavy-antlered deer
> **prove** *vb* **proved; proved/prov·en 1 :** test by experiment or by a standard . . .

When a particular sense of a word is used in a special way, such as used only in the plural form, that information is indicated after the sense number.

> **re·fresh·ment** *n* **1 :** act of refreshing **2** *pl* **:** light meal

If at a particular sense the form of the inflection is unique or not regularly formed, that information is also provided.

> **an·ten·na** *n* **1** *pl* **an·ten·nae :** one of the long slender paired sensory organs on the head of an arthropod **2** *pl* **an·ten·nas :** metallic device for sending or receiving radio waves
> **young** *adj* **1 :** being in the first or an early stage of life . . . ∼ *n* **young :** persons or animals that are young
> **up** *adv* **1 :** in or to a higher position or level . . . ∼ *vb* **1 up; upped :** act abruptly **2 upped; upped :** move or cause to move upward . . .

In the first example, the form of the plural is different for each of the two noun senses and is therefore shown. In the second example, the plural form for the noun sense is unchanged. In the third example, the verb inflections for the past tense are different for each of these two verb senses.

To show the range of entries on a page, **guide words** appear at the top, indicating the first main entry word and the last main entry word on that page.

Common **abbreviations**, including those used in this book, are shown in a separate section immediately following the dictionary proper.

Abbreviations

Most of these abbreviations are shown in one form only. Variation in use of periods, in kind of type, and in capitalization is frequent and widespread (as mph, MPH, m.p.h., Mph)

abbr abbreviation
AD in the year of our Lord
adj adjective
adv adverb
AK Alaska
AL, Ala Alabama
alt alternate, altitude
a.m., A.M. before noon
Am, Amer America, American
amt amount
anon anonymous
ans answer
Apr April
AR Arkansas
Ariz Arizona
Ark Arkansas
assn association
asst assistant
atty attorney
Aug August
ave avenue
AZ Arizona

BC before Christ
bet between
bldg building
blvd boulevard
Br, Brit Britain, British
bro brother
bros brothers
bu bushel

c carat, cent, centimeter, century, chapter, cup
C Celsius, centigrade
CA, Cal, Calif California
Can, Canad Canada, Canadian
cap capital, capitalize, capitalized
Capt captain
ch chapter, church
cm centimeter
co company, county
CO Colorado
COD cash on delivery, collect on delivery

col column
Col colonel, Colorado
Colo Colorado
conj conjunction
Conn Connecticut
cpu central processing unit
ct cent, court
CT Connecticut
cu cubic
CZ Canal Zone

d penny
DC District of Columbia
DDS doctor of dental surgery
DE Delaware
Dec December
Del Delaware
dept department
DMD doctor of dental medicine
doz dozen
Dr doctor
DST daylight saving time

E east, eastern, excellent
ea each
e.g. for example
Eng England, English
esp especially
etc et cetera

f false, female, forte
F Fahrenheit
FBI Federal Bureau of Investigation
Feb February
fem feminine
FL, Fla Florida
fr father, from
Fri Friday
ft feet, foot, fort

g gram
G good
Ga, GA Georgia
gal gallon

GB gigabyte
gen general
geog geographic, geographical, geography
gm gram
gov governor
govt government
gt great
GU Guam

HI Hawaii
hr hour
HS high school
ht height
Ia, IA Iowa
ID Idaho
i.e. that is
IL, Ill Illinois
in inch
IN Indiana
inc incorporated
Ind Indian, Indiana
interj interjection
intrans intransitive

Jan January
jr, jun junior

Kan, Kans Kansas
KB kilobyte
kg kilogram
km kilometer
KS Kansas
Ky, KY Kentucky

l left, liter
La, LA Louisiana
lb pound
Lt lieutenant
ltd limited

m male, meter, mile
MA Massachusetts
Maj major
Mar March
masc masculine
Mass Massachusetts
MB megabyte

Md Maryland
MD doctor of medicine, Maryland
Me, ME Maine
Mex Mexican, Mexico
mg milligram
MI, Mich Michigan
min minute
Minn Minnesota
Miss Mississippi
ml milliliter
mm millimeter
MN Minnesota
mo month
Mo, MO Missouri
Mon Monday
Mont Montana
mpg miles per gallon
mph miles per hour
MS Mississippi
mt mount, mountain
MT Montana

n noun
N north, northern
NC North Carolina
ND, N Dak North Dakota
NE Nebraska, northeast
Neb, Nebr Nebraska
Nev Nevada
NH New Hampshire
NJ New Jersey
NM, N Mex New Mexico
no north, number
Nov November
NV Nevada
NW northwest
NY New York

O Ohio
obj object, objective
Oct October
off office
OH Ohio
OK, Okla Oklahoma
OR, Ore, Oreg Oregon
oz ounce, ounces

p page
Pa, PA Pennsylvania
part participle
pat patent
Penn, Penna Pennsylvania

pg page
pk park, peck
pkg package
pl plural
p.m., P.M. afternoon
PO post office
poss possessive
pp pages
pr pair
PR Puerto Rico
prep preposition
pres present, president
prof professor
pron pronoun
PS postscript, public school
pt pint, point
PTA Parent-Teacher Association
PTO Parent-Teacher Organization

qt quart

r right
rd road, rod
recd received
reg region, regular
res residence
Rev reverend
RFD rural free delivery
RI Rhode Island
rpm revolutions per minute
RR railroad
RSVP please reply
rt right
rte route

S south, southern
Sat Saturday
SC South Carolina
sci science
Scot Scotland, Scottish
SD, S Dak South Dakota
SE southeast
sec second
Sept September
SI International System of Units
sing singular
so south
sq square

sr senior
Sr sister
SS steamship
st state, street
St saint
Sun Sunday
SW southwest

t true
tbs, tbsp tablespoon
TD touchdown
Tenn Tennessee
Tex Texas
Thurs, Thu Thursday
TN Tennessee
trans transitive
tsp teaspoon
Tues, Tue Tuesday
TX Texas

UN United Nations
US United States
USA United States of America
USSR Union of Soviet Socialist Republics
usu usual, usually
UT Utah

v verb
Va, VA Virginia
var variant
vb verb
VG very good
vi verb intransitive
VI Virgin Islands
vol volume
VP vice president
vs versus
vt verb transitive
Vt, VT Vermont

W west, western
WA, Wash Washington
Wed Wednesday
WI, Wis, Wisc Wisconsin
wk week
wt weight
WV, W Va West Virginia
WWW World Wide Web
WY, Wyo Wyoming

yd yard
yr year

A

¹a *n* : 1st letter of the alphabet

²a *indefinite article* : one or some — used to indicate an unspecified or unidentified individual

aard·vark *n* : ant-eating African mammal

aback *adv* : by surprise

ab·a·lo·ne *n* : large edible shellfish

aban·don *vb* : give up without intent to reclaim — **aban·don** *n* — **aban·doned** *adj* — **aban·don·ment** *n*

abase *vb* : lower in dignity — **abase·ment** *n*

abate *vb* : decrease or lessen — **abate·ment** *n*

ab·bess *n* : head of a convent

ab·bey *n* : monastery or convent

ab·bot *n* : head of a monastery

ab·bre·vi·ate *vb* : shorten — **ab·bre·vi·a·tion** *n*

ab·di·cate *vb* : renounce — **ab·di·ca·tion** *n*

ab·do·men *n* **1** : body area between chest and pelvis **2** : hindmost part of an insect — **ab·dom·i·nal** *adj* — **ab·dom·i·nal·ly** *adv*

ab·er·ra·tion *n* : deviation or distortion — **ab·er·rant** *adj*

abet *vb* : incite or encourage — **abet·tor, abet·ter** *n*

abey·ance *n* : state of inactivity

ab·hor *vb* : hate — **ab·hor·rence** *n* — **ab·hor·rent** *adj*

abide *vb* **1** : endure **2** : remain, last, or reside

abil·i·ty *n* **1** : competence **2** : natural aptitude

ab·ject *adj* : low in spirit or hope — **ab·jec·tion** *n* — **ab·ject·ly** *adv* — **ab·ject·ness** *n*

ablaze *adj or adv* : on fire

able *adj* **1** : having sufficient power, skill, or resources **2** : skilled or efficient — **ably** *adv*

ab·lu·tion *n* : washing of one's body

ab·nor·mal *adj* : deviating from the normal or average — **ab·nor·mal·i·ty** *n* — **ab·nor·mal·ly** *adv*

aboard *adv* : on, onto, or within a car, ship, or aircraft ~ *prep* : on or within

abode *n* : residence

abol·ish *vb* : do away with — **ab·o·li·tion** *n*

abom·i·na·ble *adj* : thoroughly unpleasant or revolting

abom·i·nate *vb* : hate — **abom·i·na·tion** *n*

ab·orig·i·nal *adj* **1** : original **2** : primitive

ab·orig·i·ne *n* : original inhabitant

abort *vb* : terminate prematurely — **abor·tion** *n* — **abor·tive** *adj*

abound *vb* : be plentiful

about *adv* : around ~ *prep* **1** : on every side of **2** : on the verge of **3** : having as a subject

above *adv* : in or to a higher place ~ *prep* **1** : in or to a higher place than **2** : more than

above·board *adv or adj* : without deception

abrade *vb* : wear away by rubbing — **abra·sion** *n* — **abra·sive** *adj* — **abra·sive·ly** *adv*

abreast *adv or adj* **1** : side by side **2** : up to a standard or level

abridge *vb* : shorten or condense — **abridg·ment, abridge·ment** *n*

abroad *adv or adj* **1** : over a wide area **2** : outside one's country

abrupt *adj* **1** : sudden **2** : so quick as to seem rude — **abrupt·ly** *adv*

ab·scess *n* : collection of pus surrounded by inflamed tissue — **ab·scessed** *adj*

ab·scond *vb* : run away and hide

ab·sent *adj* : not present ~ **ab·sent** *vb* : keep oneself away — **ab·sence** *n* — **absen·tee** *n*

ab·sent·mind·ed *adj* : unaware of one's surroundings or action — **ab·sent·mind·ed·ly** *adv* — **ab·sent·mind·ed·ness** *n*

ab·so·lute *adj* **1** : pure **2** : free from restriction **3** : definite — **ab·so·lute·ly** *adv*

ab·so·lu·tion *n* : remission of sins

ab·solve *vb* : set free of the consequences of guilt

ab·sorb *vb* **1** : suck up or take in as a sponge does **2** : engage (one's attention) — **ab·sor·ben·cy** *n* — **ab·sor·bent** *adj or n* — **ab·sorb·ing** *adj* — **ab·sorp·tion** *n* — **ab·sorp·tive** *adj*

ab·stain *vb* : refrain from doing something — **ab·stain·er** *n* — **ab·sten·tion** *n* — **ab·sti·nence** *n*

ab·ste·mi·ous *adj* : sparing in use of food or drink — **ab·ste·mi·ous·ly** *adv* — **ab·ste·mi·ous·ness** *n*

ab·stract *adj* **1** : expressing a quality apart from an object **2** : not representing something specific ~ *n* : summary ~ *vb* **1** : remove or separate **2** : make an abstract of — **ab·stract·ly** *adv* — **ab·stract·ness** *n* — **ab·strac·tion** *n*

ab·surd *adj* : ridiculous or unreasonable — **ab·sur·di·ty** *n* — **ab·surd·ly** *adv*

abun·dant *adj* : more than enough — **abun·dance** *n* — **abun·dant·ly** *adv*

abuse *vb* **1** : misuse **2** : mistreat **3** : attack with words ∼ *n* **1** : corrupt practice **2** : improper use **3** : mistreatment **4** : coarse and insulting speech — **abus·er** *n* — **abu·sive** *adj* — **abu·sive·ly** *adv* — **abu·sive·ness** *n*

abut *vb* : touch along a border — **abut·ter** *n* — **abut·ment** *n*

abys·mal *adj* **1** : immeasurably deep **2** : wretched — **abys·mal·ly** *adv*

abyss *n* : immeasurably deep gulf

acad·e·my *n* **1** : private high school **2** : society of scholars or artists — **ac·a·dem·ic** *adj or n* — **ac·a·dem·i·cal·ly** *adv*

ac·cede *vb* **1** : become a party to an agreement **2** : express approval **3** : enter upon an office

ac·cel·er·ate *vb* **1** : bring about earlier **2** : speed up — **ac·cel·er·a·tion** *n* — **ac·cel·er·a·tor** *n*

ac·cent *n* **1** : distinctive manner of pronunciation **2** : prominence given to one syllable of a word **3** : mark (as ´, `, ˆ) over a vowel in writing or printing to indicate pronunciation ∼ *vb* : emphasize — **ac·cen·tu·al** *adj* — **ac·cen·tu·ate** *vb* — **ac·cen·tu·a·tion** *n*

ac·cept *vb* **1** : receive willingly **2** : agree to — **ac·cept·abil·i·ty** *n* — **ac·cept·able** *adj* — **ac·cep·tance** *n*

ac·cess *n* : capability or way of approaching — **ac·ces·si·bil·i·ty** *n* — **ac·ces·si·ble** *adj*

ac·ces·so·ry *n* **1** : nonessential addition **2** : one guilty of aiding a criminal — **ac·ces·so·ry** *adj*

ac·ci·dent *n* **1** : event occurring by chance or unintentionally **2** : chance — **ac·ci·den·tal** *adj* — **ac·ci·den·tal·ly** *adv*

ac·claim *vb or n* : praise — **ac·cla·ma·tion** *n*

ac·cli·mate *vb* : acclimatize — **ac·cli·ma·tion** *n*

ac·cli·ma·tize *vb* : accustom to a new climate or situation — **ac·cli·ma·ti·za·tion** *n*

ac·co·lade *n* : expression of praise

ac·com·mo·date *vb* **1** : adapt **2** : provide with something needed **3** : hold without crowding — **ac·com·mo·da·tion** *n*

ac·com·pa·ny *vb* **1** : go or occur with **2** : play supporting music — **ac·com·pa·ni·ment** *n* — **ac·com·pa·nist** *n*

ac·com·plice *n* : associate in crime

ac·com·plish *vb* : do, fulfill, or bring about —

ac·com·plished *adj* — **ac·com·plish·er** *n* — **ac·com·plish·ment** *n*

ac·cord *vb* **1** : grant **2** : agree ∼ *n* **1** : agreement **2** : willingness to act — **ac·cor·dance** *n* — **ac·cor·dant** *adj*

ac·cord·ing·ly *adv* : consequently

according to *prep* **1** : in conformity with **2** : as stated by

ac·cor·di·on *n* : keyboard instrument with a bellows and reeds ∼ *adj* : folding like an accordion bellows — **ac·cor·di·on·ist** *n*

ac·cost *vb* : approach and speak to esp. aggressively

ac·count *n* **1** : statement of business transactions **2** : credit arrangement with a vendor **3** : report **4** : worth **5** : sum deposited in a bank ∼ *vb* : give an explanation — **ac·count·able** *adj* — **ac·count·abil·i·ty** *n* — **ac·coun·tant** *n*

ac·cou·tre·ment, ac·cou·ter·ment *n* **1** : accessory item — usu. pl. **2** : identifying characteristic

ac·cred·it *vb* **1** : approve officially **2** : attribute — **ac·cred·i·ta·tion** *n*

ac·crue *vb* : be added by periodic growth — **ac·cru·al** *n*

ac·cu·mu·late *vb* : collect or pile up — **ac·cu·mu·la·tion** *n*

ac·cu·rate *adj* : free from error — **ac·cu·ra·cy** *n* — **ac·cu·rate·ly** *adv* — **ac·cu·rate·ness** *n*

ac·cursed, ac·curst *adj* **1** : being under a curse **2** : damnable

ac·cuse *vb* : charge with an offense — **ac·cu·sa·tion** *n* — **ac·cused** *n* — **ac·cus·er** *n*

ac·cus·tom *vb* : make familiar through use or experience

ace *n* : one that excels

acer·bic *adj* : sour or biting in temper, mood, or tone

acet·amin·o·phen *n* : pain reliever

ac·e·tate *n* : fabric or plastic derived from acetic acid

ace·tic acid *n* : acid found in vinegar

ache *vb* **1** : suffer a dull persistent pain **2** : yearn — **ache** *n*

achieve *vb* : gain by work or effort — **achieve·ment** *n* — **achiev·er** *n*

ac·id *adj* **1** : sour or biting to the taste **2** : sharp in manner **3** : of or relating to an acid ∼ *n* : sour water-soluble chemical compound that reacts with a base to form a salt — **acid·ic** *adj* — **acid·i·fy** *vb* — **acid·i·ty** *n* — **ac·id·ly** *adv*

ac·knowl·edge *vb* **1** : admit as true **2** : admit the authority of **3** : express thanks for — **ac·knowl·edg·ment** *n*

ac·me *n* : highest point

ac·ne *n* : skin disorder marked esp. by pimples

acorn *n* : nut of the oak

acous·tic *adj* : relating to hearing or sound — **acous·ti·cal** *adj* — **acous·ti·cal·ly** *adv*

acous·tics *n sing or pl* **1** : science of sound **2** : qualities in a room that affect how sound is heard

ac·quaint *vb* **1** : inform **2** : make familiar — **ac·quain·tance** *n* — **ac·quain·tance·ship** *n*

ac·qui·esce *vb* : consent or submit — **ac·qui·es·cence** *n* — **ac·qui·es·cent** *adj* — **ac·qui·es·cent·ly** *adv*

ac·quire *vb* : gain — **ac·qui·sition** *n* — **ac·qui·si·tive** *adj*

ac·quit *vb* **1** : pronounce not guilty **2** : conduct (oneself) usu. well — **ac·quit·tal** *n*

acre *n* **1** *pl* : lands **2** : 4840 square yards — **acre·age** *n*

ac·rid *adj* : sharp and biting — **acrid·i·ty** *n* — **ac·rid·ly** *adv* — **ac·rid·ness** *n*

ac·ri·mo·ny *n* : harshness of language or feeling — **ac·ri·mo·ni·ous** *adj* — **ac·ri·mo·ni·ous·ly** *adv*

ac·ro·bat *n* : performer of tumbling feats — **ac·ro·bat·ic** *adj*

across *adv* : to or on the opposite side ∼ *prep* **1** : to or on the opposite side of **2** : on so as to cross

acryl·ic *n* **1** : plastic used for molded parts or in paints **2** : synthetic textile fiber

act *n* **1** : thing done **2** : law **3** : main division of a play ∼ *vb* **1** : perform in a play **2** : conduct oneself **3** : operate **4** : produce an effect — **ac·tive** *adj or n* — **ac·tive·ly** *adv* — **ac·tor** *n* — **ac·tress** *n*

ac·tion *n* **1** : legal proceeding **2** : manner or method of performing **3** : activity **4** : thing done over a period of time or in stages **5** : combat **6** : events of a literary plot **7** : operating mechanism

ac·ti·vate *vb* : make active or reactive — **ac·ti·va·tion** *n*

ac·tiv·i·ty *n* **1** : quality or state of being active **2** : what one is actively doing

ac·tu·al *adj* : really existing — **ac·tu·al·i·ty** *n* — **ac·tu·al·iza·tion** *n* — **ac·tu·al·ize** *vb* — **ac·tu·al·ly** *adv*

ac·tu·ary *n* : one who calculates insurance risks and premiums — **ac·tu·ar·i·al** *adj*

acu·men *n* : mental keenness

acu·punc·ture *n* : treatment by puncturing the body with needles — **acu·punc·tur·ist** *n*

acute *adj* **1** : sharp **2** : containing less than 90 degrees **3** : mentally alert **4** : severe — **acute·ly** *adv* — **acute·ness** *n*

ad *n* : advertisement

ad·age *n* : old familiar saying

ad·a·mant *adj* : insistent — **ad·a·mant·ly** *adv*

adapt *vb* : adjust to be suitable for a new use or condition — **adapt·abil·i·ty** *n* — **adapt·able** *adj* — **ad·ap·ta·tion** *n* — **adap·ter** *n* — **adap·tive** *adj*

add *vb* **1** : join to something else so as to increase in amount **2** : say further **3** : find a sum — **ad·di·tion** *n* — **ad·di·tion·al** *adj*

ad·der *n* **1** : poisonous European snake **2** : No. American snake

ad·dict *n* : one who is psychologically or physiologically dependent (as on a drug) ∼ *vb* : cause to become an addict — **ad·dic·tion** *n* — **ad·dic·tive** *adj*

ad·di·tive *n* : substance added to another

ad·dle *vb* : confuse

ad·dress *vb* **1** : direct one's remarks to **2** : mark an address on ∼ *n* **1** : formal speech **2** : place where a person may be reached or mail may be delivered

adept *adj* : highly skilled — **adept·ly** *adv* — **adept·ness** *n*

ad·e·quate *adj* : good or plentiful enough — **ad·e·qua·cy** *n* — **ad·e·quate·ly** *adv*

ad·here *vb* **1** : remain loyal **2** : stick fast — **ad·her·ence** *n* — **ad·her·ent** *adj or n*

ad·he·sion *n* : act or state of adhering

ad·he·sive *adj* : tending to adhere ∼ *n* : adhesive substance

adieu *n* : farewell

ad·ja·cent *adj* : situated near or next

ad·jec·tive *n* : word that serves as a modifier of a noun — **ad·jec·ti·val** *adj* — **ad·jec·ti·val·ly** *adv*

ad·join *vb* : be next to

ad·journ *vb* : end a meeting — **ad·journ·ment** *n*

ad·ju·di·cate *vb* : settle judicially — **ad·ju·di·ca·tion** *n*

ad·junct *n* : something joined or added but not essential

ad·just *vb* : fix, adapt, or set right — **ad·just·able** *adj* — **ad·just·er, ad·jus·tor** *n* — **ad·just·ment** *n*

ad–lib *vb* : speak without preparation — **ad–lib** *n or adj*

ad·min·is·ter *vb* **1** : manage **2** : give out esp. in doses — **ad·min·is·tra·ble** *adj*

ad·min·is·tra·tion *n* **1** : process of managing **2** : persons responsible for managing — **ad·min·is·tra·tive** *adj* — **ad·min·is·tra·tive·ly** *adv* — **ad·min·is·tra·tor** *n*

ad·mi·ra·ble *adj* : worthy of admiration — **ad·mi·ra·bly** *adv*

ad·mi·ral *n* : commissioned officer in the navy ranking next below a fleet admiral

ad·mire *vb* : have high regard for — **ad·mi·ra·tion** *n* — **ad·mir·er** *n* — **ad·mir·ing·ly** *adv*

ad·mis·si·ble *adj* : that can be permitted — **ad·mis·si·bil·i·ty** *n*

ad·mis·sion *n* **1** : act of admitting **2** : admittance or a fee paid for this **3** : acknowledgment of a fact

ad·mit *vb* **1** : allow to enter **2** : permit **3** : recognize as genuine — **ad·mit·ted·ly** *adv* — **ad·mit·tance** *n*

ad·mix·ture *n* **1** : thing added in mixing **2** : mixture

ad·mon·ish *vb* : rebuke — **ad·mon·ish·ment** *n* — **ad·mo·ni·tion** *n* — **ad·mon·i·to·ry** *adj*

ado *n* **1** : fuss **2** : trouble

ado·be *n* : sun-dried building brick

ad·o·les·cence *n* : period of growth between childhood and maturity — **ad·o·les·cent** *adj or n*

adopt *vb* **1** : take (a child of other parents) as one's own child **2** : take up and practice as one's own — **adop·tion** *n*

adore *vb* **1** : worship **2** : be extremely fond of — **ador·able** *adj* — **ador·ably** *adv* — **ad·o·ra·tion** *n*

adorn *vb* : decorate with ornaments — **adorn·ment** *n*

adrift *adv or adj* **1** : afloat without motive power or moorings **2** : without guidance or purpose

adroit *adj* : dexterous or shrewd — **adroit·ly** *adv* — **adroit·ness** *n*

adult *adj* : fully developed and mature ∼ *n* : grown-up person — **adult·hood** *n*

adul·ter·ate *vb* : make impure by mixture — **adul·ter·a·tion** *n*

adul·tery *n* : sexual unfaithfulness of a married person — **adul·ter·er** *n* — **adul·ter·ess** *n* — **adul·ter·ous** *adj*

ad·vance *vb* **1** : bring or move forward **2** : promote **3** : lend ∼ *n* **1** : forward movement **2** : improvement **3** : offer ∼ *adj* : being ahead of time — **ad·vance·ment** *n*

ad·van·tage *n* **1** : superiority of position **2** : benefit or gain — **ad·van·ta·geous** *adj* — **ad·van·ta·geous·ly** *adv*

ad·vent *n* **1** *cap* : period before Christmas **2** : a coming into being or use

ad·ven·ture *n* **1** : risky undertaking **2** : exciting experience — **ad·ven·tur·er** *n* — **ad·ven·ture·some** *adj* — **ad·ven·tur·ous** *adj*

ad·verb *n* : word that modifies a verb, an adjective, or another adverb — **ad·ver·bi·al** *adj* — **ad·ver·bi·al·ly** *adv*

ad·ver·sary *n* : enemy or rival — **ad·ver·sary** *adj*

ad·verse *adj* : opposing or unfavorable — **ad·verse·ly** *adv* — **ad·ver·si·ty** *n*

ad·ver·tise *vb* : call public attention to — **ad·ver·tise·ment** *n* — **ad·ver·tis·er** *n* — **ad·ver·tis·ing** *n*

ad·vice *n* : recommendation with regard to a course of action

ad·vis·able *adj* : wise or prudent — **ad·vis·abil·i·ty** *n*

ad·vise *vb* : give advice to — **ad·vis·abil·i·ty** *n* — **ad·vis·able** *adj* — **ad·vis·er, ad·vis·or** *n* — **ad·vise·ment** *n*

ad·vi·so·ry *adj* : having power to advise

ad·vo·cate *n* : one who argues or pleads for a cause or proposal ∼ *vb* : recommend — **ad·vo·ca·cy** *n*

ae·gis *n* : protection or sponsorship

aer·ate *vb* : supply or impregnate with air — **aer·a·tion** *n* — **aer·a·tor** *n*

ae·ri·al *adj* : inhabiting, occurring in, or done in the air ∼ *n* : antenna

aer·o·bic *adj* : using or needing oxygen

aer·o·bics *n sing or pl* : exercises that produce a marked increase in respiration and heart rate

aero·dy·nam·ics *n* : science of bodies in motion in a gas — **aero·dy·nam·ic** *adj* — **aero·dy·nam·i·cal·ly** *adv*

aero·nau·tics *n* : science dealing with aircraft — **aero·nau·ti·cal** *adj*

aero·sol *n* **1** : liquid or solid particles suspended in a gas **2** : substance sprayed as an aerosol

aero·space *n* : earth's atmosphere and the space beyond — **aero·space** *adj*

aes·thet·ic *adj* : relating to beauty — **aes·thet·i·cal·ly** *adv* — **aes·thet·ics** *n*

af·fa·ble *adj* : easy to talk to — **af·fa·bil·i·ty** *n* — **af·fa·bly** *adv*

af·fair *n* : something that relates to or involves one

¹af·fect *vb* : assume for effect — **af·fec·ta·tion** *n*

²affect *vb* : produce an effect on

af·fect·ed *adj* **1** : pretending to some trait **2** : artificially assumed to impress — **af·fect·ed·ly** *adv*

af·fect·ing *adj* : arousing pity or sorrow — **af·fect·ing·ly** *adv*

af·fec·tion *n* : kind or loving feeling — **af·fec·tion·ate** *adj* — **af·fec·tion·ate·ly** *adv*

af·fi·da·vit *n* : sworn statement

af·fil·i·ate *vb* : become a member or branch — **af·fil·i·ate** *n* — **af·fil·i·a·tion** *n*

af·fin·i·ty *n* : close attraction or relationship

af·firm *vb* : assert positively — **af·fir·ma·tion** *n*

af·fir·ma·tive *adj* : asserting the truth or existence of something ∼ *n* : statement of affirmation or agreement

af·flict *vb* : cause pain and distress to — **af·flic·tion** *n*

af·flu·ence *n* : wealth — **af·flu·ent** *adj*

af·ford *vb* **1** : manage to bear the cost of **2** : provide

af·front *vb or n* : insult

af·ghan *n* : crocheted or knitted blanket

aflame *adj or adv* : flaming

afloat *adj or adv* : floating

afoot *adv or adj* **1** : on foot **2** : in progress

afraid *adj* : filled with fear

afresh *adv* : anew

af·ter *adv* : at a later time ∼ *prep* **1** : behind in place or time **2** : in pursuit of ∼ *conj* : following the time when ∼ *adj* **1** : later **2** : located toward the back

af·ter·life *n* : existence after death

af·ter·math *n* : results

af·ter·noon *n* : time between noon and evening

af·ter·thought *n* : later thought

af·ter·ward, af·ter·wards *adv* : at a later time

again *adv* **1** : once more **2** : on the other hand **3** : in addition

against *prep* **1** : directly opposite to **2** : in opposition to **3** : so as to touch or strike

ag·ate *n* : quartz with bands or masses of various colors

age *n* **1** : length of time of life or existence **2** : particular time in life (as majority or the latter part) **3** : quality of being old **4** : long time **5** : period in history ∼ *vb* : become old or mature — **age·less** *adj*

aged *adj* **1** : old **2** : allowed to mature

agen·da *n* : list of things to be done

agent *n* **1** : means **2** : person acting or doing business for another — **agen·cy** *n*

ag·gra·vate *vb* **1** : make more severe **2** : irritate — **ag·gra·va·tion** *n*

ag·gre·gate *adj* : formed into a mass ∼ *vb* : collect into a mass ∼ *n* **1** : mass **2** : whole amount

ag·gres·sion *n* **1** : unprovoked attack **2** : hostile behavior — **ag·gres·sor** *n* — **ag·gres·sive** *adj* — **ag·gres·sive·ly** *adv* — **ag·gres·sive·ness** *n*

ag·grieve *vb* **1** : cause grief to **2** : inflict injury on

ag·ile *adj* : able to move quickly and easily — **agil·i·ty** *n*

ag·i·tate *vb* **1** : shake or stir back and forth **2** : excite or trouble the mind of **3** : try to arouse public feeling — **ag·i·ta·tion** *n* — **ag·i·ta·tor** *n*

ag·nos·tic *n* : one who doubts the existence of God

ago *adj or adv* : earlier than the present

agog *adj* : full of excitement

ag·o·nize *vb* : suffer mental agony — **ag·o·niz·ing·ly** *adv* — **ag·o·ny** *n*

agree *vb* **1** : be of the same opinion **2** : express willingness **3** : get along together **4** : be similar **5** : be appropriate, suitable, or healthful — **agree·able** *adj* — **agree·able·ness** *n* — **agree·ably** *adv* — **agree·ment** *n*

ag·ri·cul·ture *n* : farming — **ag·ri·cul·tur·al** *adj* — **ag·ri·cul·tur·ist, ag·ri·cul·tur·al·ist** *n*

aground *adv or adj* : on or onto the bottom or shore

ahead *adv or adj* **1** : in or toward the front **2** : into or for the future **3** : in a more advantageous position

ahead of *prep* **1** : in front or advance of **2** : in excess of

aid *vb* : provide help or support ∼ *n* : help

aide *n* : helper

AIDS *n* : serious disease of the human immune system

ail *vb* **1** : trouble **2** : be ill — **ail·ment** *n*

aim *vb* **1** : point or direct (as a weapon) **2** : direct one's efforts ∼ *n* **1** : an aiming or the direction of aiming **2** : object or purpose — **aim·less** *adj* — **aim·less·ly** *adv* — **aim·less·ness** *n*

air *n* **1** : mixture of gases surrounding the earth **2** : melody **3** : outward appearance **4** : artificial manner **5 :** compressed air **6 :** travel by or use of aircraft **7 :** medium of transmission of radio waves ∼ *vb* **1 :** expose to the air **2 :** broadcast — **air·borne** *adj*

air–condition *vb* **:** equip with an apparatus (**air conditioner**) for filtering and cooling the air

air·craft *n* (**air·craft**) **:** craft that flies

air force *n* **:** military organization for conducting warfare by air

air·lift *n* **:** a transporting of esp. emergency supplies by aircraft — **air·lift** *vb*

air·line *n* **:** air transportation system — **air·lin·er** *n*

air·mail *n* **:** system of transporting mail by airplane — **air·mail** *vb*

air·plane *n* **:** fixed-wing aircraft heavier than air

air·port *n* **:** place for landing aircraft and usu. for receiving passengers

air·tight *adj* **:** tightly sealed to prevent flow of air

air·waves *n pl* **:** medium of transmission of radio waves

airy *adj* **1 :** delicate **2 :** breezy

aisle *n* **:** passage between sections or rows

ajar *adj or adv* **:** partly open

akin *adj* **1 :** related by blood **2 :** similar in kind

al·a·bas·ter *n* **:** white or translucent mineral

alac·ri·ty *n* **:** cheerful readiness

alarm *n* **1 :** warning signal or device **2 :** fear at sudden danger ∼ *vb* **1 :** warn **2 :** frighten

alas *interj* — used to express unhappiness, pity, or concern

al·be·it *conj* **:** even though

al·bum *n* **1 :** book for displaying a collection (as of photographs) **2 :** collection of recordings

al·bu·men *n* **1 :** white of an egg **2 :** albumin

al·bu·min *n* **:** protein found in blood, milk, egg white, and tissues

al·co·hol *n* **1 :** intoxicating agent in liquor **2 :** liquor — **al·co·hol·ic** *adj or n* — **al·co·hol·ism** *n*

al·cove *n* **:** recess in a room or wall

al·der·man *n* **:** city official

ale *n* **:** beerlike beverage — **ale·house** *n*

alert *adj* **1 :** watchful **2 :** quick to perceive and act ∼ *n* **:** alarm ∼ *vb* **:** warn — **alert·ly** *adv* — **alert·ness** *n*

al·fal·fa *n* **:** cloverlike forage plant

al·ga *n* **:** any of a group of lower plants that includes seaweed — **al·gal** *adj*

al·ge·bra *n* **:** branch of mathematics — **al·ge·bra·ic** *adj* — **al·ge·bra·i·cal·ly** *adv*

alias *adv* **:** otherwise called ∼ *n* **:** assumed name

al·i·bi *n* **1 :** defense of having been elsewhere when a crime was committed **2 :** justification ∼ *vb* **:** offer an excuse

alien *adj* **:** foreign ∼ *n* **1 :** foreign-born resident **2 :** extraterrestrial

alien·ate *vb* **:** cause to be no longer friendly — **alien·ation** *n*

align *vb* **:** bring into line — **align·er** *n* — **align·ment** *n*

alike *adj* **:** identical or very similar ∼ *adv* **:** equally

al·i·men·ta·ry *adj* **:** relating to or functioning in nutrition

al·i·mo·ny *n* **:** money paid to a separated or divorced spouse

alive *adj* **1 :** having life **2 :** lively or animated

al·ka·li *n* **:** strong chemical base — **al·ka·line** *adj* — **al·ka·lin·i·ty** *n*

all *adj* **1 :** the whole of **2 :** greatest possible **3 :** every one of ∼ *adv* **1 :** wholly **2 :** so much **3 :** for each side ∼ *pron* **1 :** whole number or amount **2 :** everything or everyone

Al·lah *n* **:** God of Islam

al·lay *vb* **1 :** alleviate **2 :** calm

al·lege *vb* **:** assert without proof — **al·le·ga·tion** *n* — **al·leg·ed·ly** *adv*

al·le·giance *n* **:** loyalty

al·le·go·ry *n* **:** story in which figures and actions are symbols of general truths — **al·le·gor·i·cal** *adj*

al·ler·gen *n* **:** something that causes allergy — **al·ler·gen·ic** *adj*

al·ler·gy *n* **:** abnormal reaction to a substance — **al·ler·gic** *adj* — **al·ler·gist** *n*

al·le·vi·ate *vb* **:** relieve or lessen — **al·le·vi·a·tion** *n*

al·ley *n* **1 :** place for bowling **2 :** narrow passage between buildings

al·li·ance *n* **:** association

al·li·ga·tor *n* **:** large aquatic reptile related to the crocodiles

al·lit·er·a·tion *n* **:** repetition of initial sounds of words — **al·lit·er·a·tive** *adj*

al·lo·cate *vb* **:** assign — **al·lo·ca·tion** *n*

al·lot *vb* **:** distribute as a share — **al·lot·ment** *n*

al·low *vb* **1 :** admit or concede **2 :** permit — **al·low·able** *adj*

al·low·ance *n* **1** : allotted share **2** : money given regularly for expenses

al·loy *n* : metals melted together — **al·loy** *vb*

all right *adv or adj* **1** : satisfactorily **2** : yes **3** : certainly

al·lude *vb* : refer indirectly — **al·lu·sion** *n* — **al·lu·sive** *adj*

al·lure *vb* : entice ∼ *n* : attractive power

al·ly *vb* : enter into an alliance — **al·ly** *n*

al·ma·nac *n* : annual information book

al·mighty *adj* : having absolute power

al·most *adv* : very nearly

alms *n* : charitable gift

aloft *adv* : high in the air

alone *adj* **1** : separated from others **2** : not including anyone or anything else — **alone** *adv*

along *prep* **1** : in line with the direction of **2** : at a point on or during ∼ *adv* **1** : forward **2** : as a companion

along·side *adv or prep* : along or by the side

alongside of *prep* : alongside

aloud *adv* : so as to be heard

al·pha·bet *n* : ordered set of letters of a language — **al·pha·bet·i·cal, al·pha·bet·ic** *adj* — **al·pha·bet·i·cal·ly** *adv*

al·pha·bet·ize *vb* : arrange in alphabetical order — **al·pha·bet·iz·er** *n*

al·ready *adv* : by a given time

al·so *adv* : in addition

al·tar *n* : structure for rituals

al·ter *vb* : make different — **alter·a·tion** *n*

al·ter·ca·tion *n* : dispute

al·ter·nate *adj* **1** : arranged or succeeding by turns **2** : every other ∼ *vb* : occur or cause to occur by turns ∼ *n* : substitute — **al·ter·nate·ly** *adv* — **al·ter·na·tion** *n*

al·ter·na·tive *adj* : offering a choice — **al·ter·na·tive** *n* — **al·ter·na·tive·ly** *adv*

al·though *conj* : even though

al·ti·tude *n* **1** : distance up from the ground **2** : angular distance above the horizon

al·to *n* : lower female choral voice

al·to·geth·er *adv* **1** : wholly **2** : on the whole

al·tru·ism *n* : concern for others — **al·tru·ist** *n* — **al·tru·is·tic** *adj* — **al·tru·is·ti·cal·ly** *adv*

alu·mi·num *n* : silver-white malleable ductile light metallic element

al·ways *adv* **1** : at all times **2** : forever

am *pres 1st sing of* BE

amal·gam *n* **1** : mercury alloy **2** : mixture

amass *vb* : gather

am·a·teur *n* **1** : person who does something for pleasure rather than for pay **2** : person who is not expert — **am·a·teur·ish** *adj* — **ama·teur·ism** *n*

am·a·to·ry *adj* : of or expressing sexual love

amaze *vb* : fill with wonder — **amaze·ment** *n* — **amaz·ing·ly** *adv*

am·a·zon *n* : tall strong woman — **am·a·zo·ni·an** *adj*

am·bas·sa·dor *n* : representative esp. of a government — **am·bas·sa·do·ri·al** *adj* — **am·bas·sa·dor·ship** *n*

am·ber *n* : yellowish fossil resin or its color

am·bi·dex·trous *adj* : equally skilled with both hands — **am·bi·dex·trous·ly** *adv*

am·bi·ence, am·bi·ance *n* : pervading atmosphere

am·big·u·ous *adj* : having more than one interpretation — **am·bi·gu·i·ty** *n*

am·bi·tion *n* : eager desire for success or power — **am·bi·tious** *adj* — **am·bi·tious·ly** *adv*

am·ble *vb* : go at a leisurely gait — **am·ble** *n*

am·bu·lance *n* : vehicle for carrying injured or sick persons

am·bu·la·to·ry *adj* **1** : relating to or adapted to walking **2** : able to walk about

am·bush *n* : trap by which a surprise attack is made from a place of hiding — **am·bush** *vb*

amen *interj* — used for affirmation esp. at the end of prayers

ame·na·ble *adj* : ready to yield or be influenced

amend *vb* **1** : improve **2** : alter in writing — **amend·ment** *n*

amends *n sing or pl* : compensation for injury or loss

ame·ni·ty *n* **1** : agreeableness **2** *pl* : social conventions **3** : something serving to comfort or accommodate

ami·a·ble *adj* : easy to get along with — **ami·a·bil·i·ty** *n* — **ami·a·bly** *adv*

am·i·ca·ble *adj* : friendly — **am·i·ca·bly** *adv*

amino acid *n* : nitrogen-containing acid

am·mo·nia *n* **1** : colorless gaseous compound of nitrogen and hydrogen **2** : solution of ammonia in water

am·mu·ni·tion *n* **1** : projectiles fired from guns **2** : explosive items used in war

am·ne·sia *n* : sudden loss of memory — **am·ne·si·ac, am·ne·sic** *adj or n*

am·nes·ty *n* : a pardon for a group — **am·nes·ty** *vb*

amoe·ba *n* : tiny one-celled animal that occurs esp. in water — **amoe·bic** *adj*

amok *adv* : in a violent or uncontrolled way

among *prep* **1** : in or through **2** : in the number or class of **3** : in shares to each of

am·o·rous *adj* **1** : inclined to love **2** : being in love **3** : indicative of love — **am·o·rous·ly** *adv* — **am·o·rous·ness** *n*

am·or·tize *vb* : get rid of (as a debt) gradually with periodic payments — **amor·ti·za·tion** *n*

amount *vb* **1** : be equivalent **2** : reach a total $\sim$ *n* : total number or quantity

am·per·sand *n* : character & used for the word *and*

am·phib·i·ous *adj* **1** : able to live both on land and in water **2** : adapted for both land and water — **am·phib·i·an** *n*

am·phi·the·ater *n* : oval or circular structure with rising tiers of seats around an arena

am·ple *adj* **1** : large **2** : sufficient — **am·ply** *adv*

am·pli·fy *vb* : make louder, stronger, or more thorough — **am·pli·fi·ca·tion** *n* — **am·pli·fi·er** *n*

am·pli·tude *n* **1** : fullness **2** : extent of a vibratory movement

am·pu·tate *vb* : cut off (a body part) — **am·pu·ta·tion** *n* — **am·pu·tee** *n*

am·u·let *n* : ornament worn as a charm against evil

amuse *vb* **1** : engage the attention of in an interesting and pleasant way **2** : make laugh — **amuse·ment** *n*

an *indefinite article* : a — used before words beginning with a vowel sound

anach·ro·nism *n* : one that is chronologically out of place — **anach·ro·nis·tic** *adj*

ana·gram *n* : word or phrase made by transposing the letters of another word or phrase

anal *adj* : relating to the anus

an·al·ge·sic *n* : pain reliever

anal·o·gy *n* **1** : similarity between unlike things **2** : example of something similar — **an·a·log·i·cal** *adj* — **an·a·log·i·cal·ly** *adv* — **anal·o·gous** *adj*

anal·y·sis *n* **1** : examination of a thing to determine its parts **2** : a method of treatment of psychological problems — **an·a·lyst** *n* — **an·a·lyt·ic, an·a·lyt·i·cal** *adj* — **an·a·lyt·i·cal·ly** *adv*

an·a·lyze *vb* : make an analysis of

an·ar·chism *n* : theory that all government is undesirable — **an·ar·chist** *n or adj* — **an·ar·chis·tic** *adj*

an·ar·chy *n* : lack of government or order — **an·ar·chic** *adj* — **an·ar·chi·cal·ly** *adv* — **an-**

ar·chism *n* — **an·ar·chist** *n or adj* — **an·ar·chis·tic** *adj*

anath·e·ma *n* **1** : solemn curse **2** : person or thing accursed or intensely disliked

anat·o·my *n* : science dealing with the structure of organisms — **an·a·tom·ic, an·a·tom·i·cal** *adj* — **an·a·tom·i·cal·ly** *adv* — **anat·o·mist** *n*

an·ces·tor *n* : one from whom an individual is descended

an·ces·try *n* **1** : line of descent **2** : ancestors — **an·ces·tral** *adj*

an·chor *n* **1** : heavy device that catches in the sea bottom to hold a ship in place **2** : anchorperson $\sim$ *vb* : hold or become held in place by or as if by an anchor — **an·chor·age** *n*

an·chor·per·son *n* : news broadcast coordinator

an·cho·vy *n* : small herringlike fish

an·cient *adj* **1** : having existed for many years **2** : belonging to times long past — **an·cient** *n*

and *conj* — used to indicate connection or addition

an·drog·y·nous *adj* **1** : having characteristics of both male and female **2** : suitable for either sex

an·ec·dote *n* : brief story — **an·ec·dot·al** *adj*

ane·mia *n* : blood deficiency — **ane·mic** *adj*

an·es·the·sia *n* : loss of bodily sensation

an·es·thet·ic *n* : agent that produces anesthesia — **an·es·thet·ic** *adj* — **anes·the·tist** *n* — **anes·the·tize** *vb*

an·eu·rysm, an·eu·rism blood-filled bulge of a blood vessel

anew *adv* : over again

an·gel *n* : spiritual being superior to humans — **an·gel·ic, an·gel·i·cal** *adj* — **an·gel·i·cal·ly** *adv*

an·ger *n* : strong feeling of displeasure $\sim$ *vb* : make angry

an·gi·na *n* : painful disorder of heart muscles — **an·gi·nal** *adj*

¹an·gle *n* **1** : figure formed by the meeting of 2 lines in a point **2** : sharp corner **3** : point of view $\sim$ *vb* : turn or direct at an angle

²angle *vb* : fish with a hook and line — **an·gler** *n* — **an·gle·worm** *n* — **an·gling** *n*

an·go·ra *n* : yarn or cloth made from the hair of an Angora goat or rabbit

an·gry *adj* : feeling or showing anger — **an·gri·ly** *adv*

an·guish *n* : extreme pain or distress of mind — **an·guished** *adj*

an·gu·lar *adj* **1** : having many or sharp angles **2** : thin and bony — **an·gu·lar·i·ty** *n*

an·i·mal *n* **1** : living being capable of feeling and voluntary motion **2** : lower animal as distinguished from humans

an·i·mate *adj* : having life ∼ *vb* **1** : give life or vigor to **2** : make appear to move — **an·i·mat·ed** *adj*

an·i·ma·tion *n* **1** : liveliness **2** : animated cartoon

an·i·ma·tron·ic : relating to an electrically animated mechanical figure

an·i·mus *n* : deep-seated hostility — **an·i·mos·i·ty** *n*

an·ise *n* : herb related to the carrot with aromatic seeds (**ani·seed**) used in flavoring

an·kle *n* : joint or region between the foot and the leg — **an·kle·bone** *n*

an·nals *n pl* : chronological record of history — **an·nal·ist** *n*

an·nex *vb* : assume political control over (a territory) ∼ *n* : added building — **an·nex·a·tion** *n*

an·ni·hi·late *vb* : destroy — **an·ni·hi·la·tion** *n*

an·ni·ver·sa·ry *n* : annual return of the date of a notable event or its celebration

an·no·tate *vb* : furnish with notes — **an·no·ta·tion** *n* — **an·no·ta·tor** *n*

an·nounce *vb* : make known publicly — **an·nounce·ment** *n* — **an·nounc·er** *n*

an·noy *vb* : disturb or irritate — **an·noy·ance** *n* — **an·noy·ing·ly** *adv*

an·nu·al *adj* **1** : occurring once a year **2** : living only one year — **an·nu·al** *n* — **an·nu·al·ly** *adv*

an·nu·i·ty *n* : amount payable annually or the right to such a payment

an·nul *vb* : make legally void — **an·nul·ment** *n*

anom·a·ly *n* : something abnormal or unusual — **anom·a·lous** *adj*

anon·y·mous *adj* : of unknown origin — **anon·ym·i·ty** *n* — **anon·y·mous·ly** *adv*

an·oth·er *adj* **1** : any or some other **2** : one more ∼ *pron* **1** : one more **2** : one different

an·swer *n* **1** : something spoken or written in reply to a question **2** : solution to a problem ∼ *vb* **1** : reply to **2** : be responsible **3** : be adequate — **an·swer·er** *n* — **an·swer·able** *adj*

ant *n* : small social insect — **ant·hill** *n*

ant·ac·id : agent that counteracts acidity

an·tag·o·nize *vb* : cause to be hostile — **an·tag·o·nism** *n* — **an·tag·o·nist** *n* — **an·tag·o·nis·tic** *adj*

ant·arc·tic *adj, often cap* : relating to the region near the south pole

an·te·ced·ent *n* : one that comes before — **an·te·ced·ent** *adj*

an·te·lope *n* : deerlike mammal related to the ox

an·ten·na *n* **1** *pl* **an·ten·nae** : one of the long slender paired sensory organs on the head of an arthropod **2** *pl* **an·ten·nas** : metallic device for sending or receiving radio waves

an·them *n* : song or hymn of praise or gladness

an·thol·o·gy *n* : literary collection

an·thro·poid *n* : large ape — **an·thro·poid** *adj*

an·thro·pol·o·gy *n* : science dealing with humans — **an·thro·po·log·i·cal** *adj* — **an·thro·pol·o·gist** *n*

an·ti·bi·ot·ic *n* : substance that inhibits harmful microorganisms — **an·ti·bi·ot·ic** *adj*

an·ti·body *n* : bodily substance that counteracts the effects of a foreign substance or organism

an·tic *n* : playful act ∼ *adj* : playful

an·tic·i·pate *vb* **1** : be prepared for **2** : look forward to — **an·tic·i·pa·tion** *n* — **an·tic·i·pa·to·ry** *adj*

an·ti·dote *n* : remedy for poison

an·ti·his·ta·mine : drug for treating allergies and colds

an·tip·a·thy *n* : strong dislike

an·ti·quat·ed *adj* : out-of-date — **an·ti·quar·i·an** *n*

an·tique *adj* : very old or out-of-date — **an·tique** *n*

an·tiq·ui·ty *n* **1** : ancient times **2** *pl* : relics of ancient times

an·ti·sep·tic *adj* : killing or checking the growth of germs — **an·ti·sep·tic** *n* — **an·ti·sep·ti·cal·ly** *adv*

ant·ler *n* : solid branched horn of a deer — **ant·lered** *adj*

ant·onym *n* : word of opposite meaning

anus *n* : the rear opening of the alimentary canal

an·vil *n* : heavy iron block on which metal is shaped

anx·ious *adj* **1** : uneasy **2** : earnestly wishing — **anx·ious·ly** *adv* — **anx·i·ety** *n*

any *adj* **1** : one chosen at random **2** : of whatever number or quantity ∼ *pron* **1** : any one or ones **2** : any amount ∼ *adv* : to any extent or degree

any·body *pron* : anyone

any·how *adv* **1** : in any way **2** : nevertheless

any·more *adv* : at the present time

any·one *pron* : any person

any·place *adv* : anywhere

any·thing *pron* : any thing whatever

any·time *adv* : at any time whatever

any·way *adv* : anyhow

any·where *adv* : in or to any place

aor·ta *n* : main artery from the heart — **aor·tic** *adj*

apart *adv* **1** : separately in place or time **2** : aside **3** : to pieces

apart·ment *n* : set of usu. rented rooms

ap·a·thy *n* : lack of emotion or interest — **ap·a·thet·ic** *adj* — **ap·a·thet·i·cal·ly** *adv*

ape *n* : large tailless primate ∼ *vb* : imitate

apex *n* : highest point

aphid *n* : small insect that sucks plant juices

aph·ro·di·si·ac *n* : substance that excites sexual desire

apiece *adv* : for each one

apol·o·gize *vb* : make an apology — **apol·o·get·ic** *adj* — **apol·o·get·i·cal·ly** *adv* — **apol·o·gist** *n*

apol·o·gy *n* **1** : formal justification **2** : expression of regret for a wrong

apos·tle *n* : disciple or advocate — **apos·tle·ship** *n* — **ap·os·tolic** *adj*

apos·tro·phe *n* : punctuation mark ' to indicate the possessive case or the omission of a letter or figure

apoth·e·cary *n* : druggist

ap·pall *vb* : fill with horror or dismay

ap·pa·ra·tus *n* **1** : equipment **2** : complex machine or device

ap·par·el *n* : clothing

ap·par·ent *adj* **1** : visible **2** : obvious **3** : having the appearance of being — **ap·par·ent·ly** *adv*

ap·peal *vb* **1** : try to have a court case reheard **2** : ask earnestly **3** : have an attraction — **ap·peal** *n*

ap·pear *vb* **1** : become visible or evident **2** : come into the presence of someone **3** : seem — **ap·pear·ance** *n*

ap·pease *vb* : pacify with concessions — **ap·pease·ment** *n*

ap·pen·dec·to·my *n* : surgical removal of the appendix

ap·pen·di·ci·tis *n* : inflammation of the appendix

ap·pen·dix *n* **1** : supplementary matter **2** : narrow closed tube extending from lower right intestine

ap·pe·tite *n* **1** : natural desire esp. for food **2** : preference

ap·pe·tiz·er *n* : food or drink to stimulate the appetite — **ap·pe·tiz·ing** *adj* — **ap·pe·tiz·ing·ly** *adv*

ap·plaud *vb* : show approval esp. by clapping

ap·plause *n* : a clapping in approval

ap·ple *n* : rounded fruit with firm white flesh

ap·pli·ance *n* : household machine or device

ap·ply *vb* **1** : place in contact **2** : put to practical use **3** : devote (one's) attention or efforts to something **4** : submit a request **5** : have reference or a connection — **ap·pli·ca·ble** *adj* — **ap·pli·ca·bil·i·ty** *n* — **ap·pli·cant** *n* — **ap·pli·ca·tion** *n* — **ap·pli·ca·tor** *n*

ap·point *vb* **1** : set or assign officially **2** : equip or furnish — **ap·poin·tee** *n* — **ap·point·ment** *n*

ap·praise *vb* : set value on — **ap·prais·al** *n* — **ap·prais·er** *n*

ap·pre·ci·ate *vb* **1** : value justly **2** : be grateful for **3** : increase in value — **ap·pre·cia·ble** *adj* — **ap·pre·cia·bly** *adv* — **ap·pre·cia·tion** *n* — **ap·pre·cia·tive** *adj*

ap·pre·hen·sive *adj* : fearful — **ap·pre·hen·sive·ly** *adv* — **ap·pre·hen·sive·ness** *n*

ap·pren·tice *n* : person learning a craft ∼ *vb* : employ or work as an apprentice — **ap·pren·tice·ship** *n*

ap·proach *vb* **1** : move nearer or be close to **2** : make initial advances or efforts toward — **ap·proach** *n* — **ap·proach·able** *adj*

ap·pro·pri·ate *vb* **1** : take possession of **2** : set apart for a particular use ∼ *adj* : suitable — **ap·pro·pri·ate·ly** *adv* — **ap·pro·pri·ate·ness** *n* — **ap·pro·pria·tion** *n*

ap·prove *vb* : accept as satisfactory — **ap·prov·al** *n*

ap·prox·i·mate *adj* : nearly correct or exact ∼ *vb* : come near — **ap·prox·i·mate·ly** *adv* — **ap·prox·i·ma·tion** *n*

April *n* : 4th month of the year having 30 days

apron *n* : protective garment

apropos of *prep* : with regard to

apt *adj* **1** : suitable **2** : likely **3** : quick to learn — **apt·ly** *adv* — **apt·ness** *n*

ap·ti·tude *n* **1** : capacity for learning **2** : natural ability

aquar·i·um *n* : glass container for aquatic animals and plants

aquat·ic *adj* : of or relating to water — **aquat·ic** *n*

aq·ue·duct *n* : conduit for carrying running water

ar·bi·trary *adj* 1 : selected at random 2 : autocratic — **ar·bi·trari·ly** *adv* — **ar·bi·trari·ness** *n*

ar·bi·trate *vb* : settle a dispute as arbitrator — **ar·bi·tra·tion** *n*

ar·bi·tra·tor *n* : one chosen to settle a dispute

ar·bor *n* : shelter under branches or vines — **ar·bo·re·al** *adj*

arc *n* 1 : part of a circle 2 : bright sustained electrical discharge ∼ *vb* : form an arc

ar·cade *n* : arched passageway between shops

¹arch *n* : curved structure spanning an opening ∼ *vb* : cover with or form into an arch

²arch *adj* 1 : chief — usu. in combination 2 : mischievous — **arch·ly** *adv* — **arch·ness** *n*

ar·chae·ol·o·gy, **ar·che·ol·o·gy** *n* : study of past human life — **ar·chae·o·log·i·cal** *adj* — **ar·chae·ol·o·gist** *n*

ar·cha·ic *adj* : belonging to an earlier time — **ar·cha·i·cal·ly** *adv*

arch·an·gel *n* : angel of high rank

arch·bish·op *n* : chief bishop — **arch·bish·op·ric** *n*

arch·di·o·cese *n* : diocese of an archbishop

ar·chery *n* : shooting with bow and arrows — **ar·cher** *n*

ar·chi·pel·a·go *n* : group of islands

ar·chi·tec·ture *n* 1 : building design 2 : style of building 3 : manner of organizing elements — **ar·chi·tect** *n* — **ar·chi·tec·tur·al** *adj* — **ar·chi·tec·tur·al·ly** *adv*

ar·chives *n pl* : public records or their storage place — **archi·vist** *n*

arch·way *n* : passageway under an arch

arc·tic *adj* 1 : relating to the region near the north pole 2 : frigid

ar·dent *adj* : characterized by warmth of feeling — **ar·dent·ly** *adv*

ar·dor *n* : warmth of feeling

ar·du·ous *adj* : difficult — **ar·du·ous·ly** *adv* — **ar·du·ous·ness** *n*

are *pres 2d sing or pres pl of* BE

ar·ea *n* 1 : space for something 2 : amount of surface included 3 : region 4 : range covered by a thing or concept

area code *n* : 3-digit area-identifying telephone number

are·na *n* 1 : enclosed exhibition area 2 : sphere of activity

ar·gue *vb* 1 : give reasons for or against something 2 : disagree in words — **argu·able** *adj* — **ar·gu·ment** *n* — **ar·gu·men·ta·tive** *adj*

ar·id *adj* : very dry — **arid·i·ty** *n*

arise *vb* arose; aris·en 1 : get up 2 : originate

ar·is·toc·ra·cy *n* : upper class — **aris·to·crat** *n* — **aris·to·crat·ic** *adj*

arith·me·tic *n* : mathematics that deals with numbers — **ar·ith·met·ic, ar·ith·met·i·cal** *adj*

ark *n* : big boat

¹arm *n* 1 : upper limb 2 : branch — **armed** *adj* — **arm·less** *adj*

²arm *vb* : furnish with weapons ∼ *n* 1 : weapon 2 : branch of the military forces 3 *pl* : family's heraldic designs

armed forces *n pl* : military

ar·mor *n* : protective covering — **ar·mored** *adj*

ar·mory *n* : factory or storehouse for arms

arm·pit *n* : hollow under the junction of the arm and shoulder

ar·my *n* 1 : body of men organized for war esp. on land 2 : great number

aro·ma *n* : usu. pleasing odor — **ar·o·mat·ic** *adj*

around *adv* 1 : in or along a circuit 2 : on all sides 3 : near 4 : in an opposite direction ∼ *prep* 1 : surrounding 2 : along the circuit of 3 : to or on the other side of 4 : near

arouse *vb* 1 : awaken from sleep 2 : stir up — **arous·al** *n*

ar·raign *vb* 1 : call before a court to answer to an indictment 2 : accuse — **ar·raign·ment** *n*

ar·range *vb* 1 : put in order 2 : settle or agree on 3 : adapt (a musical composition) for voices or instruments — **ar·range·ment** *n* — **ar·rang·er** *n*

ar·ray *vb* 1 : arrange in order 2 : dress esp. splendidly ∼ *n* 1 : arrangement 2 : rich clothing 3 : imposing group

ar·rest *vb* 1 : stop 2 : take into legal custody — **ar·rest** *n*

ar·rive *vb* 1 : reach a destination, point, or stage 2 : come near in time — **ar·riv·al** *n*

ar·ro·gant *adj* : showing an offensive sense of superiority — **ar·ro·gance** *n* — **ar·ro·gant·ly** *adv*

ar·ro·gate *vb* : to claim without justification

ar·row *n* : slender missile shot from a bow — **ar·row·head** *n*

ar·se·nic *n* : solid grayish poisonous chemical element

ar·son *n* : willful or malicious burning of property — **ar·son·ist** *n*

art *n* **1** : skill **2** : branch of learning **3** : creation of things of beauty or works so produced **4** : ingenuity — **art·ful** *adj* — **art·ful·ly** *adv* — **art·ful·ness** *n* — **art·less** *adj* — **art·less·ly** *adv* — **art·less·ness** *n* — **art·ist** *n* — **ar·tis·tic** *adj* — **ar·tis·ti·cal·ly** *adv* — **ar·tis·try** *n*

ar·te·rio·scle·ro·sis *n* : hardening of the arteries — **ar·te·rio·scle·rot·ic** *adj or n*

ar·tery *n* **1** : tubular vessel carrying blood from the heart **2** : thoroughfare — **ar·te·ri·al** *adj*

ar·thri·tis *n* : inflammation of the joints — **ar·thrit·ic** *adj or n*

ar·ti·cle *n* **1** : distinct part of a written document **2** : nonfictional published piece of writing **3** : word (as *an, the*) used to limit a noun **4** : item or piece

ar·tic·u·late *adj* : able to speak effectively ⁓ *vb* **1** : utter distinctly **2** : unite by joints — **ar·tic·u·late·ly** *adv* — **ar·tic·u·late·ness** *n* — **ar·tic·u·la·tion** *n*

ar·ti·fi·cial *adj* **1** : man-made **2** : not genuine — **ar·ti·fi·ci·al·i·ty** *n* — **ar·ti·fi·cial·ly** *adv* — **ar·ti·fi·cial·ness** *n*

ar·til·lery *n* : large-caliber firearms

ar·ti·san *n* : skilled craftsman

arty *adj* : pretentiously artistic — **art·i·ly** *adv* — **art·i·ness** *n*

as *adv* **1** : to the same degree **2** : for example ⁓ *conj* **1** : in the same way or degree as **2** : while **3** : because **4** : though ⁓ *pron* — used after *same* or *such* ⁓ *prep* : in the capacity of

as·bes·tos *n* : fibrous incombustible mineral

as·cen·dant *n* : dominant position ⁓ *adj* **1** : moving upward **2** : dominant — **as·cen·dan·cy** *n*

as·cent *n* **1** : act of moving upward **2** : degree of upward slope

as·cribe *vb* : attribute — **as·crib·able** *adj* — **as·crip·tion** *n*

¹ash *n* : tree related to the olives

²ash *n* : matter left when something is burned — **ash·tray** *n*

ashamed *adj* : feeling shame — **asham·ed·ly** *adv*

ash·en *adj* : deadly pale

ashore *adv* : on or to the shore

aside *adv* **1** : toward the side **2** : out of the way

aside from *prep* **1** : besides **2** : except for

as·i·nine *adj* : foolish — **as·i·nin·i·ty** *n*

ask *vb* **1** : call on for an answer or help **2** : utter (a question or request) **3** : invite

askance *adv* **1** : with a side glance **2** : with lack of trust

askew *adv or adj* : out of line

asleep *adv or adj* **1** : sleeping **2** : numbed **3** : inactive

as of *prep* : from the time of

as·par·a·gus *n* : tall herb related to the lilies or its edible stalks

as·pect *n* **1** : way something looks to the eye or mind **2** : phase

as·phalt *n* : dark tarlike substance used in paving

as·phyx·i·ate *vb* : suffocate — **as·phyx·ia** *n* — **as·phyx·i·a·tion** *n*

as·pire *vb* : have an ambition — **as·pir·ant** *n* — **as·pi·ra·tion** *n*

as·pi·rin *n* : pain reliever

ass *n* **1** : long-eared animal related to the horse **2** : stupid person

as·sail *vb* : attack violently — **as·sail·able** *adj* — **as·sail·ant** *n*

as·sas·si·nate *vb* : murder esp. for political reasons — **as·sas·sin** *n* — **as·sas·si·na·tion** *n*

as·sault *n or vb* : attack

as·say *n* : analysis (as of an ore) to determine quality or properties — **as·say** *vb*

as·sem·ble *vb* **1** : collect into one place **2** : fit together the parts of

as·sem·bly *n* **1** : meeting **2** *cap* : legislative body **3** : a fitting together of parts — **as·sem·bly·man** *n* — **as·sem·bly·wom·an** *n*

as·sent *vb or n* : consent

as·sert *vb* **1** : declare **2** : defend — **as·ser·tion** *n* — **as·sert·ive** *adj* — **as·sert·ive·ness** *n*

as·sess *vb* **1** : impose (as a tax) **2** : evaluate for taxation — **as·sess·ment** *n* — **as·ses·sor** *n*

as·set *n* **1** *pl* : individually owned property **2** : advantage or resource

as·sid·u·ous *adj* : diligent — **as·si·du·i·ty** *n* — **as·sid·u·ous·ly** *adv* — **as·sid·u·ous·ness** *n*

as·sign *vb* **1** : transfer to another **2** : appoint to a duty **3** : designate as a task **4** : attribute — **as·sign·able** *adj* — **as·sign·ment** *n*

as·sist *vb* : help — **as·sist** *n* — **as·sis·tance** *n* — **as·sis·tant** *n*

as·so·ci·ate *vb* **1** : join in companionship or partnership **2** : connect in thought — **as·so·ci·ate** *n* — **as·so·ci·a·tion** *n*

as·sort·ed *adj* : consisting of various kinds

as·sort·ment *n* : assorted collection

as·sume *vb* **1** : take upon oneself **2** : pretend to have or be **3** : take as true — **as·sump·tion** *n*

as·sure *vb* **1** : give confidence or conviction to **2** : guarantee — **as·sur·ance** *n*

as·ter·isk *n* : a character * used as a reference mark or as an indication of omission of words

as·ter·oid *n* : small planet between Mars and Jupiter

asth·ma *n* : disorder marked by difficulty in breathing — **asth·mat·ic** *adj or n*

astig·ma·tism *n* : visual defect — **as·tig·mat·ic** *adj*

as·ton·ish *vb* : amaze — **as·ton·ish·ing·ly** *adv* — **as·ton·ish·ment** *n*

as·tound *vb* : fill with confused wonder — **as·tound·ing·ly** *adv*

astray *adv or adj* : off the right path

astride *adv* : with legs apart or one on each side ∼ *prep* : with one leg on each side of

as·trin·gent *adj* : causing shrinking or puckering of tissues — **as·trin·gen·cy** *n* — **as·trin·gent** *n*

as·trol·o·gy *n* : prediction of events by the stars — **as·trol·o·ger** *n* — **as·tro·log·i·cal** *adj*

as·tro·nau·tics *n* : construction and operation of spacecraft — **as·tro·naut** *n* — **as·tro·nau·tic, as·tro·nau·ti·cal** *adj*

as·tro·nom·i·cal *adj* **1** : relating to astronomy **2** : extremely large

as·tron·o·my *n* : study of the celestial bodies — **as·tron·o·mer** *n*

as·tute *adj* : shrewd — **as·tute·ly** *adv* — **as·tute·ness** *n*

asy·lum *n* **1** : refuge **2** : institution for care esp. of the insane

at *prep* **1** — used to indicate a point in time or space **2** — used to indicate a goal **3** — used to indicate condition, means, cause, or manner

ate *past of* EAT

athe·ist *n* : one who denies the existence of God — **athe·ism** *n* — **athe·is·tic** *adj*

ath·lete *n* : one trained to compete in athletics

ath·let·ics *n sing or pl* : exercises and games requiring physical skill — **ath·let·ic** *adj*

atlas *n* : book of maps

ATM *n* : computerized machine for performing basic bank functions

at·mo·sphere *n* **1** : mass of air surrounding the earth **2** : surrounding influence — **at·mo·spher·ic** *adj* — **at·mo·spher·i·cal·ly** *adv*

at·om *n* **1** : tiny bit **2** : smallest particle of a chemical element that can exist alone or in combination

atom·ic *adj* **1** : relating to atoms **2** : nuclear

at·om·iz·er *n* : device for dispersing a liquid as a very fine spray

atone *vb* : make amends — **atone·ment** *n*

atop *prep* : on top of ∼ *adv or adj* : on, to, or at the top

atri·um *n* **1** : open central room or court **2** : heart chamber that receives blood from the veins

atro·cious *adj* : appalling or abominable — **atro·cious·ly** *adv* — **atro·cious·ness** *n* — **atroc·i·ty** *n*

at·ro·phy *n* : wasting away of a bodily part or tissue — **at·ro·phy** *vb*

at·tach *vb* **1** : seize legally **2** : bind by personalities **3** : join — **at·tach·ment** *n*

at·ta·ché *n* : technical expert on a diplomatic staff

at·tack *vb* **1** : try to hurt or destroy with violence or words **2** : set to work on ∼ *n* **1** : act of attacking **2** : fit of sickness

at·tain *vb* **1** : achieve or accomplish **2** : reach — **at·tain·abil·i·ty** *n* — **at·tain·able** *adj* — **at·tain·ment** *n*

at·tempt *vb* : make an effort toward — **attempt** *n*

at·tend *vb* **1** : handle or provide for the care of something **2** : accompany **3** : be present at **4** : pay attention — **at·ten·dance** *n* — **at·ten·dant** *adj or n*

at·ten·tion *n* **1** : concentration of the mind on something **2** : notice or awareness — **at·ten·tive** *adj* — **at·ten·tive·ly** *adv* — **at·ten·tive·ness** *n*

at·test *vb* : certify or bear witness — **at·tes·ta·tion** *n*

at·tic *n* : space just below the roof

at·tire *vb* : dress — **at·tire** *n*

at·ti·tude *n* **1** : posture or relative position **2** : feeling, opinion, or mood

at·tor·ney *n* : legal agent

at·tract *vb* **1** : draw to oneself **2** : have emotional or aesthetic appeal for — **at·trac·tion** *n* — **at·trac·tive** *adj* — **at·trac·tive·ly** *adv* — **at·trac·tive·ness** *n*

at·tri·bute *n* : inherent characteristic ∼ *vb* **1** : regard as having a specific cause or origin **2**

20

: regard as a characteristic — **at·trib·ut·able** *adj* — **at·tri·bu·tion** *n*

auc·tion *n* : public sale of property to the highest bidder — **auc·tion** *vb* — **auc·tion·eer** *n*

au·dac·i·ty *n* : boldness or insolence — **au·da·cious** *adj*

au·di·ble *adj* : capable of being heard — **au·di·bly** *adv*

au·di·ence *n* **1** : formal interview **2** : group of listeners or spectators

au·dio *adj* : relating to sound or its reproduction ∼ *n* : television sound — **au·dio·vi·su·al** *adj*

au·dit *vb* : examine financial accounts — **au·dit** *n* — **au·di·tor** *n*

au·di·tion *n* : tryout performance — **au·di·tion** *vb*

au·di·to·ri·um *n* : room or building used for public performances

au·di·to·ry *adj* : relating to hearing

au·ger *n* : tool for boring

aug·ment *vb* : enlarge or increase — **aug·men·ta·tion** *n*

au·gur *n* : prophet ∼ *vb* : predict — **au·gu·ry** *n*

Au·gust *n* : 8th month of the year having 31 days

aunt *n* **1** : sister of one's father or mother **2** : wife of one's uncle

au·ra *n* **1** : distinctive atmosphere **2** : luminous radiation

au·ral *adj* : relating to the ear or to hearing

au·ro·ra bo·re·al·is *n* : display of light in the night sky of northern latitudes

aus·pic·es *n pl* : patronage and protection

aus·pi·cious *adj* : favorable

aus·tere *adj* : severe — **aus·tere·ly** *adv* — **aus·ter·i·ty** *n*

au·then·tic *adj* : genuine — **au·then·ti·cal·ly** *adv* — **au·then·tic·i·ty** *n*

au·then·ti·cate *vb* : prove genuine — **au·then·ti·ca·tion** *n*

au·thor *n* **1** : writer **2** : creator — **au·thor·ship** *n*

au·thor·i·tar·i·an *adj* : marked by blind obedience to authority

au·thor·i·ta·tive *adj* : being an authority — **au·thor·i·ta·tive·ly** *adv* — **au·thor·i·ta·tive·ness** *n*

au·thor·i·ty *n* **1** : expert **2** : right, responsibility, or power to influence **3** *pl* : persons in official positions

au·tho·rize *vb* : permit or give official approval for — **au·tho·ri·za·tion** *n*

au·tism *n* : mental disorder marked by impaired ability to communicate and form social relationships and by repetitive behavior patterns

au·to *n* : automobile

au·to·bi·og·ra·phy *n* : writer's own life story — **au·to·bi·og·ra·pher** *n* — **au·to·bio·graph·i·cal** *adj*

au·toc·ra·cy *n* : government by one person having unlimited power — **au·to·crat** *n* — **au·to·crat·ic** *adj* — **au·to·crat·i·cal·ly** *adv*

au·to·graph *n* : signature ∼ *vb* : write one's name on

au·to·mate *vb* : make automatic — **au·to·ma·tion** *n*

au·to·mat·ic *adj* **1** : involuntary **2** : designed to function without human intervention ∼ *n* : automatic device (as a firearm) — **au·to·mat·i·cal·ly** *adv*

au·to·mo·bile *n* : 4-wheeled passenger vehicle with its own power source

au·to·mo·tive *adj* : relating to automobiles

au·ton·o·mous *adj* : having independent existence or function — **au·ton·o·mous·ly** *adv* — **au·ton·o·my** *n*

au·top·sy *n* : medical examination of a corpse

au·tumn *n* : season between summer and winter — **au·tum·nal** *adj*

aux·il·ia·ry *adj* **1** : being a supplement or reserve **2** : accompanying a main verb form to express person, number, mood, or tense — **aux·il·ia·ry** *n*

avail·able *adj* **1** : usable **2** : accessible — **avail·abil·i·ty** *n*

av·a·lanche *n* : mass of sliding or falling snow or rock

avenge *vb* : take vengeance for — **aveng·er** *n*

av·e·nue *n* **1** : way of approach **2** : broad street

av·er·age *adj* **1** : being about midway between extremes **2** : ordinary ∼ *vb* **1** : be usually **2** : find the mean of ∼ *n* : mean

averse *adj* : feeling dislike or reluctance — **aver·sion** *n*

avert *vb* : turn away

avi·a·tion *n* : operation or manufacture of airplanes — **avi·a·tor** *n*

av·id *adj* **1** : greedy **2** : enthusiastic — **avid·i·ty** *n* — **av·id·ly** *adv*

av·o·ca·do *n* : tropical fruit with green pulp

av·o·ca·tion *n* : hobby

avoid *vb* **1** : keep away from **2** : prevent the occurrence of **3** : refrain from — **avoid·able** *adj* — **avoid·ance** *n*

av·oir·du·pois *n* : system of weight based on the pound of 16 ounces

await *vb* : wait for

awake *vb* (**awoke; awok·en**) : wake up — **awake** *adj*

awak·en *vb* : wake up

award *vb* : give (something won or deserved) ～ *n* **1** : judgment **2** : prize

aware *adj* : having realization or consciousness — **aware·ness** *n*

away *adv* **1** : from this or that place or time **2** : out of the way **3** : in another direction **4** : from one's possession ～ *adj* **1** : absent **2** : distant

awe *n* : respectful fear or wonder ～ *vb* : fill with awe — **awe·some** *adj* — **awe·struck** *adj*

aw·ful *adj* **1** : inspiring awe **2** : extremely disagreeable **3** : very great — **aw·ful·ly** *adv*

awk·ward *adj* **1** : clumsy **2** : embarrassing — **awk·ward·ly** *adv* — **awk·ward·ness** *n*

awl *n* : hole-making tool

aw·ning *n* : window cover

ax, axe *n* : chopping tool

ax·i·om *n* : generally accepted truth — **ax·i·om·at·ic** *adj*

ax·is *n* : center of rotation — **ax·i·al** *adj* — **ax·i·al·ly** *adv*

ax·le *n* : shaft on which a wheel revolves

aye *adv* : yes ～ *n* : a vote of yes

aza·lea *n* : rhododendron with funnel-shaped blossoms

az·i·muth *n* : horizontal direction expressed as an angle

azure *n* : blue of the sky — **azure** *adj*

B

b *n* : 2d letter of the alphabet

bab·ble *vb* **1** : utter meaningless sounds **2** : talk foolishly or too much — **babble** *n* — **bab·bler** *n*

ba·bel *n* : noisy confusion

ba·boon *n* : large Asian or African ape with a doglike muzzle

ba·by *n* : very young child ～ *vb* : pamper — **baby** *adj* — **ba·by·hood** *n* — **ba·by·ish** *adj*

ba·by·sit *vb* : care for children while parents are away — **baby–sit·ter** *n*

became *past of* BECOME

bac·ca·lau·re·ate *n* : bachelor's degree

bach·e·lor *n* **1** : holder of lowest 4-year college degree **2** : unmarried man — **bach·e·lor·hood** *n*

ba·cil·lus *n* : rod-shaped bacterium — **bac·il·lary** *adj*

back *n* **1** : part of a human or animal body nearest the spine **2** : part opposite the front **3** : player farthest from the opponent's goal ～ *adv* **1** : to or at the back **2** : ago **3** : to or in a former place or state **4** : in reply ～ *adj* **1** : located at the back **2** : not paid on time **3** : moving or working backward **4** : not current ～ *vb* **1** : support **2** : go or cause to go back **3** : form the back of — **back·ache** *n* — **back·er** *n* — **back·ing** *n* — **back·less** *adj* — **back·rest** *n*

back·bone *n* **1** : bony column in the back that encloses the spinal cord **2** : firm character

back·drop *n* : painted cloth hung across the rear of a stage

back·gam·mon *n* : board game

back·ground *n* **1** : scenery behind something **2** : sum of a person's experience or training

back·hand *n* : stroke (as in tennis) made with the back of the hand turned forward — **back·hand** *adj or vb* — **back·hand·ed** *adj*

back·lash *n* : adverse reaction

back·log *n* : accumulation of things to be done — **backlog** *vb*

back·pack *n* : camping pack carried on the back ～ *vb* : hike with a backpack — **back·pack·er** *n*

back·slide *vb* : lapse in morals or religious practice — **back·slid·er** *n*

back·up *n* : substitute

back·ward, back·wards *adv* **1** : toward the back **2** : with the back foremost **3** : in a reverse direction **4** : toward an earlier or worse state ～ *adj* **1** : directed, turned, or done backward **2** : retarded in development — **back·ward·ness** *n*

back·woods *n pl* : remote or isolated place

ba·con *n* : salted and smoked meat from a pig

bac·te·ri·um *n* (**bac·te·ria**) : microscopic plant — **bac·te·ri·al** *adj* — **bac·te·ri·o·log·ic,**

bac·te·ri·o·log·i·cal *adj* — **bac·te·ri·ol·o·gist** *n* — **bac·te·ri·ol·o·gy** *n*

bad *adj* **worse; worst 1 :** not good **2 :** naughty **3 :** faulty **4 :** spoiled — **bad** *n or adv* — **bad·ly** *adv* — **bad·ness** *n*

bade *past of* BID

badge *n* **:** symbol of status

bad·ger *n* **:** burrowing mammal ∼ *vb* **:** harass

bad·min·ton *n* **:** tennislike game played with a shuttlecock

baf·fle *vb* **:** perplex ∼ *n* **:** device to alter flow (as of liquid or sound) — **baf·fle·ment** *n*

bag *n* **:** flexible usu. closable container ∼ *vb* **1 :** bulge out **2 :** put in a bag **3 :** catch in hunting

ba·gel *n* **:** hard doughnut-shaped roll

bag·gage *n* **:** traveler's bags and belongings

bag·gy *adj* **:** puffed out like a bag — **bag·gi·ness** *n*

bag·pipe *n* **:** musical instrument with a bag, a tube with valves, and sounding pipes — often pl.

¹bail *n* **:** container for scooping water out of a boat — **bail** *vb* — **bail·er** *n*

²bail *n* **1 :** security given to guarantee a prisoner's appearance in court **2 :** release secured by bail ∼ *vb* **:** bring about the release of by giving bail

bai·liff *n* **1 :** British sheriff's aide **2 :** minor officer of a U.S. court

bail·out *n* **:** rescue from financial distress

bait *vb* **1 :** harass with dogs usu. for sport **2 :** furnish (a hook or trap) with bait ∼ *n* **:** lure esp. for catching animals

bake *vb* **:** cook in dry heat esp. in an oven ∼ *n* **:** party featuring baked food — **bak·er** *n* — **bak·ery** *n* — **bake·shop** *n*

bal·ance *n* **1 :** weighing device **2 :** counteracting weight, force, or influence **3 :** equilibrium **4 :** that which remains ∼ *vb* **1 :** compute the balance **2 :** equalize **3 :** bring into harmony or proportion — **bal·anced** *adj*

bal·co·ny *n* **:** platform projecting from a wall

bald *adj* **1 :** lacking a natural or usual covering (as of hair) **2 :** plain — **bald·ing** *adj* — **bald·ly** *adv* — **bald·ness** *n*

bale *n* **:** large bundle ∼ *vb* **:** pack in a bale — **bal·er** *n*

bale·ful *adj* **1 :** deadly **2 :** ominous

¹ball *n* **1 :** rounded mass **2 :** game played with a ball ∼ *vb* **:** form into a ball

²ball *n* **:** large formal dance — **ball·room** *n*

bal·lad *n* **1 :** narrative poem **2 :** slow romantic song — **bal·lad·eer** *n*

bal·last *n* **:** heavy material to steady a ship or balloon ∼ *vb* **:** provide with ballast

bal·le·ri·na *n* **:** female ballet dancer

bal·let *n* **:** theatrical dancing

bal·loon *n* **:** inflated bag ∼ *vb* **1 :** travel in a balloon **2 :** swell out — **bal·loon·ist** *n*

bal·lot *n* **1 :** paper used to cast a vote **2 :** system of voting ∼ *vb* **:** vote

balmy *adj* **:** gently soothing — **balm·i·ness** *n*

ba·lo·ney *n* **:** nonsense

bal·sam *n* **1 :** aromatic resinous plant substance **2 :** balsam-yielding plant — **bal·sam·ic** *adj*

bam·boo *n* **:** tall tropical grass with strong hollow stems

ban *vb* **:** prohibit ∼ *n* **:** legal prohibition

ba·nal *adj* **:** ordinary and uninteresting — **ba·nal·ity** *n*

ba·nana *n* **:** elongated fruit of a treelike tropical plant

¹band *n* **1 :** something that ties or binds **2 :** strip or stripe different (as in color) from nearby matter **3 :** range of radio wavelengths ∼ *vb* **1 :** enclose with a band **2 :** unite for a common end — **band·ed** *adj* — **band·er** *n*

²band *n* **1 :** group **2 :** musicians playing together — **band·stand** *n*

ban·dage *n* **:** material used esp. in dressing wounds ∼ *vb* **:** dress or cover with a bandage

ban·dan·na, ban·dana *n* **:** large colored figured handkerchief

ban·dit *n* **:** outlaw or robber — **ban·dit·ry** *n*

band·wag·on *n* **:** candidate, side, or movement gaining support

¹bang *vb* **:** strike, thrust, or move usu. with a loud noise ∼ *n* **1 :** blow **2 :** sudden loud noise ∼ *adv* **:** directly

²bang *n* **:** fringe of short hair over the forehead — usu. pl. ∼ *vb* **:** cut in bangs

ban·gle *n* **:** bracelet

ban·ish *vb* **1 :** force by authority to leave a country **2 :** expel — **ban·ish·ment** *n*

ban·is·ter *n* **1 :** upright support for a rail **2 :** handrail

ban·jo *n* **:** stringed instrument with a drumlike body — **banjo·ist** *n*

¹bank *n* **1 :** piled-up mass **2 :** rising ground along a body of water **3 :** sideways slope along a curve ∼ *vb* **1 :** form a bank **2 :** cover (as a fire) to keep inactive **3 :** incline (an airplane) laterally

²bank *n* : tier of objects

³bank *n* **1** : money institution **2** : reserve supply ∼ *vb* : conduct business in a bank — **bank·book** *n* — **bank·er** *n* — **bank·ing** *n*

bank·rupt *n* : one required by law to forfeit assets to pay off debts ∼ *adj* **1** : legally a bankrupt **2** : lacking something essential — **bankrupt** *vb* — **bank·rupt·cy** *n*

ban·ner *n* : flag ∼ *adj* : excellent

ban·quet *n* : ceremonial dinner — **banquet** *vb*

ban·shee *n* : wailing female spirit that foretells death

ban·tam *n* : miniature domestic fowl

ban·ter *n* : good-natured joking — **banter** *vb*

bap·tize *vb* : administer baptism to — **baptism** *n* — **bap·tis·mal** *adj*

bar *n* **1** : long narrow object used esp. as a lever, fastening, or support **2** : barrier **3** : body of practicing lawyers **4** : wide stripe **5** : food counter **6** : place where liquor is served **7** : vertical line across the musical staff ∼ *vb* **1** : obstruct with a bar **2** : shut out **3** : prohibit ∼ *prep* : excluding — **barred** *adj* — **barroom** *n* — **bar·tend·er** *n*

barb *n* : sharp projection pointing backward — **barbed** *adj*

bar·bar·ian *adj* **1** : relating to people considered backward **2** : not refined — **barbarian** *n* — **bar·bar·ic** *adj*

bar·ba·rous *adj* **1** : lacking refinement **2** : mercilessly cruel — **bar·bar·ism** *n* — **barbar·i·ty** *n* — **bar·ba·rous·ly** *adv*

bar·be·cue *n* : gathering at which barbecued food is served ∼ *vb* : cook over hot coals or on a spit often with a highly seasoned sauce

bar·ber *n* : one who cuts hair

bare *adj* **1** : naked **2** : not concealed **3** : empty **4** : leaving nothing to spare **5** : plain ∼ *vb* : make or lay bare — **bare·foot, barefoot·ed** *adv or adj* — **bare–hand·ed** *adv or adj* — **bare·head·ed** *adv or adj* — **bare·ly** *adv* — **bare·ness** *n*

bare·back, bare·backed *adv or adj* : without a saddle

bare·faced *adj* : open and esp. brazen

bar·gain *n* **1** : agreement **2** : something bought for less than its value ∼ *vb* **1** : negotiate **2** : barter

barge *n* : broad flat-bottomed boat ∼ *vb* : move rudely or clumsily — **barge·man** *n*

bari·tone *n* : male voice between bass and tenor

¹bark *vb* **1** : make the sound of a dog **2** : speak in a loud curt tone ∼ *n* : sound of a barking dog

²bark *n* : tough corky outer covering of a woody stem or root ∼ *vb* : remove bark or skin from

bark·er *n* : one who calls out to attract people to a show

barn *n* : building for keeping hay or livestock — **barn·yard** *n*

barn·storm *vb* : tour through rural districts giving performances

ba·rom·e·ter *n* : instrument for measuring atmospheric pressure — **baro·met·ric** *adj*

bar·racks *n sing or pl* : soldiers' housing

bar·rel *n* **1** : closed cylindrical container **2** : amount held by a barrel **3** : cylindrical part ∼ *vb* **1** : pack in a barrel **2** : move at high speed

bar·ren *adj* **1** : unproductive of life **2** : uninteresting — **bar·ren·ness** *n*

bar·rette *n* : clasp for a woman's hair

bar·ri·cade *n* : barrier — **barricade** *vb*

bar·ri·er *n* : something that separates or obstructs

bar·ter *vb* : trade by exchange of goods — **barter** *n*

¹base *n* **1** : bottom **2** : fundamental part **3** : beginning point **4** : supply source of a force **5** : compound that reacts with an acid to form a salt ∼ *vb* : establish — **base·less** *adj*

²base *adj* **1** : inferior **2** : contemptible — **base·ly** *adv* — **base·ness** *n*

base·ball *n* : game played with a bat and ball by 2 teams

base·ment *n* : part of a building below ground level

bash *vb* : strike violently ∼ *n* : heavy blow

bash·ful *adj* : self-conscious — **bash·ful·ness** *n*

ba·sic *adj* **1** : relating to or forming the base or essence **2** : relating to a chemical base — **ba·si·cal·ly** *adv* — **ba·sic·i·ty** *n*

ba·sin *n* **1** : large bowl or pan **2** : region drained by a river

ba·sis *n* **1** : something that supports **2** : fundamental principle

bask *vb* : enjoy pleasant warmth

bas·ket *n* : woven container — **bas·ket·ful** *n*

bas·ket·ball *n* : game played with a ball on a court by 2 teams

¹bass *n* : spiny-finned sport and food fish

²bass *n* **1** : deep tone **2** : lowest choral voice

bas·set hound *n* : short-legged dog with long ears

bas·soon *n* : low-pitched wind instrument

bas·tard *n* **1** : illegitimate child **2** : offensive person ∼ *adj* **1** : illegitimate **2** : inferior — **bas·tard·ize** *vb* — **bas·tardy** *n*

¹**baste** *vb* : sew temporarily with long stitches

²**baste** *vb* : moisten at intervals while cooking

¹**bat** *n* **1** : stick or club **2** : sharp blow ∼ *vb* : hit with a bat

²**bat** *n* : small flying mammal

³**bat** *vb* : wink or blink

batch *n* : quantity used or produced at one time

bath *n* **1** : a washing of the body **2** : water for washing the body **3** : liquid in which something is immersed **4** : bathroom **5** : large financial loss — **bath·robe** *n* — **bath·room** *n* — **bath·tub** *n*

bathe *vb* **1** : wash in liquid **2** : flow against so as to wet **3** : shine light over **4** : take a bath or a swim — **bath·er** *n*

bat·tal·ion *n* : military unit composed of a headquarters and two or more companies

¹**bat·ter** *vb* : beat or damage with repeated blows

²**batter** *n* : mixture of flour and liquid

³**batter** *n* : player who bats

bat·tery *n* **1** : illegal beating of a person **2** : group of artillery guns **3** : group of electric cells

bat·ting *n* : layers of cotton or wool for stuffing

bat·tle *n* : military fighting ∼ *vb* : engage in battle — **bat·tle·field** *n*

bat·tle·ship *n* : heavily armed ship of war

bau·ble *n* : a small ornament

bawdy *adj* : obscene or lewd — **bawd·i·ly** *adv* — **bawd·i·ness** *n*

bawl *vb* : cry loudly ∼ *n* : long loud cry

¹**bay** *adj* : reddish brown ∼ *n* : bay-colored animal

²**bay** *n* : European laurel

³**bay** *n* **1** : compartment **2** : area projecting out from a building and containing a window (**bay window**)

⁴**bay** *vb* : bark with deep long tones ∼ *n* **1** : position of one unable to escape danger **2** : baying of dogs

⁵**bay** *n* : body of water smaller than a gulf and nearly surrounded by land

bay·ou *n* : creek flowing through marshy land

ba·zaar *n* **1** : market **2** : fair for charity

BB *n* : small shot pellet

be *vb* **was; were; been; am; is; are 1** : equal **2** : exist **3** : occupy a certain place **4** : occur ∼ *verbal auxiliary* — used to show continuous action or to form the passive voice

beach *n* : sandy shore of a sea, lake, or river ∼ *vb* : drive ashore — **beach·comb·er** *n*

bea·con *n* : guiding or warning light or signal

bead *n* : small round body esp. strung on a thread ∼ *vb* : form into a bead — **bead·ing** *n* — **beady** *adj*

bea·gle *n* : small short-legged hound

beak *n* : bill of a bird — **beaked** *adj*

bea·ker *n* **1** : large drinking cup **2** : laboratory vessel

beam *n* **1** : large long piece of timber or metal **2** : ray of light **3** : directed radio signals for the guidance of pilots ∼ *vb* **1** : send out light **2** : smile **3** : aim a radio broadcast

bean *n* : edible plant seed borne in pods

¹**bear** *n* **1** : large heavy mammal with shaggy hair **2** : gruff or sullen person — **bear·ish** *adj*

²**bear** *vb* (**bore; borne**) **1** : carry **2** : give birth to or produce **3** : endure **4** : press **5** : go in an indicated direction — **bear·able** *adj* — **bear·er** *n*

beard *n* **1** : facial hair on a man **2** : tuft like a beard ∼ *vb* : confront boldly — **beard·ed** *adj* — **beard·less** *adj*

bear·ing *n* **1** : way of carrying oneself **2** : supporting object or purpose **3** : significance **4** : machine part in which another part turns **5** : direction with respect esp. to compass points

beast *n* **1** : animal **2** : brutal person — **beast·li·ness** *n* — **beast·ly** *adj*

beat *vb* (**beat; beat·en/beat**) **1** : strike repeatedly **2** : defeat **3** : act or arrive before **4** : throb ∼ *n* **1** : single stroke or pulsation **2** : rhythmic stress in poetry or music ∼ *adj* : exhausted — **beat·er** *n*

be·at·i·fy *vb* : make happy or blessed — **be·atif·ic** *adj* — **be·at·i·fi·ca·tion** *n*

be·at·i·tude *n* : saying in the Sermon on the Mount (Matthew 5:3-12) beginning "Blessed are"

beau·ty *n* : qualities that please the senses or mind — **beau·te·ous** *adj* — **beau·te·ous·ly** *adv* — **beau·ti·fi·ca·tion** *n* — **beau·ti·fi·er** *n* — **beau·ti·ful** *adj* — **beau·ti·ful·ly** *adv* — **beau·ti·fy** *vb*

bea·ver *n* : large fur-bearing rodent

be·cause *conj* : for the reason that

because of *prep* : by reason of

beck·on *vb* : summon esp. by a nod or gesture

be·come *vb* **became; become 1** : come to be **2** : be suitable — **be·com·ing** *adj* — **be·com·ing·ly** *adv*

bed *n* **1** : piece of furniture to sleep on **2** : flat or level surface ∼ *vb* : put or go to bed — **bed·room** *n* — **bed·spread** *n*

bed·bug *n* : wingless bloodsucking insect

bed·ding *n* **1** : sheets and blankets for a bed **2** : soft material (as hay) for an animal's bed

bed·rid·den *adj* : kept in bed by illness

bed·rock *n* : solid subsurface rock — **bedrock** *adj*

¹**bee** *n* : 4-winged honey-producing insect — **bee·hive** *n* — **bee·keep·er** *n* — **bees·wax** *n*

²**bee** *n* : neighborly work session

beech *n* : tree with smooth gray bark and edible nuts (**beech·nuts**) — **beech·en** *adj*

beef *n* : flesh of a steer, cow, or bull ∼ *vb* : strengthen — used with *up* — **beef·steak** *n*

bee·line *n* : straight course

been *past part of* BE

beep *n* : short usu. high-pitched warning sound — **beep** *vb* — **beep·er** *n*

beer *n* : alcoholic drink brewed from malt and hops — **beery** *adj*

beet *n* : garden root vegetable

bee·tle *n* : 4-winged insect

be·fore *adv* **1** : in front **2** : earlier ∼ *prep* **1** : in front of **2** : earlier than ∼ *conj* : earlier than

be·fore·hand *adv or adj* : in advance

be·fud·dle *vb* : confuse

beg *vb* : ask earnestly

beg·gar *n* : one that begs ∼ *vb* : make poor — **beg·gar·ly** *adj* — **beg·gary** *n*

be·gin *vb* **be·gan; be·gun 1** : start **2** : come into being — **be·gin·ner** *n*

be·grudge *vb* **1** : concede reluctantly **2** : look upon disapprovingly

be·guile *vb* **1** : deceive **2** : amuse

be·half *n* : benefit

be·have *vb* : act in a certain way

be·hav·ior *n* : way of behaving — **be·hav·ior·al** *adj*

be·head *vb* : cut off the head of

be·hind *adv* : at the back ∼ *prep* **1** : in back of **2** : less than **3** : supporting

be·hold *vb* : see — **be·hold·er** *n*

beige *n* : yellowish brown — **beige** *adj*

be·ing *n* **1** : existence **2** : living thing

be·lat·ed *adj* : delayed

belch *vb* **1** : expel stomach gas orally **2** : emit forcefully — **belch** *n*

be·lea·guer *vb* **1** : besiege **2** : harass

bel·fry *n* : bell tower

be·lief *n* **1** : trust **2** : something believed

be·lieve *vb* **1** : trust in **2** : accept as true **3** : hold as an opinion — **be·liev·able** *adj* — **be·liev·ably** *adv* — **be·liev·er** *n*

be·lit·tle *vb* **1** : disparage **2** : make seem less

bell *n* : hollow metallic device that rings when struck ∼ *vb* : provide with a bell

belle *n* : beautiful woman

bel·lig·er·ent *adj* **1** : waging war **2** : aggressively asserting one's own will — **bel·lig·er·ence** *n* — **bel·lig·er·en·cy** *n* — **belligerent** *n*

bel·low *vb* : make a loud deep roar or shout — **bellow** *n*

bel·lows *n sing or pl* : device with sides that can be compressed to expel air

bel·ly *n* : abdomen ∼ *vb* : bulge

be·long *vb* **1** : be suitable **2** : be owned **3** : be a part of

be·long·ings *n pl* : possessions

be·loved *adj* : dearly loved — **beloved** *n*

be·low *adv* : in or to a lower place ∼ *prep* : lower than

belt *n* **1** : strip (as of leather) worn about the waist **2** : endless band to impart motion **3** : distinct region ∼ *vb* **1** : put a belt around **2** : beat soundly

be·muse *vb* : confuse

bench *n* **1** : long seat **2** : judge's seat **3** : court

bend *vb* (**bent; bent**) **1** : curve or cause a change of shape in **2** : turn in a certain direction ∼ *n* **1** : act of bending **2** : curve

be·neath *adv or prep* : below

bene·dic·tion *n* : closing blessing

bene·fac·tor *n* : one who gives esp. charitable aid

ben·e·fit *n* **1** : something that does good **2** : help **3** : fund-raising event — **benefit** *vb* — **ben·e·fi·cial** *adj* — **ben·e·fi·cial·ly** *adv* — **ben·e·fi·cia·ry** *n*

be·nev·o·lence *n* **1** : charitable nature **2** : act of kindness — **be·nev·o·lent** *adj* — **be·nev·o·lent·ly** *adv*

be·nign *adj* **1** : gentle or kindly **2** : not malignant — **be·nig·ni·ty** *n*

bent *n* : aptitude or interest

be·numb *vb* : make numb esp. by cold

be·queath *vb* **1** : give by will **2** : hand down — **be·quest** *n*

be·rate *vb* : scold harshly

be·reaved *adj* : suffering the death of a loved one ∼ *n pl* **bereaved** : one who is bereaved — **be·reave·ment** *n*

be·ret *n* : round soft visorless cap

ber·ry *n* : small pulpy fruit

ber·serk *adj* : acting out of control or insane — **berserk** *adv*

berth *n* **1** : place where a ship is anchored **2** : place to sit or sleep esp. on a ship **3** : job ∼ *vb* : to bring or come into a berth

be·seech *vb* : entreat

be·side *prep* **1** : by the side of **2** : besides

be·sides *adv* **1** : in addition **2** : further to what has been said ∼ *prep* **1** : other than **2** : in addition to

be·siege *vb* : lay siege to — **be·sieg·er** *n*

best *adj, superlative of* GOOD **1** : excelling all others **2** : most productive **3** : largest ∼ *adv superlative of* WELL **1** : in the best way **2** : most ∼ *n* : one that is best ∼ *vb* : outdo

bes·tial *adj* **1** : relating to beasts **2** : brutish — **bes·ti·al·i·ty** *n*

best man *n* : chief male attendant at a wedding

be·stow *vb* : give — **be·stow·al** *n*

bet *n* **1** : something risked or pledged on the outcome of a contest **2** : the making of a bet ∼ *vb* **bet; bet 1** : risk (as money) on an outcome **2** : make a bet with

be·tray *vb* **1** : seduce **2** : report or reveal to an enemy by treachery **3** : abandon **4** : prove unfaithful to **5** : reveal unintentionally — **be·tray·al** *n* — **be·tray·er** *n*

be·troth *vb* : promise to marry — **be·troth·al** *n* — **be·trothed** *n*

bet·ter *adj, comparative of* GOOD **1** : more than half **2** : improved in health **3** : of higher quality ∼ *adv comparative of* WELL **1** : in a superior manner **2** : more ∼ *n* **1** : one that is better **2** : advantage ∼ *vb* **1** : improve **2** : surpass — **bet·ter·ment** *n*

bet·tor, bet·ter *n* : one who bets

be·tween *prep* **1** — used to show two things considered together **2** : in the space separating **3** — used to indicate a comparison or choice ∼ *adv* : in an intervening space or interval

bev·el *n* : slant on an edge ∼ *vb* **1** : cut or shape to a bevel **2** : incline

bev·er·age *n* : drink

be·ware *vb* : be cautious

be·wil·der *vb* : confuse — **be·wil·der·ment** *n*

be·witch *vb* **1** : affect by witchcraft **2** : charm — **be·witch·ment** *n*

be·yond *adv* **1** : farther **2** : besides ∼ *prep* **1** : on or to the farther side of **2** : out of the reach of **3** : besides

bi·an·nu·al *adj* : occurring twice a year — **bi·an·nu·al·ly** *adv*

bi·as *n* **1** : line diagonal to the grain of a fabric **2** : prejudice ∼ *vb* : prejudice

bib *n* : shield tied under the chin to protect the clothes while eating

Bi·ble *n* **1** : sacred scriptures of Christians **2** : sacred scriptures of Judaism or another religion — **bib·li·cal** *adj*

bib·li·og·ra·phy *n* : list of writings on a subject or of an author — **bib·li·og·ra·pher** *n* — **bib·li·o·graph·ic** *adj*

bi·cen·ten·ni·al *n* : 200th anniversary — **bicentennial** *adj*

bi·ceps *n* : large muscle of the upper arm

bick·er *vb or n* : squabble

bi·cus·pid *n* : double-pointed tooth

bi·cy·cle *n* : 2-wheeled vehicle moved by pedaling ∼ *vb* : ride a bicycle — **bi·cy·cler** *n* — **bi·cy·clist** *n*

bid *vb* **bade/bid; bid·den/bid 1** : order **2** : invite **3** : express **4** : make a bid ∼ *n* **1** : act of bidding **2** : buyer's proposed price — **bid·da·ble** *adj* — **bid·der** *n*

bide *vb* **1** : wait **2** : dwell

bi·en·ni·al *adj* **1** : occurring once in 2 years **2** : lasting 2 years — **biennial** *n* — **bi·en·ni·al·ly** *adv*

bifocals *n pl* : eyeglasses that correct for near and distant vision

big *adj* : large in size, amount, or scope — **big·ness** *n*

big·a·my *n* : marrying one person while still married to another — **big·a·mist** *n* — **big·a·mous** *adj*

big·ot *n* : one who is intolerant of others — **big·ot·ed** *adj* — **big·ot·ry** *n*

big shot *n* : important person

big·wig *n* : big shot

bike *n* : bicycle or motorcycle

bi·ki·ni *n* : woman's brief 2-piece bathing suit

bile *n* **1** : greenish liver secretion that aids digestion **2** : bad temper

bi·lin·gual *adj* : using 2 languages

bilk *vb* : cheat

¹bill *n* : jaws of a bird together with their horny covering ∼ *vb* : caress fondly — **billed** *adj*

²bill *n* **1** : draft of a law **2** : list of things to be paid for **3** : printed advertisement **4** : piece of paper money ∼ *vb* : submit a bill or account to

bill·board *n* : surface for displaying advertising bills

bill·fold *n* : wallet

bil·liards *n* **:** game of driving balls into one another or into pockets on a table

bil·lion *n* **:** 1000 millions — **billion** *adj* — **bil·lionth** *adj or n*

bil·low *n* **1 :** great wave **2 :** rolling mass ~ *vb* **:** swell out — **bil·lowy** *adj*

billy goat *n* **:** male goat

bin *n* **:** storage box

bi·na·ry *adj* **:** consisting of 2 things — **binary** *n*

bind *vb* **1 :** tie **2 :** obligate **3 :** unite into a mass **4 :** bandage — **bind·er** *n* — **binding** *n*

binge *n* **:** excessive indulgence

bin·go *n* **:** game of covering numbers on a card

bin·oc·u·lar *adj* **:** of or relating to both eyes ~ *n* **:** binocular optical instrument — *usu. pl.*

bio·chem·is·try *n* **:** chemistry dealing with organisms — **bio·chemi·cal** *adj or n* — **bio·chem·ist** *n*

bio·de·grad·able *adj* **:** able to be reduced to harmless products by organisms — **bio·de·grad·abil·i·ty** *n* — **bio·deg·ra·da·tion** *n* — **bio·de·grade** *vb*

bi·og·ra·phy *n* **:** written history of a person's life — **bi·og·ra·pher** *n* — **bi·o·graph·i·cal** *adj*

bi·ol·o·gy *n* **:** science of living beings and life processes — **bi·o·log·ic, bi·o·log·i·cal** *adj* — **bi·ol·o·gist** *n*

bi·on·ic *adj* **:** having normal biological capabilities enhanced by electronic or mechanical devices

bio·phys·ics *n* **:** application of physics to biological problems — **bio·phys·i·cal** *adj* — **bio·phys·i·cist** *n*

bi·op·sy *n* **:** removal of live bodily tissue for examination

bi·par·ti·san *adj* **:** involving members of 2 parties

bi·ped *n* **:** 2-footed animal

birch *n* **:** deciduous tree with close-grained wood — **birch, birch·en** *adj*

bird *n* **:** warm-blooded egg-laying vertebrate with wings and feathers — **bird·bath** *n* — **bird·house** *n* — **bird·seed** *n*

bird's–eye *adj* **1 :** seen from above **2 :** of a general or superficial nature

birth *n* **1 :** act or fact of being born or of producing young **2 :** origin — **birth·day** *n* — **birth·mark** *n* — **birth·place** *n* — **birth·rate** *n* — **birth·right** *n*

bis·cuit *n* **:** small bread made with leavening other than yeast

bi·sect *vb* **:** divide into 2 parts — **bi·sec·tion** *n* — **bi·sec·tor** *n*

bish·op *n* **:** clergy member higher than a priest

bish·op·ric *n* **1 :** diocese **2 :** office of bishop

bi·son *n pl* **bison : ** large shaggy wild ox of central U.S.

bis·tro *n* **:** small restaurant or bar

¹bit *n* **1 :** part of a bridle that goes in a horse's mouth **2 :** drilling tool

²bit *n* **1 :** small piece or quantity **2 :** small degree

bitch *n* **:** female dog ~ *vb* **:** complain

bite *vb* **bit; bit·ten 1 :** to grip or cut with teeth or jaws **2 :** dig in or grab and hold **3 :** sting **4 :** take bait ~ *n* **1 :** act of biting **2 :** bit of food **3 :** wound made by biting — **bit·ing** *adj*

bit·ten *past part of* BITE

bit·ter *adj* **1 :** having an acrid lingering taste **2 :** intense or severe **3 :** extremely harsh or resentful — **bit·ter·ly** *adv* — **bit·ter·ness** *n*

bi·valve *n* **:** animal (as a clam) with a shell of 2 parts — **bivalve** *adj*

bi·zarre *adj* **:** very strange — **bi·zarre·ly** *adv*

blab *vb* **:** talk too much

black *adj* **1 :** of the color black **2 :** having dark skin **3 :** soiled **4 :** lacking light **5 :** wicked or evil **6 :** gloomy ~ *n* **1 :** black pigment or dye **2 :** something black **3 :** color of least lightness **4 :** person of a dark-skinned race ~ *vb* **:** blacken — **black·ing** *n* — **black·ish** *adj* — **black·ly** *adv* — **black·ness** *n*

black–and–blue *adj* **:** darkly discolored from bruising

black·ball *vb* **1 :** ostracize **2 :** boycott — **blackball** *n*

black·ber·ry *n* **:** black or purple fruit of a bramble

black·board *n* **:** dark surface for writing on with chalk

black·en *vb* **1 :** make or become black **2 :** harm the reputation of

black·head *n* **:** small dark oily mass plugging the outlet of a skin gland

black hole *n* **:** invisible extremely massive celestial object

black·jack *n* **1 :** flexible leather-covered club **2 :** card game ~ *vb* **:** hit with a blackjack

black·list *n* **:** list of persons to be punished or boycotted — **blacklist** *vb*

black·mail *n* **1 :** extortion by threat of exposure **2 :** something extorted by blackmail — **blackmail** *vb* — **black·mail·er** *n*

black·out *n* **1** : darkness due to electrical failure **2** : brief fainting spell — **black out** *vb*

black·smith *n* : one who forges iron

black·top *n* : dark tarry material for surfacing roads — **blacktop** *vb*

blad·der *n* : sac into which urine passes from the kidneys

blade *n* **1** : leaf esp. of grass **2** : something resembling the flat part of a leaf **3** : cutting part of an instrument or tool — **blad·ed** *adj*

blame *vb* **1** : find fault with **2** : hold responsible or responsible for — **blam·able** *adj* — **blame** *n* — **blame·less** *adj* — **blame·lessly** *adv* — **blame·worthy** *adj*

bland *adj* **1** : smooth in manner **2** : soothing **3** : tasteless — **bland·ly** *adv* — **bland·ness** *n*

blank *adj* **1** : showing or causing a dazed look **2** : lacking expression **3** : empty **4** : free from writing **5** : downright ～ *n* **1** : an empty space **2** : form with spaces to write in **3** : unfinished form (as of a key) **4** : cartridge with no bullet ～ *vb* : cover or close up — **blank·ly** *adv* — **blank·ness** *n*

blan·ket *n* **1** : heavy covering for a bed **2** : covering layer ～ *vb* : cover ～ *adj* : applying to a group

blare *vb* : make a loud harsh sound — **blare** *n*

bla·sé *adj* : indifferent to pleasure or excitement

blas·pheme *vb* : speak blasphemy — **blasphem·er** *n* — **blas·phe·mous** *adj* — **blasphe·my** *n*

blast *n* **1** : violent gust of wind **2** : explosion ～ *vb* : shatter by or as if by explosive — **blast off** *vb* : take off esp. in a rocket

bla·tant *adj* : offensively showy — **bla·tan·cy** *n* — **bla·tant·ly** *adv*

¹blaze *n* **1** : fire **2** : intense direct light **3** : strong display ～ *vb* : burn or shine brightly

²blaze *n* **1** : white stripe on an animal's face **2** : trail marker esp. on a tree ～ *vb* : mark with blazes

bleach *vb* : whiten — **bleach** *n*

bleach·ers *n sing or pl* : spectator stand without a roof

bleak *adj* **1** : desolately barren **2** : lacking cheering qualities — **bleak·ish** *adj* — **bleak·ly** *adv* — **bleak·ness** *n*

bleary *adj* : dull or dimmed esp. from fatigue

bleat *n* : cry of a sheep or goat or a sound like it — **bleat** *vb*

bleed *vb* **1** : lose or shed blood **2** : feel distress **3** : flow from a wound **4** : draw fluid from **5** : extort money from — **bleed·er** *n*

blem·ish *vb* : spoil by a flaw ～ *n* : noticeable flaw

¹blench *vb* : flinch

²blench *vb* : grow or make pale

blend *vb* **1** : mix thoroughly **2** : combine into an integrated whole — **blend** *n* — **blend·er** *n*

bless *vb* **1** : consecrate by religious rite **2** : invoke divine care for **3** : make happy — **bless·ed, blest** *adj* — **bless·ed·ly** *adv* — **bless·ed·ness** *n* — **bless·ing** *n*

blew *past of* BLOW

blight *n* **1** : plant disorder marked by withering or an organism causing it **2** : harmful influence **3** : deteriorated condition ～ *vb* : affect with or suffer from blight

blimp *n* : airship holding form by pressure of contained gas

blind *adj* **1** : lacking or quite deficient in ability to see **2** : not intelligently controlled **3** : having no way out ～ *vb* **1** : to make blind **2** : dazzle ～ *n* **1** : something to conceal or darken **2** : place of concealment — **blind·ly** *adv* — **blind·ness** *n*

blind·fold *vb* : cover the eyes of — **blindfold** *n*

blink *vb* **1** : wink **2** : shine intermittently ～ *n* : wink

bliss *n* **1** : complete happiness **2** : heaven or paradise — **bliss·ful** *adj* — **bliss·ful·ly** *adv*

blis·ter *n* **1** : raised area of skin containing watery fluid **2** : raised or swollen spot ～ *vb* : develop or cause blisters

blithe *adj* : cheerful — **blithe·ly** *adv* — **blithe·some** *adj*

blitz *n* **1** : series of air raids **2** : fast intensive campaign — **blitz** *vb*

bliz·zard *n* : severe snowstorm

bloat *vb* : swell

blob *n* : small lump or drop

bloc *n* : group working together

block *n* **1** : solid piece **2** : frame enclosing a pulley **3** : quantity considered together **4** : large building divided into separate units **5** : a city square or the distance along one of its sides **6** : obstruction **7** : interruption of a bodily or mental function ～ *vb* : obstruct or hinder

block·ade *n* : isolation of a place usu. by troops or ships — **block·ade** *vb* — **block·ad·er** *n*

block·head *n* : stupid person

blond, blonde *adj* **1** : fair in complexion **2** : of a light color — **blond, blonde** *n*

blood *n* **1** : red liquid that circulates in the heart, arteries, and veins of animals **2** : lifeblood **3** : line of descent from common ancestors — **blood·ed** *adj* — **blood·less** *adj* — **blood·stain** *n* — **blood·stained** *adj* — **blood·suck·er** *n* — **blood·suck·ing** *n* — **bloody** *adj*

blood·hound *n* : large hound with a keen sense of smell

blood·mo·bile *n* : truck for collecting blood from donors

blood·shed *n* : slaughter

blood·shot *adj* : inflamed to redness

blood·thirsty *adj* : eager to shed blood — **blood·thirst·i·ly** *adv* — **blood·thirst·i·ness** *n*

bloom *n* **1** : flower **2** : period of flowering **3** : fresh or healthy look ~ *vb* **1** : yield flowers **2** : mature — **bloomy** *adj*

bloop·er *n* : public blunder

blos·som *n or vb* : flower

blot *n* **1** : stain **2** : blemish ~ *vb* **1** : spot **2** : dry with absorbent paper — **blot·ter** *n*

blotch *n* : large spot — **blotch** *vb* — **blotchy** *adj*

blouse *n* : loose garment reaching from the neck to the waist

¹blow *vb* **blew; blown 1** : move forcibly **2** : send forth a current of air **3** : sound **4** : shape by blowing **5** : explode **6** : bungle ~ *n* **1** : gale **2** : act of blowing — **blow·er** *n* — **blowy** *adj*

²blow *n* **1** : forcible stroke **2** *pl* : fighting **3** : calamity

blow·out *n* : bursting of a tire

blow·torch *n* : small torch that uses a blast of air

¹blub·ber *n* : fat of whales

²blub·ber *vb* : cry noisily

blud·geon *n* : short club ~ *vb* : hit with a bludgeon

blue *adj* **1** : of the color blue **2** : melancholy ~ *n* : color of the clear sky — **blu·ish** *adj*

blue·ber·ry *n* : edible blue or blackish berry

blue·bird *n* : small bluish songbird

blue jay *n* : American crested jay

blues *n pl* **1** : depression **2** : music in a melancholy style

¹bluff *adj* **1** : rising steeply with a broad flat front **2** : frank ~ *n* : cliff

²bluff *vb* : deceive by pretense ~ *n* : act of bluffing — **bluff·er** *n*

blun·der *vb* **1** : move clumsily **2** : make a stupid mistake ~ *n* : bad mistake

blunt *adj* **1** : not sharp **2** : tactless ~ *vb* : make dull — **blunt·ly** *adv* — **blunt·ness** *n*

blur *n* **1** : smear **2** : something perceived indistinctly ~ *vb* : cloud or obscure — **blur·ry** *adj*

blurb *n* : short publicity notice

blurt *vb* : utter suddenly

blush *n* : reddening of the face — **blush** *vb* — **blush·ful** *adj*

blus·ter *vb* **1** : blow violently **2** : talk or act with boasts or threats — **blus·ter** *n* — **blus·tery** *adj*

boa *n* **1** : a large snake (as the **boa con·stric·tor**) that crushes its prey **2** : fluffy scarf

boar *n* : male swine

board *n* **1** : long thin piece of sawed lumber **2** : flat thin sheet esp. for games **3** : daily meals furnished for pay **4** : official body ~ *vb* **1** : go aboard **2** : cover with boards **3** : supply meals to — **board·er** *n*

board·walk *n* : wooden walk along a beach

boast *vb* : praise oneself or one's possessions — **boast** *n* — **boast·er** *n* — **boast·ful** *adj* — **boast·ful·ly** *adv*

boat *n* : small vessel for traveling on water — **boat** *vb* — **boat·man** *n*

¹bob *vb* **1** : move up and down **2** : appear suddenly

²bob *n* **1** : float **2** : woman's short haircut ~ *vb* : cut hair in a bob

bob·bin *n* : spindle for holding thread

bob·ble *vb* : fumble — **bobble** *n*

bob·cat *n* : small American lynx

bob·sled *n* : racing sled — **bobsled** *vb*

bob·white *n* : quail

¹bode *vb* : indicate by signs

²bode *past of* BIDE

bod·ice *n* : close-fitting top of dress

bodi·ly *adj* : relating to the body ~ *adv* **1** : in the flesh **2** : as a whole

body *n* **1** : the physical whole of an organism **2** : human being **3** : main part **4** : mass of matter **5** : group — **bod·ied** *adj* — **bodi·less** *adj* — **body·guard** *n*

bog *n* : swamp ~ *vb* : sink in or as if in a bog — **bog·gy** *adj*

bo·gey *n* : someone or something frightening

bog·gle *vb* : overwhelm with amazement

bo·gus *adj* : fake

¹boil *n* : inflamed swelling

²boil *vb* **1** : heat to a temperature (**boiling point**) at which vapor forms **2** : cook in boiling liquid **3** : be agitated — **boil** *n*

boil·er *n* : tank holding hot water or steam

bois·ter·ous *adj* : noisily turbulent — **bois·ter·ous·ly** *adv*

bold *adj* **1** : courageous **2** : insolent **3** : daring — **bold·ly** *adv* — **bold·ness** *n*

boll *n* : seed pod

boll weevil *n* : small grayish weevil that infests the cotton plant

bo·lo·gna *n* : large smoked sausage

bol·ster *n* : long pillow ∼ *vb* : support

bolt *n* **1** : flash of lightning **2** : sliding bar used to fasten a door **3** : roll of cloth **4** : threaded pin used with a nut ∼ *vb* **1** : move suddenly **2** : fasten with a bolt **3** : swallow hastily

bomb *n* : explosive device ∼ *vb* : attack with bombs — **bomb·er** *n* — **bomb·proof** *adj*

bom·bard *vb* : attack with or as if with artillery — **bom·bard·ment** *n*

bom·bast *n* : pretentious language — **bom·bas·tic** *adj*

bomb·shell *n* **1** : bomb **2** : great surprise

bona fide *adj* **1** : made in good faith **2** : genuine

bo·nan·za *n* : something yielding a rich return

bon·bon *n* : piece of candy

bond *n* **1** *pl* : something that restrains **2** : uniting force **3** : obligation made binding by money **4** : interest-bearing certificate ∼ *vb* **1** : insure **2** : cause to adhere — **bond·hold·er** *n*

bond·age *n* : slavery

bonds·man *n* : slave

bone *n* : skeletal material ∼ *vb* : to free from bones — **bone·less** *adj* — **bony** *adj*

bon·er *n* : blunder

bon·fire *n* : outdoor fire

bon·net *n* : hat for a woman or infant

bo·nus *n* : extra payment

boo *n* : shout of disapproval — **boo** *vb*

book *n* **1** : paper sheets bound into a volume **2** : long literary work or a subdivision of one ∼ *vb* : reserve — **book·case** *n* — **book·ish** *adj* — **book·let** *n* — **book·mark** *n* — **book·sell·er** *n* — **book·shelf** *n*

book·ie *n* : bookmaker

book·keep·er *n* : one who keeps business accounts — **book·keep·ing** *n*

book·mak·er *n* : one who takes bets — **book·mak·ing** *n*

¹boom *n* **1** : long spar to extend the bottom of a sail **2** : beam projecting from the pole of a derrick

²boom *vb* **1** : make a deep hollow sound **2** : grow rapidly esp. in value ∼ *n* **1** : booming sound **2** : rapid growth

boo·mer·ang *n* : angular club that returns to the thrower

boon *n* : benefit

boor *n* : rude person — **boor·ish** *adj*

boost *vb* **1** : raise **2** : promote — **boost** *n* — **boost·er** *n*

boot *n* **1** : covering for the foot and leg **2** : kick ∼ *vb* : kick

boo·tee, boo·tie *n* : infant's knitted sock

booth *n* : small enclosed stall or seating area

boot·leg *vb* : make or sell liquor illegally — **bootleg** *adj or n* — **boot·leg·ger** *n*

boo·ty *n* : plunder

booze *vb* : drink liquor to excess ∼ *n* : liquor — **booz·er** *n* — **boozy** *adj*

bor·der *n* **1** : edge **2** : boundary ∼ *vb* **1** : put a border on **2** : be close

¹bore *vb* **1** : pierce **2** : make by piercing ∼ *n* : cylindrical hole or its diameter — **bor·er** *n*

²bore *past of* BEAR

³bore *n* : one that is dull ∼ *vb* : tire with dullness — **bore·dom** *n*

born *adj* **1** : brought into life **2** : being such by birth

borne *past part of* BEAR

bor·ough *n* : incorporated town or village

bor·row *vb* **1** : take as a loan **2** : take into use

bo·som *n* : breast ∼ *adj* : intimate — **bo·somed** *adj*

boss *n* : employer or supervisor ∼ *vb* : supervise — **bossy** *adj*

bot·a·ny *n* : plant biology — **bo·tan·i·cal** *adj* — **bot·a·nist** *n* — **bot·a·nize** *vb*

botch *vb* : do clumsily — **botch** *n*

both *adj or pron* : the one and the other ∼ *conj* — used to show each of two is included

both·er *vb* **1** : annoy or worry **2** : take the trouble — **bother** *n* — **both·er·some** *adj*

bot·tle *n* : container with a narrow neck and no handles ∼ *vb* : put into a bottle

bot·tle·neck *n* : place or cause of congestion

bot·tom *n* **1** : supporting surface **2** : lowest part or place — **bottom** *adj* — **bot·tom·less** *adj*

bot·u·lism *n* : acute food poisoning

bough *n* : large tree branch

bought *past of* BUY

boul·der *n* : large rounded rock — **boul·dered** *adj*

bou·le·vard *n* : broad thoroughfare

bounce *vb* **1** : spring back **2** : make bounce — **bounce** *n* — **bouncy** *adj*

¹bound *adj* : intending to go

²bound *n* : limit or boundary ⁓ *vb* : be a boundary of — **bound·less** *adj* — **bound·less·ness** *n*

³bound *adj* **1** : obliged **2** : having a binding **3** : determined **4** : incapable of failing

⁴bound *n* : leap ⁓ *vb* : move by springing

bound·ary *n* : line marking extent or separation

boun·ty *n* **1** : generosity **2** : reward — **boun·te·ous** *adj* — **boun·te·ous·ly** *adv* — **boun·ti·ful** *adj* — **boun·ti·ful·ly** *adv*

bou·quet *n* **1** : bunch of flowers **2** : fragrance

bout *n* **1** : contest **2** : outbreak

bou·tique *n* : specialty shop

bo·vine *adj* : relating to cattle — **bovine** *n*

¹bow *vb* **1** : submit **2** : bend the head or body ⁓ *n* : act of bowing

²bow *n* **1** : bend or arch **2** : weapon for shooting arrows **3** : knot with loops **4** : rod with stretched horsehairs for playing a stringed instrument ⁓ *vb* : curve or bend — **bow·man** *n* — **bow·string** *n*

³bow *n* : forward part of a ship — **bow** *adj*

bow·els *n pl* **1** : intestines **2** : inmost parts

¹bowl *n* : concave vessel or part — **bowl·ful** *n*

²bowl *n* : round ball for bowling ⁓ *vb* : roll a ball in bowling — **bowl·er** *n*

bowl·ing *n* : game in which balls are rolled to knock down pins

¹box *n* : evergreen shrub — **box·wood** *n*

²box *n* **1** : container usu. with 4 sides and a cover **2** : small compartment ⁓ *vb* : put in a box

³box *n* : slap ⁓ *vb* **1** : slap **2** : fight with the fists — **box·er** *n* — **box·ing** *n*

box·car *n* : roofed freight car

box office *n* : theater ticket office

boy *n* : male child — **boy·hood** *n* — **boy·ish** *adj* — **boy·ish·ly** *adv* — **boy·ish·ness** *n*

boy·cott *vb* : refrain from dealing with — **boy·cott** *n*

boy·friend *n* **1** : male friend **2** : woman's regular male companion

brace *n* **1** : crank for turning a bit **2** : something that resists weight or supports **3** : punctuation mark { or } ⁓ *vb* **1** : make taut or steady **2** : invigorate **3** : strengthen

brace·let *n* : ornamental band for the wrist or arm

brack·et *n* **1** : projecting support **2** : punctuation mark [or] **3** : class ⁓ *vb* **1** : furnish or fasten with brackets **2** : place within brackets **3** : group

brag *vb* : boast — **brag** *n*

brag·gart *n* : boaster

braid *vb* : weave together ⁓ *n* : something braided

braille *n* : system of writing for the blind using raised dots

brain *n* **1** : organ of thought and nervous coordination enclosed in the skull **2** : intelligence ⁓ *vb* : smash the skull of — **brained** *adj* — **brain·less** *adj* — **brainy** *adj*

braise *vb* : cook (meat) slowly in a covered dish

brake *n* : device for slowing or stopping ⁓ *vb* : slow or stop by a brake

bram·ble *n* : prickly shrub

bran *n* : edible cracked grain husks

branch *n* **1** : division of a plant stem **2** : part ⁓ *vb* **1** : develop branches **2** : diverge — **branched** *adj*

brand *n* **1** : identifying mark made by burning **2** : mark of disgrace **3** : distinctive kind (as of goods from one firm) ⁓ *vb* : mark with a brand

brand–new *adj* : unused

bran·dy *n* : liquor distilled from wine

brash *adj* **1** : impulsive **2** : aggressively self-assertive

brass *n* **1** : alloy of copper and zinc **2** : outrageous confidence in oneself **3** : high-ranking military officers — **brassy** *adj*

bras·siere *n* : woman's undergarment to support the breasts

brat *n* : ill-behaved child — **brat·ti·ness** *n* — **brat·ty** *adj*

bra·va·do *n* : false bravery

brave *adj* : showing courage ⁓ *vb* : face with courage — **brave·ly** *adv* — **brav·ery** *n*

brawl *n* : noisy quarrel or violent fight — **brawl** *vb* — **brawl·er** *n*

brawn *n* : muscular strength — **brawny** *adj* — **brawn·i·ness** *n*

bra·zen *adj* **1** : made of brass **2** : bold — **bra·zen·ly** *adv* — **bra·zen·ness** *n*

bra·zier *n* : charcoal grill

breach *n* **1** : breaking of a law, obligation, or standard **2** : gap ⁓ *vb* : make a breach in

bread *n* : baked food made of flour ∼ *vb* : cover with bread crumbs

breadth *n* : width

bread·win·ner *n* : wage earner

break *vb* **broke; bro·ken 1** : knock into pieces **2** : fail to fulfill or respect **3** : force a way into or out of **4** : exceed **5** : interrupt **6** : fail ∼ *n* **1** : act or result of breaking **2** : stroke of good luck — **break·able** *adj or n* — **break·age** *n* — **break·er** *n* — **break in** *vb* **1** : enter by force **2** : interrupt **3** : train — **break out** *vb* **1** : erupt with force **2** : develop a rash

break·down *n* : physical or mental failure — **break down** *vb*

break·fast *n* : first meal of the day — **break·fast** *vb*

breast *n* **1** : milk-producing gland esp. of a woman **2** : front part of the chest

breast·bone *n* : bone connecting the ribs in front

breath *n* **1** : slight breeze **2** : air breathed in or out — **breath·less** *adj* — **breath·less·ly** *adv* — **breath·less·ness** *n* — **breathy** *adj*

breathe *vb* **1** : draw air into the lungs and expel it **2** : live **3** : utter

breath·tak·ing *adj* : exciting

breech·es *n pl* : trousers ending near the knee

breed *vb* **1** : give birth to **2** : propagate **3** : raise ∼ *n* **1** : kind of plant or animal usu. developed by humans **2** : class — **breed·er** *n*

breeze *n* : light wind ∼ *vb* : move fast — **breezy** *adj*

brev·i·ty *n* : shortness or conciseness

brew *vb* : make by fermenting or steeping — **brew** *n* — **brew·er** *n* — **brew·ery** *n*

bri·ar *var of* BRIER

bribe *vb* : corrupt or influence by gifts ∼ *n* : something offered or given in bribing — **brib·able** *adj* — **brib·ery** *n*

bric–a–brac *n pl* : small ornamental articles

brick *n* : building block of baked clay — **brick** *vb* — **brick·lay·er** *n* — **brick·lay·ing** *n*

bride *n* : woman just married or about to be married — **brid·al** *adj*

bride·groom *n* : man just married or about to be married

brides·maid *n* : woman who attends a bride at her wedding

¹bridge *n* **1** : structure built for passage over a depression or obstacle **2** : upper part of the nose **3** : compartment from which a ship is navigated **4** : artificial replacement for missing teeth ∼ *vb* : build a bridge over — **bridge·able** *adj*

²bridge *n* : card game for 4 players

bri·dle *n* : headgear to control a horse ∼ *vb* **1** : put a bridle on **2** : restrain **3** : show hostility or scorn

brief *adj* : short or concise ∼ *n* : concise summary (as of a legal case) ∼ *vb* : give final instructions or essential information to — **brief·ly** *adv* — **brief·ness** *n*

brief·case *n* : case for papers

¹bri·er *n* : thorny plant

²brier *n* : heath of southern Europe

bri·gade *n* **1** : large military unit **2** : group organized for a special activity

bright *adj* **1** : radiating or reflecting light **2** : cheerful **3** : intelligent — **bright·en** *vb* — **bright·en·er** *n* — **bright·ly** *adv* — **bright·ness** *n*

bril·liant *adj* **1** : very bright **2** : splendid **3** : very intelligent — **bril·liance** *n* — **bril·lian·cy** *n* — **bril·liant·ly** *adv*

brim *n* : edge or rim ∼ *vb* : be or become full — **brim·ful** *adj* — **brim·less** *adj* — **brimmed** *adj*

brin·dled *adj* : gray or tawny with dark streaks or flecks

brine *n* **1** : salt water **2** : ocean — **brin·i·ness** *n* — **briny** *adj*

bring *vb* (**brought; brought**) **1** : cause to come with one **2** : persuade **3** : produce **4** : sell for — **bring·er** *n* — **bring about** *vb* : make happen — **bring up** *vb* **1** : care for and educate **2** : cause to be noticed

brink *n* : edge

bri·quette, bri·quet *n* : pressed mass (as of charcoal)

brisk *adj* **1** : lively **2** : invigorating — **brisk·ly** *adv* — **brisk·ness** *n*

bris·ket *n* : breast or lower chest of a quadruped

bris·tle *n* : short stiff hair ∼ *vb* **1** : stand erect **2** : show angry defiance **3** : appear as if covered with bristles — **bris·tly** *adj*

brit·tle *adj* : easily broken — **brit·tle·ness** *n*

broach *n* : pointed tool (as for opening casks) ∼ *vb* **1** : pierce (as a cask) to open **2** : introduce for discussion

broad *adj* **1** : wide **2** : spacious **3** : clear or open **4** : obvious **5** : tolerant in outlook **6** : widely applicable **7** : dealing with essential points — **broad·en** *vb* — **broad·ly** *adv* — **broad·ness** *n*

broad·cast *n* **1** : transmission by radio waves **2** : radio or television program ∽ *vb* **1** : scatter or sow in all directions **2** : make widely known **3** : send out on a broadcast — **broad·cast·er** *n*

broad–mind·ed *adj* : tolerant of varied opinions — **broad–mind·ed·ly** *adv* — **broad–mind·ed·ness** *n*

broad·side *n* **1** : simultaneous firing of all guns on one side of a ship **2** : verbal attack

broc·co·li *n* : green vegetable akin to cauliflower

bro·chure *n* : pamphlet

broil *vb* : cook by radiant heat — **broil** *n*

broil·er *n* **1** : utensil for broiling **2** : chicken fit for broiling

¹broke *past of* BREAK

²broke *adj* : out of money

bro·ken *adj* : imperfectly spoken — **bro·ken·ly** *adv*

bro·ken·heart·ed *adj* : overcome by grief or despair

bro·ker *n* : agent who buys and sells for a fee — **broker** *vb* — **bro·ker·age** *n*

bron·chus *n* : division of the windpipe leading to a lung — **bron·chi·al** *adj*

bronze *vb* : make bronze in color ∽ *n* **1** : alloy of copper and tin **2** : yellowish brown — **bronzy** *adj*

brooch *n* : ornamental clasp or pin

brood *n* : family of young ∽ *vb* **1** : sit on eggs to hatch them **2** : ponder ∽ *adj* : kept for breeding — **brood·er** *n* — **brood·ing·ly** *adv*

¹brook *vb* : tolerate

²brook *n* : small stream

broom *n* **1** : flowering shrub **2** : implement for sweeping — **broom·stick** *n*

broth *n* : liquid in which meat has been cooked

broth·el *n* : house of prostitutes

broth·er *n* **1** : male sharing one or both parents with another person **2** : kinsman — **broth·er·hood** *n* — **broth·er·li·ness** *n* — **broth·er·ly** *adj*

broth·er–in–law *n* **brothers–in–law** : brother of one's spouse or husband of one's sister or of one's spouse's sister

brought *past of* BRING

brow *n* **1** : eyebrow **2** : forehead **3** : edge of a steep place

brow·beat *vb* : intimidate

brown *adj* **1** : of the color brown **2** : of dark or tanned complexion ∽ *n* : a color like that of coffee ∽ *vb* : make or become brown — **brown·ish** *adj*

browse *vb* **1** : graze **2** : look over casually — **brows·er** *n*

brows·er *n* : computer program for accessing Web sites

bruise *vb* **1** : make a bruise on **2** : become bruised ∽ *n* : surface injury to flesh

brunch *n* : late breakfast, early lunch, or combination of both

bru·net, bru·nette *adj* : having dark hair and usu. dark skin — **bru·net, brunette** *n*

¹brush *n* **1** : small cut branches **2** : coarse shrubby vegetation

²brush *n* **1** : bristles set in a handle used esp. for cleaning or painting **2** : light touch ∽ *vb* **1** : apply a brush to **2** : remove with or as if with a brush **3** : dismiss in an offhand way **4** : touch lightly — **brush up** *vb* : renew one's skill

brush–off *n* : curt dismissal

brusque *adj* : curt or blunt in manner — **brusque·ly** *adv*

bru·tal *adj* : like a brute and esp. cruel — **bru·tal·i·ty** *n* — **bru·tal·ize** *vb* — **bru·tal·ly** *adv*

brute *adj* **1** : relating to beasts **2** : unreasoning **3** : purely physical ∽ *n* **1** : beast **2** : brutal person — **brut·ish** *adj*

bub·ble *vb* : form, rise in, or give off bubbles ∽ *n* : globule of gas in or covered with a liquid — **bub·bly** *adj*

buc·ca·neer *n* : pirate

buck *n* **1** : male animal (as a deer) **2** : dollar ∽ *vb* **1** : jerk forward **2** : oppose

buck·et *n* : pail — **buck·et·ful** *n*

buck·le *n* **1** : clasp (as on a belt) for two loose ends **2** : bend or fold ∽ *vb* **1** : fasten with a buckle **2** : apply oneself **3** : bend or crumple

buck·skin *n* : soft leather (as from the skin of a buck) — **buckskin** *adj*

buck·tooth *n* : large projecting front tooth — **buck–toothed** *adj*

buck·wheat *n* : herb whose seeds are used as a cereal grain or the seeds themselves

bud *n* **1** : undeveloped plant shoot **2** : partly opened flower ∽ *vb* **1** : form or put forth buds **2** : be or develop like a bud

Bud·dhism *n* : religion of eastern and central Asia — **Bud·dhist** *n or adj*

bud·dy *n* : friend

budge *vb* : move from a place

bud·get *n* **1** : estimate of income and expenses **2** : plan for coordinating income and expenses

3 : money available for a particular use —
budget *vb or adj* — **bud·get·ary** *adj*
buff *n* **1** : yellow to orange yellow color **2**
: enthusiast ⁓ *adj* : of the color buff ⁓ *vb*
: polish
buf·fa·lo *n* : wild ox (as a bison)
¹**buff·er** *n* : shield or protector
²**buffer** *n* : one that buffs
¹**buf·fet** *n* : blow or slap ⁓ *vb* : hit esp. repeatedly
²**buf·fet** *n* : meal at which people serve themselves
buf·foon *n* : clown — **buf·foon·ery** *n*
bug *n* **1** : small usu. obnoxious crawling creature **2** : 4-winged sucking insect **3** : unexpected imperfection **4** : disease-producing
germ **5** : hidden microphone ⁓ *vb* **1** : pester
2 : conceal a microphone in
bug·gy *n* : light carriage
bu·gle *n* : trumpetlike brass instrument — **bu·**
gler *n*
build *vb* (**built; built**) **1** : put together **2** : establish **3** : increase ⁓ *n* : physique — **build·er** *n*
build·ing *n* **1** : roofed and walled structure **2**
: art or business of constructing buildings
bulb *n* **1** : large underground plant bud **2**
: rounded or pear-shaped object — **bul·bous**
adj
bulge *n* : swelling projecting part ⁓ *vb* : swell
out
bulk *n* **1** : magnitude **2** : indigestible food material **3** : large mass **4** : major portion ⁓ *vb*
: cause to swell or bulge — **bulky** *adj*
bull *n* : large adult male animal (as of cattle) ⁓
adj : male
bull·dog *n* : compact short-haired dog
bull·doze *vb* **1** : move or level with a tractor
(**bull·doz·er**) having a broad blade **2** : force
bul·let *n* : missile to be shot from a gun — **bul·**
let·proof *adj*
bul·le·tin *n* **1** : brief public report **2** : periodical
bull·fight *n* : sport of taunting and killing bulls
— **bull·fight·er** *n*
bull·frog *n* : large deep-voiced frog
bul·lion *n* : gold or silver esp. in bars
bull's–eye *n* : center of a target
bul·ly *n* : one who hurts or intimidates others
⁓ *vb* : act like a bully toward
bul·rush *n* : tall coarse rush or sedge
bul·wark *n* **1** : wall-like defense **2** : strong
support or protection
bum *vb* **1** : wander as a tramp **2** : get by

begging ⁓ *n* : idle worthless person ⁓ *adj*
: bad
bum·ble·bee *n* : large hairy bee
bump *vb* : strike or knock forcibly ⁓ *n* **1**
: sudden blow **2** : small bulge or swelling —
bumpy *adj*
¹**bum·per** *adj* : unusually large
²**bump·er** *n* : shock-absorbing bar at either end
of a car
bump·kin *n* : awkward country person
bun *n* : sweet biscuit or roll
bunch *n* : group ⁓ *vb* : form into a group —
bunchy *adj*
bun·dle *n* **1** : several items bunched together
2 : something wrapped for carrying **3** : large
amount ⁓ *vb* : gather into a bundle
bun·ga·low *n* : one-story house
bun·gle *vb* : do badly — **bungle** *n* — **bun·**
gler *n*
bun·ion *n* : inflamed swelling of the first joint
of the big toe
¹**bunk** *n* : built-in bed that is often one of a tier
⁓ *vb* : sleep
²**bunk** *n* : nonsense
bun·ker *n* **1** : storage compartment **2** : protective embankment
bun·ny *n* : rabbit
¹**bun·ting** *n* : small finch
²**bunting** *n* : flag material
buoy *n* : floating marker anchored in water ⁓
vb **1** : keep afloat **2** : raise the spirits of —
buoy·an·cy *n* — **buoy·ant** *adj*
bur, burr *n* : rough or prickly covering of a fruit
— **bur·ry** *adj*
bur·den *n* **1** : something carried **2** : something oppressive **3** : cargo ⁓ *vb* : load or oppress — **bur·den·some** *adj*
bu·reau *n* **1** : chest of drawers **2** : administrative unit **3** : business office
bu·reau·cra·cy *n* **1** : body of government
officials **2** : unwieldy administrative system — **bu·reau·crat** *n* — **bu·reau·crat·ic**
adj
bur·geon *vb* : grow
bur·glary *n* : forcible entry into a building to
steal — **bur·glar** *n* — **bur·glar·ize** *vb*
Bur·gun·dy *n* : kind of table wine
buri·al *n* : act of burying
bur·lap *n* : coarse fabric usu. of jute or hemp
bur·lesque *n* **1** : witty or derisive imitation
2 : broadly humorous variety show ⁓ *vb*
: mock
bur·ly *adj* : strongly and heavily built

burn vb **1** : be on fire **2** : feel or look as if on fire **3** : alter or become altered by or as if by fire or heat **4** : cause or make by fire ⁓ n : injury or effect produced by burning — **burn·er** n

bur·nish vb : polish

burp n or vb : belch

bur·ro n : small donkey

bur·row n : hole in the ground made by an animal ⁓ vb : make a burrow — **bur·row·er** n

bur·si·tis n : inflammation of a sac (**bur·sa**) in a joint

burst vb **1** : fly apart or into pieces **2** : enter or emerge suddenly ⁓ n : sudden outbreak or effort

bury vb **1** : deposit in the earth **2** : hide

bus n : large motor-driven passenger vehicle ⁓ vb : travel or transport by bus

bus·boy n : waiter's helper

bush n **1** : shrub **2** : rough uncleared country **3** : a thick tuft or mat — **bushy** adj

bush·el n : 4 pecks

bush·ing n : metal lining used as a guide or bearing

busi·ness n **1** : vocation **2** : commercial or industrial enterprise **3** : personal concerns — **busi·ness·man** n — **busi·ness·wom·an** n

¹bust n **1** : sculpture of the head and upper torso **2** : breasts of a woman

²bust vb **1** : burst or break **2** : tame ⁓ n **1** : punch **2** : failure

bus·tle vb : move or work briskly ⁓ n : energetic activity

busy adj **1** : engaged in action **2** : being in use **3** : full of activity ⁓ vb : make or keep busy — **busi·ly** adv

busy·body n : meddler

but conj **1** : if not for the fact **2** : that **3** : without the certainty that **4** : rather **5** : yet ⁓ prep : other than

butch·er n **1** : one who slaughters animals or dresses their flesh **2** : brutal killer **3** : bungler — **butcher** vb — **butch·ery** n

but·ler n : chief male household servant

¹butt vb : strike with a butt ⁓ n : blow with the head or horns

²butt n **1** : target **2** : victim

³butt vb : join edge to edge

⁴butt n : large end or bottom

butte n : isolated steep hill

but·ter n : solid edible fat churned from cream ⁓ vb : spread with butter — **but·ter·fat** n — **but·ter·milk** n — **but·tery** adj

but·ter·cup n : yellow-flowered herb

but·ter·fly n : insect with 4 broad wings

but·ter·nut n : edible nut of a tree related to the walnut or this tree

but·ter·scotch n : candy made from sugar, corn syrup, and water

but·tocks n pl : rear part of the hips

but·ton n **1** : small knob for fastening clothing **2** : buttonlike object ⁓ vb : fasten with buttons

but·ton·hole n : hole or slit for a button ⁓ vb : hold in talk

but·tress n **1** : projecting structure to support a wall **2** : support — **buttress** vb

bux·om adj : having a large bosom

buy vb (**bought; bought**) : purchase ⁓ n : bargain — **buy·er** n

buzz vb : make a low humming sound ⁓ n : act or sound of buzzing

buz·zard n : large bird of prey

buzz·er n : signaling device that buzzes

buzz·word n : word or phrase in current popular use

by prep **1** : near **2** : through **3** : beyond **4** : throughout **5** : no later than ⁓ adv **1** : near **2** : farther

by·gone adj : past — **bygone** n

by·law, bye·law n : organization's rule

by–line n : writer's name on an article

by·pass n : alternate route ⁓ vb : go around

by–prod·uct n : product in addition to the main product

by·stand·er n : spectator

by·way n : side road

by·word n : proverb

C

c n : 3d letter of the alphabet

cab n **1** : light closed horse-drawn carriage **2** : taxi **3** : compartment for a driver — **cab·bie, cab·by** n — **cab·stand** n

ca·bana n : shelter at a beach or pool

cab·bage n : vegetable with a dense head of leaves

cab·in n **1** : private room on a ship **2** : small house **3** : airplane compartment

cab·i·net n **1** : display case or cupboard **2**

: advisory council of a head of state — **cab·i·net·mak·er** *n* — **cab·i·net·mak·ing** *n* — **cab·i·net·work** *n*

ca·ble *n* **1** : strong rope, wire, or chain **2** : telegram sent through a cable under the sea **3** : bundle of electrical wires ∼ *vb* : send a cablegram to

ca·cao *n* : So. American tree whose seeds (**cacao beans**) yield cocoa and chocolate

cack·le *vb* : make a cry or laugh like the sound of a hen — **cackle** *n* — **cack·ler** *n*

cac·tus *n* : drought-resistant flowering plant with scales or prickles

ca·dav·er *n* : dead body — **ca·dav·er·ous** *adj*

cad·die, cad·dy *n* : golfer's helper — **caddie, caddy** *vb*

ca·det *n* : student in a military academy

ca·fé *n* : restaurant

caf·e·te·ria *n* : self-service restaurant

cage *n* : box of wire or bars for confining an animal ∼ *vb* : put or keep in a cage

cake *n* **1** : food of baked or fried usu. sweet batter **2** : compacted mass ∼ *vb* **1** : form into a cake **2** : encrust

ca·lam·i·ty *n* : disaster — **ca·lam·i·tous** *adj* — **ca·lam·i·tous·ly** *adv*

cal·cu·late *vb* **1** : determine by mathematical processes **2** : judge — **cal·cu·la·ble** *adj* — **cal·cu·la·tion** *n* — **cal·cu·la·tor** *n*

cal·cu·lat·ing *adj* : shrewd

cal·en·dar *n* : list of days, weeks, and months

¹calf *n* calves : young cow or related mammal — **calf·skin** *n*

²calf *n* calves : back part of the leg below the knee

cal·i·brate *vb* : adjust precisely — **cal·i·bra·tion** *n*

cal·is·then·ics *n sing or pl* : stretching and jumping exercises — **cal·is·then·ic** *adj*

call *vb* **1** : shout **2** : summon **3** : demand **4** : telephone **5** : make a visit **6** : name — **call** *n* — **call·er** *n* — **call down** *vb* : reprimand — **call off** *vb* : cancel

call·ing *n* : vocation

cal·li·ope *n* : musical instrument of steam whistles

cal·lous *adj* **1** : thickened and hardened **2** : without apparent feelings ∼ *vb* : make callous — **cal·los·i·ty** *n* — **cal·lous·ly** *adv* — **cal·lous·ness** *n*

cal·lus *n* : callous area on skin or bark ∼ *vb* : form a callus

calm *n* **1** : period or condition of peacefulness or stillness ∼ *adj* : still or tranquil ∼ *vb* : make calm — **calm·ly** *adv* — **calm·ness** *n*

cal·o·rie *n* : unit for measuring heat and energy value of food

calves *pl of* CALF

cam *n* : machine part that slides or rotates irregularly to transmit linear motion

came *past of* COME

cam·el *n* : large hoofed mammal of desert areas

cam·eo *n* : gem carved in relief

cam·era *n* : box with a lens for taking pictures — **cam·era·man** *n*

cam·ou·flage *vb* : hide by disguising — **camouflage** *n*

camp *n* **1** : place to stay temporarily esp. in a tent **2** : group living in a camp ∼ *vb* : make or live in a camp — **camp·er** *n* — **camp·ground** *n* — **camp·site** *n*

cam·paign *n* : series of military operations or of activities meant to gain a result — **campaign** *vb*

cam·pus *n* : grounds and buildings of a college or school

¹can *vb,* (*past* **could**) **1** : be able to **2** : be permitted to by conscience or feeling **3** : have permission or liberty to

²can *n* : metal container ∼ *vb* : preserve by sealing in airtight cans or jars — **can·ner** *n* — **can·nery** *n*

ca·nal *n* **1** : tubular passage in the body **2** : channel filled with water

ca·nary *n* : yellow or greenish finch often kept as a pet

can·cel *vb* **1** : cross out **2** : destroy, neutralize, or match the force or effect of — **cancel** *n* — **can·cel·la·tion** *n* — **can·cel·er, can·cel·ler** *n*

can·cer *n* **1** : malignant tumor that tends to spread **2** : slowly destructive evil — **can·cer·ous** *adj* — **can·cer·ous·ly** *adv*

can·did *adj* **1** : frank **2** : not posed — **can·did·ly** *adv* — **can·did·ness** *n*

can·di·date *n* : one who seeks an office or membership — **can·di·da·cy** *n*

can·dle *n* : tallow or wax molded around a wick and burned to give light — **can·dle·light** *n* — **can·dle·stick** *n*

can·dy *n* : food made from sugar ∼ *vb* : encrust in sugar

cane *n* **1** : slender plant stem **2** : a tall woody grass or reed **3** : stick for walking or beating ∼ *vb* **1** : beat with a cane **2** : weave or make with cane — **can·er** *n* ca·nine *adj* : relating to dogs ∼ *n* 1 : pointed tooth next to the incisors 2 : dog

can·is·ter *n* : cylindrical container

can·ker *n* : mouth ulcer — can·ker·ous *adj*

can·ni·bal *n* : human or animal that eats its own kind — can·ni·bal·ism *n* — can·ni·bal·is·tic *adj* — can·ni·bal·ize *vb*

can·non *n* : large heavy gun — can·non·ball *n* — can·non·eer *n*

can·not : can not — cannot but : be bound to

ca·noe *n* : narrow sharp-ended boat propelled by paddles — canoe *vb* — ca·noe·ist *n*

¹can·on *n* 1 : regulation governing a church 2 : authoritative list 3 : an accepted principle

²canon *n* : clergy member in a cathedral — ca·non·i·cal *adj* — ca·non·i·cal·ly *adv*

can·on·ize *vb* : recognize as a saint — can·on·iza·tion *n*

can·o·py *n* : overhanging cover — canopy *vb*

can't : can not

can·ta·loupe *n* : muskmelon with orange flesh

can·teen *n* 1 : place of recreation for service personnel 2 : water container

can·tor *n* : synagogue official who sings liturgical music

can·vas *n* 1 : strong cloth orig. used for making tents and sails 2 : set of sails 3 : oil painting

can·vass *vb* : solicit votes, orders, or opinions from ∼ *n* : act of canvassing — can·vass·er *n*

can·yon *n* : deep valley with steep sides

cap *n* 1 : covering for the head 2 : top or cover like a cap 3 : upper limit ∼ *vb* 1 : provide or protect with a cap 2 : climax — cap·ful *n*

ca·pa·ble *adj* : able to do something — ca·pa·bil·i·ty *n* — ca·pa·bly *adv*

ca·pac·i·ty *n* 1 : ability to contain 2 : volume 3 : ability 4 : role or job ∼ *adj* : equaling maximum capacity

¹cape *n* : point of land jutting out into water

²cape *n* : garment that drapes over the shoulders

cap·il·lary *adj* 1 : resembling a hair 2 : having a very small bore ∼ *n* : tiny thin-walled blood vessel

¹cap·i·tal *adj* 1 : punishable by death 2 : being in the series A, B, C rather than a, b, c 3 : relating to capital 4 : excellent ∼ *n* 1 : capital letter 2 : seat of government 3 : wealth 4 : total face value of a company's stock 5 : investors as a group — cap·i·tal·ize *vb* — cap·i·tal·i·za·tion *n*

²capital *n* : top part of a column

cap·i·tal·ism *n* : economic system of private ownership of capital — cap·i·tal·ist *n or adj* — cap·i·tal·is·tic *adj*

cap·i·tol *n* : building in which a legislature sits

cap·size *vb* : overturn

cap·sule *n* 1 : enveloping cover (as for medicine) 2 : small pressurized compartment for astronauts ∼ *adj* : very brief or compact — cap·su·lar *adj* — cap·su·lat·ed *adj*

cap·tain *n* 1 : commander of a body of troops 2 : officer in charge of a ship 3 : commissioned officer in the navy ranking next below a rear admiral or a commodore 4 : commissioned officer (as in the army) ranking next below a major 5 : leader ∼ *vb* : be captain of — cap·tain·cy *n*

cap·tion *n* 1 : title 2 : explanation with an illustration — caption *vb*

cap·ti·vate *vb* : attract and charm — cap·ti·va·tion *n* — cap·ti·va·tor *n*

cap·tive *adj* 1 : made prisoner 2 : confined or under control — captive *n* — cap·tiv·i·ty *n*

cap·tor *n* : one that captures

cap·ture *n* : seizure by force or trickery ∼ *vb* : take captive

car *n* 1 : vehicle moved on wheels 2 : cage of an elevator

car·a·mel *n* 1 : burnt sugar used for flavoring and coloring 2 : firm chewy candy

car·bo·hy·drate *n* : compound of carbon, hydrogen, and oxygen

car·bon *n* 1 : chemical element occurring in nature esp. as diamond and graphite 2 : piece of carbon paper or a copy made with it

car·bon·ate *vb* : impregnate with carbon dioxide — car·bon·ation *n*

car·cin·o·gen *n* : agent causing cancer — car·ci·no·gen·ic *adj*

card *n* 1 : playing card 2 *pl* : game played with playing cards 3 : small flat piece of paper

card·board *n* : stiff material like paper

car·di·ac *adj* : relating to the heart

car·di·nal *n* 1 : official of the Roman Catholic Church 2 : bright red songbird

cardinal number *n* : number (as 1, 82, 357) used in counting

car·di·ol·o·gy *n* : study of the heart — car·di·ol·o·gist *n*

care *n* 1 : anxiety 2 : watchful attention 3 : supervision ∼ *vb* 1 : feel anxiety or concern 2 : like 3 : provide care — care·free *adj* — care·ful *adj* — care·ful·ly *adv* — care·ful-

ness *n* — **care·giv·er** *n* — **care·less** *adj* —
care·less·ly *adv* — **care·less·ness** *n*
ca·reer *n* : vocation ∼ *vb* : go at top speed
ca·ress *n* : tender touch ∼ *vb* : touch lovingly
or tenderly
car·go *n* : transported goods
car·i·ca·ture *n* : distorted representation for
humor or ridicule — **caricature** *vb* — **car·i·**
ca·tur·ist *n*
car·na·tion *n* : showy flower
car·ni·val *n* **1** : festival **2** : traveling enterprise
offering amusements
car·ni·vore *n* : flesh-eating animal — **car·niv·**
o·rous *adj* — **car·niv·o·rous·ly** *adv* — **car·**
niv·o·rous·ness *n*
car·ol *n* : song of joy — **carol** *vb* — **car·ol·er,**
car·ol·ler *n*
car·ou·sel, car·rou·sel *n* : merry-go-round
car·pen·ter *n* : one who builds with wood —
carpenter *vb* — **car·pen·try** *n*
car·pet *n* : fabric floor covering ∼ *vb* : cover
with a carpet — **car·pet·ing** *n*
car·riage *n* **1** : conveyance **2** : manner of
holding oneself **3** : wheeled vehicle
car·rot *n* : orange root vegetable
car·ry *vb* **1** : move while supporting **2** : hold
(oneself) in a specified way **3** : support **4**
: keep in stock **5** : reach to a distance **6** : win
— **car·ri·er** *n* — **carry on** *vb* **1** : conduct **2**
: behave excitedly — **carry out** *vb* : put into
effect
cart *n* : wheeled vehicle ∼ *vb* : carry in a cart
— **cart·age** *n* — **cart·er** *n*
car·ti·lage *n* : elastic skeletal tissue — **car·ti·**
lag·i·nous *adj*
car·ton *n* : cardboard box
car·toon *n* **1** : humorous drawing **2** : comic
strip — **cartoon** *vb* — **car·toon·ist** *n*
car·tridge *n* **1** : tube containing powder and a
bullet or shot for a firearm **2** : container of
material for insertion into an apparatus
carve *vb* **1** : cut with care **2** : cut into pieces
or slices — **carv·er** *n*
cas·cade *n* : small steep waterfall ∼ *vb* : fall
in a cascade
¹case *n* **1** : particular instance **2** : convincing
argument **3** : inflectional form esp. of a noun
or pronoun **4** : fact **5** : lawsuit **6** : instance of
disease — **in case** : as a precaution — **in**
case of : in the event of
²case *n* **1** : box **2** : outer covering ∼ *vb* **1**
: enclose **2** : inspect
cash *n pl* **cash** **1** : ready money **2** : money

paid at the time of purchase ∼ *vb* : give or get
cash for
ca·shew *n* : tropical American tree or its nut
cash·ier *n* : person who receives and records
payments
cash·mere *n* : fine goat's wool or a fabric of
this
ca·si·no *n* : place for gambling
cas·ket *n* : coffin
cas·se·role *n* : baking dish or the food cooked
in this
cas·sette *n* : case containing magnetic tape
cast *vb* (**cast; cast**) **1** : throw **2** : deposit (a
ballot) **3** : assign parts in a play **4** : mold ∼
n **1** : throw **2** : appearance **3** : rigid surgical
dressing **4** : actors in a play
cast·er *n* : small wheel on furniture
cas·tle *n* : fortified building
ca·su·al *adj* **1** : happening by chance **2**
: showing little concern **3** : informal — **ca·**
su·al·ly *adv* — **ca·su·al·ness** *n*
ca·su·al·ty *n* **1** : serious or fatal accident **2**
: one injured, lost, or destroyed
cat *n* **1** : small domestic mammal **2** : related
animal (as a lion) — **cat·like** *adj*
cat·a·log, cat·a·logue *n* **1** : list **2** : book containing a description of items ∼ *vb* **1** : make
a catalog of **2** : enter in a catalog — **cat·a·**
log·er, cat·a·logu·er *n*
cat·a·pult *n* : device for hurling or launching
— **catapult** *vb*
ca·tas·tro·phe *n* **1** : great disaster or misfortune **2** : utter failure — **cat·a·stroph·ic** *adj*
— **cat·a·stroph·i·cal·ly** *adv*
catch *vb* **caught; caught** **1** : capture esp.
after pursuit **2** : trap **3** : detect esp. by surprise **4** : grasp **5** : get entangled **6** : become
affected with or by **7** : seize and hold firmly
∼ *n* **1** : act of catching **2** : something caught
3 : something that fastens **4** : hidden difficulty
— **catch·er** *n*
catch·ing *adj* : infectious
catchy *adj* : likely to catch interest
cat·e·chism *n* : set of questions and answers
esp. to teach religious doctrine
cat·e·go·ry *n* : group or class — **cat·e·go·ri·**
za·tion *n* — **cat·e·go·rize** *vb*
ca·ter *vb* **1** : provide food for **2** : supply what
is wanted — **ca·ter·er** *n*
cat·er·cor·ner, cat·er·cor·nered *adv or adj*
: in a diagonal position
cat·er·pil·lar *n* : butterfly or moth larva
ca·the·dral *n* : principal church of a diocese

Cath·o·lic *n* : member of the Roman Catholic Church — **Ca·thol·i·cism** *n*

cat·tle *n pl* : domestic bovines — **cat·tle·man** *n*

cat·ty *adj* : mean or spiteful — **cat·ti·ly** *adv* — **cat·ti·ness** *n*

Cau·ca·sian *adj* : relating to the white race — **Caucasian** *n*

caught *past of* CATCH

cau·li·flow·er *n* : vegetable having a compact head of usu. white undeveloped flowers

caulk *vb* : make seams watertight — **caulk** *n* — **caulk·er** *n*

cause *n* **1** : something that brings about a result **2** : reason **3** : lawsuit **4** : principle or movement to support ∼ *vb* : be the cause of — **caus·al** *adj* — **cau·sal·i·ty** *n* — **caus·al·ly** *adv* — **cau·sa·tion** *n* — **caus·ative** *adj* — **cause·less** *adj* — **caus·er** *n*

caus·tic *adj* **1** : corrosive **2** : sharp or biting — **caustic** *n*

cau·tion *n* **1** : warning **2** : care or prudence ∼ *vb* : warn — **cau·tion·ary** *adj*

cau·tious *adj* : taking caution — **cau·tious·ly** *adv* — **cau·tious·ness** *n*

cave *n* : natural underground chamber — **cave in** *vb* : collapse

cav·ern *n* : large cave — **cav·ern·ous** *adj* — **cav·ern·ous·ly** *adv*

cav·i·ar, cav·i·are *n* : salted fish roe

cav·i·ty *n* **1** : unfilled place within a mass **2** : decay in a tooth

CD *n* : compact disc

cease *vb* : stop — **cease·less** *adj*

ce·dar *n* : cone-bearing tree with fragrant durable wood

ceil·ing *n* **1** : overhead surface of a room **2** : upper limit

cel·e·brate *vb* **1** : perform with appropriate rites **2** : honor with ceremonies **3** : praise highly — **cel·e·brant** *n* — **cel·e·bra·tion** *n* — **cel·e·bra·tor** *n*

cel·e·brat·ed *adj* : renowned

ce·leb·ri·ty *n* **1** : renown **2** : well-known person

cel·ery *n* : herb grown for crisp edible stalks

ce·les·tial *adj* **1** : relating to the sky **2** : heavenly

cell *n* **1** : small room **2** : tiny mass of protoplasm that forms the fundamental unit of living matter **3** : container holding an electrolyte for generating electricity — **celled** *adj*

cel·lar *n* : room or area below ground

cel·lo *n* : bass member of the violin family — **cel·list** *n*

cell phone *n* : portable cordless telephone

cel·lu·lar *adj* : relating to or consisting of cells

Cel·sius *adj* : relating to a thermometer scale on which the freezing point of water is 0° and the boiling point is 100°

ce·ment *n* **1** : powdery mixture of clay and limestone that hardens when wetted **2** : binding agent ∼ *vb* : unite or cover with cement

cem·e·tery *n* : burial ground

cen·sor *n* : one with power to suppress anything objectionable (as in printed matter) ∼ *vb* : be a censor of — **cen·so·ri·al** *adj* — **cen·sor·ship** *n*

cen·sure *n* : official reprimand ∼ *vb* : find blameworthy — **cen·sur·able** *adj*

cen·sus *n* : periodic population count — **cen·sus** *vb*

cent *n* : monetary unit equal to $\frac{1}{100}$ of a basic unit of value

cen·ten·ni·al *n* : 100th anniversary — **centen·nial** *adj*

cen·ter *n* **1** : middle point **2** : point of origin or greatest concentration **3** : region of concentrated population **4** : player near the middle of the team ∼ *vb* **1** : place, fix, or concentrate at or around a center **2** : have a center — **cen·ter·piece** *n*

cen·ti·grade *adj* : Celsius

cen·ti·me·ter *n* : $\frac{1}{100}$ meter

cen·ti·pede *n* : long flat many-legged arthropod

cen·tral *adj* **1** : constituting or being near a center **2** : essential or principal — **cen·tral·ly** *adv*

cen·tral·ize *vb* : bring to a central point or under central control — **cen·tral·i·za·tion** *n* — **cen·tral·iz·er** *n*

cen·tri·fuge *n* : machine that separates substances by spinning

cen·tu·ry *n* : 100 years

ce·ram·ic *n* **1** *pl* : art or process of shaping and hardening articles from clay **2** : product of ceramics — **ceramic** *adj*

ce·re·al *adj* : made of or relating to grain or to the plants that produce it ∼ *n* **1** : grass yielding edible grain **2** : food prepared from a cereal grain

cer·e·bel·lum *n* : part of the brain controlling muscular coordination — **cer·e·bel·lar** *adj*

ce·re·bral *adj* **1** : relating to the brain, intellect, or cerebrum **2** : appealing to the intellect ce·re·brum *n* : part of the brain that contains the higher nervous centers

cer·e·mo·ny *n* 1 : formal act prescribed by law, ritual, or convention 2 : prescribed procedures — cer·e·mo·ni·al *adj or n* — cer·e·mo·ni·ous *adj*

cer·tain *adj* 1 : settled 2 : true 3 : specific but not named 4 : bound 5 : assured ∼ *pron* : certain ones — cer·tain·ly *adv* — cer·tain·ty *n*

cer·tif·i·cate *n* : document establishing truth or fulfillment

cer·ti·fy *vb* 1 : verify 2 : endorse — cer·ti·fi·able *adj* — cer·ti·fi·ably *adv* — cer·ti·fi·ca·tion *n* — cer·ti·fi·er *n*

chafe *vb* 1 : fret 2 : make sore by rubbing

chain *n* 1 : flexible series of connected links 2 *pl* : something that restrains 3 : linked series ∼ *vb* : bind or connect with a chain

chair *n* 1 : seat with a back 2 : position of authority or dignity 3 : presiding officer ∼ *vb* : act as presiding officer of — chair·man *n* — chair·man·ship *n* — chair·wom·an *n*

chalk *n* 1 : soft limestone 2 : chalky material used as a crayon ∼ *vb* : mark with chalk — chalky *adj* — chalk up *vb* 1 : credit 2 : achieve

chalk·board *n* : blackboard

chal·lenge *vb* 1 : dispute 2 : invite or dare to act or compete — challenge *n* — chal·leng·er *n*

cham·ber *n* 1 : room 2 : enclosed space 3 : legislative meeting place or body 4 *pl* : judge's consultation room — cham·bered *adj*

champ *n* : champion

cham·pagne *n* : sparkling white wine

cham·pi·on *n* 1 : advocate or defender 2 : winning contestant ∼ *vb* : protect or fight for — cham·pi·on·ship *n*

chance *n* 1 : element of existence that cannot be predicted 2 : opportunity 3 : probability 4 : risk 5 : raffle ticket ∼ *vb* 1 : happen 2 : encounter unexpectedly 3 : risk — chance *adj*

chan·de·lier *n* : hanging lighting fixture

change *vb* 1 : make or become different 2 : exchange 3 : give or receive change for ∼ *n* 1 : a changing 2 : excess from a payment 3 : money in smaller denominations 4 : coins — change·able *adj* — change·less *adj* — chang·er *n*

chan·nel *n* 1 : deeper part of a waterway 2 : means of passage or communication 3

: strait 4 : broadcast frequency ∼ *vb* : make or direct through a channel

chant *vb* : sing or speak in one tone — chant *n* — chant·er *n*

Cha·nu·kah *var of* HANUKKAH

cha·os *n* : complete disorder — cha·ot·ic *adj* — cha·ot·i·cal·ly *adv*

¹chap *n* : fellow

²chap *vb* : dry and crack open usu. from wind and cold

cha·pel *n* : private or small place of worship

chap·er·on, chap·er·one *n* : older person who accompanies young people at a social gathering ∼ *vb* : act as chaperon at or for — chap·er·on·age *n*

chap·lain *n* : clergy member in a military unit or a prison — chap·lain·cy *n*

chap·ter *n* 1 : main book division 2 : branch of a society

char·ac·ter *n* 1 : letter or graphic mark 2 : trait or distinctive combination of traits 3 : peculiar person 4 : fictional person — char·ac·ter·i·za·tion *n* — char·ac·ter·ize *vb*

char·ac·ter·is·tic *adj* : typical ∼ *n* : distinguishing quality — char·ac·ter·is·ti·cal·ly *adv*

char·coal *n* : porous carbon prepared by partial combustion

charge *vb* 1 : give an electric charge to 2 : impose a task or responsibility on 3 : command 4 : accuse 5 : rush forward in assault 6 : assume a debt for 7 : fix as a price ∼ *n* 1 : excess or deficiency of electrons in a body 2 : tax 3 : responsibility 4 : accusation 5 : cost 6 : attack — charge·able *adj*

char·i·ot *n* : ancient 2-wheeled vehicle — char·i·o·teer *n*

cha·ris·ma *n* : special ability to lead — char·is·mat·ic *adj*

char·i·ty *n* 1 : love for mankind 2 : generosity or leniency 3 : alms 4 : institution for relief of the needy — char·i·ta·ble *adj* — char·i·ta·ble·ness *n* — char·i·ta·bly *adv*

charm *n* 1 : something with magic power 2 : appealing trait 3 : small ornament ∼ *vb* : fascinate — charm·er *n* — charm·ing *adj* — charm·ing·ly *adv*

chart *n* 1 : map 2 : diagram ∼ *vb* 1 : make a chart of 2 : plan

char·ter *n* 1 : document granting rights 2 : constitution ∼ *vb* 1 : establish by charter 2 : rent — char·ter·er *n*

chase *vb* **1** : follow trying to catch **2** : drive away — **chase** *n* — **chas·er** *n*

chasm *n* : gorge

chaste *adj* **1** : abstaining from all or unlawful sexual relations **2** : modest or decent **3** : severely simple — **chaste·ly** *adv* — **chaste·ness** *n* — **chas·ti·ty** *n*

chas·tise *vb* **1** : punish **2** : censure — **chas·tise·ment** *n*

chat *n* : informal talk — **chat** *vb* — **chat·ty** *adj*

chat·ter *vb* **1** : utter rapidly succeeding sounds **2** : talk fast or too much — **chatter** *n* — **chat·ter·er** *n*

chauf·feur *n* : hired car driver ⁓ *vb* : work as a chauffeur

cheap *adj* **1** : not expensive **2** : shoddy — **cheap** *adv* — **cheap·en** *vb* — **cheap·ly** *adv* — **cheap·ness** *n*

cheap·skate *n* : stingy person

cheat *n* **1** : act of deceiving **2** : one that cheats ⁓ *vb* **1** : deprive through fraud or deceit **2** : violate rules dishonestly — **cheat·er** *n*

check *n* **1** : sudden stoppage **2** : restraint **3** : test or standard for testing **4** : written order to a bank to pay money **5** : ticket showing ownership **6** : slip showing an amount due **7** : pattern in squares or fabric in such a pattern **8** : mark placed beside an item noted ⁓ *vb* **1** : slow down or stop **2** : restrain **3** : compare or correspond with a source or original **4** : inspect or test for condition **5** : mark with a check **6** : leave or accept for safekeeping or shipment **7** : checker — **check in** *vb* : report one's arrival — **check out** *vb* : settle one's account and leave

¹**check·er** *n* : piece in checkers ⁓ *vb* : mark with different colors or into squares

²**checker** *n* : one that checks

check·ers *n* : game for 2 played on a checkerboard — **check·er·board** *n*

check·mate *vb* : thwart completely — **checkmate** *n*

check·up *n* : physical examination

ched·dar *n* : hard smooth cheese

cheek *n* **1** : fleshy side part of the face **2** : impudence — **cheeked** *adj* — **cheeky** *adj*

cheer *n* **1** : good spirits **2** : food and drink for a feast **3** : shout of applause or encouragement ⁓ *vb* **1** : give hope or courage to **2** : make or become glad **3** : urge on or applaud with shouts — **cheer·er** *n* — **cheer·ful** *adj* — **cheer·ful·ly** *adv* — **cheer·ful·ness** *n* —

cheer·lead·er *n* — **cheer·less** *adj* — **cheer·less·ly** *adv* — **cheer·less·ness** *n*

cheery *adj* : cheerful — **cheer·i·ly** *adv* — **cheer·i·ness** *n*

cheese *n* : curd of milk usu. pressed and cured — **cheesy** *adj*

chef *n* : chief cook

chem·i·cal *adj* **1** : relating to chemistry **2** : working or produced by chemicals ⁓ *n* : substance obtained by chemistry — **chem·i·cal·ly** *adv*

chem·ist *n* : one trained in chemistry

chem·is·try *n* : science that deals with the composition and properties of substances

che·mo·ther·a·py *n* : use of chemicals in the treatment of disease — **che·mo·ther·a·peu·tic** *adj*

cher·ish *vb* : hold dear

cher·ry *n* : small fleshy fruit of a tree related to the roses or the tree or its wood

cher·ub *n* **1** *pl* **cher·u·bim** : angel **2** *pl* **cher·ubs** : chubby child — **che·ru·bic** *adj*

chess *n* : game for 2 played on a checkerboard — **chess·board** *n* — **chess·man** *n*

chest *n* **1** : boxlike container **2** : part of the body enclosed by the ribs and breastbone — **chest·ed** *adj*

chest·nut *n* : nut of a tree related to the beech or the tree

chew *vb* : crush or grind with the teeth ⁓ *n* : something to chew — **chew·able** *adj* — **chew·er** *n* — **chewy** *adj*

chic *n* : smart elegance of dress or manner ⁓ *adj* **1** : stylish **2** : currently fashionable

chick *n* : young chicken or bird

chick·a·dee *n* : small grayish American bird

chick·en *n* **1** : common domestic fowl or its flesh used as food **2** : coward

chief *n* : leader ⁓ *adj* **1** : highest in rank **2** : most important — **chief·dom** *n* — **chief·ly** *adv*

child *n* **chil·dren** **1** : unborn or recently born person **2** : son or daughter — **child·bear·ing** *n or adj* — **child·birth** *n* — **child·hood** *n* — **child·ish** *adj* — **child·ish·ly** *adv* — **child·ish·ness** *n* — **child·less** *adj* — **child·less·ness** *n* — **child·like** *adj* — **child·proof** *adj*

chili, chile, chil·li *n* **1** : hot pepper **2** : spicy stew of ground beef, chilies, and beans

chill *vb* : make or become cold or chilly ⁓ *adj* : moderately cold ⁓ *n* **1** : feeling of coldness with shivering **2** : moderate coldness

chilly *adj* : noticeably cold — **chill·i·ness** *n*

chime *n* : set of tuned bells or their sound ∼ *vb* : make bell-like sounds — **chime in** *vb* : break into or join in a conversation

chim•ney *n* 1 : passage for smoke 2 : glass tube around a lamp flame

chimp *n* : chimpanzee

chim•pan•zee *n* : small ape

chin *n* : part of the face below the mouth — **chin•less** *adj*

chi•na *n* 1 : porcelain ware 2 : domestic pottery

chip *n* 1 : small thin flat piece cut or broken off 2 : thin crisp morsel of food 3 : counter used in games 4 : flaw where a chip came off 5 : small slice of semiconductor containing electronic circuits ∼ *vb* : cut or break chips from — **chip in** *vb* : contribute

chip•munk *n* : small striped ground-dwelling rodent

chip•per *adj* : lively and cheerful

chi•ro•prac•tic *n* : system of healing based esp. on manipulation of body structures — **chi•ro•prac•tor** *n*

chirp *n* : short sharp sound like that of a bird or cricket — **chirp** *vb*

chis•el *n* : sharp-edged metal tool ∼ *vb* 1 : work with a chisel 2 : cheat — **chis•el•er** *n*

chit•chat *n* : casual conversation — **chitchat** *vb*

chiv•al•ry *n* 1 : system or practices of knighthood 2 : spirit or character of the ideal knight — **chi•val•ric** *adj* — **chiv•al•rous** *adj* — **chiv•al•rous•ly** *adv* — **chiv•al•rous•ness** *n*

chive *n* : herb related to the onion

chlo•rine *n* : chemical element that is a heavy strong-smelling greenish yellow irritating gas

chlo•ro•phyll *n* : green coloring matter of plants

chock *n* : wedge for blocking the movement of a wheel — **chock** *vb*

chock–full *adj* : full to the limit

choc•o•late *n* 1 : ground roasted cacao beans or a beverage made from them 2 : candy made of or with chocolate 3 : dark brown

choice *n* 1 : act or power of choosing 2 : one selected 3 : variety offered for selection ∼ *adj* 1 : worthy of being chosen 2 : selected with care 3 : of high quality

choir *n* : group of singers esp. in church — **choir•boy** *n* — **choir•mas•ter** *n*

choke *vb* 1 : hinder breathing 2 : clog or obstruct ∼ *n* 1 : a choking or sound of choking

2 : valve for controlling air intake in a gasoline engine

cho•les•ter•ol *n* : waxy substance in animal tissues

choose *vb* (**chose; cho•sen**) 1 : seléct after consideration 2 : decide 3 : prefer — **choos•er** *n* — **choosy** *adj*

chop *vb* 1 : cut by repeated blows 2 : cut into small pieces ∼ *n* 1 : sharp downward blow 2 : small cut of meat often with part of a rib — **chop•per** *n*

chop•py *adj* 1 : rough with small waves 2 : jerky or disconnected — **chop•pi•ly** *adv* — **chop•pi•ness** *n*

cho•ral *adj* : relating to or sung by a choir or chorus or in chorus — **cho•ral•ly** *adv*

cho•rale *n* 1 : hymn tune or harmonization of a traditional melody 2 : chorus or choir

¹chord *n* : harmonious tones sounded together

chore *n* 1 *pl* : daily household or farm work 2 : routine or disagreeable task

cho•re•og•ra•phy *n* : art of composing and arranging dances — **cho•reo•graph** *vb* — **cho•re•og•ra•pher** *n* — **cho•reo•graph•ic** *adj*

cho•rus *n* 1 : group of singers or dancers 2 : part of a song repeated at intervals 3 : composition for a chorus ∼ *vb* : sing or utter together

chose *past of* CHOOSE

cho•sen *adj* : favored

¹chow *n* : food

²chow *n* : thick-coated muscular dog

chow•der *n* : thick soup usu. of seafood and milk

chris•ten *vb* 1 : baptize 2 : name — **chris•ten•ing** *n*

Chris•tian *n* : adherent of Christianity ∼ *adj* : relating to or professing a belief in Christianity or Jesus Christ — **Chris•tian•ize** *vb*

Chris•ti•an•i•ty *n* : religion derived from the teachings of Jesus Christ

Christ•mas *n* : December 25 celebrated as the birthday of Christ

chro•mo•some *n* : part of a cell nucleus that contains the genes — **chro•mo•som•al** *adj*

chron•ic *adj* : frequent or persistent — **chron•i•cal•ly** *adv*

chron•i•cle *n* : history ∼ *vb* : record — **chron•i•cler** *n*

chro•nol•o•gy *n* : list of events in order of their occurrence — **chron•o•log•i•cal** *adj* — **chron•o•log•i•cal•ly** *adv*

chub•by *adj* : fat — **chub•bi•ness** *n*

¹**chuck** *vb* **1** : tap **2** : toss $\sim$ *n* **1** : light pat under the chin **2** : toss

²**chuck** *n* **1** : cut of beef **2** : machine part that holds work or another part

chuck·le *vb* : laugh quietly — **chuckle** *n*

chum *n* : close friend $\sim$ *vb* : be chums — **chum·my** *adj*

chump *n* : fool

chunk *n* **1** : short thick piece **2** : sizable amount

chunky *adj* **1** : thickly built **2** : containing chunks

church *n* **1** : building esp. for Christian public worship **2** : whole body of Christians **3** : denomination **4** : congregation — **church·go·er** *n* — **church·go·ing** *adj or n* — **church·yard** *n*

churn *n* : container in which butter is made $\sim$ *vb* **1** : agitate in a churn **2** : shake violently

chute *n* : trough or passage

chutz·pah *n* : nerve or insolence

ci·der *n* : apple juice

ci·gar *n* : roll of leaf tobacco for smoking

cig·a·rette *n* : cut tobacco rolled in paper for smoking

cinch *n* **1** : strap holding a saddle or pack in place **2** : sure thing — **cinch** *vb*

cin·der *n* **1** *pl* : ashes **2** : piece of partly burned wood or coal

cin·e·ma *n* : movies or a movie theater — **cin·e·mat·ic** *adj*

cin·na·mon *n* : spice from an aromatic tree bark

ci·pher *n* **1** : zero **2** : code

cir·cle *n* **1** : closed symmetrical curve **2** : cycle **3** : group with a common tie $\sim$ *vb* **1** : enclose in a circle **2** : move or revolve around

cir·cuit *n* **1** : boundary **2** : regular tour of a territory **3** : complete path of an electric current **4** : group of electronic components — **cir·cuit·ry** *n*

cir·cu·lar *adj* **1** : round **2** : moving in a circle $\sim$ *n* : advertising leaflet — **cir·cu·lar·i·ty** *n*

cir·cu·late *vb* : move or cause to move in a circle or from place to place or person to person — **cir·cu·la·tion** *n* — **cir·cu·la·to·ry** *adj*

cir·cum·cise *vb* : cut off the foreskin of — **cir·cum·ci·sion** *n*

cir·cum·fer·ence *n* : perimeter of a circle

cir·cum·stance *n* **1** : fact or event **2** *pl* : surrounding conditions **3** *pl* : financial situation — **cir·cum·stan·tial** *adj*

cir·cum·vent *vb* : get around esp. by trickery — **cir·cum·ven·tion** *n*

cir·cus *n* : show with feats of skill, animal acts, and clowns

cite *vb* **1** : summon before a court **2** : quote **3** : refer to esp. in commendation — **ci·ta·tion** *n*

cit·i·zen *n* : member of a country — **cit·i·zen·ry** *n* — **cit·i·zen·ship** *n*

cit·rus *n* : evergreen tree or shrub grown for its fruit (as the orange or lemon)

city *n* : place larger or more important than a town

civ·ics *n* : study of citizenship — **civ·ic** *adj*

civ·il *adj* **1** : relating to citizens **2** : polite **3** : relating to or being a lawsuit — **civ·il·ly** *adv*

ci·vil·ian *n* : person not in a military, police, or fire-fighting force

ci·vil·i·ty *n* : courtesy

civ·i·lize *vb* : raise from a primitive stage of cultural development — **civ·i·li·za·tion** *n* — **civ·i·lized** *adj*

civil war *n* : war among citizens of one country

clad *adj* : being covered

claim *vb* **1** : demand or take as the rightful owner **2** : maintain $\sim$ *n* **1** : demand of right or ownership **2** : declaration **3** : something claimed — **claim·ant** *n*

clair·voy·ant *adj* : able to perceive things beyond the senses — **clair·voy·ance** *n* — **clair·voy·ant** *n*

clam *n* : bivalve mollusk

clam·my *adj* : being damp, soft, and usu. cool — **clam·mi·ness** *n*

clam·or *n* **1** : uproar **2** : protest — **clamor** *vb* — **clam·or·ous** *adj*

clamp *n* : device for holding things together — **clamp** *vb*

clan *n* : group of related families — **clan·nish** *adj* — **clan·nish·ness** *n*

clan·des·tine *adj* : secret

clang *n* : loud metallic ringing — **clang** *vb*

clank *n* : brief sound of struck metal — **clank** *vb*

clap *vb* **1** : strike noisily **2** : applaud $\sim$ *n* **1** : loud crash **2** : noise made by clapping the hands

clap·per *n* : tongue of a bell

clar·i·fy *vb* : make or become clear — **clar·i·fi·ca·tion** *n*

clar·i·net *n* : woodwind instrument shaped like a tube — **clar·i·net·ist, clar·i·net·tist** *n*

clar·i·ty *n* : the quality of being clear

clash *vb* **1** : make or cause a clash **2** : be in

opposition or disharmony ∼ *n* **1** : crashing sound **2** : hostile encounter

clasp *n* **1** : device for holding things together **2** : embrace or grasp ∼ *vb* **1** : fasten **2** : embrace or grasp

class *n* **1** : group of the same status or nature **2** : social rank **3** : course of instruction **4** : group of students ∼ *vb* : classify — **class·less** *adj* — **class·mate** *n* — **class·room** *n*

clas·sic *adj* **1** : serving as a standard of excellence **2** : classical ∼ *n* : work of enduring excellence and esp. of ancient Greece or Rome — **clas·si·cal** *adj* — **clas·si·cal·ly** *adv* — **clas·si·cism** *n* — **clas·si·cist** *n*

clas·si·fied *adj* : restricted for security reasons

clas·si·fy *vb* : arrange in or assign to classes — **clas·si·fi·ca·tion** *n* — **clas·si·fi·er** *n*

clat·ter *n* : rattling sound — **clat·ter** *vb*

clause *n* **1** : separate part of a document **2** : part of a sentence with a subject and predicate

claus·tro·pho·bia *n* : fear of closed or narrow spaces — **claus·tro·pho·bic** *adj*

claw *n* : sharp curved nail or naillike part of an animal ∼ *vb* : scratch or dig — **clawed** *adj*

clay *n* : plastic earthy material — **clay·ey** *adj*

clean *adj* **1** : free from dirt or disease **2** : pure or honorable **3** : thorough ∼ *vb* : make or become clean — **clean** *adv* — **clean·er** *n* — **clean·li·ness** *n* — **clean·ly** *adv* — **clean·ness** *n*

cleanse *vb* : make clean — **cleans·er** *n*

clear *adj* **1** : bright **2** : free from clouds **3** : transparent **4** : easily heard, seen or understood **5** : free from doubt **6** : free from restriction or obstruction ∼ *vb* **1** : make or become clear **2** : go away **3** : free from accusation or blame **4** : explain or settle **5** : net **6** : jump or pass without touching ∼ *n* : clear space or part — **clear** *adv* — **clear·ance** *n* — **clear·ly** *adv*

clear·ing *n* : land cleared of wood

¹**cleave** *vb* : adhere

²**cleave** *vb* : split apart — **cleav·er** *n*

clef *n* : sign on the staff in music to show pitch

cleft *n* : crack

clench *vb* **1** : hold fast **2** : close tightly

cler·gy *n* : body of religious officials — **cler·gy·man** *n*

cler·ic *n* : member of the clergy

cler·i·cal *adj* **1** : relating to the clergy **2** : relating to a clerk or office worker

clerk *n* **1** : official responsible for record-keeping **2** : person doing general office work **3** : salesperson in a store — **clerk** *vb* — **clerk·ship** *n*

clev·er *adj* **1** : resourceful **2** : marked by wit or ingenuity — **clev·er·ly** *adv* — **clev·er·ness** *n*

cli·ché *n* : trite phrase — **cli·chéd** *adj*

click *n* : slight sharp noise ∼ *vb* : make or cause to make a click

cli·ent *n* **1** : person who engages professional services **2** : customer

cli·en·tele *n* : body of customers

cliff *n* : high steep face of rock

cli·mate *n* : average weather conditions over a period of years — **cli·mat·ic** *adj*

cli·max *n* : the highest point ∼ *vb* : come to a climax — **cli·mac·tic** *adj*

climb *vb* **1** : go up or down by use of hands and feet **2** : rise ∼ *n* : a climbing — **climb·er** *n*

clinch *vb* **1** : fasten securely **2** : settle **3** : hold fast or firmly — **clinch** *n* — **clinch·er** *n*

cling *vb* (**clung; clung**) **1** : adhere firmly **2** : hold on tightly

clin·ic *n* : facility for diagnosis and treatment of outpatients — **clin·i·cal** *adj* — **clin·i·cal·ly** *adv*

clink *vb* : make a slight metallic sound — **clink** *n*

¹**clip** *vb* : fasten with a clip ∼ *n* : device to hold things together

²**clip** *vb* **1** : cut or cut off **2** : hit ∼ *n* **1** : clippers **2** : sharp blow **3** : rapid pace

clip·per *n* **1** *pl* : implement for clipping **2** : fast sailing ship

clique *n* : small exclusive group of people

cloak *n* **1** : loose outer garment **2** : something that conceals ∼ *vb* : cover or hide with a cloak

clob·ber *vb* : hit hard

clock *n* : timepiece not carried on the person ∼ *vb* : record the time of

clock·wise *adv or adj* : in the same direction as a clock's hands move

clod *n* **1** : lump esp. of earth **2** : dull insensitive person

clog *n* **1** : restraining weight **2** : thick-soled shoe ∼ *vb* **1** : impede with a clog **2** : obstruct passage through **3** : become plugged up

clone *n* **1** : offspring produced from a single organism **2** : copy

¹**close** *vb* **1** : shut **2** : cease operation **3** : terminate **4** : bring or come together ∼ *n* : conclusion or end

²**close** *adj* **1** : confining **2** : secretive **3** : strict

4 : stuffy **5 :** having little space between items **6 :** fitting tightly **7 :** near **8 :** intimate **9 :** accurate **10 :** nearly even — **close** adv — **close·ly** adv — **close·ness** n

clos·et n **:** small compartment for household utensils or clothing

clo·sure n **1 :** act of closing **2 :** something that closes

clot n **:** dried mass of a liquid — **clot** vb

cloth n **1 :** fabric **2 :** tablecloth

clothe vb **:** dress

clothes n pl **:** clothing

cloth·ing n **:** covering for the human body

cloud n **1 :** visible mass of particles in the air **2 :** something that darkens, hides, or threatens ∼ vb **:** darken or hide — **cloud·burst** n — **cloud·i·ness** n — **cloud·less** adj — **cloudy** adj

clout n **1 :** blow **2 :** influence ∼ vb **:** hit forcefully

clove n **:** dried flower bud of an East Indian tree used as a spice

clo·ver n **:** leguminous herb with usu. 3-part leaves

clown n **:** funny costumed entertainer esp. in a circus ∼ vb **:** act like a clown — **clown·ish** adj — **clown·ish·ly** adv — **clown·ish·ness** n

cloy vb **:** disgust with excess — **cloy·ing·ly** adv

club n **1 :** heavy wooden stick **2 :** playing card of a suit marked with a black figure like a clover leaf **3 :** group associated for a common purpose ∼ vb **:** hit with a club

cluck n **:** sound made by a hen — **cluck** vb

clue n **:** piece of evidence that helps solve a problem ∼ vb **:** provide with a clue

clump n **1 :** cluster **2 :** heavy tramping sound ∼ vb **:** tread heavily

clum·sy adj **1 :** lacking dexterity, nimbleness, or grace **2 :** tactless — **clum·si·ly** adv — **clum·si·ness** n

clung past of CLING

clus·ter n **:** group ∼ vb **:** grow or gather in a cluster

clutch vb **:** grasp ∼ n **1 :** grasping hand or claws **2 :** control or power **3 :** coupling for connecting two working parts in machinery

clut·ter vb **:** fill with things that get in the way — **clutter** n

coach n **1 :** closed 2-door 4-wheeled carriage **2 :** railroad passenger car **3 :** bus **4 :** 2d-class air travel **5 :** one who instructs or trains performers ∼ vb **:** instruct or direct as a coach

coal n **1 :** glowing fragment from a fire **2 :** black solid mineral used as fuel — **coal·field** n

co·ali·tion n **:** temporary alliance

coarse adj **1 :** composed of large particles **2 :** rough or crude — **coarse·ly** adv — **coars·en** vb — **coarse·ness** n

coast n **:** seashore ∼ vb **:** move without effort — **coast·al** adj — **coast·line** n

coast·er n **1 :** one that coasts **2 :** plate or mat to protect a surface

coast guard n **:** military force that guards or patrols a coast — **coast·guards·man** n

coat n **1 :** outer garment for the upper body **2 :** external growth of fur or feathers **3 :** covering layer ∼ vb **:** cover with a coat — **coat·ed** adj — **coat·ing** n

coax vb **:** move to action or achieve by gentle urging or flattery

cob·bler n **1 :** shoemaker **2 :** deep-dish fruit pie

cob·web n **:** network spun by a spider or a similar filament

cock n **1 :** male fowl **2 :** valve or faucet ∼ vb **1 :** draw back the hammer of a firearm **2 :** tilt to one side — **cock·fight** n

cock·eyed adj **1 :** tilted to one side **2 :** slightly crazy

cock·pit n **:** place for a pilot, driver, or helmsman

cock·roach n **:** nocturnal insect often infesting houses

cock·tail n **1 :** iced drink of liquor and flavorings **2 :** appetizer

cocky adj **:** too confident in oneself — **cock·i·ly** adv — **cock·i·ness** n

co·coa n **1 :** cacao **2 :** powdered chocolate or a drink made from this

co·co·nut n **:** large nutlike fruit of a tropical palm (**coconut palm**)

co·coon n **:** case protecting an insect pupa

cod n pl **cod :** food fish of the No. Atlantic

cod·dle vb **:** pamper

code n **1 :** system of laws or rules **2 :** system of signals

co·ed n **:** female student in a coeducational institution — **coed** adj

co·ed·u·ca·tion n **:** education of the sexes together — **co·ed·u·ca·tion·al** adj

co·erce vb **:** force — **co·er·cion** n — **co·er·cive** adj

cof·fee *n* : drink made from the roasted and ground seeds (**coffee beans**) of a tropical shrub — **cof·fee·house** *n* — **cof·fee·pot** *n*

cof·fin *n* : box for burial

cog *n* : tooth on the rim of a gear — **cogged** *adj* — **cog·wheel** *n*

cog·ni·zance *n* : notice or awareness — **cog·ni·zant** *adj*

co·hab·it *vb* : live together as husband and wife — **co·hab·i·ta·tion** *n*

co·here *vb* : stick together — **co·he·sion** *n* — **co·he·sive** *adj* — **co·he·sive·ly** *adv* — **co·he·sive·ness** *n*

co·her·ent *adj* **1** : able to stick together **2** : logically consistent — **co·her·ence** *n* — **co·her·ent·ly** *adv*

coil *vb* : wind in a spiral ∼ *n* : series of loops (as of rope)

coin *n* : piece of metal used as money ∼ *vb* **1** : make (a coin) by stamping **2** : create — **coin·age** *n* — **coin·er** *n*

co·in·cide *vb* **1** : be in the same place **2** : happen at the same time **3** : be alike — **co·in·ci·dence** *n* — **co·in·ci·dent** *adj* — **co·in·ci·den·tal** *adj*

co·la *n* : carbonated soft drink

col·an·der *n* : perforated utensil for draining food

cold *adj* **1** : having a low or below normal temperature **2** : lacking warmth of feeling **3** : suffering from lack of warmth ∼ *n* **1** : low temperature **2** : minor respiratory illness — **cold·ly** *adv* — **cold·ness** *n* — **in cold blood** : with premeditation

cold–blood·ed *adj* **1** : cruel or merciless **2** : having a body temperature that varies with the temperature of the environment

cole·slaw *n* : cabbage salad

col·ic *n* : sharp abdominal pain — **col·icky** *adj*

col·i·se·um *n* : arena

col·lab·o·rate *vb* **1** : work jointly with others **2** : help the enemy — **col·lab·o·ra·tion** *n* — **col·lab·o·ra·tor** *n*

col·lapse *vb* **1** : fall in **2** : break down physically or mentally **3** : fold down ∼ *n* : breakdown — **col·laps·ible** *adj*

col·lar *n* : part of a garment around the neck ∼ *vb* **1** : seize by the collar **2** : grab — **col·lar·less** *adj*

col·lar·bone *n* : bone joining the breastbone and the shoulder blade

col·league *n* : associate

col·lect *vb* **1** : bring, come, or gather together

2 : receive payment of ∼ *adv or adj* : to be paid for by the receiver — **col·lect·ible, col·lect·able** *adj* — **col·lec·tive** *adj* — **col·lec·tive·ly** *adv* — **col·lec·tion** *n* — **col·lec·tor** *n*

col·lege *n* : institution of higher learning granting a bachelor's degree — **col·le·gian** *n* — **col·le·giate** *adj*

col·lide *vb* : strike together — **col·li·sion** *n*

col·lie *n* : large long-haired dog

col·lu·sion *n* : secret cooperation for deceit — **col·lu·sive** *adj*

co·logne *n* : perfumed liquid

¹co·lon *n* : lower part of the large intestine — **co·lon·ic** *adj*

²colon *n* : punctuation mark : used esp. to direct attention to following matter

col·o·nel *n* : commissioned officer (as in the army) ranking below a general

col·o·nize *vb* **1** : establish a colony in **2** : settle — **col·o·ni·za·tion** *n* — **col·o·niz·er** *n*

col·o·ny *n* **1** : people who inhabit a new territory or the territory itself **2** : animals of one kind (as bees) living together — **co·lo·nial** *adj or n* — **col·o·nist** *n*

col·or *n* **1** : quality of visible things distinct from shape that results from light reflection **2** *pl* : flag **3** : liveliness ∼ *vb* **1** : give color to **2** : blush — **col·or·fast** *adj* — **col·or·ful** *adj* — **col·or·less** *adj*

col·or–blind *adj* : unable to distinguish colors — **color blindness** *n*

col·ored *adj* **1** : having color **2** : of a race other than the white ∼ *n* : colored person

co·los·sus *n* : something of great size or scope — **co·los·sal** *adj*

colt *n* : young male horse — **colt·ish** *adj*

col·umn *n* **1** : vertical section of a printed page **2** : regular feature article (as in a newspaper) **3** : pillar **4** : row (as of soldiers) — **co·lum·nar** *adj* — **col·um·nist** *n*

co·ma *n* : deep prolonged unconsciousness — **co·ma·tose** *adj*

comb *n* **1** : toothed instrument for arranging the hair **2** : crest on a fowl's head — **comb** *vb* — **combed** *adj*

com·bat *vb* : fight — **com·bat** *n* — **com·bat·ant** *n* — **com·bat·ive** *adj*

com·bine *vb* : join together ∼ *n* **1** : association for business or political advantage **2** : harvesting machine — **com·bi·na·tion** *n*

com·bust *vb* : to catch fire — **com·bus·ti·bil·i·ty** *n* — **com·bus·ti·ble** *adj or n* — **com·bus·tion** *n*

come *vb* **came; come** **1** : move toward or arrive at something **2** : reach a state **3** : originate or exist **4** : amount — **come clean** *vb* : confess — **come into** *vb* : acquire, achieve — **come off** *vb* : succeed — **come to** *vb* : regain consciousness — **come to pass** : happen — **come to terms** : reach an agreement

come·back *n* **1** : retort **2** : return to a former position — **come back** *vb*

co·me·di·an *n* **1** : comic actor **2** : funny person **3** : entertainer specializing in comedy

co·me·di·enne *n* : a woman who is a comedian

com·e·dy *n* **1** : an amusing play **2** : humorous entertainment

com·et *n* : small bright celestial body having a tail

com·fort *n* **1** : consolation **2** : well-being or something that gives it ∼ *vb* **1** : give hope to **2** : console — **com·fort·able** *adj* — **comfort·ably** *adv*

com·fort·er *n* **1** : one that comforts **2** : quilt

com·ic *adj* **1** : relating to comedy **2** : funny ∼ *n* **1** : comedian **2** : sequence of cartoons — **com·i·cal** *adj*

com·ing *adj* : next

com·ma *n* : punctuation mark, used esp. to separate sentence parts

com·mand *vb* **1** : order **2** : control ∼ *n* **1** : act of commanding **2** : an order given **3** : mastery **4** : troops under a commander — **com·man·dant** *n*

com·man·deer *vb* : seize by force

com·mand·er *n* **1** : officer commanding an army or subdivision of an army **2** : commissioned officer in the navy ranking below a captain

com·mand·ment *n* : order

com·mem·o·rate *vb* : celebrate or honor — **com·mem·o·ra·tion** *n* — **com·mem·o·ra·tive** *adj*

com·mence *vb* : start

com·mence·ment *n* **1** : beginning **2** : graduation ceremony

com·mend *vb* **1** : entrust **2** : recommend **3** : praise — **com·mend·able** *adj* — **com·men·da·tion** *n*

com·ment *n* : statement of opinion or remark — **comment** *vb*

com·men·tary *n* : series of comments

com·men·ta·tor *n* : one who discusses news

com·merce *n* : business

com·mer·cial *adj* : designed for profit or for mass appeal ∼ *n* : broadcast advertisement —

com·mer·cial·ize *vb* — **com·mer·cial·ly** *adv*

com·mis·sary *n* : store esp. for military personnel

com·mis·sion *n* **1** : order granting power or rank **2** : panel to judge, approve, or act **3** : the doing of an act **4** : agent's fee ∼ *vb* **1** : confer rank or authority to or for **2** : request something be done

com·mis·sion·er *n* **1** : member of a commission **2** : head of a government department

com·mit *vb* **1** : turn over to someone for safekeeping or confinement **2** : perform or do **3** : pledge — **com·mit·ment** *n*

com·mit·tee *n* : panel that examines or acts on something

com·mod·i·ty *n* : article for sale

com·mon *adj* **1** : public **2** : shared by several **3** : widely known, found, or observed **4** : ordinary ∼ *n* : community land — **com·mon·ly** *adv* — **in common** : shared together

com·mon·place *n* : cliché ∼ *adj* : ordinary

com·mon·wealth *n* : state

com·mo·tion *n* : disturbance

com·mu·ni·cate *vb* **1** : make known **2** : transmit **3** : exchange information or opinions — **com·mu·ni·ca·ble** *adj* — **com·mu·ni·ca·tion** *n* — **com·mu·ni·ca·tive** *adj*

Com·mu·nion *n* : Christian sacrament of partaking of bread and wine

com·mu·nism *n* **1** : social organization in which goods are held in common **2** *cap* : political doctrine based on revolutionary Marxist socialism — **com·mu·nist** *n or adj, often cap* — **com·mu·nis·tic** *adj, often cap*

com·mu·ni·ty *n* : body of people living in the same place under the same laws

com·mute *vb* **1** : reduce (a punishment) **2** : travel back and forth regularly ∼ *n* : trip made in commuting — **com·mu·ta·tion** *n* — **com·mut·er** *n*

¹**com·pact** *adj* **1** : hard **2** : small or brief ∼ *vb* : pack together ∼ *n* **1** : cosmetics case **2** : small car — **com·pact·ly** *adv* — **com·pact·ness** *n*

²**com·pact** *n* : agreement

compact disc *n* : plastic-coated disc with laser-readable recorded music

com·pan·ion *n* **1** : close friend **2** : one of a pair — **com·pan·ion·able** *adj* — **com·pan·ion·ship** *n*

com·pa·ny *n* **1** : business organization **2**

: group of performers **3** : guests **4** : infantry unit

com·pare *vb* **1** : represent as similar **2** : check for likenesses or differences ⁀ *n* : comparison — **com·pa·ra·ble** *adj* — **com·par·a·tive** *adj or n* — **com·par·a·tive·ly** *adv* — **com·par·i·son** *n*

com·part·ment *n* : section or room

com·pass *n* **1** : scope **2** : device for drawing circles **3** : device for determining direction

com·pas·sion *n* : pity — **com·pas·sion·ate** *adj*

com·pat·i·ble *adj* : harmonious — **com·pat·i·bil·i·ty** *n*

com·pel *vb* : cause through necessity

com·pen·sate *vb* **1** : offset or balance **2** : repay — **com·pen·sa·tion** *n* — **com·pen·sa·to·ry** *adj*

com·pete *vb* : strive to win — **com·pe·ti·tion** *n* — **com·pet·i·tive** *adj* — **com·pet·i·tive·ness** *n* — **com·pet·i·tor** *n*

com·pe·tent *adj* : capable — **com·pe·tence** *n* — **com·pe·ten·cy** *n*

com·pile *vb* : collect or compose from several sources — **com·pi·la·tion** *n* — **com·pil·er** *n*

com·pla·cen·cy *n* : unusual satisfaction with oneself — **com·pla·cent** *adj*

com·plain *vb* **1** : express grief, pain, or discontent **2** : make an accusation — **com·plain·ant** *n* — **com·plain·er** *n* — **com·plaint** *n*

com·ple·ment *n* **1** : something that completes **2** : full number or amount ⁀ *vb* : complete — **com·ple·men·ta·ry** *adj*

com·plete *adj* **1** : having all parts **2** : finished **3** : total ⁀ *vb* **1** : make whole **2** : finish — **com·plete·ly** *adv* — **com·plete·ness** *n* — **com·ple·tion** *n*

com·plex *adj* **1** : having many parts **2** : intricate ⁀ *n* : psychological problem — **com·plex·i·ty** *n*

com·plex·ion *n* : hue or appearance of the skin esp. of the face — **com·plex·ioned** *adj*

com·pli·cate *vb* : make complex or hard to understand — **com·pli·cat·ed** *adj* — **com·pli·ca·tion** *n*

com·pli·ment *n* **1** : flattering remark **2** *pl* : greeting ⁀ *vb* : pay a compliment to

com·pli·men·ta·ry *adj* **1** : praising **2** : free

com·ply *vb* : conform or yield — **com·pli·ance** *n* — **com·pli·ant** *n*

com·po·nent *n* : part of something larger ⁀ *adj* : serving as a component

com·pose *vb* **1** : create (as by writing) or put together **2** : calm **3** : set type — **com·pos·er** *n* — **com·po·si·tion** *n*

com·pos·ite *adj* : made up of diverse parts — composite *n*

com·post *n* : decayed organic fertilizing material

com·po·sure *n* : calmness

¹**com·pound** *vb* **1** : combine or add **2** : pay (interest) on principal and accrued interest ⁀ *adj* : made up of 2 or more parts ⁀ *n* : something that is compound

²**com·pound** *n* : enclosure

com·pre·hend *vb* **1** : understand **2** : include — **com·pre·hen·si·ble** *adj* — **com·pre·hen·sion** *n* — **com·pre·hen·sive** *adj*

com·press *vb* : squeeze together ⁀ *n* : pad for pressing on a wound — **com·pres·sion** *n* — **com·pres·sor** *n*

com·prise *vb* **1** : contain or cover **2** : be made up of

com·pro·mise *vb* : settle differences by mutual concessions — **com·pro·mise** *n*

com·pul·sion *n* **1** : coercion **2** : irresistible impulse — **com·pul·sive** *adj* — **com·pul·so·ry** *adj*

com·pute *vb* : calculate — **com·pu·ta·tion** *n*

com·put·er *n* : electronic data processing machine — **com·put·er·i·za·tion** *n* — **com·put·er·ize** *vb*

com·rade *n* : companion — **com·rade·ship** *n*

con·cave *adj* : curved like the inside of a sphere — **con·cav·i·ty** *n*

con·ceal *vb* : hide — **con·ceal·ment** *n*

con·cede *vb* : grant

con·ceit *n* : excessively high opinion of oneself — **con·ceit·ed** *adj*

con·ceive *vb* **1** : become pregnant **2** : think of — **con·ceiv·able** *adj* — **con·ceiv·ably** *adv*

con·cen·trate *vb* **1** : gather together **2** : make stronger **3** : fix one's attention ⁀ *n* : something concentrated — **con·cen·tra·tion** *n*

con·cen·tric *adj* : having a common center

con·cept *n* : thought or idea

con·cep·tion *n* **1** : act of conceiving **2** : idea

con·cern *vb* **1** : relate to **2** : involve ⁀ *n* **1** : affair **2** : worry **3** : business — **con·cerned** *adj* — **con·cern·ing** *prep*

con·cert *n* **1** : agreement or joint action **2** : public performance of music — **con·cert·ed** *adj*

con·cer·to *n* : orchestral work with solo instruments

con·ces·sion *n* **1** : act of conceding **2** : something conceded **3** : right to do business on a property

con·cil·ia·to·ry *adj* : doing what's necessary to gain goodwill

con·cise *adj* : said in few words — **con·cise·ly** *adv* — **con·cise·ness** *n* — **con·ci·sion** *n*

con·clude *vb* **1** : end **2** : decide — **con·clu·sion** *n* — **con·clu·sive** *adj* — **con·clu·sive·ly** *adv*

con·coct *vb* : prepare or devise — **con·coc·tion** *n*

con·cord *n* : agreement

con·cor·dance *n* **1** : agreement **2** : index of words — **con·cor·dant** *adj*

con·course *n* : open space where crowds gather

con·crete *adj* **1** : naming something real **2** : actual or substantial **3** : made of concrete ∼ *n* : hard building material made of cement, sand, gravel, and water

con·cur *vb* : agree — **con·cur·rence** *n*

con·cur·rent *adj* : happening at the same time

con·cus·sion *n* **1** : shock **2** : brain injury from a blow

con·demn *vb* **1** : declare to be wrong, guilty, or unfit for use **2** : sentence — **con·dem·na·tion** *n*

con·dense *vb* **1** : make or become more compact **2** : change from vapor to liquid — **con·den·sa·tion** *n* — **con·dens·er** *n*

con·de·scend *vb* **1** : lower oneself **2** : act haughtily — **con·de·scen·sion** *n*

con·di·ment *n* : pungent seasoning

con·di·tion *n* **1** : necessary situation or stipulation **2** *pl* : state of affairs **3** : state of being ∼ *vb* : put into proper condition — **con·di·tion·al** *adj* — **con·di·tion·al·ly** *adv*

con·do·lence *n* : expression of sympathy — usu. pl.

con·do·min·i·um *n* : individually owned apartment

con·done *vb* : overlook or forgive

con·du·cive *adj* : tending to help or promote

con·duct *n* **1** : management **2** : behavior ∼ *vb* **1** : guide **2** : manage or direct **3** : be a channel for **4** : behave — **con·duc·tion** *n* — **con·duc·tive** *adj* — **con·duc·tiv·i·ty** *n* — **con·duc·tor** *n*

cone *n* **1** : scaly fruit of pine and related trees **2** : solid figure having a circular base and tapering sides

con·fec·tion *n* : sweet dish or candy — **con·fec·tion·er** *n*

con·fed·er·ate *adj* **1** : united in a league **2** *cap* : relating to the 11 southern states that seceded from the U.S. in 1860 and 1861 ∼ *n* **1** : ally **2** *cap* : adherent of the Confederacy ∼ *vb* : unite — **con·fed·er·a·cy** *n* — **con·fed·er·a·tion** *n*

con·fer *vb* **1** : give **2** : meet to exchange views — **con·fer·ee** *n* — **con·fer·ence** *n*

con·fess *vb* **1** : acknowledge or disclose one's misdeed, fault, or sin **2** : declare faith in — **con·fes·sion** *n* — **con·fes·sion·al** *n or adj*

con·fes·sor *n* **1** : one who confesses **2** : priest who hears confessions

con·fet·ti *n* : bits of paper or ribbon thrown in celebration

con·fide *vb* **1** : share private thoughts **2** : reveal in confidence — **con·fi·dant** *n*

con·fi·dence *n* **1** : trust **2** : certainty of one's nature or ability **3** : something confided — **con·fi·dent** *adj* — **con·fi·den·tial** *adj* — **con·fi·den·tial·ly** *adv* — **con·fi·dent·ly** *adv*

con·fig·u·ra·tion *n* : arrangement

con·fine *vb* **1** : restrain or restrict to a limited area **2** : imprison — **con·fine·ment** *n* — **con·fin·er** *n* — **con·fines** *n pl*

con·firm *vb* **1** : ratify **2** : verify **3** : admit as a full member of a church or synagogue — **con·fir·ma·tion** *n*

con·fis·cate *vb* : take by authority — **con·fis·ca·tion** *n* — **con·fis·ca·to·ry** *adj*

con·flict *n* **1** : war **2** : clash of ideas ∼ *vb* : clash

con·form *vb* **1** : make or be like **2** : obey — **con·for·mi·ty** *n*

con·front *vb* : oppose or face — **con·fron·ta·tion** *n*

con·fuse *vb* **1** : make mentally uncertain **2** : jumble — **con·fu·sion** *n*

con·geal *vb* **1** : freeze **2** : become thick and solid

con·ge·nial *adj* : kindred or agreeable — **con·ge·ni·al·i·ty** *n*

con·gest *vb* : overcrowd or overfill — **con·ges·tion** *n* — **con·ges·tive** *adj*

con·glom·er·ate *adj* : made up of diverse parts ∼ *vb* : form into a mass ∼ *n* : diversified corporation — **con·glom·er·a·tion** *n*

con·grat·u·late *vb* : express pleasure to for good fortune — **con·grat·u·la·tion** *n* — **con·grat·u·la·to·ry** *adj*

con·gre·gate *vb* : assemble — **con·gre·ga·tion** *n* — **con·gre·ga·tion·al** *adj*

con·gress *n* : assembly of delegates or of senators and representatives — **con·gres·sio·nal** *adj* — **con·gress·man** *n* — **con·gress·wom·an** *n*

co·ni·fer *n* : cone-bearing tree — **co·nif·er·ous** *adj*

con·ju·gate *vb* : give the inflected forms of (a verb) — **con·ju·ga·tion** *n*

con·junc·tion *n* 1 : combination 2 : occurrence at the same time 3 : a word that joins other words together — **con·junc·tive** *adj*

con·jure *vb* 1 : summon by sorcery 2 : practice sleight of hand 3 : entreat — **con·jur·er, con·ju·ror** *n*

con·nect *vb* : join or associate — **con·nect·able** *adj* — **con·nec·tion** *n* — **con·nec·tive** *n or adj* — **con·nec·tor** *n*

con·nive *vb* 1 : pretend ignorance of wrongdoing 2 : cooperate secretly — **con·niv·ance** *n*

con·nois·seur *n* : expert judge esp. of art

con·quer *vb* : defeat or overcome — **con·quer·or** *n*

con·quest *n* 1 : act of conquering 2 : something conquered

con·science *n* : awareness of right and wrong

con·sci·en·tious *adj* : honest and hard-working — **con·sci·en·tious·ly** *adv*

con·scious *adj* 1 : aware 2 : mentally awake or alert 3 : intentional — **con·scious·ly** *adv* — **con·scious·ness** *n*

con·se·crate *vb* 1 : declare sacred 2 : devote to a solemn purpose — **con·se·cra·tion** *n*

con·sec·u·tive *adj* : following in order — **con·sec·u·tive·ly** *adv*

con·sen·sus *n* 1 : agreement in opinion 2 : collective opinion

con·sent *vb* : give permission or approval — **consent** *n*

con·se·quence *n* 1 : result or effect 2 : importance — **con·se·quent** *adj* — **con·se·quen·tial** *adj* — **con·se·quent·ly** *adv*

con·ser·va·tive *adj* 1 : disposed to maintain the status quo 2 : cautious — **con·ser·va·tism** *n* — **con·ser·va·tive** *n* — **con·ser·va·tive·ly** *adv*

con·ser·va·to·ry *n* : school for art or music

con·serve *vb* : keep from wasting ~ *n* : candied fruit or fruit preserves — **con·ser·va·tion** *n* — **con·ser·va·tion·ist** *n*

con·sid·er *vb* 1 : think about 2 : give thought-

ful attention to 3 : think that — **con·sid·er·ate** *adj* — **con·sid·er·ation** *n*

con·sid·er·able *adj* 1 : significant 2 : noticeably large — **con·sid·er·a·bly** *adv*

con·sign *vb* 1 : transfer 2 : send to an agent for sale — **con·sign·ee** *n* — **con·sign·ment** *n* — **con·sign·or** *n*

con·sist *vb* 1 : be inherent — used with *in* 2 : be made up — used with *of*

con·sis·ten·cy *n* 1 : degree of thickness or firmness 2 : quality of being consistent

con·sis·tent *adj* : being steady and regular — **con·sis·tent·ly** *adv*

¹**con·sole** *vb* : soothe the grief of — **con·so·la·tion** *n*

²**con·sole** *n* : cabinet or part with controls

con·sol·i·date *vb* : unite or compact — **con·sol·i·da·tion** *n*

con·so·nant *n* 1 : speech sound marked by constriction or closure in the breath channel 2 : letter other than *a, e, i, o,* and *u* — **con·so·nan·tal** *adj*

con·spic·u·ous *adj* : very noticeable — **con·spic·u·ous·ly** *adv*

con·spire *vb* : secretly plan an unlawful act — **con·spir·a·cy** *n* — **con·spir·a·tor** *n* — **con·spir·a·to·ri·al** *adj*

con·sta·ble *n* : police officer

con·stant *adj* 1 : steadfast or faithful 2 : not varying 3 : continually recurring ~ *n* : something unchanging — **con·stan·cy** *n* — **con·stant·ly** *adv*

con·stel·la·tion *n* : group of stars

con·sti·pa·tion *n* : difficulty of defecation — **con·sti·pate** *vb*

con·stit·u·ent *adj* 1 : component 2 : having power to elect ~ *n* 1 : component part 2 : one who may vote for a representative — **con·stit·u·en·cy** *n*

con·sti·tute *vb* 1 : establish 2 : be all or a basic part of

con·sti·tu·tion *n* 1 : physical composition or structure 2 : the basic law of an organized body or the document containing it — **con·sti·tu·tion·al** *adj* — **con·sti·tu·tion·al·i·ty** *n*

con·strain *vb* 1 : compel 2 : confine 3 : restrain — **con·straint** *n*

con·strict *vb* : draw or squeeze together — **con·stric·tion** *n* — **con·stric·tive** *adj*

con·struct *vb* : build or make — **con·struc·tion** *n* — **con·struc·tive** *adj*

con·strue *vb* : explain or interpret

con·sul *n* 1 : Roman magistrate 2 : govern-

ment commercial official in a foreign country
— **con·sul·ar** *adj* — **con·sul·ate** *n*

con·sult *vb* **1** : ask the advice or opinion of **2** : confer — **con·sul·tant** *n* — **con·sul·ta·tion** *n*

con·sume *vb* : eat or use up — **con·sum·able** *adj* — **con·sum·er** *n*

con·sump·tion *n* **1** : act of consuming **2** : use of goods

con·tact *n* **1** : a touching **2** : association or relationship **3** : connection or communication ∼ *vb* **1** : come or bring into contact **2** : communicate with

con·ta·gion *n* **1** : spread of disease by contact **2** : disease spread by contact — **con·ta·gious** *adj*

con·tain *vb* **1** : enclose or include **2** : have or hold within **3** : restrain — **con·tain·er** *n* — **con·tain·ment** *n*

con·tam·i·nate *vb* : soil or infect by contact or association — **con·tam·i·na·tion** *n*

con·tem·plate *vb* : view or consider thoughtfully — **con·tem·pla·tion** *n* — **con·tem·pla·tive** *adj*

con·tem·po·ra·ne·ous *adj* : contemporary

con·tem·po·rary *adj* **1** : occurring or existing at the same time **2** : of the same age — **con·tem·po·rary** *n*

con·tempt *n* **1** : feeling of scorn **2** : state of being despised **3** : disobedience to a court or legislature — **con·tempt·ible** *adj*

con·temp·tu·ous *adj* : feeling or expressing contempt — **con·temp·tu·ous·ly** *adv*

con·tend *vb* **1** : strive against rivals or difficulties **2** : argue **3** : maintain or claim — **con·tend·er** *n*

¹**con·tent** *adj* : satisfied ∼ *vb* : satisfy ∼ *n* : ease of mind — **con·tent·ed** *adj* — **con·tent·ed·ly** *adv* — **con·tent·ed·ness** *n* — **con·tent·ment** *n*

²**con·tent** *n* **1** *pl* : something contained **2** *pl* : subject matter (as of a book) **3** : essential meaning **4** : proportion contained

con·ten·tion *n* : state of contending — **con·ten·tious** *adj* — **con·ten·tious·ly** *adv*

con·test *vb* : dispute or challenge ∼ *n* **1** : struggle **2** : game — **con·test·able** *adj* — **con·tes·tant** *n*

con·text *n* : words surrounding a word or phrase

con·ti·nent *n* : great division of land on the globe — **con·ti·nen·tal** *adj*

con·tin·gen·cy *n* : possible event

con·tin·gent *adj* : dependent on something else ∼ *n* : a quota from an area or group

con·tin·u·al *adj* **1** : continuous **2** : steadily recurring — **con·tin·u·al·ly** *adv*

con·tin·ue *vb* **1** : remain in a place or condition **2** : endure **3** : resume after an intermission **4** : extend — **con·tin·u·ance** *n* — **con·tin·u·ation** *n*

con·tin·u·ous *adj* : continuing without interruption — **con·ti·nu·ity** *n* — **con·tin·u·ous·ly** *adv*

con·tort *vb* : twist out of shape — **con·tor·tion** *n*

con·tour *n* **1** : outline **2** *pl* : shape

con·tra·band *n* : illegal goods

con·tract *n* : binding agreement ∼ *vb* **1** : establish or undertake by contract **2** : become ill with **3** : make shorter — **con·trac·tion** *n* — **con·trac·tor** *n* — **con·trac·tu·al** *adj* — **con·trac·tu·al·ly** *adv*

con·tra·dict *vb* : state the contrary of — **con·tra·dic·tion** *n* — **con·tra·dic·to·ry** *adj*

con·trap·tion *n* : device or contrivance

con·trary *adj* **1** : opposite in character, nature, or position **2** : mutually opposed **3** : unfavorable **4** : uncooperative or stubborn — **con·trari·ly** *adv* — **con·trari·wise** *adv* — **con·trary** *n*

con·trast *n* **1** : unlikeness shown by comparing **2** : unlike color or tone of adjacent parts ∼ *vb* **1** : show differences **2** : compare so as to show differences

con·tra·vene *vb* : go or act contrary to

con·trib·ute *vb* : give or help along with others — **con·tri·bu·tion** *n* — **con·trib·u·tor** *n* — **con·trib·u·to·ry** *adj*

con·trite *adj* : repentant — **con·tri·tion** *n*

con·trive *vb* **1** : devise or make with ingenuity **2** : bring about — **con·triv·ance** *n* — **con·triv·er** *n*

con·trol *vb* **1** : exercise power over **2** : dominate or rule ∼ *n* **1** : power to direct or regulate **2** : restraint **3** : regulating device — **con·trol·la·ble** *adj* — **con·trol·ler** *n*

con·tro·ver·sy *n* : clash of opposing views — **con·tro·ver·sial** *adj*

con·va·lesce *vb* : gradually recover health — **con·va·les·cence** *n* — **con·va·les·cent** *adj or n*

con·vec·tion *n* : circulation in fluids due to warmer portions rising and colder ones sinking — **con·vec·tion·al** *adj* — **con·vec·tive** *adj*

con·vene *vb* : assemble or meet

con·ve·nience *n* **1** : personal comfort or ease **2** : device that saves work — **con·ve·nient** *adj* — **con·ve·nient·ly** *adv*

con·vent *n* : community of nuns

con·ven·tion *n* **1** : agreement esp. between nations **2** : large meeting **3** : body of delegates **4** : accepted usage or way of behaving — **con·ven·tion·al** *adj* — **con·ven·tion·al·ly** *adv*

con·ver·sa·tion *n* : an informal talking together — **con·ver·sa·tion·al** *adj*

¹con·verse *vb* : engage in conversation — **con·verse** *n*

²con·verse *adj* : opposite — **con·verse** *n* — **con·verse·ly** *adv*

con·vert *vb* **1** : turn from one belief or party to another **2** : change ⁓ *n* : one who has adopted a religion — **con·ver·sion** *n* — **con·vert·er, con·ver·tor** *n* — **con·vert·ible** *adj*

con·vert·ible *n* : automobile with a removable top

con·vex *adj* : curved or rounded like the outside of a sphere — **con·vex·i·ty** *n*

con·vey *vb* : transport or transmit — **con·vey·ance** *n* — **con·vey·or** *n*

con·vict *vb* : find guilty ⁓ *n* : person in prison

con·vic·tion *n* **1** : act of convicting **2** : strong belief

con·vince *vb* : cause to believe — **con·vinc·ing·ly** *adv*

con·viv·ial *adj* : cheerful or festive — **con·viv·i·al·i·ty** *n*

con·vo·lut·ed *adj* **1** : intricately folded **2** : intricate

con·vo·lu·tion *n* : convoluted structure

con·voy *vb* : accompany for protection ⁓ *n* : group of vehicles or ships moving together

con·vul·sion *n* : violent involuntary muscle contraction — **con·vulse** *vb* — **con·vul·sive** *adj*

coo *n* : sound of a pigeon — **coo** *vb*

cook *n* : one who prepares food ⁓ *vb* : prepare food — **cook·book** *n* — **cook·er** *n* — **cook·ery** *n* — **cook·ware** *n*

cook·ie, cooky *n* : small sweet flat cake

cool *adj* **1** : moderately cold **2** : not excited **3** : unfriendly ⁓ *vb* : make or become cool ⁓ *n* **1** : cool time or place **2** : composure — **cool·ant** *n* — **cool·er** *n* — **cool·ly** *adv* — **cool·ness** *n*

coop *n* : enclosure usu. for poultry ⁓ *vb* : confine in or as if in a coop

co–op *n* : cooperative

co·op·er·ate *vb* : act jointly — **co·op·er·a·tion** *n* — **co·op·er·a·tive** *adj or n*

co·or·di·nate *adj* : equal esp. in rank ⁓ *n* : any of a set of numbers used in specifying the location of a point on a surface or in space ⁓ *vb* **1** : make or become coordinate **2** : work or act together harmoniously — **co·or·di·nate·ly** *adv* — **co·or·di·na·tion** *n* — **co·or·di·na·tor** *n*

cop *n* : police officer

cope *vb* : deal with difficulties

co·pi·lot *n* : assistant airplane pilot

cop·ing *n* : top layer of a wall

co·pi·ous *adj* : very abundant — **co·pi·ous·ly** *adv* — **co·pi·ous·ness** *n*

cop·per *n* **1** : malleable reddish metallic chemical element **2** : penny — **cop·pery** *adj*

copy *n* **1** : imitation or reproduction of an original **2** : writing to be set for printing ⁓ *vb* **1** : make a copy of **2** : imitate — **copi·er** *n* — **copyist** *n*

copy·right *n* : sole right to a literary or artistic work ⁓ *vb* : get a copyright on

cor·al *n* **1** : skeletal material of colonies of tiny sea polyps **2** : deep pink — **coral** *adj*

cord *n* **1** : usu. heavy string **2** : long slender anatomical structure **3** : measure of firewood equal to 128 cu. ft. **4** : small electrical cable ⁓ *vb* **1** : tie or furnish with a cord **2** : pile (wood) in cords

cor·dial *adj* : warmly welcoming — **cor·di·al·i·ty** *n* — **cor·dial·ly** *adv*

cor·du·roy *n* **1** : heavy ribbed fabric **2** *pl* : trousers of corduroy

core *n* **1** : central part of some fruits **2** : inmost part ⁓ *vb* : take out the core of — **cor·er** *n*

cork *n* **1** : tough elastic bark of a European oak (**cork oak**) **2** : stopper of cork ⁓ *vb* : stop up with a cork — **corky** *adj*

¹corn *n* : cereal grass (as Indian corn) or its seeds ⁓ *vb* : cure or preserve in brine — **corn·cob** *n* — **corn·meal** *n* — **corn·stalk** *n* — **corn·starch** *n*

²corn *n* : local hardening and thickening of skin

cor·nea *n* : transparent part of the coat of the eyeball — **cor·ne·al** *adj*

cor·ner *n* **1** : point or angle formed by the meeting of lines or sides **2** : place where two streets meet **3** : inescapable position **4** : control of the supply of something ⁓ *vb* **1** : drive into a corner **2** : get a corner on **3** : turn a corner

cor·ner·stone n **1** : stone at a corner of a wall **2** : something basic

cor·net n : trumpetlike instrument

cor·o·nary adj : relating to the heart or its blood vessels $\sim$ n **1** : thrombosis of an artery supplying the heart **2** : heart attack

cor·o·na·tion n : crowning of a monarch

cor·o·ner n : public official who investigates causes of suspicious deaths

¹cor·po·ral adj : bodily

²corporal n : noncommissioned officer ranking below a sergeant

cor·po·ra·tion n : legal creation with the rights and liabilities of a person — **cor·po·rate** adj

cor·po·re·al adj : physical or material — **cor·po·re·al·ly** adv

corps n **1** : subdivision of a military force **2** : working group

corpse n : dead body

cor·pus·cle n : blood cell

cor·ral n : enclosure for animals — **cor·ral** vb

cor·rect vb **1** : make right **2** : chastise $\sim$ adj **1** : true or factual **2** : conforming to a standard — **cor·rec·tion** n — **cor·rec·tive** adj — **cor·rect·ly** adv — **cor·rect·ness** n

cor·re·late vb : show a connection between — **cor·re·late** n — **cor·re·la·tion** n — **cor·rel·a·tive** n or adj

cor·re·spond vb **1** : match **2** : communicate by letter — **cor·re·spon·dence** n — **cor·re·spond·ing·ly** adv

cor·re·spon·dent n **1** : person one writes to **2** : reporter

cor·ri·dor n : passageway connecting rooms

cor·rode vb : wear away by chemical action — **cor·ro·sion** n — **cor·ro·sive** adj or n

cor·rupt vb **1** : change from good to bad **2** : bribe $\sim$ adj : morally debased — **cor·rupt·ible** adj — **cor·rup·tion** n

cor·sage n : bouquet worn by a woman

cos·met·ic n : beautifying preparation $\sim$ adj : relating to beautifying

cos·mic adj **1** : relating to the universe **2** : vast or grand

cos·mo·naut n : Soviet or Russian astronaut

cos·mo·pol·i·tan adj : belonging to all the world — **cos·mo·pol·i·tan** n

cos·mos n : universe

cost n **1** : amount paid for something **2** : loss or penalty $\sim$ vb **cost; cost 1** : require so

much in payment **2** : cause to pay, suffer, or lose — **cost·li·ness** n — **cost·ly** adj

cos·tume n : clothing

co·sy var of COZY

cot n : small bed

cote n : small shed or coop

cot·tage n : small house

cot·ton n : soft fibrous plant substance or thread or cloth made of it — **cot·ton·seed** n — **cot·tony** adj

cot·ton·mouth n : poisonous snake

couch vb **1** : lie or place on a couch **2** : phrase $\sim$ n : bed or sofa

couch potato n : one who spends a great deal of time watching television

cou·gar n : large tawny wild American cat

cough vb : force air from the lungs with short sharp noises — **cough** n

could past of CAN

couldn't : could not

coun·cil n **1** : assembly or meeting **2** : body of lawmakers — **coun·cil·lor, coun·cil·or** n — **coun·cil·man** n — **coun·cil·wom·an** n

coun·sel n **1** : advice **2** : deliberation together **3** pl **coun·sel** : lawyer $\sim$ vb **1** : advise **2** : consult together — **coun·sel·or, coun·sel·lor** n

¹count vb **1** : name or indicate one by one to find the total number **2** : recite numbers in order **3** : rely **4** : be of value or account $\sim$ n **1** : act of counting or the total obtained by counting **2** : charge in an indictment — **count·able** adj — **count·less** adj

²count n : European nobleman

coun·te·nance n : face or facial expression $\sim$ vb : allow or encourage

¹count·er n **1** : piece for reckoning or games **2** : surface over which business is transacted

²count·er n : one that counts

³coun·ter vb : oppose $\sim$ adv : in an opposite direction $\sim$ n : offsetting force or move $\sim$ adj : contrary

coun·ter·act vb : lessen the force of — **coun·ter·ac·tive** adj

coun·ter·bal·ance n : balancing influence or weight $\sim$ vb : oppose or balance

coun·ter·clock·wise adv or adj : opposite to the way a clock's hands move

coun·ter·feit vb **1** : copy in order to deceive **2** : pretend $\sim$ adj : not genuine $\sim$ n : fraudulent copy — **coun·ter·feit·er** n

coun·ter·part n : one that is similar or corresponds

coun·ter·sign *n* : secret signal ∼ *vb* : add a confirming signature to

count·ess *n* : wife or widow of a count or an earl or a woman holding that rank in her own right

coun·try *n* **1** : nation **2** : rural area ∼ *adj* : rural — **coun·try·man** *n*

coun·try·side *n* : rural area or its people

coun·ty *n* : local government division esp. of a state

coup *n* **1** : brilliant sudden action or plan **2** : sudden overthrow of a government

coupe *n* : 2-door automobile with an enclosed body

cou·ple *vb* : link together ∼ *n* **1** : pair **2** : two persons closely associated or married

cou·pling *n* : connecting device

cou·pon *n* : certificate redeemable for goods or a cash discount

cour·age *n* : ability to conquer fear or despair — **cou·ra·geous** *adj*

course *n* **1** : progress **2** : ground over which something moves **3** : part of a meal served at one time **4** : method of procedure **5** : subject taught in a series of classes ∼ *vb* **1** : hunt with dogs **2** : run speedily — **of course** : as might be expected

court *n* **1** : residence of a sovereign **2** : sovereign and his or her officials and advisers **3** : area enclosed by a building **4** : space marked for playing a game **5** : place where justice is administered ∼ *vb* : seek to win the affections of — **court·house** *n* — **court·room** *n* — **court·ship** *n*

cour·te·ous *adj* : showing politeness and respect for others — **cour·te·ous·ly** *adv*

cour·te·sy *n* : courteous behavior

court–mar·tial *n* **courts-mar·tial** : military trial court — **court–martial** *vb*

court·yard *n* : enclosure open to the sky that is attached to a house

cous·in *n* : child of one's uncle or aunt

cove *n* : sheltered inlet or bay

cov·e·nant *n* : binding agreement — **cov·e·nant** *vb*

cov·er *vb* **1** : place something over or upon **2** : protect or hide **3** : include or deal with ∼ *n* : something that covers — **cov·er·age** *n*

co·vert *adj* : secret ∼ *n* : thicket that shelters animals

cov·et *vb* : desire enviously — **cov·et·ous** *adj*

¹cow *n* : large adult female animal (as of cattle) — **cow·hide** *n*

²cow *vb* : intimidate

cow·ard *n* : one who lacks courage — **cow·ard·ice** *n* — **cow·ard·ly** *adv or adj*

cow·boy *n* : a mounted ranch hand who tends cattle

cow·er *vb* : shrink from fear or cold

cow·girl *n* : woman ranch hand who tends cattle

coy *adj* : shy or pretending shyness

coy·ote *n* : small No. American wolf

co·zy *adj* : snug

crab *n* : short broad shellfish with pincers

crab·by *adj* : cross

¹crack *vb* **1** : break with a sharp sound **2** : fail in tone **3** : break without completely separating ∼ *n* **1** : sudden sharp noise **2** : witty remark **3** : narrow break **4** : sharp blow **5** : try

²crack *adj* : extremely proficient

crack·down *n* : disciplinary action — **crack down** *vb*

crack·er *n* : thin crisp bakery product

crack·le *vb* **1** : make snapping noises **2** : develop fine cracks in a surface — **crack·le** *n*

crack–up *n* : crash

cra·dle *n* : baby's bed ∼ *vb* **1** : place in a cradle **2** : hold securely

craft *n* **1** : occupation requiring special skill **2** : craftiness **3** *pl usu* **craft** : structure designed to provide transportation **4** *pl usu* **craft** : small boat — **crafts·man** *n* — **crafts·man·ship** *n*

crafty *adj* : sly — **craft·i·ness** *n*

crag *n* : steep cliff — **crag·gy** *adj*

cram *vb* **1** : eat greedily **2** : pack in tight **3** : study intensely for a test

cramp *n* **1** : sudden painful contraction of muscle **2** *pl* : sharp abdominal pains ∼ *vb* **1** : affect with cramp **2** : restrain

cran·ber·ry *n* : red acid berry of a trailing plant

crane *n* **1** : tall wading bird **2** : machine for lifting heavy objects ∼ *vb* : stretch one's neck to see

crank *n* **1** : bent lever turned to operate a machine **2** : eccentric ∼ *vb* : start or operate by turning a crank

cranky *adj* : irritable

crash *vb* **1** : break noisily **2** : fall and hit something with noise and damage ∼ *n* **1** : loud sound **2** : action of crashing **3** : failure

crate *n* : wooden shipping container — **crate** *vb*

cra·ter *n* : volcanic depression

crave *vb* : long for — **crav•ing** *n*

crawl *vb* **1** : move slowly (as by drawing the body along the ground) **2** : swarm with creeping things ～ *n* : very slow pace

cray•on *n* : stick of chalk or wax used for drawing or coloring — **crayon** *vb*

craze *vb* : make or become insane ～ *n* : fad

cra•zy *adj* **1** : mentally disordered **2** : wildly impractical — **cra•zi•ly** *adv* — **cra•zi•ness** *n*

creak *vb or n* : squeak — **creaky** *adj*

cream *n* **1** : yellowish fat-rich part of milk **2** : thick smooth sauce, confection, or cosmetic **3** : choicest part ～ *vb* : beat into creamy consistency — **creamy** *adj*

cream•ery *n* : place where butter and cheese are made

crease *n* : line made by folding — **crease** *vb*

cre•ate *vb* : bring into being — **cre•ation** *n* — **cre•ative** *adj* — **cre•ativ•i•ty** *n* — **cre•a•tor** *n*

crea•ture *n* : lower animal or human being

cre•den•tials *n pl* : evidence of qualifications or authority

cred•i•ble *adj* : believable — **cred•i•bil•i•ty** *n*

cred•it *n* **1** : balance in a person's favor **2** : time given to pay for goods **3** : belief **4** : esteem **5** : source of honor ～ *vb* **1** : believe **2** : give credit to — **cred•it•able** *adj* — **cred•it•ably** *adv*

credit card *n* : a card authorizing purchases on credit

cred•i•tor *n* : person to whom money is owed

creed *n* : statement of essential beliefs

creek *n* : small stream

creep *vb* (**crept; crept**) **1** : crawl **2** : grow over a surface like ivy — **creep** *n* — **creep•er** *n*

cre•mate *vb* : burn up (a corpse) — **cre•ma•tion** *n* — **cre•ma•to•ry** *n*

cre•scen•do *adv or adj* : growing louder — **crescendo** *n*

cres•cent *n* : shape of the moon between new moon and first quarter

crest *n* **1** : tuft on a bird's head **2** : top of a hill or wave **3** : part of a coat of arms ～ *vb* : rise to a crest — **crest•ed** *adj*

cre•vasse *n* : deep fissure esp. in a glacier

crev•ice *n* : narrow fissure

crew *n* : body of workers (as on a ship) — **crew•man** *n*

crib *n* **1** : grain storage bin **2** : baby's bed ～ *vb* : put in a crib

crick•et *n* : insect noted for the chirping of the male

crime *n* : serious violation of law — **crim•i•nal** *n or adj*

crin•kle *vb* : wrinkle — **crinkle** *n* — **crin•kly** *adj*

crip•ple *n* : disabled person ～ *vb* : disable

cri•sis *n* : decisive or critical moment

crisp *adj* **1** : easily crumbled **2** : firm and fresh **3** : lively **4** : invigorating — **crisp** *vb* — **crisp•ly** *adv* — **crisp•ness** *n* — **crispy** *adj*

criss•cross *n* : pattern of crossed lines ～ *vb* : mark with or follow a crisscross

cri•te•ri•on *n* : standard

crit•ic *n* **1** : judge of literary or artistic works **2** : one who criticizes — **crit•i•cal** *adj* — **crit•i•cal•ly** *adv*

crit•i•cize *vb* **1** : judge as a critic **2** : find fault — **crit•i•cism** *n*

croak *n* : hoarse cry (as of a frog) — **croak** *vb*

crock *n* : thick earthenware pot or jar — **crock•ery** *n*

croc•o•dile *n* : large reptile of tropical waters

cro•cus *n* : herb with spring flowers

crook *n* **1** : bent or curved tool or part **2** : thief ～ *vb* : curve sharply

crook•ed *adj* **1** : bent **2** : dishonest — **crook•ed•ness** *n*

crop *n* **1** : pouch in the throat of a bird or insect **2** : short riding whip **3** : something that can be harvested ～ *vb* **1** : trim **2** : appear unexpectedly — used with *up*

cro•quet *n* : lawn game of driving balls through wickets

cross *n* **1** : figure or structure consisting of an upright and a cross piece **2** : interbreeding of unlike strains ～ *vb* **1** : intersect **2** : cancel **3** : go or extend across **4** : interbreed ～ *adj* **1** : going across **2** : contrary **3** : marked by bad temper — **cross•ing** *n* — **cross•ly** *adv*

cross—ex•am•ine *vb* : question about earlier testimony — **cross—ex•am•i•na•tion** *n*

cross—eyed *adj* : having the eye turned toward the nose

cross—re•fer *vb* : refer to another place (as in a book) — **cross—ref•er•ence** *n*

cross•roads *n* : place where two roads cross

cross section *n* : representative portion

cross•walk *n* : path for pedestrians crossing a street

crotch *n* : angle formed by the parting of 2 legs or branches

crouch *vb* : stoop over — **crouch** *n*

¹crow *n* : large glossy black bird

²crow vb **1** : make the loud sound of the cock **2** : gloat ～ n : cry of the cock

crowd vb : collect or cram together ～ n : large number of people

crown n **1** : wreath of honor or victory **2** : royal headdress **3** : top or highest part ～ vb **1** : place a crown on **2** : honor — **crowned** adj

cru·cial adj : vitally important

cru·ci·fix n : representation of Christ on the cross

cru·ci·fix·ion n : act of crucifying

cru·ci·fy vb **1** : put to death on a cross **2** : persecute

crude adj **1** : not refined **2** : lacking grace or elegance ～ n : unrefined petroleum — **crude·ly** adv — **cru·di·ty** n

cru·el adj : causing suffering to others — **cru·el·ly** adv — **cru·el·ty** n

cruise vb **1** : sail to several ports **2** : travel at the most efficient speed — **cruise** n

cruis·er n **1** : ship of war **2** : police car

crumb n : small fragment

crum·ble vb : break into small pieces — **crum·bly** adj

crum·ple vb **1** : crush together **2** : collapse

crunch vb : chew or press with a crushing noise ～ n : crunching sound — **crunchy** adj

cru·sade n **1** cap : medieval Christian expedition to the Holy Land **2** : reform movement — **crusade** vb — **cru·sad·er** n

crush vb **1** : squeeze out of shape **2** : grind or pound to bits **3** : suppress ～ n **1** : severe crowding **2** : infatuation

crust n **1** : hard outer part of bread or a pie **2** : hard surface layer — **crust·al** adj — **crusty** adj

crutch n : support for use by the disabled in walking

cry vb **1** : call out **2** : weep ～ n **1** : shout **2** : fit of weeping **3** : characteristic sound of an animal

cryp·tic adj : enigmatic

cryp·tog·ra·phy n : coding and decoding of messages — **cryp·tog·ra·pher** n

crys·tal n **1** : transparent quartz **2** : something (as glass) like crystal **3** : body formed by solidification that has a regular repeating atomic arrangement — **crys·tal·line** adj

crys·tal·lize vb : form crystals or a definite shape — **crys·tal·li·za·tion** n

cub n : young animal

cube n **1** : solid having 6 equal square sides **2** : product obtained by taking a number 3 times as a factor ～ vb **1** : raise to the 3d power **2** : form into a cube **3** : cut into cubes — **cu·bic** adj

cu·bi·cle n : small room

cuck·oo n : brown European bird ～ adj : silly

cu·cum·ber n : fleshy fruit related to the gourds

cud·dle vb : lie close

¹cue n : signal — **cue** vb

²cue n : stick used in pool

¹cuff n **1** : part of a sleeve encircling the wrist **2** : folded trouser hem

²cuff vb or n : slap

cu·li·nary adj : of or relating to cookery

cull vb : select

cul·pa·ble adj : deserving blame

cul·prit n : guilty person

cult n **1** : religious system **2** : faddish devotion — **cult·ist** n

cul·ti·vate vb **1** : prepare for crops **2** : foster the growth of **3** : refine — **cul·ti·va·tion** n

cul·ture n **1** : cultivation **2** : refinement of intellectual and artistic taste **3** : particular form or stage of civilization — **cul·tur·al** adj — **cul·tured** adj

cum·ber·some adj : awkward to handle due to bulk

cun·ning adj **1** : crafty **2** : clever **3** : appealing ～ n **1** : skill **2** : craftiness

cup n **1** : small drinking vessel **2** : contents of a cup **3** : a half pint ～ vb : shape like a cup — **cup·ful** n

cup·board n : small storage closet

cup·cake n : small cake

cu·ra·tor n : one in charge of a museum or zoo

curb n **1** : restraint **2** : raised edging along a street ～ vb : hold back

curd n : coagulated milk

cur·dle vb **1** : form curds **2** : sour

cure n **1** : recovery from disease **2** : remedy ～ vb **1** : restore to health **2** : process for storage or use — **cur·able** adj

cur·few n : requirement to be off the streets at a set hour

cu·ri·ous adj **1** : eager to learn **2** : strange — **cu·ri·os·i·ty** n — **cu·ri·ous·ly** adv — **cu·ri·ous·ness** n

curl vb **1** : form into ringlets **2** : curve ～ n **1** : ringlet of hair **2** : something with a spiral form — **curl·er** n — **curly** adj

cur·ren·cy n **1** : general use or acceptance **2** : money

cur·rent *adj* : occurring in or belonging to the present ⁓ *n* **1** : swiftest part of a stream **2** : flow of electricity

cur·ric·u·lum *n* : course of study

curse *n* **1** : a calling down of evil or harm upon one **2** : affliction ⁓ *vb* **1** : call down injury upon **2** : swear at **3** : afflict

cur·sor *n* : indicator on a computer screen

curt *adj* : rudely abrupt — **curt·ly** *adv* — **curt·ness** *n*

cur·tail *vb* : shorten — **cur·tail·ment** *n*

cur·tain *n* : hanging screen that can be drawn back or raised — **cur·tain** *vb*

curt·sy, curt·sey *n* : courteous bow made by bending the knees — **curt·sy, curt·sey** *vb*

cur·va·ture *n* : amount or state of curving

curve *vb* : bend from a straight line or course ⁓ *n* **1** : a bending without angles **2** : something curved

cush·ion *n* **1** : soft pillow **2** : something that eases or protects ⁓ *vb* **1** : provide with a cushion **2** : soften the force of

cus·tard *n* : sweetened cooked mixture of milk and eggs

cus·to·dy *n* : immediate care or charge — **cus·to·di·al** *adj* — **cus·to·di·an** *n*

cus·tom *n* **1** : habitual course of action **2** *pl* : import taxes ⁓ *adj* : made to personal order

— **cus·tom·ar·i·ly** *adv* — **cus·tom·ary** *adj* — **custom–built** *adj* — **cus·tom–made** *adj*

cus·tom·er *n* : buyer

cut *vb* (**cut; cut**) **1** : penetrate or divide with a sharp edge **2** : experience the growth of (a tooth) through the gum **3** : shorten **4** : remove by severing **5** : intersect ⁓ *n* **1** : something separated by cutting **2** : reduction — **cut·ter** *n*

— **cut in** *vb* : thrust oneself between others

cute *adj* : pretty

cut·lery *n* : cutting utensils

cut·let *n* : slice of meat

cut·throat *n* : murderer ⁓ *adj* : ruthless

cy·ber·space *n* : online world of the Internet

cy·cle *n* **1** : period of time for a series of repeated events **2** : recurring round of events **3** : long period of time **4** : bicycle or motorcycle ⁓ *vb* : ride a cycle — **cy·clic, cy·cli·cal** *adj* — **cy·clist** *n*

cy·clone *n* : tornado — **cy·clon·ic** *adj*

cyl·in·der *n* **1** : long round body or figure **2** : rotating chamber in a revolver **3** : piston chamber in an engine — **cy·lin·dri·cal** *adj*

cyn·ic *n* : one who attributes all actions to selfish motives — **cyn·i·cal** *adj* — **cyn·i·cism** *n*

cyst *n* : abnormal bodily sac — **cys·tic** *adj*

czar *n* : ruler of Russia until 1917 — **czar·ist** *n or adj*

D

d *n* : 4th letter of the alphabet

¹dab *n* : gentle touch or stroke ⁓ *vb* : touch or apply lightly

²dab *n* : small amount

dab·ble *vb* **1** : splash **2** : work without serious effort — **dab·bler** *n*

dad *n* : father

dad·dy *n* : father

daf·fo·dil *n* : narcissus with trumpetlike flowers

dag·ger *n* : knife for stabbing

dai·ly *adj* **1** : occurring, done, or used every day or every weekday **2** : computed in terms of one day ⁓ *n* : daily newspaper — **daily** *adv*

dain·ty *n* : something delicious ⁓ *adj* : delicately pretty — **dain·ti·ly** *adv* — **dain·ti·ness** *n*

dairy *n* : farm that produces or company that processes milk — **dairy·maid** *n* — **dairy·man** *n*

dai·sy *n* : tall leafy-stemmed plant bearing showy flowers

dal·ly *vb* **1** : flirt **2** : dawdle — **dal·li·ance** *n*

¹dam *n* : female parent of a domestic animal

²dam *n* : barrier to hold back water — **dam** *vb*

dam·age *n* **1** : loss or harm due to injury **2** *pl* : compensation for loss or injury ⁓ *vb* : do damage to

dame *n* : woman of rank or authority

damn *vb* **1** : condemn to hell **2** : curse — **dam·na·ble** *adj* — **dam·na·tion** *n* — **damned** *adj*

damp *n* : moisture ⁓ *vb* **1** : reduce the draft in **2** : restrain **3** : moisten ⁓ *adj* : moist — **damp·en** *vb* — **damp·ness** *n*

damp·er *n* : movable plate to regulate a flue draft

dam·sel *n* : young woman

dance *vb* : move rhythmically to music ⁓ *n*

: act of dancing or a gathering for dancing —
danc·er n

dan·de·li·on n : common yellow-flowered herb

dan·druff n : whitish thin dry scales of skin on
the scalp

dan·dy n **1** : man too concerned with clothes
2 : something excellent ∼ adj : very good

dan·ger n **1** : exposure to injury or evil **2**
: something that may cause injury — **dan·ger-
ous** adj

dan·gle vb **1** : hang and swing freely **2** : be
left without support or connection **3** : allow or
cause to hang **4** : offer as an inducement

dap·per adj : neat and stylishly dressed

dap·ple vb : mark with colored spots

dare vb **1** : have sufficient courage **2** : urge or
provoke to contend — **dare** n — **dar·ing** n or
adj

dare·dev·il n : recklessly bold person

dark adj **1** : having little or no light **2** : not
light in color **3** : gloomy ∼ n : absence of
light — **dark·en** vb — **dark·ly** adv — **darkness** n

dar·ling n **1** : beloved **2** : favorite ∼ adj **1**
: dearly loved **2** : very pleasing

dart n **1** : small pointed missile **2** pl : game of
throwing darts at a target **3** : tapering fold in a
garment **4** : quick movement ∼ vb : move
suddenly or rapidly

dash vb **1** : smash **2** : knock or hurl violently
3 : ruin **4** : perform or finish hastily **5** : move
quickly ∼ n **1** : sudden burst, splash, or
stroke **2** : punctuation mark — **3** : tiny
amount **4** : showiness or liveliness **5** : sudden
rush **6** : short race **7** : dashboard

dash·board n : instrument panel

da·ta n sing or pl : factual information

da·ta·base n : data organized for computer
search

¹date n : edible fruit of a palm

²date n **1** : day, month, or year when something is done or made **2** : historical time period **3** : social engagement or the person one
goes out with ∼ vb **1** : determine or record
the date of **2** : have a date with **3** : originate
— **to date** : up to now

dat·ed adj : old-fashioned

daub vb : smear ∼ n : something daubed on —
daub·er n

daugh·ter n : human female offspring

daugh·ter–in–law n (**daughters–in–law**)
: wife of one's son

daw·dle vb **1** : waste time **2** : loiter

dawn vb **1** : grow light as the sun rises **2**
: begin to appear, develop, or be understood ∼
n : first appearance (as of daylight)

day n **1** : period of light between one night and
the next **2** : 24 hours **3** : specified date **4**
: particular time or age **5** : period of work for
a day — **day·break** n — **day·light** n — **day-
time** n

day·dream n : fantasy of wish fulfillment —
daydream vb

daze vb **1** : stun by a blow **2** : dazzle — **daze**
n

daz·zle vb **1** : overpower with light **2** : impress greatly — **dazzle** n

dead adj **1** : lifeless **2** : unresponsive or inactive **3** : exhausted **4** : obsolete **5** : precise ∼
n **dead** **1** : one that is dead — usu. with the **2**
: most lifeless time ∼ adv **1** : completely **2**
: directly — **dead·en** vb

dead·beat n : one who will not pay debts

dead heat n : tie in a contest

dead·line n : time by which something must be
finished

dead·lock n : struggle that neither side can win
— **deadlock** vb

dead·ly adj **1** : capable of causing death **2**
: very accurate **3** : fatal to spiritual progress **4**
: suggestive of death **5** : very great ∼ adv
: extremely — **dead·li·ness** n

dead·pan adj : showing no expression —
dead·pan n or vb or adv

deaf adj : unable or unwilling to hear — **deaf-
en** vb — **deaf·ness** n

deaf–mute n : deaf person unable to speak

deal n **1** : indefinite quantity **2** : distribution
of playing cards **3** : negotiation or agreement
4 : treatment received **5** : bargain ∼ vb
dealt; dealt **1** : distribute playing cards **2**
: be concerned with **3** : administer or deliver
4 : take action **5** : sell **6** : reach a state of acceptance — **deal·er** n — **deal·ing** n

dean n **1** : head of a group of clergy members
2 : university or school administrator **3** : senior member

dear adj **1** : highly valued or loved **2** : expensive ∼ n : loved one — **dear·ly** adv — **dear-
ness** n

death n **1** : end of life **2** : cause of loss of life
3 : state of being dead **4** : destruction or extinction — **death·less** adj — **death·ly** adj or
adv

de·base vb : hurt the value or dignity of

de·bate *vb* : discuss a question by argument — **de·bat·able** *adj* — **debate** *n* — **de·bat·er** *n*

de·bil·i·tate *vb* : make ill or weak — **de·bil·i·ty** *n*

deb·it *n* : account entry of a payment or debt ∼ *vb* : record as a debit

de·bris *n* : remains of something destroyed

debt *n* **1** : sin **2** : something owed **3** : state of owing — **debt·or** *n*

de·but *n* **1** : first public appearance **2** : formal entrance into society — **debut** *vb* — **deb·u·tante** *n*

de·cade *n* : 10 years

dec·a·dence *n* : deterioration — **dec·a·dent** *adj or n*

de·cal *n* : picture or design for transfer from prepared paper

de·cap·i·tate *vb* : behead — **de·cap·i·ta·tion** *n*

de·cay *vb* **1** : decline in condition **2** : decompose — **decay** *n*

de·cease *n* : death — **decease** *vb*

de·ceit *n* **1** : deception **2** : dishonesty — **de·ceit·ful** *adj* — **de·ceit·ful·ly** *adv* — **de·ceit·ful·ness** *n*

de·ceive *vb* : trick or mislead — **de·ceiv·er** *n*

de·cel·er·ate *vb* : slow down

De·cem·ber *n* : 12th month of the year having 31 days

de·cent *adj* **1** : good, right, or just **2** : wearing clothes **3** : not obscene **4** : fairly good — **de·cen·cy** *n* — **de·cent·ly** *adv*

de·cep·tion *n* **1** : act or fact of deceiving **2** : fraud — **de·cep·tive** *adj* — **de·cep·tive·ly** *adv* — **de·cep·tive·ness** *n*

de·cide *vb* **1** : make a choice or judgment **2** : bring to a conclusion **3** : cause to decide

de·cid·ed *adj* **1** : beyond doubt or question **2** : resolute — **de·cid·ed·ly** *adv*

dec·i·mal *n* : fraction in which the denominator is a power of 10 expressed by a point (**decimal point**) placed at the left — **decimal** *adj*

de·ci·pher *vb* : make out the meaning of — **de·ci·pher·able** *adj*

de·ci·sion *n* **1** : act or result of deciding **2** : determination

de·ci·sive *adj* **1** : having the power to decide **2** : conclusive **3** : showing determination — **de·ci·sive·ly** *adv* — **de·ci·sive·ness** *n*

deck *n* **1** : floor of a ship **2** : pack of playing cards ∼ *vb* **1** : array or dress up **2** : knock down

de·clare *vb* **1** : make known formally **2** : state emphatically — **dec·la·ra·tion** *n* — **de·clar·a·tive** *adj* — **de·clar·a·to·ry** *adj* — **de·clar·er** *n*

de·cline *vb* **1** : turn or slope downward **2** : wane **3** : refuse to accept ∼ *n* **1** : gradual wasting away **2** : change to a lower state or level **3** : a descending slope — **dec·li·na·tion** *n*

de·code *vb* : decipher (a coded message) — **de·cod·er** *n*

de·com·pose *vb* **1** : separate into parts **2** : decay — **de·com·po·si·tion** *n*

de·con·ges·tant *n* : agent that relieves congestion

de·cor, dé·cor *n* : room design or decoration

dec·o·rate *vb* **1** : add something attractive to **2** : honor with a medal — **dec·o·ra·tion** *n* — **dec·o·ra·tive** *adj* — **dec·o·ra·tor** *n*

de·coy *n* : something that tempts or draws attention from another ∼ *vb* : tempt

de·crease *vb* : grow or cause to grow less — **decrease** *n*

de·cree *n* : official order — **de·cree** *vb*

de·cre·scen·do *adv or adj* : with a decrease in volume

ded·i·cate *vb* **1** : set apart for a purpose (as honor or worship) **2** : address to someone as a compliment — **ded·i·ca·tion** *n* — **ded·i·ca·to·ry** *adj*

de·duce *vb* : derive by reasoning — **de·duc·ible** *adj*

de·duct *vb* : subtract — **de·duct·ible** *adj* — **de·duc·tion** *n* — **de·duc·tive** *adj*

deed *n* **1** : exploit **2** : document showing ownership ∼ *vb* : convey by deed

deep *adj* **1** : extending far or a specified distance down, back, within, or outward **2** : occupied **3** : dark and rich in color **4** : low in tone ∼ *adv* **1** : deeply **2** : far along in time ∼ *n* : deep place — **deep·en** *vb* — **deep·ly** *adv*

deep–seat·ed *adj* : firmly established

deer *n* (**deer**) : ruminant mammal with antlers in the male — **deer·skin** *n*

de·fault *n* : failure in a duty — **default** *vb* — **de·fault·er** *n*

de·feat *vb* **1** : frustrate **2** : win victory over ∼ *n* : loss of a battle or contest

def·e·cate *vb* : discharge feces from the bowels — **def·e·ca·tion** *n*

de·fect *n* : imperfection ∼ *vb* : desert — **de·fec·tion** *n* — **de·fec·tive** *adj* — **de·fec·tor** *n*

de·fend *vb* **1** : protect from danger or harm **2** : take the side of — **de·fend·er** *n*

de·fen·dant *n* : person charged or sued in a court

de·fense *n* **1** : act of defending **2** : something that defends **3** : party, group, or team that opposes another — **de·fense·less** *adj* — **de·fen·si·ble** *adj* — **de·fen·sive** *adj or n*

de·fer *vb* : postpone — **de·fer·ment** *n* — **de·fer·ra·ble** *adj*

de·fi·ance *n* : disposition to resist — **de·fi·ant** *adj*

de·fi·cient *adj* **1** : lacking something necessary **2** : not up to standard — **de·fi·cien·cy** *n*

def·i·cit *n* : shortage esp. in money

de·fine *vb* **1** : fix or mark the limits of **2** : clarify in outline **3** : set forth the meaning of — **de·fin·able** *adj* — **de·fin·ably** *adv* — **de·fin·er** *n* — **def·i·ni·tion** *n*

def·i·nite *adj* **1** : having distinct limits **2** : clear in meaning, intent, or identity **3** : typically designating an identified or immediately identifiable person or thing — **def·i·nite·ly** *adv*

de·fin·i·tive *adj* **1** : conclusive **2** : authoritative

de·flate *vb* **1** : release air or gas from **2** : reduce — **de·fla·tion** *n*

de·flect *vb* : turn aside — **de·flec·tion** *n*

de·form *vb* **1** : distort **2** : disfigure — **de·for·ma·tion** *n* — **de·for·mi·ty** *n*

de·fraud *vb* : cheat

de·frost *vb* **1** : thaw out **2** : free from ice — **de·frost·er** *n*

de·funct *adj* : dead

de·fy *vb* **1** : challenge **2** : boldly refuse to obey

de·gen·er·ate *adj* : degraded or corrupt ∼ *n* : degenerate person ∼ *vb* : become degenerate — **de·gen·er·a·cy** *n* — **de·gen·er·a·tion** *n* — **de·gen·er·a·tive** *adj*

de·grade *vb* **1** : reduce from a higher to a lower rank or degree **2** : debase **3** : decompose — **de·grad·able** *adj* — **deg·ra·da·tion** *n*

de·gree *n* **1** : step in a series **2** : extent, intensity, or scope **3** : title given to a college graduate **4** : a 360th part of the circumference of a circle **5** : unit for measuring temperature

de·hy·drate *vb* **1** : remove water from **2** : lose liquid — **de·hy·dra·tion** *n*

de·i·fy *vb* : make a god of — **de·i·fi·ca·tion** *n*

de·i·ty *n* **1** *cap* : God **2** : a god or goddess

de·ject·ed *adj* : sad — **de·jec·tion** *n*

de·lay *n* : a putting off of something ∼ *vb* **1** : postpone **2** : stop or hinder for a time

de·lec·ta·ble *adj* : delicious

del·e·gate *n* : representative ∼ *vb* **1** : entrust to another **2** : appoint as one's delegate — **del·e·ga·tion** *n*

de·lete *vb* : eliminate something written — **de·le·tion** *n*

deli *n* : a delicatessen

de·lib·er·ate *adj* **1** : determined after careful thought **2** : intentional **3** : not hurried ∼ *vb* : consider carefully — **de·lib·er·ate·ly** *adv* — **de·lib·er·ate·ness** *n* — **de·lib·er·a·tion** *n* — **de·lib·er·a·tive** *adj*

del·i·ca·cy *n* **1** : something special and pleasing to eat **2** : fineness **3** : frailty

del·i·cate *adj* **1** : subtly pleasing to the senses **2** : dainty and charming **3** : sensitive or fragile **4** : requiring fine skill or tact — **del·i·cate·ly** *adv*

del·i·ca·tes·sen *n* : store that sells ready-to-eat food

de·li·cious *adj* : very pleasing esp. in taste or aroma — **de·li·cious·ly** *adv* — **de·li·cious·ness** *n*

de·light *n* **1** : great pleasure **2** : source of great pleasure ∼ *vb* **1** : take great pleasure **2** : satisfy greatly — **de·light·ful** *adj* — **de·light·ful·ly** *adv*

de·lin·quent *n* : delinquent person ∼ *adj* **1** : violating duty or law **2** : overdue in payment — **de·lin·quen·cy** *n*

de·liv·er *vb* **1** : set free **2** : hand over **3** : assist in birth **4** : say or speak **5** : send to an intended destination — **de·liv·er·ance** *n* — **de·liv·er·er** *n* — **de·liv·ery** *n*

del·ta *n* : triangle of land at the mouth of a river

de·lude *vb* : mislead or deceive — **de·lu·sion** *n*

de·luxe *adj* : very luxurious or elegant

de·mand *n* **1** : act of demanding **2** : something claimed as due **3** : ability and desire to buy **4** : urgent need ∼ *vb* **1** : ask for with authority **2** : require

de·mean *vb* : degrade

de·mean·or *n* : behavior

de·ment·ed *adj* : crazy

de·mer·it *n* : mark given an offender

de·mise *n* **1** : death **2** : loss of status

de·moc·ra·cy *n* **1** : government in which the supreme power is held by the people **2** : political unit with democratic government — **dem-**

o·crat *n* — dem·o·crat·ic *adj* — dem·o·crat·i·cal·ly *adv* — de·moc·ra·tize *vb*

de·mol·ish *vb* 1 : tear down or smash 2 : put an end to — de·mo·li·tion *n*

de·mon *n* : evil spirit — de·mon·ic *adj*

dem·on·strate *vb* 1 : show clearly or publicly 2 : prove 3 : explain — de·mon·stra·ble *adj* — de·mon·stra·bly *adv* — dem·on·stra·tion *n* — de·mon·stra·tive *adj or n* — dem·on·stra·tor *n*

de·mote *vb* : reduce to a lower rank — de·mo·tion *n*

den *n* 1 : animal's shelter 2 : hiding place 3 : cozy private little room

de·ni·al *n* : rejection of a request or of the validity of a statement

den·im *n* 1 : durable twilled cotton fabric 2 *pl* : pants of denim

de·nom·i·na·tion *n* 1 : religious body 2 : value or size in a series — de·nom·i·na·tion·al *adj*

de·nom·i·na·tor *n* : part of a fraction below the line

de·nounce *vb* 1 : pronounce blameworthy or evil 2 : inform against — de·nun·ci·a·tion *n*

dense *adj* 1 : thick, compact, or crowded 2 : stupid — dense·ly *adv* — dense·ness *n* — den·si·ty *n*

dent *n* : small depression — dent *vb*

den·tal *adj* : relating to teeth or dentistry

den·tist *n* : one who cares for and replaces teeth — den·tist·ry *n*

den·ture *n* : artificial teeth

de·ny *vb* 1 : declare untrue 2 : deny validity of 3 : refuse to grant

de·odor·ant *n* : preparation to prevent unpleasant odors — de·odor·ize *vb*

de·part *vb* 1 : go away or away from 2 : die — de·par·ture *n*

de·part·ment *n* 1 : area of responsibility or interest 2 : functional division — de·part·men·tal *adj*

de·pend *vb* 1 : rely for support 2 : be determined by or based on something else — de·pend·abil·i·ty *n* — de·pend·able *adj* — de·pen·dence *n* — de·pen·den·cy *n* — de·pen·dent *adj or n*

de·pict *vb* : show by or as if by a picture — de·pic·tion *n*

de·plete *vb* : use up resources of — de·ple·tion *n*

de·plore *vb* : regret strongly — de·plor·able *adj*

de·port *vb* 1 : behave 2 : send out of the country — de·por·ta·tion *n* — de·port·ment *n*

de·pos·it *vb* : place esp. for safekeeping ∼ *n* 1 : state of being deposited 2 : something deposited 3 : act of depositing 4 : natural accumulation — de·pos·i·tor *n*

de·pos·i·to·ry *n* : place for deposit

de·pot *n* 1 : place for storage 2 : bus or railroad station

de·prave *vb* : corrupt morally — de·praved *adj* — de·prav·i·ty *n*

de·pre·ci·ate *vb* 1 : lessen in value 2 : belittle — de·pre·ci·a·tion *n*

de·press *vb* 1 : press down 2 : lessen the activity or force of 3 : discourage 4 : decrease the market value of — de·pres·sant *n or adj* — de·pressed *adj* — de·pres·sive *adj or n* — de·pres·sor *n*

de·pres·sion *n* 1 : act of depressing or state of being depressed 2 : depressed place 3 : period of low economic activity

de·prive *vb* : take or keep something away from — de·pri·va·tion *n*

depth *n* 1 : something that is deep 2 : distance down from a surface 3 : distance from front to back 4 : quality of being deep

dep·u·ty *n* : person appointed to act for another — dep·u·tize *vb*

de·rail *vb* : leave the rails — de·rail·ment *n*

de·range *vb* 1 : upset an arrangement of 2 : make insane — de·range·ment *n*

der·by *n* 1 : horse race 2 : stiff felt hat with dome-shaped crown

de·reg·u·late *vb* : remove restrictions on — de·reg·u·la·tion *n*

der·e·lict *adj* 1 : abandoned 2 : negligent ∼ *n* 1 : something abandoned 2 : bum — der·e·lic·tion *n*

de·ride *vb* : make fun of — de·ri·sion *n* — de·ri·sive *adj* — de·ri·sive·ly *adv* — de·ri·sive·ness *n*

de·rive *vb* 1 : obtain from a source or parent 2 : come from a certain source 3 : infer or deduce — der·i·va·tion *n* — de·riv·a·tive *adj or n*

der·ma·tol·o·gy *n* : study of the skin and its disorders — der·ma·tol·o·gist *n*

de·rog·a·to·ry *adj* : intended to lower the reputation

de·scend *vb* 1 : move or climb down 2 : derive 3 : extend downward 4 : appear suddenly (as in an attack) — de·scen·dant, de·scen·dent *adj or n* — de·scent *n*

de·scribe *vb* : represent in words — **de·scrib·able** *adj* — **de·scrip·tion** *n* — **de·scrip·tive** *adj*

des·e·crate *vb* : treat (something sacred) with disrespect — **des·e·cra·tion** *n*

de·seg·re·gate *vb* : eliminate esp. racial segregation in — **de·seg·re·ga·tion** *n*

¹**des·ert** *n* : dry barren region — **desert** *adj*

²**de·sert** *n* : what one deserves

³**de·sert** *vb* : abandon — **de·sert·er** *n* — **de·ser·tion** *n*

de·serve *vb* : be worthy of

de·sign *vb* **1** : create and work out the details of **2** : make a pattern or sketch of ∼ *n* **1** : mental project or plan **2** : purpose **3** : preliminary sketch **4** : underlying arrangement of elements **5** : decorative pattern — **de·sign·er** *n*

des·ig·nate *vb* **1** : indicate, specify, or name **2** : appoint — **des·ig·na·tion** *n*

de·sire *vb* **1** : feel desire for **2** : request ∼ *n* **1** : strong conscious impulse to have, be, or do something **2** : something desired — **de·sir·abil·i·ty** *n* — **de·sir·able** *adj* — **de·sir·able·ness** *n* — **de·sir·ous** *adj*

de·sist *vb* : stop

desk *n* : table esp. for writing and reading

des·o·late *adj* **1** : lifeless **2** : hopelessly sad ∼ *vb* : lay waste — **des·o·la·tion** *n*

de·spair *vb* : lose all hope ∼ *n* : loss of hope

des·per·ate *adj* **1** : hopeless **2** : rash **3** : extremely intense — **des·per·ate·ly** *adv* — **des·per·a·tion** *n*

de·spise *vb* : feel contempt for — **de·spi·ca·ble** *adj*

de·spite *prep* : in spite of

de·spon·den·cy *n* : dejection — **de·spon·dent** *adj*

des·sert *n* : sweet food, fruit, or cheese ending a meal

des·ti·na·tion *n* : place where something or someone is going

des·tine *vb* **1** : designate, assign, or determine in advance **2** : direct

des·ti·ny *n* : that which is to happen in the future

des·ti·tute *adj* **1** : lacking something **2** : very poor — **des·ti·tu·tion** *n*

de·stroy *vb* : kill or put an end to — **de·stroy·er** *n* — **de·struc·ti·bil·i·ty** *n* — **de·struc·ti·ble** *adj* — **de·struc·tive** *adj* — **de·struc·tion** *n*

de·tach *vb* : separate — **de·tached** *adj* — **de·tach·ment** *n*

de·tail *n* : small item or part ∼ *vb* : give details of

de·tain *vb* **1** : hold in custody **2** : delay

de·tect *vb* : discover — **detect·able** *adj* — **de·tec·tion** *n* — **de·tec·tor** *n*

de·tec·tive *n* : one who investigates crime

de·ten·tion *n* : confinement

de·ter *vb* : discourage or prevent — **de·ter·rence** *n* — **de·ter·rent** *adj or n*

de·ter·gent *n* : cleansing agent

de·te·ri·o·rate *vb* : make or become worse — **de·te·ri·o·ra·tion** *n*

de·ter·mine *vb* **1** : decide on, establish, or settle **2** : find out **3** : bring about as a result — **de·ter·mi·na·tion** *n*

de·test *vb* : hate — **de·test·able** *adj* — **de·tes·ta·tion** *n*

det·o·nate *vb* : explode — **det·o·na·tion** *n* — **det·o·na·tor** *n*

de·tour *n* : temporary indirect route — **detour** *vb*

de·tract *vb* : take away — **de·trac·tion** *n* — **de·trac·tor** *n*

det·ri·ment *n* : damage — **det·ri·men·tal** *adj* — **det·ri·men·tal·ly** *adv*

deuce *n* **1** : 2 in cards or dice **2** : tie in tennis **3** : devil — used as an oath

de·val·ue *vb* : reduce the value of — **de·val·u·a·tion** *n*

dev·as·tate *vb* : ruin — **dev·as·ta·tion** *n*

de·vel·op *vb* **1** : grow, increase, or evolve gradually **2** : cause to grow, increase, or reach full potential — **de·vel·op·er** *n* — **de·vel·op·ment** *n* — **de·vel·op·men·tal** *adj*

de·vi·ate *vb* : change esp. from a course or standard — **de·vi·ant** *adj or n* — **de·vi·ate** *n* — **de·vi·a·tion** *n*

de·vice *n* **1** : specialized piece of equipment or tool **2** : design

dev·il *n* **1** : personified supreme spirit of evil **2** : demon **3** : wicked person ∼ *vb* **1** : season highly **2** : pester — **dev·il·ish** *adj* — **dev·il·ry, dev·il·try** *n*

de·vi·ous *adj* : tricky

de·vise *vb* **1** : invent **2** : plot **3** : give by will

de·vote *vb* : set apart for a special purpose — **de·vot·ed** *adj*

dev·o·tee *n* : ardent follower

de·vo·tion *n* **1** : prayer — *usu. pl.* **2** : loyalty and dedication — **de·vo·tion·al** *adj*

de·vour *vb* : consume ravenously — **de·vour·er** *n*

de·vout *adj* **1** : devoted to religion **2** : serious — **de·vout·ly** *adv* — **de·vout·ness** *n*

dew *n* : moisture condensed at night — **dew·drop** *n* — **dewy** *adj*

dex·ter·ous *adj* : skillful with the hands — **dex·ter·i·ty** *n* — **dex·ter·ous·ly** *adv*

di·a·be·tes *n* : disorder in which the body has too little insulin and too much sugar — **di·a·bet·ic** *adj or n*

di·ag·no·sis *n* : identifying of a disease from its symptoms — **di·ag·nose** *vb* — **di·ag·nos·tic** *adj*

di·ag·o·nal *adj* : extending from one corner to the opposite corner ∼ *n* : diagonal line, direction, or arrangement — **di·ag·o·nal·ly** *adv*

di·a·gram *n* : explanatory drawing or plan ∼ *vb* : represent by a diagram — **di·a·gram·mat·ic** *adj*

di·al *n* **1** : face of a clock, meter, or gauge **2** : control knob or wheel ∼ *vb* : turn a dial to call, operate, or select

di·a·lect *n* : variety of language confined to a region or group

di·a·logue *n* : conversation

di·am·e·ter *n* **1** : straight line through the center of a circle **2** : thickness

di·a·mond *n* **1** : hard brilliant mineral that consists of crystalline carbon **2** : flat figure having 4 equal sides, 2 acute angles, and 2 obtuse angles **3** : playing card of a suit marked with a red diamond **4** : baseball field

di·a·per *n* : baby's garment for receiving bodily wastes ∼ *vb* : put a diaper on

di·a·phragm *n* **1** : sheet of muscle between the chest and abdominal cavity **2** : contraceptive device

di·ar·rhea *n* : abnormally watery discharge from bowels

di·a·ry *n* : daily record of personal experiences — **di·a·rist** *n*

dice *n* **dice** : die or a game played with dice ∼ *vb* : cut into small cubes

dic·tate *vb* **1** : speak for a person or a machine to record **2** : command ∼ *n* : order — **dic·ta·tion** *n*

dic·ta·tor *n* : person ruling absolutely and often brutally — **dic·ta·to·ri·al** *adj* — **dic·ta·tor·ship** *n*

dic·tio·nary *n* : reference book of words with information about their meanings

did *past of* DO

didn't : did not

¹die *vb* **1** : stop living **2** : pass out of existence **3** : stop or become less active **4** : long

²die *n* **1** *pl* **dice** : small marked cube used in gambling **2** *pl* **dies** : form for stamping or cutting

die·sel *n* : engine in which high compression causes ignition of the fuel

di·et *n* : food and drink regularly consumed (as by a person) ∼ *vb* : eat less or according to certain rules — **di·etary** *adj or n* — **di·et·er** *n*

dif·fer *vb* **1** : be unlike **2** : vary **3** : disagree — **dif·fer·ence** *n* — **dif·fer·ent** *adj* — **dif·fer·ent·ly** *adv*

dif·fer·en·ti·ate *vb* **1** : make or become different **2** : attain a specialized adult form during development **3** : distinguish — **dif·fer·en·ti·a·tion** *n*

dif·fi·cul·ty *n* **1** : difficult nature **2** : great effort **3** : something hard to do, understand, or deal with — **dif·fi·cult** *adj*

dif·fuse *adj* **1** : wordy **2** : not concentrated ∼ *vb* : pour out or spread widely — **dif·fu·sion** *n*

dig *vb* **1** : turn up soil **2** : hollow out or form by removing earth **3** : uncover by turning up earth ∼ *n* **1** : thrust **2** : cutting remark — **dig in** *vb* **1** : establish a defensive position **2** : begin working or eating — **dig up** *vb* : discover

¹di·gest *n* : body of information in shortened form

²di·gest *vb* **1** : think over **2** : convert (food) into a form that can be absorbed **3** : summarize — **di·gest·ible** *adj* — **di·ges·tion** *n* — **di·ges·tive** *adj*

dig·it *n* **1** : any of the figures 1 to 9 inclusive and usu. the symbol 0 **2** : finger or toe

dig·i·tal *adj* : providing information in numerical digits — **dig·i·tal·ly** *adv*

digital camera *n* : camera that records images as digital data instead of on film

dig·ni·fy *vb* : give dignity or attention to

dig·ni·tary *n* : person of high position

dig·ni·ty *n* **1** : quality or state of being worthy or honored **2** : formal reserve (as of manner)

dike *n* : earth bank or dam

di·lap·i·dat·ed *adj* : fallen into partial ruin — **di·lap·i·da·tion** *n*

di·late *vb* : swell or expand — **dil·a·ta·tion** *n* — **di·la·tion** *n*

di·lem·ma *n* **1** : undesirable choice **2** : predicament

dil·i·gent *adj* : attentive and busy — **dil·i·gence** *n* — **dil·i·gent·ly** *adv*

dill *n* : herb with aromatic leaves and seeds

dil·ly·dal·ly *vb* : waste time by delay

di·lute *vb* : lessen the consistency or strength of by mixing with something else ∼ *adj* : weak — **di·lu·tion** *n*

dim *adj* **1** : not bright or distinct **2** : having no luster **3** : not seeing or understanding clearly — **dim** *vb* — **dim·ly** *adv* — **dim·mer** *n* — **dim·ness** *n*

dime *n* : U.S. coin worth ten cents

di·men·sion *n* **1** : measurement of extension (as in length, height, or breadth) **2** : extent — **di·men·sion·al** *adj*

di·min·ish *vb* **1** : make less or cause to appear less **2** : dwindle

dim·ple *n* : small depression esp. in the cheek or chin

dine *vb* : eat dinner

din·er *n* **1** : person eating dinner **2** : railroad dining car or restaurant resembling one

din·ghy *n* : small boat

din·gy *adj* **1** : dirty **2** : shabby — **din·gi·ness** *n*

din·ner *n* : main daily meal

di·no·saur *n* : extinct often huge reptile

di·o·cese *n* : territorial jurisdiction of a bishop — **di·oc·e·san** *adj or n*

dip *vb* **1** : plunge into a liquid **2** : take out with a ladle **3** : lower and quickly raise again **4** : sink or slope downward suddenly ∼ *n* **1** : plunge into water for sport **2** : sudden downward movement or incline — **dip·per** *n*

di·plo·ma *n* : record of graduation from a school

di·plo·ma·cy *n* **1** : business of conducting negotiations between nations **2** : tact — **dip·lo·mat** *n* — **dip·lo·mat·ic** *adj*

dire *adj* **1** : very horrible **2** : extreme

di·rect *vb* **1** : address **2** : cause to move or to follow a certain course **3** : show (someone) the way **4** : regulate the activities or course of **5** : request with authority ∼ *adj* **1** : leading to or coming from a point without deviation or interruption **2** : frank — **direct** *adv* — **di·rect·ly** *adv* — **di·rect·ness** *n* — **di·rec·tor** *n*

direct current *n* : electric current flowing in one direction only

di·rec·tion *n* **1** : supervision **2** : order **3** : course along which something moves — **di·rec·tion·al** *adj*

di·rec·tive *n* : order

di·rec·to·ry *n* : alphabetical list of names and addresses

dirt *n* **1** : mud, dust, or grime that makes something unclean **2** : soil

dirty *adj* **1** : not clean **2** : unfair **3** : extremely improper or offensive ∼ *vb* : make or become dirty — **dirt·i·ness** *n*

dis·able *vb* : make unable to function — **dis·abil·i·ty** *n*

dis·ad·van·tage *n* : something that hinders success — **dis·ad·van·ta·geous** *adj*

dis·agree *vb* **1** : fail to agree **2** : differ in opinion — **dis·agree·ment** *n*

dis·agree·able *adj* : unpleasant

dis·al·low *vb* : refuse to admit or recognize

dis·ap·pear *vb* **1** : pass out of sight **2** : cease to be — **dis·ap·pear·ance** *n*

dis·ap·point *vb* : fail to fulfill the expectation or hope of — **dis·ap·point·ment** *n*

dis·ap·prove *vb* **1** : condemn or reject **2** : feel or express dislike or rejection — **dis·ap·prov·al** *n* — **dis·ap·prov·ing·ly** *adv*

dis·arm *vb* **1** : take weapons from **2** : reduce armed forces **3** : make harmless or friendly — **dis·ar·ma·ment** *n*

di·sas·ter *n* : sudden great misfortune — **di·sas·trous** *adj*

dis·be·lieve *vb* : hold not worthy of belief — **dis·be·lief** *n*

disc *var of* DISK

dis·card *vb* : get rid of as unwanted — **dis·card** *n*

dis·cern *vb* : discover with the eyes or the mind — **dis·cern·ible** *adj* — **dis·cern·ment** *n*

dis·charge *vb* **1** : unload **2** : shoot **3** : set free **4** : dismiss from service **5** : let go or let off **6** : give forth fluid ∼ *n* **1** : act of discharging **2** : a flowing out (as of blood) **3** : dismissal

dis·ci·ple *n* : one who helps spread another's teachings

dis·ci·pline *n* **1** : field of study **2** : training that corrects, molds, or perfects **3** : punishment **4** : control gained by obedience or training ∼ *vb* **1** : punish **2** : train in self-control — **dis·ci·pli·nar·i·an** *n* — **dis·ci·plin·ary** *adj*

dis·close *vb* : reveal — **dis·clo·sure** *n*

dis·col·or *vb* : change the color of esp. for the worse — **dis·col·or·ation** *n*

dis·com·fort *n* : uneasiness

dis·con·nect *vb* : undo the connection of

dis·con·tent *n* : uneasiness of mind — **dis·con·tent·ed** *adj*

dis·con·tin·ue *vb* : end — **dis·con·tin·u·ance**

n — **dis·con·ti·nu·i·ty** *n* — **dis·con·tin·u·ous** *adj*

dis·cord *n* : lack of harmony — **dis·cor·dant** *adj* — **dis·cor·dant·ly** *adv*

dis·count *n* : reduction from a regular price ~ *vb* **1** : reduce the amount of **2** : disregard — **discount** *adj* — **dis·count·er** *n*

dis·cour·age *vb* **1** : deprive of courage, confidence, or enthusiasm **2** : dissuade — **dis·cour·age·ment** *n*

dis·cour·te·ous *adj* : lacking courtesy — **dis·cour·te·ous·ly** *adv* — **dis·cour·te·sy** *n*

dis·cov·er *vb* **1** : make known **2** : obtain the first sight or knowledge of **3** : find out — **dis·cov·er·er** *n* — **dis·cov·ery** *n*

dis·cred·it *vb* **1** : disbelieve **2** : destroy confidence in ~ *n* **1** : loss of reputation **2** : disbelief — **dis·cred·it·able** *adj*

dis·creet *adj* : capable of keeping a secret — **dis·creet·ly** *adv*

dis·crep·an·cy *n* : difference or disagreement

dis·crete *adj* : individually distinct

dis·cre·tion *n* **1** : discreet quality **2** : power of decision or choice — **dis·cre·tion·ary** *adj*

dis·crim·i·nate *vb* **1** : distinguish **2** : show favor or disfavor unjustly — **dis·crim·i·na·tion** *n* — **dis·crim·i·na·to·ry** *adj*

dis·cus *n* : disk hurled for distance in a contest

dis·cuss *vb* : talk about or present — **dis·cus·sion** *n*

dis·dain *n* : feeling of contempt ~ *vb* : look upon or reject with disdain — **dis·dain·ful** *adj* — **dis·dain·ful·ly** *adv*

dis·ease *n* : condition of a body that impairs its functioning — **dis·eased** *adj*

dis·en·chant *vb* : to free from illusion — **dis·en·chant·ment** *n*

dis·en·chant·ed *adj* : disappointed

dis·en·gage *vb* : release — **dis·en·gage·ment** *n*

dis·en·tan·gle *vb* : free from entanglement

dis·fa·vor *n* : disapproval

dis·fig·ure *vb* : spoil the appearance of — **dis·fig·ure·ment** *n*

dis·grace *vb* : bring disgrace to ~ *n* **1** : shame **2** : cause of shame — **dis·grace·ful** *adj* — **dis·grace·ful·ly** *adv*

dis·guise *vb* : hide the true identity or nature of ~ *n* : something that conceals

dis·gust *n* : strong aversion ~ *vb* : provoke disgust in — **dis·gust·ed·ly** *adv* — **dis·gust·ing·ly** *adv*

dish *n* **1** : vessel for serving food or the food it holds **2** : food prepared in a particular way ~ *vb* : put in a dish — **dish·cloth** *n* — **dish·rag** *n* — **dish·wash·er** *n* — **dish·wa·ter** *n*

dis·har·mo·ny *n* : lack of harmony — **dis·har·mo·ni·ous** *adj*

dis·heart·en *vb* : discourage

di·shev·el *vb* : throw into disorder — **di·shev·eled, di·shev·elled** *adj*

dis·hon·est *adj* : not honest — **dis·hon·est·ly** *adv* — **dis·hon·es·ty** *n*

dis·hon·or *n or vb* : disgrace — **dis·hon·or·able** *adj* — **dis·hon·or·ably** *adv*

dis·il·lu·sion *vb* : to free from illusion — **dis·il·lu·sion·ment** *n*

dis·in·fect *vb* : destroy disease germs in or on — **dis·in·fec·tant** *adj or n* — **dis·in·fec·tion** *n*

dis·in·te·grate *vb* : break into parts or small bits — **dis·in·te·gra·tion** *n*

dis·in·ter·est·ed *adj* **1** : not interested **2** : not prejudiced — **dis·in·ter·est·ed·ness** *n*

disk *n* : something round and flat

dis·like *n* : feeling that something is unpleasant and to be avoided ~ *vb* : regard with dislike

dis·lo·cate *vb* : move out of the usual or proper place — **dis·lo·ca·tion** *n*

dis·lodge *vb* : force out of a place

dis·loy·al *adj* : not loyal — **dis·loy·al·ty** *n*

dis·mal *adj* : showing or causing gloom — **dis·mal·ly** *adv*

dis·man·tle *vb* : take apart

dis·may *vb* : discourage — **dismay** *n*

dis·mem·ber *vb* : cut into pieces — **dis·mem·ber·ment** *n*

dis·miss *vb* **1** : send away **2** : remove from service **3** : put aside or out of mind — **dis·miss·al** *n*

dis·mount *vb* **1** : get down from something **2** : take apart

dis·obey *vb* : refuse to obey — **dis·obe·di·ence** *n* — **dis·obe·di·ent** *adj*

dis·or·der *n* **1** : lack of order **2** : breach of public order **3** : abnormal state of body or mind — **disorder** *vb* — **dis·or·der·li·ness** *n* — **dis·or·der·ly** *adj*

dis·or·ga·nize *vb* : throw into disorder — **dis·or·ga·ni·za·tion** *n*

dis·own *vb* : reject as not valid or not one's own

dis·par·age *vb* : say bad things about — **dis·par·age·ment** *n*

dis·patch *vb* **1** : send **2** : kill **3** : attend to rapidly **4** : defeat ~ *n* **1** : message **2** : news item from a correspondent **3** : promptness and efficiency — **dis·patch·er** *n*

dis·pense *vb* **1** : portion out **2** : make up and give out (remedies) — **dis·pen·sa·tion** *n* — **dis·pens·er** *n* — **dispense with** : do without

dis·perse *vb* : scatter — **dis·per·sal** *n* — **dis·per·sion** *n*

dis·place *vb* **1** : expel or force to flee from home or native land **2** : take the place of — **dis·place·ment** *n*

dis·play *vb* : present to view — **display** *n*

dis·please *vb* : arouse the dislike of — **dis·plea·sure** *n*

dis·pose *vb* **1** : give a tendency to **2** : settle — **dis·pos·able** *adj* — **dis·pos·al** *n* — **dis·pos·er** *n* — **dispose of 1** : determine the fate, condition, or use of **2** : get rid of

dis·po·si·tion *n* **1** : act or power of disposing of **2** : arrangement **3** : natural attitude

dis·pro·por·tion *n* : lack of proportion — **dis·pro·por·tion·ate** *adj*

dis·prove *vb* : prove false

dis·pute *vb* **1** : argue **2** : deny the truth or rightness of **3** : struggle against or over ∼ *n* : debate or quarrel — **dis·put·able** *adj* — **dis·pu·ta·tion** *n*

dis·qual·i·fy *vb* : make ineligible — **dis·qual·i·fi·ca·tion** *n*

dis·re·gard *vb* : pay no attention to ∼ *n* : neglect

dis·rep·u·ta·ble *adj* : having a bad reputation — **dis·re·pute** *n*

dis·re·spect *n* : lack of respect — **dis·re·spect·ful** *adj*

dis·rupt *vb* : throw into disorder — **dis·rup·tion** *n* — **dis·rup·tive** *adj*

dis·sat·is·fac·tion *n* : lack of satisfaction

dis·sat·is·fy *vb* : fail to satisfy

dis·sect *vb* : cut into parts esp. to examine — **dis·sec·tion** *n*

dis·sen·sion *n* : discord

dis·sent *vb* : object or disagree ∼ *n* : difference of opinion — **dis·sent·er** *n*

dis·ser·vice *n* : injury

dis·sim·i·lar *adj* : different — **dis·sim·i·lar·i·ty** *n*

dis·si·pate *vb* **1** : break up and drive off **2** : waste or lose through neglect — **dis·si·pa·tion** *n*

dis·solve *vb* **1** : break up or bring to an end **2** : pass or cause to pass into solution — **dis·so·lu·tion** *n*

dis·so·nance *n* : discord — **dis·so·nant** *adj*

dis·suade *vb* : persuade not to do something — **dis·sua·sion** *n*

dis·tance *n* **1** : measure of separation in space or time **2** : reserve

dis·tant *adj* **1** : separate in space **2** : remote in time, space, or relationship **3** : reserved — **dis·tant·ly** *adv*

dis·taste *n* : dislike — **dis·taste·ful** *adj*

dis·till *vb* : obtain by distillation — **dis·til·late** *n* — **dis·till·er** *n* — **dis·till·ery** *n*

dis·til·la·tion *n* : purification of liquid by evaporating then condensing

dis·tinct *adj* **1** : distinguishable from others **2** : readily discerned — **dis·tinc·tion** *n* — **dis·tinc·tive** *adj* — **dis·tinc·tive·ly** *adv* — **dis·tinc·tive·ness** *n* — **dis·tinct·ly** *adv* — **dis·tinct·ness** *n*

dis·tin·guish *vb* **1** : perceive as different **2** : set apart **3** : discern **4** : make outstanding — **dis·tin·guish·able** *adj* — **dis·tin·guished** *adj*

dis·tort *vb* : twist out of shape, condition, or true meaning — **dis·tor·tion** *n*

dis·tract *vb* : divert the mind or attention of — **dis·trac·tion** *n*

dis·tress *n* **1** : suffering **2** : misfortune **3** : state of danger or great need ∼ *vb* : subject to strain or distress — **dis·tress·ful** *adj*

dis·trib·ute *vb* **1** : divide among many **2** : spread or hand out — **dis·tri·bu·tion** *n* — **dis·trib·u·tive** *adj* — **dis·trib·u·tor** *n*

dis·trict *n* : territorial division

dis·trust *vb* : show lack of trust — **dis·trust** *n* — **dis·trust·ful** *adj*

dis·turb *vb* **1** : interfere with **2** : destroy the peace, composure, or order of — **dis·tur·bance** *n* — **dis·turb·er** *n*

ditch *n* : trench ∼ *vb* **1** : dig a ditch in **2** : get rid of

dit·to *n* : more of the same

dive *vb* **1** : plunge into water headfirst **2** : go or put underwater **3** : descend quickly ∼ *n* **1** : act of diving **2** : sharp decline — **div·er** *n*

di·verge *vb* **1** : move in different directions **2** : differ — **di·ver·gence** *n* — **di·ver·gent** *adj*

di·verse *adj* : involving different forms — **di·ver·si·fi·ca·tion** *n* — **di·ver·si·fy** *vb* — **di·ver·si·ty** *n*

di·vert *vb* **1** : turn from a course or purpose **2** : distract **3** : amuse — **di·ver·sion** *n*

di·vide *vb* **1** : separate **2** : distribute **3** : share **4** : subject to mathematical division — **di·vid·er** *n*

div·i·dend *n* **1** : individual share **2** : bonus **3** : number to be divided

di·vine *adj* **1** : relating to or being God or a god **2** : supremely good ∼ *n* : clergy member ∼ *vb* **1** : infer **2** : predict — **di·vine·ly** *adv* — **di·vin·er** *n* — **di·vin·i·ty** *n*

di·vis·i·ble *adj* : capable of being divided — **di·vis·i·bil·i·ty** *n*

di·vi·sion *n* **1** : distribution **2** : part of a whole **3** : disagreement **4** : process of finding out how many times one number is contained in another

di·vi·sor *n* : number by which a dividend is divided

di·vorce *n* : legal breaking up of a marriage — **di·vorce** *vb*

di·vor·cée *n* : divorced woman

di·vulge *vb* : reveal

diz·zy *adj* **1** : having a sensation of whirling **2** : causing or caused by giddiness — **diz·zi·ly** *adv* — **diz·zi·ness** *n*

DNA *n* : compound in cell nuclei that is the basis of heredity

do *vb* **did; done** **1** : work to accomplish (an action or task) **2** : behave **3** : prepare or fix up **4** : fare **5** : finish **6** : serve the needs or purpose of **7** — used as an auxiliary verb — **do·er** *n* — **do away with** **1** : get rid of **2** : destroy — **do by** : deal with — **do in** *vb* **1** : ruin **2** : kill

doc·ile *adj* : easily managed — **do·cil·i·ty** *n*

¹dock *vb* **1** : shorten **2** : reduce

²dock *n* **1** : berth between 2 piers to receive ships **2** : loading wharf or platform ∼ *vb* : bring or come into dock — **dock·work·er** *n*

doc·tor *n* **1** : person holding one of the highest academic degrees **2** : one (as a surgeon) skilled in healing arts ∼ *vb* **1** : give medical treatment to **2** : repair or alter — **doc·tor·al** *adj*

doc·trine *n* : something taught — **doc·tri·nal** *adj*

doc·u·ment *n* : paper that furnishes information or legal proof — **doc·u·ment** *vb* — **doc·u·men·ta·tion** *n* — **doc·u·ment·er** *n*

doc·u·men·ta·ry *adj* **1** : of or relating to documents **2** : giving a factual presentation — **doc·u·men·ta·ry** *n*

dodge *vb* **1** : move quickly aside or out of the way of **2** : evade — **dodge** *n*

doe *n* : adult female deer — **doe·skin** *n*

does *pres 3d sing of* DO

doesn't : does not

dog *n* : flesh-eating domestic mammal ∼ *vb* **1** : hunt down or track like a hound **2** : harass — **dog·catch·er** *n* — **dog·gy** *n or adj* — **dog·house** *n*

dog–ear *n* : turned-down corner of a page — **dog–ear** *vb* — **dog–eared** *adj*

dog·ma *n* : tenet or code of tenets

dog·ma·tism *n* : unwarranted stubbornness of opinion — **dog·ma·tic** *adj*

do·ings *n pl* : events

dol·drums *n pl* : spell of listlessness, despondency, or stagnation

dole *n* : distribution esp. of money to the needy or unemployed — **dole out** *vb* : give out esp. in small portions

dole·ful *adj* : sad — **dole·ful·ly** *adv*

doll *n* : small figure of a person used esp. as a child's toy

dol·lar *n* : any of various basic monetary units (as in the U.S. and Canada)

dol·ly *n* : small cart or wheeled platform

dol·phin *n* **1** : sea mammal related to the whales **2** : saltwater food fish

do·main *n* **1** : territory over which someone reigns **2** : sphere of activity or knowledge

dome *n* **1** : large hemispherical roof **2** : roofed stadium

do·mes·tic *adj* **1** : relating to the household or family **2** : relating and limited to one's own country **3** : tame ∼ *n* : household servant — **do·mes·ti·cal·ly** *adv*

do·mes·ti·cate *vb* : tame — **do·mes·ti·ca·tion** *n*

dom·i·nance *n* : control — **dom·i·nant** *adj*

dom·i·nate *vb* **1** : have control over **2** : rise high above — **dom·i·na·tion** *n*

dom·i·neer *vb* : exercise arbitrary control

do·min·ion *n* **1** : supreme authority **2** : governed territory

dom·i·no *n* : flat rectangular block used as a piece in a game (**dominoes**)

do·nate *vb* : make a gift of — **do·na·tion** *n*

¹done *past part of* DO

²done *adj* **1** : finished or ended **2** : cooked sufficiently

don·key *n* : sturdy domestic ass

do·nor *n* : one that gives

don't : do not

doo·dle *vb* : draw or scribble aimlessly — **doodle** *n*

doom *n* **1** : judgment **2** : fate **3** : ruin — **doom** *vb*

door *n* : passage for entrance or a movable bar-

rier that can open or close such a passage —
door·jamb *n* — **door·knob** *n* — **door·mat** *n*
— **door·step** *n* — **door·way** *n*

dope 1 : narcotic preparation 2 : stupid person 3 : information ∼ *vb* : drug

dor·mant *adj* : not actively growing or functioning — **dor·man·cy** *n*

dor·mi·to·ry *n* : residence hall (as at a college)

dose *n* : quantity (as of medicine) taken at one time ∼ *vb* : give medicine to — **dos·age** *n*

dot *n* 1 : small spot 2 : small round mark made with or as if with a pen ∼ *vb* : mark with dots

dote *vb* 1 : act feebleminded 2 : be foolishly fond

dou·ble *adj* 1 : consisting of 2 members or parts 2 : being twice as great or as many 3 : folded in two ∼ *n* 1 : something twice another 2 : one that resembles another ∼ *adv* : doubly ∼ *vb* 1 : make or become twice as great 2 : fold or bend 3 : clench

dou·ble-cross *vb* : deceive by trickery — **dou·ble-cross·er** *n*

dou·bly *adv* : to twice the degree

doubt *vb* 1 : be uncertain about 2 : show lack of trust 3 : consider unlikely ∼ *n* 1 : uncertainty 2 : lack of trust 3 : inclination not to believe — **doubt·ful** *adj* — **doubt·ful·ly** *adv* — **doubt·less** *adv*

dough *n* : stiff mixture of flour and liquid — **doughy** *adj*

dough·nut *n* : small fried ring-shaped cake

douse *vb* 1 : plunge into or drench with water 2 : extinguish

¹**dove** *n* : small wild pigeon

²**dove** *past of* DIVE

dove·tail *vb* : fit together neatly

dow·el *n* 1 : peg used for fastening two pieces 2 : wooden rod

¹**down** *adv* 1 : toward or in a lower position or state 2 : to a lying or sitting position 3 : as a cash deposit 4 : on paper ∼ *adj* 1 : lying on the ground 2 : directed or going downward 3 : being at a low level ∼ *prep* : toward the bottom of ∼ *vb* 1 : cause to go down 2 : defeat

²**down** *n* : fluffy feathers

down·cast *adj* 1 : sad 2 : directed down

down·fall *n* : ruin or cause of ruin

down·grade *n* : downward slope ∼ *vb* : lower in grade or position

down·heart·ed *adj* : sad

down·pour *n* : heavy rain

down·right *adv* : thoroughly ∼ *adj* : absolute or thorough

down·size *vb* : reduce in size

down·stairs *adv* : on or to a lower floor and esp. the main floor — **downstairs** *adj or n*

down-to-earth *adj* : practical

down·town *adv* : to, toward, or in the business center of a town — **downtown** *n or adj*

down·ward, down·wards *adv* : to a lower place or condition — **downward** *adj*

down·wind *adv or adj* : in the direction the wind is blowing

downy *adj* : resembling or covered with down

dow·ry *n* : property a woman gives her husband in marriage

dox·ol·o·gy *n* : hymn of praise to God

doze *vb* : sleep lightly — **doze** *n*

doz·en *n* : group of 12 — **doz·enth** *adj*

drab *adj* : dull — **drab·ly** *adv* — **drab·ness** *n*

draft *n* 1 : act of drawing or hauling 2 : act of drinking 3 : amount drunk at once 4 : preliminary outline or rough sketch 5 : selection from a pool or the selection process 6 : order for the payment of money 7 : air current ∼ *vb* 1 : select usu. on a compulsory basis 2 : make a preliminary sketch, version, or plan of ∼ *adj* : drawn from a container — **draft·ee** *n* — **drafty** *adj*

drag *n* 1 : something dragged over a surface or through water 2 : something that hinders progress or is boring 3 : act or an instance of dragging ∼ *vb* 1 : haul 2 : move or work with difficulty 3 : pass slowly 4 : search or fish with a drag — **drag·ger** *n*

dra·gon *n* : fabled winged serpent

drag·on·fly *n* : large 4-winged insect

drain *vb* 1 : draw off or flow off gradually or completely 2 : exhaust ∼ *n* : means or act of draining — **drain·age** *n* — **drain·er** *n* — **drain·pipe** *n*

dra·ma *n* 1 : composition for theatrical presentation esp. on a serious subject 2 : series of events involving conflicting forces — **dra·mat·ic** *adj* — **dra·mat·i·cal·ly** *adv* — **dram·a·tist** *n* — **dram·a·ti·za·tion** *n* — **dra·ma·tize** *vb*

drank *past of* DRINK

drape *vb* 1 : cover or adorn with folds of cloth 2 : cause to hang in flowing lines or folds ∼ *n* : curtain

drap•ery *n* : decorative fabric hung esp. as a heavy curtain

dras•tic *adj* : extreme or harsh — **dras•ti•cal•ly** *adj*

draw *vb* **drew; drawn** **1** : move or cause to move (as by pulling) **2** : attract or provoke **3** : extract **4** : take or receive (as money) **5** : bend a bow in preparation for shooting **6** : leave a contest undecided **7** : sketch **8** : write out **9** : deduce ∼ *n* **1** : act, process, or result of drawing **2** : tie — **draw out** : cause to speak candidly — **draw up** **1** : write out **2** : pull oneself erect **3** : bring or come to a stop

draw•back *n* : disadvantage

draw•bridge *n* : bridge that can be raised

draw•er *n* **1** : one that draws **2** : sliding box-like compartment **3** *pl* : underpants

draw•ing *n* **1** : occasion of choosing by lot **2** : act or art of making a figure, plan, or sketch with lines **3** : something drawn

drawl *vb* : speak slowly — **drawl** *n*

dread *vb* : feel extreme fear or reluctance ∼ *n* : great fear ∼ *adj* : causing dread — **dread•ful** *adj* — **dread•ful•ly** *adv*

dream *n* **1** : series of thoughts or visions during sleep **2** : dreamlike vision **3** : something notable **4** : ideal ∼ *vb* **1** : have a dream **2** : imagine — **dream•er** *n* — **dream•like** *adj* — **dreamy** *adj*

drea•ry *adj* : dismal — **drea•ri•ly** *adv*

drench *vb* : wet thoroughly

dress *vb* **1** : put clothes on **2** : decorate **3** : prepare (as a carcass) for use **4** : apply dressings, remedies, or fertilizer to ∼ *n* **1** : apparel **2** : single garment of bodice and skirt ∼ *adj* : suitable for a formal event — **dress•mak•er** *n* — **dress•mak•ing** *n*

dress•er *n* : bureau with a mirror

dress•ing *n* **1** : act or process of dressing **2** : sauce or a seasoned mixture **3** : material to cover an injury

dressy *adj* **1** : showy in dress **2** : stylish

drew *past of* DRAW

drib•ble *vb* **1** : fall or flow in drops **2** : drool — **dribble** *n*

drier *comparative of* DRY

driest *superlative of* DRY

drift *n* **1** : motion or course of something drifting **2** : mass piled up by wind **3** : general intention or meaning ∼ *vb* **1** : float or be driven along (as by a current) **2** : wander without

purpose **3** : pile up under force — **drift•er** *n* — **drift•wood** *n*

drill *vb* **1** : bore with a drill **2** : instruct by repetition ∼ *n* **1** : tool for boring holes **2** : regularly practiced exercise — **drill•er** *n*

drily *var of* DRYLY

drink *vb* **drank; drunk** **1** : swallow liquid **2** : absorb **3** : drink alcoholic beverages esp. to excess ∼ *n* **1** : beverage **2** : alcoholic liquor — **drink•able** *adj* — **drink•er** *n*

drip *vb* : fall or let fall in drops ∼ *n* **1** : a dripping **2** : sound of falling drops

drive *vb* **drove; driv•en** **1** : urge or force onward **2** : direct the movement or course of **3** : compel **4** : cause to become **5** : propel forcefully ∼ *n* **1** : trip in a vehicle **2** : intensive campaign **3** : aggressive or dynamic quality **4** : basic need — **driv•er** *n*

drive–in *adj* : accommodating patrons in cars — **drive–in** *n*

driv•el *vb* **1** : drool **2** : talk stupidly ∼ *n* : nonsense

drive•way *n* : usu. short private road from the street to a house

driz•zle *n* : fine misty rain — **drizzle** *vb*

drone *n* **1** : male honeybee **2** : deep hum or buzz ∼ *vb* : make a dull monotonous sound

drool *vb* : let liquid run from the mouth

droop *vb* **1** : hang or incline downward **2** : lose strength or spirit — **droop** *n* — **droopy** *adj*

drop *n* **1** : quantity of fluid in one spherical mass **2** *pl* : medicine used by drops **3** : decline or fall **4** : distance something drops ∼ *vb* **1** : fall in drops **2** : let fall **3** : convey **4** : go lower or become less strong or less active — **drop•let** *n* — **drop•per** *n* — **drop back** *vb* : move toward the rear — **drop behind** : fail to keep up — **drop in** *vb* : pay an unexpected visit

drought *n* : long dry spell

drove *past of* DRIVE

drown *vb* **1** : suffocate in water **2** : overpower or become overpowered

drowsy *adj* : sleepy — **drows•i•ly** *adv* — **drows•i•ness** *n*

drug *n* **1** : substance used as or in medicine **2** : narcotic ∼ *vb* : affect with drugs — **drug•gist** *n* — **drug•store** *n*

drum *n* **1** : musical instrument that is a skin-covered cylinder beaten usu. with sticks **2** : drum-shaped object (as a container) ∼ *vb* **1**

: beat a drum **2** : drive, force, or bring about by steady effort — **drum·beat** *n* — **drum·mer** *n*

drum·stick *n* **1** : stick for beating a drum **2** : lower part of a fowl's leg

drunk *adj* : having the faculties impaired by alcohol ∼ *n* : one who is drunk — **drunk·ard** *n* — **drunk·en** *adj* — **drunk·en·ly** *adv* — **drunk·en·ness** *n*

dry *adj* **1** : lacking water or moisture **2** : thirsty **3** : marked by the absence of alcoholic beverages **4** : uninteresting **5** : not sweet ∼ *vb* : make or become dry — **dry·ly** *adv* — **dry·ness** *n*

dry–clean *vb* : clean (fabrics) chiefly with solvents other than water — **dry cleaning** *n*

dry·er *n* : device for drying

du·al *adj* : twofold — **du·al·ism** *n* — **du·al·i·ty** *n*

dub *vb* : name

du·bi·ous *adj* **1** : uncertain **2** : questionable — **du·bi·ous·ly** *adv* — **du·bi·ous·ness** *n*

duch·ess *n* **1** : wife of a duke **2** : woman holding a ducal title

¹duck *n* : swimming bird related to the goose and swan ∼ *vb* **1** : thrust or plunge under water **2** : lower the head or body suddenly **3** : evade — **duck·ling** *n*

²duck *n* : cotton fabric

duct *n* : canal for conveying a fluid — **duct·less** *adj*

dude *n* **1** : dandy **2** : guy

due *adj* **1** : owed **2** : appropriate **3** : attributable **4** : scheduled ∼ *n* **1** : something due **2** *pl* : fee ∼ *adv* : directly

du·el *n* : combat between 2 persons — **du·el** *vb* — **du·el·ist** *n*

du·et *n* : musical composition for 2 performers

dug *past of* DIG

dug·out *n* **1** : boat made by hollowing out a log **2** : shelter made by digging

duke *n* : nobleman of the highest rank — **duke·dom** *n*

dull *adj* **1** : mentally slow **2** : blunt **3** : not brilliant or interesting — **dull** *vb* — **dul·lard** *n* — **dull·ness** *n* — **dul·ly** *adv*

du·ly *adv* : in a due manner or time

dumb *adj* **1** : mute **2** : stupid — **dumb·ly** *adv*

dumb·bell *n* **1** : short bar with weights on the ends used for exercise **2** : stupid person

dumb·found, dum·found *vb* : amaze

dum·my *n* **1** : stupid person **2** : imitative substitute

dump *vb* : let fall in a pile ∼ *n* : place for dumping something (as refuse) — **in the dumps** : sad

dump·ling *n* : small mass of boiled or steamed dough

dumpy *adj* : short and thick in build

¹dun *adj* : brownish gray

²dun *vb* : hound for payment of a debt

dunce *n* : stupid person

dune *n* : hill of sand

dung *n* : manure

dun·ga·ree *n* **1** : blue denim **2** *pl* : work clothes made of dungaree

dun·geon *n* : underground prison

dunk *vb* : dip temporarily into liquid

duo *n* : pair

dupe *n* : one easily deceived or cheated — **dupe** *vb*

du·plex *adj* : double ∼ *n* : 2-family house

du·pli·cate *adj* **1** : consisting of 2 identical items **2** : being just like another ∼ *n* : exact copy ∼ *vb* **1** : make an exact copy of **2** : repeat or equal — **du·pli·ca·tion** *n* — **du·pli·ca·tor** *n*

du·ra·ble *adj* : lasting a long time — **du·ra·bil·i·ty** *n*

du·ra·tion *n* : length of time something lasts

du·ress *n* : coercion

dur·ing *prep* **1** : throughout **2** : at some point in

dusk *n* : twilight — **dusky** *adj*

dust *n* : powdered matter ∼ *vb* **1** : remove dust from **2** : sprinkle with fine particles — **dust·er** *n* — **dust·pan** *n* — **dusty** *adj*

du·ty *n* **1** : action required by one's occupation or position **2** : moral or legal obligation **3** : tax — **du·te·ous** *adj* — **du·ti·able** *adj* — **du·ti·ful** *adj*

DVD *n* : digital video disk

dwarf *n* : one that is much below normal size ∼ *vb* **1** : stunt **2** : cause to seem smaller — **dwarf·ish** *adj*

dwell *vb* **1** : reside **2** : keep the attention directed — **dwell·er** *n* — **dwell·ing** *n*

dwin·dle *vb* : become steadily less

dye *n* : coloring material ∼ *vb* : give a new color to

dying *pres part of* DIE

dyke *var of* DIKE

dy·nam·ic *adj* **1** : relating to physical force producing motion **2** : energetic or forceful

dy·na·mite *n* : explosive made of nitroglycerin — **dynamite** *vb*

dy·na·mo *n* : electrical generator

dy·nas·ty *n* : succession of rulers of the same family — **dy·nas·tic** *adj*

dys·lex·ia *n* : disturbance of the ability to read — **dys·lex·ic** *adj*

dys·tro·phy *n* : disorder involving nervous and muscular tissue

E

e *n* : 5th letter of the alphabet

each *adj* : being one of the class named ∼ *pron* : every individual one ∼ *adv* : apiece

ea·ger *adj* : enthusiastic or anxious — **ea·ger·ly** *adv* — **ea·ger·ness** *n*

ea·gle *n* : large bird of prey

¹ear *n* : organ of hearing or the outer part of this — **ear·ache** *n* — **ear·drum** *n* — **eared** *adj* — **ear·lobe** *n* — **ear·phone** *n* — **ear·ring** *n*

²ear *n* : fruiting head of a cereal

earl *n* : British nobleman — **earl·dom** *n*

ear·ly *adj* **1** : relating to or occurring near the beginning or before the usual time **2** : ancient — **early** *adv*

earn *vb* **1** : receive as a return for service **2** : deserve

ear·nest *n* : serious state of mind — **earnest** *adj* — **ear·nest·ly** *adv* — **ear·nest·ness** *n*

earn·ings *n pl* : something earned

ear·shot *n* : range of hearing

earth *n* **1** : soil or land **2** : planet inhabited by man — **earth·li·ness** *n* — **earth·ly** *adj* — **earth·ward** *adv*

earth·quake *n* : shaking or trembling of the earth

earth·worm *n* : long segmented worm

earthy *adj* **1** : relating to or consisting of earth **2** : practical **3** : coarse — **earth·i·ness** *n*

ease *n* **1** : comfort **2** : naturalness of manner **3** : freedom from difficulty ∼ *vb* **1** : relieve from distress **2** : lessen the tension of **3** : make easier

ea·sel *n* : frame to hold a painter's canvas

east *adv* : to or toward the east ∼ *adj* : situated toward or at or coming from the east ∼ *n* **1** : direction of sunrise **2** *cap* : regions to the east — **east·er·ly** *adv or adj* — **east·ward** *adv or adj* — **east·wards** *adv*

Eas·ter *n* : church feast celebrating Christ's resurrection

east·ern *adj* **1** *cap* : relating to a region designated East **2** : lying toward or coming from the east — **East·ern·er** *n*

easy *adj* **1** : marked by ease **2** : lenient — **eas·i·ly** *adv* — **eas·i·ness** *n*

easy·go·ing *adj* : relaxed and casual

eat *vb* (**ate**; **eat·en**) **1** : take in as food **2** : use up or corrode — **eat·able** *adj or n* — **eat·er** *n*

eaves·drop *vb* : listen secretly — **eaves·drop·per** *n*

ebb *n* **1** : outward flow of the tide **2** : decline ∼ *vb* **1** : recede from the flood state **2** : wane

ec·cen·tric *adj* **1** : odd in behavior **2** : being off center — **eccentric** *n* — **ec·cen·tri·cal·ly** *adv* — **ec·cen·tric·i·ty** *n*

ec·cle·si·as·ti·cal, ecclesiastic *adj* : relating to a church — **ec·cle·si·as·ti·cal·ly** *adv*

echo *n* : repetition of a sound caused by a reflection of the sound waves — **echo** *vb*

éclair *n* : custard-filled pastry

eclec·tic *adj* : drawing or drawn from varied sources

eclipse *n* : total or partial obscuring of one celestial body by another — **eclipse** *vb*

ecol·o·gy *n* : science concerned with the interaction of organisms and their environment — **eco·log·i·cal** *adj* — **eco·log·i·cal·ly** *adv* — **ecol·o·gist** *n*

eco·nom·ics *n* : branch of knowledge dealing with goods and services — **econ·o·mist** *n*

econ·o·my *n* **1** : thrifty use of resources **2** : economic system — **eco·nom·ic** *adj* — **eco·nom·i·cal** *adj* — **ec·o·nom·i·cal·ly** *adv* — **econ·o·mize** *vb* — **econ·o·miz·er** *n* — **econ·o·my** *adj*

ec·sta·sy *n* : extreme emotional excitement — **ec·stat·ic** *adj* — **ec·stat·i·cal·ly** *adv*

ec·u·men·i·cal *adj* : promoting worldwide Christian unity

ed·dy *n* : whirlpool — **eddy** *vb*

Eden *n* : paradise

edge *n* **1** : cutting side of a blade **2** : line where something begins or ends ∼ *vb* **1** : give or form an edge **2** : move gradually **3** : narrowly defeat — **edg·er** *n*

edge·wise *adv* : sideways

edgy *adj* : nervous — **edg·i·ness** *n*
ed·i·ble *adj* : fit or safe to be eaten — **ed·i·bil·i·ty** *n* — **edible** *n*
ed·it *vb* **1** : revise and prepare for publication **2** : delete — **ed·i·tor** *n* — **ed·i·tor·ship** *n*
edi·tion *n* **1** : form in which a text is published **2** : total number published at one time
ed·i·to·ri·al *adj* **1** : relating to an editor or editing **2** : expressing opinion ∼ *n* : article (as in a newspaper) expressing the views of an editor — **ed·i·to·ri·al·ize** *vb* — **ed·i·to·ri·al·ly** *adv*
ed·u·cate *vb* **1** : give instruction to **2** : develop mentally and morally **3** : provide with information — **ed·u·ca·ble** *adj* — **ed·u·ca·tion** *n* — **ed·u·ca·tion·al** *adj* — **ed·u·ca·tor** *n*
eel *n* : snakelike fish
ee·rie *adj* : weird — **ee·ri·ly** *adv*
ef·fect *n* **1** : result **2** : meaning **3** : influence **4** *pl* : goods or possessions ∼ *vb* : cause to happen — **in effect** : in substance
ef·fec·tive *adj* **1** : producing a strong or desired effect **2** : being in operation — **ef·fec·tive·ly** *adv* — **ef·fec·tive·ness** *n*
ef·fec·tu·al *adj* : producing an intended effect — **ef·fec·tu·al·ly** *adv* — **ef·fec·tu·al·ness** *n*
ef·fem·i·nate *adj* : having qualities more typical of women than men — **ef·fem·i·na·cy** *n*
ef·fer·vesce *vb* **1** : bubble and hiss as gas escapes **2** : show exhilaration — **ef·fer·ves·cence** *n* — **ef·fer·ves·cent** *adj* — **ef·fer·ves·cent·ly** *adv*
ef·fi·cient *adj* : working well with little waste — **ef·fi·cien·cy** *n* — **ef·fi·cient·ly** *adv*
ef·fort *n* **1** : a putting forth of strength **2** : use of resources toward a goal **3** : product of effort — **ef·fort·less** *adj* — **ef·fort·less·ly** *adv*
¹**egg** *vb* : urge to action
²**egg** *n* **1** : rounded usu. hard-shelled reproductive body esp. of birds and reptiles from which the young hatches **2** : a female reproductive cell — **egg·shell** *n*
egg·plant *n* : edible purplish fruit of a plant related to the potato
ego *n* : self-esteem
ego·cen·tric *adj* : concerned only with one's own desires or interests
ego·tism *n* : exaggerated sense of self-importance — **ego·tist** *n* — **ego·tis·tic, ego·tis·ti·cal** *adj* — **ego·tis·ti·cal·ly** *adv*
egre·gious *adj* : notably bad — **egre·gious·ly** *adv*

ei·der·down *n* : soft down obtained from a northern sea duck (**eider**)
eight *n* **1** : one more than 7 **2** : 8th in a set or series **3** : something having 8 units — **eight** *adj or pron* — **eighth** *adj or adv or n*
eigh·teen *n* : one more than 17 — **eigh·teen** *adj or pron* — **eigh·teenth** *adj or n*
eighty *n* : 8 times 10 — **eight·i·eth** *adj or n* — **eighty** *adj or pron*
ei·ther *adj* **1** : both **2** : being the one or the other of two ∼ *pron* : one of two or more ∼ *conj* : one or the other
ejac·u·late *vb* **1** : say suddenly **2** : eject a fluid (as semen) — **ejac·u·la·tion** *n*
eject *vb* : drive or throw out — **ejec·tion** *n*
eke *vb* : barely gain with effort — usu. with *out*
elab·o·rate *adj* **1** : planned in detail **2** : complex and ornate ∼ *vb* : work out in detail — **elab·o·rate·ly** *adv* — **elab·o·rate·ness** *n* — **elab·o·ra·tion** *n*
elapse *vb* : slip by
elas·tic *adj* **1** : springy **2** : flexible ∼ *n* **1** : elastic material **2** : rubber band — **elas·tic·i·ty** *n*
elate *vb* : fill with joy — **ela·tion** *n*
el·bow *n* **1** : joint of the arm **2** : elbow-shaped bend or joint ∼ *vb* : push aside with the elbow
el·der *adj* : older ∼ *n* **1** : one who is older **2** : church officer
el·der·ly *adj* : past middle age
el·dest *adj* : oldest
elect *vb* : choose esp. by vote ∼ *adj* : elected but not yet in office ∼ *n* **elect** *pl* : exclusive group — **elec·tion** *n* — **elec·tive** *n or adj* — **elec·tor** *n* — **elec·tor·al** *adj*
elec·tric *adj* **1** *or* **elec·tri·cal** : relating to or run by electricity **2** : thrilling — **elec·tri·cal·ly** *adv*
elec·tri·cian *n* : person who installs or repairs electrical equipment
elec·tric·i·ty *n* **1** : fundamental form of energy occurring naturally (as in lightning) or produced artificially **2** : electric current
elec·tri·fy *vb* **1** : charge with electricity **2** : equip for use of electric power **3** : thrill — **elec·tri·fi·ca·tion** *n*
elec·tro·cute *vb* : kill by an electric shock — **elec·tro·cu·tion** *n*
elec·tro·mag·net *n* : magnet made using electric current
elec·tro·mag·ne·tism *n* : natural force responsible for interactions between charged parti-

cles — **elec·tro·mag·net·ic** *adj* — **elec·tro·mag·net·i·cal·ly** *adv*

elec·tron *n* : negatively charged particle within the atom

elec·tron·ic *adj* : relating to electrons or electronics — **elec·tron·i·cal·ly** *adv*

elec·tron·ics *n* : physics of electrons and their use esp. in devices

el·e·gance *n* : refined gracefulness — **el·e·gant** *adj* — **el·e·gant·ly** *adv*

el·e·ment *n* **1** *pl* : weather conditions **2** : natural environment **3** : constituent part **4** *pl* : simplest principles **5** : substance that has atoms of only one kind — **el·e·men·tal** *adj*

el·e·men·ta·ry *adj* **1** : simple **2** : relating to the basic subjects of education

el·e·phant *n* : huge mammal with a trunk and 2 ivory tusks

el·e·vate *vb* **1** : lift up **2** : exalt

el·e·va·tion *n* : height or a high place

el·e·va·tor *n* **1** : cage or platform for raising or lowering something **2** : grain storehouse

elev·en *n* **1** : one more than 10 **2** : 11th in a set or series **3** : something having 11 units — **eleven** *adj or pron* — **elev·enth** *adj or n*

elf *n* **elves** : mischievous fairy — **elf·in** *adj* — **elf·ish** *adj*

elic·it *vb* : draw forth

el·i·gi·ble *adj* : qualified to participate or to be chosen — **el·i·gi·bil·i·ty** *n*

elim·i·nate *vb* : get rid of — **elim·i·na·tion** *n*

elite *n* : choice or select group

elk *n* : large deer

el·lipse *n* : oval

el·lip·sis *n* **1** : omission of a word **2** : marks (as . . .) to show omission

el·lip·ti·cal, el·lip·tic *adj* **1** : relating to or shaped like an ellipse **2** : relating to or marked by ellipsis

elm *n* : tall shade tree

elon·gate *vb* : make or grow longer — **elon·ga·tion** *n*

elope *vb* : run away esp. to be married — **elope·ment** *n* — **elop·er** *n*

else *adv* **1** : in a different way, time, or place **2** : otherwise ～ *adj* **1** : other **2** : more

else·where *adv* : in or to another place

elude *vb* : evade — **elu·sive** *adj* — **elu·sive·ly** *adv* — **elu·sive·ness** *n*

elves *pl of* ELF

e–mail *n* : message sent or received via computers

em·bank·ment *n* : protective barrier of earth

em·bar·go *n* : ban on trade — **embargo** *vb*

em·bark *vb* **1** : go on board a ship or airplane **2** : make a start — **em·bar·ka·tion** *n*

em·bar·rass *vb* : cause distress and self-consciousness — **em·bar·rass·ment** *n*

em·bas·sy *n* : residence and offices of an ambassador

em·bel·lish *vb* : decorate — **em·bel·lish·ment** *n*

em·bez·zle *vb* : steal (money) by falsifying records — **em·bez·zle·ment** *n* — **em·bez·zler** *n*

em·blem *n* : symbol — **em·blem·at·ic** *adj*

em·body *vb* : give definite form or expression to — **em·bodi·ment** *n*

em·brace *vb* **1** : clasp in the arms **2** : welcome **3** : include — **embrace** *n*

em·broi·der *vb* : ornament with or do needlework — **em·broi·dery** *n*

em·bryo *n* : living being in its earliest stages of development — **em·bry·on·ic** *adj*

em·er·ald *n* : green gem ～ *adj* : bright green

emerge *vb* : rise, come forth, or appear — **emer·gence** *n* — **emer·gent** *adj*

emer·gen·cy *n* : condition requiring prompt action

em·i·grate *vb* : leave a country to settle elsewhere — **em·i·grant** *n* — **em·i·gra·tion** *n*

em·i·nence *n* **1** : prominence or superiority **2** : person of high rank

em·i·nent *adj* : prominent — **em·i·nent·ly** *adv*

emis·sion *n* : substance discharged into the air

emit *vb* : give off or out

emo·tion *n* : intense feeling — **emo·tion·al** *adj* — **emo·tion·al·ly** *adv*

em·per·or *n* : ruler of an empire

em·pha·sis *n* : stress

em·pha·size *vb* : stress

em·phat·ic *adj* : uttered with emphasis — **em·phat·i·cal·ly** *adv*

em·pire *n* : large state or a group of states

em·ploy *vb* **1** : use **2** : occupy ～ *n* : paid occupation — **em·ploy·ee, em·ploye** *n* — **em·ploy·er** *n* — **em·ploy·ment** *n*

em·pow·er *vb* : give power to — **em·pow·er·ment** *n*

em·press *n* **1** : wife of an emperor **2** : woman emperor

emp·ty *adj* **1** : containing nothing **2** : not occupied **3** : lacking value, sense, or purpose ～ *vb* : make or become empty — **emp·ti·ness** *n*

em·u·late *vb* : try to equal or excel — **em·u·la·tion** *n*

emul·sion *n* **1** : mixture of mutually insoluble liquids **2** : light-sensitive coating on photographic film

en·able *vb* : give power, capacity, or ability to

en·act *vb* **1** : make into law **2** : act out — **en·act·ment** *n*

enam·el *n* **1** : glasslike substance used to coat metal or pottery **2** : hard outer layer of a tooth **3** : glossy paint — **enamel** *vb*

en·chant *vb* **1** : bewitch **2** : fascinate — **en·chant·er** *n* — **en·chant·ment** *n* — **en·chant·ress** *n*

en·cir·cle *vb* : surround

en·close *vb* **1** : shut up or surround **2** : include — **en·clo·sure** *n*

en·com·pass *vb* : surround or include

en·core *n* : further performance

en·coun·ter *vb* **1** : fight **2** : meet unexpectedly — **encounter** *n*

en·cour·age *vb* **1** : inspire with courage and hope **2** : foster — **en·cour·age·ment** *n*

en·crust *vb* : coat or cover with or as if with a crust

en·cy·clo·pe·dia *n* : reference work on many subjects — **en·cy·clo·pe·dic** *adj*

end *n* **1** : point at which something stops or no longer exists **2** : process or act of stopping **3** : purpose ∼ *vb* **1** : stop or finish **2** : be at the end of — **end·less** *adj* — **end·less·ly** *adv*

en·dan·ger *vb* : bring into danger

en·dear *vb* : make dear — **en·dear·ment** *n*

en·deav·or *vb or n* : attempt

end·ing *n* : end

en·do·crine *adj* : producing secretions distributed by the bloodstream

en·dorse *vb* **1** : sign one's name to **2** : approve — **en·dorse·ment** *n*

en·dow *vb* **1** : furnish with funds **2** : furnish naturally — **en·dow·ment** *n*

en·dure *vb* **1** : last **2** : suffer patiently **3** : tolerate — **en·dur·able** *adj* — **en·dur·ance** *n*

en·e·my *n* : one that attacks or tries to harm another

en·er·get·ic *adj* : full of energy or activity — **en·er·get·i·cal·ly** *adv*

en·er·gize *vb* : give energy to

en·er·gy *n* **1** : capacity for action **2** : vigorous action **3** : capacity for doing work

en·er·vate *vb* : make weak or listless — **en·er·va·tion** *n*

en·force *vb* **1** : compel **2** : carry out — **en·force·able** *adj* — **en·force·ment** *n*

en·fran·chise *vb* : grant voting rights to — **en·fran·chise·ment** *n*

en·gage *vb* **1** : participate or cause to participate **2** : bring or come into working contact **3** : bind by a pledge to marry **4** : hire **5** : bring or enter into conflict — **en·gage·ment** *n*

en·gag·ing *adj* : attractive

en·gine *n* **1** : machine that converts energy into mechanical motion **2** : locomotive

en·gi·neer *n* **1** : one trained in engineering **2** : engine operator ∼ *vb* : lay out or manage as an engineer

en·gi·neer·ing *n* : practical application of science and mathematics

en·grave *vb* : cut into a surface — **en·grav·er** *n* — **en·grav·ing** *n*

en·gross *vb* : occupy fully

en·gulf *vb* : swallow up

en·hance *vb* : improve in value — **en·hance·ment** *n*

enig·ma *n* : puzzle or mystery — **enig·mat·ic** *adj* — **enig·mat·i·cal·ly** *adv*

en·joy *vb* : take pleasure in — **en·joy·able** *adj* — **en·joy·ment** *n*

en·large *vb* : make or grow larger — **en·large·ment** *n* — **en·larg·er** *n*

en·light·en *vb* : give knowledge or spiritual insight to — **en·light·en·ment** *n*

en·list *vb* **1** : join the armed forces **2** : get the aid of — **en·list·ee** *n* — **en·list·ment** *n*

en·liv·en *vb* : give life or spirit to

enor·mi·ty *n* **1** : great wickedness **2** : huge size

enor·mous *adj* : great in size, number, or degree — **enor·mous·ly** *adv* — **enor·mous·ness** *n*

enough *adj* : adequate ∼ *adv* **1** : in an adequate manner **2** : in a tolerable degree ∼ *pron* : adequate number, quantity, or amount

en·quire, en·qui·ry *var of* INQUIRE, INQUIRY

en·rage *vb* : fill with rage

en·rich *vb* : make rich — **en·rich·ment** *n*

en·roll, en·rol *vb* **1** : enter on a list **2** : become enrolled — **en·roll·ment** *n*

en route *adv or adj* : on or along the way

en·sem·ble *n* **1** : small group **2** : complete costume

en·shrine *vb* **1** : put in a shrine **2** : cherish

en·sign *n* **1** : flag **2** : lowest ranking commissioned officer in the navy

en·slave *vb* : make a slave of — **en·slave·ment** *n*

en·sure *vb* : guarantee

en·tail *vb* **:** involve as a necessary result

en·tan·gle *vb* **:** tangle — **en·tan·gle·ment** *n*

en·ter *vb* **1 :** go or come in or into **2 :** start **3 :** set down (as in a list)

en·ter·prise *n* **1 :** an undertaking **2 :** business organization **3 :** initiative

en·ter·pris·ing *adj* **:** showing initiative

en·ter·tain *vb* **1 :** treat or receive as a guest **2 :** hold in mind **3 :** amuse — **en·ter·tain·er** *n* — **en·ter·tain·ment** *n*

en·thrall, en·thral *vb* **:** hold spellbound

en·thu·si·asm *n* **:** strong excitement of feeling or its cause — **en·thu·si·ast** *n* — **en·thu·si·as·tic** *adj* — **en·thu·si·as·ti·cal·ly** *adv*

en·tice *vb* **:** tempt — **en·tice·ment** *n*

en·tire *adj* **:** complete or whole — **en·tire·ly** *adv* — **en·tire·ty** *n*

en·ti·tle *vb* **1 :** name **2 :** give a right to

en·ti·ty *n* **:** something with separate existence

en·tou·rage *n* **:** group of attendants

en·trails *n pl* **:** intestines

¹en·trance *n* **1 :** act of entering **2 :** means or place of entering — **en·trant** *n*

²en·trance *vb* **:** fascinate or delight

en·trap *vb* **:** trap — **en·trap·ment** *n*

en·treat *vb* **:** ask urgently — **en·treaty** *n*

en·trée, en·tree *n* **:** principal dish of the meal

en·tre·pre·neur *n* **:** organizer or promoter of an enterprise

en·trust *vb* **:** commit to another with confidence

en·try *n* **1 :** entrance **2 :** an entering in a record or an item so entered

enu·mer·ate *vb* **1 :** count **2 :** list — **enu·mer·a·tion** *n*

en·vel·op *vb* **:** surround — **en·vel·op·ment** *n*

en·ve·lope *n* **:** paper container for a letter

en·vi·ron·ment *n* **:** surroundings — **en·vi·ron·men·tal** *adj*

en·vi·ron·men·tal·ist *n* **:** person concerned about the environment

en·vi·rons *n pl* **:** vicinity

en·vi·sion *vb* **:** picture to oneself

en·vy *n* **1 :** resentful awareness of another's advantage **2 :** object of envy ⁓ *vb* **:** feel envy toward or on account of — **en·vi·able** *adj* — **en·vi·ous** *adj* — **en·vi·ous·ly** *adv*

en·zyme *n* **:** biological catalyst

eon *n* **:** indefinitely long time

ep·ic *n* **:** long poem about a hero — **epic** *adj*

ep·i·dem·ic *adj* **:** affecting many persons at one time — **epidemic** *n*

epi·der·mis *n* **:** outer layer of skin

ep·i·lep·sy *n* **:** nervous disorder marked by convulsive attacks — **ep·i·lep·tic** *adj or n*

epis·co·pal *adj* **:** governed by bishops

ep·i·sode *n* **:** occurrence — **ep·i·sod·ic** *adj*

ep·i·taph *n* **:** inscription in memory of a dead person

ep·i·thet *n* **:** characterizing often abusive word or phrase

epit·o·me *n* **1 :** summary **2 :** ideal example — **epit·o·mize** *vb*

ep·och *n* **:** extended period — **ep·och·al** *adj*

ep·oxy *n* **:** synthetic resin used esp. in adhesives ⁓ *vb* **:** glue with epoxy

equal *adj* **:** of the same quantity, value, quality, number, or status as another ⁓ *n* **:** one that is equal ⁓ *vb* **:** be or become equal to — **equal·i·ty** *n* — **equal·ize** *vb* — **equal·ly** *adv*

equate *vb* **:** treat or regard as equal

equa·tion *n* **:** mathematical statement that two things are equal

equa·tor *n* **:** imaginary circle that separates the northern and southern hemispheres — **equa·to·ri·al** *adj*

equi·lib·ri·um *n* **:** state of balance

equi·nox *n* **:** time when day and night are everywhere of equal length

equip *vb* **:** furnish with needed resources — **equip·ment** *n*

eq·ui·ta·ble *adj* **:** fair

eq·ui·ty *n* **1 :** justice **2 :** value of a property less debt

equiv·a·lent *adj* **:** equal — **equiv·a·lence** *n* — **equivalent** *n*

equiv·o·cate *vb* **1 :** use misleading language **2 :** avoid answering definitely — **equiv·o·cal** *adj* — **equiv·o·ca·tion** *n*

era *n* **:** period of time associated with something

erad·i·cate *vb* **:** do away with

erase *vb* **:** rub or scratch out — **eras·er** *n* — **era·sure** *n*

erect *adj* **:** not leaning or lying down ⁓ *vb* **1 :** build **2 :** bring to an upright position — **erec·tion** *n*

erode *vb* **:** wear away gradually

ero·sion *n* **:** process of eroding

erot·ic *adj* **:** sexually arousing — **erot·i·cal·ly** *adv* — **erot·i·cism** *n*

err *vb* **:** be or do wrong

er·rand *n* **:** short trip taken to do something often for another

er·rat·ic *adj* **1 :** eccentric **2 :** not consistent — **er·rat·i·cal·ly** *adv*

er·ro·ne·ous *adj* : wrong — **er·ro·ne·ous·ly** *adv*

er·ror *n* **1** : something that is not accurate **2** : state of being wrong

erupt *vb* : burst forth esp. suddenly and violently — **erup·tion** *n* — **erup·tive** *adj*

es·ca·late *vb* : become quickly larger or greater — **es·ca·la·tion** *n*

es·ca·la·tor *n* : moving stairs

es·ca·pade *n* : mischievous adventure

es·cape *vb* : get away or get away from ~ *n* **1** : flight from or avoidance of something unpleasant **2** : leakage **3** : means of escape ~ *adj* : providing means of escape — **es·cap·ee** *n*

es·cort *n* : one accompanying another — **es·cort** *vb*

esoph·a·gus *n* : muscular tube connecting the mouth and stomach

es·pe·cial·ly *adv* : particularly or notably

es·pi·o·nage *n* : practice of spying

espres·so *n* : strong steam-brewed coffee

es·quire *n* — used as a title of courtesy

es·say *n* : literary composition ~ *vb* : attempt — **es·say·ist** *n*

es·sence *n* **1** : fundamental nature or quality **2** : extract **3** : perfume

es·sen·tial *adj* : basic or necessary — **essential** *n* — **es·sen·tial·ly** *adv*

es·tab·lish *vb* **1** : bring into existence **2** : put on a firm basis **3** : cause to be recognized — **es·tab·lish·ment** *n*

es·tate *n* **1** : one's possessions **2** : large piece of land with a house

es·teem *n or vb* : regard

es·ti·mate *vb* : judge the approximate value, size, or cost ~ *n* **1** : rough or approximate calculation **2** : statement of the cost of a job — **es·ti·ma·tion** *n* — **es·ti·ma·tor** *n*

es·trange *vb* : make hostile — **es·trange·ment** *n*

et cet·era : and others esp. of the same kind

etch *vb* : produce by corroding parts of a surface with acid — **etch·er** *n* — **etch·ing** *n*

eter·nal *adj* : lasting forever — **eter·nal·ly** *adv*

eter·ni·ty *n* : infinite duration

eth·a·nol *n* : alcohol

eth·i·cal *adj* **1** : relating to ethics **2** : honorable — **eth·i·cal·ly** *adv*

eth·ics *n sing or pl* **1** : study of good and evil and moral duty **2** : moral principles or practice

eth·nic *adj* : relating to races or groups of people with common customs ~ *n* : member of a minority ethnic group

et·i·quette *n* : good manners

Eu·cha·rist *n* : Communion — **eu·cha·ris·tic** *adj*

eu·lo·gy *n* : speech in praise — **eu·lo·gis·tic** *adj* — **eu·lo·gize** *vb*

eu·phe·mism *n* : substitution of a pleasant expression for an unpleasant or offensive one — **eu·phe·mis·tic** *adj*

eu·pho·ria *n* : elation — **eu·phor·ic** *adj*

eu·ro *n* : common monetary unit of most of the European Union

eu·tha·na·sia *n* : mercy killing

evac·u·ate *vb* **1** : discharge wastes from the body **2** : remove or withdraw from — **evac·u·a·tion** *n*

evade *vb* : manage to avoid — **eva·sion** *n* — **eva·sive** *adj* — **eva·sive·ness** *n*

eval·u·ate *vb* : appraise — **eval·u·a·tion** *n*

evan·ge·lism *n* : the winning or revival of personal commitments to Christ — **evan·gel·i·cal** *adj* — **evan·ge·list** *n* — **evan·ge·lis·tic** *adj*

evap·o·rate *vb* **1** : pass off in or convert into vapor **2** : disappear quickly — **evap·o·ra·tion** *n* — **evap·ora·tor** *n*

even *adj* **1** : smooth **2** : equal or fair **3** : fully revenged **4** : divisible by 2 ~ *adv* **1** : already **2** — used for emphasis ~ *vb* : make or become even — **even·ly** *adv* — **even·ness** *n*

eve·ning *n* : early part of the night

event *n* **1** : occurrence **2** : noteworthy happening **3** : eventuality — **event·ful** *adj*

even·tu·al *adj* : later — **even·tu·al·ly** *adv*

even·tu·al·i·ty *n* : possible occurrence or outcome

ev·er *adv* **1** : always **2** : at any time **3** : in any case

ev·er·green *adj* : having foliage that remains green — **evergreen** *n*

ev·er·last·ing *adj* : lasting forever

ev·ery *adj* **1** : being each one of a group **2** : all possible

ev·ery·body *pron* : every person

ev·ery·day *adj* : ordinary

ev·ery·one *pron* : every person

ev·ery·thing *pron* : all that exists

ev·ery·where *adv* : in every place or part

evict *vb* : force (a person) to move from a property — **evic·tion** *n*

ev·i·dence *n* **1** : outward sign **2** : proof or testimony

ev·i·dent *adj* : clear or obvious — **ev·i·dent·ly** *adv*

evil *adj* : wicked ∼ *n* **1** : sin **2** : source of sorrow or distress — **evil·do·er** *n* — **evil·ly** *adv*

evoke *vb* : call forth or up — **evo·ca·tion** *n* — **evoc·a·tive** *adj*

evo·lu·tion *n* : process of change by degrees — **evo·lu·tion·ary** *adj*

evolve *vb* : develop or change by degrees

ewe *n* : female sheep

ex·act *vb* : compel to furnish ∼ *adj* : precisely correct — **ex·act·ing** *adj* — **ex·ac·ti·tude** *n* — **ex·act·ly** *adv* — **ex·act·ness** *n*

ex·ag·ger·ate *vb* : say more than is true — **ex·ag·ger·at·ed·ly** *adv* — **ex·ag·ger·a·tion** *n* — **ex·ag·ger·a·tor** *n*

ex·alt *vb* : glorify — **ex·al·ta·tion** *n*

ex·am *n* : examination

ex·am·ine *vb* **1** : inspect closely **2** : test by questioning — **ex·am·i·na·tion** *n*

ex·am·ple *n* **1** : representative sample **2** : model **3** : problem to be solved for teaching purposes

ex·as·per·ate *vb* : thoroughly annoy — **ex·as·per·a·tion** *n*

ex·ca·vate *vb* : dig or hollow out — **ex·ca·va·tion** *n* — **ex·ca·va·tor** *n*

ex·ceed *vb* **1** : go or be beyond the limit of **2** : do better than

ex·ceed·ing·ly *adv* : extremely

ex·cel *vb* : do extremely well or far better than

ex·cel·len·cy *n* — used as a title of honor

ex·cel·lent *adj* : very good — **ex·cel·lence** *n* — **ex·cel·lent·ly** *adv*

ex·cept *vb* : omit ∼ *prep* : excluding ∼ *conj* : but — **ex·cep·tion** *n*

ex·cep·tion·al *adj* : superior — **ex·cep·tion·al·ly** *adv*

ex·cerpt *n* : brief passage ∼ *vb* : select an excerpt

ex·cess *n* : amount left over — **excess** *adj* — **ex·ces·sive** *adj* — **ex·ces·sive·ly** *adv*

ex·change *n* **1** : the giving or taking of one thing in return for another **2** : marketplace esp. for securities ∼ *vb* : transfer in return for some equivalent — **ex·change·able** *adj*

ex·cise *n* : tax

ex·cite *vb* **1** : stir up **2** : kindle the emotions of — **ex·cit·abil·i·ty** *n* — **ex·cit·able** *adj* — **ex·ci·ta·tion** *n* — **ex·cit·ed·ly** *adv* — **ex·cite·ment** *n*

ex·claim *vb* : cry out esp. in delight — **ex·cla·ma·tion** *n* — **ex·clam·a·to·ry** *adj*

exclamation point *n* : punctuation mark ! used esp. after an interjection or exclamation

ex·clude *vb* : leave out — **ex·clu·sion** *n*

ex·clu·sive *adj* **1** : reserved for particular persons **2** : stylish **3** : sole — **exclusive** *n* — **ex·clu·sive·ly** *adv* — **ex·clu·sive·ness** *n*

ex·crete *vb* : eliminate wastes from the body — **ex·cre·ment** *n* — **ex·cre·tion** *n* — **ex·cre·to·ry** *adj*

ex·cru·ci·at·ing *adj* : intensely painful — **ex·cru·ci·at·ing·ly** *adv*

ex·cur·sion *n* : pleasure trip

ex·cuse *vb* **1** : pardon **2** : release from an obligation **3** : justify ∼ *n* **1** : justification **2** : apology

ex·e·cute *vb* **1** : carry out fully **2** : enforce **3** : put to death — **ex·e·cu·tion** *n* — **ex·e·cu·tion·er** *n*

ex·ec·u·tive *adj* : relating to the carrying out of decisions, plans, or laws ∼ *n* **1** : branch of government with executive duties **2** : administrator

ex·ec·u·tor *n* : person named in a will to execute it

ex·ec·u·trix *n* : woman executor

ex·em·pla·ry *adj* : so commendable as to serve as a model

ex·em·pli·fy *vb* : serve as an example of — **ex·em·pli·fi·ca·tion** *n*

ex·empt *adj* : being free from some liability ∼ *vb* : make exempt — **ex·emp·tion** *n*

ex·er·cise *n* **1** : a putting into action **2** : exertion to develop endurance or a skill **3** *pl* : public ceremony ∼ *vb* **1** : exert **2** : engage in exercise — **ex·er·cis·er** *n*

ex·ert *vb* : put into action — **ex·er·tion** *n*

ex·hale *vb* : breathe out — **ex·ha·la·tion** *n*

ex·haust *vb* **1** : draw out or develop completely **2** : use up **3** : tire or wear out ∼ *n* : waste steam or gas from an engine or a system for removing it — **ex·haus·tion** *n* — **ex·haus·tive** *adj*

ex·hib·it *vb* : display esp. publicly ∼ *n* **1** : act of exhibiting **2** : something exhibited — **ex·hi·bi·tion** *n* — **ex·hib·i·tor** *n*

ex·hil·a·rate *vb* : thrill — **ex·hil·a·ra·tion** *n*

ex·ile *n* **1** : banishment **2** : person banished from his or her country — **exile** *vb*

ex·ist *vb* **1** : have real or actual being **2** : live — **ex·is·tence** *n* — **ex·is·tent** *adj*

ex·it *n* **1** : departure **2** : way out of an enclosed space **3** : way off an expressway — **exit** *vb*

ex·o·dus *n* : mass departure

ex·on·er·ate *vb* : free from blame — **ex·on·er·a·tion** *n*

ex·or·bi·tant *adj* : exceeding what is usual or proper

ex·or·cise *vb* : drive out (as an evil spirit) — **ex·or·cism** *n* — **ex·or·cist** *n*

ex·ot·ic *adj* : foreign or strange — **exotic** *n* — **ex·ot·i·cal·ly** *adv*

ex·pand *vb* : enlarge — **ex·pan·sion** *n* — **ex·pan·sive** *adj* — **ex·pan·sive·ly** *adv* — **ex·pan·sive·ness** *n*

ex·panse *n* : very large area

ex·pa·tri·ate *n* : exile — **ex·pa·tri·ate** *adj or vb*

ex·pect *vb* **1** : look forward to **2** : consider probable or one's due — **ex·pec·tan·cy** *n* — **ex·pec·tant** *adj* — **ex·pec·tant·ly** *adv* — **ex·pec·ta·tion** *n*

ex·pe·di·ent *adj* : convenient or advantageous rather than right or just ~ *n* : convenient often makeshift means to an end

ex·pe·dite *vb* : carry out or handle promptly — **ex·pe·dit·er** *n* — **ex·pe·di·tious** *adj*

ex·pe·di·tion *n* : long journey for work or research or the people making this

ex·pel *vb* : force out

ex·pend *vb* **1** : pay out **2** : use up — **ex·pend·able** *adj* — **ex·pen·di·ture** *n*

ex·pense *n* : cost — **ex·pen·sive** *adj* — **ex·pen·sive·ly** *adv*

ex·pe·ri·ence *n* **1** : a participating in or living through an event **2** : an event that affects one **3** : knowledge from doing ~ *vb* : undergo

ex·per·i·ment *n* : test to discover something ~ *vb* : make experiments — **ex·per·i·men·tal** *adj* — **ex·per·i·men·ta·tion** *n* — **ex·per·i·men·ter** *n*

ex·pert *adj* : thoroughly skilled ~ *n* : person with special skill — **ex·pert·ly** *adv* — **ex·pert·ness** *n*

ex·per·tise *n* : skill

ex·pire *vb* **1** : breathe out **2** : die **3** : end — **ex·pi·ra·tion** *n*

ex·plain *vb* **1** : make clear **2** : give the reason for — **ex·plain·able** *adj* — **ex·pla·na·tion** *n* — **ex·plan·a·to·ry** *adj*

ex·ple·tive *n* : usu. profane exclamation

ex·plic·it *adj* : absolutely clear or precise — **ex·plic·it·ly** *adv* — **ex·plic·it·ness** *n*

ex·plode *vb* **1** : discredit **2** : burst or cause to burst violently **3** : increase rapidly — **ex·plo·sion** *n* — **ex·plo·sive** *adj* — **ex·plo·sive·ly** *adv*

ex·ploit *n* : heroic act ~ *vb* **1** : utilize **2** : use unfairly — **ex·ploi·ta·tion** *n*

ex·plore *vb* : examine or range over thoroughly — **ex·plo·ra·tion** *n* — **ex·plor·ato·ry** *adj* — **ex·plor·er** *n*

ex·po·nent *n* **1** : mathematical symbol showing how many times a number is to be repeated as a factor **2** : advocate — **ex·po·nen·tial** *adj* — **ex·po·nen·tial·ly** *adv*

ex·port *vb* : send to foreign countries — **ex·port** *n* — **ex·por·ta·tion** *n* — **ex·port·er** *n*

ex·pose *vb* **1** : deprive of shelter or protection **2** : subject (film) to light **3** : make known — **ex·po·sure** *n*

ex·po·sé, ex·po·se *n* : exposure of something discreditable

ex·po·si·tion *n* : public exhibition

¹ex·press *adj* **1** : clear **2** : specific **3** : traveling at high speed with few stops — **express** *adv or n* — **ex·press·ly** *adv*

²express *vb* **1** : make known in words or appearance **2** : press out (as juice)

ex·pres·sion *n* **1** : utterance **2** : mathematical symbol **3** : significant word or phrase **4** : look on one's face — **ex·pres·sive** *adj* — **ex·pres·sive·ness** *n*

ex·press·way *n* : high-speed divided highway with limited access

ex·pul·sion *n* : an expelling or being expelled

ex·qui·site *adj* **1** : flawlessly beautiful and delicate **2** : keenly discriminating

ex·tend *vb* **1** : stretch forth or out **2** : prolong **3** : enlarge — **ex·tend·able** *adj* — **ex·ten·sion** *n* — **ex·ten·sive** *adj* — **ex·ten·sive·ly** *adv*

ex·tent *n* : range, space, or degree to which something extends

ex·ten·u·ate *vb* : lessen the seriousness of — **ex·ten·u·a·tion** *n*

ex·te·ri·or *adj* : external ~ *n* : external part or surface

ex·ter·mi·nate *vb* : destroy utterly — **ex·ter·mi·na·tion** *n* — **ex·ter·mi·na·tor** *n*

ex·ter·nal *adj* : relating to or on the outside — **ex·ter·nal·ly** *adv*

ex·tinct *adj* : no longer existing — **ex·tinc·tion** *n*

ex·tin·guish *vb* : cause to stop burning — **ex·tin·guish·able** *adj* — **ex·tin·guish·er** *n*

ex·tort *vb* : obtain by force or improper pressure — **ex·tor·tion** *n* — **ex·tor·tion·er** *n* — **ex·tor·tion·ist** *n*

ex·tra *adj* **1** : additional **2** : superior — **extra** *n or adv*

ex·tract *vb* **1** : pull out forcibly **2** : withdraw (as a juice) $\sim$ n 1 : excerpt 2 : product (as a juice) obtained by extracting — **ex·tract·able** *adj* — **ex·trac·tion** *n* — **ex·trac·tor** *n*

ex·tra·cur·ric·u·lar *adj* : lying outside the regular curriculum

ex·tra·dite *vb* : bring or deliver a suspect to a different jurisdiction for trial — **ex·tra·di·tion** *n*

ex·tra·mar·i·tal *adj* : relating to sexual relations of a married person outside of the marriage

ex·tra·ne·ous *adj* : not essential or relevant — **ex·tra·ne·ous·ly** *adv*

ex·traor·di·nary *adj* : notably unusual or exceptional — **ex·traor·di·nari·ly** *adv*

ex·tra·sen·so·ry *adj* : outside the ordinary senses

ex·tra·ter·res·tri·al *n* : one existing or coming from outside the earth $\sim$ *adj* : relating to an extraterrestrial

ex·trav·a·gant *adj* : wildly excessive, lavish, or costly — **ex·trav·a·gance** *n* — **ex·trav·a·gant·ly** *adv*

ex·trav·a·gan·za *n* : spectacular event

ex·treme *adj* 1 : very great or intense 2 : very severe 3 : not moderate 4 : most remote $\sim$ *n* 1 : extreme state 2 : something located at one end or the other of a range — **ex·treme·ly** *adv*

ex·trem·i·ty *n* 1 : most remote part 2 : human hand or foot 3 : extreme degree or state (as of need)

ex·tro·vert *n* : gregarious person — **ex·tro·ver·sion** *n* — **ex·tro·vert·ed** *adj*

ex·u·ber·ant *adj* : joyously free from restraint — **ex·u·ber·ance** *n* — **ex·u·ber·ant·ly** *adv*

ex·ult *vb* : rejoice — **ex·ul·tant** *adj* — **ex·ul·tant·ly** *adv* — **ex·ul·ta·tion** *n*

eye *n* 1 : organ of sight consisting of a globular structure (**eye·ball**) in a socket of the skull with thin movable covers (**eye·lids**) bordered with hairs (**eye·lash·es**) 2 : vision 3 : judgment 4 : something suggesting an eye $\sim$ *vb* : look at — **eye·brow** *n* — **eyed** *adj* — **eye·drop·per** *n* — **eye·glass·es** *n pl* — **eye·sight** *n* — **eye·strain** *n*

eye·let *n* : hole (as in cloth) for a lacing or rope

eye–open·er *n* : something startling — **eye–open·ing** *adj*

eye·piece *n* : lens at the eye end of an optical instrument

eye·sore *n* : unpleasant sight

eye·tooth *n* : upper canine tooth

eye·wit·ness *n* : person who actually sees something happen

F

f *n* : 6th letter of the alphabet

fa·ble *n* 1 : legendary story 2 : story that teaches a lesson — **fa·bled** *adj*

fab·ric *n* 1 : structure 2 : material made usu. by weaving or knitting fibers

fab·ri·cate *vb* 1 : construct 2 : invent — **fab·ri·cation** *n*

fab·u·lous *adj* 1 : like, told in, or based on fable 2 : incredible or marvelous — **fab·u·lous·ly** *adv*

fa·cade *n* 1 : principal face of a building 2 : false or superficial appearance

face *n* 1 : front or principal surface (as of the head) 2 : presence 3 : facial expression 4 : grimace 5 : outward appearance $\sim$ *vb* 1 : challenge or resist firmly or brazenly 2 : cover with different material 3 : sit or stand with the face toward 4 : have the front oriented toward — **faced** *adj* — **face·less** *adj* — **fa·cial** *adj or n*

face–lift *n* 1 : cosmetic surgery on the face 2 : modernization

fa·ce·tious *adj* : seeking to produce laughter — **fa·ce·tious·ly** *adv* — **fa·ce·tious·ness** *n*

fa·cil·i·tate *vb* : make easier

fa·cil·i·ty *n* 1 : ease in doing or using 2 : something built or installed to serve a purpose or facilitate an activity

fac·ing *n* : lining or covering or material for this

fac·sim·i·le *n* : exact copy

fact *n* 1 : act or action 2 : something that exists or is real 3 : piece of information — **fac·tu·al** *adj* — **fac·tu·al·ly** *adv*

fac·tion *n* : part of a larger group — **fac·tion·al·ism** *n*

fac·tor *n* 1 : something that has an effect 2 : gene 3 : number used in multiplying

fac·to·ry *n* : place for manufacturing

fac·ul·ty *n* 1 : ability to act 2 : power of the mind or body 3 : body of teachers or department of instruction

fad *n* : briefly popular practice or interest — **fad·dish** *adj* — **fad·dist** *n*

fade *vb* **1** : wither **2** : lose or cause to lose freshness or brilliance **3** : grow dim **4** : vanish

Fahr·en·heit *adj* : relating to a thermometer scale with the boiling point at 212 degrees and the freezing point at 32 degrees

fail *vb* **1** : decline in health **2** : die away **3** : stop functioning **4** : fail to be successful **5** : become bankrupt **6** : disappoint **7** : neglect ∼ *n* : act of failing

fail·ing *n* : slight defect in character or conduct ∼ *prep* : in the absence or lack of

fail·ure *n* **1** : absence of expected action or performance **2** : bankruptcy **3** : deficiency **4** : one that has failed

faint *adj* **1** : cowardly or spiritless **2** : weak and dizzy **3** : lacking vigor **4** : indistinct ∼ *vb* : lose consciousness ∼ *n* : act or condition of fainting — **faint·heart·ed** *adj* — **faint·ly** *adv* — **faint·ness** *n*

¹**fair** *adj* **1** : pleasing in appearance **2** : not stormy or cloudy **3** : just or honest **4** : conforming with the rules **5** : open to legitimate pursuit or attack **6** : light in color **7** : adequate — **fair·ness** *n*

²**fair** *n* : exhibition for judging or selling — **fair-ground** *n*

fair·ly *adv* **1** : in a manner of speaking **2** : without bias **3** : somewhat

fairy *n* : usu. small imaginary being — **fairy tale** *n*

fairy·land *n* **1** : land of fairies **2** : beautiful or charming place

faith *n* **1** : allegiance **2** : belief and trust in God **3** : confidence **4** : system of religious beliefs — **faith·ful** *adj* — **faith·ful·ly** *adv* — **faith·ful·ness** *n* — **faith·less** *adj* — **faith·less·ly** *adv* — **faith·less·ness** *n*

fake *vb* **1** : falsify **2** : counterfeit ∼ *n* : copy, fraud, or impostor ∼ *adj* : not genuine — **fak·er** *n*

fal·con *n* : small long-winged hawk used esp. for hunting — **fal·con·ry** *n*

fall *vb* **fell; fall·en 1** : go down by gravity **2** : hang freely **3** : go lower **4** : be defeated or ruined **5** : commit a sin **6** : happen at a certain time ∼ *n* **1** : act of falling **2** : autumn **3** : downfall **4** *pl* : waterfall **5** : distance something falls

fal·la·cy *n* **1** : false idea **2** : false reasoning — **fal·la·cious** *adj*

fal·li·ble *adj* : capable of making a mistake — **fal·li·bly** *adv*

fall·out *n* **1** : radioactive particles from a nuclear explosion **2** : secondary effects

false *adj* **1** : not genuine, true, faithful, or permanent **2** : misleading — **false·ly** *adv* — **false·ness** *n* — **fal·si·fi·ca·tion** *n* — **fal·si·fy** *vb* — **fal·si·ty** *n*

false·hood *n* : lie

fal·ter *vb* **1** : move unsteadily **2** : hesitate — **fal·ter·ing·ly** *adv*

fame *n* : public reputation — **famed** *adj*

¹**fa·mil·iar** *n* **1** : companion **2** : guardian spirit

²**fa·mil·iar** *adj* **1** : closely acquainted **2** : forward **3** : frequently seen or experienced — **fa·mil·iar·i·ty** *n* — **fa·mil·iar·ize** *vb* — **fa·mil·iar·ly** *adv*

fam·i·ly *n* **1** : persons of common ancestry **2** : group living together **3** : parents and children **4** : group of related individuals

fam·ine *n* : extreme scarcity of food

fa·mous *adj* : widely known or celebrated

fa·mous·ly *adv* : very well

¹**fan** *n* : device for producing a current of air ∼ *vb* **1** : move air with a fan **2** : direct a current of air upon **3** : stir to activity

²**fan** *n* : enthusiastic follower or admirer

fa·nat·ic, fa·nat·i·cal *adj* : excessively enthusiastic or devoted — **fanatic** *n* — **fa·nat·i·cism** *n*

fan·ci·er *n* : one devoted to raising a particular plant or animal

fan·cy *n* **1** : liking **2** : whim **3** : imagination ∼ *vb* **1** : like **2** : imagine ∼ *adj* **1** : not plain **2** : of superior quality — **fan·ci·ful** *adj* — **fan·ci·ful·ly** *adv* — **fan·ci·ly** *adv*

fan·fare *n* **1** : a sounding of trumpets **2** : showy display

fan·tas·tic *adj* **1** : imaginary or unrealistic **2** : exceedingly or unbelievably great — **fan·tas·ti·cal·ly** *adv*

fan·ta·sy *n* **1** : imagination **2** : product of the imagination — **fan·ta·size** *vb*

FAQ *abbr* frequently asked questions

far *adv* **1** : at or to a distance **2** : much **3** : to a degree **4** : to an advanced point or extent ∼ *adj* **1** : remote **2** : long **3** : being more distant

farce *n* **1** : satirical comedy with an improbable plot **2** : ridiculous display — **far·ci·cal** *adj*

¹**fare** *vb* : get along

²**fare** *n* **1** : price of transportation **2** : range of food

fare·well *n* **1** : wish of welfare at parting **2** : departure — **fare·well** *adj*

far–fetched *adj* : improbable

farm *n* : place where something is raised for food ∼ *vb* 1 : use (land) as a farm 2 : raise plants or animals for food — **farm·er** *n* — **farm·hand** *n* — **farm·house** *n* — **farm·ing** *n* — **farm·land** *n* — **farm·yard** *n*

far·sight·ed *adj* 1 : better able to see distant things than near 2 : judicious or shrewd — **far·sight·ed·ness** *n*

far·ther *adv* 1 : at or to a greater distance or more advanced point 2 : to a greater degree or extent ∼ *adj* : more distant

far·thest *adj* : most distant ∼ *adv* 1 : to or at the greatest distance 2 : to the most advanced point 3 : by the greatest extent

fas·ci·nate *vb* : transfix and hold spellbound — **fas·ci·na·tion** *n*

fash·ion *n* 1 : manner 2 : prevailing custom or style ∼ *vb* : form or construct — **fash·ion·able** *adj* — **fash·ion·ably** *adv*

¹**fast** *adj* 1 : firmly fixed, bound, or shut 2 : faithful 3 : moving or acting quickly 4 : indicating ahead of the correct time 5 : deep and undisturbed 6 : permanently dyed 7 : wild or promiscuous ∼ *adv* 1 : so as to be secure or bound 2 : soundly or deeply 3 : swiftly

²**fast** *vb* : abstain from food or eat sparingly ∼ *n* : act or time of fasting

fas·ten *vb* : attach esp. by pinning or tying — **fas·ten·er** *n* — **fas·ten·ing** *n*

fat *adj* 1 : having much fat 2 : thick ∼ *n* : animal tissue rich in greasy or oily matter — **fat·ness** *n* — **fat·ten** *vb* — **fat·ty** *adj or n*

fa·tal *adj* : causing death or ruin — **fa·tal·ism** *n* — **fa·tal·ist** *n* — **fa·tal·is·tic** *adj* — **fa·tal·is·ti·cal·ly** *adv* — **fa·tal·i·ty** *n* — **fa·tal·ly** *adv*

fate *n* 1 : principle, cause, or will held to determine events 2 : end or outcome — **fat·ed** *adj* — **fate·ful** *adj* — **fate·ful·ly** *adv*

fa·ther *n* 1 : male parent 2 *cap* : God 3 : originator — **father** *vb* — **fa·ther·hood** *n* — **fa·ther·land** *n* — **fa·ther·less** *adj* — **fa·ther·ly** *adj*

father–in–law *n* (**fa·thers–in–law**) : father of one's spouse

fa·tigue *n* 1 : weariness from labor or use 2 : tendency to break under repeated stress ∼ *vb* : tire out

fau·cet *n* : fixture for drawing off a liquid

fault *n* 1 : weakness in character 2 : something wrong or imperfect 3 : responsibility for something wrong 4 : fracture in the earth's crust ∼ *vb* : find fault in or with — **fault·find·er** *n* — **fault·find·ing** *n* — **fault·i·ly** *adv* — **fault·less** *adj* — **fault·less·ly** *adv* — **faulty** *adj*

fau·na *n* : animals or animal life esp. of a region — **fau·nal** *adj*

fa·vor *n* 1 : approval 2 : partiality 3 : act of kindness ∼ *vb* : regard or treat with favor — **fa·vor·able** *adj* — **fa·vor·ably** *adv*

fa·vor·ite *n* : one favored — **favorite** *adj* — **fa·vor·it·ism** *n*

fawn *n* : young deer

faze *vb* : disturb the composure of

fear *n* : unpleasant emotion caused by expectation or awareness of danger ∼ *vb* : be afraid of — **fear·ful** *adj* — **fear·ful·ly** *adv* — **fear·less** *adj* — **fear·less·ly** *adv* — **fear·less·ness** *n* — **fear·some** *adj*

fea·si·ble *adj* : capable of being done — **fea·si·bil·i·ty** *n* — **fea·si·bly** *adv*

feast *n* 1 : large or fancy meal 2 : religious festival ∼ *vb* : eat plentifully

feat *n* : notable deed

feath·er *n* : one of the light horny outgrowths that form the external covering of a bird's body — **feather** *vb* — **feath·ered** *adj* — **feath·er·less** *adj* — **feath·ery** *adj*

fea·ture *n* 1 : shape or appearance of the face 2 : part of the face 3 : prominent characteristic 4 : special attraction ∼ *vb* : give prominence to — **fea·ture·less** *adj*

Feb·ru·ary *n* : 2d month of the year having 28 and in leap years 29 days

fed·er·al *adj* : of or constituting a government with power distributed between a central authority and constituent units — **fed·er·al·ism** *n* — **fed·er·al·ist** *n or adj* — **fed·er·al·ly** *adv*

fed·er·ate *vb* : join in a union of organizations — **fed·er·a·tion** *n*

fee *n* : fixed charge

fee·ble *adj* : weak or ineffective — **fee·ble-mind·ed** *adj* — **fee·ble·mind·ed·ness** *n* — **fee·ble·ness** *n* — **fee·bly** *adv*

feed *vb* 1 : give food to 2 : eat 3 : furnish ∼ *n* : food for livestock — **feed·er** *n*

feel *vb* **felt; felt** 1 : perceive or examine through physical contact 2 : think or believe 3 : be conscious of 4 : seem 5 : have sympathy ∼ *n* 1 : sense of touch 2 : quality of a thing imparted through touch — **feel·er** *n*

feel·ing *n* 1 : sense of touch 2 : state of mind 3 *pl* : sensibilities 4 : opinion

feet *pl of* FOOT

feign *vb* : pretend

fe·lic·i·tate *vb* : congratulate — **fe·lic·i·ta·tion** *n*

fe·line *adj* : relating to cats — **feline** *n*

fell *past of* FALL

fel·low *n* **1** : companion or associate **2** : man or boy — **fel·low·ship** *n*

fel·low·man *n* : kindred human being

fel·on *n* : one who has committed a felony

fel·o·ny *n* : serious crime — **fe·lo·ni·ous** *adj*

¹felt *n* : cloth made of pressed wool and fur

²felt *past of* FEEL

fe·male *adj* : relating to or being the sex that bears young — **female** *n*

fem·i·nine *adj* : relating to the female sex — **fem·i·nin·i·ty** *n* — **fem·i·nism** *n* — **fem·i·nist** *n or adj*

fence *n* : enclosing barrier esp. of wood or wire ∼ *vb* **1** : enclose with a fence **2** : practice fencing — **fenc·er** *n*

fenc·ing *n* **1** : combat with swords for sport **2** : material for building fences

fend·er *n* : guard over an automobile wheel

fer·ment *vb* : cause or undergo chemical decomposition ∼ *n* : agitation — **fer·men·ta·tion** *n*

fern *n* : flowerless seedless green plant

fe·ro·cious *adj* : fierce or savage — **fe·ro·cious·ly** *adv* — **fe·ro·cious·ness** *n* — **fe·roc·i·ty** *n*

fer·ry *vb* : carry by boat over water ∼ *n* : boat used in ferrying — **fer·ry·boat** *n*

fer·tile *adj* **1** : producing plentifully **2** : capable of developing or reproducing — **fer·til·i·ty** *n*

fer·til·ize *vb* : make fertile — **fer·til·iza·tion** *n* — **fer·til·iz·er** *n*

fes·ti·val *n* : time of celebration

fes·tive *adj* : joyous or happy — **fes·tive·ly** *adv* — **fes·tiv·i·ty** *n*

fe·tal *adj* : of, relating to, or being a fetus

fetch *vb* **1** : go or come after and bring or take back **2** : sell for

fetch·ing *adj* : attractive — **fetch·ing·ly** *adv*

fête *n* : lavish party ∼ *vb* : honor or commemorate with a fête

fe·tish *n* **1** : object believed to have magical powers **2** : object of unreasoning devotion or concern

fe·tus *n* : vertebrate not yet born or hatched

feud *n* : prolonged quarrel — **feud** *vb*

feu·dal·ism *n* : medieval political order in which land is granted in return for service — **feu·dal** *adj* — **feu·dal·is·tic** *adj*

fe·ver *n* **1** : abnormal rise in body temperature **2** : state of heightened emotion — **fe·ver·ish** *adj* — **fe·ver·ish·ly** *adv*

few *pron* : not many ∼ *adj* : some but not many — often with *a* ∼ *n* : small number — often with *a*

few·er *pron* : smaller number of things

fi·an·cé *n* : man one is engaged to

fi·an·cée *n* : woman one is engaged to

fi·as·co *n* : ridiculous failure

fib *n* : trivial lie — **fib** *vb* — **fib·ber** *n*

fi·ber, fibre *n* **1** : threadlike substance or structure (as a muscle cell or fine root) **2** : indigestible material in food **3** : element that gives texture or substance — **fi·brous** *adj*

fi·ber·glass *n* : glass in fibrous form in various products (as insulation)

fick·le *adj* : unpredictably changeable — **fick·le·ness** *n*

fic·tion *n* : a made-up story or literature consisting of these — **fic·tion·al** *adj*

fic·ti·tious *adj* : made up or pretended

fid·dle *n* : violin ∼ *vb* **1** : play on the fiddle **2** : move the hands restlessly — **fid·dler** *n*

fi·del·i·ty *n* **1** : quality or state of being faithful **2** : quality of reproduction

fid·get *n* **1** *pl* : restlessness **2** : one that fidgets ∼ *vb* : move restlessly — **fid·gety** *adj*

field *n* **1** : open country **2** : cleared land **3** : land yielding some special product **4** : sphere of activity **5** : area for sports **6** : region or space in which a given effect (as magnetism) exists ∼ *vb* : put into the field — **field** *adj* — **field·er** *n*

fiend *n* **1** : devil **2** : extremely wicked person — **fiend·ish** *adj* — **fiend·ish·ly** *adv*

fierce *adj* **1** : violently hostile or aggressive **2** : intense **3** : menacing looking — **fierce·ly** *adv* — **fierce·ness** *n*

fi·ery *adj* **1** : burning **2** : hot or passionate — **fi·eri·ness** *n*

fi·es·ta *n* : festival

fif·teen *n* : one more than 14 — **fifteen** *adj or pron* — **fif·teenth** *adj or n*

fifth *n* **1** : one that is number 5 in a countable series **2** : one of 5 equal parts of something — **fifth** *adj or adv*

fif·ty *n* : 5 times 10 — **fif·ti·eth** *adj or n* — **fifty** *adj or pron*

fif·ty–fif·ty *adv or adj* : shared equally

fig *n* : pear-shaped edible fruit

fight *vb* **fought; fought 1** : contend against another in battle **2** : box **3** : struggle ∼ *n* **1**

: hostile encounter **2** : boxing match **3** : verbal disagreement — **fight•er** *n*

fig•ment *n* : something imagined or made up

fig•u•ra•tive *adj* : metaphorical — **fig•u•ra•tive•ly** *adv*

fig•ure *n* **1** : symbol representing a number **2** *pl* : arithmetical calculations **3** : price **4** : shape or outline **5** : illustration **6** : pattern or design **7** : prominent person ⁓ *vb* **1** : be important **2** : calculate — **fig•ured** *adj*

¹**file** *n* : tool for smoothing or sharpening ⁓ *vb* : rub or smooth with a file

²**file** *vb* **1** : arrange in order **2** : enter or record officially ⁓ *n* : device for keeping papers in order

³**file** *n* : row of persons or things one behind the other ⁓ *vb* : march in file

fil•i•bus•ter *n* : long speeches to delay a legislative vote — **filibuster** *vb* — **fil•i•bus•ter•er** *n*

fill *vb* **1** : make or become full **2** : stop up **3** : feed **4** : satisfy **5** : occupy fully **6** : spread through ⁓ *n* **1** : full supply **2** : material for filling — **fill•er** *n* — **fill•ing** *n* — **fill in** *vb* **1** : provide information to or for **2** : substitute

fil•let *n* : piece of boneless meat or fish ⁓ *vb* : cut into fillets

fil•ly *n* : young female horse

film *n* **1** : thin skin or membrane **2** : thin coating or layer **3** : strip of material used in taking pictures **4** : movie ⁓ *vb* : make a movie of — **filmy** *adj*

fil•ter *n* **1** : device for separating matter from a fluid **2** : device (as on a camera lens) that absorbs light ⁓ *vb* **1** : pass through a filter **2** : remove by means of a filter — **fil•ter•able** *adj* — **fil•tra•tion** *n*

filth *n* : repulsive dirt or refuse — **filth•i•ness** *n* — **filthy** *adj*

fin *n* **1** : thin external process controlling movement in an aquatic animal **2** : fin-shaped part (as on an airplane) — **finned** *adj*

fi•nal *adj* **1** : not to be changed **2** : ultimate **3** : coming at the end — **final** *n* — **fi•nal•ist** *n* — **fi•nal•i•ty** *n* — **fi•nal•ize** *vb* — **fi•nal•ly** *adv*

fi•na•le *n* : last or climactic part

fi•nance *n* **1** *pl* : money resources **2** : management of money affairs ⁓ *vb* **1** : raise funds for **2** : give necessary funds to **3** : sell on credit — **fi•nan•cier** *n*

fi•nan•cial *adj* : relating to finance — **fi•nan•cial•ly** *adv*

finch *n* : songbird (as a sparrow or linnet) with a strong bill

find *vb* **1** : discover or encounter **2** : obtain by effort **3** : experience or feel **4** : gain or regain the use of **5** : decide on (a verdict) ⁓ *n* **1** : act or instance of finding **2** : something found — **find•er** *n* — **find•ing** *n* — **find out** *vb* : learn, discover, or verify something

fine *n* : money paid as a penalty ⁓ *vb* : impose a fine on ⁓ *adj* **1** : free from impurity **2** : small or thin **3** : not coarse **4** : superior in quality or appearance ⁓ *adv* : finely — **fine•ly** *adv* — **fine•ness** *n*

fin•ery *n* : showy clothing and jewels

fi•nesse *n* **1** : delicate skill **2** : craftiness — **fi•nesse** *vb*

fin•ger *n* **1** : one of the 5 divisions at the end of the hand and esp. one other than the thumb **2** : something like a finger **3** : part of a glove for a finger ⁓ *vb* **1** : touch with the fingers **2** : identify as if by pointing — **fin•gered** *adj* — **fin•ger•nail** *n* — **fin•ger•print** *n or vb* — **fin•ger•tip** *n*

fin•icky *adj* : excessively particular in taste or standards

fin•ish *vb* **1** : come or bring to an end **2** : use or dispose of entirely **3** : put a final coat or surface on ⁓ *n* **1** : end **2** : final treatment given a surface — **fin•ish•er** *n*

fi•nite *adj* : having definite limits

fiord *var of* FJORD

fir *n* : evergreen tree or its wood

fire *n* **1** : light or heat and esp. the flame of something burning **2** : destructive burning (as of a house) **3** : enthusiasm **4** : the shooting of weapons ⁓ *vb* **1** : kindle **2** : stir up or enliven **3** : dismiss from employment **4** : shoot **5** : bake — **fire•bomb** *n or vb* — **fire•fight•er** *n* — **fire•less** *adj* — **fire•proof** *adj or vb* — **fire•wood** *n*

fire•arm *n* : weapon (as a rifle) that works by an explosion of gunpowder

fire•ball *n* **1** : ball of fire **2** : brilliant meteor

fire•crack•er *n* : small firework that makes noise

fire•fight•er *n* : a person who fights fires

fire•fly *n* : night-flying beetle that produces a soft light

fire•place *n* : opening made in a chimney to hold an open fire

fire•side *n* **1** : place near the fire or hearth **2** : home ⁓ *adj* : having an informal quality

fire•trap *n* : place apt to catch on fire

fire•work *n* : device that explodes to produce noise or a display of light

¹firm *adj* **1** : securely fixed in place **2** : strong or vigorous **3** : not subject to change **4** : resolute ~ *vb* : make or become firm — **firm·ly** *adv* — **firm·ness** *n*

²firm *n* : business enterprise

first *adj* **1** : being number one **2** : foremost ~ *adv* **1** : before any other **2** : for the first time ~ *n* **1** : number one **2** : one that is first — **first class** *n* — **first–class** *adj or adv* — **first·ly** *adv* — **first–rate** *adj or adv*

first aid *n* : emergency care

fis·cal *adj* : relating to money — **fis·cal·ly** *adv*

fish *n* fish : water animal with fins, gills, and usu. scales ~ *vb* **1** : try to catch fish **2** : grope — **fish·er** *n* — **fish·er·man** *n* — **fish·hook** *n* — **fish·ing** *n*

fish·ery *n* : fishing business or a place for this

fishy *adj* **1** : relating to or like fish **2** : questionable

fis·sion *n* : splitting of an atomic nucleus — **fis·sion·able** *adj*

fist *n* : hand doubled up — **fist·ed** *adj* — **fist·ful** *n*

¹fit *n* : sudden attack of illness or emotion

²fit *adj* **1** : suitable **2** : qualified **3** : sound in body ~ *vb* **1** : be suitable to **2** : insert or adjust correctly **3** : make room for **4** : supply or equip **5** : belong ~ *n* : state of fitting or being fitted — **fit·ly** *adv* — **fit·ness** *n* — **fit·ter** *n*

fit·ful *adj* : restless — **fit·ful·ly** *adv*

fit·ting *adj* : suitable ~ *n* : a small part

five *n* **1** : one more than 4 **2** : 5th in a set or series **3** : something having 5 units — **five** *adj or pron*

fix *vb* **1** : attach **2** : establish **3** : make right **4** : prepare **5** : improperly influence ~ *n* **1** : predicament **2** : determination of location — **fixed** *adj* — **fixed·ly** *adv* — **fixed·ness** *n* — **fix·er** *n*

fix·a·tion *n* : obsessive attachment — **fix·ate** *vb*

fix·ture *n* : permanent part of something

fizz *vb* : make a hissing sound ~ *n* : effervescence

fiz·zle *vb* **1** : fizz **2** : fail ~ *n* : failure

fjord *n* : inlet of the sea between cliffs

flab *n* : flabby flesh

flab·by *adj* : not firm — **flab·bi·ness** *n*

¹flag *n* **1** : fabric that is a symbol (as of a country) **2** : something used to signal ~ *vb* **1** : signal with a flag — **flag·pole** *n* — **flag·staff** *n*

²flag *vb* : lose strength or spirit

flag·el·late *vb* : whip — **flag·el·la·tion** *n*

flag·on *n* : container for liquids

fla·grant *adj* : conspicuously bad — **fla·grant·ly** *adv*

flair *n* : natural aptitude

flake *n* : small flat piece ~ *vb* : separate or form into flakes

flam·boy·ant *adj* : showy — **flam·boy·ance** *n* — **flam·boy·ant·ly** *adv*

flame *n* **1** : glowing part of a fire **2** : state of combustion **3** : burning passion — **flame** *vb* — **flam·ing** *adj*

flam·ma·ble *adj* : easily ignited

flank *n* : side of something ~ *vb* **1** : attack or go around the side of **2** : be at the side of

flan·nel *n* : soft napped fabric

flap *n* **1** : slap **2** : something flat that hangs loose ~ *vb* **1** : move (wings) up and down **2** : swing back and forth noisily

flap·jack *n* : pancake

flare *vb* : become suddenly bright or excited ~ *n* : blaze of light

flash *vb* **1** : give off a sudden flame or burst of light **2** : appear or pass suddenly ~ *n* **1** : sudden burst of light or inspiration **2** : instant ~ *adj* : coming suddenly

flash·light *n* : small battery-operated light

flashy *adj* : showy — **flash·i·ly** *adv* — **flash·i·ness** *n*

flat *adj* **1** : smooth **2** : broad and thin **3** : definite **4** : uninteresting **5** : deflated **6** : below the true pitch ~ *n* **1** : level surface of land **2** : flat note in music **3** : apartment **4** : having lost air ~ *adv* **1** : exactly **2** : below the true pitch ~ *vb* : make flat — **flat·ly** *adv* — **flat·ness** *n* — **flat·ten** *vb*

flat·foot *n* flat·feet : foot condition in which the arch is flattened — **flat–foot·ed** *adj*

flat–out *adj* **1** : being maximum effort or speed **2** : downright

flat·ter *vb* **1** : praise insincerely **2** : judge or represent too favorably — **flat·ter·er** *n* — **flat·tery** *n*

flat·u·lent *adj* : full of gas — **flat·u·lence** *n*

flaunt *vb* : display ostentatiously — **flaunt** *n*

fla·vor *n* **1** : quality that affects the sense of taste **2** : something that adds flavor ~ *vb* : give flavor to — **fla·vor·ful** *adj* — **fla·vor·ing** *n* — **fla·vor·less** *adj*

flaw *n* : fault — **flaw·less** *adj* — **flaw·less·ly** *adv* — **flaw·less·ness** *n*

flea *n* : leaping bloodsucking insect

fleck *vb or n* : streak or spot

flee *vb* : run away

fleece n : sheep's wool ~ vb 1 : shear 2 : get money from dishonestly — **fleecy** adj

¹**fleet** vb : pass rapidly ~ adj : swift — **fleet·ing** adj — **fleet·ness** n

²**fleet** n : group of ships

flesh n 1 : soft parts of an animal's body 2 : soft plant tissue (as fruit pulp) — **fleshed** adj — **fleshy** adj — **flesh out** vb : make fuller

flew past of FLY

flex vb : bend

flex·i·ble adj 1 : capable of being flexed 2 : adaptable — **flex·i·bil·i·ty** n — **flex·i·bly** adv

flick n : light jerky stroke ~ vb 1 : strike lightly 2 : flutter

flick·er vb 1 : waver 2 : burn unsteadily ~ n 1 : sudden movement 2 : wavering light

fli·er n 1 : aviator 2 : advertising circular

¹**flight** n 1 : act or instance of flying 2 : ability to fly 3 : a passing through air or space 4 : series of stairs — **flight·less** adj

²**flight** n : act or instance of running away

flighty adj : capricious or silly — **flight·i·ness** n

flim·sy adj 1 : not strong or well made 2 : not believable — **flim·si·ly** adv — **flim·si·ness** n

flinch vb : shrink from pain

fling vb 1 : move brusquely 2 : throw ~ n 1 : act or instance of flinging 2 : attempt 3 : period of self-indulgence

flip vb 1 : cause to turn over quickly or many times 2 : move with a quick push ~ adj : insolent — **flip** n

flip·pant adj : not serious enough — **flip·pan·cy** n

flirt vb 1 : be playfully romantic 2 : show casual interest ~ n : one who flirts — **flir·ta·tion** n — **flir·ta·tious** adj

flit vb : dart

float n 1 : something that floats 2 : vehicle carrying an exhibit ~ vb 1 : rest on or in a fluid without sinking 2 : wander 3 : finance by issuing stock or bonds — **float·er** n

flock n : group of animals (as birds) or people ~ vb : gather or move as a group

flood n 1 : great flow of water over the land 2 : overwhelming volume ~ vb : cover or fill esp. with water — **flood·wa·ter** n

floor n 1 : bottom of a room on which one stands 2 : story of a building 3 : lower limit ~ vb 1 : furnish with a floor 2 : knock down 3 : amaze — **floor·board** n — **floor·ing** n

flop vb 1 : flap 2 : slump heavily 3 : fail — **flop** n

flop·py adj : soft and flexible

flo·ra n : plants or plant life of a region

flo·ral adj : relating to flowers

flo·rist n : flower dealer

floss n 1 : soft thread for embroidery 2 : thread used to clean between teeth — **floss** vb

flo·ta·tion n : process or instance of floating

¹**floun·der** n **flounder** : a flattened fish with both eyes on the upper side

²**flounder** vb 1 : struggle for footing 2 : proceed clumsily

flour n : finely ground meal ~ vb : coat with flour — **floury** adj

flour·ish vb 1 : thrive 2 : wave threateningly ~ n 1 : embellishment 2 : fanfare 3 : wave 4 : showiness of action

flout vb : treat with disdain

flow vb 1 : move in a stream 2 : proceed smoothly and readily ~ n : uninterrupted stream

flow·er n 1 : showy plant shoot that bears seeds 2 : state of flourishing ~ vb 1 : produce flowers 2 : flourish — **flow·ered** adj — **flow·er·less** adj — **flow·er·pot** n — **flow·ery** adj

flown past part of FLY

flu n : acute very contagious virus disease

flub vb : bungle — **flub** n

fluc·tu·ate vb : change rapidly esp. up and down — **fluc·tu·a·tion** n

flue n : smoke duct

flu·ent adj : speaking with ease — **flu·en·cy** n — **flu·ent·ly** adv

fluff n 1 : something soft and light 2 : blunder ~ vb 1 : make fluffy 2 : make a mistake — **fluffy** adj

flu·id adj : flowing ~ n : substance that can flow — **flu·id·i·ty** n — **flu·id·ly** adv

fluke n : stroke of luck

flung past of FLING

flunk vb : fail in school work

flu·o·res·cence n : emission of light after initial absorption — **flu·o·resce** vb — **flu·o·res·cent** adj

flur·ry n 1 : light snowfall 2 : bustle 3 : brief burst of activity — **flurry** vb

¹**flush** vb : cause (a bird) to fly from cover

²**flush** n 1 : sudden flow (as of water) 2 : sudden increase of emotion 3 : blush ~ vb 1 : blush 2 : wash out with a rush of liquid ~

adj **1** : filled to overflowing **2** : of a reddish healthy color **3** : smooth or level **4** : abutting — **flush** *adv*

flus·ter *vb* : upset — **fluster** *n*

flute *n* **1** : pipelike musical instrument **2** : groove — **flut·ed** *adj* — **flut·ing** *n* — **flut·ist** *n*

flut·ter *vb* **1** : flap the wings rapidly **2** : move with quick wavering or flapping motions **3** : behave in an agitated manner ∼ *n* **1** : a fluttering **2** : state of confusion — **flut·tery** *adj*

flux *n* : state of continuous change

¹**fly** *vb* (**flew; flown**) **1** : move through the air with wings **2** : float or soar **3** : flee **4** : move or pass swiftly **5** : operate an airplane

²**fly** *n* : garment closure

³**fly** *n* : winged insect

fly·er *var of* FLIER

foam *n* **1** : mass of bubbles on top of a liquid **2** : material of cellular form ∼ *vb* : form foam — **foamy** *adj*

fo·cus *n* **1** : point at which reflected or refracted rays meet **2** : adjustment (as of eyeglasses) for clear vision **3** : central point ∼ *vb* : bring to a focus — **fo·cal** *adj* — **fo·cal·ly** *adv*

foe *n* : enemy

fog *n* **1** : fine particles of water suspended near the ground **2** : mental confusion ∼ *vb* : obscure or be obscured with fog — **fog·gy** *adj* — **fog·horn** *n*

foil *n* **1** : thin sheet of metal **2** : one that sets off another by contrast

¹**fold** *n* **1** : enclosure for sheep **2** : group with a common interest

²**fold** *vb* **1** : lay one part over another **2** : embrace ∼ *n* : part folded

fold·er *n* **1** : one that folds **2** : circular **3** : folded cover or envelope for papers

fo·liage *n* : plant leaves

folk *n* **1** : people in general **2** *pl* : one's family ∼ *adj* : relating to the common people

folk·lore *n* : customs and traditions of a people — **folk·lor·ist** *n*

folksy *adj* : friendly and informal

fol·low *vb* **1** : go or come after **2** : pursue **3** : obey **4** : proceed along **5** : keep one's attention fixed on **6** : result from — **fol·low·er** *n* — **fol·low·ing** *adj or prep*

fol·ly *n* : foolishness

fond *adj* **1** : strongly attracted **2** : affectionate **3** : dear — **fond·ly** *adv* — **fond·ness** *n*

fon·dle *vb* : touch lovingly

food *n* : material eaten to sustain life

fool *n* **1** : stupid person **2** : jester ∼ *vb* **1** : waste time **2** : meddle **3** : deceive — **fool·ery** *n* — **fool·ish** *adj* — **fool·ish·ly** *adv* — **fool·ish·ness** *n* — **fool·proof** *adj*

fool·har·dy *adj* : rash — **fool·har·di·ness** *n*

foot *n* (**feet**) **1** : end part of a leg **2** : unit of length equal to ⅓ yard **3** : unit of verse meter **4** : bottom — **foot·ed** *adj* — **foot·path** *n* — **foot·print** *n* — **foot·race** *n* — **foot·rest** *n* — **foot·step** *n* — **foot·wear** *n*

foot·age *n* : size expressed in feet

foot·ball *n* : ball game played by 2 teams on a rectangular field

foot·hill *n* : hill at the foot of higher hills

foot·hold *n* : support for the feet

foot·ing *n* **1** : foothold **2** : basis

foot·lock·er *n* : small trunk

foot·loose *adj* : having no ties

foot·note *n* : note at the bottom of a page

foot·stool *n* : stool to support the feet

for *prep* **1** — used to show preparation or purpose **2** : because of **3** — used to show a recipient **4** : in support of **5** : so as to support or help cure **6** : so as to be equal to **7** : concerning **8** : through the period of ∼ *conj* : because

for·bear *vb* **1** : refrain from **2** : be patient — **for·bear·ance** *n*

for·bid *vb* **1** : prohibit **2** : order not to do something

for·bid·ding *adj* : tending to discourage

force *n* **1** : exceptional strength or energy **2** : military strength **3** : body (as of persons) available for a purpose **4** : violence **5** : influence (as a push or pull) that causes motion ∼ *vb* **1** : compel **2** : gain against resistance **3** : break open — **force·ful** *adj* — **force·ful·ly** *adv* — **in force** **1** : in great numbers **2** : valid

forc·ible *adj* **1** : done by force **2** : showing force — **forc·i·bly** *adv*

ford *n* : place to wade across a stream ∼ *vb* : wade across

fore *adv* : in or toward the front ∼ *adj* : being or coming before in time, place, or order ∼ *n* : front

fore·arm *n* : part of the arm between the elbow and the wrist

fore·bear *n* : ancestor

fore·bod·ing *n* : premonition of disaster — **fore·bod·ing** *adj*

fore·cast *vb* : predict — **forecast** *n* — **fore·cast·er** *n*

fore·close *vb* : take legal measures to terminate a mortgage — **fore·clo·sure** *n*

fore·fa·ther *n* : ancestor

fore·fin·ger *n* : finger next to the thumb

fore·foot *n* : front foot of a quadruped

fore·go *vb* : precede — **fore·go·ing** *n*

fore·gone *adj* : determined in advance

fore·ground *n* : part of a scene nearest the viewer

fore·hand *n* : stroke (as in tennis) made with the palm of the hand turned forward — **fore·hand** *adj*

fore·head *n* : part of the face above the eyes

for·eign *adj* **1** : situated outside a place or country and esp. one's own country **2** : belonging to a different place or country **3** : not pertinent **4** : related to or dealing with other nations — **for·eign·er** *n*

fore·leg *n* : front leg

fore·man *n* **1** : person who speaks for a jury **2** : workman in charge

fore·most *adj* : first in time, place, or order — **foremost** *adv*

fo·ren·sics *n pl* : art or study of speaking or debating — **fo·ren·sic** *adj*

fore·run·ner *n* : one that goes before

fore·see *vb* : see or realize beforehand — **fore·see·able** *adj*

fore·shad·ow *vb* : hint or suggest beforehand

fore·sight *n* : care or provision for the future — **fore·sight·ed** *adj* — **fore·sight·ed·ness** *n*

for·est *n* : large thick growth of trees and underbrush — **for·est·ed** *adj* — **for·est·er** *n* — **for·est·land** *n* — **for·est·ry** *n*

fore·stall *vb* : prevent by acting in advance

fore·taste *n* : advance indication or notion ∼ *vb* : anticipate

fore·tell *vb* : predict

for·ev·er *adv* **1** : for a limitless time **2** : always

for·ev·er·more *adv* : forever

fore·warn *vb* : warn beforehand

for·feit *vb* : lose or lose the right to by an error or crime ∼ *n* : something forfeited — **for·fei·ture** *n*

¹forge *vb* : workshop for shaping metal ∼ *vb* **1** : form (metal) by heating and hammering **2** : imitate falsely esp. to defraud — **forg·er** *n* — **forg·ery** *n*

²forge *vb* : move ahead steadily

for·get *vb* **1** : be unable to think of or recall **2** : fail to think of at the proper time — **for·get·ta·ble** *adj* — **for·get·ful** *adj* — **for·get·ful·ly** *adv*

for·give *vb* : pardon — **for·giv·able** *adj* — **for·give·ness** *n*

for·giv·ing *adj* **1** : able to forgive **2** : allowing room for error or weakness

for·go, fore·go *vb* : do without

fork *n* **1** : implement with prongs for lifting, holding, or digging **2** : forked part **3** : a dividing into branches or a place where something branches ∼ *vb* **1** : divide into branches **2** : move with a fork — **forked** *adj*

for·lorn *adj* **1** : deserted **2** : wretched — **for·lorn·ly** *adv*

form *n* **1** : shape **2** : set way of doing or saying something **3** : document with blanks to be filled in **4** : manner of performing with respect to what is expected **5** : mold **6** : kind or variety **7** : one of the ways in which a word is changed to show difference in use ∼ *vb* **1** : give form or shape to **2** : train **3** : develop **4** : constitute — **for·ma·tive** *adj* — **form·less** *adj*

for·mal *adj* : following established custom ∼ *n* : formal social event — **for·mal·i·ty** *n* — **for·mal·ize** *vb* — **for·mal·ly** *adv*

for·mat *n* : general style or arrangement of something — **format** *vb*

for·ma·tion *n* **1** : a giving form to something **2** : something formed **3** : arrangement

for·mer *adj* : coming before in time — **for·mer·ly** *adv*

for·mi·da·ble *adj* **1** : causing fear or dread **2** : very difficult — **for·mi·da·bly** *adv*

for·mu·la *n* **1** : set form of words for ceremonial use **2** : recipe **3** : milk mixture for a baby **4** : group of symbols or figures briefly expressing information **5** : set form or method

for·mu·late *vb* : design, devise — **for·mu·la·tion** *n*

for·sake *vb* : renounce completely

for·swear *vb* **1** : renounce under oath **2** : perjure

for·syth·ia *n* : shrub grown for its yellow flowers

fort *n* **1** : fortified place **2** : permanent army post

forte *n* : something at which a person excels

forth *adv* : forward

forth·com·ing *adj* **1** : coming or available soon **2** : open and direct

forth·right *adj* : direct — **forth·right·ly** *adv* — **forth·right·ness** *n*

for·ti·fy *vb* : make strong — **for·ti·fi·ca·tion** *n*
for·ti·tude *n* : ability to endure
fort·night *n* : 2 weeks — **fort·night·ly** *adj or adv*
for·tress *n* : strong fort
for·tu·nate *adj* **1** : coming by good luck **2** : lucky — **for·tu·nate·ly** *adv*
for·tune *n* **1** : prosperity attained partly through luck **2** : good or bad luck **3** : destiny **4** : wealth
for·tune–tel·ler *n* : one who foretells a person's future — **for·tune–tell·ing** *n or adj*
for·ty *n* : 4 times 10 — **for·ti·eth** *adj or n* — **for·ty** *adj or pron*
fo·rum *n* **1** : Roman marketplace **2** : medium for open discussion
for·ward *adj* **1** : being near or at or belonging to the front **2** : brash ~ *adv* : toward what is in front ~ *n* : player near the front of his team ~ *vb* **1** : help onward **2** : send on — **for·ward·er** *n* — **for·ward·ness** *n*
for·wards *adv* : forward
fos·sil *n* : preserved trace of an ancient plant or animal ~ *adj* : being or originating from a fossil — **fos·sil·ize** *vb*
fos·ter *adj* : being, having, or relating to substitute parents ~ *vb* : help to grow or develop
fought *past of* FIGHT
foul *adj* **1** : offensive **2** : clogged with dirt **3** : abusive **4** : wet and stormy **5** : unfair ~ *n* : a breaking of the rules in a game ~ *adv* : foully ~ *vb* **1** : make or become foul or filthy **2** : tangle — **foul·ly** *adv* — **foul·mouthed** *adj* — **foul·ness** *n*
foul–up *n* : error or state of confusion — **foul up** *vb* : bungle
found *vb* : establish — **found·er** *n*
foun·da·tion *n* **1** : act of founding **2** : basis for something **3** : endowed institution **4** : supporting structure — **foun·da·tion·al** *adj*
foun·der *vb* : sink
found·ry *n* : place where metal is cast
foun·tain *n* **1** : spring of water **2** : source **3** : artificial jet of water
four *n* **1** : one more than 3 **2** : 4th in a set or series **3** : something having 4 units — **four** *adj or pron*
four·score *adj* : eighty
four·some *n* : group of 4
four·teen *n* : one more than 13 — **four·teen** *adj or pron* — **four·teenth** *adj or n*
fourth *n* **1** : one that is 4th **2** : one of 4 equal parts of something — **fourth** *adj or adv*

fowl *n* (**fowl**) **1** : bird **2** : chicken
fox *n* **1** : small mammal related to wolves **2** : clever person ~ *vb* : trick — **foxy** *adj*
foy·er *n* : entrance hallway
frac·tion *n* **1** : number indicating one or more equal parts of a whole **2** : portion — **frac·tion·al** *adj* — **frac·tion·al·ly** *adv*
frac·ture *n* : a breaking of something — **frac·ture** *vb*
frag·ile *adj* : easily broken — **fra·gil·i·ty** *n*
frag·ment *n* : part broken off ~ *vb* : break into parts — **frag·men·tary** *adj* — **frag·men·ta·tion** *n*
fra·grant *adj* : having a sweet smell — **fra·grance** *n* — **fra·grant·ly** *adv*
frail *adj* : weak or delicate — **frail·ty** *n*
frame *vb* **1** : plan **2** : formulate **3** : construct or arrange **4** : enclose in a frame **5** : make appear guilty ~ *n* **1** : makeup of the body **2** : supporting or enclosing structure **3** : state or disposition (as of mind) — **frame·work** *n*
fran·chise *n* **1** : special privilege **2** : the right to vote — **fran·chi·see** *n*
frank *adj* : direct and sincere — **frank·ly** *adv* — **frank·ness** *n*
frank·furt·er, frank·furt *n* : cooked sausage
frank·in·cense *n* : incense resin
fran·tic *adj* : wildly excited — **fran·ti·cal·ly** *adv*
fra·ter·nal *adj* **1** : brotherly **2** : of a fraternity — **fra·ter·nal·ly** *adv*
fra·ter·ni·ty *n* : men's student social group
frat·er·nize *vb* **1** : mingle as friends **2** : associate with members of a hostile group — **frat·er·ni·za·tion** *n*
fraud *n* : trickery — **fraud·u·lent** *adj* — **fraud·u·lent·ly** *adv*
fray *vb* **1** : wear by rubbing **2** : separate the threads of **3** : irritate
fraz·zle *vb* : wear out ~ *n* : exhaustion
freak *n* **1** : something abnormal or unusual **2** : enthusiast — **freak·ish** *adj* — **freak out** *vb* **1** : experience nightmarish hallucinations from drugs **2** : distress or become distressed
freck·le *n* : brown spot on the skin — **freckle** *vb*
free *adj* **1** : having liberty or independence **2** : not taxed **3** : given without charge **4** : voluntary **5** : not in use **6** : not fastened ~ *adv* : without charge ~ *vb* : set free — **free** *adv* — **free·born** *adj* — **free·dom** *n* — **free·ly** *adv*
free·boo·ter *n* : pirate

free·load *vb* : live off another's generosity — **free·load·er** *n*

free·way *n* : expressway

freeze *vb* **froze; fro·zen** 1 : harden into ice 2 : become chilled 3 : damage by frost 4 : stick fast 5 : become motionless 6 : fix at one stage or level ~ *n* 1 : very cold weather 2 : state of being frozen — **freez·er** *n*

freeze–dry *vb* : preserve by freezing then drying — **freeze–dried** *adj*

freight *n* 1 : carrying of goods or payment for this 2 : shipped goods ~ *vb* : load or ship goods — **freigh·ter** *n*

french fry *vb* : fry in deep fat — **french fry** *n*

fre·net·ic *adj* : frantic — **fre·net·i·cal·ly** *adv*

fren·zy *n* : violent agitation — **fren·zied** *adj*

fre·quen·cy *n* 1 : frequent or regular occurrence 2 : number of cycles or sound waves per second

fre·quent *adj* : happening often ~ *vb* : go to habitually — **fre·quent·er** *n* — **fre·quent·ly** *adv*

fresh *adj* 1 : not salt 2 : pure 3 : not preserved 4 : not stale 5 : like new 6 : insolent — **fres·hen** *vb* — **fresh·ly** *adv* — **fresh·ness** *n*

fresh·man *n* : first-year student

fret *vb* 1 : worry or become irritated 2 : fray 3 : agitate ~ *n* 1 : worn spot 2 : irritation — **fret·ful** *adj* — **fret·ful·ly** *adv*

fric·tion *n* 1 : a rubbing between 2 surfaces 2 : clash of opinions — **fric·tion·al** *adj*

Fri·day *n* : 6th day of the week

friend *n* : person one likes — **friend·less** *adj* — **friend·li·ness** *n* — **friend·ly** *adj* — **friend·ship** *n*

fright *n* : sudden fear — **frigh·ten** *vb* — **fright·ful** *adj* — **fright·ful·ly** *adv* — **fright·ful·ness** *n*

frig·id *adj* : intensely cold — **fri·gid·i·ty** *n*

frill *n* 1 : ruffle 2 : pleasing but nonessential addition — **frilly** *adj*

fringe *n* 1 : ornamental border of short hanging threads or strips 2 : edge — **fringe** *vb*

frisk *vb* 1 : leap about 2 : search (a person) esp. for weapons

frisky *adj* : playful — **frisk·i·ly** *adv* — **frisk·i·ness** *n*

friv·o·lous *adj* : not important or serious — **fri·vol·i·ty** *n* — **friv·o·lous·ly** *adv*

frizz *vb* : curl tightly — **frizz** *n* — **frizzy** *adj*

frock *n* 1 : loose outer garment 2 : dress

frog *n* 1 : leaping amphibian 2 : hoarseness 3 : ornamental braid fastener 4 : small holder for flowers

frol·ic *vb* : romp ~ *n* : fun — **frol·ic·some** *adj*

from *prep* — used to show a starting point

front *n* 1 : face 2 : behavior 3 : main side of a building 4 : forward part 5 : boundary between air masses ~ *vb* 1 : have the main side adjacent to something 2 : serve as a front — **fron·tal** *adj*

front·age *n* : length of boundary line on a street

fron·tier *n* : outer edge of settled territory — **fron·tiers·man** *n*

frost *n* 1 : freezing temperature 2 : ice crystals on a surface ~ *vb* 1 : cover with frost 2 : put icing on (a cake) — **frosty** *adj*

frost·bite *n* : partial freezing of part of the body — **frost·bit·ten** *adj*

frost·ing *n* : icing

froth *n* : bubbles on a liquid — **frothy** *adj*

frown *vb or n* : scowl

frow·sy, frow·zy *adj* : untidy

froze *past of* FREEZE

frozen *past part of* FREEZE

fru·gal *adj* : thrifty — **fru·gal·i·ty** *n* — **fru·gal·ly** *adv*

fruit *n* 1 : usu. edible and sweet part of a seed plant 2 : result ~ *vb* : bear fruit — **fruit·cake** *n* — **fruit·ed** *adj* — **fruit·ful** *adj* — **fruit·ful·ness** *n* — **fruit·less** *adj* — **fruit·less·ly** *adv* — **fruity** *adj*

fru·ition *n* : completion

frus·trate *vb* 1 : block 2 : cause to fail — **frus·trat·ing·ly** *adv* — **frus·tra·tion** *n*

¹fry *vb* 1 : cook esp. with fat or oil 2 : be cooked by frying ~ *n* 1 : something fried 2 : social gathering with fried food

²fry *n* **fry** : recently hatched fish

fud·dy–dud·dy *n* : one who is old-fashioned or unimaginative

fudge *vb* : cheat or exaggerate ~ *n* : creamy candy

fu·el *n* : material burned to produce heat or power ~ *vb* : provide with or take in fuel

fu·gi·tive *adj* 1 : running away or trying to escape 2 : not lasting — **fu·gi·tive** *n*

ful·fill, ful·fil *vb* 1 : perform 2 : satisfy — **ful·fill·ment** *n*

full *adj* 1 : filled 2 : complete 3 : rounded 4 : having an abundance of something ~ *adv* : entirely ~ *n* : utmost degree — **full·ness** *n* — **ful·ly** *adv*

full–fledged *adj* : fully developed

fum·ble *vb* : fail to hold something properly — **fumble** *n*

fume *n* : irritating gas ~ *vb* 1 : give off fumes 2 : show annoyance

fu·mi·gate *vb* : treat with pest-killing fumes — **fu·mi·gant** *n* — **fu·mi·ga·tion** *n*

fun *n* 1 : something providing amusement or enjoyment 2 : enjoyment ~ *adj* : full of fun

func·tion *n* 1 : special purpose 2 : formal ceremony or social affair ~ *vb* : have or carry on a function — **func·tion·al** *adj* — **func·tion·al·ly** *adv*

func·tion·ary *n* : official

fund *n* 1 : store 2 : sum of money intended for a special purpose 3 *pl* : available money ~ *vb* : provide funds for

fun·da·men·tal *adj* 1 : basic 2 : of central importance or necessity — **fun·da·men·tal** *n* — **fun·da·men·tal·ly** *adv*

fu·ner·al *n* : ceremony for a dead person — **fu·ner·al** *adj* — **fu·ne·re·al** *adj*

fun·gus *n* **fun·gi** : lower plant that lacks chlorophyll — **fun·gal** *adj* — **fun·gous** *adj*

funk *n* : state of depression

funky *adj* : unconventional and unsophisticated

fun·nel *n* 1 : cone-shaped utensil with a tube for directing the flow of a liquid 2 : ship's smokestack ~ *vb* : move to a central point or into a central channel

fun·nies *n pl* : section of comic strips

fun·ny *adj* 1 : amusing 2 : strange

fur *n* 1 : hairy coat of a mammal 2 : article of clothing made with fur — **fur** *adj* — **furred** *adj* — **fur·ry** *adj*

fu·ri·ous *adj* : fierce or angry — **fu·ri·ous·ly** *adv*

fur·nace *n* : enclosed structure in which heat is produced

fur·nish *vb* 1 : provide with what is needed 2 : make available for use

fur·nish·ings *n pl* 1 : articles or accessories of dress 2 : furniture

fur·ni·ture *n* : movable articles for a room

fur·row *n* 1 : trench made by a plow 2 : wrinkle or groove — **fur·row** *vb*

fur·ther *adv* 1 : at or to a more advanced point 2 : more ~ *adj* : additional ~ *vb* : promote — **fur·ther·ance** *n*

fur·ther·more *adv* : in addition

fur·thest *adv or adj* : farthest

fur·tive *adj* : slyly or secretly done — **fur·tive·ly** *adv* — **fur·tive·ness** *n*

fu·ry *n* 1 : intense rage 2 : violence

¹fuse *n* 1 : cord lighted to transmit fire to an explosive 2 *usu* **fuze** : device for exploding a charge ~ *or* **fuze** *vb* : equip with a fuse

²fuse *vb* 1 : melt and run together 2 : unite ~ *n* : electrical safety device — **fus·ible** *adj*

fu·sion *n* 1 : process of merging by melting 2 : union of atomic nuclei

fuss *n* 1 : needless bustle or excitement 2 : show of attention 3 : objection or protest ~ *vb* : make a fuss

fuss·bud·get *n* : one who fusses or is fussy about trifles

fussy *adj* 1 : irritable 2 : paying very close attention to details — **fuss·i·ly** *adv* — **fuss·i·ness** *n*

fu·tile *adj* : useless or vain — **fu·til·i·ty** *n*

fu·ton *n* : a cotton-filled mattress

fu·ture *adj* : coming after the present ~ *n* 1 : time yet to come 2 : what will happen — **fu·tur·is·tic** *adj*

fuze *var of* FUSE

fuzz *n* : fine particles or fluff

fuzzy *adj* 1 : covered with or like fuzz 2 : indistinct — **fuzz·i·ness** *n*

G

g *n* 1 : 7th letter of the alphabet 2 : unit of gravitational force

gab *vb* : chatter — **gab** *n* — **gab·by** *adj*

ga·ble *n* : triangular part of the end of a building — **ga·bled** *adj*

gad·get *n* : device — **gad·get·ry** *n*

gaff *n* : metal hook for lifting fish — **gaff** *vb*

gaffe *n* : social blunder

gag *vb* 1 : prevent from speaking or crying out by stopping up the mouth 2 : retch or cause to retch ~ *n* 1 : something that stops up the mouth 2 : laugh-provoking remark or act

gag·gle *n* : flock of geese

gai·ety *n* : high spirits

gai·ly *adv* : in a gay manner

gain *n* 1 : profit 2 : obtaining of profit or possessions 3 : increase ~ *vb* 1 : get possession of 2 : win 3 : arrive at 4 : increase or increase in 5 : profit — **gain·er** *n* — **gain·ful** *adj* — **gain·ful·ly** *adv*

gait *n* : manner of walking or running — **gait-ed** *adj*

gal *n* : girl

ga·la *n* : festive celebration — **gala** *adj*

gal·axy *n* : very large group of stars — **ga·lac-tic** *adj*

gale *n* **1** : strong wind **2** : outburst

¹**gall** *n* **1** : bile **2** : insolence

²**gall** *n* **1** : skin sore caused by chafing **2** : swelling of plant tissue caused by parasites ~ *vb* **1** : chafe **2** : irritate or vex

gal·lant *n* : man very attentive to women ~ *adj* **1** : splendid **2** : brave **3** : polite and attentive to women — **gal·lant·ly** *adv* — **gal·lant-ry** *n*

gall·blad·der *n* : pouch attached to the liver in which bile is stored

gal·lery *n* **1** : outdoor balcony **2** : long narrow passage or hall **3** : room or building for exhibiting art **4** : spectators — **gal·ler·ied** *adj*

gal·ley *n* **1** : old ship propelled esp. by oars **2** : kitchen of a ship or airplane

gal·lon *n* : unit of liquid measure equal to 4 quarts

gal·lop *n* : fast 3-beat gait of a horse — **gallop** *vb* — **gal·lop·er** *n*

gall·stone *n* : abnormal concretion in the gallbladder or bile passages

ga·lore *adj* : in abundance

ga·losh *n* : overshoe — usu. pl.

gal·va·nize *vb* **1** : shock into action **2** : coat (iron or steel) with zinc — **gal·va·ni·za·tion** *n* — **gal·va·niz·er** *n*

gam·ble *vb* **1** : play a game for stakes **2** : bet **3** : take a chance ~ *n* : risky undertaking — **gam·bler** *n*

game *n* **1** : playing activity **2** : competition according to rules **3** : animals hunted for sport or food ~ *vb* : gamble ~ *adj* **1** : plucky **2** : lame — **game·ly** *adv* — **game·ness** *n*

game·keep·er *n* : person in charge of game animals or birds

gamy *or* **gam·ey** *adj* : having the flavor of game esp. when slightly tainted — **gam·i-ness** *n*

¹**gan·der** *n* : male goose

²**gander** *n* : glance

gang *n* **1** : group of persons working together **2** : group of criminals ~ *vb* : attack in a gang — with *up*

gan·gling *adj* : lanky

gang·ster *n* : member of criminal gang

gap *n* **1** : break in a barrier **2** : mountain pass **3** : empty space

gape *vb* **1** : open widely **2** : stare with mouth open — **gape** *n*

ga·rage *n* : shelter or repair shop for automobiles ~ *vb* : put or keep in a garage

garb *n* : clothing ~ *vb* : dress

gar·bage *n* **1** : food waste **2** : trash — **gar·bage·man** *n*

gar·ble *vb* : distort the meaning of

gar·den *n* **1** : plot for growing fruits, flowers, or vegetables **2** : public recreation area ~ *vb* : work in a garden — **gar·den·er** *n*

gar·de·nia *n* : tree or shrub with fragrant white or yellow flowers or the flower

gar·gan·tuan *adj* : having tremendous size or volume

gar·gle *vb* : rinse the throat with liquid — **gar·gle** *n*

gar·ish *adj* : offensively bright or gaudy

gar·lic *n* : herb with pungent bulbs used in cooking — **gar·licky** *adj*

gar·ment *n* : article of clothing

gar·nish *vb* : add decoration to (as food) — **gar·nish** *n*

gar·ru·lous *adj* : talkative — **gar·ru·li·ty** *n* — **gar·ru·lous·ly** *adv* — **gar·ru·lous·ness** *n*

gar·ter *n* : band to hold up a stocking or sock

gas *n* **1** : fluid (as hydrogen or air) that tends to expand indefinitely **2** : gasoline ~ *vb* **1** : treat with gas **2** : fill with gasoline — used with *up* — **gas·eous** *adj*

gash *n* : deep long cut — **gash** *vb*

gas·ket *n* : material or a part used to seal a joint

gas·light *n* : light of burning illuminating gas

gas·o·line *n* : flammable liquid from petroleum

gasp *vb* **1** : catch the breath audibly **2** : breathe laboriously — **gasp** *n*

gas·tric *adj* : relating to or located near the stomach

gate *n* : an opening for passage in a wall or fence — **gate·keep·er** *n* — **gate·post** *n*

gath·er *vb* **1** : bring or come together **2** : harvest **3** : pick up little by little **4** : deduce — **gath·er·er** *n* — **gath·er·ing** *n*

gaudy *adj* : tastelessly showy — **gaud·i·ly** *adv* — **gaud·i·ness** *n*

gauge *n* : instrument for measuring ~ *vb* : measure

gauze *n* : thin often transparent fabric — **gauzy** *adj*

gave *past of* GIVE

gav·el *n* : mallet of a presiding officer, auctioneer, or judge

gawk *vb* : stare stupidly

gay *adj* 1 : merry 2 : bright and lively 3 : oriented toward one's own sex — **gay** *n*

gaze *vb* : fix the eyes in a steady intent look — **gaze** *n* — **gaz·er** *n*

ga·zette *n* : newspaper

gaz·et·teer *n* : geographical dictionary

gear *n* 1 : clothing 2 : equipment 3 : toothed wheel — **gear** *vb* — **gear·shift** *n*

geek *n* : socially inept person

geese *pl of* GOOSE

gei·sha *n* : Japanese girl or woman trained to entertain men

gel·a·tin *n* : sticky substance obtained from animal tissues by boiling — **ge·lat·i·nous** *adj*

gem *n* : cut and polished valuable stone — **gem·stone** *n*

gen·der *n* 1 : sex 2 : division of a class of words (as nouns) that determines agreement of other words

gene *n* : segment of DNA that controls inheritance of a trait

ge·ne·al·o·gy *n* : study of family pedigrees — **ge·ne·a·log·i·cal** *adj* — **ge·ne·a·log·i·cal·ly** *adv* — **ge·ne·al·o·gist** *n*

gen·er·al *adj* 1 : relating to the whole 2 : applicable to all of a group 3 : common or widespread ~ *n* 1 : something that involves or is applicable to the whole 2 : commissioned officer of the highest rank in the army, air force, or marine corps — **gen·er·al·ly** *adv* — **in general** : for the most part

gen·er·al·i·ty *n* : general statement

gen·er·al·ize *vb* : reach a general conclusion esp. on the basis of particular instances — **gen·er·al·iza·tion** *n*

gen·er·ate *vb* : create or produce

gen·er·a·tion *n* 1 : living beings constituting a single step in a line of descent 2 : production — **gen·er·a·tive** *adj*

gen·er·a·tor *n* 1 : one that generates 2 : machine that turns mechanical into electrical energy

ge·ner·ic *adj* 1 : general 2 : not protected by a trademark 3 : relating to a genus — **generic** *n*

gen·er·ous *adj* : freely giving or sharing — **gen·er·os·i·ty** *n* — **gen·er·ous·ly** *adv* — **gen·er·ous·ness** *n*

ge·net·ics *n* : biology dealing with heredity and variation — **ge·net·ic** *adj* — **ge·net·i·cal·ly** *adv* — **ge·net·i·cist** *n*

ge·nial *adj* : cheerful — **ge·nial·i·ty** *n* — **ge·nial·ly** *adv*

gen·i·tal *adj* : concerned with reproduction — **gen·i·ta·lia** *n pl* — **gen·i·tal·ly** *adv* — **gen·i·tals** *n pl*

ge·nius *n* 1 : single strongly marked capacity 2 : extraordinary intellectual power or a person having such power

geno·cide *n* : systematic destruction of a racial or cultural group

gen·teel *adj* : polite or refined

gen·tile *n* : person who is not Jewish — **gentile** *adj*

gen·til·i·ty *n* 1 : good birth and family 2 : good manners

gen·tle *adj* 1 : of a family of high social station 2 : not harsh, stern, or violent 3 : soft or delicate ~ *vb* : make gentle — **gen·tle·ness** *n* — **gent·ly** *adv*

gen·tle·man *n* : man of good family or manners — **gen·tle·man·ly** *adv*

gen·try *n* 1 : people of good birth or breeding 2 : people of a certain class

gen·u·flect *vb* : bend the knee in worship — **gen·u·flec·tion** *n*

gen·u·ine *adj* : being the same in fact as in appearance — **gen·u·ine·ly** *adv* — **gen·u·ine·ness** *n*

ge·nus *n* (**gen·era**) : category of biological classification

ge·og·ra·phy *n* 1 : study of the earth and its climate, products, and inhabitants 2 : natural features of a region — **ge·og·ra·pher** *n* — **geo·graph·ic, geo·graph·i·cal** *adj* — **geo·graph·i·cal·ly** *adv*

ge·ol·o·gy *n* : study of the history of the earth and its life esp. as recorded in rocks — **geo·log·ic, geo·log·i·cal** *adj* — **geo·log·i·cal·ly** *adv* — **ge·ol·o·gist** *n*

ge·om·e·try *n* : mathematics of the relations, properties, and measurements of solids, surfaces, lines, and angles — **geo·met·ric, geo·met·ri·cal** *adj*

ge·ra·ni·um *n* : garden plant with clusters of white, pink, or scarlet flowers

ger·bil *n* : a small Old World burrowing desert rodent

ge·ri·at·ric *adj* 1 : relating to aging or the aged 2 : old

germ *n* **1** : microorganism **2** : source or rudiment

ger·mi·cide *n* : agent that destroys germs — **ger·mi·cid·al** *adj*

ger·mi·nate *vb* : begin to develop — **ger·mi·na·tion** *n*

ger·und *n* : word having the characteristics of both verb and noun

ges·ture *n* **1** : movement of the body or limbs that expresses something **2** : something said or done for its effect on the attitudes of others — **ges·tur·al** *adj* — **gesture** *vb*

ge·sund·heit *interj* — used to wish good health to one who has just sneezed

get *vb* (**got; got/got·ten**) **1** : gain or be in possession of **2** : succeed in coming or going **3** : cause to come or go or to be in a certain condition or position **4** : become **5** : be subjected to **6** : understand **7** : be obliged — **get along** *vb* **1** : get by **2** : be on friendly terms — **get by** *vb* : meet one's needs

get·away *n* **1** : escape **2** : a starting or getting under way

gey·ser *n* : spring that intermittently shoots up hot water and steam

ghast·ly *adj* : horrible or shocking

gher·kin *n* : small pickle

ghet·to *n* : part of a city in which members of a minority group live

ghost *n* : disembodied soul — **ghost·ly** *adv*

ghoul *n* : legendary evil being that feeds on corpses — **ghoul·ish** *adj*

GI *n* : member of the U.S. armed forces

gi·ant *n* **1** : huge legendary being **2** : something very large or very powerful — **giant** *adj*

gib·ber·ish *n* : unintelligible speech or language

gibe *vb* : jeer at — **gibe** *n*

gib·lets *n pl* : edible fowl viscera

gid·dy *adj* **1** : silly **2** : dizzy — **gid·di·ness** *n*

gift *n* **1** : something given **2** : talent — **gift·ed** *adj*

gi·gan·tic *adj* : very big

gig·gle *vb* : laugh in a silly manner — **giggle** *n* — **gig·gly** *adj*

gild *vb* : cover with or as if with gold

gill *n* : organ of a fish for obtaining oxygen from water

gilt *adj* : gold in color ⁓ *n* : gold or goldlike substance on the surface of an object

gim·mick *n* : new and ingenious scheme, feature, or device — **gim·mick·ry** *n* — **gim·micky** *adj*

gin·ger *n* : pungent aromatic spice from a tropical plant — **gin·ger·bread** *n*

gin·ger·ly *adv* : very cautiously

gin·seng *n* : aromatic root of a Chinese herb

gi·raffe *n* : African mammal with a very long neck

gird·er *n* : horizontal supporting beam

gir·dle *n* : woman's supporting undergarment ⁓ *vb* : surround

girl *n* **1** : female child **2** : young woman **3** : sweetheart — **girl·hood** *n* — **girl·ish** *adj*

girl·friend *n* : frequent or regular female companion of a boy or man

gist *n* : main point or part

give *vb* (**gave; giv·en**) **1** : put into the possession or keeping of another **2** : pay **3** : perform **4** : contribute or donate **5** : produce **6** : utter **7** : yield to force, strain, or pressure ⁓ *n* : capacity or tendency to yield to force or strain — **give in** *vb* : surrender — **give out** *vb* : become used up or exhausted — **give up** *vb* **1** : let out of one's control **2** : cease from trying, doing, or hoping

give·away *n* **1** : unintentional betrayal **2** : something given free

giv·en *adj* **1** : prone or disposed **2** : having been specified

gla·cial *adj* **1** : relating to glaciers **2** : very slow — **gla·cial·ly** *adv*

gla·cier *n* : large body of ice moving slowly

glad *adj* **1** : experiencing or causing pleasure, joy, or delight **2** : very willing — **glad·den** *vb* — **glad·ly** *adv* — **glad·ness** *n*

glad·i·a·tor *n* : one who fought to the death for the entertainment of ancient Romans — **glad·i·a·to·ri·al** *adj*

glad·i·o·lus *n* : plant related to the irises

glam·our, glam·or *n* : romantic or exciting attractiveness — **glam·or·ize** *vb* — **glam·or·ous** *adj*

glance *vb* **1** : strike and fly off to one side **2** : give a quick look ⁓ *n* : quick look

gland *n* : group of cells that secretes a substance — **glan·du·lar** *adj*

glare *vb* **1** : shine with a harsh dazzling light **2** : stare angrily ⁓ *n* **1** : harsh dazzling light **2** : angry stare

glar·ing *adj* : painfully obvious — **glar·ing·ly** *adv*

glass *n* **1** : hard usu. transparent material made by melting sand and other materials **2** : something made of glass **3** *pl* : lenses used to correct defects of vision — **glass** *adj* —

glass·blow·er *n* — **glass·blow·ing** *n* —
glass·ful *n* — **glass·ware** *n* — **glassy** *adj*
glau·co·ma *n* : state of increased pressure
within the eyeball
glaze *vb* **1** : furnish with glass **2** : apply glaze
to ∼ *n* : glassy surface or coating
gleam *n* **1** : transient or partly obscured light
2 : faint trace ∼ *vb* : send out gleams
glean *vb* : collect little by little — **glean·able**
adj — **glean·er** *n*
glee *n* : joy — **glee·ful** *adj*
glen *n* : narrow hidden valley
glib *adj* : speaking or spoken with ease — **glib·
ly** *adv*
glide *vb* : move or descend smoothly and ef-
fortlessly — **glide** *n*
glid·er *n* **1** : winged aircraft having no engine
2 : swinging porch seat
glim·mer *vb* : shine faintly or unsteadily ∼ *n*
1 : faint light **2** : small amount
glimpse *vb* : take a brief look at — **glimpse** *n*
glint *vb* : gleam or sparkle — **glint** *n*
glis·ten *vb* : shine or sparkle by reflection —
glisten *n*
glit·ter *vb* : shine with brilliant or metallic luster ∼ *n* : small glittering ornaments — **glit·
tery** *adj*
glitz *n* : extravagant showiness — **glitzy** *adj*
gloat *vb* : think of something with triumphant
delight
glob *n* : large rounded lump
glob·al *adj* : worldwide — **glob·al·ly** *adv*
globe *n* **1** : sphere **2** : the earth or a model of
it
glob·u·lar *adj* **1** : round **2** : made up of glob-
ules
gloom *n* **1** : darkness **2** : sadness — **gloom·i·
ly** *adv* — **gloom·i·ness** *n* — **gloomy** *adj*
glo·ry *n* **1** : praise or honor offered in worship
2 : cause for praise or renown **3** : magnificence **4** : heavenly bliss ∼ *vb* : rejoice
proudly — **glo·ri·fi·ca·tion** *n* — **glo·ri·fy** *vb*
— **glo·ri·ous** *adj* — **glo·ri·ous·ly** *adv*
gloss *n* : luster — **gloss·i·ly** *adv* — **gloss·i·
ness** *n* — **glossy** *adj* — **gloss over** *vb* **1**
: mask the true nature of **2** : deal with only su-
perficially
glos·sa·ry *n* : dictionary — **glos·sar·i·al** *adj*
glove *n* : hand covering with sections for each
finger
glow *vb* **1** : shine with or as if with intense heat
2 : show exuberance ∼ *n* : brightness or
warmth of color or feeling

glow·er *vb* : stare angrily — **glower** *n*
glue *n* : substance used for sticking things together — **glue** *vb* — **glu·ey** *adj*
glum *adj* **1** : sullen **2** : dismal
glut *vb* : fill to excess — **glut** *n*
glu·ten *n* : gluey protein substance in flour
glut·ton *n* : one who eats to excess — **glut·
ton·ous** *adj* — **glut·tony** *n*
gnarled *adj* **1** : knotty **2** : gloomy or sullen
gnat *n* : small biting fly
gnaw *vb* : bite or chew on
go *vb* (**went; gone**) **1** : move, proceed, run, or
pass **2** : leave **3** : extend or lead **4** : sell or
amount — with *for* **5** : happen **6** — used in
present participle to show intent or imminent
action **7** : become **8** : fit or harmonize **9** : belong ∼ *n* **1** : act or manner of going **2** : vigor
3 : attempt — **go back on** : betray — **go by
the board** : be discarded — **go for** : favor —
go off : explode — **go one better** : outdo —
go over 1 : examine **2** : study — **go to
town** : be very successful — **on the go** : con-
stantly active
goad *n* : something that urges — **goad** *vb*
goal *n* **1** : mark to reach in a race **2** : purpose
3 : object in a game through which a ball is
propelled
goal·ie *n* : player who defends the goal
goal·keep·er *n* : goalie
goat *n* : horned ruminant mammal related to
the sheep — **goat·skin** *n*
¹**gob·ble** *vb* : eat greedily
²**gob·ble** *vb* : make the noise of a turkey (**gob·
bler**)
gob·lin *n* : ugly mischievous sprite
god *n* **1** *cap* : supreme being **2** : being with
supernatural powers — **god·less** *adj* — **god·
less·ness** *n* — **god·like** *adj* — **god·ly** *adj*
god·child *n* : person one sponsors at baptism
— **god·daugh·ter** *n* — **god·son** *n*
god·dess *n* : female god
god·par·ent *n* : sponsor at baptism — **god·fa·
ther** *n* — **god·moth·er** *n*
goes *pres 3d sing of* GO
gog·gle *vb* : stare wide-eyed
gog·gles *n pl* : protective glasses
gold *n* : malleable yellow metallic chemical element — **gold·smith** *n*
gold·en *adj* **1** : made of, containing, or relating to gold **2** : having the color of gold **3**
: precious or favorable
gold·fish *n* : small usu. orange or golden carp
golf *n* : game played by hitting a small ball

(**golf ball**) with clubs (**golf clubs**) into holes placed in a field (**golf course**) — **golf** *vb* — **golf•er** *n*

gon•do•la *n* 1 : long narrow boat used on the canals of Venice 2 : car suspended from a cable

gon•do•lier *n* : person who propels a gondola

gone *adj* 1 : past 2 : involved

gon•er *n* : hopeless case

gong *n* : metallic disk that makes a deep sound when struck

goo *n* : thick or sticky substance — **goo•ey** *adj*

good *adj* (**bet•ter; best**) 1 : satisfactory 2 : producing a beneficial effect 3 : considerable 4 : desirable 5 : well-behaved, kind, or virtuous ∼ *n* 1 : something good 2 : benefit 3 *pl* : personal property 4 *pl* : wares ∼ *adv* : well — **good–heart•ed** *adj* — **good–look•ing** *adj* — **good–na•tured** *adj* — **good•ness** *n* — **for good** : forever

good–bye, good–by *n* : parting remark

Good Friday *n* : Friday before Easter observed as the anniversary of the crucifixion of Christ

good•ly *adj* : considerable

good•will *n* 1 : good intention 2 : kindly feeling

goody *n* : something that is good esp. to eat

goody–goody *adj* : affectedly or annoyingly sweet or self-righteous — **goody–goody** *n*

goof *vb* 1 : blunder 2 : waste time — usu. with *off* or *around* — **goof** *n* — **goof–off** *n*

goofy *adj* : crazy — **goof•i•ness** *n*

goose *n* (**geese**) : large bird with webbed feet

goose bumps *n pl* : roughening of the skin caused by fear, excitement, or cold

goose•flesh *n* : goose bumps

goose pimples *n pl* : goose bumps

go•pher *n* : burrowing rodent

¹**gore** *n* : blood — **gory** *adj*

²**gore** *vb* : pierce or wound with a horn or tusk

¹**gorge** *n* : narrow ravine

²**gorge** *vb* : eat greedily

gor•geous *adj* : supremely beautiful

go•ril•la *n* : African manlike ape

gos•pel *n* 1 : teachings of Christ and the apostles 2 : something accepted as infallible truth — **gos•pel** *adj*

gos•sip *n* 1 : person who reveals personal information 2 : rumor or report of an intimate nature ∼ *vb* : spread gossip — **gos•sipy** *adj*

got *past of* GET

gotten *past part of* GET

gouge *n* 1 : rounded chisel 2 : cavity or

groove scooped out ∼ *vb* 1 : cut or scratch a groove in 2 : to charge too much

gourd *n* 1 : any of a group of vines including the cucumber, squash, and melon 2 : inedible hard-shelled fruit of a gourd

gour•met *n* : connoisseur of food and drink

gov•ern *vb* 1 : control and direct policy in 2 : guide or influence strongly 3 : restrain — **gov•ern•ment** *n* — **gov•ern•men•tal** *adj*

gov•ern•ess *n* : female teacher in a private home

gov•er•nor *n* 1 : head of a political unit 2 : automatic speed-control device — **gov•er•nor•ship** *n*

gown *n* 1 : loose flowing outer garment 2 : woman's formal evening dress — **gown** *vb*

grab *vb* : take by sudden grasp — **grab** *n*

grace *n* 1 : unmerited divine assistance 2 : short prayer before or after a meal 3 : temporary relief 4 : ease of movement or bearing ∼ *vb* 1 : honor 2 : adorn — **graceful** *adj* — **grace•ful•ly** *adv* — **grace•ful•ness** *n* — **grace•less** *adj*

gra•cious *adj* : marked by kindness and courtesy or charm and taste — **gra•cious•ly** *adv* — **gra•cious•ness** *n*

grack•le *n* : American blackbird

grade *n* 1 : stage in a series, order, or ranking 2 : division of school representing one year's work 3 : mark of accomplishment in school 4 : degree of slope ∼ *vb* 1 : arrange in grades 2 : make level or evenly sloping 3 : give a grade to — **grad•er** *n* — **gra•da•tion** *n*

grade school *n* : school including the first six or the first eight grades

gra•di•ent *n* : slope

grad•u•al *adj* : going by steps or degrees — **grad•u•al•ly** *adv*

grad•u•ate *n* : holder of a diploma ∼ *adj* : of or relating to studies beyond the bachelor's degree ∼ *vb* 1 : grant or receive a diploma 2 : mark with degrees of measurement — **grad•u•a•tion** *n*

graf•fi•ti *n pl* : inscriptions on a wall

graft *vb* : join one thing to another so that they grow together ∼ *n* 1 : grafted plant 2 : the getting of money dishonestly or the money so gained — **graft•er** *n*

grain *n* 1 : seeds or fruits of cereal grasses 2 : small hard particle 3 : arrangement of fibers in wood — **grained** *adj* — **grainy** *adj*

gram *n* : metric unit of weight equal to $\frac{1}{1000}$ kilogram

gram·mar *n* : study of words and their functions and relations in the sentence — **gram·mar·i·an** *n* — **gram·mat·i·cal** *adj* — **gram·mat·i·cal·ly** *adv*

grammar school *n* : grade school

grand *adj* **1** : large or striking in size or scope **2** : fine and imposing **3** : very good — **grand·ly** *adv* — **grand·ness** *n*

grand·child *n* : child of one's son or daughter — **grand·daugh·ter** *n* — **grand·son** *n*

grand·par·ent *n* : parent of one's father or mother — **grand·fa·ther** *n* — **grand·moth·er** *n*

grand·stand *n* : usu. roofed stand for spectators

grant *vb* **1** : consent to **2** : give **3** : admit as true ∼ *n* **1** : act of granting **2** : something granted — **grant·ee** *n* — **grant·er** *n* — **grant·or** *n*

gran·u·late *vb* : form into grains or crystals — **gran·u·la·tion** *n*

gran·ule *n* : small particle — **gran·u·lar** *adj* — **gran·u·lar·i·ty** *n*

grape *n* : smooth juicy edible berry of a woody vine (**grape·vine**)

grape·fruit *n* : large edible yellow-skinned citrus fruit

graph *n* : diagram that shows relationships between things — **graph** *vb*

graph·ic *adj* **1** : vividly described **2** : relating to the arts (**graphic arts**) of representation and printing on flat surfaces ∼ *n* **1** : picture used for illustration **2** *pl* : computer screen display — **graph·i·cal·ly** *adv*

graph·ite *n* : soft carbon used for lead pencils and lubricants

grasp *vb* **1** : take or seize firmly **2** : understand ∼ *n* **1** : one's hold or control **2** : one's reach **3** : comprehension

grass *n* : plant with jointed stem and narrow leaves — **grass·land** *n* — **grassy** *adj*

grass·hop·per *n* : leaping plant-eating insect

¹grate *n* **1** : grating **2** : frame of iron bars to hold burning fuel

²grate *vb* **1** : pulverize by rubbing against something rough **2** : irritate — **grat·er** *n* — **grat·ing·ly** *adv*

grate·ful *adj* : thankful or appreciative — **grate·ful·ly** *adv* — **grate·ful·ness** *n*

grat·i·fy *vb* : give pleasure to — **grat·i·fi·ca·tion** *n*

grat·ing *n* : framework with bars across it

grat·i·tude *n* : state of being grateful

gra·tu·ity *n* : tip

¹grave *n* : place of burial — **grave·stone** *n* — **grave·yard** *n*

²grave *adj* **1** : threatening great harm or danger **2** : solemn — **grave·ly** *adv* — **grave·ness** *n*

grav·el *n* : loose rounded fragments of rock — **grav·el·ly** *adj*

grav·i·ta·tion *n* : natural force of attraction that tends to draw bodies together — **grav·i·ta·tion·al** *adj*

grav·i·ty *n* **1** : serious importance **2** : gravitation

gra·vy *n* : sauce made from thickened juices of cooked meat

gray *adj* **1** : of the color gray **2** : having gray hair ∼ *n* : neutral color between black and white ∼ *vb* : make or become gray — **gray·ish** *adj* — **gray·ness** *n*

¹graze *vb* : feed on herbage or pasture — **graz·er** *n*

²graze *vb* : touch lightly in passing

grease *n* : thick oily material or fat ∼ *vb* : smear or lubricate with grease — **greasy** *adj*

great *adj* **1** : large in size or number **2** : larger than usual — **great·ly** *adv* — **great·ness** *n*

greed *n* : selfish desire beyond reason — **greed·i·ly** *adv* — **greed·i·ness** *n* — **greedy** *adj*

green *adj* **1** : of the color green **2** : not yet ripe **3** : not having experience ∼ *vb* : become green ∼ *n* **1** : color between blue and yellow **2** *pl* : leafy parts of plants — **green·ish** *adj* — **green·ness** *n*

green·ery *n* : green foliage or plants

green·house *n* : glass structure for the growing of plants

greet *vb* **1** : address with expressions of kind wishes **2** : react to — **greet·er** *n*

greet·ing *n* **1** : friendly address on meeting **2** *pl* : best wishes

gre·gar·i·ous *adj* : social or companionable — **gre·gar·i·ous·ly** *adv* — **gre·gar·i·ous·ness** *n*

gre·nade *n* : small missile filled with explosive or chemicals

grew *past of* GROW

grey *var of* GRAY

grey·hound *n* : tall slender dog noted for speed

grid *n* **1** : grating **2** : evenly spaced horizontal and vertical lines (as on a map)

grid·dle *n* : flat metal surface for cooking

grid·iron *n* **1** : grate for broiling **2** : football field

grief *n* **1 :** emotional suffering caused by or as if by bereavement **2 :** disaster

griev·ance *n* **:** complaint

grieve *vb* **:** feel or cause to feel grief or sorrow

griev·ous *adj* **1 :** oppressive **2 :** causing grief or sorrow — **griev·ous·ly** *adv*

grill *vb* **1 :** cook on a grill **2 :** question intensely ∼ *n* **1 :** griddle **2 :** informal restaurant

grille, grill *n* **:** grating forming a barrier or screen — **grill·work** *n*

grim *adj* **1 :** harsh and forbidding in appearance **2 :** relentless — **grim·ly** *adv* — **grim·ness** *n*

gri·mace *n* **:** facial expression of disgust — **grimace** *vb*

grime *n* **:** embedded or accumulated dirt — **grimy** *adj*

grin *vb* **:** smile so as to show the teeth — **grin** *n*

grind *vb* (**ground; ground**) **1 :** reduce to powder **2 :** wear down or sharpen by friction **3 :** operate or produce by turning a crank ∼ *n* **:** monotonous labor or routine — **grind·er** *n* — **grind·stone** *n*

grip *vb* **:** seize or hold firmly ∼ *n* **1 :** grasp **2 :** control **3 :** device for holding

gripe *vb* **1 :** cause pains in the bowels **2 :** complain — **gripe** *n*

gris·ly *adj* **:** horrible or gruesome

grist *n* **:** grain to be ground or already ground — **grist·mill** *n*

gris·tle *n* **:** cartilage — **gris·tly** *adj*

grit *n* **1 :** hard sharp granule **2 :** material composed of granules **3 :** steadfast courage ∼ *vb* **:** press with a grating noise — **grit·ty** *adj*

groan *vb* **1 :** moan **2 :** creak under a strain — **groan** *n*

gro·cery *n* **1 :** food store **2** *pl* **:** food and commodities sold in a grocery — **gro·cer** *n*

grog·gy *adj* **:** dazed and unsteady on the feet — **grog·gi·ly** *adv* — **grog·gi·ness** *n*

groin *n* **:** juncture of the lower abdomen and inner thigh

groom *n* **1 :** one who cares for horses **2 :** bridegroom ∼ *vb* **1 :** clean and care for (as a horse) **2 :** make neat or attractive **3 :** prepare

groove *n* **1 :** long narrow channel **2 :** fixed routine — **groove** *vb*

grope *vb* **:** search for by feeling

¹gross *adj* **1 :** glaringly noticeable **2 :** bulky **3 :** consisting of an overall total exclusive of deductions **4 :** vulgar ∼ *n* **:** the whole before any deductions ∼ *vb* **:** earn as a total — **gross·ly** *adv* — **gross·ness** *n*

²gross *n* **:** 12 dozen

grouch *n* **:** complaining person — **grouch** *vb* — **grouchy** *adj*

¹ground *n* **1 :** bottom of a body of water **2** *pl* **:** sediment **3 :** basis for something **4 :** surface of the earth **5 :** conductor that makes electrical connection with the earth or a framework ∼ *vb* **1 :** force or bring down to the ground **2 :** give basic knowledge to **3 :** connect with an electrical ground — **ground·less** *adj*

²ground *past of* GRIND

ground·hog *n* **:** thick-bodied short-legged burrowing rodent

group *n* **:** number of associated individuals ∼ *vb* **:** gather or collect into groups

grove *n* **:** small group of trees

grow *vb* (**grew; grown**) **1 :** come into existence and develop to maturity **2 :** be able to grow **3 :** advance or increase **4 :** become **5 :** cultivate — **grow·er** *n*

growl *vb* **:** utter a deep threatening sound — **growl** *n*

grown–up *n* **:** adult — **grown–up** *adj*

growth *n* **1 :** stage in growing **2 :** process of growing **3 :** result of something growing

grub *vb* **1 :** root out by digging **2 :** search about ∼ *n* **1 :** thick wormlike larva **2 :** food

grub·by *adj* **:** dirty — **grub·bi·ness** *n*

grudge *vb* **:** be reluctant to give ∼ *n* **:** feeling of ill will

gru·el·ing, gru·el·ling *adj* **:** requiring extreme effort

grue·some *adj* **:** horribly repulsive

gruff *adj* **:** rough in speech or manner — **gruffly** *adv*

grum·ble *vb* **:** mutter in discontent — **grumbler** *n*

grumpy *adj* **:** cross — **grump·i·ly** *adv* — **grump·i·ness** *n*

grunge *n* **1 :** something shabby, tattered, or dirty **2 :** rock music expressing alienation and discontent — **grun·gy** *adj*

grunt *n* **:** deep guttural sound — **grunt** *vb*

guar·an·tee *n* **1 :** assurance of the fulfillment of a condition **2 :** something given or held as a security ∼ *vb* **1 :** promise to be responsible for **2 :** state with certainty — **guar·an·tor** *n*

guar·an·ty *n* **1 :** promise to answer for another's failure to pay a debt **2 :** guarantee **3 :** pledge ∼ *vb* **:** guarantee

guard *n* **1 :** defensive position **2 :** act of protecting **3** : an individual or group that guards against danger **4** : protective or safety device ~ *vb* **1** : protect or watch over **2** : take precautions — **guard·house** *n* — **guard·room** *n*

guard·ian *n* : one who has responsibility for the care of the person or property of another — **guard·ian·ship** *n*

guer·ril·la, gue·ril·la *n* : soldier engaged in small-scale harassing tactics

guess *vb* **1** : form an opinion from little evidence **2** : state correctly solely by chance **3** : think or believe — **guess** *n*

guest *n* **1** : person to whom hospitality (as of a house) is extended **2** : patron of a commercial establishment (as a hotel) **3** : person not a regular cast member who appears on a program

guide *n* **1** : one that leads or gives direction to another **2** : device on a machine to direct motion ~ *vb* **1** : show the way to **2** : direct — **guid·able** *adj* — **guid·ance** *n* — **guidebook** *n*

guide·line *n* : summary of procedures regarding policy or conduct

guild *n* : association

guile *n* : craftiness — **guile·ful** *adj* — **guileless** *adj* — **guile·less·ness** *n*

guilt *n* **1** : fact of having committed an offense **2** : feeling of responsibility for offenses — **guilt·i·ly** *adv* — **guilt·i·ness** *n* — **guilty** *adj*

guinea pig *n* : small So. American rodent

guise *n* : external appearance

gui·tar *n* : 6-stringed musical instrument played by plucking

gulf *n* **1** : extension of an ocean or a sea into the land **2** : wide gap

¹gull *n* : seabird with webbed feet

²gull *vb* : make a dupe of ~ *n* : dupe — **gullible** *adj*

gul·ly *n* : trench worn by running water

gulp *vb* : swallow hurriedly or greedily — **gulp** *n*

¹gum *n* : tissue along the jaw at the base of the teeth

²gum *n* **1** : sticky plant substance **2** : gum usu. of sweetened chicle prepared for chewing — **gum·my** *adj*

gum·drop *n* : gumlike candy

gun *n* **1** : cannon **2** : portable firearm **3** : discharge of a gun **4** : something like a gun ~ *vb* : hunt with a gun — **gun·ner** *n* — **gun·fight** *n* — **gun·fight·er** *n* — **gun·fire** *n* — **gunman** *n* — **gun·pow·der** *n* — **gun·shot** *n* — **gun·smith** *n*

gun·wale *n* : upper edge of a boat's side

gup·py *n* : tiny tropical fish

gur·gle *vb* : make a sound like that of a flowing and gently splashing liquid — **gur·gle** *n*

gu·ru *n* **1** : personal religious teacher in Hinduism **2** : expert

gush *vb* : pour forth violently or enthusiastically — **gush·er** *n*

gust *n* **1** : sudden brief rush of wind **2** : sudden outburst — **gust** *vb* — **gusty** *adj*

gus·to *n* : zest

gut *n* **1** *pl* : intestines **2** : digestive canal **3** *pl* : courage ~ *vb* : remove the intestines of

gut·ter *n* : channel for carrying off rainwater

¹guy *n* : rope, chain, or rod attached to something to steady it — **guy** *vb*

²guy *n* : person

guz·zle *vb* : drink greedily

gym *n* : gymnasium

gym·na·si·um *n* : place for indoor sports

gym·nas·tics *n* : physical exercises performed in a gymnasium — **gym·nast** *n* — **gym·nastic** *adj*

gyp *n* **1** : cheat **2** : trickery — **gyp** *vb*

gy·rate *vb* : revolve around a center — **gy·ra·tion** *n*

gy·ro·scope *n* : wheel mounted to spin rapidly about an axis that is free to turn in various directions

H

h *n* : 8th letter of the alphabet

hab·it *n* **1** : monk's or nun's clothing **2** : usual behavior **3** : addiction — **hab·it–form·ing** *adj* — **ha·bit·u·al** *adj* — **ha·bit·u·al·ly** *adv*

hab·i·tat *n* : place where a plant or animal naturally occurs

hab·i·ta·tion *n* **1** : occupancy **2** : dwelling place

hab·it·able *adj* : capable of being lived in

¹hack *vb* **1** : cut with repeated irregular blows **2** : cough in a short dry manner **3** : manage successfully — **hack** *n* — **hack·er** *n*

²**hack** *n* **1 :** horse or vehicle for hire **2 :** saddle horse **3 :** writer for hire — **hack** *adj* — **hackman** *n*

hack·saw *n* **:** saw for metal

had *past of* HAVE

hag *n* **1 :** witch **2 :** ugly old woman

hag·gard *adj* **:** worn or emaciated — **haggard·ly** *adv*

hag·gle *vb* **:** argue in bargaining — **hag·gler** *n*

¹**hail** *n* **1 :** precipitation in small lumps of ice **2 :** something like a rain of hail ⁓ *vb* **:** rain hail — **hail·stone** *n* — **hail·storm** *n*

²**hail** *vb* **1 :** greet or salute **2 :** summon ⁓ *n* **:** expression of greeting or praise — often used as an interjection

hair *n* **:** threadlike growth from the skin — **hair·brush** *n* — **hair·cut** *n* — **hair·dress·er** *n* — **haired** *adj* — **hair·i·ness** *n* — **hair·less** *adj* — **hair·line** *n* — **hair·pin** *n* — **hair·style** *n* — **hair·styl·ing** *n* — **hair·styl·ist** *n* — **hairy** *adj*

hair·breadth, hairs·breadth *n* **:** tiny distance or margin

hair·do *n* **:** style of wearing hair

hair–rais·ing *adj* **:** causing terror or astonishment

hale *adj* **:** healthy or robust

half *n* (**halves**) **:** either of 2 equal parts ⁓ *adj* **1 :** being a half or nearly a half **2 :** partial — **half** *adv*

half brother *n* **:** brother related through one parent only

half·heart·ed *adj* **:** without enthusiasm — **half·heart·ed·ly** *adv*

half–life *n* **:** time for half of something to undergo a process

half sister *n* **:** sister related through one parent only

half·way *adj* **:** midway between 2 points — **half·way** *adv*

half–wit *n* **:** foolish person — **half–wit·ted** *adj*

hal·i·but *n* (**halibut**) **:** large flattened fish with both eyes on the upper side

hall *n* **1 :** large public or college or university building **2 :** lobby **3 :** auditorium

hal·le·lu·jah *interj* — used to express praise, joy, or thanks

hall·mark *n* **:** distinguishing characteristic

hal·low *vb* **:** consecrate — **hal·lowed** *adj*

Hal·low·een *n* **:** evening of October 31 observed esp. by children in merrymaking and masquerading

hal·lu·ci·na·tion *n* **:** perception of objects that are not real — **hal·lu·ci·nate** *vb* — **hal·lu·ci·na·to·ry** *adj*

ha·lo *n* **:** circle of light appearing to surround a shining body

halt *vb* **:** stop or cause to stop — **halt** *n*

hal·ter *n* **1 :** rope or strap for leading ór tying an animal **2 :** brief blouse held up by straps ⁓ *vb* **:** catch (an animal) with a halter

halve *vb* **1 :** divide into halves **2 :** reduce to half

halves *pl of* HALF

ham *n* **1 :** thigh — usu. pl. **2 :** cut esp. of pork from the thigh **3 :** showy actor **4 :** amateur radio operator ⁓ *vb* **:** overplay a part — **ham** *adj*

ham·burg·er, ham·burg *n* **:** ground beef or a sandwich made with this

ham·mer *n* **1 :** hand tool for pounding **2 :** gun part whose striking explodes the charge ⁓ *vb* **:** beat, drive, or shape with a hammer — **hammer out** *vb* **:** produce with effort

ham·mock *n* **:** swinging bed hung by cords at each end

¹**ham·per** *vb* **:** impede

²**hamper** *n* **:** large covered basket

ham·ster *n* **:** thickly built shorttailed rodent

ham·string *vb* **1 :** cripple by cutting the leg tendons **2 :** make ineffective or powerless

hand *n* **1 :** end of a front limb adapted for grasping **2 :** side **3 :** promise of marriage **4 :** handwriting **5 :** assistance or participation **6 :** applause **7 :** cards held by a player **8 :** worker ⁓ *vb* **:** lead, assist, give, or pass with the hand — **hand·clasp** *n* — **hand·craft** *vb* — **hand·ful** *n* — **hand·gun** *n* — **hand·less** *adj* — **hand·made** *adj* — **hand·rail** *n* — **hand·saw** *n* — **hand·shake** *n* — **hand·woven** *adj* — **hand·writ·ing** *n* — **hand·written** *adj*

hand·bag *n* **:** woman's purse

hand·book *n* **:** concise reference book

hand·cuffs *n pl* **:** locking bracelets that bind the wrists together — **handcuff** *vb*

hand·i·cap *n* **1 :** advantage given or disadvantage imposed to equalize a competition **2 :** disadvantage — **handicap** *vb* — **hand·i·capped** *adj* — **hand·i·cap·per** *n*

hand·i·craft *n* **1** : manual skill **2** : article made by hand — **hand·i·craft·er** *n*

hand·ker·chief *n* : small piece of cloth carried for personal use

han·dle *n* : part to be grasped ∼ *vb* **1** : touch, hold, or manage with the hands **2** : deal with **3** : deal or trade in — **han·dle·bar** *n* — **handled** *adj* — **han·dler** *n*

hand·some *adj* **1** : sizable **2** : generous **3** : having a pleasing appearance — **hand·some·ly** *adv* — **hand·some·ness** *n*

hand·spring *n* : somersault on the hands

handy *adj* **1** : conveniently near **2** : easily used **3** : dexterous — **hand·i·ly** *adv* — **hand·i·ness** *n*

handy·man *n* : one who does odd jobs

hang *vb* **1** : fasten or remain fastened to an elevated point without support from below **2** : suspend by the neck until dead — past tense often *hanged* **3** : droop ∼ *n* **1** : way a thing hangs **2** : an understanding of something — **hang·er** *n* — **hang·ing** *n*

han·gar *n* : airplane shelter

hang·nail *n* : loose skin near a fingernail

hang·out *n* : place where one likes to spend time

han·ker *vb* : desire strongly — **han·ker·ing** *n*

han·ky–pan·ky *n* : questionable or underhanded activity

Ha·nuk·kah *n* : 8-day Jewish holiday commemorating the rededication of the Temple of Jerusalem after its defilement by Antiochus of Syria

hap·haz·ard *adj* : having no plan or order — **hap·haz·ard·ly** *adv*

hap·pen *vb* **1** : take place **2** : be fortunate to encounter something unexpectedly — often used with infinitive

hap·pen·ing *n* : occurrence

hap·py *adj* **1** : fortunate **2** : content, pleased, or joyous — **hap·pi·ly** *adv* — **hap·pi·ness** *n*

ha·rass *vb* **1** : disturb and impede by repeated raids **2** : annoy continually — **ha·rass·ment** *n*

har·bor *n* : protected body of water suitable for anchorage ∼ *vb* **1** : give refuge to **2** : hold as a thought or feeling

hard *adj* **1** : not easily penetrated **2** : firm or definite **3** : close or searching **4** : severe or without apparent feelings **5** : strenuous or difficult **6** : physically strong or intense — **hard** *adv* — **hard·ness** *n*

hard·en *vb* : make or become hard or harder — **hard·en·er** *n*

hard·head·ed *adj* **1** : stubborn **2** : realistic — **hard·head·ed·ly** *adv* — **hard·head·ed·ness** *n*

hard–heart·ed *adj* : lacking sympathy — **hard–heart·ed·ly** *adv* — **hard–heart·ed·ness** *n*

hard·ly *adv* **1** : only just **2** : certainly not

hard·ship *n* : suffering or privation

hard·ware *n* **1** : cutlery or tools made of metal **2** : physical components of a vehicle or apparatus

har·dy *adj* : able to withstand adverse conditions — **har·di·ly** *adv* — **har·di·ness** *n*

hark *vb* : listen

harm *n* **1** : physical or mental damage **2** : mischief ∼ *vb* : cause harm — **harm·ful** *adj* — **harm·ful·ly** *adv* — **harm·ful·ness** *n* — **harm·less** *adj* — **harm·less·ly** *adv* — **harm·less·ness** *n*

har·mon·i·ca *n* : small wind instrument with metallic reeds

har·mo·ny *n* **1** : musical combination of sounds **2** : pleasing arrangement of parts **3** : lack of conflict **4** : internal calm — **har·mon·ic** *adj* — **har·mon·i·cal·ly** *adv* — **har·mo·ni·ous** *adj* — **har·mo·ni·ous·ly** *adv* — **har·mo·ni·ous·ness** *n* — **har·mo·ni·za·tion** *n* — **har·mo·nize** *vb*

har·ness *n* : gear of a draft animal ∼ *vb* **1** : put a harness on **2** : put to use

harp *n* : musical instrument with many strings plucked by the fingers ∼ *vb* **1** : play on a harp **2** : dwell on a subject tiresomely — **harp·er** *n* — **harp·ist** *n*

har·row *n* : implement used to break up soil ∼ *vb* **1** : cultivate with a harrow **2** : distress

harsh *adj* **1** : disagreeably rough **2** : severe — **harsh·ly** *adv* — **harsh·ness** *n*

har·vest *n* **1** : act or time of gathering in a crop **2** : mature crop — **harvest** *vb* — **har·vest·er** *n*

has *pres 3d sing of* HAVE

hash *vb* : chop into small pieces ∼ *n* : chopped meat mixed with potatoes and browned

has·sle *n* **1** : quarrel **2** : struggle **3** : cause of annoyance — **hassle** *vb*

haste *n* **1** : rapidity of motion **2** : rash action **3** : excessive eagerness — **hast·i·ly** *adv* — **hast·i·ness** *n* — **hasty** *adj*

has·ten *vb* : hurry

hat *n* : covering for the head

¹hatch *n* : small door or opening — **hatch·way** *n*

²hatch *vb* : emerge from an egg — **hatch·ery** *n*

hatch·et *n* : short-handled ax

hate *n* : intense hostility and aversion ∼ *vb* **1** : express or feel hate **2** : dislike — **hate·ful** *adj* — **hate·ful·ly** *adv* — **hate·ful·ness** *n* — **hat·er** *n*

ha·tred *n* : hate

haugh·ty *adj* : disdainfully proud — **haugh·ti·ly** *adv* — **haugh·ti·ness** *n*

haul **1** : draw or pull **2** : transport or carry ∼ *n* **1** : amount collected **2** : load or the distance it is transported — **haul·er** *n*

haunt *vb* **1** : visit often **2** : visit or inhabit as a ghost ∼ *n* : place frequented — **haunt·er** *n* — **haunt·ing·ly** *adv*

have *vb* (**had; had**) **1** : hold in possession, service, or affection **2** : be compelled or forced — used with *to* **3** — used as an auxiliary with the past participle to form the present perfect, past perfect, or future perfect **4** : obtain or receive **5** : undergo **6** : cause to **7** : bear — **have to do with** : have in the way of connection or relation with or effect on

hav·oc *n* **1** : wide destruction **2** : great confusion

¹hawk *n* : bird of prey with a strong hooked bill and sharp talons

²hawk *vb* : offer for sale by calling out in the street — **hawk·er** *n*

hay *n* : herbs (as grass) cut and dried for use as fodder — **hay** *vb* — **hay·loft** *n* — **hay·mow** *n* — **hay·stack** *n*

hay·wire *adj* : being out of order

haz·ard *n* **1** : source of danger **2** : chance ∼ *vb* : venture or risk — **haz·ard·ous** *adj*

¹haze *n* : fine dust, smoke, or light vapor in the air that reduces visibility

²haze *vb* : harass by abusive and humiliating tricks

ha·zel *n* **1** : shrub or small tree bearing edible nuts (**ha·zel·nuts**) **2** : light brown color

hazy *adj* **1** : obscured by haze **2** : vague or indefinite — **haz·i·ly** *adv* — **haz·i·ness** *n*

he *pron* **1** : that male one **2** : a or the person

head *n* **1** : front or upper part of the body **2** : mind **3** : upper or higher end **4** : director or leader **5** : place of leadership or honor ∼ *adj* : principal or chief ∼ *vb* **1** : provide with or form a head **2** : put, stand, or be at the head **3**

: point or proceed in a certain direction — **head·ache** *n* — **head·band** *n* — **head·dress** *n* — **head·ed** *adj* — **head·first** *adv or adj* — **head·gear** *n* — **head·less** *adj* — **head·rest** *n* — **head·ship** *n* — **head·waiter** *n*

head·ing *n* **1** : direction in which a plane or ship heads **2** : something (as a title) standing at the top or beginning

head·light *n* : light on the front of a vehicle

head·line *n* : introductory line of a newspaper story printed in large type

head–on *adj* : having the front facing in the direction of initial contact — **head–on** *adv*

head·phone *n* : an earphone held on by a band over the head — usu. pl.

head·quar·ters *n sing or pl* : command or administrative center

head·strong *adj* : stubborn or willful

heady *adj* **1** : tending to make one giddy or elated **2** : shrewd

heal *vb* : make or become sound or whole — **heal·er** *n*

health *n* : sound physical or mental condition

health·ful *adj* : beneficial to health — **health·ful·ly** *adv* — **health·ful·ness** *n*

healthy *adj* : enjoying or typical of good health — **health·i·ly** *adv* — **health·i·ness** *n*

heap *n* : pile ∼ *vb* : throw or lay in a heap

hear *vb* **1** : perceive by the ear **2** : heed **3** : learn

hear·ing *n* **1** : process or power of perceiving sound **2** : earshot **3** : session in which witnesses are heard

hear·say *n* : rumor

hearse *n* : vehicle for carrying the dead to the grave

heart *n* **1** : hollow muscular organ that keeps up the circulation of the blood **2** : playing card of a suit marked with a red heart **3** : whole personality or the emotional or moral part of it **4** : courage **5** : essential part — **heart·beat** *n* — **heart·ed** *adj*

heart·ache *n* : anguish of mind

heart·break *n* : crushing grief — **heart·break·er** *n* — **heart·break·ing** *adj* — **heart·bro·ken** *adj*

heart·burn *n* : burning distress in the heart area after eating

heart·en *vb* : encourage

hearth *n* **1** : area in front of a fireplace **2** : home — **hearth·stone** *n*

heart·less *adj* : cruel

heart·warm·ing *adj* : inspiring sympathetic feeling

hearty *adj* **1** : vigorously healthy **2** : nourishing — **heart·i·ly** *adv* — **heart·i·ness** *n*

heat *vb* : make or become warm or hot ⁓ *n* **1** : condition of being hot **2** : form of energy that causes a body to rise in temperature **3** : intensity of feeling — **heat·ed·ly** *adv* — **heat·er** *n*

hea·then *n* : person who is godless or not civilized — **heathen** *adj*

heave *vb* **1** : rise or lift upward **2** : throw **3** : rise and fall ⁓ *n* **1** : an effort to lift or raise **2** : throw

heav·en *n* **1** *pl* : sky **2** : abode of the Deity and of the blessed dead **3** : place of supreme happiness — **heav·en·ly** *adj* — **heav·en·ward** *adv or adj*

heavy *adj* **1** : having great weight **2** : hard to bear **3** : greater than the average — **heav·i·ly** *adv* — **heavi·ness** *n* — **heavy·weight** *n*

heck·le *vb* : harass with gibes — **heck·ler** *n*

hec·tic *adj* : filled with excitement, activity, or confusion — **hec·ti·cal·ly** *adv*

hedge *n* **1** : fence or boundary of shrubs or small trees **2** : means of protection ⁓ *vb* **1** : protect oneself against loss **2** : evade the risk of commitment — **hedg·er** *n*

heed *vb* : pay attention ⁓ *n* : attention — **heed·ful** *adj* — **heed·ful·ly** *adv* — **heed·ful·ness** *n* — **heed·less** *adj* — **heed·less·ly** *adv* — **heed·less·ness** *n*

heel *n* **1** : back of the foot **2** : crusty end of a loaf of bread **3** : solid piece forming the back of the sole of a shoe — **heel·less** *adj*

hefty *adj* : big and bulky

height *n* **1** : highest part or point **2** : distance from bottom to top **3** : altitude

height·en *vb* : increase in amount or degree

heir *n* : one who inherits or is entitled to inherit property

heir·ess *n* : female heir esp. to great wealth

held *past of* HOLD

he·li·cop·ter *n* : aircraft supported in the air by rotors

he·li·um *n* : very light nonflammable gaseous chemical element

hell *n* **1** : nether world in which the dead continue to exist **2** : realm of the devil **3** : place or state of torment or destruction — **hell·ish** *adj*

hel·lo *n* : expression of greeting

helm *n* : lever or wheel for steering a ship — **helms·man** *n*

hel·met *n* : protective covering for the head

help *vb* **1** : supply what is needed **2** : be of use **3** : refrain from or prevent ⁓ *n* **1** : something that helps or is a source of help **2** : one who helps another — **help·er** *n* — **help·ful** *adj* — **help·ful·ly** *adv* — **help·ful·ness** *n* — **help·less** *adj* — **help·less·ly** *adv* — **help·less·ness** *n*

help·ing *n* : portion of food

hem *n* : border of an article of cloth doubled back and stitched down ⁓ *vb* **1** : sew a hem **2** : surround restrictively — **hem·line** *n*

hemi·sphere *n* : one of the halves of the earth divided by the equator into northern and southern parts (**northern hemisphere, southern hemisphere**) or by a meridian into eastern and western parts (**eastern hemisphere, western hemisphere**) — **hemi·spher·ic, hemi·spher·i·cal** *adj*

hem·or·rhage *n* : large discharge of blood — **hemorrhage** *vb* — **hem·or·rhag·ic** *adj*

hen *n* : female domestic fowl

hence *adv* **1** : away **2** : therefore **3** : from this source or origin

hence·forth *adv* : from this point on

her *adj* : of or relating to her or herself ⁓ *pron objective case of* SHE

herb *n* **1** : seed plant that lacks woody tissue **2** : plant or plant part valued for medicinal or savory qualities — **her·ba·ceous** *adj* — **herb·age** *n* — **herb·al** *n or adj* — **herb·al·ist** *n*

her·bi·cide *n* : agent that destroys plants — **her·bi·cid·al** *adj*

herd *n* : group of animals of one kind ⁓ *vb* : assemble or move in a herd — **herd·er** *n* — **herds·man** *n*

here *adv* **1** : in, at, or to this place **2** : now **3** : at or in this point or particular **4** : in the present life or state ⁓ *n* : this place — **here·abouts, here·about** *adv*

here·af·ter *adv* : in some future time or state ⁓ *n* : existence beyond earthly life

he·red·i·tary *adj* **1** : genetically passed or passable from parent to offspring **2** : passing by inheritance — **he·red·i·ty** *n*

her·e·sy *n* : opinion or doctrine contrary to church dogma — **her·e·tic** *n* — **he·re·ti·cal** *adj*

here·to·fore *adv* : up to this time

her·i·tage *n* **1** : inheritance **2** : birthright

her·mit *n* : one who lives in solitude

he·ro *n* : one that is much admired or shows great courage — **he·ro·ic** *adj* — **he·ro·i·cal·ly** *adv* — **he·ro·ics** *n pl* — **her·o·ism** *n*

her·o·in *n* : strongly addictive narcotic

her·o·ine *n* : woman of heroic achievements or qualities

her·on *n* : long-legged long-billed wading bird

hers *pron* : one or the ones belonging to her

her·self *pron* : she, her — used reflexively or for emphasis

hertz *n* **hertz** : unit of frequency equal to one cycle per second

hes·i·tant *adj* : tending to hesitate — **hes·i·tance** *n* — **hes·i·tan·cy** *n* — **hes·i·tant·ly** *adv*

hes·i·tate *vb* **1** : hold back esp. in doubt **2** : pause — **hes·i·ta·tion** *n*

hew *vb* **1** : cut or shape with or as if with an ax **2** : conform strictly — **hew·er** *n*

hex *vb* : put an evil spell on — **hex** *n*

hexa·gon *n* : 6-sided polygon — **hex·ag·o·nal** *adj*

hi·ber·nate *vb* : pass the winter in a torpid or resting state — **hi·ber·na·tion** *n* — **hi·ber·na·tor** *n*

hic·cup *vb* : to inhale spasmodically and make a peculiar sound — *n pl* : attack of hiccuping

¹hide *vb* **hid; hid·den/hid** : put or remain out of sight — **hid·er** *n*

²hide *n* : animal skin

hid·eous *adj* : very ugly — **hid·eous·ly** *adv* — **hid·eous·ness** *n*

hi·er·ar·chy *n* : persons or things arranged in a graded series — **hi·er·ar·chi·cal** *adj*

high *adj* **1** : having large extension upward **2** : elevated in pitch **3** : exalted in character **4** : of greater degree or amount than average **5** : expensive **6** : excited or stupefied by alcohol or a drug — *adv* : at or to a high place or degree — *n* **1** : elevated point or level **2** : automobile gear giving the highest speed — **high·ly** *adv* — **high·ness** *n*

high–definition *adj* : being or relating to a television system with twice as many scan lines per frame as a conventional system

high·light *n* : event or detail of major importance — *vb* **1** : emphasize **2** : be a highlight of

high school *n* : school usu. including grades 9 to 12 or 10 to 12

high–strung *adj* : very nervous or sensitive

high·way *n* : public road

hi·jack *vb* : steal esp. by commandeering a vehicle — **hijack** *n* — **hi·jack·er** *n*

hike *vb* **1** : raise quickly **2** : take a long walk — *n* **1** : long walk **2** : increase — **hik·er** *n*

hi·lar·i·ous *adj* : extremely funny — **hi·lar·i·ous·ly** *adv* — **hi·lar·i·ty** *n*

hill *n* : place where the land rises — **hill·side** *n* — **hill·top** *n* — **hilly** *adj*

him *pron, objective case of* HE

him·self *pron* : he, him — used reflexively or for emphasis

hind *adj* : back — **hind·most** *adj*

hin·der *vb* : obstruct or hold back

hin·drance *n* : something that hinders

hind·sight *n* : understanding of an event after it has happened

Hin·du·ism *n* : body of religious beliefs and practices native to India — **Hin·du** *n or adj*

hinge *n* : jointed piece on which a swinging part (as a door) turns — *vb* **1** : attach by or furnish with hinges **2** : depend

hint *n* **1** : indirect suggestion **2** : clue **3** : very small amount — **hint** *vb*

hip *n* : part of the body on either side just below the waist — **hip·bone** *n*

hip·po·pot·a·mus *n* : large thick-skinned African river animal

hire *n* **1** : payment for labor **2** : employment **3** : one who is hired — *vb* : employ for pay

his *adj* : of or belonging to him — *pron* : ones belonging to him

hiss *vb* **1** : make a sibilant sound **2** : show dislike by hissing — **hiss** *n*

his·to·ry *n* **1** : chronological record of significant events **2** : study of past events **3** : an established record — **his·to·ri·an** *n* — **his·tor·ic, his·tor·i·cal** *adj* — **his·tor·i·cal·ly** *adv*

hit *vb* **hit; hit 1** : reach with a blow **2** : come or cause to come in contact **3** : affect detrimentally — *n* **1** : blow **2** : great success — **hit·ter** *n*

hitch *vb* **1** : move by jerks **2** : catch by a hook **3** : hitchhike — *n* **1** : jerk **2** : sudden halt

hitch·hike *vb* : travel by securing free rides from passing vehicles — **hitch·hik·er** *n*

hive *n* **1** : container housing honeybees **2** : colony of bees — **hive** *vb*

HMO *n* : comprehensive health-care organization financed by clients

hoard *n* : hidden accumulation — **hoard** *vb* — **hoard·er** *n*

hoarse *adj* **1** : harsh in sound **2** : speaking in

a harsh strained voice — **hoarse·ly** *adv* — **hoarse·ness** *n*

hoax *n* : act intended to trick or dupe — **hoax** *vb* — **hoax·er** *n*

hob·ble *vb* : limp along ∼ *n* : hobbling movement

hob·by *n* : interest engaged in for relaxation — **hob·by·ist** *n*

hob·nail *n* : short nail for studding shoe soles — **hob·nailed** *adj*

hock·ey *n* : game played on ice or a field by 2 teams

hodge·podge *n* : heterogeneous mixture

hoe *n* : long-handled tool for cultivating or weeding — **hoe** *vb*

hog *n* **1** : domestic adult swine **2** : glutton ∼ *vb* : take selfishly — **hog·gish** *adj*

hoist *vb* : lift ∼ *n* **1** : lift **2** : apparatus for hoisting

hold *vb* (**held; held**) **1** : possess **2** : restrain **3** : have a grasp on **4** : remain or keep in a particular situation or position **5** : contain **6** : regard **7** : cause to occur **8** : occupy esp. by appointment or election ∼ *n* **1** : act or manner of holding **2** : restraining or controlling influence — **hold·er** *n* — **hold forth** : speak at length — **hold to** : adhere to — **hold with** : agree with

hold·up *n* **1** : robbery at the point of a gun **2** : delay

hole *n* **1** : opening into or through something **2** : hollow place (as a pit) **3** : den — **hole** *vb*

hol·i·day *n* **1** : day of freedom from work **2** : vacation — **holiday** *vb*

ho·lis·tic *adj* : relating to a whole (as the body)

hol·ler *vb* : cry out — **hol·ler** *n*

hol·low *adj* **1** : somewhat depressed **2** : having a cavity within **3** : sounding like a noise made in an empty place **4** : empty of value or meaning ∼ *vb* : make or become hollow ∼ *n* **1** : surface depression **2** : cavity — **hol·low·ness** *n*

hol·ly *n* : evergreen tree or shrub with glossy leaves

ho·lo·caust *n* : thorough destruction esp. by fire

ho·ly *adj* **1** : sacred **2** : spiritually pure — **ho·li·ness** *n*

hom·age *n* : reverent regard

home *n* **1** : residence **2** : congenial environment **3** : place of origin or refuge ∼ *vb* : go or return home — **home·bred** *adj* — **home·com·ing** *n* — **hom·ey** *adj* — **home·grown**

adj — **home·land** *n* — **home·less** *adj* — **home·made** *adj*

home·ly *adj* : plain or unattractive — **home·li·ness** *n*

home·sick *adj* : longing for home — **home·sick·ness** *n*

home·stead *n* : home and land occupied and worked by a family — **home·stead·er** *n*

home·work *n* : school lessons to be done outside the classroom

ho·mo·ge·neous *adj* : of the same or a similar kind — **ho·mo·ge·ne·i·ty** *n* — **ho·mo·ge·neous·ly** *adv*

ho·mog·e·nize *vb* : make the particles in (as milk) of uniform size and even distribution — **ho·mog·e·ni·za·tion** *n* — **ho·mog·e·niz·er** *n*

Ho·mo sa·pi·ens *n* : humankind

hon·est *adj* **1** : free from deception **2** : trustworthy **3** : frank — **hon·est·ly** *adv* — **hon·esty** *n*

hon·ey *n* : sweet sticky substance made by bees (**hon·ey·bees**) from the nectar of flowers — **hon·ey·comb** *n*

hon·ey·moon *n* : holiday taken by a newly married couple — **honeymoon** *vb*

honk *n* : cry of a goose or a similar sound — **honk** *vb* — **honk·er** *n*

hon·or *n* **1** : good name **2** : outward respect or symbol of this **3** : privilege **4** : person of superior rank or position — used esp. as a title **5** : something or someone worthy of respect **6** : integrity ∼ *vb* **1** : regard with honor **2** : confer honor on **3** : fulfill the terms of — **hon·or·able** *adj* — **hon·or·ably** *adv* — **hon·or·ari·ly** *adv* — **hon·or·ary** *adj* — **hon·or·ee** *n*

hood *n* **1** : part of a garment that covers the head **2** : covering over an automobile engine compartment — **hood·ed** *adj*

hood·wink *vb* : deceive

hoof *n* : horny covering of the toes of some mammals (as horses or cattle) — **hoofed** *adj*

hook *n* : curved or bent device for catching, holding, or pulling ∼ *vb* : seize or make fast with a hook — **hook·er** *n*

hoop *n* : circular strip, figure, or object

hoot *vb* **1** : shout in contempt **2** : make the cry of an owl — **hoot** *n* — **hoot·er** *n*

hop *vb* : move by quick springy leaps — **hop** *n*

hope *vb* : desire with expectation of fulfillment ∼ *n* **1** : act of hoping **2** : something hoped for — **hope·ful** *adj* — **hope·ful·ly** *adv* —

hope·ful·ness *n* — **hope·less** *adj* — **hope-less·ly** *adv* — **hope·less·ness** *n*

ho·ri·zon *n* : apparent junction of earth and sky — **hor·i·zon·tal** *adj* — **hor·i·zon·tal·ly** *adv*

hor·mone *n* : cell product in body fluids that has a specific effect on other cells — **hor·mon·al** *adj*

horn *n* **1** : hard bony projection on the head of a hoofed animal **2** : brass wind instrument — **horned** *adj* — **horn·less** *adj* — **horny** *adj*

hor·net *n* : large social wasp

hor·ren·dous *adj* : horrible

hor·ri·ble *adj* **1** : having or causing horror **2** : highly disagreeable — **hor·ri·ble·ness** *n* — **hor·ri·bly** *adv*

hor·ri·fy *vb* : cause to feel horror

hor·ror *n* **1** : intense fear, dread, or dismay **2** : intense repugnance **3** : something horrible

horse *n* : large solid-hoofed domesticated mammal — **horse·back** *n or adv* — **horse-hair** *n* — **horse·hide** *n* — **horse·less** *adj* — **horse·man** *n* — **horse·man·ship** *n* — **horse·wom·an** *n* — **hors·ey, horsy** *adj*

horse·play *n* : rough boisterous play

horse·pow·er *n* : unit of mechanical power

horse·shoe *n* : U-shaped protective metal plate fitted to the rim of a horse's hoof

hor·ti·cul·ture *n* : science of growing fruits, vegetables, and flowers — **hor·ti·cul·tur·al** *adj* — **hor·ti·cul·tur·ist** *n*

hose *n* **1** *pl* **hose** : stocking or sock **2** *pl* **hos-es** : flexible tube for conveying fluids ~ *vb* : spray, water, or wash with a hose

hos·pi·ta·ble *adj* : given to generous and cordial reception of guests — **hos·pi·ta·bly** *adv*

hos·pi·tal *n* : institution where the sick or injured receive medical care — **hos·pi·tal·i·za·tion** *n* — **hos·pi·tal·ize** *vb*

hos·pi·tal·i·ty *n* : hospitable treatment, reception, or disposition

¹host *n* **1** : army **2** : multitude

²host *n* : one who receives or entertains guests — **host** *vb*

³host *n* : eucharistic bread

hos·tage *n* : person held to guarantee that promises be kept or demands met

host·ess *n* : woman who is host

hos·tile *adj* : openly or actively unfriendly or opposed to someone or something — **hostile** *n* — **hos·tile·ly** *adv* — **hos·til·i·ty** *n*

hot *adj* **1** : having a high temperature **2** : giving a sensation of heat or burning **3** : ardent **4** : pungent — **hot** *adv* — **hot·ly** *adv* — **hot-ness** *n*

hot dog *n* : frankfurter

ho·tel *n* : building where lodging and personal services are provided

hound *n* : long-eared hunting dog ~ *vb* : pursue relentlessly

hour *n* **1** : 24th part of a day **2** : time of day — **hour·ly** *adv or adj*

hour·glass *n* : glass vessel for measuring time

house *n* **1** : building to live in **2** : household **3** : legislative body **4** : business firm ~ *vb* : provide with or take shelter — **house·boat** *n* — **house·clean** *vb* — **house·clean·ing** *n* — **house·ful** *n* — **house·keep·er** *n* — **house-keep·ing** *n* — **house·maid** *n* — **house-wares** *n pl* — **house·work** *n*

house·bro·ken *adj* : trained in excretory habits acceptable in indoor living

house·fly *n* : two-winged fly common about human habitations

house·hold *n* : those who dwell as a family under the same roof ~ *adj* **1** : domestic **2** : common or familiar — **house·hold·er** *n*

house·wife *n* (**house·wives**) : married woman in charge of a household — **house-wife·ly** *adj* — **house·wif·ery** *n*

hov·er *vb* **1** : remain suspended in the air **2** : move about in the vicinity

how *adv* **1** : in what way or condition **2** : for what reason **3** : to what extent ~ *conj* : the way or manner in which

how·ev·er *conj* : in whatever manner ~ *adv* **1** : to whatever degree or in whatever manner **2** : in spite of that

howl *vb* : emit a loud long doleful sound like a dog — **howl** *n* — **howl·er** *n*

hub *n* : central part of a circular object (as of a wheel) — **hub·cap** *n*

hud·dle *vb* **1** : crowd together **2** : confer — **hud·dle** *n*

hue *n* : color or gradation of color — **hued** *adj*

hug *vb* **1** : press tightly in the arms **2** : stay close to — **hug** *n*

huge *adj* : very large or extensive — **huge·ly** *adv* — **huge·ness** *n*

hulk *n* **1** : bulky or unwieldy person or thing **2** : old ship unfit for service — **hulk·ing** *adj*

hull *n* **1** : outer covering of a fruit or seed **2** : frame or body of a ship or boat ~ *vb* : remove the hulls of — **hull·er** *n*

hum *vb* **1** : make a prolonged sound like that of the speech sound /m/ **2** : be busily active **3**

: run smoothly **4** : sing with closed lips —
hum *n* — **hum•mer** *n*

hu•man *adj* **1** : of or relating to the species
people belong to **2** : by, for, or like people —
human *n* — **hu•man•kind** *n* — **hu•man•ly**
adv — **hu•man•ness** *n*

hu•mane *adj* : showing compassion or consideration for others — **hu•mane•ly** *adv* — **hu•**
mane•ness *n*

hu•man•ism *n* : doctrine or way of life cen-
tered on human interests or values — **hu•**
man•ist *n or adj* — **hu•man•is•tic** *adj*

hu•man•i•tar•i•an *n* : person promoting human
welfare — **hu•man•i•tar•i•an** *adj* — **hu•man•**
i•tari•an•ism *n*

hu•man•i•ty *n* **1** : human or humane quality or
state **2** : the human race

hum•ble *adj* **1** : not proud or haughty **2** : not
pretentious ∼ *vb* : make humble — **hum•ble•**
ness *n* — **hum•bler** *n* — **hum•bly** *adv*

hu•mid *adj* : containing or characterized by
moisture — **hu•mid•i•fi•ca•tion** *n* — **hu•mid•**
i•fi•er *n* — **hu•mid•i•fy** *vb* — **hu•mid•ly** *adv*

hu•mid•i•ty *n* : atmospheric moisture

hu•mil•i•ate *vb* : injure the self-respect of —
hu•mil•i•at•ing•ly *adv* — **hu•mil•i•ation** *n*

hu•mil•i•ty *n* : humble quality or state

hu•mor *n* **1** : mood **2** : quality of being laugh-
ably ludicrous or incongruous **3** : appreciation
of what is ludicrous or incongruous **4** : something intended to be funny ∼ *vb* : comply with
the wishes or mood of — **hu•mor•ist** *n* — **hu•**
mor•less *adj* — **hu•mor•less•ly** *adv* — **hu•**
mor•less•ness *n* — **hu•mor•ous** *adj* — **hu•**
mor•ous•ly *adv* — **hu•mor•ous•ness** *n*

hump *n* : rounded protuberance — **humped**
adj

hunch *vb* : assume or cause to assume a bent or
crooked posture ∼ *n* : strong intuitive feeling

hun•dred *n* : 10 times 10 — **hundred** *adj* —
hun•dredth *adj or n*

hun•ger *n* **1** : craving or urgent need for food
2 : strong desire — **hunger** *vb* — **hun•gri•ly**
adv — **hun•gry** *adj*

hunk *n* : large piece

hunt *vb* **1** : pursue for food or sport **2** : try to
find ∼ *n* : act or instance of hunting — **hunt•**
er *n*

hur•dle *n* **1** : barrier to leap over in a race **2**
: obstacle — **hur•dle** *vb* — **hur•dler** *n*

hurl *vb* : throw with violence — **hurl** *n* — **hurl•**
er *n*

hur•rah *interj* — used to express joy or approval

hur•ri•cane *n* : tropical storm with winds of 74
miles per hour or greater

hur•ry *vb* : go or cause to go with haste ∼ *n*
: extreme haste — **hur•ried•ly** *adv* — **hur•**
ried•ness *n*

hurt *vb* **hurt; hurt** **1** : feel or cause pain **2** : do
harm to ∼ *n* **1** : bodily injury **2** : harm —
hurt•ful *adj* — **hurt•ful•ness** *n*

hur•tle *vb* : move rapidly or forcefully

hus•band *n* : married man ∼ *vb* : manage prudently

hus•band•ry *n* **1** : careful use **2** : agriculture

hush *vb* : make or become quiet ∼ *n* : silence

husk *n* : outer covering of a seed or fruit ∼ *vb*
: strip the husk from — **husk•er** *n*

¹hus•ky *adj* : hoarse — **hus•ki•ly** *adv* — **hus•**
ki•ness *n*

²husky *adj* : burly — **husk•i•ness** *n*

hus•tle *vb* **1** : hurry **2** : work energetically —
hustle *n* — **hus•tler** *n*

hut *n* : small often temporary dwelling

hy•brid *n* : offspring of genetically differing
parents — **hybrid** *adj* — **hy•brid•iza•tion** *n*
— **hy•brid•ize** *vb* — **hy•brid•iz•er** *n*

hy•drant *n* : pipe from which water may be
drawn to fight fires

hy•dro•elec•tric *adj* : producing electricity by
waterpower — **hy•dro•elec•tric•i•ty** *n*

hy•dro•gen *n* : very light gaseous colorless
odorless flammable chemical element

hy•giene *n* : conditions or practices conducive
to health — **hy•gien•ic** *adj* — **hy•gien•i•cal•**
ly *adv* — **hy•gien•ist** *n*

hying *pres part of* HIE

hymn *n* : song of praise esp. to God — **hymn** *vb*

hym•nal *n* : book of hymns

hype *vb* : publicize extravagantly — **hype** *n*

hy•phen *n* : punctuation mark - used to divide
or compound words — **hyphen** *vb*

hy•phen•ate *vb* : connect or divide with a hyphen — **hy•phen•ation** *n*

hyp•no•sis *n* : induced state like sleep in which
the subject is responsive to suggestions of the
inducer (**hyp•no•tist**) — **hyp•no•tism** *n* —
hyp•no•tiz•able *adj* — **hyp•no•tize** *vb*

hy•poc•ri•sy *n* : a feigning to be what one is not
— **hyp•o•crite** *n* — **hyp•o•crit•i•cal** *adj* —
hyp•o•crit•i•cal•ly *adv*

hy•pot•e•nuse *n* : side of a right-angled triangle opposite the right angle

hy•poth•e•sis *n* : assumption made in order to

test its consequences — **hy·poth·e·size** *vb* — **hy·po·thet·i·cal** *adj* — **hy·po·thet·i·cal·ly** *adv*

hys·te·ria *n* : uncontrollable fear or outburst of emotion — **hys·ter·i·cal** *adj* — **hys·ter·i·cal·ly** *adv*

hys·ter·ics *n pl* : uncontrollable laughter or crying

I

i *n* : 9th letter of the alphabet

I *pron* : the speaker

ice *n* **1** : frozen water **2** : flavored frozen dessert ∼ *vb* **1** : freeze **2** : chill **3** : cover with icing

ice·berg *n* : large floating mass of ice

ice cream *n* : sweet frozen food

ice–skate *vb* : skate on ice — **ice skater** *n*

ici·cle *n* : hanging mass of ice

ic·ing *n* : sweet usu. creamy coating for baked goods

icon *n* **1** : religious image **2** : small picture on a computer screen identified with an available function

icy *adj* **1** : covered with or consisting of ice **2** : very cold — **ic·i·ly** *adv* — **ic·i·ness** *n*

idea *n* **1** : something imagined in the mind **2** : purpose or plan

ide·al *adj* **1** : imaginary **2** : perfect ∼ *n* **1** : standard of excellence **2** : model **3** : aim — **ide·al·ly** *adv*

ide·al·ize *vb* : think of or represent as ideal — **ide·al·ism** *n* — **ide·al·ist** *n* — **ide·al·is·tic** *adj* — **ide·al·is·ti·cal·ly** *adv* — **ide·al·i·za·tion** *n*

iden·ti·cal *adj* **1** : being the same **2** : exactly or essentially alike

iden·ti·fy *vb* **1** : associate **2** : establish the identity of — **iden·ti·fi·able** *adj* — **iden·ti·fi·ca·tion** *n* — **iden·ti·fi·er** *n*

iden·ti·ty *n* **1** : sameness of essential character **2** : individuality **3** : fact of being what is supposed

id·i·om *n* **1** : language peculiar to a person or group **2** : expression with a special meaning — **id·i·om·at·ic** *adj* — **id·i·om·at·i·cal·ly** *adv*

id·i·ot *n* : mentally retarded or foolish person — **id·i·o·cy** *n* — **id·i·ot·ic** *adj* — **id·i·ot·i·cal·ly** *adv*

idle *adj* **1** : worthless **2** : inactive **3** : lazy ∼ *vb* : spend time doing nothing — **idle·ness** *n* — **idler** *n* — **idly** *adv*

idol *n* **1** : image of a god **2** : object of devotion — **idol·iza·tion** *n* — **idol·ize** *vb*

idyll *n* : period of peace and contentment — **idyl·lic** *adj*

if *conj* **1** : in the event that **2** : whether **3** : even though

ig·loo *n* : hut made of snow blocks

ig·nite *vb* : set afire or catch fire — **ig·nit·able** *adj* — **ig·ni·tion** *n*

ig·no·rant *adj* **1** : lacking knowledge **2** : showing a lack of knowledge or intelligence **3** : unaware — **ig·no·rance** *n* — **ig·no·rant·ly** *adv*

ig·nore *vb* : refuse to notice

ill *adj* **worse; worst** **1** : sick **2** : bad **3** : rude or unacceptable **4** : hostile ∼ *adv* **1** : with displeasure **2** : harshly **3** : scarcely **4** : badly ∼ *n* **1** : evil **2** : misfortune **3** : sickness — **ill·ness** *n*

il·le·gal *adj* : not lawful — **il·le·gal·i·ty** *n* — **il·le·gal·ly** *adv*

il·leg·i·ble *adj* : not legible — **il·leg·i·bil·i·ty** *n* — **il·leg·i·bly** *adv*

il·le·git·i·mate *adj* **1** : born of unmarried parents **2** : illegal — **il·le·git·i·ma·cy** *n* — **il·le·git·i·mate·ly** *adv*

il·lic·it *adj* : not lawful — **il·lic·it·ly** *adv*

il·lit·er·ate *adj* : unable to read or write — **il·lit·er·a·cy** *n* — **il·lit·er·ate** *n*

il·log·i·cal *adj* : contrary to sound reasoning — **il·log·i·cal·ly** *adv*

il·lu·mi·nate *vb* **1** : light up **2** : make clear — **il·lu·mi·nat·ing·ly** *adv* — **il·lu·mi·na·tion** *n*

il·lu·sion *n* **1** : mistaken idea **2** : misleading visual image — **il·lu·so·ry** *adj*

il·lus·trate *vb* **1** : explain by example **2** : provide with pictures or figures — **il·lus·tra·tion** *n* — **il·lus·tra·tive** *adj* — **il·lus·tra·tive·ly** *adv* — **il·lus·tra·tor** *n*

il·lus·tri·ous *adj* : notably or brilliantly outstanding — **il·lus·tri·ous·ness** *n*

im·age *n* **1** : likeness **2** : visual counterpart of an object formed by a lens or mirror **3** : mental picture ∼ *vb* : create a representation of — **im·ag·ery** *n*

imag·i·nary *adj* : existing only in the imagination

imag·i·na·tion *n* **1** : act or power of forming a mental image **2** : creative ability

imag·ine *vb* : form a mental picture of something not present — **imag·in·able** *adj* — **imag·in·ably** *adv* — **imag·i·na·tive** *adj* — **imag·i·na·tive·ly** *adv*

im·be·cile *n* : idiot — **imbecile, im·be·cil·ic** *adj* — **im·be·cil·i·ty** *n*

im·i·tate *vb* **1** : follow as a model **2** : mimic — **im·i·ta·tion** *n or adj* — **im·i·ta·tive** *adj* — **im·i·ta·tor** *n*

im·mac·u·late *adj* : without stain or blemish — **im·mac·u·late·ly** *adv*

im·ma·te·ri·al *adj* **1** : spiritual **2** : not relevant — **im·ma·te·ri·al·i·ty** *n*

im·ma·ture *adj* : not yet mature — **im·ma·tu·ri·ty** *n*

im·me·di·a·cy *n* : quality or state of being urgent

im·me·di·ate *adj* **1** : direct **2** : being next in line **3** : made or done at once **4** : not distant — **im·me·di·ate·ly** *adv*

im·mense *adj* : vast — **im·mense·ly** *adv* — **im·men·si·ty** *n*

im·merse *vb* **1** : plunge or dip esp. into liquid **2** : engross — **im·mer·sion** *n*

im·mi·grate *vb* : come into a place and take up residence — **im·mi·grant** *n* — **im·mi·gra·tion** *n*

im·mo·late *vb* : offer in sacrifice — **im·mo·la·tion** *n*

im·mor·al *adj* : not moral — **im·mo·ral·i·ty** *n* — **im·mor·al·ly** *adv*

im·mor·tal *adj* **1** : not mortal **2** : having lasting fame ∼ *n* : one exempt from death or oblivion — **im·mor·tal·i·ty** *n* — **im·mor·tal·ize** *vb*

im·mune *adj* : not liable esp. to disease — **im·mu·ni·ty** *n* — **im·mu·ni·za·tion** *n* — **im·mu·nize** *vb*

im·mu·nol·o·gy *n* : science of immunity to disease — **im·mu·no·log·ic, im·mu·no·log·i·cal** *adj* — **im·mu·nol·o·gist** *n*

im·pact *vb* **1** : press close **2** : have an effect on ∼ *n* **1** : forceful contact **2** : influence

im·pair *vb* : diminish in quantity, value, or ability — **im·pair·ment** *n*

im·pale *vb* : pierce with something pointed

im·par·tial *adj* : not partial — **im·par·tial·i·ty** *n* — **im·par·tial·ly** *adv*

im·passe *n* : inescapable predicament

im·pas·sive *adj* : showing no feeling or interest — **im·pas·sive·ly** *adv* — **im·pas·siv·i·ty** *n*

im·pa·tient *adj* : not patient — **im·pa·tience** *n* — **im·pa·tient·ly** *adv*

im·peach *vb* **1** : charge (an official) with misconduct **2** : cast doubt on **3** : remove from office for misconduct — **im·peach·ment** *n*

im·pec·ca·ble *adj* : faultless — **im·pec·ca·bly** *adv*

im·pede *vb* : interfere with

im·ped·i·ment *n* **1** : hindrance **2** : speech defect

im·per·a·tive *adj* **1** : expressing a command **2** : urgent ∼ *n* **1** : imperative mood or verb form **2** : unavoidable fact, need, or obligation — **im·per·a·tive·ly** *adv*

im·per·cep·ti·ble *adj* : not perceptible — **im·per·cep·ti·bly** *adv*

im·per·fect *adj* : not perfect — **im·per·fec·tion** *n* — **im·per·fect·ly** *adv*

im·pe·ri·al *adj* **1** : relating to an empire or an emperor **2** : royal

im·pe·ri·al·ism *n* : policy of controlling other nations — **im·pe·ri·al·ist** *n or adj* — **im·pe·ri·al·is·tic** *adj* — **im·pe·ri·al·is·ti·cal·ly** *adv*

im·per·ma·nent *adj* : not permanent — **im·per·ma·nent·ly** *adv*

im·per·son·al *adj* : not involving human personality or emotion — **im·per·son·al·i·ty** *n* — **im·per·son·al·ly** *adv*

im·per·son·ate *vb* : assume the character of — **im·per·son·a·tion** *n* — **im·per·son·a·tor** *n*

im·per·ti·nent *adj* **1** : irrelevant **2** : insolent — **im·per·ti·nence** *n* — **im·per·ti·nent·ly** *adv*

im·per·vi·ous *adj* : incapable of being penetrated or affected

im·pe·tus *n* : driving force

im·plant *vb* **1** : set firmly or deeply **2** : fix in the mind or spirit ∼ *n* : something implanted in tissue — **im·plan·ta·tion** *n*

im·plau·si·ble *adj* : not plausible — **im·plau·si·bil·i·ty** *n*

im·ple·ment *n* : tool, utensil ∼ *vb* : put into practice — **im·ple·men·ta·tion** *n*

im·pli·cate *vb* : involve

im·pli·ca·tion *n* **1** : an implying **2** : something implied

im·plic·it *adj* **1** : understood though only implied **2** : complete and unquestioning — **im·plic·it·ly** *adv*

im·plode *vb* : burst inward — **im·plo·sion** *n* — **im·plo·sive** *adj*

im·ply *vb* : express indirectly

im·po·lite *adj* : not polite

im·pon·der·able *adj* : incapable of being precisely evaluated — **im·pon·der·able** *n*

im·port *vb* **1** : mean **2** : bring in from an external source ~ *n* **1** : meaning **2** : importance **3** : something imported — **im·por·ta·tion** *n* — **im·port·er** *n*

im·por·tant *adj* : having great worth, significance, or influence — **im·por·tance** *n* — **im·por·tant·ly** *adv*

im·pose *vb* **1** : establish as compulsory **2** : take unwarranted advantage of — **im·po·si·tion** *n*

im·pos·ing *adj* : impressive — **im·pos·ing·ly** *adv*

im·pos·si·ble *adj* **1** : incapable of occurring **2** : enormously difficult — **im·pos·si·bil·i·ty** *n* — **im·pos·si·bly** *adv*

im·pos·tor, im·pos·ter *n* : one who assumes an identity or title to deceive — **im·pos·ture** *n*

im·prac·ti·cal *adj* : not practical

im·pre·cise *adj* : not precise — **im·pre·cise·ly** *adv* — **im·pre·cise·ness** *n* — **im·pre·ci·sion** *n*

im·preg·nate *vb* **1** : make pregnant **2** : cause to be filled, permeated, or saturated — **im·preg·na·tion** *n*

im·press *vb* **1** : apply with or produce by pressure **2** : press, stamp, or print in or upon **3** : produce a vivid impression of **4** : affect (as the mind) forcibly — **im·pres·sive** *adj* — **im·pres·sive·ly** *adv* — **im·pres·sive·ness** *n* — **im·pres·sion** *n* — **im·pres·sion·able** *adj*

im·pris·on *vb* : put in prison — **im·pris·on·ment** *n*

im·prob·able *adj* : unlikely to be true or to occur — **im·prob·a·bil·i·ty** *n* — **im·prob·a·bly** *adv*

im·prop·er *adj* : not proper — **im·prop·er·ly** *adv*

im·prove *vb* : grow or make better — **im·prov·able** *adj* — **im·prove·ment** *n*

im·pro·vise *vb* : make, invent, or arrange without prior planning — **im·pro·vi·sa·tion** *n* — **im·pro·vis·er, im·pro·vi·sor** *n*

im·pu·dent *adj* : insolent — **im·pu·dence** *n* — **im·pu·dent·ly** *adv*

im·pugn *vb* : attack as false

im·pulse *n* **1** : moving force **2** : sudden inclination — **im·pul·sive** *adj* — **im·pul·sive·ly** *adv* — **im·pul·sive·ness** *n*

im·pure *adj* : not pure — **im·pu·ri·ty** *n*

in *prep* **1** — used to indicate location, inclusion, situation, or manner **2** : into **3** : during ~ : to or toward the inside ~ *adj* : located inside

in·ac·tive *adj* : not active or in use

in·an·i·mate *adj* : not animate or animated — **in·an·i·mate·ly** *adv* — **in·an·i·mate·ness** *n*

in·au·gu·rate *vb* **1** : install in office **2** : start — **in·au·gu·ral** *adj* — **in·au·gu·ra·tion** *n*

in·cal·cu·la·ble *adj* : too large to be calculated — **in·cal·cu·la·bly** *adv*

in·can·ta·tion *n* : use of spoken or sung charms or spells as a magic ritual

in·ca·pac·i·tate *vb* : disable

in·car·cer·ate *vb* : imprison — **in·car·cer·a·tion** *n*

in·cen·tive *n* : inducement to do something

in·cep·tion *n* : beginning

in·ces·sant *adj* : continuing without interruption — **in·ces·sant·ly** *adv*

inch *n* : unit of length equal to $\frac{1}{12}$ foot ~ *vb* : move by small degrees

in·ci·dent *n* : occurrence — **in·ci·dence** *n* — **in·ci·dent** *adj*

in·ci·den·tal *adj* **1** : subordinate, nonessential, or attendant **2** : met by chance ~ *n* **1** : something incidental **2** *pl* : minor expenses that are not itemized — **in·ci·den·tal·ly** *adv*

in·cite *vb* : arouse to action — **in·cite·ment** *n*

in·cline *vb* **1** : bow **2** : tend toward an opinion **3** : slope ~ *n* : slope — **in·cli·na·tion** *n* — **in·clin·er** *n*

in·clude *vb* : take in or comprise — **in·clu·sion** *n* — **in·clu·sive** *adj*

in·come *n* : money gained (as from work or investment)

in·com·pa·ra·ble *adj* : eminent beyond comparison

in·com·pe·tent *adj* : lacking sufficient knowledge or skill — **in·com·pe·tence** *n* — **in·com·pe·ten·cy** *n* — **in·com·pe·tent** *n*

in·con·ceiv·able *adj* **1** : impossible to comprehend **2** : unbelievable — **in·con·ceiv·ably** *adv*

in·con·se·quen·tial *adj* : not important — **in·con·se·quence** *n* — **in·con·se·quen·tial·ly** *adv*

in·con·ve·nience *n* **1** : discomfort **2** : something that causes trouble or annoyance ~ *vb*

: cause inconvenience to — **in·con·ve·nient**
adj — **in·con·ve·nient·ly** *adv*

in·cor·po·rate *vb* **1** : blend **2** : form into a
legal body — **in·cor·po·rat·ed** *adj* — **in·cor·po·ra·tion** *n*

in·cor·rect *adj* : not correct or proper — **in·cor·rect·ly** *adv*

in·crease *vb* : make or become greater ～ *n* **1**
: enlargement in size **2** : something added —
in·creas·ing·ly *adv*

in·cred·i·ble *adj* : too extraordinary to be believed — **in·cred·ibil·i·ty** *n* — **in·cred·i·bly**
adv

in·crim·i·nate *vb* : show to be guilty of a crime
— **in·crim·i·na·tion** *n* — **in·crim·i·na·to·ry**
adj

in·cur *vb* : become liable or subject to

in·deed *adv* : without question

in·def·i·nite *adj* **1** : not defining or identifying
2 : not precise **3** : having no fixed limit — **in·def·i·nite·ly** *adv*

in·den·ta·tion *n* **1** : notch, recess, or dent **2**
: action of indenting **3** : space at the beginning
of a paragraph — **in·dent** *vb*

Independence Day *n* : July 4 observed as a
legal holiday in commemoration of the adop-
tion of the Declaration of Independence in
1776

in·de·pen·dent *adj* **1** : not governed by another **2** : not requiring or relying on something
or somebody else **3** : not easily influenced —
in·de·pen·dence *n* — **in·de·pen·dent** *n* —
in·de·pen·dent·ly *adv*

in·dex *n* **1** : alphabetical list of items (as topics
in a book) **2** : a number that serves as a measure or indicator of something ～ *vb* **1** : provide with an index **2** : serve as an index of

in·di·cate *vb* **1** : point out or to **2** : show indirectly **3** : state briefly — **in·di·ca·tion** *n* —
in·dic·a·tive *adj* — **in·di·ca·tor** *n*

in·dict *vb* : charge with a crime — **in·dict·able**
adj — **in·dict·ment** *n*

in·dif·fer·ent *adj* **1** : having no preference **2**
: showing neither interest nor dislike **3**
: mediocre — **in·dif·fer·ence** *n* — **in·dif·fer·ent·ly** *adv*

in·dig·e·nous *adj* : native to a particular region

in·di·ges·tion *n* : discomfort from inability to
digest food

in·dig·na·tion *n* : anger aroused by something
unjust or unworthy — **in·dig·nant** *adj* — **in·dig·nant·ly** *adv* — **in·dig·ni·ty** *n*

in·di·rect *adj* : not straight or straightforward

— **in·di·rec·tion** *n* — **in·di·rect·ly** *adv* — **in·di·rect·ness** *n*

in·dis·crim·i·nate *adj* **1** : not careful or discriminating **2** : haphazard — **in·dis·crim·i·nate·ly** *adv*

in·dis·tinct *adj* : not clearly recognizable or
understandable — **in·dis·tinct·ly** *adv*

in·di·vid·u·al *n* **1** : single member of a cate-
gory **2** : person — **in·di·vid·u·al** *adj* — **in·di·vid·u·al·i·ty** *n* — **in·di·vid·u·al·ly** *adv*

in·di·vid·u·al·ize *vb* **1** : make individual **2**
: treat individually

in·doc·tri·nate *vb* : instruct in fundamentals
(as of a doctrine) — **in·doc·tri·na·tion** *n*

in·doors *adv* : in or into a building

in·duce *vb* **1** : persuade **2** : bring about — **in·duce·ment** *n* — **in·duc·er** *n*

in·duct *vb* **1** : put in office **2** : admit as a
member **3** : enroll (as for military service) —
in·duct·ee *n* — **in·duc·tion** *n*

in·dulge *vb* : yield to the desire of or for — **in·dul·gence** *n* — **in·dul·gent** *adj* — **in·dul·gent·ly** *adv*

in·dus·tri·ous *adj* : diligent or busy — **in·dus·tri·ous·ly** *adv* — **in·dus·tri·ous·ness** *n*

in·dus·try *n* **1** : diligence **2** : manufacturing
enterprises or activity — **in·dus·tri·al** *adj* —
in·dus·tri·al·ist *n* — **in·dus·tri·al·iza·tion** *n*
— **in·dus·tri·al·ize** *vb* — **in·dus·tri·al·ly** *adv*

in·ept *adj* **1** : inappropriate or foolish **2** : gen-
erally incompetent — **in·ep·ti·tude** *n* — **in·ept·ly** *adv* — **in·ept·ness** *n*

in·equal·i·ty *n* : quality of being unequal or uneven

in·ert *adj* **1** : powerless to move or act **2**
: sluggish — **in·ert·ly** *adv* — **in·ert·ness** *n*

in·ev·i·ta·ble *adj* : incapable of being avoided
or escaped — **in·ev·i·ta·bil·i·ty** *n* — **in·ev·i·ta·bly** *adv*

in·ex·cus·able *adj* : being without excuse or
justification — **in·ex·cus·ably** *adv*

in·fa·mous *adj* : having the worst kind of reputation — **in·fa·mous·ly** *adv* — **in·fa·my** *n*

in·fant *n* : baby — **in·fan·cy** *n* — **in·fan·tile**
adj

in·fat·u·ate *vb* : inspire with foolish love or admiration — **in·fat·u·a·tion** *n*

in·fect *vb* : contaminate with disease-
producing matter — **in·fec·tion** *n* — **in·fec·tious** *adj* — **in·fec·tive** *adj*

in·fer *vb* : deduce — **in·fer·ence** *n* — **in·fer·en·tial** *adj*

in·fe·ri·or *adj* **1** : being lower in position, degree, rank, or merit **2** : of lesser quality — **in·ferior** *n* — **in·fe·ri·or·i·ty** *n*

in·fest *vb* : swarm or grow in or over — **in·fes·ta·tion** *n*

in·fi·del·i·ty *n* : lack of faithfulness

in·fil·trate *vb* : enter or become established in without being noticed — **in·fil·tra·tion** *n*

in·fi·nite *adj* **1** : having no limit or extending indefinitely **2** : vast — **in·fi·nite** *n* — **in·fi·nite·ly** *adv* — **in·fin·i·tude** *n*

in·fin·i·tive *n* : verb form in English usu. used with *to*

in·fin·i·ty *n* **1** : quality or state of being infinite **2** : indefinitely great number or amount

in·flame *vb* **1** : excite to intense action or feeling **2** : affect or become affected with red and painful response to injury — **in·flam·ma·tion** *n* — **in·flam·ma·to·ry** *adj*

in·flam·ma·ble *adj* : flammable

in·flate *vb* **1** : swell or puff up (as with gas) **2** : expand or increase abnormally — **in·flat·able** *adj*

in·fla·tion *n* **1** : act of inflating **2** : continual rise in prices — **in·fla·tion·ary** *adj*

in·flec·tion *n* **1** : change in pitch or loudness of the voice **2** : change in form of a word — **in·flect** *vb* — **in·flec·tion·al** *adj*

in·flu·ence *n* **1** : power or capacity of causing an effect in indirect or intangible ways **2** : one that exerts influence ～ *vb* : affect or alter by influence — **in·flu·en·tial** *adj*

in·flux *n* : a flowing in

in·form *vb* : give information or knowledge to — **in·for·mant** *n* — **in·for·ma·tion** *n* — **in·for·ma·tion·al** *adj* — **in·for·ma·tive** *adj* — **in·form·er** *n*

in·for·mal *adj* **1** : without formality or ceremony **2** : for ordinary or familiar use — **in·for·mal·i·ty** *n* — **in·for·mal·ly** *adv*

in·fringe *vb* : violate another's right or privilege — **in·fringe·ment** *n*

in·fu·ri·ate *vb* : make furious — **in·fu·ri·at·ing·ly** *adv*

in·ge·nious *adj* : very clever — **in·ge·nious·ly** *adv* — **in·ge·nious·ness** *n*

in·ge·nu·ity *n* : skill or cleverness in planning or inventing

in·gen·u·ous *adj* : innocent and candid — **in·gen·u·ous·ly** *adv* — **in·gen·u·ous·ness** *n*

in·gre·di·ent *n* : one of the substances that make up a mixture

in·hab·it *vb* : live or dwell in — **in·hab·it·able** *adj* — **in·hab·it·ant** *n*

in·hale *vb* : breathe in — **in·hal·ant** *n* — **in·ha·la·tion** *n* — **in·hal·er** *n*

in·her·ent *adj* : being an essential part of something — **in·her·ent·ly** *adv*

in·her·it *vb* : receive from one's ancestors — **in·her·it·able** *adj* — **in·her·i·tance** *n* — **in·her·i·tor** *n*

in·hib·it *vb* : hold in check — **in·hi·bi·tion** *n*

in·hu·man *adj* : cruel or impersonal — **in·hu·man·i·ty** *n* — **in·hu·man·ly** *adv* — **in·hu·man·ness** *n*

ini·tial *adj* **1** : of or relating to the beginning **2** : first ～ *n* : 1st letter of a word or name ～ *vb* : put initials on — **ini·tial·ly** *adv*

ini·ti·ate *vb* **1** : start **2** : induct into membership **3** : instruct in the rudiments of something — **ini·ti·ate** *n* — **ini·ti·a·tion** *n* — **ini·tia·to·ry** *adj*

ini·tia·tive *n* **1** : first step **2** : readiness to undertake something on one's own

in·ject *vb* : force or introduce into something — **in·jec·tion** *n*

in·junc·tion *n* : court writ requiring one to do or to refrain from doing a specified act

in·jure *vb* : do damage, hurt, or a wrong to

in·ju·ry *n* **1** : act that injures **2** : hurt, damage, or loss sustained — **in·ju·ri·ous** *adj*

in·jus·tice *n* : unjust act

ink *n* : usu. liquid and colored material for writing and printing ～ *vb* : put ink on — **ink·well** *n* — **inky** *adj*

in–law *n* : relative by marriage

in·lay *vb* : set into a surface for decoration ～ *n* **1** : inlaid work **2** : shaped filling cemented into a tooth

inn *n* : hotel — **inn·keep·er** *n*

in·ner *adj* : being on the inside

in·no·cent *adj* **1** : free from guilt **2** : harmless **3** : not sophisticated — **in·no·cence** *n* — **in·no·cent** *n* — **in·no·cent·ly** *adv*

in·no·va·tion *n* : new idea or method — **in·no·vate** *vb* — **in·no·va·tive** *adj* — **in·no·va·tor** *n*

in·or·di·nate *adj* : unusual or excessive — **in·or·di·nate·ly** *adv*

in·or·gan·ic *adj* : made of mineral matter

in·put *n* : something put in — **in·put** *vb*

in·quire *vb* **1** : ask **2** : investigate — **in·quir·er** *n* — **in·quir·ing·ly** *adv* — **in·qui·ry** *n*

in·quis·i·tive *adj* : curious — **in·quis·i·tive·ly** *adv* — **in·quis·i·tive·ness** *n*

in·sane *adj* **1** : not sane **2** : absurd — **in·sane·ly** *adv* — **in·san·i·ty** *n*

in·scribe *vb* **1** : write **2** : engrave **3** : dedicate (a book) to someone — **in·scrip·tion** *n*

in·sect *n* : small usu. winged animal with 6 legs

in·sec·ti·cide *n* : insect poison — **in·sec·ti·cid·al** *adj*

in·se·cure *adj* **1** : not certain **2** : not safe **3** : fearful — **in·se·cure·ly** *adv* — **in·se·cu·ri·ty** *n*

in·sen·si·ble *adj* **1** : unconscious **2** : unable to feel **3** : unaware — **in·sen·si·bil·i·ty** *n* — **in·sen·si·bly** *adv*

in·sert *vb* : put in — **in·sert** *n* — **in·ser·tion** *n*

in·side *n* **1** : inner side **2** *pl* : internal organs ∼ *prep* **1** : in or into the inside of **2** : within ∼ *adv* **1** : on the inner side **2** : into the interior — **in·side** *adj* — **in·sid·er** *n*

in·sight *n* : understanding — **in·sight·ful** *adj*

in·sin·u·ate *vb* **1** : imply **2** : bring in artfully — **in·sin·u·a·tion** *n*

in·sist *vb* : be firmly demanding — **in·sis·tence** *n* — **in·sis·tent** *adj* — **in·sis·tent·ly** *adv*

in·so·lent *adj* : bold and contemptuous — **in·so·lence** *n*

in·sol·vent *adj* : unable or insufficient to pay debts — **in·sol·ven·cy** *n*

in·som·nia *n* : inability to sleep — **in·som·ni·ac** *n*

in·spect *vb* : view closely and critically — **in·spec·tion** *n* — **in·spec·tor** *n*

in·spire *vb* **1** : inhale **2** : influence by example **3** : bring about **4** : stir to action — **in·spi·ra·tion** *n* — **in·spi·ra·tion·al** *adj* — **in·spir·er** *n*

in·stall, in·stal *vb* **1** : induct into office **2** : set up for use — **in·stal·la·tion** *n*

in·stall·ment *n* : partial payment

in·stance *n* **1** : request or instigation **2** : example

in·stant *n* : moment ∼ *adj* **1** : immediate **2** : ready to mix — **in·stan·ta·neous** *adj* — **in·stan·ta·neous·ly** *adv* — **in·stant·ly** *adv*

in·stead *adv* : as a substitute or alternative

instead of *prep* : as a substitute for or alternative to

in·stinct *n* **1** : natural talent **2** : natural inherited or subconsciously motivated behavior — **in·stinc·tive** *adj* — **in·stinc·tive·ly** *adv* — **in·stinc·tu·al** *adj*

in·sti·tute *vb* : establish, start, or organize ∼ *n* **1** : organization promoting a cause **2** : school

in·sti·tu·tion *n* **1** : act of instituting **2** : custom **3** : corporation or society of a public character — **in·sti·tu·tion·al** *adj* — **in·sti·tu·tion·al·ize** *vb* — **in·sti·tu·tion·al·ly** *adv*

in·struct *vb* **1** : teach **2** : give an order to — **in·struc·tion** *n* — **in·struc·tion·al** *adj* — **in·struc·tive** *adj* — **in·struc·tor** *n* — **in·struc·tor·ship** *n*

in·stru·ment *n* **1** : something that produces music **2** : means **3** : device for doing work and esp. precision work **4** : legal document — **in·stru·men·tal** *adj* — **in·stru·men·tal·ist** *n* — **in·stru·men·tal·i·ty** *n* — **in·stru·men·ta·tion** *n*

in·su·late *vb* : protect from heat loss or electricity — **in·su·la·tion** *n* — **in·su·la·tor** *n*

in·sult *vb* : treat with contempt ∼ *n* : insulting act or remark — **in·sult·ing·ly** *adv*

in·sure *vb* **1** : guarantee against loss **2** : make certain — **in·sur·able** *adj* — **in·sur·ance** *n* — **in·sured** *n* — **in·sur·er** *n*

in·tact *adj* : not damaged

in·take *n* **1** : opening through which something enters **2** : act of taking in **3** : amount taken in

in·te·ger *n* : number that is not a fraction and does not include a fraction

in·te·grate *vb* **1** : unite **2** : end segregation of or at — **in·te·gra·tion** *n*

in·teg·ri·ty *n* **1** : soundness **2** : adherence to a code of values **3** : completeness

in·tel·lect *n* : power of knowing or thinking — **in·tel·lec·tu·al** *adj or n* — **in·tel·lec·tu·al·ism** *n* — **in·tel·lec·tu·al·ly** *adv*

in·tel·li·gence *n* **1** : ability to learn and understand **2** : mental acuteness **3** : information — **in·tel·li·gent** *adj* — **in·tel·li·gent·ly** *adv*

in·tend *vb* : have as a purpose — **in·tend·ed** *n or adj*

in·tense *adj* **1** : extreme **2** : deeply felt — **in·tense·ly** *adv* — **in·ten·si·fi·ca·tion** *n* — **in·ten·si·fy** *vb* — **in·ten·si·ty** *n* — **in·ten·sive** *adj* — **in·ten·sive·ly** *adv*

¹in·tent *n* : purpose — **in·ten·tion** *n* — **in·ten·tion·al** *adj* — **in·ten·tion·al·ly** *adv*

²in·tent *adj* : concentrated — **in·tent·ly** *adv* — **in·tent·ness** *n*

in·ter·ac·tion *n* : mutual influence — **in·ter·act** *vb* — **in·ter·ac·tive** *adj*

in·ter·breed *vb* : breed together

in·ter·cede *vb* : act to reconcile — **in·ter·ces·sion** *n* — **in·ter·ces·sor** *n*

in·ter·cept *vb* : interrupt the progress of — **in·ter·cept** *n* — **in·ter·cep·tion** *n* — **in·ter·cep·tor** *n* in·ter·change *vb* 1 : exchange 2 : change places ~ *n* 1 : exchange 2 : junction of highways — **in·ter·change·able** *adj*

in·ter·est *n* 1 : right 2 : benefit 3 : charge for borrowed money 4 : readiness to pay special attention 5 : quality that causes interest ~ *vb* 1 : concern 2 : get the attention of — **in·ter·est·ing** *adj* — **in·ter·est·ing·ly** *adv*

in·ter·fere *vb* 1 : collide or be in opposition 2 : try to run the affairs of others — **in·ter·fer·ence** *n*

in·te·ri·or *adj* : being on the inside ~ *n* 1 : inside 2 : inland area

in·ter·jec·tion *n* : an exclamatory word — **in·ter·jec·tion·al·ly** *adv*

in·ter·lock *vb* 1 : unite by or as by lacing together 2 : connect for mutual effect — **in·ter·lock** *n*

in·ter·me·di·ary *n* : agent between individuals or groups — **intermediary** *adj*

in·ter·me·di·ate *adj* : between extremes — **in·ter·me·di·ate** *n*

in·ter·mis·sion *n* : break in a performance

in·ter·mix *vb* : mix together — **in·ter·mix·ture** *n*

in·tern *n* : advanced student (as in medicine) gaining supervised experience ~ *vb* : act as an intern — **in·tern·ship** *n*

in·ter·nal *adj* 1 : inward 2 : inside of the body 3 : relating to or existing in the mind — **in·ter·nal·ly** *adv*

in·ter·na·tion·al *adj* : affecting 2 or more nations ~ *n* : something having international scope — **in·ter·na·tion·al·ism** *n* — **in·ter·na·tion·al·ize** *vb* — **in·ter·na·tion·al·ly** *adv*

In·ter·net *n* : network that connects computer networks worldwide

in·ter·pret *vb* : explain the meaning of — **in·ter·pre·ta·tion** *n* — **in·ter·pre·ta·tive** *adj* — **in·ter·pret·er** *n* — **in·ter·pre·tive** *adj*

in·ter·ro·gate *vb* : question — **in·ter·ro·ga·tion** *n* — **in·ter·rog·a·tive** *adj or n* — **in·ter·ro·ga·tor** *n* — **in·ter·rog·a·to·ry** *adj*

in·ter·rupt *vb* : intrude so as to hinder or end continuity — **in·ter·rupt·er** *n* — **in·ter·rup·tion** *n* — **in·ter·rup·tive** *adv*

in·ter·sect *vb* 1 : cut across or divide 2 : cross — **in·ter·sec·tion** *n*

in·ter·twine *vb* : twist together — **in·ter·twine·ment** *n*

in·ter·val *n* 1 : time between 2 : space between

in·ter·vene *vb* 1 : happen between events 2 : intercede — **in·ter·ven·tion** *n*

in·ter·view *n* : a meeting to get information — **in·ter·view** *vb* — **in·ter·view·er** *n*

in·tes·tine *n* : tubular part of the digestive system after the stomach including a long narrow upper part (**small intestine**) followed by a broader shorter lower part (**large intestine**) — **in·tes·ti·nal** *adj*

in·ti·mate *vb* : hint ~ *adj* 1 : very friendly 2 : suggesting privacy 3 : very personal ~ *n* : close friend — **in·ti·ma·cy** *n* — **in·ti·mate·ly** *adv* — **in·ti·ma·tion** *n*

in·tim·i·date *vb* : make fearful — **in·tim·i·da·tion** *n*

in·to *prep* 1 : to the inside of 2 : to the condition of 3 : against

in·to·na·tion *n* : way of singing or speaking

in·tox·i·cate *vb* : make drunk — **in·tox·i·cant** *n or adj* — **in·tox·i·ca·tion** *n*

in·tri·cate *adj* : very complex and delicate — **in·tri·ca·cy** *n* — **in·tri·cate·ly** *adv*

in·trigue *vb* 1 : scheme 2 : arouse curiosity of ~ *n* : secret scheme — **in·trigu·ing·ly** *adv*

in·tro·duce *vb* 1 : bring in esp. for the 1st time 2 : cause to be acquainted 3 : bring to notice 4 : put in — **in·tro·duc·tion** *n* — **in·tro·duc·to·ry** *adj*

in·tro·vert *n* : shy or reserved person — **in·tro·ver·sion** *n* — **in·tro·vert** *adj* — **in·tro·vert·ed** *adj*

in·trude *vb* 1 : thrust in 2 : go beyond usual or proper limits — **in·trud·er** *n* — **in·tru·sion** *n* — **in·tru·sive** *adj* — **in·tru·sive·ness** *n*

in·tu·i·tion *n* : quick and ready insight — **in·tu·it** *vb* — **in·tu·i·tive** *adj* — **in·tu·i·tive·ly** *adv*

in·vade *vb* : enter for conquest — **in·vad·er** *n* — **in·va·sion** *n*

¹in·val·id *adj* : not true or legal — **in·va·lid·i·ty** *n* — **in·val·id·ly** *adv*

²in·va·lid *adj* : sickly ~ *n* : one chronically ill

in·val·i·date *vb* : make invalid — **in·val·i·da·tion** *n*

in·valu·able *adj* : extremely valuable

in·vent *vb* 1 : think up 2 : create for the 1st time — **in·ven·tion** *n* — **in·ven·tive** *adj* — **in·ven·tive·ness** *n* — **in·ven·tor** *n*

in·ven·to·ry *n* 1 : list of goods 2 : stock — **in·ven·to·ry** *vb*

in·vert *vb* 1 : turn upside down or inside out 2 : reverse — **in·ver·sion** *n*

in·ver·te·brate *adj* : lacking a backbone ~ *n* : invertebrate animal

in·vest *vb* **1** : give power or authority to **2** : endow with a quality **3** : commit money to someone else's use in hope of profit — **in·vest·ment** *n* — **in·ves·tor** *n*

in·ves·ti·gate *vb* : study closely and systematically — **in·ves·ti·ga·tion** *n* — **in·ves·ti·ga·tive** *adj* — **in·ves·ti·ga·tor** *n*

in·vig·o·rate *vb* : give life and energy to — **in·vig·o·ra·tion** *n*

in·vis·ible *adj* : not visible

in·vite *vb* **1** : entice **2** : increase the likelihood of **3** : request the presence or participation of **4** : encourage — **in·vi·ta·tion** *n* — **in·vit·ing** *adj*

in·vo·ca·tion *n* **1** : prayer **2** : incantation

in·voice *n* : itemized bill for goods shipped ∼ *vb* : bill

in·vol·un·tary *adj* : done without control or choice — **in·vol·un·tar·i·ly** *adv*

in·volve *vb* **1** : draw in as a participant **2** : relate closely **3** : require as a necessary part **4** : occupy fully — **in·volve·ment** *n*

in·volved *adj* : intricate

in·ward, in·wards *adv* : toward the inside, center, or inner being — **in·ward·ly** *adv*

io·dine *n* **1** : nonmetallic chemical element **2** : solution of iodine used as an antiseptic

ion *n* : electrically charged particle — **ion·ic** *adj* — **ion·iz·able** *adj* — **ion·i·za·tion** *n* — **ion·ize** *vb* — **ion·iz·er** *n*

IOU *n* : acknowledgment of a debt

irate *adj* : aroused to intense anger — **irate·ly** *adv*

ire *n* : anger

iris *n* **1** : colored part around the pupil of the eye **2** : plant with long leaves and large showy flowers

irk *vb* : annoy — **irk·some** *adj* — **irk·some·ly** *adv*

iron *n* **1** : heavy metallic chemical element **2** : something made of iron **3** : heated device for pressing clothes **4** : hardness, determination ∼ *vb* : press or smooth out with an iron — **iron·ware** *n* — **iron·work** *n* — **iron·work·er** *n* — **iron·works** *n pl*

iro·ny *n* **1** : use of words to express the opposite of the literal meaning **2** : incongruity between the actual and expected result of events — **iron·ic, iron·i·cal** *adj* — **iron·i·cal·ly** *adv*

ir·ra·tio·nal *adj* **1** : incapable of reasoning **2** : not based on reason — **ir·ra·tio·nal·i·ty** *n* — **ir·ra·tio·nal·ly** *adv*

ir·reg·u·lar *adj* : not regular or normal — **ir·reg·u·lar** *n* — **ir·reg·u·lar·i·ty** *n* — **ir·reg·u·lar·ly** *adv*

ir·rel·e·vant *adj* : not relevant — **ir·rel·e·vance** *n*

ir·re·place·able *adj* : not replaceable

ir·re·sist·ible *adj* : impossible to successfully resist — **ir·re·sist·ibly** *adv*

ir·re·spon·si·ble *adj* : not responsible — **ir·re·spon·si·bil·i·ty** *n* — **ir·re·spon·si·bly** *adv*

ir·rev·er·ence *n* **1** : lack of reverence **2** : irreverent act or utterance — **ir·rev·er·ent** *adj*

ir·re·vers·ible *adj* : incapable of being reversed

ir·ri·gate *vb* : supply with water by artificial means — **ir·ri·ga·tion** *n*

ir·ri·tate *vb* **1** : excite to anger **2** : make sore or inflamed — **ir·ri·ta·bil·i·ty** *n* — **ir·ri·ta·ble** *adj* — **ir·ri·ta·bly** *adv* — **ir·ri·tant** *adj or n* — **ir·ri·tat·ing·ly** *adv* — **ir·ri·ta·tion** *n*

is *pres 3d sing of* BE

Is·lam *n* : religious faith of Muslims — **Is·lam·ic** *adj*

is·land *n* : body of land surrounded by water — **is·land·er** *n*

isle *n* : small island

iso·late *vb* : place or keep by itself — **iso·la·tion** *n*

isos·ce·les *adj* : having 2 equal sides

is·sue *vb* **1** : go, come, or flow out **2** : descend from a specified ancestor **3** : emanate or result **4** : put forth or distribute officially ∼ *n* **1** : action of issuing **2** : offspring **3** : result **4** : point of controversy **5** : act of giving out or printing **6** : quantity given out or printed — **is·su·ance** *n* — **is·su·er** *n*

it *pron* **1** : that one — used of a lifeless thing or an abstract entity **2** — used as an anticipatory subject or object ∼ *n* : player who tries to catch others (as in a game of tag)

itch *n* **1** : uneasy irritating skin sensation **2** : skin disorder **3** : persistent desire — **itch** *vb* — **itchy** *adj*

item *n* **1** : particular in a list, account, or series **2** : piece of news — **item·iza·tion** *n* — **item·ize** *vb*

itin·er·ary *n* : route or outline of a journey

its *adj* : relating to it

it·self *pron* : it — used reflexively or for emphasis

ivo·ry *n* **1** : hard creamy-white material of elephants' tusks **2** : pale yellow color

ivy *n* : trailing woody vine with evergreen leaves

J

j *n* : 10th letter of the alphabet

jab *vb* : thrust quickly or abruptly ∼ *n* : short straight punch

jab·ber *vb* : talk rapidly or unintelligibly — **jabber** *n*

jack *n* **1** : mechanical device to raise a heavy body **2** : small flag **3** : small 6-pointed metal object used in a game (**jacks**) **4** : electrical socket ∼ *vb* **1** : raise with a jack **2** : increase

jack·ass *n* **1** : male ass **2** : stupid person

jack·et *n* : garment for the upper body

jack·ham·mer *n* : pneumatic tool for drilling

jack·knife *n* **jack·knives** : pocketknife ∼ *vb* : fold like a jackknife

jack–o'–lan·tern *n* : lantern made of a carved pumpkin

jack·pot *n* : sum of money won

jade *n* : usu. green gemstone

jad·ed *adj* : dulled or bored by having too much

jag·ged *adj* : sharply notched

jail *n* : prison — **jail** *vb* — **jail·break** *n* — **jailer, jail·or** *n*

ja·la·pe·ño *n* : Mexican hot pepper

jam *vb* **1** : press into a tight position **2** : cause to become wedged and unworkable ∼ *n* **1** : crowded mass that blocks or impedes **2** : difficult situation **3** : thick sweet food made of cooked fruit

jan·gle *vb* : make a harsh ringing sound — **jan·gle** *n*

jan·i·tor *n* : person who has the care of a building — **jan·i·to·ri·al** *adj*

Jan·u·ary *n* : 1st month of the year having 31 days

¹jar *vb* **1** : have a harsh or disagreeable effect **2** : vibrate or shake ∼ *n* **1** : jolt **2** : painful effect

²jar *n* : wide-mouthed container

jar·gon *n* : special vocabulary of a group

jaw *n* **1** : either of the bony or cartilaginous structures that support the mouth **2** : one of 2 movable parts for holding or crushing ∼ *vb* : talk indignantly or at length — **jaw·bone** *n* — **jawed** *adj*

jay *n* : noisy brightly colored bird

jay·walk *vb* : cross a street carelessly — **jay·walk·er** *n*

jazz *vb* : enliven ∼ *n* **1** : kind of American music involving improvisation **2** : empty talk — **jazzy** *adj*

jeal·ous *adj* : suspicious of a rival or of one believed to enjoy an advantage — **jeal·ous·ly** *adv* — **jeal·ou·sy** *n*

jeans *n pl* : pants made of durable twilled cotton cloth

jeep *n* : 4-wheel army vehicle

jeer *vb* **1** : speak or cry out in derision **2** : ridicule ∼ *n* : taunt

Je·ho·vah *n* : God

jell *vb* **1** : come to the consistency of jelly **2** : take shape

jel·ly *n* : a substance (as food) with a soft somewhat elastic consistency — **jelly** *vb*

jel·ly·fish *n* : sea animal with a saucer-shaped jellylike body

jeop·ar·dize *vb* : exposure to death, loss, or injury — **jeop·ar·dy** *n*

jerk *vb* **1** : give a sharp quick push, pull, or twist **2** : move in short abrupt motions ∼ *n* **1** : short quick pull or twist **2** : stupid or foolish person — **jerk·i·ly** *adv* — **jerky** *adj*

jest *n* : witty remark — **jest** *vb*

jest·er *n* : one employed to entertain a court

jet *vb* **1** : spout or emit in a stream **2** : travel by jet ∼ *n* **1** : forceful rush of fluid through a narrow opening **2** : jet-propelled airplane

jet–propelled *adj* : driven by an engine (**jet engine**) that produces propulsion (**jet propulsion**) by the rearward discharge of a jet of fluid

Jew *n* : one whose religion is Judaism — **Jew·ish** *adj*

jew·el *n* **1** : ornament of precious metal **2** : gem ∼ *vb* : adorn with jewels — **jew·el·er, jew·el·ler** *n* — **jew·el·ry** *n*

jibe *vb* : be in agreement

jif·fy *n* : short time

jig·gle *vb* : move with quick little jerks — **jig·gle** *n*

jilt *vb* : drop (a lover) without apparent feelings

jim·my *n* : small crowbar ∼ *vb* : pry open

jin·gle *vb* : make a light tinkling sound ∼ *n* **1** : light tinkling sound **2** : short verse or song

jinx *n* : one that brings bad luck — **jinx** *vb*

jit·ters *n pl* : extreme nervousness — **jit·tery** *adj*

job *n* **1** : something that has to be done **2** : regular employment — **job·hold·er** n — **job·less** adj

jock·ey n : one who rides a horse in a race ∼ vb : manipulate or maneuver adroitly

jog vb **1** : give a slight shake or push to **2** : run or ride at a slow pace ∼ n **1** : slight shake **2** : slow pace — **jog·ger** n

join vb **1** : come or bring together **2** : become a member of — **join·er** n

joint n **1** : point of contact between bones **2** : place where 2 parts connect **3** : often disreputable place ∼ adj : common to 2 or more — **joint·ed** adj — **joint·ly** adv

joke n : something said or done to provoke laughter ∼ vb : make jokes — **jok·er** n — **jok·ing·ly** adv

jol·ly adj : full of high spirits — **jol·li·ty** n

jolt vb **1** : move with a sudden jerky motion **2** : give a jolt to ∼ n **1** : abrupt jerky blow or movement **2** : sudden shock — **jolt·er** n

jos·tle vb : push or shove

jot n : least bit ∼ vb : write briefly and hurriedly

jour·nal n **1** : brief account of daily events **2** : periodical (as a newspaper) — **jour·nal·ism** n — **jour·nal·ist** n — **jour·nal·is·tic** adj

jour·ney n : a going from one place to another ∼ vb : make a journey

joy n **1** : feeling of happiness **2** : source of happiness — **joy** vb — **joy·ful** adj — **joy·ful·ly** adv — **joy·less** adj — **joy·ous** adj — **joy·ous·ly** adv — **joy·ous·ness** n

joy·ride n : reckless ride for pleasure — **joy·rid·er** n — **joy·rid·ing** n

ju·bi·lant adj : expressing great joy — **ju·bi·lant·ly** adv — **ju·bi·la·tion** n

Ju·da·ism n : religion developed among the ancient Hebrews — **Ju·da·ic** adj

judge vb **1** : form an opinion **2** : decide as a judge ∼ n **1** : public official authorized to decide questions brought before a court **2** : one who gives an authoritative opinion — **judg·ment, judge·ment** n — **judg·men·tal** adj — **judg·men·tal·ly** adv — **judge·ship** n

ju·di·cial adj : relating to the judiciary — **ju·di·cial·ly** adv

ju·di·cia·ry n : system of courts of law or the judges of them — **ju·di·cial** adj — **ju·di·cial·ly** adv — **ju·di·cia·ry** adj

ju·di·cious adj : having or characterized by sound judgment — **ju·di·cious·ly** adv

ju·do n : form of wrestling — **ju·do·ist** n

jug n : large deep container with a narrow mouth and a handle

jug·gle vb **1** : keep several objects in motion in the air at the same time **2** : manipulate for an often tricky purpose — **jug·gler** n

juice n **1** : extractable fluid contents of cells or tissues **2** : electricity — **juic·er** n — **juic·i·ly** adv — **juic·i·ness** n — **juicy** adj

ju·jube n : gummy candy

juke·box n : coin-operated machine for playing music recordings

Ju·ly n : 7th month of the year having 31 days

jum·ble vb : mix in a confused mass — **jumble** n

jum·bo n : very large version — **jum·bo** adj

jump vb **1** : rise into or through the air esp. by muscular effort **2** : pass over **3** : give a start **4** : rise or increase sharply ∼ n **1** : a jumping **2** : sharp sudden increase **3** : initial advantage

[1]**jump·er** n : one that jumps

[2]**jumper** n : sleeveless one-piece dress

jumpy adj : nervous or jittery

junc·tion n **1** : a joining **2** : place or point of meeting

June n : 6th month of the year having 30 days

jun·gle n : thick tangled mass of tropical vegetation

ju·nior n **1** : person who is younger or of lower rank than another **2** : student in the next-to-last year ∼ adj : younger or lower in rank

junk n **1** : discarded articles **2** : shoddy product ∼ vb : discard or scrap — **junky** adj

ju·ris·dic·tion n **1** : right or authority to interpret and apply the law **2** : limits within which authority may be exercised — **ju·ris·dic·tion·al** adj

ju·ry n : body of persons sworn to give a verdict on a matter — **ju·ror** n

just adj **1** : reasonable **2** : correct or proper **3** : morally or legally right **4** : deserved ∼ adv **1** : exactly **2** : very recently **3** : barely **4** : only **5** : quite **6** : possibly — **just·ly** adv — **just·ness** n

jus·tice n **1** : administration of what is just **2** : judge **3** : administration of law **4** : fairness

jus·ti·fy vb : prove to be just, right, or reasonable — **jus·ti·fi·able** adj — **jus·ti·fi·ca·tion** n

ju·ve·nile adj : relating to children or young people ∼ n : young person

K

k *n* : 11th letter of the alphabet

ka·lei·do·scope *n* : device containing loose bits of colored material reflecting in many patterns — **ka·lei·do·scop·ic** *adj* — **ka·lei·do·scop·i·cal·ly** *adv*

kan·ga·roo *n* : large leaping Australian mammal

kar·a·o·ke *n* : device that plays accompaniments for singers

kar·at *n* : unit of gold content

ka·ra·te *n* : art of self-defense by crippling kicks and punches

keen *adj* **1** : sharp **2** : severe **3** : enthusiastic **4** : mentally alert — **keen·ly** *adv* — **keen·ness** *n*

keep *vb* (**kept; kept**) **1** : perform **2** : guard **3** : maintain **4** : retain in one's possession **5** : detain **6** : continue in good condition **7** : refrain ⁓ *n* **1** : fortress **2** : means by which one is kept — **keep·er** *n*

keep·sake *n* : souvenir

keg *n* : small cask or barrel

ken·nel *n* : dog shelter — **ken·nel** *vb*

ker·nel *n* **1** : inner softer part of a seed or nut **2** : whole seed of a cereal **3** : central part

ketch·up *n* : spicy tomato sauce

ket·tle *n* : vessel for boiling liquids

key *n* **1** : usu. metal piece to open a lock **2** : explanation **3** : lever pressed by a finger in playing an instrument or operating a machine **4** : leading individual or principle **5** : system of musical tones or pitch ⁓ *vb* : cause to be in tune ⁓ *adj* : basic — **key·hole** *n* — **key up** *vb* : make nervous

key·board *n* : arrangement of keys

kha·ki *n* : light yellowish brown color

kick *vb* **1** : strike out or hit with the foot **2** : object strongly ⁓ *n* : thrust with the foot **2** : stimulating effect — **kick·er** *n*

kid *n* **1** : young goat **2** : child ⁓ *vb* **1** : deceive as a joke **2** : tease — **kid·der** *n* — **kid·ding·ly** *adv*

kid·nap *vb* : carry a person away by illegal force — **kid·nap·per, kid·nap·er** *n*

kid·ney *n* : either of a pair of organs that excrete urine

kill *vb* **1** : deprive of life **2** : finish **3** : use up (time) ⁓ *n* : act of killing — **kill·er** *n*

ki·lo *n* : kilogram

ki·lo·gram *n* : metric unit of weight equal to 2.2 pounds

ki·lo·hertz *n* : 1000 hertz

ki·lo·me·ter *n* : 1000 meters

kilo·watt *n* : 1000 watts

kin *n* **1** : one's relatives **2** : kinsman

kind *n* **1** : essential quality **2** : group with common traits **3** : variety ⁓ *adj* **1** : of a sympathetic nature **2** : arising from sympathy — **kind·heart·ed** *adj* — **kind·ness** *n*

kin·der·gar·ten *n* : class for young children — **kin·der·gart·ner** *n*

kin·dle *vb* **1** : set on fire or start burning **2** : stir up — **kin·dling** *n*

kind·ly *adj* : of a sympathetic nature ⁓ *adv* **1** : sympathetically **2** : courteously — **kind·li·ness** *n*

kin·folk, kinfolks *n pl* : kin — **kins·man** *n* — **kins·wom·an** *n*

king *n* : male sovereign — **king·dom** *n* — **king·less** *adj* — **king·ly** *adj* — **king·ship** *n*

kink *n* **1** : short tight twist or curl **2** : cramp — **kinky** *adj*

kin·ship *n* : relationship

kiss *vb* **1** : touch with the lips as a mark of affection — **kiss** *n*

kit *n* : set of articles (as tools or parts)

kitch·en *n* : room with cooking facilities

kite *n* **1** : small hawk **2** : covered framework flown at the end of a string

kit·ten *n* : young cat — **kit·ten·ish** *adj*

¹kit·ty *n* : kitten

²kitty *n* : fund or pool (as in a card game)

kit·ty–cor·ner, kit·ty–cor·nered *var of* CATERCORNER

klep·to·ma·nia *n* : neurotic impulse to steal — **klep·to·ma·ni·ac** *n*

knack *n* **1** : clever way of doing something **2** : natural aptitude

knead *vb* **1** : work and press with the hands **2** : massage — **knead·er** *n*

knee *n* : joint in the middle part of the leg — **knee·cap** *n* — **kneed** *adj*

kneel *vb* (**knelt; knelt**) : rest on one's knees

knew *past of* KNOW

knick·knack *n* : small decorative object

knife *n* **knives** : sharp blade with a handle ⁓ *vb* : stab or cut with a knife

knight *n* **1** : mounted warrior of feudal times

2 : man honored by a sovereign ∼ *vb* : make a knight of — **knight·hood** *n* — **knight·ly** *adv*

knit *vb* **1** : link firmly or closely **2** : form a fabric by interlacing yarn or thread ∼ *n* : knitted garment — **knit·ter** *n*

knob *n* : rounded protuberance or handle — **knobbed** *adj* — **knob·by** *adj*

knock *vb* **1** : strike with a sharp blow **2** : collide **3** : find fault with ∼ *n* : sharp blow — **knock·er** *n* — **knock out** *vb* : make unconscious

knot *n* **1** : interlacing (as of string) that forms a lump **2** : base of a woody branch in the stem **3** : group **4** : one nautical mile per hour ∼ *vb* : tie in or with a knot — **knot·ty** *adj*

know *vb* **knew; known 1** : perceive directly or understand **2** : be familiar with — **know·able** *adj* — **know·er** *n*

know·ing *adj* : shrewdly and keenly alert — **know·ing·ly** *adv*

knowl·edge *n* **1** : understanding gained by experience **2** : range of information — **knowl·edge·able** *adj*

knuck·le *n* : rounded knob at a finger joint

Ko·ran *n* : book of Islam containing revelations made to Muhammad by Allah

ko·sher *adj* : ritually fit for use according to Jewish law

Kwan·zaa, Kwan·za *n* : African-American festival held from December 26 to January 1

L

l *n* : 12th letter of the alphabet

lab *n* : laboratory

la·bel *n* **1** : identification slip **2** : identifying word or phrase ∼ *vb* : put a label on

la·bor *n* **1** : physical or mental effort **2** : physical efforts of childbirth **3** : task **4** : people who work manually ∼ *vb* : work esp. with great effort — **la·bor·er** *n* — **la·bo·ri·ous** *adj* — **la·bo·ri·ous·ly** *adv*

lab·o·ra·to·ry *n* : place for experimental testing

Labor Day *n* : 1st Monday in September observed as a legal holiday in recognition of working people

lab·y·rinth *n* : maze — **lab·y·rin·thine** *adj*

lace *n* **1** : cord or string for tying **2** : fine net usu. figured fabric ∼ *vb* **1** : tie **2** : adorn with lace — **lacy** *adj*

lac·er·ate *vb* : tear roughly — **lac·er·a·tion** *n*

lack *vb* : be missing or deficient in ∼ *n* : deficiency

lack·lus·ter *adj* : dull

lac·tate *vb* : secrete milk — **lac·ta·tion** *n*

lad *n* : boy

lad·der *n* : device with steps or rungs for climbing

la·dle *n* : spoon with a deep bowl — **ladle** *vb*

la·dy *n* **1** : woman of rank or authority **2** : woman

lag *vb* : fail to keep up ∼ *n* **1** : a falling behind **2** : interval — **lag·gard** *n* — **lag·gard·ly** *adv or adj*

la·goon *n* : shallow sound, channel, or pond near or connecting with a larger body of water

laid *past of* LAY

lain *past part of* LIE

lair *n* : den

la·ity *n* : people of a religious faith who are not clergy members

lake *n* : inland body of water

la·ma *n* : Buddhist monk

lamb *n* : young sheep or its flesh used as food

lam·baste, lam·bast *vb* **1** : beat **2** : censure

lame *adj* **1** : having a limb disabled **2** : weak ∼ *vb* : make lame — **lame·ly** *adv* — **lame·ness** *n*

la·ment *vb* **1** : mourn **2** : express sorrow for ∼ *n* **1** : mourning **2** : complaint — **lam·en·ta·ble** *adj* — **lam·en·ta·bly** *adv* — **lam·en·ta·tion** *n*

lam·i·nat·ed *adj* : made of thin layers of material — **lam·i·nate** *vb* — **lam·i·nate** *n or adj* — **lam·i·na·tion** *n*

lamp *n* : device for producing light or heat

lam·poon *n* : satire — **lam·poon** *vb*

lance *n* : spear ∼ *vb* : pierce or open with a lancet

land *n* **1** : solid part of the surface of the earth **2** : country ∼ *vb* **1** : go ashore **2** : catch or gain **3** : touch the ground or a surface — **land·less** *adj* — **land·own·er** *n*

land·fill *n* : dump

land·ing *n* **1** : action of one that lands **2** : place for loading passengers and cargo **3** : level part of a staircase

land·lord *n* : owner of property

land·mark *n* **1** : object that marks a boundary

or serves as a guide **2** : event that marks a turning point

land·scape *n* : view of natural scenery ∼ *vb* : beautify a piece of land (as by decorative planting)

land·slide *n* **1** : slipping down of a mass of earth **2** : overwhelming victory

lane *n* : narrow way

lan·guage *n* : words and the methods of combining them for communication

lanky *adj* : tall and thin

lan·tern *n* : enclosed portable light

¹lap *n* **1** : front part of the lower trunk and thighs of a seated person **2** : overlapping part **3** : one complete circuit completing a course (as around a track or pool) ∼ *vb* : fold over

²lap *vb* **1** : scoop up with the tongue **2** : splash gently

la·pel *n* : fold of the front of a coat

lapse *n* **1** : slight error **2** : termination of a right or privilege **3** : interval ∼ *vb* **1** : slip **2** : become less **3** : cease

lap·top *adj* : of a size that may be used on one's lap

lar·ce·ny *n* : theft — **lar·ce·nous** *adj*

large *adj* : greater than average — **large·ly** *adv* — **large·ness** *n*

lar·i·at *n* : lasso

lar·va *n* : wormlike form of an insect — **lar·val** *adj*

lar·yn·gi·tis *n* : inflammation of the upper part of the throat

la·sa·gna *n* : flat noodles baked usu. with tomato sauce, meat, and cheese

la·ser *n* : device that produces an intense light beam

lash *vb* : whip ∼ *n* **1** : stroke esp. of a whip **2** : eyelash

lass *n* : girl

lass·ie *n* : girl

las·so *n* : rope with a noose for catching livestock — **las·so** *vb*

¹last *vb* : continue in existence or operation

²last *adj* **1** : final **2** : previous **3** : least likely ∼ *adv* **1** : at the end **2** : most recently **3** : in conclusion ∼ *n* : something that is last — **last·ly** *adv* — **at last** : finally

latch *vb* : catch or get hold ∼ *n* : catch that holds a door closed

late *adj* **1** : coming or staying after the proper time **2** : advanced toward the end **3** : recently deceased **4** : recent — **late** *adv* — **late·com·er** *n* — **late·ly** *adv* — **late·ness** *n*

la·tent *adj* : present but not visible or expressed — **la·ten·cy** *n*

lat·er *adv* : at some time after the present time

lat·er·al *adj* : on or toward the side — **lat·er·al·ly** *adv*

la·tex *n* : emulsion of synthetic rubber or plastic

lath·er *n* : foam ∼ *vb* : form or spread lather

lat·i·tude *n* **1** : distance north or south from the earth's equator **2** : freedom of action

lat·ter *adj* **1** : more recent **2** : being the second of 2 — **lat·ter·ly** *adv*

lat·tice *n* : framework of crossed strips

laud *vb or n* : praise — **laud·able** *adj* — **laud·ably** *adv*

laugh *vb* : show mirth, joy, or scorn with a smile and explosive sound — **laugh** *n* — **laugh·able** *adj* — **laugh·ing·ly** *adv* — **laugh·ter** *n*

laugh·ing·stock *n* : object of ridicule

launch *vb* **1** : hurl or send off **2** : set afloat **3** : start — **launch** *n* — **launch·er** *n*

laun·der *vb* : wash or iron fabrics — **laun·der·er** *n* — **laun·dress** *n* — **laun·dry** *n*

lau·rel *n* **1** : small evergreen tree **2** : honor

la·va *n* : volcanic molten rock

lav·a·to·ry *n* : bathroom

lav·ish *adj* : expended profusely ∼ *vb* : expend or give freely — **lav·ish·ly** *adv* — **lav·ish·ness** *n*

law *n* **1** : established rule of conduct **2** : body of such rules **3** : principle of construction or procedure **4** : rule stating uniform behavior under uniform conditions **5** : lawyer's profession — **law·break·er** *n* — **law·ful** *adj* — **law·ful·ly** *adv* — **law·giv·er** *n* — **law·less** *adj* — **law·less·ly** *adv* — **law·less·ness** *n* — **law·mak·er** *n* — **law·man** *n* — **law·suit** *n*

lawn *n* : grass-covered yard

law·yer *n* : legal practitioner

lax *adj* : not strict or tense — **lax·i·ty** *n* — **lax·ly** *adv*

¹lay *vb* **laid; laid 1** : put or set down **2** : produce eggs **3** : bet **4** : impose as a duty or burden **5** : put forward ∼ *n* : way something lies or is laid

²lay *past of* LIE

³lay *adj* : of the laity — **lay·man** *n* — **lay·wom·an** *n*

lay·er *n* **1** : one that lays **2** : one thickness over or under another

lay·off *n* : temporary dismissal of a worker

lay·out *n* : arrangement

la·zy *adj* : disliking activity or exertion — **la·zi·ly** *adv* — **la·zi·ness** *n*

lead led; led *vb* **1** : guide on a way **2** : direct the activity of **3** : go at the head of **4** : tend to a definite result ~ *n* : position in front — **lead·er** *n* — **lead·er·less** *adj* — **lead·er·ship** *n*

leaf *n* (**leaves**) **1** : green outgrowth of a plant stem **2** : leaflike thing ~ *vb* **1** : produce leaves **2** : turn book pages — **leaf·age** *n* — **leafed** *adj* — **leaf·less** *adj* — **leafy** *adj* — **leaved** *adj*

leaf·let *n* : pamphlet

league *n* : association for a common purpose — **league** *vb* — **leagu·er** *n*

leak *vb* **1** : enter or escape through a leak **2** : become or make known ~ *n* : opening that accidentally admits or lets out a substance — **leak·age** *n* — **leaky** *adj*

¹lean *vb* **1** : bend from a vertical position **2** : rely on for support **3** : incline in opinion — **lean** *n*

²lean *adj* **1** : lacking in flesh **2** : lacking richness — **lean·ness** *n*

leap *vb* : jump — **leap** *n*

leap year *n* : 366-day year

learn *vb* **1** : gain understanding or skill by study or experience **2** : memorize **3** : find out — **learn·er** *n*

learn·ed *adj* : having great learning — **learn·ed·ness** *n*

learn·ing *n* : knowledge

lease *n* : contract transferring real estate for a term and usu. for rent ~ *vb* : grant by or hold under a lease

leash *n* : line to hold an animal — **leash** *vb*

least *adj* **1** : lowest in importance or position **2** : smallest **3** : scantiest ~ *n* : one that is least ~ *adv* : in the smallest or lowest degree

leath·er *n* : dressed animal skin — **leath·ern** *adj* — **leath·ery** *adj*

¹leave *vb* left; left **1** : bequeath **2** : allow or cause to remain **3** : have as a remainder **4** : go away ~ *n* **1** : permission **2** : authorized absence **3** : departure

²leave *vb* : produce leaves

leaves *pl of* LEAF

lech·ery *n* : inordinate indulgence in sex — **lech·er** *n* — **lech·er·ous** *adj* — **lech·er·ous·ly** *adv* — **lech·er·ous·ness** *n*

lec·ture *n* **1** : instructive talk **2** : reprimand — **lec·ture** *vb* — **lec·tur·er** *n* — **lec·ture·ship** *n*

led *past of* LEAD

ledge *n* : shelflike projection

leery *adj* : suspicious or wary

lee·ward *adj* : situated away from the wind ~ *n* : the lee side

lee·way *n* : allowable margin

¹left *adj* : on the same side of the body as the heart ~ *n* : left hand — **left** *adv*

²left *past of* LEAVE

leg *n* **1** : limb of an animal that supports the body **2** : something like a leg **3** : clothing to cover the leg ~ *vb* : walk or run — **leg·ged** *adj* — **leg·less** *adj*

leg·a·cy *n* : inheritance

le·gal *adj* **1** : relating to law or lawyers **2** : lawful — **le·gal·is·tic** *adj* — **le·gal·i·ty** *n* — **le·gal·ize** *vb* — **le·gal·ly** *adv*

leg·end *n* **1** : story handed down from the past **2** : inscription **3** : explanation of map symbols — **leg·end·ary** *adj*

leg·i·ble *adj* : capable of being read — **leg·i·bil·i·ty** *n* — **leg·i·bly** *adv*

le·gion *n* **1** : large army unit **2** : multitude **3** : association of former servicemen — **le·gion·ary** *n* — **le·gion·naire** *n*

leg·is·late *vb* : enact or bring about with laws — **leg·is·la·tion** *n* — **leg·is·la·tive** *adj* — **leg·is·la·tor** *n* — **leg·is·la·ture** *n*

le·git·i·mate *adj* **1** : lawfully begotten **2** : genuine **3** : conforming with law or accepted standards — **le·git·i·ma·cy** *n* — **le·git·i·mate·ly** *adv* — **le·git·i·mize** *vb*

lei·sure *n* **1** : free time **2** : ease **3** : convenience — **lei·sure·ly** *adj or adv*

lem·on *n* : yellow citrus fruit — **lem·on·ade** *n* — **lem·ony** *adj*

lend *vb* (**lent**; **lent**) **1** : give for temporary use **2** : furnish — **lend·er** *n*

length *n* **1** : longest dimension **2** : duration in time **3** : piece to be joined to others — **length·en** *vb* — **length·wise** *adv or adj* — **lengthy** *adj*

le·nient *adj* : of mild and tolerant disposition or effect — **le·ni·en·cy** *n* — **le·ni·ent·ly** *adv*

lens *n* **1** : curved piece for forming an image in an optical instrument **2** : transparent body in the eye that focuses light rays

lent *past of* LEND

Lent *n* : 40-day period of penitence and fasting from Ash Wednesday to Easter — **Lent·en** *adj*

leop·ard *n* : large tawny black-spotted cat

less *adj* **1** : fewer **2** : of lower rank, degree, or importance **3** : smaller ~ *adv* : to a lesser degree $\sim$ n, pl **less** : smaller portion $\sim$ prep : minus — **less·en** vb

less·er adj : of less size, quality, or significance

les·son n **1** : reading or exercise to be studied by a pupil **2** : something learned

let vb **let; let 1** : cause to **2** : rent **3** : permit

le·thal adj : deadly — **le·thal·ly** adv

let·ter n **1** : unit of an alphabet **2** : written or printed communication **3** pl : literature or learning **4** : literal meaning $\sim$ vb : mark with letters — **let·ter·er** n

let·tuce n : garden plant with crisp leaves

lev·ee n : embankment to prevent flooding

lev·el n **1** : device for establishing a flat surface **2** : horizontal surface **3** : position in a scale $\sim$ vb **1** : make flat or level **2** : aim **3** : tear down $\sim$ adj **1** : having an even surface **2** : of the same height or rank — **lev·el·er** n — **lev·el·ly** adv — **lev·el·ness** n

le·ver n : bar for prying or dislodging something — **le·ver·age** n

li·a·ble adj **1** : legally obligated **2** : probable **3** : likely to be affected — **li·a·bil·i·ty** n

li·ar n : one who lies

li·bel n : action, crime, or an instance of injuring a person's reputation esp. by something written $\sim$ vb : make or publish a libel — **li·bel·er** n — **li·bel·ist** n — **li·bel·ous, li·bel·lous** adj

lib·er·al adj : not stingy, narrow, or conservative — **liberal** n — **lib·er·al·ism** n — **lib·er·al·i·ty** n — **lib·er·al·ize** vb — **lib·er·al·ly** adv

lib·er·ate vb : set free — **lib·er·a·tion** n — **lib·er·a·tor** n

lib·er·ty n **1** : quality or state of being free **2** : action going beyond normal limits

li·brary n **1** : place where books are kept for use **2** : collection of books — **li·brar·i·an** n

lice pl of LOUSE

li·cense, li·cence n **1** : legal permission to engage in some activity **2** : document or tag providing proof of a license **3** : irresponsible use of freedom — **license** vb — **li·cens·ee** n

lick vb **1** : draw the tongue over **2** : beat $\sim$ n **1** : stroke of the tongue **2** : small amount

lic·o·rice n : dried root of a European legume or candy flavored by it

lid n **1** : movable cover **2** : eyelid

¹lie vb **lay; lain 1** : be in, rest in, or assume a horizontal position **2** : occupy a certain relative position $\sim$ n : position in which something lies

²lie vb : tell a lie $\sim$ n : untrue statement

life n (**lives**) **1** : quality that distinguishes a vital and functional being from a dead body or inanimate matter **2** : physical and mental experiences of an individual **3** : biography **4** : period of existence **5** : way of living **6** : liveliness — **life·guard** n or vb — **life·less** adj — **life·like** adj — **life·time** n

life·blood n : basic source of strength and vitality

life·sav·ing n : art or practice of saving lives — **life·sav·er** n

lift vb **1** : move upward or cause to move upward **2** : put an end to — **lift** n — **lift·er** n

lift-off n : vertical takeoff by a rocket

¹light n **1** : radiation that makes vision possible **2** : daylight **3** : source of light **4** : public knowledge **5** : aspect **6** : celebrity **7** : flame for lighting $\sim$ adj **1** : bright **2** : weak in color $\sim$ vb **1** : make or become light **2** : cause to burn — **light·en** vb — **light·er** n — **light·ness** n — **light·proof** adj

²light adj : not heavy, serious, or abundant — **light** adv — **light·en** vb — **light·ly** adv — **light·ness** n — **light·weight** adj

light·heart·ed adj : free from worry — **light·heart·ed·ly** adv — **light·heart·ed·ness** n

light·ning n : flashing discharge of atmospheric electricity

¹like vb **1** : enjoy **2** : desire $\sim$ n : preference — **lik·able, like·able** adj

²like adj : similar $\sim$ prep **1** : similar or similarly to **2** : typical of **3** : such as $\sim$ n : counterpart $\sim$ conj : as or as if — **like·ness** n — **like·wise** adv

like·ly adj **1** : probable **2** : believable $\sim$ adv : in all probability — **like·li·hood** n

lik·en vb : compare

lily n : tall bulbous herb with funnel-shaped flowers

limb n **1** : projecting appendage used in moving or grasping **2** : tree branch — **limb·less** adj

lim·ber adj : supple or agile $\sim$ vb : make or become limber

lime n : small green lemonlike citrus fruit — **lime·ade** n

lim·er·ick n : light poem of 5 lines

lim·it n **1** : boundary **2** : something that restrains or confines $\sim$ vb : set limits on — **lim·i·ta·tion** n — **lim·it·less** adj

lim·ou·sine n : large luxurious sedan

limp vb : walk lamely $\sim$ n : limping movement

or gait $\sim$ *adj* : lacking firmness and body —
limp·ly *adv* — **limp·ness** *n*

¹**line** *vb* : cover the inner surface of — **lin·ing** *n*

²**line** *n* **1** : cord, rope, or wire **2** : row or something like a row **3** : note **4** : course of action or thought **5** : state of agreement **6** : occupation **7** : limit **8** : transportation system **9** : long narrow mark $\sim$ *vb* **1** : mark with a line **2** : place in a line **3** : form a line — **lin·er** *n*

lin·e·ar *adj* **1** : straight **2** : long and narrow

lin·en *n* **1** : cloth or thread made of flax **2** : household articles made of linen cloth

lin·ger *vb* : be slow to leave or act — **lin·ger·er** *n*

lin·guist *n* **1** : person skilled in speech or languages **2** : student of language — **lin·guis·tic** *adj* — **lin·guis·tics** *n pl*

link *n* **1** : connecting structure (as a ring of a chain) **2** : bond — **link** *vb* — **link·age** *n* — **link·er** *n*

lint *n* : fine fluff or loose short fibers from fabric

li·on *n* : large cat of Africa and Asia — **li·on·ess** *n*

lip *n* **1** : either of the 2 fleshy folds surrounding the mouth **2** : edge of something hollow — **lipped** *adj* — **lip·read·ing** *n*

lip·stick *n* : stick of cosmetic to color lips

liq·ue·fy *vb* : make or become liquid — **liq·ue·fi·er** *n*

liq·uid *adj* **1** : flowing freely like water **2** : neither solid nor gaseous **3** : of or convertible to cash — **liquid** *n* — **li·quid·i·ty** *n*

liq·ui·date *vb* **1** : pay off **2** : dispose of — **liq·ui·da·tion** *n*

li·quor *n* : usu. distilled liquid containing alcohol

lisp *vb* : pronounce *s* and *z* imperfectly — **lisp** *n*

list *n* **1** : series of names or items $\sim$ *vb* **1** : make a list of **2** : put on a list

lis·ten *vb* **1** : pay attention in order to hear **2** : heed — **lis·ten·er** *n*

list·less *adj* : having no desire to act — **list·less·ly** *adv* — **list·less·ness** *n*

lit *past of* LIGHT

li·ter *n* : unit of liquid measure equal to about 1.06 quarts

lit·er·al *adj* : being exactly as stated — **lit·er·al·ly** *adv*

lit·er·ary *adj* : relating to literature

lit·er·ate *adj* : able to read and write — **lit·er·a·cy** *n*

lit·er·a·ture *n* : writings of enduring interest

lit·i·gate *vb* : carry on a lawsuit — **lit·i·gant** *n* — **lit·i·ga·tion** *n* — **li·ti·gious** *adj* — **li·ti·gious·ness** *n*

lit·ter *n* **1** : animal offspring of one birth **2** : stretcher **3** : rubbish **4** : material to absorb animal waste $\sim$ *vb* **1** : give birth to young **2** : strew with litter

lit·tle *adj* **lit·tler/less/less·er; lit·tlest/least** **1** : not big **2** : not much **3** : not important $\sim$ *adv* **1** : slightly **2** : not often $\sim$ *n* : small amount — **lit·tle·ness** *n*

¹**live** *vb* **1** : be alive **2** : conduct one's life **3** : nourish oneself **4** : reside — **liv·able** *adj* — **liv·a·bil·i·ty** *n*

²**live** *adj* **1** : having life **2** : burning **3** : connected to electric power **4** : not exploded **5** : of continuing interest **6** : involving the actual presence of real people

live·li·hood *n* : means of supporting one's life

live·ly *adj* : full of life and vigor — **live·li·ness** *n*

liv·er *n* : organ that secretes bile

lives *pl of* LIFE

liv·ing *adj* : having life $\sim$ *n* : livelihood

load *n* **1** : cargo **2** : supported weight **3** : burden **4** : a large quantity — usu. pl. $\sim$ *vb* **1** : put a load on **2** : burden **3** : put ammunition in

¹**loaf** *n* : mass of bread

²**loaf** *vb* : waste time — **loaf·er** *n*

loan *n* **1** : money borrowed at interest **2** : something lent temporarily **3** : grant of use $\sim$ *vb* : lend

loath·ing *n* : extreme disgust

lob *vb* : throw or hit in a high arc — **lob** *n*

lob·by *n* **1** : public waiting room at the entrance of a building **2** : persons lobbying $\sim$ *vb* : try to influence legislators — **lob·by·ist** *n*

lob·ster *n* : marine crustacean with 2 large pincerlike claws

lo·cal *adj* : confined to or serving a limited area — **lo·cal** *n* — **lo·cal·i·za·tion** *n* — **lo·cal·ize** *vb* — **lo·cal·ly** *adv*

lo·cale *n* : setting for an event — **lo·cal·i·ty** *n*

lo·cate *vb* **1** : settle **2** : find a site for **3** : discover the place of — **lo·ca·tion** *n*

lock *n* **1** : fastener using a bolt **2** : enclosure in a canal to raise or lower boats $\sim$ *vb* **1** : make fast with a lock **2** : confine **3** : interlock

lock·er *n* : storage compartment

lo·co·mo·tion *n* : power of moving — **lo·co·mo·tive** *adj*

lodge *vb* **1** : provide quarters for **2** : come to rest **3** : file ～ *n* **1** : special house (as for hunters) **2** : animal's den **3** : branch of a fraternal organization — **lodg·er** *n* — **lodg·ing** *n* — **lodg·ment, lodge·ment** *n*

loft *n* **1** : attic **2** : upper floor (as of a warehouse)

lofty *adj* **1** : noble **2** : proud **3** : tall or high — **loft·i·ly** *adv* — **loft·i·ness** *n*

log *n* **1** : unshaped timber **2** : daily record of a ship's or plane's progress ～ *vb* **1** : cut (trees) for lumber **2** : enter in a log — **log·ger** *n*

log·ic *n* **1** : science of reasoning **2** : sound reasoning — **log·i·cal** *adj* — **log·i·cal·ly** *adv* — **lo·gi·cian** *n*

lo·gis·tics *n sing or pl* : procurement and movement of people and supplies — **lo·gis·tic** *adj*

loin *n* **1** : part of the body on each side of the spine between the hip and lower ribs **2** *pl* : pubic regions

loi·ter *vb* : remain around a place idly — **loi·ter·er** *n*

lol·li·pop, lol·ly·pop *n* : hard candy on a stick

lone *adj* **1** : alone or isolated **2** : only — **lone·li·ness** *n* — **lone·ly** *adj* — **lon·er** *n*

lone·some *adj* : sad from lack of company — **lone·some·ly** *adv* — **lone·some·ness** *n*

long *adj* **1** : extending far or for a considerable time **2** : having a specified length **3** : tedious **4** : well supplied — used with *on* ～ *adv* : for a long time ～ *n* : long period ～ *vb* : feel a strong desire — **long·ing** *n* — **long·ing·ly** *adv*

lon·gev·i·ty *n* : long life

lon·gi·tude *n* : angular distance east or west from a meridian

look *vb* **1** : see **2** : seem **3** : direct one's attention **4** : face ～ *n* **1** : action of looking **2** : appearance of the face **3** : aspect — **look after** : take care of — **look for 1** : expect **2** : search for

look·out *n* **1** : one who watches **2** : careful watch

¹loom *n* : frame or machine for weaving

²loom *vb* : appear large and indistinct or impressive

loop *n* **1** : doubling of a line that leaves an opening **2** : something like a loop — **loop** *vb*

loop·hole *n* : means of evading

loose *adj* **1** : not fixed tight **2** : not restrained **3** : not dense **4** : slack **5** : not exact ～ *vb* **1**

: release **2** : untie or relax — **loose** *adv* — **loose·ly** *adv* — **loos·en** *vb* — **loose·ness** *n*

loot *n or vb* : plunder — **loot·er** *n*

lop·sid·ed *adj* **1** : leaning to one side **2** : not symmetrical — **lop·sid·ed·ly** *adv* — **lop·sid·ed·ness** *n*

lord *n* **1** : one with authority over others **2** : British nobleman — **lord·ship** *n*

lord·ly *adj* : haughty

lore *n* : traditional knowledge

lose *vb* **lost; lost 1** : have pass from one's possession **2** : be deprived of **3** : waste **4** : be defeated in **5** : fail to keep to or hold **6** : get rid of — **los·er** *n*

loss *n* **1** : something lost **2** *pl* : killed, wounded, or captured soldiers **3** : failure to win

lost *adj* **1** : not used, won, or claimed **2** : unable to find the way

lot *n* **1** : object used in deciding something by chance **2** : share **3** : fate **4** : plot of land **5** : much

lo·tion *n* : liquid to rub on the skin

lot·tery *n* : drawing of lots with prizes going to winners

loud *adj* **1** : high in volume of sound **2** : noisy **3** : obtrusive in color or pattern — **loud** *adv* — **loud·ly** *adv* — **loud·ness** *n* — **loud-speak·er** *n*

lounge *vb* : act or move lazily ～ *n* : room with comfortable furniture

louse *n* **lice** : parasitic wingless usu. flat insect

lousy *adj* **1** : infested with lice **2** : not good — **lous·i·ly** *adv* — **lous·i·ness** *n*

love *n* **1** : strong affection **2** : warm attachment **3** : beloved person ～ *vb* **1** : feel affection for **2** : enjoy greatly — **lov·able** *adj* — **love·less** *adj* — **lov·er** *n* — **lov·ing·ly** *adv*

love·ly *adj* : beautiful — **love·li·ness** *n* — **lovely** *adv*

low *adj* **1** : not high or tall **2** : below normal level **3** : not loud **4** : humble **5** : sad **6** : less than usual **7** : falling short of a standard **8** : unfavorable ～ *n* **1** : something low **2** : automobile gear giving the slowest speed — **low** *adv* — **low·ness** *n*

low·er *vb* **1** : drop **2** : let descend **3** : reduce in amount

low·ly *adj* **1** : humble **2** : low in rank — **low·li·ness** *n*

loy·al *adj* : faithful to a country, cause, or friend — **loy·al·ist** *n* — **loy·al·ly** *adv* — **loy·al·ty** *n*

lu·bri·cate *vb* : apply a lubricant to — **lu·bri·cant** *n* — **lu·bri·ca·tion** *n* — **lu·bri·ca·tor** *n*

lu·cid *adj* 1 : mentally sound 2 : easily understood — **lu·cid·i·ty** *n* — **lu·cid·ly** *adv* — **lu·cid·ness** *n*

luck *n* 1 : chance 2 : good fortune — **luck·i·ly** *adv* — **luck·i·ness** *n* — **luck·less** *adj* — **lucky** *adj*

lu·cra·tive *adj* : profitable — **lu·cra·tive·ly** *adv* — **lu·cra·tive·ness** *n*

lu·di·crous *adj* : comically ridiculous — **lu·di·crous·ly** *adv* — **lu·di·crous·ness** *n*

lug *vb* : drag or carry laboriously

lug·gage *n* : baggage

lull *vb* : make or become quiet or relaxed ∼ *n* : temporary calm

lul·la·by *n* : song to lull children to sleep

lum·ber *n* : timber dressed for use ∼ *vb* : cut logs — **lum·ber·man** *n* — **lum·ber·yard** *n*

lu·mi·nous *adj* : emitting light — **lu·mi·nance** *n* — **lu·mi·nos·i·ty** *n* — **lu·mi·nous·ly** *adv*

lump *n* 1 : mass of irregular shape 2 : abnormal swelling ∼ *vb* : heap together — **lump·ish** *adj* — **lumpy** *adj*

lu·na·cy *n* : state of insanity

lu·nar *adj* : of the moon

lu·na·tic *adj* : insane — **lu·na·tic** *n*

lunch *n* : noon meal ∼ *vb* : eat lunch

lung *n* : breathing organ in the chest — **lunged** *adj*

lunge *n* 1 : sudden thrust 2 : sudden move forward — **lunge** *vb*

lurch *n* : sudden swaying — **lurch** *vb*

lure *n* 1 : something that attracts 2 : artificial fish bait ∼ *vb* : attract

lu·rid *adj* 1 : gruesome 2 : sensational — **lu·rid·ly** *adv*

lurk *vb* : lie in wait

lus·cious *adj* 1 : pleasingly sweet in taste or smell 2 : sensually appealing — **lus·cious·ly** *adv* — **lus·cious·ness** *n*

lush *adj* : covered with abundant growth

lust *n* 1 : intense sexual desire 2 : intense longing — **lust** *vb* — **lust·ful** *adj*

lus·ter, lus·tre *n* 1 : brightness from reflected light 2 : magnificence — **lus·ter·less** *adj* — **lus·trous** *adj*

lusty *adj* : full of vitality — **lust·i·ly** *adv* — **lust·i·ness** *n*

lux·u·ri·ant *adj* 1 : growing plentifully 2 : rich and varied — **lux·u·ri·ance** *n* — **lux·u·ri·ant·ly** *adv* — **lux·u·ri·ate** *vb*

lux·u·ry *n* 1 : great comfort 2 : something adding to pleasure or comfort — **lux·u·ri·ous** *adj* — **lux·u·ri·ous·ly** *adv*

lye *n* : caustic alkaline substance

lying *pres part of* LIE

lynch *vb* : put to death by mob action — **lyncher** *n*

lyr·ic *adj* 1 : suitable for singing 2 : expressing direct personal emotion ∼ *n* 1 : lyric poem 2 *pl* : words of a song — **lyr·i·cal** *adj*

M

m *n* : 13th letter of the alphabet

ma'am *n* : madam

ma·ca·bre *adj* : gruesome

mac·a·ro·ni *n* : tube-shaped pasta

mac·a·roon *n* : cookie of ground almonds or coconut

mace *n* : spice from the fibrous coating of the nutmeg

ma·chete *n* : large heavy knife

ma·chine *n* : combination of mechanical or electrical parts ∼ *vb* : modify by machine-operated tools — **ma·chin·able** *adj* — **ma·chin·ery** *n* — **ma·chin·ist** *n*

mac·ra·mé *n* : coarse lace or fringe made by knotting

mad *adj* 1 : insane or rabid 2 : rash and foolish 3 : angry 4 : carried away by enthusiasm — **mad·den** *vb* — **mad·den·ing·ly** *adv* — **mad·ly** *adv* — **mad·ness** *n*

mad·am *n* — used in polite address to a woman

made *past of* MAKE

ma·de·moi·selle *n* : an unmarried girl or woman — used as a title for a woman esp. of French nationality

mad·house *n* 1 : insane asylum 2 : place of great uproar or confusion

Ma·fia *n* : secret criminal organization

mag·a·zine *n* 1 : storehouse 2 : publication issued at regular intervals 3 : cartridge container in a gun

mag·ic *n* 1 : art of using supernatural powers

2 : extraordinary power or influence **3** : sleight of hand — **magic, mag·i·cal** *adj* — **mag·i·cal·ly** *adv* — **ma·gi·cian** *n*

mag·is·trate *n* : judge — **mag·is·te·ri·al** *adj* — **mag·is·tra·cy** *n*

mag·net *n* **1** : body that attracts iron **2** : something that attracts — **mag·net·ic** *adj* — **mag·net·i·cal·ly** *adv* — **mag·ne·tism** *n*

mag·ne·tize *vb* **1** : attract like a magnet **2** : give magnetic properties to — **mag·ne·tiz·able** *adj* — **mag·ne·ti·za·tion** *n* — **mag·ne·tiz·er** *n*

mag·nif·i·cent *adj* : splendid — **mag·nif·i·cence** *n* — **mag·nif·i·cent·ly** *adv*

mag·ni·fy *vb* **1** : intensify **2** : enlarge — **mag·ni·fi·ca·tion** *n* — **mag·ni·fi·er** *n*

mag·ni·tude *n* **1** : greatness of size or extent **2** : quantity

ma·hog·a·ny *n* : tropical evergreen tree or its reddish brown wood

maid *n* **1** : unmarried young woman **2** : female servant

mail *n* **1** : something sent or carried in the postal system **2** : postal system ∼ *vb* : send by mail — **mail·box** *n* — **mail·man** *n*

main *n* **1** : force **2** : ocean **3** : principal pipe, duct, or circuit of a utility system ∼ *adj* : chief — **main·ly** *adv*

main·land *n* : part of a country on a continent

main·stream *n* : prevailing current or direction of activity or influence — **main·stream** *adj*

main·tain *vb* **1** : keep in an existing state (as of repair) **2** : sustain **3** : declare — **main·tain·abil·i·ty** *n* — **main·tain·able** *adj* — **main·te·nance** *n*

maj·es·ty *n* **1** : sovereign power or dignity — used as a title **2** : grandeur or splendor — **ma·jes·tic** *adj* — **ma·jes·ti·cal·ly** *adv*

ma·jor *adj* **1** : larger or greater **2** : noteworthy or conspicuous ∼ *n* **1** : commissioned officer (as in the army) ranking next below a lieutenant colonel **2** : main field of study ∼ *vb* : pursue an academic major

ma·jor·i·ty *n* **1** : age of full civil rights **2** : quantity more than half

make *vb* (**made; made**) **1** : cause to exist, occur, or appear **2** : fashion or manufacture **3** : formulate in the mind **4** : constitute **5** : prepare **6** : cause to be or become **7** : carry out or perform **8** : compel **9** : gain **10** : have an effect — used with *for* ∼ *n* : brand — **mak·er** *n*

— **make do** *vb* : get along with what is available — **make good** *vb* **1** : repay **2** : succeed — **make out** *vb* **1** : draw up or write **2** : discern or understand **3** : fare — **make up** *vb* **1** : invent **2** : become reconciled **3** : compensate for

make–be·lieve *n* : a pretending to believe ∼ *adj* : imagined or pretended

make·shift *n* : temporary substitute — **makeshift** *adj*

make·up *n* **1** : way in which something is constituted **2** : cosmetics

mal·a·dy *n* : disease or disorder

male *adj* **1** : relating to the sex that performs a fertilizing function **2** : masculine ∼ *n* : male individual — **male·ness** *n*

ma·lev·o·lent *adj* : malicious or spiteful — **ma·lev·o·lence** *n*

mal·for·ma·tion *n* : distortion or faulty formation — **mal·formed** *adj*

mal·func·tion *vb* : fail to operate properly — **mal·func·tion** *n*

mal·ice *n* : desire to cause pain or injury to another — **ma·li·cious** *adj* — **ma·li·cious·ly** *adv*

ma·lig·nant *adj* **1** : harmful **2** : likely to cause death — **ma·lig·nan·cy** *n* — **ma·lig·nant·ly** *adv* — **ma·lig·ni·ty** *n*

mall *n* **1** : shaded promenade **2** : concourse providing access to rows of shops

mal·let *n* : hammerlike tool

mal·nu·tri·tion *n* : inadequate nutrition — **mal·nour·ished** *adj*

mal·prac·tice *n* : failure of professional duty

ma·ma, mam·ma *n* : mother

mam·mal *n* : warm-blooded vertebrate animal that nourishes its young with milk — **mam·ma·li·an** *adj or n*

mam·mo·gram *n* : X-ray photograph of the breasts

man *n* (**men**) **1** : human being **2** : adult male **3** : mankind ∼ *vb* : supply with people for working — **man·hood** *n* — **man·hunt** *n* — **man·like** *adj* — **man·li·ness** *n* — **man·ly** *adj or adv* — **man–made** *adj* — **man·nish** *adj* — **man·nish·ly** *adv* — **man·nish·ness** *n* — **man–size, man–sized** *adj*

man·age *vb* **1** : control **2** : direct or carry on business or affairs **3** : cope — **man·age·abil·i·ty** *n* — **man·age·able** *adj* — **man·age·able·ness** *n* — **man·age·ably** *adv* —

man•age•ment *n* — **man•ag•er** *n* — **man•a•ge•ri•al** *adj*

man•date *n* : authoritative command

man•da•to•ry *adj* : obligatory

mane *n* : animal's neck hair — **maned** *adj*

ma•neu•ver *n* **1** : planned movement of troops or ships **2** : military training exercise **3** : clever or skillful move or action — **maneuver** *vb* — **ma•neu•ver•abil•i•ty** *n*

man•gle *vb* **1** : mutilate **2** : bungle — **man•gler** *n*

man•hole *n* : entry to a sewer

ma•nia *n* **1** : insanity marked by uncontrollable emotion or excitement **2** : excessive enthusiasm — **ma•ni•ac** *n* — **ma•ni•a•cal** *adj* — **man•ic** *adj or n*

man•i•cure *n* : treatment for the fingernails ～ *vb* **1** : do manicure work on **2** : trim precisely — **man•i•cur•ist** *n*

man•i•fest *adj* : clear to the senses or to the mind ～ *vb* : make evident — **man•i•fes•ta•tion** *n* — **man•i•fest•ly** *adv*

ma•nip•u•late *vb* **1** : treat or operate manually or mechanically **2** : influence esp. by cunning — **ma•nip•u•la•tion** *n* — **ma•nip•u•la•tive** *adj* — **ma•nip•u•la•tor** *n*

man•kind *n* : human race

man•ne•quin *n* : dummy used to display clothes

man•ner *n* **1** : kind **2** : usual way of acting **3** : artistic method **4** *pl* : social conduct

man•ner•ism *n* : individual peculiarity of action

man•ner•ly *adj* : polite — **man•ner•li•ness** *n* — **mannerly** *adv*

man•or *n* : country estate — **ma•no•ri•al** *adj*

man•pow•er *n* : supply of people available for service

man•sion *n* : very big house

man•slaugh•ter *n* : unintentional killing of a person

man•tle *n* **1** : sleeveless cloak **2** : something that covers, enfolds, or envelops — **man•tle** *vb*

man•u•al *adj* : involving the hands or physical force ～ *n* : handbook — **man•u•al•ly** *adv*

man•u•fac•ture *n* : process of making atricles by hand or by machinery ～ *vb* : make from raw materials — **man•u•fac•tur•er** *n*

ma•nure *n* : animal excrement used as fertilizer

manu•script *n* **1** : something written or typed **2** : document submitted for publication

many *adj* **more; most** : consisting of a large number — **many** *n or pron*

map *n* : representation of a geographical area ～ *vb* **1** : make a map of **2** : plan in detail — **map•pa•ble** *adj* — **map•per** *n*

ma•ple *n* : tree with hard light-colored wood

mar *vb* : damage

mar•a•thon *n* **1** : long-distance race **2** : test of endurance — **mar•a•thon•er** *n*

mar•ble *n* **1** : crystallized limestone **2** : small glass ball used in a children's game (**marbles**)

march *vb* : move with regular steps or in a purposeful manner ～ *n* **1** : distance covered in a march **2** : measured stride **3** : forward movement **4** : music for marching — **march•er** *n*

March *n* : 3d month of the year having 31 days

mar•ga•rine *n* : butter substitute made usu. from vegetable oils

mar•gin *n* **1** : edge **2** : spare amount, measure, or degree — **mar•gin•al** *adj* — **mar•gin•al•ly** *adv*

ma•ri•na *n* : place for mooring pleasure boats

ma•rine *adj* **1** : relating to the sea **2** : relating to marines ～ *n* : infantry soldier associated with a navy

mar•i•tal *adj* : relating to marriage

mar•i•time *adj* : relating to the sea or commerce on the sea

mark *n* **1** : something aimed at **2** : something (as a line) designed to record position **3** : visible sign **4** : written symbol **5** : grade **6** : lasting impression **7** : blemish ～ *vb* **1** : designate or set apart by a mark or make a mark on **2** : characterize **3** : remark — **mark•er** *n*

mar•ket *n* **1** : buying and selling of goods or the place this happens **2** : demand for commodities **3** : store ～ *vb* : sell — **mar•ket•able** *adj* — **mar•ket•place** *n*

ma•roon *vb* : isolate without hope of escape

mar•riage *n* **1** : state of being married **2** : wedding ceremony — **mar•riage•able** *adj*

mar•ry *vb* **1** : join as husband and wife **2** : take or give in marriage — **mar•ried** *adj or n*

marsh *n* : soft wet land — **marshy** *adj*

mar•shal *n* **1** : leader of ceremony **2** : usu. high military or administrative officer ～ *vb* **1** : arrange in order, rank, or position **2** : lead with ceremony

marsh•mal•low *n* : spongy candy

mart *n* : market

mar•tial *adj* **1** : relating to war or an army **2** : warlike

mar•tyr *n* : one who dies or makes a great sac-

rifice for a cause ～ vb : make a martyr of —
mar•tyr•dom n

mar•vel vb : feel surprise or wonder ～ n
: something amazing — mar•vel•ous, mar•
vel•lous adj — mar•vel•ous•ly adv — mar•
vel•ous•ness n

mas•cara n : eye cosmetic

mas•cot n : one believed to bring good luck

mas•cu•line adj : relating to the male sex —
mas•cu•lin•i•ty n

mash n 1 : crushed steeped grain for fermenting 2 : soft pulpy mass ～ vb 1 : reduce to a
pulpy mass 2 : smash — mash•er n

mask n : disguise for the face ～ vb 1 : disguise 2 : cover to protect — mask•er n

mas•quer•ade n 1 : costume party 2 : disguise ～ vb 1 : disguise oneself 2 : take part
in a costume party — mas•quer•ad•er n

mass n 1 : large amount of matter or number
of things 2 : expanse or magnitude 3 : great
body of people — usu. pl. ～ vb : form into a
mass — mass•less adj — massy adj

Mass n : worship service of the Roman
Catholic Church

mas•sa•cre n : wholesale slaughter — mas•
sa•cre vb

mas•sage n : a rubbing of the body — mas•
sage vb

mas•sive adj 1 : being a large mass 2 : large
in scope — mas•sive•ly adv — mas•sive•
ness n

mast n : tall pole esp. for supporting sails —
mast•ed adj

mas•ter n 1 : male teacher 2 : holder of an academic degree between a bachelor's and a
doctor's 3 : one highly skilled 4 : one in authority ～ vb 1 : subdue 2 : become proficient in — mas•ter•ful adj — mas•ter•ful•ly
adv — mas•ter•ly adj — mas•tery n

mas•ter•piece n : great piece of work

mat n 1 : coarse woven or plaited fabric 2
: mass of tangled strands 3 : thick pad ～ vb
: form into a mat

¹match n 1 : one equal to another 2 : one able
to cope with another 3 : suitable pairing 4
: game 5 : marriage ～ vb 1 : set in competition 2 : marry 3 : be or provide the equal of 4
: fit or go together — match•less adj —
match•mak•er n

²match n : piece of wood or paper material
with a combustible tip

mate n 1 : companion 2 : subordinate officer
on a ship 3 : one of a pair ～ vb 1 : fit together 2 : come together as a pair esp. for reproduction

ma•te•ri•al adj 1 : natural 2 : relating to matter 3 : important 4 : of a physical or worldly
nature ～ n : stuff something is made of —
ma•te•ri•al•ism n — ma•te•ri•al•ist n or adj
— ma•te•ri•al•is•tic adj — ma•te•ri•al•ize vb
— ma•te•ri•al•i•za•tion n — ma•te•ri•al•ly
adv

ma•ter•nal adj : motherly — ma•ter•nal•ly adv

ma•ter•ni•ty n 1 : state of being a mother 2
: hospital's childbirth facility ～ adj 1 : worn
during pregnancy 2 : relating to the period
close to childbirth

math n : mathematics

math•e•mat•ics n pl : science of numbers and
of shapes in space — math•e•mat•i•cal adj —
math•e•mat•i•cal•ly adv — math•e•ma•ti•
cian n

mat•i•nee, mat•i•née n : afternoon performance

mat•ri•mo•ny n : marriage — mat•ri•mo•ni•al
adj — mat•ri•mo•ni•al•ly adv

ma•trix n : something (as a mold) that gives
form, foundation, or origin to something else
enclosed in it

mat•ter n 1 : subject of interest 2 pl : circumstances 3 : trouble 4 : physical substance ～
vb : be important

mat•tress n : pad to sleep on

ma•ture adj 1 : carefully considered 2 : fully
grown or developed 3 : due for payment ～ vb
: become mature — mat•u•ra•tion n — ma•
ture•ly adv — ma•tu•ri•ty n

maul n : heavy hammer ～ vb 1 : beat 2 : handle roughly

mau•so•le•um n : large above-ground tomb

max•i•mum n 1 : greatest quantity 2 : upper
limit 3 : largest number — maximum adj —
max•i•mize vb

may verbal auxiliary, past might 1 : have permission 2 : be likely to 3 — used to express
desire, purpose, or contingency

May n : 5th month of the year having 31 days

may•be adv : perhaps

may•on•naise n : creamy white sandwich
spread

may•or n : chief city official — may•or•al adj
— may•or•al•ty n

maze n : confusing network of passages —
mazy adj

me pron, objective case of I

mead·ow *n* : low-lying usu. level grassland — **mead·ow·land** *n*

mea·ger, mea·gre *adj* **1** : thin **2** : lacking richness or strength — **mea·ger·ly** *adv* — **mea·ger·ness** *n*

¹meal *n* **1** : food to be eaten at one time **2** : act of eating — **meal·time** *n*

²meal *n* : ground grain — **mealy** *adj*

¹mean *adj* **1** : humble **2** : worthy of or showing little regard **3** : stingy **4** : malicious — **mean·ly** *adv* — **mean·ness** *n*

²mean *vb* **meant; meant 1** : intend **2** : serve to convey, show, or indicate **3** : be important — **mean·ing** *n* — **mean·ing·ful** *adj* — **mean·ing·ful·ly** *adv* — **mean·ing·less** *adj*

³mean *n* **1** : middle point **2** *pl* : something that helps gain an end **3** *pl* : material resources **4** : sum of several quantities divided by the number of quantities ∼ *adj* : being a mean

mean·time *n* : intervening time — **meantime** *adv*

mean·while *n* : meantime ∼ *adv* **1** : meantime **2** : at the same time

mea·sles *n pl* : disease that is marked by red spots on the skin

mea·sure *n* **1** : moderate amount **2** : dimensions or amount **3** : something to show amount **4** : unit or system of measurement **5** : act of measuring **6** : means to an end ∼ *vb* **1** : find out or mark off size or amount of **2** : have a specified measurement — **mea·sur·able** *adj* — **mea·sur·ably** *adv* — **mea·sure·less** *adj* — **mea·sure·ment** *n* — **mea·sur·er** *n*

meat *n* **1** : food **2** : animal flesh used as food — **meat·ball** *n* — **meaty** *adj*

me·chan·ic *n* : worker who repairs machinery

me·chan·i·cal *adj* **1** : relating to machines or mechanics **2** : involuntary — **me·chan·i·cal·ly** *adv*

me·chan·ics *n sing or pl* **1** : branch of physics dealing with energy and forces in relation to bodies **2** : mechanical details

mech·a·nism *n* **1** : piece of machinery **2** : technique for gaining a result **3** : basic processes producing a phenomenon — **mech·a·nis·tic** *adj* — **mech·a·ni·za·tion** *n* — **mech·a·nize** *vb* — **mech·a·niz·er** *n*

med·al *n* **1** : religious pin or pendant **2** : coinlike commemorative metal piece

med·dle *vb* : interfere — **med·dler** *n* — **med·dle·some** *adj*

me·dia *n pl* : communications organizations

me·di·an *n* : middle value in a range — **me·di·an** *adj*

me·di·ate *vb* : help settle a dispute — **me·di·a·tion** *n* — **me·di·a·tor** *n*

med·i·cal *adj* : relating to medicine — **med·i·cal·ly** *adv*

med·i·ca·tion *n* **1** : act of medicating **2** : medicine — **med·i·cate** *vb*

med·i·cine *n* **1** : preparation used to treat disease **2** : science dealing with the cure of disease — **me·dic·i·nal** *adj* — **me·dic·i·nal·ly** *adv*

me·di·e·val, me·di·ae·val *adj* : of or relating to the Middle Ages — **me·di·e·val·ist** *n*

me·di·o·cre *adj* : not very good — **me·di·oc·ri·ty** *n*

med·i·tate *vb* : contemplate — **med·i·ta·tion** *n* — **med·i·ta·tive** *adj* — **med·i·ta·tive·ly** *adv*

me·di·um *n* **1** : middle position or degree **2** : means of effecting or conveying something **3** : surrounding substance **4** : means of communication **5** : mode of artistic expression — **me·di·um** *adj*

meek *adj* **1** : having a mild manner or personality **2** : lacking spirit — **meek·ly** *adv* — **meek·ness** *n*

meet *vb* **met; met 1** : run into **2** : join **3** : oppose **4** : assemble **5** : satisfy **6** : be introduced to ∼ *n* : sports team competition

meet·ing *n* : a getting together — **meet·ing·house** *n*

mega·byte *n* : unit of computer storage capacity

mega·hertz *n* : one million hertz

mel·an·choly *n* : depression — **mel·an·chol·ic** *adj* — **melancholy** *adj*

mel·low *adj* **1** : grown gentle or mild **2** : rich and full — **mel·low** *vb* — **mel·low·ness** *n*

mel·o·dy *n* **1** : agreeable sound **2** : succession of musical notes — **me·lod·ic** *adj* — **me·lod·i·cal·ly** *adv* — **me·lo·di·ous** *adj* — **me·lo·di·ous·ly** *adv* — **me·lo·di·ous·ness** *n*

mel·on *n* : gourdlike fruit

melt *vb* **1** : change from solid to liquid usu. by heat **2** : dissolve or disappear gradually **3** : move or be moved emotionally

mem·ber *n* **1** : part of a person, animal, or plant **2** : one of a group **3** : part of a whole — **mem·ber·ship** *n*

memo *n* : memorandum

mem·o·ra·bil·ia *n pl* **1** : memorable things **2** : souvenirs

mem·o·ra·ble *adj* : worth remembering —

mem·o·ra·bil·i·ty *n* — **mem·o·ra·ble·ness** *n*
— **mem·o·ra·bly** *adv*
mem·o·ran·dum *n* : informal note
me·mo·ri·al *n* : something (as a monument)
meant to keep remembrance alive — **memo·
rial** *adj* — **me·mo·ri·al·ize** *vb*
Memorial Day *n* : last Monday in May or formerly May 30 observed as a legal holiday in
commemoration of dead servicemen
mem·o·ry *n* **1** : power of remembering **2**
: something remembered **3** : commemoration
4 : time within which past events are remembered — **mem·o·ri·za·tion** *n* — **mem·o·rize**
vb — **mem·o·riz·er** *n*
men *pl of* MAN
men·ace *n* : threat of danger ∼ *vb* **1** : threaten
2 : endanger — **men·ac·ing·ly** *adv*
mend *vb* **1** : improve **2** : repair **3** : heal —
mend *n* — **mend·er** *n*
me·nial *adj* **1** : relating to servants **2** : humble
∼ *n* : domestic servant — **me·ni·al·ly** *adv*
meno·pause *n* : time when menstruation ends
— **meno·paus·al** *adj*
me·no·rah *n* : candelabrum used in Jewish
worship
men·stru·a·tion *n* : monthly discharge of
blood from the uterus — **men·stru·al** *adj* —
men·stru·ate *vb*
men·tal *adj* : relating to the mind or its disorders — **men·tal·i·ty** *n* — **men·tal·ly** *adv*
men·tion *vb* : refer to — **men·tion** *n*
men·tor *n* : instructor
menu *n* **1** : restaurant's list of food **2** : list of
offerings
me·ow *n* : characteristic cry of a cat — **meow**
vb
mer·chan·dise *n* : goods bought and sold ∼
vb : buy and sell — **mer·chan·dis·er** *n*
mer·chant *n* : one who buys and sells
mer·cu·ry *n* : heavy liquid metallic chemical
element
mer·cy *n* **1** : show of pity or leniency **2** : divine blessing — **mer·ci·ful** *adj* — **mer·ci·ful·
ly** *adv* — **mer·ci·less** *adj* — **mer·ci·less·ly**
adv — **mercy** *adj*
mere *adj, superlative* **mer·est** : nothing more
than — **mere·ly** *adv*
merge *vb* **1** : unite **2** : blend — **merg·er** *n*
me·rid·i·an *n* : imaginary circle on the earth's
surface passing through the poles — **me·rid·i·
an** *adj*
mer·it *n* **1** : praiseworthy quality **2** *pl* : rights
and wrongs of a legal case ∼ *vb* : deserve —

mer·i·to·ri·ous *adj* — **mer·i·to·ri·ous·ly** *adv*
— **mer·i·to·ri·ous·ness** *n*
mer·ry *adj* : full of high spirits — **mer·ri·ly** *adv*
— **mer·ri·ment** *n* — **mer·ry·mak·er** *n* —
mer·ry·mak·ing *n*
merry–go–round *n* : revolving amusement
ride
mesdames *pl of* MADAM *or of* MADAME *or of*
MRS.
mesdemoiselles *pl of* MADEMOISELLE
mesh *n* **1** : one of the openings in a net **2** : net
fabric **3** : working contact ∼ *vb* : fit together
properly — **meshed** *adj*
mes·mer·ize *vb* : hypnotize
mess *n* **1** : meal eaten by a group **2** : confused, dirty, or offensive state ∼ *vb* **1** : make
dirty or untidy **2** : work at something in a casual manner **3** : interfere — **messy** *adj*
mes·sage *n* : news, information, or a command sent by one person to another
mes·sen·ger *n* : one who carries a message or
does an errand
messieurs *pl of* MONSIEUR
Messrs. *pl of* MR.
met *past of* MEET
me·tab·o·lism *n* : biochemical processes necessary to life — **met·a·bol·ic** *adj* — **me·tab·
o·lize** *vb*
met·al *n* : shiny substance that can be melted
and shaped and conducts heat and electricity
— **me·tal·lic** *adj* — **met·al·ware** *n* — **met·
al·work** *n* — **met·al·work·er** *n* — **met·al·
work·ing** *n*
met·a·phor *n* : use of a word denoting one kind
of object or idea in place of another to suggest
a likeness between them — **met·a·phor·i·cal**
adj
me·te·or *n* : small body that produces a streak
of light as it burns up in the atmosphere
me·te·or·ic *adj* **1** : relating to a meteor **2**
: sudden and spectacular — **me·te·or·i·cal·ly**
adv
me·te·o·rol·o·gy *n* : science of weather — **me·
te·o·ro·log·ic, me·te·o·ro·log·i·cal** *adj* —
me·te·o·rol·o·gist *n*
¹me·ter *n* : unit of length equal to 39.37 inches
²me·ter *n* : measuring instrument
meth·od *n* **1** : procedure for achieving an end
2 : orderly arrangement or plan — **me·thod·i·
cal** *adj* — **me·thod·i·cal·ly** *adv* — **me·thod·
i·cal·ness** *n*
met·ric, met·ri·cal *adj* : relating to meter or the
metric system — **met·ri·cal·ly** *adv*

metric system *n* : system of weights and measures using the meter and kilogram

me·trop·o·lis *n* : major city — **met·ro·pol·i·tan** *adj*

mice *pl of* MOUSE

mi·cro·or·gan·ism *n* : very tiny living thing

mi·cro·phone *n* : instrument for changing sound waves into variations of an electric current

mi·cro·scope *n* : optical device for magnifying tiny objects — **mi·cro·scop·ic** *adj* — **mi·cro·scop·i·cal·ly** *adv* — **mi·cros·copy** *n*

mi·cro·wave *n* **1** : short radio wave **2** : oven that cooks food using microwaves ∼ *vb* : heat or cook in a microwave oven — **mi·cro·wav·able, mi·cro·wave·able** *adj*

mid *adj* : middle — **mid·point** *n* — **mid-stream** *n* — **mid·sum·mer** *n* — **mid·town** *n or adj* — **mid·week** *n* — **mid·win·ter** *n* — **mid·year** *n*

mid·air *n* : a point in the air well above the ground

mid·day *n* : noon

mid·dle *adj* **1** : equally distant from the extremes **2** : being at neither extreme ∼ *n* : middle part or point

Middle Ages *n pl* : period from about A.D. 500 to about 1500

midg·et *n* : very small person or thing

mid·night *n* : 12 o'clock at night

midst *n* : position close to or surrounded by others — **midst** *prep*

¹might *past of* MAY — used to express permission or possibility or as a polite alternative to *may*

²might *n* : power or resources

mighty *adj* **1** : very strong **2** : great — **might·i·ly** *adv* — **might·i·ness** *n* — **mighty** *adv*

mi·graine *n* : severe headache often with nausea

mi·grate *vb* **1** : move from one place to another **2** : pass periodically from one region or climate to another — **mi·grant** *n* — **mi·gra·tion** *n* — **mi·gra·to·ry** *adj*

mild *adj* **1** : gentle in nature or behavior **2** : moderate in action or effect — **mild·ly** *adv* — **mild·ness** *n*

mil·dew *n* : whitish fungal growth — **mil·dew** *vb*

mile *n* : unit of length equal to 5280 feet

mile·age *n* **1** : allowance per mile for traveling expenses **2** : amount or rate of use expressed in miles

mile·stone *n* : significant point in development

mil·i·tant *adj* : aggressively active or hostile — **mil·i·tan·cy** *n* — **militant** *n* — **mil·i·tant·ly** *adv*

mil·i·tary *adj* **1** : relating to soldiers, arms, or war **2** : relating to or performed by armed forces ∼ *n* : armed forces or the people in them — **mil·i·tar·i·ly** *adv* — **mil·i·tar·ism** *n* — **mil·i·ta·rist** *n* — **mil·i·tar·is·tic** *adj*

mi·li·tia *n* : civilian soldiers — **mi·li·tia·man** *n*

milk *n* : white nutritive fluid secreted by female mammals for feeding their young ∼ *vb* **1** : draw off the milk of **2** : draw something from as if by milking — **milk·er** *n* — **milk·i·ness** *n* — **milky** *adj*

mill *n* **1** : building in which grain is ground into flour **2** : manufacturing plant **3** : machine used esp. for forming or processing ∼ *vb* **1** : subject to a process in a mill **2** : move in a circle — **mill·er** *n*

mil·len·ni·um *n* : a period of 1000 years

mil·li·gram *n* : $\frac{1}{1000}$ gram

mil·li·li·ter *n* : $\frac{1}{1000}$ liter

mil·li·me·ter *n* : $\frac{1}{1000}$ meter

mil·lion *n* : 1000 thousands — **mil·lion** *adj* — **mil·lionth** *adj or n*

mil·lion·aire *n* : person worth a million or more (as of dollars)

mime *n* **1** : mimic **2** : pantomime — **mime** *vb*

mim·ic *n* : one that mimics ∼ *vb* **1** : imitate closely **2** : ridicule by imitation — **mim·ic·ry** *n*

mince *vb* **1** : cut into small pieces **2** : choose (one's words) carefully **3** : walk in a prim affected manner

mind *n* **1** : memory **2** : the part of an individual that feels, perceives, and esp. reasons **3** : intention **4** : normal mental condition **5** : opinion **6** : intellectual ability ∼ *vb* **1** : attend to **2** : obey **3** : be concerned about **4** : be careful — **mind·ed** *adj* — **mind·less** *adj* — **mind·less·ly** *adv* — **mind·less·ness** *n*

mind·ful *adj* : aware or attentive — **mind·ful·ly** *adv* — **mind·ful·ness** *n*

¹mine *pron* : that which belongs to me

²mine *n* **1** : excavation from which minerals are taken **2** : explosive device placed in the ground or water for destroying enemy vehicles or vessels that later pass ∼ *vb* **1** : get ore from **2** : place military mines in — **mine·field** *n* — **min·er** *n*

min·er·al *n* **1** : crystalline substance not of organic origin **2** : useful natural substance (as

coal) obtained from the ground — **min·er·al**
adj — **min·er·al·o·gy** *n* — **min·er·al·o·gist** *n*

min·gle *vb* : bring together or mix

min·ia·ture *n* : tiny copy or very small version
— **miniature** *adj* — **min·ia·tur·ist** *n* — **min·ia·tur·ize** *vb*

min·i·mal *adj* : relating to or being a minimum
— **min·i·mal·ly** *adv*

min·i·mize *vb* **1** : reduce to a minimum **2** : underestimate intentionally

min·i·mum *n* : lowest quantity or amount — **min·i·mum** *adj*

mini·skirt *n* : very short skirt

min·is·ter *n* **1** : Protestant member of the clergy **2** : high officer of state **3** : diplomatic representative ∼ *vb* : give aid or service — **min·is·te·ri·al** *adj* — **min·is·tra·tion** *n*

min·is·try *n* **1** : office or duties of a minister **2** : body of ministers **3** : government department headed by a minister

mini·van *n* : small van

mi·nor *adj* **1** : less in size, importance, or value **2** : not serious ∼ *n* **1** : person not yet of legal age **2** : secondary field of academic specialization

mi·nor·i·ty *n* **1** : time or state of being a minor **2** : smaller number (as of votes) **3** : part of a population differing from others (as in race or religion)

¹mint *n* **1** : fragrant herb that yields a flavoring oil **2** : mint-flavored piece of candy — **minty** *adj*

²mint *n* **1** : place where coins are made **2** : vast sum ∼ *adj* : unused — **mint** *vb* — **mint·er** *n*

mi·nus *prep* **1** : diminished by **2** : lacking ∼ *n* : negative quantity or quality

mi·nus·cule, min·is·cule *adj* : very small

¹min·ute *n* **1** : 60th part of an hour or of a degree **2** : short time **3** *pl* : official record of a meeting

²mi·nute *adj* **1** : very small **2** : marked by close attention to details — **mi·nute·ly** *adv* — **mi·nute·ness** *n*

mir·a·cle *n* **1** : extraordinary event taken as a sign of divine intervention in human affairs **2** : marvel — **mi·rac·u·lous** *adj* — **mi·rac·u·lous·ly** *adv*

mir·ror *n* : smooth surface (as of glass) that reflects images ∼ *vb* : reflect in or as if in a mirror

mirth *n* : gladness and laughter — **mirth·ful** *adj* — **mirth·ful·ly** *adv* — **mirth·ful·ness** *n* — **mirth·less** *adj*

mis·be·have *vb* : behave improperly — **mis·be·hav·er** *n* — **mis·be·hav·ior** *n*

mis·cel·la·neous *adj* : consisting of many things of different kinds — **mis·cel·la·ny** *n* — **mis·cel·la·neous·ly** *adv* — **mis·cel·la·neous·ness** *n*

mis·chief *n* : conduct esp. of a child that annoys or causes minor damage

mis·chie·vous *adj* **1** : causing annoyance or minor injury **2** : irresponsibly playful — **mis·chie·vous·ly** *adv* — **mis·chie·vous·ness** *n*

mis·de·mean·or *n* : crime less serious than a felony

mi·ser *n* : person who hoards and is stingy with money — **mi·ser·li·ness** *n* — **mi·ser·ly** *adj*

mis·er·a·ble *adj* **1** : wretchedly deficient **2** : causing extreme discomfort **3** : shameful — **mis·er·a·ble·ness** *n* — **mis·er·a·bly** *adv*

mis·ery *n* : suffering and want caused by distress or poverty

mis·fit *n* : person poorly adjusted to his environment

mis·for·tune *n* **1** : bad luck **2** : unfortunate condition or event

mis·giv·ing *n* : doubt or concern

mis·in·ter·pret *vb* : understand or explain wrongly — **mis·in·ter·pre·ta·tion** *n*

mis·lay *vb* : misplace

mis·lead *vb* : lead in a wrong direction or into error — **mis·lead·ing** *adj* — **mis·lead·ing·ly** *adv*

mis·place *vb* : put in a wrong or unremembered place

mis·pro·nounce *vb* : pronounce incorrectly — **mis·pro·nun·ci·a·tion** *n*

mis·quote *vb* : quote incorrectly — **mis·quo·ta·tion** *n*

mis·rep·re·sent *vb* : represent falsely or unfairly — **mis·rep·re·sen·ta·tion** *n*

¹miss *vb* **1** : fail to hit, reach, or contact **2** : notice the absence of **3** : fail to obtain **4** : avoid **5** : omit — **miss** *n*

²miss *n* : young unmarried woman or girl — often used as a title

mis·sile *n* : object (as a stone or rocket) thrown or shot

miss·ing *adj* : absent or lost

mis·sion *n* **1** : ministry sent by a church to spread its teaching **2** : group of diplomats sent to a foreign country **3** : task

mis·sion·ary *adj* : relating to religious missions ∼ *n* : person sent to spread religious faith

mis·spell *vb* : spell incorrectly — **mis·spell·ing** *n*

mis·step *n* 1 : wrong step 2 : mistake

mist *n* : particles of water falling as fine rain

mis·take *n* 1 : misunderstanding or wrong belief 2 : wrong action or statement — **mis·take** *vb* — **mis·tak·en** *adj* — **mis·tak·en·ly** *adv*

mis·ter *n* : sir — used without a name in addressing a man

mis·treat *vb* : treat badly — **mis·treat·ment** *n*

mis·tress *n* 1 : woman in control 2 : a woman not his wife with whom a married man has recurrent sexual relations

misty *adj* 1 : obscured by mist 2 : tearful — **mist·i·ly** *adv* — **mist·i·ness** *n*

mis·un·der·stand *vb* 1 : fail to understand 2 : interpret incorrectly — **mis·un·der·stand·ing** *n*

mis·use *vb* 1 : use incorrectly 2 : mistreat — **mis·use** *n*

mitt *n* : mittenlike baseball glove

mit·ten *n* : hand covering without finger sections

mix *vb* : combine or join into one mass or group ∼ *n* : commercially prepared food mixture — **mix·able** *adj* — **mix·er** *n* — **mix up** *vb* : confuse

mix·ture *n* : act or product of mixing

mix–up *n* : instance of confusion

moan *n* : low prolonged sound of pain or grief — **moan** *vb*

mob *n* 1 : large disorderly crowd 2 : criminal gang ∼ *vb* : crowd around and attack or annoy

mo·bile *adj* : capable of moving or being moved ∼ *n* : suspended art construction with freely moving parts — **mo·bil·i·ty** *n*

mo·bi·lize *vb* : assemble and make ready for war duty — **mo·bi·li·za·tion** *n*

moc·ca·sin *n* 1 : heelless shoe 2 : venomous U.S. snake

mock *vb* 1 : ridicule 2 : mimic in derision ∼ *adj* 1 : simulated 2 : phony — **mock·er** *n* — **mock·ery** *n* — **mock·ing·ly** *adv*

mode *n* 1 : particular form or variety 2 : style — **mod·al** *adj* — **mod·ish** *adj*

mod·el *n* 1 : structural design 2 : miniature representation 3 : something worthy of copying 4 : one who poses for an artist or displays clothes 5 : type or design ∼ *vb* 1 : shape 2 : work as a model ∼ *adj* 1 : serving as a pattern 2 : being a miniature representation of

mo·dem *n* : device by which a computer communicates with another computer over telephone lines

mod·er·ate *adj* : avoiding extremes ∼ *vb* 1 : lessen the intensity of 2 : act as one who presides — **mod·er·ate** *n* — **mod·er·ate·ly** *adv* — **mod·er·ate·ness** *n* — **mod·er·a·tor** *n* — **mod·er·a·tion** *n*

mod·ern *adj* : relating to or characteristic of the present — **modern** *n* — **mo·der·ni·ty** *n* — **mod·ern·i·za·tion** *n* — **mod·ern·ize** *vb* — **mod·ern·iz·er** *n* — **mod·ern·ly** *adv* — **mod·ern·ness** *n*

mod·est *adj* 1 : having a moderate estimate of oneself 2 : reserved or decent in thoughts or actions 3 : limited in size, amount, or aim — **mod·est·ly** *adv* — **mod·es·ty** *n*

mod·i·fy *vb* 1 : limit the meaning of 2 : change — **mod·i·fi·ca·tion** *n* — **mod·i·fi·er** *n*

mod·u·late *vb* 1 : keep in proper measure or proportion 2 : vary a radio wave — **mod·u·la·tion** *n* — **mod·u·la·tor** *n* — **mod·u·la·to·ry** *adj*

moist *adj* : slightly or moderately wet — **moist·en** *vb* — **moist·en·er** *n* — **moist·ly** *adv* — **moist·ness** *n*

mois·ture *n* : small amount of liquid that causes dampness — **mois·tur·ize** *vb* — **mois·tur·iz·er** *n*

mo·lar *n* : grinding tooth — **mo·lar** *adj*

mo·las·ses *n* : thick brown syrup from raw sugar

¹mold *n* : frame or cavity for forming ∼ *vb* : shape in or as if in a mold — **mold·er** *n*

²mold *n* : surface growth of fungus ∼ *vb* : become moldy — **mold·i·ness** *n* — **moldy** *adj*

¹mole *n* : spot on the skin

²mole *n* : small burrowing mammal — **mole·hill** *n*

mo·lest *vb* 1 : annoy or disturb 2 : force physical and usu. sexual contact on — **mo·les·ta·tion** *n* — **mo·lest·er** *n*

mol·li·fy *vb* : soothe in temper — **mol·li·fi·ca·tion** *n*

mom *n* : mother

mo·ment *n* 1 : tiny portion of time 2 : time of excellence 3 : importance

mo·men·tary *adj* : continuing only a moment — **mo·men·tar·i·ly** *adv* — **mo·men·tar·i·ness** *n*

mo·men·tous *adj* : very important — **mo·men·tous·ly** *adv* — **mo·men·tous·ness** *n*

mo·men·tum *n* : force of a moving body

mon·arch *n* : ruler of a kingdom or empire — **mo·nar·chi·cal** *adj* — **mon·ar·chy** *n*

mon·as·tery *n* : house for monks — **mo·nas·tic** *adj or n* — **mo·nas·ti·cal·ly** *adv* — **mo·nas·ti·cism** *n*

Mon·day *n* : 2d day of the week

mon·ey *n* **1** : something (as coins or paper currency) used in buying **2** : wealth — **mon·e·tary** *adj* — **mon·eyed** *adj* — **mon·ey·lend·er** *n*

mon·i·tor *n* **1** : student assistant **2** : television screen ∼ *vb* : watch or observe esp. for quality

monk *n* : member of a religious order living in a monastery — **monk·ish** *adj*

mon·key *n* : small long-tailed arboreal primate

mono·logue *n* : long speech — **mono·logu·ist, mo·no·lo·gist** *n*

mo·nop·o·ly *n* **1** : exclusive ownership or control of a commodity **2** : one controlling a monopoly — **mo·nop·o·list** *n* — **mo·nop·o·lis·tic** *adj* — **mo·nop·o·li·za·tion** *n* — **mo·nop·o·lize** *vb*

mo·not·o·nous *adj* **1** : sounded in one unvarying tone **2** : tediously uniform — **mo·not·o·nous·ly** *adv* — **mo·not·o·nous·ness** *n* — **mo·not·o·ny** *n*

mon·ster *n* **1** : abnormal or terrifying animal **2** : ugly, wicked, or cruel person — **mon·stros·i·ty** *n* — **mon·strous** *adj* — **mon·strous·ly** *adv*

month *n* : 12th part of a year — **month·ly** *adv or adj or n*

mon·u·ment *n* : structure erected in remembrance

mon·u·men·tal *adj* **1** : serving as a monument **2** : outstanding **3** : very great — **mon·u·men·tal·ly** *adv*

moo *vb* : make the noise of a cow — **moo** *n*

mood *n* : state of mind or emotion

moody *adj* **1** : sad **2** : subject to changing moods and esp. to bad moods — **mood·i·ly** *adv* — **mood·i·ness** *n*

moon *n* : natural satellite (as of earth) — **moon·beam** *n* — **moon·light** *n* — **moon·lit** *adj*

moor *vb* : fasten with line or anchor

moor·ing *n* : place where boat can be moored

moose *n* (**moose**) : large heavy-antlered deer

moot *adj* : open to question

mop *n* : floor-cleaning implement ∼ *vb* : use a mop on

mope *vb* : be sad or listless

mor·al *adj* **1** : relating to principles of right and wrong **2** : conforming to a standard of right behavior **3** : relating to or acting on the mind, character, or will ∼ *n* **1** : point of a story **2** *pl* : moral practices or teachings — **mor·al·ist** *n* — **mor·al·is·tic** *adj* — **mor·al·i·ty** *n* — **mor·al·ize** *vb* — **mor·al·ly** *adv*

mo·rale *n* : emotional attitude

mor·a·to·ri·um *n* : suspension of activity

mor·bid *adj* **1** : relating to disease **2** : gruesome — **mor·bid·i·ty** *n* — **mor·bid·ly** *adv* — **mor·bid·ness** *n*

more *adj* **1** : greater **2** : additional ∼ *adv* **1** : in addition **2** : to a greater degree ∼ *n* **1** : greater quantity **2** : additional amount ∼ *pron* : additional ones

morgue *n* : temporary holding place for dead bodies

morn *n* : morning

morn·ing *n* : time from sunrise to noon

mo·ron *n* **1** : mentally retarded person **2** : very stupid person — **mo·ron·ic** *adj* — **mo·ron·i·cal·ly** *adv*

mor·sel *n* : small piece or quantity

mor·tal *adj* **1** : causing or subject to death **2** : extreme — **mortal** *n* — **mor·tal·i·ty** *n* — **mor·tal·ly** *adv*

mort·gage *n* : transfer of property rights as security for a loan — **mortgage** *vb* — **mort·gag·ee** *n* — **mort·ga·gor** *n*

mo·sa·ic *n* : inlaid stone decoration — **mosaic** *adj*

Mos·lem *var of* MUSLIM

mosque *n* : building where Muslims worship

mos·qui·to *n* : biting bloodsucking insect

moss *n* : green seedless plant — **mossy** *adj*

most *adj* **1** : majority of **2** : greatest ∼ *adv* : to the greatest or a very great degree ∼ *n* : greatest amount ∼ *pron* : greatest number or part

most·ly *adv* : mainly

mo·tel *n* : hotel with rooms accessible from the parking lot

moth *n* : small pale insect related to the butterflies

moth·er *n* **1** : female parent **2** : source ∼ *vb* **1** : give birth to **2** : cherish or protect — **moth·er·hood** *n* — **moth·er·land** *n* — **moth·er·less** *adj* — **moth·er·ly** *adj*

moth·er–in–law *n* **mothers–in–law** : spouse's mother

mo·tif *n* : dominant theme

mo·tion *n* **1** : act or instance of moving **2**

: proposal for action ∼ *vb* : direct by a movement — **mo·tion·less** *adj* — **mo·tion·less·ly** *adv* — **mo·tion·less·ness** *n*

motion picture *n* : movie

mo·ti·vate *vb* : provide with a motive — **mo·ti·va·tion** *n* — **mo·ti·va·tor** *n*

mo·tive *n* : cause of a person's action ∼ *adj* **1** : moving to action **2** : relating to motion — **mo·tive·less** *adj*

mo·tor *n* : unit that supplies power or motion ∼ *vb* : travel by automobile — **mo·tor·bike** *n* — **mo·tor·boat** *n* — **mo·tor·cy·cle** *n* — **mo·tor·ist** *n* — **mo·tor·ize** *vb*

mot·to *n* : brief guiding rule

mould *var of* MOLD

mound *n* : pile (as of earth)

mount *vb* **1** : increase in amount **2** : get up on **3** : put in position ∼ *n* **1** : frame or support **2** : horse to ride — **mount·able** *adj* — **mount·er** *n*

moun·tain *n* : elevated land higher than a hill — **moun·tain·ous** *adj* — **moun·tain·top** *n*

mourn *vb* : feel or express grief — **mourn·er** *n* — **mourn·ful** *adj* — **mourn·ful·ly** *adv* — **mourn·ful·ness** *n* — **mourn·ing** *n*

mouse *n* (**mice**) **1** : small rodent **2** : device for controlling cursor movement on a computer display — **mouse·trap** *n or vb* — **mousy, mous·ey** *adj*

mousse *n* **1** : light chilled dessert **2** : foamy hair-styling preparation

mous·tache *var of* MUSTACHE

mouth *n* : opening through which an animal takes in food ∼ *vb* **1** : speak **2** : repeat without comprehension or sincerity **3** : form soundlessly with the lips — **mouthed** *adj* — **mouth·ful** *n*

mouth·piece *n* **1** : part (as of a musical instrument) held in or to the mouth **2** : person who speaks for another

move *vb* **1** : go or cause to go to another point **2** : change residence **3** : change or cause to change position **4** : take or cause to take action **5** : make a formal request **6** : stir the emotions ∼ *n* **1** : act or instance of moving **2** : step taken to achieve a goal — **mov·able, move·able** *adj* — **move·ment** *n* — **mov·er** *n*

mov·ie *n* : projected picture in which persons and objects seem to move

mow *vb* : cut with a machine — **mow·er** *n*

Mr. *n* (**Messrs.**) — conventional title for a man

Mrs. *n* (**Mes·dames**) — conventional title for a married woman

Ms. *n* — conventional title for a woman

much *adj* **more; most** : great in quantity, extent, or degree ∼ *adv* **more; most** : to a great degree or extent ∼ *n* : great quantity, extent, or degree

muck *n* : manure, dirt, or mud — **mucky** *adj*

mu·cus *n* : slippery protective secretion of membranes (**mucous membranes**) lining body cavities — **mu·cous** *adj*

mud *n* : soft wet earth — **mud·di·ly** *adv* — **mud·di·ness** *n* — **mud·dy** *adj or vb*

mud·dle *vb* **1** : make, be, or act confused **2** : make a mess of — **muddle** *n* — **mud·dle·head·ed** *adj*

muf·fin *n* : soft cake baked in a cup-shaped container

muf·fle *vb* **1** : wrap up **2** : dull the sound of — **muf·fler** *n*

¹**mug** *n* : drinking cup ∼ *vb* : make faces

²**mug** *vb* : assault with intent to rob — **mug·ger** *n*

mug·gy *adj* : hot and humid — **mug·gi·ness** *n*

¹**mule** *n* **1** : offspring of a male ass and a female horse **2** : stubborn person — **mul·ish** *adj* — **mul·ish·ly** *adv* — **mu·lish·ness** *n*

²**mule** *n* : backless shoe

mull *vb* : ponder

mul·ti·ple *adj* **1** : several or many **2** : various ∼ *n* : product of one number by another

mul·ti·pli·ca·tion *n* **1** : increase **2** : short method of repeated addition

mul·ti·ply *vb* **1** : increase in number **2** : perform multiplication — **mul·ti·pli·er** *n*

mul·ti·tude *n* : great number — **mul·ti·tu·di·nous** *adj*

mum·ble *vb* : speak indistinctly — **mum·ble** *n* — **mum·bler** *n*

mum·my *n* : embalmed body — **mum·mi·fi·ca·tion** *n* — **mum·mi·fy** *vb*

mumps *n sing or pl* : virus disease with swelling esp. of the salivary glands

munch *vb* : chew

mun·dane *adj* **1** : relating to the world **2** : lacking concern for the ideal or spiritual — **mun·dane·ly** *adv*

mu·nic·i·pal *adj* : of or relating to a town or city — **mu·nic·i·pal·i·ty** *n*

mur·der *n* : unlawful killing of a person ∼ *vb* : commit a murder — **mur·der·er** *n* — **mur·der·ess** *n* — **mur·der·ous** *adj* — **mur·der·ous·ly** *adv*

mur·mur *n* **1** : muttered complaint **2** : low indistinct sound — murmur *vb* — **mur·mur·er** *n* — **mur·mur·ous** *adj*

mus·cle *n* **1** : body tissue capable of contracting to produce motion **2** : strength ～ *vb* : force one's way — **mus·cled** *adj* — **mus·cu·lar** *adj* — **mus·cu·lar·i·ty** *n*

¹muse *vb* : ponder — **mus·ing·ly** *adv*

²muse *n* : source of inspiration

mu·se·um *n* : institution displaying objects of interest

mush *n* **1** : corn meal boiled in water or something of similar consistency **2** : sentimental nonsense — **mushy** *adj*

mush·room *n* : caplike organ of a fungus ～ *vb* : grow rapidly

mu·sic *n* : vocal or instrumental sounds — **mu·si·cal** *adj or n* — **mu·si·cal·ly** *adv*

mu·si·cian *n* : composer or performer of music — **mu·si·cian·ly** *adj* — **mu·si·cian·ship** *n*

musk *n* : strong-smelling substance from an Asiatic deer used in perfume — **musk·i·ness** *n* — **musky** *adj*

Mus·lim *n* : adherent of Islam — **Mus·lim** *adj*

mus·lin *n* : cotton fabric

muss *n* : untidy state ～ *vb* : mess up the arrangement of — **muss·i·ly** *adv* — **muss·i·ness** *n* — **mussy** *adj*

must *vb* — used as an auxiliary esp. to express a command, obligation, or necessity ～ *n* : something necessary

mus·tache *n* : hair of the human upper lip

mus·tard *n* : pungent yellow seasoning

mus·ter *vb* **1** : assemble **2** : arouse ～ *n* : assembled group

musty *adj* : stale — **must·i·ly** *adv* — **must·i·ness** *n*

mu·tate *vb* : undergo change in a hereditary character — **mu·tant** *adj or n* — **mu·ta·tion** *n* — **mu·ta·tive** *adj*

mute *adj* **1** : unable to speak **2** : silent ～ *n* **1** : one who is mute **2** : muffling device ～ *vb* : muffle — **mute·ly** *adv* — **mute·ness** *n*

mu·ti·late *vb* : damage seriously (as by cutting off or altering an essential part) — **mu·ti·la·tion** *n* — **mu·ti·la·tor** *n*

mu·ti·ny *n* : rebellion — **mu·ti·neer** *n* — **mu·ti·nous** *adj* — **mu·ti·nous·ly** *adv* — **mutiny** *vb*

mutt *n* : dog that is of mixed breed

mut·ter *vb* **1** : speak indistinctly or softly **2** : grumble — **mutter** *n*

mu·tu·al *adj* **1** : given or felt by one another in equal amount **2** : common — **mu·tu·al·ly** *adv*

muz·zle *n* **1** : nose and jaws of an animal **2** : muzzle covering to immobilize an animal's jaws **3** : discharge end of a gun ～ *vb* : restrain with or as if with a muzzle

my *adj* **1** : relating to me or myself **2** — used interjectionally esp. to express surprise

myr·i·ad *n* : indefinitely large number — **myr·iad** *adj*

my·self *pron* : I, me — used reflexively or for emphasis

mys·tery *n* **1** : religious truth **2** : something not understood **3** : puzzling or secret quality or state — **mys·te·ri·ous** *adj* — **mys·te·ri·ous·ly** *adv* — **mys·te·ri·ous·ness** *n*

mys·tic *adj* : spiritual or mysterious ～ *n* : one who has spiritual experiences — **mys·ti·cal** *adj* — **mys·ti·cal·ly** *adj* — **mys·ti·cism** *n*

mys·ti·fy *vb* : perplex — **mys·ti·fi·ca·tion** *n*

myth *n* **1** : legendary narrative explaining a belief or phenomenon **2** : imaginary person or thing — **myth·i·cal** *adj*

my·thol·o·gy *n* : body of myths — **myth·o·log·i·cal** *adj* — **my·thol·o·gist** *n*

N

n *n* : 14th letter of the alphabet

nab *vb* : seize or arrest

na·cho *n* : tortilla chip topped with a savory mixture and cheese and broiled

nag *vb* **1** : complain **2** : scold or urge continually **3** : be persistently annoying ～ *n* : one who nags habitually

nail *n* **1** : horny sheath at the end of each finger and toe **2** : pointed metal fastener ～ *vb* : fasten with a nail — **nail·er** *n*

na·ive, na·ïve *adj* **1** : innocent and unsophisticated **2** : easily deceived — **na·ive·ly** *adv* — **na·ive·ness** *n* — **na·ive·té** *n*

na·ked *adj* **1** : having no clothes on **2** : not covered **3** : plain or obvious **4** : without aid — **na·ked·ly** *adv* — **na·ked·ness** *n*

name *n* **1** : word by which a person or thing is known **2** : disparaging word for someone **3** : distinguished reputation ～ *vb* **1** : give a name to **2** : mention or identify by name **3**

: nominate or appoint ~ *adj* **1** : relating to a name **2** : prominent — **name·able** *adj* — **name·less** *adj* — **name·less·ly** *adv*

name·ly *adv* : that is to say

nap *vb* **1** : sleep briefly **2** : be off guard ~ *n* : short sleep

nape *n* : back of the neck

nap·kin *n* : small cloth for use at the table

nar·cot·ic *n* : painkilling addictive drug — **nar·cot·ic** *adj*

nar·rate *vb* : tell (a story) — **nar·ra·tion** *n* — **nar·ra·tive** *n or adj* — **nar·ra·tor** *n*

nar·row *adj* **1** : of less than standard width **2** : limited **3** : not liberal **4** : barely successful ~ *vb* : make narrow — **nar·row·ly** *adv* — **nar·row·ness** *n*

nar·row–mind·ed *adj* : shallow, provincial, or bigoted

nasal *adj* : relating to or uttered through the nose — **na·sal·ly** *adv*

nas·ty *adj* **1** : filthy **2** : extremely improper or offensive **3** : malicious or spiteful **4** : difficult or disagreeable **5** : unfair — **nas·ti·ly** *adv* — **nas·ti·ness** *n*

na·tion *n* **1** : people of similar characteristics **2** : community with its own territory and government — **na·tion·al** *adj or n* — **na·tion·al·ly** *adv* — **na·tion·hood** *n* — **na·tion·wide** *adj*

na·tion·al·ism *n* : devotion to national interests, unity, and independence — **na·tion·al·ist** *n or adj* — **na·tion·al·is·tic** *adj*

na·tion·al·i·ty *n* **1** : national character **2** : membership in a nation **3** : political independence **4** : ethnic group

na·tion·al·ize *vb* **1** : make national **2** : place under government control — **na·tion·al·i·za·tion** *n*

na·tive *adj* **1** : belonging to a person at or by way of birth **2** : born or produced in a particular place ~ *n* : one who belongs to a country by birth

Na·tiv·i·ty *n* **1** : birth of Christ **2** *not cap* : birth

nat·u·ral *adj* **1** : relating to or determined by nature **2** : not artificial **3** : simple and sincere **4** : lifelike ~ *n* : one having an innate talent — **nat·u·ral·ness** *n*

nat·u·ral·ism *n* : realism in art and literature — **nat·u·ral·ist** *n* — **nat·u·ral·is·tic** *adj*

nat·u·ral·ize *vb* **1** : become or cause to become established **2** : confer citizenship on — **nat·u·ral·i·za·tion** *n*

nat·u·ral·ly *adv* **1** : in a natural way **2** : as might be expected

na·ture *n* **1** : basic quality of something **2** : kind **3** : disposition **4** : physical universe **5** : natural environment

naugh·ty *adj* **1** : disobedient or misbehaving **2** : improper — **naught·i·ly** *adv* — **naught·i·ness** *n*

nau·sea *n* **1** : sickness of the stomach with a desire to vomit **2** : extreme disgust — **nau·se·ate** *vb* — **nau·seous** *adj*

nau·ti·cal *adj* : relating to ships and sailing — **nau·ti·cal·ly** *adv*

na·val *adj* : relating to a navy

na·vel *n* : depression in the abdomen

nav·i·gate *vb* **1** : sail on or through **2** : direct the course of — **nav·i·ga·ble** *adj* — **nav·i·ga·bil·i·ty** *n* — **nav·i·ga·tion** *n* — **nav·i·ga·tor** *n*

na·vy *n* **1** : fleet **2** : nation's organization for sea warfare

near *adv* : at or close to ~ *prep* : close to ~ *adj* **1** : not far away **2** : very much like ~ *vb* : approach — **near·ly** *adv* — **near·ness** *n*

near·by *adv or adj* : near

near·sight·ed *adj* : seeing well at short distances only — **near·sight·ed·ly** *adv* — **near·sight·ed·ness** *n*

neat *adj* **1** : not diluted **2** : tastefully simple **3** : orderly and clean — **neat** *adv* — **neat·ly** *adv* — **neat·ness** *n*

nec·es·sary *n* : indispensable item ~ *adj* **1** : inevitable **2** : compulsory **3** : positively needed — **nec·es·sar·i·ly** *adv* — **ne·ces·si·tate** *vb* — **ne·ces·si·ty** *n*

neck *n* **1** : body part connecting the head and trunk **2** : part of a garment at the neck **3** : narrow part ~ *vb* : kiss and caress — **necked** *adj*

neck·lace *n* : ornament worn around the neck

neck·tie *n* : ornamental cloth tied under a collar

nec·tar·ine *n* : smooth-skinned peach

need *n* **1** : obligation **2** : lack of something or what is lacking **3** : poverty ~ *vb* **1** : be in want **2** : have cause for **3** : be under obligation — **need·ful** *adj* — **need·less** *adj* — **need·less·ly** *adv* — **needy** *adj*

nee·dle *n* **1** : pointed sewing implement or something like it **2** : movable bar in a compass **3** : hollow instrument for injecting or withdrawing material ~ *vb* : incite to action by repeated gibes — **nee·dle·work** *n*

ne·gate *vb* **1** : deny **2** : nullify — **ne·ga·tion** *n*

neg·a·tive *adj* **1** : marked by denial or refusal **2** : showing a lack of something suspected or desirable **3** : less than zero **4** : having more electrons than protons **5** : having light and shadow images reversed ~ *n* **1** : negative word or vote **2** : a negative number **3** : negative photographic image — **neg·a·tive·ly** *adv* — **neg·a·tive·ness** *n* — **neg·a·tiv·i·ty** *n*

ne·glect *vb* **1** : disregard **2** : leave unattended to ~ *n* **1** : act of neglecting **2** : condition of being neglected — **ne·glect·ful** *adj*

neg·li·gent *adj* : marked by neglect — **neg·li·gence** *n* — **neg·li·gent·ly** *adv*

ne·go·ti·ate *vb* **1** : confer with another to settle a matter **2** : obtain cash for **3** : get through successfully — **ne·go·tia·ble** *adj* — **ne·go·ti·a·tion** *n* — **ne·go·ti·a·tor** *n*

neigh·bor *n* **1** : one living nearby **2** : fellowman ~ *vb* : be near or next to — **neigh·bor·hood** *n* — **neigh·bor·li·ness** *n* — **neigh·bor·ly** *adv*

nei·ther *pron or adj* : not the one or the other ~ *conj* **1** : not either **2** : nor

neph·ew *n* : a son of one's brother, sister, brother-in-law, or sister-in-law

nerd *n* : one who is not stylish or socially at ease — **nerdy** *adj*

nerve *n* **1** : strand of body tissue that connects the brain with other parts of the body **2** : self-control **3** : daring **4** *pl* : nervousness — **nerved** *adj* — **nerve·less** *adj* — **nervy** *adj*

ner·vous *adj* **1** : relating to or made up of nerves **2** : easily excited **3** : timid or fearful — **ner·vous·ly** *adv* — **ner·vous·ness** *n*

nest *n* **1** : shelter prepared by a bird for its eggs **2** : place where eggs (as of insects or fish) are laid and hatched **3** : snug retreat **4** : set of objects fitting one inside or under another ~ *vb* : build or occupy a nest

nes·tle *vb* : settle snugly (as in a nest)

net *n* : fabric with spaces between strands or something made of this ~ *vb* : cover with or catch in a net

net·work *n* : system of crossing or connected elements

neu·rot·ic *adj* : relating to neurosis ~ *n* : unstable person — **neu·rot·i·cal·ly** *adv*

neu·tral *adj* **1** : not favoring either side **2** : being neither one thing nor the other **3** : not decided in color **4** : not electrically charged ~ *n* **1** : one that is neutral **2** : position of gears that are not engaged — **neu·tral·i·za·tion** *n* — **neu·tral·ize** *vb*

nev·er *adv* **1** : not ever **2** : not in any degree, way, or condition

nev·er·the·less *adv* : in spite of that

new *adj* **1** : not old or familiar **2** : different from the former **3** : recently discovered or learned **4** : not accustomed **5** : refreshed or regenerated **6** : being such for the first time ~ *adv* : newly — **new·ish** *adj* — **new·ly** *adv* — **new·ness** *n*

news *n* : report of recent events — **news·cast** *n* — **news·cast·er** *n* — **news·let·ter** *n* — **news·mag·a·zine** *n* — **news·man** *n* — **news·pa·per** *n* — **news·pa·per·man** *n* — **news·stand** *n* — **news·wom·an** *n* — **news·wor·thy** *adj*

New Year's Day *n* : January 1 observed as a legal holiday

next *adj* : immediately preceding or following ~ *adv* **1** : in the time or place nearest **2** : at the first time yet to come ~ *prep* : nearest to

nib·ble *vb* : bite gently or bit by bit ~ *n* : small bite

nice *adj* **1** : exhibiting or requiring excessive care **2** : very precise or delicate **3** : pleasing **4** : respectable — **nice·ly** *adv* — **nice·ness** *n* — **nice·ty** *n*

niche *n* **1** : recess in a wall **2** : fitting place, work, or use

nick *n* **1** : small broken area or chip **2** : critical moment ~ *vb* : make a nick in

nick·el *n* **1** : hard silver-white metallic chemical element used in alloys **2** : U.S. 5-cent piece

nick·name *n* : informal substitute name — **nick·name** *vb*

niece *n* : a daughter of one's brother, sister, brother-in-law, or sister-in-law

night *n* **1** : period between dusk and dawn **2** : the coming of night — **night** *adj* — **night·ly** *adj or adv* — **night·time** *n*

night·club *n* : place for drinking and entertainment open at night

night·mare *n* : frightening dream — **night·mare** *adj* — **night·mar·ish** *adj*

nil *n* : nothing

nim·ble *adj* **1** : agile **2** : clever — **nim·ble·ness** *n* — **nim·bly** *adv*

nine *n* **1** : one more than 8 **2** : 9th in a set or series — **nine** *adj or pron* — **ninth** *adj or adv or n*

nine·teen *n* : one more than 18 — **nine·teen** *adj or pron* — **nine·teenth** *adj or n*

nine·ty *n* : 9 times 10 — **nine·ti·eth** *adj or n* — **nine·ty** *adj or pron*

nip *vb* **1** : catch hold of and squeeze tightly **2** : pinch or bite off **3** : destroy the growth or fulfillment of ∼ *n* **1** : biting cold **2** : pungent flavor **3** : pinch or bite

nip·per *n* **1** : one that nips **2** *pl* : pincers **3** : small boy

nip·py *adj* **1** : pungent **2** : chilly

ni·tro·gen *n* : tasteless odorless gaseous chemical element

nit·wit *n* : stupid person

no *adv* **1** — used to express the negative **2** : in no respect or degree **3** : not so **4** — used as an interjection of surprise or doubt ∼ *adj* **1** : not any **2** : not a ∼ *n* **1** : refusal **2** : negative vote

no·ble *adj* **1** : illustrious **2** : aristocratic **3** : marked by much dignity **4** : of outstanding character ∼ *n* : nobleman — **no·ble·ness** *n* — **no·bly** *adv*

no·ble·man *n* : a person of aristocratic rank

no·body *pron* : no person ∼ *n* : person of no influence or importance

no—brain·er : something that requires a minimum of thought

nod *vb* **1** : bend the head downward or forward (as in bowing or going to sleep or as a sign of assent) **2** : move up and down **3** : show by a nod of the head — **nod** *n*

no·el *n* **1** : Christmas carol **2** *cap* : Christmas season

noes *pl of* NO

noise *n* : loud or unpleasant sound ∼ *vb* : spread by rumor — **noise·less** *adj* — **noise·less·ly** *adv* — **noise·mak·er** *n* — **nois·i·ly** *adv* — **nois·i·ness** *n* — **noisy** *adj*

no·mad *n* : one who has no permanent home — **no·mad** *adj* — **no·mad·ic** *adj*

nom·i·nate *vb* : propose or choose as a candidate — **nom·i·na·tion** *n* — **nom·i·nee** *n*

non·cha·lant *adj* : showing indifference — **non·cha·lance** *n* — **non·cha·lant·ly** *adv*

non·con·form·ist *n* : one who does not conform to an established belief or mode of behavior — **non·con·for·mi·ty** *n*

none *pron* : not any ∼ *adv* : not at all

non·per·son *n* : person without social or legal status

non·sense *n* : foolish or meaningless words or actions — **non·sen·si·cal** *adj* — **non·sen·si·cal·ly** *adv*

noo·dle *n* : ribbon-shaped food paste

nook *n* **1** : inside corner **2** : private place

noon *n* : middle of the day — **noon** *adj* — **noon·time** *n*

noose *n* : rope loop that slips down tight

nor *conj* : and not — used esp. after *neither* to introduce and negate the 2d member of a series

norm *n* **1** : standard usu. derived from an average **2** : typical widespread practice or custom

nor·mal *adj* : average, regular, or standard — **nor·mal·cy** *n* — **nor·mal·i·ty** *n* — **nor·mal·i·za·tion** *n* — **nor·mal·ize** *vb* — **nor·mal·ly** *adv*

north *adv* : to or toward the north ∼ *adj* : situated toward, at, or coming from the north ∼ *n* **1** : direction to the left of one facing east **2** *cap* : regions to the north — **north·er·ly** *adv or adj* — **north·ern** *adj* — **North·ern·er** *n* — **north·ern·most** *adj* — **north·ward** *adv or adj* — **north·wards** *adv*

north·east *n* **1** : direction between north and east **2** *cap* : regions to the northeast — **north·east** *adj or adv* — **north·east·er·ly** *adv or adj* — **north·east·ern** *adj*

north pole *n* : northernmost point of the earth

north·west *n* **1** : direction between north and west **2** *cap* : regions to the northwest — **northwest** *adj or adv* — **north·west·er·ly** *adv or adj* — **north·west·ern** *adj*

nose *n* **1** : part of the face containing the nostrils **2** : sense of smell **3** : front part ∼ *vb* **1** : detect by smell **2** : push aside with the nose **3** : pry **4** : inch ahead — **nose·bleed** *n* — **nosed** *adj* — **nose out** *vb* : narrowly defeat

nos·tal·gia *n* : wistful yearning for something past — **nos·tal·gic** *adj*

nos·tril *n* : opening of the nose

nosy, nos·ey *adj* : tending to pry

not *adv* — used to make a statement negative

no·ta·ble *adj* **1** : noteworthy **2** : distinguished ∼ *n* : notable person — **no·ta·bil·i·ty** *n* — **no·ta·bly** *adv*

no·ta·ry public *n* : public official who attests writings to make them legally authentic

notch *n* : V-shaped hollow — **notch** *vb*

note *vb* **1** : notice **2** : write down ∼ *n* **1** : musical tone **2** : written comment or record **3** : short informal letter **4** : notice or heed — **note·book** *n*

note·wor·thy *adj* : worthy of special mention

noth·ing *pron* **1** : no thing **2** : no part **3** : one of no value or importance ∼ *adv* : not at all ∼ *n* **1** : something that does not exist **2** : zero

3 : one of little or no importance — **noth·ing·ness** *n*

no·tice *n* **1** : warning or announcement **2** : attention ∼ *vb* : take notice of — **no·tice·able** *adj* — **no·tice·ably** *adv*

no·ti·fy *vb* : give notice of or to — **no·ti·fi·ca·tion** *n*

no·tion *n* **1** : idea or opinion **2** : whim

no·to·ri·ous *adj* : widely and unfavorably known — **no·to·ri·e·ty** *n* — **no·to·ri·ous·ly** *adv*

not·with·stand·ing *prep* : in spite of ∼ *adv* : nevertheless ∼ *conj* : although

noun *n* : word that is the name of a person, place, or thing

nour·ish *vb* : promote the growth of — **nour·ish·ing** *adj* — **nour·ish·ment** *n*

nov·el *adj* : new or strange ∼ *n* : long invented prose story — **nov·el·ist** *n*

nov·el·ty *n* **1** : something new or unusual **2** : newness **3** : small manufactured article — usu. pl.

No·vem·ber *n* : 11th month of the year having 30 days

nov·ice *n* **1** : one preparing to take vows in a religious order **2** : one who does not have experience or training

now *adv* **1** : at the present time or moment **2** : immediately **3** : under these circumstances ∼ *conj* : in view of the fact ∼ *n* : present time

no·where *adv* : not anywhere — **no·where** *n*

nu·cle·ar *adj* **1** : relating to the atomic nucleus or atomic energy **2** : relating to a weapon whose power is from a nuclear reaction

nu·cle·us *n* : central mass or part (as of a cell or an atom)

nude *adj* : naked ∼ *n* : nude human figure — **nu·di·ty** *n*

nudge *vb* : touch or push gently — **nudge** *n*

nui·sance *n* : something annoying

null *adj* : having no legal or binding force — **nul·li·ty** *n*

nul·li·fy *vb* : make valueless or of no legal force — **nul·li·fi·ca·tion** *n*

numb *adj* : lacking feeling — **numb** *vb* — **numb·ly** *adv* — **numbness** *n*

num·ber *n* **1** : total of individuals taken together **2** : indefinite total **3** : unit of a mathematical system **4** : numeral **5** : one in a sequence ∼ *vb* **1** : count **2** : assign a number to **3** : comprise in number — **num·ber·less** *adj* — **nu·mer·i·cal** *adj* — **nu·mer·i·cal·ly** *adv*

nu·mer·al *n* : conventional symbol representing a number

nu·mer·a·tor *n* : part of a fraction above the line

nu·mer·ous *adj* : consisting of a great number

nun *n* : woman belonging to a religious order — **nun·nery** *n*

nurse *n* **1** : one hired to care for children **2** : person trained to care for sick people ∼ *vb* **1** : provide with milk from the breast **2** : care for

nurs·ery *n* **1** : place where children are cared for **2** : place where young plants are grown

nur·ture *n* **1** : training or upbringing **2** : food or nourishment ∼ *vb* **1** : care for or feed **2** : educate

nut *n* **1** : dry hard-shelled fruit or seed with a firm inner kernel **2** : metal block with a screw hole through it **3** : foolish, eccentric, or crazy person **4** : enthusiast — **nut·crack·er** *n* — **nut·shell** *n* — **nut·ty** *adj*

nu·tri·tion *n* : act or process of nourishing esp. with food — **nu·tri·tion·al** *adj* — **nu·tri·tious** *adj* — **nu·tri·tive** *adj*

nuts *adj* **1** : enthusiastic **2** : crazy

nuz·zle *vb* **1** : touch with or as if with the nose **2** : snuggle

ny·lon *n* **1** : tough synthetic material used esp. in textiles **2** *pl* : stockings made of nylon

O

o *n* **1** : 15th letter of the alphabet **2** : zero

oaf *n* : stupid or awkward person — **oaf·ish** *adj*

oak *n* : tree bearing a thin-shelled nut or its wood — **oak·en** *adj*

oar *n* : pole with a blade at the end used to propel a boat

oa·sis *n* : fertile area in a desert

oat *n* : cereal grass or its edible seed — **oat·cake** *n* — **oat·en** *adj* — **oat·meal** *n*

oath *n* **1** : solemn appeal to God as a pledge of sincerity **2** : profane utterance

obe·di·ent *adj* : willing to obey — **obe·di·ence** *n* — **obe·di·ent·ly** *adv*

obese *adj* : extremely fat — **obe·si·ty** *n*

obey *vb* **1** : follow the commands or guidance of **2** : behave in accordance with

obit·u·ary *n* : death notice

¹ob·ject *n* **1** : something that may be seen or felt **2** : purpose **3** : noun or equivalent toward which the action of a verb is directed or which follows a preposition

²object *vb* : offer opposition or disapproval — **ob·jec·tion** *n* — **ob·jec·tion·able** *adj* — **ob·jec·tion·ably** *adv* — **ob·jec·tor** *n*

ob·jec·tive *adj* **1** : relating to an object or end **2** : existing outside an individual's thoughts or feelings **3** : treating facts without distortion **4** : relating to or being a grammatical case marking objects ~ *n* : aim or end of action — **ob·jec·tive·ly** *adv* — **ob·jec·tive·ness** *n* — **ob·jec·tiv·i·ty** *n*

ob·li·gate *vb* : bind legally or morally — **ob·li·ga·tion** *n* — **oblig·a·to·ry** *adj*

oblige *vb* **1** : compel **2** : do a favor for — **oblig·ing** *adj* — **oblig·ing·ly** *adv*

oblit·er·ate *vb* : completely remove or destroy — **oblit·er·a·tion** *n*

obliv·i·on *n* **1** : state of having lost conscious awareness **2** : state of being forgotten

obliv·i·ous *adj* : not aware or mindful — used with *to* or *of* — **obliv·i·ous·ly** *adv* — **obliv·i·ous·ness** *n*

ob·long *adj* : longer in one direction than in the other with opposite sides parallel — **oblong** *n*

ob·nox·ious *adj* : repugnant — **ob·nox·ious·ly** *adv* — **ob·nox·ious·ness** *n*

ob·scene *adj* : repugnantly improper or offensive — **ob·scene·ly** *adv* — **ob·scen·i·ty** *n*

ob·scure *adj* **1** : dim or hazy **2** : not well known **3** : vague ~ *vb* : make indistinct or unclear — **ob·scure·ly** *adv* — **ob·scu·ri·ty** *n*

ob·ser·va·to·ry *n* : place for observing astronomical phenomena

ob·serve *vb* **1** : conform to **2** : celebrate **3** : see, watch, or notice **4** : remark — **ob·serv·able** *adj* — **ob·ser·vance** *n* — **ob·ser·vant** *adj* — **ob·ser·va·tion** *n*

ob·sess *vb* : preoccupy intensely or abnormally — **ob·ses·sion** *n* — **ob·ses·sive** *adj* — **ob·ses·sive·ly** *adv*

ob·so·lete *adj* : no longer in use

ob·sta·cle *n* : something that stands in the way or opposes

ob·sti·nate *adj* : stubborn — **ob·sti·na·cy** *n* — **ob·sti·nate·ly** *adv*

ob·struct *vb* : block or impede — **ob·struc·tion** *n* — **ob·struc·tive** *adj* — **ob·struc·tor** *n*

ob·tain *vb* **1** : gain by effort **2** : be generally recognized — **ob·tain·able** *adj*

ob·vi·ous *adj* : plain or unmistakable — **ob·vi·ous·ly** *adv* — **ob·vi·ous·ness** *n*

oc·ca·sion *n* **1** : favorable opportunity **2** : cause **3** : time of an event **4** : special event ~ *vb* : cause — **oc·ca·sion·al** *adj* — **oc·ca·sion·al·ly** *adv*

oc·cu·pa·tion *n* **1** : vocation **2** : action or state of occupying — **oc·cu·pa·tion·al** *adj* — **oc·cu·pa·tion·al·ly** *adv*

oc·cu·py *vb* **1** : engage the attention of **2** : fill up **3** : take or hold possession of **4** : reside in — **oc·cu·pan·cy** *n* — **oc·cu·pant** *n* — **oc·cu·pi·er** *n*

oc·cur *vb* **1** : be found or met with **2** : take place **3** : come to mind

oc·cur·rence *n* : something that takes place

ocean *n* **1** : whole body of salt water **2** : very large body of water — **ocean·front** *n* — **ocean·go·ing** *adj* — **oce·an·ic** *adj*

o'·clock *adv* : according to the clock

oc·ta·gon *n* : 8-sided polygon — **oc·tag·o·nal** *adj*

Oc·to·ber *n* : 10th month of the year having 31 days

oc·to·pus *n* : sea mollusk with 8 arms

odd *adj* **1** : being only one of a pair or set **2** : not divisible by two without a remainder **3** : additional to what is usual or to the number mentioned **4** : queer — **odd·i·ty** *n* — **odd·ly** *adv* — **odd·ness** *n*

odds *n pl* **1** : difference by which one thing is favored **2** : disagreement **3** : ratio between winnings and the amount of the bet

odor *n* : quality that affects the sense of smell — **odor·less** *adj* — **odor·ous** *adj*

of *prep* **1** : from **2** : distinguished by **3** : because of **4** : made or written by **5** : made with, being, or containing **6** : belonging to or connected with **7** : about **8** : that is **9** : concerning **10** : before

off *adv* **1** : from a place **2** : unattached or removed **3** : to a state of being no longer in use **4** : away from work **5** : at a distance in time or space ~ *prep* **1** : away from **2** : at the expense of **3** : not engaged in or abstaining from **4** : below the usual level of ~ *adj* **1** : not operating, up to standard, or correct **2** : remote **3** : provided for

of·fend *vb* **1** : sin or act in violation **2** : hurt, annoy, or insult — **of·fend·er** *n*

of·fense, of·fence *n* : attack, misdeed, or insult — **of·fen·sive** *adj* — **of·fen·sive·ly** *adv* — **of·fen·sive·ness** *n*

of·fer *vb* **1 :** present for acceptance **2 :** propose **3 :** put up (an effort) ∼ *n* **1 :** proposal **2 :** bid — **of·fer·ing** *n*

of·fice *n* **1 :** position of authority (as in government) **2 :** rite **3 :** place where a business is transacted — **of·fice·hold·er** *n*

of·fi·cer *n* **1 :** one charged with law enforcement **2 :** one who holds an office of trust or authority **3 :** one who holds a commission in the armed forces

of·fi·cial *n* **:** one in office ∼ *adj* **:** authorized or authoritative — **of·fi·cial·dom** *n* — **of·fi·cial·ly** *adv*

of·fi·ci·ate *vb* **:** perform a ceremony or function

off·spring *n* **offspring** **:** one coming into being through animal or plant reproduction

of·ten *adv* **:** many times — **of·ten·times, oft·times** *adv*

oh *interj* **1** — used to express an emotion **2** — used in direct address

oil *n* **1 :** greasy liquid substance **2 :** petroleum ∼ *vb* **:** put oil in or on — **oil·er** *n* — **oil·i·ness** *n* — **oily** *adj*

oint·ment *n* **:** oily medicinal preparation

OK *or* **okay** *adv or adj* **:** all right ∼ *vb* **:** approve ∼ *n* **:** approval

old *adj* **1 :** of long standing **2 :** of a specified age **3 :** relating to a past era **4 :** having existed a long time — **old·ish** *adj*

old–fash·ioned *adj* **1 :** out-of-date **2 :** conservative

ol·fac·to·ry *adj* **:** relating to the sense of smell

ol·ive *n* **1 :** evergreen tree bearing small edible fruit or the fruit **2 :** dull yellowish green color

om·e·let, om·e·lette *n* **:** beaten eggs lightly fried and folded

omen *n* **:** sign or warning of the future

om·i·nous *adj* **:** presaging evil — **om·i·nous·ly** *adv* — **om·i·nous·ness** *n*

omit *vb* **1 :** leave out **2 :** fail to perform — **omis·si·ble** *adj* — **omis·sion** *n*

om·nip·o·tent *adj* **:** almighty — **om·nip·o·tence** *n* — **om·nip·o·tent·ly** *adv*

on *prep* **1 :** in or to a position over and in contact with **2 :** at or to **3 :** about **4 :** from **5 :** with regard to **6 :** in a state or process **7 :** during the time of ∼ *adv* **1 :** in or into contact with **2 :** forward **3 :** into operation

once *adv* **1 :** one time only **2 :** at any one time **3 :** formerly ∼ *n* **:** one time ∼ *conj* **:** as soon

as ∼ *adj* **:** former — **at once 1 :** simultaneously **2 :** immediately

one *adj* **1 :** being a single thing **2 :** being one in particular **3 :** being the same in kind ∼ *pron* **1 :** certain indefinitely indicated person or thing **2 :** a person in general ∼ *n* **1 :** 1st in a series **2 :** single person or thing — **one·ness** *n*

oner·ous *adj* **:** imposing a burden

one·self *pron* **:** one's own self — usu. used reflexively or for emphasis

one·time *adj* **:** former

one–way *adj* **:** made or for use in only one direction

on·ion *n* **:** plant grown for its pungent edible bulb or this bulb

on·ly *adj* **:** alone in its class ∼ *adv* **1 :** merely or exactly **2 :** solely **3 :** at the very least **4 :** as a result ∼ *conj* **:** but

on·set *n* **:** start

on·to *prep* **:** to a position or point on

on·ward *adv or adj* **:** forward

ooze *n* **:** soft mud ∼ *vb* **:** flow or leak out slowly — **oozy** *adj*

opaque *adj* **1 :** blocking light **2 :** not easily understood — **opaque·ly** *adv*

open *adj* **1 :** not shut or shut up **2 :** not secret or hidden **3 :** frank or generous **4 :** extended **5 :** free from controls **6 :** not decided ∼ *vb* **1 :** make or become open **2 :** make or become functional **3 :** start ∼ *n* **:** outdoors — **open·er** *n* — **open·ly** *adv* — **open·ness** *n*

open·hand·ed *adj* **:** generous — **open·hand·ed·ly** *adv*

open·ing *n* **1 :** act or instance of making open **2 :** something that is open **3 :** opportunity

op·era *n* **:** drama set to music — **op·er·at·ic** *adj*

op·er·ate *vb* **1 :** perform work **2 :** perform an operation **3 :** manage — **op·er·a·ble** *adj* — **op·er·a·tive** *adj* — **op·er·a·tor** *n*

op·er·a·tion *n* **1 :** act or process of operating **2 :** surgical work on a living body **3 :** military action or mission — **op·er·a·tion·al** *adj*

opin·ion *n* **1 :** belief **2 :** judgment **3 :** formal statement by an expert

opin·ion·at·ed *adj* **:** stubborn in one's opinions

op·po·nent *n* **:** one that opposes

op·por·tune *adj* **:** suitable or timely — **op·por·tune·ly** *adv*

op·por·tun·ism *n* **:** a taking advantage of opportunities — **op·por·tun·ist** *n* — **op·por·tu·nis·tic** *adj*

op·por·tu·ni·ty *n* : favorable time

op·pose *vb* 1 : place opposite or against something 2 : resist — **op·po·si·tion** *n*

op·po·site *n* : one that is opposed ∼ *adj* 1 : set facing something that is at the other side or end 2 : opposed or contrary ∼ *adv* : on opposite sides ∼ *prep* : across from — **op·po·site·ly** *adv*

op·press *vb* 1 : persecute 2 : weigh down — **op·pres·sion** *n* — **op·pres·sive** *adj* — **op·pres·sive·ly** *adv* — **op·pres·sor** *n*

op·ti·cal *adj* : relating to optics, vision, or the eye

op·ti·mism *n* : tendency to hope for the best — **op·ti·mist** *n* — **op·ti·mis·tic** *adj* — **op·ti·mis·ti·cal·ly** *adv*

op·tion *n* 1 : ability to choose 2 : right to buy or sell a stock 3 : alternative — **op·tion·al** *adj*

or *conj* — used to indicate an alternative

oral *adj* 1 : spoken 2 : relating to the mouth — **oral·ly** *adv*

or·ange *n* 1 : reddish yellow citrus fruit 2 : color between red and yellow — **or·ange·ade** *n*

ora·tion *n* : elaborate formal speech — **or·a·tor** *n*

or·bit *n* : path made by one body revolving around another ∼ *vb* : revolve around — **or·bit·al** *adj* — **or·bit·er** *n*

or·chard *n* : place where fruit or nut trees are grown — **or·chard·ist** *n*

or·ches·tra *n* 1 : group of musicians 2 : front seats of a theater's main floor — **or·ches·tral** *adj* — **or·ches·tral·ly** *adv*

or·deal *n* : severely trying experience

or·der *n* 1 : rank, class, or special group 2 : arrangement 3 : rule of law 4 : authoritative regulation or instruction 5 : working condition 6 : special request for a purchase or what is purchased ∼ *vb* 1 : arrange 2 : give an order to 3 : place an order for

or·der·ly *adj* 1 : being in order or tidy 2 : well behaved ∼ *n* 1 : officer's attendant 2 : hospital attendant — **or·der·li·ness** *n*

or·di·nal *n* : number indicating order in a series

or·di·nance *n* : municipal law

or·di·nary *adj* : of common occurrence, quality, or ability — **or·di·nar·i·ly** *adv*

ore *n* : mineral containing a valuable constituent

or·gan *n* 1 : air-powered or electronic keyboard instrument 2 : animal or plant structure with special function 3 : periodical

or·gan·ic *adj* 1 : relating to a bodily organ 2 : relating to living things 3 : relating to or containing carbon or its compounds 4 : relating to foods produced without the use of laboratory-made products — **or·gan·i·cal·ly** *adv*

or·gan·ism *n* : a living thing

or·ga·nize *vb* : form parts into a functioning whole — **or·ga·ni·za·tion** *n* — **or·ga·ni·za·tion·al** *adj* — **or·ga·niz·er** *n*

ori·ent *vb* 1 : set in a definite position 2 : acquaint with a situation — **ori·en·ta·tion** *n*

or·i·fice *n* : opening

or·i·gin *n* 1 : ancestry 2 : rise, beginning, or derivation from a source — **orig·i·nate** *vb* — **orig·i·na·tor** *n*

orig·i·nal *n* : something from which a copy is made ∼ *adj* 1 : first 2 : not copied from something else 3 : inventive — **orig·i·nal·i·ty** *n* — **orig·i·nal·ly** *adv*

or·na·ment *n* : something that adorns ∼ *vb* : provide with ornament — **or·na·men·tal** *adj* — **or·na·men·ta·tion** *n*

or·nate *adj* : elaborately decorated — **or·nate·ly** *adv* — **or·nate·ness** *n*

or·phan *n* : child whose parents are dead — **or·phan** *vb* — **or·phan·age** *n*

or·tho·dox *adj* 1 : conforming to established doctrine 2 *cap* : of or relating to a Christian church originating in the Eastern Roman Empire — **or·tho·doxy** *n*

os·mo·sis *n* : diffusion esp. of water through a membrane — **os·mot·ic** *adj*

os·ten·ta·tion *n* : pretentious display — **os·ten·ta·tious** *adj* — **os·ten·ta·tious·ly** *adv*

os·tra·cize *vb* : exclude by common consent — **os·tra·cism** *n*

oth·er *adj* 1 : being the one left 2 : alternate 3 : additional ∼ *pron* 1 : remaining one 2 : different one

oth·er·wise *adv* 1 : in a different way 2 : in different circumstances 3 : in other respects — **oth·er·wise** *adj*

ought *verbal auxiliary* — used to express obligation, advisability, or expectation

ounce *n* 1 : unit of weight equal to about 28.3 grams 2 : unit of capacity equal to about 29.6 milliliters

our *adj* : of or relating to us

ours *pron* : that which belongs to us

our·selves *pron* : we, us — used reflexively or for emphasis

out *adv* 1 : away from the inside or center 2 : beyond control 3 : to extinction, exhaustion, or completion **4** : in or into the open ∼ *vb* : become known ∼ *adj* **1** : situated outside **2** : absent ∼ *prep* **1** : out through **2** : outward on or along — **out·bound** *adj* — **out·build·ing** *n*

out·break *n* : sudden occurrence

out·burst *n* : violent expression of feeling

out·cast *n* : person cast out by society

out·come *n* : result

out·dat·ed *adj* : out-of-date

out·do *vb* : do better than

out·doors *adv* : in or into the open air ∼ *n* : open air — **out·door** *adj*

out·er *adj* **1** : external **2** : farther out — **out·er·most** *adj*

out·fit *n* **1** : equipment for a special purpose **2** : group ∼ *vb* : equip — **out·fit·ter** *n*

out·ing *n* : excursion

outlast *vb* : last longer than

out·law *n* : lawless person ∼ *vb* : make illegal

out·lay *n* : expenditure

out·let *n* **1** : exit **2** : means of release **3** : market for goods **4** : electrical device that gives access to wiring

out·line *n* **1** : line marking the outer limits **2** : summary ∼ *vb* **1** : draw the outline of **2** : indicate the chief parts of

out·look *n* **1** : viewpoint **2** : prospect for the future

out of *prep* **1** : out from within **2** : beyond the limits of **3** : among **4** — used to indicate absence or loss **5** : because of **6** : from or with

out—of—date *adj* : no longer current or useful

out·put *n* : amount produced ∼ *vb* : produce

out·rage *n* **1** : violent or shameful act **2** : injury or insult **3** : extreme anger ∼ *vb* **1** : subject to violent injury **2** : make very angry

out·ra·geous *adj* : extremely offensive or shameful — **out·ra·geous·ly** *adv* — **out·ra·geous·ness** *n*

out·right *adv* **1** : completely **2** : instantly ∼ *adj* **1** : complete **2** : given without reservation

out·side *n* **1** : place beyond a boundary **2** : exterior **3** : utmost limit ∼ *adj* **1** : outer **2** : coming from without **3** : remote ∼ *adv* : on or to the outside ∼ *prep* **1** : on or to the outside of **2** : beyond the limits of

out·sid·er *n* : one who does not belong to a group

out·smart *vb* : outwit

out·spo·ken *adj* : direct and open in speech — **out·spo·ken·ness** *n*

out·stand·ing *adj* **1** : not yet paid **2** : very good — **out·stand·ing·ly** *adv*

out·strip *vb* **1** : go faster than **2** : surpass

out·ward *adj* **1** : being toward the outside **2** : showing outwardly — **out·ward** *adv* — **out·ward·ly** *adv*

out·wit *vb* : get the better of by superior cleverness

oval *adj* : having the shape of an egg — **oval** *n*

ova·tion *n* : enthusiastic applause

ov·en *n* : chamber (as in a stove) for baking

over *adv* **1** : across **2** : upside down **3** : in excess or addition **4** : above **5** : at an end **6** : again ∼ *prep* **1** : above in position or authority **2** : more than **3** : along, through, or across **4** : because of ∼ *adj* **1** : upper **2** : remaining **3** : ended

over·age *n* : surplus

over·all *adj* : including everything

over·alls *n pl* : pants with an extra piece covering the chest

over·bear·ing *adj* : arrogant

over·blown *adj* : pretentious

over·cast *adj* : clouded over ∼ *n* : cloud covering

over·coat *n* : outer coat

over·come *vb* **1** : defeat **2** : make helpless or exhausted

over·do *vb* : do too much

over·flow *vb* **1** : flood **2** : flow over — **over·flow** *n*

over·hang *vb* : jut out over ∼ *n* : something that overhangs

over·haul *vb* **1** : repair **2** : overtake

over·head *adv* : aloft ∼ *adj* : situated above ∼ *n* : general business expenses

over·hear *vb* : hear without the speaker's knowledge

over·joyed *adj* : filled with joy

over·lap *vb* : lap over — **overlap** *n*

over·look *vb* **1** : look down on **2** : fail to see **3** : ignore **4** : pardon **5** : supervise ∼ *n* : observation point

over·ly *adv* : excessively

over·night *adv* **1** : through the night **2** : suddenly — **overnight** *adj*

over·pass *n* : bridge over a road

over·pow·er *vb* : conquer

over·rule *vb* : rule against or set aside

over·run *vb* **1** : swarm or flow over **2** : go beyond ∼ *n* : an exceeding of estimated costs

over·see *vb* : supervise — **over·seer** *n*

over·sight *n* : inadvertent omission or error

over·take *vb* : catch up with

over·throw *vb* **1** : upset **2** : defeat — **over·throw** *n*

over·time *n* : extra working time — **overtime** *adv*

over·turn *vb* **1** : turn over **2** : nullify

over·view *n* : brief survey

over·whelm *vb* : overcome completely — **over·whelm·ing·ly** *adv*

owe *vb* **1** : have an obligation to pay **2** : be indebted to or for

owl *n* : nocturnal bird of prey — **owl·ish** *adj* — **owl·ish·ly** *adv*

own *adj* : belonging to oneself ∼ *vb* **1** : have as property **2** : acknowledge ∼ *pron* : one or ones belonging to oneself — **own·er** *n* — **own·er·ship** *n*

ox *n* (**ox·en**) : bovine mammal and esp. a castrated bull

ox·y·gen *n* : gaseous chemical element essential for life

ozone *n* : very reactive bluish form of oxygen

P

p *n* : 16th letter of the alphabet

pace *n* **1** : walking step **2** : rate of progress ∼ *vb* **1** : go at a pace **2** : cover with slow steps **3** : set the pace of

pace·mak·er *n* : electrical device to regulate heartbeat

pa·cif·ic *adj* : calm or peaceful

pac·i·fy *vb* : make calm — **pac·i·fi·ca·tion** *n* — **pac·i·fi·er** *n* — **pac·i·fism** *n* — **pac·i·fist** *n or adj* — **pac·i·fis·tic** *adj*

pack *n* **1** : compact bundle **2** : group of animals ∼ *vb* **1** : put into a container **2** : fill tightly or completely **3** : send without ceremony — **pack·er** *n*

pack·age *n* : items bundled together ∼ *vb* : enclose in a package

pack·et *n* : small package

pact *n* : agreement

pad *n* **1** : cushioning part or thing **2** : floating leaf of a water plant **3** : tablet of paper ∼ *vb* **1** : furnish with a pad **2** : expand with needless matter — **pad·ding** *n*

pad·dle *n* : implement with a flat blade ∼ *vb* : move, beat, or stir with a paddle

pad·lock *n* : lock with a U-shaped catch — **padlock** *vb*

pa·gan *n or adj* : heathen — **pa·gan·ism** *n*

¹**page** *n* : messenger ∼ *vb* : summon by repeated calls — **pag·er** *n*

²**page** *n* **1** : single leaf (as of a book) or one side of the leaf **2** : information at a single World Wide Web address

pag·eant *n* : elaborate spectacle or procession — **pag·eant·ry** *n*

pa·go·da *n* : tower with roofs curving upward

paid *past of* PAY

pail *n* : cylindrical container with a handle — **pail·ful** *n*

pain *n* **1** : punishment or penalty **2** : suffering of body or mind **3** *pl* : great care ∼ *vb* : cause or experience pain — **pain·ful** *adj* — **pain·ful·ly** *adv* — **pain·kill·er** *n* — **pain·kill·ing** *adj* — **pain·less** *adj* — **pain·less·ly** *adv*

pains·tak·ing *adj* : taking great care — **pains·tak·ing** *n* — **pains·tak·ing·ly** *adv*

paint *vb* **1** : apply color or paint to **2** : portray esp. in color ∼ *n* : mixture of pigment and liquid — **paint·brush** *n* — **paint·er** *n* — **paint·ing** *n*

pair *n* : a set of two ∼ *vb* : put or go together as a pair

pa·ja·mas *n pl* : loose suit for sleeping

pal *n* : close friend

pal·ace *n* **1** : residence of a chief of state **2** : mansion — **pa·la·tial** *adj*

pal·ate *n* **1** : roof of the mouth **2** : taste — **pal·at·able** *adj* — **pal·a·tal** *adj*

pale *adj* **1** : lacking in color or brightness **2** : light in color or shade ∼ *vb* : make or become pale — **pale·ness** *n*

pal·ette *n* : board on which paints are laid and mixed

pall *n* **1** : cloth draped over a coffin **2** : something that produces gloom

pall·bear·er *n* : one who attends the coffin at a funeral

pal·let *n* **1** : makeshift bed **2** : portable storage platform

pal·lor *n* : paleness

¹**palm** *n* **1** : tall tropical tree crowned with large leaves **2** : symbol of victory

²**palm** *n* : underside of the hand ∼ *vb* **1** : conceal in the hand **2** : impose by fraud

pal·pa·ble *adj* **1** : capable of being touched **2** : obvious — **pal·pa·bly** *adv*

pal·pi·tate *vb* : beat rapidly — **pal·pi·ta·tion** *n*

pam·per *vb* : spoil or indulge

pam·phlet *n* : unbound publication — **pamphle·teer** *n*

pan *n* : broad, shallow, and open container ∼ *vb* **1** : wash gravel in a pan to search for gold **2** : criticize severely

pan·cake *n* : fried flat cake

pan·cre·as *n* : gland that produces insulin — **pan·cre·at·ic** *adj*

pan·da *n* : black-and-white bearlike animal

pan·de·mo·ni·um *n* : wild uproar

pan·der *n* : one who caters to others' desires or weaknesses ∼ *vb* : act as a pander

pane *n* : sheet of glass

pan·el *n* **1** : list of persons (as jurors) **2** : discussion group **3** : flat piece of construction material **4** : board with instruments or controls ∼ *vb* : decorate with panels — **pan·el·ing** *n* — **pan·el·ist** *n*

pan·han·dle *vb* : ask for money on the street — **pan·han·dler** *n*

pan·ic *n* : sudden overpowering fright ∼ *vb* : affect or be affected with panic — **pan·icky** *adj*

pan·o·ra·ma *n* : view in every direction — **pan·o·ram·ic** *adj*

pant *vb* **1** : breathe with great effort **2** : yearn ∼ *n* : panting sound

pant·ies *n pl* : woman's or child's short underpants

pan·to·mime *n* **1** : play without words **2** : expression by bodily or facial movements ∼ *vb* : represent by pantomime

pan·try *n* : storage room for food and dishes

pants *n pl* **1** : 2-legged outer garment **2** : panties

pa·pal *adj* : relating to the pope

pa·per *n* **1** : pliable substance used to write or print on, to wrap things in, or to cover walls **2** : printed or written document **3** : newspaper — **paper** *adj or vb* — **pa·per·hang·er** *n* — **pa·per·weight** *n* — **pa·pery** *adj*

pa·pier–mâ·ché *n* : molding material of waste paper

par *n* **1** : stated value **2** : common level **3** : accepted standard or normal condition — **par** *adj*

para·chute *n* : large umbrella-shaped device for making a descent through air — **parachute** *vb* — **para·chut·ist** *n*

pa·rade *n* **1** : pompous display **2** : ceremonial formation and march ∼ *vb* **1** : march in a parade **2** : show off

par·a·dise *n* : place of bliss

par·a·dox *n* : statement that seems contrary to common sense yet is perhaps true — **par·a·dox·i·cal** *adj* — **par·a·dox·i·cal·ly** *adv*

para·graph *n* : unified division of a piece of writing ∼ *vb* : divide into paragraphs

par·al·lel *adj* **1** : lying or moving in the same direction but always the same distance apart **2** : similar ∼ *n* **1** : parallel line, curve, or surface **2** : line of latitude **3** : similarity ∼ *vb* **1** : compare **2** : correspond to — **par·al·lel·ism** *n*

par·al·lel·o·gram *n* : 4-sided polygon with opposite sides equal and parallel

pa·ral·y·sis *n* : loss of function and esp. of voluntary motion — **par·a·lyt·ic** *adj or n*

par·a·lyze *vb* : affect with paralysis — **par·a·lyz·ing·ly** *adv*

para·med·ic *n* : person trained to provide initial emergency medical treatment

para·noia *n* : mental disorder marked by irrational suspicion — **para·noid** *adj or n*

par·a·pher·na·lia *n sing or pl* : equipment

para·phrase *n* : restatement of a text giving the meaning in different words — **paraphrase** *vb*

par·a·site *n* : organism living on another — **par·a·sit·ic** *adj* — **par·a·sit·ism** *n*

par·cel *n* **1** : lot **2** : package ∼ *vb* : divide into portions

parch *vb* : toast or shrivel with dry heat

par·don *n* : excusing of an offense ∼ *vb* : free from penalty — **par·don·able** *adj* — **par·don·er** *n*

pare *vb* **1** : trim off an outside part **2** : reduce as if by paring — **par·er** *n*

par·ent *n* : one that begets or brings up offspring — **par·ent·age** *n* — **pa·ren·tal** *adj* — **par·ent·hood** *n*

pa·ren·the·sis *n* **1** : word or phrase inserted in a passage **2** : one of a pair of punctuation marks ( ) — **par·en·thet·ic**, **par·en·thet·i·cal** *adj* — **par·en·thet·i·cal·ly** *adv*

par·ish *n* : local church community

pa·rish·io·ner *n* : member of a parish

park *n* : land set aside for recreation or for its beauty ∼ *vb* : leave a vehicle standing

par·ka *n* : usu. hooded heavy jacket

park·way *n* : broad landscaped thoroughfare

par·lay *n* : the risking of a stake plus its winnings — **par·lay** *vb*

par·ley *n* : conference about a dispute — **parley** *vb*

par·lia·ment *n* : legislative assembly — **par·lia·men·tar·i·an** *n* — **par·lia·men·ta·ry** *adj*

par·lor *n* **1** : reception room **2** : place of business

par·o·dy *n* : humorous or satirical imitation — **par·o·dy** *vb*

pa·role *n* : conditional release of a prisoner — **pa·role** *vb* — **pa·rol·ee** *n*

par·ra·keet *var of* PARAKEET

par·rot *n* : bright-colored tropical bird

pars·ley *n* : garden plant used as a seasoning or garnish

par·son *n* : minister

par·son·age *n* : parson's house

part *n* **1** : one of the units into which a larger whole is divided **2** : function or role ~ *vb* **1** : take leave **2** : separate **3** : go away **4** : give up

par·take *vb* : have or take a share — **par·tak·er** *n*

par·tial *adj* **1** : favoring one over another **2** : affecting a part only — **par·tial·i·ty** *n* — **par·tial·ly** *adv*

par·tic·i·pate *vb* : take part in something — **par·tic·i·pant** *adj or n* — **par·tic·i·pa·tion** *n* — **par·tic·i·pa·to·ry** *adj*

par·ti·cle *n* : small bit

par·tic·u·lar *adj* **1** : relating to a specific person or thing **2** : individual **3** : hard to please ~ *n* : detail — **par·tic·u·lar·ly** *adv*

par·ti·san *n* **1** : adherent **2** : guerrilla — **par·ti·san** *adj* — **par·ti·san·ship** *n*

par·ti·tion *n* **1** : distribution **2** : something that divides — **partition** *vb*

part·ly *adv* : in some degree

part·ner *n* **1** : associate **2** : companion **3** : business associate — **part·ner·ship** *n*

part of speech : class of words distinguished esp. according to function

par·ty *n* **1** : political organization **2** : participant **3** : company of persons esp. with a purpose **4** : social gathering

pass *vb* **1** : move past, over, or through **2** : go away or die **3** : allow to elapse **4** : go unchallenged **5** : transfer or undergo transfer **6** : render a judgment **7** : occur **8** : enact **9** : undergo testing successfully **10** : be regarded **11** : decline ~ *n* **1** : low place in a mountain range **2** : act of passing **3** : accomplishment **4** : permission to leave, enter, or move about — **pass·able** *adj* — **pass·ably** *adv* — **pass·er** *n* — **pass·er·by** *n*

pas·sage *n* **1** : process of passing **2** : means

of passing **3** : voyage **4** : right to pass **5** : literary selection — **pas·sage·way** *n*

pas·sé *adj* : out-of-date

pas·sen·ger *n* : traveler in a conveyance

pas·sion *n* **1** : strong feeling esp. of anger, love, or desire **2** : object of affection or enthusiasm — **pas·sion·ate** *adj* — **pas·sion·ate·ly** *adv* — **pas·sion·less** *adj*

pas·sive *adj* **1** : not active but acted upon **2** : submissive — **pas·sive** *n* — **pas·sive·ly** *adv* — **pas·siv·i·ty** *n*

Pass·over *n* : Jewish holiday celebrated in March or April in commemoration of the Hebrews' liberation from slavery in Egypt

pass·port *n* : government document needed for travel abroad

pass·word *n* **1** : word or phrase spoken to pass a guard **2** : sequence of characters needed to get into a computer system

past *adj* **1** : ago **2** : just gone by **3** : having existed before the present **4** : expressing past time ~ *prep or adv* : beyond ~ *n* **1** : time gone by **2** : verb tense expressing time gone by **3** : past life

pas·ta *n* : fresh or dried shaped dough

paste *n* **1** : smooth ground food **2** : moist adhesive ~ *vb* : attach with paste — **pasty** *adj*

pas·tel *n* : light color — **pas·tel** *adj*

pas·teur·ize *vb* : heat (as milk) so as to kill germs — **pas·teur·i·za·tion** *n*

pas·time *n* : amusement

pas·tor *n* : priest or minister serving a church or parish — **pas·tor·ate** *n*

pas·try *n* : sweet baked goods

pas·ture *n* : land used for grazing ~ *vb* : graze

pat *n* **1** : light tap **2** : small mass ~ *vb* : tap gently ~ *adj or adv* **1** : apt or glib **2** : not yielding

patch *n* **1** : piece used for mending **2** : small area distinct from surrounding area ~ *vb* **1** : mend with a patch **2** : make of fragments **3** : repair hastily — **patchy** *adj*

pa·tent *adj* **1** : obvious **2** : protected by a patent ~ *n* : document conferring or securing a right ~ *vb* : secure by patent — **pat·ent·ly** *adv*

pa·ter·nal *adj* **1** : fatherly **2** : related through or inherited from a father — **pa·ter·nal·ly** *adv*

pa·ter·ni·ty *n* : fatherhood

path *n* **1** : trodden way **2** : route or course — **path·find·er** *n* — **path·way** *n* — **path·less** *adj*

pa·thet·ic *adj* : pitiful — **pa·thet·i·cal·ly** *adv*

pa·tience *n* : habit or fact of being patient

pa·tient *adj* : bearing pain or trials without complaint ∼ *n* : one under medical care — **pa·tient·ly** *adv*

pa·tio *n* 1 : courtyard 2 : paved recreation area near a house

pa·tri·arch *n* 1 : man revered as father or founder 2 : venerable old man — **pa·tri·ar·chal** *adj* — **pa·tri·ar·chy** *n*

pa·tri·ot *n* : one who loves his or her country — **pa·tri·ot·ic** *adj* — **pa·tri·ot·i·cal·ly** *adv* — **pa·tri·o·tism** *n*

pa·trol *n* 1 : a going around for observation or security 2 : group on patrol ∼ *vb* : carry out a patrol

pa·tron *n* 1 : special protector 2 : wealthy supporter 3 : customer — **pa·tron·age** *n*

pa·tron·ize *vb* 1 : be a customer of 2 : treat with condescension

pat·tern *n* 1 : model for imitation or for making things 2 : artistic design 3 : noticeable formation or set of characteristics ∼ *vb* : form according to a pattern

pat·ty *n* : small flat cake

paunch *n* : large belly — **paunchy** *adj*

pau·per *n* : poor person — **pau·per·ism** *n* — **pau·per·ize** *vb*

pause *n* : temporary stop ∼ *vb* : stop briefly

pave *vb* : cover to smooth or firm the surface — **pave·ment** *n* — **pav·ing** *n*

pa·vil·ion *n* 1 : large tent 2 : light structure used for entertainment or shelter

paw *n* : foot of a 4-legged clawed animal ∼ *vb* 1 : handle clumsily or rudely 2 : touch or strike with a paw

pawn *n* 1 : goods deposited as security for a loan 2 : state of being pledged ∼ *vb* : deposit as a pledge — **pawn·bro·ker** *n* — **pawn·shop** *n*

pay *vb* (**paid; paid**) 1 : make due return for goods or services 2 : discharge indebtedness for 3 : retaliate for 4 : give freely or as fitting 5 : be profitable ∼ *n* 1 : status of being paid 2 : something paid — **pay·able** *adj* — **pay·check** *n* — **pay·ee** *n* — **pay·er** *n* — **pay·ment** *n*

PC *n* : small personal computer

pea *n* : round edible seed of a leguminous vine

peace *n* 1 : state of calm and quiet 2 : absence of war or strife — **peace·able** *adj* — **peace·ably** *adv* — **peace·ful** *adj* — **peace·ful·ly** *adv* — **peace·keep·er** *n* — **peace·keep·ing** *n* — **peace·mak·er** *n* — **peace·time** *n*

peach *n* : sweet juicy fruit of a flowering tree or this tree

peak *n* 1 : pointed or projecting part 2 : top of a hill 3 : highest level ∼ *vb* : reach a maximum — **peak** *adj*

pea·nut *n* : annual herb that bears underground pods or the pod or the edible seed inside

pear *n* : fleshy fruit of a tree related to the apple

pearl *n* : gem formed within an oyster — **pearly** *adj*

peas·ant *n* : tiller of the soil — **peas·ant·ry** *n*

peat *n* : decayed organic deposit often dried for fuel — **peaty** *adj*

peb·ble *n* : small stone — **peb·bly** *adj*

pe·can *n* : hickory tree bearing a smooth-shelled nut or the nut

[1]**peck** *n* : unit of dry measure equal to 8 quarts

[2]**peck** *vb* : strike or pick up with the bill ∼ *n* : quick sharp stroke

pe·cu·liar *adj* 1 : characteristic of only one 2 : strange — **pe·cu·liar·i·ty** *n* — **pe·cu·liar·ly** *adv*

ped·al *n* : lever worked by the foot ∼ *adj* : relating to the foot ∼ *vb* : use a pedal

ped·dle *vb* : offer for sale — **ped·dler** *n*

ped·es·tal *n* : support or foot of something upright

pe·des·tri·an *adj* 1 : ordinary 2 : walking ∼ *n* : person who walks

peek *vb* 1 : look furtively 2 : glance — **peek** *n*

peel *vb* 1 : strip the skin or rind from 2 : lose the outer layer ∼ *n* : skin or rind — **peel·ing** *n*

[1]**peep** *vb* : utter faint shrill sounds — **cheep** *n*

[2]**peep** *vb* 1 : look slyly 2 : begin to emerge ∼ *n* : brief look — **peep·er** *n* — **peep·hole** *n*

[1]**peer** *n* 1 : one's equal 2 : nobleman — **peer·age** *n*

[2]**peer** *vb* : look intently or curiously

peer·less *adj* : having no equal

peeve *vb* : make resentful ∼ *n* : complaint — **peev·ish** *adj* — **peev·ish·ly** *adv* — **peev·ish·ness** *n*

peg *n* : small pinlike piece ∼ *vb* 1 : put a peg into 2 : fix or mark with or as if with pegs

pel·let *n* : little ball — **pel·let·al** *adj* — **pel·let·ize** *vb*

[1]**pelt** *n* : skin of a fur-bearing animal

[2]**pelt** *vb* : strike with blows or missiles

pel·vis *n* : cavity formed by the hip bones — **pel·vic** *adj*

¹pen *n* : enclosure for animals ∼ *vb* : shut in a pen

²pen *n* : tool for writing with ink ∼ *vb* : write

pe·nal *adj* : relating to punishment — **pe·nal·ize** *vb* — **pen·al·ty** *n*

pen·cil *n* : writing or drawing tool with a solid marking substance (as graphite) as its core ∼ *vb* : draw or write with a pencil

pen·dant *n* : hanging ornament

pen·dent, pen·dant *adj* : hanging

pend·ing *prep* : while awaiting ∼ *adj* : not yet decided

pen·du·lum *n* : a hanging weight that is free to swing

pen·e·trate *vb* **1** : enter into **2** : permeate **3** : see into — **pen·e·tra·ble** *adj* — **pen·e·tra·tion** *n* — **pen·e·tra·tive** *adj*

pen·guin *n* : short-legged flightless seabird

pen·in·su·la *n* : land extending out into the water — **pen·in·su·lar** *adj*

pen·i·ten·tia·ry *n* : state or federal prison

pen·nant *n* : nautical or championship flag

pen·ny *n* **1** : monetary unit equal to 1/100 pound **2** : cent — **pen·ni·less** *adj*

pen·sion *n* : retirement income ∼ *vb* : pay a pension to — **pen·sion·er** *n*

pen·sive *adj* : thoughtful — **pen·sive·ly** *adv*

pent·a·gon *n* : 5-sided polygon — **pen·tag·o·nal** *adj*

peo·ple *n* **1 people** *pl* : human beings in general **2 people** *pl* : human beings in a certain group (as a family) or community **3** *pl* **peoples** : tribe, nation, or race ∼ *vb* : constitute the population of

pep *n* : brisk energy ∼ *vb* : put pep into — **pep·py** *adj*

pep·per *n* **1** : pungent seasoning from the berry (**peppercorn**) of a shrub **2** : vegetable grown for its hot or sweet fruit ∼ *vb* : season with pepper — **pep·pery** *adj*

pep·per·mint *n* : pungent aromatic mint

per *prep* **1** : by means of **2** : for each **3** : according to

per·ceive *vb* **1** : realize **2** : become aware of through the senses — **per·ceiv·able** *adj* — **per·cep·ti·ble** *adj* — **per·cep·ti·bly** *adv* — **per·cep·tion** *n* — **per·cep·tive** *n* — **per·cep·tive·ly** *adv*

per·cent *adv* : in each hundred ∼ *n* **per·cent** **1** : one part in a hundred **2** : percentage

per·cent·age *n* : part expressed in hundredths

per·cen·tile *n* : a standing on a scale of 0–100

perch *n* : resting place for birds ∼ *vb* : settle on a resting place

per·co·late *vb* : trickle or filter down through a substance — **per·co·la·tor** *n*

per·cus·sion *n* **1** : sharp blow **2** : musical instrument sounded by striking

pe·ren·ni·al *adj* **1** : present at all seasons **2** : continuing from year to year **3** : recurring regularly ∼ *n* : perennial plant — **pe·ren·ni·al·ly** *adv*

per·fect *adj* **1** : being without fault or defect **2** : exact **3** : complete ∼ *vb* : make perfect — **per·fect·ibil·i·ty** *n* — **per·fect·ible** *adj* — **per·fect·ly** *adv* — **per·fect·ness** *n*

per·fec·tion *n* **1** : quality or state of being perfect **2** : highest degree of excellence — **per·fec·tion·ist** *n*

per·fo·rate *vb* : make a hole in — **per·fo·ra·tion** *n*

per·form *vb* **1** : carry out **2** : do in a set manner **3** : give a public presentation — **per·for·mance** *n* — **per·form·er** *n*

per·fume *n* **1** : pleasant odor **2** : something that gives a scent ∼ *vb* : add scent to

per·haps *adv* : possibly but not certainly

per·il *n* : danger — **per·il·ous** *adj* — **per·il·ous·ly** *adv*

pe·rim·e·ter *n* : outer boundary of a body or figure

pe·ri·od *n* **1** : punctuation mark . used esp. to mark the end of a declarative sentence or an abbreviation **2** : division of time **3** : stage in a process or development

pe·ri·od·ic *adj* : occurring at regular intervals — **pe·ri·od·i·cal** *n* — **pe·ri·od·i·cal·ly** *adv*

pe·riph·ery *n* : outer boundary — **pe·riph·er·al** *adj*

per·ish *vb* : die or spoil — **per·ish·able** *adj or n*

per·ju·ry *n* : lying under oath — **per·jure** *vb* — **per·jur·er** *n*

perk *vb* **1** : thrust (as the head) up jauntily **2** : freshen **3** : gain vigor or spirit — **perky** *adj*

per·ma·nent *adj* : lasting ∼ *n* : hair wave — **per·ma·nence** *n* — **per·ma·nent·ly** *adv*

per·me·ate *vb* **1** : seep through **2** : become spread throughout — **per·me·able** *adj* — **per·me·a·bil·i·ty** *n* — **per·me·ation** *n*

per·mit *vb* **1** : approve **2** : make possible ∼ *n* : license — **per·mis·si·ble** *adj* — **per·mis·sion** *n* — **per·mis·sive** *adj* — **per·miss·ive·ly** *adv* — **per·mis·sive·ness** *n*

per·pen·dic·u·lar *adj* **1** : vertical **2** : meeting at a right angle — **per·pen·dic·u·lar** n — **per·pen·dic·u·lar·i·ty** n — **per·pen·dic·u·lar·ly** adv

per·pe·trate vb : be guilty of doing — **per·pe·tra·tion** n — **per·pe·tra·tor** n

per·pet·u·al adj 1 : continuing forever 2 : occurring continually — **per·pet·u·al·ly** adv — **per·pet·u·ate** vb — **per·pe·tu·ity** n

per·plex vb : confuse — **per·plex·i·ty** n

per·se·cute vb : harass, afflict — **per·se·cu·tion** n — **per·se·cu·tor** n

per·se·vere vb : persist — **per·se·ver·ance** n

per·sist vb 1 : go on resolutely in spite of difficulties 2 : continue to exist — **per·sis·tence** n — **per·sis·ten·cy** n — **per·sis·tent** adj — **per·sis·tent·ly** adv

per·son n 1 : human being 2 : human being's body or individuality 3 : reference to the speaker, one spoken to, or one spoken of

per·son·able adj : having a pleasing personality

per·son·al adj 1 : relating to a particular person 2 : done in person 3 : affecting one's body 4 : offensive to a certain individual — **per·son·al·ize** vb — **per·son·al·ly** adv

per·son·al·i·ty n 1 : manner and disposition of an individual 2 : distinctive or well-known person

per·son·i·fy vb 1 : represent as a human being 2 : be the embodiment of — **per·son·i·fi·ca·tion** n

per·son·nel n : body of persons employed

per·spec·tive n 1 : apparent depth and distance in painting 2 : view of things in their true relationship or importance

per·spire vb : sweat — **per·spi·ra·tion** n

per·suade vb : win over to a belief or course of action by argument or entreaty — **per·sua·sion** n — **per·sua·sive** adj — **per·sua·sive·ly** adv — **per·sua·sive·ness** n

per·tain vb 1 : belong 2 : relate

per·ti·nent adj : relevant — **per·ti·nence** n

per·verse adj 1 : corrupt 2 : unreasonably contrary — **per·verse·ly** adv — **per·verse·ness** n — **per·ver·sion** n — **per·ver·si·ty** n

per·vert vb : corrupt or distort ~ n : one that is perverted

pes·si·mism n : inclination to expect the worst — **pes·si·mist** n — **pes·si·mis·tic** adj

pest n 1 : nuisance 2 : plant or animal detrimental to humans or their crops — **pes·ti·cide** n

pes·ter vb : harass with petty matters

pet n 1 : domesticated animal kept for pleasure 2 : favorite ~ vb : stroke gently or lovingly

pet·al n : modified leaf of a flower head

pe·ti·tion n : formal written request ~ vb : make a request — **pe·ti·tion·er** n

pet·ri·fy vb 1 : change into stony material 2 : make rigid or inactive (as from fear) — **pet·ri·fac·tion** n

pe·tro·leum n : raw oil obtained from the ground

pet·ty adj 1 : minor 2 : of no importance 3 : narrow-minded or mean — **pet·ti·ly** adv — **pet·ti·ness** n

pew n : bench with a back used in a church

pH n : number expressing relative acidity and alkalinity

phantasy var of FANTASY

phan·tom n : something that only appears to be real — **phan·tom** adj

phar·ma·ceu·ti·cal adj : relating to pharmacy or the making and selling of medicinal drugs — **phar·ma·ceu·ti·cal** n

phar·ma·cy n 1 : art or practice of preparing and dispensing medical drugs 2 : drugstore — **phar·ma·cist** n

phar·ynx n : space behind the mouth into which the nostrils, esophagus, and windpipe open — **pha·ryn·ge·al** adj

phase n 1 : particular appearance or stage in a recurring series of changes 2 : stage in a process — **phase in** vb : introduce in stages — **phase out** vb : discontinue gradually

phe·nom·e·non n 1 pl **phe·nom·e·na** : observable fact or event 2 pl **phe·nom·e·nons** : prodigy — **phe·nom·e·nal** adj

phi·los·o·phy n 1 : critical study of fundamental beliefs 2 : sciences and liberal arts exclusive of medicine, law, and theology 3 : system of ideas 4 : sum of personal convictions — **phil·o·soph·ic, phil·o·soph·i·cal** adj — **phil·o·soph·i·cal·ly** adv — **phi·los·o·phize** vb — **phi·los·o·pher** n

pho·bia n : irrational persistent fear

phone n : telephone ~ vb : call on a telephone

pho·no·graph n : instrument that reproduces sounds from a grooved disc

pho·ny, pho·ney adj : not sincere or genuine — **phony** n

pho·to n : photograph — **pho·to** vb or adj

pho·to·copy n : photographic copy (as of a printed page) — **pho·to·copy** vb

pho·to·graph n : picture taken by photography — **pho·to·graph** vb — **pho·tog·ra·pher** n

— **pho·to·graph·ic** *adj* — **pho·to·graph·i·cal·ly** *adv* — **pho·tog·ra·phy** *n*

phrase *n* **1** : brief expression **2** : group of related words that express a thought ∼ *vb* : express in a particular manner

phys·i·cal *adj* **1** : relating to nature **2** : material as opposed to mental or spiritual **3** : relating to the body ∼ *n* : medical examination — **phys·i·cal·ly** *adv*

phy·si·cian *n* : doctor of medicine

phys·i·cist *n* : specialist in physics

phys·ics *n* : science that deals with matter and motion

phy·sique *n* : build of a person's body

pi·ano *n* : musical instrument with strings sounded by hammers operated from a keyboard — **pi·a·nist** *n*

¹**pick** *vb* **1** : break up with a pointed instrument **2** : remove bit by bit **3** : gather by plucking **4** : select **5** : rob **6** : provoke **7** : unlock with a wire **8** : eat sparingly ∼ *n* **1** : act of choosing **2** : choicest one — **pick·er** *n* — **pick up** *vb* **1** : improve **2** : put in order

²**pick** *n* : pointed digging tool

pick·le *n* **1** : brine or vinegar solution for preserving foods or a food preserved in a pickle **2** : bad state — **pickle** *vb*

pick·up *n* **1** : revival or acceleration **2** : light truck with an open body

pic·nic *n* : outing with food usu. eaten in the open ∼ *vb* : go on a picnic

pic·ture *n* **1** : representation by painting, drawing, or photography **2** : vivid description **3** : copy **4** : movie ∼ *vb* : form a mental image of — **pic·to·ri·al** *adj* — **pic·tur·esque** *adj*

pie *n* : pastry crust and a filling

piece *n* **1** : part of a whole **2** : one of a group or set **3** : single item **4** : product of creative work ∼ *vb* : join into a whole

pier *n* **1** : support for a bridge span **2** : deck or wharf built out over water **3** : pillar

pierce *vb* **1** : enter or thrust into or through **2** : penetrate **3** : see through

pig *n* **1** : young swine **2** : dirty or greedy individual **3** : iron casting — **pig·gish** *adj* — **pig·let** *n* — **pig·pen** *n* — **pig·sty** *n*

pi·geon *n* : stout-bodied short-legged bird

pig·gy·back *adv or adj* : up on the back and shoulders

pig·ment *n* : coloring matter — **pig·men·ta·tion** *n*

pig·tail *n* : tight braid of hair

pike *n* : turnpike

pile *n* : quantity of things thrown on one another ∼ *vb* : heap up, accumulate

pil·grim *n* **1** : one who travels to a shrine or holy place in devotion **2** *cap* : one of the English settlers in America in 1620

pil·grim·age *n* : pilgrim's journey

pill *n* : small rounded mass of medicine — **pill·box** *n*

pil·lar *n* : upright usu. supporting column — **pil·lared** *adj*

pil·low *n* : soft cushion for the head — **pil·low·case** *n*

pi·lot *n* **1** : helmsman **2** : person licensed to take ships into and out of a port **3** : guide **4** : one that flies an aircraft or spacecraft ∼ *vb* : act as pilot of — **pi·lot·less** *adj*

pim·ple *n* : small inflamed swelling on the skin — **pim·ply** *adj*

pin *n* **1** : fastener made of a small pointed piece of wire **2** : ornament or emblem fastened to clothing with a pin **3** : wooden object used as a target in bowling ∼ *vb* **1** : fasten with a pin **2** : hold fast or immobile — **pin·hole** *n*

pin·a·fore *n* : sleeveless dress or apron fastened at the back

pin·cer *n* **1** *pl* : gripping tool with 2 jaws **2** : pincerlike claw

pinch *vb* **1** : squeeze between the finger and thumb or between the jaws of a tool **2** : compress painfully **3** : restrict **4** : steal ∼ *n* **1** : emergency **2** : painful effect **3** : act of pinching **4** : very small quantity

pin·cush·ion *n* : cushion for storing pins

¹**pine** *n* : evergreen cone-bearing tree or its wood

²**pine** *vb* **1** : lose health through distress **2** : yearn for intensely

pine·ap·ple *n* : tropical plant bearing an edible juicy fruit

pink *n* : light red color — **pink** *adj* — **pink·ish** *adj*

pin·point *vb* : locate, hit, or aim with great precision

pint *n* : one-half quart

pi·o·neer *n* **1** : one that originates or helps open up a new line of thought or activity **2** : early settler ∼ *vb* : act as a pioneer

pi·ous *adj* **1** : conscientious in religious practices **2** : affectedly religious — **pi·ous·ly** *adv*

pipe *n* **1** : tube that produces music when air is forced through **2** : bagpipe **3** : long tube for conducting a fluid **4** : smoking tool ∼ *vb* **1**

: play on a pipe **2** : speak in a high voice **3** : convey by pipes — **pip•er** n

pipe•line n **1** : line of pipe **2** : channel for information

pi•ra•cy n **1** : robbery on the seas **2** : unauthorized use of another's production or invention

pi•rate n : one who commits piracy — **pi•rate** vb — **pi•rat•i•cal** adj

pis pl of PI

pis•tol n : firearm held with one hand

pis•ton n : sliding piece that receives and transmits motion usu. inside a cylinder

¹pit n **1** : hole or shaft in the ground **2** : depressed or enclosed place for a special purpose **3** : hell **4** : hollow or indentation ∼ vb **1** : form pits in **2** : become marred with pits

²pit n : stony seed of some fruits ∼ vb : remove the pit from

pitch vb **1** : erect and fix firmly in place **2** : throw **3** : set at a particular tone level **4** : fall headlong ∼ n **1** : action or manner of pitching **2** : degree of slope **3** : relative highness of a tone **4** : sales talk — **pitched** adj

¹pitch•er n : container for liquids

²pitcher n : one that pitches (as in baseball)

pitch•fork n : long-handled fork for pitching hay

pit•tance n : small portion or amount

pity n **1** : sympathetic sorrow **2** : something to be regretted ∼ vb : feel pity for — **piti•able** adj — **piti•ful** adj — **piti•ful•ly** adv — **piti•less** adj — **piti•less•ly** adv

piv•ot n : fixed pin on which something turns ∼ vb : turn on or as if on a pivot — **piv•ot•al** adj

piz•za n : thin pie of bread dough spread with a spiced mixture (as of tomatoes, cheese, and meat)

piz•zazz, pi•zazz n : glamour

piz•ze•ria n : pizza restaurant

pla•cate vb : appease — **pla•ca•ble** adj

place n **1** : space or room **2** : indefinite area **3** : a particular building, locality, area, or part **4** : relative position in a scale or sequence **5** : seat **6** : job ∼ vb **1** : put in a place **2** : identify — **place•ment** n

plac•id adj : undisturbed or peaceful — **pla•cid•i•ty** n — **plac•id•ly** adv

pla•gia•rize vb : use (words or ideas) of another as if your own — **pla•gia•rism** n — **pla•gia•rist** n

plague n **1** : disastrous evil **2** : destructive

contagious bacterial disease ∼ vb **1** : afflict with disease or disaster **2** : harass

plaid n : woolen fabric with a pattern of crossing stripes or the pattern itself — **plaid** adj

plain n : expanse of relatively level treeless country ∼ adj **1** : lacking ornament **2** : not concealed or disguised **3** : easily understood **4** : frank **5** : not fancy or pretty — **plain•ly** adv — **plain•ness** n

plain•tiff n : complaining party in a lawsuit

plait n **1** : pleat **2** : braid of hair or straw — **plait** vb

plan n **1** : drawing or diagram **2** : method for accomplishing something ∼ vb **1** : form a plan of **2** : intend — **plan•less** adj — **plan•ner** n

plane n **1** : level surface **2** : level of existence, consciousness, or development **3** : airplane ∼ adj **1** : flat **2** : dealing with flat surfaces or figures

plan•et n : celestial body that revolves around the sun — **plan•e•tary** adj

plank n **1** : heavy thick board **2** : article in the platform of a political party — **plank•ing** n

plant vb **1** : set in the ground to grow **2** : place firmly or forcibly ∼ n **1** : living thing without sense organs that cannot move about **2** : land, buildings, and machinery used esp. in manufacture

plan•tain n : banana plant with starchy greenish fruit

plan•ta•tion n : agricultural estate usu. worked by resident laborers

plant•er n **1** : plantation owner **2** : plant container

plasma TV n : television screen in which cells of ionized gas emit light upon receiving an electric current

plas•ter n **1** : medicated dressing **2** : hardening paste for coating walls and ceilings ∼ vb : cover with plaster — **plas•ter•er** n

plas•tic adj : capable of being molded ∼ n : material that can be formed into rigid objects, films, or filaments — **plas•tic•i•ty** n

plate n **1** : flat thin piece **2** : plated metalware **3** : shallow usu. circular dish **4** : denture or the part of it that fits to the mouth **5** : something printed from an engraving ∼ vb : overlay with metal — **plat•ing** n

pla•teau n : large level area of high land

plat•form n **1** : raised flooring or stage **2** : declaration of principles for a political party

plat·i·num *n* : heavy grayish-white metallic chemical element

plat·ter *n* : large serving plate

plau·si·ble *adj* : reasonable or believeable — **plau·si·bil·i·ty** *n* — **plau·si·bly** *adv*

play *n* 1 : action in a game 2 : recreational activity 3 : light or fitful movement 4 : free movement 5 : stage representation of a drama ~ *vb* 1 : engage in recreation 2 : move or toy with aimlessly 3 : perform music 4 : act in a drama — **play·act·ing** *n* — **play·er** *n* — **play·ful** *adj* — **play·ful·ly** *adv* — **play·ful·ness** *n* — **play·ground** *n* — **play·mate** *n* — **play·pen** *n* — **play·suit** *n* — **play·thing** *n*

play·house *n* 1 : theater 2 : small house for children to play in

play·wright *n* : writer of plays

pla·za *n* 1 : public square 2 : shopping mall

plea *n* 1 : defendant's answer to charges 2 : urgent request

plead *vb* 1 : argue for or against in court 2 : answer to a charge or indictment 3 : appeal earnestly — **plead·er** *n*

pleas·ant *adj* 1 : giving pleasure 2 : marked by pleasing behavior or appearance — **pleas·ant·ly** *adv* — **pleas·ant·ness** *n* — **pleas·ant·ry** *n*

please *vb* 1 : give pleasure or satisfaction to 2 : desire or intend

pleas·ing *adj* : giving pleasure — **pleas·ing·ly** *adv*

plea·sure *n* 1 : desire or inclination 2 : enjoyment 3 : source of delight — **plea·sur·able** *adj* — **plea·sur·ably** *adv*

pleat *vb* : arrange in pleats ~ *n* : fold in cloth

pledge *n* 1 : something given as security 2 : promise or vow ~ *vb* 1 : offer as or bind by a pledge 2 : promise

plen·ty *n* : more than adequate number or amount — **plen·ti·ful** *adj* — **plen·ti·ful·ly** *adv*

pli·able *adj* : flexible

pli·ant *adj* : flexible — **pli·an·cy** *n*

pli·ers *n pl* : pinching or gripping tool

plight *n* : bad state

plod *vb* 1 : walk heavily or slowly 2 : work laboriously and monotonously — **plod·der** *n* — **plod·ding·ly** *adv*

plot *n* 1 : small area of ground 2 : ground plan 3 : main story development (as of a book or movie) 4 : secret plan for doing something ~ *vb* 1 : make a plot or plan of 2 : plan or contrive — **plot·ter** *n*

plow, plough *n* 1 : tool used to turn soil 2 : device for pushing material aside ~ *vb* 1 : break up with a plow 2 : cleave or move through like a plow — **plow·man** *n*

ploy *n* : clever maneuver

pluck *vb* 1 : pull off or out 2 : tug or twitch ~ *n* 1 : act or instance of plucking 2 : spirit or courage

plucky *adj* : courageous or spirited

plug *n* 1 : something for sealing an opening 2 : electrical connector at the end of a cord 3 : piece of favorable publicity ~ *vb* 1 : stop or make tight or secure by inserting a plug 2 : publicize

plum *n* 1 : smooth-skinned juicy fruit 2 : fine reward

plumb *n* : weight on the end of a line (**plumb line**) to show vertical direction ~ *adv* 1 : vertically 2 : completely ~ *vb* : sound or test with a plumb ~ *adj* : vertical

plumb·er *n* : one who repairs usu. water pipes and fixtures

plumb·ing *n* : system of water pipes in a building

plume *n* : large, conspicuous, or showy feather ~ *vb* 1 : provide or deck with feathers 2 : indulge in pride — **plumed** *adj*

plum·met *vb* : drop straight down

plump *adj* : having a full rounded form — **plump·ness** *n*

plun·der *vb* : rob or take goods by force (as in war) ~ *n* : something taken in plundering — **plun·der·er** *n*

plunge *vb* 1 : thrust or drive with force 2 : leap or dive into water 3 : begin an action suddenly 4 : dip or move suddenly forward or down ~ *n* : act or instance of plunging — **plung·er** *n*

plu·ral *adj* : relating to a word form denoting more than one — **plu·ral** *n* — **plu·ral·i·za·tion** *n* — **plu·ral·ize** *vb*

plu·ral·i·ty *n* : greatest number of votes cast when not a majority

plus *prep* : with the addition of ~ *n* 1 : sign + (**plus sign**) in mathematics to indicate addition 2 : added or positive quantity 3 : advantage ~ *adj* : being more or in addition ~ *conj* : and

plush *n* : fabric with a long pile ~ *adj* : luxurious — **plush·ly** *adv* — **plushy** *adj* — **plush·ness** *n*

¹**ply** *n* : fold, thickness, or strand of which something is made — **ply·wood** *n*

²ply *vb* **1** : use or work at **2** : keep supplying something to **3** : travel regularly usu. by sea

pneu·mat·ic *adj* **1** : moved by air pressure **2** : filled with compressed air — **pneu·mat·i·cal·ly** *adv*

pneu·mo·nia *n* : inflammatory lung disease

pock·et *n* **1** : small open bag sewn into a garment **2** : container or receptacle **3** : isolated area or group ∼ *vb* : put in a pocket — **pock·et·ful** *n* — **pock·et·knife** *n*

pock·et·book *n* **1** : purse **2** : financial resources

pod *n* **1** : dry fruit that splits open when ripe **2** : compartment on a ship or craft

po·et·ry *n* **1** : metrical writing **2** : poems — **po·em** *n* — **po·et** *n* — **po·et·ic, po·et·i·cal** *adj*

point *n* **1** : individual often essential detail **2** : purpose **3** : particular place, time, or stage **4** : sharp end **5** : projecting piece of land **6** : dot or period **7** : division of the compass **8** : unit of counting ∼ *vb* **1** : sharpen **2** : indicate direction by extending a finger **3** : direct attention to **4** : aim — **point·ed·ly** *adv* — **point·less** *adj*

point·er *n* **1** : one that points out **2** : large short-haired hunting dog **3** : hint or tip

poise *vb* : balance ∼ *n* : self-possessed calmness

poi·son *n* : chemical that can injure or kill ∼ *vb* **1** : injure or kill with poison **2** : apply poison to **3** : affect destructively — **poi·son·er** *n* — **poi·son·ous** *adj*

poke *vb* **1** : prod **2** : dawdle ∼ *n* : quick thrust

¹pok·er *n* : rod for stirring a fire

²poker *n* : card game for gambling

po·lar *adj* : relating to a geographical or magnetic pole

po·lar·ize *vb* **1** : cause to have magnetic poles **2** : break up into opposing groups — **po·lar·i·za·tion** *n*

¹pole *n* : long slender piece of wood or metal

²pole *n* **1** : either end of the earth's axis **2** : battery terminal **3** : either end of a magnet

po·lice *n* (**police**) **1** : department of government that keeps public order and enforces the laws **2** : members of the police ∼ *vb* : regulate and keep in order — **po·lice·man** *n* — **po·lice·wom·an** *n*

¹pol·i·cy *n* : course of action selected to guide decisions

²policy *n* : insurance contract — **pol·i·cy·hold·er** *n*

pol·ish *vb* **1** : make smooth and glossy **2** : develop or refine ∼ *n* **1** : shiny surface **2** : refinement

po·lite *adj* : marked by courteous social conduct — **po·lite·ly** *adv* — **po·lite·ness** *n*

pol·i·tics *n sing or pl* : practice of government and managing of public affairs — **po·lit·i·cal** *adj* — **po·lit·i·cal·ly** *adv* — **pol·i·ti·cian** *n*

pol·ka dot *n* : one of a series of regular dots in a pattern

poll *n* **1** : head **2** : place where votes are cast — usu. pl. **3** : a sampling of opinion ∼ *vb* **1** : cut off **2** : receive or record votes **3** : question in a poll — **poll·ster** *n*

pol·len *n* : spores of a seed plant

pol·li·na·tion *n* : the carrying of pollen to fertilize the seed — **pol·li·nate** *vb* — **pol·li·na·tor** *n*

pol·lute *vb* : contaminating with waste products — **pol·lut·ant** *n* — **pol·lut·er** *n* — **pol·lu·tion** *n*

poly·es·ter *n* : synthetic fiber

poly·gon *n* : closed plane figure with straight sides

pom·mel *n* **1** : knob on the hilt of a sword **2** : knob at the front of a saddle ∼ *vb* : pummel

pomp·ous *adj* : pretentiously dignified — **pom·pos·i·ty** *n* — **pomp·ous·ly** *adv*

pon·cho *n* : blanketlike cloak

pond *n* : small body of water

pon·der *vb* : consider

pon·der·ous *adj* **1** : very heavy **2** : clumsy **3** : oppressively dull

pon·tiff *n* : pope — **pon·tif·i·cal** *adj*

pon·tif·i·cate *vb* : talk pompously

po·ny *n* : small horse

po·ny·tail *n* : hair arrangement like the tail of a pony

poo·dle *n* : dog with a curly coat

pool *n* **1** : small body of water **2** : puddle

poor *adj* **1** : lacking material possessions **2** : less than adequate **3** : arousing pity **4** : unfavorable — **poor·ly** *adv*

¹pop *vb* **1** : move suddenly **2** : burst with or make a sharp sound **3** : protrude ∼ *n* **1** : sharp explosive sound **2** : flavored soft drink

²pop *adj* : popular

pop·corn *n* : corn whose kernels burst open into a light mass when heated

pope *n, often cap* : head of the Roman Catholic Church

pop·u·lar *adj* **1** : relating to the general public **2** : widely accepted **3** : commonly liked — **pop·u·lar·i·ty** *n* — **pop·u·lar·ize** *vb* — **pop·u·lar·ly** *adv*

pop·u·la·tion *n* : people or number of people in an area

porch *n* : covered entrance

pore *n* : tiny hole (as in the skin) — **pored** *adj*

pork *n* : pig meat

po·rous *adj* : permeable to fluids — **po·ros·i·ty** *n*

port *n* **1** : harbor **2** : city with a harbor

por·ta·ble *adj* : capable of being carried — **por·ta·ble** *n*

por·tent *n* : something that foreshadows a coming event — **por·ten·tous** *adj*

por·ter *n* : baggage carrier

port·fo·lio *n* **1** : portable case for papers **2** : office or function of a diplomat **3** : investor's securities

por·tion *n* : part or share of a whole ∼ *vb* : divide into or allot portions

por·trait *n* : picture of a person — **por·trait·ist** *n* — **por·trai·ture** *n*

por·tray *vb* **1** : make a picture of **2** : describe in words **3** : play the role of — **por·tray·al** *n*

pose *vb* **1** : assume a posture or attitude **2** : propose **3** : pretend to be what one is not ∼ *n* **1** : sustained posture **2** : pretense — **pos·er** *n*

po·si·tion *n* **1** : stand taken on a question **2** : place or location **3** : status **4** : job — **position** *vb*

pos·i·tive *adj* **1** : definite **2** : confident **3** : relating to or being an adjective or adverb form that denotes no increase **4** : greater than zero **5** : having a deficiency of electrons **6** : affirmative — **pos·i·tive·ly** *adv* — **pos·i·tive·ness** *n*

pos·sess *vb* **1** : have as property or as a quality **2** : control — **pos·ses·sion** *n* — **pos·ses·sor** *n*

pos·ses·sive *adj* **1** : relating to a grammatical case denoting ownership **2** : jealous — **pos·ses·sive** *n* — **pos·ses·sive·ness** *n*

pos·si·ble *adj* **1** : that can be done **2** : potential — **pos·si·bil·i·ty** *n* — **pos·si·bly** *adv*

¹post *n* : upright stake serving to support or mark ∼ *vb* : put up or announce by a notice

²post *vb* **1** : mail **2** : inform

³post *n* **1** : sentry's station **2** : assigned task **3** : army camp ∼ *vb* : station

post·age *n* : fee for mail

post·al *adj* : relating to the mail

post·er *n* : large usu. printed notice

post·hu·mous *adj* : occurring after one's death — **post·hu·mous·ly** *adv*

post·mark *n* : official mark on mail — **postmark** *vb*

post office *n* : agency or building for mail service

post·pone *vb* : put off to a later time — **post·pone·ment** *n*

pos·tu·late *vb* : assume as true ∼ *n* : assumption

pos·ture *n* : bearing of the body ∼ *vb* : strike a pose

pot *n* : rounded container ∼ *vb* : place in a pot — **pot·ful** *n*

po·ta·to *n* : edible plant tuber

po·tent *adj* : powerful or effective — **po·ten·cy** *n*

po·ten·tial *adj* : capable of becoming actual ∼ *n* **1** : something that can become actual **2** : degree of electrification with reference to a standard — **po·ten·ti·al·i·ty** *n* — **po·ten·tial·ly** *adv*

pot·hole *n* : large hole in a road surface

pot·luck *n* : whatever food is available

pot·pour·ri *n* **1** : mix of flowers, herbs, and spices used for scent **2** : miscellaneous collection

pot·shot *n* **1** : casual or easy shot **2** : random critical remark

pot·tery *n* : objects (as dishes) made from clay — **pot·ter** *n*

pouch *n* **1** : small bag **2** : bodily sac

poul·try *n* : domesticated fowl

pounce *vb* : spring or swoop upon and seize

¹pound *n* **1** : unit of weight equal to 16 ounces **2** : monetary unit (as of the United Kingdom) — **pound·age** *n*

²pound *vb* **1** : crush by beating **2** : strike heavily **3** : drill **4** : move along heavily

pour *vb* **1** : flow or supply esp. copiously **2** : rain hard

pout *vb* : look sullen — **pout** *n*

pov·er·ty *n* **1** : lack of money or possessions **2** : poor quality

pow·der *n* : dry material of fine particles ∼ *vb* : sprinkle or cover with powder — **pow·dery** *adj*

pow·er *n* **1** : position of authority **2** : ability to act **3** : one that has power **4** : physical might **5** : force or energy used to do work ∼ *vb*

: supply with power — **pow·er·ful** *adj* — **pow·er·ful·ly** *adv* — **pow·er·less** *adj*

prac·ti·cal *adj* **1** : relating to practice **2** : virtual **3** : capable of being put to use **4** : inclined to action as opposed to speculation — **prac·ti·cal·i·ty** *n* — **prac·ti·cal·ly** *adv*

prac·tice, prac·tise *vb* **1** : perform repeatedly to become proficient **2** : do or perform customarily **3** : be professionally engaged in ⁓ *n* **1** : actual performance **2** : habit **3** : exercise for proficiency **4** : exercise of a profession

prag·ma·tism *n* : practical approach to problems — **prag·mat·ic** *adj* — **prag·mat·i·cal·ly** *adv* — **prag·ma·tist** *n*

prai·rie *n* : broad grassy rolling tract of land

praise *vb* **1** : express approval of **2** : glorify — **praise** *n* — **praise·wor·thy** *adj*

prance *vb* **1** : spring from the hind legs **2** : swagger — **prance** *n* — **pranc·er** *n*

prank *n* : playful or mischievous act — **prank·ster** *n*

pray *vb* **1** : entreat **2** : ask earnestly for something **3** : address God or a god

prayer *n* **1** : earnest request **2** : an addressing of God or a god **3** : words used in praying — **prayer·ful** *adj* — **prayer·ful·ly** *adv*

preach *vb* **1** : deliver a sermon **2** : advocate earnestly — **preach·er** *n* — **preach·ment** *n*

pre·car·i·ous *adj* : dangerously insecure — **pre·car·i·ous·ly** *adv* — **pre·car·i·ous·ness** *n*

pre·cau·tion *n* : care taken beforehand — **pre·cau·tion·ary** *adj*

pre·cede *vb* : be, go, or come ahead of — **pre·ce·dence** *n* — **prec·e·dent** *n*

pre·cinct *n* **1** : district of a city **2** *pl* : vicinity

pre·cious *adj* **1** : of great value **2** : greatly cherished **3** : affected

pre·cip·i·tate *vb* **1** : cause to happen quickly or abruptly **2** : cause to separate out of a liquid **3** : fall as rain, snow, or hail ⁓ *n* : solid matter precipitated from a liquid ⁓ *adj* : unduly hasty — **pre·cip·i·tate·ly** *adv* — **pre·cip·i·tate·ness** *n* — **pre·cip·i·tous** *adj* — **pre·cip·i·tous·ly** *adv*

pre·cip·i·ta·tion *n* **1** : rash haste **2** : rain, snow, or hail

pre·cise *adj* **1** : definite **2** : highly accurate — **pre·cise·ly** *adv* — **pre·cise·ness** *n*

pre·ci·sion *n* : quality or state of being precise

pre·clude *vb* : make impossible

pre·co·cious *adj* : exceptionally advanced — **pre·co·cious·ly** *adv* — **pre·coc·i·ty** *n*

pred·a·to·ry *adj* : preying upon others — **pred·a·tor** *n*

pre·de·ces·sor *n* : a previous holder of a position

pre·des·tine *vb* : settle beforehand — **pre·des·ti·na·tion** *n*

pre·dic·a·ment *n* : difficult situation

pred·i·cate *n* : part of a sentence that states something about the subject ⁓ *vb* **1** : affirm **2** : establish — **pred·i·ca·tion** *n*

pre·dict *vb* : declare in advance — **pre·dict·abil·i·ty** *n* — **pre·dict·able** *adj* — **pre·dict·ably** *adv* — **pre·dic·tion** *n*

pre·dis·pose *vb* : cause to be favorable or likely to respond to something beforehand — **pre·dis·po·si·tion** *n*

pre·dom·i·nate *vb* : be superior — **pre·dom·i·nance** *n* — **pre·dom·i·nant** *adj* — **pre·dom·i·nant·ly** *adv*

pre·em·i·nent *adj* : having highest rank — **pre·em·i·nence** *n* — **pre·em·i·nent·ly** *adv*

pre·empt *vb* **1** : seize for oneself **2** : take the place of — **pre·emp·tion** *n* — **pre·emp·tive** *adj*

pre·fab·ri·cat·ed *adj* : manufactured for rapid assembly elsewhere — **pre·fab·ri·ca·tion** *n*

pref·ace *n* : introductory comments ⁓ *vb* : introduce with a preface — **pref·a·to·ry** *adj*

pre·fer *vb* **1** : like better **2** : bring (as a charge) against a person — **pref·er·a·ble** *adj* — **pref·er·a·bly** *adv* — **pref·er·ence** *n* — **pref·er·en·tial** *adj*

¹**pre·fix** *vb* : place before

²**pre·fix** *n* : affix at the beginning of a word

preg·nant *adj* **1** : containing unborn young **2** : meaningful — **preg·nan·cy** *n*

pre·his·tor·ic, pre·his·tor·i·cal *adj* : relating to the period before written history

prej·u·dice *n* **1** : damage esp. to one's rights **2** : unreasonable attitude for or against something ⁓ *vb* **1** : damage **2** : cause to have prejudice — **prej·u·di·cial** *adj*

pre·lim·i·nary *n* : something that precedes or introduces — **pre·lim·i·nary** *adj*

pre·lude *n* : introductory performance, event, or musical piece

pre·ma·ture *adj* : coming before the usual or proper time — **pre·ma·ture·ly** *adv*

pre·mier *adj* : first in rank or importance ⁓ *n* : prime minister — **pre·mier·ship** *n*

pre·miere *n* : 1st performance ⁓ *vb* : give a 1st performance of

prem·ise *n* **1** : statement made or implied as a

basis of argument **2** *pl* : piece of land with the structures on it

pre·mi·um *n* **1** : bonus **2** : sum over the stated value **3** : sum paid for insurance **4** : high value

pre·mo·ni·tion *n* : feeling that something is about to happen — **pre·mon·i·to·ry** *adj*

pre·oc·cu·py *vb* : occupy the attention of — **pre·oc·cu·pa·tion** *n* — **pre·oc·cu·pied** *adj*

pre·pare *vb* **1** : make or get ready often beforehand **2** : put together or compound — **prep·a·ra·tion** *n* — **pre·pa·ra·to·ry** *adj* — **pre·pared·ness** *n*

prep·o·si·tion *n* : word that combines with a noun or pronoun to form a phrase — **prep·o·si·tion·al** *adj*

pre·req·ui·site *n* : something required beforehand — **prerequisite** *adj*

pre·rog·a·tive *n* : special right or power

pre·scribe *vb* **1** : lay down as a guide **2** : direct the use of as a remedy

pre·scrip·tion *n* : written direction for the preparation and use of a medicine or the medicine prescribed

pres·ence *n* **1** : fact or condition of being present **2** : appearance or bearing

¹**pres·ent** *n* : gift

²**pre·sent** *vb* **1** : introduce **2** : bring before the public **3** : make a gift to or of **4** : bring before a court for inquiry — **pre·sent·able** *adj* — **pre·sen·ta·tion** *n* — **pre·sent·ment** *n*

³**pres·ent** *adj* : now existing, in progress, or attending ~ *n* : the time or moment now existing — **pres·ent·ly** *adv*

present participle *n* : participle that typically expresses present action

pre·serve *vb* **1** : keep safe from danger or spoilage **2** : maintain ~ *n* **1** : preserved fruit — often in pl. **2** : area for protection of natural resources — **pres·er·va·tion** *n* — **pre·ser·va·tive** *adj or n* — **pre·serv·er** *n*

pre·side *vb* **1** : act as chairman **2** : exercise control

pres·i·dent *n* **1** : one chosen to preside **2** : chief official (as of a company or nation) — **pres·i·den·cy** *n* — **pres·i·den·tial** *adj*

press *n* **1** : crowded condition **2** : machine or device for exerting pressure and esp. for printing **3** : pressure **4** : printing or publishing establishment **5** : news media and esp. newspapers ~ *vb* **1** : lie against and exert pressure on **2** : smooth with an iron or squeeze with some-

thing heavy **3** : urge **4** : crowd **5** : force one's way — **press·er** *n*

press·ing *adj* : urgent

pres·sure *n* **1** : burden of distress or urgent business **2** : direct application of force — **pres·sure** *vb* — **pres·sur·i·za·tion** *n* — **pres·sur·ize** *vb*

pres·tige *n* : estimation in the eyes of people — **pres·ti·gious** *adj*

pres·to *adv or adj* : quickly

pre·sume *vb* **1** : assume authority without right to do so **2** : take for granted — **pre·sum·able** *adj* — **pre·sum·ably** *adv* — **pre·sump·tion** *n* — **pre·sump·tive** *adj*

pre·sump·tu·ous *adj* : too bold or forward — **pre·sump·tu·ous·ly** *adv*

pre·sup·pose *vb* : take for granted — **pre·sup·po·si·tion** *n*

pre·tend *vb* **1** : act as if something is real or true when it is not **2** : act in a way that is false **3** : lay claim — **pre·tend·er** *n*

pre·tense, pre·tence *n* **1** : insincere effort **2** : deception — **pre·ten·sion** *n*

pre·ten·tious *adj* : overly showy or self-important — **pre·ten·tious·ly** *adv* — **pre·ten·tious·ness** *n*

pre·text *n* : falsely stated purpose

pret·ty *adj* : pleasing by delicacy or attractiveness ~ *adv* : in some degree ~ *vb* : make pretty — **pret·ti·ly** *adv* — **pret·ti·ness** *n*

pre·vail *vb* **1** : triumph **2** : urge successfully **3** : be frequent, widespread, or dominant

prev·a·lent *adj* : widespread — **prev·a·lence** *n*

pre·vent *vb* : keep from happening or acting — **pre·vent·able** *adj* — **pre·ven·tion** *n* — **pre·ven·tive** *adj or n* — **pre·ven·ta·tive** *adj or n*

pre·view *vb* : view or show beforehand — **pre·view** *n*

pre·vi·ous *adj* : having gone, happened, or existed before — **pre·vi·ous·ly** *adv*

prey *n* **1** : animal taken for food by another **2** : victim ~ *vb* **1** : seize and devour animals as prey **2** : have a harmful effect on

price *n* : cost ~ *vb* : set a price on — **pric·ey** *adj* — **price·less** *adj*

prick *n* **1** : tear or small wound made by a point **2** : something sharp or pointed ~ *vb* : pierce slightly with a sharp point — **prick·er** *n*

pride *n* : quality or state of being proud ~ *vb* : indulge in pride — **pride·ful** *adj*

priest *n* : person having authority to perform

the sacred rites of a religion — **priest·ess** n — **priest·hood** n — **priest·li·ness** n — **priest·ly** adj

pri·ma·ry adj : first in order of time, rank, or importance ∼ n : preliminary election — **pri·mar·i·ly** adv

pri·mate n **1** : highest-ranking bishop **2** : mammal of the group that includes humans and monkeys

prime n : earliest or best part or period ∼ adj : standing first (as in significance or quality) ∼ vb **1** : fill or load **2** : lay a preparatory coating on

prime minister n : chief executive of a parliamentary government

¹**prim·er** n : small introductory book

²**prim·er** n **1** : device for igniting an explosive **2** : material for priming a surface

prim·i·tive adj **1** : relating to or characteristic of an early stage of development **2** : of or relating to a tribal people or culture ∼ n : one that is primitive — **prim·i·tive·ly** adv — **prim·i·tive·ness** n

prince n **1** : ruler **2** : son of a king or queen — **prince·ly** adj

prin·cess n **1** : daughter of a king or queen **2** : wife of a prince

prin·ci·pal adj : most important ∼ n **1** : leading person **2** : head of a school **3** : sum lent at interest — **prin·ci·pal·ly** adv

prin·ci·pal·i·ty n : territory of a prince

prin·ci·ple n **1** : general or fundamental law **2** : rule or code of conduct or devotion to such a code

print n **1** : mark or impression made by pressure **2** : printed state or form **3** : printed matter **4** : copy made by printing **5** : cloth with a figure stamped on it ∼ vb **1** : produce impressions of (as from type) **2** : write in letters like those of printer's type — **print·able** adj — **print·er** n — **print·out** n — **print out** vb

prior adj : coming before in time, order, or importance — **pri·or·i·ty** n

prism n : transparent 3-sided object that separates light into colors — **pris·mat·ic** adj

pris·on n : place where criminals are confined — **pris·on·er** n

pris·sy adj : overly prim — **pris·si·ness** n

pris·tine adj : pure

pri·va·cy n : quality or state of being apart from others

pri·vate adj **1** : belonging to a particular individual or group **2** : carried on independently **3** : withdrawn from company or observation ∼ n : enlisted person of the lowest rank in the marine corps or of one of the two lowest ranks in the army — **pri·vate·ly** adv

priv·i·lege n : right granted as an advantage or favor — **priv·i·leged** adj

¹**prize** n **1** : something offered or striven for in competition or in contests of chance **2** : something very desirable — **prize** adj — **prize-win·ner** n — **prize·win·ning** adj

²**prize** vb : value highly

¹**pro** n : favorable argument or person ∼ adv : in favor

²**pro** n or adj : professional

prob·a·ble adj : seeming true or real or to have a good chance of happening — **prob·a·bil·i·ty** n — **prob·a·bly** adv

pro·bate n : judicial determination of the validity of a will ∼ vb : establish by probate

pro·ba·tion n **1** : period of testing and trial **2** : freedom for a convict during good behavior under supervision — **pro·ba·tion·ary** adj — **pro·ba·tion·er** n

probe n **1** : slender instrument for examining a cavity **2** : investigation ∼ vb **1** : examine with a probe **2** : investigate

prob·lem n **1** : question to be solved **2** : source of perplexity or vexation — **prob·lem** adj — **prob·lem·at·ic** adj — **prob·lem·at·i·cal** adj

pro·ce·dure n **1** : way of doing something **2** : series of steps in regular order — **pro·ce·dur·al** adj

pro·ceed vb **1** : come forth **2** : go on in an orderly way **3** : begin and carry on an action **4** : advance

pro·ceeds n pl : total money taken in

pro·cess n **1** : something going on **2** : natural phenomenon marked by gradual changes **3** : series of actions or operations directed toward a result **4** : summons **5** : projecting part ∼ vb : subject to a process — **pro·ces·sor** n

pro·ces·sion n : group moving along in an orderly way

pro·claim vb : announce publicly or with conviction — **proc·la·ma·tion** n

pro·cras·ti·nate vb : put something off until later — **pro·cras·ti·na·tion** n — **pro·cras·ti·na·tor** n

pro·cure vb : get possession of — **pro·cur·able** adj — **pro·cure·ment** n — **pro·cur·er** n

prod vb : push with or as if with a pointed instrument — **prod** n

prod·i·gal *adj* : recklessly extravagant or wasteful — **prodigal** *n* — **prod·i·gal·i·ty** *n*

prod·i·gy *n* : extraordinary person or thing

pro·duce *vb* 1 : present to view 2 : give birth to 3 : bring into existence ~ *n* 1 : product 2 : agricultural products — **pro·duc·er** *n*

prod·uct *n* 1 : number resulting from multiplication 2 : something produced

pro·duc·tion *n* : act, process, or result of producing — **pro·duc·tive** *adj* — **pro·duc·tive·ness** *n* — **pro·duc·tiv·i·ty** *n*

pro·fane *vb* : treat with irreverence ~ *adj* 1 : not concerned with religion 2 : serving to debase what is holy — **pro·fane·ly** *adv* — **pro·fane·ness** *n* — **pro·fan·i·ty** *n*

pro·fes·sion *n* 1 : open declaration of belief 2 : occupation requiring specialized knowledge and academic training

pro·fes·sion·al *adj* 1 : of, relating to, or engaged in a profession 2 : playing sport for pay — **pro·fes·sion·al** *n* — **pro·fes·sion·al·ism** *n* — **pro·fes·sion·al·ize** *vb* — **pro·fes·sion·al·ly** *adv*

pro·fes·sor *n* : university or college teacher — **pro·fes·so·ri·al** *adj* — **pro·fes·sor·ship** *n*

pro·fi·cient *adj* : very good at something — **pro·fi·cien·cy** *n* — **proficient** *n* — **pro·fi·cient·ly** *adv*

pro·file *n* : picture in outline — **profile** *vb*

prof·it *n* 1 : valuable return 2 : excess of the selling price of goods over cost ~ *vb* : gain a profit — **prof·it·able** *adj* — **prof·it·ably** *adv* — **prof·it·less** *adj*

pro·found *adj* 1 : marked by intellectual depth or insight 2 : deeply felt — **pro·found·ly** *adv* — **pro·fun·di·ty** *n*

prog·no·sis *n* : prospect of recovery from disease

pro·gram *n* 1 : outline of the order to be pursued or the subjects included (as in a performance) 2 : plan of procedure 3 : coded instructions for a computer ~ *vb* 1 : enter in a program 2 : provide a computer with a program — **pro·gram·ma·bil·i·ty** *n* — **pro·gram·ma·ble** *adj* — **pro·gram·mer** *n*

prog·ress *n* : movement forward or to a better condition ~ *vb* 1 : move forward 2 : improve — **pro·gres·sion** *n* — **pro·gres·sive** *adj* — **pro·gres·sive·ly** *adv*

pro·hib·it *vb* : prevent by authority — **pro·hi·bi·tion** *n* — **pro·hi·bi·tion·ist** *n* — **pro·hib·i·tive** *adj* — **pro·hib·i·tive·ly** *adv* — **pro·hib·i·to·ry** *adj*

proj·ect *n* : planned undertaking ~ *vb* 1 : design or plan 2 : protrude 3 : throw forward — **pro·jec·tion** *n*

pro·jec·tor *n* : device for projecting pictures on a screen

pro·le·tar·i·at *n* : laboring class

pro·lif·er·ate *vb* : grow or increase in number rapidly — **pro·lif·er·a·tion** *n*

pro·lif·ic *adj* : producing abundantly — **pro·lif·i·cal·ly** *adv*

pro·logue *n* : preface

pro·long *vb* : lengthen in time or extent — **pro·lon·ga·tion** *n*

prom *n* : formal school dance

prom·e·nade *n* 1 : leisurely walk 2 : place for strolling — **promenade** *vb*

prom·i·nence *n* 1 : quality, state, or fact of being readily noticeable or distinguished 2 : something that stands out — **prom·i·nent** *adj* — **prom·i·nent·ly** *adv*

prom·ise *n* 1 : statement that one will do or not do something 2 : basis for expectation — **prom·ise** *vb* — **prom·is·so·ry** *adj*

prom·is·ing *adj* : likely to succeed — **prom·is·ing·ly** *adv*

pro·mote *vb* 1 : advance in rank 2 : contribute to the growth, development, or prosperity of — **pro·mot·er** *n* — **pro·mo·tion** *n* — **pro·mo·tion·al** *adj*

¹**prompt** *vb* 1 : incite 2 : give a cue to (an actor or singer) — **prompt·er** *n*

²**prompt** *adj* : ready and quick — **prompt·ly** *adv* — **prompt·ness** *n*

prone *adj* 1 : having a tendency 2 : lying face downward — **prone·ness** *n*

pro·noun *n* : word used as a substitute for a noun

pro·nounce *vb* 1 : utter officially or as an opinion 2 : say or speak esp. correctly — **pro·nounce·able** *adj* — **pro·nounce·ment** *n* — **pro·nun·ci·a·tion** *n*

proof *n* 1 : evidence of a truth or fact 2 : trial impression or print

prop *vb* 1 : support 2 : sustain — **prop** *n*

pro·pa·gan·da *n* : the spreading of ideas or information to further or damage a cause — **pro·pa·gan·dist** *n* — **pro·pa·gan·dize** *vb*

prop·a·gate *vb* 1 : reproduce biologically 2 : cause to spread — **prop·a·ga·tion** *n*

pro·pel *vb* : drive forward — **pro·pel·lant, pro·pel·lent** *n or adj*

pro·pel·ler *n* : hub with revolving blades that propels a craft

prop·er *adj* **1** : suitable or right **2** : limited to a specified thing **3** : correct **4** : strictly adhering to standards of social manners, dignity, or good taste — **prop·er·ly** *adv*

prop·er·ty *n* **1** : quality peculiar to an individual **2** : something owned **3** : piece of real estate **4** : ownership

proph·et *n* : one who utters revelations or predicts events — **proph·e·cy** *n* — **proph·et·ess** *n* — **pro·phet·ic** *adj* — **pro·phet·i·cal·ly** *adv*

pro·por·tion *n* **1** : relation of one part to another or to the whole with respect to magnitude, quantity, or degree **2** : symmetry **3** : share ∼ *vb* : adjust in size in relation to others — **pro·por·tion·al** *adj* — **pro·por·tion·al·ly** *adv* — **pro·por·tion·ate** *adj* — **pro·por·tion·ate·ly** *adv*

pro·pose *vb* **1** : plan or intend **2** : make an offer of marriage **3** : present for consideration — **pro·pos·al** *n* — **prop·o·si·tion** *n*

pro·pri·etor *n* : owner — **pro·pri·etary** *adj* — **pro·pri·etor·ship** *n* — **pro·pri·etress** *n* — **pro·pri·ety** *n*

pro·pul·sion *n* **1** : action of propelling **2** : driving power — **pro·pul·sive** *adj*

pro·scribe *vb* : prohibit — **pro·scrip·tion** *n*

prose *n* : ordinary language

pros·e·cute *vb* **1** : follow to the end **2** : seek legal punishment of — **pros·e·cu·tion** *n* — **pros·e·cu·tor** *n*

pros·pect *n* **1** : extensive view **2** : something awaited **3** : potential buyer ∼ *vb* : look for mineral deposits — **pro·spec·tive** *adj* — **pro·spec·tive·ly** *adv* — **pros·pec·tor** *n*

pros·per *vb* : thrive or succeed — **pros·per·ous** *adj*

pros·per·i·ty *n* : economic well-being

pros·trate *adj* : stretched out with face on the ground ∼ *vb* **1** : fall or throw (oneself) into a prostrate position **2** : reduce to helplessness — **pros·tra·tion** *n*

pro·tect *vb* : shield from injury — **pro·tec·tion** *n* — **pro·tec·tive** *adj* — **pro·tec·tor** *n*

pro·tein *n* : complex combination of amino acids present in living matter

pro·test *n* **1** : organized public demonstration of disapproval ∼ *vb* **1** : assert positively **2** : object strongly — **pro·tes·ta·tion** *n* — **pro·test·er, pro·tes·tor** *n*

Prot·es·tant *n* : Christian not of a Catholic or Orthodox church — **Prot·es·tant·ism** *n*

pro·to·type *n* : original model

pro·trac·tor *n* : instrument for drawing and measuring angles

pro·trude *vb* : stick out or cause to stick out — **pro·tru·sion** *n*

pro·tu·ber·ance *n* : something that protrudes — **pro·tu·ber·ant** *adj*

proud *adj* **1** : having or showing excessive self-esteem **2** : highly pleased **3** : having proper self-respect **4** : glorious — **proud·ly** *adv*

prove *vb* (**proved; proved/prov·en**) **1** : test by experiment or by a standard **2** : establish the truth of by argument or evidence **3** : turn out esp. after trial or test — **prov·able** *adj*

prov·erb *n* : short meaningful popular saying — **pro·ver·bi·al** *adj*

pro·vide *vb* **1** : take measures beforehand **2** : make a stipulation **3** : supply what is needed — **pro·vid·er** *n*

prov·i·dence *n* **1** *often cap* : divine guidance **2** *cap* : God **3** : quality of being provident

prov·i·dent *adj* **1** : making provision for the future **2** : thrifty — **prov·i·dent·ly** *adv*

prov·ince *n* **1** : administrative district **2** *pl* : all of a country outside the metropolis **3** : sphere

pro·vin·cial *adj* **1** : relating to a province **2** : limited in outlook — **pro·vin·cial·ism** *n*

pro·vi·sion *n* **1** : act of providing **2** : stock of food — usu. in pl. **3** : stipulation ∼ *vb* : supply with provisions

pro·vi·sion·al *adj* : provided for a temporary need — **pro·vi·sion·al·ly** *adv*

pro·voke *vb* **1** : incite to anger **2** : stir up on purpose — **prov·o·ca·tion** *n* — **pro·voc·a·tive** *adj*

prowl *vb* : roam about stealthily — **prowl** *n* — **prowl·er** *n*

prox·im·i·ty *n* : nearness

proxy *n* : authority to act for another — **proxy** *adj*

prude *n* : one who shows extreme modesty — **prud·ery** *n* — **prud·ish** *adj*

pru·dent *adj* **1** : shrewd **2** : cautious **3** : thrifty — **pru·dence** *n* — **pru·den·tial** *adj* — **pru·dent·ly** *adv*

¹prune *n* : dried plum

²prune *vb* : cut off unwanted parts

¹pry *vb* : look closely or inquisitively

²pry *vb* : raise, move, or pull apart with a lever

psalm *n* : sacred song or poem — **psalm·ist** *n*

psy·che *n* : soul or mind

psy·chi·a·try *n* : branch of medicine dealing

with mental, emotional, and behavioral disorders — **psy·chi·at·ric** *adj* — **psy·chi·a·trist** *n*

psy·chic *adj* 1 : relating to the psyche 2 : sensitive to supernatural forces ~ *n* : person sensitive to supernatural forces — **psy·chi·cal·ly** *adv*

psy·chol·o·gy *n* 1 : science of mind and behavior 2 : mental and behavioral aspect (as of an individual) — **psy·cho·log·i·cal** *adj* — **psy·cho·log·i·cal·ly** *adv* — **psy·chol·o·gist** *n*

pub·lic *adj* 1 : relating to the people as a whole 2 : civic 3 : not private 4 : open to all 5 : well-known ~ *n* : people as a whole — **pub·lic·ly** *adv*

pub·lic·i·ty *n* 1 : news information given out to gain public attention 2 : public attention

pub·li·cize *vb* : bring to public attention — **pub·li·cist** *n*

pub·lish *vb* 1 : announce publicly 2 : reproduce for sale esp. by printing — **pub·li·ca·tion** *n* — **pub·lish·er** *n*

pud·ding *n* : creamy dessert

pud·dle *n* : very small pool of water

puff *vb* 1 : blow in short gusts 2 : pant 3 : enlarge ~ *n* 1 : short discharge (as of air) 2 : slight swelling 3 : something light and fluffy — **puffy** *adj*

puke *vb* : vomit — **puke** *n*

pull *vb* 1 : exert force so as to draw (something) toward or out 2 : move 3 : stretch or tear ~ *n* 1 : act of pulling 2 : influence 3 : device for pulling something — **pull·er** *n*

pul·ley *n* : wheel with a grooved rim

pulp *n* 1 : soft part of a fruit or vegetable 2 : soft moist mass (as of mashed wood) — **pulpy** *adj*

pul·pit *n* : raised desk used in preaching

pul·sate *vb* : expand and contract rhythmically — **pul·sa·tion** *n*

pulse *n* : arterial throbbing caused by heart contractions — **pulse** *vb*

pul·ver·ize *vb* : beat or grind into a powder

pum·mel *vb* : beat

¹pump *n* : device for moving or compressing fluids ~ *vb* 1 : raise (as water) with a pump 2 : fill by means of a pump — with *up* 3 : move like a pump — **pump·er** *n*

²pump *n* : woman's low shoe

pump·kin *n* : large usu. orange fruit of a vine related to the gourd

pun *n* : humorous use of a word in a way that suggests two or more interpretations — **pun** *vb*

¹punch *vb* 1 : strike with the fist 2 : perforate with a punch ~ *n* : quick blow with the fist — **punch·er** *n*

²punch *n* : mixed beverage often including fruit juice

punc·tu·al *adj* : prompt — **punc·tu·al·i·ty** *n* — **punc·tu·al·ly** *adv*

punc·tu·ate *vb* : mark with symbols to clarify meaning — **punc·tu·a·tion** *n*

punc·ture *n* : act or result of puncturing ~ *vb* : make a hole in

pun·gent *adj* : having a sharp or stinging odor or taste — **pun·gen·cy** *n* — **pun·gent·ly** *adv*

pun·ish *vb* : impose a penalty on or for — **pun·ish·able** *adj* — **pun·ish·ment** *n*

punt *vb* : kick a ball dropped from the hands ~ *n* : act of punting a ball

pu·ny *adj* : slight in power or size

pup *n* : young dog

¹pu·pil *n* : young person in school

²pu·pil *n* : dark central opening of the iris of the eye

pup·pet *n* : small doll moved by hand or by strings — **pup·pe·teer** *n*

pup·py *n* : young dog

pur·chase *vb* : obtain in exchange for money ~ *n* 1 : act of purchasing 2 : something purchased 3 : secure grasp — **pur·chas·er** *n*

pure *adj* : free of foreign matter, contamination, or corruption — **pure·ly** *adv*

purge *vb* 1 : purify esp. from sin 2 : have or cause emptying of the bowels 3 : get rid of ~ *n* 1 : act or result of purging 2 : something that purges — **pur·ga·tive** *adj or n*

pu·ri·fy *vb* : make or become pure — **pu·ri·fi·ca·tion** *n* — **pu·ri·fi·er** *n*

Pu·rim *n* : Jewish holiday celebrated in February or March in commemoration of the deliverance of the Jews from the massacre plotted by Haman

pu·ri·ty *n* : quality or state of being pure

pur·ple *n* : bluish red color — **pur·plish** *adj*

pur·pose *n* 1 : something (as a result) aimed at 2 : resolution ~ *vb* : intend — **pur·pose·ful** *adj* — **pur·pose·ful·ly** *adv* — **pur·pose·less** *adj* — **pur·pose·ly** *adv*

purse *n* 1 : bag or pouch for money and small objects 2 : financial resource 3 : prize money

pur·su·ant to *prep* : according to

pur·sue *vb* 1 : follow in order to overtake 2

: seek to accomplish **3** : proceed along **4** : engage in — **pur·su·er** *n*

pur·suit *n* **1** : act of pursuing **2** : occupation

pur·vey *vb* : supply (as provisions) usu. as a business — **pur·vey·or** *n*

push *vb* **1** : press against to move forward **2** : urge on or provoke ∼ *n* **1** : vigorous effort **2** : act of pushing — **push·cart** *n* — **push·er** *n*

pushy *adj* : objectionably aggressive

put *vb* (**put; put**) **1** : bring to a specified position or condition **2** : subject to pain, suffering, or death **3** : impose or cause to exist **4** : express **5** : cause to be used or employed — **put off** *vb* : postpone or delay — **put out** *vb* : bother or inconvenience — **put up** *vb* **1**

: prepare for storage **2** : lodge **3** : contribute or pay — **put up with** : endure

pu·tre·fy *vb* : make or become rotten — **pu·tre·fac·tion** *n* — **pu·trid** *adj* — **pu·trid·i·ty** *n*

puz·zle *vb* **1** : confuse **2** : attempt to solve — used with *out* or *over* ∼ *n* : something that confuses or tests ingenuity — **puz·zle·ment** *n* — **puz·zler** *n*

pyg·my *n* : dwarf — **pyg·my** *adj*

py·lon *n* : tower or tall post

pyr·a·mid *n* : structure with a square base and 4 triangular sides meeting at a point

py·ro·ma·nia *n* : irresistible impulse to start fires — **py·ro·ma·ni·ac** *n*

py·ro·tech·nics *n pl* : spectacular display (as of fireworks) — **py·ro·tech·nic** *adj*

Q

q *n* : 17th letter of the alphabet

[1]**quack** *vb* : make a cry like that of a duck — **quack** *n*

[2]**quack** *n* : one who pretends to have medical or healing skill — **quack** *adj* — **quack·ery** *n*

quad·ran·gle *n* : rectangular courtyard

quad·ri·lat·er·al *n* : 4-sided polygon

quad·ru·ped *n* : animal having 4 feet

qua·dru·ple *vb* : multiply by 4 ∼ *adj* : being 4 times as great or as many

qua·dru·plet *n* : one of 4 offspring born at one birth

quail *n* (**quail**) : short-winged plump game bird

quaint *adj* : pleasingly old-fashioned or odd — **quaint·ly** *adv* — **quaint·ness** *n*

quake *vb* : shake or tremble ∼ *n* : earthquake

qual·i·fy *vb* **1** : modify or limit **2** : fit by skill or training for some purpose **3** : become eligible — **qual·i·fi·ca·tion** *n* — **qual·i·fied** *adj* — **qual·i·fi·er** *n*

qual·i·ty *n* **1** : peculiar and essential character, nature, or feature **2** : excellence or distinction

quan·ti·ty *n* **1** : something that can be measured or numbered **2** : considerable amount

quar·an·tine *n* **1** : restraint on the movements of persons or goods to prevent the spread of pests or disease **2** : place or period of quarantine — **quarantine** *vb*

quar·rel *n* : basis of conflict — **quarrel** *vb* — **quar·rel·some** *adj*

[1]**quar·ry** *n* : prey

[2]**quar·ry** *n* : excavation for obtaining stone — **quar·ry** *vb*

quart *n* : unit of liquid measure equal to .95 liter or of dry measure equal to 1.10 liters

quar·ter *n* **1** : $\frac{1}{4}$ part **2** : $\frac{1}{4}$ of a dollar **3** : city district **4** *pl* : place to live esp. for a time **5** : mercy ∼ *vb* : divide into 4 equal parts

quar·ter·ly *adv or adj* : at 3-month intervals ∼ *n* : periodical published 4 times a year

quar·tet *n* **1** : music for 4 performers **2** : group of 4

quay *n* : wharf

quea·sy *adj* : nauseated — **quea·si·ly** *adv* — **quea·si·ness** *n*

queen *n* **1** : wife or widow of a king **2** : female monarch **3** : woman of rank, power, or attractiveness **4** : fertile female of a social insect — **queen·ly** *adj*

queer *adj* : differing from the usual or normal — **queer·ly** *adv* — **queer·ness** *n*

quench *vb* **1** : put out **2** : satisfy (a thirst) — **quench·able** *adj* — **quench·er** *n*

que·ry *n* : question — **que·ry** *vb*

quest *n or vb* : search

ques·tion *n* **1** : something asked **2** : subject for debate **3** : dispute ∼ *vb* **1** : ask questions **2** : doubt or dispute **3** : subject to analysis — **ques·tion·er** *n*

ques·tion·able *adj* **1** : not certain **2** : of doubtful truth or morality — **ques·tion·ably** *adv*

ques·tion·naire *n* : set of questions

queue *n* **1** : braid of hair **2** : a waiting line ∼ *vb* : line up

quib·ble *n* : minor objection — **quib·ble** *vb* — **quib·bler** *n*

quick *adj* 1 : rapid 2 : alert or perceptive ∼ *n* : sensitive area of living flesh — **quick** *adv* — **quick·ly** *adv* — **quick·ness** *n*

quick·en *vb* 1 : come to life 2 : increase in speed

qui·et *adj* 1 : marked by little motion or activity 2 : gentle 3 : free from noise 4 : not showy 5 : isolated ∼ *vb* : pacify — **quiet** *adv or n* — **qui·et·ly** *adv* — **qui·et·ness** *n*

quilt *n* : padded bedspread ∼ *vb* : stitch or sew in layers with padding in between

quin·tet *n* 1 : music for 5 performers 2 : group of 5

quin·tu·ple *adj* 1 : having 5 units or members 2 : being 5 times as great or as many — **quintuple** *n or vb*

quip *vb* : make a clever remark — **quip** *n*

quirk *n* : peculiarity of action or behavior — **quirky** *adj*

quit *vb* quit; quit 1 : stop 2 : leave — **quit·ter** *n*

quite *adv* 1 : completely 2 : to a considerable extent

quiv·er *vb* : shake or tremble — **quiv·er** *n*

quiz *n* : short test ∼ *vb* : question closely

quiz·zi·cal *adj* 1 : teasing 2 : curious

quo·rum *n* : required number of members present

quo·ta *n* : proportional part or share

quote *vb* 1 : repeat (another's words) exactly 2 : state (a price) — **quot·able** *adj* — **quo·ta·tion** *n* — **quote** *n*

quo·tient *n* : number obtained from division

R

r *n* : 18th letter of the alphabet

rab·bet *n* : groove in a board

rab·bi *n* : Jewish religious leader — **rab·bin·ate** *n* — **rab·bin·ic, rab·bin·i·cal** *adj*

rab·bit *n* : long-eared burrowing mammal

ra·bid *adj* 1 : violent 2 : fanatical 3 : affected with rabies — **ra·bid·ly** *adv*

ra·bies *n* : acute deadly virus disease

rac·coon *n* : tree-dwelling mammal with a black mask and a bushy ringed tail

¹race *n* 1 : strong current of water 2 : contest of speed 3 : election campaign ∼ *vb* 1 : run in a race 2 : rush — **race·course** *n* — **race·horse** *n* — **rac·er** *n* — **race·track** *n*

²race *n* 1 : family, tribe, people, or nation of the same stock 2 : division of mankind based on hereditary traits — **ra·cial** *adj* — **ra·cial·ly** *adv*

rac·ism *n* : discrimination based on the belief that some races are by nature superior — **rac·ist** *n*

rack *n* 1 : framework for display or storage 2 : instrument that stretches the body for torture ∼ *vb* : torture with or as if with a rack

¹rack·et *n* : bat with a tight netting across an open frame

²racket *n* 1 : confused noise 2 : fraudulent scheme — **rack·e·teer** *n* — **rack·e·teer·ing** *n*

racy *adj* : being or bordering on being highly improper or offensive — **rac·i·ly** *adv* — **rac·i·ness** *n*

ra·dar *n* : radio device for determining distance and direction of distant objects

ra·di·ant *adj* 1 : glowing 2 : beaming with happiness 3 : transmitted by radiation — **ra·di·ance** *n* — **ra·di·ant·ly** *adv*

ra·di·ate *vb* 1 : issue rays or in rays 2 : spread from a center — **ra·di·a·tion** *n*

ra·di·a·tor *n* : cooling or heating device

rad·i·cal *adj* 1 : fundamental 2 : extreme ∼ *n* : person favoring extreme changes — **rad·i·cal·ism** *n* — **rad·i·cal·ly** *adv*

radii *pl of* RADIUS

ra·dio *n* 1 : wireless transmission or reception of sound by means of electric waves 2 : radio receiving set ∼ *vb* : send a message to by radio — **radio** *adj*

ra·dio·ac·tiv·i·ty *n* : property of an element that emits energy through nuclear disintegration — **ra·dio·ac·tive** *adj*

rad·ish *n* : pungent fleshy root usu. eaten raw

ra·di·us (**ra·dii**) *n* 1 : line from the center of a circle or sphere to the circumference or surface 2 : area defined by a radius

¹raft *n* : flat floating platform ∼ *vb* : travel or transport by raft

²raft *n* : large amount or number

raf·ter *n* : beam supporting a roof

rag *n* : waste piece of cloth

rage *n* 1 : violent anger 2 : state of being currently widely popular ∼ *vb* 1 : be extremely angry or violent 2 : be out of control

rag·ged *adj* : torn — **rag·ged·ly** *adv* — **rag-ged·ness** *n*

raid *n* : sudden usu. surprise attack — **raid** *vb* — **raid·er** *n*

rail *n* **1** : bar serving as a guard or barrier **2** : bar forming a track for wheeled vehicles **3** : railroad

rail·ing *n* : rail or a barrier of rails

rail·road *n* : road for a train laid with iron rails and wooden ties ~ *vb* : force something hastily — **rail·road·er** *n* — **rail·road·ing** *n*

rain 1 : water falling in drops from the clouds **2** : shower of objects ~ *vb* : fall as or like rain — **rain·bow** *n* — **rain·coat** *n* — **rain·drop** *n* — **rain·fall** *n* — **rain·mak·er** *n* — **rain·mak·ing** — **rain·storm** *n* — **rain·water** *n* — **rainy** *adj*

raise *vb* **1** : lift **2** : arouse **3** : erect **4** : collect **5** : breed, grow, or bring up **6** : increase **7** : make light ~ *n* : increase esp. in pay — **rais·er** *n*

rai·sin *n* : dried grape

rake *n* : garden tool for smoothing or sweeping ~ *vb* **1** : gather, loosen, or smooth with or as if with a rake **2** : sweep with gunfire

ral·ly *vb* **1** : bring or come together **2** : revive or recover **3** : make a comeback ~ *n* **1** : act of rallying **2** : mass meeting

ram *n* **1** : male sheep **2** : beam used in battering down walls or doors ~ *vb* **1** : force or drive in or through **2** : strike against violently

RAM *n* : main internal storage area in a computer

ram·ble *vb* : wander — **ram·ble** *n* — **ram·bler** *n*

ramp *n* : sloping passage or connecting roadway

ram·page *vb* : rush about wildly ~ *n* : violent or riotous action or behavior

ran *past of* RUN

ranch *n* **1** : establishment for the raising of cattle, sheep, or horses **2** : specialized farm ~ *vb* : operate a ranch — **ranch·er** *n*

ran·cid *adj* : smelling or tasting as if spoiled — **ran·cid·i·ty** *n*

ran·dom *adj* : occurring by chance — **ran·dom·ize** *vb* — **ran·dom·ly** *adv* — **ran·dom·ness** *n* — **at random** : without definite aim or method

rang *past of* RING

range *n* **1** : series of things in a row **2** : open land for grazing **3** : cooking stove **4** : variation within limits **5** : place for target practice **6** : extent ~ *vb* **1** : arrange **2** : roam at large, freely, or over **3** : vary within limits

rang·er *n* : officer who manages and protects public lands

rank *n* **1** : line of soldiers **2** : orderly arrangement **3** : grade of official standing **4** : position within a group ~ *vb* **1** : arrange in formation or according to class **2** : take or have a relative position

ran·sack *vb* : search through and rob

ran·som *n* : something demanded for the freedom of a captive ~ *vb* : gain the freedom of by paying a price — **ran·som·er** *n*

rant *vb* : talk or scold violently — **rant·er** — **rant·ing·ly** *adv*

¹rap *n* : sharp blow or rebuke ~ *vb* : strike or criticize sharply

²rap *vb* : talk freely

rape *vb* : force to have sexual intercourse — **rape** *n* — **rap·er** *n* — **rap·ist** *n*

rap·id *adj* : very fast — **ra·pid·i·ty** *n* — **rap·id·ly** *adv*

rap·ture *n* : spiritual or emotional ecstasy — **rap·tur·ous** *adj* — **rap·tur·ous·ly** *adv*

¹rare *adj* : having a portion relatively uncooked

²rare *adj* **1** : not dense **2** : unusually fine **3** : seldom met with — **rare·ly** *adv* — **rare·ness** *n* — **rar·i·ty** *n*

ras·cal *n* : mean, dishonest, or mischievous person — **ras·cal·i·ty** *n* — **ras·cal·ly** *adj*

¹rash *adj* : too hasty in decision or action — **rash·ly** *adv* — **rash·ness** *n*

²rash *n* : a breaking out of the skin with red spots

rasp *vb* **1** : rub with or as if with a rough file **2** : speak in a grating tone ~ *n* : coarse file

rasp·ber·ry *n* : edible red or black berry

rat *n* : destructive rodent larger than the mouse ~ *vb* : betray or inform on

rate *n* **1** : quantity, amount, or degree measured in relation to some other quantity **2** : rank ~ *vb* **1** : estimate or determine the rank or quality of **2** : deserve — **rat·ing** *n*

rath·er *adv* **1** : preferably **2** : on the other hand **3** : more properly **4** : somewhat

rat·i·fy *vb* : approve and accept formally — **rat·i·fi·ca·tion** *n*

ra·tio *n* : relation in number, quantity, or degree between things

ra·tion *n* : share or allotment (as of food) ~ *vb* : use or allot sparingly

ra·tio·nal *adj* **1** : having reason or sanity **2** : relating to reason — **ra·tio·nal·ly** *adv*

ra·tio·nale *n* **1** : explanation of principles of belief or practice **2** : underlying reason

ra·tio·nal·ize *vb* : justify (as one's behavior or weaknesses) esp. to oneself — **ra·tio·nal·i·za·tion** *n*

rat·tle *vb* **1** : make a series of clattering sounds **2** : say briskly **3** : confuse or upset ∼ *n* **1** : series of clattering sounds **2** : something (as a toy) that rattles

rat·ty *adj* : shabby

rave *vb* **1** : talk wildly in or as if in delirium **2** : talk with extreme enthusiasm ∼ *n* **1** : act of raving **2** : enthusiastic praise

rav·el *vb* **1** : have threads become separated **2** : tangle ∼ *n* **1** : something tangled **2** : loose thread

raw *adj* **1** : not cooked **2** : not processed **3** : not trained **4** : having the surface rubbed off **5** : cold and damp **6** : vulgar — **raw·ness** *n*

ray *n* **1** : thin beam of radiant energy (as light) **2** : tiny bit

ray·on *n* : fabric made from cellulose fiber

ra·zor *n* : sharp cutting instrument used to shave off hair

reach *vb* **1** : stretch out **2** : touch or try to touch or grasp **3** : extend to or arrive at **4** : communicate with ∼ *n* **1** : act of reaching **2** : distance one can reach **3** : ability to reach — **reach·able** *adj* — **reach·er** *n*

re·act *vb* **1** : act in response to some influence or stimulus **2** : undergo chemical change — **re·ac·tion** *n* — **re·ac·tion·ary** *adj or n* — **re·ac·tive** *adj* — **re·ac·tor** *n*

read *vb* **1** : understand written language **2** : utter aloud printed words **3** : interpret **4** : study **5** : indicate ∼ *adj* : informed by reading — **read·a·bil·i·ty** *n* — **read·able** *adj* — **read·ably** *adv* — **read·er** *n* — **read·er·ship** *n* — **read·ing** *n*

ready *adj* **1** : prepared or available for use or action **2** : willing to do something ∼ *vb* : make ready ∼ *n* : state of being ready — **read·i·ly** *adv* — **read·i·ness** *n*

re·al *adj* **1** : relating to fixed or immovable things (as land) **2** : genuine **3** : not imaginary ∼ *adv* : very — **re·al·ness** *n* — **for real 1** : in earnest **2** : genuine — **re·al·i·ty** *n* — **re·al·ly** *adv*

real estate *n* : property in houses and land

re·al·ism *n* **1** : disposition to deal with facts practically **2** : faithful portrayal of reality — **re·al·ist** *adj or n* — **re·al·is·tic** *adj* — **re·al·is·ti·cal·ly** *adv*

re·al·ize *vb* **1** : make actual **2** : obtain **3** : be aware of — **re·al·iz·able** *adj* — **re·al·i·za·tion** *n*

reap *vb* : cut or clear (as a crop) with a scythe or machine — **reap·er** *n*

¹rear *vb* **1** : raise upright **2** : breed or bring up **3** : rise on the hind legs

²rear *n* **1** : back **2** : position at the back of something ∼ *adj* : being at the back — **rear·ward** *adj or adv*

rea·son *n* **1** : explanation or justification **2** : motive for action or belief **3** : power or process of thinking ∼ *vb* **1** : use the faculty of reason **2** : try to persuade another — **rea·son·er** *n* — **rea·son·ing** *n*

rea·son·able *adj* **1** : being within the bounds of reason **2** : not expensive — **rea·son·able·ness** *n* — **rea·son·ably** *adv*

re·bate *n* : return of part of a payment — **re·bate** *vb*

reb·el *n* : one that resists authority ∼ *vb* **1** : resist authority **2** : feel or exhibit anger — **reb·el** *adj* — **re·bel·lion** *n* — **re·bel·lious** *adj* — **re·bel·lious·ly** *adv* — **re·bel·lious·ness** *n*

re·bound *vb* **1** : spring back on striking something **2** : recover from a reverse ∼ *n* **1** : action of rebounding **2** : reaction to a reverse

re·buke *vb* : criticize sharply

re·call *vb* **1** : call back **2** : remember **3** : revoke ∼ *n* **1** : a summons to return **2** : remembrance **3** : act of revoking

re·cede *vb* **1** : move back or away **2** : slant backward

re·ceipt *n* **1** : act of receiving **2** : something (as payment) received — usu. in pl. **3** : writing acknowledging something received

re·ceive *vb* **1** : take in or accept **2** : greet or entertain (visitors) **3** : pick up radio waves and convert into sounds or pictures — **re·ceiv·able** *adj* — **re·ceiv·er** *n*

re·cent *adj* **1** : having lately come into existence **2** : of the present time or time just past — **re·cent·ly** *adv* — **re·cent·ness** *n*

re·cep·ta·cle *n* : container

re·cep·tion *n* **1** : act of receiving **2** : social gathering at which guests are formally welcomed

re·cep·tion·ist *n* : person employed to greet callers

re·cep·tive *adj* : open and responsive to ideas, impressions, or suggestions — **re·cep·tive·ly** *adv* — **re·cep·tive·ness** *n* — **re·cep·tiv·i·ty** *n*

re·cess *n* **1 :** indentation in a line or surface **2 :** suspension of a session for rest ∼ *vb* **1 :** make a recess in or put into a recess **2 :** interrupt a session for a recess

re·ces·sion *n* **1 :** departing procession **2 :** period of reduced economic activity

rec·i·pe *n* **:** instructions for making something

re·cip·i·ent *n* **:** one that receives

re·cip·ro·cal *adj* **1 :** affecting each in the same way **2 :** so related that one is equivalent to the other — **re·cip·ro·cal·ly** *adv* — **re·ci·proc·i·ty** *n*

re·cip·ro·cate *vb* **:** make a return for something done or given — **re·cip·ro·ca·tion** *n*

re·cit·al *n* **1 :** public reading or recitation **2 :** music or dance concert or exhibition by pupils — **re·cit·al·ist** *n*

re·cite *vb* **1 :** repeat verbatim **2 :** recount — **rec·i·ta·tion** *n* — **re·cit·er** *n*

reck·less *adj* **:** lacking caution — **reck·less·ly** *adv* — **reck·less·ness** *n*

reck·on *vb* **1 :** count or calculate **2 :** consider — **reck·on·ing** *n*

re·claim *vb* **1 :** change to a desirable condition **2 :** obtain from a waste product or by-product **3 :** demand or obtain the return of — **re·claim·able** *adj* — **rec·la·ma·tion** *n*

re·cline *vb* **:** lean backward or lie down

rec·og·nize *vb* **1 :** identify as previously known **2 :** take notice of **3 :** acknowledge esp. with appreciation — **rec·og·ni·tion** *n* — **rec·og·niz·able** *adj* — **rec·og·niz·ably** *adv*

rec·ol·lect *vb* **:** remember

rec·ol·lec·tion *n* **1 :** act or power of recollecting **2 :** something recollected

rec·om·mend *vb* **1 :** present as deserving of acceptance or trial **2 :** advise — **rec·om·mend·able** *adj* — **rec·om·men·da·tion** *n*

rec·on·cile *vb* **1 :** cause to be friendly again **2 :** adjust or settle **3 :** bring to acceptance — **rec·on·cil·able** *adj* — **rec·on·cile·ment** *n* — **rec·on·cil·er** *n* — **rec·on·cil·i·a·tion** *n*

re·con·di·tion *vb* **:** restore to good condition

re·cord *vb* **1 :** set down in writing **2 :** register permanently **3 :** indicate **4 :** preserve (as sound or images) for later reproduction ∼ *n* **1 :** something recorded **2 :** best performance — **re·cord·er** *n*

¹re·count *vb* **:** relate in detail

²re·count *vb* **:** count again — **re·count** *n*

re·cov·er *vb* **1 :** regain position, poise, or health **2 :** gain compensation for a loss — **re·cov·er·able** *adj* — **re·cov·ery** *n*

rec·re·a·tion *n* **:** a refreshing of strength or spirits as a change from work or study — **rec·re·a·tion·al** *adj*

re·cruit *n* **:** newly enlisted member ∼ *vb* **:** enlist the membership or services of — **re·cruit·er** *n* — **re·cruit·ment** *n*

rect·an·gle *n* **:** 4-sided figure with 4 right angles — **rect·an·gu·lar** *adj*

rec·ti·fy *vb* **:** make or set right — **rec·ti·fi·ca·tion** *n*

rec·tor *n* **:** pastor

rec·to·ry *n* **:** rector's residence

re·cu·per·ate *vb* **:** recover (as from illness) — **re·cu·per·a·tion** *n* — **re·cu·per·a·tive** *adj*

re·cur *vb* **1 :** return in thought or talk **2 :** occur again — **re·cur·rence** *n* — **re·cur·rent** *adj*

re·cy·cle *vb* **:** process (as glass or cans) in order to regain a material for human use — **re·cy·cla·ble** *adj*

red *n* **1 :** color of blood or of the ruby **2** *cap* **:** communist — **red** *adj* — **red·dish** *adj* — **red·ness** *n*

red·den *vb* **:** make or become red or reddish

re·deem *vb* **1 :** regain, free, or rescue by paying a price **2 :** atone for **3 :** free from sin **4 :** convert into something of value — **re·deem·able** *adj* — **re·deem·er** *n*

re·demp·tion *n* **:** act of redeeming — **re·demp·tive** *adj* — **re·demp·to·ry** *adj*

re·duce *vb* **1 :** lessen **2 :** put in a lower rank **3 :** lose weight — **re·duc·er** *n* — **re·duc·ible** *adj*

re·duc·tion *n* **1 :** act of reducing **2 :** amount lost in reducing **3 :** something made by reducing

re·dun·dant *adj* **:** using more words than necessary — **re·dun·dan·cy** *n* — **re·dun·dant·ly** *adv*

reed *n* **1 :** tall slender grass of wet areas **2 :** thin springy strip that vibrates to produce tones in certain wind instruments — **reedy** *adj*

reef *n* **:** ridge of rocks or sand at or near the surface of the water

reek *n* **:** strong or disagreeable fume or odor ∼ *vb* **:** give off a reek

reel *n* **:** revolvable device on which something flexible is wound or a quantity of something wound on it ∼ *vb* **1 :** wind on a reel **2 :** pull in by reeling — **reel·able** *adj* — **reel·er** *n*

re·fer *vb* **1 :** direct or send to some person or place **2 :** submit for consideration or action **3**

: have connection **4** : mention or allude to something — **re·fer·able** adj — **re·fer·ral** n

ref·er·ee n **1** : one to whom an issue is referred for settlement **2** : sports official ∼ vb : act as referee

ref·er·ence n **1** : act of referring **2** : a bearing on a matter **3** : consultation for information **4** : person who can speak for one's character or ability or a recommendation given by such a person

ref·er·en·dum n : a submitting of legislative measures for voters' approval or rejection

re·fill vb : fill again — **re·fill** n — **re·fill·able** adj

re·fine vb **1** : free from impurities or waste matter **2** : improve or perfect **3** : free or become free of what is coarse or uncouth — **re·fine·ment** n — **re·fin·er** n

re·flect vb **1** : bend or cast back (as light or heat) **2** : bring as a result **3** : cast reproach or blame **4** : ponder — **re·flec·tion** n — **re·flec·tive** adj — **re·flec·tor** n

re·flex n : automatic response to a stimulus ∼ adj **1** : bent back **2** : relating to a reflex — **re·flex·ly** adv

re·flex·ive adj : of or relating to an action directed back upon the doer or the grammatical subject — **reflexive** n — **re·flex·ive·ly** adv — **re·flex·ive·ness** n

re·form vb : make or become better esp. by correcting bad habits — **reform** n — **re·form·able** adj — **re·for·ma·tive** adj — **re·form·er** n

re·frac·tion n : the bending of a ray (as of light) when it passes from one medium into another — **re·frac·tive** adj

re·frain vb : hold oneself back ∼ n : verse recurring regularly in a song — **re·frain·ment** n

re·fresh vb **1** : make or become fresh or fresher **2** : supply or take refreshment — **re·fresh·er** n — **re·fresh·ing·ly** adv

re·fresh·ment n **1** : act of refreshing **2** pl : light meal

re·frig·er·ate vb : chill or freeze (food) for preservation — **re·frig·er·ant** adj or n — **re·frig·er·a·tion** n — **re·frig·er·a·tor** n

ref·uge n **1** : protection from danger **2** : place that provides protection

ref·u·gee n : person who flees for safety

re·fund vb : give or put back (money) ∼ n **1** : act of refunding **2** : sum refunded — **re·fund·able** adj

¹**re·fuse** vb : decline to accept, do, or give — **re·fus·al** n

²**ref·use** n : worthless matter

re·gal adj **1** : befitting a king **2** : marked by much dignity — **re·gal·ly** adv

re·gard n **1** : consideration **2** : feeling of approval and liking **3** pl : friendly greetings **4** : relation ∼ vb **1** : pay attention to **2** : show respect for **3** : have an opinion of **4** : look at **5** : relate to — **re·gard·ful** adj — **re·gard·less** adj

re·gard·ing prep : concerning

re·gen·er·ate adj **1** : formed or created again **2** : spiritually reborn ∼ vb **1** : reform completely **2** : replace (a lost body part) by new tissue growth **3** : give new life to — **re·gen·er·a·tion** n — **re·gen·er·a·tive** adj — **re·gen·er·a·tor** n

re·gent n **1** : person who rules during the childhood, absence, or incapacity of the sovereign **2** : member of a governing board — **re·gen·cy** n

re·gime n : government in power

reg·i·men n : systematic course of treatment or training

re·gion n : indefinitely defined area — **re·gion·al** adj — **re·gion·al·ly** adv

reg·is·ter n **1** : record of items or details or a book for keeping such a record **2** : device to regulate ventilation **3** : counting or recording device **4** : range of a voice or instrument ∼ vb **1** : enter in a register **2** : record automatically **3** : get special care for mail by paying more postage

reg·is·tra·tion n **1** : act of registering **2** : entry in a register

reg·is·try n **1** : enrollment **2** : place of registration **3** : official record book

re·gret vb **1** : mourn the loss or death of **2** : be very sorry for ∼ n **1** : sorrow or the expression of sorrow **2** pl : message declining an invitation — **re·gret·ful** adj — **re·gret·ful·ly** adv — **re·gret·ta·ble** adj — **re·gret·ta·bly** adv — **re·gret·ter** n

reg·u·lar adj **1** : conforming to what is usual, normal, or average **2** : steady, uniform, or unvarying — **regular** n — **reg·u·lar·i·ty** n — **reg·u·lar·ize** vb — **reg·u·lar·ly** adv

reg·u·late vb **1** : govern according to rule **2** : adjust to a standard — **reg·u·la·tion** n — **reg·u·la·tive** adj — **reg·u·la·tor** n — **reg·u·la·to·ry** adj

re·ha·bil·i·tate vb **1** : restore to a previous

state or position **2** : make good or usable again — **re·ha·bil·i·ta·tion** *n*

re·hearse *vb* **1** : repeat or recount **2** : engage in a practice performance of — **re·hears·al** *n* — **re·hears·er** *n*

reign *n* : sovereign's authority or rule ∼ *vb* : rule as a sovereign

re·im·burse *vb* : repay — **re·im·burs·able** *adj* — **re·im·burse·ment** *n*

rein *n* **1** : strap fastened to a bit to control an animal **2** : restraining influence ∼ *vb* : direct by reins

rein·deer *n* : large deer

re·in·force *vb* : strengthen or support — **re·in·force·ment** *n* — **re·in·forc·er** *n*

re·ject *vb* **1** : refuse to grant or consider **2** : refuse to admit, believe, or receive **3** : throw out as useless or unsatisfactory ∼ *n* : rejected person or thing — **re·jec·tion** *n*

re·joice *vb* : feel joy — **re·joic·er** *n*

re·join *vb* **1** : join again **2** : say in answer

re·ju·ve·nate *vb* : make young again — **re·ju·ve·na·tion** *n*

re·lapse *n* : recurrence of illness after a period of improvement ∼ *vb* : suffer a relapse

re·late *vb* **1** : give a report of **2** : show a connection between **3** : have a relationship — **re·lat·able** *adj* — **re·lat·er, re·la·tor** *n* — **re·la·tion** *n*

re·la·tion·ship *n* : state of being related or interrelated

rel·a·tive *n* : person connected with another by blood or marriage ∼ *adj* : considered in comparison with something else — **rel·a·tive·ly** *adv* — **rel·a·tive·ness** *n*

re·lax *vb* **1** : make or become less tense or rigid **2** : make less severe **3** : seek rest or recreation — **re·lax·er** *n*

re·lax·a·tion *n* **1** : lessening of tension **2** : recreation

re·lay *n* : fresh supply (as of horses or people) arranged to relieve others ∼ *vb* : pass along in stages

re·lease *vb* **1** : free from confinement or oppression **2** : give up claim to or control over **3** : permit publication, performance, exhibition, or sale ∼ *n* **1** : relief from trouble **2** : discharge from an obligation **3** : act of releasing or what is released

re·lent *vb* : become less severe

re·lent·less *adj* : mercilessly severe or persistent — **re·lent·less·ly** *adv* — **re·lent·less·ness** *n*

rel·e·vance *n* : relation to the matter at hand — **rel·e·vant** *adj* — **rel·e·vant·ly** *adv*

re·li·able *adj* : fit to be trusted — **re·li·abil·i·ty** *n* — **re·li·able·ness** *n* — **re·li·ably** *adv*

re·li·ant *adj* : dependent — **re·li·ance** *n*

re·lieve *vb* **1** : free from a burden or distress **2** : release from a post or duty **3** : break the monotony of — **re·lief** *n* — **re·liev·er** *n*

re·li·gion *n* **1** : service and worship of God **2** : set or system of religious beliefs — **re·li·gion·ist** *n*

re·li·gious *adj* **1** : relating or devoted to an ultimate reality or deity **2** : relating to religious beliefs or observances **3** : marked by intense feelings — **re·li·gious·ly** *adv*

rel·ish *n* **1** : keen enjoyment **2** : highly seasoned sauce (as of pickles) ∼ *vb* : enjoy — **rel·ish·able** *adj*

re·luc·tant *adj* : feeling or showing doubt or unwillingness — **re·luc·tance** *n* — **re·luc·tant·ly** *adv*

re·ly *vb* : place faith or confidence — often with *on*

re·main *vb* **1** : be left after others have been removed **2** : be something yet to be done **3** : stay behind **4** : continue unchanged — **re·mains** *n* — **re·main·der** *n*

re·mark *vb* : express as an observation ∼ *n* : passing comment

re·mark·able *adj* : extraordinary — **re·mark·able·ness** *n* — **re·mark·ably** *adv*

rem·e·dy *n* **1** : medicine that cures **2** : something that corrects an evil or compensates for a loss ∼ *vb* : provide or serve as a remedy for

re·mem·ber *vb* **1** : think of again **2** : keep from forgetting **3** : convey greetings from

re·mem·brance *n* **1** : act of remembering **2** : something that serves to bring to mind

re·mind *vb* : cause to remember — **re·mind·er** *n*

rem·nant *n* : small part or trace remaining

re·mod·el *vb* : alter the structure of

re·mon·strate *vb* : speak in protest, reproof, or opposition — **re·mon·strance** *n* — **re·mon·stra·tion** *n*

re·morse *n* : distress arising from a sense of guilt — **re·morse·ful** *adj* — **re·morse·less** *adj*

re·mote *adj* **1** : far off in place or time **2** : hard to reach or find **3** : acting, acted on, or controlled indirectly or from afar **4** : slight **5** : distant in manner — **re·mote·ly** *adv* — **re·mote·ness** *n*

re•move *vb* **1** : move by lifting or taking off or away **2** : get rid of — **re•mov•able** *adj* — **re•mov•al** *n* — **re•mov•er** *n*

re•mu•ner•ate *vb* : pay — **re•mu•ner•a•tion** *n* — **re•mu•ner•a•tor** *n*

rend *vb* (**rent; rent**) : tear apart forcibly

ren•der *vb* **1** : extract by heating **2** : hand over or give up **3** : do (a service) for another **4** : cause to be or become

ren•dez•vous *n* **1** : place appointed for a meeting **2** : meeting at an appointed place ⁓ *vb* : meet at a rendezvous

ren•e•gade *n* : deserter of one faith or cause for another

re•new *vb* **1** : make or become new, fresh, or strong again **2** : begin again **3** : grant or obtain an extension of — **re•new•able** *adj* — **re•new•al** *n* — **re•new•er** *n*

re•nounce *vb* : give up, refuse, or resign — **re•nounce•ment** *n*

ren•o•vate *vb* : make like new again — **ren•o•va•tion** *n* — **ren•o•va•tor** *n*

re•nown *n* : state of being widely known and honored — **renowned** *adj*

rent *n* : money paid or due periodically for the use of another's property ⁓ *vb* : hold or give possession and use of for rent — **rent•al** *n or adj* — **rent•er** *n*

repair *vb* : restore to good condition ⁓ *n* **1** : act or instance of repairing **2** : condition — **re•pair•er** *n* — **re•pair•man** *n*

re•pay *vb* : pay back — **re•pay•able** *adj* — **re•pay•ment** *n*

re•peal *vb* : annul by legislative action — **re•peal** *n* — **re•peal•er** *n*

re•peat *vb* : say or do again ⁓ *n* **1** : act of repeating **2** : something repeated — **re•peat•able** *adj* — **re•peat•ed•ly** *adv* — **re•peat•er** *n*

re•pel *vb* **1** : drive away **2** : disgust — **re•pel•lent** *adj or n*

re•pent *vb* **1** : turn from sin **2** : regret — **re•pen•tance** *n* — **re•pen•tant** *adj*

rep•e•ti•tion *n* : act or instance of repeating

rep•e•ti•tious *adj* : tediously repeating — **rep•e•ti•tious•ly** *adv* — **rep•e•ti•tious•ness** *n*

re•pet•i•tive *adj* : repetitious — **re•pet•i•tive•ly** *adv* — **re•pet•i•tive•ness** *n*

re•place *vb* **1** : restore to a former position **2** : take the place of **3** : put something new in the place of — **re•place•able** *adj* — **re•place•ment** *n* — **re•plac•er** *n*

re•plen•ish *vb* : stock or supply anew — **re•plen•ish•ment** *n*

rep•li•ca *n* : exact copy

rep•li•cate *vb* : duplicate or repeat — **rep•li•cate** *n* — **rep•li•ca•tion** *n*

re•ply *vb* : say or do in answer ⁓ *n* : answer

re•port *n* **1** : rumor **2** : statement of information (as events or causes) **3** : explosive noise ⁓ *vb* **1** : give an account of **2** : present an account of (an event) as news **3** : present oneself **4** : make known to authorities — **re•port•age** *n* — **re•port•ed•ly** *adv* — **re•port•er** *n* — **re•por•to•ri•al** *adj*

re•pose *vb* : lay or lie at rest ⁓ *n* **1** : state of resting **2** : calm or peace — **re•pose•ful** *adj*

re•pos•sess *vb* : regain possession and legal ownership of — **re•pos•ses•sion** *n*

rep•re•sent *vb* **1** : serve as a sign or symbol of **2** : act or speak for **3** : describe as having a specified quality or character — **rep•re•sen•ta•tion** *n*

rep•re•sen•ta•tive *adj* **1** : standing or acting for another **2** : carried on by elected representatives ⁓ *n* **1** : typical example **2** : one that represents another **3** : member of usu. the lower house of a legislature — **rep•re•sen•ta•tive•ly** *adv* — **rep•re•sen•ta•tive•ness** *n*

re•press *vb* : restrain or suppress — **re•pres•sion** *n* — **re•pres•sive** *adj*

rep•ri•mand *n* : formal or severe criticism — **rep•ri•mand** *vb*

re•proach *n* **1** : disgrace **2** : rebuke ⁓ *vb* : express disapproval to — **re•proach•ful** *adj* — **re•proach•ful•ly** *adv* — **re•proach•ful•ness** *n*

re•pro•duce *vb* **1** : produce again or anew **2** : produce offspring — **re•pro•duc•ible** *adj* — **re•pro•duc•tion** *n* — **re•pro•duc•tive** *adj*

rep•tile *n* : air-breathing scaly vertebrate — **rep•til•ian** *adj or n*

re•pub•lic *n* : country with representative government

re•pub•li•can *adj* **1** : relating to or resembling a republic **2** : supporting a republic — **republican** *n* — **re•pub•li•can•ism** *n*

re•pug•nant *adj* : contrary to one's tastes or principles — **re•pug•nance** *n* — **re•pug•nant•ly** *adv*

re•pulse *vb* **1** : drive or beat back **2** : treat with contempt **3** : be repugnant to — **repulse** *n* — **re•pul•sion** *n*

re•pul•sive *adj* : arousing aversion or disgust — **re•pul•sive•ly** *adv* — **re•pul•sive•ness** *n*

rep•u•ta•ble *adj* : having a good reputation — **rep•u•ta•bly** *adv*

rep·u·ta·tion *n* : one's character or public esteem

re·quest *n* : act or instance of asking for something or a thing asked for ∼ *vb* **1** : make a request of **2** : ask for — **re·quest·er** *n*

re·quire *vb* **1** : insist on **2** : call for as essential — **re·quire·ment** *n*

res·cue *vb* : set free from danger or confinement — **rescue** *n* — **res·cu·er** *n*

re·search *n* : careful or diligent search esp. for new knowledge — **research** *vb* — **re·search·er** *n*

re·sem·ble *vb* : be like or similar to — **re·sem·blance** *n*

re·sent *vb* : feel or show annoyance at — **re·sent·ful** *adj* — **re·sent·ful·ly** *adv* — **re·sent·ment** *n*

res·er·va·tion *n* **1** : act of reserving or something reserved **2** : limiting condition

re·serve *vb* **1** : store for future use **2** : set aside for special use ∼ *n* **1** : something reserved **2** : restraint in words or bearing **3** : military forces withheld from action or not part of the regular services — **re·served** *adj*

res·er·voir *n* : place where something (as water) is kept in store

re·side *vb* **1** : make one's home **2** : be present

res·i·dence *n* **1** : act or fact of residing in a place **2** : place where one lives — **res·i·dent** *adj or n* — **res·i·den·tial** *adj*

res·i·due *n* : part remaining — **re·sid·u·al** *adj*

re·sign *vb* **1** : give up deliberately **2** : give (oneself) over without resistance — **res·ig·na·tion** *n* — **re·sign·ed·ly** *adv*

res·in *n* : substance from the gum or sap of trees — **res·in·ous** *adj*

re·sist *vb* **1** : withstand the force or effect of **2** : fight against — **re·sist·ible** *adj* — **re·sist·less** *adj*

re·sis·tance *n* **1** : act of resisting **2** : ability of an organism to resist disease **3** : opposition to electric current

re·sis·tant *adj* : giving resistance

res·o·lute *adj* : having a fixed purpose — **res·o·lute·ly** *adv* — **res·o·lute·ness** *n*

res·o·lu·tion *n* **1** : process of resolving **2** : firmness of purpose **3** : statement of the opinion, will, or intent of a body

re·solve *vb* **1** : find an answer to **2** : make a formal resolution ∼ *n* **1** : something resolved **2** : steadfast purpose — **re·solv·able** *adj*

res·o·nant *adj* **1** : continuing to sound **2** : relating to intensification or prolongation of sound (as by a vibrating body) — **res·o·nance** *n* — **res·o·nant·ly** *adv*

re·sort *n* **1** : source of help **2** : place to go for vacation ∼ *vb* **1** : go often or habitually **2** : have recourse

re·source *n* **1** : new or reserve source **2** *pl* : available funds **3** : ability to handle situations — **re·source·ful** *adj* — **re·source·ful·ness** *n*

re·spect *n* **1** : relation to something **2** : high or special regard **3** : detail ∼ *vb* : consider deserving of high regard — **re·spect·able** *adj* — **re·spect·abil·i·ty** *n* — **re·spect·ably** *adv* — **re·spect·er** *n* — **re·spect·ful** *adj* — **re·spect·ful·ly** *adv* — **re·spect·ful·ness** *n*

re·spec·tive *adj* : individual and specific — **re·spec·tive·ly** *adv*

res·pi·ra·tion *n* : act or process of breathing — **re·spi·ra·to·ry** *adj* — **re·spire** *vb*

res·pi·ra·tor *n* : device for artificial respiration

re·spond *vb* **1** : answer **2** : react — **re·spon·dent** *n or adj* — **re·spond·er** *n*

re·sponse *n* **1** : act of responding **2** : answer

re·spon·si·ble *adj* **1** : answerable for acts or decisions **2** : able to fulfill obligations **3** : having important duties — **re·spon·si·bil·i·ty** *n* — **re·spon·si·ble·ness** *n* — **re·spon·si·bly** *adv*

re·spon·sive *adj* : quick to respond — **re·spon·sive·ly** *adv* — **re·spon·sive·ness** *n*

¹**rest** *n* **1** : sleep **2** : freedom from work or activity **3** : state of inactivity **4** : something used as a support ∼ *vb* **1** : get rest **2** : cease action or motion **3** : give rest to **4** : sit or lie fixed or supported **5** : depend — **rest·ful** *adj* — **rest·ful·ly** *adv*

²**rest** *n* : remainder

res·tau·rant *n* : public eating place

rest·less *adj* **1** : lacking or giving no rest **2** : always moving **3** : uneasy — **rest·less·ly** *adv* — **rest·less·ness** *n*

re·store *vb* **1** : give back **2** : put back into use or into a former state — **re·stor·able** *adj* — **res·to·ra·tion** *n* — **re·stor·ative** *n or adj* — **re·stor·er** *n*

re·strain *vb* : limit or keep under control — **re·strain·able** *adj* — **re·strained** *adj* — **re·strain·ed·ly** *adv* — **re·strain·er** *n* — **re·straint** *n*

re·strict *vb* **1** : confine within bounds **2** : limit use of — **re·stric·tion** *n* — **re·stric·tive** *adj* — **re·stric·tive·ly** *adv*

re·sult *vb* : come about because of something

else $\sim$ *n* **1** : thing that results **2** : something obtained by calculation or investigation — **re-sul-tant** *adj or n*

re-sume *vb* : return to or take up again after interruption — **re-sump-tion** *n*

ré-su-mé, re-su-me, re-su-mé *n* : summary of one's career and qualifications

res-ur-rect *vb* **1** : raise from the dead **2** : bring to attention or use again — **res-ur-rec-tion** *n*

re-sus-ci-tate *vb* : bring back from apparent death — **re-sus-ci-ta-tion** *n* — **re-sus-ci-ta-tor** *n*

re-tail *vb* : sell in small quantities directly to the consumer $\sim$ *n* : business of selling to consumers — **retail** *adj or adv* — **re-tail-er** *n*

re-tain *vb* **1** : keep or hold onto **2** : engage the services of

re-tain-er *n* **1** : household servant **2** : retaining fee

re-tal-i-ate *vb* : return (as an injury) in kind — **re-tal-i-a-tion** *n* — **re-tal-ia-to-ry** *adj*

re-tard *vb* : hold back — **re-tar-da-tion** *n*

re-tard-ed *adj* : slow or limited in intellectual development

retch *vb* : try to vomit

re-ten-tion *n* **1** : state of being retained **2** : ability to retain — **re-ten-tive** *adj*

ret-i-na *n* : sensory membrane lining the eye — **ret-i-nal** *adj*

re-tire *vb* **1** : withdraw for privacy **2** : end a career **3** : go to bed — **re-tir-ee** *n* — **re-tire-ment** *n*

re-tort *vb* : say in reply $\sim$ *n* : quick, witty, or cutting answer

re-trace *vb* : go over again or in reverse

re-tract *vb* **1** : draw back or in **2** : withdraw a charge or promise — **re-tract-able** *adj* — **re-trac-tion** *n*

re-treat *n* **1** : act of withdrawing **2** : place of privacy or safety or meditation and study $\sim$ *vb* : make a retreat

ret-ri-bu-tion *n* : retaliation — **re-trib-u-tive** *adj* — **re-trib-u-to-ry** *adj*

re-trieve *vb* **1** : search for and bring in game **2** : recover — **re-triev-able** *adj* — **re-triev-al** *n*

ret-ro-ac-tive *adj* : made effective as of a prior date — **ret-ro-ac-tive-ly** *adv*

ret-ro-spect *n* : review of past events — **ret-ro-spec-tion** *n* — **ret-ro-spec-tive** *adj* — **ret-ro-spec-tive-ly** *adv*

re-turn *vb* **1** : go or come back **2** : pass, give, or send back to an earlier possessor **3** : answer **4** : bring in as a profit **5** : give or do in return

$\sim$ *n* **1** : act of returning or something returned **2** *pl* : report of balloting results **3** : statement of taxable income **4** : profit — **re-turn** *adj* — **re-turn-able** *adj or n* — **re-turn-er** *n*

re-union *n* **1** : act of reuniting **2** : a meeting of persons after a separation

re-veal *vb* **1** : make known **2** : show plainly

rev-el *vb* **1** : take part in a revel **2** : take great pleasure $\sim$ *n* : wild party or celebration — **rev-el-er, rev-el-ler** *n* — **rev-el-ry** *n*

rev-e-la-tion *n* **1** : act of revealing **2** : something enlightening or astonishing

re-venge *vb* : avenge $\sim$ *n* **1** : desire for retaliation **2** : act of retaliation — **re-venge-ful** *adj* — **re-veng-er** *n*

rev-e-nue *n* : money collected by a government

re-ver-ber-ate *vb* : sound in a series of echoes — **re-ver-ber-a-tion** *n*

re-vere *vb* : show honor and devotion to — **rev-er-ence** *n* — **rev-er-ent** *adj* — **rev-er-ent-ly** *adv*

rev-er-end *adj* : worthy of reverence $\sim$ *n* : clergy member

rev-er-ie *n* : daydream

re-verse *adj* **1** : opposite to a previous or normal condition **2** : acting in an opposite way $\sim$ *vb* **1** : turn upside down or completely around **2** : change to the contrary or in the opposite direction $\sim$ *n* **1** : something contrary **2** : change for the worse **3** : back of something — **re-ver-sal** *n* — **re-verse-ly** *adv* — **re-vers-ible** *adj*

re-view *n* **1** : formal inspection **2** : general survey **3** : critical evaluation **4** : second or repeated study or examination $\sim$ *vb* **1** : examine or study again **2** : reexamine judicially **3** : look back over **4** : examine critically **5** : inspect — **re-view-er** *n*

re-vise *vb* **1** : look over something written to correct or improve **2** : make a new version of — **re-vis-able** *adj* — **revise** *n* — **re-vis-er, re-vi-sor** *n* — **re-vi-sion** *n*

re-vive *vb* : bring back to life or consciousness or into use — **re-viv-al** *n* — **re-viv-er** *n*

re-voke *vb* : annul by recalling — **re-vok-er** *n*

re-volt *vb* **1** : throw off allegiance **2** : cause or experience disgust or shock $\sim$ *n* : rebellion or revolution — **re-volt-er** *n*

re-volt-ing *adj* : extremely offensive — **re-volt-ing-ly** *adv*

rev-o-lu-tion *n* **1** : rotation **2** : progress in an orbit **3** : sudden, radical, or complete change (as overthrow of a government) — **rev·o·lu·tion·ary** *adj or n* — **rev·o·lu·tion·ize** *vb*

re·volve *vb* **1** : ponder **2** : move in an orbit **3** : rotate — **re·volv·able** *adj*

re·volv·er *n* : pistol with a revolving cylinder

re·vul·sion *n* : complete dislike or repugnance

re·ward *vb* : give a reward to or for ∼ *n* : something offered for service or achievement

re·write *vb* : revise — **rewrite** *n*

rhap·so·dy *n* **1** : expression of extravagant praise **2** : flowing free-form musical composition — **rhap·sod·ic** *adj* — **rhap·sod·i·cal·ly** *adv* — **rhap·so·dize** *vb*

rho·do·den·dron *n* : flowering evergreen shrub

rhyme *n* **1** : correspondence in terminal sounds **2** : verse that rhymes ∼ *vb* : make or have rhymes

rhythm *n* : regular succession of sounds or motions — **rhyth·mic, rhyth·mi·cal** *adj* — **rhyth·mi·cal·ly** *adv*

rib *n* **1** : curved bone joined to the spine **2** : riblike thing ∼ *vb* **1** : furnish or mark with ribs **2** : tease — **rib·ber** *n*

rib·bon *n* **1** : narrow strip of fabric used esp. for decoration **2** : strip of inked cloth (as in a typewriter)

rice *n* : starchy edible seeds of an annual cereal grass

rich *adj* **1** : having a lot of money or possessions **2** : valuable **3** : containing much sugar, fat, or seasoning **4** : abundant **5** : deep and pleasing in color or tone **6** : fertile — **rich·ly** *adv* — **rich·ness** *n*

rich·es *n pl* : wealth

rid *vb* : make free of something unwanted — **rid·dance** *n*

rid·dle *n* : puzzling question ∼ *vb* : speak in riddles

ride *vb* (**rode; rid·den**) **1** : be carried along **2** : sit on and cause to move **3** : travel over a surface **4** : tease or nag ∼ *n* **1** : trip on an animal or in a vehicle **2** : mechanical device ridden for amusement — **rid·er** *n* — **rid·er·less** *adj*

ridge *n* **1** : range of hills **2** : raised line or strip **3** : line of intersection of 2 sloping surfaces — **ridgy** *adj*

rid·i·cule *vb* : laugh at or make fun of — **ridicule** *n*

ri·dic·u·lous *adj* : arousing ridicule — **ri·dic·u·lous·ly** *adv* — **ri·dic·u·lous·ness** *n*

rifle *n* : long shoulder weapon with spiral grooves in the bore — **ri·fle·man** *n* — **ri·fling** *n*

¹rig *vb* **1** : fit out with rigging **2** : set up esp. as a makeshift ∼ *n* **1** : distinctive shape, number, and arrangement of sails and masts of a sailing ship **2** : equipment **3** : carriage with its horse

²rig *vb* : manipulate esp. by deceptive or dishonest means

right *adj* **1** : meeting a standard of conduct **2** : correct **3** : genuine **4** : normal **5** : opposite of left ∼ *n* **1** : something that is correct, just, proper, or honorable **2** : something to which one has a just claim **3** : something that is on the right side ∼ *adv* **1** : according to what is right **2** : immediately **3** : completely **4** : on or to the right ∼ *vb* **1** : restore to a proper state **2** : bring or become upright again — **right·er** *n* — **right·ness** *n* — **right·ward** *adj*

righ·teous *adj* : acting or being in accordance with what is just or moral — **righ·teous·ly** *adv* — **righ·teous·ness** *n*

rig·id *adj* : lacking flexibility — **ri·gid·i·ty** *n* — **rig·id·ly** *adv*

rig·or *n* : severity — **rig·or·ous** *adj* — **rig·or·ous·ly** *adv*

rim *n* : edge esp. of something curved ∼ *vb* : border

rind *n* : usu. hard or tough outer layer

¹ring *n* **1** : circular band used as an ornament or for holding or fastening **2** : something circular **3** : place for contest or display **4** : group with a selfish or dishonest aim ∼ *vb* : surround — **ringed** *adj* — **ring·like** *adj*

²ring *vb* **1** : sound resonantly when struck **2** : cause to make a metallic sound by striking **3** : produce a strong echoing sound **4** : call esp. by a bell ∼ *n* **1** : resonant sound or tone **2** : act or instance of ringing — **ring·er** *n*

ring·tone *n* : sound of a cell phone to indicate an incoming call

rink *n* : enclosed place for skating

rinse *vb* **1** : cleanse usu. with water only **2** : treat (hair) with a rinse ∼ *n* : liquid used for rinsing — **rins·er** *n*

ri·ot *n* **1** : violent public disorder **2** : random or disorderly lavish display — **riot** *vb* — **ri·ot·er** *n* — **ri·ot·ous** *adj*

rip *vb* : cut or tear open ∼ *n* : rent made by ripping — **rip·per** *n*

ripe *adj* : fully grown, developed, or prepared — **ripe·ly** *adv* — **rip·en** *vb* — **ripe·ness** *n*

rip·ple *vb* **1** : become lightly ruffled on the surface **2** : sound like rippling water — **ripple** *n*

rise *vb* (**rose; ris·en**) **1** : get up from sitting, kneeling, or lying **2** : take arms **3** : appear above the horizon **4** : move upward **5** : gain a higher position or rank **6** : increase ∼ *n* **1** : act of rising **2** : origin **3** : elevation **4** : increase **5** : upward slope **6** : area of high ground — **ris·er** *n*

risk *n* : exposure to loss or injury — **risk** *vb* — **risk·i·ness** *n* — **risky** *adj*

rite *n* **1** : set form for conducting a ceremony **2** : customary ceremonies of a church **3** : ceremonial action

rit·u·al *n* : rite — **ritual** *adj* — **rit·u·al·ism** *n* — **rit·u·al·is·tic** *adj* — **rit·u·al·is·ti·cal·ly** *adv* — **rit·u·al·ly** *adv*

ri·val *n* **1** : competitor **2** : peer ∼ *vb* **1** : be in competition with **2** : equal — **rival** *adj* — **ri·val·ry** *n*

riv·er *n* : large natural stream of water — **riv·er·bank** *n* — **riv·er·bed** *n* — **riv·er·boat** *n* — **riv·er·side** *n*

road *n* : open way for vehicles, persons, and animals — **road·bed** *n* — **road·block** *n* — **road·side** *n or adj* — **road·way** *n*

roam *vb* : wander

roar *vb* : utter a full loud prolonged sound — **roar** *n* — **roar·er** *n*

roast *vb* **1** : cook by dry heat **2** : criticize severely ∼ *n* : piece of meat suitable for roasting — **roast** *adj* — **roast·er** *n*

rob *vb* **1** : steal from **2** : commit robbery — **rob·ber** *n*

rob·bery *n* : theft of something from a person by use of violence or threat

robe *n* **1** : long flowing outer garment **2** : covering for the lower body ∼ *vb* : clothe with or as if with a robe

rob·in *n* : No. American thrush with a reddish breast

ro·bot *n* **1** : machine that looks and acts like a human being **2** : efficient but insensitive person — **ro·bot·ic** *adj*

¹rock *vb* : sway or cause to sway back and forth ∼ *n* **1** : rocking movement **2** : popular music marked by repetition and a strong beat

²rock *n* : mass of hard mineral material — **rock** *adj* — **rocky** *adj*

rock·er *n* **1** : curved piece on which a chair rocks **2** : chair that rocks

rock·et *n* **1** : self-propelled firework or missile **2** : jet engine that carries its own oxygen ∼ *vb* : rise abruptly and rapidly — **rock·et·ry** *n*

rod *n* **1** : straight slender stick **2** : unit of length equal to 5 yards

rode *past of* RIDE

ro·deo *n* : contest of cowboy skills

rogue *n* : dishonest or mischievous person — **rogu·ery** *n* — **rogu·ish** *adj* — **rogu·ish·ly** *adv* — **rogu·ish·ness** *n*

role *n* **1** : part to play **2** : function

roll *n* **1** : official record or list of names **2** : something rolled up or rounded **3** : bread baked in a small rounded mass **4** : sound of rapid drum strokes **5** : heavy reverberating sound **6** : rolling movement ∼ *vb* **1** : move by turning over **2** : move on wheels **3** : flow in a continuous stream **4** : swing from side to side **5** : shape or be shaped in rounded form **6** : press with a revolving cylinder — **roll·er** *n*

Ro·man Cath·o·lic *n* : member of a Christian church led by a pope — **Ro·man Cath·o·lic** *adj* — **Ro·man Ca·thol·i·cism** *n*

ro·mance *n* **1** : medieval tale of knightly adventure **2** : love story **3** : love affair ∼ *vb* **1** : have romantic fancies **2** : have a love affair with — **ro·manc·er** *n*

ro·man·tic *adj* **1** : visionary or imaginative **2** : appealing to one's emotions — **ro·man·ti·cal·ly** *adv*

romp *vb* : play actively and noisily — **romp** *n*

roof *n* : upper covering part of a building ∼ *vb* : cover with a roof — **roofed** *adj* — **roof·ing** *n* — **roof·less** *adj* — **roof·top** *n*

rook *n* : crowlike bird

rook·ie *n* : novice

room *n* **1** : sufficient space **2** : partitioned part of a building ∼ *vb* : occupy lodgings — **room·er** *n* — **room·ful** *n* — **roomy** *adj*

roost·er *n* : adult male domestic chicken

root *n* **1** : leafless underground part of a seed plant **2** : rootlike thing or part **3** : source **4** : essential core ∼ *vb* : form, fix, or become fixed by roots — **root·less** *adj* — **root·let** *n* — **root·like** *adj*

³root *vb* : applaud or encourage noisily — **root·er** *n*

rope *n* : large strong cord of strands of fiber ∼ *vb* **1** : tie with a rope **2** : lasso

ro·sa·ry *n* **1** : string of beads used in praying **2** : Roman Catholic devotion

¹rose *past of* RISE

²rose *n* **1** : prickly shrub with bright flowers **2**

: purplish red — **rose** *adj* — **rose·bud** *n* — **rose·bush** *n*

Rosh Ha·sha·nah *n* : Jewish New Year observed as a religious holiday in September or October

rosy *adj* **1** : of the color rose **2** : hopeful — **ros·i·ly** *adv* — **ros·i·ness** *n*

rot *vb* : undergo decomposition ∼ *n* **1** : decay **2** : disease in which tissue breaks down

ro·ta·ry *adj* **1** : turning on an axis **2** : having a rotating part

ro·tate *vb* **1** : turn about an axis or a center **2** : alternate in a series — **ro·ta·tion** *n* — **ro·ta·tor** *n*

ro·tor *n* **1** : part that rotates **2** : system of rotating horizontal blades for supporting a helicopter

rot·ten *adj* **1** : having rotted **2** : corrupt **3** : extremely unpleasant or inferior — **rot·ten·ness** *n*

rough *adj* **1** : not smooth **2** : not calm **3** : harsh, violent, or rugged **4** : crudely or hastily done ∼ *n* : rough state or something in that state ∼ *vb* **1** : roughen **2** : handle roughly **3** : make roughly — **rough·en** *vb* — **rough·ly** *adv* — **rough·ness** *n*

round *adj* **1** : having every part the same distance from the center **2** : cylindrical **3** : complete **4** : approximate **5** : blunt **6** : moving in or forming a circle ∼ *n* **1** : round or curved thing **2** : series of recurring actions or events **3** : period of time or a unit of action **4** : fired shot **5** : cut of beef ∼ *vb* **1** : make or become round **2** : go around **3** : finish **4** : express as an approximation — **round·ish** *adj* — **round·ly** *adv* — **round·ness** *n*

rout *n* **1** : state of wild confusion **2** : disastrous defeat ∼ *vb* : defeat decisively

route *n* : line of travel ∼ *vb* : send by a selected route

rou·tine *n* **1** : regular course of procedure **2** : an often repeated speech, formula, or part — **routine** *adj* — **rou·tine·ly** *adv*

rove *vb* : wander or roam — **rov·er** *n*

¹row *vb* **1** : propel a boat with oars **2** : carry in a rowboat ∼ *n* : act of rowing — **row·boat** *n* — **row·er** *n*

²row *n* : number of objects in a line

³row *n* : noisy quarrel — **row** *vb*

row·dy *adj* : coarse or boisterous in behavior — **row·di·ness** *n* — **rowdy** *n*

roy·al *adj* : relating to or befitting a king ∼ *n* : person of royal blood — **roy·al·ly** *adv* — **roy·al·ty** *n*

rub *vb* **1** : use pressure and friction on a body **2** : scour, polish, erase, or smear by pressure and friction **3** : chafe with friction ∼ *n* : difficulty

rub·ber *n* **1** : one that rubs **2** : waterproof elastic substance or something made of it — **rub·ber** *adj* — **rub·ber·ize** *vb* — **rub·bery** *adj*

rub·bish *n* : waste or trash

ru·by *n* : precious red stone or its color — **ruby** *adj*

rude *adj* **1** : roughly made **2** : impolite — **rude·ly** *adv* — **rude·ness** *n*

rue *vb* : feel regret for ∼ *n* : regret — **rue·ful** *adj* — **rue·ful·ly** *adv* — **rue·ful·ness** *n*

ruf·fle *vb* **1** : draw into or provide with pleats **2** : roughen the surface of **3** : irritate ∼ *n* : strip of fabric pleated on one edge — **ruf·fly** *adj*

rug *n* : piece of heavy fabric used as a floor covering

rug·ged *adj* **1** : having a rough uneven surface **2** : severe **3** : strong — **rug·ged·ly** *adv* — **rug·ged·ness** *n*

ru·in *n* **1** : complete collapse or destruction **2** : remains of something destroyed — usu. in pl. **3** : cause of destruction ∼ *vb* **1** : destroy **2** : damage beyond repair **3** : bankrupt

ru·in·ous *adj* : causing ruin — **ruin·ous·ly** *adv*

rule *n* **1** : guide or principle for governing action **2** : usual way of doing something **3** : government **4** : straight strip (as of wood or metal) marked off in units for measuring ∼ *vb* **1** : govern **2** : give as a decision — **rul·er** *n*

rum *n* : liquor made from molasses or sugarcane

rum·ble *vb* : make a low heavy rolling sound — **rumble** *n*

ru·mor *n* **1** : common talk **2** : widespread statement not authenticated — **rumor** *vb*

rump *n* : rear part of an animal

rum·ple *vb* : tousle or wrinkle — **rumple** *n*

run *vb* **ran; run 1** : go rapidly or hurriedly **2** : enter a race or election **3** : operate **4** : continue in force **5** : flow rapidly **6** : take a certain direction **7** : manage **8** : incur ∼ *n* **1** : act of running **2** : brook **3** : continuous series **4** : usual kind **5** : freedom of movement **6** : lengthwise ravel

run·away *n* : fugitive ∼ *adj* **1** : fugitive **2** : out of control

¹rung *past part of* RING

²rung *n* : horizontal piece of a chair or ladder

run·ner *n* **1** : one that runs **2** : thin piece or part on which something slides **3** : slender creeping branch of a plant

run·ning *adj* **1** : flowing **2** : continuous

runt *n* : small person or animal — **runty** *adj*

rup·ture *n* **1** : breaking or tearing apart ~ *vb* : cause or undergo rupture

ru·ral *adj* : relating to the country or agriculture

rush *vb* **1** : move forward or act with too great haste **2** : perform in a short time ~ *n* : violent forward motion ~ *adj* : requiring speed — **rush·er** *n*

rust *n* **1** : reddish coating on exposed iron **2** : reddish brown color — **rust** *vb* — **rusty** *adj*

rus·tic *adj* : relating to or suitable for the country or country dwellers ~ *n* : rustic person — **rus·ti·cal·ly** *adv*

rus·tle *vb* **1** : make or cause a rustle **2** : forage food **3** : steal cattle from the range ~ *n* : series of small sounds — **rus·tler** *n*

rut *n* **1** : track worn by wheels or feet **2** : set routine — **rut·ted** *adj*

ruth·less *adj* : having no pity — **ruth·less·ly** *adv* — **ruth·less·ness** *n*

RV *n* recreational vehicle

rye *n* **1** : cereal grass grown for grain **2** : whiskey from rye

S

s *n* : 19th letter of the alphabet

Sab·bath *n* **1** : Saturday observed as a day of worship by Jews and some Christians **2** : Sunday observed as a day of worship by Christians

sab·o·tage *n* : deliberate destruction or hampering ~ *vb* : wreck through sabotage

sack *n* : bag ~ *vb* : fire

sac·ra·ment *n* : formal religious act or rite — **sac·ra·men·tal** *adj*

sa·cred *adj* **1** : set apart for or worthy of worship **2** : worthy of reverence **3** : relating to religion — **sa·cred·ly** *adv* — **sa·cred·ness** *n*

sac·ri·fice *n* : the offering of something precious to a deity or the thing offered **2** : loss or deprivation ~ *vb* : offer or give up as a sacrifice — **sac·ri·fi·cial** *adj*

sac·ri·lege *n* : violation of something sacred — **sac·ri·le·gious** *adj*

sad *adj* **1** : affected with grief or sorrow **2** : causing sorrow — **sad·den** *vb* — **sad·ly** *adv* — **sad·ness** *n*

sad·dle *n* : seat for riding on horseback ~ *vb* : put a saddle on

sa·dism *n* : delight in cruelty — **sa·dist** *n* — **sa·dis·tic** *adj* — **sa·dis·ti·cal·ly** *adv*

sa·fa·ri *n* : hunting expedition in Africa

safe *adj* **1** : free from harm **2** : providing safety ~ *n* : container to keep valuables safe — **safe·keep·ing** *n* — **safe·ly** *adv*

safe·guard *n* : measure or device for preventing accidents — **safe·guard** *vb*

safe·ty *n* **1** : freedom from danger **2** : protective device

sag *vb* : droop, sink, or settle — **sag** *n*

sage *adj* : wise or prudent ~ *n* : wise man — **sage·ly** *adv*

said *past of* SAY

sail *n* **1** : fabric used to catch the wind and move a boat or ship **2** : trip on a sailboat ~ *vb* **1** : travel on a ship or sailboat **2** : move with ease or grace — **sail·boat** *n* — **sail·or** *n*

saint *n* : holy or godly person — **saint·ed** *adj* — **saint·hood** *n* — **saint·li·ness** *n* — **saint·ly** *adj*

sake *n* **1** : purpose or reason **2** : one's good or benefit

sal·ad *n* : dish usu. of raw lettuce, vegetables, or fruit

sa·la·mi *n* : highly seasoned dried sausage

sal·a·ry *n* : regular payment for services

sale *n* **1** : transfer of ownership of property for money **2** : selling at bargain prices **3** *pl* : activities involved in selling — **sal·able, sale·able** *adj* — **sales·man** *n* — **sales·per·son** *n* — **sales·wom·an** *n*

sa·li·va *n* : liquid secreted into the mouth — **sal·i·vary** *adj* — **sal·i·vate** *vb* — **sal·i·va·tion** *n*

salm·on *n* (**salmon**) **1** : food fish with pink or red flesh **2** : deep yellowish pink color

sa·lon *n* : elegant room or shop

sa·loon *n* **1** : public cabin on a passenger ship **2** : barroom

sal·sa *n* : spicy sauce of tomatoes, onions, and hot peppers

salt *n* **1** : white crystalline substance that consists of sodium and chlorine **2** : compound formed usu. from acid and metal — **salt** *vb or adj* — **salt·i·ness** *n* — **salty** *adj*

sa·lute *vb* : honor by ceremony or formal movement — **salute** *n*

sal·vage *n* : something saved from destruction ～ *vb* : rescue or save

sal·va·tion *n* : saving of a person from sin or danger

same *adj* : being the one referred to ～ *pron* : the same one or ones ～ *adv* : in the same manner — **same·ness** *n*

sam·ple *n* : piece or part that shows the quality of a whole ～ *vb* : judge by a sample

sanc·ti·mo·nious *adj* : hypocritically pious — **sanc·ti·mo·nious·ly** *adv*

sanc·tion *n* **1** : authoritative approval **2** : coercive measure — usu. pl ～ *vb* : approve

sanc·tu·ary *n* **1** : consecrated place **2** : place of refuge

sand *n* : loose granular particles of rock ～ *vb* : smooth with an abrasive — **sand·bank** *n* — **sand·er** *n* — **sand·storm** *n* — **sandy** *adj*

san·dal *n* : shoe consisting of a sole strapped to the foot

sand·wich *n* : bread surrounding a filling ～ *vb* : squeeze or crowd in

sane *adj* **1** : mentally healthy **2** : sensible — **sane·ly** *adv*

sang *past of* SING

san·i·tary *adj* **1** : relating to health **2** : free from filth or infective matter

san·i·ta·tion *n* : protection of health by maintenance of sanitary conditions

san·i·ty *n* : soundness of mind

sank *past of* SINK

¹sap *n* **1** : fluid that circulates through a plant **2** : gullible person

²sap *vb* **1** : undermine **2** : weaken or exhaust gradually

sap·py *adj* **1** : full of sap **2** : overly sentimental

sar·casm *n* **1** : cutting remark **2** : ironical criticism or reproach — **sar·cas·tic** *adj* — **sar·cas·ti·cal·ly** *adv*

¹sash *n* : broad band worn around the waist or over the shoulder

²sash *n* **1** : frame for a pane of glass in a door or window **2** : movable part of a window

sassy *adj* : insolent

sat *past of* SIT

Sa·tan *n* : devil — **sa·tan·ic** *adj* — **sa·tan·i·cal·ly** *adv*

satch·el *n* : small bag

sate *vb* : satisfy fully

sat·el·lite *n* : body or object that revolves around a larger celestial body

sat·in *n* : glossy fabric — **sat·iny** *adj*

sat·ire *n* : literary ridicule done with humor — **sa·tir·ic, sa·tir·i·cal** *adj* — **sa·tir·i·cal·ly** *adv* — **sat·i·rist** *n* — **sat·i·rize** *vb*

sat·is·fac·tion *n* : state of being satisfied — **sat·is·fac·to·ri·ly** *adv* — **sat·is·fac·to·ry** *adj* — **sat·is·fy** *vb* — **sat·is·fy·ing·ly** *adv*

sat·u·rate *vb* : soak or charge thoroughly — **sat·u·ra·tion** *n*

Sat·ur·day *n* : 7th day of the week

sauce *n* : fluid dressing or topping for food — **sauce·pan** *n*

sau·cer *n* : small shallow dish under a cup

sau·na *n* : steam or dry heat bath or a room or cabinet used for such a bath

sau·sage *n* : minced and highly seasoned meat

sau·té *vb* : fry in a little fat — **sauté** *n*

sav·age *adj* **1** : wild **2** : cruel ～ *n* : person belonging to a primitive society — **sav·age·ly** *adv* — **sav·age·ness** *n* — **sav·age·ry** *n*

save *vb* **1** : rescue from danger **2** : guard from destruction **3** : redeem from sin **4** : put aside as a reserve — **sav·er** *n*

sav·ior, sav·iour *n* **1** : one who saves **2** *cap* : Jesus Christ

¹saw *past of* SEE

²saw *n* : cutting tool with teeth ～ *vb* : cut with a saw — **saw·dust** *n* — **saw·mill** *n* — **saw·yer** *n*

say *vb* **said; said** **1** : express in words **2** : state positively ～ *n* **1** : expression of opinion **2** : power of decision

say·ing *n* : commonly repeated statement

scab *n* **1** : protective crust over a sore or wound **2** : worker taking a striker's job ～ *vb* **1** : become covered with a scab **2** : work as a scab — **scab·by** *adj*

scald *vb* **1** : burn with hot liquid or steam **2** : heat to the boiling point

¹scale *n* : weighing device ～ *vb* : weigh

²scale *n* **1** : thin plate esp. on the body of a fish or reptile **2** : thin coating or layer ～ *vb* : strip of scales — **scaled** *adj* — **scale·less** *adj* — **scaly** *adj*

³scale *n* **1** : graduated series **2** : size of a sample (as a model) in proportion to the size of the actual thing **3** : standard of estimation or judgment **4** : series of musical tones ～ *vb* **1** : climb by a ladder **2** : arrange in a graded series

scalp *n* : skin and flesh of the head ～ *vb* **1**

: remove the scalp from **2** : resell at a greatly increased price — **scalp·er** *n*

scam·per *vb* **1** : run nimbly — **scam·per** *n*

scan *vb* **1** : read (verses) so as to show meter **2** : examine closely or hastily **3** : examine with a sensing device — **scan** *n* — **scan·ner** *n*

scan·dal *n* **1** : disgraceful situation **2** : malicious gossip — **scan·dal·ize** *vb* — **scan·dal·ous** *adj*

scant *adj* : barely sufficient ∼ *vb* : hold back from being generous — **scant·i·ly** *adv* — **scanty** *adj*

scar *n* : mark where a wound has healed — **scar** *vb*

scarce *adj* : lacking in quantity or number — **scar·ci·ty** *n*

scarce·ly *adv* **1** : barely **2** : almost not

scare *vb* : frighten ∼ *n* : fright — **scary** *adj*

scarf *n* : cloth worn about the shoulders or the neck

scat·ter *vb* **1** : spread about irregularly **2** : disperse

scav·en·ger *n* **1** : person that collects refuse or waste **2** : animal that feeds on decayed matter — **scav·enge** *vb*

scene *n* **1** : single situation in a play or movie **2** : stage setting **3** : view **4** : display of emotion — **sce·nic** *adj*

scen·ery *n* **1** : painted setting for a stage **2** : picturesque view

scent *vb* **1** : smell **2** : fill with odor ∼ *n* **1** : odor **2** : sense of smell **3** : perfume — **scent·ed** *adj*

sched·ule *n* : list showing sequence of events ∼ *vb* : make a schedule of

scheme *n* **1** : crafty plot **2** : systematic design ∼ *vb* : form a plot — **sche·mat·ic** *adj* — **schem·er** *n*

schol·ar *n* : student or learned person — **schol·ar·ly** *adj*

schol·ar·ship *n* **1** : qualities or learning of a serious student **2** : money given to a student to pay for education

scho·las·tic *adj* : relating to schools, scholars, or scholarship

¹school *n* **1** : institution for learning **2** : pupils in a school **3** : group with shared beliefs ∼ *vb* : teach — **school·boy** *n* — **school·girl** *n* — **school·house** *n* — **school·mate** *n* — **school·room** *n* — **school·teach·er** *n*

²school *n* : large number of fish swimming together

sci·ence *n* : branch of systematic study esp. of the physical world — **sci·en·tif·ic** *adj* — **sci·en·tif·i·cal·ly** *adv* — **sci·en·tist** *n*

scis·sors *n pl* : small shears

scold *n* : person who scolds ∼ *vb* : criticize severely

scoop *n* : shovellike utensil ∼ *vb* **1** : take out with a scoop **2** : dig out

scoot·er *n* : child's foot-propelled vehicle

scope *n* **1** : extent **2** : room for development

scorch *vb* : burn the surface of

score *n* **1** *pl* **score** : twenty **2** : cut **3** : record of points made (as in a game) **4** : debt **5** : music of a composition ∼ *vb* **1** : record **2** : mark with lines **3** : gain in a game **4** : assign a grade to **5** : compose a score for — **score·less** *adj* — **scor·er** *n*

scorn *n* : emotion involving both anger and disgust ∼ *vb* : hold in contempt — **scorn·er** *n* — **scorn·ful** *adj* — **scorn·ful·ly** *adv*

scout *vb* : inspect or observe to get information ∼ *n* : person sent out to get information

scowl *vb* : make a frowning expression of displeasure — **scowl** *n*

scram *vb* : go away at once

scram·ble *vb* **1** : clamber clumsily around **2** : struggle for possession of something **3** : mix together **4** : cook (eggs) by stirring during frying — **scram·ble** *n*

scrap *n* **1** : fragment **2** : discarded material ∼ *vb* : get rid of as useless

scrape *vb* **1** : remove by drawing a knife over **2** : clean or smooth by rubbing **3** : draw across a surface with a grating sound **4** : damage by contact with a rough surface **5** : gather or proceed with difficulty ∼ *n* **1** : act of scraping **2** : predicament — **scrap·er** *n*

scratch *vb* **1** : scrape or dig with or as if with claws or nails **2** : cause to move gratingly **3** : delete by or as if by drawing a line through ∼ *n* : mark or sound made in scratching — **scratchy** *adj*

scrawl *vb* : write hastily and carelessly — **scrawl** *n*

scream *vb* : cry out loudly and shrilly ∼ *n* : loud shrill cry

screen *n* **1** : device or partition used to protect or decorate **2** : surface on which pictures appear (as in movies) ∼ *vb* : shield or separate with or as if with a screen

screw *n* **1** : grooved fastening device **2** : propeller ∼ *vb* **1** : fasten by means of a screw **2** : move spirally

screw·driv·er *n* : tool for turning screws

scrib·ble *vb* : write hastily or carelessly — **scrib·ble** *n* — **scrib·bler** *n*

script *n* : text (as of a play)

scrip·ture *n* : sacred writings of a religion — **scrip·tur·al** *adj*

scroll *n* **1** : roll of paper for writing a document **2** : spiral or coiled design

scrub *vb* : clean or wash by rubbing — **scrub** *n*

scru·ple *n* : reluctance due to ethical considerations — **scru·ple** *vb* — **scru·pu·lous** *adj* — **scru·pu·lous·ly** *adv*

scru·ti·ny *n* : careful inspection — **scru·ti·nize** *vb*

scuff *vb* : scratch, scrape, or wear away — **scuff** *n*

scuf·fle *vb* **1** : struggle at close quarters **2** : shuffle one's feet — **scuf·fle** *n*

sculp·ture *n* : work of art carved or molded ∼ *vb* : form as sculpture — **sculp·tor** *n* — **sculp·tur·al** *adj*

scum *n* : slimy film on a liquid

sea *n* **1** : large body of salt water **2** : ocean **3** : rough water — **sea** *adj* — **sea·bird** *n* — **sea·coast** *n* — **sea·food** *n* — **sea·port** *n* — **sea·shore** *n* — **sea·wa·ter** *n* — **sea·weed** *n*

¹seal *n* : large sea mammal of cold regions — **seal·skin** *n*

²seal *n* **1** : device for stamping a design **2** : something that closes ∼ *vb* **1** : affix a seal to **2** : close up securely **3** : determine finally — **seal·ant** *n* — **seal·er** *n*

seam *n* **1** : line of junction of 2 edges **2** : layer of a mineral ∼ *vb* : join by sewing — **seam·less** *adj*

search *vb* **1** : look through **2** : seek — **search** *n* — **search·er** *n* — **search·light** *n*

search engine *n* : computer software used to search for specified information on the World Wide Web

¹sea·son *n* **1** : division of the year **2** : customary time for something — **sea·son·al** *adj* — **sea·son·al·ly** *adv*

²season *vb* **1** : add spice to (food) **2** : make strong or fit for use — **sea·son·ing** *n*

seat *n* **1** : place to sit **2** : chair, bench, or stool for sitting on **3** : place that serves as a capital or center ∼ *vb* **1** : place in or on a seat **2** : provide seats for

¹sec·ond *adj* : next after the 1st ∼ *n* **1** : one that is second **2** : one who assists (as in a duel)

— **sec·ond, se·cond·ly** *adv* — **sec·ond·ary** *adj*

²sec·ond *n* **1** : 60th part of a minute **2** : moment

sec·ond·hand *adj* **1** : not original **2** : used before

se·cret *adj* **1** : hidden **2** : kept from general knowledge — **se·cre·cy** *n* — **secret** *n* — **se·cre·tive** *adj* — **se·cret·ly** *adv*

sec·re·tary *n* **1** : one hired to handle correspondence and other tasks for a superior **2** : official in charge of correspondence or records **3** : head of a government department — **sec·re·tar·i·al** *adj*

¹se·crete *vb* : produce from or as if from a gland — **se·cre·tion** *n*

²se·crete *vb* : hide

sect *n* : religious group — **sec·tar·i·an** *adj*

sec·tion *n* : distinct part — **sec·tion·al** *adj*

sec·u·lar *adj* **1** : not sacred **2** : not monastic

se·cure *adj* : free from danger or loss ∼ *vb* **1** : fasten safely **2** : get — **se·cure·ly** *adv* — **se·cu·ri·ty** *n*

se·dan *n* **1** : chair carried by 2 men **2** : enclosed automobile

¹se·date *adj* : quiet and dignified — **se·date·ly** *adv*

²sedate *vb* : dose with sedatives — **se·da·tion** *n* — **sed·a·tive** *n*

sed·i·ment *n* : material that settles to the bottom of a liquid or is deposited by water or a glacier — **sed·i·men·ta·ry** *adj* — **sed·i·men·ta·tion** *n*

se·duce *vb* **1** : lead astray **2** : entice to sexual intercourse — **se·duc·er** *n* — **se·duc·tion** *n* — **se·duc·tive** *adj*

see *vb* **saw; seen** **1** : perceive by the eye **2** : have experience of **3** : understand **4** : make sure **5** : meet with or escort

seed *n* **1** : part by which a plant is propagated **2** : source ∼ *vb* **1** : sow **2** : remove seeds from — **seed·less** *adj*

seed·ling *n* : young plant grown from seed

seedy *adj* **1** : full of seeds **2** : shabby

seek *vb* (**sought; sought**) **1** : search for **2** : try to reach or obtain — **seek·er** *n*

seem *vb* : give the impression of being — **seem·ing·ly** *adv*

seem·ly *adj* : proper or fit

seep *vb* : leak through fine pores or cracks — **seep·age** *n*

see·saw *n* : board balanced in the middle — **seesaw** *vb*

seg·ment *n* : division of a thing — **seg·ment·ed** *adj*

seg·re·gate *vb* 1 : cut off from others 2 : separate by races — **seg·re·ga·tion** *n*

seize *vb* : take by force — **sei·zure** *n*

sel·dom *adv* : not often

se·lect *adj* 1 : favored 2 : discriminating ∼ *vb* : take by preference — **se·lec·tive** *adj* — **se·lec·tion** *n*

self *n* **selves** : essential person distinct from others

self–con·fi·dent *adj* : confident in oneself and in one's powers and abilities — **self–con·fi·dence** *n*

self–con·scious *adj* : uncomfortably aware of oneself as an object of observation — **self–con·scious·ly** *adv* — **self–con·scious·ness** *n*

self–con·trol *n* : restraint over one's own impulses, emotions, or desires

self–es·teem *n* : respect for and confidence in oneself

self·ish *adj* : excessively or exclusively concerned with one's own well-being — **self·ish·ly** *adv* — **self·ish·ness** *n*

self·less *adj* : unselfish — **self·less·ness** *n*

sell *vb* (**sold; sold**) 1 : transfer (property) esp. for money 2 : deal in as a business 3 : be sold — **sell·er** *n*

selves *pl of* SELF

se·man·tic *adj* : relating to meaning in language — **se·man·tics** *n sing or pl*

se·mes·ter *n* : half a school year

semi·co·lon *n* : punctuation mark ;

semi·fi·nal *adj* : being next to the final — **semifinal** *n*

sen·ate *n* : upper branch of a legislature — **sen·a·tor** *n* — **sen·a·to·rial** *adj*

send *vb* (**sent; sent**) 1 : cause to go 2 : propel — **send·er** *n*

se·nior *adj* : older or higher ranking — **se·nior** *n* — **se·nior·i·ty** *n*

sen·sa·tion *n* 1 : bodily feeling 2 : condition of excitement or the cause of it — **sen·sa·tion·al** *adj*

sense *n* 1 : meaning 2 : faculty of perceiving something physical 3 : sound mental capacity ∼ *vb* 1 : perceive by the senses 2 : detect automatically — **sense·less** *adj* — **sense·less·ly** *adv*

sen·si·bil·i·ty *n* : delicacy of feeling

sen·si·ble *adj* 1 : capable of sensing or being sensed 2 : aware or conscious 3 : reasonable — **sen·si·bly** *adv*

sen·si·tive *adj* 1 : subject to excitation by or responsive to stimuli 2 : having power of feeling 3 : easily affected — **sen·si·tive·ness** *n* — **sen·si·tiv·i·ty** *n*

sen·si·tize *vb* : make or become sensitive

sen·so·ry *adj* : relating to sensation or the senses

sen·su·al *adj* 1 : pleasing the senses 2 : devoted to the pleasures of the senses — **sen·su·al·ist** *n* — **sen·su·al·i·ty** *n* — **sen·su·al·ly** *adv*

sen·su·ous *adj* : having strong appeal to the senses

sent *past of* SEND

sen·tence *n* 1 : judgment of a court 2 : grammatically self-contained speech unit ∼ *vb* : impose a sentence on

sen·ti·ment *n* 1 : belief 2 : feeling

sen·ti·men·tal *adj* : influenced by tender feelings — **sen·ti·men·tal·ism** *n* — **sen·ti·men·tal·ist** *n* — **sen·ti·men·tal·i·ty** *n* — **sen·ti·men·tal·ize** *vb* — **sen·ti·men·tal·ly** *adv*

sep·a·rate *vb* 1 : set or keep apart 2 : become divided or detached ∼ *adj* 1 : not connected or shared 2 : distinct from each other — **sep·a·ra·ble** *adj* — **sep·a·rate·ly** *adv* — **sep·a·ra·tion** *n* — **sep·a·ra·tor** *n*

Sep·tem·ber *n* : 9th month of the year having 30 days

se·quel *n* 1 : consequence or result 2 : continuation of a story

se·quence *n* : continuous or connected series — **se·quen·tial** *adj* — **se·quen·tial·ly** *adv*

ser·e·nade *n* : music sung or played esp. to a woman being courted — **serenade** *vb*

se·rene *adj* : tranquil — **se·rene·ly** *adv* — **se·ren·i·ty** *n*

ser·geant *n* : noncommissioned officer (as in the army)

se·ri·al *adj* : being or relating to a series or sequence ∼ *n* : story appearing in parts — **se·ri·al·ly** *adv*

se·ries *n* : number of things in order

se·ri·ous *adj* 1 : subdued in appearance or manner 2 : sincere 3 : of great importance — **se·ri·ous·ly** *adv* — **se·ri·ous·ness** *n*

ser·mon *n* : lecture on religion or behavior

ser·pent *n* : snake — **ser·pen·tine** *adj*

ser·vant *n* : person employed for domestic work

serve *vb* 1 : work through or perform a term of service 2 : be of use 3 : prove adequate 4

: hand out (food or drink) **5** : be of service to
— **serv·er** *n*

ser·vice *n* **1** : act or means of serving **2**
: meeting for worship **3** : branch of public employment or the persons in it **4** : set of dishes
or table utensils **5** : benefit ⁓ *vb* : repair —
ser·vice·able *adj* — **ser·vice·man** *n* — **ser·
vice·wom·an** *n*

ses·sion *n* : meeting

set *vb* **set; set 1** : cause to sit **2** : place **3**
: settle, arrange **4** : cause to be or do
5 : become fixed or solid **6** : sink below the
horizon ⁓ *adj* : settled ⁓ *n* **1** : group classed
together **2** : setting for the scene of a play or
film **3** : electronic apparatus **4** : collection of
mathematical elements — **set forth** : begin a
trip — **set off** *vb* : set forth — **set out** *vb*
: begin a trip or undertaking — **set up** *vb* **1**
: assemble or erect **2** : cause

set·back *n* : reverse

set·ting *n* : the time, place, and circumstances
in which something occurs

set·tle *vb* **1** : come to rest **2** : sink gradually **3**
: establish in residence **4** : adjust or arrange **5**
: calm **6** : dispose of (as by paying) **7** : decide
or agree on — **set·tle·ment** *n* — **set·tler** *n*

sev·en *n* : one more than 6 — **sev·en** *adj or
pron* — **sev·enth** *adj or adv or n*

sev·en·teen *n* : one more than 16 — **seven-
teen** *adj or pron* — **sev·en·teenth** *adj or n*

sev·en·ty *n* : 7 times 10 — **sev·en·ti·eth** *adj
or n* — **sev·en·ty** *adj or pron*

sev·er *vb* : cut off or apart — **sev·er·ance** *n*

sev·er·al *adj* **1** : distinct **2** : consisting of an
indefinite but not large number — **sev·er·al·ly**
adv

se·vere *adj* **1** : strict **2** : restrained or un-
adorned **3** : painful or distressing **4** : hard to
endure — **se·vere·ly** *adv* — **se·ver·i·ty** *n*

sew *vb* : join or fasten by stitches — **sew·ing** *n*

sew·age *n* : liquid household waste

¹sew·er *n* : one that sews

²sew·er *n* : pipe or channel to carry off waste
matter

sex *n* : either of 2 divisions into which organisms are grouped according to their reproductive roles — **sexed** *adj* — **sex·less** *adj* —
sex·u·al *adj* — **sex·u·al·i·ty** *n* — **sex·u·al·ly**
adv — **sexy** *adj*

sex·ism *n* : discrimination based on sex and
esp. against women — **sex·ist** *adj or n*

shab·by *adj* **1** : worn and faded **2** : dressed in

worn clothes **3** : not generous or fair — **shab-
bi·ly** *adv* — **shab·bi·ness** *n*

shack *n* : hut

shade *n* **1** : space sheltered from the light esp.
of the sun **2** : gradation of color **3** : small difference **4** : something that shades ⁓ *vb* **1**
: shelter from light and heat **2** : add shades of
color to **3** : show slight differences esp. in
color or meaning

shad·ow *n* **1** : shade cast upon a surface by
something blocking light **2** : trace **3** : gloomy
influence ⁓ *vb* **1** : cast a shadow **2** : follow
closely — **shad·owy** *adj*

shady *adj* **1** : giving shade **2** : of dubious
honesty

shaft *n* **1** : long slender cylindrical part **2**
: deep vertical opening (as of a mine)

shag·gy *adj* **1** : covered with long hair or wool
2 : not neat and combed

shake *vb* **shook; shak·en 1** : move or cause
to move quickly back and forth **2** : distress **3**
: clasp (hands) as friendly gesture — **shake** *n*
— **shak·er** *n*

shaky *adj* : not sound, stable, or reliable —
shak·i·ly *adv* — **shak·i·ness** *n*

shall *vb, past* **should** — used as an auxiliary
to express a command, futurity, or determination

shal·low *adj* **1** : not deep **2** : not intellectually
profound

sham·bles *n* : state of disorder

shame *n* **1** : distress over guilt or disgrace **2**
: cause of shame or regret ⁓ *vb* **1** : make
ashamed **2** : disgrace — **shame·ful** *adj* —
shame·ful·ly *adv* — **shame·less** *adj* —
shame·less·ly *adv*

sham·poo *vb* : wash one's hair ⁓ *n* : act of or
preparation used in shampooing

shape *vb* : form esp. in a particular structure or
appearance ⁓ *n* **1** : distinctive appearance or
arrangement of parts **2** : condition — **shapeless** *adj* — **shape·li·ness** *n* — **shape·ly** *adj*

share *n* **1** : portion belonging to one **2** : interest in a company's stock ⁓ *vb* : divide or use
with others — **share·hold·er** *n* — **shar·er** *n*

shark *n* : voracious sea fish

sharp *adj* **1** : having a good point or cutting
edge **2** : alert, clever, or sarcastic **3** : vigorous
or fierce **4** : having prominent angles or a sudden change in direction **5** : distinct **6** : higher
than the true pitch ⁓ *adv* : exactly ⁓ *n*
: sharp note — **shar·pen** *vb* — **sharp·en·er** *n*
— **sharp·ly** *adv* — **sharp·ness** *n*

shat·ter *vb* : smash or burst into fragments — **shat·ter·proof** *adj*

shave *vb* **1** : cut off with a razor **2** : make bare by cutting the hair from **3** : slice very thin ~ *n* : act or instance of shaving — **shav·er** *n*

shawl *n* : loose covering for the head or shoulders

she *pron* : that female one

shear *vb* **1** : trim wool from **2** : cut off with scissorlike action

shears *n pl* : cutting tool with 2 blades fastened so that the edges slide by each other

shed *vb* **1** : give off (as tears or hair) **2** : cause to flow or diffuse ~ *n* : small storage building

sheen *n* : subdued luster

sheep *n* (**sheep**) : domesticated mammal covered with wool — **sheep·skin** *n*

sheep·ish *adj* : embarrassed by awareness of a fault

sheer *adj* **1** : pure **2** : very steep **3** : very thin or transparent

sheet *n* : broad flat piece (as of cloth or paper)

shelf *n* (**shelves**) **1** : flat narrow structure used for storage or display **2** : sandbank or rock ledge

shell *n* **1** : hard or tough outer covering **2** : case holding explosive powder and projectile for a weapon **3** : light racing boat with oars ~ *vb* **1** : remove the shell of **2** : bombard — **shelled** *adj* — **shell·er** *n*

shel·ter *n* : something that gives protection ~ *vb* : give refuge to

shep·herd *n* : one that tends sheep ~ *vb* : act as a shepherd or guardian

sher·bet, sher·bert *n* : fruit-flavored frozen dessert

sher·iff *n* : county law officer

shield *n* **1** : broad piece of armor carried on the arm **2** : something that protects — **shield** *vb*

shier *comparative of* SHY

shiest *superlative of* SHY

shift *vb* **1** : change place, position, or direction **2** : get by ~ *n* **1** : loose-fitting dress **2** : an act or instance of shifting **3** : scheduled work period

shift·less *adj* : lazy

shifty *adj* : tricky or untrustworthy

shin *n* : front part of the leg below the knee ~ *vb* : climb by sliding the body close along

shine *vb* **1** : give off or cause to give off light **2** : be outstanding **3** : polish ~ *n* : brilliance

shiny *adj* : bright or polished

ship *n* **1** : large oceangoing vessel **2** : aircraft or spacecraft ~ *vb* **1** : put on a ship **2** : transport by carrier — **ship·board** *n* — **ship·build·er** *n* — **ship·per** *n* — **ship·wreck** *n or vb* — **ship·yard** *n*

ship·ment *n* : an act of shipping or the goods shipped

shirk *vb* : evade — **shirk·er** *n*

shirt *n* : garment for covering the torso — **shirt·less** *adj*

shiv·er *vb* : tremble — **shiv·er** *n* — **shiv·ery** *adj*

shock *n* **1** : forceful impact **2** : violent mental or emotional disturbance **3** : effect of a charge of electricity **4** : depression of the vital bodily processes ~ *vb* **1** : strike with surprise, horror, or disgust **2** : subject to an electrical shock — **shock·proof** *adj*

shod·dy *adj* : poorly made or done — **shod·di·ly** *adv* — **shod·di·ness** *n*

shoe *n* **1** : covering for the human foot **2** : horseshoe ~ *vb* **shod; shod:** put horseshoes on — **shoe·lace** *n* — **shoe·ma·ker** *n*

shone *past of* SHINE

shook *past of* SHAKE

shoot *vb* **shot; shot 1** : propel (as an arrow or bullet) **2** : wound or kill with a missile **3** : discharge (a weapon) **4** : drive (as a ball) at a goal **5** : photograph **6** : move swiftly ~ *n* : new plant growth — **shoot·er** *n*

shop *n* : place where things are made or sold ~ *vb* : visit stores — **shop·keep·er** *n* — **shop·per** *n*

shop·lift *vb* : steal goods from a store — **shop·lift·er** *n*

¹shore *n* : land along the edge of water — **shore·bird** *n* — **shore·line** *n*

²shore *vb* : prop up ~ *n* : something that props

short *adj* **1** : not long or tall or extending far **2** : brief in time **3** : curt **4** : not having or being enough ~ *adv* : curtly ~ *n* **1** *pl* : short drawers or trousers **2** : short circuit — **short·en** *vb* — **short·ly** *adv* — **short·ness** *n*

short·age *n* : deficiency

short·cut *n* **1** : more direct route than that usu. taken **2** : quicker way of doing something

short·hand *n* : method of speed writing

shot *n* **1** : act of shooting **2** : attempt (as at making a goal) **3** : small pellets forming a charge **4** : range or reach **5** : photograph **6** : injection of medicine **7** : small serving of liquor — **shot·gun** *n*

should *past of* SHALL — used as an auxiliary to express condition, obligation, or probability

shoul·der *n* **1 :** part of the body where the arm joins the trunk **2 :** part that projects or lies to the side ~ *vb* **:** push with or bear on the shoulder

shout *vb* **:** give voice loudly — **shout** *n*

shove *vb* **:** push along or away — **shove** *n*

shov·el *n* **:** broad tool for digging or lifting ~ *vb* **:** take up or dig with a shovel

show *vb* **1 :** present to view **2 :** reveal or demonstrate **3 :** teach **4 :** prove **5 :** conduct or escort **6 :** appear or be noticeable ~ *n* **1 :** demonstrative display **2 :** spectacle **3 :** theatrical, radio, or television program — **show·case** *n* — **show off** *vb* **1 :** display proudly **2 :** act so as to attract attention — **show up** *vb* **:** arrive

show·er *n* **1 :** brief fall of rain **2 :** bath in which water sprinkles down on the person or a facility for such a bath **3 :** party at which someone gets gifts ~ *vb* **1 :** rain or fall in a shower **2 :** bathe in a shower — **show·ery** *adj*

showy *adj* **:** very noticeable or overly elaborate — **show·i·ly** *adv* — **show·i·ness** *n*

shrank *past of* SHRINK

shred *n* **:** narrow strip cut or torn off ~ *vb* **:** cut or tear into shreds

shrewd *adj* **:** clever — **shrewd·ly** *adv* — **shrewd·ness** *n*

shriek *n* **:** shrill cry — **shriek** *vb*

shrill *adj* **:** piercing and high-pitched — **shril·ly** *adv*

shrimp *n* **:** small sea crustacean

shrine *n* **1 :** tomb of a saint **2 :** hallowed place

shrink *vb* **shrank/shrunk; shrunk/shrunk·en 1 :** draw back or away **2 :** become smaller — **shrink·able** *adj*

shriv·el *vb* **:** shrink or wither into wrinkles

shrub *n* **:** low woody plant — **shrub·by** *adj*

shrub·bery *n* **:** growth of shrubs

shrug *vb* **:** hunch the shoulders up in doubt, indifference, or uncertainty — **shrug** *n*

shrunk *past part of* SHRINK

shrunk·en *past part of* SHRINK

shud·der *vb* **:** tremble — **shud·der** *n*

shuf·fle *vb* **1 :** mix together **2 :** walk with a sliding movement — **shuf·fle** *n*

shun *vb* **:** keep away from

shut *vb* (**shut; shut**) **1 :** bar passage into or through (as by moving a lid or door) **2 :** suspend activity — **shut out** *vb* **:** exclude — **shut up** *vb* **:** stop or cause to stop talking

shut·ter *n* **1 :** movable cover for a window **2 :** camera part that exposes film

shut·tle *n* **1 :** part of a weaving machine that carries thread back and forth **2 :** vehicle traveling back and forth over a short route ~ *vb* **:** move back and forth frequently

shy *adj* **1 :** sensitive and hesitant in dealing with others **2 :** wary **3 :** lacking ~ *vb* **:** draw back (as in fright) — **shy·ly** *adv* — **shy·ness** *n*

sick *adj* **1 :** not in good health **2 :** nauseated **3 :** relating to or meant for the sick — **sick·bed** *n* — **sick·en** *vb* — **sick·ly** *adj* — **sick·ness** *n*

side *n* **1 :** part to left or right of an object or the torso **2 :** edge or surface away from the center or at an angle to top and bottom or ends **3 :** contrasting or opposing position or group — **sid·ed** *adj*

side·swipe *vb* **:** strike with a glancing blow — **side·swipe** *n*

side·track *vb* **:** lead aside or astray

side·walk *n* **:** paved walk at the side of a road

side·ways *adv or adj* **1 :** to or from the side **2 :** with one side to the front

sift *vb* **1 :** pass through a sieve **2 :** examine carefully — **sift·er** *n*

sigh *n* **:** audible release of the breath (as to express weariness) — **sigh** *vb*

sight *n* **1 :** something seen or worth seeing **2 :** process, power, or range of seeing **3 :** device used in aiming **4 :** view or glimpse ~ *vb* **:** get sight of — **sight·ed** *adj* — **sight·less** *adj* — **sight–see·ing** *adj* — **sight·seer** *n*

sign *n* **1 :** symbol **2 :** gesture expressing a command or thought **3 :** public notice to advertise or warn **4 :** trace ~ *vb* **1 :** mark with or make a sign **2 :** write one's name on — **sign·er** *n*

sig·nal *n* **1 :** sign of command or warning **2 :** electronic transmission ~ *vb* **:** communicate or notify by signals ~ *adj* **:** distinguished

sig·na·ture *n* **:** one's name written by oneself

sig·ni·fy *vb* **1 :** show by a sign **2 :** mean — **sig·nif·i·cance** *n* — **sig·nif·i·cant** *adj* — **sig·nif·i·cant·ly** *adv* — **sig·ni·fi·ca·tion** *n*

si·lence *n* **:** state of being without sound ~ *vb* **:** keep from making noise or sound — **si·lenc·er** *n* — **si·lent** *adj* — **si·lent·ly** *adv*

silk *n* **1 :** fine strong lustrous protein fiber from moth larvae (**silkworms**) **2 :** thread or cloth made from silk — **silk·en** *adj* — **silky** *adj*

sil·ly *adj* **:** foolish or stupid — **sil·li·ness** *n*

sil·ver *n* **1 :** white ductile metallic chemical element **2** : table utensils ∼ *adj* : having the color of silver — **sil·very** *adj*

sim·i·lar *adj* : resembling each other in some ways — **sim·i·lar·i·ty** *n* — **sim·i·lar·ly** *adv*

sim·ple *adj* **1** : free from dishonesty, vanity, or pretense **2** : of humble origin or modest position **3** : not complex **4** : lacking education, experience, or intelligence — **sim·ple·ness** *n* — **sim·ply** *adv*

sim·plic·i·ty *n* : state or fact of being simple

sim·pli·fy *vb* : make easier — **sim·pli·fi·ca·tion** *n*

sim·u·late *vb* : create the effect or appearance of — **sim·u·la·tion** *n* — **sim·u·la·tor** *n*

si·mul·ta·ne·ous *adj* : occurring or operating at the same time — **si·mul·ta·ne·ous·ly** *adv* — **simul·ta·ne·ous·ness** *n*

sin *n* : offense against God ∼ *vb* : commit a sin — **sin·ful** *adj* — **sin·less** *adj* — **sin·ner** *n*

since *adv* **1** : from a past time until now **2** : backward in time ∼ *prep* **1** : in the period after **2** : continuously from ∼ *conj* **1** : from the time when **2** : because

sin·cere *adj* : genuine or honest — **sin·cere·ly** *adv* — **sin·cer·i·ty** *n*

sing *vb* **sang; sung** : produce musical tones with the voice — **sing·er** *n*

sin·gle *adj* **1** : one only **2** : unmarried ∼ *n* : separate one — **sin·gle·ness** *n* — **sin·gly** *adv* — **single out** *vb* : select or set aside

sin·gu·lar *adj* **1** : relating to a word form denoting one **2** : outstanding or superior **3** : queer — **sin·gu·lar** *n* — **sin·gu·lar·i·ty** *n* — **sin·gu·lar·ly** *adv*

sink *vb* (**sank; sunk**) **1** : go or put underwater **2** : grow worse **3** : make by digging or boring **4** : invest ∼ *n* : basin with a drain

sip *vb* : drink in small quantities — **sip** *n*

sir *n* **1** — used before the first name of a knight or baronet **2** — used as a respectful form of address

si·ren *n* **1** : seductive woman **2** : wailing warning whistle

sis·sy *n* : timid or effeminate boy

sis·ter *n* : female sharing one or both parents with another person — **sis·ter·hood** *n* — **sis·ter·ly** *adj*

sis·ter–in–law *n* **sis·ters–in–law** : sister of one's spouse or wife of one's brother

sit *vb* **sat; sat** **1** : rest on the buttocks **2** : settle on a resting place **3** : hold a session **4** : pose for a portrait **5** : have a location **6** : rest or fix in place — **sit·ter** *n*

site *n* **1** : place **2** : Web site

sit·u·a·tion *n* **1** : location **2** : condition **3** : job

six *n* : one more than 5 — **six** *adj or pron* — **sixth** *adj or adv or n*

six·teen *n* : one more than 15 — **sixteen** *adj or pron* — **six·teenth** *adj or n*

six·ty *n* : 6 times 10 — **six·ti·eth** *adj or n* — **sixty** *adj or pron*

size *n* : measurement of the amount of space something takes up ∼ *vb* : grade according to size — **siz·able** *adj* — **siz·ably** *adv*

skate *n* **1** : metal runner on a shoe for gliding over ice **2** : roller skate — **skate** *vb* — **skat·er** *n*

skel·e·ton *n* : bony framework — **skel·e·tal** *adj*

skep·tic *n* : one who is critical or doubting — **skep·ti·cal** *adj* — **skep·ti·cism** *n*

sketch *n* **1** : rough drawing **2** : short story or essay — **sketch** *vb* — **sketchy** *adj*

ski *n* : long strip for gliding over snow or water — **ski** *vb* — **ski·er** *n*

skid *n* **1** : plank for supporting something or on which it slides **2** : act of skidding ∼ *vb* : slide sideways

skill *n* : developed or learned ability — **skilled** *adj* — **skill·ful** *adj* — **skill·ful·ly** *adv*

skim *vb* **1** : take off from the top of a liquid **2** : read or move over swiftly ∼ *adj* : having the cream removed — **skim·mer** *n*

skin *n* **1** : outer layer of an animal body **2** : rind ∼ *vb* : take the skin from — **skin·less** *adj* — **skinned** *adj* — **skin·tight** *adj*

skin·ny *adj* : very thin

skip *vb* **1** : move with leaps **2** : read past or ignore — **skip** *n*

skirt *n* : garment or part of a garment that hangs below the waist ∼ *vb* : pass around the edge of

skull *n* : bony case that protects the brain

sky *n* **1** : upper air **2** : heaven — **sky·line** *n* — **sky·ward** *adv or adj*

sky·scrap·er *n* : very tall building

slab *n* : thick slice

slack *adj* **1** : careless **2** : not taut **3** : not busy ∼ *n* **1** : part hanging loose **2** *pl* : casual trousers — **slack·en** *vb* — **slack·ly** *adv* — **slack·ness** *n*

slain *past part of* SLAY

slam *n* : heavy jarring impact ∼ *vb* : shut, strike, or throw violently and loudly

slang *n* : informal nonstandard vocabulary — **slangy** *adj*

slant *vb* **1** : slope **2** : present with a special

viewpoint ~ *n* : sloping direction, line, or plane

slap *vb* : strike sharply with the open hand — **slap** *n*

slash *vb* **1** : cut with sweeping strokes **2** : reduce sharply ~ *n* : gash

slaugh·ter *n* **1** : butchering of livestock for market **2** : great and cruel destruction of lives ~ *vb* : commit slaughter upon — **slaugh·ter-house** *n*

slave *n* : one owned and forced into service by another ~ *vb* : work as or like a slave — **slave** *adj* — **slav·ery** *n* — **slav·ish** *adj* — **slav·ish·ly** *adv*

slay *vb* (**slew/slayed; slain**) **1** *past slew* : kill **2** *past slayed* : overwhelm with amusement — **slay·er** *n*

sled *n* : vehicle on runners — **sled** *vb*

sleek *adj* : smooth or glossy — **sleek** *vb*

sleep *n* : natural suspension of consciousness ~ *vb* (**slept; slept**) : rest in a state of sleep — **sleep·er** *n* — **sleep·i·ly** *adv* — **sleep·i·ness** *n* — **sleep·less** *adj* — **sleep·walk·er** *n* — **sleepy** *adj*

sleeve *n* : part of a garment for the arm — **sleeve·less** *adj*

sleigh *n* : horse-drawn sled with seats ~ *vb* : drive or ride in a sleigh

slen·der *adj* **1** : thin esp. in physique **2** : scanty

slew *past of* SLAY

slice *n* : thin flat piece ~ *vb* : cut a slice from

slick *adj* **1** : very smooth **2** : clever — **slick** *vb*

slide *vb* : move smoothly along a surface ~ *n* **1** : act of sliding **2** : surface on which something slides **3** : transparent picture for projection

slier *comparative of* SLY

sliest *superlative of* SLY

slight *adj* **1** : slender **2** : frail **3** : small in degree ~ *vb* **1** : ignore or treat as not important — **slight** *n* — **slight·ly** *adv*

slim *adj* **1** : slender **2** : scanty ~ *vb* : make or become slender

slime *n* : dirty slippery film (as on water) — **slimy** *adj*

sling *vb* (**slung; slung**) : hurl with or as if with a sling ~ *n* **1** : strap for swinging and hurling stones **2** : looped strap or bandage to lift or support

slink *vb* (**slunk; slunk**) : move stealthily or sinuously — **slinky** *adj*

¹**slip** *vb* **1** : escape quietly or secretly **2** : slide along smoothly **3** : make a mistake **4** : to pass without being noticed or done **5** : fall off from a standard ~ *n* **1** : ship's berth **2** : sudden mishap **3** : mistake **4** : woman's undergarment

²**slip** *n* **1** : plant shoot **2** : small strip (as of paper)

slip·per *n* : shoe that slips on easily

slip·pery *adj* **1** : slick enough to slide on **2** : tricky — **slip·peri·ness** *n*

slit *vb* (**slit; slit**) : make a slit in ~ *n* : long narrow cut

slob *n* : untidy person

slob·ber *vb* : dribble saliva — **slob·ber** *n*

slo·gan *n* : word or phrase expressing the aim of a cause

slop *n* : food waste for animal feed ~ *vb* : spill

slope *vb* : deviate from the vertical or horizontal ~ *n* : upward or downward slant

slop·py *adj* **1** : muddy **2** : untidy

slot *n* : narrow opening

slow *adj* **1** : sluggish or stupid **2** : moving, working, or happening at less than the usual speed ~ *vb* **1** : make slow **2** : go slower — **slow** *adv* — **slow·ly** *adv* — **slow·ness** *n*

slug·gish *adj* : slow in movement or flow — **slug·gish·ly** *adv* — **slug·gish·ness** *n*

slum *n* : thickly populated area marked by poverty

slum·ber *vb or n* : sleep

slump *vb* **1** : sink suddenly **2** : assume an extremely relaxed or stooped posture — **slump** *n*

slung *past of* SLING

slunk *past of* SLINK

slur *vb* : run (words or notes) together — **slur** *n*

sly *adj* : given to or showing secrecy and deception — **sly·ly** *adv* — **sly·ness** *n*

smack *vb* **1** : move (the lips) so as to make a sharp noise **2** : kiss or slap with a loud noise ~ *n* **1** : sharp noise made by the lips **2** : noisy slap

small *adj* **1** : little in size or amount **2** : few in number **3** : trivial — **small·ish** *adj* — **small-ness** *n*

smart *vb* **1** : cause or feel stinging pain **2** : endure distress ~ *adj* **1** : intelligent or resourceful **2** : stylish — **smart** *n* — **smart·ly** *adv* — **smart·ness** *n*

smash *vb* : break or be broken into pieces ~ *n* **1** : smashing blow **2** : act or sound of smashing

smear *n* : greasy stain ∼ *vb* **1** : spread (something sticky) **2** : smudge **3** : spread malicious gossip about someone

smell *vb* **1** : perceive the odor of **2** : have or give off an odor ∼ *n* **1** : sense by which one perceives odor **2** : odor — **smelly** *adj*

smelt *vb* : melt or fuse (ore) in order to separate the metal — **smelt·er** *n*

smile *n* : facial expression with the mouth turned up usu. to show pleasure — **smile** *vb*

smog *n* : fog and smoke — **smog·gy** *adj*

smoke *n* : sooty gas from burning ∼ *vb* **1** : give off smoke **2** : inhale the fumes of burning tobacco **3** : cure (as meat) with smoke — **smoke·less** *adj* — **smok·er** *n* — **smoky** *adj*

smooth *adj* **1** : having a surface without irregularities **2** : not jarring or jolting ∼ *vb* : make smooth — **smooth·ly** *adv* — **smooth·ness** *n*

smoth·er *vb* **1** : kill by depriving of air **2** : cover thickly

smudge *vb* : soil or blur by rubbing ∼ *n* **1** : thick smoke **2** : dirty spot

smug·gle *vb* : import or export secretly or illegally — **smug·gler** *n*

snack *n* : light meal

snag *n* : unexpected difficulty ∼ *vb* : become caught on something that sticks out

snake *n* : long-bodied limbless reptile — **snake·bite** *n*

snap *vb* **1** : bite at something **2** : utter angry words **3** : break suddenly with a sharp sound ∼ *n* **1** : act or sound of snapping **2** : fastening that closes with a click **3** : something easy to do — **snap·per** *n* — **snap·pish** *adj* — **snap·py** *adj*

snap·shot *n* : casual photograph

snare *n* : trap for catching game ∼ *vb* : capture or hold with or as if with a snare

¹**snarl** *n* : tangle ∼ *vb* : cause to become knotted

²**snarl** *vb or n* : growl

snatch *vb* **1** : try to grab something suddenly **2** : seize or take away suddenly ∼ *n* **1** : act of snatching **2** : something brief or fragmentary

sneak *vb* : move or take in a furtive manner ∼ *n* : one who acts in a furtive manner — **sneak·i·ly** *adv* — **sneak·ing·ly** *adv* — **sneaky** *adj*

sneak·er *n* : sports shoe

sneer *vb* : smile scornfully — **sneer** *n*

sneeze *vb* : force the breath out with sudden and involuntary violence — **sneeze** *n*

snick·er *n* : partly suppressed laugh — **snicker** *vb*

sniff *vb* **1** : draw air audibly up the nose **2** : detect by smelling — **sniff** *n*

snob *n* : one who acts superior to others — **snob·bery** *n* — **snob·bish** *adj* — **snob·bish·ly** *adv* — **snob·bish·ness** *n*

snoop *vb* : pry in a furtive way ∼ *n* : prying person

snooze *vb* : take a nap — **snooze** *n*

snore *vb* : breathe with a hoarse noise while sleeping — **snore** *n*

snort *vb* : force air noisily through the nose — **snort** *n*

snow *n* : crystals formed from water vapor ∼ *vb* : fall as snow — **snow·ball** *n* — **snow·bank** *n* — **snow·drift** *n* — **snow·fall** *n* — **snow·plow** *n* — **snow·storm** *n* — **snowy** *adj*

snuff *vb* : put out (a candle) — **snuff·er** *n*

snug *adj* **1** : warm, secure, and comfortable **2** : fitting closely — **snug·ly** *adv* — **snug·ness** *n*

snug·gle *vb* : curl up comfortably

so *adv* **1** : in the manner or to the extent indicated **2** : in the same way **3** : therefore **4** : finally **5** : thus ∼ *conj* : for that reason

soak *vb* **1** : lie in a liquid **2** : absorb ∼ *n* : act of soaking

soap *n* : cleaning substance — **soap** *vb* — **soapy** *adj*

soar *vb* : fly upward on or as if on wings

sob *vb* : weep with convulsive heavings of the chest — **sob** *n*

so·ber *adj* **1** : not drunk **2** : serious or solemn — **so·ber·ly** *adv*

soc·cer *n* : game played by kicking a ball

so·cia·ble *adj* : friendly — **so·cia·bil·i·ty** *n* — **so·cia·bly** *adv*

so·cial *adj* **1** : relating to pleasant companionship **2** : naturally living or growing in groups **3** : relating to human society ∼ *n* : social gathering — **so·cial·ly** *adv*

so·cial·ism *n* : social system based on government control of the production and distribution of goods — **so·cial·ist** *n or adj* — **so·cial·is·tic** *adj*

so·cial·ize *vb* **1** : regulate by socialism **2** : adapt to social needs **3** : participate in a social gathering — **so·cial·i·za·tion** *n*

so·ci·ety *n* **1** : companionship **2** : community life **3** : rich or fashionable class **4** : voluntary group

so·ci·ol·o·gy *n* : study of social relationships — **so·ci·o·log·i·cal** *adj* — **so·ci·ol·o·gist** *n*

¹sock *n* : short stocking

²sock *vb or n* : punch

sock·et *n* : hollow part that holds something

so·da *n* **1** : carbonated water or a soft drink **2** : ice cream drink made with soda

so·fa *n* : wide padded chair

soft *adj* **1** : not hard, rough, or harsh **2** : containing no alcohol — **soft·en** *vb* — **soft·en·er** *n* — **soft·ly** *adv* — **soft·ness** *n*

soft·ball *n* : game like baseball

soft·ware *n* : computer programs

sog·gy *adj* : heavy with moisture — **sog·gi·ness** *n*

¹soil *vb* : make or become dirty ~ *n* : embedded dirt

²soil *n* : loose surface material of the earth

so·lar *adj* : relating to the sun or the energy in sunlight

sold *past of* SELL

sol·dier *n* : person in military service ~ *vb* : serve as a soldier — **sol·dier·ly** *adj or adv*

¹sole *n* : bottom of the foot or a shoe — **soled** *adj*

²sole *adj* : single or only — **sole·ly** *adv*

sol·emn *adj* **1** : dignified and ceremonial **2** : highly serious — **so·lem·ni·ty** *n* — **sol·emn·ly** *adv*

so·lic·it *vb* : ask for — **so·lic·i·ta·tion** *n*

so·lic·i·tor *n* **1** : one that solicits **2** : lawyer

sol·id *adj* **1** : not hollow **2** : having 3 dimensions **3** : hard **4** : of good quality **5** : of one character ~ *n* **1** : 3-dimensional figure **2** : substance in solid form — **solid** *adv* — **so·lid·i·ty** *n* — **sol·id·ly** *adv* — **sol·id·ness** *n*

sol·i·dar·i·ty *n* : unity of purpose

sol·i·tary *adj* **1** : alone **2** : isolated **3** : single

so·lo *n* : performance by only one person ~ *adv* : alone — **solo** *adj or vb* — **so·lo·ist** *n*

so·lu·tion *n* **1** : answer to a problem **2** : homogeneous liquid mixture

solve *vb* : find a solution for — **solv·able** *adj*

sol·vent *adj* **1** : able to pay all debts **2** : dissolving or able to dissolve ~ *n* : substance that dissolves or disperses another substance — **sol·ven·cy** *n*

some *adj* **1** : one unspecified **2** : unspecified or indefinite number of **3** : at least a few or a little ~ *pron* : a certain number or amount

som·er·sault *n* : body flip — **som·er·sault** *vb*

some·what *adv* : in some degree

son *n* : male offspring

song *n* : music and words to be sung

son–in–law *n* **sons–in–law** : husband of one's daughter

soon *adv* **1** : before long **2** : promptly **3** : early

soot *n* : fine black substance formed by combustion — **sooty** *adj*

soothe *vb* : calm or comfort — **sooth·er** *n*

so·phis·ti·cat·ed *adj* **1** : complex **2** : wise, cultured, or shrewd in human affairs — **so·phis·ti·ca·tion** *n*

soph·o·more *n* : 2d-year student

so·pra·no *n* : highest singing voice

sore *adj* **1** : causing pain or distress **2** : severe or intense **3** : angry ~ *n* : sore usu. infected spot on the body — **sore·ly** *adv* — **sore·ness** *n*

sor·row *n* : deep distress, sadness, or regret or a cause of this — **sor·row·ful** *adj* — **sor·row·ful·ly** *adv*

sor·ry *adj* **1** : feeling sorrow, regret, or penitence **2** : dismal

sort *n* **1** : kind **2** : nature ~ *vb* : classify — **out of sorts** : grouchy

SOS *n* : call for help

so–so *adj or adv* : barely acceptable

sought *past of* SEEK

soul *n* **1** : immaterial essence of an individual life **2** : essential part **3** : person

soul·ful *adj* : full of or expressing deep feeling — **soul·ful·ly** *adv*

¹sound *adj* **1** : free from fault, error, or illness **2** : firm or hard **3** : showing good judgment — **sound·ly** *adv* — **sound·ness** *n*

²sound *n* **1** : sensation of hearing **2** : energy of vibration sensed in hearing **3** : something heard ~ *vb* **1** : make or cause to make a sound **2** : seem — **sound·less** *adj* — **sound·less·ly** *adv* — **sound·proof** *adj or vb*

soup *n* : broth usu. containing pieces of solid food — **soupy** *adj*

sour *adj* **1** : having an acid or tart taste **2** : disagreeable ~ *vb* : become or make sour — **sour·ish** *adj* — **sour·ly** *adv* — **sour·ness** *n*

source *n* **1** : point of origin **2** : one that provides something needed

souse *vb* **1** : pickle **2** : immerse **3** : intoxicate ~ *n* **1** : something pickled **2** : drunkard

south *adv* : to or toward the south ~ *adj* : situated toward, at, or coming from the south ~ *n* **1** : direction to the right of sunrise **2** *cap* : regions to the south — **south·er·ly** *adv or adj* — **south·ern** *adj* — **South·ern·er** *n* —

south·ern·most *adj* — **southward** *adv or adj* — **south·wards** *adv*

south·east *n* **1** : direction between south and east **2** *cap* : regions to the southeast — **southeast** *adj or adv* — **south·east·er·ly** *adv or adj* — **south·east·ern** *adj*

south pole *n* : the southernmost point of the earth

south·west *n* **1** : direction between south and west **2** *cap* : regions to the southwest — **south·west** *adj or adv* — **south·west·er·ly** *adv or adj* — **south·west·ern** *adj*

sou·ve·nir *n* : something that is a reminder of a place or event

sow *vb* **1** : plant or strew with seed **2** : scatter abroad — **sow·er** *n*

sox *pl of* SOCK

space *n* **1** : period of time **2** : area in, around, or between **3** : region beyond earth's atmosphere **4** : accommodations ~ *vb* : place at intervals — **space·craft** *n* — **space·flight** *n* — **space·man** *n* — **space·ship** *n*

spa·cious *adj* : large or roomy — **spa·cious·ly** *adv* — **spa·cious·ness** *n*

¹spade *n or vb* : shovel — **spade·ful** *n*

²spade *n* : playing card marked with a black figure like an inverted heart

spa·ghet·ti *n* : pasta strings

spam *n* : unsolicited commercial e-mail

span *n* **1** : amount of time **2** : distance between supports ~ *vb* : extend across

spank *vb* : hit on the buttocks with an open hand

spare *adj* **1** : held in reserve **2** : thin or scanty ~ *vb* **1** : reserve or avoid using **2** : avoid punishing or killing — **spare** *n*

spark *n* **1** : tiny hot and glowing particle **2** : smallest beginning or germ **3** : visible electrical discharge ~ *vb* **1** : emit or produce sparks **2** : stir to activity

spar·kle *vb* **1** : flash **2** : effervesce ~ *n* : gleam — **spark·ler** *n*

sparse *adj* : thinly scattered — **sparse·ly** *adv*

spasm *n* **1** : involuntary muscular contraction **2** : sudden, violent, and temporary effort or feeling — **spas·mod·ic** *adj* — **spas·mod·i·cal·ly** *adv*

spa·tial *adj* : relating to space — **spa·tial·ly** *adv*

spat·ter *vb* : splash with drops of liquid — **spat·ter** *n*

spawn *vb* **1** : produce eggs or offspring **2** : bring forth ~ *n* : egg cluster — **spawn·er** *n*

speak *vb* (**spoke**; **spo·ken**) **1** : utter words **2**

: express orally **3** : address an audience **4** : use (a language) in talking — **speak·er** *n*

spear *n* : long pointed weapon ~ *vb* : strike or pierce with a spear

spe·cial *adj* **1** : unusual or unique **2** : particularly favored **3** : set aside for a particular use — **special** *n* — **spe·cial·ly** *adv*

spe·cial·ist *n* **1** : person who specializes in a particular branch of learning or activity **2** : any of four enlisted ranks in the army corresponding to the grades of corporal through sergeant first class

spe·cial·ize *vb* : concentrate one's efforts — **spe·cial·i·za·tion** *n*

spe·cial·ty *n* : area or field in which one specializes

spe·cies *n* : biological grouping of closely related organisms

spe·cif·ic *adj* : definite or exact — **spe·cif·i·cal·ly** *adv*

spec·i·fy *vb* : mention precisely or by name — **spec·i·fi·ca·tion** *n*

spec·i·men *n* : typical example

speck *n* : tiny particle or blemish — **speck** *vb*

spec·ta·cle *n* **1** : impressive public display **2** *pl* : eyeglasses

spec·tac·u·lar *adj* : sensational or showy

spec·ta·tor *n* : person who looks on

spec·u·late *vb* **1** : think about things yet unknown **2** : risk money in a business deal in hope of high profit — **spec·u·la·tion** *n* — **spec·u·la·tive** *adj* — **spec·u·la·tor** *n*

speech *n* **1** : power, act, or manner of speaking **2** : talk given to an audience — **speech·less** *adj*

speed *n* **1** : quality of being fast **2** : rate of motion or performance ~ *vb* **sped; sped:** go at a great or excessive rate of speed — **speed·boat** *n* — **speed·er** *n* — **speed·i·ly** *adv* — **speed·up** *n* — **speedy** *adj*

¹spell *n* : influence of or like magic

²spell *vb* **1** : name, write, or print the letters of **2** : mean — **spell·er** *n*

spend *vb* (**spent; spent**) **1** : pay out **2** : cause or allow to pass — **spend·er** *n*

sperm *n* : semen or a germ cell in it

sphere *n* **1** : figure with every point on its surface at an equal distance from the center **2** : round body **3** : range of action or influence — **spher·i·cal** *adj*

spice *n* **1** : aromatic plant product for seasoning food **2** : interesting quality — **spice** *vb* — **spicy** *adj*

spi·der *n* : small insectlike animal with 8 legs — **spi·dery** *adj*

spike *n* : very large nail ~ *vb* : fasten or pierce with a spike — **spiked** *adj*

spill *vb* **1** : fall, flow, or run out unintentionally **2** : divulge ~ *n* **1** : act of spilling **2** : something spilled — **spill·able** *adj*

spin *vb* (**spun; spun**) **1** : draw out fiber and twist into thread **2** : form thread from a sticky body fluid **3** : revolve or cause to revolve extremely fast ~ *n* : rapid rotating motion — **spin·ner** *n*

spin·ach *n* : garden herb with edible leaves

spine *n* **1** : backbone **2** : stiff sharp projection on a plant or animal — **spine·less** *adj* — **spiny** *adj*

spi·ral *adj* : circling or winding around a single point or line — **spiral** *n or vb* — **spi·ral·ly** *adv*

spire *n* : usu. tapering church tower — **spiry** *adj*

spir·it *n* **1** : life-giving force **2** *cap* : presence of God **3** : ghost **4** : mood **5** : vivacity or enthusiasm **6** *pl* : alcoholic liquor ~ *vb* : carry off secretly — **spir·it·ed** *adj* — **spir·it·less** *adj*

spir·i·tu·al *adj* **1** : relating to the spirit or sacred matters **2** : deeply religious ~ *n* : religious folk song — **spir·i·tu·al·i·ty** *n* — **spir·i·tu·al·ly** *adv*

spit *vb* (**spit/spat; spit/spat**) : eject saliva from the mouth ~ *n* **1** : saliva **2** : perfect likeness

spite *n* : petty ill will ~ *vb* : annoy or offend — **spite·ful** *adj* — **spite·ful·ly** *adv* — **in spite of** : in defiance or contempt of

splash *vb* : scatter a liquid on — **splash** *n*

splat·ter *vb* : spatter — **splat·ter** *n*

splen·did *adj* **1** : impressive in beauty or brilliance **2** : outstanding — **splen·did·ly** *adv*

splen·dor *n* **1** : brilliance **2** : magnificence

splice *vb* : join (2 things) end to end — **splice** *n*

splint *n* **1** : thin strip of wood **2** : something that keeps an injured body part in place

splin·ter *n* : thin needlelike piece ~ *vb* : break into splinters

split *vb* **split; split** : divide lengthwise or along a grain — **split** *n*

spoil *n* : plunder ~ *vb* **1** : ruin **2** : rot **3** : pamper excessively — **spoil·age** *n* — **spoil·er** *n*

spoke *past of* SPEAK

spo·ken *past part of* SPEAK

sponge *n* **1** : porous water-absorbing mass that forms the skeleton of some marine animals **2** : spongelike material used for wiping ~ *vb* **1** : wipe with a sponge **2** : live at another's expense — **spongy** *adj*

spon·sor *n* : one who assumes responsibility for another or who provides financial support — **spon·sor** *vb* — **spon·sor·ship** *n*

spon·ta·ne·ous *adj* : done, produced, or occurring naturally or without planning — **spon·ta·ne·i·ty** *n* — **spon·ta·ne·ous·ly** *adv*

spook *n* : ghost ~ *vb* : frighten — **spooky** *adj*

spool *n* : cylinder on which something is wound

spoon *n* : utensil consisting of a small shallow bowl with a handle — **spoon** *vb* — **spoon·ful** *n*

sport *vb* **1** : frolic **2** : show off ~ *n* **1** : physical activity engaged in for pleasure **2** : jest **3** : person who shows good sportsmanship — **sport·ive** *adj* — **sporty** *adj*

sports·man·ship *n* : ability to be gracious in winning or losing

spot *n* **1** : blemish **2** : distinctive small part **3** : location ~ *vb* **1** : mark with spots **2** : see or recognize ~ *adj* : made at random or in limited numbers — **spot·less** *adj* — **spot·less·ly** *adv*

spouse *n* : one's husband or wife

spout *vb* **1** : shoot forth in a stream **2** : say pompously ~ *n* **1** : opening through which liquid spouts **2** : jet of liquid

sprain *n* : twisting injury to a joint ~ *vb* : injure with a sprain

sprawl *vb* : lie or sit with limbs spread out — **sprawl** *n*

spray *n* **1** : mist **2** : device that discharges liquid as a mist — **spray** *vb* — **spray·er** *n*

spread *vb* **1** : open up or unfold **2** : scatter or smear over a surface **3** : cause to be known or to exist over a wide area ~ *n* **1** : extent to which something is spread **2** : cloth cover **3** : something intended to be spread — **spread·er** *n*

spring *vb* **1** : move or grow quickly or by elastic force **2** : come from by descent **3** : make known suddenly ~ *n* **1** : source **2** : flow of water from underground **3** : season between winter and summer **4** : elastic body or device (as a coil of wire) **5** : leap **6** : elastic power — **springy** *adj*

sprin·kle *vb* : scatter in small drops or particles ~ *n* : light rainfall — **sprin·kler** *n*

sprite *n* : elf or elfish person

sprout *vb* : send out new growth ～ *n* : plant shoot

spruce *adj* : neat and stylish in appearance ～ *vb* : make or become neat

spun *past of* SPIN

spur *n* **1** : pointed device used to urge on a horse **2** : something that urges to action **3** : projecting part ～ *vb* : urge on — **spurred** *adj*

¹**spurt** *n* : burst of effort, speed, or activity ～ *vb* : make a spurt

²**spurt** *vb* : gush out ～ *n* : sudden gush

sput·ter *vb* **1** : talk hastily and indistinctly in excitement **2** : make popping sounds — **sputter** *n*

spy *vb* : watch or try to gather information secretly — **spy** *n*

squab·ble *n or vb* : dispute

squad *n* : small group

square *n* **1** : instrument for measuring right angles **2** : flat figure that has 4 equal sides and 4 right angles **3** : open area in a city **4** : product of number multiplied by itself ～ *adj* **1** : being a square in form **2** : having sides meet at right angles **3** : multiplied by itself **4** : being a square unit of area **5** : honest ～ *vb* **1** : form into a square **2** : multiply (a number) by itself **3** : conform **4** : settle — **square·ly** *adv*

¹**squash** *vb* **1** : press flat **2** : suppress

²**squash** *n* : garden vegetable

squat *vb* **1** : stoop or sit on one's heels **2** : settle on land one does not own ～ *n* : act or posture of squatting ～ *adj* : short and thick — **squat·ter** *n*

squeak *vb* : make a thin high-pitched sound — **squeak** *n* — **squeaky** *adj*

squeal *vb* **1** : make a shrill sound or cry **2** : protest — **squeal** *n*

squeeze *vb* **1** : apply pressure to **2** : extract by pressure — **squeeze** *n* — **squeez·er** *n*

squint *vb* : look with the eyes partly closed — **squint** *n or adj*

squirm *vb* : wriggle

squir·rel *n* : rodent with a long bushy tail

squirt *vb* : eject liquid in a spurt — **squirt** *n*

stab *n* **1** : wound made by a pointed weapon **2** : quick thrust **3** : attempt ～ *vb* : pierce or wound with or as if with a pointed weapon

¹**sta·ble** *n* : building for domestic animals ～ *vb* : keep in a stable

²**stable** *adj* **1** : firmly established **2** : mentally and emotionally healthy **3** : steady — **sta·bil-i·ty** *n* — **sta·bil·iza·tion** *n* — **sta·bi·lize** *vb* — **sta·bi·liz·er** *n*

stack *n* : large pile ～ *vb* : pile up

sta·di·um *n* : outdoor sports arena

staff *n* **1** : rod or supporting cane **2** : people assisting a leader **3** : 5 horizontal lines on which music is written ～ *vb* : supply with workers — **staff·er** *n*

stag *n* : male deer ～ *adj* : only for men ～ *adv* : without a date

stage *n* **1** : raised platform for a speaker or performers **2** : theater **3** : step in a process ～ *vb* : produce (a play)

stag·ger *vb* **1** : reel or cause to reel from side to side **2** : overlap or alternate — **stagger** *n* — **stag·ger·ing·ly** *adv*

stag·nant *adj* : not moving or active — **stag·nate** *vb* — **stag·na·tion** *n*

staid *past of* STAY

stain *vb* **1** : discolor **2** : dye (as wood) **3** : disgrace ～ *n* **1** : discolored area **2** : mark of guilt **3** : coloring preparation — **stain·less** *adj*

stair *n* **1** : step in a series for going from one level to another **2** *pl* : flight of steps — **stair·way** *n* — **stair·case** *n*

stake *n* **1** : usu. small post driven into the ground **2** : bet **3** : prize in a contest ～ *vb* **1** : mark or secure with a stake **2** : bet

stale *adj* **1** : having lost good taste and quality from age **2** : no longer new, strong, or effective — **stale·ness** *n*

stale·mate *n* : deadlock — **stale·mate** *vb*

¹**stalk** *vb* **1** : walk stiffly or proudly **2** : pursue stealthily

²**stalk** *n* : plant stem — **stalked** *adj*

¹**stall** *n* **1** : compartment in a stable **2** : booth where articles are sold

²**stall** *vb* : bring or come to a standstill unintentionally

³**stall** *vb* : delay, evade, or keep a situation going to gain advantage or time

stam·i·na *n* : endurance

stam·mer *vb* : hesitate in speaking — **stammer** *n*

stamp *vb* **1** : pound with the sole of the foot or a heavy implement **2** : impress or imprint **3** : cut out with a die **4** : attach a postage stamp to ～ *n* **1** : device for stamping **2** : act of stamping **3** : government seal showing a tax or fee has been paid

stance *n* : way of standing

stand *vb* (**stood; stood**) **1** : be at rest in or assume an upright position **2** : remain unchanged **3** : be steadfast **4** : maintain a relative position or rank **5** : set upright **6** : undergo or endure ∼ *n* **1** : act or place of standing, staying, or resisting **2** : sales booth **3** : structure for holding something upright **4** : group of plants growing together **5** *pl* : tiered seats **6** : opinion or viewpoint

stan·dard *n* **1** : symbolic figure or flag **2** : model, rule, or guide **3** : upright support — **stan·dard** *adj* — **stan·dard·i·za·tion** *n* — **stan·dard·ize** *vb*

stank *past of* STINK

¹sta·ple *n* : U-shaped wire fastener — **staple** *vb* — **sta·pler** *n*

²sta·ple *n* : chief commodity or item — **sta·ple** *adj*

star *n* **1** : celestial body visible as a point of light **2** : 5- or 6-pointed figure representing a star **3** : leading performer ∼ *vb* **1** : mark with a star **2** : play the leading role — **star·dom** *n* — **star·less** *adj* — **star·light** *n* — **star·ry** *adj*

starch *n* : nourishing carbohydrate from plants also used in adhesives and laundering ∼ *vb* : stiffen with starch — **starchy** *adj*

stare *vb* : look intently with wide-open eyes — **stare** *n* — **star·er** *n*

start *vb* **1** : twitch or jerk (as from surprise) **2** : perform or show performance of the first part of an action or process ∼ *n* **1** : sudden involuntary motion **2** : beginning — **start·er** *n*

star·tle *vb* : frighten or surprise suddenly

starve *vb* **1** : suffer or die from hunger **2** : kill with hunger — **star·va·tion** *n*

stash *vb* : store in a secret place for future use — **stash** *n*

state *n* **1** : condition of being **2** : condition of mind **3** : nation or a political unit within it ∼ *vb* **1** : express in words **2** : establish — **state·hood** *n* — **state·ment** *n*

stat·ic *adj* **1** : relating to bodies at rest or forces in equilibrium **2** : not moving **3** : relating to stationary charges of electricity ∼ *n* : noise on radio or television from electrical disturbances

sta·tion *n* **1** : place of duty **2** : regular stop on a bus or train route **3** : social standing **4** : place where radio or television programs originate ∼ *vb* : assign to a station

sta·tion·ary *adj* **1** : not moving or not movable **2** : not changing

sta·tio·nery *n* : letter paper with envelopes

sta·tis·tics *n pl* : numerical facts collected for study — **sta·tis·ti·cal** *adj* — **sta·tis·ti·cal·ly** *adv* — **stat·is·ti·cian** *n*

stat·ue *n* : solid 3-dimensional likeness — **stat·u·ette** *n*

stat·ure *n* **1** : height **2** : status gained by achievement

sta·tus *n* : relative situation or condition

sta·tus quo *n* : existing state of affairs

stat·ute *n* : law — **stat·u·to·ry** *adj*

¹stay *n* : support ∼ *vb* : prop up

²stay *vb* **1** : pause **2** : remain **3** : reside **4** : stop or postpone **5** : satisfy for a time ∼ *n* : a staying

stead·fast *adj* : faithful or determined — **stead·fast·ly** *adv*

steady *adj* **1** : firm in position or sure in movement **2** : calm or reliable **3** : constant **4** : regular ∼ *vb* : make or become steady — **steadi·ly** *adv* — **steadi·ness** *n* — **steady** *adv*

steak *n* : thick slice of meat

steal *vb* (**stole; sto·len**) **1** : take and carry away wrongfully and with intent to keep **2** : move secretly or slowly

steam *n* : vapor of boiling water ∼ *vb* : give off steam — **steam·boat** *n* — **steam·ship** *n* — **steamy** *adj*

steel *n* : tough carbon-containing iron ∼ *vb* : fill with courage — **steel** *adj* — **steely** *adj*

steep *adj* : having a very sharp slope or great elevation — **steep·ly** *adv* — **steep·ness** *n*

steer *vb* **1** : direct the course of (as a ship or car) **2** : guide

stem *n* : main upright part of a plant ∼ *vb* **1** : derive **2** : make progress against — **stem·less** *adj* — **stemmed** *adj*

stem cell *n* : undifferentiated cell that may give rise to many different types of cells

step *n* **1** : single action of a leg in walking or running **2** : rest for the foot in going up or down **3** : degree, rank, or stage **4** : way of walking ∼ *vb* **1** : move by steps **2** : press with the foot

ste·reo·phon·ic *adj* : relating to a 3-dimensional effect of reproduced sound — **ste·reo** *adj or n*

ste·reo·type *n* : gross often mistaken generalization — **stereotype** *vb* — **ste·reo·typ·i·cal** *adj* — **ste·reo·typi·cal·ly** *adv*

ster·ile *adj* **1** : unable to bear fruit, crops, or offspring **2** : free from disease germs — **ste·ril·i·ty** *n* — **ster·il·i·za·tion** *n* — **ster·il·ize** *vb* — **ster·il·iz·er** *n*

stern *adj* : severe — **stern·ly** *adv* — **stern-ness** *n*

stew *n* **1** : dish of boiled meat and vegetables **2** : state of worry or agitation — **stew** *vb*

stew·ard *n* **1** : manager of an estate or an organization **2** : person on a ship or airliner who looks after passenger comfort — **stew·ard·ship** *n*

stew·ard·ess *n* : woman who is a steward (as on an airplane)

¹stick *n* **1** : cut or broken branch **2** : long thin piece of wood or something resembling it

²stick *vb* **stuck; stuck 1** : stab **2** : thrust or project **3** : hold fast to something **4** : attach **5** : become jammed or fixed

stick·er *n* : adhesive label

sticky *adj* **1** : adhesive or gluey **2** : muggy **3** : difficult

stiff *adj* **1** : not bending easily **2** : tense **3** : formal **4** : strong **5** : severe — **stiff·en** *vb* — **stiff·en·er** *n* — **stiff·ly** *adv* — **stiff·ness** *n*

still *adj* **1** : motionless **2** : silent ⁓ *vb* : make or become still ⁓ *adv* **1** : without motion **2** : up to and during this time **3** : in spite of that ⁓ *n* : silence — **still·ness** *n*

stim·u·late *vb* : make active — **stim·u·lant** *n or adj* — **stim·u·la·tion** *n*

stim·u·lus *n* : something that stimulates

sting *vb* **(stung; stung) 1** : prick painfully **2** : cause to suffer acutely ⁓ *n* **1** : act of stinging or a resulting wound — **sting·er** *n*

stin·gy *adj* : not generous — **stin·gi·ness** *n*

stink *vb* **(stank/stunk; stunk)** : have a strong offensive odor — **stink** *n* — **stink·er** *n*

stip·u·late *vb* : demand as a condition — **stip·u·la·tion** *n*

stir *vb* **1** : move slightly **2** : prod or push into activity **3** : mix by continued circular movement ⁓ *n* : act or result of stirring

stitch *n* **1** : loop formed by a needle in sewing **2** : sudden sharp pain ⁓ *vb* **1** : fasten or decorate with stitches **2** : sew

stock *n* **1** : block or part of wood **2** : original from which others derive **3** : farm animals **4** : supply of goods **5** : money invested in a large business **6** *pl* : instrument of punishment like a pillory with holes for the feet or feet and hands ⁓ *vb* : provide with stock

stock·ing *n* : close-fitting covering for the foot and leg

stock·pile *n* : reserve supply — **stockpile** *vb*

stole *past of* STEAL

stolen *past part of* STEAL

stom·ach *n* **1** : saclike digestive organ **2** : abdomen **3** : appetite or desire ⁓ *vb* : put up with — **stom·ach·ache** *n*

stomp *vb* : stamp

stone *n* **1** : hardened earth or mineral matter **2** : small piece of rock **3** : seed that is hard or has a hard covering ⁓ *vb* : pelt or kill with stones — **stony** *adj*

stood *past of* STAND

stool *n* **1** : seat usu. without back or arms **2** : footstool **3** : discharge of feces

stoop *vb* **1** : bend over **2** : lower oneself ⁓ *n* **1** : act of bending over **2** : bent position of shoulders

stop *vb* **1** : block an opening **2** : end or cause to end **3** : pause for rest or a visit in a journey ⁓ *n* **1** : plug **2** : act or place of stopping **3** : delay in a journey — **stop·light** *n* — **stop·page** *n* — **stop·per** *n*

stor·age *n* : safekeeping of goods (as in a warehouse)

store *vb* : put aside for future use ⁓ *n* **1** : something stored **2** : retail business establishment — **store·house** *n* — **store·keep·er** *n* — **store·room** *n*

storm *n* **1** : heavy fall of rain or snow **2** : violent outbreak ⁓ *vb* **1** : rain or snow heavily **2** : rage **3** : make an attack against — **stormy** *adj*

¹sto·ry *n* **1** : narrative **2** : report — **sto·ry·tell·er** *n*

²story *n* : floor of a building

stove *n* : apparatus for providing heat (as for cooking or heating)

strad·dle *vb* : stand over or sit on with legs on opposite sides — **strad·dle** *n*

strag·gle *vb* : wander or become separated from others — **strag·gler** *n*

straight *adj* **1** : having no bends, turns, or twists **2** : just, proper, or honest **3** : neat and orderly ⁓ *adv* : in a straight manner — **straight·en** *vb*

straight·for·ward *adj* : frank or honest

¹strain *n* **1** : line of descent from common ancestors **2** : trace

²strain *vb* **1** : exert to the utmost **2** : filter or remove by filtering **3** : injure by improper use ⁓ *n* **1** : excessive tension or exertion **2** : bodily injury from excessive effort — **strain·er** *n*

strait *n* **1** : narrow channel connecting 2 bodies of water **2** *pl* : distress

¹strand *vb* **1** : drive or cast upon the shore **2** : leave helpless

²**strand** *n* **1** : twisted fiber of a rope **2** : length of something ropelike

strange *adj* **1** : unusual or queer **2** : new — **strang·er** *n* — **strange·ly** *adv* — **strange-ness** *n*

stran·gle *vb* : choke to death — **stran·gler** *n* — **stran·gu·la·tion** *n*

strap *n* : narrow strip of flexible material used esp. for fastening ∼ *vb* **1** : secure with a strap **2** : beat with a strap — **strap·less** *n*

strat·e·gy *n* : carefully worked out plan of action — **stra·te·gic** *adj* — **strat·e·gist** *n*

straw *n* **1** : grass stems after grain is removed **2** : tube for drinking ∼ *adj* : made of straw

straw·ber·ry *n* : juicy red pulpy fruit

stray *vb* : wander or deviate ∼ *n* : person or animal that strays ∼ *adj* : separated from or not related to anything close by

streak *n* **1** : mark of a different color **2** : narrow band of light **3** : trace **4** : run (as of luck) or series ∼ *vb* **1** : form streaks in or on **2** : move fast

stream *n* **1** : flow of water on land **2** : steady flow (as of water or air) ∼ *vb* **1** : flow in a stream **2** : pour out streams

stream·lined *adj* **1** : made with contours to reduce air or water resistance **2** : simplified **3** : modernized — **streamline** *vb*

street *n* : thoroughfare esp. in a city or town

strength *n* **1** : quality of being strong **2** : toughness **3** : intensity

strength·en *vb* : make, grow, or become stronger — **strength·en·er** *n*

stress *n* **1** : pressure or strain that tends to distort a body **2** : relative prominence given to one thing among others **3** : state of physical or mental tension or something inducing it ∼ *vb* : put stress on — **stress·ful** *adj*

stretch *vb* **1** : spread or reach out **2** : draw out in length or breadth **3** : make taut **4** : exaggerate **5** : become extended without breaking ∼ *n* : act of extending beyond normal limits

stretch·er *n* : device for carrying a sick or injured person

strew *vb* **1** : scatter **2** : cover by scattering something over

strict *adj* **1** : allowing no escape or evasion **2** : precise — **strict·ly** *adv* — **strict·ness** *n*

stride *vb* (**strode; strid·den**) : walk or run with long steps ∼ *n* **1** : long step **2** : manner of striding

strike *vb* (**struck; struck**) **1** : hit sharply **2** : delete **3** : produce by impressing **4** : cause

to sound **5** : afflict **6** : occur to or impress **7** : cause (a match) to ignite by rubbing **8** : refrain from working **9** : find **10** : take on (as a pose) ∼ *n* **1** : act or instance of striking **2** : work stoppage **3** : military attack — **strik·er** *n* — **strike out** *vb* : start out vigorously — **strike up** *vb* : start

string *n* **1** : line usu. of twisted threads **2** : series **3** *pl* : stringed instruments ∼ *vb* **strung; strung 1** : thread on or with a string **2** : hang or fasten by a string

strin·gent *adj* : severe

stringy *adj* : tough or fibrous

¹**strip** *vb* **1** : take the covering or clothing from **2** : undress — **strip·per** *n*

²**strip** *n* : long narrow flat piece

stripe *n* : distinctive line or long narrow section ∼ *vb* : make stripes on — **striped** *adj*

strive *vb* (**strove; stri·ven/strived**) **1** : struggle **2** : try hard

strode *past of* STRIDE

stroke *vb* : rub gently ∼ *n* **1** : act of swinging or striking **2** : sudden action

stroll *vb* : walk leisurely — **stroll** *n* — **stroll·er** *n*

strong *adj* **1** : capable of exerting great force or of withstanding stress or violence **2** : healthy **3** : having intense feelings for a cause — **strong·ly** *adv*

struck *past of* STRIKE

struc·ture *n* **1** : building **2** : arrangement of elements ∼ *vb* : make into a structure — **struc·tur·al** *adj*

strug·gle *vb* **1** : make strenuous efforts to overcome an adversary **2** : proceed with great effort ∼ *n* **1** : strenuous effort **2** : intense competition for superiority

strung *past of* STRING

strut *vb* : walk in a proud or showy manner ∼ *n* **1** : proud walk **2** : supporting bar or rod

stub·born *adj* **1** : determined not to yield **2** : hard to control — **stub·born·ly** *adv* — **stub·born·ness** *n*

stuck *past of* STICK

stuck–up *adj* : conceited

¹**stud** *n* : male horse kept for breeding

²**stud** *n* **1** : upright beam for holding wall material **2** : projecting nail, pin, or rod ∼ *vb* : supply or dot with studs

stu·dent *n* : one who studies

stu·dio *n* **1** : artist's workroom **2** : place where movies are made or television or radio shows are broadcast

stu·di·ous *adj* : devoted to study — **stu·di·ous·ly** *adv*

study *n* **1** : act or process of learning about something **2** : branch of learning **3** : careful examination **4** : room for reading or studying ∼ *vb* : apply the attention and mind to a subject

stuff *n* **1** : personal property **2** : raw or fundamental material **3** : unspecified material or things ∼ *vb* : fill by packing things in — **stuff·ing** *n*

stuffy *adj* **1** : lacking fresh air **2** : unimaginative or pompous

stum·ble *vb* **1** : lose one's balance or fall in walking or running **2** : speak or act clumsily **3** : happen by chance — **stum·ble** *n*

stump *n* : part left when something is cut off ∼ *vb* : confuse — **stumpy** *adj*

stun *vb* **1** : make senseless or dizzy by or as if by a blow **2** : bewilder

stung *past of* STING

stunk *past of* STINK

stun·ning *adj* **1** : astonishing or incredible **2** : strikingly beautiful — **stun·ning·ly** *adv*

¹stunt *vb* : hinder the normal growth or progress of

²stunt *n* : spectacular feat

stu·pid *adj* : not sensible or intelligent — **stu·pid·i·ty** *n* — **stu·pid·ly** *adv*

stur·dy *adj* : strong — **stur·di·ly** *adv* — **stur·di·ness** *n*

stut·ter *vb or n* : stammer

sty *n* : pig pen

style *n* **1** : distinctive way of speaking, writing, or acting **2** : elegant or fashionable way of living ∼ *vb* **1** : name **2** : give a particular design or style to — **styl·ish** *adj* — **styl·ish·ly** *adv* — **styl·ish·ness** *n* — **styl·ist** *n* — **styl·ize** *vb*

¹sub *n or vb* : substitute

²sub *n* : submarine

sub·con·scious *adj* : existing without conscious awareness ∼ *n* : part of the mind concerned with subconscious activities — **sub·con·scious·ly** *adv*

sub·due *vb* **1** : bring under control **2** : reduce the intensity of

sub·ject *n* **1** : person under the authority of another **2** : something being discussed or studied **3** : word or word group about which something is said in a sentence ∼ *adj* **1** : being under one's authority **2** : prone **3** : dependent on some condition or act ∼ *vb* **1**

: bring under control **2** : cause to undergo — **sub·jec·tion** *n*

sub·jec·tive *adj* : deriving from an individual viewpoint or bias — **sub·jec·tive·ly** *adv* — **sub·jec·tiv·i·ty** *n*

sub·ma·rine *adj* : existing, acting, or growing under the sea ∼ *n* : underwater boat

sub·mit *vb* **1** : yield **2** : give or offer — **sub·mis·sion** *n* — **sub·mis·sive** *adj*

sub·or·di·nate *adj* : lower in rank ∼ *n* : one that is subordinate ∼ *vb* : place in a lower rank or class — **sub·or·di·na·tion** *n*

sub·scribe *vb* **1** : give consent or approval **2** : agree to support or to receive and pay for — **sub·scrib·er** *n*

sub·scrip·tion *n* : order for regular receipt of a publication

sub·se·quent *adj* : following after — **sub·se·quent·ly** *adv*

sub·sid·iary *adj* **1** : furnishing support **2** : of secondary importance ∼ *n* : company controlled by another company

sub·si·dy *n* : gift of supporting funds — **sub·si·dize** *vb*

sub·stance *n* **1** : essence or essential part **2** : physical material **3** : wealth

sub·stan·tial *adj* **1** : plentiful **2** : considerable — **sub·stan·tial·ly** *adv*

sub·stan·ti·ate *vb* : verify — **sub·stan·ti·a·tion** *n*

sub·sti·tute *n* : replacement ∼ *vb* : put or serve in place of another — **substitute** *adj* — **sub·sti·tu·tion** *n*

sub·tle *adj* **1** : hardly noticeable **2** : clever — **sub·tle·ty** *n* — **sub·tly** *adv*

sub·tract *vb* : take away (as one number from another) — **sub·trac·tion** *n*

sub·urb *n* : residential area adjacent to a city — **sub·ur·ban** *adj or n* — **sub·ur·ban·ite** *n*

sub·way *n* : underground electric railway

suc·ceed *vb* **1** : follow (someone) in a job, role, or title **2** : attain a desired object or end

suc·cess *n* **1** : favorable outcome **2** : gaining of wealth and fame **3** : one that succeeds — **suc·cess·ful** *adj* — **suc·cess·ful·ly** *adv*

suc·ces·sion *n* **1** : order, act, or right of succeeding **2** : series

such *adj* **1** : of this or that kind **2** : having a specified quality — **such** *pron or adv*

suck *vb* **1** : draw in liquid with the mouth **2** : draw liquid from by or as if by mouth — **suck** *n* — **suc·tion** *n*

sud·den *adj* **1** : happening unexpectedly **2**

: steep **3** : hasty — **sud·den·ly** *adv* — **sud·den·ness** *n*

suds *n pl* : soapy water esp. when frothy — **sudsy** *adj*

sue *vb* **1** : petition **2** : bring legal action against

suf·fer *vb* **1** : experience pain, loss, or hardship **2** : permit — **suf·fer·er** *n*

suf·fer·ing *n* : pain or hardship

suf·fi·cient *adj* : adequate — **suf·fi·cien·cy** *n* — **suf·ficient·ly** *adv*

suf·fix *n* : letters added at the end of a word — **suffix** *vb* — **suf·fix·a·tion** *n*

suf·fo·cate *vb* : suffer or die or cause to die from lack of air — **suf·fo·cat·ing·ly** *adv* — **suf·fo·ca·tion** *n*

sug·ar *n* : sweet substance ～ *vb* : mix, cover, or sprinkle with sugar — **sug·ar·cane** *n* — **sug·ary** *adj*

sug·gest *vb* **1** : put into someone's mind **2** : remind one by association of ideas — **sug·gest·ible** *adj* — **sug·ges·tion** *n* — **sug·ges·tive** *adj* — **sug·ges·tive·ly** *adv* — **sug·ges·tive·ness** *n*

sui·cide *n* **1** : act of killing oneself purposely **2** : one who commits suicide — **sui·cid·al** *adj*

suit *n* **1** : action in court to recover a right or claim **2** : number of things used or worn together **3** : one of the 4 sets of playing cards ～ *vb* **1** : be appropriate or becoming to **2** : meet the needs of — **suit·abil·i·ty** *n* — **suit·able** *adj* — **suit·ably** *adv*

suite *n* **1** : group of rooms **2** : set of matched furniture

sul·len *adj* **1** : gloomily silent **2** : dismal — **sul·len·ly** *adv* — **sul·len·ness** *n*

sum *n* **1** : amount **2** : gist **3** : result of addition ～ *vb* : find the sum of

sum·ma·ry *adj* **1** : concise **2** : done without delay or formality ～ *n* : concise statement — **sum·mar·i·ly** *adv* — **sum·ma·rize** *vb* — **sum·ma·tion** *n*

sum·mer *n* : season in which the sun shines most directly — **sum·mery** *adj*

sum·mon *vb* **1** : send for or call together **2** : order to appear in court — **sum·mon·er** *n*

sun *n* **1** : shining celestial body around which the planets revolve **2** : light of the sun ～ *vb* : expose to the sun — **sun·beam** *n* — **sun·block** *n* — **sun·burn** *n or vb* — **sun·glass·es** *n pl* — **sun·light** *n* — **sun·ny** *adj* — **sun·rise** *n* — **sun·set** *n* — **sun·shine** *n* — **sun·tan** *n*

Sun·day *n* : 1st day of the week

sung *past of* SING

sunk *past of* SINK

super *adj* : very fine

su·perb *adj* : outstanding — **su·perb·ly** *adv*

su·per·fi·cial *adj* : relating to what is only apparent — **su·per·fi·ci·al·i·ty** *n* — **su·per·fi·cial·ly** *adv*

su·per·in·tend *vb* : have charge and oversight of — **su·per·in·ten·dence** *n* — **su·per·in·ten·den·cy** *n* — **su·per·in·ten·dent** *n*

su·pe·ri·or *adj* **1** : higher, better, or more important **2** : haughty — **superior** *n* — **su·pe·ri·or·i·ty** *n*

su·per·la·tive *adj* **1** : relating to or being an adjective or adverb form that denotes an extreme level **2** : surpassing others — **superlative** *n* — **su·per·la·tive·ly** *adv*

su·per·nat·u·ral *adj* : beyond the observable physical world — **su·per·nat·u·ral·ly** *adv*

su·per·pow·er *n* : politically and militarily dominant nation

su·per·sede *vb* : take the place of

su·per·sti·tion *n* : beliefs based on ignorance, fear of the unknown, or trust in magic — **su·per·sti·tious** *adj*

su·per·vise *vb* : have charge of — **su·per·vi·sion** *n* — **su·per·vi·sor** *n* — **su·per·vi·so·ry** *adj*

sup·per *n* : evening meal

sup·ple·ment *n* : something that adds to or makes up for a lack — **supplement** *vb* — **sup·ple·men·tal** *adj* — **sup·ple·men·ta·ry** *adj*

sup·ply *vb* : furnish ～ *n* **1** : amount needed or available **2** *pl* : provisions — **sup·pli·er** *n*

sup·port *vb* **1** : take sides with **2** : provide with food, clothing, and shelter **3** : hold up or serve as a foundation for — **support** *n* — **sup·port·able** *adj* — **sup·port·er** *n*

sup·pose *vb* **1** : assume to be true **2** : expect **3** : think probable — **sup·po·si·tion** *n*

sup·press *vb* **1** : put an end to by authority **2** : keep from being known **3** : hold back — **sup·pres·sant** *n* — **sup·pres·sion** *n*

su·preme *adj* **1** : highest in rank or authority **2** : greatest possible — **su·preme·ly** *adv*

Supreme Being *n* : God

sur·charge *n* **1** : excessive load or burden **2** : extra fee or cost

sure *adj* **1** : confident **2** : reliable **3** : not to be disputed **4** : bound to happen ～ *adv* : surely — **sure·ness** *n*

sure·ly *adv* **1** : in a sure manner **2** : without doubt **3** : indeed

surf *n* : waves that break on the shore ∼ *vb* : ride the surf — **surf·board** *n* — **surf·er** *n* — **surf·ing** *n*

sur·face *n* **1** : the outside of an object **2** : outward aspect ∼ *vb* : rise to the surface

sur·geon *n* : physician who specializes in surgery

sur·gery *n* : medical treatment involving cutting open the body

sur·gi·cal *adj* : relating to surgeons or surgery — **sur·gi·cal·ly** *adv*

sur·name *n* : family name

sur·pass *vb* : go beyond or exceed — **sur·pass·ing·ly** *adv*

sur·plus *n* : quantity left over

sur·prise *vb* **1** : come upon or affect unexpectedly **2** : amaze — **surprise** *n* — **sur·pris·ing** *adj* — **sur·pris·ing·ly** *adv*

sur·ren·der *vb* : give up oneself or a possession to another ∼ *n* : act of surrendering

sur·round *vb* : enclose on all sides

sur·round·ings *n pl* : objects, conditions, or area around something

sur·veil·lance *n* : careful watch

sur·vey *vb* **1** : look over and examine closely **2** : make a survey of (as a tract of land) ∼ *n* **1** : inspection **2** : process of measuring (as land) — **sur·vey·or** *n*

sur·vive *vb* **1** : remain alive or in existence **2** : outlive or outlast — **sur·viv·al** *n* — **sur·vi·vor** *n*

sus·pect *adj* **1** : regarded with suspicion **2** : questionable ∼ *n* : one who is suspected (as of a crime) ∼ *vb* **1** : have doubts of **2** : believe guilty without proof **3** : guess

sus·pend *vb* **1** : temporarily stop or keep from a function or job **2** : withhold (judgment) temporarily **3** : hang

sus·pense *n* : excitement and uncertainty as to outcome — **sus·pense·ful** *adj*

sus·pen·sion *n* : act of suspending or the state or period of being suspended

sus·pi·cion *n* **1** : act of suspecting something **2** : trace

sus·pi·cious *adj* **1** : arousing suspicion **2** : inclined to suspect — **sus·pi·cious·ly** *adv*

sus·tain *vb* **1** : provide with nourishment **2** : keep going **3** : hold up **4** : suffer **5** : support or prove

swag·ger *vb* **1** : walk with a conceited swing **2** : boast — **swag·ger** *n*

¹**swal·low** *n* : small migratory bird

²**swal·low** *vb* **1** : take into the stomach through the throat **2** : envelop or take in **3** : accept too easily — **swal·low** *n*

swam *past of* SWIM

swamp *n* : wet spongy land ∼ *vb* : deluge (as with water) — **swampy** *adj*

swan *n* : white long-necked swimming bird

swap *vb* : trade — **swap** *n*

swat *vb* : hit sharply — **swat** *n* — **swat·ter** *n*

sway *vb* **1** : swing gently from side to side **2** : influence ∼ *n* **1** : gentle swinging from side to side **2** : controlling power or influence

swear *vb* (**swore; sworn**) **1** : make or cause to make a solemn statement under oath **2** : use profane language — **swear·er** *n* — **swear·ing** *n*

sweat *vb* **1** : excrete salty moisture from skin glands **2** : form drops of moisture on the surface **3** : work or cause to work hard — **sweat** *n* — **sweaty** *adj*

sweat·er *n* : knitted jacket or pullover

sweat·shirt *n* : loose collarless heavy cotton jersey pullover

sweep *vb* (**swept; swept**) **1** : remove or clean by a brush or a single forceful wipe (as of the hand) **2** : move over with speed and force (as of the hand) **3** : move or extend in a wide curve ∼ *n* **1** : a clearing off or away **2** : single forceful wipe or swinging movement **3** : scope — **sweep·er** *n* — **sweep·ing** *adj*

sweet *adj* **1** : being or causing the pleasing taste typical of sugar **2** : not stale or spoiled **3** : not salted **4** : pleasant **5** : much loved ∼ *n* : something sweet — **sweet·en** *vb* — **sweet·ly** *adv* — **sweet·ness** *n* — **sweet·en·er** *n*

sweet·heart *n* : person one loves

swell *vb* (**swelled; swelled/swol·len**) **1** : enlarge **2** : bulge **3** : fill or be filled with emotion ∼ *n* **1** : long rolling ocean wave **2** : condition of bulging — **swell·ing** *n*

swept *past of* SWEEP

swerve *vb* : move abruptly aside from a course — **swerve** *n*

swift *adj* **1** : moving with great speed **2** : occurring suddenly — **swift·ly** *adv* — **swift·ness** *n*

swim *vb* (**swam; swum**) **1** : propel oneself in water **2** : float in or be surrounded with a liquid **3** : be dizzy ∼ *n* : act or period of swimming — **swim·mer** *n*

swin·dle *vb* : cheat (someone) of money or property — **swindle** *n* — **swin·dler** *n*

swine *n* (**swine**) : short-legged hoofed mammal with a snout — **swin·ish** *adj*

swing *vb* (**swung; swung**) **1** : move or cause to move rapidly in an arc **2** : sway or cause to sway back and forth **3** : hang so as to sway or sag **4** : turn on a hinge or pivot **5** : manage or handle successfully ∼ *n* **1** : act or instance of swinging **2** : swinging movement (as in trying to hit something) **3** : suspended seat for swinging — **swing** *adj* — **swing·er** *n*

swipe *n* : strong sweeping blow ∼ *vb* **1** : strike or wipe with a sweeping motion **2** : steal esp. with a quick movement

swirl *vb* : move or cause to move in a circle — **swirl** *n*

switch *n* **1** : slender flexible whip or twig **2** : blow with a switch **3** : shift, change, or reversal **4** : device that opens or closes an electrical circuit ∼ *vb* **1** : punish or urge on with a switch **2** : change or reverse roles, positions, or subjects **3** : operate a switch of

switch·board *n* : panel of switches to make and break telephone connections

swiv·el *vb* : swing or turn on a pivot — **swivel** *n*

swollen *past part of* SWELL

swoop *vb* : make a swift diving attack — **swoop** *n*

sword *n* : thrusting or cutting weapon with a long blade

swore *past of* SWEAR

sworn *past part of* SWEAR

swum *past part of* SWIM

swung *past of* SWING

syl·la·ble *n* : unit of a spoken word — **syl·lab·ic** *adj*

sym·bol *n* : something that represents or suggests another thing — **sym·bol·ic** *adj* — **sym·bol·i·cal·ly** *adv* — **sym·bol·ism** *n* — **sym·bol·ize** *vb*

sym·me·try *n* : regularity and balance in the arrangement of parts — **sym·met·ri·cal** *adj* — **sym·met·ri·cal·ly** *adv*

sym·pa·thy *n* **1** : ability to understand or share the feelings of another **2** : expression of sorrow for another's misfortune — **sym·pa·thet·ic** *adj* — **sym·pa·thet·i·cal·ly** *adv* — **sym·pa·thize** *vb*

sym·pho·ny *n* : composition for an orchestra or the orchestra itself — **sym·phon·ic** *adj*

symp·tom *n* : unusual feeling or reaction that is a sign of disease — **symp·tom·at·ic** *adj*

syn·a·gogue, syn·a·gog *n* : Jewish house of worship

syn·chro·nize *vb* **1** : occur or cause to occur at the same instant **2** : cause to agree in time — **syn·chro·ni·za·tion** *n*

syn·drome *n* : particular group of symptoms

syn·onym *n* : word with the same meaning as another — **syn·on·y·mous** *adj* — **syn·on·y·my** *n*

syn·the·sis *n* : combination of parts or elements into a whole — **syn·the·size** *vb*

syn·thet·ic *adj* : artificially made — **synthetic** *n* — **syn·thet·i·cal·ly** *adv*

syr·up *n* : thick sticky sweet liquid — **syr·upy** *adj*

sys·tem *n* **1** : arrangement of units that function together **2** : regular order — **sys·tem·at·ic** *adj* — **sys·tem·at·i·cal·ly** *adv* — **sys·tem·a·tize** *vb* — **sys·tem·ic** *adj*

T

t *n* : 20th letter of the alphabet

tab·by *n* : domestic cat

ta·ble *n* **1** : piece of furniture having a smooth slab fixed on legs **2** : supply of food **3** : arrangement of data in columns **4** : short list — **ta·ble·cloth** *n* — **ta·ble·top** *n* — **ta·ble·ware** *n* — **tab·u·lar** *adj*

ta·ble·spoon *n* **1** : large serving spoon **2** : measuring spoon holding $\frac{1}{2}$ fluid ounce — **ta·ble·spoon·ful** *n*

tab·let *n* **1** : flat slab suited for an inscription **2** : collection of sheets of paper glued together at one edge **3** : disk-shaped pill

tab·loid *n* : newspaper of small page size

tack *n* **1** : small sharp nail **2** : course of action ∼ *vb* **1** : fasten with tacks **2** : add on

tack·le *n* **1** : equipment **2** : arrangement of ropes and pulleys **3** : act of tackling ∼ *vb* **1** : seize or throw down **2** : start dealing with

tacky *adj* : cheap or gaudy

tact *n* : sense of the proper thing to say or do — **tact·ful** *adj* — **tact·ful·ly** *adv* — **tact·less** *adj* — **tact·less·ly** *adv*

tac·tic *n* : action as part of a plan

taf·fy *n* : candy stretched until porous

¹**tag** *n* : piece of hanging or attached material

$\sim$ *vb* **1 :** provide or mark with a tag **2 :** follow closely

²**tag** *n* **:** children's game of trying to catch one another $\sim$ *vb* **:** touch a person in tag

tail *n* **1 :** rear end or a growth extending from the rear end of an animal **2 :** back or last part **3 :** the reverse of a coin $\sim$ *vb* **:** follow — **tailed** *adj* — **tail·less** *adj* — **tail·light** *n*

tai·lor *n* **:** one who makes or alters garments $\sim$ *vb* **1 :** fashion or alter (clothes) **2 :** make or adapt for a special purpose

take *vb* (**took; tak·en**) **1 :** get into one's possession **2 :** become affected by **3 :** receive into one's body (as by eating) **4 :** pick out or remove **5 :** use for transportation **6 :** need or make use of **7 :** lead, carry, or cause to go to another place **8 :** undertake and do, make, or perform $\sim$ *n* **:** amount taken — **take·over** *n* — **tak·er** *n* — **take advantage of :** profit by — **take exception :** object — **take off** *vb* **1 :** remove **2 :** go away **3 :** mimic **4 :** begin flight — **take over** *vb* **:** assume control or possession of or responsibility for — **take place :** happen

tale *n* **1 :** story or anecdote **2 :** falsehood

tal·ent *n* **:** natural mental or creative ability — **tal·ent·ed** *adj*

talk *vb* **1 :** express one's thoughts in speech **2 :** discuss **3 :** influence to a position or course of action by talking $\sim$ *n* **1 :** act of talking **2 :** formal discussion **3 :** rumor **4 :** informal lecture — **talk·a·tive** *adj* — **talk·er** *n*

tall *adj* **:** extending to a great or specified height — **tall·ness** *n*

tame *adj* **1 :** changed from being wild to being controllable by man **2 :** docile **3 :** dull $\sim$ *vb* **:** make or become tame — **tam·able, tame·able** *adj* — **tame·ly** *adv* — **tam·er** *n*

tan *vb* **1 :** change (hide) into leather esp. by soaking in a liquid containing tannin **2 :** make or become brown (as by exposure to the sun) $\sim$ *n* **1 :** brown skin color induced by the sun **2 :** light yellowish brown — **tan·ner** *n* — **tan·nery** *n*

tan·gi·ble *adj* **1 :** able to be touched **2 :** substantially real — **tan·gi·bly** *adv*

tan·gle *vb* **:** unite in intricate confusion $\sim$ *n* **:** tangled twisted mass

tank *n* **1 :** large artificial receptacle for liquids **2 :** armored military vehicle — **tank·ful** *n*

tank·er *n* **:** vehicle or vessel with tanks for transporting a liquid

¹**tap** *n* **1 :** faucet **2 :** act of tapping $\sim$ *vb* **1**

: pierce so as to draw off fluid **2 :** connect into — **tap·per** *n*

²**tap** *vb* **:** rap lightly $\sim$ *n* **:** light stroke or its sound

tape *n* **1 :** narrow flexible strip (as of cloth, plastic, or metal) **2 :** tape measure $\sim$ *vb* **1 :** fasten with tape **2 :** record on tape

ta·per *n* **1 :** slender wax candle **2 :** gradual lessening of width in a long object $\sim$ *vb* **1 :** make or become smaller toward one end **2 :** diminish gradually

tar *n* **:** thick dark sticky liquid distilled (as from coal) $\sim$ *vb* **:** treat or smear with tar

tar·dy *adj* **:** late — **tar·di·ly** *adv* — **tar·di·ness** *n*

tar·get *n* **1 :** mark to shoot at **2 :** goal to be achieved $\sim$ *vb* **1 :** make a target of **2 :** establish as a goal

tar·iff *n* **1 :** duty or rate of duty imposed on imported goods **2 :** schedule of tariffs, rates, or charges

¹**tart** *adj* **1 :** pleasantly sharp to the taste **2 :** caustic — **tart·ly** *adv* — **tart·ness** *n*

²**tart** *n* **:** small pie

task *n* **:** assigned work

taste *vb* **1 :** test or determine the flavor of **2 :** eat or drink in small quantities **3 :** have a specific flavor $\sim$ *n* **1 :** small amount tasted **2 :** bit **3 :** special sense that identifies sweet, sour, bitter, or salty qualities **4 :** individual preference **5 :** critical appreciation of quality — **taste·ful** *adj* — **taste·ful·ly** *adv* — **taste·less** *adj* — **taste·less·ly** *adv* — **tast·er** *n*

tasty *adj* **:** pleasing to the sense of taste — **tast·i·ness** *n*

tat·tle·tale *n* **:** one that tattles

taught *past of* TEACH

taunt *n* **:** hurtful challenge or insult — **taunt** *vb* — **taunt·er** *n*

taut *adj* **:** tightly drawn — **taut·ly** *adv* — **taut·ness** *n*

tax *vb* **1 :** impose a tax on **2 :** charge **3 :** put under stress $\sim$ *n* **1 :** charge by authority for public purposes **2 :** strain — **tax·able** *adj* — **tax·a·tion** *n* — **tax·pay·er** *n* — **tax·pay·ing** *adj*

taxi *n* **:** automobile transporting passengers for a fare $\sim$ *vb* **1 :** transport or go by taxi **2 :** move along the ground before takeoff or after landing

tea *n* **:** cured leaves of an Asian shrub or a drink made from these — **tea·cup** *n* — **tea·ket·tle** *n* — **tea·pot** *n*

teach *vb* (**taught; taught**) **1** : tell or show the fundamentals or skills of something **2** : cause to know the consequences **3** : impart knowledge of — **teach·able** *adj* — **teach·er** *n* — **teach·ing** *n*

team *n* **1** : draft animals harnessed together **2** : number of people organized for a game or work ∼ *vb* : form or work together as a team — **team** *adj* — **team·mate** *n* — **team·work** *n*

¹tear *n* : drop of salty liquid that moistens the eye — **tear·ful** *adj* — **tear·ful·ly** *adv*

²tear *vb* (**tore; torn**) **1** : separate or pull apart by force **2** : move or act with violence or haste ∼ *n* : act or result of tearing

tease *vb* : annoy by goading, coaxing, or tantalizing ∼ *n* **1** : act of teasing or state of being teased **2** : one that teases

tea·spoon *n* **1** : small spoon for stirring or sipping **2** : measuring spoon holding ⅙ fluid ounce — **tea·spoon·ful** *n*

tech·ni·cal *adj* **1** : having or relating to special mechanical or scientific knowledge **2** : by strict interpretation of rules — **tech·ni·cal·ly** *adv*

tech·ni·cal·i·ty *n* : detail meaningful only to a specialist

tech·nique *n* : manner of accomplishing something

tech·nol·o·gy *n* : applied science — **tech·no·log·i·cal** *adj*

te·dious *adj* : wearisome from length or dullness — **te·dious·ly** *adv* — **te·dious·ness** *n*

tee *n* : mound or peg on which a golf ball is placed before beginning play — **tee** *vb*

teen·age, teen·aged *adj* : relating to people in their teens — **teen·ag·er** *n*

teens *n pl* : years 13 to 19 in a person's life

tee·pee *var of* TEPEE

teeth *pl of* TOOTH

teethe *vb* : grow teeth

tele·cast *vb* : broadcast by television — **tele·cast** *n* — **tele·cast·er** *n*

tele·com·mu·ni·ca·tion *n* : communication at a distance (as by radio or telephone)

tele·phone *n* : instrument or system for electrical transmission of spoken words ∼ *vb* : communicate with by telephone — **tele·phon·er** *n*

tele·scope *n* : tube-shaped optical instrument for viewing distant objects ∼ *vb* : slide or cause to slide inside another similar section — **tele·scop·ic** *adj*

tele·vise *vb* : broadcast by television

tele·vi·sion *n* : transmission and reproduction of images by radio waves

tell *vb* (**told; told**) **1** : count **2** : relate in detail **3** : reveal **4** : give information or an order to **5** : find out by observing

tem·per *vb* **1** : dilute or soften **2** : toughen ∼ *n* **1** : characteristic attitude or feeling **2** : toughness **3** : disposition or control over one's emotions

tem·per·a·ment *n* : characteristic frame of mind — **tem·per·a·men·tal** *adj*

tem·per·a·ture *n* **1** : degree of hotness or coldness **2** : fever

¹tem·ple *n* : place of worship

²temple *n* : flattened space on each side of the forehead

tem·po·rary *adj* : lasting for a short time only — **tem·po·rar·i·ly** *adv*

tempt *vb* **1** : coax or persuade to do wrong **2** : attract or provoke — **tempt·er** *n* — **tempt·ing·ly** *adv* — **tempt·ress** *n*

temp·ta·tion *n* **1** : act of tempting **2** : something that tempts

ten *n* **1** : one more than 9 **2** : 10th in a set or series **3** : thing having 10 units — **ten** *adj or pron* — **tenth** *adj or adv or n*

ten·ant *n* : one who occupies a rented dwelling — **ten·an·cy** *n*

¹tend *vb* : take care of or supervise something

²tend *vb* **1** : move in a particular direction **2** : show a tendency

ten·den·cy *n* : likelihood to move, think, or act in a particular way

¹ten·der *adj* **1** : soft or delicate **2** : expressing or responsive to love or sympathy **3** : sensitive (as to touch) — **ten·der·ly** *adv* — **ten·der·ness** *n*

²ten·der *n* **1** : offer of a bid for a contract **2** : something that may be offered in payment — **tender** *vb*

ten·der·ize *vb* : make (meat) tender — **ten·der·iz·er** *n*

ten·nis *n* : racket-and-ball game played across a net

ten·or *n* **1** : general drift or meaning **2** : highest natural adult male voice

¹tense *n* : distinct verb form that indicates time

²tense *adj* **1** : stretched tight **2** : marked by nervous tension — **tense** *vb* — **tense·ly** *adv* — **tense·ness** *n* — **ten·si·ty** *n*

ten·sion *n* **1** : tense condition **2** : state of mental unrest or of potential hostility or opposition

tent *n* : collapsible shelter

ten·ta·tive *adj* : subject to change or discussion — **ten·ta·tive·ly** *adv*

te·pee *n* : conical tent

term *n* **1** : period of time **2** : mathematical expression **3** : special word or phrase **4** *pl* : conditions **5** *pl* : relations ∼ *vb* : name

ter·min·al *n* **1** : end **2** : device for making an electrical connection **3** : station at end of a transportation line — **ter·min·al** *adj*

ter·mi·nate *vb* : bring or come to an end — **ter·mi·na·ble** *adj* — **ter·mi·na·tion** *n*

ter·mi·nol·o·gy *n* : terms used in a particular subject

ter·race *n* **1** : balcony or patio **2** : bank with a flat top ∼ *vb* : landscape in a series of banks

ter·ri·ble *adj* **1** : exciting terror **2** : distressing **3** : intense **4** : of very poor quality — **ter·ri·bly** *adv*

ter·rif·ic *adj* **1** : exciting terror **2** : extraordinary

ter·ri·fy *vb* : fill with terror — **ter·ri·fy·ing·ly** *adv*

ter·ri·to·ry *n* : particular geographical region — **ter·ri·to·ri·al** *adj*

ter·ror *n* : intense fear and panic or a cause of it

ter·ror·ize *vb* **1** : fill with terror **2** : coerce by threat or violence — **ter·ror·ism** *n* — **ter·ror·ist** *adj or n*

test *n* : examination or evaluation ∼ *vb* : examine by a test — **test·er** *n*

tes·ti·fy *vb* **1** : give testimony **2** : serve as evidence

tes·ti·mo·ni·al *n* **1** : favorable recommendation **2** : tribute — **tes·ti·mo·ni·al** *adj*

tes·ti·mo·ny *n* : statement given as evidence in court

text *n* **1** : author's words **2** : main body of printed or written matter on a page **3** : textbook **4** : scriptural passage used as the theme of a sermon **5** : topic — **tex·tu·al** *adj*

text·book *n* : book on a school subject

tex·tile *n* : fabric

tex·ture *n* **1** : feel and appearance of something **2** : structure

than *conj or prep* — used in comparisons

thank *vb* : express gratitude to — **thank·ful** *adj* — **thank·ful·ly** *adv* — **thank·ful·ness** *n* — **thank·less** *adj* — **thanks** *n pl*

Thanks·giv·ing *n* : fourth Thursday in November observed as a legal holiday for giving thanks for divine goodness

that *pron, pl* **1** : something indicated or understood **2** : the one farther away ∼ *adj pl*

those : being the one mentioned or understood or farther away ∼ *conj or pron* — used to introduce a clause ∼ *adv* : to such an extent

the *definite article* : that particular one ∼ *adv* — used before a comparative or superlative

the·ater, the·atre *n* **1** : building or room for viewing a play or movie **2** : dramatic arts — **the·at·ri·cal** *adj*

theft *n* : act of stealing

their *adj* : relating to them

theirs *pron* : their one or ones

them *pron, objective case of* THEY

theme *n* **1** : subject matter **2** : essay **3** : melody developed in a piece of music — **the·mat·ic** *adj*

them·selves *pron pl* : they, them — used reflexively or for emphasis

then *adv* **1** : at that time **2** : soon after that **3** : in addition **4** : in that case **5** : consequently ∼ *n* : that time ∼ *adj* : existing at that time

the·o·ry *n* **1** : general principles of a subject **2** : plausible or scientifically acceptable explanation **3** : judgment, guess, or opinion — **the·o·ret·i·cal** *adj* — **the·o·rize** *vb* — **the·o·rist** *n*

ther·a·py *n* : treatment for mental or physical disorder — **ther·a·peu·tic** *adj* — **ther·a·peu·ti·cal·ly** *adv* — **ther·a·pist** *n*

there *adv* **1** : in, at, or to that place **2** : in that respect ∼ *pron* — used to introduce a sentence or clause ∼ *n* : that place or point

there·fore *adv* : for that reason

there·of *adv* **1** : of that or it **2** : from that

ther·mal *adj* : relating to, caused by, or conserving heat — **ther·mal·ly** *adv*

ther·mom·e·ter *n* : instrument for measuring temperature — **ther·mo·met·ric** *adj*

ther·mo·stat *n* : automatic temperature control — **ther·mo·stat·ic** *adj* — **ther·mo·stat·i·cal·ly** *adv*

these *pl of* THIS

the·sis *n* **1** : proposition to be argued for **2** : essay embodying results of original research

they *pron* **1** : those ones **2** : people in general

thick *adj* **1** : having relatively great mass from front to back or top to bottom **2** : having a tendency to flow very slowly ∼ *n* : most crowded or thickest part — **thick·en** *vb* — **thick·en·er** *n* — **thick·ly** *adv* — **thick·ness** *n*

thief *n* : one that steals

thigh *n* : upper part of the leg

thin *adj* **1** : having relatively little mass from

front to back or top to bottom **2** : not closely set or placed **3** : relatively free flowing **4** : lacking substance, fullness, or strength ~ *vb* : make or become thin — **thin·ly** *adv* — **thinness** *n*

thing *n* **1** : matter of concern **2** : event or act **3** : object **4** *pl* : possessions

think *vb* (**thought; thought**) **1** : form or have in the mind **2** : have as an opinion **3** : ponder **4** : devise by thinking **5** : imagine — **think·er** *n*

third *adj* : being number 3 in a countable series ~ *n* **1** : one that is third **2** : one of 3 equal parts — **third, third·ly** *adv*

thirst *n* **1** : dryness in mouth and throat **2** : intense desire ~ *vb* : feel thirst — **thirsty** *adj*

thir·teen *n* : one more than 12 — **thir·teen** *adj or pron* — **thir·teenth** *adj or n*

thir·ty *n* : 3 times 10 — **thir·ti·eth** *adj or n* — **thirty** *adj or pron*

this *pron, pl* : something close or under immediate discussion ~ *adj pl* **these** : being the one near, present, just mentioned, or more immediately under observation ~ *adv* : to such an extent or degree

thorn *n* : sharp spike on a plant or a plant bearing these — **thorny** *adj*

thor·ough *adj* : omitting or overlooking nothing — **thor·ough·ly** *adv* — **thor·ough·ness** *n*

thor·ough·fare *n* : a main road or route for passage

those *pl of* THAT

though *adv* : however ~ *conj* **1** : despite the fact that **2** : granting that

thought *past of* THINK *n* **1** : process of thinking **2** : serious consideration **3** : idea

thought·ful *adj* **1** : absorbed in or showing thought **2** : considerate of others — **thought·ful·ly** *adv* — **thought·ful·ness** *n*

thought·less *adj* **1** : careless or reckless **2** : lacking concern for others — **thought·less·ly** *adv*

thou·sand *n* : 10 times 100 — **thou·sand** *adj* — **thou·sandth** *adj or n*

thread *n* **1** : fine line of fibers **2** : train of thought **3** : ridge around a screw ~ *vb* **1** : pass thread through **2** : put together on a thread **3** : make one's way through or between

threat *n* **1** : expression of intention to harm **2** : thing that threatens

threat·en *vb* **1** : utter threats **2** : show signs of being near or impending — **threat·en·ing·ly** *adv*

three *n* **1** : one more than 2 **2** : 3d in a set or series — **three** *adj or pron*

threw *past of* THROW

thrift *n* : careful management or saving of money — **thrift·i·ly** *adv* — **thrifty** *adj*

thrill *vb* **1** : have or cause to have a sudden sharp feeling of excitement **2** : tremble — **thrill** *n* — **thrill·er** *n* — **thrill·ing·ly** *adv*

thrive *vb* **1** : grow vigorously **2** : prosper

throat *n* **1** : front part of the neck **2** : passage to the stomach — **throat·ed** *adj* — **throaty** *adj*

throb *vb* : pulsate — **throb** *n*

throne *n* : chair representing power or sovereignty

throt·tle *vb* : choke ~ *n* : valve regulating volume of fuel and air delivered to engine cylinders

through *prep* **1** : into at one side and out at the other side of **2** : by way of **3** : among, between, or all around **4** : because of **5** : throughout the time of ~ *adv* **1** : from one end or side to the other **2** : from beginning to end **3** : to the core **4** : into the open ~ *adj* **1** : going directly from origin to destination **2** : finished

through·out *adv* **1** : everywhere **2** : from beginning to end ~ *prep* **1** : in or to every part of **2** : during the whole of

throw *vb* (**threw; thrown**) **1** : propel through the air **2** : cause to fall or fall off **3** : put suddenly in a certain position or condition **4** : move quickly as if throwing **5** : put on or off hastily — **throw** *n* — **throw·er** *n* — **throw up** *vb* : vomit

thrust *vb* (**thrust; thrust**) **1** : shove forward **2** : stab or pierce — **thrust** *n*

thumb *n* **1** : short thick division of the hand opposing the fingers **2** : glove part for the thumb ~ *vb* : leaf through with the thumb — **thumb·nail** *n*

thun·der *n* : sound following lightning — **thunder** *vb* — **thun·der·clap** *n* — **thun·der·ous** *adj* — **thun·der·ous·ly** *adv*

Thurs·day *n* : 5th day of the week

thus *adv* **1** : in this or that way **2** : to this degree or extent **3** : because of this or that

[1]**tick** *n* : small 8-legged blood-sucking animal

[2]**tick** *n* **1** : light rhythmic tap or beat **2** : check mark ~ *vb* **1** : make ticks **2** : mark with a tick **3** : operate

tick·et *n* **1** : tag showing price, payment of a fee or fare, or a traffic offense **2** : list of candidates ∼ *vb* : put a ticket on

tick·le *vb* **1** : please or amuse **2** : touch lightly causing uneasiness, laughter, or spasmodic movements — **tick·le** *n*

tick·lish *adj* **1** : sensitive to tickling **2** : requiring delicate handling — **tick·lish·ness** *n*

tide *n* : alternate rising and falling of the sea ∼ *vb* : be enough to allow (one) to get by for a time — **tid·al** *adj* — **tide·wa·ter** *n*

ti·dy *adj* **1** : well ordered and cared for **2** : large or substantial — **ti·di·ness** *n* — **ti·dy** *vb*

tie *n* **1** : line or ribbon for fastening, uniting, or closing **2** : cross support to which railroad rails are fastened **3** : uniting force **4** : equality in score or tally or a deadlocked contest **5** : necktie ∼ *vb* **1** : fasten or close by wrapping and knotting a tie **2** : form a knot in **3** : gain the same score or tally as an opponent

tier *n* : one of a steplike series of rows

ti·ger *n* : very large black-striped cat — **ti·ger·ish** *adj* — **ti·gress** *n*

tight *adj* **1** : fitting close together esp. so as not to allow air or water in **2** : held very firmly **3** : taut **4** : fitting too snugly **5** : difficult **6** : stingy **7** : evenly contested **8** : low in supply — **tight** *adv* — **tight·en** *vb* — **tight·ly** *adv* — **tight·ness** *n*

tights *n pl* : skintight garments

tile *n* : thin piece of stone or fired clay used on roofs, floors, or walls ∼ *vb* : cover with tiles

¹till *prep or conj* : until

²till *vb* : cultivate (soil) — **till·able** *adj*

tilt *vb* : cause to incline ∼ *n* : slant

tim·ber *n* **1** : cut wood for building **2** : large squared piece of wood **3** : wooded land or trees for timber ∼ *vb* : cover, frame, or support with timbers — **tim·bered** *adj* — **tim·ber·land** *n*

time *n* **1** : period during which something exists or continues or can be accomplished **2** : point at which something happens **3** : customary hour **4** : age **5** : rate of speed **6** : moment, hour, day, or year as indicated by a clock or calendar **7** : one's experience during a particular period ∼ *vb* **1** : arrange or set the time of **2** : determine or record the time, duration, or rate of — **time·keep·er** *n* — **time·less** *adj* — **time·less·ness** *n* — **time·li·ness** *n* — **time·ly** *adv* — **tim·er** *n*

times *prep* : multiplied by

time·ta·ble *n* : table of departure and arrival times

tim·id *adj* : lacking in courage or self-confidence — **ti·mid·i·ty** *n* — **tim·id·ly** *adv*

tin *n* **1** : soft white metallic chemical element **2** : metal food can

tine *n* : one of the points of a fork

tin·gle *vb* : feel a ringing, stinging, or thrilling sensation — **tingle** *n*

tin·kle *vb* : make or cause to make a high ringing sound — **tinkle** *n*

tint *n* **1** : slight or pale coloration **2** : color shade ∼ *vb* : give a tint to

ti·ny *adj* : very small

¹tip *vb* **1** : overturn **2** : lean ∼ *n* : act or state of tipping

²tip *n* : pointed end of something ∼ *vb* **1** : furnish with a tip **2** : cover the tip of

³tip *n* : small sum given for a service performed ∼ *vb* : give a tip to

⁴tip *n* : piece of confidential information ∼ *vb* : give confidential information to

tip·toe *n* : the toes of the feet ∼ *adv or adj* : supported on tiptoe ∼ *vb* : walk quietly or on tiptoe

tip–top *n* : highest point ∼ *adj* : excellent

¹tire *vb* **1** : make or become weary **2** : wear out the patience of — **tire·less** *adj* — **tire·less·ly** *adv* — **tire·some** *adj* — **tire·some·ly** *adv*

²tire *n* : rubber cushion encircling a car wheel

tired *adj* : weary

tis·sue *n* **1** : soft absorbent paper **2** : layer of cells forming a basic structural element of an animal or plant body

ti·tle *n* **1** : legal ownership **2** : distinguishing name **3** : designation of honor, rank, or office **4** : championship — **ti·tled** *adj*

TNT *n* : high explosive

to *prep* **1** : in the direction of **2** : at, on, or near **3** : resulting in **4** : before or until **5** — used to show a relationship or object of a verb **6** — used with an infinitive ∼ *adv* **1** : forward **2** : to a state of consciousness

toast *vb* **1** : make (as a slice of bread) crisp and brown **2** : drink in honor of someone or something **3** : warm ∼ *n* **1** : toasted sliced bread **2** : act of drinking in honor of someone — **toast·er** *n*

to·bac·co *n* : broad-leaved herb or its leaves prepared for smoking or chewing

to·day *adv* **1** : on or for this day **2** : at the present time ∼ *n* : present day or time

to–do *n* : disturbance or fuss

toe *n* : one of the 5 end divisions of the foot — **toe·nail** *n*

tof·fee, tof·fy *n* : candy made of boiled sugar and butter

to·geth·er *adv* **1** : in or into one place or group **2** : in or into contact or association **3** : at one time **4** : as a group — **to·geth·er·ness** *n*

toil *vb* : work hard and long — **toil** *n* — **toil·er** *n* — **toil·some** *adj*

toi·let *n* **1** : dressing and grooming oneself **2** : bathroom **3** : water basin to urinate and defecate in

to·ken *n* **1** : outward sign or expression of something **2** : small part representing the whole **3** : piece resembling a coin

told *past of* TELL

tol·er·ance *n* **1** : lack of opposition for beliefs or practices differing from one's own **2** : capacity for enduring **3** : allowable deviation — **tol·er·ant** *adj* — **tol·er·ant·ly** *adv*

tol·er·ate *vb* **1** : allow to be or to be done without opposition **2** : endure or resist the action of — **tol·er·a·ble** *adj* — **tol·er·a·bly** *adv* — **tol·er·a·tion** *n*

toll *n* **1** : fee paid for a privilege or service **2** : cost of achievement in loss or suffering — **toll·booth** *n* — **toll·gate** *n*

to·ma·to *n* : tropical American herb or its fruit

tomb *n* : house, vault, or grave for burial — **tomb·stone** *n*

tom·boy *n* : girl who behaves in a manner usu. considered boyish

to·mor·row *adv* : on or for the day after today — **tomorrow** *n*

ton *n* : unit of weight equal to 2000 pounds

tone *n* **1** : vocal or musical sound **2** : sound of definite pitch **3** : manner of speaking that expresses an emotion or attitude **4** : color quality **5** : healthy condition **6** : general character or quality ~ *vb* : soften or muffle — often used with *down* — **ton·al** *adj* — **to·nal·i·ty** *n*

tongue *n* **1** : fleshy movable organ of the mouth **2** : language **3** : something long and flat and fastened at one end — **tongued** *adj* — **tongue·less** *adj*

to·night *adv* : on this night ~ *n* : present or coming night

too *adv* **1** : in addition **2** : excessively

took *past of* TAKE

tool *n* : device worked by hand ~ *vb* : shape or finish with a tool

tool·bar *n* : strip of icons on a computer display providing quick access to pictured functions

toot *vb* : sound or cause to sound esp. in short blasts — **toot** *n*

tooth *n pl* **teeth** **1** : one of the hard structures in the jaws for chewing **2** : one of the projections on the edge of a gear wheel — **tooth·ache** *n* — **tooth·brush** *n* — **toothed** *adj* — **tooth·less** *adj* — **tooth·paste** *n* — **tooth·pick** *n*

¹top *n* **1** : highest part or level of something **2** : lid or covering ~ *vb* **1** : cover with a top **2** : surpass **3** : go over the top of ~ *adj* : being at the top — **topped** *adj* — **top·most** *adj*

²top *n* : spinning toy

top·ic *n* : subject for discussion or study

top·i·cal *adj* **1** : relating to or arranged by topics **2** : relating to current or local events — **top·i·cal·ly** *adv*

top·ple *vb* : fall or cause to fall

torch *n* : flaming light — **torch·bear·er** *n* — **torch·light** *n*

tore *past of* TEAR

tor·ment *n* : extreme pain or anguish or a source of this ~ *vb* **1** : cause severe anguish to **2** : harass — **tor·men·tor** *n*

torn *past part of* TEAR

tor·na·do *n* : violent destructive whirling wind

tor·ti·lla *n* : round flat cornmeal or wheat flour bread

tor·ture *n* **1** : use of pain to punish or force **2** : agony ~ *vb* : inflict torture on — **tor·tur·er** *n*

toss *vb* **1** : move to and fro or up and down violently **2** : throw with a quick light motion **3** : move restlessly — **toss** *n*

toss–up *n* **1** : a deciding by flipping a coin **2** : even chance

to·tal *n* : entire amount ~ *vb* **1** : add up **2** : amount to — **to·tal** *adj* — **to·tal·ly** *adv*

to·tal·i·ty *n* : whole amount or entirety

tote *vb* : carry

touch *vb* **1** : make contact with so as to feel **2** : be or cause to be in contact **3** : take into the hands or mouth **4** : treat or mention a subject **5** : relate or concern **6** : move to sympathetic feeling ~ *n* **1** : light stroke **2** : act or fact of touching or being touched **3** : sense of feeling **4** : trace **5** : state of being in contact — **touch up** *vb* : improve with minor changes

touch·down *n* : scoring of 6 points in football

touchy *adj* **1** : easily offended **2** : requiring tact

tough *adj* **1** : strong but elastic **2** : not easily chewed **3** : severe or disciplined **4** : stubborn

$\sim$ *n* : rowdy — **tough·en** *vb* — **tough·ly** *adv* — **tough·ness** *n*

tour *n* **1** : period of time spent at work or on an assignment **2** : journey with a return to the starting point $\sim$ *vb* : travel over to see the sights — **tour·ist** *n*

tour·na·ment *n* **1** : medieval jousting competition **2** : championship series of games

tow *vb* : pull along behind — **tow** *n*

to·ward, to·wards *prep* **1** : in the direction of **2** : with respect to **3** : in part payment on

tow·el *n* : absorbent cloth or paper for wiping or drying

tow·er *n* : tall structure $\sim$ *vb* : rise to a great height — **tow·ered** *adj* — **tow·er·ing** *adj*

town *n* **1** : small residential area **2** : city — **towns·peo·ple** *n pl*

tox·ic *adj* : poisonous — **tox·ic·i·ty** *n*

tox·in *n* : poison produced by an organism

toy *n* : something for a child to play with $\sim$ *vb* : amuse oneself or play with something $\sim$ *adj* **1** : designed as a toy **2** : very small

trace *vb* **1** : mark over the lines of (a drawing) **2** : follow the trail or the development of $\sim$ *n* **1** : track **2** : tiny amount or residue — **trace·able** *adj* — **trac·er** *n*

track *n* **1** : trail left by wheels or footprints **2** : racing course **3** : train rails **4** : awareness of a progression **5** : looped belts propelling a vehicle $\sim$ *vb* **1** : follow the trail of **2** : make tracks on — **track·er** *n*

track–and–field *adj* : relating to athletic contests of running, jumping, and throwing events

trac·tion *n* : gripping power to permit movement — **trac·tion·al** *adj* — **trac·tive** *adj*

trac·tor *n* **1** : farm vehicle used esp. for pulling **2** : truck for hauling a trailer

trade *n* **1** : one's regular business **2** : occupation requiring skill **3** : the buying and selling of goods **4** : act of trading $\sim$ *vb* **1** : give in exchange for something **2** : buy and sell goods **3** : be a regular customer — **trades·peo·ple** *n pl*

trade·mark *n* : word or mark identifying a manufacturer — **trade·mark** *vb*

tra·di·tion *n* : belief or custom passed from generation to generation — **tra·di·tion·al** *adj* — **tra·di·tion·al·ly** *adv*

traf·fic *n* **1** : business dealings **2** : movement along a route $\sim$ *vb* : do business — **traf·fick·er** *n* — **traffic light** *n*

trag·e·dy *n* **1** : serious drama describing a conflict and having a sad end **2** : disastrous event

trag·ic *adj* : being a tragedy — **trag·i·cal·ly** *adv*

trail *vb* **1** : hang down and drag along the ground **2** : draw along behind **3** : follow the track of **4** : dwindle $\sim$ *n* **1** : something that trails **2** : path or evidence left by something

trail·er *n* **1** : vehicle intended to be hauled **2** : dwelling designed to be towed to a site

train *n* **1** : trailing part of a gown **2** : connected series **3** : group of linked railroad cars $\sim$ *vb* **1** : cause to grow as desired **2** : make or become prepared or skilled **3** : point — **train·ee** *n* — **train·er** *n* — **train·load** *n*

trai·tor *n* : one who betrays a trust or commits treason — **trai·tor·ous** *adj*

tramp *vb* **1** : walk or hike **2** : tread on $\sim$ *n* : beggar or vagrant

tram·ple *vb* : walk or step on so as to bruise or crush — **tram·ple** *n* — **tram·pler** *n*

trance *n* **1** : sleeplike condition **2** : state of mystical absorption

tran·quil *adj* : quiet and undisturbed — **tran·quil·ize** *vb* — **tran·quil·iz·er** *n* — **tran·quil·li·ty, tran·quil·i·ty** *n* — **tran·quil·ly** *adv*

trans·ac·tion *n* **1** : business deal **2** *pl* : records of proceedings — **trans·act** *vb*

trans·fer *vb* **1** : move from one person, place, or situation to another **2** : convey ownership of **3** : print or copy by contact **4** : change to another vehicle or transportation line $\sim$ *n* **1** : act or process of transferring **2** : one that transfers or is transferred **3** : ticket permitting one to transfer — **trans·fer·able** *adj* — **trans·fer·al** *n* — **trans·fer·ence** *n*

trans·form *vb* **1** : change in structure, appearance, or character **2** : change (an electric current) in potential or type — **trans·for·ma·tion** *n* — **trans·form·er** *n*

tran·sit *n* **1** : movement over, across, or through **2** : local and esp. public transportation **3** : surveyor's instrument

tran·si·tion *n* : passage from one state, stage, or subject to another — **tran·si·tion·al** *adj*

tran·si·to·ry *adj* : of brief duration

trans·late *vb* : change into another language — **trans·lat·able** *adj* — **trans·la·tion** *n* — **trans·la·tor** *n*

trans·lu·cent *adj* : not transparent but clear enough to allow light to pass through — **trans·lu·cence** *n* — **trans·lu·cen·cy** *n* — **trans·lu·cent·ly** *adv*

trans·mit *vb* **1** : transfer from one person or place to another **2** : pass on by inheritance **3**

: broadcast — **trans·mis·si·ble** *adj* — **trans·mis·sion** *n* — **trans·mit·ta·ble** *adj* — **trans·mit·tal** *n* — **trans·mit·ter** *n*

trans·par·ent *adj* **1 :** clear enough to see through **2 :** obvious — **trans·par·en·cy** *n* — **trans·par·ent·ly** *adv*

trans·plant *vb* **1 :** dig up and move to another place **2 :** transfer from one body part or person to another — **transplant** *n* — **trans·plan·ta·tion** *n*

trans·port *vb* **1 :** carry or deliver to another place **2 :** carry away by emotion ∼ *n* **1 :** act of transporting **2 :** rapture **3 :** ship or plane for carrying troops or supplies — **trans·por·ta·tion** *n* — **trans·port·er** *n*

trans·pose *vb* **:** change the position, sequence, or key — **trans·po·si·tion** *n*

trap *n* **1 :** device for catching animals **2 :** something by which one is caught unawares **3 :** device to allow one thing to pass through while keeping other things out ∼ *vb* **:** catch in a trap — **trap·per** *n*

trap·e·zoid *n* **:** plane 4-sided figure with 2 parallel sides — **trap·e·zoi·dal** *adj*

trash *n* **:** something that is no good — **trashy** *adj*

trav·el *vb* **1 :** take a trip or tour **2 :** move or be carried from point to point ∼ *n* **:** journey — often pl. — **trav·el·er, trav·el·ler** *n*

trawl *vb* **:** fish or catch with a trawl ∼ *n* **:** large cone-shaped net — **trawl·er** *n*

tray *n* **:** shallow flat-bottomed receptacle for holding or carrying something

treach·er·ous *adj* **:** disloyal or dangerous — **treach·er·ous·ly** *adv*

treach·ery *n* **:** betrayal of a trust

tread *vb* (**trod; trod·den/trod**) **1 :** step on or over **2 :** walk **3 :** press or crush with the feet ∼ *n* **1 :** way of walking **2 :** sound made in walking **3 :** part on which a thing runs

trea·son *n* **:** attempt to overthrow the government — **trea·son·able** *adj* — **trea·son·ous** *adj*

trea·sure *n* **1 :** wealth stored up **2 :** something of great value ∼ *vb* **:** keep as precious

trea·sury *n* **:** place or office for keeping and distributing funds — **trea·sur·er** *n*

treat *vb* **1 :** have as a topic **2 :** pay for the food or entertainment of **3 :** act toward or regard in a certain way **4 :** give medical care to ∼ *n* **1 :** food or entertainment paid for by another **2 :** something special and enjoyable — **treat·ment** *n*

trea·ty *n* **:** agreement between governments

tree *n* **:** tall woody plant ∼ *vb* **:** force up a tree — **tree·less** *adj*

trem·ble *vb* **1 :** shake from fear or cold **2 :** move or sound as if shaken

tre·men·dous *adj* **:** amazingly large, powerful, or excellent — **tre·men·dous·ly** *adv*

trench *n* **:** long narrow cut in land

trend *n* **:** prevailing tendency, direction, or style ∼ *vb* **:** move in a particular direction — **trendy** *adj*

tres·pass *n* **1 :** sin **2 :** unauthorized entry onto someone's property ∼ *vb* **1 :** sin **2 :** enter illegally — **tres·pass·er** *n*

tri·al *n* **1 :** hearing and judgment of a matter in court **2 :** source of great annoyance **3 :** test use or experimental effort — **trial** *adj*

tri·an·gle *n* **:** plane figure with 3 sides and 3 angles — **tri·an·gu·lar** *adj*

tribe *n* **:** social group of numerous families — **trib·al** *adj* — **tribes·man** *n* — **tribes·peo·ple** *n pl*

trib·ute *n* **1 :** payment to acknowledge submission **2 :** tax **3 :** gift or act showing respect

trick *n* **1 :** scheme to deceive **2 :** prank **3 :** deceptive or ingenious feat **4 :** mannerism **5 :** knack **6 :** tour of duty ∼ *vb* **:** deceive by cunning — **trick·ery** *n* — **trick·ster** *n*

trick·le *vb* **:** run in drops or a thin stream — **trickle** *n*

tricky *adj* **1 :** inclined to trickery **2 :** requiring skill or caution

tri·cy·cle *n* **:** 3-wheeled bicycle

tri·fle *n* **:** something of little value or importance ∼ *vb* **1 :** speak or act in a playful or flirting way **2 :** toy — **tri·fler** *n* — **tri·fling** *adj*

trig·ger *n* **:** finger-piece of a firearm lock that fires the gun ∼ *vb* **:** set into motion — **trig·ger** *adj* — **trig·gered** *adj*

tril·lion *n* **:** 1000 billions — **tril·lion** *adj* — **tril·lionth** *adj or n*

trim *vb* **1 :** decorate **2 :** make neat or reduce by cutting ∼ *adj* **:** neat and compact ∼ *n* **1 :** state or condition **2 :** ornaments — **trim·ly** *adv* — **trim·mer** *n* — **trim·ming** *n*

Trin·i·ty *n* **:** divine unity of Father, Son, and Holy Spirit

trio *n* **1 :** music for 3 performers **2 :** group of 3

trip *vb* **1 :** step lightly **2 :** stumble or cause to stumble **3 :** make or cause to make a mistake **4 :** release (as a spring or switch) ∼ *n* **1**

: journey **2** : stumble **3** : drug-induced experience

tri·ple *vb* : make 3 times as great ∼ *n* : group of 3 ∼ *adj* **1** : having 3 units **2** : being 3 times as great or as many

trip·let *n* **1** : group of 3 **2** : one of 3 offspring born together

tri·umph *n* **1** : victory or great success ∼ *vb* : obtain or celebrate victory — **tri·um·phal** *adj* — **tri·um·phant** *adj* — **tri·um·phant·ly** *adv*

triv·i·al *adj* : of little importance — **triv·i·al·i·ty** *n*

trod *past of* TREAD

trodden *past part of* TREAD

trol·ley *n* : streetcar run by overhead electric wires

troop *n* **1** : cavalry unit **2** *pl* : soldiers **3** : collection of people or things ∼ *vb* : move or gather in crowds

troop·er *n* **1** : cavalry soldier **2** : police officer on horseback or state police officer

tro·phy *n* : prize gained by a victory

trop·ic *n* **1** : either of the 2 parallels of latitude one 23½ degrees north of the equator (**tropic of Cancer**) and one 23½ degrees south of the equator (**tropic of Cap·ri·corn**) **2** *pl* : region lying between the tropics — **tropic, trop·i·cal** *adj*

trou·ble *vb* **1** : disturb **2** : afflict **3** : make an effort ∼ *n* **1** : cause of mental or physical distress **2** : effort — **trou·ble·mak·er** *n* — **trou·ble·some** *adj* — **trou·ble·some·ly** *adv*

trou·sers *n pl* : long pants — **trouser** *adj*

truce *n* : agreement to halt fighting

truck *n* **1** : wheeled frame for moving heavy objects **2** : automotive vehicle for transporting heavy loads ∼ *vb* : transport on a truck — **truck·er** *n* — **truck·load** *n*

trudge *vb* : walk or march steadily and with difficulty

true *adj* **1** : loyal **2** : in agreement with fact or reality **3** : genuine ∼ *adv* **1** : truthfully **2** : accurately ∼ *vb* : make balanced or even — **tru·ly** *adv*

trum·pet *n* : tubular brass wind instrument with a flaring end ∼ *vb* **1** : blow a trumpet **2** : proclaim loudly — **trum·pet·er** *n*

trunk *n* **1** : main part (as of a body or tree) **2** : long muscular nose of an elephant **3** : storage chest **4** : storage space in a car **5** *pl* : shorts

trust *n* **1** : reliance on another **2** : assured

hope **3** : credit **4** : property held or managed in behalf of another **5** : combination of firms that reduces competition **6** : something entrusted to another's care **7** : custody ∼ *vb* **1** : depend **2** : hope **3** : entrust **4** : have faith in — **trust·ful** *adj* — **trust·ful·ly** *adv* — **trust·ful·ness** *n* — **trust·worth·i·ness** *n* — **trust·wor·thy** *adj*

truth *n* **1** : real state of things **2** : true or accepted statement **3** : agreement with fact or reality — **truth·ful** *adj* — **truth·ful·ly** *adv* — **truth·ful·ness** *n*

try *vb* **1** : conduct the trial of **2** : put to a test **3** : strain **4** : make an effort at ∼ *n* : act of trying

try·out *n* : competitive test of performance esp. for athletes or actors — **try out** *vb*

tsar *var of* CZAR

T–shirt *n* : collarless pullover shirt with short sleeves

tub *n* **1** : wide bucketlike vessel **2** : bathtub

tube *n* **1** : hollow cylinder **2** : round container from which a substance can be squeezed **3** : airtight circular tube of rubber inside a tire — **tubed** *adj* — **tube·less** *adj* — **tu·bu·lar** *adj*

tuck *vb* **1** : pull up into a fold **2** : put into a snug often concealing place **3** : make snug in bed — used with *in* ∼ *n* : fold in a cloth

Tues·day *n* : 3d day of the week

tuft *n* : clump (as of hair or feathers) — **tuft·ed** *adj*

tug *vb* **1** : pull hard **2** : move by pulling ∼ *n* : act of tugging

tug–of–war *n* (**tugs–of–war**) : pulling contest between 2 teams

tu·ition *n* : cost of instruction

tu·lip *n* : herb with cup-shaped flowers

tum·ble *vb* **1** : perform gymnastic feats of rolling and turning **2** : fall or cause to fall suddenly **3** : toss ∼ *n* : act of tumbling

tum·my *n* : belly

tu·mor *n* : abnormal and useless growth of tissue — **tu·mor·ous** *adj*

tu·mult *n* **1** : uproar **2** : violent agitation of mind or feelings — **tu·mul·tu·ous** *adj*

tu·na *n* : large seafood fish

tune *n* **1** : melody **2** : correct musical pitch **3** : harmonious relationship ∼ *vb* **1** : bring or come into harmony **2** : adjust in musical pitch **3** : adjust a receiver so as to receive a broadcast **4** : put in first-class working order — **tun·able** *adj* — **tune·ful** *adj* — **tun·er** *n*

tun·nel *n* : underground passageway ∼ *vb* : make a tunnel through or under something

tur·bine *n* : engine turned by the force of gas or water on fan blades

tur·bu·lent *adj* **1** : causing violence or disturbance **2** : marked by agitation or tumult — **tur·bu·lence** *n* — **tur·bu·lent·ly** *adv*

turf *n* : upper layer of soil bound by grass and roots

tur·key *n* : large American bird raised for food

turn *vb* **1** : move or cause to move around an axis **2** : twist (a mechanical part) to operate **3** : wrench **4** : cause to face or move in a different direction **5** : reverse the sides or surfaces of **6** : upset **7** : go around **8** : become or cause to become **9** : seek aid from a source ∼ *n* **1** : act or instance of turning **2** : change **3** : place at which something turns **4** : place, time, or opportunity to do something in order — **turn·er** *n* — **turn down** *vb* : decline to accept — **turn in** *vb* **1** : deliver or report to authorities **2** : go to bed — **turn off** *vb* : stop the functioning of — **turn out** *vb* **1** : expel **2** : produce **3** : come together **4** : prove to be in the end — **turn over** *vb* : transfer — **turn up** *vb* **1** : discover or appear **2** : happen unexpectedly

turn·out *n* **1** : gathering of people for a special purpose **2** : size of a gathering

turn·over *n* **1** : upset or reversal **2** : filled pastry **3** : volume of business **4** : movement (as of goods or people) into, through, and out of a place

turn·pike *n* : expressway on which tolls are charged

tur·tle *n* : reptile with the trunk enclosed in a bony shell

tur·tle·neck *n* : high close-fitting collar that can be turned over or a sweater or shirt with this collar

tu·tor *n* : private teacher ∼ *vb* : teach usu. individually

TV *n* : television

tweak *vb* : pinch and pull playfully — **tweak** *n*

tweed *n* **1** : rough woolen fabric **2** *pl* : tweed clothing — **tweedy** *adj*

tweet *n* : chirping note — **tweet** *vb*

twee·zers *n pl* : small pincerlike tool

twelve *n* **1** : one more than 11 **2** : 12th in a set or series **3** : something having 12 units — **twelfth** *adj or n* — **twelve** *adj or pron*

twen·ty *n* : 2 times 10 — **twen·ti·eth** *adj or n* — **twenty** *adj or pron*

twen·ty–twen·ty, 20–20 *adj* : being vision of normal sharpness

twice *adv* **1** : on 2 occasions **2** : 2 times

twig *n* : small branch — **twig·gy** *adj*

twi·light *n* : light from the sky at dusk or dawn — **twi·light** *adj*

twin *n* : either of 2 offspring born together ∼ *adj* **1** : born with one another or as a pair at one birth **2** : made up of 2 similar parts

twine *n* : strong twisted thread ∼ *vb* **1** : twist together **2** : coil about a support — **twin·er** *n* — **twiny** *adj*

twinge *vb* : affect with or feel a sudden sharp pain ∼ *n* : sudden sharp stab (as of pain)

twin·kle *vb* : shine with a flickering light ∼ *n* **1** : wink **2** : intermittent shining — **twin·kler** *n*

twirl *vb* : whirl round ∼ *n* **1** : act of twirling **2** : coil — **twirl·er** *n*

twist *vb* **1** : unite by winding (threads) together **2** : wrench **3** : move in or have a spiral shape **4** : follow a winding course ∼ *n* **1** : act or result of twisting **2** : unexpected development

twist·er *n* : tornado

twit *n* : fool

twitch *vb* : move or pull with a sudden motion ∼ *n* : act of twitching

twit·ter *vb* : make chirping noises ∼ *n* : small intermittent noise

two *n* **1** : one more than one **2** : the 2d in a set or series **3** : something having 2 units — **two** *adj or pron*

two·fold *adj* : double — **two·fold** *adv*

two·some *n* : couple

tying *pres part of* TIE

type *n* **1** : class, kind, or group set apart by common characteristics **2** : special design of printed letters ∼ *vb* **1** : write with a typewriter **2** : identify or classify as a particular type

typ·i·cal *adj* : having the essential characteristics of a group — **typ·i·cal·i·ty** *n* — **typ·i·cal·ly** *adv* — **typ·i·cal·ness** *n*

typ·i·fy *vb* : be typical of

tyr·an·ny *n* : unjust use of absolute governmental power — **ty·ran·ni·cal** *adj* — **ty·ran·ni·cal·ly** *adv* — **tyr·an·nize** *vb*

ty·rant *n* : harsh ruler having absolute power

tzar *var of* CZAR

U

u *n* : 21st letter of the alphabet

ug·ly *adj* **1** : offensive to look at **2** : mean or quarrelsome — **ug·li·ness** *n*

uku·le·le *n* : small 4-string guitar

ul·cer *n* : eroded sore — **ul·cer·ate** *vb* — **ul·cer·a·tion** *n* — **ul·cer·ous** *adj*

ul·ti·mate *adj* : final, maximum, or extreme — **ultimate** *n* — **ul·ti·mate·ly** *adv*

ul·ti·ma·tum *n* : final proposition or demand carrying or implying a threat

um·brel·la *n* : collapsible fabric device to protect from sun or rain

um·pire *n* **1** : arbitrator **2** : sport official — **um·pire** *vb*

un·ac·cept·able *adj* : not acceptable or pleasing — **un·ac·cept·ably** *adv*

un·af·fect·ed *adj* **1** : not influenced or changed by something **2** : natural and sincere — **un·af·fect·ed·ly** *adv*

unan·i·mous *adj* **1** : showing no disagreement **2** : formed with the agreement of all — **una·nim·i·ty** *n* — **unan·i·mous·ly** *adv*

un·armed *adj* : not armed or armored

un·at·tached *adj* **1** : not attached **2** : not married or engaged

un·aware *adv* : unawares ∼ *adj* : not aware

un·awares *adv* **1** : without warning **2** : unintentionally

un·bal·anced *adj* **1** : not balanced **2** : mentally unstable

un·beat·en *adj* : not beaten

un·be·liev·able *adj* **1** : improbable **2** : superlative — **un·be·liev·ably** *adv*

un·bro·ken *adj* **1** : not damaged **2** : not interrupted

un·buck·le *vb* : unfasten the buckle of

un·but·ton *vb* : unfasten the buttons of

un·called–for *adj* : too harsh or rude for the occasion

un·cer·tain *adj* **1** : not determined, sure, or definitely known **2** : subject to chance or change — **un·cer·tain·ly** *adv* — **un·cer·tain·ty** *n*

un·cle *n* **1** : brother of one's father or mother **2** : husband of one's aunt

un·clean *adj* : not clean or pure — **un·clean·ness** *n*

un·com·mon *adj* **1** : rare **2** : superior — **un·com·mon·ly** *adv*

un·con·cerned *adj* **1** : disinterested **2** : not anxious or upset — **un·con·cerned·ly** *adv*

un·con·di·tion·al *adj* : not limited in any way — **un·con·di·tion·al·ly** *adv*

un·con·scious *adj* **1** : not awake or aware of one's surroundings **2** : not consciously done ∼ *n* : part of one's mental life that one is not aware of — **un·con·scious·ly** *adv* — **un·con·scious·ness** *n*

un·con·trol·la·ble *adj* : incapable of being controlled — **un·con·trol·la·bly** *adv*

un·cov·er *vb* **1** : reveal **2** : expose by removing a covering

un·cut *adj* **1** : not cut down, into, off, or apart **2** : not shaped by cutting **3** : not abridged

un·de·ni·able *adj* : plainly true — **un·de·ni·ably** *adv*

un·der *adv* : below or beneath something ∼ *prep* **1** : lower than and sheltered by **2** : below the surface of **3** : covered or concealed by **4** : subject to the authority of **5** : less than ∼ *adj* **1** : lying below or beneath **2** : subordinate **3** : less than usual, proper, or desired

un·der·age *adj* : of less than legal age

un·der·clothes *n pl* : underwear

un·der·cloth·ing *n* : underwear

un·der·cov·er *adj* : employed or engaged in secret investigation

un·der·de·vel·oped *adj* : not normally or adequately developed esp. economically

un·der·dog *n* : contestant given least chance of winning

un·der·es·ti·mate *vb* : estimate too low

un·der·feed *vb* : feed inadequately

un·der·foot *adv* **1** : under the feet **2** : in the way of another

un·der·go *vb* **1** : endure **2** : go through (as an experience)

un·der·grad·u·ate *n* : university or college student

un·der·ground *adv* **1** : beneath the surface of the earth **2** : in secret ∼ *adj* **1** : being or growing under the surface of the ground **2** : secret ∼ *n* : secret political movement or group

un·der·hand *adv or adj* **1** : with secrecy and deception **2** : with the hand kept below the waist

un·der·line *vb* **1** : draw a line under **2** : stress — **underline** *n*

un·der·mine *vb* **1** : excavate beneath **2** : weaken or wear away secretly or gradually

un·der·neath *prep* : directly under ∼ *adv* **1** : below a surface or object **2** : on the lower side

un·der·pants *n pl* : short undergarment for the lower trunk

un·der·priv·i·leged *adj* : poor

un·der·rate *vb* : rate or value too low

un·der·sea *adj* : being, carried on, or used beneath the surface of the sea ∼ *adv* **un·der·seas** : beneath the surface of the sea

un·der·shirt *n* : shirt worn as underwear

un·der·shorts *n pl* : short underpants

un·der·side *n* : side or surface lying underneath

un·der·stand *vb* **1** : be aware of the meaning of **2** : deduce **3** : have a sympathetic attitude — **un·der·stand·able** *adj* — **un·der·stand·ably** *adv*

un·der·stand·ing *n* **1** : intelligence **2** : ability to comprehend and judge **3** : mutual agreement ∼ *adj* : sympathetic

un·der·stood *adj* **1** : agreed upon **2** : implicit

un·der·take *vb* **1** : attempt (a task) or assume (a responsibility) **2** : guarantee — **un·der·tak·ing** *n*

un·der·tak·er *n* : one in the funeral business

un·der·wa·ter *adj* : being or used below the surface of the water — **underwater** *adv*

under way *adv* : in motion or in progress

un·der·wear *n* : clothing worn next to the skin and under ordinary clothes

un·der·write *vb* **1** : provide insurance for **2** : guarantee financial support of — **un·der·writ·er** *n*

un·dies *n pl* : underwear

un·do *vb* **1** : unfasten **2** : reverse **3** : ruin — **un·do·ing** *n*

un·dress *vb* : remove one's clothes ∼ *n* : state of being naked

un·due *adj* : excessive — **un·du·ly** *adv*

un·dy·ing *adj* : immortal or perpetual

un·earth *vb* : dig up or discover

un·easy *adj* **1** : awkward or embarrassed **2** : disturbed or worried — **un·eas·i·ly** *adv* — **un·eas·i·ness** *n*

un·em·ployed *adj* : not having a job — **un·em·ploy·ment** *n*

un·equal *adj* : not equal or uniform — **un·equal·ly** *adv*

un·equiv·o·cal *adj* : leaving no doubt — **un·equiv·o·cal·ly** *adv*

un·even *adj* **1** : not smooth **2** : not regular or consistent — **un·even·ly** *adv* — **un·even·ness** *n*

un·event·ful *adj* : lacking interesting or noteworthy incidents — **un·event·ful·ly** *adv*

un·ex·pect·ed *adj* : not expected — **un·ex·pect·ed·ly** *adv*

un·fair *adj* : marked by injustice, partiality, or deception — **un·fair·ly** *adv*

un·faith·ful *adj* : not loyal — **un·faith·ful·ly** *adv* — **un·faith·ful·ness** *n*

un·fa·mil·iar *adj* **1** : not well known **2** : not acquainted — **un·fa·mil·iar·i·ty** *n*

un·fas·ten *vb* : release a catch or lock

un·fav·or·able *adj* : not pleasing, advantageous, or agreeable — **un·fav·or·ably** *adv*

un·fit *adj* : not suitable — **un·fit·ness** *n*

un·fold *vb* **1** : open the folds of **2** : reveal **3** : develop

un·for·get·ta·ble *adj* : memorable — **un·for·get·ta·bly** *adv*

un·for·tu·nate *adj* **1** : not lucky or successful **2** : deplorable — **un·for·tu·nate** *n* — **un·for·tu·nate·ly** *adv*

un·found·ed *adj* : lacking a sound basis

un·friend·ly *adj* : not friendly or kind — **un·friend·li·ness** *n*

un·grate·ful *adj* : not thankful for favors — **un·grate·ful·ly** *adv* — **un·grate·ful·ness** *n*

un·hap·py *adj* **1** : unfortunate **2** : sad — **un·hap·pi·ly** *adv* — **un·hap·pi·ness** *n*

un·healthy *adj* **1** : not wholesome **2** : not well

un·heard—of *adj* : not known or experienced before

un·hinge *vb* **1** : take from the hinges **2** : make unstable esp. mentally

un·ho·ly *adj* : sinister or shocking — **un·ho·li·ness** *n*

uni·form *adj* : not changing or showing any variation ∼ *n* : distinctive dress worn by members of a particular group — **uni·for·mi·ty** *n* — **uni·form·ly** *adv*

uni·fy *vb* : make into a coherent whole — **uni·fi·ca·tion** *n*

un·in·hib·it·ed *adj* : free of restraint — **un·in·hib·it·ed·ly** *adv*

un·in·ten·tion·al *adj* : not done willingly — **un·in·ten·tion·al·ly** *adv*

un·in·ter·est·ing *adj* : not interesting — **un·in·ter·est·ing·ly** *adv*

union *n* **1 :** act or instance of joining two or more things into one or the state of being so joined **2 :** confederation of nations or states **3 :** organization of workers (**labor union, trade union**) — **union·ize** *vb* — **union·i·za·tion** *n*

unique *adj* **1 :** being the only one of its kind **2 :** very unusual — **unique·ly** *adv* — **unique·ness** *n*

unit *n* **1 :** smallest whole number **2 :** definite amount or quantity used as a standard of measurement **3 :** single part of a whole — **unit** *adj*

unite *vb* **:** put or join together

uni·ty *n* **1 :** quality or state of being united or a unit **2 :** harmony

uni·ver·sal *adj* **1 :** relating to or affecting everyone or everything **2 :** present or occurring everywhere — **uni·ver·sal·ly** *adv*

uni·verse *n* **:** the complete system of all things that exist

uni·ver·si·ty *n* **:** institution of higher learning

un·kind *adj* **:** not kind or sympathetic — **un·kind·li·ness** *n* — **un·kind·ly** *adv* — **un·kind·ness** *n*

un·law·ful *adj* **:** illegal — **un·law·ful·ly** *adv*

un·less *conj* **:** except on condition that

un·like *adj* **1 :** not similar **2 :** not equal ~ *prep* **:** different from — **un·like·ly** *adv* — **un·like·ness** *n* — **un·like·li·hood** *n*

un·load *vb* **1 :** take (cargo) from a vehicle, vessel, or plane **2 :** take a load from **3 :** discard

un·lock *vb* **1 :** unfasten through release of a lock **2 :** release or reveal

un·lucky *adj* **1 :** experiencing bad luck **2 :** likely to bring misfortune — **un·luck·i·ly** *adv*

un·married *adj* **:** not married

un·mis·tak·able *adj* **:** not capable of being mistaken or misunderstood — **un·mis·tak·ably** *adv*

un·nat·u·ral *adj* **1 :** not natural or spontaneous **2 :** abnormal — **un·nat·u·ral·ly** *adv* — **un·nat·u·ral·ness** *n*

un·oc·cu·pied *adj* **1 :** not busy **2 :** not occupied

un·pack *vb* **1 :** remove (things packed) from a container **2 :** remove the contents of (a package)

un·pleas·ant *adj* **:** not pleasing or agreeable

un·plug *vb* **1 :** remove a clog or plug in **2 :** disconnect from an electric circuit by removing a plug

un·re·al *adj* **:** not real or genuine — **un·re·al·i·ty** *n*

un·roll *vb* **1 :** unwind a roll of **2 :** become unrolled

un·ruly *adj* **:** not readily controlled or disciplined — **un·rul·i·ness** *n*

un·sci·en·tif·ic *adj* **:** not in accord with the principles and methods of science

un·screw *vb* **:** loosen or remove by withdrawing screws or by turning

un·self·ish *adj* **:** generous — **un·sef·ish·ly** *adv*

un·set·tle *vb* **:** disturb — **un·set·tled** *adj*

un·sta·ble *adj* **1 :** not mentally or physically balanced **2 :** tending to change

un·stop·pa·ble *adj* **:** not capable of being stopped

un·tan·gle *vb* **1 :** free from a state of being tangled **2 :** find a solution to

un·think·able *adj* **:** not to be thought of or considered possible

un·tidy *adj* **:** not neat or orderly

un·tie *vb* **:** open by releasing ties

un·til *prep* **:** up to the time of ~ *conj* **:** to the time that

un·to *prep* **:** to

un·used *adj* **1 :** not accustomed **2 :** not used

un·usu·al *adj* **:** not usual or common — **un·usu·al·ly** *adv*

un·well *adj* **:** sick

un·wind *vb* **1 :** undo something that is wound **2 :** become unwound **3 :** relax

un·wrap *vb* **:** remove the wrappings from

un·writ·ten *adj* **:** made or passed on only in speech or through tradition

un·zip *vb* **:** zip open

up *adv* **1 :** in or to a higher position or level **2 :** from beneath a surface or level **3 :** in or into an upright position **4 :** out of bed **5 :** to or with greater intensity **6 :** into existence, evidence, or knowledge **7 :** away **8** — used to indicate a degree of success, completion, or finality ~ *adj* **1 :** in the state of having risen **2 :** raised to or at a higher level **3 :** moving, inclining, or directed upward **4 :** in a state of greater intensity **5 :** at an end ~ *vb* **1 up; upped :** act abruptly **2 upped; upped :** move or cause to move upward ~ *prep* **1 :** to, toward, or at a higher point of **2 :** along or toward the beginning of

up·date *vb* **:** bring up to date — **up·date** *n*

up·grade *n* **1 :** upward slope **2 :** increase ~ *vb* **:** raise to a higher position

up·hill *adv* **:** upward on a hill or incline ~ *adj* **1 :** going up **2 :** difficult

up·hold *vb* : support or defend — **up·hold·er** *n*

up·keep *n* : act or cost of keeping up or maintaining

up·on *prep* : on

up·per *adj* : higher in position, rank, or order ∼ *n* : top part of a shoe

up·right *adj* **1** : vertical **2** : erect in posture **3** : morally correct ∼ *n* : something that stands upright — **up·right** *adv* — **up·right·ly** *adv* — **up·right·ness** *n*

up·ris·ing *n* : revolt

up·roar *n* : state of commotion or violent disturbance

up·roar·i·ous *adj* **1** : marked by uproar **2** : extremely funny — **up·roar·i·ous·ly** *adv*

up·root *vb* : remove by or as if by pulling up by the roots

up·set *vb* **1** : force or be forced out of the usual position **2** : disturb emotionally or physically ∼ *n* **1** : act of throwing into disorder **2** : minor physical disorder ∼ *adj* : emotionally disturbed or agitated

up·side down *adv* **1** : turned so that the upper and lower parts are reversed **2** : in or into confusion or disorder — **up·side–down** *adj*

up·stairs *adv* : up the stairs or to the next floor ∼ *adj* : situated on the floor above ∼ *n sing or pl* : part of a building above the ground floor

up·tight *adj* **1** : tense **2** : angry **3** : rigidly conventional

up–to–date *adj* : current — **up–to–date·ness** *n*

up·town *n* : upper part of a town or city — **up·town** *adj or adv*

up·ward, up·wards *adv* **1** : in a direction from lower to higher **2** : toward a higher or greater state or number ∼ *adj* : directed toward or situated in a higher place — **up·ward·ly** *adv*

ur·ban *adj* : characteristic of a city

ur·bane *adj* : polished in manner — **ur·ban·i·ty** *n*

ur·ban·ite *n* : city dweller

ur·chin *n* : mischievous youngster

urge *vb* **1** : earnestly plead for or insist on (an action) **2** : try to persuade **3** : impel to a course of activity ∼ *n* : force or impulse that moves one to action

ur·gent *adj* **1** : calling for immediate attention **2** : urging insistently — **ur·gen·cy** *n* — **ur·gent·ly** *adv*

urine *n* : liquid waste material from the kidneys — **uri·nary** *adj*

URL *n* : address on the Internet

urn *n* **1** : vaselike or cuplike vessel on a pedestal **2** : large coffee pot

us *pron, objective case of* WE

us·age *n* **1** : customary practice **2** : way of doing or of using something

use *n* **1** : act or practice of putting something into action **2** : state of being used **3** : way of using **4** : privilege, ability, or power to use something **5** : utility or function **6** : occasion or need to use ∼ *vb* **1** : put into action or service **2** : consume **3** : behave toward **4** : to make use of **5** — used in the past tense with *to* to indicate a former practice — **us·abil·i·ty** *n* — **us·able** *adj* — **use·ful** *adj* — **use·ful·ly** *adv* — **use·ful·ness** *n* — **use·less** *adj* — **use·less·ly** *adv* — **use·less·ness** *n* — **us·er** *n*

used *adj* **1** : not new **2** : accustomed — used with *to*

usu·al *adj* : being what is expected according to custom or habit — **usu·al·ly** *adv*

uten·sil *n* **1** : eating or cooking tool **2** : useful tool

util·i·ty *n* **1** : usefulness **2** : regulated business providing a public service (as electricity)

uti·lize *vb* : make use of — **uti·li·za·tion** *n*

ut·most *adj* **1** : most distant **2** : of the greatest or highest degree or amount — **utmost** *n*

ut·ter *adj* : absolute ∼ *vb* : express with the voice — **ut·ter·ance** *n* — **ut·ter·er** *n* — **ut·ter·ly** *adv*

V

v *n* : 22d letter of the alphabet

va·cant *adj* **1** : not occupied, filled, or in use **2** : devoid of thought or expression — **va·can·cy** *n* — **va·cant·ly** *adv*

va·cate *vb* **1** : annul **2** : leave unfilled or unoccupied

va·ca·tion *n* : period of rest from routine — **va·ca·tion** *vb* — **va·ca·tion·er** *n*

vac·ci·nate *vb* : administer a vaccine usu. by injection — **vac·ci·na·tion** *n*

vac·cine *n* : substance to induce immunity to a disease

vac·u·um *n* : empty space with no air ∼ *vb* : clean with a machine (**vacuum cleaner**) that cleans by suction

va·gi·na *n* : canal that leads out from the uterus — **vag·i·nal** *adj*

vague *adj* : not clear, definite, or distinct — **vague·ly** *adv* — **vague·ness** *n*

vain *adj* 1 : of no value 2 : not successful 3 : conceited — **vain·ly** *adv*

vale·dic·to·ri·an *n* : student giving the farewell address at commencement — **vale·dic·to·ry** *adj or n*

val·en·tine *n* : sweetheart or a card sent to a sweetheart or friend on St. Valentine's Day

val·id *adj* 1 : proper and legally binding 2 : founded on truth or fact — **va·lid·i·ty** *n* — **val·id·ly** *adv*

val·i·date *vb* : establish as valid — **val·i·da·tion** *n*

val·ley *n* : long depression between ranges of hills

val·or *n* : bravery or heroism — **val·or·ous** *adj*

valu·able *adj* 1 : worth a lot of money 2 : being of great importance or use — **valuable** *n*

val·ue *n* 1 : fair return or equivalent for something exchanged 2 : how much something is worth 3 : distinctive quality (as of a color or sound) 4 : guiding principle or ideal — usu. pl. ∼ *vb* 1 : estimate the worth of 2 : appreciate the importance of — **val·ue·less** *adj* — **val·u·er** *n*

valve *n* : structure or device to control flow of a liquid or gas — **valved** *adj* — **valve·less** *adj*

vam·pire *n* 1 : legendary night-wandering dead body that sucks human blood 2 : bat that feeds on the blood of animals

van *n* : enclosed truck

van·dal *n* : person who willfully defaces or destroys property — **van·dal·ism** *n* — **van·dal·ize** *vb*

vane *n* : bladelike device designed to be moved by force of the air or water

van·guard *n* 1 : troops moving at the front of an army 2 : forefront of an action or movement

va·nil·la *n* : a flavoring made from the pods of a tropical orchid or this orchid

van·ish *vb* : disappear suddenly

van·i·ty *n* 1 : futility or something that is futile 2 : undue pride in oneself 3 : makeup case or table

va·por *n* 1 : fine separated particles floating in and clouding the air 2 : gaseous form of an ordinarily liquid substance — **va·por·ize** *vb* — **va·por·i·za·tion** *n* — **va·por·iz·er** *n* — **va·por·ous** *adj*

vari·able *adj* : apt to vary — **var·i·abil·i·ty** *n* — **var·i·able** *n* — **var·i·ably** *adv*

vari·a·tion *n* : instance or extent of varying

var·ied *adj* : showing variety — **var·ied·ly** *adv*

va·ri·ety *n* 1 : state of being different 2 : collection of different things 3 : something that differs from others of its kind

var·i·ous *adj* : being many and unlike — **var·i·ous·ly** *adv*

var·nish *n* : liquid that dries to a hard glossy protective coating ∼ *vb* : cover with varnish

var·si·ty *n* : principal team representing a school

vary *vb* 1 : alter 2 : make or be of different kinds

vase *n* : tall usu. ornamental container to hold flowers

vast *adj* : very great in size, extent, or amount — **vast·ly** *adv* — **vast·ness** *n*

¹vault *n* 1 : masonry arch 2 : usu. underground storage or burial room ∼ *vb* : form or cover with a vault — **vault·ed** *adj* — **vaulty** *adj*

²vault *vb* : spring over esp. with the help of the hands or a pole ∼ *n* : act of vaulting — **vault·er** *n*

VCR *n* : a device that records and plays videotapes

veg·e·ta·ble *adj* 1 : relating to or obtained from plants 2 : like that of a plant ∼ *n* 1 : plant 2 : plant grown for food

veg·e·tar·i·an *n* : person who eats no meat — **veg·e·tar·i·an** *adj* — **veg·e·tar·i·an·ism** *n*

veg·e·ta·tion *n* : plant life — **veg·e·ta·tion·al** *adj* — **veg·e·ta·tive** *adj*

ve·hi·cle *n* 1 : medium through which something is expressed, applied, or administered 2 : structure for transporting something esp. on wheels — **ve·hic·u·lar** *adj*

veil *n* 1 : sheer material to hide something or to cover the face and head 2 : something that hides ∼ *vb* : cover with a veil

vein *n* 1 : rock fissure filled with deposited mineral matter 2 : vessel that carries blood toward the heart 3 : sap-carrying tube in a leaf 4 : distinctive element or style of expression — **veined** *adj*

vel·vet *n* : fabric with a short soft pile — **vel·vet** *adj* — **vel·vety** *adj*

vend *vb* : sell — **vend·ible** *adj* — **ven·dor** *n*

ven·geance *n* : punishment in retaliation for an injury or offense

venge·ful *adj* : filled with a desire for revenge — **venge·ful·ly** *adv*

ven·om *n* **1** : poison secreted by certain animals **2** : ill will — **ven·om·ous** *adj*

vent *vb* **1** : provide with or let out at a vent **2** : give expression to ∼ *n* : opening for passage or for relieving pressure

ven·ti·late *vb* : allow fresh air to circulate through — **ven·ti·la·tion** *n* — **ven·ti·la·tor** *n*

ven·ture *vb* **1** : risk or take a chance on **2** : put forward (an opinion) ∼ *n* : speculative business enterprise

ven·ture·some *adj* : brave or daring — **ven·ture·some·ly** *adv* — **ven·ture·some·ness** *n*

verb *n* : word that expresses action or existence

ver·bal *adj* **1** : having to do with or expressed in words **2** : oral **3** : relating to or formed from a verb — **ver·bal·i·za·tion** *n* — **ver·bal·ize** *vb* — **ver·bal·ly** *adv*

verbal auxiliary *n* : auxiliary verb

ver·dict *n* : decision of a jury

ver·i·fy *vb* : establish the truth, accuracy, or reality of — **ver·i·fi·able** *adj* — **ver·i·fi·ca·tion** *n*

ver·min *n* (**vermin**) : small animal pest

ver·sa·tile *adj* : having many abilities or uses — **ver·sa·til·i·ty** *n*

verse *n* **1** : line or stanza of poetry **2** : poetry **3** : short division of a chapter in the Bible

ver·sion *n* **1** : translation of the Bible **2** : account or description from a particular point of view

ver·sus *prep* : opposed to or against

ver·te·brate *n* : animal with a backbone — **verte·brate** *adj*

ver·ti·cal *adj* : rising straight up from a level surface — **vertical** *n* — **ver·ti·cal·i·ty** *n* — **ver·ti·cal·ly** *adv*

very *adj* **1** : exact **2** : exactly suitable **3** : mere or bare **4** : precisely the same ∼ *adv* **1** : to a high degree **2** : in actual fact

ves·pers *n pl* : late afternoon or evening worship service

ves·sel *n* **1** : a container (as a barrel, bottle, bowl, or cup) for a liquid **2** : craft for navigation esp. on water **3** : tube in which a body fluid is circulated

¹vest *vb* **1** : give a particular authority, right, or property to **2** : clothe with or as if with a garment

²vest *n* : sleeveless garment usu. worn under a suit coat

vet·er·an *n* **1** : former member of the armed forces **2** : person with long experience — **vet·eran** *adj*

Veterans Day *n* : 4th Monday in October or formerly November 11 observed as a legal holiday in commemoration of the end of war in 1918 and 1945

vet·er·i·nar·i·an *n* : doctor of animals — **vet·er·i·nary** *adj*

ve·to *n* **1** : power to forbid and esp. the power of a chief executive to prevent a bill from becoming law **2** : exercise of the veto ∼ *vb* **1** : forbid **2** : reject a legislative bill

vex *vb* : trouble, distress, or annoy — **vex·a·tion** *n* — **vex·a·tious** *adj*

via *prep* : by way of

vi·brant *adj* **1** : vibrating **2** : pulsing with vigor or activity **3** : sounding from vibration — **vi·bran·cy** *n*

vi·brate *vb* **1** : move or cause to move quickly back and forth or side to side **2** : respond sympathetically — **vi·bra·tion** *n* — **vi·bra·tor** *n* — **vi·bra·tory** *adj*

vice *n* **1** : immoral habit **2** : depravity

vice ver·sa *adv* : with the order reversed

vi·cin·i·ty *n* : surrounding area

vi·cious *adj* **1** : wicked **2** : savage **3** : malicious — **vi·cious·ly** *adv* — **vi·cious·ness** *n*

vic·tim *n* : person killed, hurt, or abused — **vic·tim·i·za·tion** *n* — **vic·tim·ize** *vb* — **vic·tim·iz·er** *n*

vic·tor *n* : winner

vic·to·ry *n* : success in defeating an enemy or opponent or in overcoming difficulties — **vic·to·ri·ous** *adj* — **vic·to·ri·ous·ly** *adv*

vid·eo *adj* : relating to the television image

vid·eo·tape *vb* : make a recording of (a television production) on special tape — **videotape** *n*

vie *vb* : contend — **vi·er** *n*

view *n* **1** : process of seeing or examining **2** : opinion **3** : area of landscape that can be seen **4** : range of vision **5** : purpose or object ∼ *vb* **1** : look at **2** : think about or consider — **view·er** *n*

view·point *n* : position from which something is considered

vigil *n* **1** : day of devotion before a religious feast **2** : act or time of keeping awake **3** : long period of keeping watch (as over a sick or dying person)

vig·i·lant *adj* : alert esp. to avoid danger — **vig·i·lance** *n* — **vig·i·lant·ly** *adv*

vig·or *n* **1** : energy or strength **2** : intensity or force — **vig·or·ous** *adj* — **vig·or·ous·ly** *adv* — **vig·or·ous·ness** *n*

vile *adj* : thoroughly bad or contemptible — **vile·ly** *adv* — **vile·ness** *n*

vil·la *n* : country estate

vil·lage *n* : small country town — **vil·lag·er** *n*

vil·lain *n* : bad person — **vil·lain·ess** *n* — **vil·lain·ous** *adj* — **vil·lain·ous·ly** *adv* — **vil·lain·ous·ness** *n* — **vil·lainy** *n*

vin·di·cate *vb* **1** : avenge **2** : exonerate **3** : justify — **vin·di·ca·tion** *n* — **vin·di·ca·tor** *n*

vin·dic·tive *adj* : seeking or meant for revenge — **vin·dic·tive·ly** *adv* — **vin·dic·tive·ness** *n*

vine *n* : climbing or trailing plant

vin·e·gar *n* : acidic liquid obtained by fermentation — **vin·e·gary** *adj*

vin·tage *n* **1** : season's yield of grapes or wine **2** : period of origin ∼ *adj* : of enduring interest

vi·nyl *n* : strong plastic

vi·o·late *vb* **1** : act with disrespect or disregard of **2** : rape **3** : desecrate — **vi·o·la·tion** *n* — **vi·o·la·tor** *n*

vi·o·lence *n* : intense physical force that causes or is intended to cause injury or destruction — **vi·o·lent** *adj* — **vi·o·lent·ly** *adv*

vi·o·let *n* **1** : small flowering plant **2** : reddish blue

vi·o·lin *n* : bowed stringed instrument — **vi·o·lin·ist** *n*

VIP *n* : very important person

vir·gin *n* **1** : unmarried woman **2** : a person who has never had sexual intercourse ∼ *adj* **1** : chaste **2** : natural and unspoiled — **vir·gin·al** *adj* — **vir·gin·al·ly** *adv* — **vir·gin·i·ty** *n*

vir·tu·al *adj* : being in effect but not in fact or name — **vir·tu·al·ly** *adv*

vir·tue *n* **1** : moral excellence **2** : effective or commendable quality **3** : chastity — **vir·tu·ous** *adj* — **vir·tu·ous·ly** *adv*

vi·rus *n* **1** : tiny disease-causing agent **2** : a computer program that performs a malicious action (as destroying data)

vi·sa *n* : authorization to enter a foreign country

vise *n* : device for clamping something being worked on

vis·i·ble *adj* **1** : capable of being seen **2** : manifest or apparent — **vis·i·bil·i·ty** *n* — **vis·i·bly** *adv*

vi·sion *n* **1** : vivid picture seen in a dream or trance or in the imagination **2** : foresight **3** : power of seeing ∼ *vb* : imagine

vis·it *vb* **1** : go or come to see **2** : stay with for a time as a guest **3** : cause or be a reward, affliction, or punishment ∼ *n* : short stay as a guest — **vis·it·able** *adj* — **vis·i·tor** *n*

vi·sor *n* **1** : front piece of a helmet **2** : part (as on a cap or car windshield) that shades the eyes

vis·ta *n* : distant view

vi·su·al *adj* **1** : relating to sight **2** : visible — **vi·su·al·ly** *adv*

vi·su·al·ize *vb* : form a mental image of — **vi·su·al·i·za·tion** *n* — **vi·su·al·iz·er** *n*

vi·tal *adj* **1** : relating to, necessary for, or characteristic of life **2** : full of life and vigor **3** : fatal **4** : very important — **vi·tal·ly** *adv*

vi·tal·i·ty *n* **1** : life force **2** : energy

vi·ta·min *n* : natural organic substance essential to health

viv·id *adj* **1** : lively **2** : brilliant **3** : intense or sharp — **viv·id·ly** *adv* — **viv·id·ness** *n*

vo·cab·u·lary *n* **1** : list or collection of words **2** : stock of words used by a person or about a subject

vo·cal *adj* **1** : relating to or produced by or for the voice **2** : speaking out freely and usu. emphatically — **vo·cal·ize** *vb*

vo·ca·tion *n* : regular employment — **vo·ca·tion·al** *adj*

voice *n* **1** : sound produced through the mouth by humans and many animals **2** : power of speaking **3** : right of choice or opinion ∼ *vb* : express in words — **voiced** *adj*

voice mail *n* : an electronic system for recording and playing back telephone messages

void *adj* **1** : containing nothing **2** : lacking — with *of* **3** : not legally binding ∼ *n* **1** : empty space **2** : feeling of hollowness ∼ *vb* **1** : discharge (as body waste) **2** : make (as a contract) void — **void·able** *adj* — **void·er** *n*

vol·a·tile *adj* **1** : readily vaporizing at a relatively low temperature **2** : likely to change suddenly — **vol·a·til·i·ty** *n* — **vol·a·til·ize** *vb*

vol·ca·no *n* : opening in the earth's crust from which molten rock and steam come out — **vol·ca·nic** *adj*

vol·ley *n* **1** : flight of missiles (as arrows) **2** : simultaneous shooting of many weapons

vol·ley·ball *n* : game of batting a large ball over a net

volt *n* : unit for measuring the force that moves an electric current — **volt·age** *n*

vol·ume *n* **1** : book **2** : space occupied as measured by cubic units **3** : amount **4** : loudness of a sound

vol·un·tary *adj* **1** : done, made, or given freely and without expecting compensation **2** : relating to or controlled by the will — **vol·un·tar·i·ly** *adv*

vol·un·teer *n* : person who offers to help or work without expecting payment or reward ∼ *vb* **1** : offer or give voluntarily **2** : offer oneself as a volunteer

vom·it *vb* : throw up the contents of the stomach — **vom·it** *n*

vote *n* **1** : individual expression of preference in choosing or reaching a decision **2** : right to indicate one's preference or the preference expressed ∼ *vb* **1** : cast a vote **2** : choose or defeat by vote — **vote·less** *adj* — **vot·er** *n*

vouch·er *n* : written record or receipt that serves as proof of a transaction

vow *n* : solemn promise to do something or to live or act a certain way — **vow** *vb*

vow·el *n* **1** : speech sound produced without obstruction or friction in the mouth **2** : letter representing such a sound

voy·age *n* : long journey esp. by water or through space ∼ *vb* : make a voyage — **voy·ag·er** *n*

vul·gar *adj* **1** : relating to the common people **2** : lacking refinement **3** : offensive in manner or language — **vul·gar·ism** *n* — **vul·gar·i·ty** *n* — **vul·gar·ize** *vb* — **vul·gar·ly** *adv*

vul·ner·a·ble *adj* : exposed to attack or damage — **vul·ner·a·bil·i·ty** *n* — **vul·ner·a·bly** *adv*

vul·ture *n* : large flesh-eating bird

vy·ing *pres part of* VIE

W

w *n* : 23d letter of the alphabet

wad *n* **1** : little mass **2** : soft mass of fibrous material **3** : pliable plug to retain a powder charge **4** : considerable amount ∼ *vb* **1** : form into a wad **2** : stuff with a wad

wade *vb* **1** : step in or through (as water) **2** : move with difficulty — **wade** *n* — **wad·er** *n*

wa·fer *n* **1** : thin crisp cake or cracker **2** : waferlike thing

waf·fle *n* : crisped cake of batter cooked in a hinged utensil (**waffle iron**) ∼ *vb* : hesitate in deciding

wag *vb* : sway or swing from side to side or to and fro — **wag** *n*

wage *vb* : engage in ∼ *n* **1** : payment for labor or services **2** : compensation

wa·ger *n or vb* : bet

wag·gle *vb* : wag — **waggle** *n*

wag·on *n* **1** : 4-wheeled vehicle drawn by animals **2** : child's 4-wheeled cart

waist *n* **1** : narrowed part of the body between chest and hips **2** : waistlike part — **waist·line** *n*

wait *vb* **1** : remain in readiness or expectation **2** : delay **3** : attend as a waiter ∼ *n* **1** : concealment **2** : act or period of waiting

wait·er *n* : person who serves others at tables

wait·ress *n* : woman who serves others at tables

¹wake *vb* (**woke**; **wo·ken**) **1** : keep watch **2** : bring or come back to consciousness after

sleep ∼ *n* **1** : state of being awake **2** : watch held over a dead body

²wake *n* : track left by a ship

wak·en *vb* : wake

walk *vb* **1** : move or cause to move on foot **2** : pass over, through, or along by walking ∼ *n* **1** : a going on foot **2** : place or path for walking **3** : distance to be walked **4** : way of living **5** : way of walking **6** : slow 4-beat gait of a horse — **walk·er** *n*

wall *n* **1** : structure for defense or for enclosing something **2** : upright enclosing part of a building or room **3** : something like a wall ∼ *vb* : provide, separate, surround, or close with a wall — **walled** *adj*

wal·let *n* : pocketbook with compartments

wal·low *vb* **1** : roll about in deep mud **2** : indulge oneself excessively ∼ *n* : place for wallowing

wal·nut *n* **1** : nut with a furrowed shell and adherent husk **2** : tree on which this nut grows or its brown wood

wand *n* : slender staff

wan·der *vb* **1** : move about aimlessly **2** : stray **3** : become delirious — **wan·der·er** *n*

wane *vb* **1** : grow smaller or less **2** : lose power, prosperity, or influence — **wane** *n*

want *vb* **1** : lack **2** : need **3** : desire earnestly ∼ *n* **1** : deficiency **2** : dire need **3** : something wanted

war *n* **1** : armed fighting between nations **2**

: state of hostility or conflict **3** : struggle between opposing forces or for a particular end ∼ *vb* : engage in warfare — **war·less** *adj* — **war·time** *n*

war·ble *n* **1** : melodious succession of low pleasing sounds **2** : musical trill ∼ *vb* : sing or utter in a trilling way

ward *n* **1** : a guarding or being under guard or guardianship **2** : division of a prison or hospital **3** : electoral or administrative division of a city **4** : person under protection of a guardian or a law court ∼ *vb* : turn aside — **ward·ship** *n*

war·den *n* **1** : guardian **2** : official charged with supervisory duties or enforcement of laws **3** : official in charge of a prison

ward·robe *n* **1** : clothes closet **2** : collection of wearing apparel

ware·house *n* : place for storage of merchandise — **ware·house** *vb* — **ware·house·man** *n* — **ware·hous·er** *n*

war·fare *n* **1** : military operations between enemies **2** : struggle

war·like *adj* : fond of, relating to, or used in war

warm *adj* **1** : having or giving out moderate or adequate heat **2** : serving to retain heat **3** : showing strong feeling **4** : giving a pleasant impression of warmth, cheerfulness, or friendliness ∼ *vb* **1** : make or become warm **2** : give warmth or energy to **3** : experience feelings of affection **4** : become increasingly ardent, interested, or competent — **warm·er** *n* — **warm·ly** *adv* — **warm up** *vb* : make ready by preliminary activity

warmth *n* **1** : quality or state of being warm **2** : enthusiasm

warn *vb* **1** : put on guard **2** : notify in advance — **warn·ing** *n or adj*

warp *n* **1** : lengthwise threads in a woven fabric **2** : twist ∼ *vb* **1** : twist out of shape **2** : lead astray **3** : distort

war·rant *n* **1** : authorization **2** : legal writ authorizing action ∼ *vb* **1** : declare or maintain positively **2** : guarantee **3** : approve **4** : justify

war·ran·ty *n* : guarantee of the integrity of a product

war·rior *n* : one engaged or experienced in warfare

wart *n* **1** : small projection on the skin caused by a virus **2** : wartlike protuberance — **warty** *adj*

wary *adj* : careful in guarding against danger or deception

was *past 1st & 3d sing of* BE

wash *vb* **1** : cleanse with or as if with a liquid (as water) **2** : wet thoroughly with liquid **3** : flow along the border of **4** : flow in a stream **5** : move or remove by or as if by the action of water **6** : cover or daub lightly with a liquid **7** : undergo laundering ∼ *n* **1** : act of washing or being washed **2** : articles to be washed **3** : surging action of water or disturbed air — **wash·able** *adj* — **wash·cloth** *n*

wash·er *n* **1** : machine for washing **2** : ring used around a bolt or screw to ensure tightness or relieve friction

wash·ing *n* : articles to be washed

Washington's Birthday *n* : the 3d Monday in February or formerly February 22 observed as a legal holiday

waste *n* **1** : sparsely settled or barren region **2** : act or an instance of wasting **3** : refuse (as garbage or rubbish) **4** : material (as feces) produced but not used by a living body ∼ *vb* **1** : ruin **2** : spend or use carelessly **3** : lose substance or energy ∼ *adj* **1** : wild and uninhabited **2** : being of no further use — **waste·bas·ket** *n* — **wast·er** *n* — **waste·ful** *adj* — **waste·ful·ly** *adv* — **waste·ful·ness** *n* — **waste·land** *n*

watch *vb* **1** : be or stay awake intentionally **2** : be on the lookout for danger **3** : observe **4** : keep oneself informed about ∼ *n* **1** : act of keeping awake to guard **2** : close observation **3** : one that watches **4** : period of duty on a ship or those on duty during this period **5** : timepiece carried on the person — **watch·dog** *n* — **watch·er** *n* — **watch·ful** *adj* — **watch·ful·ly** *adv* — **watch·ful·ness** *n* — **watch·man** *n*

wa·ter *n* **1** : liquid that descends as rain and forms rivers, lakes, and seas **2** : liquid containing or resembling water ∼ *vb* **1** : supply with or get water **2** : dilute with or as if with water **3** : form or secrete watery matter

wa·ter·fall *n* : steep descent of the water of a stream

wa·ter·mel·on *n* : large fruit with sweet juicy usu. red pulp

wa·ter·proof *adj* : not letting water through ∼ *vb* : make waterproof — **wa·ter·proof·ing** *n*

wa·ter·tight *adj* **1** : so tight as not to let water in **2** : allowing no possibility for doubt or uncertainty

wa·tery *adj* **1** : containing, full of, or giving out water **2** : being like water **3** : soft and soggy

watt *n* : unit of electric power — **watt·age** *n*

wave *vb* **1** : flutter **2** : signal with the hands **3** : wave to and fro with the hand **4** : curve up and down like a wave $\sim$ *n* **1** : moving swell on the surface of water **2** : wavelike shape **3** : waving motion **4** : sudden temporary increase **5** : disturbance that transfers energy from point to point — **wave·length** *n* — **wave·let** *n* — **wave·like** *adj* — **wavy** *adj*

wa·ver *vb* **1** : fluctuate in opinion, allegiance, or direction **2** : flicker **3** : falter — **waver** *n* — **wa·ver·er** *n* — **wa·ver·ing·ly** *adv*

¹wax *n* **1** : yellowish plastic substance secreted by bees **2** : substance like beeswax $\sim$ *vb* : treat or rub with wax esp. for polishing — **waxy** *adj*

²wax *vb* **1** : grow larger **2** : become

way *n* **1** : thoroughfare for travel or passage **2** : route **3** : course of action **4** : method **5** : detail **6** : usual or characteristic state of affairs **7** : condition **8** : distance **9** : progress along a course — **by the way** : in a digression — **by way of 1** : for the purpose of **2** : by the route through — **out of the way** : remote

way·ward *adj* **1** : following one's own capricious inclinations **2** : not predictable

we *pron* — used of a group that includes the speaker or writer

weak *adj* **1** : lacking strength or vigor **2** : deficient in vigor of mind or character **3** : of less than usual strength **4** : not having or exerting authority — **weak·en** *vb* — **weak·ly** *adv* — **weak·ness** *n*

weak·ling *n* : person who is physically, mentally, or morally weak

wealth *n* **1** : abundant possessions or resources **2** : great quantity

wealthy *adj* : having wealth

weap·on *n* **1** : something (as a gun) that may be used to fight with **2** : means by which one contends against another — **weap·on·less** *adj*

wear *vb* (**wore; worn**) **1** : use as an article of clothing or adornment **2** : carry on the person **3** : show an appearance of **4** : decay by use or by scraping **5** : lessen the strength of **6** : endure use $\sim$ *n* **1** : act of wearing **2** : clothing **3** : lasting quality **4** : result of use — **wear·able** *adj* — **wear·er** *n* — **wear out** *vb* **1** : make or become useless by wear **2** : tire

wea·ry *adj* **1** : worn out in strength, freshness, or patience **2** : expressing or characteristic of weariness $\sim$ *vb* : make or become weary — **wea·ri·ly** *adv* — **wea·ri·ness** *n* — **wea·ri·some** *adj* — **wea·ri·some·ly** *adv*

weath·er *n* : state of the atmosphere $\sim$ *vb* **1** : expose to or endure the action of weather **2** : endure — **weath·er·man** *n* — **weath·er·proof** *adj or vb*

weave *vb* (**wove; wo·ven**) **1** : form by interlacing strands of material **2** : to make as if by weaving together parts **3** : follow a winding course $\sim$ *n* : pattern or method of weaving — **weav·er** *n*

web *n* **1** : cobweb **2** : animal or plant membrane **3** : network **4** *cap* : World Wide Web $\sim$ *vb* : cover or provide with a web — **webbed** *adj*

web·bing *n* : strong closely woven tape

Web site *n* : group of World Wide Web pages available online

wed *vb* **1** : marry **2** : unite

wed·ding *n* : marriage ceremony and celebration

wedge *n* : V-shaped object used for splitting, raising, forcing open, or tightening $\sim$ *vb* **1** : tighten or split with a wedge **2** : force into a narrow space

Wednes·day *n* : 4th day of the week

wee *adj* : very small

weed *n* : unwanted plant $\sim$ *vb* **1** : remove weeds **2** : get rid of — **weed·er** *n* — **weedy** *adj*

weeds *n pl* : mourning clothes

week *n* **1** : 7 successive days **2** : calendar period of 7 days beginning with Sunday and ending with Saturday **3** : the working or school days of the calendar week

week·day *n* : any day except Sunday and often Saturday

week·end *n* : Saturday and Sunday $\sim$ *vb* : spend the weekend

week·ly *adj* : occurring, appearing, or done every week $\sim$ *n* : weekly publication — **week·ly** *adv*

weep *vb* (**wept; wept**) : shed tears — **weep·er** *n* — **weepy** *adj*

weigh *vb* **1** : determine the heaviness of **2** : have a specified weight **3** : consider carefully **4** : raise (an anchor) off the sea floor **5** : press down or burden

weight *n* **1** : amount that something weighs **2** : relative heaviness **3** : heavy object **4** : bur-

den or pressure **5** : importance ∼ *vb* **1** : load
with a weight **2** : oppress — **weight·less** *adj*
— **weight·less·ness** *n* — **weighty** *adj*

weird *adj* **1** : unearthly or mysterious **2**
: strange — **weird·ly** *adv* — **weird·ness** *n*

wel·come *vb* : accept or greet cordially ∼ *adj*
: received or permitted gladly ∼ *n* : cordial
greeting or reception

wel·fare *n* **1** : prosperity **2** : government aid
for those in need

¹**well** *n* **1** : spring **2** : hole sunk in the earth to
obtain a natural deposit (as of oil) **3** : source
of supply **4** : open space extending vertically
through floors ∼ *vb* : flow forth

²**well** *adv* (**bet·ter; best**) **1** : in a good or proper
manner **2** : satisfactorily **3** : fully **4** : intimately **5** : considerably ∼ *adj* **1** : satisfactory **2** : prosperous **3** : desirable **4** : healthy

well–adjusted *adj* : not psychologically troubled

well–be·ing *n* : state of being happy, healthy,
or prosperous

well–known *adj* : widely known or acknowl-
edged

well–mean·ing *adj* : having good intentions

well–off *adj* : being in good condition esp. fi-
nancially

well–to–do *adj* : prosperous

went *past of* GO

wept *past of* WEEP

were *past 2d sing, past pl, or past subjunctive
of* BE

west *adv* **1** : to or toward the west ∼ *adj* : situated toward or at or coming from the west ∼
n **1** : direction of sunset **2** *cap* : regions to the
west — **west·er·ly** *adv or adj* — **west·ward**
adv or adj — **west·wards** *adv*

west·ern *adj* **1** *cap* : of a region designated
West **2** : lying toward or coming from the
west — **West·ern·er** *n*

wet *adj* **1** : consisting of or covered or soaked
with liquid **2** : not dry ∼ *n* : moisture ∼ *vb*
: make or become moist — **wet·ly** *adv* — **wet-
ness** *n*

whack *vb* : strike sharply ∼ *n* **1** : sharp blow
2 : proper working order **3** : chance **4** : try

whale *n* : large marine mammal ∼ *vb* : hunt
for whales — **whale·boat** *n* — **whal·er** *n*

wharf *n* : structure alongside which boats lie to
load or unload

what *pron* **1** — used to inquire the identity or
nature of something **2** : that which **3** : whatever ∼ *adv* : in what respect ∼ *adj* **1** — used

to inquire about the identity or nature of something **2** : how remarkable or surprising **3**
: whatever

what·ev·er *pron* **1** : anything or everything
that **2** : no matter what ∼ *adj* : of any kind at
all

wheat *n* : cereal grain that yields flour —
wheat·en *adj*

wheel *n* **1** : disk or circular frame capable of
turning on a central axis **2** : device of which
the main part is a wheel ∼ *vb* **1** : convey or
move on wheels or a wheeled vehicle **2** : rotate **3** : turn so as to change direction —
wheeled *adj* — **wheel·er** *n* — **wheel·less**
adj

wheeze *vb* : breathe with difficulty and with a
whistling sound — **wheeze** *n* — **wheezy** *adj*

when *adv* — used to inquire about or designate
a particular time ∼ *conj* **1** : at or during the
time that **2** : every time that **3** : if **4** : although ∼ *pron* : what time

when·ev·er *conj or adv* : at whatever time

where *adv* **1** : at, in, or to what place **2** : at, in,
or to what situation, position, direction, circumstances, or respect ∼ *conj* **1** : at, in, or to
what place, position, or circumstance **2** : at,
in, or to which place ∼ *n* : place

where·abouts *adv* : about where ∼ *n sing or
pl* : place where a person or thing is

where·as *conj* **1** : while on the contrary **2**
: since

wher·ev·er *adv* : where ∼ *conj* : at, in, or to
whatever place or circumstance

whether *conj* **1** : if it is or was true that **2** : if
it is or was better **3** : whichever is the case

which *adj* **1** : being what one or ones out of a
group **2** : whichever ∼ *pron* **1** : which one or
ones **2** : whichever

which·ev·er *pron or adj* : no matter what one

whiff *n* **1** : slight gust **2** : inhalation of odor,
gas, or smoke **3** : slight trace ∼ *vb* : inhale an
odor

while *n* **1** : period of time **2** : time and effort
used ∼ *conj* **1** : during the time that **2** : as
long as **3** : although ∼ *vb* : cause to pass esp.
pleasantly

whim *n* : sudden wish, desire, or change of
mind

whim·sy, whim·sey *n* **1** : whim **2** : fanciful
creation — **whim·si·cal** *adj* — **whim·si·cal-
ly** *adv*

whine *vb* **1** : utter a usu. high-pitched plaintive

cry **2** : complain — **whine** *n* — **whin·er** *n* — **whiny** *adj*

whip *vb* **1** : move quickly **2** : strike with something slender and flexible **3** : defeat **4** : incite **5** : beat into a froth ～ *n* **1** : flexible device used for whipping **2** : party leader responsible for discipline **3** : beating motion — **whip·per** *n*

whip·lash *n* : injury from a sudden sharp movement of the neck and head

whir *vb* : move, fly, or revolve with a whir ～ *n* : continuous fluttering or vibratory sound

whirl *vb* **1** : move or drive in a circle **2** : spin **3** : move or turn quickly **4** : reel ～ *n* **1** : rapid circular movement **2** : state of commotion or confusion **3** : try

whirl·pool *n* : a current of water flowing in a circle

whisk *n* **1** : quick light sweeping or brushing motion **2** : usu. wire kitchen implement for beating ～ *vb* **1** : move or convey briskly **2** : beat **3** : brush lightly

whis·ker *n* **1** *pl* : beard **2** : long bristle or hair near an animal's mouth — **whis·kered** *adj*

whis·key, whis·ky *n* : liquor distilled from a fermented mash of grain

whis·per *vb* **1** : speak softly **2** : tell by whispering ～ *n* **1** : soft low sound **2** : rumor

whis·tle *n* **1** : device by which a shrill sound is produced **2** : shrill clear sound made by a whistle or through the lips ～ *vb* **1** : make or utter a whistle **2** : signal or call by a whistle **3** : produce by whistling — **whis·tler** *n*

white *adj* **1** : free from color **2** : of the color of new snow or milk **3** : having light skin ～ *n* **1** : color of maximum lightness **2** : white part or thing **3** : person who is light-skinned — **white·ness** *n* — **whit·ish** *adj*

white–col·lar *adj* : relating to salaried employees with duties not requiring protective or work clothing

whit·en *vb* : make or become white — **whit·en·er** *n*

whit·tle *vb* **1** : pare **2** : shape by paring **3** : reduce gradually

whiz, whizz *vb* : make a sound like a speeding object — **whiz, whizz** *n*

who *pron* **1** : what or which person or persons **2** : person or persons that **3** — used to introduce a relative clause

who·ev·er *pron* : no matter who

whole *adj* **1** : being in healthy or sound condition **2** : having all its parts or elements **3** : constituting the total sum of ～ *n* **1** : complete amount or sum **2** : something whole or entire — **on the whole 1** : considering all circumstances **2** : in general — **whole·ness** *n*

whole·heart·ed *adj* : sincere

whole·sale *n* : sale of goods in quantity usu. for resale by a retail merchant ～ *adj* **1** : of or relating to wholesaling **2** : performed on a large scale ～ *vb* : sell at wholesale — **whole·sale** *adv* — **whole·sal·er** *n*

whole·some *adj* **1** : promoting mental, spiritual, or bodily health **2** : healthy — **whole·some·ness** *n*

whol·ly *adv* **1** : totally **2** : solely

whom *pron, objective case of* WHO

whom·ev·er *pron, objective case of* WHOEVER

whoop *vb* : shout loudly ～ *n* : shout

whop·per *n* **1** : something unusually large or extreme of its kind **2** : monstrous lie

whose *adj* : of or relating to whom or which ～ *pron* : whose one or ones

why *adv* : for what reason, cause, or purpose ～ *conj* **1** : reason for which **2** : for which ～ *n* : reason ～ *interj* — used esp. to express surprise

wick *n* : cord that draws up oil, tallow, or wax to be burned

wick·ed *adj* **1** : morally bad **2** : harmful or troublesome **3** : very unpleasant **4** : very impressive — **wick·ed·ly** *adv* — **wick·ed·ness** *n*

wide *adj* **1** : covering a vast area **2** : measured at right angles to the length **3** : having a great measure across **4** : opened fully **5** : far from the thing in question ～ *adv* **1** : over a great distance **2** : so as to leave considerable space between **3** : fully — **wide·ly** *adv* — **wid·en** *vb*

wide–awake *adj* : alert

wides·pread *adj* : generally known or spread out

wid·ow *n* : woman who has lost her husband by death and has not married again ～ *vb* : cause to become a widow — **wid·ow·hood** *n*

wid·ow·er *n* : man who has lost his wife by death and has not married again

width *n* **1** : distance from side to side **2** : largeness of extent **3** : measured and cut piece of material

wield *vb* **1** : use or handle esp. effectively **2** : exert — **wield·er** *n*

wife *n* (**wives**) : married woman — **wife·hood** *n* — **wife·less** *adj* — **wife·ly** *adj*

wig *n* : manufactured covering of hair for the head

wig·gle *vb* **1** : move with quick jerky or shaking movements **2** : wriggle — **wig·gle** *n* — **wig·gler** *n*

wild *adj* **1** : living or being in a state of nature and not domesticated or cultivated **2** : showing lack of restraint **3** : turbulent **4** : crazy **5** : not civilized **6** : erratic ~ *n* **1** : wilderness **2** : undomesticated state ~ *adv* : without control — **wild·ly** *adv* — **wild·ness** *n*

wil·der·ness *n* : uncultivated and uninhabited region

wild·fire *n* : sweeping and destructive fire

wild·life *n* : undomesticated animals

will *vb past* **would** **1** : wish to **2** — used as an auxiliary verb to express (1) desire or willingness, (2) customary action, (3) simple future time, (4) capability, (5) determination, (6) probability, (7) inevitability, or (8) a command **3** : dispose of by a will ~ *n* **1** : often determined wish **2** : act, process, or experience of willing **3** : power of controlling one's actions or emotions **4** : legal document disposing of property after death

will·ful, wil·ful *adj* **1** : governed by will without regard to reason **2** : intentional — **will·ful·ly** *adv*

will·ing *adj* **1** : inclined or favorably disposed in mind **2** : prompt to act **3** : done, borne, or accepted voluntarily or without reluctance — **will·ing·ly** *adv* — **will·ing·ness** *n*

will·pow·er *n* : energetic determination

wilt *vb* **1** : lose or cause to lose freshness and become limp esp. from lack of water **2** : grow weak

win *vb* (**won; won**) **1** : get possession of esp. by effort **2** : gain victory in battle or a contest **3** : make friendly or favorable ~ *n* : victory

¹wind *n* **1** : movement of the air **2** : breath **3** : gas in the stomach or intestines **4** : air carrying a scent **5** : intimation ~ *vb* **1** : get a scent of **2** : cause to be out of breath

²wind *vb* **1** : have or follow a curving course **2** : move or lie to encircle **3** : encircle or cover with something pliable **4** : tighten the spring of ~ *n* **wound; wound** : turn or coil — **wind·er** *n*

wind·fall *n* **1** : thing blown down by wind **2** : unexpected benefit

wind·mill *n* : machine worked by the wind turning vanes

win·dow *n* **1** : opening in the wall of a building to let in light and air **2** : pane in a window **3** : span of time for something **4** : area of a computer display — **win·dow·less** *adj*

wind·shield *n* : transparent screen in front of the occupants of a vehicle

wind·up *n* : end — **wind up** *vb*

wind·ward *adj* : being in or facing the direction from which the wind is blowing ~ *n* : direction from which the wind is blowing

windy *adj* **1** : having wind **2** : indulging in useless talk

wing *n* **1** : movable paired appendage for flying **2** : winglike thing **3** *pl* : area at the side of the stage out of sight **4** : faction ~ *vb* **1** : fly **2** : propel through the air — **winged** *adj* — **wing·less** *adj* — **on the wing** : in flight — **under one's wing** : in one's charge or care

wink *vb* **1** : close and open the eyes quickly **2** : avoid seeing or noticing something **3** : twinkle **4** : close and open one eye quickly as a signal or hint ~ *n* **1** : brief sleep **2** : act of winking **3** : instant — **wink·er** *n*

win·ner *n* : one that wins

win·ning *n* **1** : victory **2** : money won at gambling ~ *adj* **1** : victorious **2** : charming

win·ter *n* : season between autumn and spring ~ *adj* : sown in autumn for harvest the next spring or summer — **win·ter·time** *n*

wipe *vb* **1** : clean or dry by rubbing **2** : remove by rubbing **3** : erase completely **4** : destroy **5** : pass over a surface ~ *n* : act or instance of wiping — **wip·er** *n*

wire *n* **1** : thread of metal **2** : work made of wire **3** : telegram or one sent through a cable under the sea ~ *vb* **1** : provide with wire **2** : bind or mount with wire — **wire·less** *adj*

wiry *adj* **1** : resembling wire **2** : slender yet strong and sinewy — **wir·i·ness** *n*

wis·dom *n* **1** : accumulated learning **2** : good sense

wise *adj* **1** : having or showing wisdom, good sense, or good judgment **2** : aware of what is going on — **wise·ly** *adv*

wise·crack *n* : clever, smart, or flippant remark ~ *vb* : make a wisecrack

wish *vb* **1** : have a desire **2** : express a wish concerning **3** : request ~ *n* **1** : a wishing or desire **2** : expressed will or desire

wish·ful *adj* **1** : expressive of a wish **2** : according with wishes rather than fact

wit *n* **1** : reasoning power **2** : mental soundness — *usu. pl.* **3** : quickness and cleverness in handling words and ideas **4** : talent for clever remarks or one noted for witty remarks — **wit·less** *adj* — **wit·less·ly** *adv* — **wit·less·ness** *n* — **wit·ted** *adj*

witch *n* **1** : person believed to have magic power **2** : ugly old woman ∼ *vb* : bewitch

witch·craft *n* : power or practices of a witch

with *prep* **1** : against, to, or toward **2** : in support of **3** : because of **4** : in the company of **5** : having **6** : despite **7** : containing **8** : by means of

with·draw *vb* **1** : take back or away **2** : call back or retract **3** : go away **4** : terminate one's participation in or use of — **with·draw·al** *n*

with·er *vb* **1** : shrivel **2** : lose or cause to lose energy, force, or freshness

with·hold *vb* **1** : hold back **2** : refrain from giving

with·in *adv* **1** : in or into the interior **2** : inside oneself ∼ *prep* **1** : in or to the inner part of **2** : in the limits or compass of

with·out *prep* **1** : outside **2** : lacking **3** : unaccompanied or unmarked by — **with·out** *adv*

wit·ness *n* **1** : testimony **2** : one who testifies **3** : one present at a transaction to testify that it has taken place **4** : one who has personal knowledge or experience **5** : something serving as proof ∼ *vb* **1** : bear witness **2** : act as legal witness of **3** : furnish proof of **4** : be a witness of **5** : be the scene of

wit·ty *adj* : marked by or full of wit — **wit·ti·ly** *adv* — **wit·ti·ness** *n*

wives *pl of* WIFE

wiz·ard *n* **1** : magician **2** : very clever person — **wiz·ard·ry** *n*

wob·ble *vb* **1** : move or cause to move with an irregular rocking motion **2** : tremble **3** : waver — **wob·ble** *n* — **wob·bly** *adj*

woe *n* **1** : deep suffering **2** : misfortune

woke *past of* WAKE

woken *past part of* WAKE

wolf *n* (**wolves**) : large doglike predatory mammal ∼ *vb* : eat greedily — **wolf·ish** *adj*

wom·an *n* (**wom·en**) **1** : adult female person **2** : women in general **3** : feminine nature — **wom·an·hood** *n* — **wom·an·ish** *adj* — **wom·an·li·ness** *n* — **wom·an·ly** *adv*

won *past of* WIN

won·der *n* **1** : cause of astonishment or surprise **2** : feeling (as of astonishment) aroused by something extraordinary ∼ *vb* **1** : feel surprise **2** : feel curiosity or doubt

won·der·ful *adj* **1** : exciting wonder **2** : un-usually good — **won·der·ful·ly** *adv* — **won·der·ful·ness** *n*

won·drous *adj* : wonderful — **won·drous·ly** *adv* — **won·drous·ness** *n*

wood *n* **1** : dense growth of trees usu. smaller than a forest — often pl. **2** : hard fibrous substance of trees and shrubs beneath the bark **3** : wood prepared for some use (as burning) ∼ *adj* **1** : wooden **2** : suitable for working with wood **3** : living or growing in woods — **wood·chop·per** *n* — **wood·pile** *n* — **wood·shed** *n*

wood·en *adj* **1** : made of wood **2** : lacking resilience **3** : lacking ease, liveliness or interest — **wood·en·ly** *adv* — **wood·en·ness** *n*

wood·work *n* : work (as interior house fittings) made of wood

woody *adj* **1** : abounding with woods **2** : of, containing, or like wood fibers — **wood·i·ness** *n*

wool *n* **1** : soft hair of some mammals and esp. the sheep **2** : something (as a textile) made of wool — **wooled** *adj*

wool·en, wool·len *adj* **1** : made of wool **2** : relating to the manufacture of woolen products ∼ *n* **1** : woolen fabric **2** : woolen garments — *usu. pl.*

wool·ly *adj* **1** : of, relating to, or bearing wool **2** : consisting of or resembling wool **3** : confused or turbulent

woo·zy *adj* **1** : confused **2** : somewhat dizzy, nauseated, or weak — **woo·zi·ness** *n*

word *n* **1** : brief remark **2** : speech sound or series of speech sounds that communicates a meaning **3** : written representation of a word **4** : order **5** : news **6** : promise **7** *pl* : dispute ∼ *vb* : express in words — **word·less** *adj*

word processing *n* : production of structured and printed documents through a computer program (**word processor**) — **word process** *vb*

wordy *adj* : using many words — **word·i·ness** *n*

wore *past of* WEAR

work *n* **1** : labor **2** : employment **3** : task **4** : something (as an artistic production) produced by mental effort or physical labor **5** *pl* : place where industrial labor is done **6** *pl* : moving parts of a mechanism **7** : workmanship ∼ *adj* **1** : suitable for wear while working **2** : used for work ∼ *vb* **1** : bring to pass **2** : create by expending labor upon **3** : bring or get into a form or condition **4** : set or keep in operation **5 :** solve **6 :** cause to labor **7 :** arrange **8 :** excite **9 :** labor **10 :** perform work regularly for wages **11 :** function according to plan or design **12 :** produce a desired effect — **work·able** *adj* — **work·bench** *n* — **work·er** *n* — **work·man** *n* — **work·room** *n* — **in the works :** in preparation

work·day *n* **1 :** day on which work is done **2 :** period of time during which one is working

work·ing *adj* **1 :** adequate to allow work to be done **2 :** adopted or assumed to help further work or activity ∼ *n* : operation — usu. used in pl.

work·man·ship *n* **1 :** art or skill of a workman **2 :** quality of a piece of work

work·out *n* **:** exercise to improve one's fitness

work out *vb* **1 :** bring about by effort **2 :** solve **3 :** develop **4 :** to be successful **5 :** perform exercises

work·shop *n* **1 :** small establishment for manufacturing or handicrafts **2 :** seminar emphasizing exchange of ideas and practical methods

world *n* **1 :** universe **2 :** earth with its inhabitants and all things upon it **3 :** people in general **4 :** great number or quantity **5 :** class of persons or their sphere of interest

world·ly *adj* **1 :** devoted to this world and its pursuits rather than to religion **2 :** sophisticated — **world·li·ness** *n*

world·wide *adj* **:** extended throughout the entire world — **worldwide** *adv*

World Wide Web *n* **:** part of the Internet accessible through a browser

worm *n* **1 :** earthworm or a similar animal **2** *pl* **:** disorder caused by parasitic worms ∼ *vb* **1 :** move or cause to move in a slow and indirect way **2 :** to free from worms — **wormy** *adj*

worn *past part of* WEAR

worn–out *adj* **:** exhausted or used up by or as if by wear

wor·ry *vb* **1 :** shake and mangle with the teeth **2 :** disturb **3 :** feel or express anxiety ∼ *n* **1 :** anxiety **2 :** cause of anxiety — **wor·ri·er** *n* — **wor·ri·some** *adj*

worse *adj, comparative of* BAD *or of* ILL **1 :** bad or evil in a greater degree **2 :** more unwell ∼ *n* **1 :** one that is worse **2 :** greater degree of badness ∼ *adv comparative of* BAD *or of* ILL : in a worse manner

wors·en *vb* **:** make or become worse

wor·ship *n* **1 :** reverence toward a divine being or supernatural power **2 :** expression of reverence **3 :** extravagant respect or devotion ∼ *vb* **1 :** honor or reverence **2 :** perform or take part in worship — **wor·ship·er, wor·ship·per** *n*

worst *adj, superlative of* BAD *or of* ILL **1 :** most bad, evil, ill, or corrupt **2 :** most unfavorable, unpleasant, or painful ∼ *n* **:** one that is worst ∼ *adv superlative of* ILL *or* BAD *or* BADLY **:** to the extreme degree of badness ∼ *vb* **:** defeat

worth *prep* **1 :** equal in value to **2 :** deserving of ∼ *n* **1 :** monetary value **2 :** value of something measured by its qualities **3 :** moral or personal merit — **worth·less** *adj*

worth·while *adj* **:** being worth the time or effort spent

wor·thy *adj* **1 :** having worth or value **2 :** having sufficient worth ∼ *n* **:** worthy person — **wor·thi·ly** *adv* — **wor·thi·ness** *n*

would *past of* WILL — used to express (1) preference, (2) intent, (3) habitual action, (4) contingency, (5) probability, or (6) a request

¹wound *n* **1 :** injury in which the skin is broken **2 :** mental hurt ∼ *vb* **:** inflict a wound to or in

²wound *past of* WIND

wove *past of* WEAVE

woven *past part of* WEAVE

wrap *vb* **1 :** cover esp. by winding or folding **2 :** envelop and secure for transportation or storage **3 :** enclose, surround, or conceal wholly **4 :** coil, fold, draw, or twine about something ∼ *n* **1 :** wrapper or wrapping **2 :** outer garment (as a shawl)

wrap·per *n* **1 :** that in which something is wrapped **2 :** one that wraps

wreath *n* **:** something (as boughs) intertwined into a circular shape

wreathe *vb* **1 :** shape into or take on the shape of a wreath **2 :** decorate or cover with a wreath

wreck *n* **1 :** broken remains (as of a ship or vehicle) after heavy damage **2 :** something disabled or in a state of ruin **3 :** an individual who has become weak or infirm **4 :** action of breaking up or destroying something ∼ *vb* **:** ruin or damage by breaking up

wreck·age *n* **1 :** act of wrecking **2 :** remains of a wreck

wreck·er *n* **1 :** automotive vehicle for removing disabled cars **2 :** one that wrecks or tears down and removes buildings

wrench *vb* **1 :** pull with violent twisting or force **2 :** injure or disable by a violent twisting or straining ∼ *n* **1 :** forcible twisting **2 :** tool for exerting a twisting force

wres·tle *vb* **1 :** scuffle with and attempt to

throw and pin an opponent **2** : compete against in wrestling **3** : struggle (as with a problem) ∼ *n* : action or an instance of wrestling — **wres·tler** *n*

wres·tling *n* : sport in which 2 opponents try to throw and pin each other

wretch·ed *adj* **1** : deeply afflicted, dejected, or distressed **2** : grievous **3** : inferior — **wretch·ed·ly** *adv* — **wretch·ed·ness** *n*

wrig·gle *vb* **1** : twist and turn restlessly **2** : move along by twisting and turning — **wrig·gle** *n* — **wrig·gler** *n*

wring *vb* **wrung; wrung** **1** : squeeze or twist out moisture **2** : get by or as if by twisting or pressing **3** : twist together in anguish **4** : pain — **wring·er** *n*

wrin·kle *n* : crease or small fold on a surface (as in the skin or in cloth) ∼ *vb* : develop or cause to develop wrinkles — **wrin·kly** *adj*

wrist *n* : joint or region between the hand and the arm

writ *n* **1** : something written **2** : legal order in writing

write *vb* (**wrote; writ·ten**) **1** : form letters or words on a surface **2** : form the letters or the words of (as on paper) **3** : make up and set down for others to read **4** : write a letter to — **write off** *vb* : cancel

writ·er *n* : one that writes esp. as a business or occupation

writ·ing *n* **1** : act of one that writes **2** : handwriting **3** : something written or printed

wrong *n* **1** : unfair or unjust act **2** : something that is contrary to justice **3** : state of being or doing wrong ∼ *adj* **1** : sinful **2** : not right according to a standard **3** : not suitable **4** : incorrect ∼ *adv* **1** : in a wrong direction or manner **2** : incorrectly ∼ *vb* **1** : do wrong to **2** : treat unjustly — **wrong·do·er** *n* — **wrong·do·ing** *n* — **wrong·ful** *adj* — **wrong·ful·ly** *adv* — **wrong·ful·ness** *n* — **wrong·ly** *adv*

wrote *past of* WRITE

wrung *past of* WRING

X

x *n* **1** : 24th letter of the alphabet **2** : unknown quantity ∼ *vb* : cancel with a series of *x*'s — usu. with *out*

Xmas *n* : Christmas

x–ray *vb* : examine, treat, or photograph with X rays

X ray *n* **1** : radiation of short wavelength that is able to penetrate solids **2** : photograph taken with X rays — **X–ray** *adj*

xy·lo·phone *n* : musical instrument with wooden bars that are struck — **xy·lo·phon·ist** *n*

Y

y *n* : 25th letter of the alphabet

yacht *n* : luxurious pleasure boat ∼ *vb* : race or cruise in a yacht

yam *n* **1** : edible root of a tropical vine **2** : deep orange sweet potato

yank *n* : strong sudden pull — **yank** *vb*

Yan·kee *n* : native or inhabitant of New England, the northern U.S., or the U.S.

¹yard *n* **1** : 3 feet **2** : long spar for supporting and spreading a sail — **yard·age** *n* — **yard·stick** *n*

²yard *n* **1** : enclosed roofless area **2** : grounds of a building **3** : work area

yar·mul·ke *n* : a small brimless cap worn by Jewish males in a synagogue

yarn *n* **1** : spun fiber for weaving or knitting **2** : tale

yawn *vb* : open the mouth wide ∼ *n* : deep breath through a wide-open mouth — **yawn·er** *n*

year *n* **1** : period of about 365 days **2** *pl* : age

year·book *n* : annual report of the year's events

year·ly *adj* : annual — **year·ly** *adv*

yearn *vb* **1** : feel desire esp. for what one cannot have **2** : feel tenderness or compassion

yearn·ing *n* : tender or urgent desire

yeast *n* : froth or sediment in sugary liquids containing a tiny fungus and used in making alcoholic liquors and as a leaven in baking — **yeasty** *adj*

yell *vb* : utter a loud cry — **yell** *n*

yel·low *adj* **1** : of the color yellow **2** : sensational **3** : cowardly ∼ *vb* : make or turn yellow ∼ *n* **1** : color of lemons **2** : yolk of an egg — **yel·low·ish** *adj*

yen *n* : strong desire

yes *adv* — used to express consent or agreement ∼ *n* : affirmative answer

ye·shi·va, ye·shi·vah *n* : Jewish school

yes·ter·day *adv* **1** : on the day preceding today **2** : only a short time ago ∼ *n* **1** : day last past **2** : time not long past

yet *adv* **1** : in addition **2** : up to now **3** : so soon as now **4** : nevertheless ∼ *conj* : but

yield *vb* **1** : surrender **2** : grant **3** : bear as a crop **4** : produce **5** : cease opposition or resistance ∼ *n* : quantity produced or returned

yo·ga *n* : system of exercises for attaining bodily or mental control and well-being

yo·gurt *n* : fermented slightly acid soft food made from milk

yoke *n* **1** : neck frame for coupling draft animals or for carrying loads **2** : clamp **3** : slavery **4** : tie or link **5** : piece of a garment esp. at the shoulder ∼ *vb* **1** : couple with a yoke **2** : join

yolk *n* : yellow part of an egg — **yolked** *adj*

Yom Kip·pur *n* : Jewish holiday observed in September or October with fasting and prayer as a day of atonement

you *pron* **1** : person or persons addressed **2** : person in general

young *adj* **1** : being in the first or an early stage of life, growth, or development **2** : recently come into being **3** : youthful ∼ *n* **young** : persons or animals that are young — **young·ish** *adj*

young·ster *n* **1** : young person **2** : child

your *adj* : relating to you or yourself

yours *pron* : the ones belonging to you

your·self *pron* (**your·selves**) : you — used reflexively or for emphasis

youth *n* **1** : period between childhood and maturity **2** : young man **3** : young persons **4** : state or quality of being young, fresh, or vigorous

youth·ful *adj* **1** : relating to or appropriate to youth **2** : young **3** : vigorous and fresh — **youth·ful·ly** *adv* — **youth·ful·ness** *n*

yo–yo *n* : toy that falls from or rises to the hand as it unwinds and rewinds on a string

yule *n* : Christmas — **yule·tide** *n*

yum·my *adj* : highly attractive or pleasing

Z

z *n* : 26th letter of the alphabet

za·ny *n* **1** : clown **2** : silly person ∼ *adj* : crazy or foolish — **za·ni·ly** *adv* — **za·ni·ness** *n*

zeal *n* : enthusiasm

ze·bra *n* : horselike African mammal marked with light and dark stripes

ze·nith *n* : highest point

ze·ro *n* **1** : number represented by the symbol 0 or the symbol itself **2** : starting point **3** : lowest point ∼ *adj* : having no size or quantity

zest *n* **1** : quality of enhancing enjoyment **2** : keen enjoyment — **zest·ful** *adj* — **zest·ful·ly** *adv* — **zest·ful·ness** *n*

zig·zag *n* : one of a series of short sharp turns or angles ∼ *adj* : having zigzags ∼ *adv* : in or by a zigzag path ∼ *vb* : proceed along a zigzag path

zil·lion *n* : large indeterminate number

¹zip *vb* : move or act with speed ∼ *n* : energy

²zip *vb* : close or open with a zipper

zip code *n* : number that identifies a U.S. postal delivery area

zip·per *n* : fastener consisting of 2 rows of interlocking teeth

zip·py *adj* : brisk

zo·di·ac *n* : imaginary belt in the heavens encompassing the paths of the planets and divided into 12 signs used in astrology — **zo·di·a·cal** *adj*

zone *n* **1** : division of the earth's surface based on latitude and climate **2** : distinctive area ∼ *vb* **1** : mark off into zones **2** : reserve for special purposes — **zon·al** *adj* — **zon·al·ly** *adv* — **zo·na·tion** *n*

zoo *n* : collection of living animals usu. for public display — **zoo·keep·er** *n*

zo·ol·o·gy *n* : science of animals — **zo·o·log·i·cal** *adj* — **zo·ol·o·gist** *n*

zoom *vb* **1** : move with a loud hum or buzz **2** : move or increase with great speed — **zoom** *n*

Thesaurus

Preface

This thesaurus is a conveniently concise guide for the understanding and selection of synonyms and antonyms. It is intended to serve as a quick reference for those who want a compact and handy thesaurus.

This thesaurus shares many details of presentation with more comprehensive works, yet unlike many thesauruses, it provides at each **main entry** a concise statement of the **meaning** shared by the listed synonyms (indicated by a ♦ symbol), and it includes an entry at its own alphabetical place for every synonym that appears at a main entry. Additionally, many entries for which there are words with directly opposite meaning show these **antonyms** to give the user additional pertinent assistance.

For those entries that are not main entries, the first word in the synonym list is in SMALL CAPITALS to indicate that this word is the main entry for the list and that at this entry you will find the shared meaning element for the list.

Words spelled the same but having different meanings are **homographs** and are given separate entries and identified with an italic part-of-speech label, as at **fair** *adj* and **fair** *n* for the adjective *fair* and the noun *fair*. Headwords that are synonyms and alphabetically close to each other are sometimes listed together, as **finicky, finicking, finical.** Multiple meanings (senses) of an entry word are distinguished by bold numerals.

Headwords ordinarily conform to normal dictionary practice: nouns are styled as singulars, verbs as infinitives. Special situations, such as plural usage, are signaled by the use of boldface, as at the entry **wage, wages** or at sense 2 of **game,** where the plural **games** is shown as the form synonymous with *athletics*.

Parentheses enclose a particle or particles usually associated with a word. They may accompany a headword, as **rely** (on *or* upon), or a word in a list, as *fail (in)* in the antonym list at **fulfill** and *fall short (of)* at another antonym list in the same entry. Parentheses also enclose material indicating a typical or, occasionally, a sole object of reference, as in the meaning core at **money** or the antonym list at **gaudy,** where the antonym *quiet* carries the parenthetical note (*in taste or style*). A semicolon separates subgroups of words which differ in their relation to the headword.

English and the Thesaurus

A Brief Look at the English Language

The English language is peculiarly rich in synonyms, which is not surprising considering its history. Over its history of more than a thousand years the language of England has woven together strands of the Celtic language, of earlier Roman words and later church Latin, and then of the Germanic tongues of the early invaders from the European continent.

Because English has so many words derived from Latin and from Greek by way of Latin, the casual observer might guess that English would be—like French, Spanish, and Italian—a Romance language derived from the Latin spoken by the ancient Romans. But although the Romans made a few visits to Britain in the first century A.D., long before the English were there (before there even was an England), English is not a Romance language. English is actually a member of the Germanic group, and thus a sister of such modern languages as Swedish, Dutch, and German.

We often speak of English as having its beginnings with the conquest and settlement of a large part of the island of Britain by Germanic tribes from the European continent in the fifth century, although the earliest written documents of the language belong to the seventh century. Of course these Germanic peoples did not suddenly begin to speak a new language the moment they arrived in England. They spoke the closely related Germanic languages of their continental homelands. And it was from these languages that the English language developed. In fact, the words *English* and *England* are derived from the name of one of these early Germanic peoples, the Angles.

From its beginnings English has been gradually changing and evolving, as language tends to do. To get a sense of how far evolution has taken us from the early tongue, we need only glance at a sample of Old English. Here is the beginning of the Lord's Prayer:

Fæder ūre, þu þe eart on heofonum: si þin nama gehālgod.
Tōbecume þin rīce. Geweorþe þin willa on eorþan swāswā on heofonum.

There is a certain continuity between the vocabularies of Old English and Modern English. Of the thousand most common Modern English words, four-fifths are of Old English origin. Think of such words as *asleep* and *awake* or *alive* and *dead*, words relating to the body, *blood, flesh, arm, leg, bone, tooth*—even words for the daily activities of farming, *acre, barn, plow, till*, or for after the harvest, *drink, eat, meal*.

Of the foreign languages affecting the Old English vocabulary, the most influential was Latin. Church terms especially, like *priest, vicar,* and *mass,* were borrowed from Latin, the language of the church. But words belonging to aspects of life other than the strictly religious, like *cap, inch, kiln, school,* and *noon,* also entered Old English from Latin. The Scandinavians, too, influenced the language of England during the Old English period. From the eighth century on, Vikings from Scandinavia raided and eventually settled in England, especially in the north and the east. In a few instances the influence of a Scandinavian word gave an English word a new meaning. Thus our *dream,* which meant "joy" in Old English, probably took on the now familiar sense "a series of thoughts, images, or emotions occurring during sleep" because its Scandinavian relative *draumr* had that meaning. A considerable number of common words, like *cross, fellow, ball,* and *raise,* also became naturalized as a result of the Viking incursions over the years. The initial consonants *sk-* often reveal the Scandinavian ancestry of words like *sky, skin,* and *skirt,* the last of which has persisted side by side with its native English relative *shirt.*

Additional foreign influence on English came about principally as a result of the Norman Conquest of 1066, which brought England under the rule of French speakers. The English language, though it did not die, was for a long time of only secondary importance in political, social, and cultural matters. French became the language of the upper classes in England. The lower classes continued to speak English, but many French words were borrowed into English. To this circumstance we owe, for example, a number of distinctions between the words used for animals in the pasture and the words for those animals prepared to be eaten. Living animals were under the care of English-speaking peasants; cooked, the animals were served to the French-speaking nobility. *Swine* in the sty became *pork* at the table, *cow* and *calf* became *beef* and *veal.* This Anglo-French also had an influence on the words used in the courts, such as *indict, jury,* and *verdict.*

English eventually reestablished itself as the major language of England, but the language did not lose its habit of borrowing. English still derives much of its learned vocabulary from Latin and Greek. We have also borrowed words from nearly all of the languages in Europe. From Modern French we have such words as *bikini, cliché,* and *discotheque;* from Dutch, *easel, gin,* and *yacht;* from German, *delicatessen, pretzel,* and *swindler;* from Swedish, *ombudsman* and *smorgasbord.* From Italian we have taken *carnival, fiasco,* and *pizza,* as well as many terms from music (including *piano*).

From the period of the Renaissance voyages of discovery through the days when the sun never set upon the British Empire and up to the present, a steady stream of new words has flowed into the language to match the new objects and experiences English speakers have encountered all over the globe. English has drawn words from India (*bandanna*), China (*gung ho*), and Japan (*tycoon*). Arabic has been a prolific source of words over the centuries, giving us *hazard, lute, magazine,* and a host of words beginning with the letter *a,* from *algebra* to *azimuth.*

How Meaning Has Developed

Whether borrowed or created, a word generally begins its life in English with one meaning. Yet no living language is static, and in time words develop new meanings and lose old ones. A word used in a specific sense may be extended, or generalized, to cover a host of similar senses. Our word *virtue* is derived from the Latin *virtus,* which originally meant "manliness." But we apply the term to any excellent quality possessed by man, woman, or beast; even inanimate objects have their *virtues.* In Latin, *decimare* meant "to select and kill a tenth part of" and described the Roman way of dealing with mutinous troops. Its English descendant, *decimate,* now simply means "to destroy a large part of."

The development of meaning can easily be followed in this example. Today when we think of the word *fast* we probably think of the sense involving great speed. But the word's oldest meaning is quite different: "firmly placed" or "immovable," as in "tent pegs set fast in the ground" and "a fast and impassable barrier." It is easy to see how this sense developed expanded uses, such as "a door that is stuck fast and won't open." We see something of this sense in the expression "fast asleep."

In time, users added senses, some of which are common today, from being "unable to leave something, as one's bed" to being "stable and unchangeable," which we find in such uses as "hard and fast rules" or "clothes that are colorfast." Then came the sense of being "steadfast" or "firmly or totally loyal," as in "they were fast friends."

The sense that is most common today, "quick, speedy," came later. It probably developed from an obsolete sense of the adverb meaning "near at hand," which may have led to another meaning "soon." From this obsolete sense of "soon" it is just a short step, in terms of language development, to the sense meaning "quick."

In addition to what could be thought of as a horizontal dimension of change—the extension or contraction of meaning—words also may rise and fall along a vertical scale of value. Perfectly unobjectionable words are sometimes used disparagingly or sarcastically. If we say, "You're a fine one to talk," we are using *fine* in a sense quite different from its usual meaning. If a word is used often enough in negative contexts, the negative coloring may eventually become an integral part of the meaning of the word. A *villain* was once a peasant. His social standing was not high, perhaps, but he was certainly not necessarily a scoundrel. *Scavenger* originally designated the collector of a particular kind of tax in late medieval England. *Puny* meant no more than "younger" when it first passed from French into English and its spelling was transformed. Only later did it acquire the derogatory meaning more familiar to us now.

The opposite process seems to take place somewhat less frequently, but change of meaning to a more positive sense does occasionally occur. In the fourteenth century *nice,* for example, meant "foolish." Its present meaning, of course, is quite different, and the attitude it conveys seems to have undergone a complete reversal from contempt to approval.

What Qualifies as a Synonym?

It is not surprising that with so much to work with, users of English have long been interested in synonyms as an element both in accuracy and in elegance in their expression. Synonyms relieve monotony and enhance expressiveness.

Earlier writers were clear on the meaning of *synonym*. They viewed synonyms as words meaning the same thing. Unfortunately, during the last century or so this simple, clear-cut meaning has become blurred. To many publishers of thesauruses the term has come to mean little more than words that are somewhat similar in meaning. But this loose definition is unsuitable for many people, since it deprives them of the guidance needed for finding the precise word in a particular context.

This thesaurus takes a different approach to describing the nature of a synonym. Groups of synonyms are organized around a segment of meaning that two or more words have in common. In order to create these groups, one has to analyze each word carefully, ignoring nonessential aspects such as connotations and implications and try to isolate the basic meaning, which we call an *elementary meaning*.

When we look at the synonymous relationship of words in terms of elementary meanings, the process of choosing synonyms is simpler and more exact. For example, it is easy to see that no term more restricted in definition than another word can be its synonym. For example, *station wagon* and *minivan* cannot be synonyms of *automobile*, nor can *biceps* be a synonym of *muscle*. Even though a very definite relationship exists between the members, *station wagon* and *minivan* are types of automobile and *biceps* is a type of muscle. So these words are narrower in their range of application. On the other hand, a word more broadly defined than another word in the dictionary may be considered a synonym of the other word so long as the two words share one or more elementary meanings. In order to pin down the area of shared meaning for you, each main entry in this work contains after its synonym list a *meaning core* which states the elementary meaning shared by all the words in that particular synonym group.

What is an Antonym?

Like the word *synonym, antonym* has been used by some writers with a great deal of vagueness and often applied loosely to words which show no real oppositeness when compared one to another. As in the case of synonyms, the relation needs to be seen as one between segments of meaning that can be isolated, rather than between words or dictionary senses of words. As is the case with synonyms, antonyms need to have one or more elementary meanings precisely opposite to or negating the same area of meaning of another word. This definition excludes from consideration as antonyms several classes of words that are sometimes treated as antonyms but that actually contain words which neither directly oppose nor directly negate the words with which they are said to be antonymous.

For example, some terms have such a relationship to each other that one can scarcely be used without suggesting the other (as *husband* and *wife, father* and *son, buyer* and *seller*), yet there is no real opposition or real negation between such pairs. These are merely *relative terms*—their relation is reciprocal or correlative rather than antonymous.

Complementary terms in a similar way are usually paired and have a reciprocal relationship to the point that one seems incomplete without the other (as in such pairs as *question* and *answer, seek* and *find*). This relation which involves no negation is better seen as sequential than antonymous.

And contrastive terms differ sharply from their "opposites" only in some parts of their meaning. They neither oppose nor negate fully, since they are significantly different in range of meaning and applicability, in emphasis, and in the suggestions they convey. An example is *destitute* (a strong word carrying suggestions of misery and distress), which is contrastive rather than antonymous with respect to *rich* (a rather neutral and matter-of-fact term), while *poor* (another neutral and matter-of-fact term) is the appropriate antonym of *rich*. Basically, contrastive words are only opposed incidentally; they do not meet head-on.

What then is considered an antonym? True antonyms can be classified in three ways:

Opposites without intermediates: What is *perfect* can be in no way *imperfect;* you cannot at the same time *accept* and *reject* or *agree* and *disagree.*

Opposites with intermediates: Such words make up the extremes in a range of difference and are so completely opposed that the language allows no wider difference. Thus, a scale of excellence might include *superiority, adequacy, mediocrity,* and *inferiority,* but only *superiority* and *inferiority* are so totally opposed that each exactly negates what its opposite affirms.

Reverse opposites: These are words that are opposed in such a way that each means the undoing or nullification of what the other affirms. Such reverse opposites exactly oppose and fully negate the special features of their opposites. Thus, *disprove* so perfectly opposes and so clearly negates the implications of *prove* that it fits the concept of antonym, as does *unkind* with respect to *kind.*

In this book, antonyms, when they fit one of these criteria, are listed after the synonym to which they apply.

A

abaft ♦ toward or at the stern (of a vessel) **Syn** aft, astern **Ant** afore

abandon *vb* 1 ♦ to quit absolutely **Syn** desert, forsake **Ant** reclaim 2 **Syn** RELINQUISH, surrender, yield, resign, leave **Ant** cherish (*hopes, opinions*); restrain (*oneself*)

abandon *n* **Syn** UNCONSTRAINT, spontaneity **Ant** self-restraint

abandoned ♦ utterly depraved **Syn** reprobate, profligate, dissolute **Ant** redeemed, regenerate

abase ♦ to lower in one's own estimation or in that of others **Syn** demean, debase, degrade, humble, humiliate **Ant** exalt; extol (*especially oneself*)

abash **Syn** EMBARRASS, discomfit, disconcert, faze, rattle **Ant** embolden; reassure

abate 1 **Syn** ABOLISH, extinguish, annihilate **Ant** perpetuate 2 **Syn** DECREASE, reduce, diminish, lessen **Ant** augment; accelerate (*pace, speed*); intensify (*hopes, fears, a fever*) 3 ♦ to die down in force or intensity **Syn** subside, wane, ebb **Ant** rise; revive

abatement **Syn** DEDUCTION, rebate, discount **Ant** addition

abbey **Syn** CLOISTER, convent, nunnery, monastery, priory

abbreviate **Syn** SHORTEN, abridge, curtail **Ant** elongate, lengthen

abdicate ♦ to give up formally or definitely a position of trust, honor, or glory **Syn** renounce, resign **Ant** assume; usurp

abdomen ♦ the part of the body between the chest and the pelvis **Syn** belly, stomach, paunch, gut

abduct ♦ to carry off (a person) surreptitiously for an illegal purpose **Syn** kidnap

aberrant **Syn** ABNORMAL, atypical **Ant** true (*to a type*)

aberration 1 **Syn** DEVIATION, deflection **Ant** conformity; regularity 2 ♦ mental disorder **Syn** derangement, alienation **Ant** soundness (*of mind*)

abet **Syn** INCITE, foment, instigate **Ant** deter (*with a personal subject*)

abettor **Syn** CONFEDERATE, accessory, accomplice, conspirator

abeyant **Syn** LATENT, dormant, quiescent, potential **Ant** operative; active; revived

abhor **Syn** HATE, abominate, loathe, detest **Ant** admire

abhorrence ♦ a feeling of extreme disgust or dislike **Syn** detestation, loathing, abomination, hatred, hate **Ant** admiration; enjoyment

abhorrent 1 **Syn** HATEFUL, abominable, detestable, odious **Ant** admirable; enjoyable 2 **Syn** REPUGNANT, repellent, obnoxious, distasteful, invidious **Ant** congenial

abide 1 **Syn** STAY, wait, remain, tarry, linger **Ant** depart 2 **Syn** CONTINUE, endure, last, persist **Ant** pass 3 **Syn** BEAR, endure, suffer, tolerate, stand, brook

ability ♦ physical, mental, or legal power to perform **Syn** capacity, capability **Ant** inability, incapacity

abject **Syn** MEAN, ignoble, sordid **Ant** exalted (*in rank, state, condition, mood, behavior*); imperious (*in manner, speech, attitude*)

abjure ♦ to abandon irrevocably and, usu., with solemnity or publicity **Syn** renounce, forswear, recant, retract **Ant** pledge (*allegiance, a vow*); elect (*a way of life, a means to an end, an end*)

able ♦ having marked power or fitness for work **Syn** capable, competent, qualified **Ant** inept; unable

abnegate **Syn** FORGO, sacrifice, eschew, forbear **Ant** indulge (in)

abnegation **Syn** RENUNCIATION, self-abnegation, self-denial **Ant** indulgence, self-indulgence

abnormal ♦ deviating markedly from the rule or standard of its kind **Syn** atypical, aberrant **Ant** normal

abode **Syn** HABITATION, dwelling, residence, domicile, home, house

abolish ♦ to make nonexistent *Syn* annihilate, extinguish, abate *Ant* establish

abominable *Syn* HATEFUL, detestable, odious, abhorrent *Ant* laudable; enjoyable, delightful

abominate *Syn* HATE, loathe, detest, abhor *Ant* esteem; enjoy

abomination 1 *Syn* ABHORRENCE, detestation, loathing, hatred, hate *Ant* esteem; enjoyment **2** ♦ a person or thing from which one shrinks with intense dislike *Syn* anathema, bugbear, bête noire *Ant* joy

aboriginal *Syn* NATIVE, indigenous, autochthonous

abortive *Syn* FUTILE, fruitless, vain, bootless *Ant* consummated

abound *Syn* TEEM, overflow, swarm *Ant* fail, fall short

about ♦ in reference to *Syn* concerning, regarding, respecting

above ♦ at a higher level *Syn* over *Ant* below

aboveboard *Syn* STRAIGHTFORWARD, forthright *Ant* underhand, underhanded

abracadabra *Syn* GIBBERISH, hocuspocus, mummery

abrade ♦ to affect a surface by rubbing, scraping, or wearing away *Syn* excoriate, chafe, fret, gall

abridge *Syn* SHORTEN, curtail, abbreviate, retrench *Ant* expand; extend

abridgment ♦ a condensation of a larger work *Syn* abstract, epitome, brief, synopsis, conspectus *Ant* expansion

abrogate 1 *Syn* ANNUL, vacate, quash, void *Ant* institute (*by enacting, decreeing*) **2** *Syn* NULLIFY, annul, negate, invalidate *Ant* establish, fix (*a right, a character, a quality, a custom*)

abrupt 1 *Syn* STEEP, precipitous, sheer *Ant* sloping **2** *Syn* PRECIPITATE, sudden, headlong, impetuous, hasty *Ant* deliberate, leisurely

abscess ♦ a localized swollen area of infection containing pus *Syn* boil, furuncle, carbuncle, pimple, pustule

abscond *Syn* ESCAPE, decamp, flee, fly *Ant* give (*oneself*) up

absence *Syn* LACK, want, dearth, defect, privation *Ant* presence

absent *Syn* ABSTRACTED, preoccupied, absentminded, distraught *Ant* attentive

absentminded *Syn* ABSTRACTED, absent, preoccupied, distraught *Ant* wide-awake

absolute 1 *Syn* PURE, simple, sheer *Ant* mixed, qualified **2** ♦ exercising power or authority without external restraint *Syn* autocratic, arbitrary, despotic, tyrannical, tyrannous *Ant* restrained; limited **3** *Syn* ULTIMATE, categorical *Ant* conditioned

absolution *Syn* PARDON, amnesty *Ant* condemnation

absolve *Syn* EXCULPATE, exonerate, acquit, vindicate *Ant* hold (*to a promise, an obligation*); charge (*with a sin, the blame, the responsibility*)

absorb 1 ♦ to take (something) in so as to become imbued with it or to make it a part of one's being *Syn* imbibe, assimilate *Ant* exude, give out **2** *Syn* MONOPOLIZE, engross, consume *Ant* dissipate (*time, attention, energies*)

absorbed *Syn* INTENT, engrossed, rapt *Ant* distracted

absorbing *Syn* INTERESTING, engrossing, intriguing *Ant* irksome

abstain *Syn* REFRAIN, forbear *Ant* indulge

abstemiousness *Syn* TEMPERANCE, abstinence, sobriety, continence *Ant* gluttony

abstinence *Syn* TEMPERANCE, continence, abstemiousness, sobriety *Ant* self-indulgence

abstract *adj* ♦ having conceptual rather than concrete existence *Syn* ideal, transcendent, transcendental *Ant* concrete

abstract *n* *Syn* ABRIDGMENT, brief, synopsis, epitome, conspectus *Ant* amplification

abstract *vb* *Syn* DETACH, disengage *Ant* insert, introduce

abstracted ♦ inattentive to what presently claims or demands consideration *Syn* preoccupied, absent, absentminded, distraught *Ant* alert

abstruse *Syn* RECONDITE, occult, esoteric *Ant* obvious, plain

absurd *Syn* FOOLISH, silly, preposterous *Ant* rational, sensible

abundant *Syn* PLENTIFUL, copious, ample, plenteous *Ant* scarce

abuse *vb* ♦ to use or treat a person or thing improperly or wrongfully *Syn* misuse, mistreat, maltreat, ill-treat, outrage *Ant* respect, honor

abuse *n* ♦ vehemently expressed condemnation or disapproval *Syn* vituperation, invective, obloquy, scurrility, billingsgate *Ant* adulation

abusive ♦ coarse, insulting, and contemptuous in character or utterance *Syn* opprobrious, vituperative, contumelious, scurrilous *Ant* complementary; respectful

abutment *Syn* BUTTRESS, pier

abutting *Syn* ADJACENT, contiguous, adjoining, tangent, conterminous, juxtaposed

abysm *Syn* GULF, chasm, abyss

abysmal *Syn* DEEP, profound

abyss *Syn* GULF, chasm, abysm

academic 1 *Syn* PEDANTIC, scholastic, bookish 2 *Syn* THEORETICAL, speculative

accede *Syn* ASSENT, acquiesce, consent, agree, subscribe *Ant* demur

accelerate *Syn* SPEED, quicken, hurry, hasten, precipitate *Ant* decelerate; retard

accent 1 *Syn* EMPHASIS, stress, accentuation 2 *Syn* INFLECTION, intonation

accentuation *Syn* EMPHASIS, accent, stress *Ant* inaccentuation

accept *Syn* RECEIVE, admit, take *Ant* reject

acceptance ♦ the act or fact of accepting or the state of being accepted *Syn* acceptation

acceptation 1 *Syn* MEANING, sense, signification, significance, import 2 *Syn* ACCEPTANCE

access 1 *Syn* ENTRANCE, ingress, entrée, entry *Ant* outlet 2 *Syn* FIT, accession, attack, paroxysm, spasm, convulsion

accession 1 *Syn* ADDITION, accretion, increment *Ant* discard 2 *Syn* FIT, access, attack, paroxysm, spasm, convulsion

accessory *n* 1 *Syn* APPENDAGE, appurtenance, adjunct 2 *Syn* CONFEDERATE, accomplice, abettor, conspirator *Ant* principal

accessory *adj Syn* AUXILIARY, contributory, subsidiary, adjuvant, ancillary, subservient *Ant* constituent, integral; principal (*in law*)

accident 1 *Syn* QUALITY, character, attribute, property *Ant* substance (*in philosophy*) 2 *Syn* CHANCE, hazard, luck, fortune, hap *Ant* design, intent 3♦ chance or a chance event bringing injury or loss *Syn* casualty, mishap

accidental ♦ not amenable to planning or prediction *Syn* casual, fortuitous, contingent, incidental *Ant* planned; essential

acclaim *vb Syn* PRAISE, extol, laud, eulogize *Ant* vituperate

acclaim *n Syn* APPLAUSE, acclamation, plaudits *Ant* vituperation

acclamation *Syn* APPLAUSE, acclaim, plaudits

acclimate *Syn* HARDEN, acclimatize, season

acclimatize *Syn* HARDEN, acclimate, season

accommodate 1 *Syn* ADAPT, adjust, conform, reconcile *Ant* constrain 2 *Syn* OBLIGE, favor *Ant* incommode 3 *Syn* CONTAIN, hold

accompaniment ♦ something attendant upon or found in association with another thing. *Syn* concomitant

accompany ♦ to go or be together with *Syn* attend, conduct, escort, convoy, chaperon

accomplice *Syn* CONFEDERATE, accessory, abettor, conspirator

accomplish *Syn* PERFORM, achieve, effect, fulfill, discharge, execute *Ant* undo

accomplished *Syn* CONSUMMATE, finished

accomplishment *Syn* ACQUIREMENT, attainment, acquisition

accord *vb* 1 *Syn* AGREE, harmonize, correspond, tally, conform, square, jibe *Ant* conflict 2 *Syn* GRANT, vouchsafe, concede, award *Ant* withhold

accord *n* 1 *Syn* HARMONY, concord, consonance *Ant* dissension, strife; antagonism 2 *Syn* AGREEMENT, understanding

accordingly *Syn* THEREFORE, SO, consequently, hence, then

accost *Syn* ADDRESS, greet, hail, salute

account *n* 1 *Syn* USE, service, advantage,

profit, avail **2** ♦ a statement of actual events or conditions or of purported occurrences or conditions **Syn** report, chronicle, version, story

account *vb* **1 Syn** CONSIDER, deem, regard, reckon **2 Syn** EXPLAIN, justify, rationalize

accountable Syn RESPONSIBLE, answerable, amenable, liable

accouter Syn FURNISH, equip, arm, outfit, appoint

accredit 1 Syn APPROVE, certify, endorse, sanction **2 Syn** AUTHORIZE, commission, license **3 Syn** ASCRIBE, credit, charge, assign, attribute, impute

accretion Syn ADDITION, increment, accession

accumulate ♦ to bring together so as to make a store or great quantity **Syn** amass, hoard **Ant** dissipate

accumulative Syn CUMULATIVE, summative, additive

accurate Syn CORRECT, exact, precise, nice, right **Ant** inaccurate

accursed Syn EXECRABLE, damnable, cursed **Ant** blessed

accuse ♦ to declare a person guilty of a fault or offense **Syn** charge, incriminate, indict, impeach, arraign **Ant** exculpate

accustom Syn HABITUATE, addict, inure **Ant** disaccustom

accustomed Syn USUAL, wonted, customary, habitual **Ant** unaccustomed

acerbity Syn ACRIMONY, asperity **Ant** mellowness

ache Syn PAIN, pang, throe, twinge, stitch

achieve 1 Syn PERFORM, accomplish, effect, fulfill, execute, discharge **Ant** fail **2 Syn** REACH, attain, gain, compass **Ant** miss (*getting or attaining*)

achievement Syn FEAT, exploit **Ant** failure

achromatic Syn COLORLESS, uncolored **Ant** chromatic

acid Syn SOUR, acidulous, tart, dry **Ant** bland; sweet; alkaline

acidulous Syn SOUR, acid, tart, dry **Ant** saccharine

acknowledge 1♦ to disclose something against one's will or inclination **Syn**

admit, own, avow, confess **Ant** deny **2**♦ to take cognizance of in some way, usually in a way dictated by custom or convention and implying acceptance or assent **Syn** recognize **Ant** ignore

acme Syn SUMMIT, apex, zenith, culmination, climax, peak, apogee, pinnacle, meridian

acoustic, acoustical Syn AUDITORY

acquaint Syn INFORM, apprise, advise, notify

acquaintance Syn FRIEND, intimate, confidant

acquiesce Syn ASSENT, consent, agree, accede, subscribe **Ant** object

acquiescence Syn compliance, resignation **Ant** rebelliousness, rebellion

acquiescent Syn COMPLIANT, resigned **Ant** rebellious

acquire Syn GET, obtain, gain, win, secure, procure **Ant** forfeit

acquirement ♦ a power or skill that is the fruit of exertion or effort **Syn** acquisition, attainment, accomplishment

acquisition Syn ACQUIREMENT, attainment, accomplishment

acquisitive Syn COVETOUS, grasping, avaricious, greedy **Ant** sacrificing, abnegating

acquit 1 Syn EXCULPATE, absolve, exonerate, vindicate **Ant** convict **2 Syn** BEHAVE, quit, conduct, demean, deport, comport

acrid 1 Syn BITTER **Ant** savory **2 Syn** CAUSTIC, mordant, scathing **Ant** benign, kindly

acrimonious Syn ANGRY, irate, indignant, wrathful, wroth, mad **Ant** irenic, peaceable

acrimony ♦ temper or language marked by irritation or some degree of anger or resentment **Syn** acerbity, asperity **Ant** suavity

across ♦ so as to intersect the length of something **Syn** crosswise, crossways, athwart

act *n* **Syn** ACTION, deed

act *vb* **1**♦ to perform esp. in an indicated way **Syn** behave, work, operate, function, react **2**♦ to assume the appearance or role of another person or character **Syn** play, impersonate

acting *Syn* TEMPORARY, ad interim, provisional

action 1 ♦ something done or effected *Syn* act, deed **2** *Syn* SUIT, cause, case, lawsuit **3** *Syn* BATTLE, engagement

activate *Syn* VITALIZE, energize *Ant* arrest

active ♦ at work or in effective action *Syn* operative, dynamic, live *Ant* inactive

actor ♦ one who, for the entertainment or edification of an audience, takes part in an exhibition simulating happenings in real life *Syn* player, performer, mummer, mime, mimic, thespian, impersonator, trouper

actual *Syn* REAL, true *Ant* ideal; imaginary

actuality *Syn* EXISTENCE, being *Ant* potentiality, possibility

actualize *Syn* REALIZE, embody, incarnate, externalize, objectify, materialize, hypostatize, reify

actuate 1 *Syn* MOVE, drive, impel **2** *Syn* ACTIVATE, motivate *Ant* deter

acumen *Syn* DISCERNMENT, penetration, insight, perception, discrimination *Ant* obtuseness

acute 1 *Syn* SHARP, keen *Ant* obtuse **2** ♦ of uncertain outcome *Syn* critical, crucial

adage *Syn* SAYING, saw, proverb, maxim, motto, epigram, aphorism, apothegm

adamant, adamantine *Syn* INFLEXIBLE, obdurate, inexorable *Ant* yielding

adapt 1 ♦ to bring into correspondence *Syn* adjust, accommodate, conform, reconcile *Ant* unfit **2** *Syn* EDIT, rewrite, revise, redact, compile

adaptable *Syn* PLASTIC, pliant, ductile, pliable, malleable *Ant* inadaptable, unadaptable

add 1 ♦ to find or represent the amount reached by putting together arithmetically a series of numbers of quantities *Syn* sum, total, tot, cast, figure, foot **2** ♦ to bring in or join on something more so as to form a larger or more inclusive whole *Syn* append, annex, subjoin, superadd *Ant* subtract, deduct

addendum *Syn* APPENDIX, supplement

addict *vb Syn* HABITUATE, accustom, inure *Ant* wean

addict *n* ♦ a person who by habit and strong inclination indulges in something or the pursuit of something *Syn* votary, devotee, habitué

addition ♦ a thing that serves to increase another in size, amount, or content *Syn* accretion, increment, accession

additive *Syn* CUMULATIVE, summative, accumulative

addle *Syn* CONFUSE, muddle, fuddle, befuddle *Ant* refresh (*mentally*)

address *vb* **1** *Syn* DIRECT, devote, apply **2** ♦ to speak to or, less often, to write or make a sign to a person in recognition or in order to obtain recognition *Syn* accost, greet, salute, hail

address *n* **1** *Syn* TACT, savoir faire, poise *Ant* maladroitness, gaucherie **2** *Syn* SPEECH, oration, harangue, lecture, talk, sermon, homily

adduce ♦ to bring forward by way of explanation, proof, illustration, or demonstration *Syn* advance, allege, cite

adept *n Syn* EXPERT, wizard, artiste, artist, virtuoso *Ant* bungler

adept *adj Syn* PROFICIENT, skilled, skillful, expert, masterly *Ant* inadept, inept; bungling

adequate *Syn* SUFFICIENT, enough, competent

adhere *Syn* STICK, cohere, cling, cleave

adherence ♦ a physical adhering *Syn* adhesion *Ant* inadherence, nonadherence

adherent *Syn* FOLLOWER, disciple, partisan, satellite, henchman, sectary *Ant* renegade

adhesion *Syn* ADHERENCE *Ant* nonadhesion, inadhesion

ad interim *Syn* TEMPORARY, provisional, acting *Ant* permanent

adjacent ♦ in close proximity *Syn* adjoining, contiguous, abutting, tangent, conterminous, juxtaposed *Ant* nonadjacent

adjoining *Syn* ADJACENT, contiguous, abutting, tangent, conterminous, juxtaposed *Ant* detached, disjoined

adjudge *Syn* JUDGE, adjudicate, arbitrate

adjudicate *Syn* JUDGE, adjudge, arbitrate

adjunct *Syn* APPENDAGE, appurtenance, accessory

adjure *Syn* BEG, entreat, beseech, implore, importune, supplicate

adjust 1 ♦ to set right or to rights *Syn* regulate, fix *Ant* derange **2** *Syn* ADAPT, accommodate, conform, reconcile

adjuvant *Syn* AUXILIARY, contributory, ancillary, accessory, subsidiary, subservient *Ant* counteractive

administer ♦ to act on the behalf of another in or as if in the capacity of a steward *Syn* dispense

admiration 1 *Syn* WONDER, wonderment, amazement **2** *Syn* REGARD, esteem, respect *Ant* abhorrence

admire *Syn* REGARD, esteem, respect *Ant* abhor

admission *Syn* ADMITTANCE

admit 1 *Syn* RECEIVE, accept, take *Ant* eject, expel **2** *Syn* ACKNOWLEDGE, own, confess, avow *Ant* gainsay; disdain **3** *Syn* ENTER, introduce *Ant* exclude

admittance ♦ permitted entrance *Syn* admission

admixture 1 *Syn* MIXTURE, composite, blend, compound, amalgam **2** ♦ an added ingredient that destroys the purity or genuineness of a substance *Syn* alloy, adulterant

admonish *Syn* REPROVE, chide, reproach, rebuke, reprimand *Ant* commend

ado *Syn* STIR, fuss, pother, flurry, bustle

adolescence *Syn* YOUTH, puberty, pubescence *Ant* senescence

adopt ♦ to make one's own what in some fashion one owes to another *Syn* embrace, espouse *Ant* repudiate; discard

adoration *Syn* REVERENCE, worship, veneration *Ant* blasphemy

adore 1 *Syn* REVERE, worship, venerate, reverence *Ant* blaspheme **2** ♦ to love or admire excessively *Syn* worship, idolize *Ant* detest

adorn ♦ to add something unessential in order to enhance the appearance *Syn* decorate, ornament, embellish, beautify, deck, bedeck, garnish *Ant* disfigure

adroit 1 *Syn* DEXTEROUS, deft, handy *Ant* maladroit **2** *Syn* CLEVER, cunning, ingenious *Ant* stolid

adulation *Syn* COMPLIMENT, flattery *Ant* abuse

adult *Syn* MATURE, grown-up, matured, ripe, mellow *Ant* juvenile; puerile

adulterant *Syn* ADMIXTURE, alloy

adulterate ♦ to alter fraudulently esp. for profit *Syn* sophisticate, load, weight, doctor *Ant* refine

adumbrate *Syn* SUGGEST, shadow

adumbration *Syn* SHADE, shadow, umbra, penumbra, umbrage *Ant* revelation

advance *vb* **1** ♦ to move or put ahead *Syn* promote, forward, further *Ant* retard; check **2** ♦ to move forward in space, in time, or in approach to a material or ideal objective *Syn* progress *Ant* recede **3** *Syn* ADDUCE, allege, cite

advance *n* **1** ♦ movement forward in space, in time, or in approach to a material or ideal objective *Syn* progress *Ant* recession, retrogression **2** *Syn* OVERTURE, approach, tender, bid

advanced 1 *Syn* PREMATURE, forward, precocious, untimely *Ant* backward **2** *Syn* LIBERAL, radical, progressive *Ant* conservative

advancement ♦ the act of raising a person in grade, rank, or dignity, or the honor that comes to one who is so raised *Syn* preferment, promotion, elevation *Ant* degradation; reduction (*in rank or status*)

advantage 1 ♦ a factor or set of factors in a competition or rivalry giving one person or side a position of superiority over the other *Syn* handicap, allowance, odds, edge *Ant* disadvantage; handicap **2** *Syn* USE, service, account, profit, avail *Ant* detriment

advantageous *Syn* BENEFICIAL, profitable *Ant* disadvantageous

advent *Syn* ARRIVAL *Ant* leaving, passing

adventure ♦ an undertaking, an exploit, or an experience involving hazards and requiring boldness *Syn* enterprise, quest

adventurous ♦ courting danger or exposing oneself to danger in a greater degree than is required for courage *Syn* venturesome, daring, daredevil, rash, reckless, foolhardy *Ant* unadventurous; cautious

adversary *Syn* OPPONENT, antagonist *Ant* ally

adverse ♦ so opposed as to cause interference, often harmful or fatal interference *Syn* antagonistic, counter, counteractive *Ant* propitious

adversity *Syn* MISFORTUNE, mischance, mishap *Ant* prosperity

advert *Syn* REFER, allude

advertise *Syn* DECLARE, publish, announce, proclaim, broadcast, promulgate

advertisement *Syn* DECLARATION, publication, announcement, broadcasting, proclamation, promulgation

advice 1 ♦ a recommendation as to a decision or a course of conduct *Syn* counsel **2** *Syn* NEWS, intelligence, tidings

advisable *Syn* EXPEDIENT, politic *Ant* inadvisable

advise ♦ to make a recommendation as to a decision or a course of conduct *Syn* counsel **2** *Syn* CONFER, consult, commune, parley, treat, negotiate **3** *Syn* INFORM, notify, apprise, acquaint

advised *Syn* DELIBERATE, considered, premeditated, designed, studied

advocate *n Syn* LAWYER, counselor, barrister, counsel, attorney, solicitor

advocate *vb Syn* SUPPORT, uphold, champion, back *Ant* impugn

aeon *Syn* PERIOD, age, era, epoch

aerial *Syn* AIRY, ethereal

aesthete ♦ a person conspicuous for his enjoyment and appreciation of the beautiful, the exquisite, or the choice *Syn* dilettante, connoisseur

affable *Syn* GRACIOUS, cordial, genial, sociable *Ant* reserved

affair 1 ♦ something done or dealt with *Syn* business, concern, matter, thing **2** *Syn* AMOUR, intrigue, liaison

affect *Syn* ASSUME, simulate, pretend, feign, counterfeit, sham

affect ♦ to produce or to have an effect upon a person or upon a thing capable of a reaction *Syn* influence, touch, impress, strike, sway

affectation *Syn* POSE, air, mannerism *Ant* artlessness

affecting *Syn* MOVING, touching, pathetic, poignant, impressive

affection 1 *Syn* FEELING, emotion, passion, sentiment *Ant* antipathy **2** *Syn* ATTACHMENT, love *Ant* coldness **3** *Syn* DISEASE, disorder, condition, ailment, malady, complaint, distemper, syndrome

affectionate *Syn* LOVING, devoted, fond, doting *Ant* cold; undemonstrative

affiliated *Syn* RELATED, allied, kindred, cognate *Ant* unaffiliated

affinity 1 *Syn* ATTRACTION, sympathy **2** *Syn* LIKENESS, resemblance, similarity, similitude, analogy

affirm *Syn* ASSERT, profess, aver, avow, protest, avouch, declare, warrant, predicate *Ant* deny

affix *Syn* FASTEN, attach, fix *Ant* detach

afflatus *Syn* INSPIRATION, fury, frenzy

afflict ♦ to inflict upon a person something which he finds hard to endure *Syn* try, torment, torture, rack *Ant* comfort

affliction *Syn* TRIAL, visitation, tribulation, cross *Ant* solace, consolation

affluent *Syn* RICH, wealthy, opulent *Ant* impecunious; straitened

afford *Syn* GIVE, confer, bestow, present, donate *Ant* deny (*something one wants*)

affray *n Syn* CONTEST, fray, fight, combat, conflict

affray *vb Syn* FRIGHTEN, fright, affright, scare, alarm, terrify, terrorize, startle

affright *Syn* FRIGHTEN, fright, affray, scare, alarm, terrify, terrorize, startle *Ant* nerve, embolden

affront *vb Syn* OFFEND, outrage, insult *Ant* gratify (*by an attention*)

affront *n* ♦ a speech or an action having for its intention or effect the dishonoring of something or someone *Syn* insult, indignity *Ant* gratification

afraid *Syn* FEARFUL, apprehensive *Ant* unafraid; sanguine

aft *Syn* ABAFT, astern *Ant* fore

after *prep, adj, adv* ♦ following upon, esp. in place or in time *Syn* behind *Ant* before

after *adj Syn* POSTERIOR, hinder, hind, rear, back

aftereffect, aftermath *Syn* EFFECT, result,

consequence, upshot, sequel, issue, outcome, event

age *n* **1 ♦** the period in one's life when one is old in years and declining in body or mind or both *Syn* senility, senescence, dotage *Ant* youth **2** *Syn* PERIOD, era, epoch, aeon

age *vb Syn* MATURE, ripen, develop

aged ♦ far advanced in years *Syn* old, elderly, superannuated *Ant* youthful

agency *Syn* MEAN, agent, instrumentality, instrument, medium, vehicle, channel, organ

agenda *Syn* PROGRAM, schedule, timetable

agent 1 *Syn* MEAN, instrument, agency, instrumentality, medium, vehicle, organ, channel *Ant* patient **2 ♦** one who performs the duties of or transacts business for another *Syn* factor, attorney, deputy, proxy *Ant* principal

agglomerate, agglomeration *Syn* AGGREGATE, conglomerate, conglomeration, aggregation

aggrandize *Syn* EXALT, magnify *Ant* belittle

aggravate 1 *Syn* INTENSIFY, heighten, enhance *Ant* alleviate **2** *Syn* IRRITATE, exasperate, provoke, rile, peeve, nettle *Ant* appease

aggregate 1 *Syn* SUM, total, whole, number, amount, quantity *Ant* individual; particular **2 ♦** a mass formed by parts or particles that are not merged into each other *Syn* aggregation, conglomerate, conglomeration, agglomerate, agglomeration *Ant* constituent

aggregation *Syn* AGGREGATE, conglomerate, conglomeration, agglomerate, agglomeration

aggression *Syn* ATTACK, offense, offensive *Ant* resistance

aggressive 1 *Syn* attacking, offensive *Ant* resisting; repelling **2 ♦** conspicuously or obtrusively active or energetic *Syn* militant, assertive, self-assertive, pushing, pushy

aggrieve *Syn* WRONG, oppress, persecute *Ant* rejoice

agile ♦ acting or moving with quickness and alacrity *Syn* nimble, brisk, spry *Ant* torpid

agitate 1 *Syn* SHAKE, rock, convulse *Ant* quiet, lull, still **2** *Syn* DISCOMPOSE, perturb, upset, fluster, flurry, disturb, disquiet *Ant* calm, tranquilize **3** *Syn* DISCUSS, argue, dispute, debate

agitation *Syn* COMMOTION, tumult, turmoil, turbulence, confusion, convulsion, upheaval *Ant* tranquillity

agnostic *Syn* ATHEIST, deist, freethinker, unbeliever, infidel

agog *Syn* EAGER, keen, anxious, avid, athirst *Ant* aloof

agonize *Syn* WRITHE, squirm

agonizing *Syn* EXCRUCIATING, racking

agony *Syn* DISTRESS, suffering, passion, misery, dolor

agrarian *Syn* agricultural

agree 1 *Syn* ASSENT, accede, consent, acquiesce, subscribe *Ant* protest (*against*); differ (*with*) **2 ♦** to come into or to be in harmony regarding a matter of opinion or a policy *Syn* concur, coincide *Ant* differ; disagree **3 ♦** to exist or go together without conflict or incongruity *Syn* square, conform, accord, harmonize, correspond, tally, jibe *Ant* differ (*from*)

agreeable *Syn* PLEASANT, grateful, pleasing, gratifying, welcome *Ant* disagreeable

agreement ♦ a reconciliation of differences as to what should be done or not done *Syn* accord, understanding

agriculture ♦ the science or the business of raising useful plants and animals *Syn* farming, husbandry

ahead *Syn* BEFORE, forward *Ant* behind

aid *vb Syn* HELP, assist *Ant* injure

aid *n* **1** *Syn* help, assistance *Ant* impediment **2** *Syn* ASSISTANT, helper, coadjutor, aide, aide-de-camp

aide *Syn* ASSISTANT, aide-de-camp, coadjutor, helper, aid

aide-de-camp *Syn* ASSISTANT, aide, aid

ail *Syn* TROUBLE, distress

ailment *Syn* DISEASE, disorder, condition, affection, malady, complaint, distemper, syndrome

aim *vb* **1** *Syn* DIRECT, point, level, train, lay

2♦ to have as a controlling desire something beyond one's present power of attainment *Syn* aspire, pant

aim *n* *Syn* INTENTION, end, goal, objective, purpose, object, intent, design

air *n* **1** *Syn* POSE, affectation, mannerism **2** *Syn* MELODY, air, tune

air *vb* *Syn* EXPRESS, ventilate, vent, utter, voice, broach

airport ♦ a place where airplanes take off and land *Syn* airdrome, airfield, airstrip, landing strip, flying field, landing field

airy ♦ as light and insubstantial as air *Syn* aerial, ethereal *Ant* substantial

aisle *Syn* PASSAGE, passageway, ambulatory, corridor, gallery, hall, hallway, cloister, arcade

akin *Syn* LIKE, alike, similar, analogous, comparable, parallel, uniform, identical *Ant* alien

alacrity *Syn* CELERITY, legerity *Ant* languor

alarm *n* **1♦** a signal that serves as a call to action or to be on guard esp. in a time of imminent danger *Syn* tocsin, alert **2** *Syn* FEAR, fright, panic, terror, horror, dismay, dread, consternation, trepidation *Ant* assurance; composure

alarm *vb* *Syn* FRIGHTEN, fright, scare, startle, terrify, affright, terrorize, affray *Ant* assure; relieve

albeit *Syn* THOUGH, although

alchemy *Syn* MAGIC, thaumaturgy, wizardry, sorcery, witchery, witchcraft

alcoholic *Syn* DRUNKARD, inebriate, dipsomaniac, sot, soak, toper, tosspot, tippler

alert *adj* **1** *Syn* WATCHFUL, wide-awake, vigilant **2** *Syn* INTELLIGENT, clever, smart, bright, quick-witted, brilliant, knowing

alert *n* *Syn* ALARM, tocsin

alias *Syn* PSEUDONYM, nom de guerre, incognito, nom de plume, pen name

alibi *Syn* APOLOGY, excuse, pretext, plea, apologia

alien *adj* *Syn* EXTRINSIC, foreign, extraneous *Ant* akin; assimilable

alien *n* *Syn* STRANGER, foreigner, outlander, outsider, immigrant, émigré *Ant* citizen

alienate 1 *Syn* TRANSFER, convey, deed **2**

Syn ESTRANGE, disaffect, wean *Ant* unite; reunite

alienation 1 *Syn* ABERRATION, derangement **2** *Syn* SOLITUDE, isolation, seclusion

alight 1 *Syn* DESCEND, dismount **2♦** to come to rest after or as if after a flight, a descent, or a fall *Syn* light, land, perch, roost

align *Syn* LINE, line up, range, array

alike *Syn* LIKE, similar, analogous, comparable, akin, parallel, uniform, identical *Ant* different

aliment *Syn* FOOD, pabulum, nutriment, nourishment, sustenance, pap

alive 1 *Syn* LIVING, animated, animate, vital *Ant* dead, defunct **2** *Syn* AWARE, awake, sensible, cognizant, conscious *Ant* blind (*to*); anesthetic (*to*)

alkaline ♦ being a compound that reacts with an acid to form a salt *Syn* basic

all 1 *Syn* WHOLE, entire, total, gross **2♦** including the entire membership of a group with no exceptions *Syn* every, each *Ant* no

all-round *Syn* VERSATILE, many-sided

allay *Syn* RELIEVE, alleviate, lighten, assuage, mitigate *Ant* intensify

allege *Syn* ADDUCE, cite, advance *Ant* contravene; (*in law*) traverse

allegiance *Syn* FIDELITY, fealty, loyalty, devotion, piety *Ant* treachery; treason

allegory 1♦ a concrete representation in art of something that is abstract or for some other reason not directly representable *Syn* symbolism **2♦** a literary form that typically tells a story for the sake of presenting a truth or of enforcing a moral *Syn* parable, myth, fable

alleviate *Syn* RELIEVE, lighten, assuage, mitigate, allay *Ant* aggravate

alliance ♦ a chiefly political combination for a common object *Syn* league, coalition, fusion, confederacy, confederation, federation

allied *Syn* RELATED, cognate, kindred, affiliated *Ant* unallied

allocate *Syn* ALLOT, assign, apportion

allot ♦ to give as one's share, portion, role, or place *Syn* assign, apportion, allocate

allow 1 *Syn* LET, permit, suffer, leave *Ant*

inhibit **2** *Syn* GRANT, concede *Ant* disallow

allowance 1 *Syn* RATION, dole, pittance **2♦** a change made by way of compromise or adjustment *Syn* concession **3** *Syn* ADVANTAGE, handicap, odds, edge

alloy *Syn* ADMIXTURE, adulterant

allude *Syn* REFER, advert

allure *Syn* ATTRACT, captivate, charm, fascinate, enchant, bewitch *Ant* repel

alluring *Syn* ATTRACTIVE, charming, fascinating, bewitching, enchanting, captivating *Ant* repulsive

ally *Syn* PARTNER, colleague, copartner, confederate *Ant* adversary

almost *Syn* NEARLY, approximately, wellnigh

alms *Syn* DONATION, benefaction, contribution

alone *adj* **1♦** isolated from others *Syn* solitary, lonely, lonesome, lone, lorn, forlorn, desolate *Ant* accompanied **2** *Syn* ONLY

alone *adv Syn* ONLY

aloof *Syn* INDIFFERENT, detached, uninterested, disinterested, unconcerned, incurious *Ant* familiar, close

alp *Syn* MOUNTAIN, peak, mount

also *Syn* too, likewise, besides, moreover, furthermore

alter 1 *Syn* CHANGE, vary, modify *Ant* fix **2** *Syn* STERILIZE, castrate, spay, emasculate, mutilate, geld

alteration *Syn* CHANGE, variation, modification *Ant* fixation; fixity

altercate *vb Syn* QUARREL, wrangle, squabble, bicker, spat, tiff *Ant* concur

altercation *Syn* QUARREL, wrangle, squabble, bickering, spat, tiff *Ant* concurrence; accord

alternate *adj Syn* INTERMITTENT, recurrent, periodic *Ant* consecutive

alternate *vb Syn* ROTATE

alternate *n Syn* SUBSTITUTE, supply, understudy, double, stand-in, pinch hitter, locum tenens

alternation *Syn* CHANGE, vicissitude, mutation, permutation

alternative *Syn* CHOICE, option, preference, selection, election

although *Syn* THOUGH, albeit

altitude *Syn* HEIGHT, elevation

altruistic *Syn* CHARITABLE, benevolent, humanitarian, philanthropic, eleemosynary *Ant* egoistic

amalgam *Syn* MIXTURE, admixture, compound, blend, composite

amalgamate *Syn* MIX, blend, commingle, merge, coalesce, fuse, mingle

amalgamation *Syn* CONSOLIDATION, merger

amass *Syn* ACCUMULATE, hoard *Ant* distribute

amateur ♦ a person who follows a pursuit without attaining proficiency or a professional status *Syn* dilettante, dabbler, tyro *Ant* professional; expert

amative *Syn* EROTIC, amorous, amatory

amatory *Syn* EROTIC, aphrodisiac, amative, amorous

amaze *Syn* SURPRISE, astound, flabbergast, astonish

amazement *Syn* WONDER, wonderment, admiration

amazon *Syn* VIRAGO, termagant

ambassador ♦ a diplomatic agent serving his or her sovereign or government in a foreign country *Syn* legate, nuncio, minister, envoy, internuncio, chargé d'affaires

ambiguity ♦ expression or, more often, an expression capable of more than one interpretation *Syn* equivocation, tergiversation, double entendre *Ant* lucidity; explicitness

ambiguous *Syn* OBSCURE, equivocal, cryptic, enigmatic, vague, dark *Ant* explicit

ambition ♦ strong desire for advancement *Syn* aspiration, pretension

ambitious 1♦ extremely desirous of something that will give one power, fame, success, or riches *Syn* emulous *Ant* unambitious **2♦** straining or exceeding the capacity of their authors or executants *Syn* pretentious, utopian *Ant* modest

amble *Syn* SAUNTER, stroll

ambulant *Syn* ITINERANT, ambulatory, peripatetic, nomadic, vagrant *Ant* bedridden

ambulatory *adj Syn* ITINERANT, ambulant, peripatetic, nomadic, vagrant

ambulatory *n* *Syn* PASSAGE, passageway, aisle, gallery, cloister, arcade, hall, hallway, corridor

ambuscade *Syn* AMBUSH

ambush *vb* *Syn* SURPRISE, waylay

ambush *n* ♦ a device to entrap an enemy by lying in wait under cover for an opportune moment to make a surprise attack *Syn* ambuscade

ameliorate *Syn* IMPROVE, better, help *Ant* worsen; deteriorate

amenable 1 *Syn* RESPONSIBLE, answerable, liable, accountable *Ant* independent (*of*); autonomous **2** *Syn* OBEDIENT, tractable, docile, biddable *Ant* recalcitrant, refractory

amend *Syn* CORRECT, reform, rectify, revise, emend, remedy, redress *Ant* debase; impair

amends *Syn* REPARATION, redress, indemnity, restitution

amenity 1 ♦ something that gives refined or exquisite pleasure or is exceedingly pleasing to the mind or senses *Syn* luxury *Ant* rigor **2** *Syn* COURTESY, attention, gallantry *Ant* acerbity, asperity; rudeness

amerce *Syn* PENALIZE, fine, mulct

amercement *Syn* FINE

amiable ♦ having or manifesting the desire or disposition to please *Syn* good-natured, obliging, complaisant *Ant* unamiable; surly

amicable ♦ marked by or exhibiting goodwill or absence of antagonism *Syn* neighborly, friendly *Ant* antagonistic

amiss ♦ otherwise than intended *Syn* astray *Ant* aright, right

amity *Syn* FRIENDSHIP, comity, goodwill *Ant* enmity

amnesty *Syn* PARDON, absolution

among *Syn* BETWEEN

amorous *Syn* EROTIC, amative, amatory *Ant* frigid

amount *Syn* SUM, total, quantity, number, aggregate, whole

amour ♦ an instance of illicit sexual relationship *Syn* liaison, intrigue, affair

amour propre *Syn* CONCEIT, self-esteem, self-love, egoism, egotism

ample 1 *Syn* SPACIOUS, capacious, commodious *Ant* meager; circumscribed **2** *Syn* PLENTIFUL, abundant, plenteous, copious *Ant* scant, meager

amplify *Syn* EXPAND, swell, distend, dilate, inflate *Ant* abridge, condense

amplitude *Syn* EXPANSE, spread, stretch *Ant* straitness; limitation

amulet *Syn* FETISH, charm, talisman

amuse ♦ to cause or enable one to pass one's time in pleasant or agreeable activity *Syn* divert, entertain, recreate *Ant* bore

amusement ♦ an agreeable activity or its effect *Syn* diversion, entertainment, recreation *Ant* boredom

anagogic *Syn* MYSTICAL, mystic, cabalistic

analgesic *Syn* ANODYNE, anesthetic *Ant* irritant

analogous *Syn* LIKE, alike, similar, comparable, akin, parallel, uniform, identical

analogue *Syn* PARALLEL, counterpart, correlate

analogy 1 *Syn* LIKENESS, similitude, resemblance, similarity, affinity **2** ♦ a comparison between things essentially or generically different but strikingly alike in one or more pertinent aspects *Syn* simile, metaphor

analysis ♦ separation of a whole into its fundamental elements or constituent parts *Syn* resolution, dissection, breakdown *Ant* synthesis

analytical *Syn* LOGICAL, subtle *Ant* creative, inventive, constructive

analyze ♦ to divide a complex whole or unit into its component parts or constituent elements *Syn* resolve, dissect, break down *Ant* compose, compound; construct

anarchy ♦ absence, suspension, breakdown, or widespread defiance of government, law, and order *Syn* chaos, lawlessness *Ant* order; discipline

anathema 1 *Syn* ABOMINATION, bête noire, bugbear **2** *Syn* CURSE, malediction, imprecation

anathematize *Syn* EXECRATE, curse, damn, objurgate

anatomy *Syn* STRUCTURE, skeleton, framework

ancestor ♦ a person from whom one is descended **Syn** progenitor, forefather, forebear **Ant** descendant

ancestry ♦ one's progenitors or their character or quality as a whole **Syn** lineage, pedigree **Ant** descendants; posterity

anchor **Syn** SECURE, rivet

anchorite **Syn** RECLUSE, hermit, eremite, cenobite

ancient **Syn** OLD, venerable, antediluvian, antique, antiquated, archaic, obsolete **Ant** modern

ancillary **Syn** AUXILIARY, contributory, subsidiary, adjuvant, subservient, accessory

androgynous **Syn** BISEXUAL, hermaphroditic, hermaphrodite, epicene

anecdote **Syn** STORY, tale, yarn, narrative

anemic **Syn** PALE, bloodless **Ant** full-blooded; florid

anesthetic *adj* **Syn** INSENSIBLE, insensitive, impassible **Ant** alive

anesthetic *n* **Syn** ANODYNE, analgesic **Ant** stimulant

angel **Syn** SPONSOR, backer, patron, surety, guarantor

anger *n* ♦ emotional excitement induced by intense displeasure **Syn** ire, rage, fury, indignation, wrath **Ant** pleasure, gratification; forbearance

anger *vb* ♦ to make angry **Syn** incense, enrage, infuriate, madden **Ant** please, gratify; pacify

angle 1 **Syn** POINT OF VIEW, viewpoint, standpoint, slant 2 **Syn** PHASE, aspect, facet, side

angry ♦ feeling or showing strong displeasure or bad temper **Syn** irate, indignant, wrathful, wroth, acrimonious, mad

anguish **Syn** SORROW, woe, heartache, heartbreak, grief, regret **Ant** relief

angular **Syn** LEAN, gaunt, rawboned, lank, lanky, spare, scrawny, skinny **Ant** rotund

animadversion ♦ a remark or statement that is an adverse criticism **Syn** stricture, aspersion, reflection **Ant** commendation

animadvert **Syn** REMARK, comment, commentate

animal **Syn** CARNAL, fleshly, sensual **Ant** rational

animalism **Syn** ANIMALITY

animality ♦ the animal aspect or quality of human beings or human nature **Syn** animalism

animate *adj* **Syn** LIVING, alive, animated, vital **Ant** inanimate

animate *vb* 1 **Syn** QUICKEN, vivify, enliven 2 **Syn** INFORM, inspire, fire **Ant** inhibit

animated 1 **Syn** LIVING, alive, animate, vital **Ant** inert 2 **Syn** LIVELY, vivacious, sprightly, gay **Ant** depressed, dejected

animosity **Syn** ENMITY, animus, rancor, hostility, antipathy, antagonism **Ant** goodwill

animus **Syn** ENMITY, animosity, rancor, hostility, antipathy, antagonism **Ant** favor

annals **Syn** HISTORY, chronicle

annex *vb* **Syn** ADD, append, subjoin, superadd

annex *n* ♦ an addition to a main (and, often, the original) building **Syn** extension, wing, ell

annihilate **Syn** ABOLISH, extinguish, abate

annotate ♦ to add or append comment **Syn** gloss

annotation ♦ added or appended comment intended to be helpful in interpreting a passage or text **Syn** gloss

announce **Syn** DECLARE, publish, proclaim, promulgate, advertise, broadcast

announcement **Syn** DECLARATION, publication, proclamation, promulgation, advertisement, broadcasting

annoy 1 ♦ to disturb and nervously upset a person **Syn** vex, irk, bother **Ant** soothe 2 **Syn** WORRY, pester, plague, tantalize, tease, harass, harry

annul 1 **Syn** NULLIFY, negate, invalidate, abrogate 2 ♦ to deprive of legal validity, force, or authority **Syn** abrogate, void, vacate, quash

anodyne 1 ♦ something used to relieve or prevent pain **Syn** analgesic, anesthetic 2 ♦ something used to dull or deaden one's senses or one's sensibility **Syn** opiate, narcotic, nepenthe **Ant** stimulant; irritant

anoint **Syn** OIL, cream, grease, lubricate

anomalous **Syn** IRREGULAR, unnatural

anomaly **Syn** PARADOX, antinomy

answer *n* ♦ something spoken or written by way of return to a question or demand *Syn* reply, response, rejoinder, retort

answer *vb* 1♦ to say, write, or do something in response *Syn* respond, reply, rejoin, retort 2 *Syn* SATISFY, meet, fulfill

answerable *Syn* RESPONSIBLE, accountable, amenable, liable

antagonism *Syn* ENMITY, antipathy, hostility, animosity, rancor, animus *Ant* accord; comity

antagonist *Syn* OPPONENT, adversary *Ant* supporter

antagonistic *Syn* ADVERSE, counteractive, counter *Ant* favoring, favorable

antagonize *Syn* RESIST, withstand, contest, oppose, fight, combat, conflict *Ant* conciliate

ante *Syn* BET, stake, pot, wager

antecedent *n Syn* CAUSE, determinant, reason, occasion *Ant* consequence

antecedent *adj Syn* PRECEDING, precedent, foregoing, previous, prior, former, anterior *Ant* subsequent; consequent

antediluvian *Syn* OLD, ancient, antiquated, obsolete, antique, venerable, archaic

anterior *Syn* PRECEDING, precedent, previous, prior, foregoing, antecedent, former *Ant* posterior

anthropoid ♦ resembling man *Syn* anthropomorphic, anthropomorphous

anthropomorphic, anthropomorphous *Syn* ANTHROPOID

antic *n Syn* PRANK, monkeyshine, caper, dido

antic *adj Syn* FANTASTIC, grotesque, bizarre

anticipate 1 *Syn* PREVENT, forestall *Ant* consummate 2 *Syn* FORESEE, apprehend, foreknow, divine

anticipation *Syn* PROSPECT, foretaste, outlook *Ant* retrospect

antidote *Syn* CORRECTIVE, check, control

antinomy *Syn* PARADOX, anomaly

antipathetic ♦ arousing marked aversion or dislike *Syn* unsympathetic *Ant* congenial

antipathy 1 *Syn* ENMITY, antagonism, hostility, animosity, rancor, animus *Ant*

taste (*for*); affection (*for*) 2♦ the state of mind created by what is antipathetic *Syn* aversion

antipodal, antipodean *Syn* OPPOSITE, antithetical, contrary, contradictory, antonymous

antipode *Syn* OPPOSITE, antithesis, contrary, opposite, contradictory, antonym

antiquated *Syn* OLD, archaic, obsolete, antediluvian, antique, ancient, venerable *Ant* modernistic; modish

antique *Syn* OLD, ancient, venerable, antiquated, antediluvian, obsolete, archaic *Ant* modern; current

antisocial *Syn* UNSOCIAL, asocial, nonsocial *Ant* social

antithesis 1 *Syn* COMPARISON, contrast, parallel, collation 2 *Syn* OPPOSITE, antipode, contradictory, contrary, antonym

antithetical *Syn* OPPOSITE, contrary, contradictory, antonymous, antipodal, antipodean

antonym *Syn* OPPOSITE, contradictory, contrary, antithesis, antipode

antonymous *Syn* OPPOSITE, contradictory, contrary, antithetical, antipodal, antipodean

anxiety *Syn* CARE, worry, concern, solicitude *Ant* security

anxious 1 *Syn* WORRIED, concerned, solicitous *Ant* composed 2 *Syn* EAGER, keen, agog, avid *Ant* loath

apartment *Syn* ROOM, chamber

apathetic *Syn* IMPASSIVE, phlegmatic, stolid, stoic *Ant* alert; aghast

apathy *Syn* IMPASSIVITY, impassiveness, phlegm, stolidity, stoicism *Ant* zeal; enthusiasm

ape *Syn* COPY, imitate, mimic, mock

aperçu *Syn* COMPENDIUM, sketch, précis, survey, digest, pandect, syllabus

aperitif *Syn* APPETIZER

aperture ♦ an opening allowing passage through or in and out *Syn* interstice, orifice

apex *Syn* SUMMIT, peak, culmination, pinnacle, climax, acme, meridian, zenith, apogee

aphorism *Syn* SAYING, apothegm, epigram, saw, maxim, adage, proverb, motto

aphrodisiac *Syn* EROTIC, amatory, amorous *Ant* anaphrodisiac

apiece *Syn* EACH, severally, individually, respectively

aplomb *Syn* CONFIDENCE, assurance, self-assurance, self-possession, self-confidence *Ant* shyness

apocalypse *Syn* REVELATION, vision, prophecy

apocryphal *Syn* FICTITIOUS, mythical, legendary, fabulous

apogee *Syn* SUMMIT, climax, peak, culmination, apex, acme, meridian, zenith, pinnacle *Ant* perigee

apologia *Syn* APOLOGY, excuse, plea, alibi, pretext

apology ♦ the reason or reasons offered in explanation or defense of something (as an act, a policy, or a view) *Syn* apologia, excuse, plea, pretext, alibi

apostasy *Syn* DEFECTION, desertion

apostate *Syn* RENEGADE, turncoat, recreant, backslider

apothecary *Syn* DRUGGIST, pharmacist, chemist

apothegm *Syn* SAYING, aphorism, epigram, saw, maxim, adage, proverb, motto

apotheosis *Syn* PARAGON, nonpareil, nonesuch

appall *Syn* DISMAY, horrify, daunt *Ant* nerve, embolden

appalling *Syn* FEARFUL, dreadful, terrible, horrible, frightful, shocking, awful, terrific, horrific *Ant* reassuring

appanage *Syn* RIGHT, prerogative, privilege, perquisite, birthright

apparatus 1 *Syn* EQUIPMENT, gear, tackle, outfit, paraphernalia, machinery, matériel **2** *Syn* MACHINE, mechanism, machinery, engine, motor

apparel *vb Syn* CLOTHE, attire, dress, array, robe *Ant* divest

apparel *n Syn* CLOTHES, clothing, dress, attire, raiment

apparent 1 *Syn* EVIDENT, manifest, patent, distinct, obvious, palpable, plain, clear *Ant* unintelligible **2** ♦ not actually being what appearance indicates *Syn* illusory, seeming, ostensible *Ant* real

apparition ♦ a visible but immaterial appearance of a person or thing, esp. a likeness of a dead person or of a person or thing that is not physically present *Syn* phantasm, phantom, wraith, ghost, spirit, specter, shade, revenant

appeal *n Syn* PRAYER, plea, petition, suit

appeal *vb Syn* PRAY, plead, sue, petition

appear 1 ♦ to come out into view *Syn* loom, emerge *Ant* disappear; vanish **2** *Syn* SEEM, look

appearance ♦ the outward show presented by a person or thing *Syn* look, aspect, semblance

appease *Syn* PACIFY, placate, mollify, propitiate, conciliate *Ant* exasperate, aggravate

appellation *Syn* NAME, title, designation, denomination, style

append *Syn* ADD, subjoin, annex, superadd

appendage ♦ something regarded as additional and at the same time as subsidiary to another object *Syn* appurtenance, accessory, adjunct

appendix ♦ additional matter subjoined to a book *Syn* addendum, supplement

apperception *Syn* RECOGNITION, assimilation, identification

appertain *Syn* BEAR, pertain, belong, relate, apply

appetite *Syn* DESIRE, lust, passion, urge

appetizer *Syn* hors d'oeuvre, aperitif

appetizing *Syn* PALATABLE, relishing, tasty, toothsome, flavorsome, savory, sapid *Ant* nauseating

applaud 1 ♦ to demonstrate one's feeling, esp. one's approbation or joy, audibly and enthusiastically *Syn* cheer, root *Ant* hiss; boo **2** *Syn* COMMEND, compliment, recommend *Ant* disparage; criticize

applause ♦ public expression of approbation *Syn* acclamation, acclaim, plaudits *Ant* hisses; boos

appliance *Syn* IMPLEMENT, tool, instrument, utensil

applicable *Syn* RELEVANT, pertinent, apposite, apropos, germane, material *Ant* inapplicable

applicant *Syn* CANDIDATE, aspirant

application *Syn* ATTENTION, concentration, study *Ant* indolence

appliqué *Syn* OVERLAY, superpose, superimpose

apply 1 *Syn* USE, employ, utilize, avail **2** *Syn* DIRECT, devote, address **3** *Syn* RESORT, go, turn, refer **4** *Syn* BEAR, relate, pertain, appertain

appoint 1 *Syn* DESIGNATE, name, nominate, elect **2** *Syn* FURNISH, equip, accouter, outfit, arm

appointment *Syn* ENGAGEMENT, rendezvous, tryst, assignation, date

apportion 1 *Syn* ALLOT, allocate, assign **2♦** to divide something carefully and distribute it among a number *Syn* portion, parcel, ration, prorate

apposite *Syn* RELEVANT, pertinent, germane, apropos, applicable, material *Ant* inapposite, inapt

appraise *Syn* ESTIMATE, value, evaluate, assay, rate, assess

appreciable *Syn* PERCEPTIBLE, sensible, ponderable, palpable, tangible *Ant* inappreciable

appreciate 1 *Syn* UNDERSTAND, comprehend *Ant* depreciate **2♦** to hold in high estimation *Syn* value, prize, treasure, cherish *Ant* despise

apprehend 1 *Syn* ARREST, detain, attach **2♦** to lay hold of something with the mind so as to know it *Syn* comprehend **3** *Syn* FORESEE, divine, anticipate, foreknow

apprehension 1 *Syn* ARREST, detention, attachment **2♦** something that is known *Syn* comprehension **3♦** fear (or an instance of it) that something is going wrong or will go wrong *Syn* foreboding, misgiving, presentiment *Ant* confidence

apprehensive *Syn* FEARFUL, afraid *Ant* confident

apprentice *Syn* NOVICE, novitiate, probationer, postulant, neophyte

apprise *Syn* INFORM, advise, notify, acquaint

approach *vb* **1♦** to come or draw close (to) *Syn* near, approximate **2** *Syn* MATCH, touch, equal, rival

approach *n* *Syn* OVERTURE, advance, tender, bid *Ant* repulse

approbation ♦ warmly commending acceptance or agreement *Syn* approval *Ant* disapprobation

appropriate *vb* *Syn* ARROGATE, preempt, confiscate, usurp

appropriate *adj* *Syn* FIT, fitting, proper, suitable, apt, meet, happy, felicitous *Ant* inappropriate

appropriation ♦ money or property given or set apart by an authorized body for a predetermined use by others *Syn* grant, subvention, subsidy

approval *Syn* APPROBATION *Ant* disapproval

approve ♦ to have or to express a favorable opinion of *Syn* endorse, sanction, accredit, certify *Ant* disapprove

approximate *Syn* APPROACH, near

approximately *Syn* NEARLY, almost, wellnigh *Ant* precisely, exactly

appurtenance *Syn* APPENDAGE, accessory, adjunct

apropos *Syn* RELEVANT, apposite, pertinent, germane, applicable, material *Ant* unapropos

apt 1 *Syn* FIT, happy, felicitous, appropriate, fitting, suitable, meet, proper *Ant* inapt, inept **2** *Syn* likely, liable **3** *Syn* QUICK, prompt, ready

aptitude *Syn* GIFT, bent, turn, talent, faculty, knack, genius *Ant* inaptitude

aqueduct *Syn* CHANNEL, canal, conduit, duct

arbiter *Syn* JUDGE, arbitrator, umpire, referee

arbitrary *Syn* ABSOLUTE, autocratic, despotic, tyrannical, tyrannous *Ant* legitimate

arbitrate *Syn* JUDGE, adjudicate, adjudge

arbitrator *Syn* JUDGE, referee, arbiter, umpire

arc *Syn* CURVE, arch, bow

arcade *Syn* PASSAGE, gallery, cloister, ambulatory, passageway, corridor, hall, hallway, aisle

arcane *Syn* MYSTERIOUS, inscrutable

arch *n* *Syn* CURVE, bow, arc

arch *adj* *Syn* SAUCY, pert

archaic *Syn* OLD, obsolete, antiquated, antique, ancient, antediluvian, venerable *Ant* up-to-date

architect *Syn* ARTIST, artificer, artisan

archive *Syn* DOCUMENT, record, monument

arctic *Syn* COLD, frigid, freezing, frosty, icy, gelid, glacial, chilly, cool *Ant* torrid

ardent *Syn* IMPASSIONED, passionate, fervid, perfervid, fervent *Ant* cool

ardor *Syn* PASSION, fervor, enthusiasm, zeal *Ant* coolness; indifference

arduous *Syn* HARD, difficult *Ant* light, facile

area 1 ♦ a distinguishable extent of surface and esp. of the earth's surface *Syn* tract, region, zone, belt **2** *Syn* SIZE, extent, dimensions, magnitude, volume

argot *Syn* DIALECT, cant, jargon, slang, lingo, vernacular, patois

argue 1 *Syn* DISCUSS, debate, dispute, agitate **2** *Syn* INDICATE, bespeak, prove, attest, betoken

argument 1 *Syn* REASON, proof, ground **2** ♦ a vigorous and often heated discussion of a moot question *Syn* dispute, controversy **3** *Syn* SUBJECT, theme, matter, subject matter, topic, text, motive, motif, leitmotiv

argumentation ♦ the act or art of argument or an exercise of one's powers of argument *Syn* disputation, debate, forensic, dialectic

arid *Syn* DRY *Ant* moist; verdant

arise 1 *Syn* RISE, ascend, mount, soar, levitate, surge, tower, rocket *Ant* recline; slump **2** *Syn* SPRING, rise, originate, derive, flow, issue, emanate, proceed, stem

aristocracy 1 *Syn* OLIGARCHY, plutocracy **2** ♦ a body of persons who constitute a socially superior caste *Syn* nobility, gentry, county, elite, society *Ant* people, proletariat

aristocrat *Syn* GENTLEMAN, patrician *Ant* commoner

arm *Syn* FURNISH, accouter, outfit, equip, appoint *Ant* disarm

armistice *Syn* TRUCE, cease-fire, peace

army *Syn* MULTITUDE, host, legion

aroma *Syn* SMELL, odor, scent *Ant* stink, stench

aromatic *Syn* ODOROUS, balmy, redolent, fragrant *Ant* acrid (*of odors*)

arouse *Syn* STIR, rouse, awaken, waken, rally *Ant* quiet, calm

arraign *Syn* ACCUSE, charge, impeach, indict, incriminate

arrange 1 *Syn* ORDER, marshal, organize, systematize, methodize *Ant* derange, disarrange **2** *Syn* NEGOTIATE, concert

arrant *Syn* OUTRIGHT, out-and-out, unmitigated

array *vb* **1** *Syn* LINE, line up, range, align *Ant* disarray **2** *Syn* CLOTHE, apparel, attire, robe, dress

array *n* *Syn* DISPLAY, parade, pomp

arrear *Syn* DEBT, indebtedness, debit, obligation, liability

arrest *vb* **1** ♦ to stop in midcourse *Syn* check, interrupt *Ant* activate; quicken **2** ♦ to seize and hold under restraint or in custody by authority of the law *Syn* apprehend, attach, detain

arrest *n* ♦ seizing and holding under restraint or in custody by authority of the law *Syn* apprehension, detention, attachment

arresting *Syn* NOTICEABLE, striking, remarkable, outstanding, salient, signal, prominent, conspicuous

arrival ♦ the reaching of a destination *Syn* advent *Ant* departure

arrive *Syn* COME *Ant* depart

arrogant *Syn* PROUD, haughty, lordly, insolent, overbearing, supercilious, disdainful *Ant* meek; unassuming

arrogate ♦ to seize or take over in a highhanded manner *Syn* usurp, preempt, appropriate, confiscate *Ant* renounce; yield

art 1 ♦ the faculty of performing or executing expertly what is planned or devised *Syn* skill, cunning, artifice, craft **2** *Syn* TRADE, craft, handicraft, profession

artery *Syn* WAY, route, course, passage, pass

artful *Syn* SLY, wily, guileful, crafty, cunning, tricky, foxy, insidious *Ant* artless

article 1 *Syn* PARAGRAPH, clause, plank, count, verse **2** *Syn* THING, object **3** *Syn* ESSAY, paper, theme, composition

articled *Syn* BOUND, indentured, bond

articulate *adj* **1** *Syn* VOCAL, oral *Ant* inarticulate, dumb **2** *Syn* VOCAL, fluent, eloquent, voluble, glib *Ant* inarticulate, dumb

articulate *vb* **1** *Syn* INTEGRATE, concatenate **2♦** to form speech sounds *Syn* pronounce, enunciate

articulation 1 *Syn* INTEGRATION, concatenation **2** *Syn* JOINT, suture

artifact *Syn* WORK, product, production, opus

artifice 1 *Syn* ART, cunning, craft, skill **2** *Syn* TRICK, ruse, wile, stratagem, maneuver, gambit, ploy, feint

artificer *Syn* ARTIST, artisan, architect

artificial ♦ not brought into being by nature but by human art or effort or by some process of manufacture *Syn* factitious, synthetic, ersatz *Ant* natural

artisan 1 *Syn* ARTIST, artificer, architect **2** *Syn* WORKER, mechanic, workman, workingman, operative, craftsman, handicraftsman, hand, laborer, roustabout

artist 1♦ one who makes something beautiful or useful or both *Syn* artificer, artisan, architect **2** *Syn* EXPERT, artiste, virtuoso, adept, wizard

artiste *Syn* EXPERT, artist, virtuoso, adept, wizard

artless *Syn* NATURAL, simple, ingenuous, naïve, unsophisticated, unaffected *Ant* artful; affected

as *Syn* BECAUSE, since, for, inasmuch as

ascend 1 *Syn* RISE, arise, mount, soar, tower, rocket, levitate, surge *Ant* descend **2♦** to move upward to or toward a summit *Syn* mount, climb, scale *Ant* descend

ascendancy *Syn* SUPREMACY

ascension ♦ the act of moving upward or the movement upward *Syn* ascent

ascent *Syn* ASCENSION

ascertain *Syn* DISCOVER, determine, unearth, learn

ascetic *Syn* SEVERE, austere, stern *Ant* luxurious, voluptuous, sensuous

ascribe ♦ to lay something (creditable, discreditable, or neutral) to the account of a person or thing *Syn* attribute, impute, assign, refer, credit, accredit, charge

ash ♦ the remains of combustible material after it has been destroyed by fire *Syn* cinders, clinkers, embers

ashamed ♦ acutely or manifestly conscious of embarrassment and humiliation *Syn* mortified, chagrined *Ant* proud

ashen *Syn* PALE, ashy, livid, pallid, wan

ashy *Syn* PALE, ashen, livid, pallid, wan

asinine *Syn* SIMPLE, fatuous, silly, foolish *Ant* sensible, judicious

ask 1♦ to address a person in an attempt to elicit information *Syn* question, interrogate, query, inquire, catechize, quiz, examine **2♦** to seek to obtain by making one's wants or desires known *Syn* request, solicit

askance *Syn* AWRY, askew *Ant* straightforwardly, directly

askew *Syn* AWRY, askance *Ant* straight

asocial *Syn* UNSOCIAL, antisocial, nonsocial *Ant* social

aspect 1 *Syn* APPEARANCE, look, semblance **2** *Syn* PHASE, side, facet, angle

asperity *Syn* ACRIMONY, acerbity *Ant* amenity

asperse *Syn* MALIGN, vilify, traduce, calumniate, slander, defame, libel

aspersion *Syn* ANIMADVERSION, reflection, stricture

asphyxiate *Syn* SUFFOCATE, stifle, smother, choke, strangle, throttle

aspirant *Syn* CANDIDATE, applicant, nominee

aspiration *Syn* AMBITION, pretension

aspire *Syn* AIM, pant

assail *Syn* ATTACK, bombard, assault, storm

assassin ♦ one who can be hired to murder *Syn* cutthroat, gunman, bravo

assassinate *Syn* KILL, murder, slay, dispatch, execute

assault *n* *Syn* ATTACK, onslaught, onset

assault *vb* *Syn* ATTACK, storm, bombard, assail

assay *Syn* ESTIMATE, assess, evaluate, appraise, value, rate

assemblage *Syn* GATHERING, assembly, collection, congregation

assemble *Syn* GATHER, congregate, collect *Ant* disperse

assembly *Syn* GATHERING, assemblage, congregation, collection

assent ♦ concurrence with what someone else has stated or proposed **Syn** consent, accede, acquiesce, agree, subscribe **Ant** dissent

assert 1 ♦ to state positively usu. either in anticipation of denial or objection or in the face of it **Syn** declare, profess, affirm, aver, protest, avouch, avow, predicate, warrant **Ant** deny; controvert **2 Syn** MAINTAIN, vindicate, justify, defend

assertive Syn AGGRESSIVE, self-assertive, pushing, pushy, militant **Ant** retiring; acquiescent

assess Syn ESTIMATE, assay, appraise, value, evaluate, rate

asset 1 assets *pl* **Syn** POSSESSIONS, resources, means, effects, belongings **Ant** liabilities **2 Syn** CREDIT **Ant** handicap

assiduous Syn BUSY, sedulous, diligent, industrious **Ant** desultory

assign 1 Syn ALLOT, allocate, apportion **2 Syn** ASCRIBE, refer, attribute, impute, credit, accredit, charge **3 Syn** PRESCRIBE, define

assignation Syn ENGAGEMENT, rendezvous, tryst, date, appointment

assignment Syn TASK, duty, job, stint, chore

assimilate 1 Syn IDENTIFY, incorporate, embody **2 Syn** ABSORB, imbibe

assimilation Syn RECOGNITION, apperception, identification

assist Syn HELP, aid **Ant** hamper; impede

assistance Syn HELP, aid **Ant** impediment; obstruction

assistant ♦ a person who takes over part of the duties of another, esp. in a subordinate capacity **Syn** helper, coadjutor, aid, aide, aide-de-camp

associate *vb* **Syn** JOIN, connect, relate, link, conjoin, combine, unite

associate *n* ♦ a person frequently found in the company of another **Syn** companion, comrade, crony

association ♦ a body of persons who unite in the pursuit of a common aim or object **Syn** society, club, order

assort ♦ to arrange in systematic order or according to some definite method of arrangement or distribution **Syn** sort, classify, pigeonhole

assorted Syn MISCELLANEOUS, heterogeneous, motley, promiscuous **Ant** jumbled

assuage Syn RELIEVE, alleviate, mitigate, lighten, allay **Ant** exacerbate; intensify

assume 1 ♦ to put on a false or deceptive appearance **Syn** affect, pretend, simulate, feign, counterfeit, sham **2 Syn** PRESUPPOSE, postulate, presume, premise, posit

assumption ♦ something that is taken for granted or advanced as fact **Syn** presupposition, postulate, posit, presumption, premise

assurance 1 Syn CERTAINTY, certitude, conviction **Ant** mistrust; dubiousness **2 Syn** CONFIDENCE, self-assurance, self-confidence, self-possession, aplomb **Ant** diffidence; alarm

assure Syn ENSURE, insure, secure **Ant** alarm

assured Syn CONFIDENT, sanguine, sure, presumptuous **Ant** abashed; timorous

astern Syn ABAFT, aft **Ant** ahead

astonish Syn SURPRISE, astound, amaze, flabbergast

astound Syn SURPRISE, astonish, amaze, flabbergast

astral Syn STARRY, stellar, sidereal

astray Syn AMISS

astute Syn SHREWD, perspicacious, sagacious **Ant** gullible

asylum Syn SHELTER, refuge, retreat, sanctuary, cover

atavism Syn REVERSION, throwback

atavistic Syn REVERSIONARY

atheist ♦ a person who rejects some or all of the essential doctrines of religion and particularly the existence of God **Syn** agnostic, deist, freethinker, unbeliever, infidel **Ant** theist

athirst Syn EAGER, avid, keen, anxious, agog

athletic Syn MUSCULAR, husky, sinewy, brawny, burly

athletics ♦ physical activities engaged in for exercise or play **Syn** sports, games

athwart Syn ACROSS, crosswise, crossways

atmosphere ♦ an intangible and usually unanalyzable quality or aggregate of qualities which gives something an individual and distinctly recognizable character **Syn** feeling, feel, aura

atom *Syn* PARTICLE, bit, mite, smidgen, jot, tittle, iota, whit

atone *Syn* EXPIATE

atonement *Syn* EXPIATION

atrabilious *Syn* MELANCHOLIC, hypochondriac, melancholy *Ant* blithe

atrocious *Syn* OUTRAGEOUS, heinous, monstrous *Ant* humane; noble, moral

attach 1 *Syn* ARREST, apprehend, detain **2** *Syn* FASTEN, affix, fix *Ant* detach

attachment 1 *Syn* ARREST, apprehension, detention **2 ♦** the feeling which animates a person who is genuinely fond of someone or something *Syn* affection, love *Ant* aversion

attack *vb* **♦** to make an onslaught upon *Syn* assail, assault, bombard, storm

attack *n* **1 ♦** an attempt made on another or on others to injure, destroy, or defame *Syn* assault, onslaught, onset **2 ♦** action in a struggle for supremacy which must be met with defense or by means of defenses *Syn* aggression, offense, offensive **3** *Syn* FIT, access, accession, paroxysm, spasm, convulsion

attacking ♦ initiating hostile action in a struggle for supremacy *Syn* aggressive, offensive

attain *Syn* REACH, compass, gain, achieve

attainment *Syn* ACQUIREMENT, accomplishment, acquisition

attaint *Syn* CONTAMINATE, taint, pollute, defile

attempt *vb* **♦** to make an effort to do something that may or may not be successful *Syn* try, endeavor, essay, strive, struggle *Ant* succeed

attempt *n* **♦** an effort made to do or accomplish something *Syn* endeavor, essay, try, striving, struggle

attend 1 *Syn* TEND, mind, watch **2** *Syn* ACCOMPANY, escort, chaperon, convoy

attention 1♦ the direct focusing of the mind esp. on something to be learned, worked out, or dealt with *Syn* study, concentration, application *Ant* inattention **2** *Syn* COURTESY, gallantry, amenity

attentive *Syn* THOUGHTFUL, considerate *Ant* inattentive; neglectful

attenuate *Syn* THIN, rarefy, dilute, extenuate *Ant* enlarge; dilate; enrich

attest 1 *Syn* CERTIFY, witness, vouch **2** *Syn* INDICATE, argue, prove, bespeak, betoken *Ant* belie

attire *vb* *Syn* CLOTHE, apparel, array, dress, robe *Ant* divest

attire *n* *Syn* CLOTHES, clothing, apparel, raiment, dress

attitude 1 *Syn* POSTURE, pose **2** *Syn* POSITION, stand

attorney 1 *Syn* AGENT, deputy, proxy, factor **2** *Syn* LAWYER, solicitor, counselor, barrister, counsel, advocate

attract ♦ to draw another by exerting an irresistible or compelling influence *Syn* allure, charm, fascinate, bewitch, enchant, captivate *Ant* repel

attraction ♦ the relationship between persons or things that are involuntarily or naturally drawn together *Syn* affinity, sympathy

attractive ♦ drawing another by exerting a compelling influence *Syn* alluring, charming, fascinating, bewitching, enchanting, captivating *Ant* repellent; forbidding

attribute *n* **1** *Syn* QUALITY, property, character, accident **2** *Syn* SYMBOL, emblem, type

attribute *vb* *Syn* ASCRIBE, impute, assign, credit, accredit, refer, charge

attrition *Syn* PENITENCE, contrition, repentance, remorse, compunction

attune *Syn* HARMONIZE, tune

atypical *Syn* ABNORMAL, aberrant *Ant* typical; representative

audacious *Syn* BRAVE, courageous, unafraid, fearless, intrepid, valiant, valorous, dauntless, undaunted, doughty, bold *Ant* circumspect

audacity *Syn* TEMERITY, hardihood, effrontery, nerve, cheek, gall *Ant* circumspection

audience 1 *Syn* HEARING, audition **2** *Syn* FOLLOWING, public, clientele

audit *n* *Syn* SCRUTINY, examination, inspection, scrutiny, scanning

audit *vb* *Syn* SCRUTINIZE, examine, inspect, scan

audition *Syn* HEARING, audience

auditory ♦ of or relating to the hearing of sounds *Syn* acoustic, acoustical

augment *Syn* INCREASE, enlarge, multiply *Ant* abate

augur *Syn* FORETELL, prognosticate, presage, portend, forebode, prophesy, forecast, predict

augury *Syn* FORETOKEN, omen, portent, presage, prognostic

august *Syn* GRAND, majestic, imposing, stately, noble, grandiose, magnificent *Ant* unimpressive; unimposing

aura *Syn* ATMOSPHERE, feeling, feel

aureate *Syn* RHETORICAL, euphuistic, flowery, grandiloquent, magniloquent, bombastic *Ant* austere (*in style*)

auspicious *Syn* FAVORABLE, propitious, benign *Ant* inauspicious; ill-omened

austere *Syn* SEVERE, stern, ascetic *Ant* luscious (*of fruits*); warm, ardent (*of persons, feelings*); exuberant (*of style, quality*)

autarchic *Syn* FREE, autarkic, autonomous, independent, sovereign

autarchy *Syn* FREEDOM, autarky, autonomy, independence, sovereignty

autarkic *Syn* FREE, autarchic, autonomous, independent, sovereign

autarky *Syn* FREEDOM, autarchy, autonomy, independence, sovereignty

authentic ♦ being exactly as appears or is claimed *Syn* genuine, veritable, bona fide *Ant* spurious

authenticate *Syn* CONFIRM, validate, verify, substantiate, corroborate *Ant* impugn

author *Syn* MAKER, creator

authoritarian *Syn* DICTATORIAL, dogmatic, magisterial, doctrinaire, oracular *Ant* liberal, libertarian; anarchistic, anarchic

authority 1 *Syn* POWER, jurisdiction, command, control, dominion, sway 2 *Syn* INFLUENCE, weight, credit, prestige

authorize ♦ to invest with power or the right to act *Syn* commission, accredit, license

autobiography *Syn* BIOGRAPHY, memoir, life, confessions

autochthonous *Syn* NATIVE, indigenous, aboriginal, endemic *Ant* naturalized

autocratic *Syn* ABSOLUTE, arbitrary, despotic, tyrannical, tyrannous

automatic *Syn* SPONTANEOUS, mechanical, instinctive, impulsive

autonomous *Syn* FREE, independent, sovereign, autarchic, autarkic

autonomy *Syn* FREEDOM, independence, sovereignty, autarchy, autarky

auxiliary ♦ supplying aid or support *Syn* subsidiary, accessory, contributory, subservient, ancillary, adjuvant

avail *vb* 1 *Syn* BENEFIT, profit 2 *Syn* USE, utilize, employ, apply

avail *n* *Syn* USE, service, account, advantage, profit

avarice *Syn* CUPIDITY, greed, rapacity *Ant* prodigality

avaricious *Syn* COVETOUS, acquisitive, grasping, greedy *Ant* generous

avenge ♦ to inflict punishment by way of repayment for *Syn* revenge

aver *Syn* ASSERT, declare, avouch, avow, profess, affirm, protest *Ant* deny

average *n* ♦ something (as a number, quantity, or condition) that represents a middle point between extremes *Syn* mean, median, norm, par *Ant* maximum; minimum

average *adj* *Syn* MEDIUM, middling, indifferent, fair, moderate, mediocre, secondrate *Ant* exceptional; extraordinary

averse *Syn* DISINCLINED, indisposed, loath, reluctant, hesitant *Ant* avid (*of* or *for*); athirst (*for*)

aversion 1 *Syn* DISLIKE, distaste, disfavor *Ant* predilection 2 *Syn* ANTIPATHY *Ant* attachment, predilection

avert 1 *Syn* TURN, deflect, sheer, divert 2 *Syn* PREVENT, ward, obviate, preclude

avid *Syn* EAGER, keen, anxious, agog, athirst *Ant* indifferent; averse

avoid *Syn* ESCAPE, shun, eschew, evade, elude *Ant* face; meet

avouch *Syn* ASSERT, aver, affirm, avow, profess, declare, protest, warrant, predicate

avow 1 *Syn* ASSERT, affirm, profess, declare, aver, avouch, warrant, protest, predicate 2 *Syn* ACKNOWLEDGE, own, confess, admit *Ant* disavow

await *Syn* EXPECT, hope, look *Ant* despair

awake *Syn* AWARE, alive, cognizant, conscious, sensible

awaken *Syn* STIR, waken, rouse, arouse, rally *Ant* subdue

award *vb Syn* GRANT, accord, vouchsafe, concede

award *n Syn* PREMIUM, prize, reward, guerdon, meed, bonus, bounty

aware ♦ having knowledge of something *Syn* cognizant, conscious, sensible, alive, awake *Ant* unaware

awe *Syn* REVERENCE, fear

awful *Syn* FEARFUL, dreadful, frightful, terrible, horrible, shocking, appalling, terrific, horrific

awkward ♦ not marked by ease (as of performance, movement, or social conduct) *Syn* clumsy, maladroit, inept, gauche *Ant* handy, deft; graceful

awry ♦ deviating from a straight line or direction *Syn* askew, askance

axiom *Syn* PRINCIPLE, fundamental, law, theorem

B

babble *Syn* CHAT, gabble, jabber, prattle, chatter, patter, prate, gibber, gab

babel *Syn* DIN, hubbub, clamor, racket, uproar, hullabaloo, pandemonium

baby *Syn* INDULGE, mollycoddle, humor, pamper, spoil

back *n Syn* SPINE, backbone, vertebrae, chine

back *adj Syn* POSTERIOR, rear, hind, hinder, after *Ant* front

back *vb* 1 *Syn* SUPPORT, uphold, champion, advocate 2 *Syn* RECEDE, retrograde, retreat, retract

backbiting *Syn* DETRACTION, slander, scandal, calumny *Ant* vindication

backbone 1 *Syn* SPINE, back, vertebrae, chine 2 *Syn* FORTITUDE, grit, guts, sand, pluck *Ant* spinelessness

backdrop *Syn* BACKGROUND, setting, milieu, mise-en-scène, environment

backer *Syn* SPONSOR, surety, guarantor, patron, angel

background ♦ the place, time, and circumstances in which something occurs *Syn* setting, environment, milieu, mise-en-scène, backdrop

backslide *Syn* LAPSE, relapse

backslider *Syn* RENEGADE, apostate, recreant, turncoat

backsliding *Syn* LAPSE, relapse

backward ♦ not moving or going ahead *Syn* retrograde, retrogressive, regressive *Ant* advanced

bad 1 ♦ deviating from the dictates of moral law *Syn* evil, ill, wicked, naughty *Ant* good 2 ♦ not measuring up to a standard of what is satisfactory *Syn* poor, wrong *Ant* good

badge *Syn* SIGN, token, mark, note, symptom

badger *Syn* BAIT, hound, chivy, hector, ride, heckle

badinage ♦ animated back-and-forth exchange of remarks *Syn* persiflage, raillery

badlands *Syn* WASTE, desert, wilderness

baffle *Syn* FRUSTRATE, balk, circumvent, outwit, foil, thwart

bag *n* ♦ a container made of a flexible material and open or opening at the top *Syn* sack, pouch

bag *vb Syn* CATCH, capture, trap, snare, entrap, ensnare

bail *n Syn* GUARANTEE, bond, surety, security, guaranty

bail *vb Syn* DIP, ladle, scoop, spoon, dish

bailiwick *Syn* FIELD, province, domain, territory, sphere

bait *vb* ♦ to persist in tormenting or harassing another *Syn* badger, heckle, hector, chivy, hound, ride

bait *n Syn* LURE, snare, trap, decoy

bake *Syn* DRY, parch, desiccate, dehydrate

balance *n* 1 ♦ the stability or efficiency resulting from the equalization or exact adjustment of opposing forces *Syn* equilibrium, equipoise, poise, tension 2 *Syn* SYMMETRY, proportion, harmony 3 *Syn* REMAINDER, rest, residue, residuum, leavings, remnant, remains

balance *vb* 1 *Syn* COMPENSATE, counterpoise, counterbalance, countervail, offset 2 *Syn* STABILIZE, poise, ballast, trim, steady

bald *Syn* BARE, barren, naked, nude

balderdash *Syn* NONSENSE, twaddle, drivel, bunk, poppycock, gobbledygook, trash, rot, bull

bale *Syn* BUNDLE, package, pack, parcel, bunch, packet

baleful *Syn* SINISTER, maleficent, malefic, malign *Ant* beneficent

balk 1 *Syn* FRUSTRATE, thwart, foil, baffle, circumvent, outwit *Ant* forward 2 *Syn* DEMUR, jib, shy, boggle, stickle, scruple, strain, stick

balky *Syn* CONTRARY, restive, perverse, froward, wayward

ballast *Syn* STABILIZE, steady, balance, trim, poise

ballot *Syn* SUFFRAGE, vote, franchise

ballyhoo *Syn* PUBLICITY, promotion, propaganda

balmy 1 *Syn* ODOROUS, aromatic, fragrant, redolent *Ant* rank, noisome 2 *Syn* SOFT, gentle, smooth, bland, mild, lenient

bamboozle *Syn* DUPE, trick, hoodwink, gull, hoax, befool

ban *Syn* FORBID, prohibit, interdict, inhibit, enjoin

banal *Syn* INSIPID, flat, jejune, inane, vapid, wishy-washy *Ant* original; recherché

band 1 *Syn* BOND, tie 2 *Syn* STRIP, stripe, ribbon, fillet 3 *Syn* COMPANY, troop, troupe, party

bandy *Syn* EXCHANGE, interchange

bane *Syn* POISON, venom, virus, toxin

baneful *Syn* PERNICIOUS, noxious, deleterious, detrimental *Ant* beneficial

banish ♦ to remove by authority or force from a country, state, or sovereignty *Syn* exile, expatriate, ostracize, deport, transport, extradite

bank *n* 1 *Syn* SHOAL, bar, reef 2 *Syn* SHORE, strand, coast, beach, foreshore, littoral 3 *Syn* HEAP, mass, pile, stack, shock, cock

bank *vb* *Syn* HEAP, mass, pile, stack, shock, cock

bank *vb* *Syn* RELY, count, reckon, trust, depend

bankrupt *Syn* DEPLETE, impoverish, exhaust, drain

banner *Syn* FLAG, standard, ensign, color, streamer, pennant, pendant, pennon, jack

banquet *Syn* DINNER, feast

banter ♦ to make fun of good-naturedly *Syn* chaff, kid, rag, rib, josh, jolly

baptize ♦ to administer the rite of baptism *Syn* christen

bar *n* 1 ♦ something which hinders or obstructs *Syn* barrier, barricade 2 *Syn* OBSTACLE, obstruction, impediment, snag *Ant* advantage 3 *Syn* SHOAL, bank, reef

bar *vb* *Syn* HINDER, obstruct, block, dam, impede *Ant* admit; open

barbarian ♦ of, relating to, or characteristic of people that are not fully civilized *Syn* barbaric, barbarous, savage *Ant* civilized

barbaric *Syn* BARBARIAN, savage, barbarous *Ant* restrained; refined; subdued

barbarism ♦ a word or expression which offends against standards of correctness *Syn* corruption, impropriety, solecism, vernacularism, vulgarism

barbarous 1 *Syn* BARBARIAN, savage, barbaric *Ant* civilized; humane 2 *Syn* FIERCE, savage, inhuman, ferocious, cruel, fell, truculent *Ant* clement

bard *Syn* POET, minstrel, troubadour, rhymer, rhymester, versifier, poetaster

bare *adj* 1 ♦ lacking naturally or conventionally appropriate covering or clothing *Syn* naked, nude, bald, barren *Ant* covered 2 *Syn* MERE, very

bare *vb* *Syn* STRIP, denude, divest, dismantle *Ant* cover

barefaced *Syn* SHAMELESS, brazen, brash, impudent *Ant* furtive

bargain *Syn* CONTRACT, compact, pact

bark *vb* ♦ to make the sound of or a sound suggestive of a dog *Syn* bay, howl, growl, snarl, yelp, yap

bark *n* *Syn* SKIN, rind, peel, hide, pelt

baroque *Syn* ORNATE, florid, rococo, flamboyant

barren 1 *Syn* STERILE, unfruitful, infertile, impotent *Ant* fecund **2** *Syn* BARE, bald, naked, nude

barricade *Syn* BAR, barrier

barrier *Syn* BAR, barricade

barrister *Syn* LAWYER, counselor, counsel, advocate, attorney, solicitor

basal 1 *Syn* FUNDAMENTAL, basic, underlying, radical **2** *Syn* ELEMENTARY, beginning, elemental, rudimentary

base *n* ♦ something on which another thing is reared or built or by which it is supported or fixed in place *Syn* basis, foundation, ground, groundwork *Ant* top

base *vb* ♦ to supply or to serve as a basis *Syn* found, ground, bottom, stay, rest

base *adj* ♦ deserving of contempt because of the absence of higher values *Syn* low, vile *Ant* noble

baseless ♦ not justified or justifiable in any way *Syn* groundless, unfounded, unwarranted

bashful *Syn* SHY, diffident, modest, coy *Ant* forward; brazen

basic 1 *Syn* FUNDAMENTAL, basal, underlying, radical *Ant* top; peak **2** *Syn* ALKALINE *Syn* ELEMENTAL, elementary, essential, fundamental, primitive, underlying

basis *Syn* BASE, foundation, ground, groundwork

baste *Syn* BEAT, pummel, thrash, buffet, pound, belabor

bastion *Syn* BULWARK, breastwork, parapet, rampart

bathos *Syn* PATHOS, poignancy

batter *Syn* MAIM, mangle, mutilate, cripple

battle *n* ♦ a hostile meeting between opposing military forces *Syn* engagement, action

battle *vb* *Syn* CONTEND, war, fight

bawl *vb* **1** *Syn* ROAR, bellow, bluster, vociferate, clamor, howl, ululate **2** *Syn* SCOLD, rate, berate, tongue-lash, upbraid, chew out, wig, rail, revile, vituperate

bawl *n* *Syn* ROAR, bellow, bluster, vociferation, ululation

bay *Syn* BARK, howl, growl, snarl, yelp, yap

be ♦ to have actuality or reality *Syn* exist, live, subsist

beach *Syn* SHORE, strand, coast, foreshore, bank, littoral

beak *Syn* BILL, neb, nib

beam *Syn* RAY

beaming *Syn* BRIGHT, radiant, refulgent, effulgent, brilliant, luminous, lustrous, lambent, lucent, incandescent

bear 1 *Syn* CARRY, convey, transport, transmit **2** ♦ to bring forth as products *Syn* produce, yield, turn out **3** ♦ to sustain something trying or painful *Syn* suffer, endure, abide, tolerate, stand, brook **4** *Syn* PRESS, bear down, squeeze, crowd, jam **5** ♦ to have a connection especially logically *Syn* relate, pertain, appertain, belong, apply

beard *Syn* FACE, brave, challenge, dare, defy

bear down *Syn* PRESS, bear, squeeze, crowd, jam

bearing ♦ the way in which or the quality by which a person outwardly manifests personality *Syn* deportment, demeanor, mien, port, presence

beastly *Syn* BRUTAL, bestial, brute, brutish, feral

beat *vb* **1** ♦ to strike repeatedly *Syn* pound, pummel, thrash, buffet, baste, belabor **2** *Syn* CONQUER, defeat, lick, vanquish, subdue, subjugate, reduce, overcome, surmount, overthrow, rout **3** *Syn* PULSATE, throb, pulse, palpitate

beat *n* *Syn* PULSATION, pulse, throb, palpitation

beatitude *Syn* HAPPINESS, blessedness, bliss, felicity *Ant* despair; dolor

beau *Syn* FOP, exquisite, dandy, coxcomb, dude, buck

beau ideal *Syn* MODEL, ideal, exemplar, pattern, example, mirror, standard

beauteous *Syn* BEAUTIFUL, pulchritudinous, fair, good-looking, handsome, pretty, comely, bonny, lovely

beautiful ♦ very pleasing or delightful to look at *Syn* lovely, handsome, pretty, bonny, comely, fair, beauteous, pulchritudinous, good-looking *Ant* ugly

beautify *Syn* ADORN, embellish, deck, bedeck, ornament, decorate, garnish *Ant* uglify

because ♦ for the reason that *Syn* for, since, as, inasmuch as

becloud *Syn* OBSCURE, cloud, eclipse, fog, befog, dim, bedim, darken, obfuscate

bedeck *Syn* ADORN, deck, garnish, embellish, beautify, decorate, ornament

bedim *Syn* OBSCURE, dim, eclipse, cloud, becloud, fog, befog, obfuscate, darken

beetle *Syn* BULGE, overhang, jut, project, protrude, stick out

befall *Syn* HAPPEN, betide, occur, chance, transpire

befog *Syn* OBSCURE, fog, cloud, becloud, eclipse, darken, dim, bedim, obfuscate

befool *Syn* DUPE, trick, hoax, hoodwink, gull, bamboozle

before ♦ in advance, especially in place or in time *Syn* ahead, forward *Ant* after

beforehand *Syn* EARLY, betimes, soon *Ant* behindhand

befoul *Syn* SOIL, foul, dirty, sully, smirch, besmirch, grime, begrime, tarnish

befuddle *Syn* CONFUSE, fuddle, addle, muddle *Ant* clarify, clear

beg ♦ to ask or request urgently *Syn* entreat, beseech, implore, supplicate, adjure, importune

beget *Syn* GENERATE, get, sire, procreate, engender, breed, propagate, reproduce

beggarly *Syn* CONTEMPTIBLE, cheap, scurvy, shabby, sorry, despicable, pitiable

begin ♦ to take the first step in a course, process, or operation *Syn* commence, start, initiate, inaugurate *Ant* end

beginning *n* ♦ the first part or stage of a process or development *Syn* genesis, rise, initiation

beginning *adj Syn* ELEMENTARY, basal, elemental, rudimentary

begrime *Syn* SOIL, grime, smirch, besmirch, dirty, sully, foul, befoul, tarnish

begrudge *Syn* COVET, envy, grudge

beguile 1 *Syn* DECEIVE, delude, mislead, betray, double-cross 2 *Syn* WHILE, wile, beguile, fleet

behave 1 ♦ to act or to cause oneself to do something in a certain way *Syn* conduct, comport, demean, deport, acquit, quit *Ant* misbehave 2 *Syn* ACT, react, operate, work, function

behavior ♦ one's actions in general or on a particular occasion *Syn* conduct, deportment

behest *Syn* COMMAND, bidding, dictate, injunction, order, mandate

behind *Syn* AFTER *Ant* ahead

behindhand *Syn* TARDY, late, overdue *Ant* beforehand

behold *Syn* SEE, view, survey, observe, descry, espy, notice, perceive, discern, remark, note, contemplate

beholder *Syn* SPECTATOR, onlooker, looker-on, observer, witness, eyewitness, bystander, kibitzer

being 1 *Syn* EXISTENCE, actuality *Ant* becoming; nonbeing 2 *Syn* ENTITY, creature, individual, person

belabor *Syn* BEAT, pound, pummel, thrash, buffet, baste

belch ♦ to eject (gas) from the stomach by way of the mouth or matter from a containing cavity by way of an opening *Syn* burp, vomit, disgorge, regurgitate, spew, throw up

beleaguer *Syn* BESIEGE, invest, blockade

belie *Syn* MISREPRESENT, falsify, garble *Ant* attest

belief 1 ♦ the act of one who assents intellectually to something proposed or offered for acceptance as true or the state of mind of one who so assents *Syn* faith, credence, credit *Ant* unbelief, disbelief 2 *Syn* OPINION, conviction, persuasion, view, sentiment

believable *Syn* PLAUSIBLE, credible, colorable, specious *Ant* unbelievable

belittle *Syn* DECRY, depreciate, disparage, derogate, detract, minimize *Ant* aggrandize, magnify

bellicose *Syn* BELLIGERENT, pugnacious,

combative, contentious, quarrelsome **Ant** pacific; amicable

belligerent ♦ having or taking an aggressive or fighting attitude **Syn** bellicose, pugnacious, combative, quarrelsome, contentious **Ant** friendly

bellow *vb* **Syn** ROAR, bluster, bawl, vociferate, clamor, howl, ululate

bellow *n* **Syn** ROAR, bluster, bawl, vociferation, ululation

belly **Syn** ABDOMEN, stomach, paunch, gut

belong **Syn** BEAR, pertain, appertain, relate, apply

belongings **Syn** POSSESSIONS, effects, means, resources, assets

below ♦ in a lower position relative to some other object or place **Syn** under, beneath, underneath **Ant** above

belt **Syn** AREA, zone, tract, region

bemoan **Syn** DEPLORE, bewail, lament **Ant** exult

bemuse **Syn** DAZE, stun, stupefy, benumb, paralyze, petrify

bend **Syn** CURVE, twist **Ant** straighten

beneath **Syn** BELOW, underneath, under **Ant** above, over

benefaction **Syn** DONATION, contribution, alms

beneficial ♦ bringing good or gain **Syn** advantageous, profitable **Ant** harmful; detrimental

benefit ♦ to do good or to be of advantage to someone **Syn** profit, avail **Ant** harm

benevolent **Syn** CHARITABLE, philanthropic, eleemosynary, humanitarian, humane, altruistic **Ant** malevolent

benign 1 **Syn** KIND, benignant, kindly **Ant** malign **2** **Syn** FAVORABLE, auspicious, propitious **Ant** malign

benignant **Syn** KIND, benign, kindly **Ant** malignant

bent **Syn** GIFT, turn, talent, aptitude, knack, faculty, genius

benumb **Syn** DAZE, stun, bemuse, stupefy, paralyze, petrify

bequeath **Syn** WILL, devise, leave, legate

berate **Syn** SCOLD, rate, tongue-lash, up-

braid, jaw, bawl, chew out, wig, rail, revile, vituperate

berth 1 **Syn** ROOM, play, elbowroom, leeway, margin, clearance **2** **Syn** WHARF, dock, pier, quay, slip, jetty, levee

beseech **Syn** BEG, entreat, implore, supplicate, importune, adjure

beset **Syn** INFEST, overrun

besides **Syn** ALSO, moreover, furthermore, too, likewise

besiege ♦ to surround an enemy in a fortified or strong position so as to prevent ingress or egress **Syn** beleaguer, invest, blockade

besmirch **Syn** SOIL, smirch, dirty, sully, foul, befoul, grime, begrime, tarnish **Ant** cleanse

besotted **Syn** FOND, infatuated, insensate

bespangle **Syn** SPOT, spangle, spatter, sprinkle, mottle, fleck, stipple, marble, speckle

bespangled **Syn** SPOTTED, spangled, spattered, sprinkled, mottled, flecked, stippled, marbled, speckled

bespeak **Syn** INDICATE, betoken, attest, argue, prove

bestial **Syn** BRUTAL, brutish, brute, feral, beastly

bestow **Syn** GIVE, confer, present, donate, afford

bet ♦ something (as money) staked on a winner-take-all basis on the outcome of an uncertainty **Syn** wager, stake, pot, ante

bête noire **Syn** ABOMINATION, bugbear, anathema

bethink **Syn** REMEMBER, recollect, remind, recall, reminisce, mind

betide **Syn** HAPPEN, befall, chance, occur, transpire

betimes **Syn** EARLY, soon, beforehand **Ant** unseasonably, inopportunely

betoken **Syn** INDICATE, bespeak, attest, argue, prove

betray 1 **Syn** DECEIVE, mislead, delude, beguile, double-cross **2** **Syn** REVEAL, discover, disclose, divulge, tell

better *adj* ♦ more worthy or more pleasing than another or others **Syn** superior, preferable

better *vb Syn* IMPROVE, ameliorate, help
Ant worsen

between ♦ in common to (as in position,
in a distribution, or in participation) *Syn*
among

bewail *Syn* DEPLORE, lament, bemoan *Ant*
rejoice

bewilder *Syn* PUZZLE, mystify, perplex,
distract, confound, nonplus, dumbfound

bewitch *Syn* ATTRACT, enchant, captivate,
fascinate, charm, allure

bewitching *Syn* ATTRACTIVE, enchanting, captivating, fascinating, charming, alluring

beyond *Syn* FARTHER further

bias *n Syn* PREDILECTION, prejudice, prepossession, partiality

bias *vb Syn* INCLINE, dispose, predispose

bicker *Syn* QUARREL, squabble, spat, tiff,
wrangle, altercate

bickering *Syn* QUARREL, spat, tiff, squabble, wrangle, altercation

bid *vb* **1** *Syn* COMMAND, order, enjoin, direct, instruct, charge *Ant* forbid **2** *Syn* IN-
VITE, solicit, court, woo

bid *n Syn* OVERTURE, tender, advance,
approach

biddable *Syn* OBEDIENT, docile, amenable, tractable *Ant* willful

bidding *Syn* COMMAND, behest, order,
injunction, mandate, dictate

big *Syn* LARGE, great *Ant* little

bigot *Syn* ENTHUSIAST, fanatic, zealot

bigoted *Syn* ILLIBERAL, narrow-minded,
narrow, intolerant, hidebound

bill ♦ the jaws of a bird together with their
horny covering *Syn* beak, neb, nib

billingsgate *Syn* ABUSE, scurrility, vituperation, invective, obloquy

bind *Syn* TIE *Ant* loose; unbind

biography ♦ an account of the events and
circumstances of a person's life *Syn* life,
memoir, autobiography, confessions

biologic *Syn* DRUG, simple, medicinal,
pharmaceutical

biotope *Syn* HABITAT, range, station

birthright **1** *Syn* RIGHT, appanage, prerogative, privilege, perquisite **2** *Syn* HER-
ITAGE, patrimony, inheritance

bisexual ♦ combining male and female
qualities *Syn* hermaphroditic, hermaphrodite, androgynous, epicene

bit *Syn* PARTICLE, mite, smidgen, whit,
atom, iota, jot, tittle

bite ♦ to attack with or as if with the teeth
Syn gnaw, champ, gnash

biting *Syn* INCISIVE, cutting, crisp, trenchant, clear-cut

bitter ♦ having or being an unusually unpleasant flavor or odor *Syn* acrid *Ant* delicious

bizarre *Syn* FANTASTIC, grotesque, antic
Ant chaste; subdued

blab *Syn* GOSSIP, tattle

blackball *Syn* EXCLUDE, debar, shut out,
eliminate, rule out, disbar, suspend

blackguard *Syn* VILLAIN, scoundrel,
knave, rascal, rogue, scamp, rapscallion,
miscreant

blame *vb Syn* CRITICIZE, reprehend, reprobate, condemn, denounce, censure

blame *n* ♦ responsibility for misdeed or
delinquency *Syn* culpability, guilt, fault

blameworthy ♦ deserving reproach and
punishment for a wrong, sinful, or criminal
act, practice, or condition *Syn* guilty, culpable *Ant* blameless

blanch *Syn* WHITEN, bleach, decolorize,
etiolate

bland **1** *Syn* SUAVE, smooth, urbane,
diplomatic, politic *Ant* brusque **2** *Syn*
SOFT, mild, gentle, smooth, balmy, lenient
Ant pungent, piquant; savory, tasty, palatable

blandish *Syn* COAX, wheedle, cajole

blank *Syn* EMPTY, void, vacant, vacuous

blasé *Syn* SOPHISTICATED, worldly-wise,
worldly, disillusioned

blasphemous *Syn* IMPIOUS, profane, sacrilegious *Ant* reverent

blasphemy **1** ♦ impious or irreverent
speech *Syn* profanity, swearing, cursing
Ant adoration **2** *Syn* PROFANATION, desecration, sacrilege

blast *n* ♦ severe, sudden, or surprising ruin
or injury *Syn* blight, nip

blast *vb* ♦ to ruin or to injure severely, suddenly, or surprisingly *Syn* blight, nip

blatant *Syn* VOCIFEROUS, clamorous, strident, boisterous, obstreperous *Ant* decorous; reserved

blaze *n* ♦ brightly burning light or fire *Syn* flare, flame, glare, glow

blaze *vb* ♦ to burn or appear to burn brightly *Syn* flame, flare, glare, glow

bleach *Syn* WHITEN, etiolate, decolorize, blanch *Ant* dye

bleak *Syn* DISMAL, cheerless, dispiriting, dreary, desolate

blemish ♦ an imperfection (as a spot or crack) *Syn* defect, flaw *Ant* immaculateness

blench *Syn* RECOIL, quail, shrink, flinch, wince

blend *vb Syn* MIX, fuse, merge, coalesce, mingle, commingle, amalgamate *Ant* resolve

blend *n Syn* MIXTURE, admixture, compound, composite, amalgam

blessed *Syn* HOLY, sacred, divine, spiritual, religious *Ant* accursed

blessedness *Syn* HAPPINESS, beatitude, bliss, felicity *Ant* misery, dolor

blight *n Syn* BLAST, nip

blight *vb Syn* BLAST, nip

blind *adj* ♦ lacking or deficient in the power to see or to discriminate objects *Syn* sightless, purblind

blind *n* ♦ a device that serves as a screen for a window *Syn* shade, shutter

blink *Syn* WINK

bliss *Syn* HAPPINESS, beatitude, blessedness, felicity *Ant* anguish; bale

blithe *Syn* MERRY, jocund, jovial, jolly *Ant* morose; atrabilious

bloc *Syn* COMBINATION, party, faction, ring, combine

block *Syn* HINDER, obstruct, bar, dam, impede

blockade *n* ♦ the isolation of an enemy area by a belligerent force to prevent the passage of persons or supplies *Syn* siege

blockade *vb Syn* BESIEGE, beleaguer, invest

bloodless *Syn* PALE, anemic *Ant* sanguine; plethoric

bloody ♦ affected by or involving the shedding of blood *Syn* sanguinary, sanguine, sanguineous, gory

bloom *n Syn* BLOSSOM, flower, blow

bloom *vb Syn* BLOSSOM, flower, blow

blossom *n* ♦ the period or state of florescence of a seed plant *Syn* flower, bloom, blow

blossom *vb* ♦ to become florescent *Syn* bloom, flower, blow

blot *Syn* STIGMA, brand, stain

blot out *Syn* ERASE, delete, obliterate, expunge, cancel, efface

blow *vb Syn* BLOSSOM, bloom, flower

blow *n Syn* BLOSSOM, bloom, flower

blowsy *Syn* SLATTERNLY, frowzy, dowdy *Ant* smart, spruce; dainty

blubber *Syn* CRY, weep, wail, keen, whimper

bluejacket *Syn* MARINER, sailor, seaman, tar, gob

blueprint *n Syn* SKETCH, draft, tracing, plot, diagram, delineation, outline

blueprint *vb Syn* SKETCH, draft, trace, plot, diagram, delineate, outline

blues *Syn* SADNESS, dejection, depression, melancholy, gloom, dumps

bluff ♦ abrupt and unceremonious in speech or manner *Syn* blunt, brusque, curt, crusty, gruff *Ant* suave, smooth

blunder *Syn* STUMBLE, lurch, flounder, trip, lumber, galumph, lollop, bumble

blunder *Syn* ERROR, mistake, bull, howler, boner, slip, lapse, faux pas

blunt 1 *Syn* DULL, obtuse *Ant* keen, sharp **2** *Syn* BLUFF, brusque, curt, gruff, crusty *Ant* tactful; subtle

blurb *Syn* CRITICISM, puff, review, critique

blush *vb* ♦ to turn or grow red in the face *Syn* flush

blush *n* ♦ reddening of the face *Syn* flush

bluster *vb Syn* ROAR, bellow, bawl, vociferate, clamor, howl, ululate

bluster *n Syn* ROAR, bellow, bawl, vociferation, ululation

board *Syn* HARBOR, house, lodge, shelter, entertain

boast ♦ to give vent in speech to one's pride in oneself or something intimately connected with oneself *Syn* brag, vaunt, crow, gasconade *Ant* depreciate (*oneself, one's accomplishments*)

boat ♦ a floating structure designed to carry persons or goods over water *Syn* vessel, ship, craft

bodily ♦ of or relating to the human body *Syn* physical, corporeal, corporal, somatic

body ♦ the dead physical substance of a human being or animal *Syn* corpse, carcass, cadaver

boggle *Syn* DEMUR, stickle, stick, strain, scruple, balk, jib, shy *Ant* subscribe (*to*)

bogus *Syn* COUNTERFEIT, spurious, fake, sham, pseudo, pinchbeck, phony

boil *n* *Syn* ABSCESS, furuncle, carbuncle, pimple, pustule

boil *vb* ♦ to prepare (as food) in a liquid heated to the point where it emits considerable steam *Syn* seethe, simmer, parboil, stew

boisterous *Syn* VOCIFEROUS, obstreperous, clamorous, blatant, strident

bold *Syn* BRAVE, courageous, unafraid, fearless, intrepid, valiant, valorous, dauntless, undaunted, doughty, audacious *Ant* cowardly

bolster *Syn* SUPPORT, prop, sustain, buttress, brace

bombard *Syn* ATTACK, assail, storm, assault

bombast ♦ speech or writing characterized by high-flown pomposity or pretentiousness of language disproportionate to the thought or subject matter *Syn* rhapsody, rant, fustian, rodomontade

bombastic *Syn* RHETORICAL, grandiloquent, magniloquent, aureate, flowery, euphuistic

bona fide *Syn* AUTHENTIC, genuine, veritable *Ant* counterfeit, bogus

bond *adj* *Syn* BOUND, indentured, articled *Ant* free

bond *n* **1** ♦ something which serves to bind or bring two or more things firmly together *Syn* band, tie **2** *Syn* GUARANTEE, surety, security, bail, guaranty

bondage *Syn* SERVITUDE, slavery

boner *Syn* ERROR, blunder, mistake, howler, bull, slip, lapse, faux pas

bonny *Syn* BEAUTIFUL, comely, pretty, good-looking, fair, lovely, handsome, beauteous, pulchritudinous *Ant* homely

bonus *Syn* PREMIUM, bounty, reward, guerdon, award, prize, meed

bon vivant *Syn* EPICURE, gastronome, gourmet, gourmand, glutton *Ant* ascetic

bookish *Syn* PEDANTIC, academic, scholastic

boon *Syn* GIFT, favor, present, gratuity, largess *Ant* calamity

boor ♦ an uncouth ungainly person *Syn* churl, lout, clown, clodhopper, bumpkin, hick, yokel, rube *Ant* gentleman

boorish ♦ uncouth in manners, or appearance *Syn* loutish, clownish, churlish *Ant* gentlemanly

boost *Syn* LIFT, raise, elevate, hoist, rear, heave

bootleg *Syn* SMUGGLED, contraband

bootless *Syn* FUTILE, fruitless, vain, abortive

bootlicker *Syn* PARASITE, sycophant, toady, lickspittle, hanger-on, favorite, leech, sponge, sponger

booty *Syn* SPOIL, loot, plunder, prize, swag

border ♦ the line or relatively narrow space which marks the limit or outermost bound of something *Syn* margin, verge, edge, rim, brim, brink

bore *Syn* PERFORATE, drill, puncture, punch, prick

boredom *Syn* TEDIUM, ennui, doldrums

boring *Syn* IRKSOME, tiresome, wearisome, tedious

botch ♦ to handle or treat awkwardly or unskillfully *Syn* bungle, fumble, muff, cobble

bother *Syn* ANNOY, vex, irk *Ant* comfort

bottom *Syn* BASE, found, ground, stay, rest

bough *Syn* SHOOT, branch, limb

bounce *Syn* DISMISS, drop, sack, fire, discharge, cashier

bound *n* *Syn* LIMIT, confine, end, term

bound *adj* ♦ obliged to serve a master or in a clearly defined capacity for a certain number of years by the terms of a contract or mutual agreement *Syn* bond, indentured, articled

bound *n Syn* JUMP, leap, spring, vault

bound *vb* **1** *Syn* JUMP, leap, spring, vault **2** *Syn* SKIP, ricochet, hop, curve, lope, lollop

bounder *Syn* CAD, rotter

boundless *Syn* INFINITE, uncircumscribed, illimitable, eternal, sempiternal

bountiful, bounteous *Syn* LIBERAL, generous, openhanded, munificent, handsome *Ant* niggardly

bounty *Syn* PREMIUM, award, reward, meed, guerdon, prize, bonus

bouquet *Syn* FRAGRANCE, perfume, redolence, incense

bout *Syn* SPELL, stint, turn, trick, tour, shift, go

bow *vb Syn* YIELD, defer, submit, capitulate, succumb, relent, cave

bow *n Syn* CURVE, arc, arch

bow *vb Syn* FLEX, crook, buckle

box *Syn* STRIKE, hit, smite, punch, slug, slog, swat, clout, slap, cuff

boyish *Syn* YOUTHFUL, juvenile, puerile, maiden, virgin, virginal

brace *n Syn* COUPLE, pair, yoke

brace *vb Syn* SUPPORT, sustain, buttress, prop, bolster

brag *Syn* BOAST, vaunt, crow, gasconade *Ant* apologize

braid *Syn* WEAVE, plait, knit, crochet, tat

brain *Syn* MIND, intellect, intelligence, wit, psyche, soul

branch *Syn* SHOOT, limb, bough

brand *n* **1** *Syn* MARK, stamp, label, tag, ticket **2** *Syn* STIGMA, blot, stain

brand *vb Syn* MARK, stamp, label, tag, ticket

brandish *Syn* SWING, flourish, shake, wave, trash

brash *Syn* SHAMELESS, brazen, barefaced, impudent *Ant* wary

brave *adj* ♦ having or showing no fear when faced with something dangerous, difficult, or unknown *Syn* courageous, unafraid, fearless, intrepid, valiant, valorous, dauntless, undaunted, doughty, bold, audacious *Ant* craven

brave *vb Syn* FACE, dare, defy, beard, challenge

bravo *Syn* ASSASSIN, cutthroat, gunman

brawl ♦ a noisy fight or quarrel *Syn* broil, fracas, melee, row, rumpus, scrap

brawny *Syn* MUSCULAR, burly, husky, sinewy, athletic *Ant* scrawny

brazen *Syn* SHAMELESS, brash, impudent *Ant* bashful

breach **1** ♦ the act or the offense of failing to keep the law or to do what the law, duty, or obligation requires *Syn* infraction, violation, transgression, trespass, infringement, contravention *Ant* observance **2** ♦ a pulling apart in relations or in connections *Syn* break, split, schism, rent, rupture, rift

bread, bread and butter *Syn* LIVING, sustenance, livelihood, subsistence, maintenance, support, keep

break *vb* ♦ to come apart or cause to come apart *Syn* crack, burst, bust, snap, shatter, shiver *Ant* cleave (*together*); keep (*of laws*)

break *n* **1** ♦ a lapse in continuity *Syn* gap, interruption, interval, interim, hiatus, lacuna **2** *Syn* BREACH, split, schism, rent, rupture, rift **3** *Syn* OPPORTUNITY, chance, occasion, time

break down *Syn* ANALYZE, resolve, dissect

breakdown *Syn* ANALYSIS, resolution, dissection

breastwork *Syn* BULWARK, bastion, parapet, rampart

breed *vb Syn* GENERATE, engender, propagate, reproduce, procreate, beget, sire, get

breed *n Syn* VARIETY, subspecies, race, cultivar, strain, clone, stock

breeding *Syn* CULTURE, cultivation, refinement *Ant* vulgarity

breeze *Syn* WIND, gale, hurricane, zephyr

bridle **1** *Syn* RESTRAIN, check, curb, inhibit *Ant* vent **2** *Syn* STRUT, bristle, swagger

brief *adj* ♦ not long *Syn* short *Ant* prolonged, protracted

brief *n Syn* ABRIDGMENT, abstract, epitome, synopsis, conspectus

bright 1 ♦ actually or seemingly shining or glowing with light *Syn* brilliant, radiant, luminous, lustrous, effulgent, refulgent, beaming, lambent, lucent, incandescent *Ant* dull; dim **2** *Syn* INTELLIGENT, smart, quick-witted, brilliant, clever, knowing, alert *Ant* dense, dull

brilliant 1 *Syn* BRIGHT, radiant, luminous, effulgent, lustrous, refulgent, beaming, lambent, lucent, incandescent *Ant* subdued (*of light, color*) **2** *Syn* INTELLIGENT, clever, bright, smart, alert, quick-witted, knowing *Ant* crass

brim *Syn* BORDER, rim, edge, brink, verge, margin

bring ♦ to convey from one place to another *Syn* take, fetch *Ant* withdraw, remove

brink *Syn* BORDER, rim, brim, verge, edge, margin

brisk *Syn* AGILE, nimble, spry *Ant* sluggish

bristle *Syn* STRUT, bridle, swagger

brittle *Syn* FRAGILE, crisp, frangible, short, friable *Ant* supple

broach *Syn* EXPRESS, voice, utter, vent, air, ventilate

broad ♦ having horizontal extent *Syn* wide, deep *Ant* narrow

broadcast 1 *Syn* STREW, straw, scatter, sow **2** *Syn* DECLARE, promulgate, publish, advertise, announce, proclaim

broadcasting *Syn* DECLARATION, promulgation, publication, advertisement, announcement, proclamation

Brobdingnagian *Syn* HUGE, vast, immense, enormous, elephantine, mammoth, giant, gigantic, gigantean, colossal, gargantuan, Herculean, cyclopean, titanic *Ant* lilliputian

broil *Syn* BRAWL, fracas, melee, row, rumpus, scrap

bromide *Syn* COMMONPLACE, cliché, platitude, truism

brook *Syn* BEAR, stand, abide, tolerate, suffer, endure

browbeat *Syn* INTIMIDATE, bulldoze, bully, cow

bruise *vb* *Syn* CRUSH, mash, smash, squash, macerate

bruise *n* *Syn* WOUND, contusion, trauma, traumatism, lesion

brush *vb* ♦ to touch lightly in passing *Syn* graze, glance, shave, skim

brush *n* *Syn* ENCOUNTER, skirmish

brusque *Syn* BLUFF, curt, blunt, gruff, crusty *Ant* unctuous; bland

brutal ♦ characteristic of an animal in nature, action, or instinct *Syn* brute, brutish, bestial, beastly, feral

brute *Syn* BRUTAL, brutish, bestial, beastly, feral

brutish *Syn* BRUTAL, brute, bestial, beastly, feral

buccaneer *Syn* PIRATE, freebooter, privateer, corsair

buck *Syn* FOP, dude, dandy, beau, coxcomb, exquisite

buckle *Syn* FLEX, crook, bow

bucolic *Syn* RURAL, pastoral, rustic *Ant* urbane

buffet *Syn* BEAT, baste, pummel, pound, belabor, thrash

bugbear *Syn* ABOMINATION, bête noire, anathema

build *vb* ♦ to form or fashion a structure or something comparable to a structure *Syn* construct, erect, frame, raise, rear *Ant* unbuild, destroy

build *n* *Syn* PHYSIQUE, habit, constitution

building ♦ a construction (as of wood, brick, or stone) intended to house a family, a business, or an institution *Syn* edifice, structure, pile

bulge *vb* ♦ to extend outward beyond the usual and normal line *Syn* jut, stick out, protrude, project, overhang, beetle

bulge *n* *Syn* PROJECTION, protuberance, protrusion

bulk ♦ a body of usually material substance that constitutes a thing or unit *Syn* mass, volume

bulky *Syn* MASSIVE, massy, monumental, substantial

bull 1 *Syn* ERROR, blunder, howler,

boner, mistake, slip, lapse, faux pas **2 *Syn*** NONSENSE, twaddle, drivel, bunk, balderdash, poppycock, gobbledygook, trash, rot

bulldoze *Syn* INTIMIDATE, bully, browbeat, cow

bullheaded *Syn* OBSTINATE, pigheaded, stiff-necked, stubborn, mulish, dogged, pertinacious

bully *Syn* INTIMIDATE, bulldoze, browbeat, cow ***Ant*** coax

bulwark ♦ an aboveground defensive structure that forms part of a fortification ***Syn*** breastwork, rampart, parapet, bastion

bum *Syn* VAGABOND, vagrant, tramp, hobo, truant

bumble *Syn* STUMBLE, trip, blunder, lurch, flounder, lumber, galumph, lollop

bump ♦ to come or cause to come into violent contact or close or direct opposition ***Syn*** clash, collide, conflict

bumpkin *Syn* BOOR, hick, yokel, rube, clodhopper, clown, lout, churl

bunch 1 *Syn* GROUP, cluster, parcel, lot **2 *Syn*** BUNDLE, bale, parcel, pack, package, packet

bundle ♦ things done up for storage, sale, or carriage ***Syn*** bunch, bale, parcel, pack, package, packet

bungle *Syn* BOTCH, fumble, muff, cobble

bunk *Syn* NONSENSE, twaddle, drivel, balderdash, poppycock, gobbledygook, trash, rot, bull

buoyant *Syn* ELASTIC, volatile, expansive, resilient, effervescent ***Ant*** depressed, dejected

burden *n* ***Syn*** LOAD, cargo, freight, lading

burden *vb* ♦ to lay a heavy load upon or to lie like a heavy load upon a person or thing ***Syn*** encumber, cumber, weigh, weight, load, lade, tax, charge, saddle

burden *n* ***Syn*** SUBSTANCE, purport, gist, core, pith

burdensome *Syn* ONEROUS, oppressive, exacting ***Ant*** light

burglar *Syn* THIEF, robber, larcener, larcenist

burglarize *Syn* ROB, plunder, rifle, loot

burglary *Syn* THEFT, larceny, robbery

burlesque *n* ***Syn*** CARICATURE, parody, travesty

burlesque *vb* ***Syn*** CARICATURE, parody, travesty

burly *Syn* MUSCULAR, husky, brawny, athletic, sinewy ***Ant*** lanky, lank

burn ♦ to injure by exposure to fire or intense heat ***Syn*** scorch, char, sear, singe

burp *Syn* BELCH, vomit, disgorge, regurgitate, spew, throw up

burst *Syn* BREAK, crack, bust, snap, shatter, shiver

bury *Syn* HIDE, secrete, cache, conceal, screen, ensconce

business 1 *Syn* WORK, occupation, pursuit, calling, employment **2 *Syn*** AFFAIR, concern, matter, thing **3** ♦ one of the forms or branches of human endeavor which have for their objective the supplying of commodities ***Syn*** commerce, trade, industry, traffic

bust *Syn* BREAK, crack, burst, snap, shatter, shiver

bustle *Syn* STIR, flurry, ado, fuss, pother

busy ♦ actively engaged or occupied in work or in accomplishing a purpose or intention ***Syn*** industrious, diligent, assiduous, sedulous ***Ant*** idle; unoccupied

butchery *Syn* MASSACRE, slaughter, carnage, pogrom

butt in *Syn* INTRUDE, obtrude, interlope

buttress *n* ♦ auxiliary structures designed to serve as a prop, shore, or support for a wall (as of a building) ***Syn*** pier, abutment

buttress *vb* ***Syn*** SUPPORT, sustain, prop, bolster, brace

buy ♦ to acquire something for money or an equivalent ***Syn*** purchase

by ♦ using as a means of approach or action ***Syn*** through, with

bystander *Syn* SPECTATOR, onlooker, looker-on, witness, eyewitness, observer, beholder

byword *Syn* CATCHWORD, shibboleth, slogan

C

cabal *Syn* PLOT, intrigue, conspiracy, machination

cabalistic *Syn* MYSTICAL, anagogic, mystic

cache *Syn* HIDE, secrete, bury, conceal, ensconce, screen

cad ♦ one who shows himself to be no gentleman *Syn* bounder, rotter

cadaver *Syn* BODY, corpse, carcass

cadaverous *Syn* HAGGARD, wasted, pinched, worn, careworn *Ant* plump, stout

cadence *Syn* RHYTHM, meter

cage *Syn* ENCLOSE, envelop, fence, pen, coop, corral, wall

cajole *Syn* COAX, wheedle, blandish

cake *Syn* HARDEN, solidify, indurate, petrify

calamitous *Syn* UNLUCKY, disastrous, ill-starred, ill-fated, unfortunate, luckless, hapless

calamity *Syn* DISASTER, catastrophe, cataclysm *Ant* boon

calculate ♦ to determine something (as cost, speed, or quantity) by mathematical processes *Syn* compute, estimate, reckon

calculating *Syn* CAUTIOUS, circumspect, wary, chary *Ant* reckless, rash

calculation *Syn* CAUTION, circumspection, wariness, chariness *Ant* recklessness, rashness

caliber *Syn* QUALITY, stature

call *vb Syn* SUMMON, summons, cite, convoke, convene, muster

call *n Syn* VISIT, visitation

caller *Syn* VISITOR, visitant, guest

calling *Syn* WORK, occupation, pursuit, business, employment

callous *Syn* HARDENED, indurated *Ant* tender

callow *Syn* RUDE, green, crude, raw, rough, uncouth *Ant* full-fledged, grown-up

calm *adj* ♦ quiet and free from all that disturbs or excites *Syn* tranquil, serene, placid, peaceful, halcyon *Ant* stormy; agitated

calm *vb* ♦ to relieve or to bring to an end

whatever distresses, agitates, or disturbs *Syn* compose, quiet, quieten, still, lull, soothe, settle, tranquilize *Ant* agitate, arouse

calumniate *Syn* MALIGN, defame, slander, asperse, traduce, vilify, libel *Ant* eulogize; vindicate

calumny *Syn* DETRACTION, slander, backbiting, scandal *Ant* eulogy; vindication

camouflage *Syn* DISGUISE, cloak, mask, dissemble

canal *Syn* CHANNEL, conduit, duct, aqueduct

cancel *Syn* ERASE, efface, obliterate, expunge, delete, blot out

candid *Syn* FRANK, open, plain *Ant* evasive

candidate ♦ one who seeks an office, honor, position, or award *Syn* aspirant, nominee, applicant

canon *Syn* LAW, precept, regulation, rule, statute, ordinance

cant 1 *Syn* DIALECT, jargon, argot, lingo, vernacular, slang, patois **2** *Syn* HYPOCRISY, sanctimony, pharisaism

canting *Syn* HYPOCRITICAL, sanctimonious, pharisaical

capability *Syn* ABILITY, capacity *Ant* incapability, incompetence

capable *Syn* ABLE, competent, qualified *Ant* incapable

capacious *Syn* SPACIOUS, commodious, ample *Ant* exiguous

capacity *Syn* ABILITY, capability *Ant* incapacity

caper *Syn* PRANK, monkeyshine, antic, dido

capital *Syn* CHIEF, principal, main, leading, foremost

capitulate *Syn* YIELD, submit, succumb, relent, defer, bow, cave

capitulation *Syn* SURRENDER, submission

caprice ♦ an arbitrary notion that usually lacks a logical basis and therefore may be unsound, impractical, or even irrational

Syn freak, fancy, whim, whimsy, conceit, vagary, crotchet

capricious *Syn* INCONSTANT, mercurial, unstable, fickle *Ant* steadfast

capsize *Syn* OVERTURN, upset, overthrow, subvert

caption *Syn* INSCRIPTION, legend

captious *Syn* CRITICAL, caviling, carping, hypercritical, faultfinding, censorious *Ant* appreciative

captivate *Syn* ATTRACT, fascinate, bewitch, enchant, charm, allure *Ant* repulse

captivating *Syn* ATTRACTIVE, fascinating, bewitching, enchanting, charming, alluring *Ant* repulsive

captive *Syn* PRISONER

capture *Syn* CATCH, trap, snare, entrap, ensnare, bag

carbon copy *Syn* REPRODUCTION, copy, duplicate, transcript, facsimile, replica

carbuncle *Syn* ABSCESS, boil, furuncle, pimple, pustule

carcass *Syn* BODY, corpse, cadaver

cardinal *Syn* ESSENTIAL, vital, fundamental *Ant* negligible

care ♦ a troubled or engrossed state of mind or the thing that causes this *Syn* concern, solicitude, anxiety, worry

careful ♦ marked by close attention to details or care in execution or performance *Syn* meticulous, scrupulous, punctilious, punctual *Ant* careless

careless ♦ showing lack of concern or attention *Syn* heedless, thoughtless, inadvertent *Ant* careful

caress ♦ to show affection or love by touching or handling *Syn* fondle, pet, cosset, cuddle, dandle

careworn *Syn* HAGGARD, worn, pinched, wasted, cadaverous *Ant* carefree

cargo *Syn* LOAD, burden, freight, lading

caricature *n* ♦ a grotesque or bizarre imitation of something *Syn* burlesque, parody, travesty

caricature *vb* ♦ to make a grotesque or bizarre imitation of something *Syn* burlesque, parody, travesty

carnage *Syn* MASSACRE, slaughter, butchery, pogrom

carnal ♦ characterized by physical rather than intellectual or spiritual orientation *Syn* fleshly, sensual, animal *Ant* spiritual; intellectual

carol *Syn* SING, toll, descant, warble, trill, hymn, chant, intone

carping *Syn* CRITICAL, caviling, faultfinding, captious, hypercritical, censorious *Ant* fulsome

carry ♦ to be the agent or the means whereby something or someone is moved from one place to another *Syn* bear, convey, transport, transmit

cartel 1 *Syn* CONTRACT, compact, pact, convention, bargain, concordat, treaty, entente 2 *Syn* MONOPOLY, pool, syndicate, corner, trust

carve 1 *Syn* CUT, slit, hew, chop, slash 2 ♦ to cut an outline or a shape out of or into some substance *Syn* incise, engrave, etch, chisel, sculpture, sculpt, sculp

case 1 *Syn* INSTANCE, illustration, example, specimen, sample 2 *Syn* SUIT, cause, action, lawsuit

casement *Syn* WINDOW, dormer, oriel

cash *Syn* MONEY, currency, legal tender, specie, coin, coinage

cashier *Syn* DISMISS, discharge, drop, fire, sack, bounce

cast 1 *Syn* THROW, fling, hurl, pitch, toss, sling 2 *Syn* DISCARD, shed, molt, slough, scrap, junk 3 *Syn* ADD, figure, foot, sum, total, tot

castaway *Syn* OUTCAST, derelict, reprobate, pariah, untouchable

castigate *Syn* PUNISH, chastise, chasten, discipline, correct

castrate *Syn* STERILIZE, spay, emasculate, alter, mutilate, geld

casual 1 *Syn* ACCIDENTAL, incidental, contingent, fortuitous 2 *Syn* RANDOM, desultory, haphazard, chancy, hit-or-miss, happy-go-lucky *Ant* deliberate

casualty *Syn* ACCIDENT, mishap

casuistical *Syn* FALLACIOUS, sophistical

casuistry *Syn* FALLACY, sophistry, sophism

cataclysm *Syn* DISASTER, catastrophe, calamity

catalog *n* **Syn** LIST, inventory, table, schedule, register, roll, roster

catalog *vb* **Syn** RECORD, register, list, enroll

cataract **Syn** FLOOD, deluge, inundation, torrent, spate

catastrophe **Syn** DISASTER, calamity, cataclysm

catch 1 ♦ to come to possess or control by or as if by seizing **Syn** capture, trap, snare, entrap, ensnare, bag **Ant** miss **2 Syn** INCUR, contract

catching **Syn** INFECTIOUS, contagious, communicable

catchword ♦ a phrase that catches the eye or the ear and is repeated so often that it becomes a formula **Syn** byword, shibboleth, slogan

catechize **Syn** ASK, interrogate, quiz, examine, question, query, inquire

categorical 1 **Syn** ULTIMATE, absolute **2 Syn** EXPLICIT, express, definite, specific

category **Syn** CLASS,

cater ♦ to furnish with what satisfies the appetite or desires **Syn** purvey, pander

catholic **Syn** UNIVERSAL, cosmic, ecumenical, cosmopolitan **Ant** parochial; provincial

catnap **Syn** SLEEP, nap, snooze, slumber, drowse, doze

cause ♦ that (as a person, fact, or condition) which is responsible for an effect **Syn** determinant, antecedent, reason, occasion **2 Syn** SUIT, lawsuit, action, cause, case

caustic ♦ stingingly incisive **Syn** mordant, acrid, scathing **Ant** genial

caution *n* ♦ careful prudence esp. in reducing or avoiding risk or danger **Syn** circumspection, wariness, chariness, calculation **Ant** temerity; adventurousness

caution *vb* **Syn** WARN, forewarn

cautious ♦ prudently watchful and discreet in the face of danger or risk **Syn** circumspect, wary, chary, calculating **Ant** adventurous, temerarious

cavalcade **Syn** PROCESSION, parade, cortege, motorcade

cave **Syn** YIELD, succumb, submit, capitulate, relent, defer, bow

caviling **Syn** CRITICAL, captious, faultfinding, censorious, carping, hypercritical

cavity **Syn** HOLE, hollow, pocket, void, vacuum

cease **Syn** STOP, quit, discontinue, desist

cease-fire **Syn** TRUCE, armistice, peace

cede **Syn** RELINQUISH, surrender, abandon, waive, resign, yield, leave

celebrate **Syn** KEEP, commemorate, solemnize, observe

celebrated **Syn** FAMOUS, renowned, famed, eminent, illustrious **Ant** obscure

celebrity **Syn** FAME, renown, glory, honor, éclat, reputation, repute, notoriety **Ant** obscurity

celerity ♦ quickness in movement or action **Syn** alacrity, legerity **Ant** leisureliness

celestial ♦ of, relating to, or fit for heaven or the heavens **Syn** heavenly, empyrean, empyreal **Ant** terrestrial

celibate **Syn** UNMARRIED, single, virgin, maiden

cenobite **Syn** RECLUSE, eremite, hermit, anchorite

censorious **Syn** CRITICAL, faultfinding, hypercritical, captious, carping, caviling **Ant** eulogistic

censure **Syn** CRITICIZE, reprehend, blame, condemn, denounce, reprobate **Ant** commend

center *n* ♦ the point, spot, or portion of a thing which is comparable to a point around which a circle is described **Syn** middle, midst, core, hub, focus, nucleus, heart

center *vb* ♦ to draw to or fix upon a center **Syn** focus, centralize, concentrate

central ♦ dominant or most important **Syn** focal, pivotal

centralize **Syn** CENTER, focus, concentrate

cerebral **Syn** MENTAL, intellectual, psychic, intelligent

ceremonial *adj* ♦ characterized or marked by attention to the forms, procedures, and details prescribed as right, proper, or requisite **Syn** ceremonious, formal, conventional, solemn

ceremonial *n Syn* FORM, ceremony, ritual, rite, liturgy, formality

ceremonious *Syn* CEREMONIAL, formal, solemn, conventional *Ant* unceremonious, informal

ceremony *Syn* FORM, ceremonial, ritual, liturgy, rite, formality

certain 1 *Syn* SURE, positive, cocksure *Ant* uncertain **2** ♦ bound to follow in obedience to the laws of nature or of thought *Syn* inevitable, necessary *Ant* probable; supposed

certainty ♦ a state of mind in which one is free from doubt *Syn* certitude, assurance, conviction *Ant* uncertainty

certify 1 ♦ to testify to the truth or genuineness of something *Syn* attest, witness, vouch **2** *Syn* APPROVE, endorse, accredit, sanction

certitude *Syn* CERTAINTY, assurance, conviction *Ant* doubt

chafe *Syn* ABRADE, excoriate, fret, gall

chaff *Syn* BANTER, kid, rag, jolly, rib, josh

chagrined *Syn* ASHAMED, mortified

chain *Syn* SUCCESSION, series, train, string, sequence, progression

challenge *Syn* FACE, brave, dare, defy, beard

chamber *Syn* ROOM, apartment

champ *Syn* BITE, gnaw, gnash

champion *n Syn* VICTOR, vanquisher, winner, conqueror

champion *vb Syn* SUPPORT, back, advocate, uphold *Ant* combat

chance *n* **1** ♦ something that happens without an apparent or determinable cause or as a result of unpredictable forces *Syn* accident, fortune, luck, hap, hazard *Ant* law, principle **2** *Syn* OPPORTUNITY, occasion, break, time

chance *vb* **1** *Syn* HAPPEN, befall, betide, occur, transpire **2** *Syn* VENTURE, hazard, risk, jeopardize, endanger, imperil

chance *adj Syn* RANDOM, haphazard, chancy, casual, desultory, hit-or-miss, happy-go-lucky

chancy *Syn* RANDOM, haphazard, chance, hit-or-miss, happy-go-lucky, casual, desultory

change *vb* ♦ to make or become different *Syn* alter, vary, modify

change *n* **1** ♦ a making different *Syn* alteration, variation, modification *Ant* uniformity; monotony **2** ♦ a result of a making different *Syn* mutation, permutation, vicissitude, alternation

changeable ♦ having or showing a marked capacity for changes or a marked tendency to alter under slight provocation *Syn* changeful, variable, mutable, protean *Ant* stable; unchangeable

changeful *Syn* CHANGEABLE, variable, protean, mutable *Ant* changeless; stereotyped

channel 1 *Syn* STRAIT, passage, narrows, sound **2** ♦ something through which a fluid (as water) is led or flows *Syn* canal, conduit, duct, aqueduct **3** *Syn* MEAN, vehicle, instrument, instrumentality, organ, agency, agent, medium

chant *Syn* SING, troll, carol, descant, warble, trill, hymn, intone

chaos 1 *Syn* CONFUSION, disorder, disarray, jumble, clutter, snarl, muddle *Ant* system **2** *Syn* ANARCHY, lawlessness

chaperon *Syn* ACCOMPANY, attend, escort, convoy, conduct

char *Syn* BURN, scorch, sear, singe

character 1 ♦ an arbitrary or conventional device that is used in writing and in printing, but is neither a word nor a phrase nor a picture *Syn* symbol, sign, mark **2** *Syn* QUALITY, property, attribute, accident **3** *Syn* DISPOSITION, individuality, personality, complexion, temperament, temper **4** *Syn* TYPE, nature, description, kind, ilk, sort, stripe, kidney **5** *Syn* CREDENTIAL, reference, recommendation, testimonial

characteristic *adj* ♦ being or revealing a quality specific or identifying to an individual or group *Syn* individual, peculiar, distinctive

characteristic *n* ♦ something that marks or sets apart a person or thing *Syn* trait, feature

characterize ♦ to be a peculiar or significant quality or feature of something *Syn* distinguish, mark, qualify

charge *vb* **1** *Syn* BURDEN, encumber, cumber, weigh, weight, load, lade, tax, saddle **2** *Syn* COMMAND, direct, instruct, bid, enjoin, order **3** *Syn* ACCUSE, incriminate, indict, impeach, arraign *Ant* absolve **4** *Syn* ASCRIBE, attribute, impute, assign, refer, credit, accredit **5** *Syn* RUSH, dash, tear, shoot

charge *n Syn* PRICE, cost, expense

chargé d'affaires *Syn* AMBASSADOR, legate, nuncio, minister, envoy, internuncio

chariness *Syn* CAUTION, circumspection, wariness, calculation

charitable ♦ having or showing interest in or being concerned with the welfare of others *Syn* benevolent, humane, humanitarian, philanthropic, eleemosynary, altruistic *Ant* uncharitable

charity **1** *Syn* MERCY, clemency, grace, lenity *Ant* malice, ill will **2** ♦ love for one's fellowmen and a disposition to help those who are in need *Syn* philanthropy

charlatan *Syn* IMPOSTOR, mountebank, quack, faker

charm *n Syn* FETISH, talisman, amulet

charm *vb Syn* ATTRACT, fascinate, allure, captivate, enchant, bewitch *Ant* disgust

charming *Syn* ATTRACTIVE, fascinating, alluring, captivating, enchanting, bewitching *Ant* forbidding

chart *n* ♦ a stylized or symbolic depiction of something incapable of direct verbal or pictorial representation *Syn* map, graph

chart *vb* ♦ to make a representation of something with a chart *Syn* map, graph

charter *Syn* HIRE, let, lease, rent

chary *Syn* CAUTIOUS, circumspect, wary, calculating

chase *Syn* FOLLOW, pursue, trail, tag, tail

chasm *Syn* GULF, abyss, abysm

chaste ♦ free from all taint of what is lewd or salacious *Syn* pure, modest, decent *Ant* lewd, wanton, immoral; bizarre (*of style, effect*)

chasten *Syn* PUNISH, discipline, correct, chastise, castigate *Ant* pamper, mollycoddle

chastise *Syn* PUNISH, discipline, correct, castigate, chasten

chat ♦ to emit a loose and ready flow of inconsequential talk *Syn* gab, chatter, patter, prate, prattle, babble, gabble, jabber, gibber

chatter *Syn* CHAT, gab, patter, prate, babble, gabble, jabber, gibber

cheap *Syn* CONTEMPTIBLE, beggarly, shabby, pitiable, sorry, despicable, scurvy *Ant* noble

cheat *n Syn* IMPOSTURE, fraud, fake, deceit, deception, counterfeit, sham, humbug

cheat *vb* ♦ to obtain something and esp. money or valuables from or an advantage over another by dishonesty and trickery *Syn* cozen, defraud, swindle, overreach

check *n Syn* CORRECTIVE, control, antidote

check *vb* **1** *Syn* ARREST, interrupt **2** *Syn* RESTRAIN, bridle, curb, inhibit *Ant* accelerate (*of speed*); advance (*of movements, plans, hopes*); release (*of feelings, energies*)

checked, checkered *Syn* VARIEGATED, parti-colored, motley, pied, piebald, skewbald, dappled, freaked

cheek *Syn* TEMERITY, nerve, effrontery, hardihood, gall, audacity *Ant* diffidence

cheep *vb Syn* CHIRP, chirrup, peep, tweet, twitter, chitter

cheep *n Syn* CHIRP, chirrup, peep, tweet, twitter, chitter

cheer **1** *Syn* ENCOURAGE, inspirit, hearten, embolden, nerve, steel *Ant* deject; dismay **2** *Syn* APPLAUD, root

cheerful *Syn* GLAD, lighthearted, joyful, joyous, happy *Ant* glum, gloomy

cheerless *Syn* DISMAL, dreary, dispiriting, bleak, desolate *Ant* cheerful

cheeseparing *Syn* STINGY, close, closefisted, tight, tightfisted, niggardly, pennypinching, parsimonious, penurious, miserly

chemist *Syn* DRUGGIST, apothecary, pharmacist

cherish **1** *Syn* APPRECIATE, prize, treasure, value *Ant* neglect **2** *Syn* NURSE, foster, nurture, cultivate *Ant* abandon

chew out *Syn* SCOLD, upbraid, rate, berate, tongue-lash, jaw, bawl, wig, rail, revile, vituperate

chic *Syn* STYLISH, smart, fashionable, modish, dashing

chicane, chicanery *Syn* DECEPTION, trickery, double-dealing, fraud

chide *Syn* REPROVE, reproach, rebuke, reprimand, admonish *Ant* commend

chief *n* ♦ the person in whom resides authority or ruling power *Syn* chieftain, head, headman, leader, master

chief *adj* ♦ first in importance or in standing *Syn* principal, main, leading, foremost, capital *Ant* subordinate

chiefly *Syn* LARGELY, greatly, mostly, mainly, principally, generally

chieftain *Syn* CHIEF, head, leader, master

childish *Syn* CHILDLIKE *Ant* mature, grown-up

childlike ♦ having or showing the manner, spirit, or disposition of a child *Syn* childish

chilly *Syn* COLD, cool, frigid, freezing, frosty, gelid, icy, glacial, arctic *Ant* balmy

chimerical *Syn* IMAGINARY, fantastic, fanciful, visionary, quixotic *Ant* feasible

chine *Syn* SPINE, backbone, back, vertebrae

chink *Syn* CRACK, cleft, fissure, crevasse, crevice, cranny

chirp *vb* ♦ to make a short, sharp, and usu. repetitive sound *Syn* chirrup, cheep, peep, tweet, twitter, chitter

chirp *n* ♦ the little sounds characteristic of small animals or sounds that suggest such small animal sounds *Syn* chirrup, cheep, peep, tweet, twitter, chitter

chirrup *vb* *Syn* CHIRP, cheep, peep, tweet, twitter, chitter

chirrup *n* *Syn* CHIRP, cheep, peep, tweet, twitter, chitter

chisel *Syn* CARVE, sculpture, sculpt, sculp, incise, engrave, etch

chitter *vb* *Syn* CHIRP, chirrup, cheep, peep, tweet, twitter

chitter *n* *Syn* CHIRP, chirrup, cheep, peep, tweet, twitter

chivalrous *Syn* CIVIL, gallant, courtly, courteous, polite *Ant* churlish

chivy *Syn* BAIT, badger, heckle, hector, hound, ride

choice *n* ♦ the act or opportunity of choosing or the thing chosen *Syn* option, alternative, preference, selection, election

choice *adj* ♦ having qualities that appeal to a fine or highly refined taste *Syn* exquisite, elegant, recherché, rare, dainty, delicate *Ant* indifferent, medium

choke *Syn* SUFFOCATE, asphyxiate, stifle, smother, strangle, throttle

choleric *Syn* IRASCIBLE, splenetic, testy, touchy, cranky, cross *Ant* placid; imperturbable

choose ♦ to fix upon one of a number of things as the one to be taken, accepted, or adopted *Syn* select, elect, opt, pick, cull, prefer, single *Ant* reject; eschew

chop *Syn* CUT, hew, slit, slash, carve

chore *Syn* TASK, duty, assignment, job, stint

christen *Syn* BAPTIZE

chronic *Syn* INVETERATE, confirmed, deep-seated, deep-rooted *Ant* acute (*of illness*)

chronicle 1 *Syn* HISTORY, annals **2** *Syn* ACCOUNT, story, report, version

chthonic, chthonian *Syn* INFERNAL, Hadean, stygian, hellish, Tartarean

chubby *Syn* FLESHY, rotund, plump, fat, stout, portly, corpulent, obese *Ant* slim

chummy *Syn* FAMILIAR, intimate, close, thick, confidential

chunky *Syn* STOCKY, thickset, thick, stubby, squat, dumpy

church *Syn* RELIGION, denomination, sect, communion, creed, faith, cult, persuasion

churl *Syn* BOOR, lout, clown, clodhopper, bumpkin, hick, yokel, rube

churlish *Syn* BOORISH, loutish, clownish *Ant* courtly

cinders *Syn* ASH, clinkers, embers

circadian *Syn* DAILY, diurnal, quotidian

circle *n* *Syn* SET, coterie, clique

circle *vb* **1** *Syn* SURROUND, environ, encircle, encompass, compass, hem, gird, girdle, ring **2** *Syn* TURN, revolve, rotate, gyrate, wheel, spin, twirl, whirl, eddy, swirl, pirouette

circuit *Syn* CIRCUMFERENCE, compass, perimeter, periphery

circuitous *Syn* INDIRECT, roundabout *Ant* straight

circulate *Syn* SPREAD, disseminate, diffuse, propagate, radiate

circumference ♦ a continuous line enclosing an area or space *Syn* perimeter, periphery, circuit, compass

circumlocution *Syn* VERBIAGE, periphrasis, pleonasm, redundancy, tautology

circumscribe *Syn* LIMIT, confine, restrict *Ant* expand, dilate

circumspect *Syn* CAUTIOUS, wary, calculating, chary *Ant* audacious

circumspection *Syn* CAUTION, wariness, calculation, chariness *Ant* audacity

circumstance *Syn* OCCURRENCE, event, incident, episode

circumstantial ♦ dealing with a matter fully and usu. point by point *Syn* minute, particular, particularized, detailed, itemized *Ant* abridged; summary

circumvent *Syn* FRUSTRATE, outwit, baffle, balk, thwart, foil *Ant* conform (to *laws*, *orders*); cooperate (with *persons*)

citadel *Syn* FORT, stronghold, fortress, fastness

citation *Syn* ENCOMIUM, eulogy, tribute, panegyric

cite 1 *Syn* SUMMON, summons, call, convoke, convene, muster **2** *Syn* QUOTE, repeat **3** *Syn* ADDUCE, advance, allege

citizen 1 *Syn* INHABITANT, resident, denizen **2** ♦ a person who is regarded as a member of a sovereign state, entitled to its protection, and subject to its laws *Syn* subject, national *Ant* alien

civil ♦ observant of the forms required by good breeding *Syn* polite, courteous, courtly, gallant, chivalrous *Ant* uncivil, rude

claim *vb Syn* DEMAND, exact, require *Ant* disclaim; renounce

claim *n* ♦ an actual or alleged right to demand something as one's possession, quality, power, or prerogative *Syn* title, pretension, pretense

clamor *n Syn* DIN, uproar, pandemonium, hullabaloo, babel, hubbub, racket

clamor *vb Syn* ROAR, bellow, bluster, bawl, vociferate, howl, ululate

clamorous *Syn* VOCIFEROUS, blatant, strident, boisterous, obstreperous *Ant* taciturn

clandestine *Syn* SECRET, covert, surreptitious, furtive, underhand, underhanded, stealthy *Ant* open

clash *vb Syn* BUMP, collide, conflict *Ant* blend

clash *n Syn* IMPACT, collision, impingement, shock, concussion, percussion, jar, jolt

class *n* ♦ a group including all individuals with a common characteristic *Syn* category

class *vb* ♦ to order a number of things according to a scale or to place a thing in its due order *Syn* grade, rank, rate, graduate, gradate

classify *Syn* ASSORT, pigeonhole, sort

clause *Syn* PARAGRAPH, verse, article, plank, count

clean ♦ to remove whatever soils, stains, or contaminates *Syn* cleanse *Ant* soil

cleanse *Syn* CLEAN *Ant* defile, besmirch

clear *adj* **1** ♦ having the property of being literally or figuratively seen through *Syn* transparent, translucent, lucid, pellucid, diaphanous, limpid *Ant* turbid; confused **2** ♦ quickly and easily understood *Syn* perspicuous, lucid *Ant* unintelligible; abstruse **3** *Syn* EVIDENT, manifest, obvious, distinct, apparent, patent, palpable, plain

clear *vb Syn* RID, unburden, disabuse, purge

clearance *Syn* ROOM, berth, play, elbowroom, leeway, margin

clear-cut *Syn* INCISIVE, trenchant, cutting, biting, crisp

cleave *vb Syn* STICK, cling, adhere, cohere *Ant* part

cleave *vb Syn* TEAR, split, rive, rend, rip

cleft *Syn* CRACK, fissure, crevasse, crevice, cranny, chink

clemency 1 *Syn* MERCY, lenity, charity, grace *Ant* harshness **2** *Syn* FORBEARANCE, mercifulness, leniency, indulgence, tolerance

clement *Syn* FORBEARING, merciful, lenient, indulgent, tolerant *Ant* harsh; barbarous

clemently *Syn* FORBEARINGLY, tolerantly, mercifully, leniently, indulgently

clever 1 *Syn* INTELLIGENT, quick-witted, brilliant, bright, smart, alert, knowing *Ant* dull **2** ♦ having or showing a high degree of practical intelligence or skill in contrivance *Syn* adroit, cunning, ingenious

cliché *Syn* COMMONPLACE, platitude, truism, bromide

clientele *Syn* FOLLOWING, public, audience

climax *Syn* SUMMIT, culmination, peak, apex, acme, zenith, apogee, pinnacle, meridian

climb *Syn* ASCEND, mount, scale *Ant* descend

cling *Syn* STICK, cleave, adhere, cohere

clinkers *Syn* ASH, cinders, embers

clip *Syn* SHEAR, poll, trim, prune, lop, snip, crop

clique *Syn* SET, circle, coterie

cloak *Syn* DISGUISE, mask, dissemble, camouflage *Ant* uncloak

clodhopper *Syn* BOOR, bumpkin, hick, yokel, rube, lout, clown, churl

clog *Syn* HAMPER, fetter, hog-tie, shackle, manacle, trammel *Ant* expedite, facilitate

cloister 1 ♦ a place of retirement from the world for members of a religious community *Syn* convent, monastery, nunnery, abbey, priory **2** *Syn* PASSAGE, arcade, passageway, ambulatory, gallery, corridor, aisle, hall, hallway

clone *Syn* VARIETY, subspecies, race, breed, cultivar, strain, stock

close *vb* **1** ♦ to stop or fill in an opening by means of a closure *Syn* shut *Ant* open **2** ♦ to bring or come to a limit or a natural or appropriate stopping point *Syn* end, conclude, finish, complete, terminate

close *adj* **1** ♦ not far (as in place, time, or relationship) from the point, position, or relation that is indicated or understood *Syn* near, nigh, nearby *Ant* remote, remotely **2** ♦ having constituent parts that are massed tightly together *Syn* dense, compact, thick *Ant* open **3** *Syn* SILENT, close-lipped, closemouthed, tight-lipped, secretive, reserved, taciturn, reticent, un-

communicative *Ant* open, frank **4** *Syn* FAMILIAR, intimate, confidential, chummy, thick *Ant* aloof **5** *Syn* STINGY, closefisted, tight, tightfisted, niggardly, parsimonious, penurious, cheeseparing, penny-pinching *Ant* liberal

closefisted *Syn* STINGY, close, tight, tightfisted, niggardly, parsimonious, penurious, miserly, cheeseparing, penny-pinching

close-lipped *Syn* SILENT, close, closemouthed, uncommunicative, taciturn, reserved, reticent, secretive, tight-lipped

closemouthed *Syn* SILENT, close, close-lipped, tight-lipped, reticent, reserved, uncommunicative, taciturn, secretive

clot *Syn* COAGULATE, congeal, curdle, set, jelly, jell

clothe ♦ to cover with or as if with garments *Syn* attire, dress, apparel, array, robe *Ant* unclothe

clothes ♦ a person's garments considered collectively *Syn* clothing, dress, attire, apparel, raiment

clothing *Syn* CLOTHES, dress, attire, apparel, raiment

cloud *Syn* OBSCURE, dim, bedim, darken, eclipse, becloud, fog, befog, obfuscate

clout *Syn* STRIKE, hit, smite, punch, slug, slog, swat, slap, cuff, box

clown *Syn* BOOR, clodhopper, lout, bumpkin, hick, yokel, rube, churl

clownish *Syn* BOORISH, loutish, churlish *Ant* urbane

cloy *Syn* SATIATE, sate, surfeit, pall, glut, gorge

club *Syn* ASSOCIATION, society, order

clumsy *Syn* AWKWARD, gauche, maladroit, inept *Ant* dexterous, adroit; facile

cluster *Syn* GROUP, bunch, parcel, lot

clutch *vb* *Syn* TAKE, grasp, grab, seize, snatch

clutch *n* *Syn* HOLD, grip, grasp

clutter *Syn* CONFUSION, disorder, disarray, jumble, chaos, muddle, snarl

coadjutor *Syn* ASSISTANT, helper, aid, aide, aide-de-camp

coagulate ♦ to alter by chemical reaction from a liquid to a more or less firm jelly *Syn* congeal, set, curdle, clot, jelly, jell

coalesce *Syn* MIX, merge, fuse, blend, mingle, commingle, amalgamate

coalition *Syn* ALLIANCE, fusion, confederacy, confederation, federation, league

coarse ♦ offensive to good taste or morals *Syn* vulgar, gross, obscene, ribald *Ant* fine; refined

coast *n Syn* SHORE, strand, beach, bank, foreshore, littoral

coast *vb Syn* SLIDE, toboggan, glide, slip, skid, glissade, slither

coax ♦ to use ingratiating art in persuading or attempting to persuade *Syn* cajole, wheedle, blandish *Ant* bully

cobble *Syn* BOTCH, bungle, fumble, muff

cock *vb Syn* HEAP, stack, shock, pile, mass, bank

cock *n Syn* HEAP, stack, shock, pile, mass, bank

cocksure *Syn* SURE, positive, certain *Ant* dubious, doubtful

coerce *Syn* FORCE, compel, constrain, oblige

coercion *Syn* FORCE, compulsion, violence, duress, constraint, restraint

coetaneous *Syn* CONTEMPORARY, coeval, contemporaneous, synchronous, simultaneous, coincident, concomitant, concurrent

coeval *Syn* CONTEMPORARY, coetaneous, synchronous, concurrent, simultaneous, coincident, concomitant, contemporaneous

cogent *Syn* VALID, convincing, compelling, telling, sound

cogitate *Syn* THINK, reflect, deliberate, reason, speculate

cognate *Syn* RELATED, allied, kindred, affiliated

cognizant *Syn* AWARE, conscious, sensible, alive, awake *Ant* ignorant

cohere *Syn* STICK, adhere, cleave, cling

coherence ♦ the quality or character of a whole all of whose parts cohere or stick together *Syn* cohesion *Ant* incoherence

cohesion *Syn* COHERENCE

coil *Syn* WIND, curl, twist, twine, wreathe, entwine

coin *Syn* MONEY, coinage, currency, specie, legal tender, cash

coinage *Syn* MONEY, coin, currency, cash, specie, legal tender

coincide *Syn* AGREE, concur *Ant* differ

coincident *Syn* CONTEMPORARY, synchronous, simultaneous, concurrent, concomitant, coeval, coetaneous, contemporaneous

cold ♦ having a temperature below that which is normal or comfortable *Syn* cool, chilly, frigid, freezing, frosty, gelid, icy, glacial, arctic *Ant* hot

collate *Syn* COMPARE, contrast

collateral *Syn* SUBORDINATE, secondary, dependent, subject, tributary

collation *Syn* COMPARISON, parallel, contrast, antithesis

colleague *Syn* PARTNER, copartner, ally, confederate

collect *Syn* GATHER, assemble, congregate *Ant* disperse; distribute

collected *Syn* COOL, composed, unruffled, imperturbable, unflappable, nonchalant *Ant* distracted, distraught

collection *Syn* GATHERING, assemblage, assembly, congregation

collide *Syn* BUMP, clash, conflict

collision *Syn* IMPACT, impingement, clash, shock, concussion, percussion, jar, jolt

color 1 ♦ a property or attribute of a visible thing recognizable only when rays of light fall upon it and serving to distinguish things otherwise visually identical (as shape or size) *Syn* hue, shade, tint, tinge, tone 2 *usu pl* colors *Syn* FLAG, ensign, standard, banner, streamer, pennant, pendant, pennon, jack

colorable *Syn* PLAUSIBLE, credible, believable, specious

colorless ♦ without color *Syn* uncolored, achromatic *Ant* colorful

colossal *Syn* HUGE, vast, immense, enormous, elephantine, mammoth, giant, gigantic, gigantean, gargantuan, Herculean, cyclopean, titanic, Brobdingnagian

column *Syn* PILLAR, pilaster

comatose *Syn* LETHARGIC, torpid, sluggish *Ant* awake

comb *Syn* SEEK, search, scour, hunt, ferret out, ransack, rummage

combat *vb* *Syn* RESIST, withstand, contest, oppose, fight, conflict, antagonize *Ant* champion; defend

combat *n* *Syn* CONTEST, conflict, fight, affray, fray

combative *Syn* BELLIGERENT, bellicose, pugnacious, quarrelsome, contentious *Ant* pacifistic

combination ♦ a union, either of individuals or of organized interests, for mutual support in obtaining common political or private ends *Syn* combine, party, bloc, faction, ring

combine *vb* 1 *Syn* JOIN, unite, associate, link, conjoin, connect, relate *Ant* separate 2 *Syn* UNITE, cooperate, concur, conjoin

combine *n* *Syn* COMBINATION, party, bloc, faction, ring

combustible ♦ showing a tendency to catch or be set on fire *Syn* inflammable, flammable, incendiary, inflammatory

come ♦ to get to one point from another more or less distant in space, time, relation, or development *Syn* arrive *Ant* go

comely *Syn* BEAUTIFUL, fair, pretty, bonny, handsome, lovely, good-looking, beauteous, pulchritudinous *Ant* homely

comestibles *Syn* FOOD, provisions, viands, victuals, feed, provender, fodder, forage

comfort *n* *Syn* REST, ease, repose, relaxation, leisure *Ant* discomfort

comfort *vb* ♦ to give or offer a person help or assistance in relieving his suffering or sorrow *Syn* console, solace *Ant* afflict; bother

comfortable ♦ enjoying or providing condition or circumstances which make for one's contentment and security *Syn* cozy, snug, easy, restful *Ant* uncomfortable; miserable

comic *Syn* LAUGHABLE, comical, farcical, funny, droll, risible, ludicrous, ridiculous *Ant* tragic

comical *Syn* LAUGHABLE, comic, farcical, ludicrous, ridiculous, risible, droll, funny *Ant* pathetic

comity *Syn* FRIENDSHIP, amity, goodwill

command *vb* ♦ to issue orders to someone to give, get, or do something *Syn* order, bid, enjoin, direct, instruct, charge *Ant* comply, obey

command *n* 1 ♦ a direction that must or should be obeyed *Syn* order, injunction, bidding, behest, mandate, dictate 2 *Syn* POWER, control, authority, jurisdiction, sway, dominion

commemorate *Syn* KEEP, celebrate, observe, solemnize

commence *Syn* BEGIN, start, initiate, inaugurate

commend ♦ to voice or otherwise manifest to others one's warm approval *Syn* recommend, applaud, compliment *Ant* censure; admonish

commensurable *Syn* PROPORTIONAL, commensurate, proportionate *Ant* incommensurable

commensurate *Syn* PROPORTIONAL, commensurable, proportionate *Ant* incommensurate

comment *n* *Syn* REMARK, commentary, observation, note, obiter dictum

comment *vb* *Syn* REMARK, commentate, animadvert

commentary *Syn* REMARK, comment, observation, note, obiter dictum

commentate *Syn* REMARK, comment, animadvert

commerce 1 *Syn* BUSINESS, trade, industry, traffic 2 *Syn* INTERCOURSE, traffic, dealings, communication, communion, conversation, converse, correspondence

commercial ♦ of, relating to, or dealing with the supplying of commodities *Syn* mercantile

commingle *Syn* MIX, mingle, blend, merge, coalesce, fuse, amalgamate

commiseration *Syn* SYMPATHY, compassion, pity, condolence, ruth, empathy *Ant* ruthlessness, pitilessness

commission *Syn* AUTHORIZE, accredit, license

commit 1 ♦ to assign to a person or place for some definite end or purpose (as custody or safekeeping) *Syn* entrust, confide, consign, relegate **2** ♦ to be responsible for or to be guilty of some offense or mistake *Syn* perpetrate

commodious *Syn* SPACIOUS, capacious, ample

common 1 *Syn* UNIVERSAL, general, generic *Ant* individual **2** *Syn* RECIPROCAL, mutual **3** ♦ generally met with and not in any way special, strange, or unusual *Syn* ordinary, familiar, popular, vulgar *Ant* uncommon; exceptional

commonplace ♦ an idea or expression lacking in originality or freshness *Syn* platitude, truism, bromide, cliché

common sense *Syn* — see SENSE 2

commotion ♦ great physical, mental, or emotional excitement *Syn* agitation, tumult, turmoil, turbulence, confusion, convulsion, upheaval

commune *Syn* CONFER, consult, advise, parley, treat, negotiate

communicable *Syn* INFECTIOUS, contagious, catching

communicate ♦ to convey or transfer something (as information, feelings, or qualities) neither tangible nor concrete *Syn* impart

communication *Syn* INTERCOURSE, commerce, traffic, dealings, conversation, converse, correspondence, communion

communion 1 *Syn* INTERCOURSE, commerce, traffic, converse, dealings, communication, conversation, correspondence **2** *Syn* RELIGION, denomination, faith, church, creed, sect, cult, persuasion

compact *adj Syn* CLOSE, dense, thick

compact *vb* ♦ to bring or gather together the parts, particles, elements, or units of a thing so as to form a close mass or an integral whole *Syn* consolidate, unify, concentrate

compact *n Syn* CONTRACT, pact, entente, convention, concordat, treat, cartel, bargain

companion *Syn* ASSOCIATE, comrade, crony

companionable *Syn* SOCIAL, cooperative, convivial, gregarious, hospitable

company ♦ a group of persons who are associated in a joint endeavor or who are assembled for a common end *Syn* party, band, troop, troupe

comparable *Syn* LIKE, alike, similar, analogous, akin, parallel, uniform, identical *Ant* disparate

compare ♦ to set two or more things side by side in order to show likenesses and differences *Syn* contrast, collate

comparison ♦ a setting of things side by side so as to discover or exhibit their likenesses and differences *Syn* contrast, antithesis, collation, parallel

compass *vb* **1** *Syn* SURROUND, environ, encircle, circle, encompass, hem, gird, girdle, ring **2** *Syn* REACH, gain, attain, achieve

compass *n* **1** *Syn* CIRCUMFERENCE, perimeter, periphery, circuit **2** *Syn* RANGE, gamut, reach, radius, sweep, scope, orbit, horizon, ken, purview

compassion *Syn* SYMPATHY, pity, commiseration, ruth, empathy, condolence

compassionate *Syn* TENDER, sympathetic, warmhearted, warm, responsive

compatible *Syn* CONSONANT, congruous, consistent, congenial, sympathetic *Ant* incompatible

compel *Syn* FORCE, coerce, constrain, oblige

compelling *Syn* VALID, telling, convincing, cogent, sound

compendious *Syn* CONCISE, summary, pithy, succinct, terse, laconic

compendium ♦ a condensed treatment of a subject *Syn* syllabus, digest, pandect, survey, sketch, précis, aperçu

compensate 1 ♦ to make up for or to undo the effects of *Syn* countervail, balance, offset, counterbalance, counterpoise **2** *Syn* PAY, remunerate, recompense, repay, reimburse, satisfy, indemnify

compete 1 ♦ to strive to gain the mastery or upper hand *Syn* contend, contest **2** *Syn* RIVAL, vie, emulate

competent 1 *Syn* ABLE, capable, qualified *Ant* incompetent **2** *Syn* sufficient, enough, adequate

compile *Syn* EDIT, revise, redact, rewrite, adapt

complacent ♦ feeling or showing an often excessive or unjustified satisfaction in one's possessions, attainments, accomplishments, or virtues *Syn* self-complacent, self-satisfied, smug, priggish

complaint *Syn* DISEASE, ailment, disorder, condition, affection, malady, distemper, syndrome

complaisant *Syn* AMIABLE, obliging, good-natured *Ant* contrary, perverse

complement *n* ♦ something that makes up for a want or deficiency in another thing *Syn* supplement

complement *vb* ♦ to supply what is needed to make up for a want or deficiency *Syn* supplement

complementary, complemental *Syn* RECIPROCAL, correlative, corresponding, convertible

complete *adj Syn* FULL, plenary, replete *Ant* incomplete

complete *vb Syn* CLOSE, finish, conclude, end, terminate

complex *adj* ♦ having parts or elements that are more or less confusingly interrelated *Syn* complicated, intricate, involved, knotty *Ant* simple

complex *n Syn* SYSTEM, network, organism, scheme *Ant* component

complexion *Syn* DISPOSITION, temperament, temper, character, personality, individuality

compliance ♦ passive or weak agreement to what is asked or demanded *Syn* acquiescence, resignation *Ant* forwardness

compliant ♦ manifesting acceptance (as of another's will or something disagreeable) *Syn* acquiescent, resigned *Ant* forward

complicated *Syn* COMPLEX, intricate, involved, knotty *Ant* simple

compliment *n* ♦ praise addressed directly to a person *Syn* flattery, adulation *Ant* taunt

compliment *vb Syn* COMMEND, applaud, recommend

comply *Syn* OBEY, mind *Ant* command, enjoin

component *Syn* ELEMENT, constituent, ingredient, factor *Ant* composite; complex

comport *Syn* BEHAVE, acquit, quit, demean, conduct, deport

compose *Syn* CALM, quiet, quieten, still, lull, soothe, settle, tranquilize *Ant* discompose

composed *Syn* COOL, collected, unruffled, imperturbable, unflappable, nonchalant *Ant* discomposed; anxious

composite *Syn* MIXTURE, admixture, blend, compound, amalgam

composition *Syn* ESSAY, theme, paper, article

composure *Syn* EQUANIMITY, sangfroid, phlegm *Ant* discomposure, perturbation

compound *Syn* MIXTURE, amalgam, composite, admixture, blend *Ant* element

comprehend 1 *Syn* UNDERSTAND, appreciate **2** *Syn* APPREHEND **3** *Syn* INCLUDE, embrace, involve, imply, subsume

comprehension *Syn* APPREHENSION,

compress *Syn* CONTRACT, constrict, deflate, condense, shrink *Ant* stretch; spread

compulsion *Syn* FORCE, coercion, constraint, duress, violence, restraint

compunction 1 *Syn* PENITENCE, remorse, repentance, contrition, attrition **2** *Syn* QUALM, scruple, demur

compute *Syn* CALCULATE, reckon, estimate

comrade *Syn* ASSOCIATE, companion, crony

conation *Syn* WILL, volition

concatenate *Syn* INTEGRATE, articulate

concatenation *Syn* INTEGRATION, articulation

conceal *Syn* HIDE, screen, secrete, bury, cache, ensconce *Ant* reveal

concede 1 *Syn* GRANT, allow *Ant* dispute **2** *Syn* GRANT, vouchsafe, accord, award *Ant* deny (*something to somebody*)

conceit 1 ♦ an attitude of regarding oneself with favor *Syn* egotism, egoism, self-esteem, self-love, amour propre *Ant* humility **2** *Syn* CAPRICE, freak, fancy, whim, whimsy, vagary, crotchet

conceive *Syn* THINK, imagine, fancy, realize, envisage, envision

concentrate 1 *Syn* CENTER, focus, centralize **2** *Syn* COMPACT, consolidate, unify *Ant* dissipate

concentration *Syn* ATTENTION, application, study *Ant* distraction

concept *Syn* IDEA, conception, notion, thought, impression

conception *Syn* IDEA, concept, thought, notion, impression

concern 1 *Syn* AFFAIR, business, matter, thing **2** *Syn* CARE, solicitude, anxiety, worry *Ant* unconcern

concerned *Syn* WORRIED, solicitous, anxious *Ant* unconcerned

concerning *Syn* ABOUT, regarding, respecting

concert *Syn* NEGOTIATE, arrange

concession *Syn* ALLOWANCE

conciliate *Syn* PACIFY, appease, placate, propitiate, mollify *Ant* antagonize

concise ♦ presented with or given to brevity of expression *Syn* terse, succinct, laconic, summary, pithy, compendious *Ant* redundant

conclude 1 *Syn* CLOSE, finish, terminate, end, complete *Ant* open **2** *Syn* INFER, judge, gather, deduce

concluding *Syn* LAST, final, terminal, latest, ultimate *Ant* opening

conclusion *Syn* INFERENCE, judgment, deduction

conclusive ♦ having or manifesting qualities that bring something to a finish or end *Syn* decisive, determinative, definitive *Ant* inconclusive

concoct *Syn* CONTRIVE, devise, invent, frame

concomitant *adj* *Syn* CONTEMPORARY, coincident, concurrent, synchronous, simultaneous, contemporaneous, coeval, coetaneous

concomitant *n* *Syn* ACCOMPANIMENT

concord *Syn* HARMONY, consonance, accord *Ant* discord

concordat *Syn* CONTRACT, compact, pact, treaty, entente, convention, cartel, bargain

concourse *Syn* JUNCTION, confluence

concur 1 *Syn* UNITE, conjoin, combine, cooperate **2** *Syn* AGREE, coincide *Ant* contend; altercate

concurrent *Syn* CONTEMPORARY, coincident, simultaneous, synchronous, concomitant, contemporaneous, coeval, coetaneous

concussion *Syn* IMPACT, shock, percussion, impingement, collision, clash, jar, jolt

condemn 1 *Syn* CRITICIZE, denounce, censure, blame, reprobate, reprehend **2** *Syn* SENTENCE, doom, damn, proscribe

condense *Syn* CONTRACT, shrink, compress, constrict, deflate *Ant* amplify

condescend *Syn* STOOP, deign *Ant* presume

condign *Syn* DUE, rightful

condition *n* **1** ♦ something that limits or qualifies an agreement or offer *Syn* stipulation, terms, provision, proviso, reservation, strings **2** *Syn* STATE, situation, mode, posture, status **3** *Syn* DISEASE, disorder, affection, ailment, malady, complaint, distemper, syndrome

condition *vb* *Syn* PREPARE, fit, qualify, ready

conditional *Syn* DEPENDENT, contingent, relative *Ant* unconditional

condolence *Syn* SYMPATHY, pity, commiseration, compassion, ruth, empathy

condone *Syn* EXCUSE, forgive, pardon, remit

conduct *n* *Syn* BEHAVIOR, deportment

conduct *vb* **1** *Syn* ACCOMPANY, escort, convoy, attend, chaperon **2** ♦ to use one's skill, authority, or other powers in order to lead, guide, command, or dominate persons or things *Syn* manage, control, direct **3** *Syn* BEHAVE, demean, deport, comport, acquit, quit

conduit *Syn* CHANNEL, canal, duct, aqueduct

confederacy, confederation *Syn* ALLIANCE, federation, coalition, fusion, league

confederate 1 *Syn* PARTNER, copartner,

colleague, ally 2 ♦ one associated with another or others in a wrong or unlawful act *Syn* conspirator, accessory, abettor, accomplice

confer 1 *Syn* GIVE, bestow, present, donate, afford 2 ♦ to carry on a conversation or discussion esp. in order to reach a decision or settlement *Syn* commune, consult, advise, parley, treat, negotiate

confess *Syn* ACKNOWLEDGE, avow, admit, own *Ant* renounce (*one's beliefs, principles*)

confessions *Syn* BIOGRAPHY, life, memoir, autobiography

confidant *Syn* FRIEND, intimate, acquaintance

confide *Syn* COMMIT, entrust, consign, relegate

confidence 1 *Syn* TRUST, reliance, dependence, faith *Ant* doubt; apprehension 2 ♦ a feeling or showing of adequacy or reliance on oneself and one's powers *Syn* self-confidence, assurance, self-assurance, self-possession, aplomb *Ant* diffidence

confident ♦ not inhibited by doubts, fears, or a sense of inferiority *Syn* assured, sanguine, sure, presumptuous *Ant* apprehensive; diffident

confidential *Syn* FAMILIAR, close, intimate, chummy, thick

configuration *Syn* FORM, conformation, figure, shape

confine *vb Syn* LIMIT, circumscribe, restrict

confine *n Syn* LIMIT, bound, end, term

confirm 1 *Syn* RATIFY 2 ♦ to attest to the truth, genuineness, accuracy, or validity of something *Syn* corroborate, substantiate, verify, authenticate, validate *Ant* deny; contradict

confirmed *Syn* INVETERATE, chronic, deep-seated, deep-rooted

confiscate *Syn* ARROGATE, appropriate, usurp, preempt

conflagration *Syn* FIRE, holocaust

conflict *n* 1 *Syn* CONTEST, combat, fight, affray, fray 2 *Syn* DISCORD, strife, contention, dissension, difference, variance *Ant* harmony

conflict *vb* 1 *Syn* RESIST, withstand, contest, oppose, fight, combat, antagonize 2 *Syn* BUMP, clash, collide *Ant* accord

confluence *Syn* JUNCTION, concourse

conform 1 *Syn* ADAPT, adjust, accommodate, reconcile 2 *Syn* AGREE, accord, harmonize, correspond, square, tally, jibe *Ant* diverge

conformation *Syn* FORM, configuration, shape, figure

confound 1 *Syn* PUZZLE, dumbfound, nonplus, bewilder, mystify, perplex, distract 2 *Syn* MISTAKE, confuse *Ant* distinguish, discriminate

confront *Syn* MEET, face, encounter *Ant* recoil

confuse 1 ♦ to make unclear in mind or purpose *Syn* muddle, addle, fuddle, befuddle *Ant* enlighten 2 *Syn* MISTAKE, confound *Ant* differentiate

confusion 1 ♦ a condition in which things are not in their normal or proper places or relationships *Syn* disorder, chaos, disarray, jumble, clutter, snarl, muddle 2 *Syn* COMMOTION, agitation, tumult, turmoil, turbulence, convulsion, upheaval

confute *Syn* DISPROVE, controvert, refute, rebut

congeal *Syn* COAGULATE, set, curdle, clot, jelly, jell

congenial *Syn* CONSONANT, consistent, compatible, congruous, sympathetic *Ant* uncongenial; antipathetic (*of persons*); abhorrent (*of tasks, duties*)

congenital *Syn* INNATE, inborn, hereditary, inherited, inbred

conglomerate, conglomeration *Syn* AGGREGATE, agglomerate, agglomeration, aggregation

congratulate *Syn* FELICITATE

congregate *Syn* GATHER, assemble, collect *Ant* disperse

congregation *Syn* GATHERING, assembly, assemblage, collection

congruous *Syn* CONSONANT, compatible, congenial, sympathetic, consistent *Ant* incongruous

conjectural *Syn* SUPPOSED, hypothetical, supposititious, reputed, putative, purported

conjecture *vb* ♦ to draw an inference from slight evidence **Syn** surmise, guess

conjecture *n* ♦ an inference based on slight evidence **Syn** surmise, guess **Ant** fact

conjoin 1 **Syn** JOIN, combine, unite, connect, link, associate, relate 2 **Syn** UNITE, combine, concur, cooperate

conjugal **Syn** MATRIMONIAL, marital, connubial, nuptial, hymeneal **Ant** single

connect **Syn** JOIN, link, associate, relate, unite, conjoin, combine **Ant** disconnect

connoisseur **Syn** AESTHETE, dilettante

connubial **Syn** MATRIMONIAL, conjugal, marital, nuptial, hymeneal

conquer ♦ to get the better of or to bring into subjection by force or strategy **Syn** defeat, vanquish, overcome, surmount, subdue, subjugate, reduce, overthrow, rout, beat, lick

conqueror **Syn** VICTOR, vanquisher, winner, champion

conquest **Syn** VICTORY, triumph

conscientious **Syn** UPRIGHT, scrupulous, honorable, honest, just **Ant** unconscientious, unscrupulous

conscious **Syn** AWARE, sensible, cognizant, alive, awake **Ant** unconscious

consecrate **Syn** DEVOTE, hallow, dedicate

consecutive ♦ following one after the other in order **Syn** successive, sequent, sequential, serial **Ant** inconsecutive

consent **Syn** ASSENT, accede, acquiesce, agree, subscribe **Ant** dissent

consequence 1 **Syn** EFFECT, result, upshot, aftereffect, aftermath, sequel, issue, outcome, event **Ant** antecedent 2 **Syn** IMPORTANCE, moment, weight, significance, import

consequently **Syn** THEREFORE, hence, then, accordingly, so

conserve **Syn** SAVE, preserve **Ant** waste, squander

consider 1 ♦ to give serious thought to **Syn** study, contemplate, weigh, excogitate 2 ♦ to come to view, judge, or classify **Syn** regard, account, reckon, deem

considerate **Syn** THOUGHTFUL, attentive **Ant** inconsiderate

considered **Syn** DELIBERATE, premeditated, advised, designed, studied **Ant** unconsidered

consign **Syn** COMMIT, entrust, confide, relegate

consistent **Syn** CONSONANT, congruous, compatible, congenial, sympathetic **Ant** inconsistent

console **Syn** COMFORT, solace

consolidate **Syn** COMPACT, unify, concentrate

consolidation ♦ a union of two or more business corporations **Syn** merger, amalgamation **Ant** dissolution

consonance **Syn** HARMONY, concord, accord **Ant** dissonance (*in music*); discord

consonant ♦ conforming (as to a pattern, standard, or relationship) without discord or difficulty **Syn** consistent, compatible, congruous, congenial, sympathetic **Ant** inconstant; dissonant (*in music*)

conspectus **Syn** ABRIDGMENT, synopsis, epitome, abstract, brief

conspicuous **Syn** NOTICEABLE, prominent, salient, signal, remarkable, striking, arresting, outstanding **Ant** inconspicuous

conspiracy **Syn** PLOT, cabal, intrigue, machination

conspirator **Syn** CONFEDERATE, accessory, accomplice, abettor

constant 1 **Syn** FAITHFUL, true, loyal, staunch, steadfast, resolute **Ant** inconstant, fickle 2 **Syn** STEADY, uniform, even, equable **Ant** variable 3 **Syn** CONTINUAL, incessant, unremitting, continuous, perpetual, perennial **Ant** fitful

consternation **Syn** FEAR, panic, terror, alarm, fright, dread, dismay, horror, trepidation

constituent **Syn** ELEMENT, component, ingredient, factor **Ant** whole, aggregate

constitution **Syn** PHYSIQUE, build, habit

constitutional **Syn** INHERENT, intrinsic, essential, ingrained

constrain **Syn** FORCE, oblige, coerce, compel

constraint **Syn** FORCE, compulsion, coercion, duress, restraint, violence

constrict *Syn* CONTRACT, compress, shrink, condense, deflate

construct *Syn* BUILD, erect, frame, raise, rear *Ant* demolish; analyze

constructive *Syn* IMPLICIT, virtual *Ant* manifest

construe *Syn* EXPLAIN, explicate, elucidate, interpret, expound

consult *Syn* CONFER, advise, parley, commune, treat, negotiate

consume 1 *Syn* WASTE, squander, dissipate, fritter **2** *Syn* EAT, swallow, ingest, devour **3** *Syn* MONOPOLIZE, engross, absorb

consummate ♦ brought to completion or perfection *Syn* finished, accomplished *Ant* crude

contact ♦ the state of coming into direct connection or close association *Syn* touch

contagious *Syn* INFECTIOUS, communicable, catching

contain ♦ to have or be capable of having within *Syn* hold, accommodate

contaminate ♦ to debase by making impure or unclean *Syn* taint, attaint, pollute, defile

contemn *Syn* DESPISE, disdain, scorn, scout

contemplate 1 *Syn* CONSIDER, study, weigh, excogitate **2** *Syn* SEE, observe, survey, notice, remark, note, perceive, discern, view, behold, decry, espy

contemplative *Syn* THOUGHTFUL, meditative, reflective, speculative, pensive

contemporaneous *Syn* CONTEMPORARY, coeval, coetaneous, synchronous, simultaneous, coincident, concomitant, concurrent

contemporary ♦ existing, living, or occurring at the same time *Syn* contemporaneous, coeval, coetaneous, synchronous, simultaneous, coincident, concomitant, concurrent

contempt *Syn* DESPITE, disdain, scorn *Ant* respect

contemptible ♦ arousing or deserving scorn or disdain *Syn* despicable, pitiable, sorry, scurvy, cheap, beggarly, shabby *Ant* admirable, estimable; formidable

contend 1 ♦ to strive in opposition to someone or something *Syn* fight, battle, war **2** *Syn* COMPETE, contest

content contented *adj Syn* SATISFIED,

content *vb Syn* SATISFY

contention *Syn* DISCORD, dissension, difference, variance, strife, conflict

contentious *Syn* BELLIGERENT, quarrelsome, bellicose, pugnacious, combative *Ant* peaceable

conterminous *Syn* ADJACENT, contiguous, abutting, adjoining, tangent, juxtaposed

contest 1 *Syn* COMPETE, contend **2** *Syn* RESIST, withstand, oppose, fight, combat, conflict, antagonize

contest *n* ♦ a battle between opposing forces for supremacy, for power, or for possessions *Syn* conflict, combat, fight, affray, fray

contiguous *Syn* ADJACENT, adjoining, abutting, conterminous, tangent, juxtaposed

continence *Syn* TEMPERANCE, abstemiousness, sobriety, abstinence *Ant* incontinence

continent *Syn* SOBER, temperate, unimpassioned *Ant* incontinent

contingency *Syn* JUNCTURE, emergency, exigency, pinch, pass, strait, crisis

contingent 1 *Syn* ACCIDENTAL, fortuitous, casual, incidental **2** *Syn* DEPENDENT, conditional, relative

continual ♦ characterized by continued occurrence or recurrence over a relatively long period of time *Syn* continuous, constant, incessant, unremitting, perpetual, perennial *Ant* intermittent

continuance *Syn* CONTINUATION, continuity

continuation ♦ the quality, the act, or the state of continuing or of being continued *Syn* continuance, continuity *Ant* cessation

continue ♦ to remain indefinitely in existence or in a given condition or course *Syn* last, endure, abide, persist

continuity *Syn* CONTINUATION, continuance

continuous *Syn* CONTINUAL, constant, perpetual, perennial, incessant, unremitting *Ant* interrupted

contort *Syn* DEFORM, distort, warp

contour *Syn* OUTLINE, silhouette, skyline, profile

contraband *Syn* SMUGGLED, bootleg

contract *n* ♦ an agreement reached after negotiation and ending in an exchange of promises between the parties concerned *Syn* bargain, compact, pact, treaty, entente, convention, cartel, concordat

contract *vb* **1** *Syn* PROMISE, pledge, covenant, engage, plight **2** *Syn* INCUR, catch **3** ♦ to decrease in bulk, volume, or content *Syn* shrink, condense, compress, constrict, deflate *Ant* expand

contradict *Syn* DENY, gainsay, negative, contravene, traverse, impugn *Ant* corroborate

contradictory *n* *Syn* OPPOSITE, contrary, antithesis, antonym, antipode

contradictory *adj* *Syn* OPPOSITE, contrary, antithetical, antonymous, antipodal, antipodean, converse, counter, reverse

contraption *Syn* DEVICE, gadget, contrivance

contrary *n* *Syn* OPPOSITE, antithesis, contradictory, antonym, antipode

contrary *adj* **1** *Syn* OPPOSITE, antithetical, contradictory, antonymous, antipodal, antipodean, converse, counter, reverse **2** ♦ given to opposing or resisting wishes, commands, conditions, or circumstances *Syn* perverse, restive, balky, froward, wayward *Ant* good-natured, complaisant

contrast *n* *Syn* COMPARISON, collation, parallel, antithesis

contrast *vb* *Syn* COMPARE, collate

contravene *Syn* DENY, contradict, traverse, impugn, negative *Ant* uphold (*law, principle*); allege (*right, claim, privilege*)

contravention *Syn* BREACH, trespass, transgression, violation, infringement, infraction

contribution *Syn* DONATION, benefaction, alms

contributory *Syn* AUXILIARY, ancillary, adjuvant, subservient, accessory

contrition *Syn* PENITENCE, attrition, repentance, compunction, remorse

contrivance *Syn* DEVICE, gadget, contraption

contrive ♦ to find a way of making or doing something or of achieving an end by the exercise of one's mind *Syn* devise, invent, frame, concoct

control *vb* *Syn* CONDUCT, direct, manage

control *n* **1** *Syn* POWER, command, dominion, authority, jurisdiction, sway **2** *Syn* CORRECTIVE, check, antidote

controversy *Syn* ARGUMENT, dispute

controvert *Syn* DISPROVE, rebut, refute, confute *Ant* assert

contumacious *Syn* INSUBORDINATE, rebellious, mutinous, seditious, factious *Ant* obedient

contumelious *Syn* ABUSIVE, opprobrious, vituperative, scurrilous *Ant* obsequious

contusion *Syn* WOUND, bruise, trauma, traumatism, lesion

conundrum *Syn* MYSTERY, puzzle, riddle, enigma, problem

convalesce *Syn* IMPROVE, recover, recuperate, gain

convenance *Syn* FORM, convention, usage

convene *Syn* SUMMON, convoke, muster, summons, call, cite *Ant* adjourn

convent *Syn* CLOISTER, nunnery, monastery, abbey, priory

convention **1** *Syn* CONTRACT, entente, compact, pact, treaty, cartel, concordat, bargain **2** *Syn* FORM, convenance, usage

conventional *Syn* CEREMONIAL, formal, ceremonious, solemn *Ant* unconventional

conversant ♦ familiar with something *Syn* versed *Ant* ignorant

conversation, converse *Syn* INTERCOURSE, communion, communication, commerce, traffic, dealings, correspondence

converse *vb* *Syn* SPEAK, talk

converse *n* *Syn* OPPOSITE, contrary, antithesis, contradictory, antipode, antonym, counter, reverse

conversion *Syn* TRANSFORMATION, metamorphosis, transmutation, transmogrification, transfiguration

convert *vb* **Syn** TRANSFORM, metamorphose, transmute, transmogrify, transfigure

convert *n* ♦ a person who has embraced another creed, opinion, or doctrine than the one he or she has previously accepted or adhered to **Syn** proselyte

convertible Syn RECIPROCAL, corresponding, correlative, complementary, complemental

convey 1 Syn CARRY, transport, transmit, bear **2 Syn** TRANSFER, deed, alienate

convict Syn CRIMINAL, felon, malefactor, culprit, delinquent

conviction 1 Syn CERTAINTY, assurance, certitude **2 Syn** OPINION, belief, persuasion, view, sentiment

convincing Syn VALID, compelling, telling, cogent, sound

convivial Syn SOCIAL, companionable, gregarious, hospitable, cooperative **Ant** taciturn; staid

convoke Syn SUMMON, convene, muster, summons, call, cite **Ant** prorogue, dissolve

convoy Syn ACCOMPANY, escort, conduct, attend, chaperon

convulse Syn SHAKE, rock, agitate

convulsion 1 Syn FIT, spasm, paroxysm, attack, access, accession **2 Syn** COMMOTION, agitation, tumult, turmoil, turbulence, confusion, upheaval

convulsive Syn FITFUL, spasmodic

cool 1 Syn COLD, chilly, frigid, freezing, frosty, gelid, icy, glacial, arctic **Ant** warm **2** ♦ showing or seeming to show freedom from agitation or excitement **Syn** composed, collected, unruffled, imperturbable, unflappable, nonchalant **Ant** ardent; agitated

coop Syn ENCLOSE, envelop, fence, pen, corral, cage, wall

cooperate Syn UNITE, conjoin, combine **Ant** counteract

cooperative Syn SOCIAL, companionable, gregarious, convivial, hospitable **Ant** uncooperative

cop Syn STEAL, filch, pinch, snitch, swipe, lift, pilfer, purloin

copartner Syn PARTNER, colleague, ally, confederate

copious Syn PLENTIFUL, abundant, ample, plenteous **Ant** meager

copy *n* **Syn** REPRODUCTION, duplicate, carbon, carbon copy, transcript, facsimile, replica **Ant** original

copy *vb* ♦ to make something like an already existing thing in form, appearance, or obvious or salient characteristics **Syn** imitate, mimic, ape, mock **Ant** originate

coquet Syn TRIFLE, flirt, dally, toy

cordial Syn GRACIOUS, genial, affable, sociable

core 1 Syn CENTER, middle, midst, hub, focus, nucleus, heart **2 Syn** SUBSTANCE, purport, gist, burden, pith

corner Syn MONOPOLY, pool, syndicate, trust, cartel

corporal Syn BODILY, corporeal, physical, somatic

corporeal 1 Syn MATERIAL, physical, sensible, phenomenal, objective **Ant** incorporeal **2 Syn** BODILY, physical, corporal, somatic

corpse Syn BODY, carcass, cadaver

corpulent Syn FLESHY, portly, fat, stout, obese, rotund, plump, chubby **Ant** spare

corral Syn ENCLOSE, envelop, fence, pen, coop, cage, wall

correct *vb* **1** ♦ to set or make right something which is wrong **Syn** rectify, emend, remedy, redress, amend, reform, revise **2 Syn** PUNISH, discipline, chastise, chasten, castigate

correct *adj* ♦ conforming to standard, fact, or truth **Syn** accurate, exact, precise, nice, right **Ant** incorrect

corrective *adj* **Syn** CURATIVE, remedial, restorative, sanative

corrective *n* ♦ something which serves to keep another thing in its desired place or condition **Syn** control, check, antidote

correlate Syn PARALLEL, analogue, counterpart

correlative Syn RECIPROCAL, corresponding, complementary, complemental, convertible

correspond Syn AGREE, square, accord, tally, jibe, harmonize, conform

correspondence *Syn* INTERCOURSE, communication, conversation, converse, communion, commerce, traffic, dealings

corresponding *Syn* RECIPROCAL, correlative, complementary, complemental, convertible

corridor *Syn* PASSAGE, passageway, hall, hallway, gallery, arcade, cloister, aisle, ambulatory

corroborate *Syn* CONFIRM, substantiate, verify, authenticate, validate *Ant* contradict

corrupt *vb Syn* DEBASE, deprave, debauch, pervert

corrupt *adj Syn* VICIOUS, iniquitous, nefarious, flagitious, infamous, villainous, degenerate

corrupted *Syn* DEBASED, corrupt, vitiated, depraved, debauched, perverted

corruption *Syn* BARBARISM, impropriety, solecism, vulgarism, vernacular

corsair *Syn* PIRATE, freebooter, buccaneer, privateer

cortege *Syn* PROCESSION, cavalcade, parade, motorcade

coruscate *Syn* FLASH, gleam, scintillate, glance, glint, sparkle, glitter, glisten, twinkle

cosmic *Syn* UNIVERSAL, catholic, ecumenical, cosmopolitan

cosmopolitan *Syn* UNIVERSAL, catholic, ecumenical, cosmic *Ant* provincial; insular; parochial

cosset *Syn* CARESS, fondle, pet, cuddle, dandle

cost *Syn* PRICE, expense, charge

costly ♦ having a high value or valuation, esp. in terms of money *Syn* expensive, dear, valuable, precious, invaluable, priceless *Ant* cheap

coterie *Syn* SET, circle, clique

couchant *Syn* PRONE, recumbent, dormant, supine, prostrate

counsel *n* 1 *Syn* ADVICE 2 *Syn* LAWYER, counselor, barrister, advocate, attorney, solicitor

counsel *vb Syn* ADVISE,

counselor *Syn* LAWYER, barrister, counsel, advocate, attorney, solicitor

count *vb* 1 ♦ to ascertain the total of units in a collection by noting one after another *Syn* tell, enumerate, number 2 *Syn* RELY, depend, bank, trust, reckon

count *n Syn* PARAGRAPH, verse, article, clause, plank

countenance *n Syn* FACE, visage, physiognomy, mug, puss

countenance *vb Syn* FAVOR, encourage

counter *adj Syn* ADVERSE, antagonistic, counteractive

counter *n Syn* OPPOSITE, contradictory, contrary, antithesis, antipode, antonym, converse, reverse

counteract *Syn* NEUTRALIZE, negative *Ant* cooperate

counteractive *Syn* ADVERSE, counter, antagonistic

counterbalance *Syn* COMPENSATE, offset, countervail, balance, counterpoise

counterfeit *vb Syn* ASSUME, feign, sham, simulate, pretend, affect

counterfeit *adj* ♦ being an imitation intended to mislead or deceive *Syn* spurious, bogus, fake, sham, pseudo, pinchbeck, phony *Ant* bona fide, genuine

counterfeit *n Syn* IMPOSTURE, fraud, sham, fake, cheat, humbug, deceit, deception

counterpart *Syn* PARALLEL, correlate, analogue

counterpoise *Syn* COMPENSATE, balance, countervail, counterbalance, offset

countervail *Syn* COMPENSATE, offset, balance, counterbalance, counterpoise

county *Syn* ARISTOCRACY, gentry, elite, nobility, society

coup, coup d'etat *Syn* REBELLION, revolution, uprising, revolt, insurrection, mutiny, putsch

couple ♦ two things of the same kind *Syn* pair, brace, yoke

courage ♦ a quality of mind or temperament that enables one to stand fast in the face of opposition, danger, or hardship *Syn* mettle, spirit, resolution, tenacity *Ant* cowardice

courageous *Syn* BRAVE, unafraid, fearless, intrepid, valiant, valorous, dauntless, undaunted, doughty, bold, audacious *Ant* pusillanimous

course *Syn* WAY, route, passage, pass, artery

court *Syn* INVITE, woo, bid, solicit

courteous *Syn* CIVIL, polite, courtly, gallant, chivalrous *Ant* discourteous

courtesy ♦ a manner or an act which promotes agreeable or pleasant social relations *Syn* amenity, attention, gallantry *Ant* discourtesy

courtly *Syn* CIVIL, courteous, gallant, chivalrous, polite *Ant* churlish

covenant *Syn* PROMISE, pledge, engage, plight, contract

cover *vb* ♦ to put or place or to be put or placed over or around *Syn* overspread, envelop, wrap, shroud, veil *Ant* bare

cover *n* *Syn* SHELTER, retreat, refuge, asylum, sanctuary *Ant* exposure

covert *Syn* SECRET, clandestine, surreptitious, underhand, underhanded, stealthy, furtive *Ant* overt

covet 1 ♦ to desire selfishly to have something for one's own *Syn* envy, grudge, begrudge 2 *Syn* DESIRE, crave, wish, want *Ant* renounce (*something desirable*)

covetous ♦ having or manifesting a strong desire for esp. material possessions *Syn* greedy, acquisitive, grasping, avaricious

cow *Syn* INTIMIDATE, browbeat, bulldoze, bully

cower *Syn* FAWN, cringe, truckle, toady

coxcomb *Syn* FOP, dandy, beau, exquisite, dude, buck

coy *Syn* SHY, bashful, diffident, modest *Ant* pert

cozen *Syn* CHEAT, defraud, swindle, overreach

cozy *Syn* COMFORTABLE, snug, easy, restful

crabbed *Syn* SULLEN, surly, glum, morose, gloomy, sulky, saturnine, dour

crack *vb* *Syn* BREAK, burst, bust, snap, shatter, shiver

crack *n* 1 ♦ an opening, break, or discontinuity made by or as if by splitting or rupture *Syn* cleft, fissure, crevasse, crevice, cranny, chink 2 *Syn* JOKE, wisecrack, witticism, jest, jape, quip, gag

craft 1 *Syn* ART, skill, cunning, artifice 2 *Syn* TRADE, handicraft, art, profession 3 *Syn* BOAT, ship, vessel

craftsman *Syn* WORKER, handicraftsman, mechanic, artisan, workman, workingman, laborer, hand, operative, roustabout

crafty *Syn* SLY, tricky, cunning, insidious, foxy, guileful, wily, artful

cram *Syn* PACK, crowd, stuff, ram, tamp

cranky *Syn* IRASCIBLE, cross, choleric, splenetic, testy, touchy

cranny *Syn* CRACK, cleft, fissure, crevasse, crevice, chink

crass *Syn* STUPID, dense, slow, dull, dumb *Ant* brilliant

crave *Syn* DESIRE, covet, wish, want *Ant* spurn

crawl *Syn* CREEP

craze *Syn* FASHION, vogue, fad, rage, style, mode, dernier cri, cry

crazy, crazed *Syn* INSANE, mad, demented, lunatic, maniac, deranged, non compos mentis

cream *Syn* OIL, grease, lubricate, anoint

create *Syn* ESTABLISH, institute, organize

creator *Syn* MAKER, author

creature *Syn* ENTITY, being, individual, person

credence *Syn* BELIEF, credit, faith

credential ♦ something presented by one person to another in proof that he is what or who he claims to be *Syn* testimonial, recommendation, character, reference

credible *Syn* PLAUSIBLE, believable, colorable, specious *Ant* incredible

credit *n* 1 *Syn* BELIEF, faith, credence 2 *Syn* INFLUENCE, prestige, authority, weight *Ant* discredit 3 ♦ a person or thing that enhances another *Syn* asset

credit *vb* *Syn* ASCRIBE, accredit, assign, attribute, impute, refer, charge

credulity ♦ undue trust or confidence *Syn* gullibility *Ant* incredulity; skepticism

credulous ♦ unduly trusting or confiding *Syn* gullible *Ant* incredulous; skeptical

creed *Syn* RELIGION, faith, persuasion, denomination, sect, cult, communion, church

creep ♦ to move slowly along a surface in a prone or crouching position *Syn* crawl

crevasse *Syn* CRACK, cleft, fissure, crevice, cranny, chink

crevice *Syn* CRACK, cleft, fissure, crevasse, cranny, chink

crime *Syn* OFFENSE, vice, sin, scandal

criminal ♦ one who has committed a usu. serious offense esp. against the law *Syn* felon, convict, malefactor, culprit, delinquent

cringe *Syn* FAWN, cower, truckle, toady

cripple 1 *Syn* MAIM, mutilate, batter, mangle **2** *Syn* WEAKEN, disable, enfeeble, debilitate, undermine, sap

crisis *Syn* JUNCTURE, exigency, emergency, pinch, pass, contingency, strait

crisp 1 *Syn* FRAGILE, brittle, short, friable, frangible **2** *Syn* INCISIVE, clear-cut, cutting, trenchant, biting

criterion *Syn* STANDARD, touchstone, yardstick, gauge

critical 1 ♦ exhibiting the spirit of one who detects and points out faults or defects *Syn* hypercritical, faultfinding, captious, caviling, carping, censorious *Ant* uncritical **2** *Syn* ACUTE, crucial

criticism ♦ a discourse presenting one's conclusions after examining a work of art and esp. of literature *Syn* critique, review, blurb, puff

criticize ♦ to find fault with someone or something openly, often publicly, and with varying degrees of severity *Syn* reprehend, blame, censure, reprobate, condemn, denounce

critique *Syn* CRITICISM, review, blurb, puff

crochet *Syn* WEAVE, knit, plait, braid, tat

crony *Syn* ASSOCIATE, comrade, companion

crook *Syn* FLEX, bow, buckle

crooked ♦ not straight or straightforward *Syn* devious, oblique *Ant* straight

crop *Syn* SHEAR, poll, clip, trim, prune, lop, snip

cross *n Syn* TRIAL, tribulation, affliction, visitation

cross *adj Syn* IRASCIBLE, cranky, testy, touchy, choleric, splenetic

crosswise, crossways *Syn* ACROSS, athwart

crotchet *Syn* CAPRICE, freak, fancy, whim, whimsy, conceit, vagary

crow *Syn* BOAST, brag, vaunt, gasconade

crowd *vb* **1** *Syn* PRESS, bear, bear down, squeeze, jam **2** *Syn* PACK, cram, stuff, ram, tamp

crowd *n* ♦ a more or less closely assembled multitude usually of persons *Syn* throng, press, crush, mob, rout, horde

crucial *Syn* ACUTE, critical

crude *Syn* RUDE, rough, uncouth, raw, callow, green *Ant* consummate, finished

cruel *Syn* FIERCE, inhuman, fell, truculent, ferocious, barbarous, savage *Ant* pitiful

cruise *Syn* JOURNEY, voyage, tour, trip, jaunt, excursion, expedition, pilgrimage

crumble *Syn* DECAY, disintegrate, decompose, rot, putrefy, spoil

crush *vb* **1** ♦ to reduce or be reduced to a pulpy or broken mass *Syn* mash, smash, bruise, squash, macerate **2** ♦ to bring to an end by destroying or defeating *Syn* quell, extinguish, suppress, quench, quash

crush *n Syn* CROWD, press, throng, horde, mob, rout

crusty *Syn* BLUFF, brusque, gruff, blunt, curt

cry *vb* ♦ to show grief, pain, or distress by tears and usu. inarticulate utterances *Syn* weep, wail, keen, whimper, blubber

cry *Syn* FASHION, vogue, rage, style, mode, fad, craze, dernier cri

crying *Syn* PRESSING, urgent, imperative, importunate, insistent, exigent, instant

cryptic *Syn* OBSCURE, enigmatic, dark, vague, ambiguous, equivocal

cuddle *Syn* CARESS, fondle, dandle, pet, cosset

cuff *Syn* STRIKE, hit, smite, punch, slug, slog, swat, clout, slap, box

cull *Syn* CHOOSE, pick, single, select, elect, opt, prefer

culmination *Syn* SUMMIT, peak, climax, apex, acme, pinnacle, meridian, zenith, apogee

culpability *Syn* BLAME, guilt, fault

culpable *Syn* BLAMEWORTHY, guilty

culprit *Syn* CRIMINAL, felon, convict, malefactor, delinquent

cult *Syn* RELIGION, sect, denomination, communion, faith, creed, persuasion, church

cultivar *Syn* VARIETY, subspecies, race, breed, strain, clone, stock

cultivate *Syn* NURSE, nurture, foster, cherish

cultivation *Syn* CULTURE, breeding, refinement

culture ♦ enlightenment and excellence of taste acquired by intellectual and aesthetic training *Syn* cultivation, breeding, refinement

cumber *Syn* BURDEN, encumber, weigh, weight, load, lade, tax, charge, saddle

cumbersome, cumbrous *Syn* HEAVY, ponderous, weighty, hefty

cumulative ♦ increasing or produced by the addition of like or assimilable things *Syn* accumulative, additive, summative

cunning *adj* **1** *Syn* CLEVER, ingenious, adroit **2** *Syn* SLY, crafty, tricky, artful, foxy, insidious, wily, guileful *Ant* ingenuous

cunning *n* **1** *Syn* ART, skill, craft, artifice **2** *Syn* DECEIT, guile, duplicity, dissimulation *Ant* ingenuousness

cupidity ♦ intense desire for wealth or possessions *Syn* greed, rapacity, avarice

curative ♦ returning or tending to return to a state of normalcy or health *Syn* sanative, restorative, remedial, corrective

curb *Syn* RESTRAIN, check, bridle, inhibit *Ant* spur

curdle *Syn* COAGULATE, congeal, set, clot, jelly, jell

cure *n* *Syn* REMEDY, medicine, medicament, medication, specific, physic

cure *vb* ♦ to rectify an unhealthy or undesirable condition especially by some specific treatment *Syn* heal, remedy

curious **1** ♦ interested in what is not one's personal or proper concern *Syn* inquisitive, prying, snoopy, nosy *Ant* incurious; uninterested **2** *Syn* STRANGE, singular, peculiar, unique, odd, queer, quaint, outlandish, eccentric, erratic

curl *Syn* WIND, coil, twist, twine, wreathe, entwine

currency *Syn* MONEY, cash, legal tender, specie, coin, coinage

current *adj* *Syn* PREVAILING, prevalent, rife *Ant* antique, antiquated; obsolete

current *n* *Syn* FLOW, stream, flood, tide, flux

curse *n* ♦ a denunciation that conveys a wish or threat of evil *Syn* imprecation, malediction, anathema *Ant* blessing

curse *vb* *Syn* EXECRATE, damn, anathematize, objurgate *Ant* bless

cursed *Syn* EXECRABLE, accursed, damnable

cursing *Syn* BLASPHEMY, profanity, swearing

cursory *Syn* SUPERFICIAL, shallow, uncritical *Ant* painstaking

curt *Syn* BLUFF, brusque, blunt, crusty, gruff *Ant* voluble

curtail *Syn* SHORTEN, abbreviate, abridge, retrench *Ant* protract, prolong

curve *vb* ♦ to swerve or cause to swerve from a straight line or course *Syn* bend, twist

curve *n* ♦ a line or something which follows a line that is neither straight nor angular but rounded *Syn* arc, bow, arch

curvet *Syn* SKIP, bound, hop, lope, lollop, ricochet

custom *Syn* HABIT, usage, habitude, practice, use, wont

customary *Syn* USUAL, wonted, accustomed, habitual *Ant* occasional

cut ♦ to penetrate and divide something with a sharp-bladed tool or instrument *Syn* hew, chop, carve, slit, slash

cutthroat *Syn* ASSASSIN, gunman, bravo

cutting *Syn* INCISIVE, trenchant, clear-cut, biting, crisp

cyclone *Syn* TORNADO, twister

cyclopean *Syn* HUGE, vast, immense, enormous, elephantine, mammoth, giant, gigantic, gigantean, colossal, gargantuan, Herculean, titanic, Brobdingnagian

cynical ♦ deeply and often contemptuously distrustful *Syn* misanthropic, pessimistic

D

dabbler *Syn* AMATEUR, tyro, dilettante

daily ♦ of each or every day *Syn* diurnal, quotidian, circadian

dainty 1 *Syn* CHOICE, delicate, exquisite, elegant, recherché, rare *Ant* gross **2** *Syn* NICE, fastidious, finicky, finicking, finical, particular, fussy, squeamish, persnickety, pernickety

dally *Syn* TRIFLE, flirt, coquet, toy

dam *Syn* HINDER, bar, block, obstruct, impede

damage *n* *Syn* INJURY, harm, hurt, mischief

damage *vb* *Syn* INJURE, harm, impair, mar, hurt, spoil

damn 1 *Syn* SENTENCE, doom, condemn, proscribe *Ant* save (*from eternal punishment*) **2** *Syn* EXECRATE, curse, anathematize, objurgate

damnable *Syn* EXECRABLE, accursed, cursed

damp *Syn* WET, moist, dank, humid

dandle *Syn* CARESS, cuddle, pet, cosset, fondle

dandy *Syn* FOP, beau, coxcomb, exquisite, dude, buck *Ant* sloven

danger ♦ the state of being exposed to injury, pain, or loss *Syn* peril, jeopardy, hazard, risk *Ant* security

dangerous ♦ attended by or involving the possibility of loss, evil, injury, or harm *Syn* hazardous, precarious, perilous, risky *Ant* safe, secure

dangle *Syn* HANG, suspend, sling

dank *Syn* WET, damp, humid, moist

dappled *Syn* VARIEGATED, parti-colored, motley, checkered, checked, pied, piebald, skewbald, freaked

dare *Syn* FACE, brave, challenge, defy, beard

daredevil *Syn* ADVENTUROUS, daring, rash, reckless, foolhardy, venturesome

daring *Syn* ADVENTUROUS, rash, reckless, daredevil, foolhardy, venturesome

dark 1 ♦ deficient in light *Syn* dim, dusky, obscure, murky, gloomy *Ant* light **2** *Syn* OBSCURE, vague, enigmatic, cryptic, ambiguous, equivocal *Ant* lucid

darken *Syn* OBSCURE, dim, bedim, eclipse, cloud, becloud, fog, befog, obfuscate *Ant* illuminate

dart *Syn* FLY, scud, skim, float, shoot, sail

dash *vb* *Syn* RUSH, tear, shoot, charge

dash *n* **1** *Syn* VIGOR, vim, spirit, esprit, verve, punch, élan, drive **2** *Syn* TOUCH, suggestion, suspicion, soupçon, tincture, tinge, shade, smack, spice, vein, strain, streak

dashing *Syn* STYLISH, smart, fashionable, modish, chic

date *Syn* ENGAGEMENT, rendezvous, tryst, appointment, assignation

daunt *Syn* DISMAY, appall, horrify

dauntless *Syn* BRAVE, courageous, unafraid, fearless, intrepid, valiant, valorous, undaunted, doughty, bold, audacious *Ant* poltroon

dawdle *Syn* DELAY, procrastinate, loiter, lag

daydream *Syn* FANCY, dream, fantasy, phantasy, phantasm, vision, nightmare

daze ♦ to dull or deaden the powers of the mind through some disturbing experience or influence *Syn* stun, bemuse, stupefy, benumb, paralyze, petrify

dazzled *Syn* GIDDY, dizzy, vertiginous, swimming

dead ♦ devoid of life *Syn* defunct, deceased, departed, late, lifeless, inanimate

deadlock *Syn* DRAW, tie, stalemate, standoff

deadly ♦ causing or causative of death *Syn* mortal, fatal, lethal

deal 1 *Syn* DISTRIBUTE, divide, dispense, dole **2** *Syn* TREAT, handle

dealings *Syn* INTERCOURSE, commerce, traffic, communication, communion, conversation, converse, correspondence

dear *Syn* COSTLY, expensive, precious, valuable, invaluable, priceless *Ant* cheap

dearth *Syn* LACK, want, absence, defect, privation *Ant* excess

death ♦ the end or the ending of life **Syn** decease, demise, passing **Ant** life

deathless **Syn** IMMORTAL, undying, unfading

debar **Syn** EXCLUDE, blackball, disbar, suspend, shut out, eliminate, rule out

debase 1 ♦ to cause a person or thing to become impaired and lowered in quality or character **Syn** vitiate, deprave, corrupt, debauch, pervert **Ant** elevate (*taste, character*); amend (*morals, way of life*) **2 Syn** ABASE, degrade, demean, humble, humiliate

debased ♦ being lowered in quality or character **Syn** vitiated, depraved, corrupted, debauched, perverted

debate *n* **Syn** ARGUMENTATION, disputation, forensic, dialectic

debate *vb* **Syn** DISCUSS, dispute, argue, agitate

debauch **Syn** DEBASE, corrupt, deprave, pervert, vitiate

debauched **Syn** DEBASED, corrupted, depraved, perverted, vitiated

debilitate **Syn** WEAKEN, enfeeble, undermine, sap, cripple, disable **Ant** invigorate

debit **Syn** DEBT, indebtedness, liability, obligation, arrear **Ant** credit

debris **Syn** REFUSE, waste, rubbish, trash, garbage, offal

debt ♦ something, and esp. a sum of money, that is owed **Syn** indebtedness, obligation, liability, debit, arrear

decadence **Syn** DETERIORATION, decline, declension, degeneration, devolution **Ant** rise; flourishing

decamp **Syn** ESCAPE, flee, fly, abscond

decay ♦ to undergo or to cause to undergo destructive changes **Syn** decompose, rot, putrefy, spoil, disintegrate, crumble

decease **Syn** DEATH, demise, passing

deceased **Syn** DEAD, departed, late, defunct, lifeless, inanimate

deceit 1 ♦ the act or practice of imposing upon the credulity of others by dishonesty, fraud, or trickery **Syn** duplicity, dissimulation, cunning, guile **2 Syn** IMPOSTURE, cheat, fraud, sham, fake, deception, counterfeit, humbug

deceitful **Syn** DISHONEST, mendacious, lying, untruthful **Ant** trustworthy

deceive ♦ to lead astray or into evil or to frustrate by underhandedness or craft **Syn** mislead, delude, beguile, betray, double-cross **Ant** undeceive; enlighten

decency **Syn** DECORUM, propriety, dignity, etiquette

decent 1 **Syn** DECOROUS, seemly, proper, nice **2 Syn** CHASTE, modest, pure **Ant** indecent; obscene

deception 1 ♦ the act or practice of deliberately deceiving **Syn** fraud, double-dealing, trickery, chicane, chicanery **2 Syn** IMPOSTURE, cheat, fraud, sham, fake, humbug, counterfeit, deceit

deceptive **Syn** MISLEADING, delusory, delusive

decide ♦ to come or to cause to come to a conclusion **Syn** determine, settle, rule, resolve

decided ♦ free from any doubt, wavering, or ambiguity **Syn** decisive, determined, resolved

decipher **Syn** SOLVE, resolve, unfold, unravel

decisive 1 **Syn** CONCLUSIVE, determinative, definitive **Ant** indecisive **2 Syn** DECIDED, determined, resolved **Ant** irresolute

deck **Syn** ADORN, bedeck, decorate, ornament, garnish, embellish, beautify

declaration ♦ the act of making known openly or publicly **Syn** announcement, publication, advertisement, proclamation, promulgation, broadcasting

declare 1 ♦ to make known explicitly or plainly **Syn** announce, publish, advertise, proclaim, promulgate, broadcast **2 Syn** ASSERT, profess, affirm, aver, avouch, avow, protest, predicate, warrant

declass **Syn** DEGRADE, demote, reduce, disrate

declension **Syn** DETERIORATION, decline, decadence, degeneration, devolution

decline *vb* ♦ to turn away by not accepting, receiving, or considering **Syn** refuse, reject, repudiate, spurn **Ant** accept

decline *n* **Syn** DETERIORATION, declension, decadence, degeneration, devolution

decolorize *Syn* WHITEN, blanch, bleach, etiolate

decompose *Syn* DECAY, rot, putrefy, spoil, disintegrate, crumble

decorate *Syn* ADORN, ornament, embellish, beautify, deck, bedeck, garnish

decorous ♦ conforming to an accepted standard of what is right or fitting or is regarded as good form *Syn* decent, seemly, proper, nice *Ant* indecorous; blatant

decorticate *Syn* SKIN, peel, pare, flay

decorum ♦ the quality or character of rightness, fitness, or honorableness in behavior or conduct *Syn* decency, propriety, dignity, etiquette *Ant* indecorum; license

decoy *n* *Syn* LURE, bait, snare, trap

decoy *vb* *Syn* LURE, entice, inveigle, tempt, seduce

decrease ♦ to make or grow less esp. gradually *Syn* lessen, diminish, reduce, abate, dwindle *Ant* increase

decree *Syn* DICTATE, prescribe, ordain, impose

decrepit *Syn* WEAK, infirm, feeble, frail, fragile *Ant* sturdy

decry ♦ to indicate one's low opinion of something *Syn* deprecate, disparage, derogate, detract, belittle, minimize *Ant* extol

dedicate *Syn* DEVOTE, consecrate, hallow

deduce *Syn* INFER, gather, conclude, judge

deduct ♦ to take away one quantity from another *Syn* subtract *Ant* add

deduction 1 ♦ an amount subtracted from a gross sum *Syn* abatement, rebate, discount 2 *Syn* INFERENCE, conclusion, judgment

deed *n* *Syn* ACTION, act

deed *vb* *Syn* TRANSFER, convey, alienate

deem *Syn* CONSIDER, regard, account, reckon

deep 1 ♦ having great extension downward or inward *Syn* profound, abysmal 2 *Syn* BROAD, wide

deep-rooted *Syn* INVETERATE, deepseated, chronic, confirmed

deep-seated *Syn* INVETERATE, chronic, deep-rooted, confirmed

deface ♦ to mar the appearance of *Syn* disfigure

defame *Syn* MALIGN, vilify, calumniate, traduce, asperse, slander, libel

default *Syn* FAILURE, neglect, miscarriage, dereliction

defeat *Syn* CONQUER, beat, vanquish, lick, subdue, subjugate, reduce, overcome, surmount, overthrow, rout

defect 1 *Syn* LACK, want, dearth, absence, privation 2 *Syn* BLEMISH, flaw

defection ♦ conscious abandonment of allegiance or duty *Syn* desertion, apostasy

defective *Syn* DEFICIENT *Ant* intact

defend 1 ♦ to keep secure from danger or against attack *Syn* protect, shield, guard, safeguard *Ant* combat; attack 2 *Syn* MAINTAIN, assert, vindicate

defer *vb* ♦ to a delay an action, activity, or proceeding *Syn* postpone, intermit, suspend, stay

defer *vb* *Syn* YIELD, bow, submit, cave, capitulate, succumb, relent

deference *Syn* HONOR, reverence, homage, obeisance *Ant* disrespect

deficiency *Syn* IMPERFECTION, shortcoming, fault *Ant* excess

deficient ♦ showing lack of something necessary *Syn* defective *Ant* sufficient, adequate; excessive

defile *Syn* CONTAMINATE, pollute, taint, attaint *Ant* cleanse; purify

define *Syn* PRESCRIBE, assign

definite *Syn* EXPLICIT, express, specific, categorical *Ant* indefinite; equivocal

definitive *Syn* CONCLUSIVE, determinative, decisive *Ant* tentative, provisional

deflate *Syn* CONTRACT, compress, shrink, condense, constrict *Ant* inflate

deflect *Syn* TURN, divert, avert, sheer

deflection *Syn* DEVIATION, aberration, divergence

deform ♦ to mar or spoil by or as if by twisting *Syn* distort, contort, warp

defraud *Syn* CHEAT, swindle, overreach, cozen

deft *Syn* DEXTEROUS, adroit, handy *Ant* awkward

defunct *Syn* DEAD, deceased, departed, late, lifeless, inanimate *Ant* alive; live

defy *Syn* FACE, brave, challenge, dare, beard *Ant* recoil

degenerate *Syn* VICIOUS, corrupt, infamous, villainous, iniquitous, nefarious, flagitious

degeneration *Syn* DETERIORATION, devolution, decadence, decline, declension

degrade 1 ♦ to lower in station, rank, or grade *Syn* demote, reduce, declass, disrate *Ant* elevate **2** *Syn* ABASE, debase, demean, humble, humiliate *Ant* uplift

dehydrate *Syn* DRY, desiccate, parch, bake

deign *Syn* STOOP, condescend

deject *Syn* DISCOURAGE, dishearten, dispirit *Ant* exhilarate; cheer

dejected *Syn* DOWNCAST, depressed, dispirited, disconsolate, woebegone

dejection *Syn* SADNESS, depression, melancholy, melancholia, gloom, blues, dumps *Ant* exhilaration

delay 1 ♦ to cause to be late or behind in movement or progress *Syn* retard, slow, slacken, detain *Ant* expedite; hasten **2** ♦ to move or act slowly so that progress is hindered or work remains undone or unfinished *Syn* procrastinate, lag, loiter, dawdle *Ant* hasten, hurry

delectable *Syn* DELIGHTFUL, delicious, luscious

delectation *Syn* PLEASURE, enjoyment, delight, joy, fruition

delegate ♦ a person who stands in place of another or others *Syn* deputy, representative

delete *Syn* ERASE, cancel, efface, obliterate, blot out, expunge

deleterious *Syn* PERNICIOUS, detrimental, baneful, noxious *Ant* salutary

deliberate *adj* **1** *Syn* VOLUNTARY, willful, intentional, willing *Ant* impulsive **2** ♦ arrived at after due thought *Syn* considered, advised, premeditated, designed, studied *Ant* casual **3** *Syn* SLOW, leisurely, dilatory, laggard *Ant* precipitate, abrupt

deliberate *vb Syn* THINK, reflect, cogitate, reason, speculate

delicate *Syn* CHOICE, exquisite, dainty, rare, recherché, elegant *Ant* gross

delicious *Syn* DELIGHTFUL, delectable, luscious

delight *n Syn* PLEASURE, delectation, enjoyment, joy, fruition *Ant* disappointment; discontent

delight *vb Syn* PLEASE, gratify, rejoice, gladden, tickle, regale *Ant* distress; bore

delightful ♦ highly pleasing to the senses or to aesthetic taste *Syn* delicious, delectable, luscious *Ant* distressing; boring; horrid

delineate 1 *Syn* SKETCH, trace, outline, diagram, draft, plot, blueprint **2** *Syn* REPRESENT, depict, portray, picture, limn

delineation *Syn* SKETCH, tracing, outline, sketch, diagram, plot, blueprint

delinquent *Syn* CRIMINAL, felon, convict, malefactor, culprit

deliquesce *Syn* LIQUEFY, melt, fuse, thaw

delirious *Syn* FURIOUS, frantic, frenzied, wild, frenetic, rabid

delirium *Syn* MANIA, frenzy, hysteria

deliver *Syn* RESCUE, redeem, save, ransom, reclaim

delude *Syn* DECEIVE, beguile, mislead, betray, double-cross *Ant* enlighten

deluge *Syn* FLOOD, inundation, torrent, spate, cataract

delusion ♦ something which is believed to be or is accepted as being true or real but which is actually false or unreal *Syn* illusion, hallucination, mirage

delusive, delusory *Syn* MISLEADING, deceptive

delve *Syn* DIG, spade, grub, excavate

demand ♦ to ask or call for something as due or as necessary or as strongly desired *Syn* claim, require, exact

demarcate *Syn* DISTINGUISH, differentiate, discriminate

demean *vb Syn* BEHAVE, deport, comport, conduct, acquit, quit

demean *vb Syn* ABASE, degrade, debase, humble, humiliate

demeanor *Syn* BEARING, deportment, mien, port, presence

demented *Syn* INSANE, mad, crazy, crazed, deranged, lunatic, maniac, non compos mentis *Ant* rational

dementia *Syn* INSANITY, lunacy, mania, psychosis

demise *Syn* DEATH, decease, passing

demolish *Syn* DESTROY, raze *Ant* construct

demoniac demonic *Syn* FIENDISH, diabolic, diabolical, devilish

demonstrate 1 *Syn* SHOW, manifest, evince, evidence **2** *Syn* PROVE, try, test

demonstration *Syn* PROOF, trial, test

demote *Syn* DEGRADE, reduce, declass, disrate *Ant* promote (*in rank, grade*)

demur *vb* ♦ to hesitate or show reluctance because of difficulties in the way *Syn* scruple, balk, jib, shy, boggle, stick, stickle, strain *Ant* accede

demur *n* *Syn* QUALM, compunction, scruple

denizen *Syn* INHABITANT, resident, citizen

denomination 1 *Syn* NAME, designation, appellation, title, style **2** *Syn* RELIGION, sect, communion, faith, creed, cult, persuasion, church

denote *Syn* MEAN, signify, import

denounce *Syn* CRITICIZE, condemn, censure, reprobate, reprehend, blame *Ant* eulogize

dense 1 *Syn* CLOSE, compact, thick *Ant* sparse (*of population, forests*); tenuous (*of clouds, air, masses*) **2** *Syn* STUPID, crass, slow, dull, dumb *Ant* subtle; bright

denude *Syn* STRIP, bare, divest, dismantle *Ant* clothe

deny ♦ to refuse to accept as true or valid *Syn* gainsay, contradict, negative, traverse, impugn, contravene *Ant* confirm; concede

depart 1 *Syn* GO, leave, withdraw, retire, quit *Ant* arrive; remain, abide **2** *Syn* SWERVE, digress, deviate, diverge, veer

departed *Syn* DEAD, deceased, late, defunct, lifeless, inanimate

depend 1 ♦ (on *or* upon) *Syn* RELY, trust, count, reckon, bank **2** ♦ to rest or to be contingent upon something uncertain, variable, or indeterminable *Syn* hinge, hang, turn

dependable *Syn* RELIABLE, trustworthy, trusty, tried

dependence *Syn* TRUST, reliance, confidence, faith

dependent 1 ♦ determined or conditioned by another *Syn* contingent, conditional, relative *Ant* absolute; infinite; original **2** *Syn* SUBORDINATE, subject, tributary, secondary, collateral *Ant* independent

depict *Syn* REPRESENT, portray, delineate, picture, limn

deplete ♦ to bring to a low estate by depriving of something essential *Syn* drain, exhaust, impoverish, bankrupt

deplore ♦ to manifest grief or sorrow for something *Syn* lament, bewail, bemoan

deport 1 *Syn* BEHAVE, demean, comport, conduct, acquit, quit **2** *Syn* BANISH, transport, exile, expatriate, ostracize, extradite

deportment 1 *Syn* BEHAVIOR, conduct **2** *Syn* BEARING, demeanor, mien, port, presence

deposit ♦ matter which settles to the bottom of a liquid *Syn* precipitate, sediment, dregs, lees, grounds

deprave *Syn* DEBASE, vitiate, corrupt, debauch, pervert

depraved *Syn* DEBASED, vitiated, corrupted, debauched, perverted

deprecate *Syn* DISAPPROVE *Ant* endorse

depreciate *Syn* DECRY, disparage, derogate, detract, belittle, minimize *Ant* appreciate

depreciative, depreciatory *Syn* DEROGATORY, disparaging, slighting, pejorative

depress ♦ to lower in spirit or mood *Syn* weigh, oppress *Ant* elate; cheer

depressed *Syn* DOWNCAST, dejected, dispirited, disconsolate, woebegone

depression *Syn* SADNESS, dejection, gloom, blues, dumps, melancholy, melancholia *Ant* buoyancy

deputy 1 *Syn* AGENT, attorney, factor, proxy **2** *Syn* DELEGATE, representative

deracinate *Syn* EXTERMINATE, uproot, eradicate, extirpate, wipe

derange *Syn* DISORDER, disarrange, unsettle, disturb, disorganize *Ant* arrange; adjust

deranged *Syn* INSANE, demented, non compos mentis, crazed, crazy, mad, lunatic, maniac

derangement *Syn* ABERRATION, alienation

derelict *Syn* OUTCAST, castaway, reprobate, pariah, untouchable

dereliction *Syn* FAILURE, neglect, default, miscarriage

deride *Syn* RIDICULE, mock, taunt, twit, rally

derive *Syn* SPRING, originate, arise, rise, emanate, issue, stem, flow, proceed

dernier cri *Syn* FASHION, style, mode, vogue, fad, rage, craze, cry

derogate *Syn* DECRY, disparage, detract, belittle, minimize, depreciate

derogatory ♦ designed or tending to belittle *Syn* depreciatory, depreciative, disparaging, slighting, pejorative

descant 1 *Syn* SING, troll, carol, warble, trill, hymn, chant, intone **2** *Syn* DISCOURSE, expatiate, dilate

descend ♦ to get or come down from a height *Syn* dismount, alight *Ant* ascend, climb

descendant *Syn* OFFSPRING, young, progeny, issue, posterity

describe *Syn* RELATE, narrate, state, report, rehearse, recite, recount

description *Syn* TYPE, kind, sort, character, nature, stripe, kidney, ilk

descry *Syn* SEE, espy, behold, observe, notice, remark, note, perceive, discern, view, survey, contemplate

desecration *Syn* PROFANATION, sacrilege, blasphemy

desert *n Syn* WASTE, badlands, wilderness

desert *n Syn* DUE, merit

desert *vb Syn* ABANDON, forsake *Ant* stick to, cleave to

desertion *Syn* DEFECTION, apostasy

deserve ♦ to be or become worthy of *Syn* merit, earn, rate

desiccate *Syn* DRY, dehydrate, parch, bake

design *vb* **1** *Syn* INTEND, mean, propose, purpose **2** *Syn* PLAN, plot, scheme, project

design *n* **1** *Syn* PLAN, plot, scheme, project **2** *Syn* INTENTION, intent, purpose, aim, end, object, objective, goal *Ant* accident **3** *Syn* FIGURE, pattern, motif, device

designate ♦ to declare a person one's choice *Syn* name, nominate, elect, appoint

designation *Syn* NAME, denomination, appellation, title, style

designed *Syn* DELIBERATE, premeditated, considered, advised, studied *Ant* accidental

desire *vb* ♦ to have a longing for something *Syn* wish, want, crave, covet

desire *n* ♦ a longing for something that promises enjoyment or satisfaction *Syn* appetite, lust, passion, urge *Ant* distaste

desist *Syn* STOP, discontinue, cease, quit *Ant* persist

desolate 1 *Syn* ALONE, forlorn, lorn, lonesome, lone, solitary, lonely **2** *Syn* DISMAL, dreary, cheerless, dispiriting, bleak

despair *Syn* DESPONDENCY, hopelessness, desperation, forlornness *Ant* hope; optimism; beatitude

despairing *Syn* DESPONDENT, hopeless, desperate, forlorn *Ant* hopeful

desperate *Syn* DESPONDENT, hopeless, despairing, forlorn

desperation *Syn* DESPONDENCY, hopelessness, despair, forlornness

despicable *Syn* CONTEMPTIBLE, pitiable, sorry, scurvy, cheap, beggarly, shabby *Ant* praiseworthy, laudable

despise ♦ to regard as beneath one's notice and as unworthy of attention or interest *Syn* contemn, scorn, disdain, scout *Ant* appreciate

despite *n* **1** *Syn* MALICE, spite, ill will, malevolence, spleen, grudge, malignity, malignancy *Ant* appreciation; regard **2** ♦ the feeling or attitude of despising *Syn* contempt, scorn, disdain

despite *prep Syn* NOTWITHSTANDING, in spite of

despoil *Syn* RAVAGE, devastate, waste, sack, pillage, spoliate

despondency ♦ the state or feeling of having lost hope *Syn* despair, desperation, hopelessness, forlornness *Ant* lightheartedness

despondent ♦ having lost all or nearly all hope *Syn* despairing, desperate, hopeless, forlorn *Ant* lighthearted

despotic *Syn* ABSOLUTE, tyrannical, tyrannous, arbitrary, autocratic

destiny *Syn* FATE, lot, doom, portion

destitute 1 *Syn* DEVOID, void **2** *Syn* POOR, indigent, needy, penniless, impecunious, poverty-stricken, necessitous *Ant* opulent

destitution *Syn* POVERTY, want, indigence, penury, privation *Ant* opulence

destroy ♦ to bring to ruin *Syn* demolish, raze

destruction *Syn* RUIN, havoc, devastation

desultory *Syn* RANDOM, casual, hit or miss, haphazard, happy-go-lucky, chance, chancy *Ant* assiduous; methodical

detach ♦ to remove one thing from another with which it is in union or association *Syn* disengage, abstract *Ant* attach, affix

detached *Syn* INDIFFERENT, aloof, uninterested, disinterested, unconcerned, incurious *Ant* interested; selfish

detail 1 *Syn* ITEM, particular **2** *Syn* PART, portion, piece, parcel, member, division, segment, sector, fraction, fragment

detailed *Syn* CIRCUMSTANTIAL, itemized, particularized, minute, particular

detain 1 *Syn* ARREST, apprehend, attach **2** *Syn* KEEP, withhold, hold, hold back, keep back, keep out, retain, reserve **3** *Syn* DELAY, retard, slow, slacken

detention *Syn* ARREST, apprehension, attachment

deter *Syn* DISSUADE, discourage, divert *Ant* abet; actuate, motivate

deterioration ♦ a falling from a higher to a lower level in quality, character, or vitality *Syn* degeneration, devolution, decadence, decline, declension *Ant* improvement, amelioration

determinant *Syn* CAUSE, antecedent, reason, occasion

determinative *Syn* CONCLUSIVE, decisive, definitive

determine 1 *Syn* DECIDE, settle, rule, resolve **2** *Syn* DISCOVER, ascertain, unearth, learn

determined *Syn* DECIDED, decisive, resolved

detest *Syn* HATE, abhor, abominate, loathe *Ant* adore

detestable *Syn* HATEFUL, odious, abominable, abhorrent

detestation *Syn* ABHORRENCE, hate, hatred, abomination, loathing

detract *Syn* DECRY, belittle, minimize, disparage, derogate, depreciate

detraction ♦ the expression of damaging or malicious opinions *Syn* backbiting, calumny, slander, scandal

detriment *Syn* DISADVANTAGE, handicap, drawback *Ant* advantage, benefit

detrimental *Syn* PERNICIOUS, deleterious, noxious, baneful *Ant* beneficial

devastate *Syn* RAVAGE, waste, sack, pillage, despoil, spoliate

devastation *Syn* RUIN, havoc, destruction

develop 1 *Syn* UNFOLD, evolve, elaborate, perfect **2** *Syn* MATURE, ripen, age

development ♦ advance from a lower to a higher form *Syn* evolution

deviate *Syn* SWERVE, digress, diverge, veer, depart

deviation ♦ departure from a straight course or procedure or from a norm or standard *Syn* aberration, divergence, deflection

device 1 ♦ something usu. of a mechanical character that performs a function or effects a desired end *Syn* contrivance, gadget, contraption **2** *Syn* FIGURE, design, motif, pattern

devilish *Syn* FIENDISH, diabolical, diabolic, demoniac, demonic *Ant* angelic

devious *Syn* CROOKED, oblique *Ant* straightforward

devise 1 *Syn* CONTRIVE, invent, frame, concoct **2** *Syn* WILL, bequeath, leave, legate

devoid ♦ showing a want or lack *Syn* void, destitute

devolution *Syn* DETERIORATION, decadence, decline, declension, degeneration *Ant* evolution

devote 1 ♦ to set apart for a particular and often a better or higher use or end *Syn* dedicate, consecrate, hallow **2** *Syn* DI-RECT, apply, address

devoted *Syn* LOVING, affectionate, fond, doting

devotee *Syn* ADDICT, votary, habitué

devotion *Syn* FIDELITY, loyalty, fealty, piety, allegiance

devour *Syn* EAT, swallow, ingest, consume

devout ♦ showing fervor and reverence in the practice of religion *Syn* pious, religious, pietistic, sanctimonious

dexterity *Syn* READINESS, facility, ease *Ant* clumsiness

dexterous ♦ ready and skilled in physical movements *Syn* adroit, deft, handy *Ant* clumsy

diabolical, diabolic *Syn* FIENDISH, demonic, devilish, demoniac

diagram *n Syn* SKETCH, outline, draft, tracing, delineation, plot, blueprint

diagram *vb Syn* SKETCH, outline, plot, blueprint, draft, trace, delineate

dialect 1 ♦ a form of language that is not recognized as standard *Syn* vernacular, patois, lingo, jargon, cant, argot, slang **2** *Syn* LANGUAGE, tongue, speech, idiom

dialectic *Syn* ARGUMENTATION, disputation, debate, forensic

diaphanous *Syn* CLEAR, limpid, pellucid, transparent, translucent, lucid

diatribe *Syn* TIRADE, jeremiad, philippic

dictate *vb* ♦ to lay down expressly something to be followed, observed, obeyed, or accepted *Syn* prescribe, ordain, decree, impose

dictate *n Syn* COMMAND, behest, bidding, injunction, order, mandate

dictatorial ♦ imposing one's will or opinions on others *Syn* magisterial, authoritarian, dogmatic, doctrinaire, oracular

diction *Syn* LANGUAGE, vocabulary, phraseology, phrasing, style

dido *Syn* PRANK, caper, antic, monkeyshine

differ ♦ to be unlike or out of harmony *Syn* vary, disagree, dissent *Ant* agree

difference 1 *Syn* DISSIMILARITY, unlikeness, divergence, divergency, distinction *Ant* resemblance **2** *Syn* DISCORD, strife, conflict, contention, dissension, variance

different ♦ unlike in kind or character *Syn* diverse, divergent, disparate, various *Ant* identical, alike, same

differentiate *Syn* DISTINGUISH, discriminate, demarcate *Ant* confuse

difficult *Syn* HARD, arduous *Ant* simple

difficulty ♦ something which demands effort and endurance if it is to be overcome or one's end achieved *Syn* hardship, rigor, vicissitude

diffident *Syn* SHY, modest, bashful, coy *Ant* confident

diffuse *adj Syn* WORDY, prolix, redundant, verbose *Ant* succinct

diffuse *vb Syn* SPREAD, circulate, disseminate, propagate, radiate *Ant* concentrate

dig ♦ to loosen and turn over or remove (as soil) with or as if with a spade *Syn* delve, spade, grub, excavate

digest *Syn* COMPENDIUM, syllabus, pandect, survey, sketch, précis, aperçu

digit *Syn* NUMBER, numeral, figure, integer

dignify ♦ to enhance the status of or raise in human estimation *Syn* ennoble, honor, glorify

dignity 1 *Syn* DECORUM, decency, propriety, etiquette **2** *Syn* ELEGANCE, grace

digress *Syn* SWERVE, deviate, diverge, depart, veer

digression ♦ a departure from a subject or theme *Syn* episode, excursus, divagation

dilapidate *Syn* RUIN, wreck

dilapidated *Syn* SHABBY, dingy, faded, seedy, threadbare

dilate 1 *Syn* DISCOURSE, expatiate, descant **2** *Syn* EXPAND, distend, swell, amplify, inflate *Ant* constrict; circumscribe; attenuate

dilatory *Syn* SLOW, laggard, deliberate, leisurely *Ant* diligent

dilemma *Syn* PREDICAMENT, quandary, plight, scrape, fix, jam, pickle

dilettante 1 *Syn* AMATEUR, dabbler, tyro **2** *Syn* AESTHETE, connoisseur

diligent *Syn* BUSY, assiduous, sedulous, industrious *Ant* dilatory

dilute *Syn* THIN, attenuate, rarefy *Ant* condense; concentrate

dim *adj* *Syn* DARK, dusky, obscure, murky, gloomy *Ant* bright; distinct

dim *vb* *Syn* OBSCURE, bedim, darken, eclipse, cloud, becloud, fog, befog, obfuscate *Ant* illustrate

dimensions *Syn* SIZE, extent, area, magnitude, volume

diminish *Syn* DECREASE, reduce, lessen, abate, dwindle

diminutive *Syn* SMALL, little, wee, tiny, minute, miniature

din *n* ♦ a disturbing or confusing welter of sounds *Syn* uproar, pandemonium, hullabaloo, babel, hubbub, clamor, racket *Ant* quiet

dingy *Syn* SHABBY, dilapidated, faded, seedy, threadbare

dinner ♦ a usu. elaborate meal served to guests or to a group often to mark an occasion or honor an individual *Syn* banquet, feast

dip 1 ♦ to plunge a person or thing into or as if into liquid *Syn* immerse, submerge, duck, souse, dunk **2** ♦ to remove a liquid or a loose or soft substance from a container by means of an implement shaped to hold liquid *Syn* bail, scoop, ladle, spoon, dish

diplomatic *Syn* SUAVE, politic, smooth, bland, urbane

dipsomaniac *Syn* DRUNKARD, alcoholic, inebriate, sot, soak, toper, tosspot, tippler

direct *vb* **1** ♦ to turn or bend one's attention or efforts toward a certain object or objective *Syn* address, devote, apply **2** ♦ to turn something toward its appointed or intended mark or goal *Syn* aim, point, level, train, lay *Ant* misdirect **3** *Syn* CONDUCT, manage, control **4** *Syn* COMMAND, order, bid, enjoin, instruct, charge

direct *adj* ♦ marked by the absence of interruption (as between the cause and the effect, the source and the issue, or the beginning and the end) *Syn* immediate

directly *Syn* PRESENTLY, shortly, soon

dirty *adj* ♦ conspicuously unclean or impure *Syn* filthy, foul, nasty, squalid *Ant* clean

dirty *vb* *Syn* SOIL, sully, tarnish, foul, befoul, smirch, besmirch, grime, begrime

disable *Syn* WEAKEN, cripple, undermine, enfeeble, debilitate, sap *Ant* rehabilitate

disabuse *Syn* RID, clear, unburden, purge

disadvantage ♦ something which interferes with the success or well-being of a person or thing *Syn* detriment, handicap, drawback *Ant* advantage

disaffect *Syn* ESTRANGE, alienate, wean *Ant* win over

disagree *Syn* DIFFER, vary, dissent *Ant* agree

disallow *Syn* DISCLAIM, disavow, repudiate, disown *Ant* allow

disappear *Syn* VANISH, evanesce, evaporate, fade *Ant* appear

disapprove ♦ to feel or to express an objection to or condemnation of *Syn* deprecate *Ant* approve

disarrange *Syn* DISORDER, derange, disorganize, unsettle, disturb *Ant* arrange

disarray *Syn* CONFUSION, disorder, chaos, jumble, clutter, snarl, muddle

disaster ♦ an event bringing great damage, loss, or destruction *Syn* calamity, catastrophe, cataclysm

disastrous *Syn* UNLUCKY, ill-starred, ill-fated, unfortunate, calamitous, luckless, hapless

disavow *Syn* DISCLAIM, repudiate, disown, disallow *Ant* avow

disbar *Syn* EXCLUDE, shut out, eliminate, rule out, suspend, debar, blackball

disbelief *Syn* UNBELIEF, incredulity *Ant* belief

disburse *Syn* SPEND, expend

discard ♦ to get rid of *Syn* cast, shed, molt, slough, scrap, junk

discern *Syn* SEE, perceive, descry, observe, notice, remark, note, espy, behold, view, survey, contemplate

discernment ♦ a power to see what is not evident to the average mind **Syn** discrimination, perception, penetration, insight, acumen

discharge 1 Syn FREE, release, liberate, emancipate, manumit **2 Syn** DISMISS, cashier, drop, sack, fire, bounce **3 Syn** PERFORM, execute, accomplish, achieve, effect, fulfill

disciple Syn FOLLOWER, adherent, henchman, satellite, sectary, partisan

discipline *n* **Syn** MORALE, esprit de corps **Ant** anarchy, lawlessness

discipline *vb* **1 Syn** TEACH, train, educate, instruct, school **2 Syn** PUNISH, chastise, castigate, chasten, correct

disclaim ♦ to refuse to admit, accept, or approve **Syn** disavow, repudiate, disown, disallow **Ant** claim

disclose Syn REVEAL, divulge, tell, discover, betray

discomfit Syn EMBARRASS, disconcert, faze, abash, rattle

discommode Syn INCONVENIENCE, incommode, trouble

discompose ♦ to excite one so as to destroy one's capacity for clear or collected thought or prompt action **Syn** disquiet, disturb, perturb, agitate, upset, fluster, flurry

disconcert Syn EMBARRASS, rattle, faze, discomfit, abash

disconsolate Syn DOWNCAST, woebegone, dejected, depressed, dispirited

discontinue Syn STOP, desist, cease, quit **Ant** continue

discord ♦ a state or condition marked by disagreement and lack of harmony **Syn** strife, conflict, contention, dissension, difference, variance

discordant Syn INCONSONANT, incongruous, uncongenial, unsympathetic, incompatible, inconsistent, discrepant

discount Syn DEDUCTION, rebate, abatement

discourage 1 ♦ to weaken the stamina, interest, or zeal of **Syn** dishearten, dispirit, deject **Ant** encourage **2 Syn** DISSUADE, deter, divert

discourse *n* ♦ a systematic, serious, and often learned exposition of a subject or topic **Syn** treatise, disquisition, dissertation, thesis, monograph

discourse *vb* ♦ to talk or sometimes write esp. formally and at length upon a subject **Syn** expatiate, dilate, descant

discourteous Syn RUDE, impolite, uncivil, ungracious, ill-mannered **Ant** courteous

discover 1 Syn REVEAL, disclose, divulge, tell, betray **2** ♦ to find out something not previously known **Syn** ascertain, determine, unearth, learn

discreet Syn PRUDENT, forethoughtful, foresighted, provident **Ant** indiscreet

discrepant Syn INCONSONANT, inconsistent, discordant, incompatible, incongruous, uncongenial, unsympathetic **Ant** identical (*as accounts, explanations*)

discrete Syn DISTINCT, separate, several

discretion Syn PRUDENCE, forethought, foresight, providence **Ant** indiscretion

discriminate Syn DISTINGUISH, differentiate, demarcate **Ant** confound

discrimination Syn DISCERNMENT, penetration, insight, perception, acumen

discuss ♦ to exchange views about something in order to arrive at the truth or to convince others **Syn** argue, debate, dispute, agitate

disdain *n* **Syn** DESPITE, scorn, contempt

disdain *vb* **Syn** DESPISE, scorn, scout, contemn **Ant** favor; admit

disdainful Syn PROUD, supercilious, overbearing, insolent, arrogant, lordly, haughty

disease ♦ an impairment of the normal state of the living body that interferes with normal bodily functions **Syn** disorder, condition, affection, ailment, malady, complaint, distemper, syndrome

diseased Syn UNWHOLESOME, morbid, sickly, pathological

disembarrass Syn EXTRICATE, disencumber, disentangle, untangle

disencumber Syn EXTRICATE, disembarrass, disentangle, untangle

disengage Syn DETACH, abstract **Ant** engage

disentangle *Syn* EXTRICATE, untangle, disembarrass, disencumber *Ant* entangle

disfavor *Syn* DISLIKE, distaste, aversion

disfigure *Syn* DEFACE, *Ant* adorn

disgorge *Syn* BELCH, burp, vomit, regurgitate, spew, throw up

disgrace ◆ the state of suffering loss of esteem and of enduring reproach *Syn* dishonor, disrepute, shame, infamy, ignominy, opprobrium, obloquy, odium *Ant* respect, esteem

disguise ◆ to alter so as to hide the true appearance or character of *Syn* cloak, mask, dissemble, camouflage

disgust ◆ to arouse an extreme distaste in *Syn* sicken, nauseate *Ant* charm

dish *Syn* DIP, ladle, spoon, bail, scoop

dishearten *Syn* DISCOURAGE, dispirit, deject *Ant* hearten

disheveled *Syn* SLIPSHOD, unkempt, sloppy, slovenly

dishonest ◆ unworthy of trust or belief *Syn* DECEITFUL, mendacious, lying, untruthful *Ant* honest

dishonor *Syn* DISGRACE, disrepute, shame, infamy, ignominy, opprobrium, obloquy, odium *Ant* honor

disillusioned *Syn* SOPHISTICATED, worldly-wise, worldly, blasé

disinclined ◆ lacking the will or the desire to do something *Syn* indisposed, hesitant, reluctant, loath, averse

disinfect *Syn* STERILIZE, sanitize, fumigate *Ant* infect

disintegrate *Syn* DECAY, crumble, decompose, rot, putrefy, spoil *Ant* integrate

disinterested *Syn* INDIFFERENT, uninterested, detached, aloof, unconcerned, incurious *Ant* interested; prejudiced, biased

dislike ◆ a feeling of aversion or disapproval *Syn* distaste, aversion, disfavor *Ant* liking

disloyal *Syn* FAITHLESS, false, perfidious, traitorous, treacherous *Ant* loyal

dismal ◆ devoid of all that makes for cheer or comfort *Syn* dreary, cheerless, dispiriting, bleak, desolate

dismantle *Syn* STRIP, divest, denude, bare

dismay *vb* ◆ to unnerve and check by arousing fear, apprehension, or aversion *Syn* appall, horrify, daunt *Ant* cheer

dismay *n* *Syn* FEAR, alarm, consternation, panic, dread, fright, terror, horror, trepidation

dismiss 1 ◆ to let go from one's employ or service *Syn* discharge, cashier, drop, sack, fire, bounce **2** *Syn* EJECT, oust, expel, evict

dismount *Syn* DESCEND, alight

disorder *vb* ◆ to undo the fixed or proper order of something *Syn* derange, disarrange, disorganize, unsettle, disturb

disorder *n* **1** *Syn* CONFUSION, disarray, clutter, jumble, chaos, snarl, muddle *Ant* order **2** *Syn* DISEASE, condition, affection, ailment, malady, complaint, distemper, syndrome

disorganize *Syn* DISORDER, disturb, unsettle, derange, disarrange

disown *Syn* DISCLAIM, disavow, repudiate, disallow *Ant* own

disparage *Syn* DECRY, depreciate, derogate, detract, belittle, minimize *Ant* applaud

disparaging *Syn* DEROGATORY, depreciatory, depreciative, slighting, pejorative

disparate *Syn* DIFFERENT, diverse, divergent, various *Ant* comparable, analogous

dispassionate *Syn* FAIR, unbiased, impartial, objective, uncolored, just, equitable *Ant* passionate; intemperate

dispatch *vb* **1** *Syn* SEND, forward, transmit, remit, route, ship **2** *Syn* KILL, slay, murder, assassinate, execute

dispatch *n* **1** *Syn* HASTE, speed, expedition, hurry *Ant* delay **2** *Syn* LETTER, message, note, epistle, report, memorandum, missive

dispel *Syn* SCATTER, dissipate, disperse

dispense *Syn* DISTRIBUTE, divide, deal, dole **2** *Syn* ADMINISTER

disperse *Syn* SCATTER, dissipate, dispel *Ant* assemble, congregate; collect

dispirit *Syn* DISCOURAGE, dishearten, deject *Ant* inspirit

dispirited *Syn* DOWNCAST, depressed, dejected, disconsolate, woebegone *Ant* high-spirited

dispiriting *Syn* DISMAL, dreary, cheerless, bleak, desolate *Ant* inspiriting

displace *Syn* REPLACE, supplant, supersede

display *vb Syn* SHOW, exhibit, expose, parade, flaunt

display *n* ♦ a striking or spectacular show or exhibition for the sake of effect *Syn* parade, array, pomp

disport *n Syn* PLAY, sport, frolic, rollick, romp, gambol

disport *vb Syn* PLAY, sport, frolic, rollick, romp, gambol

disposal ♦ the act or the power of disposing of something *Syn* disposition

dispose *Syn* INCLINE, predispose, bias

disposition 1 *Syn* DISPOSAL 2 ♦ the prevailing and dominant quality or qualities which distinguish or identify a person or group *Syn* temperament, temper, complexion, character, personality, individuality

disprove ♦ to show by presenting evidence that something is not true *Syn* refute, confute, rebut, controvert *Ant* prove, demonstrate

disputation *Syn* ARGUMENTATION, debate, forensic, dialectic

dispute *vb Syn* DISCUSS, argue, debate, agitate *Ant* concede

dispute *n Syn* ARGUMENT, controversy

disquiet *Syn* DISCOMPOSE, disturb, agitate, perturb, upset, fluster, flurry *Ant* tranquilize, soothe

disquisition *Syn* DISCOURSE, dissertation, thesis, treatise, monograph

disrate *Syn* DEGRADE, demote, reduce, declass

disregard *Syn* NEGLECT, ignore, overlook, slight, forget, omit

disrepute *Syn* DISGRACE, dishonor, shame, infamy, ignominy, opprobrium, obloquy, odium

dissect *Syn* ANALYZE, break down, resolve

dissection *Syn* ANALYSIS, breakdown, resolution

dissemble *Syn* DISGUISE, mask, cloak, camouflage *Ant* betray

disseminate *Syn* SPREAD, circulate, diffuse, propagate, radiate

dissension *Syn* DISCORD, difference, variance, strife, conflict, contention *Ant* accord; comity

dissent *Syn* DIFFER, vary, disagree *Ant* concur; assent; consent

dissenter *Syn* HERETIC, nonconformist, sectarian, sectary, schismatic

dissertation *Syn* DISCOURSE, disquisition, thesis, treatise, monograph

dissimilarity ♦ lack of agreement or correspondence or an instance of this *Syn* unlikeness, difference, divergence, divergency, distinction *Ant* similarity

dissimulation *Syn* DECEIT, duplicity, cunning, guile

dissipate 1 *Syn* SCATTER, dispel, disperse *Ant* accumulate; absorb; concentrate 2 *Syn* WASTE, squander, fritter, consume

dissolute *Syn* ABANDONED, profligate, reprobate

dissuade ♦ to turn one aside from a purpose, a project, or a plan *Syn* deter, discourage, divert *Ant* persuade

distant ♦ not close in space, time, or relationship *Syn* far, faraway, far-off, remote, removed

distaste *Syn* DISLIKE, aversion, disfavor *Ant* taste

distasteful *Syn* REPUGNANT, obnoxious, repellent, abhorrent, invidious *Ant* agreeable; palatable

distemper *Syn* DISEASE, complaint, syndrome, malady, ailment, disorder, condition, affection

distend *Syn* EXPAND, swell, dilate, inflate, amplify *Ant* constrict

distinct 1 ♦ capable of being distinguished as differing *Syn* separate, several, discrete 2 *Syn* EVIDENT, manifest, patent, obvious, apparent, palpable, plain, clear *Ant* indistinct; nebulous

distinction *Syn* DISSIMILARITY, difference, divergence, divergency, unlikeness

distinctive *Syn* CHARACTERISTIC, peculiar, individual *Ant* typical

distinguish 1 ♦ to recognize the differences between *Syn* differentiate, discriminate, demarcate *Ant* confound **2** *Syn* CHARACTERIZE, mark, qualify

distort *Syn* DEFORM, contort, warp

distract *Syn* PUZZLE, bewilder, nonplus, confound, dumbfound, mystify, perplex *Ant* collect (*one's thoughts, one's powers*)

distraught *Syn* ABSTRACTED, absentminded, absent, preoccupied *Ant* collected

distress *n* ♦ the state of being in great trouble or in mental or physical anguish *Syn* suffering, misery, agony, dolor, passion

distress *vb Syn* TROUBLE, ail

distribute ♦ to give out, usu. in shares, to each member of a group *Syn* dispense, divide, deal, dole *Ant* collect; amass

district *Syn* LOCALITY, vicinity, neighborhood

distrust *vb* ♦ to lack trust or confidence in *Syn* mistrust, doubt, misdoubt, suspect

distrust *n* ♦ a lack of trust or confidence *Syn* mistrust

disturb 1 *Syn* DISORDER, unsettle, derange, disarrange, disorganize **2** *Syn* DISCOMPOSE, perturb, upset, disquiet, agitate, fluster, flurry

dither *Syn* SHAKE, tremble, quake, quiver, shiver, quaver, wobble, teeter, shimmy, shudder, totter

diurnal *Syn* DAILY, quotidian

divagation *Syn* DIGRESSION, episode, excursus

dive *Syn* PLUNGE, pitch

diverge *Syn* SWERVE, veer, deviate, depart, digress *Ant* converge; conform

divergence 1 *Syn* DEVIATION, deflection, aberration *Ant* convergence **2** *Syn* DISSIMILARITY, divergency, difference, unlikeness, distinction *Ant* conformity, correspondence

divergency *Syn* DISSIMILARITY, divergence, difference, unlikeness, distinction

divergent *Syn* DIFFERENT, diverse, disparate, various *Ant* convergent

divers *Syn* MANY, several, sundry, various, numerous, multifarious

diverse *Syn* DIFFERENT, divergent, disparate, various *Ant* identical, selfsame

diversion *Syn* AMUSEMENT, recreation, entertainment

diversity *Syn* VARIETY *Ant* uniformity; identity

divert 1 *Syn* TURN, deflect, avert, sheer **2** *Syn* AMUSE, entertain, recreate **3** *Syn* DISSUADE, deter, discourage

divest *Syn* STRIP, denude, bare, dismantle *Ant* invest, vest (*in robes of office, with power or authority*); apparel, clothe

divide 1 *Syn* SEPARATE, part, sever, sunder, divorce *Ant* unite **2** *Syn* DISTRIBUTE, dispense, deal, dole

divine *adj Syn* HOLY, sacred, spiritual, religious, blessed

divine *vb Syn* FORESEE, foreknow, apprehend, anticipate

division *Syn* PART, section, segment, sector, portion, piece, detail, member, fraction, fragment, parcel

divorce *Syn* SEPARATE, sever, sunder, part, divide

divulge *Syn* REVEAL, tell, disclose, betray, discover

dizzy *Syn* GIDDY, vertiginous, swimming, dazzled

docile *Syn* OBEDIENT, biddable, tractable, amenable *Ant* indocile; unruly, ungovernable

dock *Syn* WHARF, pier, quay, slip, berth, jetty, levee

doctor *Syn* ADULTERATE, sophisticate, load, weight

doctrinaire *Syn* DICTATORIAL, dogmatic, magisterial, oracular, authoritarian

doctrine ♦ a principle accepted as valid and authoritative *Syn* dogma, tenet

document ♦ something preserved and serving as evidence (as of an event, a situation, or the culture of the period) *Syn* monument, record, archive

dodge ♦ to avoid or evade by some maneuver or shift *Syn* parry, sidestep, duck, shirk, fence, malinger *Ant* face

dogged *Syn* OBSTINATE, pertinacious, mulish, stubborn, stiff-necked, pigheaded, bullheaded *Ant* faltering

dogma *Syn* DOCTRINE, tenet

dogmatic *Syn* DICTATORIAL, magisterial, doctrinaire, oracular, authoritarian

doldrums *Syn* TEDIUM, boredom, ennui *Ant* spirits, high spirits

dole *n Syn* RATION, allowance, pittance

dole *vb Syn* DISTRIBUTE, dispense, deal, divide

doleful *Syn* MELANCHOLY, lugubrious, dolorous, plaintive, rueful *Ant* cheerful, cheery

dolor *Syn* DISTRESS, agony, suffering, passion, misery *Ant* beatitude, blessedness

dolorous *Syn* MELANCHOLY, doleful, plaintive, lugubrious, rueful

domain *Syn* FIELD, sphere, province, territory, bailiwick

domicile *Syn* HABITATION, dwelling, abode, residence, house, home

dominant ♦ superior to all others in power, influence, position, or rank *Syn* predominant, paramount, preponderant, preponderating, sovereign *Ant* subordinate

domineering *Syn* MASTERFUL, imperious, imperative, peremptory *Ant* subservient

dominion *Syn* POWER, control, command, sway, authority, jurisdiction

donate *Syn* GIVE, present, bestow, confer, afford

donation ♦ a gift of money or its equivalent for a charitable, philanthropic, or humanitarian object *Syn* benefaction, contribution, alms

doom *n Syn* FATE, destiny, lot, portion

doom *vb Syn* SENTENCE, damn, condemn, proscribe

door ♦ an entrance to a place *Syn* gate, portal, postern, doorway, gateway

doorway *Syn* DOOR, portal, postern, gate, gateway

dormant 1 *Syn* LATENT, quiescent, abeyant, potential *Ant* active, live 2 *Syn* PRONE, couchant, recumbent, supine, prostrate

dormer *Syn* WINDOW, casement, oriel

dotage *Syn* AGE, senility, senescence *Ant* infancy

dote *Syn* LIKE, love, relish, enjoy, fancy *Ant* loathe

doting *Syn* LOVING, fond, devoted, affectionate

double *Syn* SUBSTITUTE, understudy, stand-in, supply, locum tenens, alternate, pinch hitter

double-cross *Syn* DECEIVE, delude, betray, beguile, mislead

double-dealing *Syn* DECEPTION, chicanery, chicane, trickery, fraud

double entendre *Syn* AMBIGUITY, equivocation, tergiversation

doubt *n Syn* UNCERTAINTY, skepticism, suspicion, mistrust, dubiety, dubiosity *Ant* certitude; confidence

doubt *vb Syn* DISTRUST, mistrust, misdoubt, suspect

doubtful ♦ not affording assurance of the worth, soundness, success, or certainty of something or someone *Syn* dubious, problematic, questionable *Ant* cocksure, positive

doughty *Syn* BRAVE, courageous, unafraid, fearless, intrepid, valiant, valorous, dauntless, undaunted, bold, audacious

dour *Syn* SULLEN, saturnine, glum, gloomy, morose, surly, sulky, crabbed

dowdy *Syn* SLATTERNLY, frowzy, blowsy *Ant* smart (*in dress, appearance*)

dower ♦ to furnish or provide with a gift *Syn* endow, endue

downcast ♦ very low in spirits *Syn* dispirited, dejected, depressed, disconsolate, woebegone *Ant* elated

downright *Syn* FORTHRIGHT

doze *Syn* SLEEP, drowse, snooze, slumber, nap, catnap

draft *n Syn* SKETCH, outline, diagram, delineation, tracing, plot, blueprint

draft *vb Syn* SKETCH, outline, diagram, delineate, trace, plot, blueprint

drag *Syn* PULL, draw, haul, hale, tug, tow

drain *Syn* DEPLETE, exhaust, impoverish, bankrupt

dramatic ♦ of, relating to, or suggestive of plays, or the performance of a play *Syn* theatrical, dramaturgic, melodramatic, histrionic

dramaturgic *Syn* DRAMATIC, theatrical, histrionic, melodramatic

draw *vb Syn* PULL, drag, tug, tow, haul, hale

draw *n* ♦ an indecisive ending to a contest or competition *Syn* tie, stalemate, deadlock, standoff

drawback *Syn* DISADVANTAGE, detriment, handicap

dread *Syn* FEAR, horror, terror, fright, alarm, trepidation, panic, consternation, dismay

dreadful *Syn* FEARFUL, horrible, horrific, appalling, awful, frightful, terrible, terrific, shocking

dream *Syn* FANCY, fantasy, phantasy, phantasm, vision, daydream, nightmare

dreary 1 *Syn* DISMAL, cheerless, dispiriting, bleak, desolate 2 *Syn* DULL, humdrum, monotonous, pedestrian, stodgy

dregs *Syn* DEPOSIT, sediment, precipitate, lees, grounds

drench *Syn* SOAK, saturate, sop, steep, impregnate, waterlog

dress *vb Syn* CLOTHE, attire, apparel, array, robe *Ant* undress

dress *n Syn* CLOTHES, clothing, attire, apparel, raiment

drift *Syn* TENDENCY, trend, tenor

drill *vb* 1 *Syn* PERFORATE, bore, punch, puncture, prick 2 *Syn* PRACTICE, exercise

drill *n Syn* PRACTICE, exercise

drive *vb Syn* MOVE, impel, actuate

drive *n* 1 *Syn* RIDE 2 *Syn* VIGOR, vim, spirit, dash, esprit, verve, punch, élan

drivel *Syn* NONSENSE, twaddle, bunk, balderdash, poppycock, gobbledygook, trash, rot, bull

droll *Syn* LAUGHABLE, risible, comic, comical, funny, ludicrous, ridiculous, farcical

droop ♦ to become literally or figuratively limp through loss of vigor or freshness *Syn* wilt, flag, sag

drop 1 *Syn* FALL, sink, slump, subside *Ant* mount 2 *Syn* DISMISS, discharge, cashier, sack, fire, bounce

drowse *Syn* SLEEP, doze, snooze, slumber, nap, catnap

drowsy *Syn* SLEEPY, somnolent, slumberous

drudgery *Syn* WORK, toil, travail, labor, grind

drug ♦ a substance used by itself or in a mixture for the treatment or in the diagnosis of disease *Syn* medicinal, pharmaceutical, biologic, simple

druggist ♦ one who deals in medicinal drugs *Syn* pharmacist, apothecary, chemist

drunk ♦ having the faculties impaired by alcohol *Syn* drunken, intoxicated, inebriated, tipsy, tight *Ant* sober

drunkard ♦ one who is habitually drunk *Syn* inebriate, alcoholic, dipsomaniac, sot, soak, toper, tosspot, tippler *Ant* teetotaler

drunken *Syn* DRUNK, intoxicated, inebriated, tipsy, tight

dry *adj* 1 ♦ devoid of moisture *Syn* arid *Ant* wet 2 *Syn* SOUR, acid, acidulous, tart *Ant* sweet (*wine*)

dry *vb* ♦ to treat or to affect so as to deprive of moisture *Syn* desiccate, dehydrate, bake, parch *Ant* moisten, wet

dubiety *Syn* UNCERTAINTY, dubiosity, doubt, skepticism, suspicion, mistrust *Ant* decision

dubiosity *Syn* UNCERTAINTY, dubiety, doubt, skepticism, suspicion, mistrust *Ant* decidedness

dubious *Syn* DOUBTFUL, questionable, problematic *Ant* cocksure; reliable; trustworthy

duck 1 *Syn* DIP, immerse, submerge, souse, dunk 2 *Syn* DODGE, parry, shirk, sidestep, fence, malinger

duct *Syn* CHANNEL, canal, conduit, aqueduct

ductile *Syn* PLASTIC, pliable, pliant, malleable, adaptable

dude *Syn* FOP, dandy, beau, coxcomb, exquisite, buck

dudgeon *Syn* OFFENSE, umbrage, huff, pique, resentment

due *adj* ♦ being in accordance with what is just and appropriate *Syn* rightful, condign

due *n* ♦ what is justly owed to a person (sometimes a thing), esp. as a recompense or compensation *Syn* desert, merit

dulcet *Syn* SWEET, engaging, winning, winsome *Ant* grating

dull 1 *Syn* STUPID, slow, dumb, dense, crass *Ant* clever, bright **2** ♦ lacking sharpness of edge or point *Syn* blunt, obtuse *Ant* sharp; poignant (*sensation, feeling, reaction*) **3** ♦ being so unvaried and uninteresting as to provoke boredom or tedium *Syn* humdrum, dreary, monotonous, pedestrian, stodgy *Ant* lively

dumb 1 ♦ lacking the power to speak *Syn* mute, speechless, inarticulate **2** *Syn* STUPID, dull, slow, dense, crass *Ant* articulate

dumbfound *Syn* PUZZLE, confound, nonplus, bewilder, distract, mystify, perplex

dumps *Syn* SADNESS, dejection, gloom, blues, depression, melancholy, melancholia

dumpy *Syn* STOCKY, thickset, thick, chunky, stubby, squat

dunk *Syn* DIP, immerse, souse, submerge, duck

dupe ♦ mean to delude by underhanded means or methods *Syn* gull, befool, trick, hoax, hoodwink, bamboozle

duplicate *Syn* REPRODUCTION, facsimile, copy, carbon copy, transcript, replica

duplicity *Syn* DECEIT, dissimulation, cunning, guile

durable *Syn* LASTING, perdurable, permanent, stable, perpetual

duress *Syn* FORCE, constraint, coercion, compulsion, violence, restraint

dusky *Syn* DARK, dim, obscure, murky, gloomy

duty 1 *Syn* OBLIGATION **2** *Syn* FUNCTION, office, province **3** *Syn* TASK, assignment, job, stint, chore

dwarf ♦ an individual and usu. a person of very small size *Syn* pygmy, midget, manikin, homunculus, runt

dwell *Syn* RESIDE, live, lodge, sojourn, stay, put up, stop

dwelling *Syn* HABITATION, abode, residence, domicile, home, house

dwindle *Syn* DECREASE, diminish, lessen, reduce,

dynamic *Syn* ACTIVE, live, operative

E

each *adj Syn* ALL, every

each *adv* ♦ by, for, or to every one of the many *Syn* apiece, severally, individually, respectively

eager ♦ moved by a strong and urgent desire or interest *Syn* avid, keen, anxious, agog, athirst *Ant* listless

early ♦ at or nearly at the beginning of a specified or implied period of time *Syn* soon, beforehand, betimes *Ant* late

earn *Syn* DESERVE, merit, rate

earnest *adj Syn* SERIOUS, solemn, grave, somber, sober, sedate, staid *Ant* frivolous

earnest *n Syn* PLEDGE, token, pawn, hostage

earsplitting *Syn* LOUD, stentorian, hoarse, raucous, strident, stertorous

earth ♦ the entire area or extent of space in which human beings think of themselves as living and acting *Syn* world, globe, planet

earthly ♦ of, belonging to, or characteristic of the earth or life on earth *Syn* terrestrial, earthy, mundane, worldly, sublunary

earthy *Syn* EARTHLY, mundane, worldly, terrestrial, sublunary

ease 1 *Syn* REST, comfort, relaxation, repose, leisure **2** *Syn* READINESS, facility, dexterity *Ant* effort

easy 1 *Syn* COMFORTABLE, restful, cozy, snug *Ant* disquieting, disquieted **2** ♦ causing or involving little or no difficulty *Syn* facile, simple, light, effortless, smooth *Ant* hard

eat ♦ to take food into the stomach through the mouth *Syn* swallow, ingest, devour, consume

ebb *Syn* ABATE, subside, wane *Ant* flow

eccentric *Syn* STRANGE, erratic, odd, queer, peculiar, singular, unique, quaint, outlandish, curious

eccentricity ♦ an act, a practice, or a characteristic that impresses the observer as strange or singular *Syn* idiosyncrasy

echelon *Syn* LINE, row, rank, file, tier

éclat *Syn* FAME, renown, glory, celebrity, notoriety, repute, reputation, honor

eclipse *Syn* OBSCURE, dim, bedim, darken, cloud, becloud, fog, befog, obfuscate

economical *Syn* SPARING, frugal, thrifty *Ant* extravagant

ecstasy ♦ a feeling or a state of intense, sometimes excessive or extreme, mental and emotional exaltation *Syn* rapture, transport

ecumenical *Syn* UNIVERSAL, cosmic, catholic, cosmopolitan *Ant* provincial; diocesan

eddy *n* ♦ a swirling mass esp. of water *Syn* whirlpool, maelstrom, vortex

eddy *vb* *Syn* TURN, rotate, gyrate, circle, spin, whirl, revolve, twirl, wheel, swirl, pirouette

edge 1 *Syn* BORDER, verge, rim, brink, margin, brim **2** *Syn* ADVANTAGE, odds, handicap, allowance

edifice *Syn* BUILDING, structure, pile

edit ♦ to prepare material for publication *Syn* compile, revise, redact, rewrite, adapt

edition ♦ the total number of copies of the same work printed during a stretch of time *Syn* impression, reprinting, printing, reissue

educate *Syn* TEACH, train, discipline, school, instruct

educe ♦ to bring or draw out what is hidden, latent, or reserved *Syn* evoke, elicit, extract, extort

eerie *Syn* WEIRD, uncanny

efface *Syn* ERASE, obliterate, expunge, blot out, delete, cancel

effect *n* **1** ♦ a condition, situation, or occurrence, ascribable to a cause *Syn* result, consequence, upshot, aftereffect, aftermath, sequel, issue, outcome, event *Ant* cause **2** *pl* **effects** *Syn* POSSESSIONS, belongings, means, resources, assets

effect *vb* *Syn* PERFORM, accomplish, achieve, execute, discharge, fulfill

effective ♦ producing or capable of producing a result *Syn* effectual, efficient, efficacious *Ant* ineffective; futile

effectual *Syn* EFFECTIVE, efficacious, efficient *Ant* ineffectual; fruitless

effervescent *Syn* ELASTIC, volatile, buoyant, expansive, resilient *Ant* subdued

efficacious *Syn* EFFECTIVE, effectual, efficient *Ant* inefficacious; powerless

efficient *Syn* EFFECTIVE, effectual, efficacious *Ant* inefficient

effort ♦ the active use or expenditure of physical or mental power to produce a desired result *Syn* exertion, pains, trouble *Ant* ease

effortless *Syn* EASY, smooth, facile, simple, light *Ant* painstaking

effrontery *Syn* TEMERITY, audacity, hardihood, nerve, cheek, gall

effulgent *Syn* BRIGHT, radiant, luminous, brilliant, lustrous, refulgent, beaming, lambent, lucent, incandescent

egg *Syn* URGE, exhort, goad, spur, prod, prick, sic

egoism *Syn* CONCEIT, egotism, amour propre, self-love, self-esteem *Ant* altruism

egotism *Syn* CONCEIT, egoism, self-love, amour propre, self-esteem *Ant* modesty

eject ♦ to force or thrust something or someone out *Syn* expel, oust, evict, dismiss *Ant* admit

elaborate *Syn* UNFOLD, evolve, develop, perfect

élan *Syn* VIGOR, vim, spirit, dash, esprit, verve, punch, drive

elapse *Syn* PASS, pass away, expire

elastic 1 ♦ able to endure strain without being permanently affected or injured *Syn* resilient, springy, flexible, supple *Ant* rigid **2** ♦ able to recover quickly from depression and maintain high spirits *Syn* expansive, resilient, buoyant, volatile, effervescent *Ant* depressed

elbowroom *Syn* ROOM, berth, play, leeway, margin, clearance

elderly *Syn* AGED, old, superannuated *Ant* youthful

elect *adj* *Syn* SELECT, picked, exclusive *Ant* reprobate (*in theology*)

elect *vb* **1** *Syn* CHOOSE, select, pick, prefer, single, opt, cull *Ant* abjure **2** *Syn* DESIGNATE, name, nominate, appoint

election *Syn* CHOICE, selection, option, preference, alternative

electrify *Syn* THRILL, enthuse

eleemosynary *Syn* CHARITABLE, benevolent, humane, humanitarian, philanthropic, altruistic

elegance ♦ impressive beauty of form, appearance, or behavior *Syn* grace, dignity

elegant *Syn* CHOICE, exquisite, recherché, rare, dainty, delicate

element ♦ one of the parts of a compound or complex whole *Syn* component, constituent, ingredient, factor *Ant* compound (*in science*); composite

elemental 1 ♦ of, relating to, or being an ultimate or irreducible element *Syn* basic, elementatry, essential, fundamental, primitive, underlying **2** *Syn* ELEMENTARY, basal, beginning, rudimentary

elementary 1 ♦ of, relating to, or dealing with the simplest principles *Syn* basal, beginning, elemental, rudimentary **2** *Syn* ELEMENTAL, basic, essential, fundamental, primitive, underlying

elephantine *Syn* HUGE, vast, immense, enormous, mammoth, giant, gigantic, gigantean, colossal, gargantuan, Herculean, cyclopean, titanic, Brobdingnagian

elevate *Syn* LIFT, raise, rear, hoist, heave, boost *Ant* lower

elevation 1 *Syn* HEIGHT, altitude **2** *Syn* ADVANCEMENT, promotion, preferment *Ant* degradation

elicit *Syn* EDUCE, evoke, extract, extort

eliminate *Syn* EXCLUDE, rule out, debar, blackball, disbar, suspend, shut out

elite *Syn* ARISTOCRACY, society, nobility, gentry, county *Ant* rabble

ell *Syn* ANNEX, wing, extension

elongate *Syn* EXTEND, lengthen, prolong, protract *Ant* abbreviate, shorten

eloquent 1 *Syn* VOCAL, articulate, voluble, fluent, glib **2** *Syn* EXPRESSIVE, significant, meaningful, pregnant, sententious

elucidate *Syn* EXPLAIN, interpret, construe, expound, explicate

elude *Syn* ESCAPE, evade, avoid, shun, eschew

emanate *Syn* SPRING, issue, proceed, rise, arise, originate, derive, flow, stem

emancipate *Syn* FREE, manumit, liberate, release, discharge

emasculate 1 *Syn* STERILIZE, castrate, spay, alter, mutilate, geld **2** *Syn* UNNERVE, enervate, unman

embarrass ♦ to distress by confusing or confounding *Syn* discomfit, abash, disconcert, rattle, faze *Ant* relieve; facilitate

embellish *Syn* ADORN, beautify, deck, bedeck, garnish, decorate, ornament

embers *Syn* ASH, cinders, clinkers

emblem *Syn* SYMBOL, attribute, type

embody 1 *Syn* REALIZE, incarnate, materialize, externalize, objectify, actualize, hypostatize, reify *Ant* disembody **2** *Syn* IDENTIFY, incorporate, assimilate

embolden *Syn* ENCOURAGE, inspirit, hearten, cheer, nerve, steel *Ant* abash

embrace 1 *Syn* ADOPT, espouse *Ant* spurn **2** *Syn* INCLUDE, comprehend, involve, imply, subsume

emend *Syn* CORRECT, rectify, revise, amend, remedy, redress, reform *Ant* corrupt (*a text, passage*)

emerge *Syn* APPEAR, loom

emergency *Syn* JUNCTURE, exigency, contingency, crisis, pass, pinch, strait

emigrant ♦ a person who leaves one country in order to settle in another *Syn* immigrant, migrant

emigrate *Syn* MIGRATE immigrate

émigré *Syn* STRANGER, immigrant, alien, foreigner, outlander, outsider

eminent *Syn* FAMOUS, illustrious, renowned, celebrated, famed

emolument *Syn* WAGE, stipend, salary, fee, pay, hire

emotion *Syn* FEELING, affection, passion, sentiment

empathy *Syn* SYMPATHY, pity, compassion, commiseration, ruth, condolence

emphasis ♦ exerted force or special stress that gives impressiveness or importance to something *Syn* stress, accent, accentuation

employ *Syn* USE, utilize, apply, avail

employment *Syn* WORK, occupation, business, calling, pursuit

empower *Syn* ENABLE

empty 1 ♦ lacking the contents that could or should be present *Syn* vacant, blank, void, vacuous *Ant* full **2** *Syn* VAIN, idle, hollow, nugatory, otiose

empyrean empyreal *Syn* CELESTIAL, heavenly

emulate *Syn* RIVAL, compete, vie

emulous *Syn* AMBITIOUS

enable ♦ to render able often by giving power, strength, or means to *Syn* empower

enamored ♦ possessed by a strong or unreasoning love or admiration *Syn* infatuated

enchant *Syn* ATTRACT, charm, captivate, allure, fascinate, bewitch *Ant* disenchant

enchanting *Syn* ATTRACTIVE, charming, captivating, alluring, fascinating, bewitching,

encircle *Syn* SURROUND, environ, circle, encompass, compass, hem, gird, girdle, ring

enclose ♦ to shut in or confine by or as if by barriers *Syn* envelop, fence, pen, coop, corral, cage, wall

encomium ♦ a more or less formal and public expression of praise *Syn* eulogy, panegyric, tribute, citation

encompass *Syn* SURROUND, environ, encircle, circle, compass, hem, gird, girdle, ring

encounter *vb* *Syn* MEET, face, confront

encounter *n* ♦ a sudden, hostile, and usu. brief confrontation or dispute between factions or persons *Syn* skirmish, brush

encourage 1 ♦ to fill with courage or strength of purpose esp. in preparation for a hard task *Syn* inspirit, hearten, embolden, cheer, nerve, steel *Ant* discouage **2** *Syn* FAVOR, countenance *Ant* discourage

encroach *Syn* TRESPASS, entrench, infringe, invade

encumber *Syn* BURDEN, cumber, weigh, weight, load, lade, tax, charge, saddle

end *n* **1** *Syn* LIMIT, bound, term, confine **2** ♦ the point at which something ceases *Syn* termination, ending, terminus *Ant* be-

ginning **3** *Syn* INTENTION, objective, goal, aim, object, intent, purpose, design

end *vb* *Syn* CLOSE, conclude, terminate, finish, complete *Ant* begin

endanger *Syn* VENTURE, hazard, risk, chance, jeopardize, imperil

endeavor *vb* *Syn* ATTEMPT, try, essay, strive, struggle

endeavor *n* *Syn* ATTEMPT, essay, striving, struggle, try

endemic *Syn* NATIVE, indigenous, autochthonous, aboriginal *Ant* exotic; pandemic

ending *Syn* END, terminus, termination

endless *Syn* EVERLASTING, interminable, unceasing

endorse *Syn* APPROVE, sanction, accredit, certify

endow *Syn* DOWER, endue

endue *Syn* DOWER, endow

endure 1 *Syn* CONTINUE, last, abide, persist *Ant* perish **2** *Syn* BEAR, abide, tolerate, suffer, stand, brook

enemy ♦ an individual or a group that is hostile toward another *Syn* foe

energetic *Syn* VIGOROUS, strenuous, lusty, nervous *Ant* lethargic

energize 1 *Syn* VITALIZE, activate **2** *Syn* STRENGTHEN, invigorate, fortify, reinforce

energy *Syn* POWER, force, strength, might, puissance *Ant* inertia

enervate *Syn* UNNERVE, emasculate, unman *Ant* harden, inure

enervated *Syn* LANGUID, languishing, languorous, lackadaisical, spiritless, listless

enfeeble *Syn* WEAKEN, debilitate, sap, undermine, cripple, disable *Ant* fortify

enforce ♦ to put something into effect or operation *Syn* implement *Ant* relax (*discipline, rules, demands*)

engage *Syn* PROMISE, pledge, plight, covenant, contract

engagement 1 ♦ a promise to be in an agreed place at a specified time, usu. for a particular purpose *Syn* appointment, rendezvous, tryst, assignation, date **2** *Syn* BATTLE, action

engaging *Syn* SWEET, winning, winsome, dulcet *Ant* loathsome

engender *Syn* GENERATE, breed, beget, get, sire, procreate, propagate, reproduce

engine *Syn* MACHINE, mechanism, machinery, apparatus, motor

engineer *Syn* GUIDE, pilot, lead, steer

engrave *Syn* CARVE, incise, etch, sculpture, sculpt, sculp, chisel

engross *Syn* MONOPOLIZE, absorb, consume

engrossed *Syn* INTENT, absorbed, rapt

engrossing *Syn* INTERESTING, absorbing, intriguing *Ant* irksome

enhance *Syn* INTENSIFY, heighten, aggravate

enigma *Syn* MYSTERY, riddle, puzzle, conundrum, problem

enigmatic *Syn* OBSCURE, cryptic, dark, vague, ambiguous, equivocal *Ant* explicit

enjoin 1 *Syn* COMMAND, direct, order, bid, instruct, charge **2** *Syn* FORBID, interdict, prohibit, inhibit, ban

enjoy 1 *Syn* LIKE, love, relish, fancy, dote *Ant* loathe, abhor, abominate **2** *Syn* HAVE, possess, own, hold

enjoyment *Syn* PLEASURE, delight, joy, delectation, fruition *Ant* abhorrence

enlarge *Syn* INCREASE, augment, multiply

enlighten *Syn* ILLUMINATE, illustrate, illume, light, lighten *Ant* confuse, muddle

enliven *Syn* QUICKEN, animate, vivify *Ant* deaden; subdue

enmesh *Syn* ENTANGLE, involve

enmity ♦ deep-seated dislike or ill will or a manifestation of such a feeling *Syn* hostility, antipathy, antagonism, animosity, rancor, animus *Ant* amity

ennoble *Syn* DIGNIFY, honor, glorify

ennui *Syn* TEDIUM, doldrums, boredom

enormous *Syn* HUGE, vast, immense, elephantine, mammoth, giant, gigantic, gigantean, colossal, gargantuan, Herculean, cyclopean, titanic, Brobdingnagian

enough *Syn* SUFFICIENT, adequate, competent

enrage *Syn* ANGER, infuriate, madden, incense *Ant* placate

enrapture *Syn* TRANSPORT, ravish, entrance

enroll *Syn* RECORD, register, list, catalog

ensconce *Syn* HIDE, screen, secrete, conceal, cache, bury

ensign *Syn* FLAG, standard, banner, color, streamer, pennant, pendant, pennon, jack

ensnare *Syn* CATCH, snare, entrap, trap, bag, capture

ensue *Syn* FOLLOW, succeed, supervene

ensure ♦ to make a person or thing certain or sure *Syn* insure, assure, secure

entangle ♦ to catch or hold as if in a net from which it is difficult to escape *Syn* involve, enmesh *Ant* disentangle

entente *Syn* CONTRACT, treaty, pact, compact, concordat, convention, cartel, bargain

enter 1 ♦ to make way into something so as to reach or pass through the interior *Syn* penetrate, pierce, probe *Ant* issue from **2** ♦ to cause or permit to go in or get in *Syn* introduce, admit

enterprise *Syn* ADVENTURE, quest

entertain 1 *Syn* HARBOR, shelter, lodge, house, board **2** *Syn* AMUSE, divert, recreate

entertainment *Syn* AMUSEMENT, diversion, recreation

enthuse *Syn* THRILL, electrify

enthusiasm *Syn* PASSION, fervor, ardor, zeal *Ant* apathy

enthusiast ♦ a person who manifests excessive ardor, fervor, or devotion in an attachment to some cause, idea, party, or church *Syn* fanatic, zealot, bigot

entice *Syn* LURE, inveigle, decoy, tempt, seduce *Ant* scare

entire 1 *Syn* WHOLE, total, all, gross *Ant* partial **2** *Syn* PERFECT, whole, intact *Ant* impaired

entity ♦ one that has real and independent existence *Syn* being, creature, individual, person

entrance *n* ♦ the act or fact of going in or coming in *Syn* entry, entrée, ingress, access *Ant* exit

entrance *vb* *Syn* TRANSPORT, ravish, enrapture

entrap ***Syn*** CATCH, trap, snare, ensnare, bag, capture
entreat ***Syn*** BEG, beseech, implore, supplicate, importune, adjure
entrée ***Syn*** ENTRANCE, entry, ingress, access
entrench ***Syn*** TRESPASS, encroach, infringe, invade
entrust ***Syn*** COMMIT, confide, consign, relegate
entry ***Syn*** ENTRANCE, entrée, ingress, access
entwine ***Syn*** WIND, coil, curl, twist, twine, wreathe
enumerate ***Syn*** COUNT, tell, number
enunciate ***Syn*** ARTICULATE, pronounce
envelop **1** ***Syn*** COVER, overspread, wrap, shroud, veil **2** ***Syn*** ENCLOSE, fence, pen, coop, corral, cage, wall
envious ♦ maliciously grudging another's advantages ***Syn*** jealous
environ ***Syn*** SURROUND, encircle, circle, encompass, compass, hem, gird, girdle, ring
environment ***Syn*** BACKGROUND, setting, milieu, backdrop, mise-en-scène
envisage envision ***Syn*** THINK, conceive, imagine, realize, fancy
envoy ***Syn*** AMBASSADOR, legate, minister, nuncio, internuncio, chargé d'affaires
envy ***Syn*** COVET, grudge, begrudge
ephemeral ***Syn*** TRANSIENT, transitory, passing, fugitive, fleeting, evanescent, momentary, short-lived
epicene ***Syn*** BISEXUAL, hermaphroditic, hermaphrodite, androgynous
epicure ♦ one who takes great pleasure in eating and drinking ***Syn*** gourmet, gourmand, glutton, bon vivant, gastronome
epicurean ***Syn*** SENSUOUS, sybaritic, luxurious, sensual, voluptuous ***Ant*** gross
epigram ***Syn*** SAYING, aphorism, apothegm, saw, maxim, adage, proverb, motto
episode **1** ***Syn*** DIGRESSION, divagation, excursus **2** ***Syn*** OCCURRENCE, incident, event, circumstance
epistle ***Syn*** LETTER, missive, note, message, dispatch, report, memorandum
epitome ***Syn*** ABRIDGMENT, conspectus, synopsis, abstract, brief
epoch ***Syn*** PERIOD, era, age, aeon
equable ***Syn*** STEADY, even, constant, uniform ***Ant*** variable, changeable
equal *adj* ***Syn*** SAME, equivalent, very, identical, identic, tantamount ***Ant*** unequal
equal *vb* ***Syn*** MATCH, rival, approach, touch
equanimity ♦ the characteristic quality of one who is self-possessed or not easily disturbed or perturbed ***Syn*** composure, sangfroid, phlegm
equilibrium ***Syn*** BALANCE, equipoise, poise, tension
equip ***Syn*** FURNISH, outfit, appoint, accouter, arm
equipment ♦ items needed for the performance of a task or useful in effecting a given end ***Syn*** apparatus, machinery, paraphernalia, outfit, tackle, gear, matériel
equipoise ***Syn*** BALANCE, equilibrium, poise, tension
equitable ***Syn*** FAIR, just, impartial, unbiased, dispassionate, uncolored, objective ***Ant*** inequitable, unfair
equity ***Syn*** JUSTICE
equivalent ***Syn*** SAME, equal, identical, identic, selfsame, very, tantamount ***Ant*** different
equivocal ***Syn*** OBSCURE, ambiguous, dark, vague, enigmatic, cryptic ***Ant*** unequivocal
equivocate ***Syn*** LIE, prevaricate, palter, fib
equivocation ***Syn*** AMBIGUITY, tergiversation, double entendre
era ***Syn*** PERIOD, age, epoch, aeon
eradicate ***Syn*** EXTERMINATE, uproot, deracinate, extirpate, wipe
erase ♦ to strike, rub, or scrape out something so that it no longer has effect or existence ***Syn*** expunge, cancel, efface, obliterate, blot out, delete
erect ***Syn*** BUILD, construct, frame, raise, rear ***Ant*** raze
eremite ***Syn*** RECLUSE, hermit, anchorite, cenobite
erotic ♦ of, devoted to, affected by, or tending to arouse sexual love or desire

Syn amatory, amorous, amative, aphrodisiac

erratic *Syn* STRANGE, eccentric, odd, queer, singular, peculiar, unique, quaint, outlandish, curious

error ♦ something (as an act, statement, or belief) that departs from what is or is generally held to be acceptable *Syn* mistake, blunder, slip, lapse, faux pas, bull, howler, boner

errorless *Syn* IMPECCABLE, flawless, faultless

ersatz *Syn* ARTIFICIAL, synthetic, factitious

erudite *Syn* LEARNED, scholarly

erudition *Syn* KNOWLEDGE, learning, scholarship, science, information, lore

escape 1 ♦ to run away esp. from something that limits one's freedom or threatens one's well-being *Syn* flee, fly, decamp, abscond **2** ♦ to get away or keep away from what one does not wish to incur, endure, or encounter *Syn* avoid, evade, elude, shun, eschew

eschew 1 *Syn* ESCAPE, shun, elude, avoid, evade *Ant* choose **2** *Syn* FORGO, forbear, abnegate, sacrifice

escort *Syn* ACCOMPANY, conduct, convoy, chaperon, attend

esoteric *Syn* RECONDITE, occult, abstruse

especial *Syn* SPECIAL, specific, particular, individual

espousal *Syn* MARRIAGE, matrimony, nuptial, wedding, wedlock

espouse *Syn* ADOPT, embrace

esprit *Syn* VIGOR, vim, spirit, dash, verve, punch, élan, drive

esprit de corps *Syn* MORALE, discipline

espy *Syn* SEE, descry, behold, perceive, discern, notice, remark, note, observe, survey, view, contemplate

essay *vb Syn* ATTEMPT, endeavor, strive, struggle, try

essay *n* **1** *Syn* ATTEMPT, endeavor, striving, struggle, try **2** ♦ a relatively brief discourse written for others' reading or consideration *Syn* article, paper, theme, composition

essential 1 *Syn* INHERENT, intrinsic, constitutional, ingrained *Ant* accidental **2** ♦ so important as to be indispensable *Syn* fundamental, vital, cardinal **3** *Syn* NEEDFUL, indispensable, requisite, necessary *Ant* nonessential **4** *Syn* ELEMENTAL, basic, elementary, fundamental, primitive, underlying

establish 1 *Syn* SET, settle, fix *Ant* uproot; abrogate **2** *Syn* FOUND, institute, organize, create *Ant* abolish

esteem *n Syn* REGARD, respect, admiration *Ant* abomination; contempt

esteem *vb Syn* REGARD, respect, admire *Ant* abominate

estimate *vb* **1** ♦ to judge a thing with respect to its worth *Syn* appraise, evaluate, value, rate, assess, assay **2** *Syn* CALCULATE, reckon, compute

estimate *n Syn* ESTIMATION

estimation ♦ the act of valuing or appraising *Syn* estimate

estrange ♦ to cause one to break a bond or tie of affection or loyalty *Syn* alienate, disaffect, wean *Ant* reconcile

etch *Syn* CARVE, incise, engrave, chisel, sculpture, sculpt, sculp

eternal *Syn* INFINITE, sempiternal, boundless, illimitable, uncircumscribed *Ant* mortal

ethereal *Syn* AIRY, aerial *Ant* substantial

ethical *Syn* MORAL, righteous, virtuous, noble *Ant* unethical

etiolate *Syn* WHITEN, decolorize, blanch, bleach

etiquette *Syn* DECORUM, propriety, decency, dignity

eulogize *Syn* PRAISE, extol, acclaim, laud *Ant* calumniate, vilify

eulogy *Syn* ENCOMIUM, panegyric, tribute, citation *Ant* calumny; tirade

euphuistic *Syn* RHETORICAL, flowery, aureate, grandiloquent, magniloquent, bombastic

evade *Syn* ESCAPE, elude, avoid, shun, eschew

evaluate *Syn* ESTIMATE, appraise, value, rate, assess, assay

evanesce *Syn* VANISH, evaporate, disappear, fade

evanescent *Syn* TRANSIENT, ephemeral, passing, fugitive, fleeting, transitory, momentary, short-lived

evaporate *Syn* VANISH, evanesce, disappear, fade

even 1 *Syn* LEVEL, smooth, flat, plane, plain, flush *Ant* uneven **2** *Syn* STEADY, uniform, equable, constant

event 1 *Syn* OCCURRENCE, incident, episode, circumstance **2** *Syn* EFFECT, result, consequence, upshot, aftereffect, aftermath, sequel, issue, outcome

eventual *Syn* LAST, ultimate, concluding, terminal, final, latest

everlasting ♦ continuing on and on without end *Syn* endless, interminable, unceasing *Ant* transitory

every *Syn* ALL, each

evict *Syn* EJECT, oust, expel, dismiss

evidence *Syn* SHOW, evince, manifest, demonstrate

evident ♦ readily perceived or apprehended *Syn* manifest, patent, distinct, obvious, apparent, palpable, plain, clear

evil *adj* *Syn* BAD, ill, wicked, naughty *Ant* exemplary; salutary

evil *n* ♦ whatever is harmful or disastrous to morals or well-being *Syn* ill *Ant* good

evince *Syn* SHOW, manifest, evidence, demonstrate

evoke *Syn* EDUCE, elicit, extract, extort

evolution *Syn* DEVELOPMENT

evolve *Syn* UNFOLD, develop, elaborate, perfect

exact *vb* *Syn* DEMAND, require, claim

exact *adj* *Syn* CORRECT, accurate, right, precise, nice

exacting *Syn* ONEROUS, burdensome, oppressive *Ant* easy; lenient

exaggeration ♦ an overstepping of the bounds of truth, especially in describing the goodness or badness or the greatness or the smallness of something *Syn* overstatement, hyperbole

exalt ♦ to increase in importance or in prestige *Syn* magnify, aggrandize *Ant* abase

examination *Syn* SCRUTINY, inspection, scanning, audit

examine 1 *Syn* SCRUTINIZE, inspect, scan, audit **2** *Syn* ASK, question, interrogate, quiz, catechize, query, inquire

example 1 *Syn* INSTANCE, sample, specimen, case, illustration **2** *Syn* MODEL, exemplar, pattern, ideal, standard, beau ideal, mirror

exasperate *Syn* IRRITATE, provoke, nettle, aggravate, rile, peeve *Ant* mollify

excavate *Syn* DIG, delve, spade, grub

exceed ♦ to go or to be beyond a stated or implied limit, measure, or degree *Syn* surpass, transcend, excel, outdo, outstrip

excel *Syn* EXCEED, surpass, transcend, outdo, outstrip

excellence ♦ the quality of especial worth or value *Syn* merit, virtue, perfection *Ant* fault

exceptionable *Syn* OBJECTIONABLE, unacceptable, undesirable, unwanted, unwelcome *Ant* unexceptionable; exemplary

exceptional ♦ being out of the ordinary *Syn* extraordinary, phenomenal, unusual, unwonted *Ant* common; average

excerpt *Syn* EXTRACT

excess ♦ whatever exceeds a limit, measure, bound, or usual degree *Syn* superfluity, surplus, surplusage, overplus *Ant* deficiency; dearth, paucity

excessive ♦ going beyond a normal or acceptable limit *Syn* immoderate, inordinate, extravagant, exorbitant, extreme *Ant* deficient

exchange ♦ to give and receive reciprocally *Syn* interchange, bandy

excitant *Syn* STIMULUS, stimulant, incitement, impetus

excite *Syn* PROVOKE, stimulate, pique, quicken, galvanize *Ant* soothe, quiet; allay (*fears, anxiety*)

exclude ♦ to prevent the participation, consideration, or inclusion of *Syn* debar, blackball, eliminate, rule out, shut out, disbar, suspend *Ant* admit; include

exclusive *Syn* SELECT, elect, picked *Ant* inclusive

excogitate *Syn* CONSIDER, weigh, study, contemplate

excoriate *Syn* ABRADE, chafe, fret, gall

excruciating ♦ intensely or unbearably painful *Syn* agonizing, racking

exculpate ♦ to free from alleged fault or guilt *Syn* absolve, exonerate, acquit, vindicate *Ant* inculpate; accuse

excursion *Syn* JOURNEY, trip, jaunt, tour, cruise, voyage, expedition, pilgrimage

excursus *Syn* DIGRESSION, divagation, episode

excuse *vb* ♦ to exact neither punishment nor redress for or from *Syn* condone, pardon, forgive, remit *Ant* punish

excuse *n* *Syn* APOLOGY, plea, pretext, apologia, alibi

execrable ♦ so odious as to be utterly detestable *Syn* damnable, accursed, cursed

execrate ♦ to denounce violently *Syn* curse, damn, anathematize, objurgate

execute 1 *Syn* PERFORM, effect, fulfill, discharge, accomplish, achieve **2** *Syn* KILL, dispatch, slay, murder, assassinate

exemplar *Syn* MODEL, pattern, ideal, beau ideal, example, mirror, standard

exemplify ♦ to use examples or show instances of in order to clarify *Syn* illustrate

exemption ♦ freeing or the state of being free or freed from a charge or obligation to which others are subject *Syn* immunity

exercise *n* ♦ repeated activity or exertion *Syn* practice, drill

exercise *vb* *Syn* PRACTICE, drill

exertion *Syn* EFFORT, pains, trouble

exhaust 1 *Syn* DEPLETE, drain, impoverish, bankrupt **2** *Syn* TIRE, fatigue, jade, weary, fag, tucker

exhibit *vb* *Syn* SHOW, display, expose, parade, flaunt

exhibit *n* *Syn* EXHIBITION, show, exposition, fair

exhibition ♦ a public display of objects of interest *Syn* show, exhibit, exposition, fair

exhort *Syn* URGE, egg, goad, spur, prod, prick, sic

exigency 1 *Syn* JUNCTURE, pass, emergency, pinch, strait, crisis, contingency **2** *Syn* NEED, necessity

exigent *Syn* PRESSING, urgent, imperative, crying, importunate, insistent, instant

exiguous *Syn* MEAGER, scant, scanty, skimpy, scrimpy, spare, sparse *Ant* capacious, ample

exile *Syn* BANISH, expatriate, ostracize, deport, transport, extradite

exist *Syn* BE, live, subsist

existence ♦ the state or fact of having independent reality *Syn* being, actuality *Ant* nonexistence

exonerate *Syn* EXCULPATE, acquit, vindicate, absolve *Ant* charge

exorbitant *Syn* EXCESSIVE, inordinate, extravagant, immoderate, extreme *Ant* just

exordium *Syn* INTRODUCTION, preamble, preface, foreword, prologue, prelude

expand ♦ to increase or become increased in size, bulk, or volume *Syn* amplify, swell, distend, inflate, dilate *Ant* contract; abridge; circumscribe

expanse ♦ a significantly large area or range *Syn* amplitude, spread, stretch

expansive *Syn* ELASTIC, resilient, buoyant, volatile, effervescent *Ant* tense; reserved

expatiate *Syn* DISCOURSE, descant, dilate

expatriate *Syn* BANISH, exile, ostracize, deport, transport, extradite *Ant* repatriate

expect ♦ to anticipate in the mind *Syn* hope, look, await *Ant* despair of

expedient *adj* ♦ dictated by practical wisdom or by motives of prudence *Syn* politic, advisable *Ant* inexpedient

expedient *n* *Syn* RESOURCE, resort, shift, makeshift, stopgap, substitute, surrogate

expedition 1 *Syn* HASTE, dispatch, speed, hurry *Ant* procrastination **2** *Syn* JOURNEY, voyage, tour, trip, jaunt, excursion, cruise, pilgrimage

expeditious *Syn* FAST, speedy, swift, rapid, fleet, quick, hasty *Ant* sluggish

expel *Syn* EJECT, oust, dismiss, evict *Ant* admit

expend *Syn* SPEND, disburse

expense *Syn* PRICE, cost, charge

expensive *Syn* COSTLY, dear, valuable, precious, invaluable, priceless *Ant* inexpensive

experience ♦ to pass through the process of actually coming to know or to feel **Syn** undergo, sustain, suffer

expert *adj* **Syn** PROFICIENT, adept, skilled, skillful, masterly **Ant** amateurish

expert *n* ♦ one who shows mastery in a subject, an art, or a profession or who reveals extraordinary skill in execution, performance, or technique **Syn** adept, artist, artiste, virtuoso, wizard **Ant** amateur

expiate ♦ to make amends or give satisfaction for wrong done **Syn** atone

expiation ♦ the making of amends or the giving of satisfaction for wrongs done **Syn** atonement

expire **Syn** PASS, pass away, elapse

explain 1 ♦ to make the meaning of something understood or more comprehensible **Syn** expound, explicate, elucidate, interpret, construe **2** ♦ to give the reason for or cause of **Syn** account, justify, rationalize

explicate **Syn** EXPLAIN, expound, elucidate, interpret, construe

explicit ♦ characterized by full precise expression and meaning that is perfectly clear **Syn** express, specific, definite, categorical **Ant** ambiguous

exploit **Syn** FEAT, achievement

expose **Syn** SHOW, display, exhibit, parade, flaunt

exposé **Syn** EXPOSITION, exposure

exposed **Syn** LIABLE, open, subject, prone, susceptible, sensitive

exposition 1 **Syn** EXHIBITION, fair, exhibit, show **2** ♦ a setting forth or laying open of a thing or things hitherto not known or fully understood **Syn** exposure, exposé

expostulate **Syn** OBJECT, remonstrate, protest, kick

exposure **Syn** EXPOSITION, exposé **Ant** cover; covering

expound **Syn** EXPLAIN, explicate, elucidate, interpret, construe

express *adj* **Syn** EXPLICIT, definite, specific, categorical

express *vb* ♦ to let out what one feels or thinks **Syn** vent, utter, voice, broach, air, ventilate **Ant** imply

expression **Syn** PHRASE, locution, idiom

expressive ♦ clearly conveying or manifesting a thought, idea, or feeling or a combination of these **Syn** eloquent, significant, meaningful, pregnant, sententious

expunge **Syn** ERASE, cancel, efface, obliterate, blot out, delete

exquisite *adj* **1** **Syn** CHOICE, recherché, rare, dainty, delicate, elegant **2** **Syn** INTENSE, vehement, fierce, violent

exquisite *n* **Syn** FOP, coxcomb, beau, dandy, dude, buck

extemporaneous ♦ composed, devised, or done at the moment rather than beforehand **Syn** extempore, extempory, improvised, impromptu, offhand, unpremeditated

extempory, extempore **Syn** EXTEMPORANEOUS, improvised, impromptu, offhand, unpremeditated

extend ♦ to make or become longer **Syn** lengthen, elongate, prolong, protract **Ant** abridge, shorten

extension **Syn** ANNEX, wing, ell

extent **Syn** SIZE, dimensions, area, magnitude, volume

extenuate **Syn** THIN, attenuate, dilute, rarefy **Ant** intensify **2** **Syn** PALLIATE, gloze, gloss, whitewash, whiten

exterior **Syn** OUTER, external, outward, outside **Ant** interior

exterminate ♦ to destroy utterly **Syn** extirpate, eradicate, uproot, deracinate, wipe

external **Syn** OUTER, exterior, outward, outside **Ant** internal

externalize **Syn** REALIZE, materialize, actualize, embody, incarnate, objectify, hypostatize, reify

extinguish 1 **Syn** CRUSH, quell, suppress, quench, quash **Ant** inflame **2** **Syn** ABOLISH, annihilate, abate

extirpate **Syn** EXTERMINATE, eradicate, uproot, deracinate, wipe out

extol **Syn** PRAISE, laud, eulogize, acclaim **Ant** decry; abase (*oneself*)

extort **Syn** EDUCE, extract, elicit, evoke

extra **Syn** SUPERFLUOUS, supernumerary, spare, surplus

extract *vb* **Syn** EDUCE, extort, elicit, evoke

extract *n* ♦ a passage transcribed or quoted from a book or document *Syn* excerpt

extradite *Syn* BANISH, deport, transport, expatriate, exile, ostracize

extraneous *Syn* EXTRINSIC, foreign, alien *Ant* relevant

extraordinary *Syn* EXCEPTIONAL, phenomenal, unusual, unwonted

extravagant *Syn* EXCESSIVE, inordinate, immoderate, exorbitant, extreme *Ant* restrained

extreme *adj Syn* EXCESSIVE, exorbitant, inordinate, immoderate, extravagant

extreme *n* ♦ the utmost limit or degree of something *Syn* extremity

extremity *Syn* EXTREME

extricate ♦ to free or release from what binds or holds back *Syn* disentangle, untangle, disencumber, disembarrass

extrinsic ♦ external to a thing, its essential nature, or its original character *Syn* extraneous, foreign, alien *Ant* intrinsic

exuberant *Syn* PROFUSE, lavish, prodigal, luxuriant, lush *Ant* austere; sterile

eyewitness *Syn* SPECTATOR, witness, onlooker, looker-on, observer, beholder, bystander, kibitzer

F

fable 1 *Syn* FICTION, fabrication, figment **2** *Syn* ALLEGORY, myth, parable

fabricate *Syn* MAKE, fashion, forge, form, shape, manufacture

fabrication *Syn* FICTION, figment, fable

fabulous *Syn* FICTITIOUS, mythical, legendary, apocryphal

face *n* ♦ the front part of a human or, sometimes, animal head including the mouth, nose, eyes, forehead, and cheeks *Syn* countenance, visage, physiognomy, mug, puss

face *vb* **1** *Syn* MEET, encounter, confront **2** ♦ to confront with courage or boldness *Syn* brave, challenge, dare, defy, beard *Ant* avoid

facet *Syn* PHASE, aspect, side, angle

facetious *Syn* WITTY, humorous, jocose, jocular *Ant* lugubrious

facile *Syn* EASY, smooth, light, simple, effortless *Ant* arduous; constrained, clumsy

facility *Syn* READINESS, ease, dexterity

facsimile *Syn* REPRODUCTION, copy, carbon copy, duplicate, replica, transcript

faction *Syn* COMBINATION, bloc, party, combine, ring

factious *Syn* INSUBORDINATE, contumacious, seditious, mutinous, rebellious *Ant* cooperative

factitious *Syn* ARTIFICIAL, synthetic, ersatz *Ant* bona fide, veritable

factor 1 *Syn* AGENT, attorney, deputy, proxy **2** *Syn* ELEMENT, constituent, component, ingredient

faculty 1 *Syn* POWER, function **2** *Syn* GIFT, aptitude, knack, bent, turn, genius, talent

fad *Syn* FASHION, vogue, style, rage, craze, mode, dernier cri, cry

fade *Syn* VANISH, evanesce, evaporate, disappear

faded *Syn* SHABBY, dilapidated, dingy, seedy, threadbare

fag *Syn* TIRE, exhaust, jade, fatigue, weary, tucker

failing *Syn* FAULT, frailty, foible, vice *Ant* perfection

failure ♦ an omission on the part of someone or something of what is expected or required *Syn* neglect, default, miscarriage, dereliction

faineant *Syn* LAZY, indolent, slothful

fair *adj* **1** *Syn* BEAUTIFUL, comely, lovely, pretty, bonny, handsome, beauteous, pulchritudinous, good-looking *Ant* foul; ill-favored **2** ♦ characterized by honesty, justice, and freedom from improper influence *Syn* just, equitable, impartial, unbiased, dispassionate, uncolored, objective *Ant* unfair **3** *Syn* MEDIUM, average, middling, mediocre, second-rate, moderate, indifferent

fair *n Syn* EXHIBITION, exposition, show, exhibit

faith 1 *Syn* BELIEF, credence, credit *Ant* doubt **2** *Syn* TRUST, dependence, reliance, confidence **3** *Syn* RELIGION, creed, persuasion, church, denomination, sect, cult, communion

faithful ♦ firm in adherence to whatever one is bound to by duty or promise *Syn* loyal, true, constant, staunch, steadfast, resolute *Ant* faithless

faithless ♦ not true to allegiance or duty *Syn* false, disloyal, traitorous, treacherous, perfidious *Ant* faithful

fake *n Syn* IMPOSTURE, sham, humbug, counterfeit, cheat, fraud, deceit, deception

fake *adj Syn* COUNTERFEIT, spurious, bogus, sham, pseudo, pinchbeck, phony

faker *Syn* IMPOSTOR, mountebank, charlatan, quack

fall ♦ to go or to let go downward freely *Syn* drop, sink, slump, subside *Ant* rise

fallacious ♦ contrary to or devoid of logic *Syn* sophistical, casuistical *Ant* sound, valid

fallacy ♦ unsound and misleading reasoning or line of argument *Syn* sophism, sophistry, casuistry

false 1 ♦ not in conformity with what is true or right *Syn* wrong *Ant* true **2** *Syn* FAITHLESS, perfidious, disloyal, traitorous, treacherous *Ant* true

falsehood *Syn* LIE, untruth, fib, misrepresentation, story *Ant* truth

falsify *Syn* MISREPRESENT, belie, garble

falter *Syn* HESITATE, waver, vacillate

fame ♦ the state of being widely known for one's deeds *Syn* renown, honor, glory, celebrity, reputation, repute, notoriety, éclat *Ant* infamy; obscurity

famed *Syn* FAMOUS, renowned, celebrated, eminent, illustrious *Ant* obscure

familiar 1 ♦ near to one another because of frequent association or shared interests *Syn* intimate, close, confidential, chummy, thick *Ant* aloof **2** *Syn* COMMON, ordinary, popular, vulgar *Ant* unfamiliar; strange

famous ♦ widely known and honored for achievement *Syn* famed, renowned, celebrated, eminent, illustrious *Ant* obscure

fanatic *Syn* ENTHUSIAST, bigot, zealot

fanciful *Syn* IMAGINARY, visionary, fantastic, chimerical, quixotic *Ant* realistic

fancy *n* **1** *Syn* CAPRICE, freak, whim, whimsy, conceit, vagary, crotchet **2** *Syn* IMAGINATION, fantasy *Ant* experience **3** ♦ a vivid idea or image present in the mind but having no concrete or objective reality *Syn* fantasy, phantasy, phantasm, vision, dream, daydream, nightmare *Ant* reality

fancy *vb* **1** *Syn* LIKE, dote, love, enjoy, relish **2** *Syn* THINK, imagine, conceive, envisage, envision, realize

fantastic 1 *Syn* IMAGINARY, chimerical, visionary, fanciful, quixotic **2** ♦ conceived or made without reference to reality *Syn* bizarre, grotesque, antic

fantasy 1 *Syn* IMAGINATION, fancy **2** *Syn* FANCY, phantasy, phantasm, vision, dream, daydream, nightmare

far faraway, far-off *Syn* DISTANT, remote, removed *Ant* near, nigh, nearly

farcical *Syn* LAUGHABLE, comical, comic, ludicrous, ridiculous, risible, droll, funny

farfetched *Syn* FORCED, labored, strained

farming *Syn* AGRICULTURE, husbandry

farther ♦ at or to a greater distance or more avanced point *Syn* further, beyond

fascinate *Syn* ATTRACT, charm, bewitch, enchant, captivate, allure

fascinating *Syn* ATTRACTIVE, charming, bewitching, enchanting, captivating, alluring

fashion *n* **1** *Syn* METHOD, manner, way, mode, system **2** ♦ the prevailing or accepted custom *Syn* style, mode, vogue, fad, rage, craze, dernier cri, cry

fashion *vb Syn* MAKE, form, shape, fabricate, manufacture, forge

fashionable *Syn* STYLISH, modish, smart, chic, dashing *Ant* unfashionable; old-fashioned

fast ♦ moving, proceeding, or acting with great celerity *Syn* rapid, swift, fleet, quick, speedy, hasty, expeditious *Ant* slow

fasten ♦ to cause one thing to hold to another *Syn* fix, attach, affix *Ant* unfasten; loosen, loose

fastidious *Syn* NICE, finicky, finicking, finical, particular, fussy, dainty, squeamish, persnickety, pernickety

fastness *Syn* FORT, stronghold, fortress, citadel

fat *Syn* FLESHY, stout, portly, plump, corpulent, obese, rotund, chubby *Ant* lean

fatal *Syn* DEADLY, mortal, lethal

fate ♦ whatever is destined or inevitably decreed for one *Syn* destiny, lot, portion, doom

fateful *Syn* OMINOUS, portentous, inauspicious, unpropitious

fathom ♦ to measure depth typically with a weighted line *Syn* sound, plumb

fatigue *Syn* TIRE, exhaust, jade, weary, fag, tucker *Ant* rest

fatuous *Syn* SIMPLE, asinine, silly, foolish *Ant* sensible

fault 1 *Syn* IMPERFECTION, deficiency, shortcoming *Ant* excellence **2** ♦ an imperfection in character or an ingrained moral weakness *Syn* failing, frailty, foible, vice *Ant* merit **3** *Syn* BLAME, culpability, guilt

faultfinding *Syn* CRITICAL, captious, caviling, carping, censorious, hypercritical

faultless *Syn* IMPECCABLE, flawless, errorless *Ant* faulty

faux pas *Syn* ERROR, blunder, slip, mistake, lapse, bull, howler, boner

favor *n Syn* GIFT, boon, largess, present, gratuity

favor *vb* **1** ♦ to give the support of one's approval to *Syn* countenance, encourage *Ant* disapprove **2** *Syn* OBLIGE, accommodate

favorable ♦ being of good omen or presaging a happy or successful outcome *Syn* benign, auspicious, propitious *Ant* unfavorable; antagonistic

favorite *Syn* PARASITE, sycophant, toady, lickspittle, bootlicker, hanger-on, leech, sponge, sponger

fawn ♦ to behave abjectly before a superior *Syn* toady, truckle, cringe, cower *Ant* domineer

faze *Syn* EMBARRASS, disconcert, discomfit, rattle, abash

fealty *Syn* FIDELITY, loyalty, devotion, allegiance, piety *Ant* perfidy

fear 1 ♦ agitation or dismay which overcomes one in the anticipation or in the presence of danger *Syn* dread, fright, alarm, dismay, consternation, panic, terror, horror, trepidation *Ant* fearlessness **2** *Syn* REVERENCE, awe *Ant* contempt

fearful 1 ♦ inspired or moved by fear *Syn* apprehensive, afraid *Ant* fearless; intrepid **2** ♦ causing fear *Syn* awful, dreadful, frightful, terrible, terrific, horrible, horrific, shocking, appalling

fearless *Syn* BRAVE, unafraid, dauntless, undaunted, bold, intrepid, audacious, courageous, valiant, valorous, doughty *Ant* fearful

feasible *Syn* POSSIBLE, practicable *Ant* unfeasible, infeasible; chimerical

feast *Syn* DINNER, banquet

feat ♦ a remarkable deed or performance *Syn* exploit, achievement

feature *Syn* CHARACTERISTIC, trait

fecund *Syn* FERTILE, fruitful, prolific *Ant* barren

fecundity *Syn* FERTILITY, fruitfulness, prolificacy *Ant* barrenness

federation *Syn* ALLIANCE, confederacy, confederation, coalition, fusion

fee *Syn* WAGE, stipend, emolument, salary, wages, pay, hire

feeble *Syn* WEAK, infirm, decrepit, frail, fragile *Ant* robust

feed *vb* ♦ to provide the food that one needs or desires *Syn* nourish, pasture, graze *Ant* starve

feed *n Syn* FOOD, fodder, forage, provender, victuals, viands, provisions, comestibles

feel *vb Syn* TOUCH, palpate, handle, paw

feel *n Syn* ATMOSPHERE, feeling, aura

feeling 1 *Syn* SENSATION, sensibility, sense **2** ♦ subjective response or reaction *Syn* affection, emotion, sentiment, passion **3** *Syn* ATMOSPHERE, feel, aura

feign *Syn* ASSUME, simulate, counterfeit, sham, pretend, affect

feint *Syn* TRICK, artifice, wile, ruse, gambit, ploy, stratagem, maneuver

felicitate ♦ to express one's pleasure in the joy, success, elevation, or prospects of another *Syn* congratulate

felicitous *Syn* FIT, happy, apt, fitting, appropriate, suitable, meet, proper *Ant* infelicitous; inept, maladroit

felicity *Syn* HAPPINESS, bliss, beatitude, blessedness *Ant* misery

fell *Syn* FIERCE, cruel, inhuman, savage, barbarous, ferocious, truculent

felon *Syn* CRIMINAL, convict, malefactor, culprit, delinquent

female *n* ♦ a person and esp. an adult who belongs to the sex that is the counterpart of the male sex *Syn* woman, lady

female *adj* ♦ of, characteristic of, or like a female esp. of the human species *Syn* feminine, womanly, womanlike, womanish, ladylike *Ant* male

feminine *Syn* FEMALE, womanly, womanish, ladylike, womanlike *Ant* masculine

fence 1 *Syn* ENCLOSE, envelop, pen, coop, corral, cage, wall **2** *Syn* DODGE, parry, sidestep, duck, shirk, malinger

feral *Syn* BRUTAL, brute, brutish, bestial, beastly

ferocious *Syn* FIERCE, truculent, barbarous, savage, inhuman, cruel, fell

ferret out *Syn* SEEK, search, scour, hunt, comb, ransack, rummage

fertile ♦ marked by abundant productivity *Syn* fecund, fruitful, prolific *Ant* infertile, sterile

fertility ♦ the quality or state of being fertile *Syn* fruitfulness, fecundity, prolificacy *Ant* infertility, sterility

fervent *Syn* IMPASSIONED, ardent, fervid, perfervid, passionate

fervid *Syn* IMPASSIONED, fervent, ardent, perfervid, passionate

fervor *Syn* PASSION, ardor, enthusiasm, zeal

fetch *Syn* BRING, take

fetid *Syn* MALODOROUS, noisome, stinking, putrid, rank, rancid, fusty, musty *Ant* fragrant

fetish ♦ an object believed to be endowed with the virtue of averting evil or of bringing good fortune *Syn* talisman, charm, amulet

fetter *Syn* HAMPER, shackle, trammel, clog, manacle, hog-tie

fib *n* *Syn* LIE, untruth, falsehood, misrepresentation, story

fib *vb* *Syn* LIE, equivocate, palter, prevaricate

fickle *Syn* INCONSTANT, unstable, capricious, mercurial *Ant* constant, true

fiction ♦ a story, account, explanation, or conception which is an invention of the human mind *Syn* figment, fabrication, fable

fictitious ♦ having the character of something invented or imagined as opposed to something true or genuine *Syn* fabulous, legendary, mythical, apocryphal *Ant* historical

fidelity ♦ faithfulness to something to which one is bound by a pledge or duty *Syn* allegiance, fealty, loyalty, devotion, piety *Ant* faithlessness; perfidy

fidgety *Syn* IMPATIENT, restless, restive, uneasy, jumpy, jittery, nervous, unquiet

field ♦ a limited area of knowledge or endeavor to which pursuits, activities, and interests are confined *Syn* domain, province, sphere, territory, bailiwick

fiendish ♦ having or manifesting qualities associated with devils, demons, and fiends *Syn* devilish, diabolical, diabolic, demoniac, demonic

fierce 1 ♦ displaying fury or malignity in looks or actions *Syn* truculent, ferocious, barbarous, savage, inhuman, cruel, fell *Ant* tame; mild **2** *Syn* INTENSE, vehement, exquisite, violent

fiery *Syn* SPIRITED, high-spirited, peppery, gingery, mettlesome, spunky

fight *vb* **1** *Syn* CONTEND, battle, war **2** *Syn* RESIST, withstand, contest, oppose, combat, conflict, antagonize

fight *n* *Syn* CONTEST, combat, fray, affray, conflict

figment *Syn* FICTION, fabrication, fable

figure *n* **1** *Syn* NUMBER, numeral, digit, integer **2** *Syn* FORM, shape, configuration, conformation **3** ♦ a unit in a decorative composition (as in fabric) *Syn* pattern, design, motif, device

figure *vb* **Syn** ADD, cast, sum, total, tot, foot

filch **Syn** STEAL, purloin, lift, pilfer, pinch, snitch, swipe, cop

file **Syn** LINE, row, rank, echelon, tier

fillet **Syn** STRIP, band, ribbon, stripe

filthy **Syn** DIRTY, foul, squalid, nasty **Ant** neat, spick-and-span

final **Syn** LAST, terminal, concluding, latest, ultimate, eventual

financial ♦ of or relating to the possession, making, borrowing, lending, or expenditure of money **Syn** monetary, pecuniary, fiscal

fine *n* ♦ a pecuniary penalty exacted by an authority **Syn** amercement

fine *vb* **Syn** PENALIZE, amerce, mulct

finicky, finicking, finical **Syn** NICE, particular, fussy, fastidious, dainty, squeamish, persnickety, pernickety

finish **Syn** CLOSE, complete, conclude, end, terminate

finished **Syn** CONSUMMATE, accomplished **Ant** crude

fire *n* ♦ a destructive burning **Syn** conflagration, holocaust

fire *vb* **1** **Syn** LIGHT, kindle, ignite **2** **Syn** INFORM, animate, inspire **Ant** daunt **3** **Syn** DISMISS, discharge, cashier, drop, sack, bounce

firm ♦ having a texture or consistency that resists deformation by external force **Syn** hard, solid **Ant** loose, flabby

fiscal **Syn** FINANCIAL, monetary, pecuniary

fish ♦ to attempt to catch fish **Syn** angle

fissure **Syn** CRACK, cleft, crevasse, crevice, cranny, chink

fit *n* ♦ an episode of bodily or mental disorder or excess **Syn** attack, access, accession, paroxysm, spasm, convulsion

fit *adj* ♦ right with respect to some end, need, use, or circumstances **Syn** suitable, meet, proper, appropriate, fitting, apt, happy, felicitous **Ant** unfit

fit *vb* **Syn** PREPARE, qualify, condition, ready

fitful ♦ lacking steadiness or regularity in course, movement, or succession **Syn** spasmodic, convulsive **Ant** constant

fitting **Syn** FIT, appropriate, proper, meet, suitable, apt, happy, felicitous **Ant** unfitting

fix *vb* **1** **Syn** SET, settle, establish **Ant** alter; abrogate (*a custom, rule, law*) **2** **Syn** FASTEN, attach, affix **3** **Syn** ADJUST, regulate

fix *n* **Syn** PREDICAMENT, plight, dilemma, quandary, scrape, jam, pickle

flabbergast **Syn** SURPRISE, amaze, astound, astonish

flabby **Syn** LIMP, flaccid, floppy, flimsy, sleazy **Ant** firm

flaccid **Syn** LIMP, flabby, floppy, flimsy, sleazy **Ant** resilient

flag *n* ♦ a piece of fabric that is used as a symbol (as of a nation) or as a signaling device **Syn** ensign, standard, banner, color, streamer, pennant, pendant, pennon, jack

flag *vb* **Syn** DROOP, wilt, sag

flagitious **Syn** VICIOUS, nefarious, infamous, iniquitous, villainous, corrupt, degenerate

flagrant ♦ bad or objectionable **Syn** glaring, gross, rank

flair **Syn** LEANING, proclivity, propensity, penchant

flamboyant **Syn** ORNATE, florid, rococo, baroque

flame *n* **Syn** BLAZE, flare, glare, glow

flame *vb* **Syn** BLAZE, flare, glare, glow

flammable **Syn** COMBUSTIBLE, inflammable, incendiary, inflammatory

flare *vb* **Syn** BLAZE, glare, flame, glow **Ant** gutter out

flare *n* **Syn** BLAZE, glare, flame, glow

flash *vb* ♦ to shoot forth light (as in rays or sparks) **Syn** gleam, glance, glint, sparkle, glitter, glisten, scintillate, coruscate, twinkle

flash *n* **Syn** INSTANT, second, moment, minute, jiffy, twinkling, split second

flashy **Syn** GAUDY, garish, tawdry, meretricious

flat **1** **Syn** LEVEL, plane, plain, even, smooth, flush **2** **Syn** INSIPID, vapid, jejune, banal, wishy-washy, inane

flattery **Syn** COMPLIMENT, adulation

flatulent *Syn* INFLATED, tumid, turgid

flaunt *Syn* SHOW, parade, expose, display, exhibit

flavor *Syn* TASTE, savor, tang, relish, smack

flavorsome *Syn* PALATABLE, toothsome, tasty, savory, sapid, relishing, appetizing

flaw *Syn* BLEMISH, defect

flawless *Syn* IMPECCABLE, faultless, errorless

flay *Syn* SKIN, decorticate, peel, pare

fleck *Syn* SPOT, spatter, sprinkle, mottle, stipple, marble, speckle, spangle, bespangle

flecked *Syn* SPOTTED, spattered, sprinkled, mottled, stippled, marbled, speckled, spangled, bespangled

flee *Syn* ESCAPE, fly, decamp, abscond

fleer *Syn* SCOFF, jeer, gibe, gird, sneer, flout

fleet *vb Syn* WHILE, wile, beguile

fleet *adj Syn* FAST, swift, rapid, quick, speedy, hasty, expeditious

fleeting *Syn* TRANSIENT, evanescent, fugitive, passing, transitory, ephemeral, momentary, short-lived *Ant* lasting

fleshly *Syn* CARNAL, sensual, animal

fleshy ♦ thick and heavy in body because of superfluous fat *Syn* fat, stout, portly, plump, rotund, chubby, corpulent, obese *Ant* skinny, scrawny

flex ♦ to bend *Syn* crook, bow, buckle *Ant* extend

flexible *Syn* ELASTIC, supple, resilient, springy *Ant* inflexible

flexuous *Syn* WINDING, sinuous, serpentine, tortuous

flicker *Syn* FLIT, flutter, flitter, hover

flightiness *Syn* LIGHTNESS, lightmindedness, volatility, levity, frivolity, flippancy *Ant* steadiness; steadfastness

flimsy *Syn* LIMP, sleazy, floppy, flaccid, flabby

flinch *Syn* RECOIL, shrink, wince, blench, quail

fling *Syn* THROW, hurl, sling, toss, cast, pitch

flippancy *Syn* LIGHTNESS, levity, light-

mindedness, frivolity, volatility, flightiness *Ant* seriousness

flirt *Syn* TRIFLE, coquet, dally, toy

flit ♦ to move or fly briskly, irregularly, and usu. intermittently *Syn* flutter, flitter, flicker, hover

flitter *Syn* FLIT, flutter, flicker, hover

float *Syn* FLY, skim, sail, dart, scud, shoot

flood 1 *Syn* FLOW, stream, current, tide, flux **2** ♦ a great or overwhelming flow of or as if of water *Syn* deluge, inundation, torrent, spate, cataract

floppy *Syn* LIMP, flabby, flaccid, flimsy, sleazy

florid *Syn* ORNATE, flamboyant, rococo, baroque *Ant* chaste (*in style, decoration*)

flounder *Syn* STUMBLE, trip, blunder, lurch, lumber, galumph, lollop, bumble

flourish 1 *Syn* SUCCEED, prosper, thrive *Ant* languish **2** *Syn* SWING, brandish, shake, wave, thrash

flout *Syn* SCOFF, jeer, gibe, fleer, gird, sneer *Ant* revere

flow *vb Syn* SPRING, issue, emanate, proceed, stem, derive, arise, rise, originate

flow *n* ♦ something suggestive of running water *Syn* stream, current, flood, tide, flux

flower *n Syn* BLOSSOM, bloom, blow

flower *vb Syn* BLOSSOM, bloom, blow

flowery *Syn* RHETORICAL, aureate, grandiloquent, magniloquent, euphuistic, bombastic

fluctuate *Syn* SWING, oscillate, sway, vibrate, pendulate, waver, undulate

fluent *Syn* VOCAL, eloquent, voluble, glib, articulate

fluid *Syn* LIQUID

flurry *n Syn* STIR, bustle, fuss, ado, pother

flurry *vb Syn* DISCOMPOSE, fluster, agitate, perturb, disturb, disquiet

flush *n Syn* BLUSH

flush *vb Syn* BLUSH

flush *adj Syn* LEVEL, even, flat, plane, plain, smooth

fluster *Syn* DISCOMPOSE, upset, agitate, perturb, flurry, disturb, disquiet

flutter *Syn* FLIT, flitter, flicker, hover

flux *Syn* FLOW, current, tide, stream, flood

fly 1 ♦ to pass lightly or quickly over or above a surface *Syn* dart, float, skim, scud, shoot, sail **2** *Syn* ESCAPE, flee, decamp, abscond

flying field *Syn* AIRPORT, airdrome, airfield, airstrip, landing strip, landing field

foam ♦ a mass of bubbles gathering in or on the surface of a liquid or something as insubstantial as such a mass *Syn* froth, spume, scum, lather, suds, yeast

focal *Syn* CENTRAL, pivotal

focus *n* *Syn* CENTER, heart, nucleus, core, middle, midst, hub

focus *vb* *Syn* CENTER, centralize, concentrate

fodder *Syn* FOOD, forage, feed, provender, provisions, comestibles, victuals, viands

foe *Syn* ENEMY *Ant* friend

fog *n* *Syn* HAZE, smog, mist

fog *vb* *Syn* OBSCURE, dim, bedim, darken, eclipse, cloud, becloud, befog, obfuscate

foible *Syn* FAULT, failing, frailty, vice

foil *Syn* FRUSTRATE, thwart, circumvent, balk, baffle, outwit

follow 1 ♦ to come after in time *Syn* succeed, ensue, supervene **2** ♦ to go after or on the trail of *Syn* pursue, chase, trail, tag, tail *Ant* precede; forsake (*a teacher or teachings*)

follower ♦ one who attaches himself to another *Syn* adherent, disciple, sectary, partisan, henchman, satellite *Ant* leader

following ♦ the body of persons who attach themselves to another esp. as disciples, patrons, or admirers *Syn* clientele, public, audience

foment *Syn* INCITE, abet, instigate *Ant* quell

fond 1 ♦ made blindly or stupidly foolish *Syn* infatuated, besotted, insensate **2** *Syn* LOVING, devoted, affectionate, doting

fondle *Syn* CARESS, pet, cosset, cuddle, dandle

food 1 ♦ things that are edible for human beings or animals *Syn* feed, victuals, viands, provisions, comestibles, proven-der, fodder, forage **2** ♦ material which feeds and supports the mind or the spirit *Syn* aliment, pabulum, nutriment, nourishment, sustenance, pap

fool ♦ one regarded as lacking sense or good judgment *Syn* idiot, imbecile, moron, simpleton, natural

foolhardy *Syn* ADVENTUROUS, daring, daredevil, rash, reckless, venturesome *Ant* wary

foolish 1 *Syn* SIMPLE, silly, fatuous, asinine **2** ♦ felt to be ridiculous because not exhibiting good sense *Syn* silly, absurd, preposterous *Ant* sensible

foot *Syn* ADD, figure, cast, sum, total, tot

fop ♦ a man who is conspicuously fashionable or elegant in dress or manners *Syn* dandy, beau, coxcomb, exquisite, dude, buck

for *Syn* BECAUSE, since, as, inasmuch as

forage *Syn* FOOD, fodder, provender, feed, provisions, comestibles, victuals, viands

forbear 1 *Syn* FORGO, abnegate, eschew, sacrifice **2** *Syn* REFRAIN, abstain

forbearance 1 *Syn* PATIENCE, long-suffering, longanimity, resignation **2** ♦ a disinclination to be severe or rigorous *Syn* tolerance, clemency, mercifulness, leniency, indulgence *Ant* vindictiveness; anger

forbearing ♦ disinclined by nature, disposition, or circumstances to be severe or rigorous *Syn* tolerant, clement, merciful, lenient, indulgent *Ant* unrelenting

forbearingly ♦ in a forbearing manner *Syn* tolerantly, clemently, mercifully, leniently, indulgently

forbid ♦ to debar one from using, doing, or entering or something from being used, done, or entered *Syn* prohibit, enjoin, interdict, inhibit, ban *Ant* permit; bid

force *n* **1** *Syn* POWER, energy, strength, might, puissance **2** ♦ the exercise of power in order to impose one's will on a person or to have one's will with a thing *Syn* violence, compulsion, coercion, duress, constraint, restraint

force *vb* ♦ to cause a person or thing to

yield to pressure *Syn* compel, coerce, constrain, oblige

forced ♦ produced or kept up through effort *Syn* labored, strained, farfetched

forceful *Syn* POWERFUL, potent, forcible, puissant *Ant* feeble

forcible *Syn* POWERFUL, forceful, potent, puissant

forebear *Syn* ANCESTOR, forefather, progenitor

forebode *Syn* FORETELL, portend, presage, augur, prognosticate, predict, forecast, prophesy

foreboding *Syn* APPREHENSION, misgiving, presentiment

forecast *Syn* FORETELL, predict, prophesy, prognosticate, augur, presage, portend, forebode

forefather *Syn* ANCESTOR, forebear, progenitor

foregoing *Syn* PRECEDING, antecedent, precedent, previous, prior, former, anterior *Ant* following

foreign *Syn* EXTRINSIC, alien, extraneous *Ant* germane

foreigner *Syn* STRANGER, alien, outlander, outsider, immigrant, émigré

foreknow *Syn* FORESEE, divine, anticipate, apprehend

foremost *Syn* CHIEF, leading, principal, main, capital

forensic *Syn* ARGUMENTATION, debate, disputation, dialectic

forerunner ♦ one that goes before or in some way announces the coming of another *Syn* precursor, harbinger, herald

foresee ♦ to know or expect in advance that something will happen or come into existence or be made manifest *Syn* foreknow, divine, apprehend, anticipate

foreshore *Syn* SHORE, beach, strand, coast, littoral

foresight *Syn* PRUDENCE, forethought, providence, discretion *Ant* hindsight

foresighted *Syn* PRUDENT, forethoughtful, provident, discreet *Ant* hindsighted

forestall *Syn* PREVENT, anticipate

foretaste *Syn* PROSPECT, anticipation, outlook

foretell ♦ to tell something before it happens through special knowledge or occult power *Syn* predict, forecast, prophesy, prognosticate, augur, presage, portend, forebode

forethought *Syn* PRUDENCE, foresight, providence, discretion

forethoughtful *Syn* PRUDENT, foresighted, provident, discreet

foretoken ♦ something that serves as a sign of future happenings *Syn* presage, prognostic, omen, augury, portent

forewarn *Syn* WARN, caution

foreword *Syn* INTRODUCTION, preface, exordium, prologue, prelude, preamble

forge *Syn* MAKE, fabricate, fashion, manufacture, form, shape

forget *Syn* NEGLECT, overlook, ignore, disregard, omit, slight *Ant* remember

forgetful ♦ losing or letting go from one's mind something once known or learned *Syn* oblivious, unmindful

forgive *Syn* EXCUSE, pardon, remit, condone

forgo ♦ to deny oneself something for the sake of an end *Syn* forbear, abnegate, eschew, sacrifice

forlorn 1 *Syn* ALONE, lorn, lone, desolate, lonesome, lonely, solitary **2** *Syn* DESPONDENT, hopeless, despairing, desperate

forlornness *Syn* DESPONDENCY, hopelessness, despair, desperation

form *n* **1** ♦ outward appearance of something as distinguished from the substance of which it is made *Syn* figure, shape, conformation, configuration **2** ♦ conduct regulated by an external control (as custom or a formal protocol of procedure) *Syn* formality, ceremony, ceremonial, rite, ritual, liturgy **3** ♦ a fixed or accepted way of doing or sometimes of expressing something *Syn* usage, convention, convenance

form *vb Syn* MAKE, shape, fashion, fabricate, manufacture, forge

formal *Syn* CEREMONIAL, conventional, ceremonious, solemn *Ant* informal

formality *Syn* FORM, ceremony, ceremonial, rite, liturgy, ritual

former *Syn* PRECEDING, prior, previous, antecedent, precedent, foregoing, anterior *Ant* latter

formless ♦ having no definite or recognizable form *Syn* unformed, shapeless

forsake *Syn* ABANDON, desert *Ant* return to; revert to

forswear 1 *Syn* ABJURE, renounce, recant, retract **2** *Syn* PERJURE

fort ♦ a structure or place offering resistance to a hostile force *Syn* fortress, citadel, stronghold, fastness

forth *Syn* ONWARD, forward

forthright *Syn* STRAIGHTFORWARD, aboveboard *Ant* furtive

fortify *Syn* STRENGTHEN, invigorate, energize, reinforce *Ant* enfeeble

fortitude ♦ a quality of character combining courage and staying power *Syn* grit, backbone, pluck, guts, sand *Ant* pusillanimity

fortress *Syn* FORT, citadel, stronghold, fastness

fortuitous *Syn* ACCIDENTAL, contingent, casual, incidental

fortunate *Syn* LUCKY, providential, happy *Ant* unfortunate; disastrous

fortune *Syn* CHANCE, accident, luck, hap, hazard

forward *adj Syn* PREMATURE, advanced, untimely, precocious *Ant* backward

forward *adv* **1** *Syn* BEFORE, ahead *Ant* backward **2** *Syn* ONWARD, forth *Ant* backward

forward *vb* **1** *Syn* ADVANCE, promote, further *Ant* hinder; balk **2** *Syn* SEND, dispatch, transmit, remit, route, ship

foster *Syn* NURSE, nurture, cherish, cultivate

foul *adj Syn* DIRTY, filthy, nasty, squalid *Ant* fair; undefiled

foul *vb Syn* SOIL, dirty, sully, tarnish, befoul, smirch, besmirch, grime, begrime

found 1 *Syn* BASE, ground, bottom, stay, rest **2** ♦ to set going or to bring into existence *Syn* establish, institute, organize, create

foundation *Syn* BASE, basis, ground, groundwork *Ant* superstructure

foxy *Syn* SLY, insidious, wily, guileful, tricky, crafty, cunning, artful

fracas *Syn* BRAWL, broil, melee, row, rumpus, scrap

fraction *Syn* PART, fragment, piece, portion, section, segment, sector, detail, member, division, parcel

fractious *Syn* IRRITABLE, peevish, snappish, waspish, petulant, pettish, huffy, fretful, querulous

fragile 1 ♦ easily broken *Syn* frangible, brittle, crisp, short, friable *Ant* tough **2** *Syn* WEAK, frail, feeble, decrepit, infirm *Ant* durable

fragment *Syn* PART, fraction, piece, portion, section, segment, sector, division, detail, member, parcel

fragrance ♦ a sweet or pleasant odor *Syn* perfume, incense, redolence, bouquet *Ant* stench, stink

fragrant *Syn* ODOROUS, aromatic, redolent, balmy *Ant* fetid

frail *Syn* WEAK, fragile, feeble, infirm, decrepit *Ant* robust

frailty *Syn* FAULT, failing, foible, vice

frame 1 *Syn* BUILD, construct, erect, raise, rear **2** *Syn* CONTRIVE, devise, invent, concoct

framework *Syn* STRUCTURE, skeleton, anatomy

franchise *Syn* SUFFRAGE, vote, ballot

frangible *Syn* FRAGILE, brittle, crisp, short, friable

frank ♦ marked by free, forthright, and sincere expression *Syn* candid, open, plain *Ant* reticent

frantic *Syn* FURIOUS, frenzied, wild, frenetic, delirious, rabid

fraud 1 *Syn* DECEPTION, trickery, chicanery, chicane, double-dealing **2** *Syn* IMPOSTURE, cheat, sham, fake, humbug, deceit, deception, counterfeit

fray *Syn* CONTEST, affray, fight, conflict, combat

freak *Syn* CAPRICE, fancy, whim, whimsy, conceit, vagary, crotchet

freaked *Syn* VARIEGATED, parti-colored, motley, checkered, checked, pied, piebald, skewbald, dappled

free *adj* ♦ not subject to the rule or control of another **Syn** independent, sovereign, autonomous, autarchic, autarkic **Ant** bond

free *vb* **Syn** ♦ to relieve from constraint or restraint **Syn** release, liberate, emancipate, manumit, discharge

freebooter Syn PIRATE, buccaneer, privateer, corsair

freedom 1 ♦ the state or condition of not being subject to external rule or control **Syn** independence, autonomy, sovereignty, autarchy, autarky **Ant** bondage **2** ♦ the power or condition of acting without compulsion **Syn** liberty, license **Ant** necessity

freethinker Syn ATHEIST, unbeliever, agnostic, deist, infidel

freezing Syn COLD, frigid, frosty, gelid, icy, glacial, arctic, chilly, cool

freight Syn LOAD, cargo, burden, lading

frenetic Syn FURIOUS, frantic, frenzied, wild, delirious, rabid

frenzied Syn FURIOUS, frantic, wild, frenetic, delirious, rabid

frenzy 1 Syn MANIA, delirium, hysteria **2 Syn** INSPIRATION, fury, afflatus

frequently Syn OFTEN, oft, oftentimes **Ant** rarely, seldom

fresh Syn NEW, novel, new-fashioned, newfangled, modern, modernistic, original **Ant** stale

fret Syn ABRADE, excoriate, chafe, gall

fretful Syn IRRITABLE, peevish, petulant, querulous, fractious, snappish, waspish, pettish, huffy

friable Syn FRAGILE, short, frangible, crisp, brittle

friar Syn RELIGIOUS, monk, nun

friend ♦ a person, esp. not related by blood, with whom one is on good and usu. familiar terms **Syn** acquaintance, intimate, confidant **Ant** foe

friendly Syn AMICABLE, neighborly **Ant** unfriendly; belligerent

friendship ♦ the relation existing between persons, communities, states, or peoples that are in accord and in sympathy with each other **Syn** amity, comity, goodwill **Ant** animosity

fright *n* **Syn** FEAR, alarm, consternation, panic, dread, dismay, terror, horror, trepidation

fright *vb* **Syn** FRIGHTEN, scare, alarm, terrify, terrorize, startle, affray, affright

frighten ♦ to strike or to fill with fear or dread **Syn** fright, scare, alarm, terrify, terrorize, startle, affray, affright

frightful Syn FEARFUL, dreadful, awful, terrible, terrific, horrible, horrific, shocking, appalling

frigid Syn COLD, freezing, gelid, icy, glacial, arctic, cool, chilly, frosty **Ant** torrid (*temperature*); amorous (*persons*)

fritter Syn WASTE, squander, dissipate, consume

frivolity Syn LIGHTNESS, levity, flippancy, light-mindedness, volatility, flightiness **Ant** seriousness, staidness

frolic *vb* **Syn** PLAY, sport, disport, rollick, romp, gambol

frolic *n* **Syn** PLAY, sport, disport, rollick, romp, gambol

frolicsome Syn PLAYFUL, sportive, roguish, waggish, impish, mischievous

frosty Syn COLD, chilly, cool, frigid, freezing, gelid, icy, glacial, arctic

froth Syn FOAM, spume, scum, lather, suds, yeast

froward Syn CONTRARY, perverse, balky, restive, wayward **Ant** compliant

frown ♦ to put on a dark or malignant countenance or aspect **Syn** scowl, glower, lower, gloom **Ant** smile

frowzy Syn SLATTERNLY, blowsy, dowdy **Ant** trim; smart

frugal Syn SPARING, thrifty, economical **Ant** wasteful

fruitful Syn FERTILE, fecund, prolific **Ant** unfruitful; fruitless

fruitfulness Syn FERTILITY, prolificacy, fecundity

fruition Syn PLEASURE, enjoyment, delectation, delight, joy

fruitless Syn FUTILE, vain, bootless, abortive **Ant** fruitful

frustrate ♦ to come between a person and his or her aim or desire or to defeat another's plan **Syn** thwart, foil, baffle, balk, circumvent, outwit **Ant** fulfill

fuddle *Syn* CONFUSE, muddle, addle

fugitive *Syn* TRANSIENT, evanescent, transitory, fleeting, passing, ephemeral, momentary, short-lived

fulfill 1 *Syn* PERFORM, effect, achieve, accomplish, execute, discharge *Ant* frustrate; fail (in) **2** *Syn* SATISFY, meet, answer *Ant* fall short (of)

full ♦ containing all that is wanted or needed or possible *Syn* complete, plenary, replete *Ant* empty

fulsome ♦ too obviously extravagant or ingratiating to be accepted as genuine or sincere *Syn* oily, unctuous, oleaginous, slick, soapy

fumble *Syn* BOTCH, bungle, muff, cobble

fumigate *Syn* STERILIZE, disinfect, sanitize

fun ♦ action or speech that is intended to amuse or arouse laughter *Syn* jest, sport, game, play

function *n* **1** ♦ acts or operations expected of a person or thing *Syn* office, duty, province **2** *Syn* POWER, faculty

function *vb* *Syn* ACT, operate, work, behave, react

fundamental *adj* **1** ♦ forming or affecting the groundwork, roots, or lowest part of something *Syn* basic, basal, underlying, radical **2** *Syn* ESSENTIAL, vital, cardinal **3** *Syn* ELEMENTAL, basic, elementary, essential, primitive, underlying

fundamental *n* *Syn* PRINCIPLE, axiom, law, theorem

funny *Syn* LAUGHABLE, risible, ludicrous, ridiculous, comic, comical, farcical, droll

furious ♦ marked by uncontrollable excitement esp. under the stress of a powerful emotion *Syn* frantic, frenzied, wild, frenetic, delirious, rabid

furnish 1 *Syn* PROVIDE, supply *Ant* strip **2** ♦ to supply one with what is needed (as for daily living or a particular activity) *Syn* equip, outfit, appoint, accouter, arm

further *adv* *Syn* FARTHER, beyond

further *vb* *Syn* ADVANCE, forward, promote *Ant* hinder; retard

furthermore *Syn* ALSO, moreover, besides, likewise, too

furtive *Syn* SECRET, stealthy, clandestine, surreptitious, underhand, underhanded, covert *Ant* forthright; brazen

furuncle *Syn* ABSCESS, boil, carbuncle, pimple, pustule

fury 1 *Syn* ANGER, rage, ire, wrath, indignation **2** *Syn* INSPIRATION, frenzy, afflatus

fuse 1 *Syn* LIQUEFY, melt, deliquesce, thaw **2** *Syn* MIX, amalgamate, merge, coalesce, blend, mingle, commingle

fusion *Syn* ALLIANCE, coalition, league, federation, confederation, confederacy

fuss *Syn* STIR, pother, ado, flurry, bustle

fussy *Syn* NICE, finicky, finicking, finical, particular, persnickety, pernickety, dainty, fastidious, squeamish

fustian *Syn* BOMBAST, rant, rodomontade, rhapsody

fusty *Syn* MALODOROUS, musty, rancid, putrid, fetid, stinking, noisome, rank

futile ♦ barren of result *Syn* vain, fruitless, bootless, abortive

G

gab *Syn* CHAT, chatter, patter, prate, prattle, babble, gabble, jabber, gibber

gabble *Syn* CHAT, babble, gab, chatter, patter, prate, prattle, jabber, gibber

gad *Syn* WANDER, stray, roam, ramble, rove, range, prowl, gallivant, traipse, meander

gadget *Syn* DEVICE, contraption, contrivance

gag *Syn* JOKE, jest, jape, quip, witticism, wisecrack, crack

gain 1 *Syn* GET, win, obtain, procure, secure, acquire *Ant* forfeit; lose **2** *Syn* REACH, compass, achieve, attain **3** *Syn* IMPROVE, recover, recuperate, convalesce

gainful *Syn* PAYING, remunerative, lucrative, profitable

gainsay *Syn* DENY, contradict, impugn, contravene, negative, traverse *Ant* admit

gall *n* *Syn* TEMERITY, effrontery, nerve, cheek, hardihood, audacity

gall *vb* Syn ABRADE, chafe, excoriate, fret

gallant *Syn* CIVIL, courtly, chivalrous, courteous, polite

gallantry 1 *Syn* HEROISM, valor, prowess *Ant* dastardliness **2** *Syn* COURTESY, attention, amenity

gallery *Syn* PASSAGE, passageway, corridor, arcade, cloister, ambulatory, aisle, hall, hallway

gallivant *Syn* WANDER, stray, roam, ramble, rove, range, prowl, gad, traipse, meander

galumph *Syn* STUMBLE, trip, blunder, lurch, flounder, lumber, lollop, bumble

galvanize *Syn* PROVOKE, excite, stimulate, quicken, pique

gambit *Syn* TRICK, ruse, stratagem, maneuver, ploy, artifice, wile, feint

gambol *n* *Syn* PLAY, frolic, disport, sport, rollick, romp

gambol *vb* *Syn* PLAY, frolic, disport, sport, rollick, romp

game 1 *Syn* FUN, sport, play, jest **2** *pl* **games** *Syn* ATHLETICS, sports

gamut *Syn* RANGE, reach, radius, compass, sweep, scope, orbit, horizon, ken, purview

gap *Syn* BREAK, interruption, interval, interim, hiatus, lacuna

gape *Syn* GAZE, stare, glare, gloat, peer

garbage *Syn* REFUSE, waste, offal, rubbish, trash, debris

garble *Syn* MISREPRESENT, falsify, belie

gargantuan *Syn* HUGE, vast, immense, enormous, elephantine, mammoth, giant, gigantic, gigantean, colossal, Herculean, cyclopean, titanic, Brobdingnagian

garish *Syn* GAUDY, tawdry, flashy, meretricious *Ant* somber

garner *Syn* REAP, glean, gather, harvest

garnish *Syn* ADORN, embellish, beautify, deck, bedeck, decorate, ornament

garrulity, garrulousness *Syn* TALKATIVENESS, loquacity, volubility, glibness

garrulous *Syn* TALKATIVE, loquacious, voluble, glib *Ant* taciturn

gasconade *Syn* BOAST, vaunt, brag, crow

gastronome *Syn* EPICURE, gourmet, gourmand, bon vivant, glutton

gate *Syn* DOOR, portal, gateway, postern, doorway

gateway *Syn* DOOR, gate, portal, postern, doorway

gather 1 ◆ to come or bring together *Syn* collect, assemble, congregate **2** *Syn* REAP, glean, garner, harvest **3** *Syn* INFER, deduce, conclude, judge

gathering ◆ a number of individuals come or brought together *Syn* collection, assemblage, assembly, congregation

gauche *Syn* AWKWARD, maladroit, clumsy, inept

gaudy ◆ vulgar or cheap in its showiness *Syn* tawdry, garish, flashy, meretricious *Ant* quiet (*in taste or style*)

gauge *Syn* STANDARD, criterion, yardstick, touchstone

gaunt *Syn* LEAN, rawboned, angular, lank, lanky, spare, scrawny, skinny

gay *Syn* LIVELY, vivacious, sprightly, animated *Ant* grave, sober

gaze ◆ to look at long and attentively *Syn* gape, stare, glare, peer, gloat

gear *Syn* EQUIPMENT, tackle, paraphernalia, outfit, apparatus, machinery

geld *Syn* STERILIZE, castrate, spay, emasculate, alter, mutilate

gelid *Syn* COLD, icy, frigid, freezing, frosty, glacial, arctic, cool, chilly

general *Syn* UNIVERSAL, generic, common

generally *Syn* LARGELY, mostly, chiefly, mainly, principally, greatly

generate ◆ to give life or origin to or to bring into existence by or as if by natural processes *Syn* engender, breed, beget, get, sire, procreate, propagate, reproduce

generic *Syn* UNIVERSAL, general, common

generous *Syn* LIBERAL, bountiful, bounteous, openhanded, munificent, handsome *Ant* stingy

genesis *Syn* BEGINNING, rise, initiation

genial *Syn* GRACIOUS, sociable, affable, cordial *Ant* saturnine; caustic

genius *Syn* GIFT, talent, faculty, aptitude, knack, bent, turn

gentle *Syn* SOFT, mild, smooth, lenient, bland, balmy *Ant* rough, harsh

gentleman ♦ a person of good or noble birth *Syn* patrician, aristocrat *Ant* boor

gentry *Syn* ARISTOCRACY, county, nobility, elite, society

genuine *Syn* AUTHENTIC, bona fide, veritable *Ant* counterfeit; fraudulent

germane *Syn* RELEVANT, pertinent, material, apposite, applicable, apropos *Ant* foreign

gesticulation *Syn* GESTURE

gesture ♦ an expressive movement of the body or the use of such a movement *Syn* gesticulation

get 1 ♦ to come into possession of *Syn* obtain, procure, secure, acquire, gain, win **2** *Syn* GENERATE, beget, procreate, sire, engender, breed, propagate, reproduce **3** *Syn* INDUCE, persuade, prevail

ghastly ♦ horrifying and repellent in appearance or aspect *Syn* grisly, gruesome, macabre, grim, lurid

ghost *Syn* APPARITION, spirit, specter, shade, phantasm, phantom, wraith, revenant

giant *Syn* HUGE, vast, immense, enormous, elephantine, mammoth, gigantic, gigantean, colossal, gargantuan, Herculean, cyclopean, titanic, Brobdingnagian

gibber *Syn* CHAT, prate, chatter, gab, patter, prattle, babble, gabble, jabber

gibberish ♦ speech or actions that are esoteric in nature and suggest the magical, strange, or unknown *Syn* mummery, hocus-pocus, abracadabra

gibe *Syn* SCOFF, jeer, sneer, flout, gird, fleer

giddy ♦ affected by a sensation of being whirled about or around *Syn* dizzy, vertiginous, swimming, dazzled

gift 1 ♦ something, often of value but not necessarily material, given freely to another for his benefit or pleasure *Syn* present, gratuity, favor, boon, largess **2** ♦ a special ability or a capacity for a definite kind of activity or achievement *Syn* faculty, aptitude, genius, talent, knack, bent, turn

gigantic, gigantean *Syn* HUGE, vast, immense, enormous, elephantine, mammoth, giant, colossal, gargantuan, Herculean, cyclopean, titanic, Brobdingnagian

gingery *Syn* SPIRITED, fiery, peppery, high-spirited, mettlesome, spunky

gird *vb Syn* SURROUND, environ, encircle, circle, encompass, compass, hem, girdle, ring

gird *vb Syn* SCOFF, sneer, flout, jeer, gibe, fleer

girdle *Syn* SURROUND, environ, encircle, circle, encompass, compass, hem, gird, ring

gist *Syn* SUBSTANCE, purport, burden, core, pith

give ♦ to convey something or make something over or available to another *Syn* present, donate, bestow, confer, afford

glacial *Syn* COLD, arctic, icy, gelid, frigid, freezing, frosty, cool, chilly

glad ♦ characterized by or expressing the mood of one who is pleased or delighted *Syn* happy, cheerful, lighthearted, joyful, joyous *Ant* sad

gladden *Syn* PLEASE, delight, rejoice, gratify, tickle, regale *Ant* sadden

glance *vb* **1** *Syn* BRUSH, graze, shave, skim **2** *Syn* FLASH, glint, gleam, sparkle, glitter, glisten, scintillate, coruscate, twinkle

glance *n Syn* LOOK, glimpse, peep, peek, sight, view

glare *vb* **1** *Syn* BLAZE, glow, flare, flame **2** *Syn* GAZE, stare, peer, gloat, gape

glare *n Syn* BLAZE, flare, glow, flame

glaring *Syn* FLAGRANT, gross, rank

glaze *Syn* LUSTER, gloss, sheen

gleam *Syn* FLASH, glance, glint, sparkle, glitter, glisten, scintillate, coruscate, twinkle

glean *Syn* REAP, gather, garner, harvest

glee *Syn* MIRTH, jollity, hilarity *Ant* gloom

glib 1 *Syn* VOCAL, fluent, voluble, articulate, eloquent **2** *Syn* TALKATIVE, loquacious, garrulous, voluble

glibness *Syn* TALKATIVENESS, loquacity, garrulity, volubility

glide *Syn* SLIDE, slip, skid, glissade, slither, coast, toboggan

glimpse *Syn* LOOK, glance, peep, peek, sight, view

glint *Syn* FLASH, glance, gleam, sparkle, glitter, glisten, scintillate, coruscate, twinkle

glissade *Syn* SLIDE, glide, slip, skid, slither, coast, toboggan

glisten *Syn* FLASH, sparkle, glitter, gleam, glance, glint, scintillate, coruscate, twinkle

glitter *Syn* FLASH, glisten, sparkle, gleam, glance, glint, scintillate, coruscate, twinkle

gloat *Syn* GAZE, gape, stare, glare, peer

globe *Syn* EARTH, world, planet

gloom *vb Syn* FROWN, lower, glower, scowl

gloom *n Syn* SADNESS, dejection, depression, melancholy, melancholia, blues, dumps *Ant* glee

gloomy 1 *Syn* DARK, murky, obscure, dim, dusky *Ant* brilliant **2** *Syn* SULLEN, glum, morose, saturnine, dour, surly, sulky, crabbed *Ant* cheerful

glorify *Syn* DIGNIFY, ennoble, honor

glorious *Syn* SPLENDID, resplendent, sublime, superb, gorgeous *Ant* inglorious

glory *Syn* FAME, renown, honor, celebrity, éclat, reputation, repute, notoriety *Ant* ignominy, shame

gloss *n Syn* LUSTER, sheen, glaze

gloss *vb Syn* PALLIATE, gloze, extenuate, whitewash, whiten

gloss *n Syn* ANNOTATION

gloss *vb Syn* ANNOTATE

glossy *Syn* SLEEK, slick, velvety, silken, silky, satiny

glow *vb Syn* BLAZE, flame, flare, glare

glow *n Syn* BLAZE, flame, flare, glare

glower *Syn* FROWN, lower, scowl, gloom

gloze *Syn* PALLIATE, gloss, whitewash, extenuate, whiten

glum *Syn* SULLEN, gloomy, morose, saturnine, dour, surly, sulky, crabbed *Ant* cheerful

glut *Syn* SATIATE, gorge, surfeit, sate, cloy, pall

glutton *Syn* EPICURE, gourmand, gastronome, bon vivant, gourmet

gluttonous *Syn* VORACIOUS, ravenous, ravening, rapacious *Ant* abstemious

gnash *Syn* BITE, gnaw, champ

gnaw *Syn* BITE, champ, gnash

go *vb* **1** ♦ to move out of or away from where one is *Syn* leave, depart, quit, withdraw, retire *Ant* come **2** *Syn* RESORT, refer, apply, turn

go *n Syn* SPELL, shift, tour, trick, turn, stint, bout

goad *n Syn* MOTIVE, spur, incentive, inducement, spring, impulse *Ant* curb

goad *vb Syn* URGE, egg, exhort, spur, prod, prick, sic

goal *Syn* INTENTION, objective, object, end, aim, intent, purpose, design

gob *Syn* MARINER, sailor, seaman, tar, bluejacket

gobbledygook *Syn* NONSENSE, twaddle, drivel, bunk, balderdash, poppycock, trash, rot, bull

godless *Syn* IRRELIGIOUS, ungodly, unreligious, nonreligious

good ♦ in accordance with one's standard of what is satisfactory *Syn* right *Ant* bad; poor

good-looking *Syn* BEAUTIFUL, comely, pretty, bonny, fair, beauteous, pulchritudinous, handsome, lovely

good-natured *Syn* AMIABLE, obliging, complaisant *Ant* contrary

goodness ♦ moral excellence *Syn* virtue, rectitude, morality *Ant* badness, evil

good sense *Syn* SENSE

goodwill *Syn* FRIENDSHIP, amity, comity *Ant* animosity

gorge *Syn* SATIATE, surfeit, sate, glut, cloy, pall

gorgeous *Syn* SPLENDID, resplendent, glorious, sublime, superb

gory *Syn* BLOODY, sanguinary, sanguine, sanguineous

gossip *n Syn* REPORT, rumor, hearsay

gossip *vb* ♦ to disclose something, often of questionable veracity, that is better kept to oneself *Syn* blab, tattle

gourmand *Syn* EPICURE, glutton, gastronome, bon vivant, gourmet

gourmet *Syn* EPICURE, bon vivant, gastronome, gourmand, glutton

govern ♦ to exercise sovereign authority *Syn* rule

grab *Syn* TAKE, grasp, clutch, seize, snatch

grace 1 *Syn* MERCY, clemency, lenity, charity **2** *Syn* ELEGANCE, dignity

gracious ♦ marked by kindly courtesy *Syn* cordial, affable, genial, sociable *Ant* ungracious

gradate *Syn* CLASS, grade, rank, rate, graduate

gradation ♦ difference or variation between two things that are nearly alike *Syn* shade, nuance

grade *Syn* CLASS, rank, rate, graduate, gradate

graduate *Syn* CLASS, grade, rank, rate, gradate

grand ♦ large, handsome, dignified, and impressive *Syn* magnificent, imposing, stately, majestic, august, noble, grandiose

grandiloquent *Syn* RHETORICAL, magniloquent, aureate, flowery, euphuistic, bombastic

grandiose *Syn* GRAND, imposing, stately, august, magnificent, majestic, noble

grant *vb* **1** ♦ to give as a favor or as a right *Syn* concede, vouchsafe, accord, award **2** ♦ to admit something in question, esp. a contention of one's opponent in an argument *Syn* concede, allow

grant *n* *Syn* APPROPRIATION, subvention, subsidy

graph *n* *Syn* CHART, map

graph *vb* *Syn* CHART, map

graphic ♦ giving a clear visual impression esp. in words *Syn* vivid, picturesque, pictorial

grapple *Syn* WRESTLE, tussle, scuffle

grasp *vb* *Syn* TAKE, clutch, grab, seize, snatch

grasp *n* *Syn* HOLD, grip, clutch

grasping *Syn* COVETOUS, greedy, avaricious, acquisitive

grate *Syn* SCRAPE, scratch, rasp, grind

grateful 1 ♦ feeling or expressing gratitude *Syn* thankful *Ant* ungrateful **2** *Syn* PLEASANT, agreeable, gratifying, pleasing, welcome *Ant* obnoxious

gratify *Syn* PLEASE, delight, rejoice, gladden, tickle, regale *Ant* anger; offend, affront; disappoint

gratifying *Syn* PLEASANT, grateful, agreeable, pleasing, welcome

gratuitous *Syn* SUPEREROGATORY, uncalled-for, wanton

gratuity *Syn* GIFT, largess, boon, favor, present

grave *Syn* SERIOUS, solemn, somber, sedate, sober, earnest, staid *Ant* gay

graze *vb* *Syn* FEED, pasture, nourish

graze *vb* *Syn* BRUSH, glance, shave, skim

grease *Syn* OIL, lubricate, anoint, cream

great *Syn* LARGE, big *Ant* little

greatly *Syn* LARGELY, mostly, chiefly, mainly, principally, generally

greed *Syn* CUPIDITY, rapacity, avarice

greedy *Syn* COVETOUS, acquisitive, grasping, avaricious

green *Syn* RUDE, callow, raw, crude, rough, uncouth *Ant* experienced; seasoned

greet *Syn* ADDRESS, salute, hail, accost

greeting ♦ the ceremonial words or acts of one who meets, welcomes, or formally addresses another *Syn* salutation, salute

gregarious *Syn* SOCIAL, cooperative, convivial, companionable, hospitable

grief *Syn* SORROW, anguish, woe, heartache, heartbreak, regret

grievance *Syn* INJUSTICE, wrong, injury

grieve ♦ to feel or express sorrow or grief *Syn* mourn, sorrow *Ant* rejoice

grim 1 ♦ being extremely obdurate or firm in action or purpose *Syn* implacable, relentless, unrelenting, merciless *Ant* lenient **2** *Syn* GHASTLY, grisly, gruesome, macabre, lurid

grime *Syn* SOIL, dirty, sully, tarnish, foul, befoul, smirch, besmirch, begrime

grin *vb* *Syn* SMILE, smirk, simper

grin *n* *Syn* SMILE, smirk, simper

grind *vb* *Syn* SCRAPE, scratch, grate, rasp

grind *n* *Syn* WORK, drudgery, toil, travail, labor

grip *Syn* HOLD, grasp, clutch

grisly *Syn* GHASTLY, gruesome, macabre, grim, lurid

grit *Syn* FORTITUDE, pluck, backbone, guts, sand *Ant* faintheartedness

groan *vb* *Syn* SIGH, moan, sob

groan *n* *Syn* SIGH, moan, sob

gross 1 *Syn* WHOLE, total, entire, all *Ant* net **2** *Syn* COARSE, vulgar, obscene, ribald *Ant* delicate, dainty; ethereal **3** *Syn* FLAGRANT, glaring, rank *Ant* petty

grotesque *Syn* FANTASTIC, bizarre, antic

ground *n* **1** *Syn* BASE, basis, foundation, groundwork **2** *Syn* REASON, argument, proof **3** *pl* **grounds** *Syn* DEPOSIT, precipitate, sediment, dregs, lees

ground *vb* *Syn* BASE, found, bottom, stay, rest

groundless *Syn* BASELESS, unfounded, unwarranted

groundwork *Syn* BASE, foundation, basis, ground *Ant* superstructure

group ♦ a collection or assemblage of persons or things *Syn* cluster, bunch, parcel, lot

grovel *Syn* WALLOW, welter

growl *Syn* BARK, bay, howl, snarl, yelp, yap

grown-up *Syn* MATURE, adult, matured, ripe, mellow *Ant* childish; callow

grub *Syn* DIG, delve, spade, excavate

grudge *vb* *Syn* COVET, begrudge, envy

grudge *n* *Syn* MALICE, ill will, malevolence, spite, despite, malignity, malignancy, spleen

gruesome *Syn* GHASTLY, macabre, grisly, grim, lurid

gruff *Syn* BLUFF, crusty, brusque, blunt, curt

guarantee ♦ an assurance for the fulfillment of a condition or a person who provides such assurance *Syn* guaranty, surety, security, bond, bail

guarantor *Syn* SPONSOR, surety, patron, backer, angel

guaranty *Syn* GUARANTEE, surety, security, bond, bail

guard *Syn* DEFEND, shield, protect, safeguard

guerdon *Syn* PREMIUM, reward, meed, bounty, award, prize, bonus

guess *vb* *Syn* CONJECTURE, surmise

guess *n* *Syn* CONJECTURE, surmise *Ant* certainty

guest *Syn* VISITOR, caller, visitant

guide ♦ to put or lead on a course or into the way to be followed *Syn* lead, steer, pilot, engineer *Ant* misguide

guile *Syn* DECEIT, duplicity, dissimulation, cunning *Ant* ingenuousness; candor

guileful *Syn* SLY, cunning, crafty, tricky, foxy, insidious, wily, artful

guilt *Syn* BLAME, culpability, fault *Ant* innocence; guiltlessness

guilty *Syn* BLAMEWORTHY, culpable *Ant* innocent

gulf ♦ a hollow place of vast width and depth *Syn* chasm, abysm, abyss

gull *Syn* DUPE, befool, trick, hoax, hoodwink, bamboozle

gullibility *Syn* CREDULITY *Ant* astuteness

gullible *Syn* CREDULOUS *Ant* astute

gumption *Syn* SENSE, common sense, good sense, judgment, wisdom

gunman *Syn* ASSASSIN, cutthroat, bravo

gush *Syn* POUR, stream, sluice

gusto *Syn* TASTE, relish, zest, palate

gut 1 *Syn* ABDOMEN, belly, stomach, paunch **2** *pl* **guts** *Syn* FORTITUDE, grit, pluck, backbone, sand

gyrate *Syn* TURN, rotate, revolve, spin, whirl, wheel, circle, twirl, eddy, swirl, pirouette

H

habit 1 ♦ a mode of behaving or doing that has become fixed by constant repetition *Syn* habitude, practice, usage, custom, use, wont **2** *Syn* PHYSIQUE, build, constitution

habitat ♦ the place in which a particular kind of organism lives or grows *Syn* biotope, range, station

habitation ♦ the place where one lives *Syn* dwelling, abode, residence, domicile, home, house

habitual *Syn* USUAL, customary, wonted, accustomed *Ant* occasional

habituate ♦ to make used to something *Syn* accustom, addict, inure

habitude *Syn* HABIT, practice, usage, custom, use, wont

habitué *Syn* ADDICT, votary, devotee

hack *Syn* MERCENARY, hireling, venal

hackneyed *Syn* TRITE, stereotyped, threadbare, shopworn

Hadean *Syn* INFERNAL, chthonian, Tartarean, stygian, hellish, chthonic

haggard ♦ thin and drawn by or as if by worry, fatigue, hunger, or illness *Syn* worn, careworn, pinched, wasted, cadaverous

hail *Syn* ADDRESS, salute, greet, accost

halcyon *Syn* CALM, serene, placid, tranquil, peaceful

hale *adj Syn* HEALTHY, robust, sound, wholesome, well *Ant* infirm

hale *vb Syn* PULL, haul, draw, drag, tug, tow

hall hallway *Syn* PASSAGE, passageway, corridor, gallery, arcade, cloister, aisle, ambulatory

hallow *Syn* DEVOTE, consecrate, dedicate

hallucination *Syn* DELUSION, mirage, illusion

hamper ♦ to hinder or impede in moving, progressing, or acting freely *Syn* trammel, clog, fetter, shackle, manacle, hog-tie *Ant* assist (*persons*); expedite (*work, projects*)

hand *Syn* WORKER, operative, workman, workingman, laborer, craftsman, handicraftsman, mechanic, artisan, roustabout

handicap 1 *Syn* ADVANTAGE, allowance, odds, edge **2** *Syn* DISADVANTAGE, detriment, drawback *Ant* asset, advantage

handicraft *Syn* TRADE, craft, art, profession

handicraftsman *Syn* WORKER, craftsman, workman, artisan, mechanic, workingman, laborer, operative, hand, roustabout

handle 1 ♦ to deal with or manage usu. with dexterity or efficiency *Syn* manipulate, wield, swing, ply **2** *Syn* TREAT, deal **3** *Syn* TOUCH, feel, palpate, paw

handsome 1 *Syn* LIBERAL, generous, bountiful, bounteous, openhanded, munificent **2** *Syn* BEAUTIFUL, pulchritudinous, beauteous, comely, good-looking, lovely, pretty, bonny, fair

handy *Syn* DEXTEROUS, deft, adroit

hang 1 ♦ to place or be placed so as to be supported at one point or side usu. at the top *Syn* suspend, sling, dangle **2** *Syn* DEPEND, hinge, turn

hanger-on *Syn* PARASITE, sycophant, leech, sponge, sponger, favorite, toady, lickspittle, bootlicker

hanker *Syn* LONG, yearn, pine, hunger, thirst

hap *Syn* CHANCE, fortune, luck, accident, hazard

haphazard *Syn* RANDOM, chance, chancy, casual, desultory, hit-or-miss, happy-go-lucky

hapless *Syn* UNLUCKY, disastrous, ill-starred, ill-fated, unfortunate, calamitous, luckless

happen ♦ to come to pass or to come about *Syn* chance, occur, befall, betide, transpire

happiness ♦ a state of well-being or pleasurable satisfaction *Syn* felicity, beatitude, blessedness, bliss *Ant* unhappiness

happy 1 *Syn* LUCKY, fortunate, providential *Ant* unhappy **2** *Syn* FIT, felicitous, apt, appropriate, fitting, suitable, meet, proper *Ant* unhappy **3** *Syn* GLAD, cheerful, light-hearted, joyful, joyous *Ant* unhappy; disconsolate

happy-go-lucky *Syn* RANDOM, haphazard, hit-or-miss, chance, chancy, casual, desultory

harangue *Syn* SPEECH, oration, address, lecture, talk, sermon, homily

harass *Syn* WORRY, harry, annoy, plague, pester, tease, tantalize

harbinger *Syn* FORERUNNER, precursor, herald

harbor *n* ♦ a place where seacraft may ride secure *Syn* haven, port

harbor *vb* ♦ to provide with shelter or refuge *Syn* shelter, entertain, lodge, house, board

hard 1 *Syn* FIRM, solid *Ant* soft **2** ♦ demanding great toil or effort *Syn* difficult, arduous *Ant* easy

harden 1 ♦ to make or to become physically hard or solid *Syn* solidify, indurate, petrify, cake *Ant* soften **2** ♦ to make proof against hardship, strain, or exposure *Syn* season, acclimatize, acclimate *Ant* soften

hardened ♦ grown or become hard *Syn* indurated, callous *Ant* softened.

hardihood *Syn* TEMERITY, audacity, effrontery, nerve, cheek, gall

hardship *Syn* DIFFICULTY, rigor, vicissitude

harm *n Syn* INJURY, damage, hurt, mischief *Ant* benefit

harm *vb Syn* INJURE, impair, hurt, damage, mar, spoil *Ant* benefit

harmless ♦ not having hurtful or injurious qualities *Syn* innocuous, innocent, inoffensive, unoffending *Ant* harmful

harmonize 1 *Syn* AGREE, accord, correspond, square, conform, tally, jibe *Ant* clash; conflict **2** ♦ to bring into consonance or accord *Syn* tune, attune

harmony 1 ♦ the effect produced when different things come together without clashing or disagreement *Syn* consonance, accord, concord *Ant* conflict **2** *Syn* SYMMETRY, proportion, balance

harry *Syn* WORRY, harass, annoy, plague, pester, tease, tantalize

harsh *Syn* ROUGH, rugged, scabrous, uneven *Ant* pleasant; mild

harvest *Syn* REAP, glean, gather, garner

haste ♦ rapidity of motion or action *Syn* hurry, speed, expedition, dispatch *Ant* deliberation

hasten *Syn* SPEED, accelerate, quicken, hurry, precipitate *Ant* delay

hasty 1 *Syn* FAST, speedy, quick, expeditious, rapid, swift, fleet **2** *Syn* PRECIPITATE, headlong, abrupt, impetuous, sudden

hate *n Syn* ABHORRENCE, hatred, detestation, abomination, loathing

hate *vb* ♦ to feel extreme enmity or dislike *Syn* detest, abhor, abominate, loathe *Ant* love

hateful ♦ deserving of or arousing hate *Syn* odious, abhorrent, detestable, abominable *Ant* lovable; sympathetic

hatred *Syn* ABHORRENCE, hate, detestation, abomination, loathing

haughty *Syn* PROUD, arrogant, insolent, lordly, overbearing, supercilious, disdainful *Ant* lowly

haul *Syn* PULL, hale, draw, drag, tug, tow

have ♦ to keep, control, or experience as one's own *Syn* hold, own, possess, enjoy

haven *Syn* HARBOR, port

havoc *Syn* RUIN, devastation, destruction

hazard *n* **1** *Syn* CHANCE, accident, fortune, luck, hap **2** *Syn* DANGER, jeopardy, peril, risk

hazard *vb Syn* VENTURE, risk, chance, jeopardize, endanger, imperil

hazardous *Syn* DANGEROUS, precarious, risky, perilous

haze ♦ an atmospheric condition that is characterized by the presence of fine particulate material in the air and that deprives the air of its transparency *Syn* mist, fog, smog

head, headman *Syn* CHIEF, leader, chieftain, master

headlong *Syn* PRECIPITATE, impetuous, abrupt, hasty, sudden

headstrong *Syn* UNRULY, ungovernable, intractable, refractory, recalcitrant, willful

headway *Syn* SPEED, pace, velocity, momentum, impetus

heal *Syn* CURE, remedy

healthful ♦ conducive or beneficial to the health or soundness of body or mind *Syn* healthy, wholesome, salubrious, salutary, hygienic, sanitary

healthy 1 *Syn* HEALTHFUL, wholesome, salubrious, salutary, hygienic, sanitary **2** ♦ having or manifesting health of mind or body or indicative of such health *Syn* sound, wholesome, robust, hale, well *Ant* unhealthy

heap *n* ♦ a quantity of things brought together into a more or less compact group *Syn* pile, stack, shock, cock, mass, bank

heap *vb* ♦ to bring a number of things together into a more or less compact group or collection *Syn* pile, stack, shock, cock, mass, bank

hearing ♦ an opportunity to be heard *Syn* audience, audition

hearsay *Syn* REPORT, rumor, gossip

heart *Syn* CENTER, middle, core, hub, nucleus, midst, focus

heartache, heartbreak *Syn* SORROW, grief, anguish, woe, regret

hearten *Syn* ENCOURAGE, inspirit, embolden, cheer, nerve, steel *Ant* dishearten

heartfelt *Syn* SINCERE, hearty, unfeigned, wholehearted, whole-souled

hearty *Syn* SINCERE, heartfelt, unfeigned, wholehearted, whole-souled *Ant* hollow

heave *Syn* LIFT, raise, hoist, elevate, boost, rear

heavenly *Syn* CELESTIAL, empyrean, empyreal

heavy ♦ having great weight *Syn* weighty, ponderous, cumbrous, cumbersome, hefty *Ant* light

heckle *Syn* BAIT, badger, hector, chivy, hound, ride

hector *Syn* BAIT, badger, chivy, heckle, hound, ride

heedless *Syn* CARELESS, thoughtless, inadvertent *Ant* heedful

hefty *Syn* HEAVY, weighty, ponderous, cumbrous, cumbersome

height ♦ the distance a thing rises above the level on which it stands *Syn* altitude, elevation

heighten *Syn* INTENSIFY, enhance, aggravate

heinous *Syn* OUTRAGEOUS, atrocious, monstrous *Ant* venial

hellish *Syn* INFERNAL, chthonian, chthonic, Hadean, Tartarean, stygian

help *vb* **1** ♦ to give assistance or support *Syn* aid, assist *Ant* hinder **2** *Syn* IMPROVE, better, ameliorate

help *n* ♦ an act or instance of giving what will benefit or assist *Syn* aid, assistance

helper *Syn* ASSISTANT, coadjutor, aid, aide, aide-de-camp

hem *Syn* SURROUND, environ, encircle, circle, encompass, compass, gird, girdle, ring

hence *Syn* THEREFORE, consequently, then, accordingly, so

henchman *Syn* FOLLOWER, adherent, disciple, partisan, satellite, sectary

herald *Syn* FORERUNNER, harbinger, precursor

Herculean *Syn* HUGE, vast, immense, enormous, elephantine, mammoth, giant, gigantic, gigantean, colossal, gargantuan, cyclopean, titanic, Brobdingnagian

hereditary *Syn* INNATE, congenital, inborn, inherited, inbred

heretic ♦ one who is not orthodox in his beliefs *Syn* schismatic, sectarian, sectary, dissenter, nonconformist

heretical *Syn* HETERODOX

heritage ♦ something which one receives or is entitled to receive by succession *Syn* inheritance, patrimony, birthright

hermaphroditic, hermaphrodite *Syn* BISEXUAL, androgynous, epicene

hermit *Syn* RECLUSE, eremite, anchorite, cenobite

heroism ♦ conspicuous courage or bravery *Syn* valor, prowess, gallantry

hesitancy *Syn* HESITATION

hesitant *Syn* DISINCLINED, reluctant, loath, averse, indisposed

hesitate ♦ to show irresolution or uncertainty *Syn* waver, vacillate, falter

hesitation ♦ an act or action of hesitating *Syn* hesitancy

heterodox ♦ not in conformity with orthodox beliefs or teachings *Syn* heretical *Ant* orthodox

heterogeneous *Syn* MISCELLANEOUS, motley, promiscuous, assorted *Ant* homogeneous

hew *Syn* CUT, chop, carve, slit, slash

hiatus *Syn* BREAK, gap, interruption, interval, interim, lacuna

hick *Syn* BOOR, bumpkin, yokel, rube, clodhopper, clown, lout, churl

hide *vb* ♦ to withdraw or to withhold from sight or observation *Syn* conceal, screen, secrete, cache, bury, ensconce

hide *n* *Syn* SKIN, pelt, rind, bark, peel

hidebound *Syn* ILLIBERAL, narrow-minded, narrow, intolerant, bigoted

hideous *Syn* UGLY, ill-favored, unsightly *Ant* fair

high ♦ having a relatively great upward extension *Syn* tall, lofty *Ant* low

high-spirited *Syn* SPIRITED, mettlesome, spunky, fiery, peppery, gingery

hilarity *Syn* MIRTH, jollity, glee

hind *Syn* POSTERIOR, hinder, rear, after, back *Ant* fore, front

hinder *vb* ♦ to put obstacles in the way *Syn* impede, obstruct, block, bar, dam *Ant* further

hinder *adj Syn* POSTERIOR, hind, rear, after, back *Ant* front, fore

hinge *Syn* DEPEND, hang, turn

hint *Syn* SUGGEST, intimate, insinuate, imply

hire *n Syn* WAGE, wages, pay, salary, stipend, fee, emolument

hire *vb* ♦ to take or engage something or grant the use of something for a stipulated price or rate *Syn* let, lease, rent, charter

hireling *Syn* MERCENARY, venal, hack

history ♦ a chronological record of events *Syn* chronicle, annals

histrionic *Syn* DRAMATIC, theatrical, dramaturgic, melodramatic

hit *Syn* STRIKE, smite, punch, slug, slog, swat, clout, slap, cuff, box

hit-or-miss *Syn* RANDOM, haphazard, happy-go-lucky, desultory, casual, chance, chancy

hoard *Syn* ACCUMULATE, amass

hoarse *Syn* LOUD, raucous, strident, stentorian, earsplitting, stertorous

hoax *Syn* DUPE, hoodwink, bamboozle, gull, befool, trick

hobo *Syn* VAGABOND, tramp, vagrant, truant, bum

hocus-pocus *Syn* GIBBERISH, mummery, abracadabra

hog-tie *Syn* HAMPER, trammel, clog, fetter, shackle, manacle

hoist *Syn* LIFT, raise, elevate, boost, heave, rear

hold *vb* **1** *Syn* KEEP, hold back, withhold, reserve, detain, retain, keep back, keep out **2** *Syn* CONTAIN, accommodate **3** *Syn* HAVE, own, possess, enjoy

hold *n* ♦ the act or manner of grasping or holding *Syn* grip, grasp, clutch

hold back *Syn* KEEP, hold, withhold, reserve, detain, retain, keep back, keep out

hole ♦ a space within the substance of a body or mass *Syn* hollow, cavity, pocket, void, vacuum

holiness ♦ a state of spiritual soundness and unimpaired virtue *Syn* sanctity

holler *vb Syn* SHOUT, yell, shriek, scream, screech, squeal, whoop

holler *n Syn* SHOUT, yell, shriek, scream, screech, squeal, whoop

hollow *adj Syn* VAIN, empty, nugatory, otiose, idle

hollow *n Syn* HOLE, cavity, pocket, void, vacuum

holocaust *Syn* FIRE, conflagration

holy ♦ dedicated to the service of or set apart by religion *Syn* sacred, divine, spiritual, religious, blessed *Ant* unholy

homage *Syn* HONOR, reverence, deference, obeisance

home *Syn* HABITATION, house, dwelling, abode, residence, domicile

homely *Syn* PLAIN, simple, unpretentious *Ant* comely, bonny

homily *Syn* SPEECH, sermon, talk, address, oration, harangue, lecture

homunculus *Syn* DWARF, manikin, midget, pygmy, runt

honest *Syn* UPRIGHT, just, conscientious, scrupulous, honorable *Ant* dishonest

honesty ♦ uprightness as evidenced in character and actions *Syn* honor, integrity, probity *Ant* dishonesty

honor *n* **1** *Syn* FAME, glory, renown, celebrity, éclat, reputation, repute, notoriety *Ant* dishonor **2** ♦ respect or esteem shown one as his or her due or claimed by one as a right *Syn* homage, reverence, deference, obeisance **3** *Syn* HONESTY, integrity, probity

honor *vb Syn* DIGNIFY, ennoble, glorify

honorable *Syn* UPRIGHT, just, scrupulous, conscientious, honest *Ant* dishonorable

hoodwink *Syn* DUPE, hoax, trick, gull, befool, bamboozle

hop *Syn* SKIP, bound, curvet, lope, lollop, ricochet

hope *Syn* EXPECT, look, await *Ant* despair (*of*); despond

hopeful ♦ having or showing confidence that the end or outcome will be favorable *Syn* optimistic, roseate, rose-colored *Ant* hopeless, despairing

hopeless *Syn* DESPONDENT, despairing, desperate, forlorn *Ant* hopeful

hopelessness *Syn* DESPONDENCY, despair, desperation, forlornness *Ant* hopefulness

horde *Syn* CROWD, mob, throng, crush, press, rout

horizon *Syn* RANGE, gamut, reach, radius, compass, sweep, scope, orbit, ken, purview

horrendous *Syn* HORRIBLE, horrific, horrid

horrible 1 ♦ inspiring horror or abhorrence *Syn* horrid, horrific, horrendous *Ant* fascinating **2** *Syn* FEARFUL, horrific, shocking, appalling, awful, dreadful, frightful, terrible, terrific

horrid *Syn* HORRIBLE, horrific, horrendous *Ant* delightful

horrific 1 *Syn* HORRIBLE, horrid, horrendous **2** *Syn* FEARFUL, horrible, terrible, terrific, shocking, appalling, awful, dreadful, frightful

horrify *Syn* DISMAY, daunt, appall

horror *Syn* FEAR, terror, dread, fright, alarm, dismay, consternation, panic, trepidation *Ant* fascination

hors d'oeuvre *Syn* APPETIZER, aperitif

horse sense *Syn* SENSE, common sense, good sense, gumption, judgment, wisdom

hospitable *Syn* SOCIAL, gregarious, convivial, cooperative, companionable *Ant* inhospitable

host *Syn* MULTITUDE, army, legion

hostage *Syn* PLEDGE, pawn, earnest, token

hostility *Syn* ENMITY, animosity, antagonism, antipathy, rancor, animus

hound *Syn* BAIT, ride, hector, badger, heckle, chivy

house *n* *Syn* HABITATION, home, dwelling, abode, residence, domicile

house *vb* *Syn* HARBOR, lodge, board, shelter, entertain

hover *Syn* FLIT, flutter, flitter, flicker

howl 1 *Syn* BARK, bay, growl, snarl, yelp, yap **2** *Syn* ROAR, bellow, bluster, bawl, vociferate, clamor, ululate

howler *Syn* ERROR, boner, mistake, blunder, slip, lapse, faux pas, bull

hub *Syn* CENTER, core, middle, nucleus, heart, focus, midst

hubbub *Syn* DIN, uproar, pandemonium, hullabaloo, babel, clamor, racket

hue *Syn* COLOR, shade, tint, tinge, tone

huff *Syn* OFFENSE, dudgeon, pique, resentment, umbrage

huffy *Syn* IRRITABLE, petulant, pettish, fractious, peevish, snappish, waspish, fretful, querulous

huge ♦ exceedingly or excessively large *Syn* vast, immense, enormous, elephantine, mammoth, giant, gigantic, gigantean, colossal, gargantuan, Herculean, cyclopean, titanic, Brobdingnagian

hullabaloo *Syn* DIN, uproar, pandemonium, babel, hubbub, clamor, racket

humane *Syn* CHARITABLE, humanitarian, benevolent, philanthropic, eleemosynary, altruistic *Ant* barbarous, inhuman; atrocious

humanitarian *Syn* CHARITABLE, humane, benevolent, philanthropic, eleemosynary, altruistic

humble *adj* ♦ lacking all signs of pride, aggressiveness, or self-assertiveness *Syn* meek, modest, lowly

humble *vb* *Syn* ABASE, humiliate, demean, debase, degrade

humbug *Syn* IMPOSTURE, fake, sham, cheat, fraud, deceit, deception, counterfeit

humdrum *Syn* DULL, dreary, monotonous, pedestrian, stodgy

humid *Syn* WET, moist, damp, dank

humiliate *Syn* ABASE, humble, degrade, debase, demean

humor *n* **1** *Syn* MOOD, temper, vein **2** *Syn* WIT, irony, satire, sarcasm, repartee

humor *vb Syn* INDULGE, pamper, spoil, baby, mollycoddle

humorous *Syn* WITTY, facetious, jocular, jocose

hunger *Syn* LONG, yearn, hanker, pine, thirst

hunt *Syn* SEEK, search, ransack, rummage, scour, comb, ferret out

hurl *Syn* THROW, fling, cast, pitch, toss, sling

hurricane ♦ a violent rotating storm originating in the tropics and often moving into temperate latitudes *Syn* tropical storm, typhoon

hurry *vb Syn* SPEED, quicken, precipitate, hasten *Ant* delay

hurry *n Syn* HASTE, speed, dispatch, expedition

hurt *vb Syn* INJURE, harm, damage, impair, mar, spoil

hurt *n Syn* INJURY, harm, damage, mischief

husbandry *Syn* AGRICULTURE, farming

husky *Syn* MUSCULAR, brawny, sinewy, athletic, burly

hygienic *Syn* HEALTHFUL, sanitary, healthy, wholesome, salubrious, salutary

hymeneal *Syn* MATRIMONIAL, nuptial, marital, connubial, conjugal

hymn *Syn* SING, troll, carol, descant, warble, trill, chant, intone

hyperbole *Syn* EXAGGERATION, overstatement

hypercritical *Syn* CRITICAL, captious, caviling, carping, censorious, faultfinding

hypochondriac *Syn* MELANCHOLIC, melancholy, atrabilious

hypocrisy ♦ the pretense or affectation of having virtues, principles, or beliefs that one does not actually have *Syn* sanctimony, pharisaism, cant

hypocritical ♦ characterized by hypocrisy *Syn* sanctimonious, pharisaical, canting

hypostatize *Syn* REALIZE, reify, externalize, materialize, incarnate, actualize, embody, objectify

hypothetical *Syn* SUPPOSED, conjectural, supposititious, reputed, putative, purported

hysteria *Syn* MANIA, delirium, frenzy

I

icon *Syn* IMAGE, portrait, effigy, statue, photograph, mask

iconoclast *Syn* REBEL, insurgent

icy *Syn* COLD, glacial, arctic, gelid, frigid, freezing, frosty, cool, chilly *Ant* fiery

idea ♦ what exists in the mind as a representation as of something comprehended or as a formulation as of a plan *Syn* concept, conception, thought, notion, impression

ideal *adj Syn* ABSTRACT, transcendent, transcendental *Ant* actual

ideal *n Syn* MODEL, pattern, exemplar, example, standard, beau ideal, mirror

identical 1 *also* **identic** *Syn* SAME, selfsame, very, equivalent, equal, tantamount *Ant* diverse 2 *Syn* LIKE, alike, similar, analogous, comparable, akin, parallel, uniform *Ant* different

identification *Syn* RECOGNITION, apperception, assimilation

identify ♦ to bring (one or more things) into union with another thing *Syn* incorporate, embody, assimilate

idiom 1 *Syn* LANGUAGE, dialect, speech, tongue 2 *Syn* PHRASE, expression, locution

idiosyncrasy *Syn* ECCENTRICITY

idiot *Syn* FOOL, imbecile, moron, simpleton, natural

idle *adj* 1 *Syn* VAIN, nugatory, otiose, empty, hollow 2 *Syn* INACTIVE, inert, passive, supine *Ant* busy

idle *vb* ♦ to spend time not in work but in idleness *Syn* loaf, lounge, loll, laze

idolize *Syn* ADORE, worship

ignite *Syn* LIGHT, kindle, fire *Ant* stifle; extinguish

ignoble *Syn* MEAN, sordid, abject *Ant* noble; magnanimous

ignominy *Syn* DISGRACE, infamy, shame, opprobrium, dishonor, disrepute, obloquy, odium

ignorant ♦ lacking knowledge or education *Syn* illiterate, unlettered, uneducated, untaught, untutored, unlearned *Ant* cognizant (*of something*); conversant; informed

ignore *Syn* NEGLECT, disregard, overlook, slight, omit, forget *Ant* heed (*a warning, a sign, a symptom*); acknowledge

ilk *Syn* TYPE, kind, sort, nature, description, character, stripe, kidney

ill *adj Syn* BAD, evil, wicked, naughty *Ant* good

ill *n Syn* EVIL *Ant* good

illegal *Syn* UNLAWFUL, illegitimate, illicit *Ant* legal

illegitimate *Syn* UNLAWFUL, illegal, illicit *Ant* legitimate

ill-fated *Syn* UNLUCKY, ill-starred, disastrous, unfortunate, calamitous, luckless, hapless

ill-favored *Syn* UGLY, hideous, unsightly *Ant* well-favored; fair

illiberal ♦ unwilling or unable to understand the point of view of others *Syn* narrow-minded, narrow, intolerant, bigoted, hidebound *Ant* liberal

illicit *Syn* UNLAWFUL, illegal, illegitimate *Ant* licit

illimitable *Syn* INFINITE, boundless, uncircumscribed, eternal, sempiternal

illiterate *Syn* IGNORANT, unlettered, uneducated, untaught, untutored, unlearned *Ant* literate

ill-mannered *Syn* RUDE, uncivil, ungracious, impolite, discourteous *Ant* well-bred

ill-starred *Syn* UNLUCKY, ill-fated, disastrous, unfortunate, calamitous, luckless, hapless

ill-treat *Syn* ABUSE, maltreat, mistreat, misuse, outrage

illuminate, illumine ♦ to fill with or to throw light upon *Syn* light, lighten, enlighten, illustrate *Ant* darken, obscure

illusion *Syn* DELUSION, mirage, hallucination

illusory *Syn* APPARENT, seeming, ostensible *Ant* factual; matter-of-fact

illustrate 1 *Syn* ILLUMINATE, enlighten, illumine, light, lighten *Ant* dim **2** *Syn* EXEMPLIFY

illustration *Syn* INSTANCE, example, case, sample, specimen

illustrious *Syn* FAMOUS, eminent, renowned, celebrated, famed *Ant* infamous

ill will *Syn* MALICE, malevolence, malignity, malignancy, spite, despite, spleen, grudge *Ant* goodwill; charity

image 1 ♦ a lifelike representation esp. of a living being *Syn* effigy, statue, icon, portrait, photograph, mask **2** *Syn* SENSATION, percept, sense-datum, sensum

imaginary ♦ unreal or unbelievable or conceiving such unreal or unbelievable things *Syn* fanciful, visionary, fantastic, chimerical, quixotic *Ant* real, actual

imagination ♦ the power or function of the mind by which mental images of things are formed or the exercise of that power *Syn* fancy, fantasy

imagine *Syn* THINK, conceive, fancy, realize, envisage, envision

imbecile *Syn* FOOL, idiot, moron, simpleton, natural

imbibe *Syn* ABSORB, assimilate *Ant* ooze, exude

imbue *Syn* INFUSE, inoculate, leaven, ingrain, suffuse

imitate *Syn* COPY, mimic, ape, mock

immaterial ♦ not composed of matter *Syn* spiritual, incorporeal *Ant* material

immature ♦ not fully developed *Syn* unmatured, unripe, unmellow *Ant* mature

immediate *Syn* DIRECT *Ant* mediate (*knowledge, relation, operation*); distant (*relatives*)

immense *Syn* HUGE, vast, enormous, elephantine, mammoth, giant, gigantic, gigantean, colossal, gargantuan, Herculean, cyclopean, titanic, Brobdingnagian

immerse *Syn* DIP, submerge, duck, souse, dunk

immigrant 1 *Syn* STRANGER, alien, foreigner, outlander, outsider, émigré **2** *Syn* EMIGRANT, migrant

immigrate *Syn* MIGRATE, emigrate

imminent *Syn* IMPENDING

immobile *Syn* IMMOVABLE, immotive *Ant* mobile

immoderate *Syn* EXCESSIVE, inordinate, exorbitant, extreme, extravagant *Ant* moderate

immortal ♦ not subject to death or decay *Syn* deathless, undying, unfading *Ant* mortal

immotive *Syn* IMMOVABLE, immobile

immovable ♦ incapable of moving or being moved *Syn* immobile, immotive *Ant* movable

immunity *Syn* EXEMPTION *Ant* susceptibility

immure *Syn* IMPRISON, incarcerate, jail, intern

impact ♦ a forcible or enforced contact between two or more things *Syn* impingement, collision, clash, shock, concussion, percussion, jar, jolt

impair *Syn* INJURE, damage, mar, harm, hurt, spoil *Ant* improve, amend; repair

impalpable *Syn* IMPERCEPTIBLE, insensible, intangible, inappreciable, imponderable *Ant* palpable

impart *Syn* COMMUNICATE

impartial *Syn* FAIR, equitable, unbiased, objective, just, dispassionate, uncolored *Ant* partial

impassable ♦ not allowing passage *Syn* impenetrable, impervious, impermeable *Ant* passable

impassible *Syn* INSENSIBLE, insensitive, anesthetic

impassioned ♦ actuated by or showing intense feeling *Syn* passionate, ardent, fervent, fervid, perfervid *Ant* unimpassioned

impassive ♦ unresponsive to what might normally excite interest or emotion *Syn* stoic, phlegmatic, apathetic, stolid *Ant* responsive

impassivity, impassiveness ♦ unresponsiveness to something that might normally excite interest or emotion *Syn* apathy, stolidity, phlegm, stoicism

impatient ♦ manifesting signs of unrest or an inability to keep still or quiet *Syn* nervous, unquiet, restless, restive, uneasy, fidgety, jumpy, jittery *Ant* patient

impeach *Syn* ACCUSE, indict, incriminate, charge, arraign

impeccable ♦ absolutely correct and beyond criticism *Syn* faultless, flawless, errorless

impecunious *Syn* POOR, indigent, needy, destitute, penniless, poverty-stricken, necessitous *Ant* flush

impede *Syn* HINDER, obstruct, block, bar, dam *Ant* assist; promote

impediment *Syn* OBSTACLE, obstruction, bar, snag *Ant* aid, assistance; advantage

impel *Syn* MOVE, drive, actuate *Ant* restrain

impending ♦ likely to occur soon or without further warning *Syn* imminent

impenetrable *Syn* IMPASSABLE, impervious, impermeable *Ant* penetrable

impenetrate *Syn* PERMEATE, interpenetrate, penetrate, pervade, impregnate, saturate

imperative 1 *Syn* MASTERFUL, peremptory, imperious, domineering **2** *Syn* PRESSING, urgent, crying, importunate, insistent, exigent, instant

imperceptible ♦ incapable of being apprehended by the senses or intellect *Syn* insensible, impalpable, intangible, inappreciable, imponderable *Ant* perceptible

imperfection ♦ an instance of failure to reach a standard of excellence or perfection *Syn* deficiency, shortcoming, fault *Ant* perfection

imperial *Syn* KINGLY, regal, royal, queenly, princely

imperil *Syn* VENTURE, hazard, risk, chance, jeopardize, endanger

imperious *Syn* MASTERFUL, domineering, peremptory, imperative *Ant* abject

impermeable *Syn* IMPASSABLE, impervious, impenetrable

impersonate *Syn* ACT, play

impersonator *Syn* ACTOR, player, mummer, mime, mimic, performer, thespian, trouper

impertinent ♦ given to thrusting oneself into the affairs of others *Syn* officious, meddlesome, intrusive, obtrusive

imperturbable *Syn* COOL, composed, collected, unruffled, unflappable, nonchalant *Ant* choleric, touchy

impervious *Syn* IMPASSABLE, impenetrable, impermeable

impetuous *Syn* PRECIPITATE, headlong, abrupt, hasty, sudden

impetus 1 *Syn* SPEED, momentum, velocity, pace **2** *Syn* STIMULUS, excitant, incitement, stimulant

impingement *Syn* IMPACT, collision, clash, shock, concussion, percussion, jar, jolt

impious ♦ lacking in reverence for what is sacred or divine *Syn* profane, blasphemous, sacrilegious *Ant* pious; reverent

impish *Syn* PLAYFUL, roguish, waggish, mischievous, frolicsome, sportive

implacable *Syn* GRIM, relentless, unrelenting, merciless

implant ♦ to introduce into the mind *Syn* inculcate, instill

implement *n* ♦ a relatively simple device for performing work *Syn* tool, instrument, appliance, utensil

implement *vb* *Syn* ENFORCE

implicate *Syn* INVOLVE

implication ♦ something hinted at but not explicitly stated *Syn* inference

implicit ♦ understood though not directly stated *Syn* virtual, constructive *Ant* explicit

implore *Syn* BEG, entreat, beseech, supplicate, importune, adjure

imply 1 *Syn* INCLUDE, involve, comprehend, embrace, subsume **2** *Syn* SUGGEST, hint, intimate, insinuate *Ant* express

impolite *Syn* RUDE, uncivil, discourteous, ill-mannered, ungracious *Ant* polite

imponderable *Syn* IMPERCEPTIBLE, impalpable, inappreciable, insensible, intangible *Ant* ponderable, appreciable

import *vb* *Syn* MEAN, denote, signify

import *n* **1** *Syn* MEANING, significance, sense, acceptation, signification **2** *Syn* IMPORTANCE, significance, consequence, moment, weight

importance ♦ the quality or state of being of notable worth or influence *Syn* consequence, moment, weight, significance, import *Ant* unimportance

importunate *Syn* PRESSING, urgent, imperative, crying, insistent, exigent, instant

importune *Syn* BEG, entreat, beseech, implore, supplicate, adjure

impose *Syn* DICTATE, prescribe, ordain, decree

imposing *Syn* GRAND, stately, majestic, august, noble, magnificent, grandiose *Ant* unimposing

impostor ♦ a person who fraudulently pretends to be someone or something else *Syn* faker, quack, mountebank, charlatan

imposture ♦ a thing made to seem other than it is *Syn* cheat, fraud, sham, fake, humbug, deceit, deception, counterfeit

impotent 1 *Syn* POWERLESS *Ant* potent **2** *Syn* STERILE, barren, unfruitful, infertile *Ant* virile

impoverish *Syn* DEPLETE, bankrupt, exhaust, drain *Ant* enrich

imprecation *Syn* CURSE, malediction, anathema *Ant* prayer

impregnable *Syn* INVINCIBLE, inexpugnable, unassailable, invulnerable, unconquerable, indomitable

impregnate 1 *Syn* PERMEATE, saturate, pervade, penetrate, impenetrate, interpenetrate **2** *Syn* SOAK, saturate, drench, steep, sop, waterlog

impress *vb* *Syn* AFFECT, touch, strike, influence, sway

impress *n* *Syn* IMPRESSION, imprint, print, stamp

impressible *Syn* SENTIENT, sensitive, impressionable, responsive, susceptible

impression 1 ♦ the perceptible trace or traces left by pressure *Syn* impress, imprint, print, stamp **2** *Syn* IDEA, notion, thought, concept, conception **3** *Syn* EDITION, reprinting, printing, reissue

impressionable *Syn* SENTIENT, sensitive, impressible, responsive, susceptible

impressive *Syn* MOVING, affecting, poignant, touching, pathetic *Ant* unimpressive

imprint *Syn* IMPRESSION, print, impress, stamp

imprison ♦ to confine closely so that escape is impossible or unlikely *Syn* incarcerate, jail, immure, intern

impromptu *Syn* EXTEMPORANEOUS, unpremeditated, offhand, improvised, extempore, extemporary

improper 1 *Syn* UNFIT, inappropriate, unfitting, unsuitable, inapt, unhappy, infelicitous *Ant* proper **2** *Syn* INDECOROUS, indecent, unseemly, unbecoming, indelicate *Ant* proper

impropriety *Syn* BARBARISM, corruption, solecism, vulgarism, vernacular

improve 1 ♦ to make more acceptable or bring nearer to some standard *Syn* better, help, ameliorate *Ant* impair; worsen **2** ♦ to grow or become better (as in health or well-being) *Syn* recover, recuperate, convalesce, gain

improvised *Syn* EXTEMPORANEOUS, unpremeditated, impromptu, offhand, extempore, extemporary

impudent *Syn* SHAMELESS, brazen, barefaced, brash *Ant* respectful

impugn *Syn* DENY, gainsay, contradict, negative, traverse, contravene *Ant* authenticate; advocate

impulse *Syn* MOTIVE, spring, incentive, inducement, spur, goad

impulsive *Syn* SPONTANEOUS, instinctive, automatic, mechanical *Ant* deliberate

impute *Syn* ASCRIBE, attribute, assign, refer, credit, accredit, charge

inactive ♦ not engaged in work or activity *Syn* idle, inert, passive, supine *Ant* active, live

inadvertent *Syn* CARELESS, heedless, thoughtless

inane *Syn* INSIPID, banal, wishy-washy, jejune, vapid, flat

inanimate *Syn* DEAD, lifeless, defunct, deceased, departed, late *Ant* animate

inappreciable *Syn* IMPERCEPTIBLE, imponderable, impalpable, insensible, intangible *Ant* appreciable, ponderable

inappropriate *Syn* UNFIT, unfitting, inapt, improper, unsuitable, unhappy, infelicitous *Ant* appropriate

inapt *Syn* UNFIT, unhappy, infelicitous, inappropriate, unfitting, unsuitable, improper *Ant* apt

inarticulate *Syn* DUMB, speechless, mute *Ant* articulate

inasmuch as *Syn* BECAUSE, since, for, as

inaugurate 1 *Syn* INITIATE, install, induct, invest **2** *Syn* BEGIN, start, commence

inauspicious *Syn* OMINOUS, unpropitious, portentous, fateful *Ant* auspicious

inborn *Syn* INNATE, congenital, hereditary, inherited, inbred *Ant* acquired

inbred *Syn* INNATE, inborn, congenital, hereditary, inherited

incapable ♦ mentally or physically unfit, or untrained to do a given kind of work *Syn* incompetent, unqualified *Ant* capable

incarcerate *Syn* IMPRISON, jail, immure, intern

incarnate *Syn* REALIZE, embody, hypostatize, materialize, externalize, objectify, actualize, reify

incendiary *Syn* COMBUSTIBLE, inflammable, flammable, inflammatory

incense *n Syn* FRAGRANCE, redolence, perfume, bouquet

incense *vb Syn* ANGER, enrage, infuriate, madden *Ant* placate

incentive *Syn* MOTIVE, inducement, spring, spur, goad, impulse

inception *Syn* ORIGIN, source, root, provenance, provenience *Ant* termination

incessant *Syn* CONTINUAL, continuous, constant, unremitting, perpetual, perennial *Ant* intermittent

incident *Syn* OCCURRENCE, episode, event, circumstance

incidental *Syn* ACCIDENTAL, casual, fortuitous, contingent *Ant* essential

incise *Syn* CARVE, engrave, etch, chisel, sculpture, sculpt, sculp

incisive ♦ having, manifesting, or suggesting a keen alertness of mind *Syn* trenchant, clear-cut, cutting, biting, crisp

incite ♦ to spur to action *Syn* instigate, abet, foment *Ant* restrain

incitement *Syn* STIMULUS, stimulant, excitant, impetus *Ant* restraint; inhibition

incline 1 *Syn* SLANT, lean, slope **2** ♦ to influence one to have or to take an attitude toward something *Syn* bias, dispose, predispose *Ant* disincline, indispose

include ♦ to contain within as part of the whole *Syn* comprehend, embrace, involve, imply, subsume *Ant* exclude

incognito *Syn* PSEUDONYM, alias, nom de guerre, pen name, nom de plume

incommode *Syn* INCONVENIENCE, discommode, trouble *Ant* accommodate

incomparable *Syn* SUPREME, peerless, superlative, transcendent, surpassing, preeminent

incompatible *Syn* INCONSONANT, incongruous, inconsistent, discordant, discrepant, uncongenial, unsympathetic *Ant* compatible

incompetent *Syn* INCAPABLE, unqualified *Ant* competent

incongruous *Syn* INCONSONANT, uncongenial, incompatible, inconsistent, discordant, discrepant, unsympathetic *Ant* congruous

inconsistent *Syn* INCONSONANT, incompatible, incongruous, uncongenial, unsympathetic, discordant, discrepant *Ant* consistent

inconsonant ♦ not in agreement with or not agreeable to *Syn* inconsistent, incompatible, incongruous, uncongenial, unsympathetic, discordant, discrepant *Ant* consonant

inconstant ♦ lacking firmness or steadiness (as in purpose or devotion) *Syn* fickle, capricious, mercurial, unstable *Ant* constant

inconvenience ♦ to subject to disturbance or discomfort *Syn* incommode, discommode, trouble

incorporate *Syn* IDENTIFY, embody, assimilate

incorporeal *Syn* IMMATERIAL, spiritual *Ant* corporeal

increase ♦ to make or become greater *Syn* enlarge, augment, multiply *Ant* decrease

incredulity *Syn* UNBELIEF, disbelief *Ant* credulity

increment *Syn* ADDITION, accretion, accession

incriminate *Syn* ACCUSE, impeach, indict, charge, arraign

inculcate *Syn* IMPLANT, instill

incur ♦ to bring upon oneself something usu. unpleasant or injurious *Syn* contract, catch

incurious *Syn* INDIFFERENT, unconcerned, aloof, detached, uninterested, disinterested *Ant* curious, inquisitive

incursion *Syn* INVASION, raid, inroad

indebtedness *Syn* DEBT, debit, obligation, liability, arrear

indecent *Syn* INDECOROUS, unseemly, indelicate, improper, unbecoming *Ant* decent

indecorous ♦ not conforming to what is accepted as right, fitting, or in good taste *Syn* improper, unseemly, indecent, unbecoming, indelicate *Ant* decorous

indefatigable ♦ capable of prolonged and arduous effort *Syn* tireless, weariless, untiring, unwearying, unwearied, unflagging

indefinable *Syn* UNUTTERABLE, inexpressible, unspeakable, ineffable, indescribable

indelicate *Syn* INDECOROUS, indecent, unseemly, improper, unbecoming *Ant* delicate, refined

indemnify *Syn* PAY, reimburse, recompense, compensate, remunerate, repay, satisfy

indemnity *Syn* REPARATION, redress, amends, restitution

indentured *Syn* BOUND, articled, bond

independence *Syn* FREEDOM, autonomy, sovereignty, autarchy, autarky *Ant* dependence

independent *Syn* FREE, autonomous, sovereign, autarchic, autarkic *Ant* dependent

indescribable *Syn* UNUTTERABLE, inexpressible, ineffable, unspeakable, indefinable

indicate ♦ to give evidence of or to serve as ground for a valid or reasonable inference *Syn* betoken, attest, bespeak, argue, prove

indict *Syn* ACCUSE, incriminate, impeach, charge, arraign

indifferent 1 ♦ not showing or feeling interest *Syn* unconcerned, incurious, aloof, detached, uninterested, disinterested *Ant* avid **2** *Syn* MEDIUM, average, moderate, middling, fair, mediocre, second-rate *Ant* choice **3** *Syn* NEUTRAL

indigence *Syn* POVERTY, penury, want, destitution, privation *Ant* affluence, opulence

indigenous *Syn* NATIVE, autochthonous, endemic, aboriginal *Ant* naturalized; exotic

indigent *Syn* POOR, needy, destitute, penniless, impecunious, poverty-stricken, necessitous *Ant* opulent

indignant *Syn* ANGRY, irate, wrathful, wroth, acrimonious, mad

indignation *Syn* ANGER, wrath, ire, rage, fury

indignity *Syn* AFFRONT, insult

indirect ♦ deviating from a direct line or straightforward course *Syn* circuitous, roundabout *Ant* direct; forthright; straightforward

indiscriminate ♦ including all or nearly all within the range of choice, operation, or effectiveness *Syn* wholesale, sweeping *Ant* selective; discriminating

indispensable *Syn* NEEDFUL, essential, necessary, requisite *Ant* dispensable

indisposed *Syn* DISINCLINED, loath, averse, hesitant, reluctant *Ant* disposed

individual *adj* **1** *Syn* SPECIAL, particular, specific, especial *Ant* general **2** *Syn* CHARACTERISTIC, peculiar, distinctive *Ant* common

individual *n* *Syn* ENTITY, being, creature, person

individuality *Syn* DISPOSITION, personality, temperament, temper, complexion, character

individually *Syn* EACH, apiece, severally, respectively

indolent *Syn* LAZY, faineant, slothful *Ant* industrious

indomitable *Syn* INVINCIBLE, unconquerable, impregnable, inexpugnable, unassailable, invulnerable

induce ♦ to move another to do or agree to something *Syn* persuade, prevail, get

inducement *Syn* MOTIVE, incentive, spur, goad, spring, impulse

induct *Syn* INITIATE, inaugurate, install, invest

indulge ♦ to show undue favor to a person's desires and feelings *Syn* pamper, humor, spoil, baby, mollycoddle *Ant* discipline (*others*); abstain (*with reference to oneself, one's appetite*)

indulgence *Syn* FORBEARANCE, tolerance, clemency, mercifulness, leniency *Ant* strictness

indulgent *Syn* FORBEARING, lenient, tolerant, clement, merciful *Ant* strict

indulgently *Syn* FORBEARINGLY, tolerantly, clemently, mercifully, leniently

indurate *Syn* HARDEN, solidify, petrify, cake

indurated *Syn* HARDENED, callous *Ant* pliable

industrious *Syn* BUSY, diligent, assiduous, sedulous *Ant* slothful, indolent

industry *Syn* BUSINESS, trade, commerce, traffic

inebriate *Syn* DRUNKARD, alcoholic, dipsomaniac, sot, soak, toper, tosspot, tippler *Ant* teetotaler

inebriated *Syn* DRUNK, drunken, intoxicated, tipsy, tight

ineffable *Syn* UNUTTERABLE, inexpressible, unspeakable, indescribable, indefinable

ineffective ♦ not producing or incapable of producing an intended result *Syn* ineffectual, inefficient, inefficacious *Ant* effective

ineffectual *Syn* INEFFECTIVE, inefficacious, inefficient *Ant* effectual

inefficacious *Syn* INEFFECTIVE, ineffectual, inefficient *Ant* efficacious

inefficient *Syn* INEFFECTIVE, ineffectual, inefficacious *Ant* efficient

ineluctable *Syn* INEVITABLE, inescapable, unescapable, unavoidable

inept *Syn* AWKWARD, clumsy, maladroit, gauche *Ant* apt; adept; able

inerrable *Syn* INFALLIBLE, inerrant, unerring

inerrant *Syn* INFALLIBLE, unerring

inert *Syn* INACTIVE, passive, idle, supine *Ant* dynamic; animated

inescapable *Syn* INEVITABLE, ineluctable, unescapable, unavoidable *Ant* escapable

inevitable 1 ♦ incapable of being avoided or escaped *Syn* ineluctable, inescapable, unescapable, unavoidable *Ant* evitable **2** *Syn* CERTAIN, necessary

inexorable *Syn* INFLEXIBLE, obdurate, adamant, adamantine *Ant* exorable

inexpressible *Syn* UNUTTERABLE, ineffable, unspeakable, indescribable, indefinable *Ant* expressible

inexpugnable *Syn* INVINCIBLE, unassailable, impregnable, unconquerable, invulnerable, indomitable *Ant* expugnable

infallible ♦ incapable of making mistakes or errors *Syn* inerrable, inerrant, unerring *Ant* fallible

infamous *Syn* VICIOUS, nefarious, flagitious, iniquitous, villainous, corrupt, degenerate *Ant* illustrious

infamy *Syn* DISGRACE, ignominy, shame, dishonor, disrepute, opprobrium, obloquy, odium

infancy ♦ the state or period of being under the age established by law for the attainment of full civil rights *Syn* minority, nonage

infatuated 1 *Syn* FOND, besotted, insensate **2** *Syn* ENAMORED

infectious 1 ♦ transmissible by infection *Syn* contagious, communicable, catching **2** ♦ capable of infecting or tending to infect *Syn* infective

infective *Syn* INFECTIOUS

infelicitous *Syn* UNFIT, unhappy, inapt, inappropriate, unfitting, unsuitable, improper *Ant* felicitous

infer ♦ to arrive at by reasoning from evidence or from premises *Syn* deduce, conclude, judge, gather

inference 1 ♦ the deriving of a conclusion by reasoning *Syn* deduction, conclusion, judgment **2** ♦ the process of arriving at conclusions from data or premises *Syn* ratiocination **3** *Syn* IMPLICATION

inferential ♦ deduced or deducible by reasoning *Syn* ratiocinative

inferior ♦ one who is lower than another esp. in station or rank *Syn* underling, subordinate *Ant* superior

infernal ♦ of or relating to a nether world of the dead *Syn* chthonian, chthonic, hellish, Hadean, Tartarean, stygian *Ant* supernal

infertile *Syn* STERILE, barren, impotent, unfruitful *Ant* fertile

infest ♦ to spread or swarm over in a troublesome manner *Syn* overrun, beset *Ant* disinfest

infidel *Syn* ATHEIST, unbeliever, freethinker, agnostic, deist

infinite ♦ being without known limits *Syn* eternal, sempiternal, boundless, illimitable, uncircumscribed *Ant* finite

infirm *Syn* WEAK, feeble, decrepit, frail, fragile *Ant* hale

inflammable *Syn* COMBUSTIBLE, flammable, incendiary, inflammatory *Ant* extinguishable

inflammatory *Syn* COMBUSTIBLE, inflammable, flammable, incendiary

inflate *Syn* EXPAND, distend, swell, amplify, dilate *Ant* deflate

inflated ♦ swollen with or as if with something insubstantial *Syn* flatulent, tumid, turgid *Ant* pithy

inflection ♦ a particular manner of employing the sounds of the voice in speech *Syn* intonation, accent

inflexible 1 *Syn* STIFF, rigid, tense, stark, wooden *Ant* flexible **2** ♦ unwilling to alter a predetermined course or purpose *Syn* inexorable, obdurate, adamant, adamantine *Ant* flexible

influence *n* ♦ power exerted over the minds or behavior of others *Syn* authority, prestige, weight, credit

influence *vb* *Syn* AFFECT, sway, impress, touch, strike

inform 1 ♦ to stimulate (as mental powers) to higher or more intense activity *Syn* animate, inspire, fire **2** ♦ to make one aware of something *Syn* acquaint, apprise, advise, notify

information *Syn* KNOWLEDGE, lore, learning, science, erudition, scholarship

infraction *Syn* BREACH, violation, transgression, infringement, trespass, contravention *Ant* observance

infrequent ♦ not common or abundant *Syn* uncommon, scarce, rare, occasional, sporadic *Ant* frequent

infringe *Syn* TRESPASS, encroach, entrench, invade

infringement *Syn* BREACH, infraction, violation, trespass, transgression, contravention

infuriate *Syn* ANGER, enrage, incense, madden

infuse ♦ to introduce one thing into another so as to affect it throughout *Syn* suffuse, imbue, ingrain, inoculate, leaven

ingeminate *Syn* REPEAT, iterate, reiterate

ingenious *Syn* CLEVER, cunning, adroit

ingenuous *Syn* NATURAL, simple, naïve, unsophisticated, artless *Ant* disingenuous; cunning

ingest *Syn* EAT, swallow, devour, consume

ingrain *Syn* INFUSE, suffuse, imbue, inoculate, leaven

ingrained *Syn* INHERENT, constitutional, essential, intrinsic

ingredient *Syn* ELEMENT, constituent, component, factor

ingress *Syn* ENTRANCE, entry, entrée, access *Ant* egress

inhabitant ♦ one that occupies a particular place regularly *Syn* denizen, resident, citizen

inherent ♦ being a part, element, or quality of a thing's inmost being *Syn* ingrained, intrinsic, essential, constitutional *Ant* adventitious

inheritance *Syn* HERITAGE, patrimony, birthright

inherited *Syn* INNATE, hereditary, inborn, inbred, congenital

inhibit 1 *Syn* FORBID, prohibit, interdict, ban, enjoin *Ant* allow **2** *Syn* RESTRAIN, curb, check, bridle *Ant* animate; activate

inhuman *Syn* FIERCE, savage, barbarous, truculent, ferocious, cruel, fell *Ant* humane

iniquitous *Syn* VICIOUS, nefarious, flagitious, villainous, infamous, corrupt, degenerate *Ant* righteous

initial ♦ marking a beginning or constituting a start *Syn* original, primordial *Ant* final

initiate 1 *Syn* BEGIN, commence, start, inaugurate *Ant* consummate **2** ♦ to put through the formalities for becoming a member or an official *Syn* induct, inaugurate, install, invest

initiation *Syn* BEGINNING, genesis, rise

initiative *Syn* MANDATE, referendum, plebiscite

injunction *Syn* COMMAND, order, bidding, behest, mandate, dictate

injure ♦ to deplete the soundness, strength, effectiveness, or perfection of something *Syn* harm, hurt, damage, impair, mar, spoil *Ant* aid

injury 1 ♦ the act or the result of inflicting something that causes loss or pain *Syn* hurt, damage, harm, mischief **2** *Syn* INJUSTICE, wrong, grievance

injustice ♦ an act that inflicts undeserved hurt *Syn* injury, wrong, grievance

innate ♦ not acquired after birth *Syn* inborn, inbred, congenital, hereditary, inherited *Ant* acquired

inner ♦ situated further in *Syn* inward, inside, interior, internal, intestine *Ant* outer

innocent *Syn* HARMLESS, innocuous, inoffensive, unoffending

innocuous *Syn* HARMLESS, innocent, inoffensive, unoffending *Ant* pernicious

innuendo *Syn* INSINUATION

inoculate *Syn* INFUSE, imbue, ingrain, leaven, suffuse

inoffensive *Syn* HARMLESS, innocuous, innocent, unoffending *Ant* offensive

inordinate *Syn* EXCESSIVE, immoderate, exorbitant, extreme, extravagant *Ant* temperate

inquest *Syn* INQUIRY, investigation, probe, inquisition, research

inquire *Syn* ASK, query, question, interrogate, catechize, quiz, examine

inquiry ♦ a search for truth, knowledge, or information *Syn* inquisition, investigation, inquest, probe, research

inquisition *Syn* INQUIRY, inquest, probe, investigation, research

inquisitive *Syn* CURIOUS, prying, snoopy, nosy *Ant* incurious

inroad *Syn* INVASION, incursion, raid

insane ♦ afflicted by or manifesting unsoundness of mind or an inability to control one's rational processes *Syn* mad, crazy, crazed, demented, deranged, lunatic, maniac, non compos mentis *Ant* sane

insanity ♦ a deranged state of mind or serious mental disorder *Syn* lunacy, psychosis, mania, dementia *Ant* sanity

inscription ♦ something written, printed, or engraved (as on a coin or a medal or under or over a picture) to indicate or describe the purpose or the nature of the thing *Syn* legend, caption

inscrutable *Syn* MYSTERIOUS, arcane

insensate *Syn* FOND, besotted, infatuated

insensible 1 ♦ unresponsive to stimuli or to external influences *Syn* insensitive, impassible, anesthetic *Ant* sensible (*to or of something*) **2** *Syn* IMPERCEPTIBLE, impalpable, intangible, inappreciable, imponderable *Ant* sensible, palpable

insensitive *Syn* INSENSIBLE, impassible, anesthetic *Ant* sensitive

insert *Syn* INTRODUCE, interpolate, intercalate, insinuate, interpose, interject *Ant* abstract; extract

inside *Syn* INNER, interior, internal, intestine, inward *Ant* outside

insidious *Syn* SLY, cunning, crafty, tricky, foxy, wily, guileful, artful

insight *Syn* DISCERNMENT, penetration, acumen, discrimination, perception *Ant* obtuseness

insinuate 1 *Syn* INTRODUCE, insert, interject, interpolate, intercalate, interpose **2** *Syn* SUGGEST, intimate, hint, imply

insinuation ♦ a subtle or covert hinting or suggestion *Syn* innuendo

insipid ♦ devoid of qualities that make for spirit and character *Syn* vapid, flat, jejune, banal, wishy-washy, inane *Ant* sapid; zestful

insistent *Syn* PRESSING, urgent, imperative, crying, importunate, exigent, instant

insolent *Syn* PROUD, arrogant, overbearing, supercilious, disdainful, haughty, lordly *Ant* deferential

inspect *Syn* SCRUTINIZE, examine, scan, audit

inspection *Syn* SCRUTINY, examination, scanning, audit

inspiration ♦ a divine or seemingly divine imparting of knowledge or power *Syn* afflatus, fury, frenzy

inspire *Syn* INFORM, animate, fire

inspirit *Syn* ENCOURAGE, hearten, embolden, cheer, nerve, steel *Ant* dispirit

in spite of *Syn* NOTWITHSTANDING, despite

install *Syn* INITIATE, induct, inaugurate, invest

instance *n* ♦ something that exhibits distinguishing characteristics in its category *Syn* case, illustration, example, sample, specimen

instance *vb Syn* MENTION, name, specify

instant *n* ♦ an almost imperceptible point or stretch of time *Syn* moment, minute, second, flash, jiffy, twinkling, split second

instant *adj Syn* PRESSING, urgent, imperative, crying, importunate, insistent, exigent

instigate *Syn* INCITE, abet, foment

instill *Syn* IMPLANT, inculcate

instinctive 1 ♦ prompted by natural instinct or propensity *Syn* intuitive *Ant* reasoned **2** *Syn* SPONTANEOUS, impulsive, automatic, mechanical *Ant* intentional

institute *Syn* FOUND, establish, organize, create *Ant* abrogate

instruct 1 *Syn* TEACH, train, educate, discipline, school **2** *Syn* COMMAND, direct, enjoin, bid, order, charge

instrument 1 *Syn* MEAN, instrumentality, agency, medium, agent, organ, vehicle, channel **2** *Syn* IMPLEMENT, tool, appliance, utensil **3** *Syn* PAPER, document

instrumentality *Syn* MEAN, agent,

agency, instrument, medium, organ, vehicle, channel

insubordinate ♦ unwilling to submit to authority *Syn* rebellious, mutinous, seditious, factious, contumacious

insular ♦ having the narrow and limited outlook characteristic of geographic isolation *Syn* provincial, parochial, local, small-town

insulate *Syn* ISOLATE, segregate, seclude, sequester

insult *vb Syn* OFFEND, affront, outrage *Ant* honor

insult *n Syn* AFFRONT, indignity

insure *Syn* ENSURE, assure, secure

insurgent *Syn* REBEL, iconoclast

insurrection *Syn* REBELLION, uprising, revolt, mutiny, revolution, putsch, coup

intact *Syn* PERFECT, whole, entire *Ant* defective

intangible *Syn* IMPERCEPTIBLE, impalpable, insensible, inappreciable, imponderable *Ant* tangible

integer *Syn* NUMBER, numeral, figure, digit

integrate ♦ to join together systematically *Syn* articulate, concatenate *Ant* disintegrate

integration ♦ the act or process of operating as a unit or whole *Syn* articulation, concatenation

integrity 1 *Syn* UNITY, solidarity, union 2 *Syn* HONESTY, probity, honor *Ant* duplicity

intellect *Syn* MIND, soul, psyche, brain, intelligence, wit

intellectual *Syn* MENTAL, psychic, cerebral, intelligent *Ant* carnal

intelligence 1 *Syn* MIND, brain, intellect, soul, psyche, wit 2 *Syn* NEWS, tidings, advice

intelligent 1 *Syn* MENTAL, intellectual, cerebral, psychic 2 ♦ mentally quick or keen *Syn* clever, alert, quick-witted, bright, smart, knowing, brilliant *Ant* unintelligent

intend ♦ to have in mind as a purpose or goal *Syn* mean, design, propose, purpose

intense ♦ extreme in degree, power, or effect *Syn* vehement, fierce, exquisite, violent *Ant* subdued

intensify ♦ to increase markedly in degree or measure *Syn* aggravate, heighten, enhance *Ant* temper; mitigate, allay; abate

intent *n Syn* INTENTION, purpose, design, aim, end, object, objective, goal *Ant* accident

intent *adj* ♦ having one's mind or attention deeply fixed *Syn* engrossed, absorbed, rapt *Ant* distracted

intention ♦ what one intends to accomplish or attain *Syn* intent, purpose, design, aim, end, object, objective, goal

intentional *Syn* VOLUNTARY, deliberate, willful, willing *Ant* instinctive

intercalate *Syn* INTRODUCE, interpolate, insert, interpose, interject, insinuate

intercede *Syn* INTERPOSE, mediate, intervene, interfere

interchange *Syn* EXCHANGE, bandy

intercourse ♦ connection or dealing between persons or groups *Syn* commerce, traffic, dealings, communication, communion, conversation, converse, correspondence

interdict *Syn* FORBID, ban, inhibit, enjoin, prohibit *Ant* sanction

interesting ♦ holding the attention for some time *Syn* engrossing, absorbing, intriguing *Ant* boring

interfere 1 *Syn* INTERPOSE, intervene, mediate, intercede 2 *Syn* MEDDLE, intermeddle, tamper

interim *Syn* BREAK, gap, interruption, interval, hiatus, lacuna

interior *Syn* INNER, inside, internal, inward, intestine *Ant* exterior

interject *Syn* INTRODUCE, interpolate, interpose, insert, intercalate, insinuate

interlope *Syn* INTRUDE, butt in, obtrude

intermeddle *Syn* MEDDLE, interfere, tamper

interminable *Syn* EVERLASTING, unceasing, endless

intermission *Syn* PAUSE, recess, respite, lull

intermit *Syn* DEFER, suspend, stay, postpone

intermittent ♦ occurring or appearing in interrupted sequence *Syn* recurrent, periodic, alternate *Ant* incessant, continual

intern *Syn* IMPRISON, immure, incarcerate, jail

internal *Syn* INNER, interior, intestine, inward, inside *Ant* external

internuncio *Syn* AMBASSADOR, nuncio, legate, minister, envoy, chargé d'affaires

interpenetrate *Syn* PERMEATE, impenetrate, penetrate, pervade, impregnate, saturate

interpolate *Syn* INTRODUCE, insert, intercalate, insinuate, interpose, interject

interpose 1 *Syn* INTRODUCE, interject, insert, insinuate, interpolate, intercalate **2** ♦ to come or go between *Syn* interfere, intervene, mediate, intercede

interpret *Syn* EXPLAIN, elucidate, construe, expound, explicate

interrogate *Syn* ASK, question, catechize, quiz, examine, query, inquire

interrupt *Syn* ARREST, check

interruption *Syn* BREAK, gap, interval, interim, hiatus, lacuna

interstice *Syn* APERTURE, orifice

interval *Syn* BREAK, gap, interruption, interim, hiatus, lacuna

intervene *Syn* INTERPOSE, mediate, intercede, interfere

intestine *Syn* INNER, internal, interior, inside *Ant* foreign

intimate *vb Syn* SUGGEST, imply, hint, insinuate

intimate *adj Syn* FAMILIAR, close, confidential, chummy, thick

intimate *n Syn* FRIEND, confidant, acquaintance *Ant* stranger, outsider

intimidate ♦ to frighten into submission *Syn* cow, bulldoze, bully, browbeat

intolerant *Syn* ILLIBERAL, narrowminded, narrow, bigoted, hidebound *Ant* tolerant

intonation *Syn* INFLECTION, accent

intone *Syn* SING, troll, carol, descant, warble, trill, hymn, chant

intoxicated *Syn* DRUNK, drunken, inebriated, tipsy, tight

intractable *Syn* UNRULY, ungovernable, refractory, recalcitrant, willful, headstrong *Ant* tractable

intrepid *Syn* BRAVE, courageous, unafraid, fearless, valiant, valorous, dauntless, undaunted, doughty, bold, audacious

intricate *Syn* COMPLEX, complicated, involved, knotty

intrigue 1 *Syn* PLOT, conspiracy, machination, cabal **2** *Syn* AMOUR, liaison, affair

intriguing *Syn* INTERESTING, engrossing, absorbing

intrinsic *Syn* INHERENT, ingrained, constitutional, essential *Ant* extrinsic

introduce 1 *Syn* ENTER, admit **2** ♦ to put among or between others *Syn* insert, insinuate, interpolate, intercalate, interpose, interject *Ant* withdraw; abstract

introduction ♦ something that serves as a preliminary or antecedent *Syn* prologue, prelude, preface, foreword, exordium, preamble

introductory *Syn* PRELIMINARY, preparatory, prefatory *Ant* closing, concluding

intrude ♦ to thrust or force in or upon without permission, welcome, or fitness *Syn* obtrude, interlope, butt in *Ant* stand off

intrusive *Syn* IMPERTINENT, officious, meddlesome, obtrusive *Ant* retiring; unintrusive

intuition *Syn* REASON, understanding *Ant* ratiocination

intuitive *Syn* INSTINCTIVE *Ant* ratiocinative

inundation *Syn* FLOOD, deluge, torrent, spate, cataract

inure *Syn* HABITUATE, accustom, addict

invade *Syn* TRESPASS, encroach, entrench, infringe

invalidate *Syn* NULLIFY, negate, annul, abrogate *Ant* validate

invaluable *Syn* COSTLY, priceless, precious, valuable, dear, expensive *Ant* worthless

invasion ♦ a hostile entrance into the territory of another *Syn* incursion, raid, inroad

invective *Syn* ABUSE, vituperation, obloquy, scurrility, billingsgate

inveigle *Syn* LURE, decoy, entice, tempt, seduce

invent *Syn* CONTRIVE, devise, frame, concoct

inventory *Syn* LIST, register, schedule, catalog, table, roll, roster

invert *Syn* REVERSE, transpose

invest 1 *Syn* INITIATE, induct, install, inaugurate *Ant* divest, strip; unfrock **2** *Syn* BESIEGE, beleaguer, blockade

investigation *Syn* INQUIRY, probe, inquest, inquisition, research

inveterate ♦ so firmly established that change is almost impossible *Syn* confirmed, chronic, deep-seated, deep-rooted

invidious *Syn* REPUGNANT, distasteful, obnoxious, repellent, abhorrent

invigorate *Syn* STRENGTHEN, fortify, energize, reinforce *Ant* debilitate

invincible ♦ incapable of being conquered *Syn* unconquerable, indomitable, impregnable, inexpugnable, unassailable, invulnerable

inviolable *Syn* SACRED, inviolate, sacrosanct

inviolate *Syn* SACRED, sacrosanct, inviolable *Ant* violated

invite ♦ to request the presence or participation of *Syn* bid, solicit, court, woo

involve 1 *Syn* ENTANGLE, enmesh **2** *Syn* INCLUDE, comprehend, embrace, imply, subsume **3** ♦ to bring a person or thing into circumstances or a situation from which extrication is difficult *Syn* implicate

involved *Syn* COMPLEX, intricate, complicated, knotty

invunerable *Syn* INVINCIBLE, impregnable, inexpugnable, unassailable, unconquerable, indomitable *Ant* vulnerable

inward *Syn* INNER, interior, internal, inside, intestine *Ant* outward

iota *Syn* PARTICLE, jot, tittle, whit, bit, mite, smidgen, atom

irascible ♦ easily aroused to anger *Syn* choleric, splenetic, testy, touchy, cranky, cross

irate *Syn* ANGRY, wrathful, wroth, mad, indignant, acrimonious

ire *Syn* ANGER, rage, fury, indignation, wrath

irenic *Syn* PACIFIC, peaceable, peaceful, pacifist, pacifistic *Ant* acrimonious

iridescent *Syn* PRISMATIC, opalescent, opaline

irk *Syn* ANNOY, vex, bother

irksome ♦ tending to cause boredom or tedium *Syn* tiresome, wearisome, tedious, boring *Ant* absorbing, engrossing

ironic *Syn* SARCASTIC, satiric, sardonic

irony *Syn* WIT, satire, sarcasm, humor, repartee

irrational ♦ not governed or guided by reason *Syn* unreasonable *Ant* rational

irregular ♦ not conforming to rule, law, or custom *Syn* anomalous, unnatural *Ant* regular

irreligious ♦ lacking religious emotions, doctrines, or practices *Syn* unreligious, nonreligious, ungodly, godless *Ant* religious

irritable ♦ easily exasperated *Syn* fractious, peevish, snappish, waspish, petulant, pettish, huffy, fretful, querulous *Ant* easygoing

irritate ♦ to excite a feeling of anger or annoyance *Syn* exasperate, nettle, provoke, aggravate, rile, peeve

isolate ♦ to set apart from others *Syn* segregate, seclude, insulate, sequester

isolation *Syn* SOLITUDE, alienation, seclusion

issue *n* **1** *Syn* EFFECT, outcome, result, consequence, upshot, aftereffect, aftermath, sequel, event **2** *Syn* OFFSPRING, young, progeny, descendant, posterity

issue *vb* *Syn* SPRING, emanate, proceed, flow, derive, originate, arise, rise, stem

item ♦ one of the distinct parts of a whole *Syn* detail, particular

itemized *Syn* CIRCUMSTANTIAL, detailed, particularized, minute, particular *Ant* summarized

iterate *Syn* REPEAT, reiterate, ingeminate

itinerant ♦ traveling from place to place *Syn* peripatetic, ambulatory, ambulant, nomadic, vagrant

J

jabber *Syn* CHAT, chatter, gab, patter, prate, prattle, babble, gabble, gibber

jack *Syn* FLAG, ensign, standard, banner, color, streamer, pennant, pendant, pennon

jade *Syn* TIRE, exhaust, fatigue, weary, fag, tucker *Ant* refresh

jail *Syn* IMPRISON, incarcerate, immure, intern

jam *vb Syn* PRESS, crowd, squeeze, bear, bear down

jam *n Syn* PREDICAMENT, plight, fix, dilemma, quandary, scrape, pickle

jape *Syn* JOKE, jest, quip, witticism, wisecrack, crack, gag

jar *Syn* IMPACT, jolt, impingement, collision, clash, shock, concussion, percussion

jargon *Syn* DIALECT, vernacular, patois, lingo, cant, argot, slang

jaunt *Syn* JOURNEY, excursion, trip, tour, voyage, cruise, expedition, pilgrimage

jaw *Syn* SCOLD, upbraid, rate, berate, tongue-lash, bawl, chew out, wig, rail, revile, vituperate

jealous *Syn* ENVIOUS

jeer *Syn* SCOFF, gibe, fleer, gird, sneer, flout

jejune *Syn* INSIPID, vapid, flat, wishy-washy, inane, banal

jell jelly *Syn* COAGULATE, congeal, set, curdle, clot

jeopardize *Syn* VENTURE, hazard, risk, chance, endanger, imperil

jeopardy *Syn* DANGER, peril, hazard, risk

jeremiad *Syn* TIRADE, diatribe, philippic

jerk ♦ to make a sudden sharp quick movement *Syn* snap, twitch, yank

jest 1 *Syn* JOKE, jape, quip, witticism, wisecrack, crack, gag **2** *Syn* FUN, sport, game, play

jetty *Syn* WHARF, dock, pier, quay, slip, berth, levee

jib *Syn* DEMUR, balk, shy, boggle, stickle, stick, strain, scruple

jibe *Syn* AGREE, harmonize, accord, conform, square, tally, correspond

jiffy *Syn* INSTANT, moment, minute, second, flash, twinkling, split second

jittery *Syn* IMPATIENT, jumpy, nervous, unquiet, restless, restive, uneasy, fidgety

job *Syn* TASK, duty, assignment, stint, chore

jocose *Syn* WITTY, jocular, facetious, humorous

jocular *Syn* WITTY, jocose, humorous, facetious

jocund *Syn* MERRY, blithe, jolly, jovial

jog *vb Syn* POKE, prod, nudge

jog *n Syn* POKE, prod, nudge

join ♦ to bring or come together into some manner of union *Syn* conjoin, combine, unite, connect, link, associate, relate *Ant* disjoin; part

joint ♦ a place where two or more things are united *Syn* articulation, suture

joke ♦ something said or done to provoke laughter *Syn* jest, jape, quip, witticism, wisecrack, crack, gag

jollity *Syn* MIRTH, hilarity, glee

jolly *adj Syn* MERRY, jovial, jocund, blithe

jolly *vb Syn* BANTER, chaff, kid, rag, rib, josh

jolt *Syn* IMPACT, jar, shock, impingement, collision, clash, concussion, percussion

josh *Syn* BANTER, chaff, kid, rag, rib, jolly

jot *Syn* PARTICLE, tittle, iota, bit, mite, smidgen, whit, atom

journal ♦ a publication that appears at regular intervals *Syn* periodical, newspaper, magazine, review, organ

journey ♦ travel or a passage from one place to another *Syn* voyage, tour, trip, jaunt, excursion, cruise, expedition, pilgrimage

jovial *Syn* MERRY, jolly, jocund, blithe

joy *Syn* PLEASURE, delight, enjoyment, delectation, fruition *Ant* sorrow; misery; abomination

joyful *Syn* GLAD, joyous, cheerful, happy, lighthearted *Ant* joyless

joyous *Syn* GLAD, joyful, happy, cheerful, lighthearted *Ant* lugubrious

judge *vb* 1 ♦ to decide something in dispute or controversy upon its merits and upon evidence *Syn* adjudge, adjudicate, arbitrate 2 *Syn* INFER, conclude, deduce, gather

judge *n* ♦ a person who impartially decides unsettled questions or controversial issues *Syn* arbiter, arbitrator, referee, umpire

judgment 1 *Syn* INFERENCE, conclusion, deduction 2 *Syn* SENSE, wisdom, gumption

judicious *Syn* WISE, sage, sapient, prudent, sensible, sane *Ant* injudicious; asinine

jumble *Syn* CONFUSION, disorder, chaos, disarray, clutter, snarl, muddle

jump *vb* ♦ to move suddenly through space by or as if by muscular action *Syn* leap, spring, bound, vault

jump *n* ♦ a sudden move through space *Syn* leap, spring, bound, vault

jumpy *Syn* IMPATIENT, jittery, nervous, restless, uneasy, fidgety, unquiet, restive *Ant* steady

junction ♦ the act, state, or place of meeting or uniting *Syn* confluence, concourse

juncture ♦ a critical or crucial time or state of affairs *Syn* pass, exigency, emergency, contingency, pinch, strait, crisis

junk *Syn* DISCARD, scrap, cast, shed, molt, slough

jurisdiction *Syn* POWER, authority, control, command, sway, dominion

just 1 *Syn* UPRIGHT, honorable, conscientious, scrupulous, honest 2 *Syn* FAIR, equitable, impartial, unbiased, dispassionate, uncolored, objective *Ant* unjust

justice ♦ awarding each what is rightly due *Syn* equity

justify 1 *Syn* MAINTAIN, vindicate, defend, assert 2 *Syn* EXPLAIN, account, rationalize 3 ♦ to constitute sufficient grounds *Syn* warrant

jut *Syn* BULGE, stick out, protrude, project, overhang, beetle

juvenile *Syn* YOUTHFUL, puerile, boyish, virgin, virginal, maiden *Ant* adult; senile

juxtaposed *Syn* ADJACENT, adjoining, contiguous, abutting, tangent, conterminous

K

keen *adj* 1 *Syn* SHARP, acute *Ant* blunt 2 *Syn* EAGER, avid, agog, athirst, anxious

keen *vb* *Syn* CRY, wait, weep, whimper, blubber

keep *vb* 1 ♦ to notice or honor a day, occasion, or deed *Syn* observe, celebrate, solemnize, commemorate *Ant* break 2 ♦ to hold in one's possession or under one's control *Syn* keep back, keep out, retain, detain, withhold, reserve, hold back *Ant* relinquish

keep *n* *Syn* LIVING, livelihood, subsistence, sustenance, maintenance, support, bread

keep back, keep out *Syn* KEEP, retain, detain, withhold, reserve, hold, hold back

keepsake *Syn* REMEMBRANCE, remembrancer, reminder, memorial, memento, token, souvenir

ken *Syn* RANGE, gamut, reach, radius, compass, sweep, scope, orbit, horizon, purview

kibitzer *Syn* SPECTATOR, onlooker, looker-on, bystander, observer, beholder, witness, eyewitness

kick *Syn* OBJECT, protest, remonstrate, expostulate

kid *Syn* BANTER, chaff, rag, rib, josh, jolly

kidnap *Syn* ABDUCT

kidney *Syn* TYPE, kind, sort, nature, description, character, stripe, ilk

kill ♦ to deprive of life *Syn* slay, murder, assassinate, dispatch, execute

kind *n* *Syn* TYPE, sort, stripe, kidney, ilk, description, nature, character

kind *adj* ♦ showing or having a gentle considerate nature *Syn* kindly, benign, benignant *Ant* unkind

kindle *Syn* LIGHT, ignite, fire *Ant* smother, stifle

kindly *Syn* KIND, benign, benignant *Ant* unkindly; acrid (*of temper, attitudes, comments*)

kindred *Syn* RELATED, cognate, allied, affiliated *Ant* alien

kingly ♦ of, relating to, or befitting one who occupies a throne *Syn* regal, royal, queenly, imperial, princely

knack *Syn* GIFT, bent, turn, faculty, aptitude, genius, talent *Ant* ineptitude

knave *Syn* VILLAIN, scoundrel, blackguard, rascal, rogue, scamp, rapscallion, miscreant

knit *Syn* WEAVE, crochet, braid, plait, tat

knock *vb Syn* TAP, rap, thump, thud

knock *n Syn* TAP, rap, thump, thud

knotty *Syn* COMPLEX, intricate, involved, complicated

knowing *Syn* INTELLIGENT, alert, bright, smart, clever, quick-witted, brilliant

knowledge ♦ what is or can be known by an individual or by mankind *Syn* science, learning, erudition, scholarship, information, lore *Ant* ignorance

L

label *n Syn* MARK, brand, stamp, tag, ticket

label *vb Syn* MARK, brand, stamp, tag, ticket

labor *Syn* WORK, toil, travail, drudgery, grind

labored *Syn* FORCED, strained, farfetched

laborer *Syn* WORKER, working man, workman, craftsman, handicraftsman, mechanic, artisan, operative, hand, roustabout

lack *vb* ♦ to be without something, esp. something essential or greatly needed *Syn* want, need, require

lack *n* ♦ the fact or state of being wanting or deficient *Syn* want, dearth, absence, defect, privation

lackadaisical *Syn* LANGUID, listless, spiritless, enervated, languishing, languorous

laconic *Syn* CONCISE, succinct, terse, summary, pithy, compendious *Ant* verbose

lacuna *Syn* BREAK, gap, hiatus, interruption, interval, interim

lade *Syn* BURDEN, load, encumber, cumber, weigh, weight, tax, charge, saddle *Ant* unlade

lading *Syn* LOAD, freight, cargo, burden

ladle *Syn* DIP, scoop, spoon, dish, bail

lady *Syn* FEMALE, woman

ladylike *Syn* FEMALE, feminine, womanly, womanlike, womanish

lag *Syn* DELAY, loiter, dawdle, procrastinate

laggard *Syn* SLOW, dilatory, leisurely, deliberate *Ant* prompt, quick

lambent *Syn* BRIGHT, beaming, luminous, brilliant, radiant, lustrous, effulgent, refulgent, lucent, incandescent

lament *Syn* DEPLORE, bewail, bemoan *Ant* exult; rejoice

lampoon *Syn* LIBEL, skit, squib, pasquinade

land *Syn* ALIGHT, light, perch, roost

landing field, landing strip *Syn* AIRPORT, airdrome, airfield, airstrip, flying field

language 1 ♦ a body or system of words and phrases used by a large community or by a people, a nation, or a group of nations *Syn* dialect, tongue, speech, idiom **2** ♦ oral or written expression or a quality of such expression that is dependent on the variety, or arrangement, or expressiveness of words *Syn* vocabulary, phraseology, phrasing, diction, style

languid ♦ lacking in vim or energy *Syn* languishing, languorous, lackadaisical, listless, spiritless, enervated *Ant* vivacious; chipper

languishing *Syn* LANGUID, languorous, lackadaisical, listless, spiritless, enervated *Ant* thriving, flourishing; unaffected

languor *Syn* LETHARGY, lassitude, stupor, torpor, torpidity *Ant* alacrity

languorous *Syn* LANGUID, languishing, lackadaisical, listless, spiritless, enervated *Ant* vigorous; strenuous (*of times, seasons*)

lank lanky *Syn* LEAN, gaunt, rawboned, spare, angular, scrawny, skinny *Ant* burly

lapse *n* **1** *Syn* ERROR, slip, mistake, blunder, faux pas, bull, howler, boner **2** ♦ a fall back into a state or condition from which one has been raised **Syn** relapse, backsliding

lapse *vb* ♦ to fall from a better or higher state into a lower or poorer one **Syn** relapse, backslide

larcener, larcenist **Syn** THIEF, robber, burglar

larceny **Syn** THEFT, robbery, burglary

large ♦ above the average of its kind in magnitude **Syn** big, great **Ant** small

largely ♦ in a reasonably inclusive manner **Syn** greatly, mostly, chiefly, mainly, principally, generally

largesse, largess **Syn** GIFT, boon, present, gratuity, favor

lascivious **Syn** LICENTIOUS, lewd, libertine, lustful, libidinous, lecherous, wanton

lassitude **Syn** LETHARGY, languor, stupor, torpor, torpidity **Ant** vigor

last *vb* **Syn** CONTINUE, endure, abide, persist **Ant** fleet

last *adj* ♦ following all others as in time, order, or importance **Syn** latest, final, terminal, concluding, eventual, ultimate **Ant** first

lasting ♦ enduring so long as to seem fixed or established **Syn** permanent, perdurable, durable, stable, perpetual **Ant** fleeting

late 1 **Syn** TARDY, behindhand, overdue **Ant** early; punctual, prompt **2** **Syn** DEAD, departed, deceased, defunct, lifeless, inanimate **3** **Syn** MODERN, recent

latent ♦ not now showing signs of activity or existence **Syn** dormant, quiescent, potential, abeyant **Ant** patent

latest **Syn** LAST, final, terminal, concluding, eventual, ultimate **Ant** earliest

lather **Syn** FOAM, suds, froth, spume, scum, yeast

laud **Syn** PRAISE, extol, eulogize, acclaim **Ant** revile

laughable ♦ provoking laughter or mirth **Syn** risible, ludicrous, ridiculous, comic, comical, farcical, droll, funny

lavish **Syn** PROFUSE, prodigal, luxuriant, lush, exuberant **Ant** sparing

law 1 ♦ a principle governing action or procedure **Syn** rule, regulation, precept, statute, ordinance, canon **2** **Syn** PRINCIPLE, axiom, fundamental, theorem **Ant** chance

lawful ♦ being in accordance with law **Syn** legal, legitimate, licit **Ant** unlawful

lawlessness **Syn** ANARCHY, chaos **Ant** discipline; order

lawsuit **Syn** SUIT, action, cause, case

lawyer ♦ a person authorized to practice law in the courts or to serve clients in the capacity of legal agent or adviser **Syn** counselor, barrister, counsel, advocate, attorney, solicitor

lax 1 **Syn** LOOSE, relaxed, slack **Ant** rigid **2** **Syn** NEGLIGENT, remiss, neglectful **Ant** strict, stringent

lay *vb* **Syn** DIRECT, aim, point, level, train

lay *adj* **Syn** PROFANE, secular, temporal

laze **Syn** IDLE, loaf, lounge, loll

lazy ♦ not easily aroused to activity **Syn** indolent, slothful, faineant

lead **Syn** GUIDE, pilot, engineer, steer **Ant** follow

leader **Syn** CHIEF, head, chieftain, master **Ant** follower

leading **Syn** CHIEF, principal, main, foremost, capital **Ant** subordinate

league **Syn** ALLIANCE, coalition, fusion, confederacy, confederation, federation

lean *vb* **Syn** SLANT, slope, incline

lean *adj* ♦ thin because of an absence of excess flesh **Syn** spare, lank, lanky, gaunt, rawboned, angular, scrawny, skinny **Ant** fleshy

leaning ♦ a strong instinct or liking for something **Syn** propensity, proclivity, penchant, flair **Ant** distaste

leap *vb* **Syn** JUMP, spring, bound, vault

leap *n* **Syn** JUMP, spring, bound, vault

learn **Syn** DISCOVER, ascertain, determine, unearth

learned ♦ possessing or manifesting unusually wide and deep knowledge **Syn** scholarly, erudite

learning **Syn** KNOWLEDGE, erudition, scholarship, science, information, lore

lease *Syn* HIRE, let, charter, rent

leave *vb* **1** *Syn* WILL, bequeath, devise, legate **2** *Syn* RELINQUISH, resign, surrender, abandon, yield, cede, waive **3** *Syn* GO, depart, quit, withdraw, retire **4** *Syn* LET, allow, permit, suffer

leave *n* *Syn* PERMISSION, sufferance

leaven *Syn* INFUSE, imbue, inoculate, ingrain, suffuse

leavings *Syn* REMAINDER, remains, residue, residuum, rest, balance, remnant

lecherous *Syn* LICENTIOUS, libidinous, lascivious, lustful, lewd, wanton, libertine

lecture *Syn* SPEECH, address, oration, harangue, talk, sermon, homily

leech *Syn* PARASITE, sponge, sponger, sycophant, toady, lickspittle, bootlicker, hanger-on, favorite

lees *Syn* DEPOSIT, precipitate, sediment, dregs, grounds

leeway *Syn* ROOM, berth, play, elbowroom, margin, clearance

legal *Syn* LAWFUL, legitimate, licit *Ant* illegal

legal tender *Syn* MONEY, cash, currency, specie, coin, coinage

legate *n* *Syn* AMBASSADOR, nuncio, internuncio, chargé d'affaires, minister, envoy

legate *vb* *Syn* WILL, bequeath, devise, leave

legend 1 *Syn* MYTH, saga **2** *Syn* INSCRIPTION, caption

legendary *Syn* FICTITIOUS, mythical, apocryphal, fabulous

legerity *Syn* CELERITY, alacrity *Ant* deliberateness; sluggishness

legion *Syn* MULTITUDE, host, army

legitimate *Syn* LAWFUL, legal, licit *Ant* illegitimate; arbitrary

leisure *Syn* REST, relaxation, repose, ease, comfort *Ant* toil

leisurely *Syn* SLOW, deliberate, dilatory, laggard *Ant* hurried; abrupt

leitmotiv *Syn* SUBJECT, motive, motif, theme, matter, subject matter, argument, topic, text

lengthen *Syn* EXTEND, elongate, prolong, protract *Ant* shorten

leniency *Syn* FORBEARANCE, clemency, mercifulness, tolerance, indulgence

lenient 1 *Syn* SOFT, gentle, smooth, mild, bland, balmy *Ant* caustic **2** *Syn* FORBEARING, indulgent, merciful, clement, tolerant *Ant* stern; exacting

leniently *Syn* FORBEARINGLY, tolerantly, clemently, mercifully, indulgently

lenity *Syn* MERCY, clemency, charity, grace *Ant* severity

lesion *Syn* WOUND, trauma, traumatism, bruise, contusion

lessen *Syn* DECREASE, diminish, reduce, abate, dwindle

let 1 *Syn* HIRE, lease, rent, charter **2** ♦ to neither forbid nor prevent *Syn* allow, permit, suffer, leave

lethal *Syn* DEADLY, fatal, mortal

lethargic ♦ deficient in alertness or activity *Syn* sluggish, torpid, comatose *Ant* energetic, vigorous

lethargy ♦ physical or mental inertness *Syn* languor, lassitude, stupor, torpor, torpidity *Ant* vigor

letter ♦ a direct or personal written or printed message addressed to a person or organization *Syn* epistle, missive, note, message, dispatch, report, memorandum

levee *Syn* WHARF, dock, pier, quay, slip, berth, jetty

level *vb* *Syn* DIRECT, point, train, aim, lay

level *adj* ♦ having a surface without bends, curves, or irregularities *Syn* flat, plane, plain, even, smooth, flush

levitate *Syn* RISE, arise, ascend, mount, soar, tower, rocket, surge *Ant* gravitate, sink

levity *Syn* LIGHTNESS, light-mindedness, frivolity, flippancy, volatility, flightiness *Ant* gravity

lewd *Syn* LICENTIOUS, lustful, lascivious, libidinous, lecherous, wanton, libertine *Ant* chaste

liability *Syn* DEBT, indebtedness, obligation, debit, arrear *Ant* asset (*or plural* assets)

liable 1 *Syn* RESPONSIBLE, amenable, answerable, accountable **2** ♦ being by nature or through circumstances likely to experience something adverse **Syn** open, exposed, subject, prone, susceptible, sensitive **Ant** exempt, immune **3** **Syn** APT, likely

liaison **Syn** AMOUR, intrigue, affair

libel *n* ♦ a public and often satirical presentation of the faults or weaknesses, esp. of an individual **Syn** skit, squib, lampoon, pasquinade

libel *vb* **Syn** MALIGN, defame, slander, traduce, asperse, vilify, calumniate

liberal 1 ♦ giving or given freely and unstintingly **Syn** generous, bountiful, bounteous, openhanded, munificent, handsome **Ant** close **2** ♦ not bound by what is orthodox, established, or traditional **Syn** progressive, advanced, radical **Ant** authoritarian

liberate **Syn** FREE, release, emancipate, manumit, discharge

libertine **Syn** LICENTIOUS, lewd, wanton, lustful, lascivious, libidinous, lecherous **Ant** straitlaced

liberty **Syn** FREEDOM, license **Ant** restraint

libidinous **Syn** LICENTIOUS, lecherous, lustful, lascivious, lewd, wanton, libertine

license *n* **Syn** FREEDOM, liberty **Ant** decorum

license *vb* **Syn** AUTHORIZE, commission, accredit **Ant** ban

licentious ♦ lacking moral restraint esp. in a disregarding of sexual restraints **Syn** libertine, lewd, wanton, lustful, lascivious, libidinous, lecherous **Ant** continent

licit **Syn** LAWFUL, legitimate, legal **Ant** illicit

lick **Syn** CONQUER, beat, defeat, vanquish, subdue, subjugate, reduce, overcome, surmount, overthrow, rout

lickspittle **Syn** PARASITE, sycophant, toady, bootlicker, hanger-on, leech, sponge, sponger, favorite

lie *vb* ♦ to tell an untruth **Syn** prevaricate, equivocate, palter, fib

lie *n* ♦ a statement or declaration that is not true **Syn** falsehood, untruth, fib, misrepresentation, story **Ant** truth

life **Syn** BIOGRAPHY, memoir, autobiography, confessions

lifeless **Syn** DEAD, inanimate, defunct, deceased, departed, late **Ant** living

lift 1 ♦ to move from a lower to a higher place or position **Syn** raise, rear, elevate, hoist, heave, boost **Ant** lower **2** **Syn** STEAL, purloin, filch, pilfer, pinch, snitch, swipe, cop

light *vb* **1** ♦ to cause something to start burning **Syn** kindle, ignite, fire **2** **Syn** ILLUMINATE, lighten, illumine, enlighten, illustrate

light *adj* **Syn** EASY, simple, facile, effortless, smooth **Ant** heavy; arduous; burdensome

light *vb* **Syn** ALIGHT, land, perch, roost

lighten *vb* **Syn** ILLUMINATE, illumine, light, enlighten, illustrate **Ant** darken

lighten *vb* **Syn** RELIEVE, alleviate, mitigate, assuage, allay

lighthearted **Syn** GLAD, cheerful, happy, joyful, joyous **Ant** despondent

light-mindedness **Syn** LIGHTNESS, levity, frivolity, flippancy, volatility, flightiness

lightness ♦ gaiety or indifference where seriousness and attention are called for **Syn** light-mindedness, levity, frivolity, flippancy, volatility, flightiness **Ant** seriousness

like *vb* ♦ to feel attraction toward or take pleasure in **Syn** love, enjoy, relish, fancy, dote **Ant** dislike

like *adj* ♦ the same or nearly the same (as in appearance, character, or quantity) **Syn** alike, similar, analogous, comparable, akin, parallel, uniform, identical **Ant** unlike

likely 1 **Syn** PROBABLE, possible **Ant** unlikely **2** **Syn** APT, liable

likeness ♦ agreement or correspondence in details **Syn** similarity, resemblance, similitude, analogy, affinity **Ant** unlikeness

likewise **Syn** ALSO, too, besides, moreover, furthermore

limb **Syn** SHOOT, bough, branch

limber **Syn** SUPPLE, lithe, lithesome, lissome

limit *n* ♦ a material or immaterial point beyond which something does not or cannot extend *Syn* bound, confine, end, term

limit *vb* ♦ to set bounds for *Syn* restrict, circumscribe, confine *Ant* widen

limn *Syn* REPRESENT, depict, portray, delineate, picture

limp ♦ deficient in firmness of texture, substance, or structure *Syn* floppy, flaccid, flabby, flimsy, sleazy

limpid *Syn* CLEAR, transparent, translucent, lucid, pellucid, diaphanous *Ant* turbid

line *n* ♦ a series of things arranged in continuous or uniform order *Syn* row, rank, file, echelon, tier

line *vb* ♦ to arrange in a line or in lines *Syn* line up, align, range, array

lineage *Syn* ANCESTRY, pedigree

line up *Syn* LINE, align, range, array

linger *Syn* STAY, tarry, wait, remain, abide

lingo *Syn* DIALECT, vernacular, patois, jargon, cant, argot, slang

link *Syn* JOIN, connect, relate, associate, conjoin, combine, unite *Ant* sunder

liquefy ♦ to convert or to become converted to a liquid state *Syn* melt, deliquesce, fuse, thaw

lissome *Syn* SUPPLE, lithesome, lithe, limber

list *n* ♦ a series of items (as names) written down or printed as a memorandum or record *Syn* table, catalog, schedule, register, roll, roster, inventory

list *vb* *Syn* RECORD, register, enroll, catalog

listless *Syn* LANGUID, spiritless, languishing, languorous, lackadaisical, enervated *Ant* eager

lithe, lithesome *Syn* SUPPLE, lissome, limber

little *Syn* SMALL, diminutive, wee, tiny, minute, miniature *Ant* big

littoral *Syn* SHORE, coast, beach, strand, bank, foreshore

liturgy *Syn* FORM, ritual, rite, ceremony, ceremonial, formality

live *vb* 1 *Syn* BE, exist, subsist 2 *Syn* RESIDE, dwell, sojourn, lodge, stay, put up, stop

live *adj Syn* ACTIVE, operative, dynamic *Ant* inactive, inert; dormant; defunct

livelihood *Syn* LIVING, subsistence, sustenance, maintenance, support, keep, bread

lively ♦ keenly alive and spirited *Syn* animated, vivacious, sprightly, gay *Ant* dull

livid *Syn* PALE, ashen, ashy, pallid, wan

living *adj* ♦ having or showing life *Syn* alive, animate, animated, vital *Ant* lifeless

living *n* ♦ supplies or resources needed to live *Syn* livelihood, subsistence, sustenance, maintenance, support, keep, bread, bread and butter

load *n* ♦ something which is carried, conveyed, or transported from one place to another *Syn* burden, freight, cargo, lading

load *vb* 1 *Syn* BURDEN, encumber, cumber, weigh, weight, lade, tax, charge, saddle *Ant* unload 2 *Syn* ADULTERATE, weight, sophisticate, doctor

loaf *Syn* IDLE, lounge, loll, laze

loath *Syn* DISINCLINED, indisposed, averse, hesitant, reluctant *Ant* anxious

loathe *Syn* HATE, abominate, detest, abhor *Ant* dote on

loathing *Syn* ABHORRENCE, detestation, abomination, hate, hatred *Ant* tolerance

loathsome *Syn* OFFENSIVE, repulsive, repugnant, revolting *Ant* engaging, inviting

local *Syn* INSULAR, provincial, parochial, small-town *Ant* cosmopolitan

locality ♦ a more or less definitely circumscribed place or region *Syn* district, vicinity, neighborhood

location *Syn* PLACE, position, situation, site, spot, station

locomotion *Syn* MOTION, movement, move, stir

locum tenens *Syn* SUBSTITUTE, supply, alternate, understudy, pinch hitter, double, stand-in

locution *Syn* PHRASE, idiom, expression

lodge 1 *Syn* HARBOR, house, board, shelter, entertain 2 *Syn* RESIDE, live, dwell, sojourn, stay, put up, stop

lofty *Syn* HIGH, tall

logical ♦ having or showing skill in thinking or reasoning *Syn* analytical, subtle *Ant* illogical

logistic, logistical *Syn* STRATEGIC, tactical

logistics *Syn* STRATEGY, tactics

loiter *Syn* DELAY, dawdle, lag, procrastinate

loll *Syn* IDLE, loaf, lounge, laze

lollop 1 *Syn* SKIP, bound, hop, curvet, lope, ricochet **2** *Syn* STUMBLE, trip, blunder, lurch, flounder, lumber, galumph, bumble

lone 1 *Syn* ALONE, lonely, lonesome, forlorn, lorn, solitary, desolate **2** *Syn* SINGLE, sole, unique, solitary, separate, particular

lonely *Syn* ALONE, lonesome, lone, solitary, forlorn, lorn, desolate

lonesome *Syn* ALONE, lonely, lone, solitary, forlorn, lorn, desolate

long ♦ to have a strong desire for something *Syn* yearn, hanker, pine, hunger, thirst

longanimity *Syn* PATIENCE, longsuffering, forbearance, resignation

long-suffering *Syn* PATIENCE, resignation, forbearance

look *vb* **1** *Syn* SEE, watch **2** *Syn* SEEM, appear **3** *Syn* EXPECT, hope, await

look *n* **1** ♦ the directing of one's eyes in order to see *Syn* sight, view, glance, glimpse, peep, peek **2** *Syn* APPEARANCE, aspect, semblance

looker-on *Syn* SPECTATOR, onlooker, beholder, observer, witness, eyewitness, bystander, kibitzer

loom *Syn* APPEAR, emerge *Ant* vanish

loose ♦ not tightly bound, held, restrained, or stretched *Syn* relaxed, slack, lax *Ant* tight; strict

loot *n* *Syn* SPOIL, booty, plunder, swag, prize

loot *vb* *Syn* ROB, plunder, rifle, burglarize

lop *Syn* SHEAR, poll, clip, trim, prune, snip, crop

lope *Syn* SKIP, bound, hop, curvet, lollop, ricochet

loquacious *Syn* TALKATIVE, garrulous, voluble, glib

loquacity, loquaciousness *Syn* TALKATIVENESS, garrulity, volubility, glibness

lordly *Syn* PROUD, haughty, arrogant, overbearing, insolent, supercilious, disdainful

lore *Syn* KNOWLEDGE, science, learning, erudition, scholarship, information

lorn *Syn* ALONE, forlorn, lonely, lonesome, lone, solitary, desolate

lot 1 *Syn* FATE, destiny, portion, doom **2** *Syn* GROUP, cluster, bunch, parcel

loud ♦ marked by intensity or volume of sound *Syn* stentorian, earsplitting, hoarse, raucous, strident, stertorous *Ant* low-pitched, low

lounge *Syn* IDLE, loaf, loll, laze

lout *Syn* BOOR, churl, clown, clodhopper, bumpkin, hick, yokel, rube

loutish *Syn* BOORISH, churlish, clownish

love *n* *Syn* ATTACHMENT, affection *Ant* hate

love *vb* *Syn* LIKE, enjoy, dote, relish, fancy *Ant* hate

lovely *Syn* BEAUTIFUL, fair, comely, pretty, bonny, handsome, beauteous, pulchritudinous, good-looking *Ant* unlovely; plain

loving ♦ feeling or expressing love *Syn* affectionate, devoted, fond, doting *Ant* unloving

low *Syn* BASE, vile

lower *Syn* FROWN, glower, scowl, gloom

lowly *Syn* HUMBLE, meek, modest *Ant* pompous

loyal *Syn* FAITHFUL, true, constant, staunch, steadfast, resolute *Ant* disloyal

loyalty *Syn* FIDELITY, allegiance, fealty, devotion, piety *Ant* disloyalty

lubricate *Syn* OIL, grease, anoint, cream

lucent *Syn* BRIGHT, brilliant, radiant, luminous, lustrous, effulgent, refulgent, beaming, lambent, incandescent

lucid 1 *Syn* CLEAR, pellucid, transparent, translucent, diaphanous, limpid **2** *Syn* CLEAR, perspicuous *Ant* obscure, vague, dark

luck *Syn* CHANCE, fortune, hap, accident, hazard

luckless *Syn* UNLUCKY, disastrous, ill-starred, ill-fated, unfortunate, calamitous, hapless

lucky ♦ meeting with unforeseen success *Syn* fortunate, happy, providential *Ant* unlucky

lucrative *Syn* PAYING, gainful, remunerative, profitable

ludicrous *Syn* LAUGHABLE, risible, ridiculous, comic, comical, farcical, droll, funny

lugubrious *Syn* MELANCHOLY, doleful, dolorous, rueful, plaintive *Ant* joyous; facetious

lull *vb* *Syn* CALM, compose, quiet, quieten, still, soothe, settle, tranquilize *Ant* agitate

lull *n* *Syn* PAUSE, recess, respite, intermission

lumber *Syn* STUMBLE, trip, blunder, lurch, flounder, galumph, lollop, bumble

luminous *Syn* BRIGHT, brilliant, radiant, lustrous, effulgent, lucent, refulgent, beaming, lambent, incandescent

lunacy *Syn* INSANITY, psychosis, mania, dementia

lunatic *Syn* INSANE, mad, crazy, crazed, demented, deranged, maniac, non compos mentis

lurch *Syn* STUMBLE, trip, blunder, flounder, lumber, galumph, lollop, bumble

lure *n* ♦ something that leads an animal or a person into a place or situation from which escape is difficult *Syn* bait, decoy, snare, trap

lure *vb* ♦ to lead astray from one's true course *Syn* entice, inveigle, decoy, tempt, seduce *Ant* revolt, repel

lurid *Syn* GHASTLY, grisly, gruesome, macabre, grim

lurk ♦ to behave so as to escape attention *Syn* skulk, slink, sneak

luscious *Syn* DELIGHTFUL, delicious, delectable *Ant* austere; tasteless

lush *Syn* PROFUSE, luxuriant, lavish, prodigal, exuberant

lust *Syn* DESIRE, appetite, passion, urge

luster ♦ the quality or condition of shining by reflected light *Syn* sheen, gloss, glaze

lustful *Syn* LICENTIOUS, lascivious, libidinous, lecherous, wanton, lewd, libertine

lustrous *Syn* BRIGHT, luminous, radiant, brilliant, effulgent, refulgent, beaming, lambent, lucent, incandescent

lusty *Syn* VIGOROUS, energetic, strenuous, nervous *Ant* effete

luxuriant *Syn* PROFUSE, lush, exuberant, lavish, prodigal

luxurious 1 *Syn* SENSUOUS, voluptuous, sybaritic, epicurean, sensual *Ant* ascetic **2** ♦ ostentatiously rich or magnificent *Syn* sumptuous, opulent

luxury *Syn* AMENITY *Ant* hardship

lying *Syn* DISHONEST, mendacious, untruthful, deceitful *Ant* truthtelling

M

macabre *Syn* GHASTLY, gruesome, grisly, grim, lurid

macerate *Syn* CRUSH, mash, smash, bruise, squash

machination *Syn* PLOT, intrigue, conspiracy, cabal

machine ♦ a device or system by which energy can be converted into useful work *Syn* mechanism, machinery, apparatus, engine, motor

machinery 1 *Syn* EQUIPMENT, apparatus, paraphernalia, outfit, tackle, gear, matériel **2** *Syn* MACHINE, mechanism, apparatus, engine, motor

mad 1 *Syn* INSANE, crazy, crazed, demented, deranged, lunatic, maniac, non compos mentis **2** *Syn* ANGRY, irate, wrathful, wroth, indignant, acrimonious

madden *Syn* ANGER, incense, enrage, infuriate

maelstrom *Syn* EDDY, whirlpool, vortex

magazine ♦ *Syn* JOURNAL, periodical, review, organ, newspaper

magic ♦ the use of means (as charms or spells) believed to have supernatural power over natural forces *Syn* sorcery, witchcraft, witchery, wizardry, alchemy, thaumaturgy

magisterial *Syn* DICTATORIAL, authoritarian, dogmatic, doctrinaire, oracular

magnificent *Syn* GRAND, imposing, stately, majestic, august, noble, grandiose *Ant* modest

magnify *Syn* EXALT, aggrandize *Ant* minimize, belittle

magniloquent *Syn* RHETORICAL, grandiloquent, aureate, flowery, euphuistic, bombastic

magnitude *Syn* SIZE, volume, extent, dimensions, area

maiden 1 *Syn* UNMARRIED, single, celibate, virgin **2** *Syn* YOUTHFUL, juvenile, virgin, virginal, puerile, boyish *Ant* experienced

maim ♦ to injure so severely as to cause lasting damage *Syn* cripple, mutilate, batter, mangle

main *Syn* CHIEF, principal, leading, foremost, capital

mainly *Syn* LARGELY, greatly, mostly, chiefly, principally, generally

maintain ♦ to uphold as true, right, just, or reasonable *Syn* assert, defend, vindicate, justify

maintenance *Syn* LIVING, sustenance, support, livelihood, subsistence, keep, bread

majestic *Syn* GRAND, stately, august, noble, magnificent, imposing, grandiose

make ♦ to bring something into being by forming, shaping, combining, or altering materials *Syn* form, shape, fashion, fabricate, manufacture, forge

make-believe *Syn* PRETENSE, pretension

maker ♦ one who brings something into being or existence *Syn* creator, author

makeshift *Syn* RESOURCE, shift, expedient, resort, stopgap, substitute, surrogate

maladroit *Syn* AWKWARD, clumsy, gauche, inept *Ant* adroit

malady *Syn* DISEASE, ailment, disorder, condition, affection, complaint, distemper, syndrome

male ♦ of, characteristic of, or like a male, esp. of the human species *Syn* masculine, manly, manlike, mannish, manful, virile *Ant* female

malediction *Syn* CURSE, imprecation, anathema *Ant* benediction

malefactor *Syn* CRIMINAL, felon, convict, culprit, delinquent *Ant* benefactor; welldoer

malefic, maleficent *Syn* SINISTER, malign, baleful

malevolence *Syn* MALICE, ill will, malignity, malignancy, spite, despite, spleen, grudge *Ant* benevolence

malevolent *Syn* MALICIOUS, malignant, malign, spiteful *Ant* benevolent

malice ♦ the desire to see another experience pain, injury, or distress *Syn* ill will, malevolence, spite, despite, malignity, malignancy, spleen, grudge *Ant* charity

malicious ♦ having, showing, or indicative of intense often vicious ill will *Syn* malevolent, malignant, malign, spiteful

malign *adj* **1** *Syn* MALICIOUS, malignant, malevolent, spiteful *Ant* benign **2** *Syn* SINISTER, baleful, malefic, maleficent *Ant* benign

malign *vb* ♦ to injure by speaking ill of *Syn* traduce, asperse, vilify, calumniate, defame, slander, libel *Ant* defend

malignancy *Syn* MALICE, malignity, ill will, malevolence, spite, despite, spleen, grudge

malignant *Syn* MALICIOUS, malign, malevolent, spiteful *Ant* benignant

malignity *Syn* MALICE, malignancy, ill will, malevolence, spite, despite, spleen, grudge *Ant* benignity

malinger *Syn* DODGE, parry, sidestep, duck, shirk, fence

malleable *Syn* PLASTIC, pliable, pliant, ductile, adaptable *Ant* refractory

malodorous ♦ having an unpleasant smell *Syn* stinking, fetid, noisome, putrid, rank, rancid, fusty, musty *Ant* odorous

maltreat *Syn* ABUSE, mistreat, ill-treat, misuse, outrage

mammoth *Syn* HUGE, vast, immense, enormous, elephantine, giant, gigantic, gigantean, colossal, gargantuan, Herculean, cyclopean, titanic, Brobdingnagian

manacle *Syn* HAMPER, trammel, clog, fetter, shackle, hog-tie

manage *Syn* CONDUCT, control, direct

mandate 1 *Syn* COMMAND, dictate, order, injunction, bidding, behest **2** ♦ an authorization to take a political action given to a representative *Syn* initiative, referendum, plebiscite

maneuver *Syn* TRICK, stratagem, ruse, gambit, ploy, artifice, wile, feint

manful *Syn* MALE, virile, mannish, manlike, manly, masculine

mangle *Syn* MAIM, batter, mutilate, cripple

mania 1 *Syn* INSANITY, lunacy, psychosis, dementia *Ant* lucidity **2** ♦ a state of mind in which there is loss of control over emotional, nervous, or mental processes *Syn* delirium, frenzy, hysteria

maniac *Syn* INSANE, mad, crazy, crazed, demented, deranged, lunatic, non compos mentis

manifest *adj Syn* EVIDENT, patent, distinct, obvious, apparent, palpable, plain, clear *Ant* latent; constructive

manifest *vb Syn* SHOW, evidence, evince, demonstrate *Ant* suggest

manikin *Syn* DWARF, midget, pygmy, homunculus, runt *Ant* giant

manipulate *Syn* HANDLE, wield, swing, ply

manlike *Syn* MALE, mannish, manful, virile, manly, masculine

manly *Syn* MALE, manlike, manful, virile, masculine, mannish *Ant* unmanly, womanly

manner *Syn* METHOD, mode, way, fashion, system

mannerism *Syn* POSE, air, affectation

mannish *Syn* MALE, manlike, virile, masculine, manful, manly *Ant* womanish

manufacture *Syn* MAKE, fabricate, forge, form, shape, fashion

manumit *Syn* FREE, emancipate, enfranchise, deliver, discharge, release, liberate *Ant* enslave

many ♦ amounting to or being one at a large indefinite number *Syn* several, sundry, various, divers, numerous, multifarious *Ant* few

many-sided *Syn* VERSATILE, all-around

map *Syn* CHART, graph

mar *Syn* INJURE, damage, hurt, harm, impair, spoil

marble *Syn* SPOT, spatter, sprinkle, mottle, fleck, stipple, speckle, spangle, bespangle

marbled *Syn* SPOTTED, spattered, sprinkled, mottled, flecked, stippled, speckled, spangled, bespangled

margin 1 *Syn* BORDER, verge, edge, rim, brim, brink **2** *Syn* ROOM, berth, play, elbowroom, leeway, clearance

marine ♦ of or relating to the navigation of the sea *Syn* maritime, nautical, naval

mariner ♦ a person engaged in sailing or handling a ship *Syn* sailor, seaman, tar, gob, bluejacket

marital *Syn* MATRIMONIAL, conjugal, connubial, nuptial, hymeneal

maritime *Syn* MARINE, nautical, naval

mark *n* **1** *Syn* SIGN, symptom, note, token, badge **2** *Syn* CHARACTER, symbol, sign **3** ♦ a symbol or device used for identification or indication of ownership *Syn* brand, stamp, label, tag, ticket

mark *vb* **1** ♦ to affix, attach, or impress something which serves for identification *Syn* brand, stamp, label, tag, ticket **2** *Syn* CHARACTERIZE, distinguish, qualify

marriage ♦ acts by which a man and woman become husband and wife or the state of being husband and wife *Syn* matrimony, wedlock, wedding, nuptial, espousal

marshal *Syn* ORDER, arrange, organize, systematize, methodize

martial ♦ of, relating to, or suited for war or a warrior *Syn* warlike, military

marvel *Syn* WONDER, prodigy, miracle, phenomenon

masculine *Syn* MALE, virile, manful, manly, manlike, mannish *Ant* feminine

mash *Syn* CRUSH, smash, bruise, squash, macerate

mask *Syn* DISGUISE, cloak, dissemble, camouflage

mass *n* **1** *Syn* BULK, volume **2** *Syn* HEAP, pile, stack, shock, cock, bank

mass *vb Syn* HEAP, pile, stack, shock, cock, bank

massacre ♦ the act or an instance of killing a number of usu. helpless or unresisting human beings under circumstances of atrocity or cruelty *Syn* slaughter, butchery, carnage, pogrom

massive ♦ impressively large or heavy *Syn* massy, bulky, monumental, substantial

massy *Syn* MASSIVE, bulky, monumental, substantial

master *Syn* CHIEF, chieftain, head, leader

masterful ♦ tending to impose one's will on others *Syn* domineering, imperious, peremptory, imperative

masterly *Syn* PROFICIENT, adept, skilled, skillful, expert

match ♦ to come up to or nearly up to the level or standard of *Syn* rival, equal, approach, touch

material *adj* 1 ♦ of or belonging to actuality *Syn* physical, corporeal, phenomenal, sensible, objective *Ant* immaterial 2 *Syn* RELEVANT, germane, pertinent, apposite, applicable, apropos *Ant* immaterial

material *n Syn* MATTER, substance, stuff

materialize *Syn* REALIZE, externalize, objectify, incarnate, embody, actualize, hypostatize, reify

matériel *Syn* EQUIPMENT, apparatus, machinery, paraphernalia, outfit, tackle, gear

matrimonial ♦ of, relating to, or characteristic of marriage *Syn* marital, conjugal, connubial, nuptial, hymeneal

matrimony *Syn* MARRIAGE, wedlock, wedding, nuptial, espousal

matter 1 ♦ what goes into the makeup or forms the being of a thing whether physical or not *Syn* substance, material, stuff 2 *Syn* AFFAIR, business, concern, thing 3 *Syn* SUBJECT, subject matter, argument, topic, text, theme, motive, motif, leitmotiv

matter-of-fact *Syn* PROSAIC, prosy

mature *adj* ♦ having attained the normal peak of natural growth and development *Syn* matured, ripe, mellow, adult, grown-up *Ant* immature; childish

mature *vb* ♦ to become fully developed or ripe *Syn* develop, ripen, age

matured *Syn* MATURE, ripe, mellow, adult, grown-up *Ant* unmatured; premature

maudlin *Syn* SENTIMENTAL, mawkish, romantic, soppy, mushy, slushy

mawkish *Syn* SENTIMENTAL, maudlin, romantic, soppy, mushy, slushy

maxim *Syn* SAYING, saw, adage, proverb, motto, epigram, aphorism, apothegm

meager ♦ falling short of what is normal, necessary, or desirable *Syn* scanty, scant, skimpy, scrimpy, exiguous, spare, sparse *Ant* ample; copious

mean *adj* ♦ being below the normal standards of human decency and dignity *Syn* ignoble, abject, sordid

mean *vb* 1 *Syn* INTEND, design, propose, purpose 2 ♦ to convey (as an idea) to the mind *Syn* denote, signify, import

mean *n* 1 *Syn* AVERAGE, median, norm, par 2 ♦ one by which work is accomplished or an end effected *Syn* instrument, instrumentality, agent, agency, medium, organ, vehicle, channel 3 *pl* **means** *Syn* POSSESSIONS, resources, assets, effects, belongings

mean *adj Syn* AVERAGE, median, par *Ant* extreme

meander *Syn* WANDER, stray, roam, ramble, rove, range, prowl, gad, gallivant, traipse

meaning ♦ the idea that something conveys to the mind *Syn* sense, acceptation, signification, significance, import

meaningful *Syn* EXPRESSIVE, significant, pregnant, sententious, eloquent *Ant* meaningless

measly *Syn* PETTY, paltry, trifling, trivial, puny, picayunish, picayune

mechanic *Syn* WORKER, workman, workingman, artisan, operative, hand, laborer, craftsman, handicraftsman, roustabout

mechanical *Syn* SPONTANEOUS, automatic, instinctive, impulsive

mechanism *Syn* MACHINE, machinery, apparatus, engine, motor

meddle ♦ to interest oneself in what is not one's concern *Syn* interfere, intermeddle, tamper

meddlesome *Syn* IMPERTINENT, intrusive, obtrusive, officious

median *n* *Syn* AVERAGE, mean, norm, par

median *adj* *Syn* AVERAGE, mean, par

mediate *Syn* INTERPOSE, intercede, intervene, interfere

medicament, medication *Syn* REMEDY, medicine, cure, specific, physic

medicinal *Syn* DRUG, pharmaceutical, biologic, simple

medicine *Syn* REMEDY, cure, medicament, medication, specific, physic

mediocre *Syn* MEDIUM, middling, second-rate, moderate, average, fair, indifferent

meditate *Syn* PONDER, muse, ruminate

meditative *Syn* THOUGHTFUL, contemplative, speculative, reflective, pensive

medium *n* *Syn* MEAN, instrument, instrumentality, agent, agency, organ, vehicle, channel

medium *adj* ♦ about midway between the extremes of a scale, measurement, or evaluation *Syn* middling, mediocre, second-rate, moderate, average, fair, indifferent

meed *Syn* PREMIUM, guerdon, prize, award, reward, bounty, bonus

meek *Syn* HUMBLE, modest, lowly *Ant* arrogant

meet *vb* **1** ♦ to come together face-to-face or as if face-to-face *Syn* face, encounter, confront *Ant* avoid **2** *Syn* SATISFY, fulfill, answer *Ant* disappoint

meet *adj* *Syn* FIT, suitable, proper, appropriate, fitting, apt, happy, felicitous *Ant* unmeet

melancholia *Syn* SADNESS, melancholy, depression, dejection, gloom, blues, dumps

melancholic ♦ gloomy or depressed, esp. as a manifestation of one's temperament or state of health *Syn* melancholy, atrabilious, hypochondriac

melancholy *n* *Syn* SADNESS, melancholia, dejection, gloom, depression, blues, dumps *Ant* exhilaration

melancholy *adj* **1** *Syn* MELANCHOLIC, atrabilious, hypochondriac **2** ♦ expressing or suggesting sorrow or mourning *Syn* dolorous, doleful, lugubrious, rueful, plaintive

melee *Syn* BRAWL, fracas, row, broil, rumpus, scrap

mellow *Syn* MATURE, ripe, matured, adult, grown-up *Ant* unmellow; green

melodramatic *Syn* DRAMATIC, histrionic, theatrical, dramaturgic

melody ♦ a rhythmic succession of single tones organized as an aesthetic whole *Syn* air, tune

melt *Syn* LIQUEFY, deliquesce, fuse, thaw

member *Syn* PART, portion, piece, detail, division, section, segment, sector, fraction, fragment, parcel

memento *Syn* REMEMBRANCE, remembrancer, reminder, memorial, token, keepsake, souvenir

memoir *Syn* BIOGRAPHY, life, autobiography, confessions

memorable *Syn* NOTEWORTHY, notable

memorandum *Syn* LETTER, epistle, missive, note, message, dispatch, report

memorial *Syn* REMEMBRANCE, remembrancer, reminder, memento, token, keepsake, souvenir

memory ♦ the capacity for or the act of remembering, or the thing remembered *Syn* remembrance, recollection, reminiscence, mind, souvenir *Ant* oblivion

menace *Syn* THREATEN

mend ♦ to put into good order something that is injured, damaged, or defective *Syn* repair, patch, rebuild

mendacious *Syn* DISHONEST, lying, untruthful, deceitful *Ant* veracious

menial *Syn* SUBSERVIENT, servile, slavish, obsequious

mental ♦ of or relating to the mind *Syn* intellectual, psychic, intelligent, cerebral

mention ♦ to refer to someone or something in a clear unmistakable manner *Syn* name, instance, specify

mephitic *Syn* POISONOUS, toxic, venomous, virulent, pestilent, pestilential, miasmic, miasmatic, miasmal

mercantile *Syn* COMMERCIAL

mercenary ♦ serving merely for pay or sordid advantage *Syn* hireling, venal, hack

merciful *Syn* FORBEARING, clement, tolerant, lenient, indulgent *Ant* merciless

mercifully *Syn* FORBEARINGLY, tolerantly, clemently, leniently, indulgently

mercifulness *Syn* FORBEARANCE, clemency, tolerance, leniency, indulgence

merciless *Syn* GRIM, implacable, relentless, unrelenting *Ant* merciful

mercurial *Syn* INCONSTANT, fickle, capricious, unstable *Ant* saturnine

mercy ♦ a disposition to show compassion or kindness *Syn* charity, grace, clemency, lenity

mere ♦ being as stated with nothing more added or extra *Syn* bare, very

meretricious *Syn* GAUDY, tawdry, garish, flashy

merge *Syn* MIX, blend, fuse, coalesce, amalgamate, commingle, mingle

merger *Syn* CONSOLIDATION, amalgamation

meridian *n* *Syn* SUMMIT, culmination, zenith, apogee, peak, pinnacle, climax, apex, acme

merit *n* 1 *Syn* DUE, desert 2 *Syn* EXCELLENCE, virtue, perfection *Ant* fault; defect

merit *vb* *Syn* DESERVE, earn, rate

merry ♦ showing high spirits or lightheartedness *Syn* blithe, jocund, jovial, jolly

mesa *Syn* MOUNTAIN, mount, peak, alp, volcano

message *Syn* LETTER, missive, note, epistle, dispatch, report, memorandum

metamorphose *Syn* TRANSFORM, transmute, convert, transmogrify, transfigure

metamorphosis *Syn* TRANSFORMATION, transmutation, conversion, transmogrification, transfiguration

metaphor *Syn* ANALOGY, simile

metaphrase *Syn* TRANSLATION, version, paraphrase

meter *Syn* RHYTHM, cadence

method ♦ the means taken or procedure followed in achieving an end *Syn* mode, manner, way, fashion, system

methodical *Syn* ORDERLY, systematic, regular *Ant* unmethodical; desultory

methodize *Syn* ORDER, systematize, organize, arrange, marshal

meticulous *Syn* CAREFUL, scrupulous, punctilious, punctual

mettle *Syn* COURAGE, spirit, resolution, tenacity

mettlesome *Syn* SPIRITED, high-spirited, spunky, fiery, peppery, gingery

miasmic, miasmatic, miasmal *Syn* POISONOUS, toxic, venomous, virulent, pestilent, pestilential, mephitic

microscopic *Syn* SMALL, minute, little, diminutive, miniature, petite, wee, tiny, teeny, weeny

middle *Syn* CENTER, midst, core, hub, focus, nucleus, heart

middling *Syn* MEDIUM, mediocre, second-rate, moderate, average, fair, indifferent

midget *Syn* DWARF, manikin, pygmy, homunculus, runt

midst *Syn* CENTER, middle, core, hub, focus, nucleus, heart

mien *Syn* BEARING, demeanor, deportment, port, presence

might *Syn* POWER, strength, energy, force, puissance

migrant *Syn* EMIGRANT, immigrant

migrate ♦ to move from one country, place, or locality to another *Syn* emigrate, immigrate

mild *Syn* SOFT, gentle, smooth, lenient, bland, balmy *Ant* harsh; fierce

milieu *Syn* BACKGROUND, environment, setting, mise-en-scène, backdrop

militant *Syn* AGGRESSIVE, assertive, self-assertive, pushing, pushy

military *Syn* MARTIAL, warlike

mime *Syn* ACTOR, player, performer, mummer, mimic, thespian, impersonator, trouper

mimic *n* *Syn* ACTOR, player, performer, mummer, mime, thespian, impersonator, trouper

mimic *vb* *Syn* COPY, imitate, ape, mock

mind *n* 1 *Syn* MEMORY, remembrance, recollection, reminiscence, souvenir 2 ♦ the element or complex of elements in an individual that feels, perceives, thinks, wills, and esp. reasons *Syn* intellect, soul, psyche, brain, intelligence, wit

mind *vb* **1** *Syn* REMEMBER, recollect, recall, remind, reminisce, bethink **2** *Syn* OBEY, comply **3** *Syn* TEND, attend, watch

mingle *Syn* MIX, commingle, blend, merge, coalesce, amalgamate, fuse

miniature *Syn* SMALL, minute, diminutive, little, wee, tiny, teeny, weeny

minimize *Syn* DECRY, depreciate, belittle, disparage, derogate, detract *Ant* magnify

minister *Syn* AMBASSADOR, envoy, legate, nuncio, internuncio, chargé d'affaires

minority *Syn* INFANCY, nonage *Ant* majority

minstrel *Syn* POET, bard, troubadour, versifier, rhymer, rhymester, poetaster

minute *n* *Syn* INSTANT, moment, second, flash, jiffy, twinkling, split second

minute *adj* **1** *Syn* SMALL, little, diminutive, miniature, wee, tiny, teeny, weeny **2** *Syn* CIRCUMSTANTIAL, particular, particularized, detailed, itemized

miracle *Syn* WONDER, marvel, prodigy, phenomenon

miraculous *Syn* SUPERNATURAL, supranatural, preternatural, superhuman

mirage *Syn* DELUSION, hallucination, illusion

mirror *Syn* MODEL, example, pattern, exemplar, ideal, standard, beau ideal

mirth ♦ a mood or temper characterized by joy and high spirits and usu. manifested in laughter and merrymaking *Syn* glee, jollity, hilarity

misanthropic *Syn* CYNICAL, pessimistic *Ant* philanthropic

miscarriage *Syn* FAILURE, neglect, default, dereliction

miscellaneous ♦ consisting of diverse things or members *Syn* assorted, heterogeneous, motley, promiscuous

mischance *Syn* MISFORTUNE, adversity, mishap

mischief *Syn* INJURY, hurt, damage, harm

mischievous *Syn* PLAYFUL, roguish, waggish, impish, frolicsome, sportive

miscreant *Syn* VILLAIN, scoundrel, blackguard, knave, rascal, rogue, scamp, rapscallion

misdoubt *Syn* DISTRUST, mistrust, doubt, suspect

mise-en-scène *Syn* BACKGROUND, setting, environment, milieu, backdrop

miserable ♦ being in a pitiable state of distress or unhappiness (as from want or shame) *Syn* wretched *Ant* comfortable

miserly *Syn* STINGY, penurious, parsimonious, niggardly, tight, tightfisted, close, closefisted, cheeseparing, penny-pinching

misery *Syn* DISTRESS, suffering, agony, dolor, passion *Ant* felicity, blessedness

misfortune ♦ adverse fortune or an instance of this *Syn* mischance, adversity, mishap *Ant* happiness; prosperity

misgiving *Syn* APPREHENSION, foreboding, presentiment

mishap **1** *Syn* MISFORTUNE, mischance, adversity **2** *Syn* ACCIDENT, casualty

mislay *Syn* MISPLACE

mislead *Syn* DECEIVE, delude, beguile, betray, double-cross

misleading ♦ having an appearance or character that leads one astray or into error *Syn* deceptive, delusive, delusory

misplace ♦ to put in the wrong place *Syn* mislay

misrepresent ♦ to give a false or misleading representation of usu. with an intent to deceive *Syn* falsify, belie, garble

misrepresentation *Syn* LIE, falsehood, untruth, fib, story

missive *Syn* LETTER, epistle, note, message, dispatch, report, memorandum

mist *Syn* HAZE, fog, smog

mistake *vb* ♦ to take one thing to be another *Syn* confuse, confound *Ant* recognize

mistake *n* *Syn* ERROR, slip, lapse, blunder, faux pas, bull, howler, boner

mistreat *Syn* ABUSE, maltreat, ill-treat, misuse, outrage

mistrust *n* **1** *Syn* UNCERTAINTY, suspi-

cion, skepticism, doubt, dubiety, dubiosity
Ant trust; assurance **2** *Syn* DISTRUST

mistrust *vb Syn* DISTRUST, doubt, suspect,
misdoubt

misuse *Syn* ABUSE, mistreat, maltreat, ill-
treat, outrage *Ant* respect

mite *Syn* PARTICLE, bit, smidgen, whit,
atom, iota, jot, tittle

mitigate *Syn* RELIEVE, allay, alleviate,
lighten, assuage *Ant* intensify

mix ♦ to combine or be combined into a
more or less uniform whole *Syn* mingle,
commingle, blend, merge, coalesce, amalgamate, fuse

mixture ♦ a product formed by the combination of two or more things *Syn* admixture, blend, compound, composite, amalgam

moan *n Syn* SIGH, groan, sob

moan *vb Syn* SIGH, groan, sob

mob *Syn* CROWD, throng, press, crush,
rout, horde

mobile *Syn* MOVABLE, motive *Ant* immobile

mock 1 *Syn* RIDICULE, taunt, deride,
twit, rally **2** *Syn* COPY, imitate, mimic,
ape

mode *n* **1** *Syn* STATE, condition, situation,
posture, status **2** *Syn* METHOD, manner,
way, fashion, system

mode *n Syn* FASHION, style, vogue, fad,
rage, craze, dernier cri, cry

model ♦ someone or something set before
one for guidance or imitation *Syn* example, pattern, exemplar, ideal, standard,
beau ideal, mirror

moderate *adj* **1** ♦ not excessive in degree,
amount, or intensity *Syn* temperate *Ant*
immoderate **2** *Syn* MEDIUM, middling,
mediocre, second-rate, average, fair, indifferent

moderate *vb* ♦ to modify something so as
to avoid an extreme or to keep within
bounds *Syn* qualify, temper

modern 1 ♦ having taken place, existed, or
developed in times close to the present
Syn recent, late **2** *Syn* NEW, modernistic,
novel, new-fashioned, newfangled, original, fresh *Ant* antique; ancient

modernistic *Syn* NEW, new-fashioned,
newfangled, novel, modern, original, fresh
Ant antiquated

modest 1 *Syn* HUMBLE, meek, lowly *Ant*
ambitious **2** *Syn* SHY, bashful, diffident,
coy **3** *Syn* CHASTE, decent, pure *Ant* im-
modest

modification *Syn* CHANGE, alteration,
variation

modify *Syn* CHANGE, alter, vary

modish *Syn* STYLISH, fashionable, smart,
chic, dashing *Ant* antiquated

moist *Syn* WET, damp, humid, dank

mollify *Syn* PACIFY, appease, placate, propitiate, conciliate *Ant* exasperate

mollycoddle *Syn* INDULGE, humor, pamper, spoil, baby

molt *Syn* DISCARD, cast, shed, slough,
scrap, junk

moment 1 *Syn* INSTANT, minute, second,
flash, jiffy, twinkling, split second **2** *Syn*
IMPORTANCE, consequence, significance,
import, weight

momentary *Syn* TRANSIENT, transitory,
passing, ephemeral, fugitive, fleeting,
evanescent, short-lived *Ant* agelong

momentum *Syn* SPEED, impetus, velocity,
pace, headway

monastery *Syn* CLOISTER, convent, nunnery, abbey, priory

monetary *Syn* FINANCIAL, pecuniary, fiscal

money ♦ something (as pieces of stamped
metal or paper certificates) customarily
and legally used as a medium of exchange
Syn cash, currency, legal tender, specie,
coin, coinage

monk *Syn* RELIGIOUS, friar, nun

monkeyshine *Syn* PRANK, caper, antic,
dido

monograph *Syn* DISCOURSE, treatise, disquisition, dissertation, thesis

monopolize ♦ to take up completely *Syn*
engross, absorb, consume

monopoly ♦ exclusive possession or control *Syn* corner, pool, syndicate, trust, cartel

monotonous *Syn* DULL, dreary, pedestrian, humdrum, stodgy

monstrous 1 ♦ extremely impressive *Syn* prodigious, tremendous, stupendous, monumental **2** *Syn* OUTRAGEOUS, heinous, atrocious

monument *Syn* DOCUMENT, record, archive

monumental 1 *Syn* MONSTROUS, prodigious, tremendous, stupendous **2** *Syn* MASSIVE, massy, bulky, substantial

mood ♦ a state of mind in which an emotion or set of emotions gains ascendancy *Syn* humor, temper, vein

moor *Syn* SECURE, anchor, rivet

moral ♦ conforming to a standard of what is right and good *Syn* ethical, virtuous, righteous, noble

morale ♦ a sense of common purpose or dedication with respect to a group *Syn* discipline, esprit de corps

morality *Syn* GOODNESS, virtue, rectitude

morally *Syn* VIRTUALLY, practically

morbid *Syn* UNWHOLESOME, sickly, diseased, pathological *Ant* sound

mordant *Syn* CAUSTIC, acrid, scathing

moreover *Syn* ALSO, besides, furthermore, likewise, too

moron *Syn* FOOL, imbecile, idiot, simpleton, natural

morose *Syn* SULLEN, glum, gloomy, saturnine, dour, surly, sulky, crabbed

mortal *Syn* DEADLY, fatal, lethal *Ant* venial (*esp. of a sin*)

mortified *Syn* ASHAMED, chagrined

mostly *Syn* LARGELY, greatly, chiefly, mainly, principally, generally

motif 1 *Syn* FIGURE, device, design, pattern **2** *Syn* SUBJECT, matter, subject matter, argument, topic, text, theme, motive, leitmotiv

motion ♦ the act or an instance of moving *Syn* movement, move, locomotion, stir

motivate *Syn* ACTIVATE, actuate

motive *n* **1** ♦ a stimulus to action *Syn* spring, impulse, incentive, inducement, spur, goad **2** *Syn* SUBJECT, matter, subject matter, argument, topic, text, theme, motif, leitmotiv

motive *adj Syn* MOVABLE, mobile

motley 1 *Syn* VARIEGATED, parti-colored, checkered, checked, pied, piebald, skewbald, dappled, freaked **2** *Syn* MISCELLANEOUS, heterogeneous, assorted, promiscuous

motor *Syn* MACHINE, mechanism, machinery, apparatus, engine

motorcade *Syn* PROCESSION, parade, cortege, cavalcade

mottle *Syn* SPOT, spatter, sprinkle, fleck, stipple, marble, speckle, spangle, bespangle

mottled *Syn* SPOTTED, spattered, sprinkled, flecked, stippled, marbled, speckled, spangled, bespangled

motto *Syn* SAYING, proverb, adage, saw, maxim, epigram, aphorism, apothegm

mount *n Syn* MOUNTAIN, peak, alp, volcano, mesa

mount *vb* **1** *Syn* RISE, ascend, soar, arise, tower, rocket, levitate, surge *Ant* drop **2** *Syn* ASCEND, climb, scale *Ant* dismount

mountain ♦ a relatively steep and high elevation of land *Syn* mount, peak, alp, volcano, mesa

mountebank *Syn* IMPOSTOR, faker, charlatan, quack

mourn *Syn* GRIEVE, sorrow

movable ♦ capable of moving or of being moved *Syn* mobile, motive *Ant* immovable; stationary

move *vb* **1** ♦ to set or keep in motion *Syn* actuate, drive, impel **2** ♦ to change or to cause to change from one place to another *Syn* remove, shift, transfer

move *n Syn* MOTION, movement, locomotion, stir

movement *Syn* MOTION, move, locomotion, stir

moving ♦ having the power to produce deep emotion *Syn* impressive, poignant, affecting, touching, pathetic

muddle *vb Syn* CONFUSE, addle, fuddle, befuddle *Ant* enlighten

muddle *n Syn* CONFUSION, disorder, chaos, disarray, jumble, clutter, snarl

muddy *Syn* TURBID, roily

muff *Syn* BOTCH, bungle, fumble, cobble

mug *Syn* FACE, countenance, visage, physiognomy, puss

mulct *Syn* PENALIZE, fine, amerce

mulish *Syn* OBSTINATE, dogged, stubborn, pertinacious, stiff-necked, pigheaded, bullheaded

multifarious *Syn* MANY, divers, numerous, various, several, sundry

multiply *Syn* INCREASE, augment, enlarge

multitude ♦ a very large number of individuals or things *Syn* army, host, legion

mummer *Syn* ACTOR, performer, mime, mimic, player, thespian, impersonator, trouper

mummery *Syn* GIBBERISH, hocus-pocus, abracadabra

mundane *Syn* EARTHLY, worldly, earthy, terrestrial, sublunary *Ant* eternal

munificent *Syn* LIBERAL, bountiful, bounteous, openhanded, generous, handsome

murder *Syn* KILL, slay, assassinate, dispatch, execute

murky *Syn* DARK, obscure, gloomy, dim, dusky

muscular ♦ strong and powerful in build or action *Syn* brawny, sinewy, athletic, burly, husky

muse *Syn* PONDER, meditate, ruminate

mushy *Syn* SENTIMENTAL, romantic, mawkish, maudlin, soppy, slushy

muster *Syn* SUMMON, summons, call, cite, convoke, convene

musty *Syn* MALODOROUS, fusty, stinking, fetid, noisome, putrid, rank, rancid

mutable *Syn* CHANGEABLE, changeful, variable, protean *Ant* immutable

mutation *Syn* CHANGE, permutation, vicissitude, alternation

mute *Syn* DUMB, speechless, inarticulate

mutilate 1 *Syn* MAIM, cripple, batter, mangle **2** *Syn* STERILIZE, castrate, spay, emasculate, alter, geld

mutinous *Syn* INSUBORDINATE, rebellious, seditious, factious, contumacious

mutiny *Syn* REBELLION, revolution, uprising, revolt, insurrection, putsch, coup

mutual *Syn* RECIPROCAL, common

mysterious ♦ being beyond one's power to discover, understand, or explain *Syn* inscrutable, arcane

mystery ♦ something which baffles or perplexes *Syn* problem, enigma, riddle, puzzle, conundrum

mystic *Syn* MYSTICAL, anagogic, cabalistic

mystical ♦ having a spiritual meaning or reality that is neither apparent to the senses nor obvious to the intelligence *Syn* mystic, anagogic, cabalistic

mystify *Syn* PUZZLE, bewilder, perplex, distract, nonplus, confound, dumbfound *Ant* enlighten

myth 1 ♦ a traditional story of ostensibly historical content whose origin has been lost *Syn* legend, saga **2** *Syn* ALLEGORY, parable, fable

mythical *Syn* FICTITIOUS, fabulous, legendary, apocryphal

N

naïve *Syn* NATURAL, unsophisticated, artless, ingenuous, simple

naked *Syn* BARE, nude, bald, barren

name *n* ♦ the word or combination of words by which something is called and by means of which it can be distinguished or identified *Syn* designation, denomination, appellation, title, style

name *vb* **1** *Syn* DESIGNATE, nominate, elect, appoint **2** *Syn* MENTION, instance, specify

nap *Syn* SLEEP, catnap, doze, drowse, snooze, slumber

narcotic *Syn* ANODYNE, opiate, nepenthe

narrate *Syn* RELATE, rehearse, recite, recount, describe, state, report

narrative *Syn* STORY, tale, anecdote, yarn

narrow, narrow-minded *Syn* ILLIBERAL, intolerant, bigoted, hidebound *Ant* broad, broad-minded

narrows *Syn* STRAIT, sound, channel, passage

nasty *Syn* DIRTY, filthy, squalid, foul

national *Syn* CITIZEN, subject

native ♦ belonging to a particular place by birth or origin *Syn* indigenous, endemic, aboriginal, autochthonous *Ant* alien, foreign

natural *adj* 1 *Syn* REGULAR, normal, typical *Ant* unnatural; artificial; adventitious 2 ♦ free from pretension or calculation *Syn* simple, ingenuous, naïve, unsophisticated, artless, unaffected

natural *n* *Syn* FOOL, idiot, imbecile, moron, simpleton

nature *Syn* TYPE, kind, sort, stripe, kidney, ilk, description, character

naughty *Syn* BAD, evil, ill, wicked

nauseate *Syn* DISGUST, sicken

nautical *Syn* MARINE, maritime, naval

naval *Syn* MARINE, nautical, maritime

near *adj & adv* *Syn* CLOSE, nigh, nearby *Ant* far

near *vb* *Syn* APPROACH, approximate

nearby *Syn* CLOSE, near, nigh *Ant* far off

nearly ♦ very close to *Syn* almost, approximately, well-nigh

neat ♦ manifesting care and orderliness *Syn* tidy, trim, trig, snug, shipshape, spick-and-span *Ant* filthy

neb *Syn* BILL, beak, nib

necessary 1 *Syn* NEEDFUL, requisite, indispensable, essential 2 *Syn* CERTAIN, inevitable

necessitous *Syn* POOR, indigent, needy, destitute, penniless, impecunious, poverty-stricken

necessity *Syn* NEED, exigency

need *n* ♦ a pressing lack of something essential *Syn* necessity, exigency

need *vb* *Syn* LACK, want, require

needful ♦ required for supply or relief *Syn* necessary, requisite, indispensable, essential

needy *Syn* POOR, indigent, destitute, penniless, impecunious, poverty-stricken, necessitous

nefarious *Syn* VICIOUS, iniquitous, flagitious, infamous, corrupt, degenerate, villainous

negate *Syn* NULLIFY, annul, abrogate, invalidate

negative 1 *Syn* DENY, gainsay, traverse, contradict, impugn, contravene 2 *Syn* NEUTRALIZE, counteract

neglect *vb* ♦ to pass over without giving due attention *Syn* omit, disregard, ignore, overlook, slight, forget *Ant* cherish

neglect *n* 1 *Syn* FAILURE, default, miscarriage, dereliction 2 *Syn* NEGLIGENCE

neglectful *Syn* NEGLIGENT, lax, slack, remiss *Ant* attentive

negligence ♦ a failure to exercise proper or due care *Syn* neglect *Ant* attention; solicitude

negligent ♦ culpably careless or indicative of such carelessness *Syn* neglectful, lax, slack, remiss

negotiate 1 *Syn* CONFER, parley, treat, commune, consult, advise 2 ♦ to bring about by mutual agreement *Syn* arrange, concert

neighborhood *Syn* LOCALITY, district, vicinity

neighborly *Syn* AMICABLE, friendly *Ant* unneighborly; ill-disposed

neophyte *Syn* NOVICE, novitiate, probationer, postulant, apprentice

nepenthe *Syn* ANODYNE, opiate, narcotic

nerve *n* *Syn* TEMERITY, effrontery, audacity, hardihood, cheek, gall

nerve *vb* *Syn* ENCOURAGE, inspirit, hearten, embolden, cheer, steel *Ant* unnerve

nervous 1 *Syn* VIGOROUS, lusty, energetic, strenuous 2 *Syn* IMPATIENT, restless, restive, unquiet, uneasy, fidgety, jumpy, jittery *Ant* steady

nettle *Syn* IRRITATE, provoke, exasperate, aggravate, rile, peeve

network *Syn* SYSTEM, scheme, complex, organism

neutral ♦ lacking decisiveness or distinctiveness in character, quality, action, or effect *Syn* indifferent

neutralize ♦ to make inoperative or ineffective usu. by means of an opposite force, influence, or effect *Syn* counteract, negative

new ♦ having recently come into existence or use **Syn** novel, new-fashioned, newfangled, modern, modernistic, original, fresh **Ant** old

newfangled **Syn** NEW, novel, new-fashioned, modernistic, modern, original, fresh

new-fashioned **Syn** NEW, novel, newfangled, modernistic, modern, original, fresh

news ♦ a report of events or conditions not previously known **Syn** tidings, intelligence, advice

newspaper **Syn** JOURNAL, periodical, magazine, review, organ

nib **Syn** BILL, beak, neb

nice 1 ♦ having or displaying exacting standards **Syn** dainty, fastidious, finicky, finicking, finical, particular, fussy, squeamish, persnickety, pernickety **2 Syn** CORRECT, precise, exact, accurate, right **3 Syn** DECOROUS, proper, seemly, decent

niggardly **Syn** STINGY, parsimonious, penurious, miserly, close, closefisted, tight, tightfisted, cheeseparing, penny-pinching **Ant** bountiful

nigh **Syn** CLOSE, near, nearby **Ant** far

night **Syn** NIGHTLY, nocturnal

nightly ♦ of, relating to, or associated with the night **Syn** nocturnal, night **Ant** daily

nightmare **Syn** FANCY, dream, vision, fantasy, phantasy, phantasm, daydream

nimble **Syn** AGILE, brisk, spry

nip *vb* **Syn** BLAST, blight

nip *n* **Syn** BLAST, blight

nobility **Syn** ARISTOCRACY, gentry, county, elite, society

noble 1 **Syn** GRAND, stately, majestic, imposing, august, magnificent, grandiose **Ant** ignoble; cheap **2 Syn** MORAL, virtuous, righteous, ethical **Ant** base (*of actions*); atrocious (*of acts, deeds*)

nocturnal **Syn** NIGHTLY **Ant** diurnal

noise **Syn** SOUND

noiseless **Syn** STILL, silent, quiet, stilly

noisome **Syn** MALODOROUS, fetid, stinking, putrid, rank, rancid, fusty, musty **Ant** balmy

nomadic **Syn** ITINERANT, peripatetic, ambulatory, ambulant, vagrant

nom de guerre, nom de plume **Syn** PSEUDONYM, alias, pen name, incognito

nominate **Syn** DESIGNATE, name, elect, appoint

nominee **Syn** CANDIDATE, aspirant, applicant

nonage **Syn** INFANCY, minority **Ant** age

nonchalant **Syn** COOL, unruffled, imperturbable, unflappable, composed, collected

non compos mentis **Syn** INSANE, mad, crazy, crazed, demented, deranged, lunatic, maniac

nonconformist **Syn** HERETIC, dissenter, sectary, sectarian, schismatic

nonesuch **Syn** PARAGON, apotheosis, nonpareil

nonpareil **Syn** PARAGON, apotheosis, nonesuch

nonplus **Syn** PUZZLE, bewilder, distract, confound, dumbfound, mystify, perplex

nonreligious **Syn** IRRELIGIOUS, unreligious, ungodly, godless

nonsense ♦ something said or proposed that seems senseless or absurd **Syn** twaddle, drivel, bunk, balderdash, poppycock, gobbledygook, trash, rot, bull

nonsocial **Syn** UNSOCIAL, asocial, antisocial

norm **Syn** AVERAGE, mean, median, par

normal **Syn** REGULAR, typical, natural **Ant** abnormal

nosy **Syn** CURIOUS, inquisitive, prying, snoopy

notable **Syn** NOTEWORTHY, memorable

note *vb* **Syn** SEE, remark, notice, perceive, discern, observe, contemplate, survey, view, behold, descry, espy

note *n* **1 Syn** SIGN, mark, token, badge, symptom **2 Syn** REMARK, observation, comment, commentary, obiter dictum **3 Syn** LETTER, epistle, missive, message, dispatch, report, memorandum

noteworthy ♦ having some quality that attracts one's attention **Syn** notable, memorable

notice **Syn** SEE, remark, observe, note, perceive, discern, behold, descry, espy, view, survey, contemplate

noticeable ♦ attracting notice or attention **Syn** remarkable, prominent, outstanding, conspicuous, salient, signal, striking, arresting

notify **Syn** INFORM, apprise, advise, acquaint

notion **Syn** IDEA, concept, conception, thought, impression

notoriety **Syn** FAME, reputation, repute, éclat, celebrity, renown, honor, glory

notwithstanding ♦ without being prevented or obstructed by **Syn** in spite of, despite

nourish **Syn** FEED, pasture, graze

nourishment **Syn** FOOD, nutriment, sustenance, aliment, pabulum, pap

novel **Syn** NEW, new-fashioned, newfangled, modern, modernistic, original, fresh

novice ♦ one who is just entering a field in which he or she has no previous experience **Syn** novitiate, apprentice, probationer, postulant, neophyte

novitiate **Syn** NOVICE, apprentice, probationer, postulant, neophyte

noxious **Syn** PERNICIOUS, baneful, deleterious, detrimental **Ant** wholesome, sanitary

nuance **Syn** GRADATION, shade

nucleus **Syn** CENTER, middle, midst, core, hub, focus, heart

nude **Syn** BARE, naked, bald, barren **Ant** clothed

nudge *vb* **Syn** POKE, prod, jog

nudge *n* **Syn** POKE, prod, jog

nugatory **Syn** VAIN, otiose, idle, empty, hollow

nullify ♦ to deprive of effective or continued existence **Syn** negate, annul, abrogate, invalidate

number *n* **1** **Syn** SUM, quantity, whole, total, aggregate, amount **2** ♦ a character by which an arithmetical value is designated **Syn** numeral, figure, digit, integer

number *vb* **Syn** COUNT, tell, enumerate

numeral **Syn** NUMBER, figure, digit, integer

numerous **Syn** MANY, several, sundry, various, divers, multifarious

nun **Syn** RELIGIOUS, monk, friar

nuncio **Syn** AMBASSADOR, legate, internuncio, chargé d'affaires, minister, envoy

nunnery **Syn** CLOISTER, monastery, convent, abbey, priory

nuptial *adj* **Syn** MATRIMONIAL, conjugal, connubial, hymeneal, marital

nuptial *n* **Syn** MARRIAGE, matrimony, wedlock, wedding, espousal

nurse ♦ to promote the growth, development, or progress of **Syn** nurture, foster, cherish, cultivate

nurture **Syn** NURSE, foster, cherish, cultivate

nutriment **Syn** FOOD, nourishment, sustenance, aliment, pabulum, pap

O

obdurate **Syn** INFLEXIBLE, inexorable, adamant, adamantine

obedient ♦ submissive to the will of another **Syn** docile, tractable, amenable, biddable **Ant** disobedient; contumacious

obeisance **Syn** HONOR, deference, homage, reverence

obese **Syn** FLESHY, corpulent, rotund, chubby, fat, stout, portly, plump **Ant** scrawny

obey ♦ to follow the wish, direction, or command of another **Syn** comply, mind **Ant** command, order

obfuscate **Syn** OBSCURE, dim, bedim, darken, eclipse, cloud, becloud, fog, befog

obiter dictum **Syn** REMARK, observation, comment, commentary, note

object *n* **1** **Syn** THING, article **2** **Syn** INTENTION, objective, goal, end, aim, design, purpose, intent

object *vb* ♦ to oppose by arguing against **Syn** protest, remonstrate, expostulate, kick **Ant** acquiesce

objectify **Syn** REALIZE, externalize, materialize, incarnate, embody, actualize, hypostatize, reify

objectionable ♦ arousing or likely to arouse objection **Syn** exceptionable, unacceptable, undesirable, unwanted, unwelcome

objective *adj* **1** *Syn* MATERIAL, physical, corporeal, phenomenal, sensible *Ant* subjective **2** *Syn* FAIR, impartial, unbiased, dispassionate, uncolored, just, equitable

objective *n* *Syn* INTENTION, object, end, goal, aim, design, purpose, intent

objurgate *Syn* EXECRATE, curse, damn, anathematize

obligation 1 ♦ something one is bound to do or forbear *Syn* duty **2** *Syn* DEBT, indebtedness, liability, debit, arrear

oblige 1 *Syn* FORCE, constrain, coerce, compel **2** ♦ to do a service or courtesy *Syn* accommodate, favor *Ant* disoblige

obliging *Syn* AMIABLE, good-natured, complaisant *Ant* disobliging; inconsiderate

oblique *Syn* CROOKED, devious

obliterate *Syn* ERASE, efface, cancel, expunge, blot out, delete

oblivious *Syn* FORGETFUL, unmindful

obloquy 1 *Syn* ABUSE, vituperation, invective, scurrility, billingsgate **2** *Syn* DISGRACE, dishonor, disrepute, shame, infamy, ignominy, opprobrium, odium

obnoxious *Syn* REPUGNANT, distasteful, invidious, abhorrent, repellent *Ant* grateful

obscene *Syn* COARSE, gross, vulgar, ribald *Ant* decent

obscure *adj* **1** *Syn* DARK, murky, gloomy, dim, dusky **2** ♦ not clearly understandable *Syn* dark, vague, enigmatic, cryptic, ambiguous, equivocal *Ant* distinct, obvious

obscure *vb* ♦ to make dark, dim, or indistinct *Syn* dim, bedim, darken, eclipse, cloud, becloud, fog, befog, obfuscate *Ant* illuminate, illumine

obsequious *Syn* SUBSERVIENT, servile, slavish, menial *Ant* contumelious

observation *Syn* REMARK, comment, commentary, note, obiter dictum

observe 1 *Syn* KEEP, celebrate, solemnize, commemorate *Ant* violate **2** *Syn* SEE, survey, view, contemplate, notice, remark, note, perceive, discern, behold, descry, espy

observer *Syn* SPECTATOR, beholder, looker-on, onlooker, witness, eyewitness, bystander, kibitzer

obsolete *Syn* OLD, antiquated, archaic, antique, ancient, venerable, antediluvian *Ant* current

obstacle ♦ something that seriously hampers action or progress *Syn* obstruction, impediment, bar, snag

obstinate ♦ fixed and unyielding in course or purpose *Syn* dogged, stubborn, pertinacious, mulish, stiff-necked, pigheaded, bullheaded *Ant* pliant, pliable

obstreperous *Syn* VOCIFEROUS, clamorous, blatant, strident, boisterous

obstruct *Syn* HINDER, impede, block, bar, dam

obstruction *Syn* OBSTACLE, impediment, bar, snag *Ant* assistance

obtain *Syn* GET, procure, secure, acquire, gain, win

obtrude *Syn* INTRUDE, interlope, butt in

obtrusive *Syn* IMPERTINENT, intrusive, meddlesome, officious *Ant* unobtrusive; shy

obtuse *Syn* DULL, blunt *Ant* acute

obviate *Syn* PREVENT, preclude, avert, ward

obvious *Syn* EVIDENT, manifest, patent, distinct, apparent, palpable, plain, clear *Ant* obscure; abstruse

occasion 1 *Syn* OPPORTUNITY, chance, break, time **2** *Syn* CAUSE, determinant, antecedent, reason

occasional *Syn* INFREQUENT, uncommon, scarce, rare, sporadic *Ant* customary

occult *Syn* RECONDITE, esoteric, abstruse

occupation *Syn* WORK, employment, calling, pursuit, business

occur *Syn* HAPPEN, chance, befall, betide, transpire

occurrence ♦ something that happens or takes place *Syn* event, incident, episode, circumstance

odd *Syn* STRANGE, queer, quaint, singular, unique, peculiar, eccentric, erratic, outlandish, curious

odds *Syn* ADVANTAGE, handicap, allowance, edge

odious *Syn* HATEFUL, abhorrent, abominable, detestable

odium *Syn* DISGRACE, obloquy, opprobrium, ignominy, infamy, dishonor, disrepute, shame

odor *Syn* SMELL, scent, aroma

odorous ♦ emitting and diffusing scent *Syn* fragrant, redolent, aromatic, balmy *Ant* malodorous; odorless

offal *Syn* REFUSE, waste, rubbish, trash, debris, garbage

offend ♦ to cause hurt feelings or deep resentment *Syn* outrage, affront, insult

offense 1 *Syn* ATTACK, offensive, aggression **2** ♦ an emotional response to a slight or indignity *Syn* resentment, umbrage, pique, dudgeon, huff **3** ♦ a transgression of law *Syn* sin, vice, crime, scandal

offensive *adj* **1** *Syn* ATTACKING, aggressive **2** ♦ utterly distasteful or unpleasant to the senses or sensibilities *Syn* loathsome, repulsive, repugnant, revolting

offensive *n* *Syn* ATTACK, aggression, offense

offer ♦ to put something before another for acceptance or consideration *Syn* proffer, tender, present, prefer

offhand *Syn* EXTEMPORANEOUS, extempore, extemporary, improvised, impromptu, unpremeditated

office *Syn* FUNCTION, duty, province

officious *Syn* IMPERTINENT, meddlesome, intrusive, obtrusive

offset *Syn* COMPENSATE, countervail, balance, counterbalance, counterpoise

offspring ♦ those who follow in direct parental line *Syn* young, progeny, issue, descendants, posterity

oft *Syn* OFTEN, frequently, oftentimes

often ♦ many times *Syn* frequently, oft, oftentimes

oftentimes *Syn* OFTEN, frequently, oft

oil ♦ to smear, rub over, or lubricate with oil or an oily substance *Syn* grease, lubricate, anoint, cream

oily *Syn* FULSOME, unctuous, oleaginous, slick, soapy

old 1 *Syn* AGED, elderly, superannuated *Ant* young **2** ♦ having come into existence or use in the more or less distant past *Syn* ancient, venerable, antique, antiquated, antediluvian, archaic, obsolete *Ant* new

oleaginous *Syn* FULSOME, oily, unctuous, slick, soapy

oligarchy ♦ government by, or a state governed by, the few *Syn* aristocracy, plutocracy

omen *Syn* FORETOKEN, augury, portent, presage, prognostic

ominous ♦ having a menacing or threatening aspect *Syn* portentous, fateful, inauspicious, unpropitious

omit *Syn* NEGLECT, disregard, ignore, overlook, slight, forget

omnipresent ♦ present at all places at all times *Syn* ubiquitous

onerous ♦ imposing great hardship or strain *Syn* burdensome, oppressive, exacting

onlooker *Syn* SPECTATOR, looker-on, observer, beholder, witness, eyewitness, bystander, kibitzer

only ♦ being one or more of which there are no others *Syn* alone

onset *Syn* ATTACK, assault, onslaught

onslaught *Syn* ATTACK, assault, onset

onward ♦ toward or at a point lying ahead in space or time *Syn* forward, forth

opalescent, opaline *Syn* PRISMATIC, iridescent

open 1 *Syn* LIABLE, exposed, subject, prone, susceptible, sensitive *Ant* closed **2** *Syn* FRANK, plain, candid *Ant* close, closemouthed, close-lipped; clandestine

openhanded *Syn* LIBERAL, bountiful, bounteous, generous, munificent, handsome *Ant* closefisted, tightfisted

operate *Syn* ACT, behave, work, function, react

operative *adj* *Syn* ACTIVE, dynamic, live *Ant* abeyant

operative *n* *Syn* WORKER, mechanic, artisan, hand, workman, workingman, laborer, craftsman, handicraftsman, roustabout

opiate *Syn* ANODYNE, narcotic, nepenthe

opinion ♦ a judgment one holds as true *Syn* view, belief, conviction, persuasion, sentiment

opponent ♦ one who expresses or manifests opposition *Syn* antagonist, adversary

opportune *Syn* SEASONABLE, timely, well-timed, pat *Ant* inopportune

opportunity ♦ a state of affairs or a combination of circumstances favorable to some end *Syn* occasion, chance, break, time

oppose *Syn* RESIST, contest, fight, combat, conflict, antagonize, withstand

opposite *n* ♦ something that is exactly opposed or contrary *Syn* contradictory, contrary, antithesis, antipode, antonym, converse, counter, reverse

opposite *adj* ♦ so far apart as to be or to seem irreconcilable *Syn* contradictory, contrary, antithetical, antipodal, antipodean, antonymous

oppress 1 *Syn* DEPRESS, weigh 2 *Syn* WRONG, persecute, aggrieve

oppressive *Syn* ONEROUS, burdensome, exacting

opprobrious *Syn* ABUSIVE, vituperative, contumelious, scurrilous

opprobrium *Syn* DISGRACE, obloquy, odium, ignominy, infamy, shame, dishonor, disrepute

opt *Syn* CHOOSE, select, elect, pick, cull, prefer, single

optimistic *Syn* HOPEFUL, roseate, rose-colored *Ant* pessimistic

option *Syn* CHOICE, alternative, preference, selection, election

opulent 1 *Syn* RICH, affluent, wealthy *Ant* destitute; indigent 2 *Syn* LUXURIOUS, sumptuous

opus *Syn* WORK, product, production, artifact

oracular *Syn* DICTATORIAL, doctrinaire, dogmatic, authoritarian, magisterial

oral *Syn* VOCAL, articulate *Ant* written

oration *Syn* SPEECH, address, harangue, lecture, talk, sermon, homily

orbit *Syn* RANGE, gamut, reach, radius, compass, sweep, scope, horizon, ken, purview

ordain *Syn* DICTATE, prescribe, decree, impose

order *n* 1 *Syn* ASSOCIATION, society, club 2 *Syn* COMMAND, injunction, bidding, behest, mandate, dictate

order *vb* 1 ♦ to put persons or things into their proper places in relation to each other *Syn* arrange, marshal, organize, systematize, methodize 2 *Syn* COMMAND, bid, enjoin, direct, instruct, charge

orderly ♦ following a set arrangement, design, or pattern *Syn* methodical, systematic, regular *Ant* disorderly; chaotic

ordinance *Syn* LAW, canon, precept, rule, regulation, statute

ordinary *Syn* COMMON, familiar, popular, vulgar *Ant* extraordinary

organ 1 *Syn* MEAN, medium, vehicle, channel, instrument, instrumentality, agent, agency 2 *Syn* JOURNAL, periodical, newspaper, magazine, review

organism *Syn* SYSTEM, scheme, network, complex

organize 1 *Syn* ORDER, systematize, methodize, arrange, marshal *Ant* disorganize 2 *Syn* FOUND, institute, establish, create

oriel *Syn* WINDOW, casement, dormer

orifice *Syn* APERTURE, interstice

origin ♦ the point at which something begins its course or its existence *Syn* source, inception, root, provenance, provenience, prime mover

original 1 *Syn* INITIAL, primordial 2 *Syn* NEW, fresh, novel, new-fashioned, newfangled, modern, modernistic *Ant* dependent; banal; trite

originate *Syn* SPRING, rise, derive, arise, flow, issue, emanate, proceed, stem

ornament *Syn* ADORN, decorate, embellish, beautify, deck, bedeck, garnish

ornate ♦ elaborately and often pretentiously decorated or designed *Syn* rococo, baroque, flamboyant, florid *Ant* chaste; austere

orotund *Syn* RESONANT, sonorous, ringing, resounding, vibrant

oscillate *Syn* SWING, sway, vibrate, fluctuate, pendulate, waver, undulate

ostensible *Syn* APPARENT, seeming, illusory

ostentatious *Syn* SHOWY, pretentious

ostracize *Syn* BANISH, exile, expatriate, deport, transport, extradite

otiose *Syn* VAIN, nugatory, idle, empty, hollow

oust *Syn* EJECT, expel, evict, dismiss

out-and-out *Syn* OUTRIGHT, unmitigated, arrant

outcast ♦ one that is cast out or refused acceptance by society *Syn* castaway, derelict, reprobate, pariah, untouchable

outcome *Syn* EFFECT, result, consequence, upshot, aftereffect, aftermath, sequel, issue, event

outdo *Syn* EXCEED, excel, outstrip, transcend, surpass

outer ♦ being or located outside something *Syn* outward, outside, external, exterior *Ant* inner

outfit *n Syn* EQUIPMENT, apparatus, paraphernalia, tackle, machinery, gear, matériel

outfit *vb Syn* FURNISH, equip, appoint, accouter, arm

outlander *Syn* STRANGER, foreigner, alien, outsider, immigrant, émigré

outlandish *Syn* STRANGE, singular, unique, peculiar, eccentric, erratic, odd, queer, quaint, curious

outlast *Syn* OUTLIVE, survive

outline *n* 1 ♦ the line that bounds and gives form to something *Syn* contour, profile, skyline, silhouette 2 *Syn* SKETCH, diagram, delineation, draft, tracing, plot, blueprint

outline *vb Syn* SKETCH, diagram, delineate, draft, trace, plot, blueprint

outlive ♦ to remain in existence longer than *Syn* outlast, survive

outlook *Syn* PROSPECT, anticipation, foretaste

outrage 1 *Syn* ABUSE, misuse, mistreat, maltreat, ill-treat 2 *Syn* OFFEND, affront, insult

outrageous ♦ enormously or flagrantly bad or horrible *Syn* monstrous, heinous, atrocious

outright ♦ being exactly what is stated *Syn* out-and-out, unmitigated, arrant

outside *Syn* OUTER, outward, external, exterior *Ant* inside

outsider *Syn* STRANGER, foreigner, alien, outlander, immigrant, émigré

outstanding *Syn* NOTICEABLE, prominent, conspicuous, salient, signal, striking, arresting, remarkable *Ant* commonplace

outstrip *Syn* EXCEED, outdo, surpass, transcend, excel

outward *Syn* OUTER, outside, external, exterior *Ant* inward

outwit *Syn* FRUSTRATE, thwart, foil, baffle, balk, circumvent

over *Syn* ABOVE *Ant* beneath

overbearing *Syn* PROUD, supercilious, disdainful, lordly, arrogant, haughty, insolent *Ant* subservient

overcome *Syn* CONQUER, surmount, overthrow, subjugate, rout, vanquish, defeat, beat, lick, subdue

overdue *Syn* TARDY, behindhand, late

overflow *Syn* TEEM, swarm, abound

overhang *Syn* BULGE, jut, stick out, protrude, project, beetle

overlay ♦ to lay or spread over or across *Syn* superpose, superimpose, appliqué

overlook *Syn* NEGLECT, slight, forget, ignore, disregard, omit

overplus *Syn* EXCESS, superfluity, surplus, surplusage

overreach *Syn* CHEAT, cozen, defraud, swindle

overrun *Syn* INFEST, beset

oversight ♦ the function or duty of watching or guarding for the sake of proper control or direction *Syn* supervision, surveillance

overspread *Syn* COVER, envelop, wrap, shroud, veil

overstatement *Syn* EXAGGERATION, hyperbole *Ant* understatement

overthrow 1 *Syn* OVERTURN, subvert, upset, capsize 2 *Syn* CONQUER, rout, surmount, overcome, vanquish, defeat, beat, lick, subdue, subjugate, reduce

overture ♦ an action taken to win the favor or approval of another person or party *Syn* approach, advance, tender, bid

overturn ♦ to turn from an upright or proper position *Syn* upset, capsize, overthrow, subvert

own 1 *Syn* HAVE, possess, hold, enjoy 2 *Syn* ACKNOWLEDGE, avow, admit, confess *Ant* disown; repudiate

P

pabulum *Syn* FOOD, aliment, nutriment, nourishment, sustenance, pap

pace *Syn* SPEED, velocity, momentum, impetus, headway

pacific ♦ affording or promoting peace *Syn* peaceable, peaceful, irenic, pacifist, pacifistic *Ant* bellicose

pacifist, pacifistic *Syn* PACIFIC, peaceable, peaceful, irenic

pacify ♦ to ease the anger or disturbance of *Syn* appease, placate, mollify, propitiate, conciliate *Ant* anger

pack *n* *Syn* BUNDLE, bunch, package, packet, bale, parcel

pack *vb* ♦ to fill a limited space with more than is practicable or fitting *Syn* crowd, cram, stuff, ram, tamp

package *Syn* BUNDLE, packet, bunch, bale, parcel, pack

packet *Syn* BUNDLE, package, pack, bunch, bale, parcel

pact *Syn* CONTRACT, compact, bargain, treaty, entente, convention, cartel, concordat

pain 1 ♦ a bodily sensation that causes acute discomfort or suffering *Syn* ache, pang, throe, twinge, stitch 2 *pl* **pains** *Syn* EFFORT, exertion, trouble

pair *Syn* COUPLE, brace, yoke

palatable ♦ agreeable or pleasant to the taste *Syn* appetizing, savory, sapid, tasty, toothsome, flavorsome, relishing *Ant* unpalatable; distasteful

palate *Syn* TASTE, relish, gusto, zest

pale 1 ♦ deficient in color or in intensity of color *Syn* pallid, ashen, ashy, wan, livid 2 ♦ being weak and thin in substance or in vital qualities *Syn* anemic, bloodless

pall *Syn* SATIATE, cloy, surfeit, sate, glut, gorge

palliate ♦ to give a speciously fine appearance to what is base, evil, or erroneous *Syn* extenuate, gloze, gloss, whitewash, whiten

pallid *Syn* PALE, ashen, ashy, wan, livid

palpable 1 *Syn* PERCEPTIBLE, sensible, tangible, appreciable, ponderable *Ant* insensible 2 *Syn* EVIDENT, plain, clear, apparent, manifest, patent, obvious, distinct *Ant* impalpable

palpate *Syn* TOUCH, feel, handle, paw

palpitate *Syn* PULSATE, beat, throb, pulse

palpitation *Syn* PULSATION, beat, throb, pulse

palter *Syn* LIE, prevaricate, equivocate, fib

paltry *Syn* PETTY, trifling, trivial, puny, measly, picayunish, picayune

pamper *Syn* INDULGE, humor, spoil, baby, mollycoddle *Ant* chasten

pandect *Syn* COMPENDIUM, syllabus, digest, survey, sketch, précis, aperçu

pandemonium *Syn* DIN, uproar, hullabaloo, babel, hubbub, clamor, racket

pander *Syn* CATER, purvey

panegyric *Syn* ENCOMIUM, tribute, eulogy, citation

pang *Syn* PAIN, ache, throe, twinge, stitch

panic *Syn* FEAR, terror, horror, trepidation, consternation, dismay, alarm, fright, dread

pant *Syn* AIM, aspire

pap *Syn* FOOD, aliment, pabulum, nutriment, nourishment, sustenance

paper 1 ♦ a written or printed statement that is of value as a source of information or proof of a right, contention, or claim *Syn* instrument, document 2 *Syn* ESSAY, article, theme, composition

par *n* *Syn* AVERAGE, norm, mean, median

par *adj* *Syn* AVERAGE, mean, median

parable *Syn* ALLEGORY, myth, fable

parade *n* 1 *Syn* DISPLAY, array, pomp 2 *Syn* PROCESSION, cavalcade, cortege, motorcade

parade *vb* *Syn* SHOW, flaunt, expose, display, exhibit

paradox ♦ an expression or revelation of an inner or inherent contradiction *Syn* antinomy, anomaly

paragon ♦ a model of excellence or perfection *Syn* apotheosis, nonpareil, nonesuch

paragraph ♦ one of the several and individually distinct statements of a discourse or instrument, each of which deals with a particular point or item *Syn* verse, article, clause, plank, count

parallel *adj Syn* LIKE, alike, similar, analogous, comparable, akin, uniform, identical

parallel *n* **1** *Syn* COMPARISON, contrast, antithesis, collation **2** ♦ one that corresponds to or closely resembles another *Syn* counterpart, analogue, correlate

paralyze *Syn* DAZE, stun, bemuse, stupefy, benumb, petrify

paramount *Syn* DOMINANT, preponderant, preponderating, predominant, sovereign

parapet *Syn* BULWARK, rampart, breastwork, bastion

paraphernalia *Syn* EQUIPMENT, apparatus, machinery, outfit, tackle, gear, matériel

paraphrase *Syn* TRANSLATION, metaphrase, version

parasite ♦ a usu. obsequious flatterer or self-seeker *Syn* sycophant, favorite, toady, lickspittle, bootlicker, hanger-on, leech, sponge, sponger

parboil *Syn* BOIL, seethe, simmer, stew

parcel *n* **1** *Syn* PART, portion, piece, detail, member, division, section, segment, sector, fraction, fragment **2** *Syn* BUNDLE, bunch, pack, package, packet, bale **3** *Syn* GROUP, cluster, bunch, lot

parcel *vb Syn* APPORTION, portion, ration, prorate

parch *Syn* DRY, desiccate, dehydrate, bake

pardon *n* ♦ a remission of penalty or punishment *Syn* amnesty, absolution

pardon *vb Syn* EXCUSE, forgive, remit, condone *Ant* punish

pardonable *Syn* VENIAL

pare *Syn* SKIN, peel, decorticate, flay

pariah *Syn* OUTCAST, castaway, derelict, reprobate, untouchable

parley *Syn* CONFER, treat, negotiate, commune, consult, advise

parochial *Syn* INSULAR, provincial, local, small-town *Ant* catholic

parody *n Syn* CARICATURE, travesty, burlesque

parody *vb Syn* CARICATURE, travesty, burlesque

paroxysm *Syn* FIT, spasm, convulsion, attack, access, accession

parry *Syn* DODGE, shirk, sidestep, duck, fence, malinger

parsimonious *Syn* STINGY, niggardly, penurious, close, closefisted, tight, tightfisted, miserly, cheeseparing, penny-pinching *Ant* prodigal

part *n* ♦ something less than the whole *Syn* portion, piece, detail, member, division, section, segment, sector, fraction, fragment, parcel *Ant* whole

part *vb Syn* SEPARATE, divide, sever, sunder, divorce

partake *Syn* SHARE, participate

partiality *Syn* PREDILECTION, prepossession, prejudice, bias *Ant* impartiality

participate *Syn* SHARE, partake

particle ♦ a tiny or insignificant amount, part, or piece *Syn* bit, mite, smidgen, whit, atom, iota, jot, tittle

parti-colored *Syn* VARIEGATED, motley, checkered, checked, pied, piebald, skewbald, dappled, freaked

particular *adj* **1** *Syn* SINGLE, sole, separate, unique, lone, solitary *Ant* general **2** *Syn* SPECIAL, individual, specific, especial *Ant* general, universal **3** *Syn* CIRCUMSTANTIAL, particularized, detailed, itemized, minute **4** *Syn* NICE, fussy, squeamish, dainty, fastidious, finicky, finicking, finical, persnickety, pernickety

particular *n Syn* ITEM, detail *Ant* universal; whole; aggregate

particularized *Syn* CIRCUMSTANTIAL, particular, detailed, itemized, minute *Ant* generalized

partisan *Syn* FOLLOWER, adherent, disciple, sectary, henchman, satellite

partner ♦ one associated in action with another *Syn* copartner, colleague, ally, confederate *Ant* rival

party **1** *Syn* COMPANY, band, troop, troupe **2** *Syn* COMBINATION, combine, bloc, faction, ring

pasquinade *Syn* LIBEL, lampoon, squib, skit

pass *vb* ♦ move or come to a termination or end *Syn* pass away, elapse, expire

pass *n Syn* WAY, passage, route, course, artery

pass *n Syn* JUNCTURE, exigency, emergency, contingency, pinch, strait, crisis

passage 1 *Syn* WAY, pass, route, course, artery **2** ♦ a typically long narrow way connecting parts of a building *Syn* passageway, corridor, hall, hallway, gallery, arcade, cloister, aisle, ambulatory **3** *Syn* STRAIT, sound, channel, narrows

passageway *Syn* PASSAGE, corridor, hall, hallway, gallery, arcade, cloister, aisle, ambulatory

pass away *Syn* PASS, elapse, expire

passing *n Syn* DEATH, decease, demise

passing *adj Syn* TRANSIENT, transitory, ephemeral, momentary, fugitive, fleeting, evanescent, short-lived

passion 1 *Syn* DISTRESS, suffering, agony, dolor, misery **2** *Syn* FEELING, emotion, affection, sentiment **3** *Syn* DESIRE, lust, appetite, urge **4** ♦ intense emotion compelling action *Syn* fervor, ardor, enthusiasm, zeal

passionate *Syn* IMPASSIONED, ardent, fervent, fervid, perfervid

passive *Syn* INACTIVE, inert, idle, supine *Ant* active

pastoral *Syn* RURAL, rustic, bucolic

pasture *Syn* FEED, graze, nourish

pat *Syn* SEASONABLE, timely, well-timed, opportune

patch *Syn* MEND, repair, rebuild

patent *Syn* EVIDENT, manifest, distinct, obvious, apparent, palpable, plain, clear *Ant* latent

pathetic *Syn* MOVING, poignant, affecting, touching, impressive *Ant* comical

pathological *Syn* UNWHOLESOME, morbid, sickly, diseased

pathos ♦ a quality that moves one to pity and sorrow *Syn* poignancy, bathos

patience ♦ the power or capacity to endure without complaint something difficult or disagreeable *Syn* long-suffering, longanimity, forbearance, resignation *Ant* impatience

patois *Syn* DIALECT, vernacular, lingo, jargon, cant, argot, slang

patrician *Syn* GENTLEMAN, aristocrat

patrimony *Syn* HERITAGE, inheritance, birthright

patron *Syn* SPONSOR, surety, guarantor, backer, angel *Ant* client; protégé

patter *Syn* CHAT, chatter, prate, gab, prattle, babble, gabble, jabber, gibber

pattern 1 *Syn* MODEL, exemplar, example, ideal, standard, beau ideal, mirror **2** *Syn* FIGURE, design, motif, device

paunch *Syn* ABDOMEN, belly, stomach, gut

pause ♦ a temporary cessation of activity or of an activity *Syn* recess, respite, lull, intermission

paw *Syn* TOUCH, feel, palpate, handle

pawn *Syn* PLEDGE, hostage, earnest, token

pay *vb* ♦ to give money or its equivalent in return for something *Syn* compensate, remunerate, satisfy, reimburse, indemnify, repay, recompense

pay *n Syn* WAGE, wages, salary, stipend, fee, hire, emolument

paying ♦ yielding a profit *Syn* gainful, remunerative, lucrative, profitable

peace *Syn* TRUCE, cease-fire, armistice

peaceable *Syn* PACIFIC, peaceful, pacifist, pacifistic, irenic *Ant* contentious; acrimonious

peaceful 1 *Syn* CALM, tranquil, serene, placid, halcyon *Ant* turbulent **2** *Syn* PACIFIC, peaceable, pacifist, pacifistic, irenic

peak 1 *Syn* MOUNTAIN, mount, alp, volcano, mesa **2** *Syn* SUMMIT, pinnacle, climax, apex, acme, culmination, meridian, zenith, apogee

peculiar 1 *Syn* CHARACTERISTIC, individual, distinctive **2** *Syn* STRANGE, eccentric, odd, queer, singular, unique, quaint, outlandish, curious

pecuniary *Syn* FINANCIAL, monetary, fiscal

pedantic ♦ too narrowly concerned with scholarly matters *Syn* academic, scholastic, bookish

pedestrian *Syn* DULL, humdrum, dreary, monotonous, stodgy

pedigree *Syn* ANCESTRY, lineage

peek *Syn* LOOK, peep, glimpse, glance, sight, view

peel *vb Syn* SKIN, decorticate, pare, flay

peel *n Syn* SKIN, bark, rind, hide, pelt

peep *vb Syn* CHIRP, chirrup, cheep, tweet, twitter, chitter

peep *n Syn* CHIRP, chirrup, cheep, tweet, twitter, chitter

peep *n Syn* LOOK, glance, glimpse, peek, sight, view

peer *Syn* GAZE, gape, stare, glare, gloat

peerless *Syn* SUPREME, surpassing, preeminent, superlative, transcendent, incomparable

peeve *Syn* IRRITATE, exasperate, nettle, provoke, aggravate, rile

peevish *Syn* IRRITABLE, fractious, snappish, waspish, petulant, pettish, huffy, fretful, querulous

pejorative *Syn* DEROGATORY, depreciatory, depreciative, disparaging, slighting

pellucid *Syn* CLEAR, transparent, translucent, lucid, diaphanous, limpid

pelt *Syn* SKIN, hide, rind, bark, peel

pen *Syn* ENCLOSE, envelop, fence, coop, corral, cage, wall

penalize ♦ to inflict a penalty on *Syn* fine, amerce, mulct

penchant *Syn* LEANING, propensity, proclivity, flair

pendant *Syn* FLAG, ensign, standard, banner, color, streamer, pennant, pennon, jack

pendent *Syn* SUSPENDED, pendulous

pendulate *Syn* SWING, sway, oscillate, vibrate, fluctuate, waver, undulate

pendulous *Syn* SUSPENDED, pendent

penetrate 1 *Syn* ENTER, pierce, probe **2** *Syn* PERMEATE, pervade, impenetrate, interpenetrate, impregnate, saturate

penetration *Syn* DISCERNMENT, insight, acumen, discrimination, perception

penitence ♦ regret for sin or wrongdoing *Syn* repentance, contrition, attrition, compunction, remorse

pen name *Syn* PSEUDONYM, nom de plume, alias, nom de guerre, incognito

pennant *Syn* FLAG, ensign, standard,

banner, color, streamer, pendant, pennon, jack

penniless *Syn* POOR, indigent, needy, destitute, impecunious, poverty-stricken, necessitous

pennon *Syn* FLAG, ensign, standard, banner, color, streamer, pennant, pendant, jack

penny-pinching *Syn* STINGY, close, closefisted, tight, tightfisted, niggardly, parsimonious, penurious, miserly, cheeseparing

pensive *Syn* THOUGHTFUL, reflective, speculative, contemplative, meditative

penumbra *Syn* SHADE, umbra, adumbration, umbrage, shadow

penurious *Syn* STINGY, parsimonious, niggardly, close, closefisted, tight, tightfisted, miserly, cheeseparing, penny-pinching

penury *Syn* POVERTY, indigence, want, destitution, privation *Ant* luxury

peppery *Syn* SPIRITED, fiery, gingery, high-spirited, mettlesome, spunky

perceive *Syn* SEE, discern, note, remark, notice, observe, contemplate, behold, descry, espy, view, survey

percept *Syn* SENSATION, sense-datum, sensum, image

perceptible ♦ apprehensible as real or existent *Syn* sensible, palpable, tangible, appreciable, ponderable *Ant* imperceptible

perception *Syn* DISCERNMENT, penetration, insight, acumen, discrimination

perch *Syn* ALIGHT, light, land, roost

percussion *Syn* IMPACT, concussion, clash, shock, impingement, collision, jar, jolt

perdurable *Syn* LASTING, durable, permanent, stable, perpetual *Ant* fleeting

peremptory *Syn* MASTERFUL, imperative, imperious, domineering

perennial *Syn* CONTINUAL, perpetual, incessant, unremitting, constant, continuous

perfect *adj* ♦ not lacking or faulty in any particular *Syn* whole, entire, intact *Ant* imperfect

perfect *vb Syn* UNFOLD, evolve, develop, elaborate

perfection *Syn* EXCELLENCE, virtue, merit *Ant* failing

perfervid *Syn* IMPASSIONED, fervid, passionate, ardent, fervent

perfidious *Syn* FAITHLESS, false, disloyal, traitorous, treacherous

perforate ♦ to pierce through so as to leave a hole *Syn* puncture, punch, prick, bore, drill

perform ♦ to carry out or into effect *Syn* execute, discharge, accomplish, achieve, effect, fulfill

performer *Syn* ACTOR, player, mummer, mime, mimic, thespian, impersonator, trouper

perfume *Syn* FRAGRANCE, bouquet, redolence, incense

peril *Syn* DANGER, jeopardy, hazard, risk

perilous *Syn* DANGEROUS, hazardous, risky, precarious

perimeter *Syn* CIRCUMFERENCE, periphery, circuit, compass

period ♦ a division of time *Syn* epoch, era, age, aeon

periodic *Syn* INTERMITTENT, recurrent, alternate

periodical *Syn* JOURNAL, magazine, newspaper, review, organ

peripatetic *Syn* ITINERANT, ambulatory, ambulant, nomadic, vagrant

periphery *Syn* CIRCUMFERENCE, perimeter, circuit, compass

periphrasis *Syn* VERBIAGE, redundancy, tautology, pleonasm, circumlocution

perjure ♦ to make a false swearer of oneself by violating one's oath to tell the truth *Syn* forswear

permanent *Syn* LASTING, perdurable, durable, stable, perpetual *Ant* temporary; ad interim (*of persons*)

permeate ♦ to pass or cause to pass through every part of a thing *Syn* pervade, penetrate, impenetrate, interpenetrate, impregnate, saturate

permission ♦ a sanctioning to act or do something that is granted by one in authority *Syn* leave, sufferance *Ant* prohibition

permit *Syn* LET, allow, suffer, leave *Ant* prohibit, forbid

permutation *Syn* CHANGE, mutation, vicissitude, alternation

pernicious ♦ exceedingly harmful or destructive *Syn* baneful, noxious, deleterious, detrimental *Ant* innocuous

pernickety *Syn* NICE, persnickety, fastidious, finicky, finicking, finical, dainty, particular, fussy, squeamish

perpendicular *Syn* VERTICAL, plumb *Ant* horizontal

perpetrate *Syn* COMMIT

perpetual 1 *Syn* LASTING, permanent, perdurable, durable, stable **2** *Syn* CONTINUAL, continuous, constant, incessant, unremitting, perennial *Ant* transitory, transient

perplex *Syn* PUZZLE, mystify, bewilder, distract, nonplus, confound, dumbfound

perquisite *Syn* RIGHT, prerogative, privilege, appanage, birthright

persecute *Syn* WRONG, oppress, aggrieve

persevere ♦ to continue in a given course in the face of difficulty or opposition *Syn* persist

persiflage *Syn* BADINAGE, raillery

persist 1 *Syn* PERSEVERE *Ant* desist **2** *Syn* CONTINUE, last, endure, abide *Ant* desist

persnickety *Syn* NICE, pernickety, fastidious, finicky, finicking, finical, dainty, particular, fussy, squeamish

person *Syn* ENTITY, being, creature, individual

personality *Syn* DISPOSITION, character, individuality, temperament, temper, complexion

perspicacious *Syn* SHREWD, sagacious, astute *Ant* dull

perspicuous *Syn* CLEAR, lucid

persuade *Syn* INDUCE, prevail, get *Ant* dissuade

persuasion 1 *Syn* OPINION, conviction, belief, view, sentiment **2** *Syn* RELIGION, denomination, sect, cult, communion, faith, creed, church

pert *Syn* SAUCY, arch *Ant* coy

pertain *Syn* BEAR, relate, appertain, belong, apply

pertinacious *Syn* OBSTINATE, stubborn, dogged, mulish, stiff-necked, pigheaded, bullheaded

pertinent *Syn* RELEVANT, germane, material, apposite, applicable, apropos *Ant* impertinent; foreign

perturb *Syn* DISCOMPOSE, disturb, agitate, upset, disquiet, fluster, flurry

pervade *Syn* PERMEATE, penetrate, impenetrate, interpenetrate, impregnate, saturate

perverse *Syn* CONTRARY, restive, balky, froward, wayward

pervert *Syn* DEBASE, deprave, corrupt, vitiate, debauch

perverted *Syn* DEBASED, corrupted, depraved, vitiated, debauched

pessimistic *Syn* CYNICAL, misanthropic *Ant* optimistic

pester *Syn* WORRY, plague, tease, tantalize, annoy, harass, harry

pestilent, pestilential *Syn* POISONOUS, venomous, virulent, toxic, mephitic, miasmic, miasmatic, miasmal

pet *Syn* CARESS, fondle, cosset, cuddle, dandle

petite *Syn* SMALL, little, diminutive, wee, tiny, teeny, weeny, minute, microscopic, miniature

petition *n Syn* PRAYER, suit, plea, appeal

petition *vb Syn* PRAY, sue, plead, appeal

petrify 1 *Syn* HARDEN, solidify, indurate, cake 2 *Syn* DAZE, stun, bemuse, stupefy, benumb, paralyze

pettish *Syn* IRRITABLE, fractious, peevish, petulant, snappish, waspish, huffy, fretful, querulous

petty ♦ being often contemptibly insignificant or unimportant *Syn* puny, trivial, trifling, paltry, measly, picayunish, picayune *Ant* important, momentous; gross

petulant *Syn* IRRITABLE, fractious, peevish, pettish, snappish, waspish, huffy, fretful, querulous

phantasm 1 *Syn* APPARITION, phantom, wraith, ghost, spirit, specter, shade, revenant 2 *Syn* FANCY, fantasy, phantasy, vision, dream, daydream, nightmare

phantasy *Syn* FANCY, fantasy, phantasm, vision, dream, daydream, nightmare

phantom *Syn* APPARITION, phantasm, wraith, ghost, spirit, specter, shade, revenant

pharisaical *Syn* HYPOCRITICAL, sanctimonious, canting

pharisaism *Syn* HYPOCRISY, sanctimony, cant

pharmaceutical *Syn* DRUG, medicinal, biologic, simple

pharmacist *Syn* DRUGGIST, apothecary, chemist

phase ♦ one of the possible ways of viewing or being presented to view *Syn* aspect, side, facet, angle

phenomenal 1 *Syn* MATERIAL, physical, corporeal, sensible, objective *Ant* noumenal 2 *Syn* EXCEPTIONAL, extraordinary, unusual, unwonted

phenomenon *Syn* WONDER, marvel, prodigy, miracle

philanthropic *Syn* CHARITABLE, benevolent, humane, humanitarian, eleemosynary, altruistic *Ant* misanthropic

philanthropy *Syn* CHARITY *Ant* misanthropy

philippic *Syn* TIRADE, diatribe, jeremiad

phlegm 1 *Syn* IMPASSIVITY, impassiveness, stolidity, apathy, stoicism 2 *Syn* EQUANIMITY, composure, sangfroid

phlegmatic *Syn* IMPASSIVE, stolid, apathetic, stoic

phony *Syn* COUNTERFEIT, spurious, bogus, fake, sham, pseudo, pinchbeck

phrase ♦ a group of words which, taken together, express a notion and may be used as a part of a sentence *Syn* idiom, expression, locution

phraseology, phrasing *Syn* LANGUAGE, vocabulary, diction, style

physic *Syn* REMEDY, cure, medicine, medicament, medication, specific

physical 1 *Syn* BODILY, corporeal, corporal, somatic 2 *Syn* MATERIAL, corporeal, phenomenal, sensible, objective

physiognomy *Syn* FACE, countenance, visage, mug, puss

physique ♦ bodily makeup or type *Syn* build, habit, constitution

picayunish, picayune *Syn* PETTY, trivial, trifling, puny, paltry, measly

pick *Syn* CHOOSE, select, elect, opt, cull, prefer, single

picked *Syn* SELECT, elect, exclusive

pickle *Syn* PREDICAMENT, plight, dilemma, quandary, scrape, fix, jam

pictorial *Syn* GRAPHIC, vivid, picturesque

picture *Syn* REPRESENT, depict, portray, delineate, limn

picturesque *Syn* GRAPHIC, vivid, pictorial

piece *Syn* PART, portion, detail, member, division, section, segment, sector, fraction, fragment, parcel

pied, piebald *Syn* VARIEGATED, particolored, motley, checkered, checked, skewbald, dappled, freaked

pier 1 *Syn* BUTTRESS, abutment 2 *Syn* WHARF, dock, quay, slip, berth, jetty, levee

pierce *Syn* ENTER, penetrate, probe

pietistic *Syn* DEVOUT, sanctimonious, pious, religious

piety *Syn* FIDELITY, devotion, allegiance, fealty, loyalty *Ant* impiety

pigeonhole *Syn* ASSORT, sort, classify

pigheaded *Syn* OBSTINATE, stubborn, mulish, stiff-necked, bullheaded, dogged, pertinacious

pilaster *Syn* PILLAR, column

pile *n* 1 *Syn* HEAP, stack, mass, bank, shock, cock 2 *Syn* BUILDING, edifice, structure

pile *vb* *Syn* HEAP, stack, mass, bank, shock, cock

pilfer *Syn* STEAL, filch, purloin, lift, pinch, snitch, swipe, cop

pilgrimage *Syn* JOURNEY, voyage, tour, trip, jaunt, excursion, cruise, expedition

pillage *Syn* RAVAGE, devastate, waste, sack, despoil, spoliate

pillar ♦ a firm upright support for a superstructure *Syn* column, pilaster

pilot *Syn* GUIDE, steer, lead, engineer

pimple *Syn* ABSCESS, boil, furuncle, carbuncle, pustule

pinch *vb* *Syn* STEAL, pilfer, filch, purloin, lift, snitch, swipe, cop

pinch *n* *Syn* JUNCTURE, pass, exigency, emergency, contingency, strait, crisis

pinchbeck *Syn* COUNTERFEIT, spurious, bogus, fake, sham, pseudo, phony

pinched *Syn* HAGGARD, cadaverous, worn, careworn, wasted

pinch hitter *Syn* SUBSTITUTE, supply, locum tenens, alternate, understudy, double, stand-in

pine *Syn* LONG, yearn, hanker, hunger, thirst

pinnacle *Syn* SUMMIT, peak, apex, acme, climax, culmination, meridian, zenith, apogee

pious *Syn* DEVOUT, religious, pietistic, sanctimonious *Ant* impious

piquant *Syn* PUNGENT, poignant, racy, spicy, snappy *Ant* bland

pique *n* *Syn* OFFENSE, resentment, umbrage, dudgeon, huff

pique *vb* 1 *Syn* PROVOKE, excite, stimulate, quicken, galvanize 2 *Syn* PRIDE, plume, preen

pirate ♦ a robber on the high seas *Syn* freebooter, buccaneer, privateer, corsair

pirouette *Syn* TURN, revolve, rotate, gyrate, circle, spin, twirl, whirl, wheel, eddy, swirl

pitch 1 *Syn* THROW, hurl, fling, cast, toss, sling 2 *Syn* PLUNGE, dive

piteous *Syn* PITIFUL, pitiable

pith *Syn* SUBSTANCE, purport, gist, burden, core

pithy *Syn* CONCISE, summary, compendious, terse, succinct, laconic

pitiable 1 *Syn* PITIFUL, piteous 2 *Syn* CONTEMPTIBLE, despicable, sorry, scurvy, cheap, beggarly, shabby

pitiful ♦ arousing or deserving pity *Syn* piteous, pitiable *Ant* cruel

pittance *Syn* RATION, allowance, dole

pity *Syn* SYMPATHY, compassion, commiseration, condolence, ruth, empathy

pivotal *Syn* CENTRAL, focal

placate *Syn* PACIFY, appease, mollify, propitiate, conciliate *Ant* enrage

place ♦ the portion of space occupied by or chosen for something *Syn* position, location, situation, site, spot, station

placid *Syn* CALM, tranquil, serene, peaceful, halcyon *Ant* choleric (*of persons*); ruffled (*of things*)

plague *Syn* WORRY, pester, tease, tantalize, harry, harass, annoy

plain 1 *Syn* LEVEL, plane, flat, even, smooth, flush *Ant* solid **2** *Syn* EVIDENT, clear, distinct, obvious, manifest, patent, apparent, palpable *Ant* abstruse **3** ♦ free from all ostentation or superficial embellishment *Syn* homely, simple, unpretentious *Ant* lovely **4** *Syn* FRANK, candid, open

plaintive *Syn* MELANCHOLY, dolorous, doleful, lugubrious, rueful

plait *Syn* WEAVE, knit, crochet, braid, tat

plan *n* ♦ a method devised for making or doing something or achieving an end *Syn* design, plot, scheme, project

plan *vb* ♦ to formulate a plan for arranging, realizing, or achieving something *Syn* design, plot, scheme, project

plane *Syn* LEVEL, plain, flat, even, smooth, flush *Ant* solid

planet *Syn* EARTH, world, globe

plank *Syn* PARAGRAPH, verse, article, clause, count

plastic ♦ susceptible of being modified in form or nature *Syn* pliable, pliant, ductile, malleable, adaptable

platitude *Syn* COMMONPLACE, truism, bromide, cliché

plaudits *Syn* APPLAUSE, acclamation, acclaim

plausible ♦ appearing worthy of belief *Syn* credible, believable, colorable, specious

play *n* **1** ♦ activity engaged in for amusement *Syn* sport, disport, frolic, rollick, romp, gambol *Ant* work **2** *Syn* FUN, jest, sport, game *Ant* earnest **3** *Syn* ROOM, berth, elbowroom, leeway, margin, clearance

play *vb* **1** ♦ to engage in an activity for amusement or recreation *Syn* sport, disport, frolic, rollick, romp, gambol **2** *Syn* ACT, impersonate

player *Syn* ACTOR, performer, mummer, mime, mimic, thespian, impersonator, trouper

playful ♦ given to or characterized by play, jests, or tricks *Syn* frolicsome, sportive, roguish, waggish, impish, mischievous

plea 1 *Syn* APOLOGY, apologia, excuse, pretext, alibi **2** *Syn* PRAYER, suit, petition, appeal

plead *Syn* PRAY, sue, petition, appeal

pleasant ♦ highly acceptable to the mind or the senses *Syn* pleasing, agreeable, grateful, gratifying, welcome *Ant* unpleasant; distasteful; harsh

please ♦ to give or be a source of pleasure to *Syn* gratify, delight, rejoice, gladden, tickle, regale *Ant* displease; anger; vex

pleasing *Syn* PLEASANT, agreeable, grateful, gratifying, welcome *Ant* displeasing; repellent

pleasure ♦ the agreeable emotion accompanying the expectation, acquisition, or possession of something good or greatly desired *Syn* delight, joy, delectation, enjoyment, fruition *Ant* displeasure; anger; vexation

plebiscite *Syn* MANDATE, initiative, referendum

pledge *n* ♦ something given or held as a sign of another's good faith or intentions *Syn* earnest, token, pawn, hostage

pledge *vb* *Syn* PROMISE, engage, plight, covenant, contract *Ant* abjure

plenary *Syn* FULL, complete, replete *Ant* limited

plenteous *Syn* PLENTIFUL, ample, abundant, copious

plentiful ♦ more than sufficient without being excessive *Syn* plenteous, ample, abundant, copious *Ant* scanty, scant

pleonasm *Syn* VERBIAGE, redundancy, tautology, circumlocution, periphrasis

pliable *Syn* PLASTIC, pliant, ductile, malleable, adaptable *Ant* obstinate

pliant *Syn* PLASTIC, pliable, ductile, malleable, adaptable

plight *vb* *Syn* PROMISE, engage, pledge, covenant, contract

plight *n* *Syn* PREDICAMENT, dilemma, quandary, scrape, fix, jam, pickle

plot *n* **1** *Syn* PLAN, design, scheme, project **2** ♦ a plan secretly devised to accomplish an evil or treacherous end *Syn* in-

trigue, machination, conspiracy, cabal **3
Syn** SKETCH, outline, diagram, delineation, draft, tracing, blueprint

plot *vb* **1 Syn** PLAN, design, scheme, project **2 Syn** SKETCH, outline, diagram, delineate, draft, trace, blueprint

ploy Syn TRICK, ruse, stratagem, maneuver, gambit, artifice, wile, feint

pluck Syn FORTITUDE, grit, backbone, guts, sand

plumb *vb* **Syn** FATHOM, sound

plumb *adj* **Syn** VERTICAL, perpendicular

plume Syn PRIDE, pique, preen

plump Syn FLESHY, stout, portly, rotund, chubby, fat, corpulent, obese **Ant** cadaverous

plunder *vb* **Syn** ROB, rifle, loot, burglarize

plunder *n* **Syn** SPOIL, booty, prize, loot, swag

plunge ♦ to thrust or cast oneself or something into or as if into deep water **Syn** dive, pitch

plutocracy Syn OLIGARCHY, aristocracy

ply Syn HANDLE, manipulate, wield, swing

pocket Syn HOLE, hollow, cavity, void, vacuum

poet ♦ a writer of verse **Syn** versifier, rhymer, rhymester, poetaster, bard, minstrel, troubadour

poetaster Syn POET, versifier, rhymer, rhymester, bard, minstrel, troubadour

pogrom Syn MASSACRE, slaughter, butchery, carnage

poignancy Syn PATHOS, bathos

poignant 1 Syn PUNGENT, piquant, racy, spicy, snappy **Ant** dull **2 Syn** MOVING, touching, pathetic, impressive, affecting

point Syn DIRECT, aim, level, train, lay

point of view ♦ a position from which something is considered or evaluated **Syn** viewpoint, standpoint, angle, slant

poise *vb* **Syn** STABILIZE, steady, balance, ballast, trim

poise *n* **1 Syn** BALANCE, equilibrium, equipoise, tension **2 Syn** TACT, address, savoir faire

poison ♦ something that harms, interferes with, or destroys the activity, progress, or welfare of something else **Syn** venom, virus, toxin, bane

poisonous ♦ having the properties or effects of poison **Syn** venomous, virulent, toxic, mephitic, pestilent, pestilential, miasmic, miasmatic, miasmal

poke *vb* ♦ to thrust something into so as to stir up, urge on, or attract attention **Syn** prod, nudge, jog

poke *n* ♦ a quick thrust with or as if with the hand **Syn** prod, nudge, jog

polite Syn CIVIL, courteous, courtly, gallant, chivalrous **Ant** impolite

politic 1 Syn EXPEDIENT, advisable **2 Syn** SUAVE, diplomatic, bland, smooth, urbane

politician ♦ a person engaged in the art or science of government **Syn** statesman, politico

politico Syn POLITICIAN, statesman

poll Syn SHEAR, clip, trim, prune, lop, snip, crop

pollute Syn CONTAMINATE, defile, taint, attaint

pomp Syn DISPLAY, parade, array

ponder ♦ to consider or examine attentively or deliberately **Syn** meditate, muse, ruminate

ponderable Syn PERCEPTIBLE, appreciable, sensible, palpable, tangible

ponderous Syn HEAVY, cumbrous, cumbersome, weighty, hefty

pool Syn MONOPOLY, corner, syndicate, trust, cartel

poor 1 ♦ lacking money or material possessions **Syn** indigent, needy, destitute, penniless, impecunious, poverty-stricken, necessitous **Ant** rich **2 Syn** BAD, wrong

poppycock Syn NONSENSE, twaddle, drivel, bunk, balderdash, gobbledygook, trash, rot, bull

popular Syn COMMON, ordinary, familiar, vulgar **Ant** unpopular; esoteric

port *n* **Syn** HARBOR, haven

port *n* **Syn** BEARING, presence, deportment, demeanor, mien

portal Syn DOOR, gate, doorway, gateway, postern

portend *Syn* FORETELL, presage, augur, prognosticate, predict, forecast, prophesy, forebode

portent *Syn* FORETOKEN, presage, prognostic, omen, augury

portentous *Syn* OMINOUS, unpropitious, inauspicious, fateful

portion *n* 1 *Syn* PART, piece, detail, member, division, section, segment, sector, fraction, fragment, parcel 2 *Syn* FATE, destiny, lot, doom

portion *vb* *Syn* APPORTION, parcel, ration, prorate

portly *Syn* FLESHY, stout, plump, rotund, chubby, fat, corpulent, obese

portray *Syn* REPRESENT, depict, delineate, picture, limn

pose *vb* 1 *Syn* PROPOSE, propound

pose *n* 1 ♦ an adopted way of speaking or behaving *Syn* air, affectation, mannerism 2 *Syn* POSTURE, attitude

posit *vb* *Syn* PRESUPPOSE, presume, assume, postulate, premise

posit *n* *Syn* ASSUMPTION, presupposition, presumption, postulate, premise

position 1 ♦ a firmly held point of view or way of regarding something *Syn* stand, attitude 2 *Syn* PLACE, location, situation, site, spot, station

positive *Syn* SURE, certain, cocksure *Ant* doubtful

possess *Syn* HAVE, own, enjoy, hold

possessions ♦ all the items that taken together constitute a person's or group's property or wealth *Syn* belongings, effects, means, resources, assets

possible 1 ♦ capable of being realized *Syn* practicable, feasible 2 *Syn* PROBABLE, likely

posterior ♦ situated at or toward the back *Syn* rear, hind, hinder, after, back *Ant* anterior

posterity *Syn* OFFSPRING, young, progeny, issue, descendant *Ant* ancestry

postern *Syn* DOOR, gate, gateway, doorway, portal

postpone *Syn* DEFER, suspend, stay, intermit

postulant *Syn* NOVICE, novitiate, probationer, neophyte, apprentice

postulate *vb* *Syn* PRESUPPOSE, presume, assume, premise, posit

postulate *n* *Syn* ASSUMPTION, presupposition, presumption, premise, posit

posture 1 ♦ the position or bearing of the body *Syn* attitude, pose 2 *Syn* STATE, situation, condition, mode, status

pot *Syn* BET, wager, stake, ante

potent *Syn* POWERFUL, puissant, forceful, forcible *Ant* impotent

potential *Syn* LATENT, dormant, quiescent, abeyant *Ant* active, actual

pother *Syn* STIR, flurry, fuss, ado, bustle

pouch *Syn* BAG, sack

pound *Syn* BEAT, pummel, buffet, baste, belabor, thrash

pour ♦ to send forth or come forth abundantly *Syn* stream, gush, sluice

poverty ♦ the state of one with insufficient resources *Syn* indigence, penury, want, destitution, privation *Ant* riches

poverty-stricken *Syn* POOR, indigent, needy, destitute, penniless, impecunious, necessitous

power 1 ♦ the ability to exert effort *Syn* force, energy, strength, might, puissance *Ant* impotence 2 ♦ the ability of a living being to perform in a given way or a capacity for a particular kind of performance *Syn* faculty, function 3 ♦ the right to govern or rule or determine *Syn* authority, jurisdiction, control, command, sway, dominion

powerful ♦ having or manifesting power to effect great or striking results *Syn* potent, puissant, forceful, forcible *Ant* powerless; inefficacious

powerless ♦ unable to effect one's purpose, intention, or end *Syn* impotent *Ant* powerful; efficacious

practicable *Syn* POSSIBLE, feasible *Ant* impracticable

practically *Syn* VIRTUALLY, morally

practice *vb* ♦ to perform or cause one to perform an act or series of acts repeatedly in order to master or strengthen a skill or ability *Syn* exercise, drill

practice *n* 1 *Syn* HABIT, habitude, usage, custom, use, wont 2 ♦ repeated activity or exertion in order to develop or improve a strength or skill **Syn** exercise, drill **Ant** theory; precept

praise ♦ to express approval of or esteem for **Syn** laud, acclaim, extol, eulogize **Ant** blame

prank ♦ a playful, often a mischievous, act or trick **Syn** caper, antic, monkeyshine, dido

prate **Syn** CHAT, chatter, gab, patter, prattle, babble, gabble, jabber, gibber

prattle **Syn** CHAT, chatter, patter, prate, gab, babble, gabble, jabber, gibber

pray ♦ to request or make a request for in a humble, beseeching manner **Syn** plead, petition, appeal, sue

prayer ♦ an earnest and usu. a formal request for something **Syn** suit, plea, petition, appeal

preamble **Syn** INTRODUCTION, prologue, prelude, preface, foreword, exordium

precarious **Syn** DANGEROUS, hazardous, perilous, risky

precedence **Syn** PRIORITY

precedent **Syn** PRECEDING, antecedent, foregoing, previous, prior, former, anterior

preceding ♦ being before, esp. in time or in arrangement **Syn** antecedent, precedent, foregoing, previous, prior, former, anterior **Ant** following

precept **Syn** LAW, rule, canon, regulation, statute, ordinance **Ant** practice; counsel

precious **Syn** COSTLY, expensive, dear, valuable, invaluable, priceless

precipitate *vb* **Syn** SPEED, accelerate, quicken, hasten, hurry

precipitate *n* **Syn** DEPOSIT, sediment, dregs, lees, grounds

precipitate *adj* ♦ showing undue haste or unexpectedness **Syn** headlong, abrupt, impetuous, hasty, sudden **Ant** deliberate

precipitous **Syn** STEEP, abrupt, sheer

précis **Syn** COMPENDIUM, sketch, aperçu, survey, syllabus, digest, pandect

precise **Syn** CORRECT, exact, accurate, nice, right **Ant** loose

preciseness **Syn** PRECISION

precision ♦ the quality or character of what is precise **Syn** preciseness

preclude **Syn** PREVENT, obviate, avert, ward

precocious **Syn** PREMATURE, untimely, forward, advanced **Ant** backward

precursor **Syn** FORERUNNER, harbinger, herald

predicament ♦ a difficult, perplexing, or trying situation **Syn** dilemma, quandary, plight, scrape, fix, jam, pickle

predicate **Syn** ASSERT, affirm, declare, profess, aver, protest, avouch, avow, warrant

predict **Syn** FORETELL, forecast, prophesy, prognosticate, augur, presage, portend, forebode

predilection ♦ an attitude of mind that predisposes one to favor something **Syn** partiality, prepossession, prejudice, bias **Ant** aversion

predispose **Syn** INCLINE, dispose, bias

predominant **Syn** DOMINANT, paramount, preponderant, preponderating, sovereign

preeminent **Syn** SUPREME, surpassing, transcendent, superlative, peerless, incomparable

preempt **Syn** ARROGATE, usurp, appropriate, confiscate

preen **Syn** PRIDE, plume, pique

preface **Syn** INTRODUCTION, prologue, prelude, foreword, exordium, preamble

prefatory **Syn** PRELIMINARY, introductory, preparatory

prefer 1 **Syn** CHOOSE, select, elect, opt, pick, cull, single **2** **Syn** OFFER, proffer, tender, present

preferable **Syn** BETTER, superior

preference **Syn** CHOICE, selection, election, option, alternative

preferment **Syn** ADVANCEMENT, promotion, elevation

pregnant **Syn** EXPRESSIVE, meaningful, significant, eloquent, sententious

prejudice **Syn** PREDILECTION, bias, partiality, prepossession

preliminary ♦ serving to make ready the way for something that follows **Syn** introductory, preparatory, prefatory

prelude **Syn** INTRODUCTION, prologue, preface, foreword, exordium, preamble

premature ♦ unduly early in coming, happening, or developing *Syn* untimely, forward, advanced, precocious *Ant* matured

premeditated *Syn* DELIBERATE, considered, advised, designed, studied *Ant* unpremeditated; casual, accidental

premise *n Syn* ASSUMPTION, postulate, posit, presupposition, presumption

premise *vb Syn* PRESUPPOSE, postulate, posit, presume, assume

premium ♦ something that is offered or given for some service or attainment *Syn* prize, award, reward, meed, guerdon, bounty, bonus

preoccupied *Syn* ABSTRACTED, absent, absentminded, distraught

preparatory *Syn* PRELIMINARY, introductory, prefatory

prepare ♦ to make ready beforehand usu. for some purpose, use, or activity *Syn* fit, qualify, condition, ready

preponderant, preponderating *Syn* DOMINANT, predominant, paramount, sovereign

prepossession *Syn* PREDILECTION, partiality, prejudice, bias

preposterous *Syn* FOOLISH, absurd, silly

prerequisite *Syn* REQUIREMENT, requisite

prerogative *Syn* RIGHT, privilege, perquisite, appanage, birthright

presage *n Syn* FORETOKEN, prognostic, omen, augury, portent

presage *vb Syn* FORETELL, augur, portend, forebode, prognosticate, predict, forecast, prophesy

prescribe 1 *Syn* DICTATE, ordain, decree, impose **2** ♦ to fix arbitrarily or authoritatively for the sake of order or of a clear understanding *Syn* assign, define

prescription *Syn* RECEIPT, recipe

presence *Syn* BEARING, deportment, demeanor, mien, port

present *n Syn* GIFT, gratuity, favor, boon, largesse

present *vb* **1** *Syn* GIVE, bestow, confer, donate, afford **2** *Syn* OFFER, tender, proffer, prefer

presentiment *Syn* APPREHENSION, misgiving, foreboding

presently ♦ without undue time lapse *Syn* shortly, soon, directly

preserve *Syn* SAVE, conserve

press *n Syn* CROWD, throng, crush, mob, rout, horde

press *vb* ♦ to act upon through steady pushing or thrusting force exerted in contact *Syn* bear, bear down, squeeze, crowd, jam

pressing ♦ demanding or claiming esp. immediate attention *Syn* urgent, imperative, crying, importunate, insistent, exigent, instant

pressure *Syn* STRESS, strain, tension

prestige *Syn* INFLUENCE, authority, weight, credit

presume *Syn* PRESUPPOSE, postulate, premise, posit, assume

presumption *Syn* ASSUMPTION, presupposition, postulate, premise, posit

presumptuous *Syn* CONFIDENT, assured, sanguine, sure

presuppose ♦ to take something for granted or as true or existent esp. as a basis for action or reasoning *Syn* presume, assume, postulate, premise, posit

presupposition *Syn* ASSUMPTION, presumption, postulate, premise, posit

pretend *Syn* ASSUME, affect, simulate, feign, counterfeit, sham

pretense 1 *Syn* CLAIM, pretension, title **2** ♦ the offering of something false as real or true *Syn* pretension, make-believe

pretension 1 *Syn* CLAIM, title, pretense **2** *Syn* PRETENSE, make-believe **3** *Syn* AMBITION, aspiration

pretentious 1 *Syn* SHOWY, ostentatious *Ant* unpretentious **2** *Syn* AMBITIOUS, utopian

preternatural *Syn* SUPERNATURAL, supranatural, miraculous, superhuman

pretext *Syn* APOLOGY, excuse, plea, alibi, apologia

pretty *Syn* BEAUTIFUL, bonny, comely, fair, lovely, handsome, good-looking, beauteous, pulchritudinous

prevail *Syn* INDUCE, persuade, get

prevailing

prevailing ♦ general (as in circulation, acceptance, or use) in a given place or at a given time *Syn* prevalent, rife, current

prevalent *Syn* PREVAILING, rife, current

prevaricate *Syn* LIE, equivocate, palter, fib

prevent 1 ♦ to deal with beforehand *Syn* anticipate, forestall **2** ♦ to stop from advancing or occurring *Syn* preclude, obviate, avert, ward *Ant* permit

previous *Syn* PRECEDING, foregoing, prior, antecedent, precedent, former, anterior *Ant* subsequent; consequent

prey *Syn* VICTIM, quarry

price ♦ the quantity of one thing that is exchanged or demanded in barter or sale for another *Syn* charge, cost, expense

priceless *Syn* COSTLY, invaluable, precious, expensive, dear, valuable

prick 1 *Syn* PERFORATE, punch, puncture, bore, drill **2** *Syn* URGE, egg, exhort, goad, spur, prod, sic

pride *n* ♦ an attitude of inordinate self-esteem or superiority *Syn* vanity, vainglory *Ant* humility; shame

pride *vb* ♦ to congratulate oneself because of something one is, has, or has done or achieved *Syn* plume, pique, preen

priggish 1 *Syn* COMPLACENT, smug, self-complacent, self-satisfied **2** *Syn* PRIM, prissy, prudish, puritanical, straitlaced, stuffy

prim ♦ excessively concerned with what one regards as proper or right *Syn* priggish, prissy, prudish, puritanical, straitlaced, stuffy

primal *Syn* PRIMARY, primordial, primitive, pristine, primeval, prime

primary ♦ first in some respect (as order, character, or importance) *Syn* primal, primordial, primitive, pristine, primeval, prime

prime *Syn* PRIMARY, primal, primordial, primitive, pristine, primeval

prime mover *Syn* ORIGIN, source, provenance, provenience, inception, root

primeval *Syn* PRIMARY, pristine, primitive, primordial, primal, prime

primitive 1 *Syn* PRIMARY, primal, primordial, pristine, primeval, prime **2** *Syn* ELE-MENTAL, basic, elementary, essential, fundamental, underlying

primordial 1 *Syn* PRIMARY, primeval, pristine, primitive, primal, prime **2** *Syn* INITIAL, original

princely *Syn* KINGLY, regal, royal, queenly, imperial

principal *Syn* CHIEF, main, leading, foremost, capital

principally *Syn* LARGELY, mainly, chiefly, mostly, greatly, generally

principle ♦ a comprehensive and fundamental rule, doctrine, or assumption *Syn* axiom, fundamental, law, theorem

print *Syn* IMPRESSION, impress, imprint, stamp

printing *Syn* EDITION, impression, reprinting, reissue

prior *Syn* PRECEDING, previous, foregoing, precedent, anterior, former, antecedent

priority ♦ the act, the fact, or the right of preceding another *Syn* precedence

priory *Syn* CLOISTER, monastery, nunnery, convent, abbey

prismatic ♦ marked by or displaying a variety of colors *Syn* iridescent, opalescent, opaline

prisoner ♦ one who is deprived of liberty and kept under involuntary restraint *Syn* captive

prissy *Syn* PRIM, priggish, prudish, puritanical, straitlaced, stuffy

pristine *Syn* PRIMARY, primeval, primordial, primitive, primal, prime

privateer *Syn* PIRATE, freebooter, buccaneer, corsair

privation 1 *Syn* LACK, want, dearth, absence, defect **2** *Syn* POVERTY, want, destitution, indigence, penury

privilege *Syn* RIGHT, prerogative, birthright, perquisite, appanage

prize *n* *Syn* PREMIUM, award, reward, meed, guerdon, bounty, bonus *Ant* forfeit

prize *vb* *Syn* APPRECIATE, value, treasure, cherish

prize *n* *Syn* SPOIL, booty, plunder, loot, swag

probable ♦ almost sure to be or to become true or real *Syn* possible, likely *Ant* certain; improbable

probationer *Syn* NOVICE, novitiate, apprentice, postulant, neophyte

probe *n Syn* INQUIRY, investigation, inquisition, inquest, research

probe *vb Syn* ENTER, pierce, penetrate

probity *Syn* HONESTY, honor, integrity

problem *Syn* MYSTERY, enigma, fiddle, puzzle, conundrum *Ant* solution

problematic *Syn* DOUBTFUL, dubious, questionable

procedure *Syn* PROCESS, proceeding

proceed *Syn* SPRING, issue, emanate, stem, flow, derive, arise, rise, originate

proceeding *Syn* PROCESS, procedure

process ♦ the series of actions, operations, or motions involved in the accomplishment of an end *Syn* procedure, proceeding

procession ♦ a body (as of persons and vehicles) moving along in a usu. ceremonial order *Syn* parade, cortege, cavalcade, motorcade

proclaim *Syn* DECLARE, announce, publish, advertise, promulgate, broadcast

proclamation *Syn* DECLARATION, announcement, publication, advertisement, promulgation, broadcasting

proclivity *Syn* LEANING, propensity, penchant, flair

procrastinate *Syn* DELAY, lag, dawdle, loiter *Ant* hasten, hurry

procreate *Syn* GENERATE, engender, beget, get, sire, breed, propagate, reproduce

procure *Syn* GET, obtain, secure, acquire, gain, win

prod *vb* 1 *Syn* POKE, nudge, jog 2 *Syn* URGE, egg, exhort, goad, spur, prick, sic

prod *n Syn* POKE, nudge, jog

prodigal *adj Syn* PROFUSE, lavish, exuberant, luxuriant, lush *Ant* parsimonious; frugal

prodigal *n Syn* SPENDTHRIFT, profligate, waster, wastrel

prodigious *Syn* MONSTROUS, tremendous, stupendous, monumental

prodigy *Syn* WONDER, marvel, miracle, phenomenon

produce *vb Syn* BEAR, yield, turn out

produce *n Syn* PRODUCT, production

product 1 *Syn* WORK, production, opus, artifact 2 ♦ something produced by physical labor or intellectual effort *Syn* production, produce

production 1 *Syn* WORK, product, opus, artifact 2 *Syn* PRODUCT, produce

profanation ♦ a violation or a misuse of something normally held sacred *Syn* desecration, sacrilege, blasphemy

profane 1 ♦ not concerned with religion or religious purposes *Syn* secular, lay, temporal *Ant* sacred 2 *Syn* IMPIOUS, blasphemous, sacrilegious

profanity *Syn* BLASPHEMY, cursing, swearing

profess *Syn* ASSERT, declare, affirm, aver, protest, avouch, avow, predicate, warrant

profession *Syn* TRADE, art, handicraft, craft

proffer *Syn* OFFER, tender, present, prefer

proficient ♦ having great knowledge and experience in a trade or profession *Syn* adept, skilled, skillful, expert, masterly

profile *Syn* OUTLINE, contour, silhouette, skyline

profit *n Syn* USE, service, advantage, account, avail

profit *vb Syn* BENEFIT, avail

profitable 1 *Syn* BENEFICIAL, advantageous *Ant* unprofitable 2 *Syn* PAYING, gainful, remunerative, lucrative

profligate *adj Syn* ABANDONED, dissolute, reprobate

profligate *n Syn* SPENDTHRIFT, prodigal, wastrel, waster

profound *Syn* DEEP, abysmal *Ant* shallow

profuse ♦ giving or given out in great abundance *Syn* lavish, prodigal, luxuriant, lush, exuberant *Ant* spare, scanty, scant

progenitor *Syn* ANCESTOR, forefather, forebear *Ant* progeny

progeny *Syn* OFFSPRING, young, issue, descendant, posterity *Ant* progenitor

prognostic *Syn* FORETOKEN, presage, omen, augury, portent

prognosticate *Syn* FORETELL, predict, forecast, prophesy, augur, presage, portend, forebode

program ♦ a formulated plan listing things to be done or to take place esp. in chronological order *Syn* schedule, timetable, agenda

progress *n* **1** *Syn* ADVANCE **2** ♦ a movement forward (as in time or space) *Syn* progression

progress *vb* *Syn* ADVANCE *Ant* retrogress

progression **1** *Syn* SUCCESSION, series, sequence, chain, train, string **2** *Syn* PROGRESS

progressive *Syn* LIBERAL, advanced, radical *Ant* reactionary

prohibit *Syn* FORBID, inhibit, enjoin, interdict, ban *Ant* permit

project *n* *Syn* PLAN, scheme, design, plot

project *vb* **1** *Syn* PLAN, scheme, design, plot **2** *Syn* BULGE, jut, stick out, protrude, overhang, beetle

projection ♦ an extension beyond the normal line or surface *Syn* protrusion, protuberance, bulge

prolific *Syn* FERTILE, fruitful, fecund *Ant* barren, unfruitful

prolificacy *Syn* FERTILITY, fruitfulness, fecundity *Ant* barrenness, unfruitfulness

prolix *Syn* WORDY, verbose, diffuse, redundant

prologue *Syn* INTRODUCTION, prelude, preface, foreword, exordium, preamble

prolong *Syn* EXTEND, protract, lengthen, elongate *Ant* curtail

prominent *Syn* NOTICEABLE, remarkable, conspicuous, salient, outstanding, signal, striking, arresting

promiscuous *Syn* MISCELLANEOUS, heterogeneous, motley

promise ♦ to give one's word to do, bring about, or provide *Syn* engage, pledge, plight, covenant, contract

promote *Syn* ADVANCE, forward, further *Ant* impede

promotion **1** *Syn* ADVANCEMENT, preferment, elevation *Ant* demotion **2** *Syn* PUBLICITY, ballyhoo, propaganda

prompt *Syn* QUICK, ready, apt

promulgate *Syn* DECLARE, proclaim, announce, publish, advertise, broadcast

promulgation *Syn* DECLARATION, proclamation, announcement, publication, advertisement, broadcasting

prone **1** *Syn* LIABLE, subject, exposed, open, susceptible, sensitive **2** ♦ lying down *Syn* supine, prostrate, recumbent, couchant, dormant *Ant* erect

pronounce *Syn* ARTICULATE, enunciate

proof **1** *Syn* REASON, ground, argument **2** ♦ something that serves as evidence compelling the acceptance of a truth or fact *Syn* demonstration, test, trial *Ant* disproof

prop *Syn* SUPPORT, sustain, bolster, buttress, brace

propaganda *Syn* PUBLICITY, ballyhoo, promotion

propagate **1** *Syn* GENERATE, engender, breed, beget, procreate, sire, reproduce **2** *Syn* SPREAD, circulate, disseminate, diffuse, radiate

propel *Syn* PUSH, shove, thrust

propensity *Syn* LEANING, proclivity, penchant, flair *Ant* antipathy

proper **1** *Syn* FIT, meet, appropriate, fitting, apt, happy, felicitous, suitable *Ant* improper **2** *Syn* DECOROUS, seemly, decent, nice

property *Syn* QUALITY, character, attribute, accident

prophecy *Syn* REVELATION, vision, apocalypse

prophesy *Syn* FORETELL, predict, forecast, prognosticate, augur, presage, portend, forebode

propinquity *Syn* PROXIMITY

propitiate *Syn* PACIFY, appease, placate, mollify, conciliate

propitious *Syn* FAVORABLE, auspicious, benign *Ant* unpropitious; adverse

proportion *Syn* SYMMETRY, balance, harmony

proportional ♦ corresponding in size, degree, or intensity *Syn* proportionate, commensurate, commensurable

proportionate *Syn* PROPORTIONAL, commensurate, commensurable *Ant* disproportionate

proposal ♦ something put forward, offered, or otherwise stated for consideration *Syn* proposition

propose 1 *Syn* INTEND, purpose, mean, design **2** ♦ to set before the mind for consideration *Syn* propound, pose

proposition *Syn* PROPOSAL

propound *Syn* PROPOSE, pose

propriety *Syn* DECORUM, decency, etiquette, dignity

prorate *Syn* APPORTION, portion, parcel, ration

prosaic ♦ having a plain, practical, everyday character or quality *Syn* prosy, matter-of-fact

proscribe *Syn* SENTENCE, condemn, damn, doom

proselyte *Syn* CONVERT

prospect ♦ an advance realization of something to come *Syn* outlook, anticipation, foretaste

prosper *Syn* SUCCEED, thrive, flourish

prostrate *Syn* PRONE, supine, recumbent, couchant, dormant

prosy *Syn* PROSAIC, matter-of-fact

protean *Syn* CHANGEABLE, changeful, variable, mutable

protect *Syn* DEFEND, shield, guard, safeguard

protest 1 *Syn* ASSERT, avouch, avow, profess, affirm, aver, declare, predicate, warrant **2** *Syn* OBJECT, remonstrate, expostulate, kick *Ant* agree

protract *Syn* EXTEND, prolong, lengthen, elongate *Ant* curtail

protrude *Syn* BULGE, jut, stick out, project, overhang, beetle

protrusion *Syn* PROJECTION, protuberance, bulge

protuberance *Syn* PROJECTION, protrusion, bulge

protuberate *Syn* BULGE, jut, stick out, protrude, project, overhang, beetle

proud 1 ♦ showing scorn for inferiors *Syn* arrogant, haughty, lordly, insolent, overbearing, supercilious, disdainful *Ant* humble; ashamed **2** ♦ having or exhibiting undue or excessive pride esp. in one's appearance or achievements *Syn* vain, vainglorious *Ant* ashamed; humble

prove 1 ♦ to establish a point by appropriate objective means *Syn* try, test, demonstrate *Ant* disprove **2** *Syn* INDICATE, betoken, attest, bespeak, argue

provenance, provenience *Syn* ORIGIN, source, inception, root, prime mover

provender *Syn* FOOD, fodder, forage, feed, victuals, viands, provisions, comestibles

proverb *Syn* SAYING, maxim, adage, motto, saw, epigram, aphorism, apothegm

provide ♦ to give or acquire and make available something wanted or needed *Syn* supply, furnish

providence *Syn* PRUDENCE, foresight, forethought, discretion *Ant* improvidence

provident *Syn* PRUDENT, foresighted, forethoughtful, discreet *Ant* improvident

providential *Syn* LUCKY, fortunate, happy

providing *Syn* IF

province 1 *Syn* FIELD, domain, sphere, territory, bailiwick **2** *Syn* FUNCTION, office, duty

provincial *Syn* INSULAR, parochial, local, small-town *Ant* catholic

provision 1 *Syn* CONDITION, stipulation, terms, proviso, reservation, strings **2** *pl*

provisions *Syn* FOOD, feed, victuals, viands, comestibles, provender, fodder, forage

provisional 1 ♦ not final or definitive *Syn* tentative *Ant* definitive **2** *Syn* TEMPORARY, ad interim, acting

proviso *Syn* CONDITION, stipulation, terms, provision, reservation, strings

provoke 1 ♦ to arouse as if pricking *Syn* excite, stimulate, pique, quicken, galvanize **2** *Syn* IRRITATE, exasperate, nettle, aggravate, rile, peeve *Ant* gratify

prowess *Syn* HEROISM, valor, gallantry

prowl *Syn* WANDER, stray, roam, ramble, rove, range, gad, gallivant, traipse, meander

proximity ♦ the quality or state of being near *Syn* propinquity *Ant* distance

proxy *Syn* AGENT, deputy, attorney, factor

prudence ♦ good sense or shrewdness in

the management of affairs *Syn* providence, foresight, forethought, discretion

prudent 1 *Syn* WISE, judicious, sensible, sane, sage, sapient **2** ♦ making provision for the future *Syn* provident, foresighted, forethoughtful, discreet

prudish *Syn* PRIM, priggish, prissy, puritanical, straitlaced, stuffy

prune *Syn* SHEAR, trim, lop, poll, clip, snip, crop

prying *Syn* CURIOUS, inquisitive, snoopy, nosy

pseudo *Syn* COUNTERFEIT, spurious, bogus, fake, sham, pinchbeck, phony

pseudonym ♦ a fictitious or assumed name *Syn* alias, nom de guerre, pen name, nom de plume, incognito

psyche *Syn* MIND, intellect, soul, brain, intelligence, wit

psychic *Syn* MENTAL, intellectual, intelligent, cerebral

psychosis *Syn* INSANITY, lunacy, mania, dementia

puberty, pubescence *Syn* YOUTH, adolescence

public *Syn* FOLLOWING, clientele, audience

publication *Syn* DECLARATION, announcement, advertisement, proclamation, promulgation, broadcasting

publicity ♦ an act or device designed to attract public interest and to mold public opinion *Syn* ballyhoo, promotion, propaganda

publish *Syn* DECLARE, announce, advertise, proclaim, promulgate, broadcast

puerile *Syn* YOUTHFUL, juvenile, boyish, virgin, virginal, maiden *Ant* adult

puff *Syn* CRITICISM, critique, review, blurb

pugnacious *Syn* BELLIGERENT, combative, bellicose, quarrelsome, contentious *Ant* pacific

puissance *Syn* POWER, might, strength, force, energy

puissant *Syn* POWERFUL, potent, forceful, forcible *Ant* impuissant

pulchritudinous *Syn* BEAUTIFUL, beauteous, good-looking, comely, bonny, pretty, handsome, fair, lovely

pull ♦ to cause to move toward or after an applied force *Syn* draw, drag, haul, hale, tug, tow

pulsate ♦ to course or move with or as if with rhythmic strokes *Syn* pulse, beat, throb, palpitate

pulsation ♦ a rhythmical movement or one single step in recurring rhythmic steps *Syn* pulse, beat, throb, palpitation

pulse *n* *Syn* PULSATION, beat, throb, palpitation

pulse *vb* *Syn* PULSATE, beat, throb, palpitate

pummel *Syn* BEAT, pound, buffet, baste, belabor, thrash

punch *vb* **1** *Syn* STRIKE, hit, smite, slug, slog, swat, clout, slap, box, cuff **2** *Syn* PERFORATE, puncture, prick, bore, drill

punch *n* *Syn* VIGOR, vim, spirit, dash, esprit, verve, élan, drive

punctilious *Syn* CAREFUL, punctual, meticulous, scrupulous

punctual *Syn* CAREFUL, punctilious, meticulous, scrupulous

puncture *Syn* PERFORATE, punch, prick, bore, drill

pungent ♦ sharp and stimulating to the mind or the senses *Syn* piquant, poignant, racy, spicy, snappy *Ant* bland

punish ♦ to inflict a penalty on in requital for wrongdoing *Syn* chastise, castigate, chasten, discipline, correct *Ant* excuse; pardon

puny *Syn* PETTY, trivial, trifling, paltry, measly, picayunish, picayune

purblind *Syn* BLIND, sightless

purchase *Syn* BUY

pure 1 ♦ containing nothing that does not properly belong *Syn* absolute, simple, sheer *Ant* contaminated, polluted; adulterated; applied (*of science*) **2** *Syn* CHASTE, modest, decent *Ant* impure; immoral

purge *Syn* RID, clear, unburden, disabuse

puritanical *Syn* PRIM, priggish, prissy, prudish, straitlaced, stuffy

purloin *Syn* STEAL, pilfer, filch, lift, pinch, snitch, swipe, cop

purport *Syn* SUBSTANCE, gist, burden, core, pith

purported *Syn* SUPPOSED, supposititious, supposititious, reputed, putative, conjectural, hypothetical

purpose *n* *Syn* INTENTION, intent, design, aim, end, object, objective, goal

purpose *vb* *Syn* INTEND, propose, design, mean

pursue *Syn* FOLLOW, chase, trail, tag, tail

pursuit *Syn* WORK, calling, occupation, employment, business

purvey *Syn* CATER, pander

purview *Syn* RANGE, gamut, reach, radius, compass, sweep, scope, orbit, horizon, ken

push ♦ to press against with force so as to cause to move ahead or aside *Syn* shove, thrust, propel

pushing, pushy *Syn* AGGRESSIVE, militant, assertive, self-assertive

puss *Syn* FACE, countenance, visage, physiognomy, mug

pustule *Syn* ABSCESS, boil, furuncle, carbuncle, pimple

putative *Syn* SUPPOSED, supposititious, supposititious, reputed, purported, conjectural, hypothetical

putrefy *Syn* DECAY, rot, decompose, spoil, disintegrate, crumble

putrid *Syn* MALODOROUS, fetid, noisome, stinking, rank, rancid, fusty, musty

putsch *Syn* REBELLION, revolution, uprising, revolt, insurrection, mutiny, coup

put up *Syn* RESIDE, live, dwell, sojourn, lodge, stay, stop

puzzle *vb* ♦ to baffle and disturb mentally *Syn* perplex, mystify, bewilder, distract, nonplus, confound, dumbfound

puzzle *n* *Syn* MYSTERY, problem, enigma, riddle, conundrum

pygmy *Syn* DWARF, midget, manikin, homunculus, runt

Q

quack *Syn* IMPOSTOR, faker, mountebank, charlatan

quail *Syn* RECOIL, shrink, flinch, wince, blench

quaint *Syn* STRANGE, odd, queer, outlandish, curious, peculiar, eccentric, erratic, singular, unique

quake *Syn* SHAKE, tremble, totter, quiver, shiver, shudder, quaver, wobble, teeter, shimmy, dither

qualified *Syn* ABLE, competent, capable *Ant* unqualified

qualify 1 *Syn* MODERATE, temper 2 *Syn* CHARACTERIZE, distinguish, mark 3 *Syn* PREPARE, fit, condition, ready

quality 1 ♦ an intelligible feature by which a thing may be identified *Syn* property, character, attribute, accident 2 ♦ a usu. high level of merit or superiority *Syn* stature, caliber

qualm ♦ a misgiving about what one is doing or is going to do *Syn* scruple, compunction, demur

quandary *Syn* PREDICAMENT, dilemma, plight, scrape, fix, jam, pickle

quantity *Syn* SUM, amount, aggregate, total, whole, number

quarrel *n* ♦ a usu. verbal dispute marked by anger or discord *Syn* wrangle, altercation, squabble, bickering, spat, tiff

quarrel *vb* *Syn* wrangle, altercate, squabble, bicker, spat, tiff

quarrelsome *Syn* BELLIGERENT, pugnacious, combative, bellicose, contentious

quarry *Syn* VICTIM, prey

quash 1 *Syn* ANNUL, abrogate, void, vacate 2 *Syn* CRUSH, quell, extinguish, suppress, quench

quaver *Syn* SHAKE, tremble, shudder, quake, totter, quiver, shiver, wobble, teeter, shimmy, dither

quay *Syn* WHARF, dock, pier, slip, berth, jetty, levee

queenly *Syn* KINGLY, regal, royal, imperial, princely

queer *Syn* STRANGE, odd, erratic, eccentric, peculiar, quaint, outlandish, curious

quell *Syn* CRUSH, extinguish, suppress, quench, quash *Ant* foment

quench *Syn* CRUSH, quell, extinguish, suppress, quash

querulous *Syn* IRRITABLE, fretful, petulant, pettish, huffy, peevish, fractious, snappish, waspish

query *Syn* ASK, question, interrogate, inquire, examine, quiz, catechize

quest *Syn* ADVENTURE, enterprise

question *Syn* ASK, interrogate, query, inquire, examine, quiz, catechize *Ant* answer

questionable *Syn* DOUBTFUL, dubious, problematic *Ant* authoritative; unquestioned

quick 1 *Syn* FAST, fleet, swift, rapid, speedy, expeditious, hasty **2** ♦ able to respond without delay or hesitation or indicative of such ability *Syn* prompt, ready, apt *Ant* sluggish

quicken 1 ♦ to make alive or lively *Syn* animate, enliven, vivify *Ant* deaden **2** *Syn* PROVOKE, excite, stimulate, pique, galvanize *Ant* arrest **3** *Syn* SPEED, hasten, hurry, accelerate, precipitate *Ant* slacken

quick-witted *Syn* INTELLIGENT, clever, bright, smart, alert, knowing, brilliant

quiescent *Syn* LATENT, dormant, potential, abeyant

quiet *adj Syn* STILL, silent, noiseless, stilly *Ant* unquiet

quiet, quieten *vb Syn* CALM, compose, still, lull, soothe, settle, tranquilize *Ant* disquiet; arouse, rouse

quip *Syn* JOKE, jest, jape, witticism, wisecrack, crack, gag

quit 1 *Syn* BEHAVE, acquit, comport, deport, demean, conduct **2** *Syn* GO, leave, depart, withdraw, retire **3** *Syn* STOP, cease, discontinue, desist

quiver *Syn* SHAKE, shiver, shudder, quaver, totter, tremble, quake, wobble, teeter, shimmy, dither

quixotic *Syn* IMAGINARY, chimerical, fantastic, visionary, fanciful

quiz *Syn* ASK, question, interrogate, examine, catechize, query, inquire

quote ♦ to speak or write again something already said or written by another *Syn* cite, repeat

quotidian *Syn* DAILY, diurnal, circadian

R

rabid *Syn* FURIOUS, frantic, frenzied, wild, frenetic, delirious

race *Syn* VARIETY, subspecies, breed, cultivar, strain, clone, stock

rack *Syn* AFFLICT, torment, torture, try

racket *Syn* DIN, uproar, pandemonium, hullabaloo, babel, hubbub, clamor

racking *Syn* EXCRUCIATING, agonizing

racy *Syn* PUNGENT, piquant, poignant, spicy, snappy

radiant *Syn* BRIGHT, brilliant, luminous, lustrous, effulgent, refulgent, beaming, lambent, lucent, incandescent

radiate *Syn* SPREAD, circulate, disseminate, diffuse, propagate

radical 1 *Syn* FUNDAMENTAL, basic, basal, underlying *Ant* superficial **2** *Syn* LIBERAL, advanced, progressive

radius *Syn* RANGE, gamut, reach, compass, sweep, scope, orbit, horizon, ken, purview

rag *Syn* BANTER, chaff, kid, rib, josh, jolly

rage 1 *Syn* ANGER, ire, fury, indignation, wrath **2** *Syn* FASHION, style, mode, vogue, craze, cry, dernier cri, fad

raid *Syn* INVASION, incursion, inroad

rail *Syn* SCOLD, revile, vituperate, rate, berate, upbraid, tongue-lash, jaw, bawl, chew out, wig

raillery *Syn* BADINAGE, persiflage

raiment *Syn* CLOTHES, apparel, attire, clothing, dress

raise 1 *Syn* LIFT, elevate, hoist, heave, rear, boost **2** *Syn* BUILD, construct, erect, frame, rear *Ant* raze

rally *vb Syn* STIR, rouse, arouse, awaken, waken

rally *vb Syn* RIDICULE, deride, mock, taunt, twit

ram *Syn* PACK, crowd, cram, stuff, tamp

ramble *Syn* WANDER, stray, roam, rove, range, prowl, gad, gallivant, traipse, meander

rampant *Syn* RANK

rampart *Syn* BULWARK, breastwork, parapet, bastion

rancid *Syn* MALODOROUS, stinking, fetid, rank, noisome, putrid, fusty, musty

rancor *Syn* ENMITY, antagonism, animosity, animus, antipathy, hostility

random ♦ determined by accident rather than by design *Syn* haphazard, chance, chancy, casual, desultory, hit-or-miss, happy-go-lucky

range *n* **1** *Syn* HABITAT, biotope, station **2** ♦ the extent that lies within the powers of something to cover or control *Syn* gamut, reach, radius, compass, sweep, scope, orbit, horizon, ken, purview

range *vb* **1** *Syn* LINE, line up, align, array **2** *Syn* WANDER, rove, ramble, roam, stray, prowl, gad, gallivant, traipse, meander

rank *adj* **1** ♦ growing or increasing at an immoderate rate *Syn* rampant **2** *Syn* MALODOROUS, fusty, musty, rancid, stinking, fetid, noisome, putrid *Ant* balmy **3** *Syn* FLAGRANT, glaring, gross

rank *n Syn* LINE, row, file, echelon, tier

rank *vb Syn* CLASS, grade, rate, graduate, gradate

ransack *Syn* SEEK, search, hunt, rummage, scour, comb, ferret out

ransom *Syn* RESCUE, deliver, redeem, reclaim, save

rant *Syn* BOMBAST, fustian, rodomontade, rhapsody

rap *n Syn* TAP, knock, thump, thud

rap *vb Syn* TAP, knock, thump, thud

rapacious *Syn* VORACIOUS, ravening, ravenous, gluttonous

rapacity *Syn* CUPIDITY, greed, avarice

rapid *Syn* FAST, swift, fleet, quick, speedy, hasty, expeditious *Ant* deliberate; leisurely

rapscallion *Syn* VILLAIN, scoundrel, blackguard, knave, rascal, rogue, scamp, miscreant

rapt *Syn* INTENT, absorbed, engrossed

rapture *Syn* ECSTASY, transport

rare **1** *Syn* THIN, tenuous, slight, slender, slim **2** *Syn* CHOICE, delicate, dainty, exquisite, elegant, recherché **3** *Syn* INFREQUENT, scarce, uncommon, occasional, sporadic

rarefy *Syn* THIN, attenuate, extenuate, dilute

rascal *Syn* VILLAIN, scoundrel, blackguard, knave, rogue, scamp, rapscallion, miscreant

rash *Syn* ADVENTUROUS, daring, daredevil, reckless, foolhardy, venturesome *Ant* calculating

rasp *Syn* SCRAPE, scratch, grate, grind

rate *vb Syn* SCOLD, berate, upbraid, tongue-lash, jaw, bawl, chew out, wig, rail, revile, vituperate

rate *vb* **1** *Syn* ESTIMATE, value, evaluate, appraise, assess, assay **2** *Syn* CLASS, grade, rank, graduate, gradate

ratify ♦ to make something legally valid or operative usu. by formal approval or sanctioning *Syn* confirm

ratiocination *Syn* INFERENCE *Ant* intuition

ratiocinative *Syn* INFERENTIAL *Ant* intuitive

ration *n* ♦ an amount allotted or made available esp. from a limited supply *Syn* allowance, dole, pittance

ration *vb Syn* APPORTION, portion, prorate, parcel

rational ♦ relating to, based on, or agreeable to reason *Syn* reasonable *Ant* irrational; animal (*of nature*); demented (*of state of mind*); absurd (*of actions, behavior*)

rationalize *Syn* EXPLAIN, account, justify

rattle *Syn* EMBARRASS, faze, discomfit, disconcert, abash

raucous *Syn* LOUD, stentorian, earsplitting, hoarse, strident, stertorous

ravage ♦ to lay waste by plundering or destroying *Syn* devastate, waste, sack, pillage, despoil, spoliate

ravening *Syn* VORACIOUS, rapacious, ravenous, gluttonous

ravenous *Syn* VORACIOUS, ravening, rapacious, gluttonous

ravish *Syn* TRANSPORT, enrapture, entrance

raw *Syn* RUDE, crude, callow, green, rough, uncouth

rawboned *Syn* LEAN, gaunt, angular, lank, lanky, spare, scrawny, skinny

ray ♦ a shaft of light *Syn* beam

raze *Syn* DESTROY, demolish

reach *vb* ♦ to arrive at a point by effort or work *Syn* gain, compass, achieve, attain

reach *n* *Syn* RANGE, gamut, radius, compass, sweep, scope, orbit, horizon, ken, purview

react *Syn* ACT, operate, work, function, behave

readiness ♦ the power of doing something without evidence of effort *Syn* ease, facility, dexterity

ready *adj* *Syn* QUICK, prompt, apt

ready *vb* *Syn* PREPARE, fit, qualify, condition

real ♦ corresponding to known facts *Syn* actual, true *Ant* unreal; apparent; imaginary

realize 1 ♦ to bring into concrete existence something that has existed as an abstraction or a conception or a possibility *Syn* actualize, embody, incarnate, materialize, externalize, objectify, hypostatize, reify **2** *Syn* THINK, conceive, imagine, fancy, envisage, envision

reap ♦ to do the work of collecting ripened crops *Syn* glean, gather, garner, harvest

rear *vb* **1** *Syn* BUILD, construct, erect, frame, raise **2** *Syn* LIFT, raise, elevate, hoist, heave, boost

rear *adj* *Syn* POSTERIOR, after, back, hind, hinder *Ant* front

reason *n* **1** ♦ a point or points that support something open to question *Syn* ground, argument, proof **2** *Syn* CAUSE, determinant, antecedent, occasion **3** ♦ the power of the mind by which man attains truth or knowledge *Syn* understanding, intuition

reason *vb* *Syn* THINK, reflect, deliberate, speculate, cogitate

reasonable *Syn* RATIONAL *Ant* unreasonable

rebate *Syn* DEDUCTION, abatement, discount

rebel ♦ one who rises up against constituted authority or the established order *Syn* insurgent, iconoclast

rebellion ♦ an outbreak against authority *Syn* revolution, uprising, revolt, insurrection, mutiny, putsch, coup

rebellious *Syn* INSUBORDINATE, mutinous, seditious, factious, contumacious *Ant* acquiescent, resigned; submissive

rebound ♦ to spring back to an original position or shape *Syn* reverberate, recoil, resile, repercuss

rebuild *Syn* MEND, repair, patch

rebuke *Syn* REPROVE, reprimand, admonish, reproach, chide

rebut *Syn* DISPROVE, refute, confute, controvert

recalcitrant *Syn* UNRULY, refractory, intractable, headstrong, willful, ungovernable *Ant* amenable

recall 1 *Syn* REMEMBER, recollect, remind, reminisce, bethink, mind **2** *Syn* REVOKE, reverse, repeal, rescind

recant *Syn* ABJURE, retract, renounce, forswear

recede ♦ to move backward *Syn* retreat, retrograde, retract, back *Ant* proceed; advance

receipt ♦ a formula or set of directions for the compounding of ingredients esp. in cookery and medicine *Syn* recipe, prescription

receive ♦ to bring and accept into one's possession, one's presence, a group, or the mind *Syn* accept, admit, take

recent *Syn* MODERN, late

recess *Syn* PAUSE, respite, lull, intermission

recherché *Syn* CHOICE, elegant, exquisite, delicate, dainty, rare *Ant* banal

recipe *Syn* RECEIPT, prescription

reciprocal 1 ♦ shared, felt, or shown by both sides concerned **Syn** mutual, common **2** ♦ like, equivalent, or similarly related to each other (as in kind, quality, or value) **Syn** corresponding, correlative, complementary, complemental, convertible

reciprocate ♦ to give back usu. in kind or in quantity **Syn** retaliate, requite, return

recite **Syn** RELATE, rehearse, recount, narrate, describe, state, report

reckless **Syn** ADVENTUROUS, daring, daredevil, rash, foolhardy, venturesome **Ant** calculating

reckon 1 **Syn** CALCULATE, compute, estimate **2** **Syn** CONSIDER, regard, account, deem **3** **Syn** RELY, count, bank, trust, depend

reclaim **Syn** RESCUE, save, ransom, redeem, deliver **Ant** abandon

recluse ♦ a person who leads a secluded or solitary life **Syn** hermit, eremite, anchorite, cenobite

recognition ♦ a learning process that relates a perception of something new to knowledge already possessed **Syn** identification, assimilation, apperception

recognize **Syn** ACKNOWLEDGE

recoil 1 ♦ to draw back in fear or distaste **Syn** shrink, flinch, wince, blench, quail **Ant** confront; defy **2** **Syn** REBOUND, reverberate, resile, repercuss

recollect **Syn** REMEMBER, recall, remind, reminisce, bethink, mind

recollection **Syn** MEMORY, remembrance, reminiscence, mind, souvenir

recommend **Syn** COMMEND, compliment, applaud

recommendation **Syn** CREDENTIAL, testimonial, character, reference

recompense **Syn** PAY, reimburse, indemnify, repay, satisfy, remunerate, compensate

reconcile **Syn** ADAPT, conform, accommodate, adjust

recondite ♦ beyond the reach of the average intelligence **Syn** abstruse, occult, esoteric

record *vb* ♦ to set down in writing usu. for the purpose of written evidence or official record of **Syn** register, list, enroll, catalog

record *n* **Syn** DOCUMENT, monument, archive

recount **Syn** RELATE, recite, rehearse, narrate, describe, state, report

recoup **Syn** RECOVER, recruit, retrieve, regain

recover 1 ♦ to get back again **Syn** regain, retrieve, recoup, recruit **2** **Syn** IMPROVE, recuperate, convalesce, gain

recreant **Syn** RENEGADE, apostate, turncoat, backslider

recreate **Syn** AMUSE, divert, entertain

recreation **Syn** AMUSEMENT, diversion, entertainment

recrudesce **Syn** RETURN, revert, recur

recrudescence **Syn** RETURN, reversion, recurrence

recruit **Syn** RECOVER, regain, retrieve, recoup

rectify **Syn** CORRECT, emend, amend, reform, revise, remedy, redress

rectitude **Syn** GOODNESS, virtue, morality

recumbent **Syn** PRONE, supine, prostrate, couchant, dormant **Ant** upright, erect

recuperate **Syn** IMPROVE, recover, convalesce, gain

recur **Syn** RETURN, revert, recrudesce

recurrence **Syn** RETURN, reversion, recrudescence

recurrent **Syn** INTERMITTENT, periodic, alternate

redact **Syn** EDIT, compile, revise, rewrite, adapt

redeem **Syn** RESCUE, deliver, ransom, save, reclaim

redolence **Syn** FRAGRANCE, perfume, incense, bouquet

redolent **Syn** ODOROUS, aromatic, balmy, fragrant

redress *vb* **Syn** CORRECT, emend, remedy, amend, rectify, reform, revise

redress *n* **Syn** REPARATION, amends, restitution, indemnity

reduce 1 **Syn** DECREASE, lessen, diminish, abate, dwindle **2** **Syn** CONQUER, vanquish, defeat, subjugate, beat, overcome, lick, subdue, surmount, overthrow, rout **3** **Syn** DEGRADE, demote, declass, disrate

redundancy *Syn* VERBIAGE, tautology, pleonasm, circumlocution, periphrasis

redundant *Syn* WORDY, verbose, prolix, diffuse *Ant* concise

reef *Syn* SHOAL, bank, bar

reel ♦ to move uncertainly or uncontrollably or unsteadily (as from weakness or intoxication) *Syn* whirl, stagger, totter

refer 1 *Syn* ASCRIBE, assign, credit, accredit, attribute, impute, charge **2** *Syn* RESORT, apply, go, turn **3** ♦ to call or direct attention to something *Syn* allude, advert

referee *Syn* JUDGE, umpire, arbiter, arbitrator

reference *Syn* CREDENTIAL, testimonial, recommendation, character

referendum *Syn* MANDATE, initiative, plebiscite

refinement *Syn* CULTURE, cultivation, breeding *Ant* vulgarity

reflect *Syn* THINK, cogitate, reason, speculate, deliberate

reflection *Syn* ANIMADVERSION, stricture, aspersion

reflective *Syn* THOUGHTFUL, contemplative, meditative, pensive, speculative

reform *Syn* CORRECT, rectify, emend, amend, remedy, redress, revise

refractory *Syn* UNRULY, recalcitrant, intractable, ungovernable, headstrong, willful *Ant* malleable; amenable

refrain ♦ to hold oneself back from doing or indulging in *Syn* abstain, forbear

refresh *Syn* RENEW, restore, rejuvenate, renovate, refurbish *Ant* jade, addle

refuge *Syn* SHELTER, asylum, sanctuary, cover, retreat

refulgent *Syn* BRIGHT, effulgent, luminous, radiant, lustrous, brilliant, beaming, lambent, lucent, incandescent

refurbish *Syn* RENEW, renovate, refresh, restore, rejuvenate

refuse *vb Syn* DECLINE, reject, repudiate, spurn

refuse *n* ♦ matter that is regarded as worthless and fit only for throwing away *Syn* waste, rubbish, trash, debris, garbage, offal

refute *Syn* DISPROVE, confute, rebut, controvert

regain *Syn* RECOVER, recruit, recoup, retrieve

regal *Syn* KINGLY, royal, queenly, imperial, princely

regale *Syn* PLEASE, tickle, gratify, delight, rejoice, gladden *Ant* vex

regard *n* ♦ a feeling of deferential approval and liking *Syn* respect, esteem, admiration *Ant* despite

regard *vb* **1** ♦ to recognize the worth of a person or thing *Syn* respect, esteem, admire *Ant* despise **2** *Syn* CONSIDER, account, reckon, deem

regarding *Syn* ABOUT, concerning, respecting

region *Syn* AREA, tract, zone, belt

register *n Syn* LIST, table, catalog, schedule, roll, roster, inventory

register *vb Syn* RECORD, list, enroll, catalog

regressive *Syn* BACKWARD, retrogressive, retrograde *Ant* progressive

regret *Syn* SORROW, grief, heartache, heartbreak, anguish, woe

regular 1 ♦ being of the sort or kind that is expected as usual, ordinary, or average *Syn* normal, typical, natural *Ant* irregular **2** *Syn* ORDERLY, methodical, systematic, regular *Ant* irregular

regulate *Syn* ADJUST, fix

regulation *Syn* LAW, rule, precept, statute, ordinance, canon

regurgitate *Syn* BELCH, burp, vomit, disgorge, spew, throw up

rehearse *Syn* RELATE, narrate, describe, recite, recount, state, report

reify *Syn* REALIZE, actualize, embody, incarnate, materialize, externalize, objectify, hypostatize

reimburse *Syn* PAY, indemnify, repay, recompense, compensate, remunerate, satisfy

reinforce *Syn* STRENGTHEN, invigorate, fortify, energize

reissue *Syn* EDITION, impression, reprinting, printing

reiterate *Syn* REPEAT, iterate, ingeminate

reject *Syn* DECLINE, repudiate, spurn, refuse *Ant* accept; choose, select

rejoice *Syn* PLEASE, delight, gladden, gratify, tickle, regale *Ant* grieve; aggrieve; bewail

rejoin *Syn* ANSWER, respond, reply, retort

rejoinder *Syn* ANSWER, response, reply, retort

rejuvenate *Syn* RENEW, restore, refresh, renovate, refurbish

relapse *n Syn* LAPSE, backsliding

relapse *vb Syn* LAPSE, backslide

relate 1 ♦ to tell orally or in writing the details or circumstances of a situation *Syn* rehearse, recite, recount, narrate, describe, state, report **2** *Syn* JOIN, associate, link, connect, conjoin, combine, unite **3** *Syn* BEAR, pertain, appertain, belong, apply

related ♦ connected by or as if by family ties *Syn* cognate, kindred, allied, affiliated

relative *Syn* DEPENDENT, contingent, conditional *Ant* absolute

relaxation *Syn* REST, repose, leisure, ease, comfort

relaxed *Syn* LOOSE, slack, lax *Ant* stiff

release *Syn* FREE, liberate, emancipate, manumit, discharge, *Ant* detain; check; oblige

relegate *Syn* COMMIT, entrust, confide, consign

relent *Syn* YIELD, submit, capitulate, succumb, defer, bow, cave

relentless *Syn* GRIM, unrelenting, merciless, implacable

relevant ♦ relating to or bearing upon the matter in hand *Syn* germane, material, pertinent, apposite, applicable, apropos *Ant* extraneous

reliable ♦ having qualities that merit confidence or trust *Syn* dependable, trustworthy, trusty, tried *Ant* dubious

reliance *Syn* TRUST, confidence, dependence, faith

relieve ♦ to make something more tolerable or less grievous *Syn* alleviate, lighten, assuage, mitigate, allay *Ant* intensify; embarrass; alarm

religion ♦ a system of religious belief or the body of persons who accept such a system *Syn* denomination, sect, cult, communion, faith, creed, persuasion, church

religious *adj* **1** *Syn* DEVOUT, pious, pietistic, sanctimonious *Ant* irreligious **2** *Syn* HOLY, spiritual, sacred, divine, blessed *Ant* secular; profane

religious *n* ♦ a member of a religious order usu. bound by monastic vows of poverty, chastity, and obedience *Syn* monk, friar, nun

relinquish ♦ to give up completely *Syn* yield, leave, resign, surrender, cede, abandon, waive *Ant* keep

relish *n* **1** *Syn* TASTE, savor, tang, flavor, smack **2** *Syn* TASTE, palate, gusto, zest

relish *vb Syn* LIKE, fancy, dote, enjoy, love

relishing *Syn* PALATABLE, appetizing, savory, sapid, tasty, toothsome, flavorsome

reluctant *Syn* DISINCLINED, indisposed, hesitant, loath, averse

rely on, rely upon ♦ to have or place full confidence *Syn* trust, depend, count, reckon, bank

remain *Syn* STAY, wait, abide, tarry, linger *Ant* depart

remainder ♦ a remaining or left-over group, part, or trace *Syn* residue, residuum, remains, leavings, rest, balance, remnant

remains *Syn* REMAINDER, leavings, residue, residuum, rest, balance, remnant

remark *vb* **1** *Syn* SEE, notice, note, observe, perceive, discern, behold, descry, espy, view, survey, contemplate **2** ♦ to make observations and pass judgment thereon *Syn* comment, commentate, animadvert

remark *n* ♦ an expression of opinion or judgment *Syn* observation, comment, commentary, note, obiter dictum

remarkable *Syn* NOTICEABLE, prominent, outstanding, conspicuous, salient, signal, striking, arresting

remedial *Syn* CURATIVE, restorative, sanative, corrective

remedy *n* ♦ something prescribed or used for the treatment of disease *Syn* cure, medicine, medicament, medication, specific, physic

remedy *vb* **1** *Syn* CURE, heal **2** *Syn* CORRECT, rectify, emend, amend, redress, reform, revise

remember ♦ to bring an image or idea from the past into the mind **Syn** recollect, recall, remind, reminisce, bethink, mind **Ant** forget

remembrance 1 Syn MEMORY, recollection, reminiscence, mind, souvenir **Ant** forgetfulness **2** ♦ something that serves to keep a person or thing in mind **Syn** remembrancer, reminder, memorial, memento, token, keepsake, souvenir

remembrancer Syn REMEMBRANCE, reminder, memorial, memento, token, keepsake, souvenir

remind Syn REMEMBER, recollect, recall, reminisce, bethink, mind

reminder Syn REMEMBRANCE, remembrancer, memorial, memento, token, keepsake, souvenir

reminisce Syn REMEMBER, recollect, recall, remind, bethink, mind

reminiscence Syn MEMORY, remembrance, recollection, mind, souvenir

remiss Syn NEGLIGENT, lax, slack, neglectful **Ant** scrupulous

remit 1 Syn EXCUSE, pardon, forgive, condone **2 Syn** SEND, forward, transmit, route, ship, dispatch

remnant Syn REMAINDER, residue, residuum, remains, leavings, rest, balance

remonstrate Syn OBJECT, expostulate, protest, kick

remorse Syn PENITENCE, repentance, contrition, attrition, compunction

remote Syn DISTANT, far, faraway, far-off, removed **Ant** close

remove Syn MOVE, shift, transfer

removed Syn DISTANT, remote, far-off, faraway, far

remunerate Syn PAY, compensate, satisfy, reimburse, indemnify, repay, recompense

remunerative Syn PAYING, gainful, lucrative, profitable

rend Syn TEAR, split, cleave, rive, rip

rendezvous Syn ENGAGEMENT, tryst, appointment, assignation, date

renegade ♦ a person who forsakes his or her faith, party, cause, or allegiance and aligns with another **Syn** apostate, turncoat, recreant, backslider **Ant** adherent

renew ♦ to make like new **Syn** restore, refresh, renovate, refurbish, rejuvenate

renounce 1 Syn ABDICATE, resign **Ant** arrogate; covet **2 Syn** ABJURE, forswear, recant, retract **Ant** confess; claim

renovate Syn RENEW, refurbish, rejuvenate, restore, refresh

renown Syn FAME, honor, glory, celebrity, reputation, repute, notoriety, éclat

renowned Syn FAMOUS, famed, celebrated, eminent, illustrious

rent vb **Syn** HIRE, let, lease, charter

rent n **Syn** BREACH, break, split, schism, rupture, rift

renunciation ♦ voluntary surrender or putting aside of something desired or desirable **Syn** abnegation, self-abnegation, self-denial

repair Syn MEND, patch, rebuild

reparation ♦ a return for something lost or suffered, usu. through the fault of another **Syn** redress, amends, restitution, indemnity

repartee Syn WIT, humor, irony, sarcasm, satire

repay Syn PAY, compensate, remunerate, recompense, satisfy, reimburse, indemnify

repeal Syn REVOKE, reverse, rescind, recall

repeat 1 ♦ to say or do again **Syn** iterate, reiterate, ingeminate **2 Syn** QUOTE, cite

repellent Syn REPUGNANT, abhorrent, distasteful, obnoxious, invidious **Ant** attractive; pleasing

repentance Syn PENITENCE, contrition, attrition, remorse, compunction

repercuss Syn REBOUND, reverberate, recoil, resile

replace ♦ to put out of a usual or proper place or into the place of another **Syn** displace, supplant, supersede

replete Syn FULL, complete, plenary

replica Syn REPRODUCTION, facsimile, duplicate, copy, carbon copy, transcript

reply vb **Syn** ANSWER, respond, rejoin, retort

reply n **Syn** ANSWER, response, rejoinder, retort

report n **1** ♦ common talk or an instance of it that spreads rapidly **Syn** rumor, gossip, hearsay 2 *Syn* ACCOUNT, story, chronicle, version 3 *Syn* LETTER, dispatch, message, note, epistle, missive, memorandum

report *vb Syn* RELATE, narrate, describe, state, recite, recount, rehearse

repose *Syn* REST, relaxation, leisure, ease, comfort

reprehend *Syn* CRITICIZE, censure, reprobate, condemn, denounce, blame

represent ♦ to present an image or lifelike imitation of (as in art) *Syn* depict, portray, delineate, picture, limn

representative *Syn* DELEGATE, deputy

repress *Syn* SUPPRESS

reprimand *Syn* REPROVE, rebuke, reproach, admonish, chide

reprinting *Syn* EDITION, impression, printing, reissue

reprisal *Syn* RETALIATION, retribution, revenge, vengeance

reproach *Syn* REPROVE, chide, admonish, rebuke, reprimand

reprobate *vb Syn* CRITICIZE, censure, reprehend, blame, condemn, denounce

reprobate *adj Syn* ABANDONED, profligate, dissolute *Ant* elect (*in theology*)

reprobate *n Syn* OUTCAST, castaway, derelict, pariah, untouchable

reproduce *Syn* GENERATE, propagate, engender, breed, beget, get, sire, procreate

reproduction ♦ a thing made to closely resemble another *Syn* duplicate, copy, carbon copy, facsimile, replica, transcript

reprove ♦ to criticize adversely *Syn* rebuke, reprimand, admonish, reproach, chide

repudiate 1 *Syn* DECLINE, spurn, reject, refuse *Ant* adopt 2 *Syn* DISCLAIM, disavow, disown, disallow *Ant* own

repugnant 1 ♦ so alien or unlikable as to arouse antagonism and aversion *Syn* repellent, abhorrent, distasteful, obnoxious, invidious *Ant* congenial 2 *Syn* OFFENSIVE, repulsive, revolting, loathsome

repulsive *Syn* OFFENSIVE, repugnant, revolting, loathsome *Ant* alluring, captivating

reputation *Syn* FAME, repute, renown, honor, glory, celebrity, éclat, notoriety

repute *Syn* FAME, reputation, renown,

celebrity, notoriety, éclat, honor, glory *Ant* disrepute

reputed *Syn* SUPPOSED, supposititious, suppositious, putative, purported, conjectural, hypothetical

request *Syn* ASK, solicit

require 1 *Syn* DEMAND, exact, claim 2 *Syn* LACK, want, need

requirement ♦ something essential to the existence or occurrence of something else *Syn* requisite, prerequisite

requisite *adj Syn* NEEDFUL, necessary, indispensable, essential

requisite *n Syn* REQUIREMENT, prerequisite

requite *Syn* RECIPROCATE, retaliate, return

rescind *Syn* REVOKE, reverse, repeal, recall

rescue ♦ to set free from confinement or danger *Syn* deliver, redeem, ransom, reclaim, save

research *Syn* INQUIRY, investigation, inquisition, inquest, probe

resemblance *Syn* LIKENESS, similarity, similitude, analogy, affinity *Ant* difference; distinction

resentment *Syn* OFFENSE, umbrage, pique, dudgeon, huff

reservation *Syn* CONDITION, stipulation, terms, provision, proviso, strings

reserve *Syn* KEEP, keep back, keep out, hold, hold back, retain, withhold, detain

reserved *Syn* SILENT, reticent, uncommunicative, taciturn, secretive, close, closelipped, closemouthed, tight-lipped *Ant* affable; expansive; blatant

reside ♦ to have as one's habitation or domicile *Syn* live, dwell, sojourn, lodge, stay, put up, stop

residence *Syn* HABITATION, dwelling, abode, domicile, home, house

resident *Syn* INHABITANT, denizen, citizen

residue, residuum *Syn* REMAINDER, remains, leavings, rest, balance, remnant

resign 1 *Syn* RELINQUISH, yield, surrender, leave, abandon, cede, waive 2 *Syn* ABDICATE, renounce

resignation 1 *Syn* COMPLIANCE, acquiescence **2** *Syn* PATIENCE, long-suffering, longanimity, forbearance

resigned *Syn* COMPLIANT, acquiescent *Ant* rebellious

resile *Syn* REBOUND, recoil, reverberate, repercuss

resilient 1 *Syn* ELASTIC, springy, flexible, supple **2** *Syn* ELASTIC, expansive, buoyant, volatile, effervescent *Ant* flaccid

resist ♦ to stand firm against a person or influence *Syn* withstand, contest, oppose, fight, combat, conflict, antagonize *Ant* submit; abide

resolute *Syn* FAITHFUL, steadfast, staunch, true, loyal

resolution 1 *Syn* ANALYSIS, dissection, breakdown **2** *Syn* COURAGE, mettle, spirit, tenacity

resolve 1 *Syn* ANALYZE, dissect, break down *Ant* blend **2** *Syn* DECIDE, determine, settle, rule **3** *Syn* SOLVE, unfold, unravel, decipher

resolved *Syn* decided, decisive, determined

resonant ♦ marked by conspicuously full and rich sounds or tones (as of speech or music) *Syn* sonorous, ringing, resounding, vibrant, orotund

resort *n* *Syn* RESOURCE, expedient, shift, makeshift, stopgap, substitute, surrogate

resort *vb* ♦ to betake oneself or to have recourse when in need of help or relief *Syn* refer, apply, go, turn

resounding *Syn* RESONANT, sonorous, ringing, vibrant, orotund

resource 1 *pl* **resources** *Syn* POSSESSIONS, assets, belongings, effects, means **2** ♦ something one turns to in the absence of the usual means or source of supply *Syn* resort, expedient, shift, makeshift, stopgap, substitute, surrogate

respect *n* *Syn* REGARD, esteem, admiration *Ant* contempt

respect *vb* *Syn* REGARD, esteem, admire *Ant* abuse; misuse

respecting *Syn* ABOUT, concerning, regarding

respectively *Syn* EACH, apiece, severally, individually

respite *Syn* PAUSE, recess, lull, intermission

resplendent *Syn* SPLENDID, gorgeous, glorious, sublime, superb

respond *Syn* ANSWER, reply, rejoin, retort

response *Syn* ANSWER, reply, rejoinder, retort

responsible ♦ subject to being held to account *Syn* answerable, accountable, amenable, liable

responsive 1 *Syn* SENTIENT, sensitive, impressible, impressionable, susceptible *Ant* impassive **2** *Syn* TENDER, sympathetic, warm, warmhearted, compassionate

rest *n* ♦ freedom from toil or strain *Syn* repose, relaxation, leisure, ease, comfort

rest *vb* *Syn* BASE, found, ground, bottom, stay

rest *n* *Syn* REMAINDER, residue, residuum, remains, leavings, balance, remnant

restful *Syn* COMFORTABLE, cozy, snug, easy

restitution *Syn* REPARATION, amends, redress, indemnity

restive 1 *Syn* CONTRARY, perverse, balky, froward, wayward **2** *Syn* IMPATIENT, restless, nervous, unquiet, uneasy, fidgety, jumpy, jittery

restless *Syn* IMPATIENT, restive, nervous, unquiet, uneasy, fidgety, jumpy, jittery

restorative *Syn* CURATIVE, remedial, corrective, sanative

restore 1 *Syn* RENEW, refresh, rejuvenate, renovate, refurbish **2** ♦ to help or cause to regain signs of life and vigor *Syn* revive, revivify, resuscitate

restrain ♦ to hold back from or control in doing something *Syn* curb, check, bridle, inhibit *Ant* impel; incite; activate; abandon (*oneself*)

restraint *Syn* FORCE, constraint, compulsion, coercion, duress, violence *Ant* incitement; liberty

restrict *Syn* LIMIT, circumscribe, confine

result *Syn* EFFECT, consequence, upshot, aftereffect, aftermath, sequel, issue, outcome, event

resuscitate *Syn* RESTORE, revive, revivify

retain *Syn* KEEP, keep back, keep out, detain, withhold, reserve, hold, hold back

retaliate *Syn* RECIPROCATE, requite, return

retaliation ♦ the act of inflicting or the intent to inflict injury in return for injury *Syn* reprisal, revenge, vengeance, retribution

retard *Syn* DELAY, slow, slacken, detain *Ant* accelerate; advance, further

reticent *Syn* SILENT, reserved, uncommunicative, taciturn, secretive, close, close-lipped, closemouthed, tight-lipped *Ant* frank

retire *Syn* GO, withdraw, leave, depart, quit

retort *vb Syn* ANSWER, rejoin, reply, respond

retort *n Syn* ANSWER, rejoinder, reply, response

retract 1 *Syn* RECEDE, retrograde, back, retreat *Ant* protract 2 *Syn* ABJURE, recant, renounce, forswear

retreat *n Syn* SHELTER, cover, refuge, asylum, sanctuary

retreat *vb Syn* RECEDE, retrograde, back, retract

retrench *Syn* SHORTEN, curtail, abridge, abbreviate

retribution *Syn* RETALIATION, reprisal, vengeance, revenge

retrieve *Syn* RECOVER, regain, recoup, recruit *Ant* lose

retrograde *adj Syn* BACKWARD, retrogressive, regressive

retrograde *vb Syn* RECEDE, retreat, back, retract

retrogressive *Syn* BACKWARD, regressive, retrograde *Ant* progressive

return *vb* 1 ♦ to go or come back (as to a person, place, or condition) *Syn* revert, recur, recrudesce 2 *Syn* RECIPROCATE, retaliate, requite

return *n* ♦ the act of coming back to or from a place or condition *Syn* reversion, recurrence, recrudescence

reveal ♦ to make known what has been or should be concealed *Syn* discover, disclose, divulge, tell, betray *Ant* conceal

revelation ♦ disclosure or something disclosed by or as if by divine or preternatural means *Syn* vision, apocalypse, prophecy *Ant* adumbration

revenant *Syn* APPARITION, phantasm, phantom, wraith, ghost, spirit, specter, shade

revenge *vb Syn* AVENGE

revenge *n Syn* RETALIATION, vengeance, retribution, reprisal

revengeful *Syn* VINDICTIVE, vengeful

reverberate *Syn* REBOUND, repercuss, recoil, resile

revere ♦ to honor and admire profoundly and respectfully *Syn* reverence, venerate, worship, adore *Ant* flout

reverence *n* 1 *Syn* HONOR, homage, deference, obeisance 2 ♦ a feeling of worshipful respect *Syn* veneration, worship, adoration 3 ♦ the emotion inspired by what arouses one's deep respect or veneration *Syn* awe, fear

reverence *vb Syn* REVERE, venerate, worship, adore

reverse *vb* 1 ♦ to change to the opposite position *Syn* transpose, invert 2 *Syn* REVOKE, repeal, rescind, recall

reverse *n Syn* OPPOSITE, contradictory, contrary, antithesis, antipode, antonym, converse, counter

reversion 1 *Syn* RETURN, recurrence, recrudescence 2 ♦ a return to an ancestral type or condition or an instance of such return *Syn* atavism, throwback

reversionary ♦ relating to a return to an ancestral type *Syn* atavistic

revert *Syn* RETURN, recur, recrudesce

review 1 *Syn* CRITICISM, critique, blurb, puff 2 *Syn* JOURNAL, periodical, magazine, organ, newspaper

revile *Syn* SCOLD, vituperate, rail, berate, rate, upbraid, tongue-lash, jaw, bawl, chew out, wig *Ant* laud

revise 1 *Syn* CORRECT, rectify, emend, remedy, redress, amend, reform 2 *Syn* EDIT, compile, redact, rewrite, adapt

revive *Syn* RESTORE, revivify, resuscitate

revivify *Syn* RESTORE, revive, resuscitate

revoke ♦ to annul by recalling or taking back *Syn* reverse, repeal, rescind, recall

revolt *Syn* REBELLION, revolution, uprising, insurrection, mutiny, putsch, coup

revolting *Syn* OFFENSIVE, loathsome, repulsive, repugnant

revolution *Syn* REBELLION, uprising, revolt, insurrection, mutiny, putsch, coup

revolve *Syn* TURN, rotate, gyrate, circle, spin, twirl, whirl, wheel, eddy, swirl, pirouette

reward *Syn* PREMIUM, prize, award, meed, guerdon, bounty, bonus

rewrite *Syn* EDIT, compile, revise, redact, adapt

rhapsody *Syn* BOMBAST, rant, fustian, rodomontade

rhetorical ♦ emphasizing style often at the expense of thought *Syn* grandiloquent, magniloquent, aureate, flowery, euphuistic, bombastic

rhymer, rhymester *Syn* POET, versifier, poetaster, bard, minstrel, troubadour

rhythm ♦ the regular rise and fall in intensity of sounds that is associated chiefly with poetry and music *Syn* meter, cadence

rib *Syn* BANTER, chaff, kid, rag, josh, jolly

ribald *Syn* COARSE, obscene, gross, vulgar

ribbon *Syn* STRIP, fillet, band, stripe

rich ♦ having goods, property, and money in abundance *Syn* wealthy, affluent, opulent *Ant* poor

ricochet *Syn* SKIP, bound, hop, curvet, lope, lollop

rid ♦ to set a person or thing free of something that encumbers *Syn* clear, unburden, disabuse, purge

riddle *Syn* MYSTERY, puzzle, conundrum, enigma, problem

ride *vb* 1 ♦ to travel by automobile or other conveyance *Syn* drive 2 *Syn* BAIT, badger, heckle, hector, chivy, hound

ride *n* ♦ a usu. short trip in a vehicle or by other conveyance *Syn* drive

ridicule ♦ to make an object of laughter of *Syn* deride, mock, taunt, twit, rally

ridiculous *Syn* LAUGHABLE, risible, ludi-

crous, droll, funny, comic, comical, farcical

rife *Syn* PREVAILING, prevalent, current

rifle *Syn* ROB, plunder, loot, burglarize

rift *Syn* BREACH, break, split, schism, rent, rupture

right *adj* 1 *Syn* GOOD *Ant* wrong 2 *Syn* CORRECT, accurate, exact, precise, nice *Ant* wrong

right *n* ♦ something to which one has a just claim *Syn* prerogative, privilege, perquisite, appanage, birthright

righteous *Syn* MORAL, virtuous, noble, ethical *Ant* iniquitous

rightful *Syn* DUE, condign

rigid 1 *Syn* STIFF, inflexible, tense, stark, wooden *Ant* elastic 2 ♦ extremely severe or stern *Syn* rigorous, strict, stringent *Ant* lax

rigor *Syn* DIFFICULTY, hardship, vicissitude *Ant* amenity

rigorous *Syn* RIGID, strict, stringent

rile *Syn* IRRITATE, exasperate, nettle, provoke, aggravate, peeve

rim *Syn* BORDER, brim, brink, margin, verge, edge

rind *Syn* SKIN, bark, peel, hide, pelt

ring *n Syn* COMBINATION, combine, party, bloc, faction

ring *vb Syn* SURROUND, environ, encircle, circle, encompass, compass, hem, gird, girdle

ringing *Syn* RESONANT, sonorous, resounding, vibrant, orotund

rip *Syn* TEAR, rend, split, cleave, rive

ripe *Syn* MATURE, matured, mellow, adult, grown-up *Ant* green; unripe

ripen *Syn* MATURE, develop, age

rise *vb* 1 *Syn* SPRING, arise, originate, derive, flow, issue, emanate, proceed, stem *Ant* abate 2 ♦ to move or come up from a lower to a higher level *Syn* arise, ascend, mount, soar, tower, rocket, levitate, surge *Ant* decline; set (*as the sun*)

rise *n Syn* BEGINNING, genesis, initiation *Ant* fall

risible *Syn* LAUGHABLE, droll, funny, ludicrous, ridiculous, comic, comical, farcical

risk *n Syn* DANGER, hazard, peril, jeopardy

risk *vb* **Syn** VENTURE, hazard, chance, jeopardize, endanger, imperil

risky **Syn** DANGEROUS, precarious, hazardous, perilous

rite, ritual **Syn** FORM, liturgy, ceremonial, ceremony, formality

rival 1 ♦ to strive to equal or surpass **Syn** compete, vie, emulate **2** **Syn** MATCH, equal, approach, touch

rive **Syn** TEAR, cleave, split, rend, rip

rivet **Syn** SECURE, anchor, moor

roam **Syn** WANDER, stray, ramble, rove, range, prowl, gad, gallivant, traipse, meander

roar *vb* ♦ to make a very loud and often a continuous or protracted noise **Syn** bellow, bluster, bawl, vociferate, clamor, howl, ululate

roar *n* ♦ a very loud and often a continuous noise **Syn** bellow, bluster, bawl, vociferation, ululation

rob ♦ to take possessions unlawfully **Syn** plunder, rifle, loot, burglarize

robber **Syn** THIEF, burglar, larcener, larcenist

robbery **Syn** THEFT, larceny, burglary

robe **Syn** CLOTHE, attire, dress, apparel, array

robust **Syn** HEALTHY, sound, wholesome, hale, well **Ant** frail, feeble

rock **Syn** SHAKE, agitate, convulse

rocket **Syn** RISE, arise, ascend, mount, soar, tower, levitate, surge

rococo **Syn** ORNATE, baroque, flamboyant, florid

rodomontade **Syn** BOMBAST, rhapsody, rant, fustian

rogue **Syn** VILLAIN, scoundrel, blackguard, knave, rascal, scamp, rapscallion, miscreant

roguish **Syn** PLAYFUL, frolicsome, sportive, waggish, impish, mischievous

roily **Syn** TURBID, muddy

roll **Syn** LIST, table, catalog, schedule, register, roster, inventory

rollick *vb* **Syn** PLAY, frolic, disport, sport, romp, gambol

rollick *n* **Syn** PLAY, frolic, disport, sport, romp, gambol

romantic **Syn** SENTIMENTAL, mawkish, maudlin, soppy, mushy, slushy

romp *n* **Syn** PLAY, frolic, rollick, gambol, disport, sport

romp *vb* **Syn** PLAY, frolic, rollick, gambol, disport, sport

room 1 ♦ space in a building enclosed or set apart by a partition **Syn** chamber, apartment **2** ♦ enough space or range for free movement **Syn** berth, play, elbowroom, leeway, margin, clearance

roost **Syn** ALIGHT, perch, light, land

root *n* **Syn** ORIGIN, source, inception, provenance, provenience, prime mover

root *vb* **Syn** APPLAUD, cheer

roseate **Syn** HOPEFUL, optimistic, rosecolored

rose-colored **Syn** HOPEFUL, optimistic, roseate

roster **Syn** LIST, table, catalog, schedule, register, roll, inventory

rot *vb* **Syn** DECAY, decompose, putrefy, spoil, disintegrate, crumble

rot *n* **Syn** NONSENSE, twaddle, drivel, bunk, balderdash, poppycock, gobbledygook, trash, bull

rotate 1 **Syn** TURN, revolve, gyrate, circle, spin, twirl, whirl, wheel, eddy, swirl, pirouette **2** ♦ to succeed or cause to succeed each other in turn **Syn** alternate

rotter **Syn** CAD, bounder

rotund **Syn** FLESHY, plump, chubby, portly, stout, fat, corpulent, obese **Ant** angular

rough 1 ♦ not smooth or even **Syn** harsh, uneven, rugged, scabrous **Ant** smooth **2** **Syn** RUDE, crude, uncouth, raw, callow, green **Ant** gentle

roundabout **Syn** INDIRECT, circuitous

rouse **Syn** STIR, arouse, awaken, rally, waken

roustabout **Syn** WORKER, workman, workingman, laborer, mechanic, artisan, operative, hand, craftsman, handicraftsman

rout *n* **Syn** CROWD, throng, press, crush, mob, horde

rout *vb* **Syn** CONQUER, vanquish, defeat, subdue, subjugate, reduce, overcome, surmount, overthrow, beat, lick

route *n Syn* WAY, course, passage, pass, artery

route *vb Syn* SEND, forward, transmit, remit, ship, dispatch

rove *Syn* WANDER, stray, roam, ramble, range, prowl, gad, gallivant, traipse, meander

row *n Syn* LINE, rank, file, echelon, tier

row *n Syn* BRAWL, broil, fracas, melee, rumpus, scrap

royal *Syn* KINGLY, regal, queenly, imperial, princely

rubbish *Syn* REFUSE, waste, trash, debris, garbage, offal

rube *Syn* BOOR, bumpkin, hick, yokel, clodhopper, clown, lout, churl

rude 1 ♦ lacking in social refinement *Syn* rough, crude, raw, callow, green, uncouth **2** ♦ offensive in manner or action *Syn* illmannered, impolite, discourteous, uncivil, ungracious *Ant* civil; urbane

rudimentary *Syn* ELEMENTARY, basal, beginning, elemental

rueful *Syn* MELANCHOLY, dolorous, doleful, lugubrious, plaintive

rugged *Syn* ROUGH, scabrous, harsh, uneven *Ant* fragile

ruin *n* ♦ the bringing about of or the results of disaster *Syn* havoc, devastation, destruction

ruin *vb* ♦ to subject to forces that are destructive of soundness, worth, or usefulness *Syn* wreck, dilapidate

rule *n Syn* LAW, regulation, precept, statute, ordinance, canon

rule *vb* **1** *Syn* GOVERN **2** *Syn* DECIDE, determine, settle, resolve

rule out *Syn* EXCLUDE, eliminate, debar, shut out, suspend, disbar, blackball

ruminate *Syn* PONDER, muse, meditate

rummage *Syn* SEEK, comb, ransack, search, hunt, scour, ferret out

rumor *Syn* REPORT, gossip, hearsay

rumpus *Syn* BRAWL, broil, fracas, melee, row, scrap

runt *Syn* DWARF, pygmy, midget, manikin, homunculus

rupture *Syn* BREACH, break, split, schism, rent, rift

rural ♦ relating to or characteristic of the country *Syn* rustic, pastoral, bucolic

ruse *Syn* TRICK, stratagem, maneuver, gambit, ploy, artifice, wile, feint

rush ♦ to move or cause to move quickly, impetuously, and often heedlessly *Syn* dash, tear, shoot, charge

rustic *Syn* RURAL, pastoral, bucolic

ruth *Syn* SYMPATHY, commiseration, compassion, pity, condolence, empathy

S

sack *n Syn* BAG, pouch

sack *vb Syn* DISMISS, discharge, cashier, drop, fire, bounce

sack *vb Syn* RAVAGE, pillage, despoil, spoliate, devastate, waste

sacred 1 *Syn* HOLY, divine, blessed, spiritual, religious *Ant* profane **2** ♦ protected (as by law, custom, or human respect) against abuse *Syn* sacrosanct, inviolate, inviolable

sacrifice *Syn* FORGO, abnegate, forbear, eschew

sacrilege *Syn* PROFANATION, desecration, blasphemy

sacrilegious *Syn* IMPIOUS, blasphemous, profane

sacrosanct *Syn* SACRED, inviolate, inviolable

saddle *Syn* BURDEN, encumber, cumber, weigh, weight, load, lade, tax, charge

sadness ♦ the quality, state, or instance of being unhappy or low in spirits *Syn* depression, melancholy, melancholia, dejection, gloom, blues, dumps *Ant* gladness

safe ♦ affording security from threat of danger, harm, or loss *Syn* secure *Ant* dangerous

safeguard *Syn* DEFEND, guard, shield, protect

sag *Syn* DROOP, wilt, flag

saga *Syn* MYTH, legend

sagacious *Syn* SHREWD, perspicacious, astute

sage *Syn* WISE, sapient, judicious, prudent, sensible, sane

sail *Syn* FLY, float, skim, scud, shoot, dart

sailor *Syn* MARINER, seaman, tar, gob, bluejacket

salary *Syn* WAGE, wages, stipend, pay, hire, emolument, fee

salient *Syn* NOTICEABLE, conspicuous, outstanding, signal, striking, arresting, prominent, remarkable

salubrious *Syn* HEALTHFUL, healthy, wholesome, salutary, hygienic, sanitary

salutary *Syn* HEALTHFUL, wholesome, healthy, salubrious, hygienic, sanitary *Ant* deleterious; evil

salutation *Syn* GREETING, salute

salute *vb Syn* ADDRESS, greet, hail, accost

salute *n Syn* GREETING, salutation

same ♦ not different or not differing from one another *Syn* selfsame, very, identical, identic, equivalent, equal, tantamount *Ant* different

sample *Syn* INSTANCE, specimen, example, case, illustration

sanative *Syn* CURATIVE, remedial, restorative, corrective

sanctimonious 1 *Syn* DEVOUT, pietistic, religious, pious 2 *Syn* HYPOCRITICAL, pharisaical, canting

sanctimony *Syn* HYPOCRISY, pharisaism, cant

sanction *Syn* APPROVE, endorse, accredit, certify *Ant* interdict

sanctity *Syn* HOLINESS

sanctuary *Syn* SHELTER, refuge, asylum, cover, retreat

sand *Syn* FORTITUDE, grit, backbone, pluck, guts

sane *Syn* WISE, judicious, prudent, sensible, sage, sapient *Ant* insane

sangfroid *Syn* EQUANIMITY, phlegm, composure

sanguinary *Syn* BLOODY, sanguine, sanguineous, gory

sanguine 1 *also* **sanguineous** *Syn* BLOODY, sanguinary, gory *Ant* bloodless 2 *Syn* CONFIDENT, assured, sure, presumptuous *Ant* afraid

sanitary *Syn* HEALTHFUL, hygienic, salutary, salubrious, healthy, wholesome *Ant* noxious

sanitize *Syn* STERILIZE, disinfect, fumigate

sap *Syn* WEAKEN, undermine, enfeeble, debilitate, cripple, disable

sapid *Syn* PALATABLE, appetizing, savory, tasty, toothsome, flavorsome, relishing *Ant* insipid

sapient *Syn* WISE, sage, judicious, prudent, sensible, sane

sarcasm *Syn* WIT, satire, irony, humor, repartee

sarcastic ♦ marked by bitterness and a power or will to cut or sting *Syn* satiric, ironic, sardonic

sardonic *Syn* SARCASTIC, ironic, satiric

sate *Syn* SATIATE, surfeit, cloy, pall, glut, gorge

satellite *Syn* FOLLOWER, adherent, henchman, partisan, disciple, sectary

satiate ♦ to fill to repletion *Syn* sate, surfeit, cloy, pall, glut, gorge

satiny *Syn* SLEEK, silky, silken, velvety, glossy, slick

satire *Syn* WIT, irony, humor, sarcasm, repartee

satiric *Syn* SARCASTIC, ironic, sardonic

satisfied ♦ showing or expressing satisfaction from the fulfillment of one's desires *Syn* content, contented

satisfy 1 ♦ to appease desires or longings *Syn* content *Ant* tantalize 2 *Syn* PAY, recompense, compensate, remunerate, repay, reimburse, indemnify 3 ♦ to measure up to a set of criteria or requirements *Syn* fulfill, meet, answer

saturate 1 *Syn* SOAK, steep, impregnate, drench, sop, waterlog 2 *Syn* PERMEATE, impregnate, impenetrate, interpenetrate, penetrate, pervade

saturnine *Syn* SULLEN, dour, gloomy, glum, morose, surly, sulky, crabbed *Ant* genial; mercurial

saucy ♦ flippant and bold in manner or attitude **Syn** pert, arch

saunter ♦ to walk slowly in an idle or aimless manner **Syn** stroll, amble

savage 1 Syn FIERCE, ferocious, barbarous, inhuman, cruel, fell, truculent **2 Syn** BARBARIAN, barbaric, barbarous

save 1 Syn RESCUE, deliver, redeem, ransom, reclaim **Ant** lose; waste; damn (*in theology*) **2** ♦ to keep secure or maintain intact from injury, decay, or loss **Syn** preserve, conserve **Ant** spend; consume

savoir faire Syn TACT, poise, address

savor Syn TASTE, flavor, tang, relish, smack

savory Syn PALATABLE, appetizing, sapid, tasty, toothsome, flavorsome, relishing **Ant** bland; acrid

saw Syn SAYING, adage, proverb, maxim, motto, epigram, aphorism, apothegm

say ♦ to express in words **Syn** utter, tell, state

saying ♦ an often repeated statement that usu. is brief and expresses a common observation or general truth **Syn** saw, adage, proverb, maxim, motto, epigram, aphorism, apothegm

scabrous Syn ROUGH, harsh, uneven, rugged **Ant** glabrous; smooth

scale Syn ASCEND, climb, mount

scamp Syn VILLAIN, scoundrel, blackguard, knave, rascal, rogue, rapscallion, miscreant

scamper Syn SCUTTLE, scurry, skedaddle, sprint

scan Syn SCRUTINIZE, examine, inspect, audit

scandal 1 Syn OFFENSE, sin, vice, crime **2 Syn** DETRACTION, calumny, slander, backbiting

scanning Syn SCRUTINY, examination, inspection, audit

scant, scanty Syn MEAGER, skimpy, scrimpy, exiguous, spare, sparse **Ant** plentiful; profuse

scarce Syn INFREQUENT, rare, uncommon, occasional, sporadic **Ant** abundant

scare Syn FRIGHTEN, alarm, fright, terrify, terrorize, startle, affray, affright **Ant** entice

scathing Syn CAUSTIC, mordant, acrid **Ant** scorching, searing, burning; fierce, ferocious, truculent, savage; incisive, biting, cutting, trenchant

scatter 1 ♦ to cause to separate or break up **Syn** disperse, dissipate, dispel **2 Syn** STREW, straw, broadcast, sow

scent Syn SMELL, odor, aroma

schedule 1 Syn LIST, table, catalog, register, roll, roster, inventory **2 Syn** PROGRAM, timetable, agenda

scheme *n* **1 Syn** PLAN, design, plot, project **2 Syn** SYSTEM, network, complex, organism

scheme *vb* **Syn** PLAN, design, plot, project

schism Syn BREACH, split, rupture, break, rent, rift

schismatic Syn HERETIC, sectarian, dissenter, nonconformist

scholarly Syn LEARNED, erudite

scholarship Syn KNOWLEDGE, learning, erudition, science, information, lore

scholastic Syn PEDANTIC, academic, bookish

school Syn TEACH, discipline, train, instruct, educate

science Syn KNOWLEDGE, learning, erudition, scholarship, information, lore

scintillate Syn FLASH, gleam, glance, glint, sparkle, glitter, glisten, coruscate, twinkle

scoff ♦ to show one's contempt in derision or mockery **Syn** jeer, gibe, fleer, gird, sneer, flout

scold *n* **Syn** VIRAGO, shrew, vixen, termagant, amazon

scold *vb* ♦ to reproach angrily and abusively **Syn** upbraid, rate, berate, tonguelash, jaw, bawl, chew out, wig, rail, revile, vituperate

scoop Syn DIP, bail, ladle, spoon, dish

scope Syn RANGE, gamut, reach, radius, compass, sweep, orbit, horizon, ken, purview

scorch Syn BURN, char, sear, singe

scorn *n* **Syn** DISDAIN, contempt, despite

scorn *vb* **Syn** DESPISE, disdain, scout, contemn

scoundrel *Syn* VILLAIN, blackguard, knave, rascal, rogue, scamp, rapscallion, miscreant

scour *Syn* SEEK, search, hunt, ransack, rummage, comb, ferret out

scout *Syn* DESPISE, scorn, contemn, disdain

scowl *Syn* FROWN, glower, lower, gloom

scrap *vb Syn* DISCARD, junk, cast, shed, molt, slough

scrap *n Syn* BRAWL, broil, fracas, melee, row, rumpus

scrape *vb* ♦ to rub or slide against something that is harsh, rough, or sharp *Syn* scratch, grate, rasp, grind

scrape *n Syn* PREDICAMENT, dilemma, quandary, plight, fix, jam, pickle

scratch *Syn* SCRAPE, grate, rasp, grind

scrawny *Syn* LEAN, skinny, lank, lanky, spare, gaunt, rawboned, angular *Ant* brawny; fleshy; obese

scream *vb Syn* SHOUT, shriek, screech, yell, squeal, holler, whoop

scream *n Syn* SHOUT, shriek, screech, yell, squeal, holler, whoop

screech *vb Syn* SHOUT, scream, shriek, yell, squeal, holler, whoop

screech *n Syn* SHOUT, scream, shriek, yell, squeal, holler, whoop

screen *Syn* HIDE, conceal, secrete, cache, bury, ensconce

scrimpy *Syn* MEAGER, scanty, scant, skimpy, exiguous, spare, sparse

scruple *n Syn* QUALM, demur, compunction

scruple *vb Syn* DEMUR, balk, jib, shy, boggle, stickle, stick, strain

scrupulous 1 *Syn* CAREFUL, meticulous, punctilious, punctual *Ant* remiss **2** *Syn* UPRIGHT, conscientious, honest, just, honorable *Ant* unscrupulous

scrutinize ♦ to look at or over *Syn* scan, inspect, examine, audit

scrutiny ♦ a close study, inquiry, or visual inspection *Syn* examination, scanning, inspection, audit

scud *Syn* FLY, skim, shoot, sail, dart, float

scuffle *Syn* WRESTLE, tussle, grapple

sculpture, sculpt, sculp *Syn* CARVE, chisel, engrave, incise, etch

scum *Syn* FOAM, froth, spume, lather, suds, yeast

scurrility *Syn* ABUSE, billingsgate, invective, vituperation, obloquy

scurrilous *Syn* ABUSIVE, opprobrious, vituperative, contumelious

scurry *Syn* SCUTTLE, scamper, skedaddle, sprint

scurvy *Syn* CONTEMPTIBLE, despicable, pitiable, sorry, cheap, beggarly, shabby

scuttle ♦ to move with or as if with short brisk steps *Syn* scurry, scamper, skedaddle, sprint

seaman *Syn* MARINER, sailor, tar, gob, bluejacket

sear *Syn* BURN, scorch, char, singe

search *Syn* SEEK, scour, hunt, comb, ransack, rummage, ferret out

season *Syn* HARDEN, acclimatize, acclimate

seasonable ♦ done or occurring at a good, suitable, or proper time *Syn* timely, well-timed, opportune, pat *Ant* unseasonable

seclude *Syn* ISOLATE, segregate, insulate, sequester

seclusion *Syn* SOLITUDE, isolation, alienation

second *Syn* INSTANT, moment, minute, flash, jiffy, twinkling, split second

secondary *Syn* SUBORDINATE, dependent, subject, tributary, collateral *Ant* primary

second-rate *Syn* MEDIUM, mediocre, middling, moderate, average, fair, indifferent

secret ♦ done without attracting observation *Syn* covert, stealthy, furtive, clandestine, surreptitious, underhand, underhanded

secrete *Syn* HIDE, conceal, screen, cache, bury, ensconce

secretive *Syn* SILENT, close, close-lipped, closemouthed, tight-lipped, uncommunicative, taciturn, reticent, reserved

sect *Syn* RELIGION, denomination, cult, communion, faith, creed, persuasion, church

sectary 1 *Syn* FOLLOWER, adherent, disciple, partisan, henchman, satellite **2** *also* **sectarian** *Syn* HERETIC, schismatic, dissenter, nonconformist

section *Syn* PART, sector, segment, division, portion, piece, detail, member, fraction, fragment, parcel

sector *Syn* PART, segment, section, division, portion, piece, detail, member, fraction, fragment, parcel

secular *Syn* PROFANE, temporal, lay *Ant* religious; sacred; regular

secure *adj Syn* SAFE *Ant* precarious, dangerous

secure *vb* **1** ♦ to fasten or fix firmly *Syn* anchor, moor, rivet **2** *Syn* ENSURE, insure, assure **3** *Syn* GET, procure, obtain, acquire, gain, win

security *Syn* GUARANTEE, surety, guaranty, bond, bail

sedate *Syn* SERIOUS, grave, staid, earnest, sober, solemn, somber *Ant* flighty

sediment *Syn* DEPOSIT, precipitate, dregs, lees, grounds

sedition ♦ an offense against a ruling authority to which one owes allegiance *Syn* treason

seditious *Syn* INSUBORDINATE, mutinous, rebellious, factious, contumacious

seduce *Syn* LURE, tempt, entice, inveigle, decoy

sedulous *Syn* BUSY, assiduous, diligent, industrious

see 1 ♦ to take cognizance of by physical or mental vision *Syn* behold, descry, espy, view, survey, contemplate, observe, notice, remark, note, perceive, discern **2** ♦ to perceive something by means of the eyes *Syn* look, watch

seedy *Syn* SHABBY, dilapidated, dingy, faded, threadbare

seek ♦ to look for *Syn* search, scour, hunt, comb, ferret out, ransack, rummage

seem ♦ to give the impression of being without necessarily being so in fact *Syn* look, appear

seeming *Syn* APPARENT, illusory, ostensible

seemly *Syn* DECOROUS, proper, nice, decent *Ant* unseemly

seethe *Syn* BOIL, simmer, parboil, stew

segment *Syn* PART, section, sector, division, portion, piece, detail, member, fraction, fragment, parcel

segregate *Syn* ISOLATE, seclude, insulate, sequester

seize *Syn* TAKE, grasp, clutch, snatch, grab

select *adj* ♦ chosen from a number or group by fitness, superiority, or preference *Syn* elect, picked, exclusive *Ant* indiscriminate

select *vb Syn* CHOOSE, elect, prefer, opt, pick, cull, single *Ant* reject

selection *Syn* CHOICE, preference, election, option, alternative *Ant* rejection

self-abnegation *Syn* RENUNCIATION, abnegation, self-denial

self-assertive *Syn* AGGRESSIVE, assertive, pushing, pushy, militant

self-assurance *Syn* CONFIDENCE, assurance, self-confidence, aplomb, self-possession

self-complacent *Syn* COMPLACENT, self-satisfied, smug, priggish

self-confidence *Syn* CONFIDENCE, assurance, self-assurance, self-possession, aplomb

self-denial *Syn* RENUNCIATION, self-abnegation, abnegation

self-esteem *Syn* CONCEIT, self-love, egotism, egoism, amour propre *Ant* self-distrust

self-love *Syn* CONCEIT, self-esteem, egotism, egoism, amour propre *Ant* self-forgetfulness

self-possession *Syn* CONFIDENCE, self-confidence, assurance, self-assurance, aplomb

selfsame *Syn* SAME, very, identical, identic, equivalent, equal, tantamount *Ant* diverse

self-satisfied *Syn* COMPLACENT, self-complacent, smug, priggish

semblance *Syn* APPEARANCE, look, aspect

sempiternal *Syn* INFINITE, eternal, boundless, illimitable, uncircumscribed

send ♦ to cause to go or be taken from one place, person or condition to another *Syn* dispatch, forward, transmit, remit, route, ship

senescence *Syn* AGE, senility, dotage *Ant* adolescence

senility *Syn* AGE, dotage, senescence

sensation 1 ♦ awareness (as of heat or pain) due to stimulation of a sense organ *Syn* percept, sense-datum, sensum, image **2** ♦ the power to respond or an act of responding to stimuli *Syn* sense, feeling, sensibility

sense 1 *Syn* SENSATION, feeling, sensibility **2** ♦ the ability to reach intelligent conclusions *Syn* common sense, good sense, horse sense, gumption, judgment, wisdom **3** *Syn* MEANING, acceptation, signification, significance, import

sense-datum *Syn* SENSATION, sensum, percept, image

sensibility *Syn* SENSATION, feeling, sense

sensible 1 *Syn* MATERIAL, physical, corporeal, phenomenal, objective *Ant* intelligible **2** *Syn* PERCEPTIBLE, palpable, tangible, appreciable, ponderable *Ant* insensible **3** *Syn* AWARE, conscious, cognizant, alive, awake *Ant* insensible (of *or* to) **4** *Syn* WISE, prudent, sane, judicious, sage, sapient *Ant* absurd, foolish; fatuous, asinine

sensitive 1 *Syn* LIABLE, susceptible, subject, exposed, open, prone *Ant* insensitive **2** *Syn* SENTIENT, impressible, impressionable, responsive, susceptible

sensual 1 *Syn* CARNAL, fleshly, animal **2** *Syn* SENSUOUS, luxurious, voluptuous, sybaritic, epicurean

sensum *Syn* SENSATION, sense-datum, percept, image

sensuous ♦ relating to or providing pleasure through gratification of the senses *Syn* sensual, luxurious, voluptuous, sybaritic, epicurean

sentence ♦ to decree the fate or punishment of one adjudged guilty, unworthy, or unfit *Syn* condemn, damn, doom, proscribe

sententious *Syn* EXPRESSIVE, pregnant, meaningful, significant, eloquent

sentient ♦ readily affected by external stimuli *Syn* sensitive, impressible, impressionable, responsive, susceptible

sentiment 1 *Syn* FEELING, emotion, affection, passion **2** *Syn* OPINION, view, belief, conviction, persuasion

sentimental ♦ unduly or affectedly emotional *Syn* romantic, mawkish, maudlin, soppy, mushy, slushy

separate *vb* ♦ to become or cause to become disunited or disjoined *Syn* part, divide, sever, sunder, divorce *Ant* combine

separate *adj* **1** *Syn* DISTINCT, several, discrete **2** *Syn* SINGLE, solitary, particular, unique, sole, lone

sequel *Syn* EFFECT, outcome, issue, result, consequence, upshot, aftereffect, aftermath, event

sequence *Syn* SUCCESSION, series, progression, chain, train, string

sequent, sequential *Syn* CONSECUTIVE, successive, serial

sequester *Syn* ISOLATE, segregate, seclude, insulate

serene *Syn* CALM, tranquil, peaceful, placid, halcyon

serial *Syn* CONSECUTIVE, successive, sequent, sequential

series *Syn* SUCCESSION, progression, sequence, chain, train, string

serious ♦ not light or frivolous (as in disposition, appearance, or manner) *Syn* grave, solemn, somber, sedate, staid, sober, earnest *Ant* light, flippant

sermon *Syn* SPEECH, homily, address, oration, harangue, talk, lecture

serpentine *Syn* WINDING, sinuous, tortuous, flexuous

service *Syn* USE, advantage, profit, account, avail

servile *Syn* SUBSERVIENT, menial, slavish, obsequious *Ant* authoritative

servitude ♦ the state of subjection to a master *Syn* slavery, bondage

set *vb* **1** ♦ to position (something) in a specified place *Syn* settle, fix, establish **2** *Syn* COAGULATE, congeal, curdle, clot, jelly, jell

set *n* ♦ a group of persons associated by

common interest *Syn* circle, coterie, clique

setting *Syn* BACKGROUND, environment, milieu, mise-en-scène, backdrop

settle 1 *Syn* SET, fix, establish *Ant* unsettle **2** *Syn* CALM, compose, quiet, quieten, still, lull, soothe, tranquilize *Ant* unsettle **3** *Syn* DECIDE, determine, rule, resolve

sever *Syn* SEPARATE, sunder, part, divide, divorce

several 1 *Syn* DISTINCT, separate, discrete **2** *Syn* MANY, sundry, various, divers, numerous, multifarious

severally *Syn* EACH, individually, respectively, apiece

severe ♦ given to or marked by strict discipline and firm restraint *Syn* stern, austere, ascetic *Ant* tolerant; tender

shabby 1 ♦ being ill-kept and showing signs of wear and tear *Syn* dilapidated, dingy, faded, seedy, threadbare **2** *Syn* CONTEMPTIBLE, despicable, pitiable, sorry, scurvy, cheap, beggarly

shackle *Syn* HAMPER, fetter, clog, trammel, manacle, hog-tie

shade 1 ♦ comparative darkness or obscurity due to interception of light rays *Syn* shadow, umbrage, umbra, penumbra, adumbration **2** *Syn* APPARITION, ghost, spirit, specter, phantasm, phantom, wraith, revenant **3** *Syn* BLIND, shutter **4** *Syn* COLOR, tint, hue, tinge, tone **5** *Syn* GRADATION, nuance **6** *Syn* TOUCH, suggestion, suspicion, soupçon, tinge, smack, spice, dash, vein, strain, tincture, streak

shadow *n Syn* SHADE, umbrage, umbra, penumbra, adumbration

shadow *vb Syn* SUGGEST, adumbrate

shake 1 ♦ to exhibit vibratory, wavering, or oscillating movement often as an evidence of instability *Syn* tremble, quake, totter, quiver, shiver, shudder, quaver, wobble, teeter, shimmy, dither **2** ♦ to move up and down or to and fro with some violence *Syn* agitate, rock, convulse **3** *Syn* SWING, wave, flourish, brandish, thrash

shallow *Syn* SUPERFICIAL, cursory, uncritical

sham *n Syn* IMPOSTURE, cheat, fake, humbug, fraud, deceit, deception, counterfeit

sham *vb Syn* ASSUME, feign, simulate, counterfeit, pretend, affect

sham *n Syn* COUNTERFEIT, spurious, bogus, fake, pseudo, pinchbeck, phony

shame *Syn* DISGRACE, dishonor, disrepute, infamy, ignominy, opprobrium, obloquy, odium *Ant* glory; pride

shameless ♦ characterized by or exhibiting boldness and a lack of shame *Syn* brazen, barefaced, brash, impudent

shape *vb Syn* MAKE, form, fashion, fabricate, manufacture, forge

shape *n Syn* FORM, figure, conformation, configuration

shapeless *Syn* FORMLESS, unformed *Ant* shapely

share ♦ to have, get, or use in common with another or others *Syn* participate, partake

sharp ♦ having or showing alert competence and clear understanding *Syn* keen, acute *Ant* dull; blunt

shatter *Syn* BREAK, shiver, crack, burst, bust, snap

shave *Syn* BRUSH, graze, glance, skim

shear ♦ to cut or cut off with or as if with shears *Syn* poll, clip, trim, prune, lop, snip, crop

shed *Syn* DISCARD, cast, molt, slough, scrap, junk

sheen *Syn* LUSTER, gloss, glaze

sheer *adj* **1** *Syn* PURE, simple, absolute **2** *Syn* STEEP, precipitous, abrupt

sheer *vb Syn* TURN, divert, deflect, avert

shelter *n* ♦ something that covers or affords protection *Syn* cover, retreat, refuge, asylum, sanctuary

shelter *vb Syn* HARBOR, lodge, house, entertain, board

shibboleth *Syn* CATCHWORD, byword, slogan

shield *Syn* DEFEND, protect, guard, safeguard

shift *vb Syn* MOVE, remove, transfer

shift *n* **1** *Syn* RESOURCE, makeshift, expedient, resort, stopgap, substitute, surrogate **2** *Syn* SPELL, tour, trick, turn, stint, bout, go

shimmy *Syn* SHAKE, tremble, quake, totter, quiver, shiver, shudder, quaver, wobble, teeter, dither

ship *n Syn* BOAT, vessel, craft

ship *vb Syn* SEND, forward, transmit, remit, route, dispatch

shipshape *Syn* NEAT, tidy, trim, trig, snug, spick-and-span

shirk *Syn* DODGE, parry, sidestep, duck, fence, malinger

shiver *vb Syn* BREAK, shatter, crack, burst, bust, snap

shiver *vb Syn* SHAKE, quiver, shudder, quaver, tremble, quake, totter, wobble, teeter, shimmy, dither

shoal ♦ a shallow place in a body of water *Syn* bank, reef, bar

shock *n Syn* HEAP, cock, stack, pile, mass, bank

shock *vb Syn* HEAP, cock, stack, pile, mass, bank

shock *n Syn* IMPACT, collision, clash, concussion, impingement, percussion, jar, jolt

shocking *Syn* FEARFUL, appalling, awful, dreadful, frightful, terrible, terrific, horrible, horrific

shoot *vb* **1** *Syn* FLY, dart, float, skim, scud, sail **2** *Syn* RUSH, dash, tear, charge

shoot *n* ♦ a branch or a part of a plant that is an outgrowth from a main stem *Syn* branch, bough, limb

shopworn *Syn* TRITE, hackneyed, stereotyped, threadbare

shore ♦ land bordering a usu. large body of water *Syn* coast, beach, strand, bank, littoral, foreshore

short **1** *Syn* BRIEF *Ant* long **2** *Syn* FRAGILE, crisp, brittle, friable, frangible

shortcoming *Syn* IMPERFECTION, deficiency, fault

shorten ♦ to reduce in extent *Syn* curtail, abbreviate, abridge, retrench *Ant* lengthen, elongate; extend

short-lived *Syn* TRANSIENT, transitory, passing, ephemeral, momentary, fugitive, fleeting, evanescent *Ant* agelong

shortly *Syn* PRESENTLY, soon, directly

shout *vb* ♦ to utter a sudden loud cry (as to attract attention) *Syn* yell, shriek, scream, screech, squeal, holler, whoop

shout *n* ♦ a sudden loud cry *Syn* yell, shriek, scream, screech, squeal, holler, whoop

shove *Syn* PUSH, thrust, propel

show *vb* **1** ♦ to reveal outwardly or make apparent *Syn* manifest, evidence, evince, demonstrate **2** ♦ to present so as to invite notice or attention *Syn* exhibit, display, expose, parade, flaunt *Ant* disguise

show *n Syn* EXHIBITION, exhibit, exposition, fair

showy ♦ given to excess outward display *Syn* pretentious, ostentatious

shrew *Syn* VIRAGO, scold, vixen, termagant, amazon

shrewd ♦ acute in perception and sound in judgment *Syn* sagacious, perspicacious, astute

shriek *vb Syn* SHOUT, yell, scream, screech, squeal, holler, whoop

shriek *n Syn* SHOUT, yell, scream, screech, squeal, holler, whoop

shrink **1** *Syn* CONTRACT, constrict, compress, condense, deflate *Ant* swell **2** *Syn* RECOIL, flinch, quail, blench, wince

shrivel *Syn* WITHER, wizen

shroud *Syn* COVER, overspread, envelop, wrap, veil

shudder *Syn* SHAKE, shiver, quiver, quaver, tremble, quake, totter, wobble, teeter, shimmy, dither

shun *Syn* ESCAPE, avoid, evade, elude, eschew *Ant* habituate

shut *Syn* CLOSE

shut out *Syn* EXCLUDE, eliminate, debar, rule out, blackball, disbar

shutter *Syn* BLIND, shade

shy *adj* ♦ not inclined to be forward *Syn* bashful, diffident, modest, coy *Ant* obtrusive

shy *vb Syn* DEMUR, balk, boggle, scruple, jib, stickle, stick, strain

sic *Syn* URGE, egg, exhort, goad, spur, prod, prick

sicken *Syn* DISGUST, nauseate

sickly *Syn* UNWHOLESOME, morbid, diseased, pathological *Ant* robust

side *Syn* PHASE, aspect, facet, angle

sidereal *Syn* STARRY, stellar, astral

sidestep *Syn* DODGE, parry, shirk, duck, fence, malinger

siege *Syn* BLOCKADE

sigh *vb* ♦ to let out a deep audible breath (as in weariness or sorrow) *Syn* sob, moan, groan

sigh *n* ♦ a usu. inarticulate sound indicating mental or physical pain or distress *Syn* groan, moan, sob

sight *Syn* LOOK, view, glance, glimpse, peep, peek

sightless *Syn* BLIND, purblind

sign 1 ♦ a discernible indication of what is not itself directly perceptible *Syn* mark, token, badge, note, symptom 2 ♦ a motion, action, gesture, or word by which a command, thought, or wish is expressed *Syn* signal 3 *Syn* CHARACTER, symbol, mark

signal *n Syn* SIGN

signal *adj Syn* NOTICEABLE, salient, striking, arresting, outstanding, prominent, remarkable, conspicuous

significance 1 *Syn* MEANING, signification, import, sense, acceptation 2 *Syn* IMPORTANCE, import, consequence, moment, weight

significant *Syn* EXPRESSIVE, meaningful, pregnant, eloquent, sententious

signification *Syn* MEANING, significance, import, sense, acceptation

signify *Syn* MEAN, import, denote

silent 1 ♦ showing restraint in speaking *Syn* uncommunicative, taciturn, reticent, reserved, secretive, close, close-lipped, closemouthed, tight-lipped *Ant* talkative 2 *Syn* STILL, stilly, quiet, noiseless

silhouette *Syn* OUTLINE, contour, profile, skyline

silken, silky *Syn* SLEEK, slick, glossy, velvety, satiny

silly 1 *Syn* SIMPLE, foolish, fatuous, asinine 2 *Syn* FOOLISH, absurd, preposterous

similar *Syn* LIKE, alike, analogous, comparable, akin, parallel, uniform, identical *Ant* dissimilar

similarity *Syn* LIKENESS, resemblance, similitude, analogy, affinity *Ant* dissimilarity

simile *Syn* ANALOGY, metaphor

similitude *Syn* LIKENESS, similarity, resemblance, analogy, affinity *Ant* dissimilitude, dissimilarity

simmer *Syn* BOIL, seethe, parboil, stew

simper *vb Syn* SMILE, smirk, grin

simper *n Syn* SMILE, smirk, grin

simple *adj* 1 *Syn* PURE, absolute, sheer *Ant* compound; complex 2 *Syn* EASY, facile, light, effortless, smooth *Ant* complicated; difficult 3 *Syn* PLAIN, homely, unpretentious 4 *Syn* NATURAL, ingenuous, naïve, unsophisticated, artless 5 ♦ actually or apparently deficient in intelligence *Syn* foolish, silly, fatuous, asinine *Ant* wise

simple *n Syn* DRUG, medicinal, pharmaceutical, biologic

simpleton *Syn* FOOL, moron, imbecile, idiot, natural

simulate *Syn* ASSUME, feign, counterfeit, sham, pretend, affect

simultaneous *Syn* CONTEMPORARY, synchronous, coincident, contemporaneous, coeval, coetaneous, concomitant, concurrent

sin *Syn* OFFENSE, vice, crime, scandal

since *Syn* BECAUSE, for, as, inasmuch as

sincere ♦ genuine in feeling *Syn* wholehearted, whole-souled, heartfelt, hearty, unfeigned *Ant* insincere

sinewy *Syn* MUSCULAR, athletic, husky, brawny, burly

sing ♦ to produce musical tones by or as if by means of the voice *Syn* troll, carol, descant, warble, trill, hymn, chant, intone

singe *Syn* BURN, sear, scorch, char

single *adj* 1 *Syn* UNMARRIED, celibate, virgin, maiden 2 ♦ one as distinguished from two or more or all others *Syn* sole, unique, lone, solitary, separate, particular *Ant* accompanied; supported; conjugal

single *vb Syn* CHOOSE, prefer, select, elect, opt, pick, cull

singular *Syn* STRANGE, unique, peculiar, eccentric, erratic, odd, queer, quaint, outlandish, curious

sinister ♦ seriously threatening evil or disaster *Syn* baleful, malign, malefic, maleficent

sink *Syn* FALL, drop, slump, subside

sinuous *Syn* WINDING, flexuous, serpentine, tortuous

sire *Syn* GENERATE, beget, get, procreate, engender, breed, propagate, reproduce

site *Syn* PLACE, position, location, situation, spot, station

situation 1 *Syn* PLACE, position, location, site, spot, station **2** *Syn* STATE, condition, mode, posture, status

size ♦ the amount of measurable space or area occupied by a thing *Syn* dimensions, area, extent, magnitude, volume

skedaddle *Syn* SCUTTLE, scurry, scamper, sprint

skeleton *Syn* STRUCTURE, anatomy, framework

skepticism *Syn* UNCERTAINTY, doubt, dubiety, mistrust

sketch *n* **1** ♦ a rough drawing representing the chief features of an object or scene *Syn* outline, diagram, delineation, draft, tracing, plot, blueprint **2** *Syn* COMPENDIUM, précis, aperçu, syllabus, digest, pandect, survey

sketch *vb* ♦ to make a sketch, rough draft, or outline of *Syn* outline, diagram, delineate, draft, trace, plot, blueprint

skewbald *Syn* VARIEGATED, parti-colored, motley, checkered, checked, pied, piebald, dappled, freaked

skid *Syn* SLIDE, slip, glide, glissade, slither, coast, toboggan

skill *Syn* ART, cunning, craft, artifice

skilled *Syn* PROFICIENT, skillful, adept, expert, masterly *Ant* unskilled

skillful *Syn* PROFICIENT, adept, expert, skilled, masterly *Ant* unskillful

skim 1 *Syn* FLY, float, dart, scud, shoot, sail **2** *Syn* BRUSH, graze, glance, shave

skimpy *Syn* MEAGER, scrimpy, exiguous, scanty, scant, spare, sparse

skin *n* ♦ an outer or surface layer esp. the outer limiting layer of an animal body *Syn* hide, pelt, rind, bark, peel

skin *vb* ♦ to remove the surface, skin, or thin outer covering of *Syn* decorticate, peel, pare, flay

skinny *Syn* LEAN, scrawny, rawboned, angular, gaunt, lank, lanky, spare *Ant* fleshy

skip ♦ to move or advance with successive springs or leaps *Syn* bound, hop, curvet, lope, lollop, ricochet

skirmish *Syn* ENCOUNTER, brush

skit *Syn* LIBEL, squib, lampoon, pasquinade

skulk *Syn* LURK, couch, slink, sneak

skyline *Syn* OUTLINE, profile, contour, silhouette

slack 1 *Syn* NEGLIGENT, lax, remiss, neglectful **2** *Syn* LOOSE, relaxed, lax

slacken *Syn* DELAY, retard, slow, detain *Ant* quicken

slander *n* *Syn* DETRACTION, calumny, backbiting, scandal

slander *vb* *Syn* MALIGN, defame, libel, calumniate, traduce, asperse, vilify

slang *Syn* DIALECT, vernacular, patois, lingo, jargon, cant, argot

slant *vb* ♦ to set or be set at an angle *Syn* slope, incline, lean

slant *n* *Syn* POINT OF VIEW, viewpoint, standpoint, angle

slap *Syn* STRIKE, hit, smite, punch, slug, slog, swat, clout, cuff, box

slash *Syn* CUT, slit, hew, chop, carve

slatternly ♦ being habitually untidy and very dirty esp. in dress or appearance *Syn* dowdy, frowzy, blowsy

slaughter *Syn* MASSACRE, butchery, carnage, pogrom

slavery *Syn* SERVITUDE, bondage

slavish *Syn* SUBSERVIENT, servile, menial, obsequious

slay *Syn* KILL, murder, assassinate, dispatch, execute

sleazy *Syn* LIMP, flimsy, floppy, flaccid, flabby

sleek ♦ having a smooth bright surface or appearance *Syn* slick, glossy, velvety, silken, silky, satiny

sleep ♦ to take rest by a suspension of consciousness *Syn* slumber, drowse, doze, nap, catnap, snooze

sleepy ♦ affected by or inducing of a desire to sleep *Syn* drowsy, somnolent, slumberous

slender *Syn* THIN, slim, slight, tenuous, rare

slick 1 *Syn* SLEEK, glossy, velvety, silken, satiny, silky **2** *Syn* FULSOME, oily, unctuous, oleaginous, soapy

slide ♦ to go or progress with a smooth continuous motion *Syn* slip, glide, skid, glissade, slither, coast, toboggan

slight *adj Syn* THIN, tenuous, rare, slender, slim

slight *vb Syn* NEGLECT, ignore, overlook, disregard, omit, forget

slighting *Syn* DEROGATORY, depreciatory, depreciative, disparaging, pejorative

slim *Syn* THIN, slender, slight, tenuous, rare *Ant* chubby

sling *vb Syn* THROW, hurl, fling, pitch, toss, cast

sling *vb Syn* HANG, suspend, dangle

slink *Syn* LURK, skulk, sneak

slip *vb Syn* SLIDE, glide, skid, glissade, slither, coast, toboggan

slip *n* **1** *Syn* WHARF, dock, pier, quay, berth, jetty, levee **2** *Syn* ERROR, lapse, mistake, blunder, faux pas, bull, howler, boner

slipshod ♦ negligent of or marked by lack of neatness and order esp. in appearance or dress *Syn* slovenly, unkempt, disheveled, sloppy

slit *Syn* CUT, slash, hew, chop, carve

slither *Syn* SLIDE, slip, glide, skid, glissade, coast, toboggan

slog *Syn* STRIKE, hit, smite, punch, slug, swat, clout, slap, cuff, box

slogan *Syn* CATCHWORD, byword, shibboleth

slope *Syn* SLANT, incline, lean

sloppy *Syn* SLIPSHOD, slovenly, unkempt, disheveled

slothful *Syn* LAZY, indolent, faineant *Ant* industrious

slough *Syn* DISCARD, cast, shed, molt, scrap, junk

slovenly *Syn* SLIPSHOD, unkempt, disheveled, sloppy

slow *adj* **1** *Syn* STUPID, dull, dense, crass, dumb **2** ♦ moving, flowing, or proceeding at less than the usual, desirable, or required speed *Syn* dilatory, laggard, deliberate, leisurely *Ant* fast

slow *vb Syn* DELAY, slacken, retard, detain *Ant* speed

slug *Syn* STRIKE, hit, smite, punch, slog, swat, clout, slap, cuff, box

sluggish *Syn* LETHARGIC, torpid, comatose *Ant* brisk; expeditious; quick

sluice *Syn* POUR, stream, gush

slumber *Syn* SLEEP, drowse, doze, nap, catnap, snooze

slumberous *Syn* SLEEPY, drowsy, somnolent

slump *Syn* FALL, drop, sink, subside

slushy *Syn* SENTIMENTAL, mushy, romantic, mawkish, maudlin, soppy

sly ♦ attaining or seeking to attain one's ends by devious means *Syn* cunning, crafty, tricky, foxy, insidious, wily, guileful, artful

smack 1 *Syn* TASTE, flavor, savor, tang, relish **2** *Syn* TOUCH, suggestion, suspicion, soupçon, tincture, tinge, shade, spice, dash, vein, strain, streak

small ♦ noticeably below average in size *Syn* little, diminutive, petite, wee, tiny, teeny, weeny, minute, microscopic, miniature *Ant* large

small-town *Syn* INSULAR, provincial, parochial, local *Ant* cosmopolitan

smart 1 *Syn* INTELLIGENT, bright, knowing, quick-witted, clever, alert *Ant* dull (*of mind*) **2** *Syn* STYLISH, modish, fashionable, chic, dashing *Ant* dowdy, frowzy, blowsy

smash *Syn* CRUSH, mash, bruise, squash, macerate

smell ♦ the quality that makes a thing perceptible to the olfactory sense *Syn* scent, odor, aroma

smidgen *Syn* PARTICLE, bit, mite, whit, atom, iota, jot, tittle

smile *vb* ♦ to have, produce, or exhibit a smile *Syn* grin, simper, smirk *Ant* frown

smile *n* ♦ a facial expression in which the lips curve slightly upward esp. in expression of pleasure or amusement **Syn** simper, smirk, grin **Ant** frown

smirch **Syn** SOIL, dirty, sully, tarnish, foul, befoul, besmirch, grime, begrime

smirk *vb* **Syn** SMILE, simper, grin

smirk *n* **Syn** SMILE, simper, grin

smite **Syn** STRIKE, hit, punch, slug, slog, swat, clout, slap, cuff, box

smog **Syn** HAZE, fog, mist

smooth 1 **Syn** LEVEL, even, plane, plain, flat, flush **Ant** rough 2 **Syn** EASY, effortless, light, simple, facile **Ant** labored 3 **Syn** SUAVE, bland, diplomatic, politic, urbane **Ant** bluff 4 **Syn** SOFT, bland, mild, gentle, lenient, balmy

smother **Syn** SUFFOCATE, asphyxiate, stifle, choke, strangle, throttle

smug **Syn** COMPLACENT, self-complacent, self-satisfied, priggish

smuggled ♦ imported or exported secretly and in violation of the law **Syn** bootleg, contraband

snag **Syn** OBSTACLE, obstruction, impediment, bar

snap 1 **Syn** JERK, twitch, yank 2 **Syn** BREAK, crack, burst, bust, shatter, shiver

snappish **Syn** IRRITABLE, fractious, peevish, waspish, petulant, pettish, huffy, fretful, querulous

snappy **Syn** PUNGENT, piquant, poignant, racy, spicy

snare *n* **Syn** LURE, trap, bait, decoy

snare *vb* **Syn** CATCH, ensnare, trap, entrap, bag, capture

snarl *n* **Syn** CONFUSION, disorder, chaos, disarray, jumble, clutter, muddle

snarl *vb* **Syn** BARK, bay, howl, growl, yelp, yap

snatch **Syn** TAKE, grasp, grab, clutch, seize

sneak **Syn** LURK, slink, skulk

sneer **Syn** SCOFF, jeer, gird, flout, gibe, fleer

snip **Syn** SHEAR, poll, clip, trim, prune, lop, crop

snitch **Syn** STEAL, pilfer, filch, purloin, lift, pinch, swipe, cop

snoopy **Syn** CURIOUS, inquisitive, prying, nosy

snooze **Syn** SLEEP, slumber, drowse, doze, nap, catnap

snug 1 **Syn** NEAT, trim, trig, shipshape, tidy, spick-and-span 2 **Syn** COMFORTABLE, cozy, easy, restful

so **Syn** THEREFORE, hence, consequently, then, accordingly

soak *vb* ♦ to permeate or be permeated with a liquid **Syn** saturate, drench, steep, impregnate, sop, waterlog

soak *n* **Syn** DRUNKARD, inebriate, alcoholic, dipsomaniac, sot, toper, tosspot, tippler

soapy **Syn** FULSOME, slick, oily, unctuous, oleaginous

soar **Syn** RISE, arise, ascend, mount, tower, rocket, levitate, surge

sob *vb* **Syn** SIGH, moan, groan

sob *n* **Syn** SIGH, moan, groan

sober 1 ♦ having or exhibiting self-control and avoiding extremes of behavior **Syn** temperate, continent, unimpassioned **Ant** drunk; excited 2 **Syn** SERIOUS, grave, sedate, staid, solemn, somber, earnest **Ant** gay

sobriety **Syn** TEMPERANCE, abstinence, abstemiousness, continence **Ant** drunkenness; excitement

sociable **Syn** GRACIOUS, cordial, affable, genial **Ant** unsociable

social ♦ inclined to seek or enjoy the company of others **Syn** gregarious, cooperative, convivial, companionable, hospitable **Ant** unsocial, antisocial, asocial

society 1 **Syn** ARISTOCRACY, elite, nobility, gentry, county 2 **Syn** ASSOCIATION, order, club

soft ♦ free from all harshness, roughness, or intensity **Syn** bland, mild, gentle, smooth, lenient, balmy **Ant** hard; stern

soil ♦ to make or become unclean **Syn** dirty, sully, tarnish, foul, befoul, smirch, besmirch, grime, begrime

sojourn **Syn** RESIDE, lodge, stay, put up, stop, live, dwell

solace **Syn** COMFORT, console

sole **Syn** SINGLE, unique, solitary, lone, separate, particular

solecism **Syn** BARBARISM, corruption, impropriety, vulgarism, vernacular

solemn 1 *Syn* CEREMONIAL, ceremonious, formal, conventional **2** *Syn* SERIOUS, grave, somber, sedate, earnest, staid, sober

solemnize *Syn* KEEP, celebrate, observe, commemorate

solicit 1 *Syn* ASK, request **2** *Syn* INVITE, bid, court, woo

solicitor *Syn* LAWYER, attorney, counselor, barrister, counsel, advocate

solicitous *Syn* WORRIED, concerned, anxious *Ant* unmindful; negligent

solicitude *Syn* CARE, concern, anxiety, worry *Ant* negligence; unmindfulness

solid *Syn* FIRM, hard *Ant* fluid, liquid

solidarity *Syn* UNITY, union, integrity

solidify *Syn* HARDEN, indurate, petrify, cake

solitary 1 *Syn* ALONE, lonely, lonesome, lone, forlorn, lorn, desolate **2** *Syn* SINGLE, sole, unique, lone, separate, particular

solitude ♦ the state of one who is alone *Syn* isolation, alienation, seclusion

solve ♦ to find an explanation or solution for something obscure, mysterious, or incomprehensible *Syn* resolve, unfold, unravel, decipher

somatic *Syn* BODILY, physical, corporeal, corporal

somber *Syn* SERIOUS, grave, solemn, sedate, staid, sober, earnest *Ant* garish

somnolent *Syn* SLEEPY, drowsy, slumberous

sonorous *Syn* RESONANT, ringing, resounding, vibrant, orotund

soon 1 *Syn* PRESENTLY, shortly, directly **2** *Syn* EARLY, beforehand, betimes

soothe *Syn* CALM, compose, quiet, quieten, still, lull, settle, tranquilize *Ant* annoy; excite

sop *Syn* SOAK, saturate, drench, steep, impregnate, waterlog

sophism *Syn* FALLACY, sophistry, casuistry

sophistical *Syn* FALLACIOUS, casuistical *Ant* valid

sophisticate *Syn* ADULTERATE, load, weight, doctor

sophisticated ♦ experienced in the ways of the world *Syn* worldly-wise, worldly, blasé, disillusioned *Ant* unsophisticated

sophistry *Syn* FALLACY, sophism, casuistry

soppy *Syn* SENTIMENTAL, romantic, mawkish, maudlin, mushy, slushy

sorcery *Syn* MAGIC, witchcraft, witchery, wizardry, alchemy, thaumaturgy

sordid *Syn* MEAN, ignoble, abject

sorrow *n* ♦ distress of mind *Syn* grief, heartache, heartbreak, anguish, woe, regret *Ant* joy

sorrow *vb* *Syn* GRIEVE, mourn

sorry *Syn* CONTEMPTIBLE, pitiable, despicable, scurvy, cheap, beggarly, shabby

sort *n* *Syn* TYPE, kind, stripe, kidney, ilk, description, nature, character

sort *vb* *Syn* ASSORT, classify, pigeonhole

sot *Syn* DRUNKARD, inebriate, alcoholic, dipsomaniac, soak, toper, tosspot, tippler

soul 1 *Syn* MIND, intellect, psyche, brain, intelligence, wit **2** ♦ the immortal part of a human being believed to have permanent individual existence *Syn* spirit *Ant* body

sound *adj* **1** *Syn* HEALTHY, wholesome, robust, hale, well **2** *Syn* VALID, cogent, convincing, compelling, telling *Ant* fallacious

sound *n* ♦ a sensation or effect produced by stimulation of the auditory receptors *Syn* noise *Ant* silence

sound *n* *Syn* STRAIT, channel, passage, narrows

sound *vb* *Syn* FATHOM, plumb

soupçon *Syn* TOUCH, suspicion, suggestion, tincture, tinge, shade, smack, spice, dash, vein, strain, streak

sour ♦ having a taste devoid of sweetness *Syn* acid, acidulous, tart, dry

source *Syn* ORIGIN, root, inception, provenance, provenience, prime mover *Ant* termination; outcome

souse *Syn* DIP, immerse, submerge, duck, dunk

souvenir 1 *Syn* REMEMBRANCE, remembrancer, reminder, memorial, memento, token, keepsake **2** *Syn* MEMORY, remembrance, recollection, reminiscence, mind

sovereign 1 *Syn* DOMINANT, predominant, paramount, preponderant, preponderating **2** *Syn* FREE, independent, autonomous, autarchic, autarkic

sovereignty *Syn* FREEDOM, independence, autonomy, autarky, autarchy

sow *Syn* STREW, straw, scatter, broadcast

spacious ♦ larger in extent or capacity than the average *Syn* commodious, capacious, ample

spade *Syn* DIG, delve, grub, excavate

spangle *Syn* SPOT, spatter, sprinkle, mottle, fleck, stipple, marble, speckle, bespangle

spangled *Syn* SPOTTED, spattered, sprinkled, mottled, flecked, stippled, marbled, speckled, bespangled

spare 1 *Syn* SUPERFLUOUS, extra, surplus, supernumerary **2** *Syn* LEAN, lank, lanky, skinny, scrawny, gaunt, rawboned, angular *Ant* corpulent **3** *Syn* MEAGER, exiguous, sparse, scanty, scant, skimpy, scrimpy *Ant* profuse

sparing ♦ careful in the use of one's money or resources *Syn* frugal, thrifty, economical *Ant* lavish

sparkle *Syn* FLASH, gleam, glance, glint, glitter, glisten, scintillate, coruscate, twinkle

sparse *Syn* MEAGER, spare, exiguous, scanty, scant, skimpy, scrimpy *Ant* dense

spasm *Syn* FIT, paroxysm, convulsion, attack, access, accession

spasmodic *Syn* FITFUL, convulsive

spat *n Syn* QUARREL, bickering, squabble, wrangle, altercation, tiff

spat *vb Syn* QUARREL, bicker, squabble, wrangle, altercate, tiff

spate *Syn* FLOOD, deluge, inundation, torrent, cataract

spatter *Syn* SPOT, sprinkle, mottle, fleck, stipple, marble, speckle, spangle, bespangle

spattered *Syn* SPOTTED, sprinkled, mottled, flecked, stippled, marbled, speckled, spangled, bespangled

spay *Syn* STERILIZE, castrate, emasculate, alter, mutilate, geld

speak ♦ to articulate words so as to express thoughts *Syn* talk, converse

special ♦ of or relating to one thing or class *Syn* especial, specific, particular, individual

specie *Syn* MONEY, cash, currency, legal tender, coin, coinage

specific *adj* **1** *Syn* SPECIAL, especial, particular, individual *Ant* generic **2** *Syn* EXPLICIT, definite, express, categorical *Ant* vague

specific *n Syn* REMEDY, cure, medicine, medicament, medication, physic

specify *Syn* MENTION, name, instance

specimen *Syn* INSTANCE, example, sample, illustration, case

specious *Syn* PLAUSIBLE, believable, colorable, credible

speckle *Syn* SPOT, spatter, sprinkle, mottle, fleck, stipple, marble, spangle, bespangle

speckled *Syn* SPOTTED, spattered, sprinkled, mottled, flecked, stippled, marbled, spangled, bespangled

spectator ♦ one who looks on or watches *Syn* observer, beholder, looker-on, onlooker, witness, eyewitness, bystander, kibitzer

specter *Syn* APPARITION, spirit, ghost, phantasm, phantom, wraith, shade, revenant

speculate *Syn* THINK, reason, reflect, cogitate, deliberate

speculative 1 *Syn* THOUGHTFUL, contemplative, meditative, reflective, pensive **2** *Syn* THEORETICAL, academic

speech 1 *Syn* LANGUAGE, tongue, dialect, idiom **2** ♦ a usu. formal discourse delivered to an audience *Syn* address, oration, harangue, lecture, talk, sermon, homily

speechless *Syn* DUMB, mute, inarticulate

speed *n* **1** *Syn* HASTE, hurry, expedition, dispatch **2** ♦ rate of motion, performance, or action *Syn* velocity, momentum, impetus, pace, headway

speed *vb* ♦ to go or make go fast or faster *Syn* accelerate, quicken, hasten, hurry, precipitate

speedy *Syn* FAST, expeditious, quick, swift, fleet, rapid, hasty *Ant* dilatory

spell ♦ a limited period or amount of activity *Syn* shift, tour, trick, turn, stint, bout, go

spend ♦ to use up or pay out *Syn* expend, disburse *Ant* save

spendthrift ♦ a person who spends foolishly and wastefully *Syn* prodigal, profligate, waster, wastrel

spew *Syn* BELCH, burp, vomit, disgorge, regurgitate, throw up

sphere *Syn* FIELD, domain, province, territory, bailiwick

spice *Syn* TOUCH, suggestion, suspicion, soupçon, tincture, tinge, shade, smack, dash, vein, strain, streak

spick-and-span *Syn* NEAT, tidy, trim, trig, snug, shipshape *Ant* filthy

spicy *Syn* PUNGENT, piquant, poignant, racy, snappy

spin *Syn* TURN, revolve, rotate, gyrate, circle, twirl, whirl, wheel, eddy, swirl, pirouette

spine ♦ the articulated column of bones that is the central and axial feature of a vertebrate skeleton *Syn* backbone, back, vertebrae, chine

spirit 1 *Syn* SOUL 2 *Syn* APPARITION, ghost, phantasm, phantom, wraith, specter, shade, revenant 3 *Syn* COURAGE, mettle, resolution, tenacity 4 *Syn* VIGOR, vim, dash, esprit, verve, punch, élan, drive

spirited ♦ full of energy, animation, or courage *Syn* high-spirited, mettlesome, spunky, fiery, peppery, gingery *Ant* spiritless

spiritless *Syn* LANGUID, languishing, languorous, listless, enervated, lackadaisical *Ant* spirited

spiritual 1 *Syn* IMMATERIAL, incorporeal *Ant* physical 2 *Syn* HOLY, sacred, divine, religious, blessed *Ant* physical; carnal; material; temporal

spite *Syn* MALICE, despite, malignity, malignancy, spleen, grudge, ill will, malevolence

spiteful *Syn* MALICIOUS, malignant, malevolent, malign

spleen *Syn* MALICE, malignity, malignancy, grudge, spite, despite, malevolence, ill will

splendid ♦ extraordinarily or transcendently impressive *Syn* resplendent, gorgeous, glorious, sublime, superb

splenetic *Syn* IRASCIBLE, choleric, testy, touchy, cranky, cross

split *vb* *Syn* TEAR, rend, cleave, rive, rip

split *n* *Syn* BREACH, break, schism, rent, rupture, rift

split second *Syn* INSTANT, moment, second, minute, flash, jiffy, twinkling

spoil *n* ♦ something taken from another by force or craft *Syn* plunder, booty, prize, loot, swag

spoil *vb* 1 *Syn* INJURE, harm, hurt, damage, impair, mar 2 *Syn* INDULGE, pamper, humor, baby, mollycoddle 3 *Syn* DECAY, decompose, rot, putrefy, disintegrate, crumble

spoliate *Syn* RAVAGE, despoil, devastate, waste, sack, pillage

sponge, sponger *Syn* PARASITE, sycophant, favorite, toady, lickspittle, bootlicker, hanger-on, leech

sponsor ♦ one who assumes responsibility for some other person or thing *Syn* patron, surety, guarantor, backer, angel

spontaneity *Syn* UNCONSTRAINT, abandon

spontaneous ♦ acting or activated without deliberation *Syn* impulsive, instinctive, automatic, mechanical

spoon *Syn* DIP, ladle, dish, bail, scoop

sporadic *Syn* INFREQUENT, occasional, rare, scarce, uncommon

sport *vb* *Syn* PLAY, disport, frolic, rollick, romp, gambol

sport *n* 1 *Syn* PLAY, disport, frolic, rollick, romp, gambol 2 *Syn* FUN, jest, game, play 3 *pl* **sports** *Syn* ATHLETICS, games

sportive *Syn* PLAYFUL, frolicsome, roguish, waggish, impish, mischievous

spot *n* *Syn* PLACE, position, location, situation, site, station

spot *vb* ♦ to mark or become marked with or as if with spots or sometimes streaks

Syn spatter, sprinkle, mottle, fleck, stipple, marble, speckle, spangle, bespangle

spotted ♦ marked with spots or streaks *Syn* spattered, sprinkled, mottled, flecked, stippled, marbled, speckled, spangled, bespangled

sprain *n Syn* STRAIN

sprain *vb Syn* STRAIN

spread *vb* ♦ to extend or cause to extend over an area or space *Syn* circulate, disseminate, diffuse, propagate, radiate

spread *n Syn* EXPANSE, amplitude, stretch

sprightly *Syn* LIVELY, animated, vivacious, gay

spring *vb* 1 ♦ to come up or out of something into existence *Syn* arise, rise, originate, derive, flow, issue, emanate, proceed, stem 2 *Syn* JUMP, leap, bound, vault

spring *n* 1 *Syn* MOTIVE, impulse, incentive, inducement, spur, goad 2 *Syn* JUMP, leap, bound, vault

springy *Syn* ELASTIC, resilient, flexible, supple

sprinkle *Syn* SPOT, spatter, mottle, fleck, stipple, marble, speckle, spangle, bespangle

sprinkled *Syn* SPOTTED, spattered, mottled, flecked, stippled, marbled, speckled, spangled, bespangled

sprint *Syn* SCUTTLE, scurry, scamper, skedaddle

spry *Syn* AGILE, brisk, nimble *Ant* doddering

spume *Syn* FOAM, froth, scum, lather, suds, yeast

spunky *Syn* SPIRITED, high-spirited, mettlesome, fiery, peppery, gingery

spur *n Syn* MOTIVE, goad, spring, impulse, incentive, inducement

spur *vb Syn* URGE, egg, exhort, goad, prod, prick, sic *Ant* curb

spurious *Syn* COUNTERFEIT, bogus, fake, sham, pseudo, pinchbeck, phony *Ant* genuine

spurn *Syn* DECLINE, reject, repudiate, refuse *Ant* crave; embrace

squabble *n Syn* QUARREL, wrangle, altercation, bickering, spat, tiff

squabble *vb Syn* QUARREL, wrangle, altercate, bicker, spat, tiff

squalid *Syn* DIRTY, nasty, filthy, foul

squander *Syn* WASTE, dissipate, fritter, consume

square *Syn* AGREE, conform, accord, harmonize, correspond, tally, jibe

squash *Syn* CRUSH, mash, smash, bruise, macerate

squat *Syn* STOCKY, thickset, thick, chunky, stubby, dumpy *Ant* lanky

squeal *vb Syn* SHOUT, yell, shriek, scream, screech, holler, whoop

squeal *n Syn* SHOUT, yell, shriek, scream, screech, holler, whoop

squeamish *Syn* NICE, finicky, finicking, finical, particular, fussy, persnickety, pernickety, fastidious, dainty

squeeze *Syn* PRESS, bear, bear down, crowd, jam

squib *Syn* LIBEL, skit, lampoon, pasquinade

squirm *Syn* WRITHE, agonize

stabilize ♦ to make or become stable, steadfast, or firm *Syn* steady, poise, balance, ballast, trim

stable *Syn* LASTING, durable, perdurable, permanent, perpetual *Ant* unstable; changeable

stack *n Syn* HEAP, pile, mass, bank, shock, cock

stack *vb Syn* HEAP, pile, mass, bank, shock, cock

stagger *Syn* REEL, whirl, totter

staid *Syn* SERIOUS, sedate, grave, somber, sober, earnest *Ant* jaunty

stain *Syn* STIGMA, blot, brand

stake *Syn* BET, wager, pot, ante

stalemate *Syn* DRAW, tie, deadlock, standoff

stalwart *Syn* STRONG, stout, sturdy, tough, tenacious

stammer ♦ to make involuntary stops and repetitions in speaking *Syn* stutter

stamp *vb Syn* MARK, brand, label, tag, ticket

stamp *n* 1 *Syn* IMPRESSION, impress, imprint, print 2 *Syn* MARK, brand, label, tag, ticket

stand *vb* *Syn* BEAR, tolerate, brook, suffer, endure, abide

stand *n* *Syn* POSITION, attitude

standard 1 *Syn* FLAG, ensign, banner, color, streamer, pennant, pendant, pennon, jack **2** ♦ a means of determining what a thing should be *Syn* criterion, gauge, yardstick, touchstone **3** *Syn* MODEL, ideal, beau ideal, pattern, exemplar, example, mirror

stand-in *Syn* SUBSTITUTE, supply, understudy, double, locum tenens, alternate, pinch hitter

standoff *Syn* DRAW, tie, stalemate, deadlock

standpoint *Syn* POINT OF VIEW, viewpoint, angle, slant

stare *Syn* GAZE, gape, glare, peer, gloat

stark *Syn* STIFF, rigid, inflexible, tense, wooden

starry ♦ of, relating to, or suggestive of a star or group of stars *Syn* stellar, astral, sidereal

start *Syn* BEGIN, commence, initiate, inaugurate

startle *Syn* FRIGHTEN, scare, alarm, terrify, terrorize, fright, affray, affright

state *n* ♦ the way in which one manifests existence or the circumstances under which one exists or by which one is given distinctive character *Syn* condition, mode, situation, posture, status

state *vb* **1** *Syn* SAY, utter, tell **2** *Syn* RELATE, report, rehearse, recite, recount, narrate, describe

stately *Syn* GRAND, magnificent, imposing, majestic, august, noble, grandiose

statesman *Syn* POLITICIAN, politico

station 1 *Syn* PLACE, position, location, situation, site, spot **2** *Syn* HABITAT, biotope, range

stature *Syn* QUALITY, caliber

status *Syn* STATE, situation, posture, condition, mode

statute *Syn* LAW, ordinance, regulation, rule, precept, canon

staunch *Syn* FAITHFUL, loyal, true, constant, steadfast, resolute

stay *vb* **1** ♦ to continue to be in one place for a noticeable time *Syn* remain, wait, abide, tarry, linger **2** *Syn* RESIDE, sojourn, lodge, put up, stop, live, dwell **3** *Syn* DEFER, postpone, suspend, intermit

stay *vb* *Syn* BASE, found, ground, bottom, rest

steadfast *Syn* FAITHFUL, staunch, resolute, constant, true, loyal **Ant** capricious

steady *adj* ♦ not varying throughout a course or extent *Syn* uniform, even, equable, constant **Ant** unsteady; nervous, jumpy

steady *vb* *Syn* STABILIZE, poise, balance, ballast, trim

steal ♦ to take from another without right or without detection *Syn* pilfer, filch, purloin, lift, pinch, snitch, swipe, cop

stealthy *Syn* SECRET, covert, furtive, clandestine, surreptitious, underhand, underhanded

steel *Syn* ENCOURAGE, inspirit, hearten, embolden, cheer, nerve

steep *adj* ♦ having an incline approaching the perpendicular *Syn* abrupt, precipitous, sheer

steep *vb* *Syn* SOAK, saturate, impregnate, drench, sop, waterlog

steer *Syn* GUIDE, lead, pilot, engineer

stellar *Syn* STARRY, sidereal, astral

stem *Syn* SPRING, proceed, issue, emanate, derive, flow, originate, arise, rise

stentorian *Syn* LOUD, earsplitting, hoarse, raucous, strident, stertorous

stereotyped *Syn* TRITE, hackneyed, threadbare, shopworn **Ant** changeful

sterile ♦ not able to bear fruit, crops, or offspring *Syn* barren, impotent, unfruitful, infertile **Ant** fertile; exuberant

sterilize 1 ♦ to make incapable of producing offspring *Syn* castrate, spay, emasculate, alter, mutilate, geld **Ant** fertilize **2** ♦ to free from living microorganisms *Syn* disinfect, sanitize, fumigate

stern *Syn* SEVERE, austere, ascetic **Ant** soft; lenient

stertorous *Syn* LOUD, stentorian, earsplitting, hoarse, raucous, strident

stew *Syn* BOIL, seethe, simmer, parboil

stick 1 ♦ to become or cause to become closely and firmly attached *Syn* adhere, cohere, cling, cleave **2** *Syn* DEMUR, stickle, balk, shy, boggle, scruple, jib, strain

stickle *Syn* DEMUR, balk, shy, boggle, jib, scruple, stick, strain

stick out *Syn* BULGE, jut, protrude, project, overhang, beetle

stiff ♦ difficult to bend *Syn* rigid, inflexible, tense, stark, wooden *Ant* relaxed; supple

stiff-necked *Syn* OBSTINATE, stubborn, mulish, dogged, pertinacious, pigheaded, bullheaded

stifle *Syn* SUFFOCATE, asphyxiate, smother, choke, strangle, throttle

stigma ♦ a mark of shame or discredit *Syn* brand, blot, stain

still *adj* ♦ making no stir or noise *Syn* stilly, quiet, silent, noiseless *Ant* stirring; noisy

still *vb* *Syn* CALM, compose, quiet, quieten, lull, soothe, settle, tranquilize *Ant* agitate

stilly *Syn* STILL, quiet, silent, noiseless

stimulant *Syn* STIMULUS, excitant, incitement, impetus *Ant* anesthetic; anodyne

stimulate *Syn* PROVOKE, excite, quicken, pique, galvanize *Ant* unnerve; deaden

stimulus ♦ something that rouses or incites to activity *Syn* stimulant, excitant, incitement, impetus

stingy ♦ being unwilling or showing unwillingness to share with others *Syn* close, closefisted, tight, tightfisted, niggardly, parsimonious, penurious, miserly, cheeseparing, penny-pinching *Ant* generous

stinking *Syn* MALODOROUS, fetid, noisome, putrid, rank, rancid, fusty, musty

stint 1 *Syn* TASK, duty, assignment, job, chore **2** *Syn* SPELL, bout, shift, tour, trick, turn, go

stipend *Syn* WAGE, wages, salary, fee, emolument, pay, hire

stipple *Syn* SPOT, spatter, sprinkle, mottle, fleck, marble, speckle, spangle, bespangle

stippled *Syn* SPOTTED, spattered, sprinkled, mottled, flecked, marbled, speckled, spangled, bespangled

stipulation *Syn* CONDITION, terms, provision, proviso, reservation, strings

stir *vb* ♦ to cause to shift from quiescence or torpor into activity *Syn* rouse, arouse, awaken, waken, rally

stir *n* **1** *Syn* MOTION, movement, move, locomotion **2** ♦ signs of excited activity, hurry, or commotion *Syn* bustle, flurry, pother, fuss, ado *Ant* tranquillity

stitch *Syn* PAIN, twinge, ache, pang, throe

stock *Syn* VARIETY, subspecies, race, breed, cultivar, strain, clone

stocky ♦ compact, sturdy, and relatively thick in build *Syn* thickset, thick, chunky, stubby, squat, dumpy

stodgy *Syn* DULL, humdrum, dreary, monotonous, pedestrian

stoic *Syn* IMPASSIVE, phlegmatic, apathetic, stolid

stoicism *Syn* IMPASSIVITY, impassiveness, phlegm, apathy, stolidity

stolid *Syn* IMPASSIVE, phlegmatic, apathetic *Ant* adroit

stolidity *Syn* IMPASSIVITY, impassiveness, phlegm, apathy, stoicism

stomach *Syn* ABDOMEN, belly, paunch, gut

stoop ♦ to descend from one's real or pretended level of dignity *Syn* condescend, deign

stop 1 ♦ to suspend or cause to suspend activity *Syn* cease, quit, discontinue, desist **2** *Syn* RESIDE, stay, put up, lodge, sojourn, live, dwell

stopgap *Syn* RESOURCE, makeshift, shift, expedient, resort, substitute, surrogate

storm *Syn* ATTACK, bombard, assault, assail

story 1 *Syn* ACCOUNT, report, chronicle, version **2** ♦ a recital of happenings less elaborate than a novel *Syn* narrative, tale, anecdote, yarn **3** *Syn* LIE, falsehood, untruth, fib, misrepresentation

stout 1 *Syn* STRONG, sturdy, stalwart, tough, tenacious **2** *Syn* FLESHY, fat, portly, corpulent, obese, plump, rotund, chubby *Ant* cadaverous

straightforward ♦ free from all that is dishonest or secretive **Syn** forthright, aboveboard **Ant** devious; indirect

strain *n* 1 **Syn** VARIETY, subspecies, race, breed, cultivar, clone, stock 2 **Syn** TOUCH, streak, vein, suggestion, suspicion, soupçon, tincture, tinge, shade, smack, spice, dash

strain *vb* ♦ to injure (as a body part) by overuse or misuse **Syn** sprain 2 **Syn** DEMUR, scruple, balk, jib, shy, boggle, stickle, stick

strain *n* 1 **Syn** STRESS, pressure, tension 2 ♦ an injury to a part of the body from undue stretching **Syn** sprain

strained **Syn** FORCED, labored, farfetched

strait 1 ♦ a comparatively narrow stretch of water connecting two larger bodies of water **Syn** sound, channel, passage, narrows 2 **Syn** JUNCTURE, pass, exigency, pinch, emergency, contingency, crisis

straitlaced **Syn** PRIM, priggish, prissy, prudish, puritanical, stuffy **Ant** libertine

strand **Syn** SHORE, coast, beach, bank, littoral, foreshore

strange ♦ departing from what is ordinary, usual, and to be expected **Syn** singular, unique, peculiar, eccentric, erratic, odd, queer, quaint, outlandish, curious **Ant** familiar

stranger ♦ a nonresident or an unknown person in a community **Syn** foreigner, alien, outlander, outsider, immigrant, émigré

strangle **Syn** SUFFOCATE, asphyxiate, stifle, smother, choke, throttle

stratagem **Syn** TRICK, ruse, maneuver, gambit, ploy, artifice, wile, feint

strategic ♦ of, relating to, or marked by strategy **Syn** tactical, logistic

strategy ♦ the art of devising or employing plans toward a usu. military goal **Syn** tactics, logistics

straw **Syn** STREW, scatter, sow, broadcast

stray **Syn** WANDER, roam, ramble, rove, range, prowl, gad, gallivant, traipse, meander

streak **Syn** TOUCH, strain, vein, suggestion, suspicion, soupçon, tincture, tinge, shade, smack, spice, dash

stream *n* **Syn** FLOW, current, flood, tide, flux

stream *vb* **Syn** POUR, gush, sluice

streamer **Syn** FLAG, pennant, pendant, pennon, banner, ensign, standard, color

strength **Syn** POWER, force, might, energy, puissance

strengthen ♦ to make strong or stronger **Syn** invigorate, fortify, energize, reinforce **Ant** weaken

strenuous **Syn** VIGOROUS, energetic, lusty, nervous

stress 1 ♦ the action or effect of force exerted within or upon a thing **Syn** strain, pressure, tension 2 **Syn** EMPHASIS, accent, accentuation

stretch **Syn** EXPANSE, amplitude, spread

strew ♦ to throw loosely or at intervals **Syn** straw, scatter, sow, broadcast

strict **Syn** RIGID, stringent, rigorous **Ant** lax; loose; lenient, indulgent

stricture **Syn** ANIMADVERSION, aspersion, reflection **Ant** commendation

strident 1 **Syn** LOUD, stentorian, earsplitting, hoarse, raucous, stertorous 2 **Syn** VOCIFEROUS, blatant, clamorous, boisterous, obstreperous

strife **Syn** DISCORD, conflict, contention, dissension, difference, variance **Ant** peace; accord

strike 1 ♦ to deliver (a blow) in a strong, vigorous manner **Syn** hit, smite, punch, slug, slog, swat, clout, slap, cuff, box 2 **Syn** AFFECT, impress, touch, influence, sway

striking **Syn** NOTICEABLE, arresting, signal, salient, conspicuous, outstanding, remarkable, prominent

string 1 **Syn** SUCCESSION, progression, series, sequence, chain, train 2 *pl* **strings** **Syn** CONDITION, stipulation, terms, provision, proviso, reservation

stringent **Syn** RIGID, strict, rigorous

strip *vb* ♦ to remove what clothes, furnishes, or invests a person or thing **Syn** divest, denude, bare, dismantle **Ant** furnish; invest

strip *n* ♦ long narrow piece or area *Syn* stripe, band, ribbon, fillet

stripe 1 *Syn* STRIP, band, ribbon, fillet **2** *Syn* TYPE, character, description, nature, kind, sort, kidney, ilk

strive *Syn* ATTEMPT, struggle, endeavor, essay, try

striving *Syn* ATTEMPT, struggle, endeavor, essay, try

stroll *Syn* SAUNTER, amble

strong ♦ showing power to resist or to endure *Syn* stout, sturdy, stalwart, tough, tenacious *Ant* weak

stronghold *Syn* FORT, citadel, fortress, fastness

structure 1 *Syn* BUILDING, edifice, pile **2** ♦ something made up of interdependent parts in a definite pattern of organization *Syn* anatomy, framework, skeleton

struggle *vb Syn* ATTEMPT, strive, endeavor, essay, try

struggle *n Syn* ATTEMPT, striving, endeavor, essay, try

strut ♦ to walk with an air of pomposity or affected dignity *Syn* swagger, bristle, bridle

stubborn *Syn* OBSTINATE, dogged, pertinacious, mulish, stiff-necked, pigheaded, bullheaded

stubby *Syn* STOCKY, thickset, thick, chunky, squat, dumpy

studied *Syn* DELIBERATE, considered, advised, premeditated, designed

study *n Syn* ATTENTION, concentration, application

study *vb Syn* CONSIDER, contemplate, weigh, excogitate

stuff *n Syn* MATTER, substance, material

stuff *vb Syn* PACK, crowd, cram, ram, tamp

stuffy *Syn* PRIM, priggish, prissy, prudish, puritanical, straitlaced

stumble ♦ to move so clumsily or unsteadily as to fall or nearly fall *Syn* trip, blunder, lurch, flounder, lumber, galumph, lollop, bumble

stun *Syn* DAZE, bemuse, stupefy, benumb, paralyze, petrify

stupefy *Syn* DAZE, stun, bemuse, benumb, paralyze, petrify

stupendous *Syn* MONSTROUS, tremendous, prodigious, monumental

stupid ♦ lacking in power to absorb ideas or impressions *Syn* slow, dull, dense, crass, dumb *Ant* intelligent

stupor *Syn* LETHARGY, torpor, torpidity, lassitude, languor

sturdy *Syn* STRONG, stout, stalwart, tough, tenacious *Ant* decrepit

stutter *Syn* STAMMER

stygian *Syn* INFERNAL, chthonic, chthonian, Hadean, Tartarean, hellish

style 1 *Syn* LANGUAGE, diction, phraseology, phrasing, vocabulary **2** *Syn* FASHION, mode, vogue, fad, rage, craze, dernier cri, cry **3** *Syn* NAME, designation, title, denomination, appellation

stylish ♦ conforming to current fashion *Syn* fashionable, modish, smart, chic, dashing

suave ♦ pleasantly tactful and well-mannered *Syn* urbane, diplomatic, bland, smooth, politic *Ant* bluff

subdue *Syn* CONQUER, subjugate, reduce, overcome, surmount, overthrow, rout, vanquish, defeat, beat, lick *Ant* awaken, waken

subdued *Syn* TAME, submissive *Ant* intense; barbaric (*of taste*); bizarre (*of effects*); effervescent (*of character and temperament*)

subject *n* **1** *Syn* CITIZEN, national *Ant* sovereign **2** ♦ the basic idea or the principal object of attention in a discourse or artistic composition *Syn* matter, subject matter, argument, topic, text, theme, motive, motif, leitmotiv

subject *adj* **1** *Syn* SUBORDINATE, dependent, secondary, tributary, collateral *Ant* sovereign, dominant **2** *Syn* LIABLE, open, exposed, prone, susceptible, sensitive *Ant* exempt

subject matter *Syn* SUBJECT, matter, argument, topic, text, theme, motive, motif, leitmotiv

subjoin *Syn* ADD, append, annex, superadd

subjugate *Syn* CONQUER, subdue, reduce, overcome, surmount, overthrow, rout, vanquish, defeat, beat, lick

sublime *Syn* SPLENDID, glorious, superb, resplendent, gorgeous

sublunary *Syn* EARTHLY, terrestrial, earthy, mundane, worldly

submerge *Syn* DIP, immerse, duck, souse, dunk

submission *Syn* SURRENDER, capitulation *Ant* resistance

submissive *Syn* TAME, subdued *Ant* rebellious

submit *Syn* YIELD, capitulate, succumb, relent, defer, bow, cave *Ant* resist, withstand

subordinate *adj* ♦ placed in or occupying a lower class, rank, or status *Syn* secondary, dependent, subject, tributary, collateral *Ant* chief, leading; dominant

subordinate *n* *Syn* INFERIOR, underling *Ant* chief

subscribe *Syn* ASSENT, agree, acquiesce, consent, accede *Ant* boggle

subservient 1 *Syn* AUXILIARY, subsidiary, contributory, ancillary, adjuvant, accessory **2** ♦ showing or characterized by extreme compliance or abject obedience *Syn* servile, slavish, menial, obsequious *Ant* domineering; overbearing

subside 1 *Syn* FALL, drop, sink, slump **2** *Syn* ABATE, wane, ebb

subsidiary *Syn* AUXILIARY, contributory, subservient, ancillary, adjuvant, accessory

subsidy *Syn* APPROPRIATION, grant, subvention

subsist *Syn* BE, exist, live

subsistence *Syn* LIVING, livelihood, sustenance, maintenance, support, keep, bread, bread and butter

subspecies *Syn* VARIETY, race, breed, cultivar, strain, clone, stock

substance 1 ♦ the inner significance or central meaning of something written or said *Syn* purport, gist, burden, core, pith **2** *Syn* MATTER, material, stuff

substantial *Syn* MASSIVE, massy, bulky, monumental *Ant* airy, ethereal

substantiate *Syn* CONFIRM, verify, corroborate, authenticate, validate

substitute 1 *Syn* RESOURCE, surrogate, resort, expedient, shift, makeshift, stopgap **2** ♦ a person who takes the place of or acts instead of another *Syn* supply, locum tenens, alternate, understudy, double, stand-in, pinch hitter

subsume *Syn* INCLUDE, comprehend, embrace, involve, imply

subtle *Syn* LOGICAL, analytical *Ant* dense; blunt

subtract *Syn* DEDUCT *Ant* add

subvention *Syn* APPROPRIATION, grant, subsidy

subvert *Syn* OVERTURN, overthrow, capsize, upset *Ant* uphold, sustain

succeed 1 *Syn* FOLLOW, ensue, supervene *Ant* precede **2** ♦ to attain or be attaining a desired end *Syn* prosper, thrive, flourish *Ant* fail; attempt

succession ♦ a number of things that follow each other in some order *Syn* progression, series, sequence, chain, train, string

successive *Syn* CONSECUTIVE, sequent, sequential, serial

succinct *Syn* CONCISE, terse, laconic, summary, pithy, compendious *Ant* discursive

succumb *Syn* YIELD, submit, capitulate, relent, defer, bow, cave

sudden *Syn* PRECIPITATE, hasty, headlong, abrupt, impetuous

suds *Syn* FOAM, froth, spume, lather, scum, yeast

sue *Syn* PRAY, plead, petition

suffer 1 *Syn* BEAR, endure, abide, tolerate, stand, brook **2** *Syn* EXPERIENCE, undergo, sustain **3** *Syn* LET, permit, allow, leave

sufferance *Syn* PERMISSION, leave

suffering *Syn* DISTRESS, misery, agony, dolor, passion

sufficient ♦ being what is necessary or desirable *Syn* enough, adequate, competent

suffocate ♦ to stop the respiration of *Syn* asphyxiate, stifle, smother, choke, strangle, throttle

suffrage ♦ the right, privilege, or power of expressing one's choice or wish (as in an election or in the determination of policy) *Syn* franchise, vote, ballot

suffuse *Syn* INFUSE, imbue, ingrain, inoculate, leaven

suggest 1 ♦ to convey an idea indirectly *Syn* imply, hint, intimate, insinuate *Ant* express **2** ♦ to call to mind by thought, through close connection, or by association *Syn* adumbrate, shadow *Ant* manifest

suggestion *Syn* TOUCH, suspicion, soupçon, tincture, tinge, shade, smack, spice, dash, vein, strain, streak

suit 1 *Syn* PRAYER, plea, petition, appeal **2** ♦ a legal proceeding instituted for the sake of demanding justice or enforcing a right *Syn* lawsuit, action, cause, case

suitable *Syn* FIT, meet, proper, appropriate, fitting, apt, happy, felicitous *Ant* unsuitable; unbecoming

sulky *Syn* SULLEN, surly, morose, glum, crabbed, saturnine, dour, gloomy

sullen ♦ showing a forbidding or disagreeable mood *Syn* glum, morose, surly, sulky, crabbed, saturnine, dour, gloomy

sully *Syn* SOIL, dirty, tarnish, foul, befoul, smirch, besmirch, grime, begrime

sum *n* ♦ the result of simple addition of all the numbers or particulars in a given group *Syn* amount, number, aggregate, total, whole, quantity

sum *vb Syn* ADD, total, tot, cast, figure, foot

summary *Syn* CONCISE, pithy, compendious, terse, succinct, laconic *Ant* circumstantial

summative *Syn* CUMULATIVE, accumulative, additive

summit ♦ the highest point attained or attainable *Syn* peak, pinnacle, climax, apex, acme, culmination, meridian, zenith, apogee

summon, summons ♦ to demand or request the presence or service of *Syn* call, cite, convoke, convene, muster

sumptuous *Syn* LUXURIOUS, opulent

sunder *Syn* SEPARATE, sever, divide, part, divorce *Ant* link

sundry *Syn* MANY, several, various, divers, numerous, multifarious

superadd *Syn* ADD, annex, append, subjoin

superannuated *Syn* AGED, old, elderly

superb *Syn* SPLENDID, resplendent, glorious, gorgeous, sublime

supercilious *Syn* PROUD, disdainful, overbearing, arrogant, haughty, lordly, insolent

supererogatory ♦ given or done without compulsion, need, or warrant *Syn* gratuitous, uncalled-for, wanton

superficial ♦ lacking in depth or solidity *Syn* shallow, cursory, uncritical *Ant* radical

superfluity *Syn* EXCESS, surplus, surplusage, overplus

superfluous ♦ exceeding what is needed or necessary *Syn* surplus, supernumerary, extra, spare

superhuman *Syn* SUPERNATURAL, preternatural, miraculous, supranatural

superimpose *Syn* OVERLAY, superpose, appliqué

superior *Syn* BETTER, preferable *Ant* inferior

superlative *Syn* SUPREME, transcendent, surpassing, peerless, incomparable, preeminent

supernatural ♦ of or relating to an order of existence beyond the visible observable universe *Syn* supranatural, preternatural, miraculous, superhuman

supernumerary *Syn* SUPERFLUOUS, surplus, extra, spare

superpose *Syn* OVERLAY, superimpose, appliqué

supersede *Syn* REPLACE, displace, supplant

supervene *Syn* FOLLOW, succeed, ensue

supervision *Syn* OVERSIGHT, surveillance

supine 1 *Syn* PRONE, prostrate, recumbent, couchant, dormant **2** *Syn* INACTIVE, inert, passive, idle

supplant *Syn* REPLACE, displace, supersede

supple 1 *Syn* ELASTIC, flexible, resilient, springy *Ant* stiff **2** ♦ able to bend or twist with ease and grace *Syn* limber, lithe, lithesome, lissome

supplement *n* **1** *Syn* COMPLEMENT **2** *Syn*

APPENDIX, addendum, addenda

supplement *vb Syn* COMPLEMENT

supplicate *Syn* BEG, implore, beseech, entreat, importune, adjure

supply *vb Syn* PROVIDE, furnish

supply *n Syn* SUBSTITUTE, locum tenens, alternate, understudy, pinch hitter, double, stand-in

supply *adj Syn* TEMPORARY, provisional, ad interim, acting

support *vb* **1** ♦ to hold up in position by serving as a foundation or base for *Syn* sustain, prop, bolster, buttress, brace **2** ♦ to favor actively one that meets opposition *Syn* uphold, advocate, back, champion

support *n Syn* LIVING, maintenance, sustenance, livelihood, subsistence, keep, bread *Ant* adversary, antagonist

supposed ♦ accepted or advanced as true or real on the basis of less than conclusive evidence *Syn* supposititious, suppositious, reputed, putative, purported, conjectural, hypothetical *Ant* certain

supposititious, suppositious *Syn* SUPPOSED, reputed, putative, purported, conjectural, hypothetical

suppress **1** *Syn* CRUSH, quell, extinguish, quench, quash **2** ♦ to hold back more or less forcefully someone or something that seeks an outlet *Syn* repress

supranatural *Syn* SUPERNATURAL, miraculous, preternatural, superhuman

supremacy ♦ the position of being first (as in rank, power, or influence) *Syn* ascendancy

supreme ♦ developed to the utmost and not exceeded by any other in degree, quality, or intensity *Syn* superlative, transcendent, surpassing, preeminent, peerless, incomparable

sure **1** *Syn* CONFIDENT, assured, sanguine, presumptuous **2** ♦ having no doubt or uncertainty *Syn* certain, positive, cocksure *Ant* unsure

surety **1** *Syn* GUARANTEE, security, bond, guaranty, bail **2** *Syn* SPONSOR, guarantor, backer, patron, angel

surfeit *Syn* SATIATE, sate, cloy, pall, glut, gorge *Ant* whet

surge *Syn* RISE, arise, ascend, mount, soar, tower, rocket, levitate

surly *Syn* SULLEN, morose, glum, crabbed, sulky, saturnine, dour, gloomy *Ant* amiable

surmise *vb Syn* CONJECTURE, guess

surmise *n Syn* CONJECTURE, guess

surmount *Syn* CONQUER, overcome, overthrow, rout, vanquish, defeat, subdue, subjugate, reduce, beat, lick

surpass *Syn* EXCEED, transcend, excel, outdo, outstrip

surpassing *Syn* SUPREME, transcendent, superlative, preeminent, peerless, incomparable

surplus *n Syn* EXCESS, superfluity, surplusage, overplus *Ant* deficiency

surplus *adj Syn* SUPERFLUOUS, supernumerary, extra, spare

surplusage *Syn* EXCESS, surplus, superfluity, overplus

surprise **1** ♦ to attack unawares *Syn* waylay, ambush **2** ♦ to impress forcibly through unexpectedness *Syn* astonish, astound, amaze, flabbergast

surrender *vb Syn* RELINQUISH, abandon, resign, yield, leave, cede, waive

surrender *n* ♦ the yielding of one's person, forces, or possessions to another *Syn* submission, capitulation

surreptitious *Syn* SECRET, underhand, underhanded, covert, stealthy, furtive, clandestine

surrogate *Syn* RESOURCE, substitute, shift, makeshift, expedient, resort, stopgap

surround ♦ to close in or as if in a ring about something *Syn* environ, encircle, circle, encompass, compass, hem, gird, girdle, ring

surveillance *Syn* OVERSIGHT, supervision

survey *vb Syn* SEE, view, espy, descry, behold, observe, notice, remark, note, perceive, discern

survey *n Syn* COMPENDIUM, syllabus, digest, pandect, sketch, précis, aperçu

survive *Syn* OUTLIVE, outlast

susceptible 1 *Syn* LIABLE, sensitive, subject, exposed, prone, open *Ant* immune **2** *Syn* SENTIENT, sensitive, impressible, impressionable, responsive

suspect *Syn* DISTRUST, mistrust, doubt, misdoubt

suspend 1 *Syn* EXCLUDE, disbar, shut out, eliminate, debar, blackball, rule out **2** *Syn* DEFER, stay, intermit, postpone **3** *Syn* HANG, sling, dangle

suspended ♦ hanging from or remaining in place as if hanging from a support *Syn* pendent, pendulous

suspicion 1 *Syn* UNCERTAINTY, mistrust, doubt, dubiety, dubiosity, skepticism **2** *Syn* TOUCH, suggestion, soupçon, tincture, tinge, shade, smack, spice, dash, vein, strain, streak

sustain 1 *Syn* SUPPORT, prop, bolster, buttress, brace *Ant* subvert **2** *Syn* EXPERIENCE, undergo, suffer

sustenance 1 *Syn* FOOD, nourishment, nutriment, aliment, pabulum, pap **2** *Syn* LIVING, maintenance, support, livelihood, subsistence, keep, bread

suture *Syn* JOINT, articulation

swag *Syn* SPOIL, plunder, loot, booty, prize

swagger *Syn* STRUT, bristle, bridle

swallow *Syn* EAT, ingest, devour, consume

swarm *Syn* TEEM, abound, overflow

swat *Syn* STRIKE, hit, smite, punch, slug, slog, clout, slap, cuff, box

sway *vb* **1** *Syn* SWING, oscillate, fluctuate, pendulate, vibrate, waver, undulate **2** *Syn* AFFECT, influence, impress, strike, touch

sway *n* *Syn* POWER, dominion, control, command, authority

swearing *Syn* BLASPHEMY, profanity, cursing

sweep *Syn* RANGE, gamut, reach, radius, compass, scope, orbit, horizon, ken, purview

sweeping *Syn* INDISCRIMINATE, wholesale

sweet ♦ distinctly pleasing or charming *Syn* engaging, winning, winsome, dulcet *Ant* sour; bitter

swell *Syn* EXPAND, amplify, distend, inflate, dilate *Ant* shrink

swerve ♦ to turn aside from a straight course *Syn* veer, deviate, depart, digress, diverge

swift *Syn* FAST, rapid, fleet, quick, speedy, hasty, expeditious

swimming *Syn* GIDDY, dizzy, vertiginous, dazzled

swindle *Syn* CHEAT, overreach, cozen, defraud

swing 1 ♦ to wield or cause to move to and fro or up and down *Syn* wave, flourish, brandish, shake, thrash **2** ♦ to move from one direction to its opposite *Syn* sway, oscillate, vibrate, fluctuate, pendulate, waver, undulate **3** *Syn* HANDLE, wield, manipulate, ply

swipe *Syn* STEAL, pilfer, filch, purloin, lift, pinch, snitch, cop

swirl *Syn* TURN, circle, spin, twirl, whirl, wheel, eddy, revolve, rotate, gyrate, pirouette

sybaritic *Syn* SENSUOUS, sensual, luxurious, voluptuous, epicurean

sycophant *Syn* PARASITE, favorite, toady, lickspittle, bootlicker, hanger-on, leech, sponge, sponger

syllabus *Syn* COMPENDIUM, digest, pandect, survey, sketch, précis, aperçu

symbol 1 ♦ something concrete that represents or suggests another thing that cannot in itself be pictured *Syn* emblem, attribute, type **2** *Syn* CHARACTER, sign, mark

symbolism *Syn* ALLEGORY

symmetry ♦ beauty of form or arrangement arising from balanced proportions *Syn* proportion, balance, harmony

sympathetic 1 *Syn* CONSONANT, congenial, congruous, compatible, consistent **2** *Syn* TENDER, compassionate, warm, warmhearted, responsive *Ant* unsympathetic

sympathy 1 *Syn* ATTRACTION, affinity *Ant* antipathy **2** ♦ the act or capacity for sharing in the interests and esp. in the painful experiences of another *Syn* pity, compassion, commiseration, condolence, ruth, empathy

symptom *Syn* SIGN, mark, token, badge

synchronous *Syn* CONTEMPORARY, coeval, coetaneous, contemporaneous, simultaneous, coincident, concomitant, concurrent

syndicate *Syn* MONOPOLY, corner, pool, trust, cartel

syndrome *Syn* DISEASE, disorder, condition, affection, ailment, malady, complaint, distemper

synopsis *Syn* ABRIDGMENT, brief, conspectus, epitome, abstract

synthetic *Syn* ARTIFICIAL, ersatz, factitious

system 1 ♦ an organized integrated whole made up of diverse but interrelated and interdependent parts *Syn* scheme, network, complex, organism *Ant* chaos **2** *Syn* METHOD, mode, manner, way, fashion

systematic *Syn* ORDERLY, methodical, regular

systematize *Syn* ORDER, organize, methodize, arrange, marshal

T

table *Syn* LIST, catalog, schedule, register, roll, roster, inventory

taciturn *Syn* SILENT, uncommunicative, reserved, reticent, secretive, close, close-lipped, closemouthed, tight-lipped *Ant* garrulous; clamorous (*esp. of crowds*); convivial

tackle *Syn* EQUIPMENT, apparatus, machinery, paraphernalia, outfit, gear, matériel

tact ♦ skill and grace in dealing with others *Syn* address, poise, savoir faire *Ant* awkwardness

tactical *Syn* STRATEGIC, logistic

tactics *Syn* STRATEGY, logistics

tag *n* *Syn* MARK, brand, stamp, label, ticket

tag *vb* **1** *Syn* MARK, brand, stamp, label, ticket **2** *Syn* FOLLOW, pursue, chase, trail, tail

tail *Syn* FOLLOW, pursue, chase, trail, tag

taint *Syn* CONTAMINATE, pollute, defile

take 1 ♦ to get hold of by or as if by catching up with the hand *Syn* seize, grasp, clutch, snatch, grab **2** *Syn* RECEIVE, accept, admit **3** *Syn* BRING, fetch

tale *Syn* STORY, narrative, anecdote, yarn

talent *Syn* GIFT, genius, faculty, aptitude, knack, bent, turn

talisman *Syn* FETISH, charm, amulet

talk *vb* *Syn* SPEAK, converse

talk *n* *Syn* SPEECH, address, oration, harangue, lecture, sermon, homily

talkative ♦ given to talk or talking *Syn* loquacious, garrulous, voluble, glib *Ant* silent

talkativeness ♦ the inclination to talk or to talking *Syn* loquacity, loquaciousness, garrulity, garrulousness, volubility, glibness *Ant* silence

tall *Syn* HIGH, lofty *Ant* short

tally *Syn* AGREE, square, accord, harmonize, correspond, conform, jibe

tame ♦ made docile and tractable *Syn* subdued, submissive *Ant* fierce

tamp *Syn* PACK, crowd, cram, stuff, ram

tamper *Syn* MEDDLE, interfere, intermeddle

tang *Syn* TASTE, flavor, savor, relish, smack

tangent *Syn* ADJACENT, abutting, adjoining, contiguous, conterminous, juxtaposed

tangible *Syn* PERCEPTIBLE, sensible, palpable, appreciable, ponderable *Ant* intangible

tantalize *Syn* WORRY, tease, harass, harry, annoy, plague, pester *Ant* satisfy

tantamount *Syn* SAME, selfsame, very, identical, identic, equivalent, equal

tap *vb* ♦ to strike or hit audibly *Syn* knock, rap, thump, thud

tap *n* ♦ a light usu. audible blow or the sound made by such a blow *Syn* rap, knock, thump, thud

tar *Syn* MARINER, sailor, seaman, gob, bluejacket

tardy ♦ not arriving, occurring, or done at the set, due, or expected time *Syn* late, behindhand, overdue *Ant* prompt

tarnish *Syn* SOIL, dirty, sully, foul, befoul, smirch, besmirch, grime, begrime *Ant* polish

tarry *Syn* STAY, remain, wait, abide, linger

tart *Syn* SOUR, acid, acidulous, dry

Tartarean *Syn* INFERNAL, chthonian, chthonic, Hadean, stygian, hellish

task ♦ a piece of work to be done *Syn* duty, assignment, job, stint, chore

taste 1 ♦ the property of a substance which makes it perceptible to the gustatory sense *Syn* flavor, savor, tang, relish, smack **2** ♦ a liking for or enjoyment of something because of the pleasure it gives *Syn* palate, relish, gusto, zest *Ant* antipathy

tasty *Syn* PALATABLE, savory, sapid, appetizing, toothsome, flavorsome, relishing *Ant* bland

tat *Syn* WEAVE, knit, crochet, braid, plait

tattle *Syn* GOSSIP, blab

taunt *Syn* RIDICULE, mock, deride, twit, rally

taut *Syn* TIGHT, tense

tautology *Syn* VERBIAGE, redundancy, pleonasm, circumlocution, periphrasis

tawdry *Syn* GAUDY, garish, flashy, meretricious

tax *Syn* BURDEN, encumber, cumber, weigh, weight, load, lade, charge, saddle

teach ♦ to cause to acquire knowledge or skill *Syn* instruct, educate, train, discipline, school

tear ♦ to separate forcibly *Syn* rip, rend, split, cleave, rive **2** *Syn* RUSH, dash, shoot, charge

tease *Syn* WORRY, tantalize, pester, plague, harass, harry, annoy

tedious *Syn* IRKSOME, tiresome, wearisome, boring *Ant* exciting

tedium ♦ a state of dissatisfaction and weariness *Syn* boredom, ennui, doldrums

teem ♦ to be present in large quantity *Syn* abound, swarm, overflow

teeny *Syn* SMALL, tiny, little, diminutive, petite, wee, weeny, minute, microscopic, miniature

teeter *Syn* SHAKE, tremble, quake, totter, quiver, shiver, shudder, quaver, wobble, shimmy, dither

tell 1 *Syn* COUNT, enumerate, number **2** *Syn* SAY, utter, state **3** *Syn* REVEAL, divulge, discover, disclose, betray

telling *Syn* VALID, compelling, convincing, cogent, sound

temerity ♦ conspicuous or flagrant boldness *Syn* audacity, hardihood, effrontery, nerve, cheek, gall *Ant* caution

temper *vb* *Syn* MODERATE, qualify *Ant* intensify

temper *n* **1** *Syn* MOOD, humor, vein **2** *Syn* DISPOSITION, temperament, complexion, character, personality, individuality

temperament *Syn* DISPOSITION, temper, complexion, character, personality, individuality

temperance ♦ self-restraint in the gratification of appetites or passions *Syn* sobriety, abstinence, abstemiousness, continence

temperate 1 *Syn* MODERATE *Ant* intemperate; inordinate **2** *Syn* SOBER, continent, unimpassioned

temporal *Syn* PROFANE, secular, lay *Ant* spiritual

temporary ♦ lasting, continuing, or serving for a limited time *Syn* provisional, ad interim, acting, *Ant* permanent

tempt *Syn* LURE, entice, inveigle, decoy, seduce

tenacious *Syn* STRONG, tough, stout, sturdy, stalwart

tenacity *Syn* COURAGE, resolution, spirit, mettle

tend ♦ to supervise or take charge of *Syn* attend, mind, watch

tendency ♦ movement in a particular direction *Syn* trend, drift, tenor

tender *adj* ♦ showing or expressing interest in another *Syn* compassionate, sympathetic, warm, warmhearted, responsive *Ant* callous; severe

tender *vb* *Syn* OFFER, proffer, present, prefer

tender *n* *Syn* OVERTURE, approach, advance, bid

tenet *Syn* DOCTRINE, dogma

tenor *Syn* TENDENCY, drift, trend

tense 1 *Syn* TIGHT, taut *Ant* slack **2** *Syn* STIFF, rigid, inflexible, stark, wooden *Ant* expansive

tension 1 *Syn* STRESS, strain, pressure **2** *Syn* BALANCE, equilibrium, equipoise, poise

tentative *Syn* PROVISIONAL *Ant* definitive

tenuous *Syn* THIN, rare, slender, slim, slight *Ant* dense

tergiversation *Syn* AMBIGUITY, equivocation, double entendre

term 1 *Syn* LIMIT, end, confine, bound **2** *Syn* WORD, vocable **3** *pl* **terms** *Syn* CONDITION, stipulation, provision, proviso, reservation, strings

termagant *Syn* VIRAGO, scold, shrew, vixen, amazon

terminal *Syn* LAST, final, concluding, latest, eventual, ultimate *Ant* initial

terminate *Syn* CLOSE, end, conclude, finish, complete

termination *Syn* END, ending, terminus *Ant* inception; source

terminus *Syn* END, termination, ending *Ant* starting point

terrestrial *Syn* EARTHLY, earthy, mundane, worldly, sublunary *Ant* celestial

terrible *Syn* FEARFUL, terrific, frightful, dreadful, awful, horrible, horrific, shocking, appalling

terrific *Syn* FEARFUL, terrible, frightful, dreadful, horrible, horrific, awful, shocking, appalling

terrify *Syn* FRIGHTEN, fright, scare, alarm, terrorize, startle

territory *Syn* FIELD, domain, province, sphere, bailiwick

terror *Syn* FEAR, panic, consternation, dread, fright, alarm, dismay, horror, trepidation

terrorize *Syn* FRIGHTEN, terrify, fright, alarm, scare, startle, affray, affright

terse *Syn* CONCISE, succinct, laconic, summary, pithy, compendious

test *n* *Syn* PROOF, trial, demonstration

test *vb* *Syn* PROVE, try, demonstrate

testimonial *Syn* CREDENTIAL, recommendation, character, reference

testy *Syn* IRASCIBLE, choleric, splenetic, touchy, cranky, cross

text *Syn* SUBJECT, topic, argument, theme, matter, subject matter, motive, motif, leitmotiv

thankful *Syn* GRATEFUL *Ant* thankless

thaumaturgy *Syn* MAGIC, sorcery, witchcraft, witchery, wizardry, alchemy

thaw *Syn* LIQUEFY, melt, deliquesce, fuse *Ant* freeze

theatrical *Syn* DRAMATIC, dramaturgic, melodramatic, histrionic

theft ♦ an unlawful taking of property esp. personal property stolen from its rightful owner *Syn* larceny, robbery, burglary

theme 1 *Syn* SUBJECT, text, topic, argument, matter, subject matter, motive, motif, leitmotiv **2** *Syn* ESSAY, composition, paper, article

then *Syn* THEREFORE, hence, consequently, accordingly, so

theorem *Syn* PRINCIPLE, axiom, fundamental, law

theoretical ♦ concerned principally with abstractions and theories *Syn* speculative, academic

therefore ♦ for this or that reason *Syn* hence, consequently, then, accordingly, so

thesis *Syn* DISCOURSE, dissertation, treatise, monograph, disquisition

thespian *Syn* ACTOR, player, impersonator, trouper, performer, mummer, mime, mimic

thick 1 *Syn* STOCKY, thick, thickset, chunky, stubby, squat, dumpy *Ant* thin **2** *Syn* CLOSE, compact, dense **3** *Syn* FAMILIAR, close, confidential, chummy, intimate

thickset *Syn* STOCKY, thick, chunky, stubby, squat, dumpy

thief ♦ one that steals esp. stealthily or secretly *Syn* robber, burglar, larcener, larcenist

thin *adj* ♦ not thick, broad, abundant, or dense *Syn* slender, slim, slight, tenuous, rare *Ant* thick

thin *vb* ♦ to make thin or thinner or less dense *Syn* attenuate, extenuate, dilute, rarefy *Ant* thicken

thing 1 *Syn* AFFAIR, matter, concern, business **2** ◆ whatever is apprehended as having actual, distinct, and demonstrable existence *Syn* object, article

think 1 ◆ to form an idea of *Syn* conceive, imagine, fancy, realize, envisage, envision **2** ◆ to use one's powers of conception, judgment, or inference *Syn* cogitate, reflect, reason, speculate, deliberate

thirst *Syn* LONG, hunger, pine, yearn, hanker

though ◆ in spite of the fact that *Syn* although, albeit

thought *Syn* IDEA, concept, conception, notion, impression

thoughtful 1 ◆ characterized by or exhibiting the power to think *Syn* reflective, speculative, contemplative, meditative, pensive **2** ◆ mindful of others *Syn* considerate, attentive *Ant* thoughtless

thoughtless *Syn* CARELESS, heedless, inadvertent *Ant* thoughtful

thrash 1 *Syn* BEAT, pound, pummel, buffet, baste, belabor **2** *Syn* SWING, flourish, brandish, shake, wave

threadbare 1 *Syn* SHABBY, dilapidated, dingy, faded, seedy **2** *Syn* TRITE, shopworn, hackneyed, stereotyped

threaten ◆ to announce or forecast impending danger or evil *Syn* menace

thrifty *Syn* SPARING, economical, frugal *Ant* wasteful

thrill ◆ to thrill with emotions that stir or excite or to be so excited *Syn* electrify, enthuse

thrive *Syn* SUCCEED, prosper, flourish *Ant* languish

throb *vb Syn* PULSATE, beat, pulse, palpitate

throb *n Syn* PULSATION, beat, pulse, palpitation

throe *Syn* PAIN, ache, pang, twinge, stitch

throng *Syn* CROWD, press, crush, mob, rout, horde

throttle *Syn* SUFFOCATE, asphyxiate, stifle, smother, choke, strangle

through *Syn* BY, with

throw ◆ to cause to move swiftly through space by a propulsive movement or a propelling force *Syn* cast, fling, hurl, pitch, toss, sling

throwback *Syn* REVERSION, atavism

throw up *Syn* BELCH, burp, vomit, disgorge, regurgitate, spew

thrust *Syn* PUSH, shove, propel

thud *vb Syn* TAP, thump, knock, rap

thud *n Syn* TAP, thump, knock, rap

thump *vb Syn* TAP, thud, knock, rap

thump *n Syn* TAP, thud, knock, rap

thwart *Syn* FRUSTRATE, foil, baffle, balk, circumvent, outwit

ticket *n Syn* MARK, brand, stamp, label, tag

ticket *vb Syn* MARK, brand, stamp, label, tag

tickle *Syn* PLEASE, regale, gratify, delight, rejoice, gladden

tide *Syn* FLOW, flood, stream, current, flux

tidings *Syn* NEWS, intelligence, advice

tidy *Syn* NEAT, trim, trig, snug, shipshape, spick-and-span *Ant* untidy

tie *n* **1** *Syn* BOND, band **2** *Syn* DRAW, stalemate, deadlock, standoff

tie *vb* ◆ to make fast and secure *Syn* bind *Ant* untie

tier *Syn* LINE, row, rank, file, echelon

tiff *n Syn* QUARREL, bickering, spat, squabble, wrangle, altercation

tiff *vb Syn* QUARREL, spat, bicker, squabble, wrangle, altercate

tight 1 ◆ fitting, drawn, or stretched so that there is no slackness or looseness *Syn* taut, tense *Ant* loose **2** *also* **tightfisted** *Syn* STINGY, close, closefisted, niggardly, parsimonious, penurious, miserly, cheeseparing, penny-pinching **3** *Syn* DRUNK, tipsy, intoxicated, drunken, inebriated

tight-lipped *Syn* SILENT, uncommunicative, taciturn, close, close-lipped, closemouthed, reticent, reserved, secretive

time *Syn* OPPORTUNITY, occasion, chance, break

timely *Syn* SEASONABLE, well-timed, opportune, pat *Ant* untimely

timetable *Syn* PROGRAM, schedule, agenda

timid ◆ marked by or exhibiting a lack of

boldness, courage, or determination **Syn** timorous

timorous *Syn* TIMID *Ant* assured

tincture *Syn* TOUCH, suggestion, tinge, suspicion, soupçon, shade, smack, spice, dash, vein, strain, streak

tinge 1 *Syn* COLOR, tint, shade, hue, tone **2** *Syn* TOUCH, tincture, suggestion, shade, suspicion, soupçon, smack, spice, dash, vein, strain, streak

tint *Syn* COLOR, hue, shade, tinge, tone

tiny *Syn* SMALL, minute, miniature, diminutive, wee, little, teeny, weeny

tippler *Syn* DRUNKARD, inebriate, alcoholic, dipsomaniac, sot, soak, toper, tosspot

tipsy *Syn* DRUNK, intoxicated, inebriated, drunken, tight

tirade ♦ a violent, often long-winded, and usu. denunciatory speech or writing **Syn** diatribe, jeremiad, philippic *Ant* eulogy

tire ♦ to make or become unable or unwilling to continue (as from a loss of physical strength or endurance) **Syn** weary, fatigue, exhaust, jade, fag, tucker

tireless *Syn* INDEFATIGABLE, weariless, untiring, unwearying, unwearied, unflagging

tiresome *Syn* IRKSOME, wearisome, tedious, boring

titanic *Syn* HUGE, vast, immense, enormous, elephantine, mammoth, giant, gigantic, gigantean, colossal, gargantuan, Herculean, cyclopean, Brobdingnagian

title 1 *Syn* CLAIM, pretension, pretense **2** *Syn* NAME, designation, denomination, appellation, style

tittle *Syn* PARTICLE, bit, mite, smidgen, whit, atom, iota, jot

toady *n Syn* PARASITE, sycophant, favorite, lickspittle, bootlicker, hanger-on, leech, sponge, sponger

toady *vb Syn* FAWN, truckle, cringe, cower

toboggan *Syn* SLIDE, coast, slip, glide, skid, glissade, slither

tocsin *Syn* ALARM, alert

toil *Syn* WORK, labor, travail, drudgery, grind *Ant* leisure

token 1 *Syn* SIGN, mark, symptom,

badge, note **2** *Syn* PLEDGE, pawn, hostage **3** *Syn* REMEMBRANCE, remembrancer, reminder, memorial, memento, keepsake, souvenir

tolerance *Syn* FORBEARANCE, leniency, indulgence, clemency, mercifulness *Ant* intolerance; loathing

tolerant *Syn* FORBEARING, lenient, indulgent, clement, merciful *Ant* intolerant; severe

tolerantly *Syn* FORBEARINGLY, clemently, mercifully, leniently, indulgently

tolerate *Syn* BEAR, endure, abide, suffer, stand, brook

tone *Syn* COLOR, hue, shade, tint, tinge

tongue *Syn* LANGUAGE, dialect, speech, idiom

tongue-lash *Syn* SCOLD, upbraid, rate, berate, jaw, bawl, chew out, wig, rail, revile, vituperate

too *Syn* ALSO, likewise, besides, moreover, furthermore

tool *Syn* IMPLEMENT, instrument, appliance, utensil

toothsome *Syn* PALATABLE, appetizing, savory, sapid, tasty, flavorsome, relishing

toper *Syn* DRUNKARD, inebriate, alcoholic, dipsomaniac, sot, soak, tosspot, tippler

topic *Syn* SUBJECT, matter, subject matter, argument, text, theme, motive, motif, leitmotiv

torment *Syn* AFFLICT, torture, rack, try

tornado ♦ a violent whirling wind accompanied by a funnel-shaped cloud **Syn** cyclone, twister

torpid *Syn* LETHARGIC, sluggish, comatose *Ant* agile

torpidity *Syn* LETHARGY, torpor, stupor, languor, lassitude

torpor *Syn* LETHARGY, torpidity, stupor, languor, lassitude *Ant* animation

torrent *Syn* FLOOD, deluge, inundation, spate, cataract

tortuous *Syn* WINDING, sinuous, serpentine, flexuous

torture *Syn* AFFLICT, rack, torment, try

toss *Syn* THROW, pitch, sling, cast, fling, hurl

tosspot *Syn* DRUNKARD, inebriate, alcoholic, dipsomaniac, sot, soak, toper, tippler

tot *Syn* ADD, total, sum, cast, figure, foot

total *adj Syn* WHOLE, entire, all, gross

total *n Syn* SUM, aggregate, whole, amount, number, quantity

total *vb Syn* ADD, tot, sum, figure, cast, foot

totter 1 *Syn* SHAKE, tremble, quake, quaver, quiver, shiver, shudder, wobble, teeter, shimmy, dither **2** *Syn* REEL, stagger, whirl

touch *vb* **1** ♦ to probe with a sensitive part of the body (as a finger) so as to get or produce a sensation often in the course of examining or exploring *Syn* feel, palpate, handle, paw **2** *Syn* AFFECT, influence, impress, strike, sway **3** *Syn* MATCH, approach, rival, equal

touch *n* **1** *Syn* CONTACT **2** ♦ a very small amount or perceptible trace of something added *Syn* suggestion, suspicion, soupçon, tincture, tinge, shade, smack, spice, dash, vein, strain, streak

touching *Syn* MOVING, affecting, impressive, poignant, pathetic

touchstone *Syn* STANDARD, criterion, gauge, yardstick

touchy *Syn* IRASCIBLE, choleric, splenetic, testy, cranky, cross *Ant* imperturbable

tough *Syn* STRONG, tenacious, stout, sturdy, stalwart *Ant* fragile

tour 1 *Syn* SPELL, shift, trick, turn, stint, bout, go **2** *Syn* JOURNEY, voyage, trip, cruise, expedition, jaunt, excursion, pilgrimage

tow *Syn* PULL, tug, haul, hale, draw, drag

tower *Syn* RISE, mount, ascend, soar, rocket, arise, levitate, surge

toxic *Syn* POISONOUS, venomous, virulent, mephitic, pestilent, pestilential, miasmic, miasmatic, miasmal

toxin *Syn* POISON, venom, virus, bane

toy *Syn* TRIFLE, dally, flirt, coquet

trace *n* ♦ a perceptible sign made by something that has passed *Syn* vestige, track

trace *vb Syn* SKETCH, outline, diagram, delineate, draft, plot, blueprint

tracing *Syn* SKETCH, outline, diagram, delineation, draft, plot, blueprint

track *Syn* TRACE, vestige

tract *Syn* AREA, region, zone, belt

tractable *Syn* OBEDIENT, amenable, biddable, docile *Ant* intractable; unruly

trade 1 ♦ a pursuit followed as an occupation or means of livelihood and requiring technical knowledge and skill *Syn* craft, handicraft, art, profession **2** *Syn* BUSINESS, commerce, industry, traffic

traduce *Syn* MALIGN, asperse, vilify, calumniate, defame, slander, libel

traffic 1 *Syn* BUSINESS, commerce, trade, industry **2** *Syn* INTERCOURSE, commerce, dealings, communication, communion, conversation, converse, correspondence

trail *Syn* FOLLOW, pursue, chase, tag, tail

train *n Syn* SUCCESSION, progression, series, sequence, chain, string

train *vb* **1** *Syn* TEACH, discipline, school, instruct, educate **2** *Syn* DIRECT, aim, point, level, lay

traipse *Syn* WANDER, stray, roam, ramble, rove, range, prowl, gad, gallivant, meander

trait *Syn* CHARACTERISTIC, feature

traitorous *Syn* FAITHLESS, treacherous, perfidious, false, disloyal

trammel *Syn* HAMPER, fetter, shackle, clog, manacle, hog-tie

tramp *Syn* VAGABOND, vagrant, hobo, truant, bum

tranquil *Syn* CALM, serene, placid, peaceful, halcyon *Ant* troubled

tranquilize *Syn* CALM, compose, quiet, quieten, still, lull, soothe, settle *Ant* agitate

transcend *Syn* EXCEED, surpass, excel, outdo, outstrip

transcendent 1 *Syn* SUPREME, surpassing, superlative, peerless, preeminent, incomparable **2** *Syn* ABSTRACT, transcendental, ideal

transcendental *Syn* ABSTRACT, transcendent, ideal

transcript *Syn* REPRODUCTION, copy, carbon copy, duplicate, facsimile, replica

transfer 1 *Syn* MOVE, remove, shift **2** ♦ to shift title or possession from one owner to another *Syn* convey, alienate, deed

transfiguration

transfiguration *Syn* TRANSFORMATION, metamorphosis, transmutation, conversion, transmogrification

transfigure *Syn* TRANSFORM, metamorphose, transmute, convert, transmogrify

transform ♦ to change a thing into a different thing *Syn* metamorphose, transmute, convert, transmogrify, transfigure

transformation ♦ change of one thing into another different thing *Syn* metamorphosis, transmutation, conversion, transmogrification, transfiguration

transgression *Syn* BREACH, trespass, violation, infraction, infringement, contravention

transient ♦ lasting or staying only a short time *Syn* transitory, passing, ephemeral, momentary, fugitive, fleeting, evanescent, short-lived *Ant* perpetual

transitory *Syn* TRANSIENT, passing, ephemeral, momentary, fugitive, fleeting, evanescent, short-lived *Ant* everlasting; perpetual

translation ♦ a restating often in a simpler language of something previously stated or written *Syn* version, paraphrase, metaphrase

translucent *Syn* CLEAR, lucid, pellucid, diaphanous, limpid, transparent

transmit 1 *Syn* SEND, forward, remit, route, ship, dispatch 2 *Syn* CARRY, bear, convey, transport

transmogrification *Syn* TRANSFORMATION, metamorphosis, transmutation, conversion, transfiguration

transmogrify *Syn* TRANSFORM, metamorphose, transmute, convert, transfigure

transmutation *Syn* TRANSFORMATION, metamorphosis, conversion, transmogrification, transfiguration

transmute *Syn* TRANSFORM, metamorphose, convert, transmogrify, transfigure

transparent *Syn* CLEAR, lucid, pellucid, diaphanous, translucent, limpid *Ant* opaque

transpire *Syn* HAPPEN, occur, chance, befall, betide

transport *vb* 1 *Syn* CARRY, bear, convey, transmit 2 ♦ to carry away by strong and usu. pleasurable emotion *Syn* ravish, enrapture, entrance 3 *Syn* BANISH, deport, exile, expatriate, ostracize, extradite

transport *n Syn* ECSTASY, rapture

transpose *Syn* REVERSE, invert

trap *n Syn* LURE, bait, decoy, snare

trap *vb Syn* CATCH, entrap, snare, ensnare, bag, capture

trash 1 *Syn* REFUSE, waste, rubbish, debris, garbage, offal 2 *Syn* NONSENSE, twaddle, drivel, bunk, balderdash, poppycock, gobbledygook, rot, bull

trauma, traumatism *Syn* WOUND, lesion, bruise, contusion

travail *Syn* WORK, labor, toil, drudgery, grind

traverse *Syn* DENY, gainsay, contradict, negative, impugn, contravene *Ant* allege

travesty *n Syn* CARICATURE, parody, burlesque

travesty *vb Syn* CARICATURE, parody, burlesque

treacherous *Syn* FAITHLESS, perfidious, traitorous, false, disloyal

treason *Syn* SEDITION *Ant* allegiance

treasure *Syn* APPRECIATE, prize, value, cherish

treat 1 *Syn* CONFER, parley, negotiate, commune, consult, advise 2 ♦ to have to do with or behave toward (a person or thing) in a specified manner *Syn* deal, handle

treatise *Syn* DISCOURSE, disquisition, dissertation, thesis, monograph

treaty *Syn* CONTRACT, bargain, compact, pact, entente, convention, cartel, concordat

tremble *Syn* SHAKE, quake, quiver, shiver, shudder, quaver, totter, wobble, teeter, shimmy, dither

tremendous *Syn* MONSTROUS, stupendous, monumental, prodigious

trenchant *Syn* INCISIVE, clear-cut, cutting, biting, crisp

trend *Syn* TENDENCY, drift, tenor

trepidation *Syn* FEAR, horror, terror, panic, consternation, dread, fright, alarm, dismay

trespass *n Syn* BREACH, transgression, violation, infraction, infringement, contravention

trespass *vb* ♦ to make inroads upon the property, territory, or rights of another *Syn* encroach, entrench, infringe, invade

trial 1 *Syn* PROOF, test, demonstration **2** ♦ the state or fact of being tested (as by suffering) *Syn* tribulation, affliction, visitation, cross

tribulation *Syn* TRIAL, affliction, visitation, cross *Ant* consolation

tributary *Syn* SUBORDINATE, secondary, dependent, subject, collateral

tribute *Syn* ENCOMIUM, eulogy, panegyric, citation

trick *n* **1** ♦ an indirect means to gain an end *Syn* ruse, stratagem, maneuver, gambit, ploy, artifice, wile, feint **2** *Syn* SPELL, turn, tour, shift, stint, bout, go

trick *vb* *Syn* DUPE, gull, befool, hoax, hoodwink, bamboozle

trickery *Syn* DECEPTION, double-dealing, chicanery, chicane, fraud

tricky *Syn* SLY, crafty, foxy, insidious, cunning, wily, guileful, artful

tried *Syn* RELIABLE, dependable, trustworthy, trusty

trifle ♦ to deal with or act toward without serious purpose *Syn* toy, dally, flirt, coquet

trifling *Syn* PETTY, trivial, puny, paltry, measly, picayunish, picayune

trig *Syn* NEAT, trim, tidy, spick-and-span, snug, shipshape

trill *Syn* SING, troll, carol, descant, warble, hymn, chant, intone

trim *vb* **1** *Syn* SHEAR, poll, clip, prune, lop, snip, crop **2** *Syn* STABILIZE, steady, poise, balance, ballast

trim *adj* *Syn* NEAT, tidy, trig, snug, shipshape, spick-and-span *Ant* frowzy

trip *vb* *Syn* STUMBLE, blunder, lurch, flounder, lumber, galumph, lollop, bumble

trip *n* *Syn* JOURNEY, voyage, tour, excursion, cruise, expedition, jaunt, pilgrimage

trite ♦ lacking the freshness that evokes attention or interest *Syn* hackneyed, stereotyped, threadbare, shopworn *Ant* original; fresh

triumph *Syn* VICTORY, conquest

trivial *Syn* PETTY, trifling, puny, paltry, measly, picayunish, picayune *Ant* weighty; momentous

troll *Syn* SING, carol, descant, warble, trill, hymn, chant, intone

troop *Syn* COMPANY, band, troupe, party

troubadour *Syn* POET, versifier, rhymer, rhymester; poetaster, bard, minstrel

trouble *vb* **1** ♦ to cause to be uneasy or upset *Syn* distress, ail **2** *Syn* INCONVENIENCE, incommode, discommode

trouble *n* *Syn* EFFORT, exertion, pains

troupe *Syn* COMPANY, troop, band, party

trouper *Syn* ACTOR, player, performer, mummer, mime, mimic, thespian, impersonator

truant *Syn* VAGABOND, vagrant, tramp, hobo, bum

truce ♦ a suspension of or an agreement for suspending hostilities *Syn* cease-fire, armistice, peace

truckle *Syn* FAWN, toady, cringe, cower

truculent *Syn* FIERCE, ferocious, barbarous, savage, inhuman, cruel, fell

true 1 *Syn* FAITHFUL, loyal, constant, staunch, steadfast, resolute *Ant* false; fickle **2** *Syn* REAL, actual *Ant* false

truism *Syn* COMMONPLACE, platitude, bromide, cliche

trust *n* **1** ♦ assured reliance on the character, ability, strength, or truth of someone or something *Syn* confidence, reliance, dependence, faith *Ant* mistrust **2** *Syn* MONOPOLY, corner, pool, syndicate, cartel

trust *vb* *Syn* RELY, depend, count, reckon, bank

trustworthy *Syn* RELIABLE, dependable, trusty, tried *Ant* deceitful; dubious

trusty *Syn* RELIABLE, trustworthy, tried, dependable

truth ♦ the quality or state of keeping close to fact and avoiding distortion or misrepresentation *Syn* veracity, verity, verisimilitude *Ant* untruth; lie, falsehood

try *vb* **1** *Syn* PROVE, test, demonstrate **2** *Syn* AFFLICT, torment, torture, rack **3** *Syn* ATTEMPT, endeavor, essay, strive, struggle

try *n* *Syn* ATTEMPT, endeavor, essay, striving, struggle

tryst *Syn* ENGAGEMENT, rendezvous, assignation, appointment, date

tucker *Syn* TIRE, fatigue, exhaust, jade, fag, weary

tug *Syn* PULL, tow, hale, haul, drag, draw

tumid *Syn* INFLATED, flatulent, turgid

tumult *Syn* COMMOTION, agitation, turmoil, turbulence, confusion, convulsion, upheaval

tune *n Syn* MELODY, air

tune *vb Syn* HARMONIZE, attune

turbid ♦ not clear or translucent but clouded with or as if with sediment *Syn* muddy, roily *Ant* clear; limpid

turbulence *Syn* COMMOTION, agitation, tumult, turmoil, confusion, convulsion, upheaval

turgid *Syn* INFLATED, tumid, flatulent

turmoil *Syn* COMMOTION, agitation, tumult, turbulence, confusion, convulsion, upheaval

turn *vb* 1 ♦ to move or cause to move in a curved or circular path on or as if on an axis *Syn* revolve, rotate, gyrate, circle, spin, twirl, whirl, wheel, eddy, swirl, pirouette 2 ♦ to change or cause to change course or direction *Syn* divert, deflect, avert, sheer 3 *Syn* RESORT, refer, apply, go 4 *Syn* DEPEND, hinge, hang

turn *n* 1 *Syn* SPELL, trick, tour, shift, stint, bout, go 2 *Syn* GIFT, bent, faculty, aptitude, genius, talent, knack

turncoat *Syn* RENEGADE, apostate, recreant, backslider

turn out *Syn* BEAR, produce, yield

tussle *Syn* WRESTLE, grapple, scuffle

twaddle *Syn* NONSENSE, drivel, bunk, balderdash, poppycock, gobbledygook, trash, rot, bull

tweet *n Syn* CHIRP, chirrup, cheep, peep, twitter, chitter

tweet *vb Syn* CHIRP, chirrup, cheep, peep, twitter, chitter

twine *Syn* WIND, coil, curl, twist, wreathe, entwine

twinge *Syn* PAIN, ache, pang, throe, stitch

twinkle *Syn* FLASH, gleam, glance, glint, sparkle, glitter, glisten, scintillate, coruscate

twinkling *Syn* INSTANT, moment, minute, second, flash, jiffy, split second

twirl *Syn* TURN, revolve, rotate, gyrate, circle, spin, whirl, wheel, eddy, swirl, pirouette

twist 1 *Syn* WIND, coil, curl, twine, wreathe, entwine 2 *Syn* CURVE, bend

twister *Syn* TORNADO, cyclone

twit *Syn* RIDICULE, deride, mock, taunt, rally

twitch *Syn* JERK, snap, yank

twitter *vb Syn* CHIRP, chirrup, cheep, peep, tweet, chitter

twitter *n Syn* CHIRP, chirrup, cheep, peep, tweet, chitter

type 1 *Syn* SYMBOL, emblem, attribute *Ant* antitype 2 ♦ a number of individuals thought of as a group because of a common quality or qualities *Syn* kind, sort, stripe, kidney, ilk, description, nature, character

typhoon *Syn* HURRICANE, tropical storm

typical *Syn* REGULAR, natural, normal *Ant* atypical; distinctive

tyrannical, tyrannous *Syn* ABSOLUTE, despotic, arbitrary, autocratic

tyro *Syn* AMATEUR, dilettante, dabbler

U

ubiquitous *Syn* OMNIPRESENT

ugly ♦ unpleasing to the sight *Syn* hideous, ill-favored, unsightly *Ant* beautiful

ultimate 1 *Syn* LAST, latest, final, terminal, concluding, eventual 2 ♦ being so fundamental as to represent the extreme limit of actual or possible knowledge *Syn* absolute, categorical

ululate *Syn* ROAR, bellow, bluster, bawl, vociferate, clamor, howl

ululation *Syn* ROAR, bellow, bluster, bawl, vociferation

umbra *Syn* SHADE, penumbra, shadow, umbrage, adumbration

umbrage 1 *Syn* SHADE, shadow, umbra, penumbra, adumbration 2 *Syn* OFFENSE, resentment, pique, dudgeon, huff

umpire *Syn* JUDGE, referee, arbiter, arbitrator

unacceptable *Syn* OBJECTIONABLE, undesirable, unwanted, unwelcome

unaffected *Syn* NATURAL, artless, simple, ingenuous, naïve, unsophisticated

unafraid *Syn* BRAVE, fearless, dauntless, undaunted, bold, intrepid, audacious, courageous, valiant, valorous, doughty *Ant* afraid

unassailable *Syn* INVINCIBLE, impregnable, inexpugnable, invulnerable, unconquerable, indomitable

unavoidable *Syn* INEVITABLE, ineluctable, inescapable, unescapable

unbecoming *Syn* INDECOROUS, improper, unseemly, indecent, indelicate

unbelief ♦ the attitude or state of mind of one who does not believe *Syn* disbelief, incredulity *Ant* belief

unbeliever *Syn* ATHEIST, freethinker, agnostic, infidel, deist

unbiased *Syn* FAIR, impartial, dispassionate, just, equitable, uncolored, objective *Ant* biased

unburden *Syn* RID, clear, disabuse, purge *Ant* burden

uncalled-for *Syn* SUPEREROGATORY, gratuitous, wanton

uncanny *Syn* WEIRD, eerie

unceasing *Syn* EVERLASTING, endless, interminable

uncertainty ♦ lack of sureness about someone or something *Syn* doubt, dubiety, dubiosity, skepticism, suspicion, mistrust *Ant* certainty

uncircumscribed *Syn* INFINITE, boundless, illimitable, sempiternal, eternal *Ant* circumscribed

uncivil *Syn* RUDE, ill-mannered, impolite, discourteous, ungracious *Ant* civil

uncolored 1 *Syn* COLORLESS, achromatic **2** *Syn* FAIR, dispassionate, impartial, objective, unbiased, just, equitable

uncommon *Syn* INFREQUENT, scarce, rare, occasional, sporadic *Ant* common

uncommunicative *Syn* SILENT, taciturn, reticent, reserved, secretive, close, closelipped, closemouthed, tight-lipped *Ant* communicative

unconcerned *Syn* INDIFFERENT, incurious, aloof, detached, uninterested, disinterested *Ant* concerned

uncongenial *Syn* INCONSONANT, unsympathetic, incompatible, inconsistent, incongruous, discordant, discrepant *Ant* congenial

unconquerable *Syn* INVINCIBLE, indomitable, impregnable, inexpugnable, unassailable, invulnerable *Ant* conquerable

unconstraint ♦ freedom from constraint or pressure *Syn* abandon, spontaneity

uncouth *Syn* RUDE, rough, crude, raw, callow, green

uncritical *Syn* SUPERFICIAL, shallow, cursory *Ant* critical

unctuous *Syn* FULSOME, oily, oleaginous, slick, soapy *Ant* brusque

undaunted *Syn* BRAVE, courageous, unafraid, fearless, intrepid, valiant, valorous, dauntless, doughty, bold, audacious *Ant* afraid

under *Syn* BELOW, beneath, underneath

undergo *Syn* EXPERIENCE, sustain, suffer

underhand, underhanded *Syn* SECRET, covert, stealthy, furtive, clandestine, surreptitious *Ant* aboveboard

underling *Syn* INFERIOR, subordinate *Ant* leader, master

underlying 1 *Syn* FUNDAMENTAL, basic, basal, radical **2** *Syn* ELEMENTAL, basic, elementary, essential, fundamental, primitive

undermine *Syn* WEAKEN, enfeeble, debilitate, sap, cripple, disable *Ant* reinforce

underneath *Syn* BELOW, under, beneath

understand ♦ to have a clear or complete idea of *Syn* comprehend, appreciate

understanding 1 *Syn* REASON, intuition **2** *Syn* AGREEMENT, accord

understudy *Syn* SUBSTITUTE, supply,

locum tenens, alternate, pinch hitter, double, stand-in

undesirable *Syn* OBJECTIONABLE, unacceptable, unwanted, unwelcome

undulate *Syn* SWING, waver, sway, oscillate, vibrate, fluctuate, pendulate

undying *Syn* IMMORTAL, deathless, unfading

unearth *Syn* DISCOVER, ascertain, determine, learn

uneasy *Syn* IMPATIENT, nervous, unquiet, restless, restive, fidgety, jumpy, jittery

uneducated *Syn* IGNORANT, illiterate, unlettered, untaught, untutored, unlearned *Ant* educated

unerring *Syn* INFALLIBLE, inerrable, inerrant

unescapable *Syn* INEVITABLE, ineluctable, inescapable, unavoidable

uneven *Syn* ROUGH, harsh, rugged, scabrous *Ant* even

unfading *Syn* IMMORTAL, deathless, undying

unfeigned *Syn* SINCERE, wholehearted, whole-souled, heartfelt, hearty

unfit ◆ not adapted or appropriate to a particular end or purpose *Syn* unsuitable, improper, inappropriate, unfitting, inapt, unhappy, infelicitous *Ant* fit

unfitting *Syn* UNFIT, inappropriate, improper, unsuitable, inapt, unhappy, infelicitous *Ant* fitting

unflagging *Syn* INDEFATIGABLE, unwearied, unwearying, tireless, untiring, weariless

unflappable *Syn* COOL, composed, collected, unruffled, imperturbable, nonchalant

unfold 1 ◆ to disclose by degrees to the sight or understanding *Syn* evolve, develop, elaborate, perfect **2** *Syn* SOLVE, resolve, unravel, decipher

unformed *Syn* FORMLESS, shapeless *Ant* formed

unfortunate *Syn* UNLUCKY, disastrous, ill-starred, ill-fated, calamitous, luckless, hapless *Ant* fortunate

unfounded *Syn* BASELESS, groundless, unwarranted

unfruitful *Syn* STERILE, barren, infertile, impotent *Ant* fruitful, prolific

ungodly *Syn* IRRELIGIOUS, godless, unreligious, nonreligious

ungovernable *Syn* UNRULY, intractable, refractory, recalcitrant, willful, headstrong *Ant* governable; docile

ungracious *Syn* RUDE, ill-mannered, impolite, discourteous, uncivil *Ant* gracious

unhappy *Syn* UNFIT, infelicitous, inapt, unsuitable, improper, inappropriate, unfitting *Ant* happy

uniform 1 *Syn* LIKE, alike, similar, analogous, comparable, akin, parallel, identical *Ant* various **2** *Syn* STEADY, constant, even, equable *Ant* multiform

unify *Syn* COMPACT, consolidate, concentrate

unimpassioned *Syn* SOBER, temperate, continent *Ant* impassioned

uninterested *Syn* INDIFFERENT, unconcerned, incurious, aloof, detached, disinterested

union *Syn* UNITY, solidarity, integrity

unique 1 *Syn* SINGLE, sole, lone, solitary, separate, particular **2** *Syn* STRANGE, singular, peculiar, eccentric, erratic, odd, queer, quaint, outlandish, curious

unite 1 *Syn* JOIN, conjoin, combine, connect, link, associate, relate *Ant* divide; alienate **2** ◆ to join forces or act in concert *Syn* combine, conjoin, cooperate, concur *Ant* part

unity ◆ the character of a thing that is a whole composed of many parts *Syn* solidarity, integrity, union

universal 1 ◆ present or significant throughout the world *Syn* cosmic, ecumenical, catholic, cosmopolitan **2** ◆ of, belonging, or relating to all or the whole *Syn* general, generic, common *Ant* particular

unkempt *Syn* SLIPSHOD, slovenly, sloppy, disheveled

unlawful ◆ contrary to or prohibited by the

law *Syn* illegal, illegitimate, illicit *Ant* lawful

unlearned *Syn* IGNORANT, illiterate, unlettered, uneducated, untaught, untutored

unlettered *Syn* IGNORANT, illiterate, uneducated, untaught, untutored, unlearned

unlikeness *Syn* DISSIMILARITY, difference, divergence, divergency, distinction *Ant* likeness

unlucky ♦ involving or suffering misfortune that results from chance *Syn* disastrous, ill-starred, ill-fated, unfortunate, calamitous, luckless, hapless *Ant* lucky

unman *Syn* UNNERVE, emasculate, enervate

unmarried ♦ being without a spouse *Syn* single, celibate, virgin, maiden

unmatured *Syn* IMMATURE, unripe, unmellow *Ant* matured

unmellow *Syn* IMMATURE, unmatured, unripe *Ant* mellow, mellowed

unmindful *Syn* FORGETFUL, oblivious *Ant* mindful; solicitous

unmitigated *Syn* OUTRIGHT, out-and-out, arrant

unnatural *Syn* IRREGULAR, anomalous *Ant* natural

unnerve ♦ to deprive of strength or vigor and the capacity for effective action *Syn* enervate, unman, emasculate

unoffending *Syn* HARMLESS, innocuous, innocent, inoffensive

unpremeditated *Syn* EXTEMPORANEOUS, extempore, extemporary, improvised, impromptu, offhand *Ant* premeditated

unpretentious *Syn* PLAIN, homely, simple

unpropitious *Syn* OMINOUS, portentous, fateful, inauspicious *Ant* propitious

unqualified *Syn* INCAPABLE, incompetent *Ant* qualified

unquiet *Syn* IMPATIENT, nervous, restless, restive, uneasy, fidgety, jumpy, jittery *Ant* quiet

unravel *Syn* SOLVE, resolve, unfold, decipher

unreasonable *Syn* IRRATIONAL *Ant* reasonable

unrelenting *Syn* GRIM, implacable, relentless, merciless *Ant* forbearing

unreligious *Syn* IRRELIGIOUS, ungodly, godless, nonreligious

unremitting *Syn* CONTINUAL, constant, incessant, continuous, perpetual, perennial

unripe *Syn* IMMATURE, unmatured, unmellow *Ant* ripe

unruffled *Syn* COOL, imperturbable, unflappable, nonchalant, composed, collected *Ant* ruffled; excited

unruly ♦ not submissive to government or control *Syn* ungovernable, intractable, refractory, recalcitrant, willful, headstrong *Ant* tractable, docile

unseemly *Syn* INDECOROUS, improper, unbecoming, indecent, indelicate *Ant* seemly

unsettle *Syn* DISORDER, derange, disarrange, disorganize, disturb *Ant* settle

unsightly *Syn* UGLY, hideous, ill-favored

unsocial ♦ disliking or avoiding the company of others *Syn* asocial, antisocial, nonsocial *Ant* social

unsophisticated *Syn* NATURAL, simple, ingenuous, naïve, artless *Ant* sophisticated

unspeakable *Syn* UNUTTERABLE, inexpressible, ineffable, indescribable, indefinable

unstable *Syn* INCONSTANT, fickle, capricious, mercurial *Ant* stable

unsuitable *Syn* UNFIT, improper, inappropriate, unfitting, inapt, unhappy, infelicitous *Ant* suitable

unsympathetic 1 *Syn* INCONSONANT, uncongenial, discordant, incongruous, incompatible, inconsistent, discrepant *Ant* sympathetic **2** *Syn* ANTIPATHETIC *Ant* sympathetic

untangle *Syn* EXTRICATE, disentangle, disencumber, disembarrass

untaught *Syn* IGNORANT, illiterate, unlettered, uneducated, untutored, unlearned *Ant* taught

untimely *Syn* PREMATURE, forward, advanced, precocious *Ant* timely

untiring *Syn* INDEFATIGABLE, tireless, weariless, unwearying, unwearied, unflagging

untouchable *Syn* OUTCAST, castaway, derelict, reprobate, pariah

untruth *Syn* LIE, falsehood, fib, misrepresentation, story *Ant* truth

untruthful *Syn* DISHONEST, lying, mendacious, deceitful *Ant* truthful

untutored *Syn* IGNORANT, illiterate, unlettered, uneducated, untaught, unlearned *Ant* tutored

unusual *Syn* exceptional, extraordinary, phenomenal, unwonted

unutterable ♦ not capable of being put into words *Syn* inexpressible, unspeakable, ineffable, indescribable, indefinable

unwanted *Syn* OBJECTIONABLE, unacceptable, undesirable, unwelcome

unwarranted *Syn* BASELESS, groundless, unfounded *Ant* warranted

unwearied *Syn* INDEFATIGABLE, tireless, weariless, untiring, unwearying, unflagging

unwearying *Syn* INDEFATIGABLE, tireless, weariless, untiring, unwearied, unflagging

unwelcome *Syn* OBJECTIONABLE, unacceptable, undesirable, unwanted

unwholesome ♦ detrimental to physical, mental, or moral well-being *Syn* morbid, sickly, diseased, pathological *Ant* wholesome

unwonted *Syn* EXCEPTIONAL, extraordinary, phenomenal, unusual

upbraid *Syn* SCOLD, rate, berate, tonguelash, revile, vituperate, jaw, bawl, chew out, wig, rail

upheaval *Syn* COMMOTION, agitation, tumult, turmoil, turbulence, confusion, convulsion

uphold *Syn* SUPPORT, advocate, back, champion *Ant* contravene; subvert

upright ♦ having or showing a strict regard for what is morally right *Syn* honest, just, conscientious, scrupulous, honorable

uprising *Syn* REBELLION, revolution, revolt, insurrection, mutiny, putsch, coup

uproar *Syn* DIN, pandemonium, hullabaloo, babel, hubbub, clamor, racket

uproot *Syn* EXTERMINATE, eradicate, deracinate, extirpate, wipe *Ant* establish; inseminate

upset 1 *Syn* OVERTURN, capsize, overthrow, subvert **2** *Syn* DISCOMPOSE, agitate, perturb, disturb, disquiet, fluster, flurry

upshot *Syn* EFFECT, outcome, issue, result, consequence, aftereffect, aftermath, event, sequel

urbane *Syn* SUAVE, smooth, diplomatic, bland, politic *Ant* rude; clownish, bucolic

urge *vb* ♦ to press or impel to action, effort, or speed *Syn* egg, exhort, goad, spur, prod, prick, sic

urge *n* *Syn* DESIRE, lust, passion, appetite

urgent *Syn* PRESSING, imperative, crying, importunate, insistent, exigent, instant

usage 1 *Syn* HABIT, practice, custom, use, habitude, wont **2** *Syn* FORM, convention, convenance

use *n* **1** ♦ a useful or valuable end, result, or purpose *Syn* service, advantage, profit, account, avail **2** ♦ a capacity for serving an end or purpose *Syn* usefulness, utility **3** *Syn* HABIT, wont, practice, usage, custom, habitude

use *vb* ♦ to put into service esp. to attain an end *Syn* employ, utilize, apply, avail

usefulness *Syn* USE, utility

usual ♦ familiar through frequent or regular repetition *Syn* customary, habitual, wonted, accustomed

usurp *Syn* ARROGATE, preempt, appropriate, confiscate *Ant* abdicate

utensil *Syn* IMPLEMENT, tool, instrument, appliance

utility *Syn* USE, usefulness

utilize *Syn* USE, employ, apply, avail

utopian *Syn* AMBITIOUS, pretentious

utter 1 *Syn* SAY, tell, state **2** *Syn* EXPRESS, vent, voice, broach, air, ventilate

V

vacant *Syn* EMPTY, blank, vacuous

vacate *Syn* ANNUL, abrogate, void, quash

vacillate *Syn* HESITATE, waver, falter

vacuous *Syn* EMPTY, vacant, blank, void

vacuum *Syn* HOLE, void, cavity, hollow, pocket

vagabond ♦ a person who wanders at will or as a habit *Syn* vagrant, truant, tramp, bum, hobo

vagary *Syn* CAPRICE, freak, fancy, whim, whimsy, conceit, crotchet

vagrant *n* *Syn* VAGABOND, truant, tramp, hobo, bum

vagrant *adj* *Syn* ITINERANT, peripatetic, ambulatory, ambulant, nomadic

vague *Syn* OBSCURE, dark, enigmatic, cryptic, ambiguous, equivocal *Ant* definite; specific; lucid

vain **1** ♦ being without worth or significance *Syn* nugatory, otiose, idle, empty, hollow **2** *Syn* FUTILE, fruitless, bootless, abortive **3** *Syn* PROUD, vainglorious

vainglorious *Syn* PROUD, vain

vainglory *Syn* PRIDE, vanity

valiant *Syn* BRAVE, courageous, unafraid, fearless, intrepid, valorous, dauntless, undaunted, doughty, bold, audacious *Ant* timid; dastardly

valid ♦ having such force as to compel serious attention and usu. acceptance *Syn* sound, cogent, convincing, compelling, telling *Ant* fallacious, sophistical

validate *Syn* CONFIRM, authenticate, substantiate, verify, corroborate *Ant* invalidate

valor *Syn* HEROISM, prowess, gallantry

valorous *Syn* BRAVE, courageous, unafraid, fearless, intrepid, valiant, dauntless, undaunted, doughty, bold, audacious

valuable *Syn* COSTLY, precious, invaluable, priceless, expensive, dear

value *n* *Syn* WORTH

value *vb* **1** *Syn* ESTIMATE, appraise, evaluate, rate, assess, assay **2** *Syn* APPRECIATE, prize, treasure, cherish

vanish ♦ to pass from view or out of existence *Syn* evanesce, evaporate, disappear, fade *Ant* appear; loom

vanity *Syn* PRIDE, vainglory

vanquish *Syn* CONQUER, defeat, beat, lick, subdue, subjugate, reduce, overcome, surmount, overthrow, rout

vanquisher *Syn* VICTOR, conqueror, winner, champion

vapid *Syn* INSIPID, flat, jejune, banal, wishy-washy, inane

variable *Syn* CHANGEABLE, protean, changeful, mutable *Ant* constant; equable

variance *Syn* DISCORD, contention, dissension, difference, strife, conflict

variation *Syn* CHANGE, alteration, modification

variegated ♦ having a pattern involving different colors or shades of color *Syn* parti-colored, motley, checkered, checked, pied, piebald, skewbald, dappled, freaked

variety **1** ♦ the quality or state of being composed of different parts, elements, or individuals *Syn* diversity **2** ♦ a group of related plants or animals narrower in scope than a species *Syn* subspecies, race, breed, cultivar, strain, clone, stock

various **1** *Syn* DIFFERENT, diverse, divergent, disparate *Ant* uniform; cognate **2** *Syn* MANY, several, sundry, divers, numerous, multifarious

vary **1** *Syn* CHANGE, alter, modify **2** *Syn* DIFFER, disagree, dissent

vast *Syn* HUGE, immense, enormous, elephantine, mammoth, giant, gigantic, gigantean, colossal, gargantuan, Herculean, cyclopean, titanic, Brobdingnagian

vault *vb* *Syn* JUMP, leap, spring, bound

vault *n* *Syn* JUMP, leap, spring, bound

vaunt *Syn* BOAST, brag, crow, gasconade

veer *Syn* SWERVE, deviate, depart, digress, diverge

vehement *Syn* INTENSE, fierce, exquisite, violent

vehicle *Syn* MEAN, instrument, instrumentality, agent, agency, medium, organ, channel

veil *Syn* COVER, overspread, envelop, wrap, shroud

vein 1 *Syn* MOOD, humor, temper **2** *Syn* TOUCH, strain, streak, suggestion, suspicion, soupçon, tincture, tinge, shade, smack, spice, dash

velocity *Syn* SPEED, momentum, impetus, pace, headway

velvety *Syn* SLEEK, silken, silky, satiny, glossy, slick

venal *Syn* MERCENARY, hireling, hack

venerable *Syn* OLD, ancient, antique, antiquated, archaic, obsolete, antediluvian

venerate *Syn* REVERE, reverence, worship, adore

veneration *Syn* REVERENCE, worship, adoration

vengeance *Syn* RETALIATION, revenge, retribution, reprisal

vengeful *Syn* VINDICTIVE, revengeful

venial ♦ not warranting punishment or the imposition of a penalty *Syn* pardonable *Ant* heinous; mortal

venom *Syn* POISON, toxin, virus, bane

venomous *Syn* POISONOUS, virulent, toxic, mephitic, pestilent, pestilential, miasmic, miasmatic, miasmal

vent *Syn* EXPRESS, utter, voice, broach, air, ventilate *Ant* bridle

ventilate *Syn* EXPRESS, vent, air, utter, voice, broach

venture ♦ to expose to risk or loss *Syn* hazard, risk, chance, jeopardize, endanger, imperil

venturesome *Syn* ADVENTUROUS, daring, daredevil, rash, reckless, foolhardy

veracity *Syn* TRUTH, verity, verisimilitude

verbiage ♦ an excess of words usu. of little or obscure content *Syn* redundancy, tautology, pleonasm, circumlocution, periphrasis

verbose *Syn* WORDY, prolix, diffuse, redundant *Ant* laconic

verge *Syn* BORDER, edge, rim, brim, brink, margin

verify *Syn* CONFIRM, corroborate, substantiate, authenticate, validate

verisimilitude *Syn* TRUTH, veracity, verity

veritable *Syn* AUTHENTIC, genuine, bona fide *Ant* factitious

verity *Syn* TRUTH, veracity, verisimilitude

vernacular 1 *Syn* DIALECT, patois, lingo, jargon, cant, argot, slang **2** *Syn* BARBARISM, corruption, impropriety, solecism, vulgarism

versatile ♦ having a wide range of skills or abilities or many different uses *Syn* many-sided, all-around

verse *Syn* PARAGRAPH, article, clause, plank, count

versed *Syn* CONVERSANT

versifier *Syn* POET, rhymer, rhymester, poetaster, bard, minstrel, troubadour

version 1 *Syn* TRANSLATION, paraphrase, metaphrase **2** *Syn* ACCOUNT, report, story, chronicle

vertebrae *Syn* SPINE, backbone, back, chine

vertical ♦ being at right angles to a base line *Syn* perpendicular, plumb *Ant* horizontal

vertiginous *Syn* GIDDY, dizzy, swimming, dazzled

verve *Syn* VIGOR, vim, spirit, dash, esprit, punch, élan, drive

very 1 *Syn* SAME, selfsame, identical, identic, equivalent, equal, tantamount **2** *Syn* MERE, bare

vessel *Syn* BOAT, ship, craft

vestige *Syn* TRACE, track

vex *Syn* ANNOY, irk, bother *Ant* please, regale

viands *Syn* FOOD, provisions, comestibles, feed, victuals, provender, fodder, forage

vibrant *Syn* RESONANT, sonorous, ringing, resounding, orotund

vibrate *Syn* SWING, sway, oscillate, fluctuate, pendulate, waver, undulate

vice 1 *Syn* FAULT, failing, frailty, foible **2** *Syn* OFFENSE, sin, crime, scandal *Ant* virtue

vicinity *Syn* LOCALITY, neighborhood, district

vicious ♦ highly reprehensible or offensive in character, nature, or conduct *Syn* villainous, iniquitous, nefarious, flagitious, infamous, corrupt, degenerate *Ant* virtuous

vicissitude 1 *Syn* CHANGE, alteration, mutation, permutation 2 *Syn* DIFFICULTY, hardship, rigor

victim ♦ one killed or injured for the ends of the one who kills or injures *Syn* prey, quarry

victor ♦ one that defeats an enemy or opponent *Syn* winner, conqueror, champion, vanquisher

victory ♦ a successful outcome in a contest or struggle *Syn* conquest, triumph *Ant* defeat

victuals *Syn* FOOD, feed, viands, provisions, comestibles, provender, fodder, forage

vie *Syn* RIVAL, compete, emulate

view *n* 1 *Syn* LOOK, sight, glance, glimpse, peep, peek 2 *Syn* OPINION, belief, conviction, persuasion, sentiment

view *vb Syn* SEE, survey, contemplate, observe, note, remark, notice, perceive, discern, behold, descry, espy

viewpoint *Syn* POINT OF VIEW, standpoint, angle, slant

vigilant *Syn* WATCHFUL, alert, wide-awake

vigor ♦ a quality of force, forcefulness, or energy *Syn* vim, spirit, dash, esprit, verve, punch, élan, drive

vigorous ♦ having or showing great vitality and force *Syn* energetic, strenuous, lusty, nervous *Ant* languorous; lethargic

vile *Syn* BASE, low

vilify *Syn* MALIGN, traduce, asperse, calumniate, defame, slander, libel *Ant* eulogize

villain ♦ a low, mean, reprehensible person utterly lacking in principles *Syn* scoundrel, blackguard, knave, rascal, rogue, scamp, rapscallion, miscreant

villainous *Syn* VICIOUS, iniquitous, nefarious, flagitious, infamous, corrupt, degenerate

vim *Syn* VIGOR, spirit, dash, esprit, verve, punch, élan, drive

vindicate 1 *Syn* MAINTAIN, justify, defend, assert 2 *Syn* EXCULPATE, exonerate, absolve, acquit *Ant* calumniate

vindictive ♦ showing or motivated by a desire for vengeance *Syn* revengeful, vengeful

violation *Syn* BREACH, infraction, transgression, trespass, infringement, contravention

violence *Syn* FORCE, compulsion, coercion, duress, constraint, restraint

violent *Syn* INTENSE, vehement, fierce, exquisite

virago ♦ a loud, overbearing, ill-tempered woman *Syn* amazon, termagant, scold, shrew, vixen

virgin *Syn* UNMARRIED, single, celibate, maiden

virginal *Syn* YOUTHFUL, maiden, boyish, juvenile, puerile

virile *Syn* MALE, manful, manly, masculine, manlike, mannish *Ant* effeminate; impotent

virtual *Syn* IMPLICIT, constructive *Ant* actual

virtually ♦ not absolutely or actually, yet so nearly so that the difference is negligible *Syn* practically, morally

virtue 1 *Syn* GOODNESS, morality, rectitude *Ant* vice 2 *Syn* EXCELLENCE, merit, perfection

virtuoso *Syn* EXPERT, adept, artist, artiste, wizard

virtuous *Syn* MORAL, ethical, righteous, noble *Ant* vicious

virulent *Syn* POISONOUS, venomous, toxic, mephitic, pestilent, pestilential, miasmic, miasmatic, miasmal

visage *Syn* FACE, countenance, physiognomy, mug, puss

vision 1 *Syn* REVELATION, prophecy, apocalypse 2 *Syn* FANCY, fantasy, phantasy, phantasm, dream, daydream, nightmare

visionary *Syn* IMAGINARY, fanciful, fantastic, chimerical, quixotic

visit ♦ a usu. brief stay with another as an act of friendship or courtesy *Syn* visitation, call

visitant *Syn* VISITOR, guest, caller

visitation 1 *Syn* VISIT, call 2 *Syn* TRIAL, tribulation, affliction, cross

visitor ♦ one who visits another *Syn* visitant, guest, caller

vital 1 *Syn* LIVING, alive, animate, animated 2 *Syn* ESSENTIAL, fundamental, cardinal

vitalize ♦ to arouse to activity, animation, or life *Syn* energize, activate *Ant* atrophy

vitiate *Syn* DEBASE, deprave, corrupt, pervert, debauch

vitiated *Syn* DEBASED, depraved, corrupted, debauched, perverted

vituperate *Syn* SCOLD, revile, berate, rate, upbraid, tongue-lash, jaw, bawl, chew out, wig, rail

vituperation *Syn* ABUSE, invective, obloquy, scurrility, billingsgate *Ant* acclaim, praise

vituperative *Syn* ABUSIVE, opprobrious, contumelious, scurrilous

vivacious *Syn* LIVELY, animated, gay, sprightly *Ant* languid

vivid *Syn* GRAPHIC, picturesque, pictorial

vivify *Syn* QUICKEN, animate, enliven

vixen *Syn* VIRAGO, shrew, scold, termagant, amazon

vocable *Syn* WORD, term

vocabulary *Syn* LANGUAGE, phraseology, diction, phrasing, style

vocal 1 ♦ uttered by the voice or having to do with such utterance *Syn* articulate, oral 2 ♦ being able to express oneself clearly or easily *Syn* articulate, fluent, eloquent, voluble, glib

vociferate *Syn* ROAR, bellow, bluster, bawl, clamor, howl, ululate

vociferation *Syn* ROAR, bellow, bluster, bawl, ululation

vociferous ♦ so loud or insistent as to compel attention *Syn* clamorous, blatant, strident, boisterous, obstreperous

vogue *Syn* FASHION, mode, style, fad, rage, craze, dernier cri, cry

voice *Syn* EXPRESS, utter, vent, broach, air, ventilate

void *adj* 1 *Syn* EMPTY, vacant, blank, vacuous 2 *Syn* DEVOID, destitute

void *n* *Syn* HOLE, vacuum, hollow, cavity, pocket

void *vb* *Syn* ANNUL, vacate, abrogate, quash

volatile *Syn* ELASTIC, effervescent, buoyant, expansive, resilient

volatility *Syn* LIGHTNESS, light-mindedness, levity, frivolity, flippancy, flightiness

volcano *Syn* MOUNTAIN, mount, peak, alp, mesa

volition *Syn* WILL, conation

volubility *Syn* TALKATIVENESS, glibness, garrulity, loquacity

voluble 1 *Syn* VOCAL, fluent, glib, eloquent, articulate *Ant* stuttering, stammering 2 *Syn* TALKATIVE, glib, garrulous, loquacious *Ant* curt

volume 1 *Syn* SIZE, magnitude, extent, dimensions, area 2 *Syn* BULK, mass

voluntary ♦ done or brought about of one's own will *Syn* intentional, deliberate, willful, willing *Ant* involuntary; instinctive

voluptuous *Syn* SENSUOUS, luxurious, sybaritic, epicurean, sensual *Ant* ascetic

vomit *Syn* BELCH, burp, disgorge, regurgitate, spew, throw up

voracious ♦ excessively greedy *Syn* gluttonous, ravenous, ravening, rapacious

vortex *Syn* EDDY, whirlpool, maelstrom

votary *Syn* ADDICT, devotee, habitué

vote *Syn* SUFFRAGE, franchise, ballot

vouch *Syn* CERTIFY, attest, witness

vouchsafe *Syn* GRANT, accord, concede, award

voyage *Syn* JOURNEY, tour, trip, excursion, cruise, expedition, jaunt, pilgrimage

vulgar 1 *Syn* COMMON, ordinary, familiar, popular 2 *Syn* COARSE, gross, obscene, ribald

vulgarism *Syn* BARBARISM, corruption, impropriety, solecism, vernacular

W

wage, wages ♦ the price paid a person for his or her labor or services *Syn* salary, stipend, fee, pay, hire, emolument

wager *Syn* BET, stake, pot, ante

waggish *Syn* PLAYFUL, sportive, frolicsome, impish, mischievous, roguish

wail *Syn* CRY, weep, whimper, blubber, keen

wait *Syn* STAY, remain, abide, tarry, linger

waive *Syn* RELINQUISH, cede, yield, resign, abandon, surrender, leave

waken *Syn* STIR, awaken, arouse, rouse, rally *Ant* subdue

wall *Syn* ENCLOSE, envelop, fence, pen, coop, corral, cage

wallow ♦ to move clumsily and in a debased or pitable condition *Syn* welter, grovel

wan *Syn* PALE, pallid, ashen, ashy, livid

wander ♦ to move about from place to place more or less aimlessly and without a plan *Syn* stray, roam, ramble, rove, range, prowl, gad, gallivant, traipse, meander

wane *Syn* ABATE, subside, ebb *Ant* wax

want *vb* **1** *Syn* LACK, need, require **2** *Syn* DESIRE, wish, crave, covet

want *n* **1** *Syn* LACK, dearth, absence, defect, privation **2** *Syn* POVERTY, destitution, indigence, privation, penury

wanton 1 *Syn* LICENTIOUS, libertine, lewd, lustful, lascivious, libidinous, lecherous *Ant* chaste **2** *Syn* SUPEREROGATORY, uncalled-for, gratuitous

war *Syn* CONTEND, battle, fight

warble *Syn* SING, troll, carol, descant, trill, hymn, chant, intone

ward *Syn* PREVENT, avert, preclude, obviate *Ant* conduce to

wariness *Syn* CAUTION, chariness, circumspection, calculation *Ant* foolhardiness; brashness

warlike *Syn* MARTIAL, military

warm *Syn* TENDER, warmhearted, sympathetic, compassionate, responsive *Ant* cool; austere

warmhearted *Syn* TENDER, warm, sympathetic, compassionate, responsive *Ant* coldhearted

warn ♦ to let one know of approaching danger or risk *Syn* forewarn, caution

warp *Syn* DEFORM, distort, contort

warrant 1 *Syn* ASSERT, declare, profess, affirm, aver, protest, avouch, avow, predicate **2** *Syn* JUSTIFY

wary *Syn* CAUTIOUS, chary, circumspect, calculating *Ant* foolhardy; brash

waspish *Syn* IRRITABLE, snappish, fractious, peevish, petulant, pettish, huffy, fretful, querulous

waste *n* **1** ♦ an area of the earth unsuitable for cultivation or general habitation *Syn* desert, badlands, wilderness **2** *Syn* REFUSE, rubbish, trash, debris, garbage, offal

waste *vb* **1** *Syn* RAVAGE, devastate, sack, pillage, despoil, spoliate *Ant* conserve, save **2** ♦ to spend or expend freely and usu. foolishly or futilely *Syn* squander, dissipate, fritter, consume *Ant* save; conserve

wasted *Syn* HAGGARD, pinched, cadaverous, worn, careworn

waster *Syn* SPENDTHRIFT, profligate, prodigal, wastrel

wastrel *Syn* SPENDTHRIFT, profligate, prodigal, waster

watch 1 *Syn* TEND, mind, attend **2** *Syn* SEE, look

watchful ♦ on the lookout esp. for danger or for opportunities *Syn* vigilant, wideawake, alert

waterlog *Syn* SOAK, drench, saturate, steep, impregnate, sop

wave *Syn* SWING, flourish, brandish, shake, thrash

waver 1 *Syn* SWING, fluctuate, oscillate, pendulate, vibrate, sway, undulate **2** *Syn* HESITATE, falter, vacillate

way 1 ♦ a track or path traversed in going from one place to another *Syn* route, course, passage, pass, artery **2** *Syn* METHOD, mode, manner, fashion, system

waylay *Syn* SURPRISE, ambush

wayward *Syn* CONTRARY, perverse, froward, restive, balky

weak ♦ lacking physical, mental, or moral strength *Syn* feeble, frail, fragile, infirm, decrepit *Ant* strong

weaken ♦ to lose or cause to lose strength, vigor, or energy *Syn* enfeeble, debilitate, undermine, sap, cripple, disable *Ant* strengthen

wealthy *Syn* RICH, affluent, opulent *Ant* indigent

wean *Syn* ESTRANGE, alienate, disaffect *Ant* addict

weariless *Syn* INDEFATIGABLE, unwearying, unwearied, tireless, untiring, unflagging

wearisome *Syn* IRKSOME, tiresome, tedious, boring

weary *Syn* TIRE, fatigue, exhaust, jade, fag, tucker

weave ♦ to make a textile or to form an article by interlacing threads or strands of material *Syn* knit, crochet, braid, plait, tat

wedding *Syn* MARRIAGE, matrimony, nuptial, espousal, wedlock

wedlock *Syn* MARRIAGE, matrimony, nuptial, espousal, wedding

wee *Syn* SMALL, diminutive, tiny, teeny, weeny, little, minute, microscopic, miniature, petite

weeny *Syn* SMALL, tiny, teeny, wee, diminutive, minute, microscopic, miniature, little

weep *Syn* CRY, wail, keen, whimper, blubber

weigh 1 *Syn* CONSIDER, study, contemplate, excogitate **2** *Syn* BURDEN, encumber, cumber, weight, load, lade, tax, charge, saddle **3** *Syn* DEPRESS, oppress

weight *n* **1** *Syn* IMPORTANCE, significance, moment, consequence, import **2** *Syn* INFLUENCE, authority, prestige, credit

weight *vb* **1** *Syn* ADULTERATE, load, sophisticate **2** *Syn* BURDEN, encumber, cumber, weigh, load, lade, tax, charge, saddle

weighty *Syn* HEAVY, ponderous, cumbrous, cumbersome, hefty

weird ♦ fearfully and mysteriously strange or fantastic *Syn* eerie, uncanny

welcome *Syn* PLEASANT, pleasing, agreeable, grateful, gratifying *Ant* unwelcome

well *Syn* HEALTHY, sound, wholesome, robust, hale *Ant* unwell, ill

well-nigh *Syn* NEARLY, almost, approximately

well-timed *Syn* SEASONABLE, timely, opportune, pat

welter *Syn* WALLOW, grovel

wet ♦ covered or more or less soaked with liquid *Syn* damp, dank, moist, humid *Ant* dry

wharf ♦ a structure used by boats and ships for taking on or landing cargo or passengers *Syn* dock, pier, quay, slip, berth, jetty, levee

wheedle *Syn* COAX, blandish, cajole

wheel *Syn* TURN, revolve, rotate, gyrate, circle, spin, twirl, whirl, swirl, pirouette, eddy

while ♦ to pass time, esp. leisure time, without boredom or in pleasant ways *Syn* wile, beguile, fleet

whim *Syn* CAPRICE, freak, fancy, whimsy, conceit, vagary, crotchet

whimper *Syn* CRY, weep, blubber, wail, keen

whimsy *Syn* CAPRICE, freak, fancy, whim, conceit, vagary, crotchet

whirl 1 *Syn* TURN, twirl, spin, wheel, swirl, revolve, rotate, gyrate, circle, pirouette, eddy **2** *Syn* REEL, stagger, totter

whirlpool *Syn* EDDY, maelstrom, vortex

whirlwind ♦ a rotating windstorm of limited extent *Syn* whirly

whirly *Syn* WHIRLWIND

whit *Syn* PARTICLE, mite, jot, iota, bit, smidgen, tittle, atom

whiten 1 ♦ to change from an original color to white or almost to white *Syn* blanch, bleach, decolorize, etiolate *Ant* blacken **2** *Syn* PALLIATE, whitewash, gloze, gloss, extenuate

whitewash *Syn* PALLIATE, whiten, gloze, gloss, extenuate

whole *adj* **1** *Syn* PERFECT, entire, intact **2** ♦ having every constituent element or individual *Syn* entire, total, all, gross *Ant* partial

whole *n* *Syn* SUM, total, aggregate, amount, number, quantity *Ant* part; constituent; particular

wholehearted *Syn* SINCERE, whole-souled, heartfelt, hearty, unfeigned

wholesale *Syn* INDISCRIMINATE, sweeping

wholesome 1 *Syn* HEALTHFUL, healthy, salubrious, salutary, hygienic, sanitary *Ant* noxious **2** *Syn* HEALTHY, sound, robust, hale, well

whole-souled *Syn* SINCERE, whole-hearted, heartfelt, hearty, unfeigned

whoop *vb* *Syn* SHOUT, yell, shriek, scream, screech, squeal, holler

whoop *n* *Syn* SHOUT, yell, shriek, scream, screech, squeal, holler

wicked *Syn* BAD, evil, ill, naughty

wide *Syn* BROAD, deep *Ant* strait

wide-awake *Syn* WATCHFUL, vigilant, alert

wield *Syn* HANDLE, swing, manipulate, ply

wig *Syn* SCOLD, tongue-lash, jaw, bawl, chew out, berate, upbraid, rate, rail, revile, vituperate

wild *Syn* FURIOUS, frantic, frenzied, frenetic, delirious, rabid

wilderness *Syn* WASTE, desert, badlands

wile *n* *Syn* TRICK, artifice, feint, ruse, maneuver, stratagem, gambit, ploy

wile *vb* *Syn* WHILE, beguile, fleet

will *n* ♦ the power or act of making or effecting a choice or decision *Syn* volition, conation

will *vb* ♦ to give to another by will *Syn* bequeath, devise, leave, legate

willful 1 *Syn* VOLUNTARY, deliberate, intentional, willing **2** *Syn* UNRULY, headstrong, intractable, refractory, recalcitrant, ungovernable *Ant* biddable

willing *Syn* VOLUNTARY, intentional, deliberate, willful *Ant* unwilling

wilt *Syn* DROOP, flag, sag

wily *Syn* SLY, cunning, crafty, tricky, foxy, insidious, guileful, artful

win *Syn* GET, gain, acquire, obtain, procure, secure *Ant* lose

wince *Syn* RECOIL, flinch, shrink, blench, quail

wind ♦ to follow a circular, spiral, or writhing course *Syn* coil, curl, twist, twine, wreathe, entwine

winding ♦ curving repeatedly first one way and then another *Syn* sinuous, serpentine, tortuous, flexuous *Ant* straight

window ♦ an opening in the wall of a building that is usu. covered with glass and serves to admit light and air *Syn* casement, oriel

wing *Syn* ANNEX, ell, extension

wink ♦ to close and open one's eyelids quickly *Syn* blink

winner *Syn* VICTOR, conqueror, champion, vanquisher *Ant* loser

winning *Syn* SWEET, engaging, winsome, dulcet

winsome *Syn* SWEET, engaging, winning, dulcet

wipe *Syn* EXTERMINATE, extirpate, eradicate, uproot, deracinate

wisdom *Syn* SENSE, judgment, gumption *Ant* folly; injudiciousness

wise ♦ exercising or involving sound judgment *Syn* sage, sapient, judicious, prudent, sensible, sane *Ant* simple

wisecrack *Syn* JOKE, crack, gag, jest, jape, quip, witticism

wish *Syn* DESIRE, want, crave, covet

wishy-washy *Syn* INSIPID, vapid, flat, jejune, banal, inane

wit 1 *Syn* MIND, intelligence, brain, intellect, soul, psyche **2** ♦ a mode of expression intended to arouse amusement *Syn* humor, irony, sarcasm, satire, repartee

witchcraft *Syn* MAGIC, wizardry, witchery, sorcery, alchemy, thaumaturgy

witchery *Syn* MAGIC, sorcery, witchcraft, wizardry, alchemy, thaumaturgy

with *Syn* BY, through

withdraw *Syn* GO, leave, depart, quit, retire

wither ♦ to lose freshness and substance by or as if by loss of natural moisture *Syn* shrivel, wizen

withhold *Syn* KEEP, detain, keep back, keep out, retain, hold, hold back, reserve

withstand *Syn* RESIST, contest, oppose, fight, combat, conflict, antagonize

witness *n Syn* SPECTATOR, observer, beholder, looker-on, onlooker, eyewitness, bystander, kibitzer

witness *vb Syn* CERTIFY, attest, vouch

witticism *Syn* JOKE, jest, jape, quip, wisecrack, crack, gag

witty ♦ provoking or intended to provoke laughter *Syn* humorous, facetious, jocular, jocose

wizard *Syn* EXPERT, adept, artist, artiste, virtuoso

wizardry *Syn* MAGIC, witchcraft, witchery, sorcery, alchemy, thaumaturgy

wizen *Syn* WITHER, shrivel

wobble *Syn* SHAKE, teeter, totter, shimmy, quiver, shiver, shudder, quaver, quake, tremble, dither

woe *Syn* SORROW, grief, anguish, heartache, heartbreak, regret

woebegone *Syn* DOWNCAST, disconsolate, dispirited, dejected, depressed

woman *Syn* FEMALE, lady

womanish *Syn* FEMALE, womanlike, womanly, ladylike, feminine *Ant* mannish

womanlike *Syn* FEMALE, womanly, womanish, ladylike, feminine

womanly *Syn* FEMALE, womanlike, ladylike, womanish, feminine *Ant* unwomanly, manly

wonder 1 ♦ something that causes astonishment or admiration *Syn* marvel, prodigy, miracle, phenomenon **2** ♦ the complex emotion aroused by the incomprehensible and esp. the awe-inspiring *Syn* wonderment, amazement, admiration

wonderment *Syn* WONDER, amazement, admiration

wont *Syn* HABIT, habitude, practice, usage, custom, use

wonted *Syn* USUAL, accustomed, customary, habitual

woo *Syn* INVITE, court, solicit, bid

wooden *Syn* STIFF, rigid, inflexible, tense, stark

word ♦ a pronounceable sound or combination of sounds that expresses and symbolizes an idea *Syn* vocable, term

wordy ♦ using or marked by the use of more words than are necessary to express the thought *Syn* verbose, prolix, diffuse, redundant

work *n* **1** ♦ strenuous activity that involves difficulty and effort and usually affords no pleasure *Syn* labor, travail, toil, drudgery, grind *Ant* play **2** ♦ a sustained activity that affords one a livelihood *Syn* employment, occupation, calling, pursuit, business **3** ♦ something brought into being by the exertion of effort and the exercise of skill *Syn* product, production, opus, artifact

work *vb Syn* ACT, operate, function, behave, react

worker ♦ one who earns his living by labor, esp. by manual labor *Syn* workman, workingman, laborer, craftsman, handicraftsman, mechanic, artisan, hand, operative, roustabout *Ant* idler

workingman *Syn* WORKER, workman, laborer, craftsman, handicraftsman, mechanic, artisan, operative, hand, roustabout

workman *Syn* WORKER, workingman, laborer, craftsman, handicraftsman, mechanic, artisan, operative, hand, roustabout

world *Syn* EARTH, globe, planet

worldly 1 *Syn* EARTHLY, mundane, terrestrial, earthy, sublunary **2** *Syn* SOPHISTICATED, worldly-wise, blasé, disillusioned

worldly-wise *Syn* SOPHISTICATED, worldly, blasé, disillusioned

worn *Syn* HAGGARD, careworn, pinched, wasted, cadaverous

worried ♦ distressed or troubled usu. about something anticipated *Syn* anxious, concerned, careful, solicitous

worry *vb* ♦ to disturb one or destroy one's peace of mind by repeated or persistent tormenting attacks *Syn* annoy, harass, harry, plague, pester, tease, tantalize

worry *n Syn* CARE, anxiety, concern, solicitude

worship *n* **Syn** REVERENCE, adoration, veneration

worship *vb* 1 **Syn** REVERE, adore, venerate, reverence 2 **Syn** ADORE, idolize

worth ♦ equivalence in good qualities expressed or implied **Syn** value

wound ♦ an injury to the body **Syn** trauma, traumatism, lesion, bruise, contusion

wraith **Syn** APPARITION, phantasm, phantom, ghost, spirit, specter, shade, revenant

wrangle *vb* **Syn** QUARREL, altercate, squabble, bicker, spat, tiff

wrangle *n* **Syn** QUARREL, altercation, squabble, bickering, spat, tiff

wrap **Syn** COVER, overspread, envelop, shroud, veil

wrath **Syn** ANGER, rage, indignation, ire, fury

wrathful **Syn** ANGRY, irate, indignant, mad, wroth, acrimonious

wreathe **Syn** WIND, coil, curl, twist, twine, entwine

wreck **Syn** RUIN, dilapidate

wrench ♦ to turn or twist forcibly **Syn** wrest, wring

wrest **Syn** WRENCH, wring

wrestle ♦ to struggle with an opponent at close quarters **Syn** tussle, grapple, scuffle

wretched **Syn** MISERABLE

wring **Syn** WRENCH, wrest

writhe ♦ to twist or turn in physical or mental distress **Syn** agonize, squirm

wrong *n* **Syn** INJUSTICE, injury, grievance

wrong *adj* 1 **Syn** FALSE *Ant* right 2 **Syn** BAD, poor

wrong *vb* ♦ to inflict injury without just cause or in an outrageous manner **Syn** oppress, persecute, aggrieve

wroth **Syn** ANGRY, irate, indignant, wrathful, acrimonious, mad

Y

yank **Syn** JERK, snap, twitch

yap **Syn** BARK, bay, howl, growl, snarl, yelp

yardstick **Syn** STANDARD, criterion, gauge, touchstone

yarn **Syn** STORY, tale, narrative, anecdote

yearn **Syn** LONG, pine, hanker, hunger, thirst

yeast **Syn** FOAM, froth, spume, scum

yell *vb* **Syn** SHOUT, shriek, scream, screech, squeal, holler, whoop

yell *n* **Syn** SHOUT, shriek, scream, screech, squeal, holler, whoop

yap **Syn** BARK, bay, howl, growl, snarl, yap

yield 1 **Syn** BEAR, produce, turn out 2 **Syn** RELINQUISH, surrender, cede, abandon, leave, resign, waive 3 ♦ to give way before a force that one cannot further resist **Syn** submit, capitulate, succumb, relent, defer, bow, cave

yoke **Syn** COUPLE, pair, brace

yokel **Syn** BOOR, bumpkin, hick, rube, clodhopper, lout, churl

young **Syn** OFFSPRING, progeny, issue, descendant, posterity

youth ♦ the period in life when one passes from childhood to maturity **Syn** adolescence, puberty, pubescence *Ant* age

youthful ♦ relating to or characteristic of one who is between childhood and adulthood **Syn** juvenile, puerile, boyish, virgin, virginal, maiden *Ant* aged

Z

zeal **Syn** PASSION, enthusiasm, fervor, ardor *Ant* apathy

zealot **Syn** ENTHUSIAST, fanatic, bigot

zenith **Syn** SUMMIT, apogee, culmination, meridian, peak, pinnacle, climax, apex, acme *Ant* nadir

zest **Syn** TASTE, relish, gusto, palate

zone **Syn** AREA, belt, tract, region